Genealogies of
PENNSYLVANIA *F*AMILIES

From The Pennsylvania
Genealogical Magazine

Genealogies of
PENNSYLVANIA FAMILIES

From The Pennsylvania
Genealogical Magazine

Volume II

Hinman – Sotcher

Indexed by
Thomas Hollowak & Eleanor Antoniak

Baltimore
GENEALOGICAL PUBLISHING CO., INC.
1982

Excerpted and reprinted from *The Pennsylvania
Genealogical Magazine,* with added Publisher's
Note, Contents, Index, and textual notes, by
Genealogical Publishing Co., Inc., Baltimore, 1982.
Copyright © 1982, Genealogical Publishing Co., Inc.,
Baltimore, Maryland, all rights reserved.
Library of Congress Catalogue Card Number 81-85694.
International Standard Book Number, Volume II:
0-8063-0972-5. Set Number: 0-8063-0974-1.
Made in the United States of America.

Note to the Reader

THIS VOLUME is composed of articles which have been excerpted from *The Pennsylvania Genealogical Magazine.* It is one of three volumes of genealogies extracted from the *Magazine* and published under the title *Genealogies of Pennsylvania Families.* The three volumes together contain every family history article published in the *Magazine* from its founding in 1895—as *Publications of the Genealogical Society of Pennsylvania*—through the year 1980. Also included in this work are Bible records and genealogical memoranda as well as the lengthy "Van Nieuwkirk, Nieukirk, Newkirk" article which had originally been published as an out-of-series special number. (To avoid any mischance in the indexing of Dutch names we have retained the original index to this article as well as the original pagination.)

The reader might note that we recently published another book under the title *Genealogies of Pennsylvania Families.* This was compiled from an entirely different source, however—*The Pennsylvania Magazine of History and Biography*—and stands as a separate and independent work. Nevertheless, as their characteristics are identical, the four volumes may be viewed as forming a series.

Our thanks for their cooperation in the production of this work go to the Executive Committee of The Genealogical Society of Pennsylvania and to Mr. Charles B. Barclay, President of the Society, for so generously consenting to our request to reproduce articles from the *Magazine;* to Don Yoder, Fellow of The Genealogical Society of Pennsylvania and Professor of Folklife Studies at the University of Pennsylvania, for the splendid Introduction; and to Thomas L. Hollowak and Eleanor R. Antoniak for the new name index.

Genealogical Publishing Company

Contents

Genealogies of
PENNSYLVANIA FAMILIES

From The Pennsylvania
Genealogical Magazine

NAOMI HINMAN OF LEWES, DELAWARE, AND HER SIX MARRIAGES: ROADES, FASSET, LAYFIELD, NEW-BOLD, SHANKLAND, WARRINGTON

By Helene C. (Mrs. D. Anthony) Potter

In the register of the United Presbyterian Churches of Lewes, Indian River, and Cool Spring, is found the burial record: " 28 Feb. 1768: Naomi Warranton (who had six husbands!) " [1]

This lady of matrimonial distinction was born Naomi Hinman,[2] daughter of Richard Hinman, a vestryman of St. Peter's Episcopal Church, Lewes, Delaware, as early as 1731.[3] His Will dated 30 January 1740/1 and proved 13 August 1742, named his " daughter Naomy Roades widow of John Roades decd." and his " two grandsons Hinman Roads and John Roads, sons of my abovesaid daughter Naomy." [4]

Naomi's first husband, John Roades, died intestate before 30 January 1740/1, the date of her father's Will above quoted, and she was the administratrix of the former and the executrix of the latter estate.[5] By John Roades she had the two sons named above, Hinman and John, who were still minors in 1748 when the Orphans Court appointed Nehmiah Field and Jacob Phillips as their guardians.[6] Hinman Roades died without issue in 1754,[7] and John Roades the younger married on 22 February 1763 Elon (Helen) McIlvaine,[1] and died from " consumption from strong drink," [1] and was buried 6 November 1768, leaving one son Hinman Roades.[8] The widow Elon Roades married David Hazzard and had further issue;[9] she died, and was buried 5 March 1793.[1] See Bible records, *postea*.[18]

The surname Roades is found variously spelled in the public records as Roots, Roads, Roades, Rhoads, and Rhodes. John Roades Sr., the first husband named above, was a grandson of John Roads, a Judge of the early Court in Sussex County, and great grandson of Dr. Jan Roots, also a judge, who came from England prior to 1664, first to Virginia, and later to Maryland, moving to Delaware by 1671, where he perished in the burning of the Whorekill in 1673.[10]

Naomi Hinman Roades married secondly Capt. William Fasset, or Fassit, of Worcester County, Maryland, by 1743, in which year Nehemiah Field complained to the Orphans Court that " Ye widow and administratrix of ye said John Roades was now married to Capt. Fassit of Worcester County, Maryland, and removed there without securing the portion and estates due to Hinman Roads and John Roads, minors and

1

children of the aforesaid John Roades and grandchildren of Richard Hinman decd." [11]

Mary Fassit, daughter of Capt. William and Naomi (Hinman-Roades) Fassit, was born after her father's death in 1744/5. In his Will dated 14 December 1744 and proved 26 January 1745, William Fassit listed his children, presumably by a former marriage, his wife Naomi and the " child she bears." The executors were the wife Naomi and testator's brother Rouse Fassit.[12] On 3 March 1763 Mary Fassit married WILLIAM THOMPSON and had issue, Margaret, James, Naomi, and William Thompson.[1] Mary (Fassit) Thompson was buried 18 February 1775, and her husband William Thompson on 13 November 1809, " an aged rich man in this world's goods." [1]

Naomi Hinman Roades Fassit married thirdly THOMAS LAYFIELD in 1745-1747. Their only child Thomas Layfield Jr. died unmarried and was buried 3 April 1774, the funeral being held " at William Thompson's, Rehoboth." [1]

Naomi Hinman Roades Fasset Layfield married fourthly, by July 1748, CAPTAIN JOHN NEWBOLD of Worcester County, Maryland, on which date he, describing himself as " intermarried with Naomi Layfield, one of the executors of the estate of William Fasset, decd.," petitioned the Orphans Court to settle the distribution of the estates of John Roades Sr. and Jr., Richard Hinman, and William Fasset.[13] Capt. John Newbold and Wife Naomi had two sons, James and Francis Newbold,[7] of whom Francis died unmarried in 1771,[1] and James married Hannah Jacobs who died in 1825,[1] himself died intestate on 25 August 1831 leaving " no widow or children." His heirs were the heirs of his half-brother John Roads Jr. and of his half-sister Mary Thompson.[14] No record of Capt. John Newbold's death has been found.

Naomi Hinman Roades, Fasset, Layfield, Newbold, as the " Widow Newbold ", married fifthly on 12 March 1761 ROBERT SHANKLAND.[1] This marriage was brief, as her husband was deceased by 4 August 1761, on which date a Deed passed between the Administrators of Capt. John Newbold decd. to Peter Marsh, in which a recital of title mentions " Naomi Shankland, widow of Robert Shankland and formerly widow of Capt. John Newbold," and refers to the settlement of the accounts of the Newbold estate in the Orphans Court of 5 February 1761.[15]

Naomi Hinman Roades, Fasset, Layfield, Newbold, Shankland, married sixthly THOMAS WARRINGTON, and he was appointed the administrator on the estate of her minor son Francis Newbold, in the record of which it is stated that " The said Naomi afterwards intermarried with the said Thomas Warrington." [16] Record of this marriage has not been found. But there was evidently one child of this final union, Naomi, who is named as "sister Naomi Warrington" in the Will of John Roads Jr., dated 24 November 1768 and proved 11 February 1769.[17] This child may have died young, as she is not listed with the heirs in the Petition made to the Orphans Court of 12 May 1773 in the continued settlement of the estate of John Roades Sr., the first husband of Naomi the subject hereof. It is interesting to notice, in conclusion, that her grandson Hinman Roads, son of John and Elon (McIlvaine) Roads, married on 13 June 1787, Margaret Thompson,[1] her grand-daughter, daughter of William and Mary (Fassit) Thompson, abovesaid.

References:

[1] Records of the United Presbyterian Churches of Lewes, Indian River, and Cool Spring in custody of the Lewes Presbyterian Church. (A transcript is in the collections of the Genealogical Society of Penna., Phila.)

[2] Richard Hinman was the son of Richard and Mary (Avery) Hinman. The latter was daughter of Capt. John Avery, and she married firstly Hercules Shepheard.

[3] Minutes of the Vestry beginning 1731, St. Peter's Church, Lewes.

[4] Sussex County, Del., Will Book A, page 373.

[5] Sussex County Orphans Court Book 1728-1744, pages 136 and 145, in Delaware State Archives, Dover, Del.

[6] Ibid. 1744-1751, page 57.

[7] Ibid. Book A, pages 131-134, at the Court House, Georgetown, Del.

[8] Sussex County, Del., Will Book B, page 373, at the Court House supra.

[9] Volume A-75, page 53, of Wills, in Delaware State Archives, supra.

[10] Pennsylvania Magazine of History and Biography, October 1950, page 477.

[11] Sussex County Orphans Court Book 1728-1744, page 145, in Archives, supra.

[12] Volume A-71, page 57, of Wills, in Archives, supra.

[13] Sussex County Orphans Court Book 1744-1751, pages 54-55, supra.

[14] Ibid., Book Q, page 28, at the Court House, supra.

[15] Sussex County Deed Book I, page 338, ditto.

[16] Sussex County Orphans Court Book A, page 84, at the Court House, supra.

[17] Sussex County Will Book B, page 373, at the Court House, supra.

[18] Family records from a Bible printed and published by M. Carey & Son, no. 126 Chestnut Street, Philadelphia, 1821, and quoted here by the courtesy of the present owners, Mr. Thomas P. Hazzard and his sister Miss Penelope Hazzard of Lewes, Delaware:

John A. Marsh & Lydia Ann was married November 28th 1848.
David Hazzard, son of Cord & Rachel Hazzard, was born May ye 13th A.D. 1749.
Elon McIlvain, daughter of Andrew & Edy McIlvain, was born Sept. 21st A.D. 1746.
Hinmon Roades, son of Jno. & Elon Roades, was born Sept. ye 28th A.D. 1765.

Cord Hazzard, son of David & Elon Hazzard, was born July ye 8th A.D. 1771.

David Hazzard, son of David & Elon Hazzard, was born June ye 4th A.D. 1773.

William Hazzard, son of David & Elon Hazzard, was born June ye 23d A.D. 1775.

James Hazzard, son of David & Elon Hazzard, was born March ye 28th 1778.

John Hazzard, son of David & Elon Hazzard, was born January ye 28th A.D. 1780.

Roades Hazzard, son of David & Elon Hazzard, was born April ye 18th A.D. 1783.

Ebenezer Hazzard, son of David & Elon Hazzard, was born July ye 2nd A.D. 1786.

Cord Hazzard, son of David & Elon Hazzard, died March ye 20th A.D. 1793.

William Hazzard, son of David & Elon Hazzard, died July 6th A.D. 1776.

Roades Hazzard, son of David & Elon Hazzard, died Oct. ye 16th A.D. 1783.

Ebenezer Hazzard, son of David & Elon Hazzard, died Octr. ye 31st A.D. 1786.

David Hazzard, son of Cord and Rachel Hazzard, died about 4 o'clock P.M., July ye 17th in the 42 year of his age A.D. 1790.

John Hazzard, son of David & Elon Hazzard, died February the 20th 1823.

David Hazzard, son of David and Elon his wife, departed this life July 22nd 1842 at 8 o'clock (in the) morning, aged 69 years 1 month 18 days.

Lydia Hazzard, daughter of Marnex and Lydia Virden, departed this life March 3rd 1848.

The Family of Thomas Holme

MARY IRMA CORCORAN *

IN VIEW of the continuing interest in Thomas Holme and the general confusion concerning his background and family relationships, it seems appropriate at this time to bring together in one article whatever documents regarding his forebears and immediate family are currently available.

At the time of Thomas's birth at the Waterhead at Monk Coniston in upper Lancashire,[1] the name Holme was widely dispersed from Yorkshire to Scotland, through Westmorland, Lancashire and Cheshire. It appeared in various spellings — Holme, Holmes, Hulme, Hume — but probably all of the Lancashire families of the name had a common ancestor in the John of Stockholm who is said to have received a large tract of land in Yorkshire as a reward for his part in William's conquest of England. According to legend, one of his descendants ran afoul of John Lackland and fled to the secluded valley of Mardale beside Hawes Water in Westmorland.[2] All of this is plausible but conjectural. The earliest records of the parish of Shap,[3] which originally included Mardale, yield many Christian names that reappear in the records of the not-far-distant parish of Hawkshead to the southwest in northernmost

---

* Sister Mary Irma Corcoran, a descendant of the Holme and Whitaker families of Philadelphia, is a professor of English at Mundelein College, Chicago. This article is based upon some of the materials collected at home and abroad for the life of Thomas Holme upon which she is currently engaged. Her research was made possible by a fellowship from the American Association of University Women and a grant from the American Philosophical Society.

[1] The revealing clues to the parentage of Thomas Holme and his wife, his birth and marriage, are in his personal record in the manuscript volume, Wexford Registers of Births, Marriages, and Deaths, 1640-1720, (F. 1), Item 2, Friends' Library, Dublin.

[2] J. Whiteside, "The Holmes of Mardale," *Transactions of the Cumberland-Westmorland Archeological Society*, N.S., II (1902), 143.

[3] These records are unpublished, but have been microfilmed.

Lancashire: William, George, Christopher, Reginald, Thomas, Agnes, Ann, Isabella, Ellen.

The earliest unmistakable evidence concerning Thomas Holme's family commences late in the reign of Queen Elizabeth I with two wills preserved in the County Library of Lancashire at Preston: those of his great-grandfathers, Michael Holme and Myles Sawrey. Michael Holme, by his will, dated 13 March 1598, left to his son George all his tenements and other property at Yewdall with the rent of Mr. Fleming, the almshouse, his interests in Skellwith Bridge, the "great arke," [4] and, to be shared with George's mother Agnes, all the meal in it. His brothers-in-law shared in two corn mills and, among other beneficiaries, his father's man David was remembered, receiving the pair of blue breeches — all-in-all, a considerable estate. Michael Holme was buried at Hawkshead, according to the parish record, on 20 February 1600.[5]

One of Michael's executors was Myles Sawrey, father-in-law of Michael's son George. Sawrey was a member of a substantial mining family who employed full or part time many of their neighbors to work in the iron mills, or fell and cut wood that fired the furnaces where the ore was smelted.[6] Myles outlived his son-in-law George Holme by ten years,[7] but he was solicitous for his grandchildren. His will, dated 24 August 1613, is an impressive document engrossed on vellum. In it he bequeathed to his sons William and Henry Sawrey tenements and farmholds at the Waterhead and elsewhere in the parish of Hawkshead, together with grounds in "farre Coniston" on the opposite side of Coniston Water, as well as sundry other properties. He left cash legacies to the children of Robert Jopson and Richard Hodgson, as well as to Elsabeth Holme, daughter of George, "wch I am grandfather unto," to Mabel Holme, her sister, and "lykewise to George Holme there brother [8] ...." A supervisor of his will was his "welbeloved in Christ Mr Edwyn Sands," probably, it would appear from the Hawkshead registers, a nephew of

---

[4] An obsolete term for a large chest or coffer.

[5] H. S. Cowper, ed., *The Oldest Register Book of the Parish of Hawkshead in Lancashire, 1568-1704* (London, 1897), 94. The baptisms, marriages and burials in these registers are listed by years, each year beginning 25 March or later, under the Julian calendar and ending no later than the following 25 March. Since the historical year actually began 1 January, the dates in these records between 1 January and 25 March need to be double-dated. Thus, the burial of Michael Holme actually was in 1601 (1600/1). The wife of Michael Holme was bur. 11 October 1607, "in the church." *Ibid.*, 109.

[6] This and other information about the Sawrey family was communicated to the writer by a local driver and business man in the Lake District.

[7] According to the *Hawkshead Register*, 126, cited above, Myles Sawrey was bur. "in the church" 12 October 1613.

[8] George Holme was bapt. 16 April 1592, Elsabeth on 29 March 1593, and Mabel on 24 March 1599 [/1600], according to *Hawkshead Register*, 70, 74, 93.

6

the Bishop Sands who founded the Hawkshead grammar school. From the will of Myles' son, William Sawrey, we know that Richard Hodgson and Robert Jopson were the husbands of Ellen and Mabel Sawrey.

According to the Hawkshead register, George Holme, son of Michael, was baptized 7 March 1568.[9] He married Ann Sawrey on 26 August 1586, when they both were only seventeen years old.[10] They had been married only sixteen years when his will was written on 2 December 1602, and he died five months later. His burial record identifies him as George Holme of Waterhead,[11] a distinguishing title sometimes applied to his son George (second of the name), to whom he willed property inherited from his own father, Michael Holme. This included the tenement and farmhold at Yewdall, and the rent of his tenement and farmhold at Waterhead when young George should arrive at the age of twenty-one. After he had attained his majority, he was to render their shares to his three sisters, Agnes,[12] Elsabeth and Mabel, when they reached twenty-one or married. Other legatees in the will of George Holme of Waterhead were his wife Ann (Sawrey) and miscellaneous relatives and friends.

George's widow Ann seems to have remarried within the year; there is no record of the death of an Ann Holme or of the widow of George Holme. An Ann Holme, not otherwise accounted for in the Hawkshead registers, married one William Middlefall on 27 November 1603,[13] exactly six months after the inventory of George Holme's estate was made.

George, son of George Holme of Waterhead, came of age in April, 1613. On the following 18 May he married Alice Whitesyde, according to the parish register of Coniston.[14] His sisters' marriages, in the autumn of the same year, were entered in the Hawkshead register.[15]

Just where young George Holme met his bride is not known. She may have been the daughter of William Whiteside of Poulton, the Alice whose baptism is recorded in the Poulton-le-Fylde register as hav-

[9] Actually 1568/9; it was entered at the end of the entries for the year 1568, the same year the register was opened. *Ibid.*, 2.

[10] She was bapt. 29 April 1569. *Ibid.*, 4, 56.

[11] He was bur. 10 May 1603. *Ibid.*, 100. George's will, like those of his father and father-in-law, is in the County Library at Preston.

[12] Agnes's baptism is not found in the *Hawkshead Register*.

[13] *Ibid.*, 102.

[14] The Rev. Hector Maclean and Henry Brierly, eds., "The Registers of the Parish Church of Coniston, Lancashire. Christenings, Burials and Weddings, 1599-1700," *Lancashire Parish Register Society* (Wigan, 1907), Vol. XXX, 42. These records contain entries supplementing those in the Hawkshead register.

[15] *Hawkshead Register*, 127.

ing taken place on 21 April 1598.[16] The Whiteside name does not occur in either Hawkshead or Coniston registers prior to this date, but does appear frequently in the Poulton register. George and Alice Holme's son Thomas identifies his parents only as George and Alice Holme of the Waterhead at Monk Coniston.

Two unmistakable offspring of George and Alice are known: Thomas, son of George Holme of Waterhead, baptized at Coniston 3 November 1624, and Mary, daughter of George Holme of Waterhead, baptized at Hawkshead 13 September 1627.[17] The identification of other children is complicated by the existence of at least two other George Holmes within the parish of Hawkshead.[18] All one can do is list, as possible siblings of Thomas Holme and his sister Mary, those children of a George Holme not identified with any specific locale, whose baptisms were entered in the Hawkshead register between 1614 and 1630. These were, with the dates of their baptisms:

> Ealse, 20 April 1614
> William, 29 June 1615
> Agnes, 26 May 1616
> Agnes, 8 March 1617 [/18]
> Michael, 9 December 1618
> Elsabeth, 22 July 1621
> Christopher, 27 August 1626
> Michael, 27 October 1628
> Agnes, 20 March 1630 [/31]

During this same period, the only offspring of a George Holme whose burial is recorded at Hawkshead was John, son of a George, who was buried 7 June 1618. The repetition of names — three Agneses and two Michaels — with no record of the burial of any of them intervening between their baptisms, suggests that at least three families are represented in the list. This is further born out by the burial in Hawkshead church on 5 March 1623, of a George Holme, tanner (of Coulthouse) ; the burial "in templo" on 27 December 1630, of George Holme of the Waterhead, and the burial "in the church" on the following 17

---

[16] Wm. Edward Robinson, ed., "The Registers of the Parish Church of Poulton-le-Fylde," *Lancashire Parish Register Society* (Wigan, 1907), Vol. XIX, 14. Poulton is about three miles inland from Blackpool on the west coast of Lancashire, due south of Hawkshead and across Morecombe Bay.

[17] *Coniston Register*, cited above, 7; *Hawkshead Register*, 165. In the latter register there are only five entries for 1624; presumably there was no one available for the baptism there, and hence Thomas's baptism at Coniston.

[18] A George Holme and Elsabeth Banke were m. 24 September 1614, and a George Holme and Margaret Rooke were m. 12 December 1619, according to the *Hawkshead Register*, 130, 144. The identity of the wife of one of these George Holmes, who was buried in the Hawkshead church on 5 April 1618, has not been established.

January 1630[/31] of a George Holme, not otherwise identified.[19] Of these three, George of the Waterhead is undoubtedly the father of Thomas and Mary. Of his other children, the most·certain name among the possible siblings of Thomas and Mary for the present record is Michael, of whom more will be said later.

Between Thomas Holme's baptism at Coniston in 1624, at the age of three days, and his marriage on 5 August 1649, to Sarah Croft of Tewkesbury in Gloucestershire, we have no datable information about the career of the future Surveyor General of Pennsylvania. But during this period two events important to his life occurred: England was involved in two civil wars between 1642 and 1648, and a young man named George Fox was beginning to draw large crowds to hear sermons of overwhelming simplicity and conviction. Both events displaced large numbers of people and split families, in the one case, between King and Parliament, in the other, between the Established Church and the religiously disestablished, of whom Fox's group soon would begin to be called "Quakers" in derision.

We know that Thomas Holme was in the Parliamentary army before 1649, since he described himself that year as being a member "of the English Army," a technical term used to denote an army of veterans. Very probably he was in a group garrisoned at Tewkesbury, for it was there that he married in 1649 the daughter of William and Maudlin Croft. The marriage of these parents-in-law, William Crafte (also written Crofte) and Maudlin White on 13 June 1613, was recorded in the Registers of Tewkesbury Abbey, Volume II, now in Shire Hall, Gloucester. Other than Thomas Holme's own record in the Wexford Friends' Registry at Dublin, there seems to be no record of his marriage to Sarah Croft. A book containing such may have been lost in one of a number of accidents that befell the Tewkesbury registers or, conceivably, it may have been performed privately according to an independent ritual and so not registered in the books of the Established Church.

A month after their marriage, Thomas, as "a member of the English Army," and his wife Sarah went to Ireland where, between 1651 and 1665, eight of their ten children were born. The first, Thomas's namesake, was born in Tewkesbury in 1651, where it would seem that Thomas had sent Sarah home to her family to preserve her from the dangers of embattled Limerick, where he presumably was stationed. No doubt she had been with him up to this time, both for

---

[19] *Ibid.*, 157, 175.

9

companionship and because the wives of soldiers were encouraged to accompany them in order to help care for the sick and wounded. The next three, Sarah (1653), Hester (1654), and Mary (1656), were all born in Limerick where their parents continued to live in the interval between the end of the war and the establishment of veterans on Irish land. The next two, Susanna in 1657, and Samuel in 1658, were both born at the family's first home in County Wexford — Dungiar, as their father wrote it — across Ireland on the east coast. Elinor, the seventh child, was born in Tewkesbury in 1659. Since the later children, Hester (second of the name) in 1661, Tryall in 1663, and William in 1665, were all born in a new home in Wexford, Brigurteen, the change of residence may have been the reason for Sarah's return to England for Elinor's birth.

Of these children, five died in Ireland: the first Hester and Mary in infancy, Hester at fifteen months and Mary at five months. Thomas died aged seventeen, Susanna at fourteen, and Samuel, at seventeen, shortly after the death of his mother in 1676. The first two burials were in Limerick, the others "in the burial place of the people of God at Corlecane," [20] a peaceful circular plot enclosed by a moat and earthenwork, shaded by myrtle, not far from the road down which the army had come from Dublin to Wexford.

Of the surviving children, Sarah, the second child and eldest daughter, married Richard Holcomb of Dulverton, Somersetshire, and went back to England with him. [21] The remaining children, the second Esther, as she was known in Pennsylvania, Elinor, Tryall and William, all accompanied their father to Pennsylvania on the *Amity* in 1682. They constituted the family for whose entertainment during their first six months' residence Thomas Fairman billed William Penn after the death of Thomas Holme. [22] The subsequent history of the two daughters is well known. Soon after her arrival Esther married Silas Crispin,

---

[20] The births and burials of Thomas Holme's children and wife are from his personal record in the Wexford Registry, noted above.

[21] The births of two children of Richard and Sarah Holcomb are entered in the records of Bristol and Somerset Meetings; Susannah b. 25 4m 1673, and Richard, b. 5 5m 1675. They belonged to the Withill and "Dilverton" Meeting, in the Western Division of Somerset. Neither the death of Sarah nor of her husband has been found. Abstracts of Records of the Quarterly Meeting of Bristol and Somerset, Marriages and Births, 122, in Collections of the Genealogical Society of Pennsylvania. This corrects and supplements the account by Richard C. Holcomb, "The Descendants of Sarah Holme," *The Pennsylvania Magazine of History and Biography (PMHB)*, XLIV (1920), 158-169, and *ibid.*, XLVII (1923), 277. There may have been other children of Richard and Sarah Holcomb, as indicated in a letter from one Richard Holcomb, written in 1734, who claimed to be the only child of his father who was the "eldest son" of his grandfather who had married Sarah Holme. See M. Jackson Crispin Mss, Am.04851, Historical Society of Pennsylvania (HSP).✻

[22] Recited in Philadelphia Deed Book D-13, 474, Department of Records, City Hall: 10 December 1713, Release of Thomas Fairman: "to Lodging Captn Holme his two Sons & two Daughters with their and other Friends Accomodation in the Proprietaries Service, £50."

✻The article on Sarah Holmes' descendants is reprinted in *Genealogies of Pennsylvania Families: From The Pennsylvania Magazine of History and Biography* (Baltimore: Genealogical Publishing Co., Inc., 1981), 434-446.

son of the deceased William Crispin whom Penn had hoped would be his Chief Justice. Various accounts of her descendants have been published,[23] and further information is included in the volumes of Crispiniana in the Collections of the Genealogical Society of Pennsylvania. Elinor Holme, Esther's sister, married Joseph Moss, was widowed in 1687, and later married Joseph Smallwood.

Tryall and William Holme are not so well known. Both seem to have been employed as assistants to their father. The meager evidence that has so far come to light in support of Tryall's position consists of his signature on a few documents, notably Indian deeds of 7 4m (June) 1684, and of 30 5m (July) 1685; a somewhat rough sketch of a field map, apparently made in 1684, of three adjoining properties near Concord in Chester County, and a page of doodling.[24] Below the map is a cryptic comment signed by Deputy Surveyor Robert Longshore: "Tryall Holme Concordance of Neighbors in good design is a thing commendable."

In 1684, five hundred acres of land in Dublin Township, Philadelphia County, were laid out and surveyed "unto Richard Corsley for the use of Tryall Holme." The following year one thousand acres were surveyed and laid out for Tryall adjoining lands of William Stanley and Nicholas More in Philadelphia County.[25] In 1701, however, when Silas Crispin was attempting to close his father-in-law's estate, he found no record of a regular return into the Secretary's office of the 500-acre tract. He requested Penn to order a return made into the Secretary's office, and to permit the sale of the tract, with all of which Penn promptly complied.[26] Since Tryall took no part in the transaction, was not mentioned in his father's will, and was not referred to as either "late" or "deceased," it is possible that he was still alive but absent.

One more reference to Tryall in relation to his father concerns an incident that must have been somewhat embarrassing to the Surveyor General when he learned of it. On the "1ᵗʰ 3ᵈ day in yᵉ first

[23] See for example, Oliver Hough, "Captain Holme, Surveyor General of Pennsylvania and Provincial Councillor," *PMHB*, XIX (1895), 413 and *ibid.*, XX (1896), 128, *passim.*

[24] *Pennsylvania Archives* [1st Series (1852)], I, 92, 93; Old Rights Book D-85, 80, 101ᵛ, Land Office, Department of Internal Affairs, Harrisburg, Pa. Tryall also witnessed the conveyance by his father of 80 acres of Liberty Land to Nicholas More, for which see Philadelphia Deed Book E-1-5, 134: 3 9m (November) 1685, Thomas Holme to Nicholas More.

[25] Warrants and Surveys of the Province of Pennsylvania including the Three Lower Counties, I, 439; III, 516, Municipal Archives, City Hall, Philadelphia. Corsley's name is variously given in the records as Corslett, Croslet, Crosley and Crosby.

[26] Old Rights Book D-85, 4, 14, 16, cited in Note 24. For Crispin's sale of the 500 acres, in which recital no mention is made of Tryall, see *Pennsylvania Archives*, 2nd Series, XIX, 301, 332.

weeke in ye 7th month 1690," at Chester County Court, Thomas Holme, by his attornies, Charles Pickering and Patrick Robinson, brought suit against Charles Ashcom, deputy surveyor for Chester County, for withheld fees due Holme amounting to some £205, of which only four pounds had been received. In the course of the testimony, Ashcom produced a receipt for four pounds which Tryall at some past date had borrowed from him and never repaid.[27] Where Tryall was at the time was not disclosed, nor is there any further record of him. He may have disappeared into the interior of the Province, gone to sea, or returned to Ireland or England. Perhaps he was disowned by his father, if he did not die in Thomas's lifetime.

William Holme, Thomas's youngest son, appears to have served even more briefly than his brother in their father's office, entering documents with the careful notation, "Intra. *per* Wm. Holme."[28] It was he, seemingly the more responsible of the two sons, who was the first to die, just eight months past his eighteenth birthday. In the Wexford Friends' Register is the record that William, son of Thomas and Sarah Holme, died in Philadelphia on 8 9m (November) 1683. Whether his father was bitter or merely brusque in his reference to the event in a letter to William Penn on the day of the funeral, it is hard to say. He wrote, "Governour — Please to excuse my further attendance on thee ^{to}day [*sic*] 3. ^{a}clock one hour hence this afternoon, Being appointed for ye buriall of my son's corps."[29]

The identification of Thomas Holme's sons leaves a Michael Holme still to be accounted for. Some relationship to Thomas is strongly suggested by his signature as witness to the will of Joseph Moss, Thomas's son-in-law.[30] Beyond this, nothing pertaining to him has been found in the public domain in America. However, other items draw him into a narrower circle of probability as a brother of Thomas. Two refer to the latter's position in Ireland.

Two years after the restoration of Charles II, on 11 November 1662, from Dublin Castle, Captain Michael Holme[31] addressed a peti-

---

[27] *Record of the Courts of Chester County, Pennsylvania, 1681-1697* (Philadelphia, 1910), 92, 214, 215, 217.

[28] See for example, Thomas Holme's orders to Thomas Fairman and Charles Ashcom to survey land, in Albert Cook Myers Collection, Penn Papers, Vol. 59, 144, 165, 183; Vol. 62A, 97, Chester County Historical Society, West Chester, Pa.

[29] Penn Manuscripts, 4, Friends' Library, London. The identification of William as Thomas Holme's son thus corrects the account in *PMHB*, XX, 251, cited in Note 23.

[30] Philadelphia Will Book A, 71, #35:1687, will of Joseph Moss.

[31] He hardly seems to be identical with the Michael Holme who received three months pay — £8 8s. — as a private in Col. Daniel Redman's troop on the musters of 7 May, 4 June, and 2 July 1662. Historical Manuscripts Commission, *Calendar of the Manuscripts of the Marquess of Ormonde, K.P., Preserved at Kilkenny Castle*, New Series, III (London, 1904), 419.

tion to James, Duke of Ormonde, Governor of Ireland. In view of faithful service to "His late Ma^te in England and his Ma^te y^t now is wth yor Grace in this Kingdome beyond Seas after the yeare 1650," and the lack of subsistence for his servant and his poor wife since his discharge from the army on 17 July of that year, he prayed that he be granted the Duke's particular warrant "to receive the seasonable comfitt of his and his servants stated arrears out of his Ma^tis Treasury at Dublin or by way of Assignment on his brother in the County of Wexford . . ." until re-employment in the King's service.[32] Ormonde ordered an examination of Michael's claim. Then on 10 March 1664, Michael Holme was admitted as Captain-Lieutenant to Lord Caulfield's troop.[33] The signature to the 1662 petition to Ormonde and that of the witness "Michaell Holme" on Moss's will in 1687, are beyond any reasonable doubt by the same hand. Moreover, meticulous records of residents in Ireland were kept during this period and, although the original registers perished by fire, the published volumes containing the Deputy Keeper's copies are available. Thomas Holme was the only land holder of the name residing in Wexford at that time.[34]

That a troublesome brother of Thomas years later haunted his erstwhile home in Wexford is attested in a letter which John Tottenham, the friend who looked after Thomas's Irish interests, sent to Thomas in London in 1692. "I find thy Brother," Tottenham wrote, "a great plague to thee," from which he went on to many discreditable details.[35]

Thomas Holme died between the time his will was written on "10th day of 12th month [10 February] 1694/5," when he was "aged full seventie years," and 8 April 1695, when the will was admitted to probate in Philadelphia.[36] It caps the list of recovered documents which set forth, from the beginning of the pertinent parish records in England, his ancestry and family.

---

[32] Manuscript Letters and Papers of James, Duke of Ormonde, Vol. 27, 209, National Library, Dublin.

[33] Historical Manuscripts Commission, *Ninth Report of The Royal Commission on Historical Manuscripts, Part II, Appendix* (London, 1884), 161.

[34] For example, see the entry for "Shelmaleer Barrony, Wexford County, Carrick Parish, Townlands: Bragurteen, 6 people: Thomas Holmes, gent., 2 English, 4 Irish," in Seamus Pender, ed., *A Census of Ireland, circa 1659, with Supplementary Material from the Poll Money Ordinances, 1660-1661* (Dublin, 1939), 542-543.

[35] Society Miscellaneous Papers, Am.3841, 11, HSP.

[36] Philadelphia Will Book A, 308, #123:1695. In his will Thomas Holme left a bequest to one Susanna James, "his niece," who remains unidentified. She may have been the Susanna James, wife of John James, to whom Philip Theodore Lehnmann, Penn's secretary, left 300 acres to be laid out in Pennsylvania, in his will in 1687. Silas Crispin, Elinor Moss, and Thomas Holme were also legatees under Lehnmann's will. Philadelphia Will Book A, 72, #37:1687.

Thomas Holme's Personal Record[37]

Thomas Holme, son of George & Alice Holme of Waterhead, Monk Coniston, in the parish of Haukshead in ffourness fells in Lancashire, born the first of ye 9 mon 1624, & marryed Sarah the daughter of William & Maudlin Craft of Tewksbury in Gloucestershire ye 5th of the 6 month 1649 and came over into Ireland ye 7th month following, a member of the English Army, and by his said wife had these children following, and (for consceince sake) did not suffer any of his said children to be sprinkled or as some call it to be baptized, their being no Scripture for such a practise, but was introduced by the pope & papists or other Apostates, in the right of Apostacy

Births		Where and when	Ano
Thomas	1	Holme the son of the sd Thomas & Sarah Holme was born in ye psh of Tewksbury in Gloucestershire ye 19th of the 4th month	1651
Sarah	2	Holme daughter of the sd Thomas & Sarah Holme was born in Limerick City in Ireland ye 4th of 7 mon	1653
Hester	3	Holme daughter of ye said Thomas & Sarah Holme was born in ye sd Limerick ye 8th of the 12th month	1654
Mary	4	Holme daughter of the said Thomas & Sarah Holme was born in ye sd Limerick ye 29th of 2d month	1656
Susanna	5	Holme daughter of the said Thomas & Sarah Holme was born at Dungiar psh County Wexford 19th 5 mo	1657
Samuel	6	Holme the son of the said Thomas & Sarah Holme was born at Dungiar aforesaid ye 20th of ye 7th month	1658
Elinor	7	Holme daughter of the sd Thomas & Sarah Holme was born at Tewksbury aforesaid ye 26th of ye 7th month	1659
Hester	8	Holme daughter of the sd Thomas & Sarah Holme was born at Brigurteen in Kilbride pish in Wexford Countie 27 2 mon	1661
Tryall	9	Holme son of ye sd Thomas & Sarah Holme was born at Brigurteen aforesaid the 25th 2 mo	1663
William	10	Holme the son of the sd Thomas & Sarah Holme was born at the sd Brigurteen ye 5th of the first month	1665

The Burials of the said family

Burials	When and where	Ano
Hester	Holme daughter of the said Thomas & Sarah Holme deceased ye 10th of 3d mon in Limerick City	1656
Mary	Holme daughter of ye sd Thomas & Sarah Holme deceased in the 7th month in Limerick & there buryed	1656
Thomas	Holme son of the said Thomas & Sarah Holme deceased at Brigurteen in ye County of Wexford on the [blank] day of ye [blank] month & was buryed in the burying place of the people of God at Corlecane	1668

[37] Reproduced here with the kind permission of Mrs. Olive Goodbody, Librarian of Friends' Library, Dublin, from a photo-copy of the Wexford Registry of Births, Marriages and Burials, 1640-1720 (F. 1), Thomas Holme Summary #2, ff 2, 3.

14

Susanna	Holme daughter of the sd Thomas & Sarah Holme deceased at Brigurteen aforsd ye 17th of 6th month & was buried in ye burying place of the people of God at Corlecane	1671
Sarah	Holme the wife of the said Thomas Holme deceased at Brigurteen aforesaid the 30th of the 2d month & was buryed in the burial place of the people of god at Corlecane the first of ye 3d month	1676
Samuel	Holme the son of the said Thomas & Sarah Holme deceased at Brigurteen aforesd the 11th day of the fiveth [?] month & was buried in friends buriall place aforesaid	1676
William	Holme son of the sd Thomas & Sarah Holme deceased at philadelphia pensilvania the 8th day of the ninth month in the year	1683

Thomas Holme's Commission as Surveyor General

To all, whom this may come, and more especially to all such as are or may be concerned as adventurers, Purchasers Planters & Inhabitants in the Province of Pensilvania in America Whereas King Charles the second by his Letters Pattents under the great seal of England for the considerations therein mentioned hath given, granted and confirmed unto me William Penn (by the name of William Penn Esquire son and heir of Sir William Penn deceased) the absolute proprietary of the said Province of Pennsilvania, with ample jurisdictions and powers necessary for the well being ordering and government thereof as by the said Letters Pattents do appeare. Now know ye, that I the said William Penn reposeing special confidence in the Integrity and ability of my Loveing friend Captain Thomas Holme of the City of Waterford in the Kingdom of Ireland, do by these presents elect, empower and establish him the said Thomas Holme in the office, Trust and employment of Surveyor Generall of all the said Province of Pennsilvania for and dureing his Natural life, he behaveing himself honestly and faithfully in the said Office, Trust and employment, Hereby giveing and granting unto the said Thomas Holme full power and Authority to enter into, survey and admeasure, or cause to be entered into, surveyed and admeasured (with all reasonable expedition) all the said Province of Pennsilvania, and all and every parts, Islands and territories thereof, which by the said Letters Pattents do or may of right belong and appertaine unto me my heirs and assignes. And to the end, I the said William Penn as absolute proprietary of the said Province by Letters Pattents aforesaid, may have and obtaine a true and certaine knowledge of the exact quantities of every distinct & individual part and parcell of Land in the said Province that already is or hereafter may be granted and disposed of

15

by me, my heirs and assignes, unto any person or persons whatsoever, and to whom and for what use or purpose soever, the said Thomas Holme as Surveyor Generall, is hereby empowered from time to time to cause all persons employed in the survey, and admeasurement of any part or parcell of land in the said Province, to return a true duplicate of all their originall fieldworks and the protractions and quantities of their operations unto his said office, there to be examined, and tryed, and what there shall be approved of the same, and no other to be fairely entred in the said office and there to remaine upon record as a standing rule, conclusive & binding to me my heirs and assignes as absolute Proprietary and also to all the Adventurers, Purchasers, Planters and Inhabitants concerned in the said Province, in relation to the respective quantities, meers and bounds of their Lands Lotts and holdings. And if any person or persons whatsoever that now are, or hereafter may be concerned, in the said Province shall survey and admeasure or cause to be surveyed and admeasured any part or parcell of Land in order to be taken up and planted without orders & directions from the said Thomas Holme that all such surveys and admeasurements shall by me my heires and Assignes be held and deemed invalid, and no wayes hinder the due disposal thereof. And the said Thomas Holme is to observe such orders and directions about the method of proceeding in the survey and admeasurement of the Lands in the said province, and also of the allottments and distribution thereof, as he shall from time to time receive from me my heirs or assignes, and according to such Concessions as are or may be agreed upon betweene me and the persons concerned in the said Province, And to keep his publique office of Surveyor Generall in the Capitall City or Town in the said Province that so if any difference happen about the quantities, meers or bounds of Lands, the same may be there regulated and composed. And I hereby grant to the said Thomas Holme to take, receive and to his own use enjoy, all and every such profitts and benefits for the Surveys and admeasurements of the said Province, or any part thereof, and keeping his office of Surveyor Generall there as are allowable in the like cases in America. Given under my hand & seal of the province of Pennsilvania this eighteenth day of the second Month one thousand six hundred Eighty two.

/s/ Wm Penn

Recorded y^e 27th of the $\frac{mo}{3}$ 1684 in Patent Book A-1, 7, and transcribed therefrom verbatim ac literatim

JOHN HOLMES, PHILADELPHIA PAPER-MAKER, AND HIS WIFE MARY HOOPER

By WALTER LEE SHEPPARD, JR., F.A.S.G.

Elizabeth Ralph Holmes, born 12 November 1823, prepared two statements of what she knew of her family. The first was written about 1880 for her nephew, Franklin Lawrence Sheppard:

Mary Hooper, born May 7, 1790, in Tiverton, Devonshire, married John Holmes of Mirfield, Yorkshire, August 1820, at Ainderby Steeple Church. It is near North Allerton, in Yorkshire, England. Sailed for Philadelphia in October 1820. John Holmes died in Philadelphia January 1828.

Her father's name was Robert Hooper. He was killed in an explosion of gunpowder on board a vessel at Plymouth where he had gone to meet a brother who was returning from East India. They were both lost.

Her mother's name was Grace Vinicomb of Tiverton. Mother had two brothers, John who died with a white swelling, and Samuel who was living in London when she left England, and one sister Elizabeth Hooper who married Joseph Ralph who was in the Army and started for India about the time mother left England.

Their grandmother Hooper married for her second husband Abraham Duckham of Tiverton.

Mother had an uncle Tucker, the husband of mother's [grandmother's?] sister all of Tiverton, Devonshire. They had one daughter, Sallie Tucker. I have forgotten her married name.

Mother died April 9, 1879, in Philadelphia; buried in Odd Fellow's Ground, Philadelphia.

The second statement was prepared by Elizabeth Ralph Holmes after 1900 for her nephew, Howard Reynolds Sheppard:

My father's name was John Holmes of Mirfield, Yorkshire, England. His mother's name Elizabeth Barron, her father's name William Barron.

My mother's name, Mary Hooper of Tiverton, Devonshire, England, her father's name, Samuel Hooper. He was lost at sea; his mother for her second husband married a man named Abraham Duckham. On mother's side her name was Grace Vinicomb. Mother had two brothers, John and Samuel, and one sister Elizabeth who married one Joseph Ralph. They went out to India.

Mother and father were married August 1820 in a church called Ainderby Steeple or Enderby Steeple, near North Allerton, Yorkshire, England. Came to America 1820.

Mother had an uncle named Tucker, he had a daughter named Sallie Tucker, can't

17

remember the name of her husband. They lived in Tiverton. Mother's brothers Samuel and John I think went to London to live.

I do not think you can read this as my hand trembles so I can hardly hold the pencil.[1]

With the above information as a starting point, the following account has been assembled, reconstructing the family from substantiating documents.

JOHN HOLMES was born, probably between the years 1792 and 1794, at Mirfield, West Riding of Yorkshire, England, son of John Holmes and his wife Elizabeth Barron, the probable daughter of William Barron. On 8 August 1820, John Holmes "of Leeds," was married at Ainderby Steeple, near North Allerton, Yorkshire, to MARY HOOPER, born at Tiverton, Devonshire, on 7 May 1790, daughter of Robert Hooper and his wife Grace Vinicomb.[2] John and Mary Holmes set sail for America the September following their marriage, and by winter were probably living in Philadelphia. The ship and date of arrival have so far not been discovered.

The Philadelphia City Directory for 1824—the first in which he can be identified—shows John Holmes at 412 North Second Street, Northern Liberties, near the corner of Second and Coats Streets (now Fairmount Avenue), where he had a "paper store."[3] The directories continued to list him at this address, selling "stationary," through 1827, but not in that of 1828, which probably went to press after his death.

Possibly before 1824 he started to manufacture paper, and though the directories do not show him as such, when he joined Masonic Lodge No. 3 in February, 1826, he was called a "paper manufacturer," and was stated to be 34 years old.[4] Little more is known of him. He died either on 11 January 1828, according to the family Bible and the inscription on his tombstone, or on 10 January 1828, "of an inflamatory fever, aged 34," and was buried in St. John's Methodist North Burial Ground sometime "between 5th and 12th January 1828."[5]

---

[1] The writing is quite legible, and is now in the possession of the present author.

[2] The copy of the marriage certificate, in the possession of the author, shows that the ceremony took place at the church of St. Helen, Parish of Ainderby Steeple, and that Mary Hooper was "of this parish." William Hutchinson and Ann Hildereth, the witnesses, both signed the register. For the birth date of Mary Hooper, see the Holmes-Maxwell Bible record, presented following the text, and for the year of birth of John Holmes, the text, *infra*.

[3] In earlier Philadelphia directories, a John Holmes, labourer, is listed. But as the name was a common one, it is not possible to show that he was identical with the John Holmes, formerly "of Leeds."

[4] His membership certificate is in the possession of the author.

[5] St. John's Methodist Cemetery, at "7th and Poplar," was opened in 1817. Part of the cemetery, including the Holmes' lot, was sold in 1858, and the balance of the property in 1864. See Charles R. Barker, A Register of the Burying Grounds of Philadelphia, II, 73, Collections of the Genealogical Society of Pennsylvania (GSP). On 14 Jan. 1857, Elizabeth Ralph Holmes purchased by deed #7244,

John Holmes, "stationer and paper maker," left no will. Letters of administration on his estate were granted 15 January 1828, to his widow Mary Holmes.[6] Sureties for the $32,000 bond posted were James Lupton of 438 N. Treat [Front?] Street, Philadelphia County, Joseph Holmes, grocer, Northern Liberties, Philadelphia County, and the widow Mary Holmes. Separate inventories were taken of his personal and business effects, the latter including materials "at the mill in Delaware County." This mill, and the store and home in Philadelphia apparently were all rented properties since no deeds in either Philadelphia or Delaware County have been found in his name. Efforts to identify the mill have so far been unsuccessful.

The store inventory, dated 12 February 1828, and taken by Isaac Pugh and Joseph McDowell, totalled $5,020.12. It lists a wide variety of paper products and books, including "readers" and "spelling books." The household inventory, made on 4 February 1828, by Daniel Miller and John Engard, totalled $236.62. Since it did not state in which rooms the items were found, the size of the house and the number of rooms remain uncertain. The mill inventory totalling $4,224.87¾, was sworn to on 7 February 1828, by John B. Duckett and Joseph Hall. It included rags of various kinds, lead, starch and other raw materials, as well as a variety of finished paper ranging from fine through sized and glazed to felts and boards. It also included molds, kettles, stoves, wheels, nails, presses, pumps, etc., and would be of interest to students of paper making in this period.

A preliminary account showed payments on immediate debts of $1,356.98, the largest of which was $483.19 to "J. Hall wages for labour at the mill as per bill." Receipts totalled $286.61. The final accounting, submitted 17 December 1828, showed a total estate of $11,276.46, of which $3,573.79 remained for distribution after settlement. Apparently the business was operated chiefly on borrowed money. The bulk of the payments shown were on twenty-two notes held by a num-

---

Lot 189, Section O, in the American Mechanics' Cemetery at 23rd and Diamond Sts., from the Odd Fellows' Cemetery Co., to which the remains of John Holmes and his young son William B. Holmes, according to Mechanics' Cemetery records, were removed in 1856. Their stones, also removed to Mechanics' Cemetery, were transcribed in 1940 by the author: "John Holmes died January 11, 1828 aged 34," and "William B. Holmes son of John and Mary died November 28, 1824 aged 2 years 11 months." For the burial record, see Burial Records, Board of Health, Philadelphia, 29 Dec. 1827–8 March 1828, 50, GSP. In 1950, both Mechanics' and the original ground of the Odd Fellows' Cemetery were closed out to make room for a housing development. All interments were removed to Lawnview Cemetery, Huntington Pike, Fox Chase. The old tombstones were destroyed as the Lawnview rules require that all markers be uniform in size and design and of bronze. The Holmes' graves, now in Glenwood Lawn, Section 54, graves 27, 28 and 29, are now unmarked.

[6] For the letters of administration on the estate of John Holmes, see Philadelphia Administration Book N, 178, #8:1828. Data relating to his estate is from the original papers in the docket. Settlement was accepted by the Court on 20 Feb. 1829, for which see Philadelphia Orphans Court Book 31, 433.

ber of persons. Chief of these was John B. Duckett, who had taken the mill inventory with Joseph Hall. Duckett held about one-third of the notes. He might have been a partner.

No baptisms for the children of John and Mary Holmes have been found, nor has their church affiliation, if any, been established. However, the Holmes-Maxwell family Bible, kept by John Holmes and continued by his widow's second husband, has survived and provides the record of their children, all born in Philadelphia.

Issue of John Holmes by his wife Mary Hooper: [7]

i. WILLIAM B[arron] HOLMES, b. 20 December 1821; d. 27 November 1824. His tombstone gave the date as "November 28, 1824, aged 2 years 11 months."

ii. ELIZABETH RALPH HOLMES, b. 12 November 1823; d. unm. 22 May 1906.[8] She was the author of the two records cited first above.

iii. CAROLINE PRESTON MARY HOLMES, b. 5 February 1826; d. 24 May 1897; m. 5 February 1850, ISAAC APPLIN SHEPPARD, b. 11 July 1827, in Cumberland County, N. J., son of Ephraim and Mary (Westcott) Sheppard; d. at Philadelphia, 6 March 1898; both buried at Laurel Hill Cemetery, as were their children.[9]

After the death of her husband, Mary (Hooper) Holmes apparently continued to operate the store, but not the paper mill. She was listed in the directories from 1829 to 1833 as "Mary Holmes, Bookstore, 416 N. Second." [10] But though she was so listed, she had in fact married a second time. On 3 October 1830, she was married at the Second Baptist Church in Philadelphia by Reverend Thomas J. Kitts to WILLIAM REMINGTON MAXWELL. The marriage record stated they were both of the Northern Liberties, and that the groom was "a Minister of the Gospel of the Baptist denomination," and a member of "N. Market." [11]

---

7 See the Bible record, cited in Note 2 above, photostats of which, and of the Christie Bible, are in GSP. The original Bibles are owned by Mrs. Andrew Jackson of Wynnewood, a Christie descendant.

8 Records of Mechanics' Cemetery give her age as 82½. The inscription on her stone was read in 1940 as "Elizabeth R. Holmes died May 22 1906 aged 83."

9 They had issue: 1. *Applin Holmes Sheppard*, b. 28 Nov. 1850; d. 21 Jan. 1851. 2. *Franklin Lawrence Sheppard*, b. 7 Aug. 1852; d. 14 Feb. 1930, who had issue. 3. *Mary Ball Sheppard*, b. 7 June 1858; d. 2 May 1872, without issue. 4. *Heber Judson Sheppard*, b. 8 June 1863; d. 28 Oct. 1886, without issue. 5. *Howard Reynolds Sheppard*, b. 31 Dec. 1865; d. 24 Dec. 1934, with issue but line extinct. See also the Autobiographical Sketch of Isaac Applin Sheppard, GSP, and the *Vineland Historical Magazine*, Vols. 32, 80, and 31, 28.

10 A Joseph Holmes, perhaps John Holmes' brother, and her fellow bondsman, was first listed in the Philadelphia directory for 1828 as "2nd above Coates," and continued to be so listed through 1833. Neither name appeared in the 1835-6 volume.

11 For the marriage, see *Publications of the Genealogical Society of Pennsylvania* (PGSP), XII, 130, "Marriages of Rev. Thomas J. Kitts," wherein the Baptist Church, of which Mr. Maxwell was a member, is erroneously given as "North Market," properly *New Market* Street Baptist Church, then above Noble Street.

20

Born "about 30 June 1793," at "Haslingden," Lancashire, England, William Maxwell had been married before. His first wife Lydia had died 6 September 1822, at Woodstown, Salem County, N.J. A year later on 20 August 1823, he had married secondly, one Hannah Paul, possibly a widow, who died in Philadelphia 14 June 1829, aged thirty-seven.[12] He had no issue by either wife.

A little over three months after his marriage to the widow Mary Holmes, William Maxwell appeared before the Philadelphia Court of Quarter Sessions on 17 January 1831, presenting his declaration of intent to become a citizen of the United States. In his declaration he stated he had sailed from Liverpool, arriving in the "Port of Philadelphia about 1 September 1821." He was granted his final papers of citizenship by the Philadelphia District Court on 13 May 1832 [1834], "aged 38, in the country 12 Years." His sponsor was his brother Francis Maxwell, who must have been naturalized earlier, although no record of such has been seen.[13]

Although he was a Baptist clergyman, a check of clergy lists has failed to show where he was ordained, or what charges he filled.[14] He appears in many of the city directories, 1876-1879, usually listed as a clergyman, but with no affiliation shown. According to information passed down through the family, in his later years he was without a charge, and apparently was not a well man.

Mary (Hooper) Holmes Maxwell died in Philadelphia 9 April 1879, her second husband, William Remington Maxwell, less than a year later, on 6 January 1880. Both were buried in Mechanics' Cemetery.[15]

[12] A family Bible notation possibly referring to Hannah Paul, reads "Hannah B. Warner, born 6 September 1791 in Philadelphia." William Maxwell's first two marriages are from an outline of a biographical sketch of him, giving dates only, now in the possession of Mrs. Andrew Jackson, for whom see Note 7 above.

[13] The index for Philadelphia District Court Naturalizations gives 1832 as the year in which William Maxwell received his final papers, but the records themselves show it was 1834. Francis Maxwell, William's brother, was born in Haslingen 8 Feb. 1797, and died in Philadelphia 24 Jan. 1838. He may be the Francis Maxwell, weaver, who appeared in the 1830 directory at 489 N. Third St., at which time William R. Maxwell was at "Second near Germantown Rd." A James Hincliffe Maxwell submitted a declaration of intent to the District Court of Philadelphia Co. on 6 Feb. 1828. In this he stated he was born in the county of Lancaster, England about 1 Mar. 1790, and had sailed from Liverpool to New York on 28 May 1820. Sponsored by one Anthony Davis, he was "admitted" by the District Court on 6 Mar. 1830, "aged about 37, resided 5 years." Perhaps he was a relative.

[14] His only known affiliation was with the Odd Fellows' to which order he was admitted in Philadelphia 26 July 1826.

[15] Mechanics' Cemetery records give Mary Maxwell's age as 86 at the time of burial, and William Maxwell's as 87 in 1880, when he was buried. Their stones, however, as read in 1940, stated that "Mary Maxwell died April 9 1879 aged 87," and that "William R. Maxwell died January 6 1880 aged 88." Their son "John H. Maxwell died March 9 1867 aged 36," according to his stone.

Issue of William Remington Maxwell by his 3rd wife Mary
(Hooper) Holmes:

i. JOHN H. MAXWELL, b. 17 September 1831; d. unm. 9 March 1867.

ii. MARY JANE MAXWELL, b. 13 November 1835; d. 2 January 1904; m. 4 June 1866, JAMES CHRISTIE, b. 28 August 1840; d. 24 August 1911, aged 71. He m. 2nd, 10 November 1904, JOSEPHINE JANNEY. He had issue by both wives.[16]

The first probable ancestor of the above-noted Mary (Hooper) Holmes Maxwell appears to be one ROBERT HOOPER, JR., who married at St. Peter's, Tiverton, Devonshire, on 8 August 1720, one AMEY GILL.[17] She was either the Amey Gill, daughter of Francis Gill, baptized at St. Peter's 29 July 1698, or the Amey Gill, daughter of Richard Gill, who was baptized at St. Peter's 15 September 1698. One of these two children was buried 7 November 1707. Robert Hooper, Jr., husband of the one which survived, was buried at St. Peter's on 17 October 1743, and his wife Amey (Gill) Hooper on 21 December 1748. Since probate records at Exeter in Devonshire were destroyed by a direct hit during the bombings in World War II, it is not possible to supplement either the Hooper or Gill lines by wills, and the parish records are by no means complete. Only one child of Robert and Amey Hooper is recorded.

This was HENRY HOOPER, born 28 January, baptized 31 January 1721[1721/2], son of Robert and Amey Gill, at St. Peter's Church. He married MELLONY (or Meller) PIERCY at St. Peter's on 4 July 1742. Neither her baptism nor her death record have been found.[18] Henry Hooper was buried 17 December 1764.

Known Issue of Henry Hooper by his wife Mellony Piercy:

i. ROBERT HOOPER, b. 21 January, bapt. 1 February 1759, at St. Peter's, Tiverton, for whom see below.

---

[16] James Christie's issue by his 1st wife Mary Jane Maxwell, were: 1. *Mary Christie*, b. 28 Mar. 1867; d. 20 Dec. 1881. 2. *Charles Cameron Christie*, b. 1 July 1868; d. 5 Nov. 1868. 3. *Alexander James Christie*, b. 5 Oct. 1869; m. and had issue. 4. *Elizabeth Ralph Christie*, b. 17 Jan. 1872; d. 28 Jan. 1935. 5. *Herbert Maxwell Christie*, b. 27 Oct. 1873; no issue. By his 2nd wife, Josephine Janney, James Christie had issue two children: 6. *Josephine Christie*. 7. *Henry Christie*.

[17] The parish registers of St. Peter's, Tiverton, from which this and following records were extracted, were first searched for Howard Reynolds Sheppard fifty years ago, and have been again examined at the request of the author. The records do not appear to have been well kept during the eighteenth century, and are not complete. Few deaths or burials appear.

[18] From St. Peter's registers, it appears that Joan, daughter of a Humphrey Piercy, was baptized in 1694. No second marriage for Mellony (Piercy) Hooper, presumably the "grandmother Hooper" mentioned by Elizabeth Ralph Holmes, has been found. But St. Peter's registers do show the marriage on 15 Aug. 1795, of "Abraham Duckham of this parish, widower, to Elizabeth Clove of this parish, spinster." Was he the same Abraham Duckham whom Elizabeth R. Holmes claimed married her great-grandmother Hooper?

ii. CHRISTOPHER HOOPER, b. 11 July, bapt. 19 July 1743, at St. Peter's; bur. 3 September 1747.

iii. CHRISTOPHER HOOPER (2nd), b. 13 June, bapt. 13 August 1748, at St. Peter's.

iv. JOHN HOOPER, b. 26 March, bapt. 4 April 1752, at St. Peter's.

v. AB^M (Abraham or Absolom?) HOOPER, b. *ca.* 1764, for whom see below.

ROBERT HOOPER, son of the above-mentioned Henry Hooper and his wife Mellony Piercy, married at St. Peter's, Tiverton, 30 January 1780, GRACE VINICOMB. She was probably the Grace Vinicomb, born 5 December 1752, who was the daughter of William and Elizabeth Vinicomb of the same parish.[19]

Robert Hooper's trade or business is not known, but his younger brother, "Ab^m" according to Admiralty records, entered the Royal Navy as a seaman on 9 July 1793, aged 29, "born in Tiverton." [20] In 1796 he was attached as "Able Seaman," to His Majesty's frigate *Amphion* which had been cruising in the North Sea with Admiral Duncan's squadron, under the command of Captain (later Admiral) Israel Pellew.

On orders to join Admiral Sir Edward Pellew's squadron, *Amphion* put into the Royal dockyard fronting the Hamoaze, an estuary of the Tamar River opposite Plymouth, for refitting and victualling. While she was in harbor many visitors came aboard. On 22 September, a farewell dinner was given by Captain Pellew for his officers and a guest, Captain Swaffield, master of the Dutch ship *Overryssel*, then also in port. On deck, seamen entertained their guests, among whom apparently was Robert Hooper, come to see his brother. In the midst of these festivities, and without any warning, the ship blew up.[21]

"At the moment of the explosion, the signal lieutenant on board the Admiral's ship, which lay a short distance off, happened to be looking at the *Amphion* and described afterwards how he saw her rise out of the

<hr/>

19 William and Elizabeth Vinicomb had another daughter, Ruth, b. 26 June, bapt. 12 July 1747, at St. Peter's. Ruth may have been the sister who married a Tucker, and had a daughter Sallie, but no records have been found to substantiate the supposition. Nor have any baptisms been found for Ruth's and Grace's parents, William and Elizabeth Vinicomb. In an earlier generation, a William Vinicomb had children baptized between 1714 and 1726: Joan, bapt. 1 Jan. 1714; Ann, bapt. 13 Sept. 1717, but no William was found in the registers. The marriage record is also missing. Registers examined for the years 1736-1755, at the request of Mr. Sheppard included, beside those of St. Peter's, those of Uploman, St. Mary's Washfield, Halburton and Bickleigh, with negative reports from all. At Bickleigh, the rector did find the marriage of a John Vinicomb to an Alice Woodbury on 4 Apr. 1754.

20 The author is indebted to Mr. Kenneth Timings of the Public Record Office in London who located this entry in an early muster book of the *Amphion*, for which see the text *infra*.

21 A check with the Lord Mayor of Plymouth has resulted in the initial identification of this occurrence. See also Llewellyn Jewitt, *A History of Plymouth* (London, 1873), 373-375; Henry Francis Whitfeld, *Plymouth and Devonport: In times of War and Peace* (Plymouth, 1900), 202; Charles Bracken, *A History of Plymouth and her Neighbors* (Plymouth, 1934), 214, all of which contain accounts of the tragedy. The quotation in the text was furnished by the Admiralty.

water until her keel was visible. The strangeness of the sight made him feel that he was giddy. The next moment she blew up. The whole fore part of the ship was torn to pieces and the remaining hulk sank directly in about ten fathoms of water.

"Captain Pellew and his first lieutenant were blown out of the windows of the cabin, the captain onto the deck of the sheer hulk (the repair ship close to which *Amphion* was lying), and the lieutenant into the water, whence he was able to swim to shore. Neither was seriously injured. Captain Swaffield was killed." His head had been crushed.

Apparently little or no effect of the explosion was felt ashore, or even aboard nearby vessels, but the loss of life on the *Amphion* was tremendous. Out of a crew of some 220, only 15 men survived, and of the officers, only Captain Pellew and his first lieutenant. The death toll of visitors was never accurately determined, nor was the Court of Enquiry able to fix the blame. The general consensus was that it had been caused by a gunner who, while stealing ammunition, had dropped a match in the magazine.

The pay book of the *Amphion* was recovered, and in it was subsequently entered "Ab^m Hooper, Able Seaman, Discharged Dead on 22 September 1796." [22] According to the parish register of Charles Church, Plymouth, his brother Robert Hooper was buried 4 October 1796.[23] Whether the delay in burial was due to delay in recovering his body, or whether he lingered a few days before dying, is not known.

The burial record of a Grace Hooper of Tiverton appears in the same St. Peter's records under the date of 28 September 1815. Her age, given in the record as 66, places her birth in 1749. If, then, she was indeed Grace Vinicomb, widow of Robert Hooper, her age was in error by three years. No other Grace Hoopers were found.

Issue of Robert Hooper by his wife Grace Vinicomb:

i. JOHN HOOPER, b. 25 July 1781; bapt. 7 September 1783, at St. Peter's, Tiverton; "died with a white swelling."

ii. ELIZABETH HOOPER, b. 28 August, bapt. 7 September 1783, at St. Peter's; m. JOSEPH RALPH, said to be in the British army; went to India between 1815 and 1820.

---

[22] The current muster book was not recovered, but Mr. Timings found this record in the pay book, and kindly supplied the illustration of the explosion accompanying the text. It is from a pamphlet entitled "The Dreadful explosion of His Majesty's frigate *Amphion* . . . September 22, 1796," published by T. Tegg in 1809, and is bound with other accounts of marine disasters in Volume LV, *The Mariners' Magazine*, in the National Maritime Museum, Greenwich, England.

[23] The City Librarian of Plymouth, Mr. W. Best Harris, located this entry for the author in the parish register. He also noted a memorial tablet in the Totnes (Tiverton) Church for "William Harvey Hooper, R.N., Secretary of the Royal Navy Hospital at Greenwich, 2nd son of Thomas Hooper of Totnes. He was at the capture of Java, and made four voyages of discovery in the Polar seas, and died at Paignton, 8 Nov. 1835, aged 41." Perhaps he was a relative.

iii. SAMUEL HOOPER, baptism not found; said to be living in London in 1820.

iv. MARY HOOPER, b. 4 May, bapt. 12 May 1788, at St. Peter's, Tiverton.

This last above-named Mary Hooper may have been the one who married first, John Holmes, as noted above, and second, William R. Maxwell. However, since the family Bible states that Mary Hooper, wife of John Holmes, was born 7 May 1790, it is possible the Mary, born in 1788, was an elder sister who died in infancy. On the other hand, if the Mary, born in 1788, was identical with Mary, wife of John Holmes and William Maxwell, both of whom were younger than she, it would not be unnatural for her to lessen the difference in age by a few years. Whatever the true date of her birth was, there seems little reason to doubt that a Mary, daughter of Robert and Grace (Vinicomb) Hooper of Tiverton, Devonshire, eventually became the wife of John Holmes in Yorkshire. What took her to Yorkshire remains unexplained. Left fatherless before she was ten years old, she may have been bound out as a child. Since she did not marry until she was about thirty, she may have been "in service" with some county family in the West Riding, and there met her future husband.

JOHN HOLMES FAMILY BIBLE RECORD

[Printed by C. Ewer and T. Bedlington, Boston, 1827; now in the possession of Mrs. Andrew Jackson, Wynnewood, Pa. The record, first kept by Mary Hooper, wife of John Holmes, was continued by her second husband, William Remington Maxwell.]

Marriages

John Holmes to Mary Hooper August 8th 1820 at Ainderby Steeple Near North Allerton Yorkshire England

William R. Maxwell to Mary Holmes Octbr 3th 1830 Philadelphia America

Married on the 4th of June 1866 Mary Jane Maxwell Daughter of the Above to James Christie at Pittsburg Pa

Married on the 5th Feby 1850 Caroline P. M. Holmes to Isaac A. Sheppard of Philadelphia Pa.

Births

William B. Holmes Son of John & Mary Holmes was born Decr 20th 1821

Elizabeth R. Holmes Daughter of Jno & Mary Holmes was born Nov 12th 1823

Caroline Preston M. Holmes Daughter of Jno & Mary Holmes was born Feby 5th 1826

John H. Maxwell Son of William R & Mary Maxwell was born Sept 17 1831

Mary Jane Maxwell Daughter of William R & Mary Maxwell was born Novr 13th 1835

Mary Hooper Born May 7th 1793 Tiverton Devonshire in England
Robert Hooper the Father of the above and Grace hir Mother
John & Samuel Hooper Sons of Robt & Grace and Elisabeth Ralph hir Daughter
John Holmes Husband of Mary Hooper was born in Murfield Yorkshire — England

Deaths

William B. Holmes Died Nov 27th 1824

John Holmes Died Jany 11th 1828

John H. Maxwell Son of W R & Mary Maxwell Died March 7th 1867

Died on the 2 May 1872 Mary B. Sheppard Daughter of Isaac A & Caroline M. Sheppard In the 14th year of hir age

Elizabeth Ralph Holmes Daughter of John and Mary Holmes Died May 22nd 1906

Agnes Ashworth Daughter of Francis & Elizabeth Maxwell Died June 24 1836 in Haslingden Lancashire England. She was born 19 June 1791 Haslingden Lancashire England

Francis Son of Francis & Elizabeth Maxwell was Born Feby 8th 1797 in Haslingden, Lanc. England. The above died Jany 24th 1838 in Phil^d North America

Betsey Maxwell Daughter of Francis & Elizabeth Maxwell Died 6 March 1843 — Haslingden England

In Memory of The Late Mrs. Jane Schofield of Haslingden — Lancashire who died Jany 20th 1848 age^d 53 Years Daughter of F & E Maxwell England

THE HUBER-HOOVER FAMILY OF AESCH, SWIT-
ZERLAND AND TRIPPSTADT, PALATINATE.
WITH SOME ACCENT ON MIGRATIONS
TO PENNSYLVANIA.

BY RICARDO W. STAUDT OF BUENOS AIRES.

SOON after *The Story of a Research upon the Origin of the Huber-Hoover Families in the Palatinate* by me, had gone to Press,* Professor Herm. Friedr. Macco of Berlin-Steglitz, discovered that the Huber family, which appears at the end of the 17th century in Trippstadt in the Palatinate, and to which the records published by Mrs. Eula K. Woodward of Washington, D. C. and Miss E. Adele Affleck of Winchester, Virginia, in March 1927,† refer, is not that to which the former President of the United States, Herbert C. Hoover, belongs, and which had emigrated to the Palatinate from Oberkulm in the Canton of Bern. As stated in that article, the greater number of the Swiss emigrants to the Palatinate came from Bern, but there were a few emigrants from the

---

* *National Genealogical Society Quarterly*, Volume XVII, No. 1, March, 1929.

† *Ibid.*, Volume XV, No. 1, March, 1927.

canton of Zürich. In the meantime genealogies of two different Huber families of Swiss origin who emigrated to the Palatinate, one from Bern and one from Zürich, have been completed.

While Prof. Macco has investigated, of his own accord, the former President's ancestry in the canton of Bern as far back as the 13th century, a study which has not been published, I have taken an interest in investigating the ancestors of my great-great-great-grand-mother, Anna Maria Huber, born at Trippstadt, 1711, died at Gemünd / Eifel, 1773, who married in 1730, at Trippstadt, Johann David Staudt. With the help of Prof. Macco I have been able to trace the genealogy of this Huber family of Trippstadt to about the year 1500, in Aesch near Neftenbach, in the canton Zürich.

I am grateful to The Genealogical Society of Pennsylvania for putting at my disposal space in its *Publications* for the German and Swiss ancestry of several colonial emigrants, whose descendants are now spread over the United States. Hereafter only that part of the Huber genealogy in Europe will be given which can be of interest to the American branches. I am sorry to say that I have not been in personal contact with any of these descendants bearing the Huber name. All my efforts in this respect have so far been in vain. Nevertheless, I beg to express the hope that my aim to awaken in America the interest of the Hoover descendants of these Hubers may yet be realized, and that the American part of the genealogy will soon be compiled.

The Name Huber. Families bearing the name of Huber will generally be found to originate from those parts of the German speaking countries where the "Hube" or hufe, was the unit to measure farm land,—i. e. in Southern Germany and the German parts of Switzerland. In Switzerland a "hub" or huob, huebe, used to be a plot of land of about 48 acres. In the middle ages the person possessing and working a "hube" or farm was called "huber" i. e. farmer, and sometimes this characterization became the name of such farmer's family. This explains the relative frequency of the name Huber used by families with no interrelation whatsoever. While this name appears rather often in the eastern cantons, it is not indigenous to the so-called "Urschweiz" (the cantons Schwyz, Uri and Unterwalden), nor in Fribourg and Wallis. Huber families now there have emigrated from other cantons.

In the canton of Bern, especially in the Emmenthal, or Valley of the river Emme, "Hub" or Huob has gradually become a frequent name for fields and there, and in the neighboring cantons especially, the round top of a hill, or place from which a good view can be obtained, is also called a Hub. A site on the Riesberg, about one mile west from Neftenbach, is still called the Hub. Very likely the Hubers of the text obtained this family name because of their residence.

Early Swiss Emigration. For many centuries the soil of Switzerland was not fertile enough to support its increasing population. Thus many of the young males were forced to look abroad for work and food; for instance, serving as lansquenets in foreign armies. But, about the middle fifties of the 17th century, bad harvests caused such a famine in Switzerland that an emigration, the so called "reislaufen" at first but temporary, became permanent. Many of the Swiss who left their country and accepted seasonal work in the neighbouring parts of Germany along the Rhine, (Alsatia, Swabia, the margravate of Baden, Wurttemberg and the Palatinate), settled down, married, and never again returned to Switzerland.

This emigration movement could not be checked, not even by the most severe decrees, which the cantonal authorities issued one after the other, and its importance is often evidenced in contemporaneous parish reports of the canton of Zürich. There the ministers were always emphasizing the failure of crops as reason for the "reislaufen", or emigration, frequently giving quite large lists of parishioners who had moved away.

With due consideration of such reliable documents, it cannot be maintained that religious persecution, so often made responsible for this emigration, was its motivating force. Religious difficulties were, if at all, of rather minor importance, as many Protestants migrating to Catholic communities were there soon converted, just as people moving from Catholic cantons to Protestant ones easily accepted the Protestant faith. Scarcely any difference was made between Lutherans and Calvinists; thus Calvinist Hubers from Neftenbach in canton Zürich became Lutherans after their emigration to Trippstadt in the Palatinate.

Aesch, the Cradle of Hubers of the text. It is a country town 1400 feet above sea level on the south-east side of the

Riesberg, where it slopes towards Wiesenbach Valley. It belongs to the parish of Neftenbach at the end of Wiesenbach Valley, protected by the Riesberg mountain and the Taggenberg and almost touching the valley of the Toess River, which, six miles further down, flows into the Rhine. For many centuries the wine produced from the yield of vineyards on the hills of Neftenbach has been considered the best of the whole district.

The Hubers in Basel. As time went on, all the Hubers moved from their ancestral homesteads at Aesch-Neftenbach; but only the genealogies of the branches at Basel, Switzerland, and Trippstadt, Palatinate, have so far been made matters of investigation. Among the thirty-two persons mentioned in *Lists of Swiss Emigrants in the Eighteenth Century to The American Colonies, Between 1734-1744,* as having left Neftenbach in order to travel to Carolina and Pennsylvania, the name of Huber is recorded only once: Elizabeth Huber, from Neftenbach, who left in 1738, aged 30 years with her husband Gottfried Scherer von der hintere Hub. As several Elisabeth Hubers are recorded in Neftenbach parish register as born in 1708, it has not been possible to identify her.

In Basel, the Hubers produced several eminent business men and scientists. Among the most prominent was the astronomer, John Jacob Huber, 1733-1798, called to Berlin by King Frederic the Great and made a member of the Royal Academy of Sciences. He lived there many years as director of the Potsdam Observatory, returning to Basel with his family after the death of the King. This family has borne, since the 17th century, the following coat of arms: Or, a triple hill vert, in chief a gothic "h" sable. No member of this Huber branch of Basel is recorded as having emigrated to America. Hans Rudolf Huber, son of Dr. Joh. Werner Huber and Marg. Besk, of Basel, who is mentioned in the Faust & Brumbaugh Lists,† as having "left British military service near Halifax in 1754," apparently belongs to a different Huber family.

---

* *Lists of Swiss Emigrants in The Eighteenth Century to The American Colonies, From the State Archives of Bern and Basel, Switzerland.* Compiled and edited by Albert Bernhardt Faust, A.B., Ph.D., and Gaius Marcus Brumbaugh, M.S., M.D., Litt.D. Published by The National Genealogical Society, Washington, D. C., 1920, Volume II, p. 67.

† *Ibid.*, Volume II, p. 208.

The Hubers in Trippstadt, Palatinate. In present times many families bearing the name Huber are living in the Palatinate; the name is especially frequent in the hilly region of the Holzwald, in the district of Kaiserslautern. Nevertheless, before the second half of the 17th century there were no Hubers in the Palatinate. The name of Huber does not appear among those persons recorded in the well-kept minutes of the Protestant Parochial Visitations of the beginning of the 17th century, although these contain exact lists of the inhabitants of the various parishes.*

According to a parish document, a "roedel" from the Latin word rotula, presented † on October 14, 1657, concerning the twenty-one persons belonging to the parish of Neftenbach, who left the country in 1656 and 1657, eleven went to the Palatinate, four left for the "Lutheran", one for the "Catholic" country, and the traces of five were lost. No names are mentioned, but one is certainly correct in assuming that several Hubers joined these emigrants, because, just ten years later, their names appear for the first time in the church register at Trippstadt. The first one entered and recorded as Swiss, is Martin Huber, born at Aesch, August 11, 1639, died at Trippstadt, between 1689 and 1692, the ancestor of the Huber family still flourishing at the latter place. Martin, the sixth of the eleven children of Hans Huber by his wife Barbara Braetscher, is mentioned in the "soul register" of Neftenbach in 1649, but not in the following one of 1670. Furthermore, there is no record whether Martin, before settling in Trippstadt, had first emigrated elsewhere.

Trippstadt is a straggling village situated in the immense leafy woods of Holzwald, six miles south of Kaiserslautern. Its Lutheran parish has existed since the days of the Reformation. On account of the various French invasions, and especially the terrible devastation of the Palatinate by Louis XIV of France in 1688, the parish registers were nearly all destroyed. Thus, the parish register of Trippstadt beginning in 1688 is the first that has been preserved to the present day. However, Engelhard Gillhausen, vicar of Wallhalben, father-in-law of the youngest son of Peter Huber (1726), miller at the Mausmühle, made inquiries in order to obtain an exact

---

* See *Special Number of the Publications of The Genealogical Society of Pennsylvania*, 1930.

† By the Reformed minister of Neftenbach to the Church inspection.

record as far back as 1665. This record contains the baptism of Martin Huber's son, Heinrich Philipp, in January 1666. Furthermore, he undertook to complete the Protestant parish register of his district. When starting, about 1710, a new parish register for the villages belonging to his parish such as Saalstadt, Landstuhl, Wallhalben etc., he tried to obtain statements from old inhabitants for the period before 1710. Therefore, it is to Engelhard Gillhausen that the Huber genealogy in the Palatinate is indebted for its earliest dates.

Contemporary with Martin Huber, were other persons in Trippstadt evidently of Swiss origin, like Buschi, Busi, Buchon, Luddig, Racket, Rochi, while others, like the families May and Stadler of Bern, are especially mentioned in the registers as having come from Switzerland.

The social development of Martin Huber's immediate family concerned not only himself, but his kin, who remained in Switzerland. While his forefathers were free peasants, he became a forester in the service of Baron von Hack, one of the innumerable independent land-noblemen of the old German empire. In later years Martin Huber is also mentioned as mayor of Trippstadt. His sons, as well as many of his descendants, held office under the Barons von Hack; among the latter, Adolf Huber is present mayor of Trippstadt.

When in the 18th century the stream of emigration from the Continent to the North American colonies increased, several Hubers were caught by its force. They all adopted the spelling Hoover, as their name was recorded phonetically by the colonial authorities. Rupp's * indications are often too laconic to provide for identification, while documents dealing with emigration to North America and other over-sea countries are rare in Germany.

Nevertheless, as relates to Huber-Hoovers, absolute identification of several of the arrivals in Philadelphia with those who are either registered in the Palatinate as having left for Pennsylvania, or, who completely disappeared from the Church registers, is beyond question. The documents, passports and manumissions by Freiherr von Hack's Court, pub-

---

* *Names of Foreigners who took the Oath of Allegiance to the Province and State of Pennsylvania 1727-1775, With the Foreign Arrivals, 1786-1808.* Edited by William Henry Egle, M.D., Harrisburg, 1892. *Pennsylvania Archives, Second Series,* Volume XVII.

lished by The National Genealogical Society * clearly show that "Henrich, Johann Nicol, Johann Adam, Johann Philipp and Maria Elizabetha, five children of Johann Konrath Huber, made suitable request for the purchase of freedom from bondage", and "obtained release upon payment of the usual price", in Trippstadt, on May 12, 1767. A passport was . . . granted to them on that date "to journey from there to Holland and further to Pennsylvania". On October 5 of the same year, 1767, on the ship *Sally,* from Rotterdam, John Osman, Master, 116 passengers arrive at Philadelphia, amongst whom "Nickel Huber, Adam Huber and Phillipp Huber" are registered.† Female passengers were never registered, thus no Maria Elizabeth is listed.

Henrich Huber, the eldest brother is also not registered. At an earlier date he had come to Pennsylvania; a discharging certificate to the same Henry Huber states: that he had served in His Majesty's 48th Regiment of Foot three years and eight months, that he was discharged at Fairfield, Connecticut, the 25th day of November, 1758, and that he was twenty-five years of age (he was born December 5, 1732). Therefore, his arrival at Philadelphia, in 1767, was in the nature of a return from his native country to the land of his adoption. Documentary evidence of November 8, 1766, shows that a passport was issued for him by the mayor of Rotterdam for a journey from there to the Palatinate. This voyage to Europe and to the Palatinate had doubtless been caused by the news of the death of his father, Johann Konrath Huber, April 10, 1766, and by the need of his assistance at the distribution of the father's estate. Another passport, issued in Trippstadt on January 29, 1767, states, that "Henry Huber from Pennsylvania had undertaken to travel to his native country to visit his friends and that, after a prolonged sojourn he wished to make a business tour to Baaden-Durlach and other places". Probably only a visit to Gräfenstein and Rothalben was meant, a little county belonging to the Markgraf of Baden and bordering to the south of his native county.

---

* *National Genealogical Society Quarterly,* March 1927, Volume XV, pp. 2-4.

† *Pennsylvania German Pioneers. A Publication of the Original Lists of Arrivals In the Port of Philadelphia From 1727 to 1808.* By Ralph Beaver Strassburger, LL.D. Edited by William John Heinke, LL.D., D.D. In three volumes. Norristown, Pennsylvania, 1934. Volume I, p. 714.

Henry Huber must have remained longer in the Palatinate that he at first intended, always in engaged in settling his father's estate. But finally all these proceedings were finished and when the "Loos-Zettel" (document of inheritance) had been made out by Baron von Hack's Office, on May 12, 1767, every one of the ten children (six from the first marriage and four from the second) and the widow inherited from the estate, which had been estimated as worth: fl. 2522, less liabilities of fl. 341—net fl. 2181, the sum of fl. 195.

Under the same date a passport was granted to the four brothers and the sister who wished to emigrate to Pennsylvania and they immediately set out on their journey. Johann Jacob Kinn, who was to travel together and on the same passport with the Hubers, is also unmentioned in the *Sally's* passenger list. It may therefore be presumed that he, like Henrich Huber, was not arriving for the first time, or that he had either changed his mind and remained in Europe, or perished on the journey, as was then so frequently the fate of the emigrant.

Henrich Huber may well be identified with Johann Heinrich Huber, a passenger on the ship *Isaac,* who together with 206 others, entered the Port of Philadelphia, September 27, 1749;* all designated as protestants from the Palatinate with the exception of five Roman Catholics and one Mennonite.

Three other Huber arrivals can easily be identified as coming from Trippstadt. Two brothers: Johann Adam, born April 14, 1729, arrived August 13, 1750, on the *Edinburgh,* whilst his younger brother Johann, born April 22, 1731, came four years later on the same ship, September 30, 1754. Their father, Johann Jacob Huber, born July 19, 1699, is likely to be the one who arrived August 21, 1750, on the ship *Andersen.†*

It has not yet been possible to prove the genealogical connection between the Huber Family of Trippstadt and Johannes Huber, who is mentioned in 1720-1722 as a miller on the Mausmühle near Thaleischweiler, ten miles east of Zweibrücken. He died as miller on the Weissmühle, near Wallhalben, September 1, 1728, aged 74 years and three weeks, hence born about August 11, 1654. He is recorded as an emigrant from Switzerland, and was probably a close relative,

---

* *Pennsylvania German Pioneers, op. cit.,* Volume I, p. 431.

† *Ibid.,* p. 435.

perhaps cousin of Martin Huber. The genealogy of this branch follows hereafter, as three grandsons of his, George, Daniel and Johann Huber, came on the sailing vessel *Friendship* * and subscribed to the usual oaths in Philadelphia, October 12, 1741. Further descendants in Germany are so far unknown.

With these three Huber brothers, several others of the parish of Thaleischweiler are mentioned as having emigrated to Pennsylvania on the same sailing vessel:

David Dreher, who in one list is named David Dicker (?), 29 years of age, the son of the shoemaker Bernhard Dreher, whose death certificate of 1738 bears his signature. Valentin Hochwarter, whose name in one list was changed into Hohwerder and in another one into Huberter, was married at Thaleischweiler in 1735 and reported in the register as "having gone to Pennsylvania". Jacob Diehl was a son of the assistant judge Peter Diehl of Thaleischweiler. The passenger list Peter Baul, is Peter Bohl, son of Johann Peter Bohl, mentioned in 1732 at Herschberg, near Wallhalben. Jacob Domdeur of Eischweiler, had his name changed on the list into Jacob Dundier.† The foregoing are but a few characteristic names. From other notes in the parish registers of Eischweiler it can be seen that a large number of persons from that parish emigrated to Pennsylvania: Joh. Adam Fischer, born 1720; Anna Maria Allenbach born 1726, emigrated in 1752; Joh. Heinrich Bruder, born 1730, emigrated in 1749; Joh. Martin Zaun, married in 1736; Reinhard Alspach, married in 1737; Heinrich Kiefer, married in 1737, etc. In each case the fact of the emigration is stated by special entry.‡

If the entries of baptisms supplemented by such a "nota" were compared with the lists of passengers who took the Oath of Allegiance, the number of emigrants from the parish of Thaleischweiler would be considerable.

---

* Jurgan Huber, aged 24; Daniel Huber, 22, and Andreas Huber, 20. —*Pennsylvania Archives, Second Series*, Volume XVII, p. 217.

† *Ibid.*, pp. 217-8.

‡ *Cf. Origin of The Hoover Families.* By Ricardo W. Staudt, NATIONAL GENEALOGICAL SOCIETY QUARTERLY, March, 1929.

HANS ? HUBER, born *circa* 1480-1490, ancestor of this Huber family, lived in Aesch,* near Neftenbach, situated in the former County of Kyburg, which now belongs to the canton of Zurich, Switzerland. His christian name cannot be definitely determined; but, as, for several generations, the eldest son in the family was always christened Hans, it is quite probable that this was also his name.

He married *circa* 1518, and had issue, order uncertain:

    i.   HANS,[2] born *circa* 1520. His descendants for five generations remained at Aesch. By about 1700, they had died out, or emigrated.

2. ii.   MARTIN.

    iii. MARGARETHE, born *circa* 1525; mentioned as married.

    iv. MAGDALENA, born *circa* 1530; no further record.

2. MARTIN [2] HUBER (Hans?), born circa 1522; died after 1575; resided at Aesch. He married (1), *circa* 1548, Anna Schmidlin, who is mentioned 1553-1557. He married (2), at Neftenbach, 1 mo. 29, 1559, Agathe Wipf from Seuzach, three miles north-east of Neftenbach; and (3) at Neftenbach 11 mo. 16, 1569, Catharine Schaub.

Children, born in Aesch; baptized in Neftenbach.

    i.   HANS,[3] born *circa* 1550; married Veronica Waser; had four daughters and eight sons, of whom only Martin Huber is recorded as married. The latter was the father of seven children whose descendants are unknown.

    ii. CHRISTIAN, bapt. 1 mo. 10, 1553; no further record.

    iii. CATHARINA, bapt. 10 mo. 21, 1554; probably died young.

    iv. BARBARA, bapt. 12 mo. 8, 1555; married 1 mo. 25, 1575, Martin Fritschi.

    v. VERONIKA (Verena), bapt. 9 mo. 5, 1557; died in infancy.

    vi. FRONEGG, bapt. 6 mo. 1560.†

    vii. MAGDALENA, bapt. 11 mo. 12, 1561.†

    viii. CATHARINE, bapt. 7 mo. 2, 1564; died in infancy.

    ix. CATHARINE, bapt. 8 mo. 5, 1565.†

    x. HEINRICH, bapt. 10 mo. 19, 1567.†

    xi. VERONIKA (Verena), bapt. 8 mo. 20, 1570; married 2 mo. 23, 1589, Christopher Waser.

3. xii. MARTIN, bapt. 3 mo. 2, 1572.

    xiii. ANNA, bapt. 2 mo. 20, 1575; married 7 mo. 17, 1599, Hans Waser of Hünikon.

3. MARTIN [3] HUBER (*Martin,*[2] *Hans?*[1]), baptized at Neftenbach, 3 mo. 2, 1572; died in 1634; resided in Aesch. He married at Neftenbach, 1 mo. 30, 1592, Catharine Erb, from Oberwinterthur near Winterthur.

---

* The little village of Aesch belongs to the parish of Neftenbach, and is situated three and half miles north of Winterthur, and eleven south of Schaffhausen. In former times Aesch was frequently spelled Aisch.

† No further record.

Children, born in Aesch, baptized in Neftenbach:

i. JACOB,[4] bapt. 1 mo. 30, 1593.*
ii. MARTIN, bapt. 4 mo. 13, 1594; was a taylor by trade; went to Basle, where he was admitted to citizenship June 20, 1621. Descendants of his branch are still resident in Basle.
4. iii. HANS, bapt. 9 mo. 21, 1595.
iv. GEORG (Jörg) bapt. 8 mo. 28, 1597; died at Aesch, 3 mo. 23, 1663. Like his brother, Martin, he was taylor. From three marriages, eight children are recorded in the church books of Neftenbach. His male descendants, all taylors by trade, are, for three generations to be found in Neftenbach, after which there is no further record of this branch. As one of Georg Huber's daughters, Anna Huber, born 1638, is recorded as having removed to the Palatinate, it is not unlikely that a Johannes Huber, who appears in the Palatinate is also his son. According to the death record of the latter he was born in Switzerland, in August, 1654. Four of his children went to America.*
v. MORITZ (Mauritius), bapt. 2 mo. 4, 1599.†
vi. ABRAHAM, bapt. 8 mo. 16, 1601; married at Neftenbach, 4 mo. 29, 1628, Anna Waser; had one daughter.
vii. BARBARA, bapt. 12 mo. 26, 1602, married at Neftenbach, 3 mo. 3, 1623, Jacob Brätscher.
viii. VERONIKA (Verena), bapt. 5 mo. 20, 1604; died an infant.
ix. ANNA, bapt. 3 mo. 23, 1606.†
x. VERONIKA, bapt. 5 mo. 23, 1607; married at Neftenbach, 2 mo. 17, 1629, Heinrich Brätscher.

4. HANS [4] HUBER (*Martin,*[3] *Martin,*[2] *Hans* [1]?), baptized at Neftenbach, 9 mo. 21, 1595; died at Aesch, where he was a farmer, 7 mo. 19, 1653; married at Neftenbach, 4 mo. 30, 1627, Barbara Brätscher, born Aesch, 9 mo. 13, 1607; died there, 9 mo. 1, 1662; daughter of Heinrich Brätscher and Barbara Klingen of Aesch.

Children, born in Aesch, baptized in Neftenbach.

i. ANNA,[5] born 1628; died Aesch 1 mo. 5, 1710; married Neftenbach, 5 mo. 2, 1651, Hans Klinger.
ii. HANS JACOB, bapt. 2 mo. 6, 1631; lived on his father's farm in Aesch, where he died 1 mo. 1, 1694, unmarried.
iii. MARTIN, bapt. 8 mo. 26, 1632; died between 1637 and 1643.
iv. JACOB, bapt. 3 mo. 1, 1634; died Aesch, 12 mo. 27, 1715. He was a schoolmaster and inherited his father's farm, where he lived and died. He was twice married and had 5 children; two boys were married; but their descendants are unknown.
v. VERONIKA (Verena), bapt. 8 mo. 21, 1636; living in 1649.
5. vi. MARTIN, bapt. 8 mo. 11, 1639.
vii. HANS HEINRICH, bapt. 4 mo. 16, 1641; died Aesch, 3 mo. 8, 1694. He married in Neftenbach, January 28, 1668, Susanne Ellicker, with whom he had seven children. Three sons married, but their descendants are unknown.
viii. BARBARA, bapt. 3 mo. 5, 1643; mentioned in the Visitation Register of 1649, but no further record.

---

* As to three of his sons on the *Friendship*, cf. page 231.

† No further record.

37

ix. JOHANNES, known as Hans, bapt. 7 mo. 26, 1646; died Aesch,
     2 mo. 21, 1714; was twice married and had five children,
     all by first wife, of whom all seem to have died in their
     nonage.
x.   SUSANNA, bapt. 3 mo. 4, 1649; died in infancy.
xi. ABRAHAM, bapt. 2 mo. 10, 1652; died in infancy.

5. MARTIN [5] HUBER (*Hans*,[4] *Martin*,[3] *Martin*,[2] *Hans?*[1]),
born at Aesch, baptized at Neftenbach 8 mo. 11, 1639; died
at Trippstadt (Palatinate) between 1689 and 1692; married
circa 1664, Katharina . . ., born about 1644; died after 1692,
probably before 1698. In 1683 she was god-mother to Anna
Maria, daughter of Johannes Hopf and Anna Elisabeth from
Gauersheim, near Kirchheimbolanden. In 1692 she is mentioned as widow.

In the Visitation Register of 1649 Martin Huber is mentioned as living with his parents at Aesch. Owing to bad
harvests in the years 1656-60, and the thereby resulting lack
of employment in Switzerland, he emigrated, as did so many
of his countrymen, to the Palatinate. According to a report
by the Reformed Minister of Neftenbach, dated 14th of
October, 1657, which unfortunately gives no names, twenty-
one persons removed from that parish during the years
1656/57; eleven of whom went to the Palatinate.

From about 1665, Martin Huber is recorded in Trippstadt,
formerly belonging to the territory of the Count of Flörsheim.
In 1669 he was manorial forester and in 1683, he is mentioned
as Schultheiss, village mayor, of Trippstadt. The Lutheran
Church Registers of Trippstadt begin in the year 1688, but
in 1725 supplements were compiled for the period 1665-98.

Children, born and baptized in Trippstadt:

i.   HEINRICH PHILIPP,[6] bapt. 1 mo. 14, 1666.*
ii.   JOHANN NIKOLAUS, bapt. 3 mo. 10, 1667; married Anna
      Katharina . . . by whom he had six children. Later on he
      is mentioned as juror in Trippstadt. None of his descend-
      ants are recorded as emigrants to America, and after three
      generations his branch became extinct.
iii. ANNA CHRISTINA, bapt. 12 mo. 27, 1668.*
6. iv. HANS BARTHOLOMAUS, born *circa* 1670.
v.   ANNA MARIA KATHARINA, born *circa* 1671, married 1696
      Nicolaus Wagner.
vi.   ANNA BARBARA, born *circa* 1672; buried before 1 mo. 25, 1711;
      married in 1694, Joh. Jacob Schaaf.
7. vii. JOHANN PHILIPP, born *circa* 1675.
8. viii. CIRIACUS (ZILLIOX, ZILLJACOB), bapt. 12 mo. 24, 1680.
ix.   ANNA MARGARETA, born *circa* 1682; died at Trippstadt,
      10 mo. 4, 1747; married 2 mo. 23, 1700, Hans Philipp
      Schmalenberger.

---

* No further record.

x. JOHANN HEINRICH, bapt. 1 mo. 15, 1683. He is probably the ancestor of the Huber family in Linden, near Thaleischweiler, Palatinate; none of whom are recorded as emigrants to America.

xi. JOHANN ANDREAS, born *circa* 1684, died Trippstadt, 3 mo. 21, 1754; married September 25, 1703, Maria Elisabeth Linden. He was inn-keeper of Zum weissen Schwan, Trippstadt. This inn still exists in the same house which bears his wife's and his name on one of the beams of the woodwork. None of his descendants, who can be traced in Trippstadt for four generations, emigrated to America.

xii. MARIA KATHARINA, born *circa* 1686; died in Trippstadt, 9 mo. 23, 1759; married 1 mo. 30, 1703, Joh. Heinr. Schmalenberger, inn-keeper of the Sheep-Inn in Trippstadt.

xiii. HANS GEORG, bapt. 9 mo. 5, 1688.*

6. HANS [6] BARTHOLOMAUS HUBER (*Martin,*[5] *Hans,*[4] *Martin,*[3] *Martin,*[2] *Hans?*[1]), born at Trippstadt, *circa* 1670; buried there, 7 mo. 24, 1721; was forester in the service of Baron von Hack of Trippstadt. He married, *circa* 1692, Anna Maria ————, born *circa* 1671; died at Trippstadt, 4 mo. 29, 1730, aged fifty-nine years. She married (2) in Trippstadt, 11 mo. 5, 1726, Frederick Knauth, who died before 1730, son of Philipp Knauth (died before 1726), citizen and glazier-master in Halle / Saale.

Children, born and baptized in Trippstadt:

i. JOHANN JACOB,[7] bapt. 5 mo. 21, 1693; died in infancy.

ii. JOHANN PETER, born 9 mo. 30, 1694; died Trippstadt 4 mo. 9, 1758; succeeded his father as forester of Baron von Hack. He was twice married; first to Eva Buschon at Trippstadt, 9 mo. 22, 1722; second, to Maria Margareta Mag, 2 mo. 9, 1745, and had twelve children. None of his issue emigrated to America: descendants of his grandchildren could not be traced.

iii. CLARA ELISABETH, bapt. in the Spring of 1697; married (1) Hans Jacob Buschon; (2) Johannes Feickert.

9. iv. JOHANN JACOB, bapt. 7 mo. 19, 1699.

v. JOHANN GEORG, born 1 mo. 11, 1702; died at Trippstadt, 3 mo. 13, 1778. He was also a forester in the service of Baron von Hack, and is recorded as presbyter. He married Maria Elisabeth Stadler, by whom he had eight children, none of whom emigrated to America. His youngest daughter married Joh. Lorenz Staudt, schoolmaster at Trippstadt.

vi. JOHANN ADAM, bapt. 11 mo. 4, 1703; died 4 mo. 22, 1773; married Maria Magdalena Linn, by whom he had ten children, nearly all dying in infancy. None of his issue emigrated to America. No further record of his grand children has been ascertained.

vii. ANNA KATHARINE, bapt. 7 mo. 17, 1707.

viii. ANNA MARIA, bapt. 12 mo. 13, 1711; died Gemünd / Eifel, 8 mo. 26, 1773; married at Trippstadt, 7 mo. 4, 1730, Joh. David Staudt, Lutheran schoolmaster.*

7. JOHANN PHILLIP [6] HUBER (*Martin,*[5] *Hans,*[4] *Martin,*[3] *Martin,*[2] *Hans?*[1]), born at Trippstadt, *circa* 1675; died there

---

* *Cf. ante*, p. 224.

3 mo. 15, 1718. In 1698, he is recorded as a member of the Trippstadt Church Congregation, and in 1713, Palatinate tax collector in his native town.

He married (1), *circa* 1696, Anna Katharina (Burkhardt?), who was buried at Trippstadt, 3 mo. 22, 1711, (Epitaph: "Today we are fresh, healthy and strong"). His second marriage was also at Trippstadt, 6 mo. 30, 1711, to Eva Margareta Linn, daughter of Johann Nikolaus and Maria Magdalena Linn.*

Children born and baptized in Trippstadt, the first six by first marriage. Two more children are recorded in the Church Book without further mention. The death of a child of Johann Philipp Huber is entered on 4 April, 1718, without name or age.

    i.   HANS JOBST,[7] bapt. 2mo. 23, 1697; died in infancy.
    ii. JOHANN PETER, bapt. 2 mo. 22, 1699; died in infancy.
    iii. JOHANN HEINRICH, bapt. 1 mo. 24, 1702. No further record in Trippstadt. Possibly he is to be identified with Heinrich Huber who, in the summer of 1747, sailed from Rotterdam to Pennsylvania. No age recorded upon his arrival. Rudolf Huber and Heinrich Huber jr. were passengers on the same vessel.
    iv. ANNA MARGARETA, bapt. 9 mo. 2, 1704.†
    v. JOHANN PHILIPP, bapt. 12 mo. 5, 1706; died in infancy.
10. vi. JOHANN PHILIPP, bapt. 7 mo. 1, 1708.
    vii. EVA MARGARETA, bapt. 3 mo. 29, 1712; died Mölschbach 2 mo. 21, 1786; married in Trippstadt 10 mo. 3, 1730, Johann Heinrich Edinger, bapt. in Trippstadt 7 mo. 3, 1702; died Mölschbach, 2 mo. 24, 1764, son of Johann Martin and Maria Sibilla Edinger.
    viii. ANNA KATHARINA, bapt. 5 mo. 6, 1714; died Mölschbach, 4 mo. 9, 1769; married at Mölschbach, 1 mo. 19, 1734, Johann Heinrich May, born *circa* 1704; died Willstein near Trippstadt 1 mo. 20, 1780; aged seventy-six years.‡
    ix. CLARA ELIZABETH, bapt. 10 mo. 13, 1715.
    x. JOHANN GEORGE, bapt. 3 mo. 14, 1717.

8. CIRIACUS [6] (ZILLIOX, ZILLJACOB) HUBER (*Martin*,[5] *Hans*,[4] *Martin*,[3] *Martin*,[2] *Hans?*[1]), baptized at Trippstadt, 12 mo.

---

* Eva Margareta (Linn) Huber married (2) Johann Buschi, born in Switzerland in 1681; d. Mölschbach, 9 mo. 3, 1728; married (3) at Mölschbach, 6 mo. 1, 1734, Johann Casper Becker of Morlautern, one and a half miles north of Kaiserslautern.

† No further record.

‡ Johann Heinrich May had married (1) in Mölschbach, 7 mo. 29, 1732, Maria Susanna des Armes, daughter of David des Arms, citizen and cooper in Otterberg near Kaiserslautern, and widow of Johann Ludwig Wagner, who died at Trippstadt, 12 mo. 5, 1731, aged twenty-eight years, son of Heinrich Wagner of Kirckenback. She died before 1734.

24, 1680; died there 7 mo. 17, 1761; married *circa* 1706, Anna Maria ————, from Hohenecken, three and a half miles southwest of Kaiserslautern to which parish it belonged. She was born 10 mo. 7, 1683, and died, at Trippstadt, on her birthday, in her eighty-seventh year, buried there 10 mo. 9, 1770. She lived to see seventy-four grand-children, and forty-eight great grandchildren, with her children, 129 descendants.

Ciriacus or Zilljacob Huber was inn-keeper of Zum Hirschen; from 1734, Palatine Schultheiss (village mayor) and territorial tax collector in Trippstadt. He possessed, besides arable land, meadows and fields, two houses in Trippstadt, situated one behind the other, in front of Zum Hirschen with 17 poles 6½ feet frontage to the street, bearing the arms of the inn, which became the property of his son-in-law Peter Keffer.

Children all born in Trippstadt:

11. i.   JOHANN KONRATH,[7] born *circa* 1707.
    ii.   ANNA KATHARINA, born *circa* 1708; married in Trippstadt, 11 mo. 18, 1727, Hans Adam Edinger jr., bapt. Trippstadt 11 mo. 29, 1699; died Trippstadt, 3 mo. 21, 1766, son of Johann Martin and Maria Sibilla Edinger, from Heltersberg, four and half miles south-west of Trippstadt.
    iii.   MARIA SIBILLA, born *circa* 1710; died Trippstadt, 1 mo. 1, 1746, aged thirty-six years; married Trippstadt, 1 mo. 23, 1731, Johann Peter Mang, linen-weaver in Trippstadt, bapt. Trippstadt, 11 mo. 27, 1707; son of Joh. Theobald Mang and Maria Linn, married in Trippstadt 7 mo. 14, 1705.
    iv.   JOHANN PAUL, born 8mo. 27, 1713; was a blacksmith in Trippstadt, where he died on the 29th March 1798. He married there 1 mo. 11, 1735, Anna Elisabeth Burghart, youngest daughter of Johann Caspar Burghart, hereditary tenant on the Stüterhof, one mile east of Mölschbach. None of their descendants are recorded as emigrants to America, nor have they been elsewhere traced.
    v.   MARIA ELISABETH, born *circa* 1715; died Trippstadt 3 mo. 7, 1766, aged forty-eight years. She was inn-keeper of Zum Hirschen, and married (1), in Trippstadt, 11 mo. 10, 1736, Johann Valentin Heintz, who died *circa* 1750, son of Adam Heintz of Oberarnbach, nine and half miles south-west of Kaiserslautern. She married (2), in Trippstadt, *circa* 1752, Peter Keffer (Keber) from Oberarnbach, who died at Trippstadt, 7 mo. 13, 1767 aged 39 years and 4 months; inn-keeper of the Zum Hirschen.*

---

* Peter Keffer (Keber) married, secondly, at Trippstadt, 10 mo. 7, 1766, Anna Maria Edinger, bapt. Trippstadt, 10 mo. 20, 1737, daughter of Johann Heinrich Edinger of Mölschbach, bapt. Trippstadt 7 mo. 3, 1702; died Mölschbach 2 mo. 24, 1764, and Eva Margareta Huber, bapt. Trippstadt 3 mo. 29, 1712; died Mölschbach 2 mo. 21, 1786. The latter was daughter of Johann Philipp Huber of Trippstadt (see p. 236). Anna Maria Edinger, widow of Peter Keffer, married (2) at Mölschbach, 11 mo. 22, 1768, George Peter Rothmüller, son of Karl Ludwig Rothmüller.

vi. MARIA BARBARA, born *circa* 1718; inherited the second house on the street in Trippstadt. She married (1) at Trippstadt, 4 mo. 7, 1739, Johann Michael Frölich, saddler in Trippstadt, who died at Trippstadt 7 mo. 4, 1766, either in his 56th or 66th year. Her second marriage was to Heinrich Alt, from Schmalenberg, near Trippstadt, 1 mo. 9, 1770.

12. vii. JOHANN PHILIPP, born 11 mo. 10, 1726.

9. JOHANN[7] JACOB HUBER (*Hans[6] Bartholomaus, Martin,[5] Hans,[4] Martin,[3] Martin,[2] Hans?[1]*), born at Trippstadt; baptized there, 7 mo. 19, 1699; died in Pennsylvania; married in Trippstadt, 10 mo. 31, 1724, Maria Barbara Edinger, baptized Trippstadt, 3 mo. 9, 1704; died probably in Pennsylvania, daughter of Hans Adam Edinger of Trippstadt and Anna Maria Kerr.

He lived in his native town until 1750, in which year he sailed on the ship *Anderson* from Rotterdam via Cowes, for America, arriving in Philadelphia, August 21, 1750, when he is of record as taking the Oath of Allegiance. His wife's death is not registered at Trippstadt; presumably she accompanied him, as did their daughters, of whom there are no entries save their births in the church book.

Children, born and baptized at Trippstadt:

i. EVA ELISABETH,[8] bapt. 8 mo. 1, 1725; married at Mölschbach 11 mo. 11, 1749, Johann George Fleck, son of Johann Philipp Fleck and Anna Margareta Eberle.
ii. MARIA KATHARINA, born 7 mo. 20, 1727; died Trippstadt, 10 mo. 5, 1728.
iii. JOHANN ADAM, born 4 mo. 14, 1729; he sailed in the ship *Edinburgh*, from Rotterdam, via Portsmouth, to Philadelphia, where he took the Oath of Allegiance, 13 August, 1750.
iv. JOHANNES HUBER, born 4 mo. 22, 1731. He followed his brother and father to America, crossing the ocean four years later than his brother Johann Adam, but travelled on the same ship *Edinburgh*, from Rotterdam, via Portsmouth, to Philadelphia, where he is of record as taking the Oath of Allegiance, 30 September, 1754.
v. JOHANN PETER, born 3 mo. 14, 1734; died Trippstadt 8 mo. 1, 1784, in his fifty-first year; unmarried.
vi. MARIA DOROTHEA, born 9 mo. 19, 1736.
vii. CLARA ELISABETH, born 2mo. 26, 1739.
viii. MARIA KATHARINA, born 7 mo. 1, 1742.

10. JOHANN PHILIPP[7] HUBER (*Johann Philipp,[6] Martin,[5] Hans,[4] Martin,[3] Martin,[2] Hans?[1]*), baptized at Trippstadt, 7 mo. 1, 1708; died at Mölschbach, of which he had long been a resident, 5 mo. 7, 1793. He married at the latter place, 7 mo. 20, 1734, Maria Elizabeth Buschi, born at Trippstadt, 2 mo. 3, 1715; died at Mölschbach 5 mo. 2, 1789; daughter of Johannes Buschi, who died before 1734, and Maria Susana Eberle.

Children, born in Mölschbach, baptized at Trippstadt:

i. MARIA ELISABETH,[8] born 8 mo. 5, 1736; died Mölschbach
    5 mo. 2, 1808; married there 2 mo. 13, 1764, Christoph
    Eberle, who died at Mölschbach, 12 mo. 26, 1783, in his
    fifty-third year, son of Peter Eberle who died before 1764.
ii. JOHANN PETER, born 10 mo. 2, 1738; died Stelzenberg, 1 mo.
    9, 1798; married Mölschbach, 1 mo. 19, 1768, Maria Philip-
    pina Georgi, born Trippstadt 6 mo. 8, 1750; died
    Stelzenberg, 3 mo. 30, 1794; daughter of Johann Caspar
    Georgi of Trippstadt. They lived at Trippstadt and had
    eight children. There is no record of the issue of their
    grandchildren.
iii. JOHANN GEORG, born 12 mo. 23, 1740. No further record in
    the Palatinate. Thus he probably emigrated to America
    and is to be identified with Joh. Georg Huber, who sailed
    from Rotterdam to Philadelphia on the *Betsey* and took
    the Oath of Allegiance on the (16?) 26th October, 1768.
iv. JOHANN PAUL, born 12 mo. 18, 1741; died in infancy.
v. MARIA KATHARINA, born 1 mo. 26, 1742; died Mölschbach
    6 mo. 27, 1794; married in Trippstadt, 4 mo. 26, 1768,
    Johann Peter Huber, bapt. Trippstadt, 6 mo. 3, 1725; died
    Mölschbach, 11 mo. 20, 1793; son of Johann Caspar Huber.
vi. JOHANN NIKOLAS, born 8 mo. 1, 1744; died in infancy.
vii. ANNA MARIA, born 2 mo. 22, 1749; died before 1788, after
    April 1786; married Stelzenberg, 4 mo. 26, 1768 Johann
    Jacob Lüttich,* born in Stelzenberg, 9 mo. 17, 1744; son of
    Johann Nikolaus Lüttich.
viii. ANNA MARGARETA, born 9 mo. 10, 1753; married in Mölsch-
    bach, 4 mo. 30, 1771, Johann Philipp Eberle, weaver in
    Mölschbach, born there 1 mo. 19, 1743, son of Johann Adam
    Eberle.
ix. JOHANN HEINRICH, born 3 mo. 23, 1755. After serving in the
    Bavarian army he lived as a farmer in Mölschbach, where
    he died March 4, 1836. He married, Mölschbach, 1 mo.
    12, 1779, Katharina Assel from Stüterhof, one mile east of
    Mölschbach, born Stüterhof, 2 mo. 4, 1756; daughter of
    Johann Adam Assel of Stüterhof and Maria Elisabeth
    Jacobs. They had two sons. No record of their grand-
    children.

11. JOHANN KONRATH [7] HUBER (*Ciriacus,*[6] *Martin,*[5] *Hans,*[4]
Martin,[3] *Martin,*[2] *Hans?*[1]), born at Trippstadt, *circa* 1707;
died there 4 mo. 10, 1766. He married there, 2 mo. 26, 1732,
as first wife, Anna Elizabeth Edinger, born at Trippstadt,
11 mo. 1, 1705; died there 8 mo. 5, 1751; daughter of Johann
Martin Edinger of Heltersberg.† He married (2) at Trippstadt, 2 mo. 8, 1752, Maria Appolonia Scheuermann, who died
there, 7 mo. 2, 1781, in her fifty-fourth year. She was a
daughter of Joh. Peter Scheuermann, who died before 1752,
in Kottweiler, ten and half miles west of Kaiserslautern, belonging to the parish of Steinwenden.

---

* Johann Jacob Lüttich, married (2) at Stelzenberg, 5 mo. 3, 1788,
Anna Barbara Fuchs.

† *Ante*, p. 236.

Children, born and baptized at Trippstadt:

i. JOHANN HEINRICH,[8] born 12 mo. 5, 1732. He is not further
recorded in the parish register of Trippstadt and may well
be identified as the Johann Heinrich Huber, who arrived at
the port of Philadelphia, on the ship, *Isaac* from Rotterdam, and took the Oath of Allegiance, 27 September, 1749.*
In any case he is the same for whom "the manumission
from bondage and passports" were extended by Baron
von Hack's Court at Trippstadt, in 1767.† These documents all evidence that Johann Hienrich Huber had
been living in Pennsylvania at the time of his father's
death in 1766, and that, receiving news thereof, he returned to his home in the Palatinate. After a brief stay
there he again journeyed to Pennsylvania, this time on the
ship *Sally*, accompanied by his three younger brothers and
one sister: Johann Nikolaus, Johann Adam, Johann Philipp
and Maria Elizabeth. The three brothers are shown to
have taken the Oath of Allegiance in Philadelphia, after
the arrival of the *Sally* from Rotterdam, October 5, 1767.
As elsewhere stated, Johann Jacob Kinn, mentioned in the
Huber passport, does not appear as having arrived in
America.

ii. JOHANN NIKOLAUS, born 12 mo. 17, 1734; emigrated to Pennsylvania. His descendants are still undetermined.

iii. ANNA MARIA, born 11 mo. 22, 1736; died in infancy.

iv. MARIA KATHARINE, born 10 mo. 27, 1737; died at Mölschbach,
4 mo. 30, 1788; married at Mölschbach, 2 mo. 8, 1763,
Johann Philipp May, churchwarden in Mölschbach, born
there 11 mo. 24, 1736, son of Johann Heinrich May, who
died at Willstein, near Trippstadt, 1 mo. 20, 1780, in his
seventy-sixth year and Anna Katharina Huber, bapt. Trippstadt, 5 mo. 6, 1714, daughter of Johann Philipp Huber.‡
Johann Philipp May married (2) at Mölschbach, 11 mo.
27, 1788, Charlotte Luise Huber, born Willstein, 11 mo.
30, 1769; baptized at Trippstadt; daughter of Johann
Jacob Huber, weaver-master on the Willsteiner Hoff, near
Trippstadt.

v. JOHANN PHILIPP, born 5 mo. 29, 1740; emigrated to Pennsylvania. His descendants not yet ascertained.

vi. MARIA ELISABETH, born Mölschbach 1 mo. 20, 1743; emigrated to America.

vii. JOHANN ADAM, born 7 mo. 8, 1745; emigrated to America.
His descendants still untraced.

viii. ANNA MARIA, born 4 mo. 30, 1750; died in infancy.

ix. JOHANN MICHAEL, born 11 mo. 24, 1752; died Trippstadt, 10
mo. 8, 1832; married (1) at Trippstadt, 11 mo. 26, 1776, Eva
Elisabeth Kallenbach, born Trippstadt, 8 mo. 15, 1753; died

---

* It is doubtful whether the *Isaac's* passenger can be identified with
the Heinrich Huber who died in Winchester, Virginia, 28 August, 1828,
aged 89 years, 8 months and 7 days, hence December 21, 1738, should be
his birthday. The six years difference in age makes this combination
the less likely. This Henry Huber, or Hoover, married Charity Barrick,
born 1740, and had: i. *John Huber*, born January 6, 1764. ii. *Juliann
Catherin Huber*, born March 1, 1766. iii. *Philipp Huber*, born June
21, 1770.

† *Ante*, p. 229.

‡ *Ante*, p. 236.

44

circa 1783; daughter of Carl Kilian Kallenbach and Eva Rosina Bucher. He married (2) at Trippstadt, 2 mo. 17, 1784, Fredrika Elisabeth Huber, born Trippstadt, 12 mo. 10, 1768; daughter of Johann Caspar Huber, smith in Trippstadt and Maria Elisabeth Huber. None of his descendants are recorded as emigrants to America, and are untraced.

 x. ANNA MARGARETE, born 10 mo. 31, 1754; died Trippstadt, 12 mo. 1, 1783; unmarried.

 xi. ELISABETH BARBARA, born 1 mo. 6, 1757; died in infancy.

 xii. MARIA DOROTHEA, born 4 mo. 12, 1759; married at Trippstadt, 1 mo. 3, 1779, Johann Heinrich Jülich.

 xiii. JOHANN JACOB, born 7 mo. 9, 1761; died in infancy.

 xiv. JOHANN CONRAD, born 10 mo. 3, 1762; died in infancy.

 xv. ANNA KATHARINA, born 4 mo. 21, 1765. No further record.

12. JOHANN PHILIPP [7] HUBER (*Ciriacus,*[6] *Martin,*[5] *Hans,*[4] *Martin,*[3] *Martin,*[2] *Hans?*[1]), born at Trippstadt, 11 mo. 10, 1726, and there baptized; died there, 2 mo. 26, 1804; having been inn-keeper of Zur Krone and baker in Trippstadt. He married, 4 mo. 7, 1750, Anna Margareta Huber, baptized Trippstadt, 8 mo. 24, 1727; daughter of Johann Caspar Huber, inn-keeper of Zum Löwen in Trippstadt.

Children, born and baptized in Trippstadt:

 i. MARIA ELISABETH,[8] born 11 mo. 29, 1750; died in infancy.

 ii. JOHANN PHILIPP, born 11 mo. 20, 1751; died in infancy.

 iii. ROSINA LUISE, born 12 mo. 16, 1753; died Stüterhof, near Mölschbach, 1 mo. 24, 1829; married Stüterhof, 5 mo. 10, 1774, Conrad Eberle, born Stüterhof, 3 mo. 27, 1754; died before 1829; son of Conrad Eberle, who died before 1774.

 iv. ANNA BARBARA, born 10 mo. 8, 1755; married at Trippstadt, 5 mo. 28, 1776, Johannes Huber, forester in Heltersberg and Waldfischbach, bapt. Trippstadt, 11 mo. 18, 1732; died Schmalenberg, 10 mo. 10, 1784; son of Johann Peter Huber and Eva Buschon.*

 v. ANNA MARIA, born 1 mo. 1, 1758.*

 vi. MARIA ELISABETH, born 2 mo. 2, 1760; married at Trippstadt, 1 mo. 21, 1784, Johann Michael, forester and game-keeper at the hunting lodge near Trippstadt; from about 1790, on the Stüterhof, near Trippstadt.

13. vii. JOHN CASPAR HUBER, born 2 mo. 23, 1762.

 viii. ANNA KATHARINA, born 11 mo. 8, 1764.*

 ix. JOHANN GEORG, born 9 mo. 16, 1767; died Trippstadt, 1 mo. 15, 1803; married at Trippstadt, 4 mo. 9, 1792, Magdalena Mang, born Aschbach, two and half miles north of Trippstadt, 4 mo. 3, 1773; died Trippstadt, 10 mo. 22, 1834, daughter of Jacob Mang, forester, and Anna Katharina . . . , Johann Georg Huber was baker and inn-keeper of Zur Krone in Trippstadt; and died in his thirty-sixth year, leaving no male descendants.

 x. JOHANN CARL, born 3 mo. 1, 1770; died in infancy.

 xi. JOHANN BERNHARD, born 6mo. 14, 1772.*

13. JOHANN CASPAR [8] HUBER (*Johann Philipp,*[7] *Ciriacus,*[6] *Martin,*[5] *Hans,*[4] *Martin,*[3] *Martin,*[2] *Hans?*[1]), born at Tripp-

---

* No further record.

stadt, 2 mo. 23, 1762, and there died, 3 mo. 21, 1838. He married at Herschberg, five miles north-west of Waldfischbach, before 1787, Henriette Katharina Margareta Köhler, born Herschberg, 9 mo. 10, 1765, died at Trippstadt, 4 mo. 25, 1827. He was a brew master in Trippstadt and in 1820, is mentioned as Royal Bavarian tax-receiver.

Children, born and baptized at Trippstadt:

    i.   ANNA MARIA,[9] born 12 mo. 22, 1790; died Trippstadt 11 mo. 4, 1825; married *circa* 1812, Johann Jacob Kaspary, citizen and tradesman in Trippstadt, foreman at the iron works near there.

14. ii.   JOHANN PETER, born 8 mo. 27, 1792.

    iii.   MARIA KATHARINA, born 5 mo. 27, 1795; died after 1830; married *circa* 1814, Heinrich Schäfer, inn-keeper of Zum Goldenen Hirsch in Trippstadt; alive in 1830.

    iv.   KARL THEODOR, born 2 mo. 24, 1797; inn-keeper of Zum Hirschen in Thaleischweiler; lived in Waldfischbach, 1827; was married. No further record.

    v.   SOPHIE MARGARETE, born 6 mo. 11, 1799; married at Trippstadt 12 mo. 3, 1822, Johannes Peter Fröhlich, protestant minister in Trippstadt.

15. JOHANN PETER [9] HUBER (*Johann Caspar,*[8] *Johann Philipp,*[7] *Ciriacus,*[6] *Martin,*[5] *Hans,*[4] *Martin,*[3] *Martin,*[2] *Hans?*[1]), baker and inn-keeper at Trippstadt, was born there 8 mo. 27, 1792. He married there, 8 mo. 19, 1813, Wilhelmina Luise Müller, daughter of Johannes Müller, forester on the Leichhof.*

Children, born and baptized at Trippstadt:

    i.   KATHARINA MARGARETA,[10] born 7 mo. 25, 1814; married at Trippstadt, 10 mo. 13, 1836, Johann Michael Kirchner of Trippstadt, widower of Anna Maria Gumpe.

    ii.   KARL, born 8 mo, 6, 1817.†

16. iii.   KASPAR, born 4 mo. 23, 1819.

    iv.   PHILIP, born 10 mo. 21, 1820; died Trippstadt 10 mo. 22, 1820.

    v.   FRIEDRICH, born 2 mo. 1, 1822.‡

    vi.   PHILIPP LORENZ, born 11 mo. 4, 1823.‡

16. KASPAR [10] HUBER (*Johann Peter,*[9] *Johann Caspar,*[8] *Johann Philipp,*[7] *Ciriacus,*[6] *Martin,*[5] *Hans,*[4] *Martin,*[3] *Martin,*[2] *Hans?*[1]), was born at Trippstadt, 4 mo. 23, 1819, and died there, 2 mo. 25, 1873. He married, *circa* 1845, Christina Eber, born at Haardt, 7 mo. 7, 1819; died Trippstadt, 6 mo.

---

* Probably Leinhof near Enkenbach, six miles north-east of Kaiserslautern.

† No further record.

‡ No further record.

1, 1901; daughter of Salomon Eber of Haardt, one mile north of Neustadt.

Children, born at Trippstadt:

i. JOHANN PHILIPP,[11] born 12 mo. 9, 1847; died at Trippstadt, 12 mo. 10, 1902. He married (1) at Trippstadt, 6 mo. 10, 1876, Lina Kettenring, born Hermersberg, 9 mo. 8, 1857; died Trippstadt, 7 mo. 29, 1890. His second wife, Emma Höh, whom he married 2 mo. 9, 1891, at Neustadt, was born at Steinalben, 8 mo. 19, 1866, daughter of Michael Höh of Steinalben, six miles south-west of Trippstadt. Johann Philipp Huber was postmaster at Trippstadt. His descendants are still living in the Palatinate.

ii. WILHELM, born 7 mo. 22, 1849; emigrated to the United States; married and had issue.*

iii. FRANZ KARL, born 4 mo. 6, 1851; died at Augsburg, 2 mo. 14, 1904. He married at Augsburg, 8 mo. 5, 1880, Johanna (known as Jeanette) Würth, born Augsburg, 6 mo. 7, 1860; daughter of Leonhard Würth, owner of a brewery in Augsburg, and Katharina Döbler. Franz Karl Huber was a merchant in Augsburg where his descendants still reside.

iv. LUISE, born *circa* 1853; married *circa* 1875, . . . Müller.†

v. VALENTIN, born *circa* 1855.†

vi. MARIA, born *circa* 1857.†

vii. SUSANNA, married *circa* 1885, . . . Jacob.†

---

* A son C.... Huber, gardener in Brooklyn, New York, was living in 1930, at 1279 Bedford Avenue, in that city.

† No further record.

HOOVER—SCARBOROUGH

HOOVER—SCARBOROUGH. Descent of Herbert Hoover, President of the United States, from the Scarborough Family of Bucks County, Pennsylvania and London, England:

Herbert Hoover,[10] son of

Jesse Clark Hoover and Huldah [9] Minthorn, daughter of

Theodore Minthorne and Mary [8] Wasley, daughter of

Henry Wasley and Ann [7] Tool, daughter of

Aaron Tool and Rachel [6] Haworth, daughter of

Mary and John [5] Haworth, son of

George Haworth and Sarah [4] Scarborough, daughter of

John [3] Scarborough, a settler of Bucks County, in 1682, son of

John [2] Scarborough of Hoosier Lane, London, son of

William [1] Scarborough of Hoosier Lane, London, who was born in 1598, belonged to Peel Monthly Meeting of Friends and is buried at Bunhill Fields.—Henry W. Scarborough, of Philadelphia.

A HOUSTON CORRECTION

By Walter Lee Sheppard, Jr., F.A.S.G.

The Houstons of Pequea, by Margaret E. Houston, undated but published about 1921 and cited as an authoritative source in at least one subsequent Houston genealogy,[1] contains many errors, some careless misspelling of names and others, more serious, statements of facts made on slim or no evidence, or without discernable authority. Since this book is certainly not authoritative, no effort at a comprehensive correction is here made. However, one widely quoted statement on page 16 is here reexamined. On this page it is said that the Scotch-Irish immigrant, John Houston, born about 1705, came to Pennsylvania sometime about 1730, took up a patent for 430 acres of land in Lancaster County immediately after his arrival and died in 1769 between August 10 and December 6. The controversial statement is then made that he married Martha, " one of the daughters of George Stewart," who took up land adjoining his.

The facts that can be supported with documents are these: George Stewart received his patent from the Proprietaries on August 11, 1741,[2] for land in Leacock Township. John Houston's first patent which appears in the *Pennsylvania Archives* was for only 25 acres, surveyed June 4, 1742, in Strasburg Township.[3] On April 12, 1751, as miller, of Strasburg, he purchased for £7 an acre on Pequea Creek and a right of way across George Stewart's land to his mill, for his mill race, with access rights in order to repair dam and race.[4] When he became George Stewart's neighbor is not clear, but it would appear to be subsequent to Stewart's original patent, on which he lived, and which he left to his son.

George Stewart, of Leacock Township, left a will dated April 1, 1769, proved April 24, 1769, in which he left to his wife Jean 1/3 of his personal estate. His only son George received the other 2/3 of the personal and all the real estate, amounting to 330 acres, during his lifetime and subject to the wife's privileges. His daughter Esther McCausland, wife of John McCausland, received £100, and in case of her death this was to be divided evenly between her children, George's two granddaughters, Esther and Jean McCausland; they were each to receive £20 in addition when of age. The real estate was entailed on George's sons, grandsons of the testator. If George Stewart predeceased his wife Sarah, she was to have £100. The will was signed by mark, a scroll G, and witnessed by Stewart Herbert, James M. Math and William Scott.[5] On November 12, 1785, George Stewart, the son, sold his rights in the 330 acre plantation to John Pitzer, of Earl Township.[6] By a separate deed on the same day, his two sons, George, Jr., and John Stewart, also of Leacock Township, concurred in the sale and sold their shares.[7] These deeds recite the will quoted above and the first adds the data on the original patent quoted in the second paragraph above. On March 9, 1789, David and Robert Stewart, of Robinson Township, two other grandsons of the testator and also sons of George the younger, sold their rights to Pitzer for £300.[8]

Nowhere in the foregoing is there any mention of a daughter Martha, nor in fact of any daughter other than Esther. Although they were neighbors, John Houston did not witness the will nor was he in any way concerned in the estate. John Houston did not name any of his numerous sons George, or Robert, which latter was a common Stewart name. This does not prove that John Houston's wife Martha was *not* " a daughter of George Stewart," but without positive proof that she *was*, the probability is certainly slight.

Who, then, was Martha? The writer cannot say. The deeds name many families whose properties adjoined John Houston. Most of these have been checked through records of wills and deeds, without obtaining any lead. It can only be hoped that an unrecorded deed or family Bible record will some day identify the wife of John Houston.

Other Houston deeds of interest to the family, but not elsewhere noted are:

> 1744, December 8. John Houston sold to Evan Morgan land in Salisbury Township. Recorded May 1, 1745. (*Lancaster County Deed Book* B, p. 240).

> 1751, June 19. John Houston, miller, of Strasburg Township, purchased from William Blyth, miller, and Christian (or Catrin), his wife, 20 acres including a grist mill on Pequea Creek, part of an original patent of 126 acres made April 18, 1741, to Samuel Blyth. (*Ibid.,* D, p. 336).

> 1759, November 21. John Houston secured from Sebastian Graff a £600 mortgage on the grist mill and 20 acres on Pequea Creek bought from William Blyth. Repayment by Houston was acknowledged March 1, 1797, by John Hopson, executor, and Andrew Graff, one of the heirs of Sebastian Graff. (*Ibid.,* D, p. 553).

> 1762, May 1. John Houston purchased land from William Clark, and Anne, his wife. Recorded December 10, 1762. (*Ibid.,* G, p. 420).

1763, October 14.   John Houston, of Leacock Township, and Martha, his wife, granted to the Trustees of the College, Academy and Charitable School of Philadelphia, in payment of a debt of £1500 or 370 Spanish gold pistoles and 10 shillings, two tracts of land, one containing 190 acres in Strasburg Township on Pequea Creek, bounded by George Stewart, Samuel Davison, John McCally, Samuel Blyth and Humphrey Fullerton, purchased June 10, 1752, from Thomas and Mary Cookson; the second, 180½ acres in Strasburg Township, bounded by William White, John McCawley and Isaac Taylor, part of 361 acres purchased April 29, 1763, from the Pennsylvania Land Company.   The deed contains a recapture clause in case the money is paid back.   (*Ibid.*, K, p. 59).

1767, June 13.   John Houston purchased from William Young and Matthew Young land in Strasburg and Leacock Townships.   Recorded October 9, 1767.   (*Ibid.*, M, p. 242).

1785, June 17.   John Houston (Estate settlement), to John Houston, et al., Recorded June 17, 1785.   (*Ibid.*, U, p. 743).

1790, May 3.   William Houston and Jane, his wife, to Daniel Houston, land in Strasburg Township left by their father, bounded by George Stewart. (*Ibid.*, LL, p. 214).

FOOTNOTES AND REFERENCES

[1] Thomas H. Bateman, comp., *Houston and Allied Families* (New York: American Historical Company, Inc., 1950), which on page 4 contains the statement corrected in this article.

[2] *Lancaster County Deed Book* DD, pp. 419-420.   *Pennsylvania Archives* do not index this patent. On June 1, 1741 a survey of 450 acres was made to Stewart and Mackerel.

[3] *Pennsylvania Archives,* 3rd Series, XXIV, 429.

[4] Recorded June 20, 1751.   *Lancaster County Deed Book* C, p. 67.

[5] *Lancaster County Will Book* C-1, p. 81.   In *Deed Book* KK, p. 362 is recorded a mortgage given by John McCausland and Esther, his wife, to his brother-in-law, George Stewart, November 3, 1772, recorded December 30, 1772.   A good signature of George Stewart appears in the record as a receipt for repayment.

[6] *Lancaster County Deed Book* DD, p. 419.

[7] *Ibid.*, p. 420.

[8] *Ibid.*, KK, p. 1.

HOWARD, AN EARLY PHILADELPHIA FAMILY

By Ralph Dornfeld Owen, F.A.S.G., F.G.S.P.

Note: The thoughtfulness of Mr. George H. S. King of Fredericksburg, Virginia, in transcribing and submitting the Howard Family Bible Record, stimulated the writer to search Pennsylvania records concerning the Howard family.

Thomas Howard, according to the inscription on his tombstone, was born in the year 1697. There seems to be no record of the names of his parents or the place of his birth. The name Howard does not occur in the list of " First Purchasers " of 1682, either in Hazard: *Annals* or in Reed's List of First Purchasers.[1]

Thomas Howard could not have been the man of that name to whom a 49½ ft. lot on the north side of Mulberry (Arch) Street was patented in 1687. This lot, between Fifth and Sixth Streets, is shown in William Parson's Plan of Philadelphia which depicts the lots of First Purchasers. The lot was devised by the earlier Thomas Howard to his son Benjamin Howard " who left it to his Wid'w, with whom Geo. Harmar Intermarried, And upon this, sold to Wm. Oxely," all of which occurred before 1705 and is recorded in Minute Book " G " of the Commissioners of Property. Whether Thomas Howard, born in 1697, was the son of the above-mentioned Benjamin Howard can only be conjectured until further search is undertaken.[2]

Thanks to a fortunate coincidence, another article in this issue includes a reproduction of a part of Nicholas Scull's *Map of Philadelphia,* published in 1762.[3] It shows the area in which three generations of this Howard family lived.

On 16 September 1723 Thomas Howard married Grace Beaks. The date is recorded in the Family Bible. It does not appear in either the published church records or in the list of licenses, probably because " the earlier records were lost." [4]

[1] Samuel Hazard, *Annals of Pennsylvania 1609-1682* (Philadelphia, 1850), 637-642. John Reed, *Map of the City and Liberties of Philadelphia, With the Catalogue of Purchasers* . . . (1774). *Pennsylvania Magazine of History and Biography,* LXXX (1956), 173, 218, hereafter *PMHB.*

[2] " Minutes of the Board of Property of the Province of Pennsylvania," *Pennsylvania Archives,* 2nd Series, XIX, 472. For an additional reference to this lot see " Philadelphia Rent Rolls," *Internal Affairs Monthly Bulletin,* XXII (April 1954), 28, wherein the two lots of Thomas Rutter and Thomas Howard in Mulberry Street were by 1703 in the possession of William Oxley.

[3] " Taxables in Chestnut, Middle and South Wards, Philadelphia: 1754," annotated by Hannah Benner Roach, 160 of this Magazine. *

[4] *Pennsylvania Archives,* 2nd Series, II, 13 ff.

*The map referred to appears in *The Pennsylvania Genealogical Magazine,* Volume XXI:2 (1959), 160.

Grace Beaks, who was born in 1695, was very probably the daughter of John and Grace Beaks, who lived on the Barbadoes Lot a few doors south of the Howard lot. This assumption is supported by the following entries:

" Grace, wife of John Beaks, of Barbeddes, died 10–4–1702 " [5]

" John Howard son of Thomas in 1754 paid the tax on his house and also the tax on the Barbadoes lot." [6]

John Beeks (or Beaks) probably had come to Philadelphia from the Barbadoes, where there was a settlement of English Friends. Besse lists some 240 individuals who were persecuted by the British authorities in the islands.[7]

Grace was the granddaughter of William Beaks, who had come from Somerset County, England. The Friends' Meeting of Portishead, Somerset County, issued a certificate to him under date of 25 June 1682. On 2 March 1683 he and six other men organized the Falls Monthly Meeting of Friends in Bucks County.[8]

William Beaks was one of the First Purchasers in Pennsylvania, having bought 1000 acres in Bucks County.[9] This entitled him to lots in the city of Philadelphia. By an indenture of sale dated 29 July 1681, William Penn granted to William Beaks of Bradwell, Somerset, Great Britain, the following lot " situate between the eighth and ninth street, from Delaware river, containing in breadth in High Street twenty-six feet, six inches, and in length three hundred and six feet, bounded Southward with High Street, Eastward with Thomas Howard's ground, Northward and Westward with vacant ground." [10]

William Beaks also owned a lot 20 ft. wide, running from Front to Second Street, lying between a 20 ft. lot on the south, owned by John Clowes, and a 110 ft. lot on the north, owned by Thomas Callowhill.[11]

In 1742 Thomas Howard petitioned the Provincial government to grant to him, the husband of a granddaughter of the late William Beaks, the lot on High Street, between Eighth and Ninth Streets. Under date of

---

[5] William Wade Hinshaw, *Encyclopedia of American Quaker Genealogy* (Ann Arbor, Mich., 1938), II, 951, 978, hereafter Hinshaw, *Encyclopedia.*

[6] " Taxables . . . in Philadelphia," *op. cit.,* 190.

[7] Joseph Besse, *Collection of the Sufferings of the People Called Quakers* (London, 1753), II, index to Volume I.

[8] Hinshaw, *Encyclopedia, op. cit.*

[9] Hazard, *Annals of Pennsylvania, op. cit.,* Appendix, 639.

[10] Philadelphia County Exemplification Book II, 626-629, Department of Records, Philadelphia City Hall.

[11] See Nicholas B. Wainwright, " Plan of Philadelphia," *PMHB,* LXXX (1956), 206.

2 September 1742 a patent for the lot was granted to Thomas Howard:

" John Penn, Thomas Penn, and Richard Penn, Esquires, true and absolute Proprietors and Governors in chief of the Province of Pennsylvania . . . to all unto whom these Presents shall come Greeting:

" Know ye that in consideration of the grant to the said William Beaks and for the yearly Quit rent hereinafter mentioned and received, we have granted, and by these presents do give, grant, release, and confirm to the said Thomas Howard and his heirs the said lot of ground . . . for the sole use, benefit and behoof of the several heirs of the said William Beaks—

" To be holden of us, our Heirs and Successors, Proprietors of Pennsylvania, as of our Manor of Springetsbury in the County of Philadelphia, in free and common soccage by fealty only, in lieu of all other services, Yielding and paying therefor yearly to us, our Heirs and Successors at the city of Philadelphia upon the first day of March in every year one English silver Shilling or the value thereof in coin current according as the Exchange shall then be between our said Province and the City of London.

" Witness: George Thomas, Esq., Lt Governor of the Province, who hath hereunto set his hand and has caused the Great Seal of the Province to be affixed at Philadelphia this second day of September in the year of our Lord one thousand seven hundred forty-two, in the sixteenth year of the reign of King George the Second over Great Britain . . . " [11a]

Recorded 11th Sept. 1742 in Patent Book A, Vol. 10, pp. 479-481.

Grace Beeks, six months before her marriage, requested and received a certificate from the Friends' Women's Meeting of Friends dated 1 March 1723.[12]

Thomas and Grace Howard made their home in the house on Second Street. Between 1724 and 1737 they had born to them seven children. While Grace was a Friend, Thomas evidently was not. In 1735 and 1736 he was elected a vestryman in Christ Church. All the children were baptized there. Four lived to survive their parents. Grace Howard died on 19 August 1742, at the age of forty-seven. She was buried in Christ Church cemetery. Her death was recorded in Friends' Meeting.[13]

Of the children, John was fifteen, Joanna, eleven, Grace, nine, and Mary, seven years old at the time of their mother's death. It was no wonder that Thomas married again before two years had elapsed. His second wife was a widow Susanna —— whose maiden name was either Bickingsale or Screven. She had children of her own.[14]

Thomas practiced the trade of joiner (joyner), that is, a maker of furniture. His shop was at his home on Second Street. He died at the

---

11a See *Exemplification Book* II, 626-629.

12 Statement of Records Department, Friends' Yearly Meeting, Philadelphia.

13 Hinshaw, *Encyclopedia*, II, 332.

14 See will of her sister Mrs. Sarah Smith who leaves something to " the children of the present wife of Thomas Howard." Abstract of Philadelphia Wills, 1680-1726, 836 in Collections of the Genealogical Society of Pennsylvania.

age of fifty-one on 25 December 1748, after having made and signed his will on the previous day. It consisted of two pages 16" x 10", witnessed by Edmond Skinner and Thomas Riley.[15] From his will one learns that he had acquired property in addition to that already mentioned: " two messuages with ground belonging to them on High Street." He willed the eastern one to his daughter Joanna, then 17 years old; the western one to his daughter Mary, then 13 years old; also a piece of ground, 90 ft. on High Street and 202 ft. on the west side of Eighth Street (a part of the site of the Strawbridge and Clothier Store today). He willed the north half to Joanna and the south half to Mary.

To his only son John he willed his house and shop and stock in trade, also " the residue of my real estate consisting of Lots, Lands, Ground rents, and Herediments."

In another section of his will he leaves to John 1000 foot of walnut lumber, 1000 foot of cedar, 1000 foot of poplar, and " all of my mahogany plank; " also " one-half of all the bedsteads in the yard belonging to the workshop," on condition that " the said John pay all the outstanding debts connected with the business." Further he gives him all the tools belonging to the business.

After disposing of the real estate he wills to each child some keepsakes, e.g.,

" I give to my daughter Mary my silver half-pint Can and a large silver soop spoon, three . . . silver spoons; also the bed, Bolster and Pillos and Callico Curtains wherein I now lye in my great Chamber and the Looking Glass in my back chamber a bit whereof is broke at the top." [16]

Concerning his second wife he writes:

" I give and devise unto my beloved wife Susanna all and singular the Household goods plate Furniture and implements of Household with all the Tools and Utensils which I received with her at the time of intermarriage with her. Moreover I give her the Looking Glass which . . . also the Chest; . . . and the sum of One hundred pounds lawful money of Pennsylvania within nine months after my decease over and besides what I have given her in and by my marriage Settlement." [17]

---

[15] Recorded in Philadelphia *Will Book* I, 30 #19. The original has broken into twelve parts and is being repaired. The Philadelphia Department of Records, Archives Division, courteously furnished the writer a photostatic copy.

[16] A Mary Howard was married to Thomas Calvert in Christ Church 29 Oct. 1755. There is no record of Joanna's marriage.

[17] The widow Susanna Howard was still living in 1808, when the City Directory gave her address as Lombard Street. She died in 1816.

He instructs his executor, his son John, " to sell and dispose of my two servant men for the best price that can be gotten." To carry out this directive, John Howard placed the following advertisement in the *Pennsylvania Gazette*, 24 January 1748/49:

To be Sold

Two lots of ground, fronting Market Street, containing in breadth about 33 feet and about 100 feet deep, or therabouts. Enquire of John Howard, in Second-street.

All persons indebted to the estate of Thomas Howard, late of this city, deceased, are desired to make speedy payment; and those who have any demands against said estate, are desired to bring in their accounts, that they may be adjusted by the above John Howard, executor.

N.B. Said Howard has to sell a likely negro boy, about 17 years of age, this country born and has had the small-pox and measles.[18]

Thomas and his first wife were buried in the cemetery of Christ Church, Section A. Following are the inscriptions:

XLVIII
In Memory of Grace
the wife of Thomas
Howard who departed
this life Aug. the 17th, 1742
aged 47 years.

XLIX
Here lyeth the body of
Thomas Howard
who departed this life
Dec. 25th 1748
Aged 51 years.

SECOND GENERATION

JOHN HOWARD, son of Thomas and Grace (Beeks) Howard, was born 13 March 1727 in the house on Second Street. He was baptized 30 March 1731 in Christ Church. He was married, according to the family record, 16 October 1749 to Sarah Bunting.[19]

Sarah Bunting, born in 1732, was the sixth child of John Bunting (b. 1685) and his wife Alice Lord Nicholson, who were married in 1722.

Her father John Bunting was the son of Samuel Bunting from Matlack, Derbyshire, England, who on 18 September 1684 married according to Friends' custom Mary Foulks at Chesterfield (now Trenton), N. J.

---

[18] Courtesy of Hannah Benner Roach.

[19] Not recorded either in Philadelphia Marriage Licenses or Christ Church Marriage Records.

Both the Buntings and the Nicholsons were active in Friends' Meetings.[20]

Four years after her marriage to John Howard, Sarah Bunting Howard was received into the Philadelphia Monthly Meeting on a certificate from the Chesterfield Meeting, dated 1753–3–30. It is evident that she retained her membership, for according to the record " Sarah Howard and children, Charles, John, Luke, and Deborah, were received into the Philadelphia Monthly Meeting by request, 1782–2–22."

Again: " Sarah Howard died at the age of 52 and was buried 10–9–1784." [21]

John and Sarah had twelve children born to them between October 1750 and December 1775. Four died young. Of the survivors four were received into the Friends' Meeting. But three, namely Grace, b. 1750, Sarah, b. 1758, and Alice, b. 1762 were baptized in Christ Church.

The family probably was divided in its religious affiliations. The Friends' Meeting House, located on the west side of Second Street at the corner of High Street, and Christ Church, located on the same side of Second Street, just north of High, were equally close to the Howard home.

Sarah (Bunting) Howard evidently was a more zealous Friend than her mother-in-law Grace Beeks Howard had been. John, like his father, was not a Friend.

John first lived in the house on Second Street, between Market and Chestnut Streets and next door but one to Joseph Trotter's house. In 1752 there was organized the Philadelphia Contributionship to protect the homes of its members from loss through fire. Its twelve-member Board of Directors was headed by Benjamin Franklin. One of the directors, Samuel Rhoads, on 22 July 1752 made a survey of John Howard's dwelling house on Second Street (Survey No. 96). It showed that the building had

14 feet front, 32 feet back, 3 Storys; a Joint Party Wall on the south, and a joint ditto on the north.

Board newal stairs with ramp and twise(?) Rail and Ballisters in the lower Room.

Wooden partitions, enveloping the Shops and lights. Ditto above. 3 Storys painted.

Piazza and Kitchen 8 feet by 25½ feet one story.

Board newal Stairs. Shingling about 18 years old.

" He (Howard) has since desired to make him out a new account for £200 only." [22]

---

[20] Granville Malcolm, Ancestors and Descendants of Howard Malcolm, Ms, in Historical Society of Pennsylvania.

[21] Hinshaw, *Encyclopedia*, II, 555, 377.

[22] Courtesy of Hannah Benner Roach.

John Howard took over the joiner and furniture business of his father and carried it on for about thirty years. Just as his father had before him, John made furniture, everything from cradles to coffins. Witness an item in the account of the executors of the estate of John Lukens, deceased, under date of 4 September 1776: " debtor to a mahogany coffing for his wife, to John Howard £8–0–0." [23]

John Howard's name appears frequently in tax lists—1769 Proprietary tax: " John Howard, joiner, Middle Ward, 58 £–17 Shillings "; State tax: " John Howard 41 £."; Provincial tax: " John Howard 62 £." [24]

On 20 August 1754 the four assessors of the city levied certain taxes on property holders. " A tax of two pence on the pound and six shillings per head on the Estates of the Freeholders and Inhabitants of the City." William Savery was the collector. Susannah Howard (widow of Thomas), living between Owen Fling and Hannah Brentnal in Second Street, was assessed at £24 and paid 4 shillings tax.

John Howard, living next door to Joseph Trotter, was assessed at £24 and also for the Barbados Lott another £30. He paid 9 shillings total tax. [25]

The *Pennsylvania Gazette* 31 January 1765 contains a notice: " Robert Ferguson has lately moved his shop from the Corner of Chestnut and Second-streets, to the house of Mr. John Howard, in Second Street, between Market and Chestnut-streets, and next door, but one, to Trotter's Alley."

Some time after 1765 John and his family removed to a house in Strawberry Alley, which lay parallel to Second, one half block to the West, and between Market and Chestnut.

In 1780 John Howard changed his business. In the tax lists his name appears between those of Moore and Wilson thus: " John Howard, Middle Ward, fishtacker." The city collected in 1780 an " Effective Supply Tax " at the rate of five shillings and six pence on every Hundred Pounds. Evidently it was a tax on the stock which a merchant had on hand. Howard was assessed at £103,500 and he paid a tax of £84." [26]

In 1781 he was taxed on a valuation of £2563, evidently the value of the real estate, at the rate of 25 shillings per Hundred £. He paid 29£–9 sh.–5 d. [27]

---

[23] " Some Items From the Account of the Executors of John Lukens, Deceased," *PMHB*, XXIV (1900), 122.

[24] *Pennsylvania Archives*, 3rd Series, XIV, 154, 775.

[25] " Taxables . . . in Philadelphia," 163.

[26] *Pennsylvania Archives*, 3rd Series, XV, 189-190.

[27] *Ibid.*, 697.

A transaction typical of eighteenth century business was his releasing a man from his status as an apprentice or redemptioner. On 13 January 1773 John Howard released an indentured servant "Assigned before Hon. John Gibson, Mayor of Philadelphia, Patrick Taafe, indentured to John Howard 19 July 1771, now cancelled, to James Lee of Philadelphia. 13 January 1773." [28]

Howard was a speculator in land. On 17 August 1781 he received a warrant for land in Bedford County, Penna., 168 acres and 158 perches (slightly under one acre) of land. It lacked one square rod of being 169 acres.

On the same date his son Thomas Howard received a warrant for 139¼ acres of land in Bedford County. [29]

In 1785 a John Howard paid a state tax of eight shillings on land in Union Township, Fayette County, Penna.

In 1786 a John Howard paid a state tax in Wharton Township, Fayette County, Penna. [30]

About 1790 John Howard retired from business. The City Directory of 1791, edited by Francis White, lists him as " Howard, John, Gentleman, 27 Strawberry Street." All directories thereafter list him thus. Strawberry Street lay between Second and Third and between High and Chestnut Streets. From his will we learn that he spent some time in Orange County, Virginia.

He died on 31 July 1809. According to the family Bible he was eighty-two at the time of his death, but according to the inscription on his tombstone he was eighty-four. Inspection of the Bible record clearly indicates that the latter is incorrect.

He was buried near his parents in Section A of Christ Church cemetery. His tombstone bore the inscription

JOHN HOWARD
departed this life
July 31st 1809

Aged 84 years.

Of John's children eight grew to adulthood.

1. Thomas (see Third Generation).
2. Sarah, b. 4 Feb. 1758; d. 29 Jan. 1786; m. in Christ Church 22 Aug. 1782 to Lawrence Slater, who died 5 Sept. 1783; daughter Sarah, b. 22 June 1783; d. 20 Dec. 1784.

---

[28] " Record of Servants and Apprentices Bound and Assigned Before Hon. John Gibson, Mayor . . . ," *PMHB*, XXXIV (1910), 102.

[29] *Pennsylvania Archives*, 3rd Series, XXV, 531.

[30] *Ibid.*, XXII, 551, 639.

3. Elizabeth, b. 30 July 1760; d. 22 May 1786.
4. Alice (see Third Generation).
5. Charles Pitt (see Third Generation).
6. John, b. 15 April 1769; d. unm. 12 May 1815. He served in the U S Navy. " Appointed Captain to command a galley. 20 March 1799."[31] He served as a captain in Tripoli in 1804, according to family information. He was disowned by the Philadelphia Monthly Meeting of Friends " for accepting a commission on board a ship of war," 1800, Jan. 31.[32] On 23 April 1801 John and his sister Deborah Howard were appointed administrators of the estate of their brother-in-law John James Malcolm. Thomas Howard, iron monger, and Samuel Baker, shopkeeper, were sureties in the amount of $3000.00.[33]
7. Luke, b. 1 Feb. 1772; unm; d. 25 March 1793.
8. Deborah, b. 7 Dec. 1775 (see Third Generation).

John Howard made his will in Philadelphia 26 January 1809. It is a beautifully engrossed document of seven sheets 14" x 9", containing about 1500 words. He named his friends Peter Browne, shipsmith, John Riley, watchmaker, and John Hart, druggist, as executors and trustees. They witnessed the will, the first two by oath, the last by affirmation.[34]

Of the twelve children born to him and Sarah (Bunting) Howard between 1750 and 1775, eight grew to adulthood, but only four survived him, namely Thomas, Charles Pitt, John, and Deborah.

He mentions the following pieces of property in Philadelphia:

1. His largest messuage or tenement on the north side of Callowhill Street, in Spring Garden in the North Liberties;
   devised to his grandson Caleb Howard, son of Thomas.
2. A messuage and lot on the north side of Callowhill Street, adjoining the preceding on the west;
   devised to his granddaughter Sarah Howard, daughter of Thomas.
3. A messuage and lot on the north side of Callowhill Street, adjoining the preceding on the west;
   devised to his granddaughter Edith Howard, daughter of Thomas.
4. His shop on the south side of Callowhill Street, " now (1809) occupied by Nathaniel Hillborn," (337 Callowhill?);
   devised to his granddaughter Deborah Howard, daughter of Thomas.
5. " The messuage and lot of ground on the east side of Strawberry Street which I now occupy; "
   devised to his grandson Charles Howard, son of Thomas.

---

[31] Edward W. Callahan, *List of Officers of the Navy of the United States and of the Marine Corps from 1775 to 1900* (New York, 1901).

[32] Hinshaw, *Encyclopedia, op. cit.*

[33] Philadelphia *Administration Book* K, 21.

[34] Philadelphia *Will Book* 2, 523 #73.

6. " The messuage and lot of ground on the west side of Delaware Second Street between Chestnut and High Streets, which James Musgrave now (1809) occupies," (44 South 2d St.) ;

> devised to his son John with the provision that if John should die without issue, the property should go to Caleb Howard, son of Thomas.

7. " The yearly rent charge of one hundred dollars issuing out of the lot adjoining the one last named, where Musgrave lives, originally payable by one Harbeson; "

> devised to his son John Howard during his life and immediately after his decease to Deborah Malcolm and her heirs.

8. The messuage and lot of ground on the west side of Delaware Second Street between Chestnut and High Streets, adjoining that " late of David Bacon; "

> devised to his daughter Deborah Malcolm for the term of her life, and then to her son Howard Malcom and his heirs.

John Howard may be said to have been a champion of women's rights. This is indicated in the provisions he made in his will for his unmarried granddaughters, e.g.,

" I give and devise to the executors my Messuage and Lot of Ground on the North Side of Callowhill Street . . . with the Appurtenances in trust to permit and suffer my Granddaughter Sarah Howard to receive all the Rents . . . and Profits during all the Term of her natural Life for her own sole and separate Use notwithstanding any Coverture and from and immediately after her Decease in trust for the Use of any Child or Children which the said Sarah may leave . . . forever."

Note: First he prevents the common law rule of Coverture from applying to Sarah. Second, by using the phrase " immediately after her Decease " he prevents her husband from retaining her inheritance for the rest of his life under the common law rule of Curtesy.

Under the rule of Coverture a woman at marriage lost her property rights because her husband exercised protection or guardianship over her. Under the rule of Curtesy the husband, if he survived her, enjoyed the use and benefit of her property for the rest of his life, even if she had left it to her children.

In Pennsylvania the former was repealed by the Legislature by the Act of 11th April 1848, P.L. 536. The latter was repealed by the Act of 7th June 1917, P.L. 429.[35]

Third Generation

1. THOMAS HOWARD, son of John and Sarah (Bunting) Howard, was born 1 January 1754. He died 21 April 1815.

About 1 January 1787 he married (1) Edith Newbold, daughter of Caleb and Sarah (Haines) Newbold. She was born 31 August 1766 in Burlington County, N. J. She was descended in the fourth generation

---

[35] Courtesy of Ledyard Hart Heckscher, Esq.

from Michael Newbold, who in 1681 had come from Sheffield, Yorkshire, England, and had bought a large tract of land in Burlington County, West Jersey. He was the ancestor of the Newbold family of Philadelphia.

Thomas Howard had been received by request by the Philadelphia Monthly Meeting of Friends on 3 January 1777.[36] But on 27 April 1787 that Meeting adopted the following resolution:

" Thomas Howard, of this city, Clock and Watch-maker, . . . hath deviated from the good order of our Discipline by accomplishing his marriage contrary to the Rules thereof, therefore we testify that we do no longer esteem him in religious membership with us. We desire that he may properly acknowledge his deviation and become rightly restored to membership again." [37]

Thomas did not conform. But the Monthly Meeting of Upper Springfield, Burlington County, N. J., on 9 April 1788 sent the following communication to the Philadelphia Monthly Meeting:

" Application having been made to us on behalf of Edith Howard, who hath removed to live with her husband within the verge of your Meeting . . . we recommend her to your care and notice . . . " [38]

Edith (Newbold) Howard died and was buried 20 March 1799.[39] On 27 March 1801 Thomas Howard did penance and was re-instated by the Meeting. On 29 May 1801 the Southern District (Pine Street) granted him a certificate to marry (2) Sarah Powell (Buckley) Cooper, daughter of William and Sarah (Powell) Buckley, and widow of Joseph Cooper of Gloucester, N. J. Howard and Sarah were married 1 July 1801 at the Pine Street Meeting.[40]

Thomas learned the trade of a clock and watch maker. The following advertisement probably marks the beginning of his business:

" Thomas Howard, Second Street, between Market and Chestnut,
Clocks and Watches sold."

Pennsylvania Packet, 20 May 1777.

The city directory of 1791 lists him as a clock and watch-maker, living at 26 Second Street. But by 1794 he had changed his business, for in the city directory of that year he appears as an iron-monger, living at 40 South Second Street.

---

[36] Hinshaw, *Encyclopedia*, II, 555.

[37] Philadelphia Monthly Meeting, Minutes, E 11, 313.

[38] Philadelphia Monthly Meeting, Southern District, Certificates Received, G 13, 56.

[39] Hinshaw, *Encyclopedia*, II, 377.

[40] *Ibid*.

After 1800 he changed his business once more, for the city directories list him as a lumber merchant. Thus in 1814 Kite's Philadelphia Directory states "Thomas Howard, lumber merchant, 143 and 179 Pine Street."

In 1780, when the City of Philadelphia levied an "Effective Supply Tax," he was taxed £38. In 1782 on a valuation of £750, he paid 5 £–7 shillings–6 pence.[41]

On 17 August 1781 Thomas received a warrant for land in Bedford County, containing 139 acres of land.[42]

In his father's will, made in 1809, there occur the following provisions:

"I give to my son Thomas my silver Tankard, two silver Tumblers, and my Looking Glass now in my Parlour which was my father's.

"My executors shall collect the bond of my son Thomas for three hundred thirty-three and a third of a Dollar, when it becomes due. They shall spend a part of it to purchase for Sarah Howard, daughter Thomas, a silver Slop Bowl and six silver Spoons to complete the set of Plate which I have given her. The rest of the money they shall divide between Edith and Deborah, daughters of Thomas, to buy for themselves sets of Plate."

Thomas Howard 2d made his own will on 18 April 1815.[43] It consists of two sheets 18″ x 10″, engrossed. It begins with the following words: "Be it remembered that I Thomas Howard, Lumber Merchant, being of weak and declining State of Health but sound Memory and Understanding, do make and ordain this my Last Will and Testament."

He bequeaths to his son Caleb N. Howard, who already had received his proportionate part of the father's estate, the sum of seventy-five dollars to be retained by the Executors to be laid out for a casimere coat and pantaloons and such other clothing suitable either for sea or land, as Caleb may want. He also gives him the best part of his wearing apparel.

Other personal bequests include: To his daughter Sarah Newbold Conway his silver pint Can marked T.E.H. To his daughter Edith Newbold Howard the scalloped silver waiter marked E.N. which was given by her grandmother with the intent that it be handed down in the family, also two silver tumblers, ten silver teaspoons marked "T.E.H." To his daughter Deborah Howard six large silver tablespoons and a silver ladle all marked T.E.H. He gives to his beloved wife Sarah one-third of the rest of his personal estate. He gives to her also one-third of the income of all his real estate for the rest of her natural life.

[41] *Pennsylvania Archives,* 3rd Series, XV, 6.

[42] *Ibid.,* XXV, 351.

[43] Philadelphia *Will Book* 6, 37 #56.

The rest of his personal and real estate he ordered to be divided equally among his six children, with this exception: since Charles was treated handsomely in his grandfather's will (he got John Howard's home on Strawberry Street), four hundred dollars should be taken from his share and divided among his five sisters.

He appoints Samuel Newbold, brother of his first wife, and Anthony M. Buckley, brother of his present wife, as executors, instructing them to sell all his real estate, but to use their discretion in the best interest of his wife and children.

The will was witnessed by Benjamin Cooper and Howard Malcolm, who both solemnly affirmed, and by Peter Thomas, who solemnly swore, that it was signed by the testator.

Thomas had the following children:

By his first wife, Edith Newbold: [43a]

Caleb Newbold, b. *ca.* 1788.
Sarah Newbold, b. *ca.* 1790; m. George Conway and removed to Alabama.
Edith Newbold, b. *ca.* 1792; m. a Govett; she d. 1832.
Deborah Newbold (" Debby "), b. *ca.* 1794; she never married.

By his second wife, Sarah Buckley: [43b]

Charles Powell, b. 14 July 1802.
Eliza, b. 1803, d. 1808, aged 4 yrs.
Emma Buckley, b. 8 Nov. 1810; m. 11 Oct. 1848 at Friends' Meeting House to William L. Edwards of Philadelphia, son of Griffith and Sarah Edwards, both deceased.
Elizabeth Buckley, b. 28 April 1812; m. 2 Oct. 1832 to Samuel H. Edwards of Philadelphia, son of Griffith Edwards, deceased, and his wife Sarah.

4. ALICE HOWARD, daughter of John and Sarah (Bunting) Howard, was born 5 January 1762 and was baptized in Christ Church. She was married 3 March 1791 in Christ Church to Humphrey Hill. The latter was born in 1763, probably in Chester, Pa. In 1787 the Chester M.M. issued him a certificate to the Philadelphia M.M. Here he worked as an apprentice and became an apothecary. He died 7 December 1811.[44] Alice died 15 January 1792 a week after giving birth to their only child, John Howard Hill. (See Fourth Generation.)

5. CHARLES PITT HOWARD, son of John and Sarah (Bunting) Howard, was born 25 November 1765, as their eighth child. The fact that

---

[43a] Granville Malcolm, *op. cit.*

[43b] Philadelphia Friends' Yearly Meeting, Southern District, Department of Records, G 18, 4 and G 17, 152.

[44] Hinshaw, *Encyclopedia*, II, 174.

his parents gave him the middle name " Pitt " illustrates the admiration which the English colonists felt for William Pitt, the Prime Minister who had turned near-defeat into a decisive victory in the war with the French and Indians.

On 22 February 1782 Charles Pitt, at the age of sixteen was received " by request into the Philadelphia Friends' Monthly Meeting."

Some ten years later Charles Pitt was settled in Orange County, Virginia, and he was to spend the rest of a long life there. He married 11 March 1793 Jane Taylor, who was born 2 March 1766 and died 13 January 1849.[45] Her immigrant ancestor was James Taylor I. Her grandfather was James Taylor II. Her father was Erasmus Taylor (1715-1794), who was a vestryman in St. Thomas Parish, Orange County, Virginia. His family was related to that of William Henry Harrison (1773-1841), the ninth President of the United States, and that of Zachary Taylor (1784-1850), twelfth President of the United States. Her mother was Jane Moore (1728-1812).[46]

Charles Pitt Howard played a prominent role in the affairs of Orange County, as can be seen from a few entries in the Minute Book:

24 February 1795 Francis Taylor, Francis Cowherd, Charles P. Howard, and James Bell, or any three of them, to settle with the Sheriff for the County Levy from the year 1782 to the present time." (Minute Bk. 3, p. 282)

25 June 1798, Charles P. Howard, Charles Taylor, James Bell, and Francis Taylor, appointed to appraise the estate of Thomas Bell, deceased. (Minute Bk. 4, p. 83)

24 February 1800. John Henshaw and Charles P. Howard be appointed to let to the lowest bidder to repair or rebuild the Blue Run Bridge. (Minute Bk. 4, p. 806)

27 February 1804 Charles P. Howard commissioned as Justice by a commission dated 21 Jan. 1804. (Minute Bk. 4, p. 536)

Charles P. Howard listed as magistrate for the years 1803, 1804, and 1805. (Minute Bk. 4, p. 2911)

In 1799 Charles Pitt Howard purchased from Prettyman Merry for $3,733.00 a tract of 529 acres. A few years later he sold nine acres of it. It is probable that his father, John Howard, advanced some money to pay for this estate, with the understanding that the amount would represent the son's share in his father's estate at the latter's death. Two sections of John Howard's will suggest this:

(on sheet 4) " I give and devise the Plantation and Tract of land in Orange County, Virginia, containing about five hundred and thirty acres, whereon my son Charles P. Howard resides, with the appurtenances, unto him my son Charles P. Howard, his heirs

---

[45] Granville Malcolm, op. cit.

[46] Horace Edwin Hayden: *Virginia Genealogies*, reprinted in 1931, contains a meager account of the Taylor family and gives no dates for Jane Taylor.

and assigns forever. I also give to my said son Charles P. Howard all the plate, furniture, and other personal estate soever which I left at the said plantation when I removed from there; "

(sheet 6) " My will is that whatever I have advanced or given to any or either of my said children or grandchildren during my life shall not be accounted for by them or either of them in any way either one to another or to my estate."

In 1810 Charles P. Howard and his wife Jane sold the remaining 520 acres to John Henshaw. The deed recites " and being the land whereon the said Howard now resides."

In 1811 Charles P. Howard purchased a tract of 532½ acres from the administrator of the estate of John Baylor. This land was located in what is now Orange County. It is located about one mile west of the town of Orange on the old Orange-Stanardsville Pike, now Route 20, just to the east of Montpelier, the home of James Madison.[47]

Charles Pitt Howard and his wife are buried in the Taylor Family Lot.[48]

> In Memory of
> Charles Pitt Howard
> Born Nov. 25, 1765
> Died at his late residence in this County
> the 18th March 1856
>
> In Memory of
> Jane Taylor
> the beloved wife of
> Charles Pitt Howard
> Born M'ch 2, 1766
> Died Jan. 13 1849.

Charles Pitt Howard lived to be ninety-one years old. His will, dated 23 August 1853, is a document of fifteen sheets, 14½" x 8½" with a text of 1500 words in a handwriting which is rather difficult to decipher. It is recorded in Orange County.[49] It was proved 24 March 1856. In Item No. 1 he directs that all his debts and funeral expenses be paid. In Item No. 2 that he be buried beside his wife in the Taylor family cemetery and that suitable marble monuments be erected to himself and his wife.

---

[47] Letter from H. C. De Jarnette, Clerk, Circuit Court of Orange County, Orange, Virginia, June 1959.

[48] Granville Malcolm, *op. cit.*

[49] *Will Book* 12, 211, Orange County, Va.

In Item No. 8 he bequeaths to his nephew John Howard Hill, son of his deceased sister Alice, late of Philadelphia, the sum of three thousand dollars. In Item No. 9 the like sum to his nephew Howard Malcolm, son of his sister Deborah. In Item No. 10 he bequeaths to his sister Deborah, mother of Howard Malcolm and now wife of Chandler Hollbrook, all his silver plate.

In Item No. 12 he bequeaths the residue of his estate to his great nephew Charles Howard Malcolm, son of Howard Malcolm and grandson of Deborah (Howard) Malcolm, now the wife of Chandler Hollbrook.

In Items Nos. 5 to 6 he makes bequests to " Willis Dangerfield, whom I emancipated some years since, . . . living in Allegany City, Pennsylvania, the sum of four hundred dollars; to Polly McNeale, whom I also emancipated some years ago, the like sum of four hundred dollars; to Mary Ann Pittman, now residing near Mt. Holly, N. Y. the like sum."

More than one-half of the text (Item No. 3) is devoted to his plan of freeing his forty slaves and making provision for them:

> " I hereby manumit and free all the slaves and servants that I may die possessed of or entitled to . . . . Feeling an anxious concern for their welfare and an earnest desire to put them in situations wherever they may be comfortable and enjoy the benefits intended for them, I have appropriated the sum of four thousand dollars to be divided among them."

He appoints his friend William O. Moore, Sr., to take charge of the matter and to try to move them in a body to some one of the states or territories of the United States in which slavery is not legal. He directs that a sum of five thousand dollars may be used for that purpose. But he has an alternative to offer (sheet 3, line 9):

> " Those of my said freedmen who desire not to remove . . . , may choose for themselves if, in the judgment of my executors they shall be of an age and discretion fit to judge on that subject for themselves, . . . to them shall be paid their respective shares of the sums due and to be divided . . . . "

If it should prove impractical to move any of his freedmen to another state, then the agent, Mr. William O. Moore, Sr., could fall back on this provision. There seems to be no report on file concerning the execution of the plan to re-settle these freedmen outside of Virginia.

Charles P. Howard names as his executors six men: Philip S. Fry, Thomas S. Slaughter, John Willis, Lewis B. Williams, William Moore, Sr., and William Green.

On 15 November 1856 three executors, " the only acting executors," sold to Richard S. Baulware two lots in Orange County Court House which the said C. P. Howard had bought 8 October 1832 from Daniel Hord for $530.00. (Recorded 17 Nov. 1856, Orange County Deed Bk. 44, p. 211.)

On 1 April 1862 the executors of the late C. P. Howard sold to John Willis of Orange County 889.59 acres, survey made by George S. Newman, less 5.59 acres conveyed to the railroad, leaving 884 acres, sold at $23.75 per acre, same being the land on which the said C. P. Howard resided at the time of his death, near the town of Orange Court House (Orange County Deed Bk. 45, p. 373.)

Charles Howard Malcolm was named the heir of Charles Pitt Howard's residual estate. (See Fourth Generation.)

8. DEBORAH HOWARD, daughter of John and Sarah (Bunting) Howard, was born 7 December 1775. She was married 22 February 1798 in Christ Church to John James Malcolm, who was born 27 June 1775, son of John and Hannah (Roberts) Malcolm. As a child she had joined the Friends with her mother. Now, for " marrying out of unity " she was disowned by the Philadelphia Monthly Meeting on 25 May 1798.

The Philadelphia City Directory of 1798 lists " John J. Malcolm & Co., druggists, 78 South Second Street." The 1799 directory lists the firm as located at 26 South Second Street, probably a property belonging to her father John Howard. John James Malcolm contracted consumption and died 16 April 1801, leaving his wife Deborah with a son Howard Malcolm, born 19 January 1799. She was married (2) on 7 November 1820 to Chandler Hollbrook, who was born in Massachusetts. The ceremony was performed by her son the Rev. Howard Malcolm.

Deborah's father, John Howard, when he made his will, made generous provision for Deborah:

" I give the Messuage and Lot of Ground on the East side of Strawberry Street which I now occupy unto the executors in trust to permit and suffer my daughter Deborah Malcolm to receive all Profits thereof or to occupy the same for her own use until my Grandson Charles Howard (son of Thomas) arrive to the Age of twenty-one Years, etc (sheet 5) I assign the annual rent of one hundred dollars on a lot in Second Street between Chestnut and High, payable originally by one Harbeson, to my son John Howard, but after his death to Deborah Malcolm and her heirs forever."

He assigns another messuage and lot on Second Street between Chestnut and High Streets to the trustees for the benefit of his daughter Deborah Malcolm " for her own sole and separate use notwithstanding any coverture for the term of her natural life and thereafter to her son Howard and his heirs forever; " (sheet 6) " the sum of one thousand dollars to my daughter Deborah Malcolm; " (sheet 6) all the rest of the plate, household and kitchen furniture and linens and woolens which shall be in his house at the time of his death to his daughter Deborah Malcolm.

FOURTH GENERATION

JOHN HOWARD HILL, son of Humphrey and 4. Alice (Howard) Hill, was born 9 January 1792 in Philadelphia.

His grandfather John Howard in his will, made in 1809, declared:

"I give and devise all that my Plantation and Tract of land on Sideling Hill Gap in Bedford County in the State of Pennsylvania, afore called 'Howard's Plantation,' containing one hundred and sixty-eight acres and one hundred and fifty-eight Perches . . . unto my Grandson John Howard Hill, son of my daughter Alice, deceased, to hold, to him, his Assigns and Heirs forever . . . I also give and bequeath to the said John Howard Hill the sum of Three Thousand five Hundred Dollars . . . "

He entered the School of Medicine of the University of Pennsylvania in 1810 and remained two years. He did not graduate,[50] but he practiced medicine in Philadelphia until 1840. His name appears the last time in the 1840 city directory as living at 100 N. Eighth Street. " He was a successful physician in Pennsylvania," wrote Granville Malcolm. Later he removed to California and died there at the age of ninety-four on 7 May 1886.

He married (1) 16 December 1813 Elizabeth Louisa Davis, daughter of Nathaniel Davis and Catherine Cornog; (2) 8 October 1835 Cynthia Craig, daughter of Daniel Craig of Montgomery County and Jane Jamieson of Bucks County.[51]

HOWARD MALCOLM, son of John J. and 8. Deborah (Howard) Malcolm, was born 19 January 1799 in Philadelphia.

In 1814, at the age of fifteen, he entered Dickinson Academy at Carlisle, Pa., but at the end of the academic year the school was closed. In January 1816 he was converted and he joined the Sansom Street Baptist Church. In 1818, at the age of nineteen, he was licensed to preach by the Baptist Association. He then studied for two years, 1818-20, in Princeton Theological Seminary.

Ordained as a Baptist minister, he accepted a call to Hudson, some fifty miles north of New York City, and remained there seven years. He was called to Boston, Mass., and he served there from 1827 to 1835. The

---

[50] Not until 1875 did the legislature of Pennsylvania pass a law making a degree from a medical school a prerequisite for a person's being admitted to the practice of medicine. See George P. Donehoo, *Pennsylvania: A History* (New York, 1926), IV.

[51] Granville Malcolm, *op. cit.*, 43.

next ten years he did field work for the church. For two years, 1849-51, he was pastor of his home church, the Sansom Street Baptist Church in Philadelphia.

From 1851 to 1857 he was president of Bucknell University in Lewisburg, Pa. " He was a persuasive preacher and a voluminous writer of religious books." [52] Upon retirement he settled in Philadelphia. He died 25 March 1879 at 1520 Mt. Vernon Street, and was buried in Laurel Hill Cemetery.[53]

He married (1) in 1820 Lydia Morris Sheilds, daughter of Robert and Mary Sheilds, who was born in Philadelphia in 1797. She died in January 1833 in Boston; (2) 26 June 1838 Ruth Anne Dyer, daughter of Ezra and Anne (Jennings) Dyer, who was born in Boston, Mass., 11 November 1808. She died 2 February 1878 in Philadelphia.

Children by the first marriage:

    i. Thomas Sheilds, b. 1821 in Philadelphia. He graduated from Brown University and Princeton Theological Seminary. He married in 1844 Margaret Nevius Van Dyke of Princeton, N. J. He died in 1888 in Philadelphia.

    ii. Louisa, b. 1828 at Hudson, N. Y.; married to Robert Stenton of New York, N. Y. 8 Oct. 1858.

    iii. Charles Howard, b. 1831 in Boston, Mass. He graduated from Bucknell University in 1852, from Princeton Theological Seminary in 1856. He married 5 Feb. 1856 Margaret McKay of Philadelphia. He died 19 August 1899 at Newport, R. I. In 1856 he was named residual heir to the estate of his great uncle Charles Pitt Howard of Orange County, Va.

Children by second marriage:

    iv. Granville, b. 2 April 1839, Boston, Mass. He graduated from Georgetown Medical College, Washington, D. C. in 1867. He prepared a manuscript of sixty pages entitled " The Ancestors and Descendants of Howard Malcolm," which in 1894 he deposited with the Historical Society of Pennsylvania.

    v. Arthur, b. 1842.

Howard Malcolm early evinced an interest in his family history. Upon retirement he did some research, which was to be continued by his son Granville. Howard wrote to Granville:

" Thomas and Grace Howard and all their children are interred in the NW corner of Christ Church Yard, as are all the rest of the Howard family down to 1823.

" I examined this spot in 1826 and found but few stones visible. In 1814 I visited the same yard and found fifteen or twenty stones quite legible and bearing inscriptions highly honorable to the family and indicating longevity."

---

[52] Rev. William Cathcart, *Baptist Encyclopedia* (Philadelphia).

[53] Granville Malcolm, *op. cit.*

Corrections

Corrections on "Howard, An Early Philadelphia Family," *PGM*, XXI, 197-215, by Ralph Dornfeld Owen. See page 198, re: *Grace Beaks* — *

Grace Beaks, wife of Thomas Howard of Philadelphia, born in 1695, daughter of *Stephen and Elizabeth (Biles) Beaks* of Falls Township, Bucks County, Pennsylvania; granddaughter of William and Mary (Walle) Beaks of Backwell, County Somerset, England, who arrived in Bucks County, Pennsylvania, 12 February 1682, and settled in Middletown Twsp. See *The American Genealogist,* 51: 205; 52: 35. See page 199, 4th paragraph should read: "Grace *Beaks, four* months before her marriage, (to Thomas Howard) requested and received a certificate (for removal) from *Falls Monthly Meeting of Friends,* Bucks County, Pennsylvania, dated *1st of 3rd mo. (May) 1723." Hinshaw,* 2: 978. 6th paragraph should be added — "(Thomas Howard's) second wife was a widow Susanna _____". Thomas Howard of Philadelphia and *Susanna* Edgecomb, *widow,* were married 22 October 1745, Trinity Church, Oxford Township, Philadelphia County. She was his 2nd wife, widow of Nathaniel Edgecomb of Philadelphia, who died intestate shortly before 10 Nov. 1741, (*PGM*, XXVIII, 263), and whom as Susannah Skinner, she had married 2 February 1729 at Christ Church, Philadelphia.

Lewis D. Cook, FASG, FGSP.

---

*Page 52, this volume.

HOWARD BIBLE RECORD

TRANSCRIBED AND SUBMITTED BY

GEORGE H. S. KING, F.A.S.G., Fredericksburg, Virginia

Bible published by Andrus and Judd, New York, N. Y., 1832.
Bible is in the Clerk's Office, Orange County, Virginia, Court.
Fly leaf: " Charles P. Howard near Orange Court House, Virginia."

Thomas Howard and Grace Beeks were married September 16, 1723.
Grace Howard born 15 October 1725; died 10 June 1728.
John Howard born 13 March 1727; died 31 July 1809.
Grace Howard born 18 October 1729; died 31 March 1731.
Joanna Howard born 11 October 1731.
Grace Howard born 29 October 1733.
Mary Howard born 11 March 1735.
Sarah Howard born 13 March 1737; died 13 June 1737.
Grace Howard died 19 August 1742. } Father and mother of the above.
Thomas Howard died 25 December 1748. }

All of the foregoing individuals were interred in the Cemetery of
Christ Church in the City of Philadelphia.

John J. Malcom and Deborah Howard were married 22 February 1798.
Howard Malcom born 19 January 1799.
John J. Malcom died 16 April 1801.

John Howard Hill son of Humphrey Hill and Alice [Howard] Hill, born 9 January
1792.

Charles P. Howard and Jane Taylor were married 11 March 1793. [This marriage is of
record in Orange County, Va. Marriage Register No. One, page 32.]

John Howard and Sarah Bunting were married 16 October 1749.
Grace Howard was born 4 October 1750; died 9 April 1761.
Thomas Howard was born 1 January 1754; died 21 April 1815.
John Howard was born 12 May 1756; died 6 September 1757.
Sarah Howard was born 4 February 1758; married 22 August 1782 Laurence Slater who
died 5 September 1783. She died 29 January 1786. Sarah L. Slater was born 22
June 1783 and died 20 December 1784.
Elizabeth Howard born 30 July 1760 and died 22 May 1786.
Alice Howard born 5 January 1762, married Humphrey Hill and died 15 January 1792.
Joshua Howard born 1 July 1764; died 8 July 1764.
Charles Pitt Howard born 25 November 1765; died 20 March 1856, aged 91 years,
3 months and 25 days.
Mary Howard born 28 October 1767; died 16 March 1773.
John Howard born 15 April 1769; died 12 May 1815.
Luke Howard born 1 Feb. 1772; died 25 March 1793.
Deborah Howard born 7 December 1775.
Sarah Howard died 8 October 1784. } Father and mother of the above.
John Howard died 31 July 1809. }

71

THE HUMPHREYS FAMILY.

BY THE HONORABLE HAMPTON L. CARSON.

An Address Delivered before The Genealogical Society of Pennsylvania, at the Annual Meeting, March 6, 1922.

Ladies and Gentlemen: Your Presiding Officer's introduction is embarrassing, because I noted that he was uncertain as to the particular subject he wished me to talk upon. I recollect being at a University gathering, where the Reverend George Dana Boardman proposed as a subject, ''The Founding of the University of Bologna in the Eleventh Century, with Personal Reminiscences by Mr. Carson.'' You, Sir, have saved me from such a situation by carrying notes which, though in your pocket, commit me to a definite theme. I do not know who it was, perhaps it was your Secretary, who suggested that I should talk about the Humphreys Family. At all events that is my subject.

I am not going to give a genealogical table nor attempt to draw a genealogical tree. We all know what such trees look like, and there are only certain particular buds on distant branches which can be of interest to each individual in an audience. I shall confine myself to representatives of six generations of the Humphreys Family, illustrating the sturdiness of the parent stock and the character of the achievements in each generation of that remarkable family.

In order that you may have before you in a general way a picture of the Humphreys Family, it occurs to me that I can appeal to the recollection of everybody in the room of the old house which long stood on the east side of Thirteenth Street just above Spruce, and which gave way but eighteen months ago to a garage. For many years, prior to its occupation by the Junkers, Miss Borie lived there. Prior to Miss Borie's occupancy, an old gentleman of the name of Charles Humphreys, who died in the year 1873, had lived there for over fifty years. It was an old-fashioned three-story brick dwelling house, with dormer garret windows, somewhat moderate in its rooms and but two rooms in depth, with a low two-story back building, all bordered on the south by a garden of exceeding beauty. When you passed along Thirteenth Street and looked through the perforated iron grill that was set in the gate, you would observe old-fashioned flower-beds bordered by box-wood, a clinging and fragrant yellow jasmine vine on the southern wall, grape vines and trellis-work of wistaria, in the rear; in the spring, beautiful beds of tulips, succeeded by flowers in season, and a bit of turf that was kept closely cropped, rivaling any of our finest lawns. That garden was a source of perpetual delight to those who were privileged to enter it. My own childish recollection runs back to it with affection. I have seen there not only Mr. Humphreys, who was a flour merchant, and his genial wife, a dame of the olden school, but his guests who frequently were his opponents in a game of backgammon, Commodore Dale, a son of Richard Dale who was first lieutenant under Paul Jones on the deck of the *Bon Homme Richard* as she grappled with the *Serapis;* Admiral Turner of the Civil War, General Humphreys and General Isaac J. Wistar; so that, during my boyish days, I would hear stories of the sea and of the land, of the Army and of the Navy. Mr. Humphreys would drive twice a week, on Sundays and on Thursdays, out to his father's place, the Humphreys farm on the Haverford Road directly back of Ardmore, with an old-fashioned pebble-dashed house which many of you have admired, where the Tilghmans have been in residence for so many years that it is almost thought to be a Tilghman possession, but it still belongs to the Humphreys' Estate. Between the house on Thirteenth Street and the old pebble-dashed house on the Haverford Road Mr. Humphreys spent his life. He had there a model farm, with a wonderful herd of cattle, whose cows and calves were curried twice a day as though they had been horses. Not a weed was permitted to grow in any spot of the place. Crops were exceedingly fine, the clover crops particularly so. There was a wonderful semicircle of great beech trees in a dense woods which even now cuts the western sky like a half-moon, presenting to our State Forester, if he should go there at this hour, a specimen of an old Colonial grove still flourishing in its primeval strength.

All through the Township of Haverford, as it was called in Delaware County, the Humphreys were numerous. The old name of Bryn Mawr was Humphreyville, many of the family residing in that neighborhood, and if you should ascend the hill of the Quaker Meeting House, which was the second Meeting House erected in this part of the State, the first being at Merion, you will find along the wall of the burying ground the gravestones of members of the Humphreys family, extending in double rows. There they sleep, still ruling our spirits with their sceptres from their urns. You cannot enter that old Quaker burying-ground without being impressed by the fact that in former days the Humphreys family dominated that section of Delaware County. It is of that family that I shall speak.

You, Mr. Chairman, well remember certain members of the family. Old Miss "Patty" Humphreys, was within your recollection. I am getting back, you see, somewhat to the last century. I belong to the last century myself, that is the greater part of me. Miss Patty Humphreys was the maiden sister of the old gentleman whom I have described. I am quite sure that if Mr. Sayres ever tasted her scrapple, her sausages and her pumpkin pies he would be more anxious to leave this earth in search of where she now is and repeat his experiences than his present quiet attitude indicates.

The name of Humphreys is of Norman origin and can be traced for a thousand years. In Domesday Book it appears as *Humfridus,* with a Latin termination, afterwards spelled H-u-m-f-r-e-y and sometimes H-u-m-p-h-r-y. I have seen it also "i-e-s", but the particular branch of the family I am speaking of to-night spells it "e-y-s". About the year 1340, when the Herald's College was established, there were at least six coats-of-arms relating to branches of the Humphreys Family registered. One of those, a lion rampant with dexter paw on the head of a nag, represented the Conquest of Wales by one branch of the family, and there for six hundred years the family held possession of lands which their ancestors had got by force of arms and by valor.

The first ancestor to whom I intend to allude was Samuel Humphreys, the son of Hugh Ap Humphreys, who in 1606 had married Elizabeth Powell, daughter of John Powell and Sibill Gwyn of Llanwdlwn. Samuel Humphreys died in Merionethshire in Wales. He had married Elizabeth Rhys or Rees, according to a difference in spelling. They had six or seven children, the oldest son being Daniel, whose line of descent is the only one that I intend to illustrate because, although the family has had numerous branches, it is only in running down the direct line of Daniel that I find public services rendered by members of the family. The other branches, while estimable in private life, were not prominent in the affairs of the world. Daniel Humphreys, in 1682, his father being dead five years, came to this country. He carried with him a certificate of good character from the Quarterly Meeting in Wales. In the following year, 1683, he was followed by his widowed mother, Elizabeth, with her remaining children, and they all settled in the Township of Haverford, the name Haverford being derived from *Aber Ford,* which means above the ford or above the confluence of streams. The township in South Wales which bears that name had a castle dating back as far as 1113, which was visited by Bishop Baldwin in the year 1152, so it appears that they were people of substance and character as well as of achievement. Daniel welcomed his mother, his brothers and his sisters and established them about seven miles west of our City Hall.

To get the exact position in your minds: go directly south of Ardmore and strike the Haverford Road; turn down to the left and find this old pebble-dashed house standing on the north side of Cobb's Creek, below the new Golf Grounds which have been placed there in recent years. Daniel married Mary, the daughter of Thomas Wynne, the first Speaker of the First Provincial Assembly of Pennsylvania and the ancestor of Hugh Wynne, about whom Doctor S. Weir Mitchell has written so charmingly. He built a very substantial house, long known as "The Mansion House," of brick and of stone with a hipped roof, with windows scattered about in very irregular fashion, with small glass panes in leaden frames. That house stayed in the possession of the family until 1810, when Dennis Kelly, a miller, who had mills along the line of Cobb's Creek, purchased it, and about the year 1860 or 1862 the house was torn down and that memorial of the Humphreys Family vanished. Daniel and Mary had six or seven children. One of them, Edward, was particularly distinguished as a doctor, who practiced physics and surgery with much success and public approval. He left no descendants.

Before alluding to the son who carried the line down into the next generation, which is the one on which I particularly wish to dwell, let me call your attention to another childless son of Daniel who reached great distinction, a man of high integrity, character and purpose, free from the arts of the politician, but, differing in judgment from many of his countrymen, abruptly terminated his public career. I refer to Charles Humphreys, who in 1763 was chosen a member of the Provincial Assembly and remained such until 1776. He was one of the seven delegates chosen to represent Pennsylvania in the first Continental Congress, which met in Old Carpenter's Hall in September, 1774. He served also in the Continental Congress of 1775 and the early one of 1776, with John Dickinson, Edward Biddle, Thomas Willing, Andrew Allen, Robert Morris and James Wilson. He participated actively in all the measures which the Continental Congress found it necessary to adopt. He signed with others the Declaration of Rights representing the grievances of which the Colonies complained. He also signed the Non-intercourse Proclamation, and in every way participated until it came to the crucial point of voting for the Declaration of Independence. Those of you who have read the records will recall that, in November 1775, the Pennsylvania Legislature by express resolution instructed its members in Congress not to sanction or support any measure which looked towards a separation of the Colonies from the Crown, and that restriction was not removed until the 8th of June, 1776. I cannot stop to go into the niceties of Pennsylvania history, but Pennsylvania's position in the matter of the Declaration of Independence is entirely misunderstood and misapprehended by people outside of the State and sometimes by people within it. They forget that the battle for popular rights had been waged and won in the long struggle between the people, represented by David Lloyd and Benjamin Franklin, on the one side, and on the other by the representatives of governors appointed by the Penns who owned the soil in fee as well as possessing limited sovereignty under the charter. That battle had raged for over seventy years on our soil. We had won in Pennsylvania a recognition of popular rights which the other Colonies did not possess, so we had not the same grievances the other Colonies had and were not suffering from weight of oppression in the same sense. Besides that, there was in the charter of William Penn a distinct reservation which did not exist anywhere else, of the right of the Crown to tax the colonists without their consent. With that background, you can easily understand the attitude of a man like John Dickinson, who happened to be Charles Humphreys' third cousin because his mother traced back descent from Thomas Wynne. John Dickinson expressly stated the reason why he did not vote for the Declaration. So did Edward Biddle, and Mr. Thomas Willing Balch explained this matter last November when talking about Thomas Willing in this hall. These men were not unpatriotic, not at all. They gave everything they had to the cause, but they differed in judgment from the majority as to the time or necessity for the act of Independence. They said that without a French alliance, without some preparation on the part of the Colonies for an effective resistance to the power of the Crown, it was an act of madness to sever precipitately the tie of the Colonies to the Throne. Therefore they declined to sign. Bancroft declares that it was an act of the highest moral courage. Charles Humphreys was one of that kind. He erred in judgment you may say, because the tide of popular opinion went the other way, but he was not a politician and refused to surrender his convictions. For this reason he was left out of Congress on a new election. I ought to say also that Robert Morris and James Wilson, both of them signers of the Declaration of Independence, originally agreed in sentiment with Dickinson, Willing, Allen, Humphreys and Biddle. Charles Humphreys passed from the public service, but lived a long life highly respected. I have seen some of his books and read some of his letters but he did not enter upon the discussion of the question I have touched. The family has always cherished a high regard for his memory, and his grave is in the old Haverford burying ground.

His elder brother, Joshua, was not remarkable for any act of public service, though highly esteemed in private life. I mention him because he was the father of Joshua Humphreys, born in 1751, who lived until 1838, dying at the ripe age of eighty-seven. The younger Joshua is the man to whom we are indebted for the American Navy, for he was the first naval constructor in the United States, the man who made it possible for our seamen to carry the flag unashamed and victorious on the sea. His was the house—that old pebble-dashed house now standing on Haverford Road — and it was to that house that his son Charles went, leaving his garden gate at Thirteenth and Spruce Streets to drive out to Haverford Road. Joshua Humphreys as a young man was apprenticed to a shipbuilder and displayed remarkable talent even in the early years of the Revolutionary War. He planned the frigate *Randolph*, that gallant little American ship which, carrying the flag under Captain Nicholas Biddle, in September, 1777, was attacked by the *Yarmouth*, a British ship twice her size. In a desperate battle when Biddle found himself doomed to defeat, because overpowered by a more powerful adversary, rather than strike his flag he blew up his ship and perished with all his crew. Humphreys also designed many of those little ships commanded by the first of our American admirals, Esek Hopkins, who carried the Rattlesnake Flag with Paul Jones as one of his subordinate officers. Think of what that little fleet did, designed in part by this Philadelphia Quaker who was put out of Meeting because of the support he was giving to the cause of the Colonies. The American fleet captured 800 British vessels of all kinds during the War of the Revolution, with five thousand prisoners. What splendid exploits! When the Revolution was over, the French Revolution soon followed, and later the Berlin and Milan Decrees were beginning to agitate the world; the Tripolitan War hung like a dark cloud over us. At this time Humphreys foresaw the absolute necessity for building up an American navy. He addressed a letter to Robert Morris in which he sketched out his plans. I have facsimiles of all his letters, and his correspondence in this book which I have on the desk beside me; the originals are upstairs in our treasury vaults. His letters justify the claim that is made for him as being the founder of the American Navy. Without going into technical niceties—I am not a naval man nor a ship carpenter, so I can only explain the general idea—his thought was this, a bold thought and one characteristic of his genius. He knew perfectly well that the English navy was the most powerful afloat, that it could overpower us in any part of the world. We could not build ships fast enough to match them ship for ship, so Humphreys' thought was this: build six frigates and let each one of those frigates be more than a match for any two English ships that she can meet. Let them also have special sailing qualities so that if chased or overpowered by more powerful squadrons they can "show their heels", in nautical phrase, or sail right away, or else, if obliged to face the guns of British men-of-war, let them be capable of so acting in rolling seas or in blowing weather, that when the English gun-deck is half-submerged, the American deck will be steadily above water and can rake the English ship with its fire. Those were his three objects, fast sailing qualities, steadiness of gun-deck, and heavier armament for the raking of hostile ships. In effect he said, "If we can accomplish that as builders, then we can safely leave it to our captains to do the rest." Such was his genius. The Act of 1794, passed by the Congress of the United States in Washington's Administration, authorized Henry Knox, the Secretary of War, because in those days there was no Secretary of the Navy, to have Humphreys plan those frigates. He planned them, *The Constitution* or *Old Ironsides, The Congress, The United States, The Constellation, The Chesapeake* and *The President.* Hear what those six ships did. The War of 1812 had not yet opened, but those ships carried Decatur, Truxton, Bainbridge, Hull, Stewart and Jones through the glories of the war with Tripoli, and later crowned themselves with victory in the War of 1812, although ten or fifteen years old. They were built of live oak and red cedar, bolted and riveted together, and were not brittle shells, as ships had been prior to that time. They were a little over-weighted as to their guns. It was found necessary to diminish the number of guns on their decks because they rolled too heavily in a rough sea, and hog-backed the ships. In the War of 1812 there was captured 1500 British ships and 12,000 prisoners.

When I was a boy I saw over the entrance to the old dining room in the rear of Joshua Humphreys' house a model that he had carved with his own penknife of one of his model ships. The exquisite curvature of lines was such that below the water the ship's keel cut the water like a knife. Hence they were as swift as they could be. Above, they were steadied against rolling by bulging sides which gave them a steady gun-deck, and they carried a weight of metal which the British did not expect. In other words, the British imagined that they were going to fight eighteen-pound guns and found they were really fighting twenty-fours. They thought they were fighting thirty-five guns. In point of fact they were fighting fifty, and the crushing effect on the British Navy was a surprise. When the ships first appeared in the Mediterranean, modelled on the Humphreys' plan, Nelson said, "Those American ships will cost the British Navy very anxious thought in the future." Nelson did not live to be engaged in the War of 1812 and face those ships but his prophecy came true.

Just an instance or two I will take of their behavior. *Old Ironsides* was the most glorious ship in the Navy as to her sailing and fighting qualities. You often see pictures of her in her fight with the *Guerriere*. When the *Constitution* first encountered the *Guerriere*, the *Guerriere* was part of an English squadron of six large ships. Captain Isaac Hull, who then commanded her, saw at a glance that he could not fight a squadron, so he determined to put the sailing qualities of his vessel to the test. He drew off and ran away from them. They pursued in line. Soon they were spread out. He saw then that he could pick his antagonist if he could get the British ships at a sufficient distance from each other so as to give him the advantage of the wind. Think of what it was to command a ship in those days. I am talking of sailing vessels, not of steam. There is comparatively little merit now in selecting positions for a battleship because steam will put a ship against wind and waves in any position desired, but before the days of steam, when the wind blew hard and a captain had to get the weather gauge of his enemy and manoeuvre in such a way as to rake him with a broadside and not be raked in turn, it required the supremest degree of seamanship. Hull had it, and he had the ship, and he had the builder of Philadelphia behind him who had planned it all. The result was that he was drawing away from the British squadron just to his own taste, when a dead calm fell upon him. Of course, even swift ships cannot sail in a calm, and the difficulty was double, for the calm had not struck the pursuing squadron; the British began to overtake him. Hull, with quick thought, looked ahead and saw rough water, indicating a breeze, ahead of him a mile away; instantly he put out his boats, put strong men in them carrying anchors and long ropes; the boats were rowed until the lines were taut, anchors were dropped, and the ship was then kedged or pulled right up to the anchors; the operation was repeated and the ship was drawn through the smooth water before the British got on to the device. Hull got into the ruffled water and began to recover the wind. By that time the British squadron was becalmed. Later, when the *Guerriere* was far ahead, Hull wheeled and in less than an hour knocked the

81

British frigate all to pieces. The *Constitution,* "Old Iron-sides," had achieved her first victory. Under Bainbridge she scored again by capturing *The Java.* Her greatest exploit was, when commanded by Captain Charles Stewart, she fought two British ships—*The Cyane* and *The Levant*—at the same time, and was manoeuvered in such a way that she sailed between them, raking first one and then the other before they could wheel and rake her. All that was due to the sailing qualities of the vessel, and the seamanship that directed her.

The other ships had glorious records. Decatur's ship, the *United States,* conquered the *Macedonian,* after bitter battle. *The President,* commanded by Truxton, conquered the *Insurgent.* I need not dwell on these, but these achievements are largely to be credited to Joshua Humphreys, the first naval constructor of the United States. He remained in office until President Jefferson came in, and Jefferson, being strongly opposed to the Navy, practically asked him to retire. Robert Smith, Secretary of the Navy, wrote a letter of regret to Humphreys on his retirement couched in graceful terms, especially so considering that it came from a reluctant Secretary. I will not stop to read this letter, but I will now read one of Humphreys' own letters, to indicate the dignity of the man and how he insisted on his claim to be recognized as the Constructor of the Navy. I dwell on this for the reason that occasionally there springs from some other part of the country a claim that Josiah Fox was the real constructor of the Navy of the United States and that Humphreys was not entitled to priority. Here is a letter which Humphreys addressed to Josiah Fox on the 25th of July, 1797. Fox was a clerk in the Marine Department. He was under orders from Humphreys. Being a bumptious individual, he undertook to usurp authority that did not belong to him, and wrote a letter to Humphreys, which was answered in this way: "Sir, I received your letter of yesterday purporting to tell me that the Secretary of War is very desirous that the frigate *Constellation* should be launched in the safest manner and with as little expense to the United States as possible. Judging that your [my] advice may be necessary to assist Mr. Stoddard, acting for the Navy, in the performance of that service, he desires me," etc. . . . "I have waited on the Secretary. It is with pleasure and with alacrity I shall always receive and obey while in the service of the United States any orders of the Secretary of War, but, Sir, *I cannot receive hereafter or attend to any directions from you,* although directed by the Secretary of War, while *you style yourself naval constructor.* You must know that my station in the service of the United States requires no direction from a naval constructor. You also know that I am the head of that Department. *When you direct a letter hereafter to me let it be done in your own proper style as clerk in the Marine Department."* Listen to the closing sentence: *"Whenever the Secretary deems my services no longer necessary, you may then, to other persons, assume such title as your vanity may suggest.* I am. Sir, Joshua Humphreys."

I return to the old house in which Mr. Humphreys after his retirement (he retired in 1803) lived until 1838. The house, which is on Haverford Road, as I have already said, is an exceedingly interesting one, built in three parts. The rear consisted of the original cabin dating back to about 1730. The second part was of later date, about the time of the Revolution, and the pebble-dashed front, which is three stories high with a garret beneath the roof, was built in the year 1812. The stairways, the walls, and the deep window panelings are of curled maple, beautifully polished. All the doors are of solid curled maple. The house itself was furnished with exquisite mahogany highboys, lowboys, pie-crust tables and mirrors, which latter were brought from France by Clement Humphreys, the elder brother of Joshua, who had been sent by John Adams on a mission to France, and who later perished at sea. As I have mentioned Clement, let me give you one little instance of his spirit when a boy. While the frigate *United States* was building, the editor of the *Aurora*, a newspaper in Philadelphia, came out with a furious attack on President Washington. Clement Humphreys, who was but nineteen years of age at that time, finding the editor of the paper, Mr. Duane, walking about the shipyard, caned him for the libel. He was prosecuted, brought into court and tried for assault and battery. He said, "Yes, I am guilty. I caned the editor, undoubtedly." A verdict was rendered against him, and a fine imposed. Citizens of Philadelphia paid it for the boy, and you will find a glowing account of the incident in the papers of the day. It is said that he was sent later to France by John Adams out of admiration for a young Federalist who had courage enough to cane a Democratic editor.

While Joshua Humphreys lived in the old house until 1838, he had a son Samuel, who was the Chief of Construction in the Navy Yards of the United States from 1816 until 1846. Samuel Humphreys inherited all the talents of his father for shipbuilding. He planned many of the successful ships of the period, one of them the famous fighting frigate *Franklin*, which at the time was the largest fighting craft afloat. Let me give a sample of the character of Samuel. The morning after one of the Wistar parties (and we all know what Wistar parties are) in the year 1824, Mr. Richard Peters, the son of Judge Peters, and Reporter of the decisions of the Supreme Court of the United States, with his office on South Sixth Street, was visited in his office by a young law student in somebody else's office. I wish I knew who the young law student was. He has not disclosed his personal identity but he wrote a most remarkable account of this visit. He was sent by his preceptor to Mr. Peters and found with him Judge Hopkinson of the United States District Court and Mr. Izakoff, the Russian Ambassador. After talking over some unfinished conversation which had been started the night before at the Wistar party, the Ambassador said to Mr. Peters, "How is it that American ships are superior to those of any other navy in the world so far as their sailing qualities are concerned?" Mr. Peters replied, "Better built, and better planned." "Well," said the Ambassador, "the Czar, Alexander, who sent me here, is very anxious to build up a navy, and has commissioned me to find the finest shipbuilder in the world. Do you know who the builder of those ships happens to be?" "Yes," said Mr. Peters. "He is a client of mine, Sam Humphreys." "Can I meet him?" "Yes, you can meet him, if you wish to."

"Won't you make an appointment, Mr. Peters?" "What hour will suit you?" "Ten o'clock to-morrow morning." The student was asked to carry a note to Sam Humphreys. He begged to be permitted to be present at the time the interview took place, and he says he was there. At ten o'clock Mr. Humphreys came in. A minute or two afterwards came the Ambassador. They were introduced to each other. The Ambassador said: "Mr. Humphreys, I am commissioned to employ a shipbuilder for the Russian Government. I can offer you a salary of sixty thousand dollars a year, a town house, a country house, a coach and all supplies." Humphreys said: "This is a very great surprise to me. Let me think it over until to-morrow morning," and he bowed his way out. The Ambassador thought that was a favorable omen. Mr. Peters remarked, "Perhaps, you think so." The next morning Humphreys returned, bowed very politely to the Ambassador and said: "The salary is far larger than I could earn. It is beyond my desires. I have but one house. That is where I do my work at the Navy Yard. I always walk and have no need of a coach. I do not know whether my talents are as great as my friend Mr. Peters has described, but I do know, that whether they be great or small, they belong to my country and I will not sell them." The writer asks, "In the history of dazzling offers, where is there a match for this patriotic and dignified refusal?" Remember that it was in a time of peace. There was no international objection to acceptance. Had Humphreys been an ordinary commercial contractor, he would have said, "Yes, I can build ships for a foreign nation. We are not at war." The Ambassador was staggered. Mr. Peters mentioned it to Judge Hopkinson. Judge Hopkinson said, "I knew it. He would not have been his father's boy if he had accepted that offer." Such was Samuel Humphreys.

Up to this time the successive generations of the Humphreys Family had been represented by men and women of pure Welsh blood, men of Welsh descent but of Norman origin, transmuted through the conquest of Wales and by long residence in Wales and intermarriage with Welsh women into pure Welsh blood. A new strain now appears.

Samuel Humphreys married Letitia Atkinson, a rather striking name. The circumstances of the marriage are romantic. Andrew Atkinson, the father of Letitia, was of Irish blood. His father was Thomas Atkinson of Cavan Garden, Bally Shannon, County Donegal, who had married Jean Murray, a descendant of Sir Archibald Murray of Scotland, the Seventh Baron in line from that James Murray who had been of the Black Barony that adhered to the Pretender. It is said that young Thomas Atkinson, then an ensign in the British service, as he marched past Edinburgh Castle saw Jean Murray on the battlements, a girl of sixteen, he a boy of nineteen, and instantly fell in love with her. They were introduced. They eloped in less than six months. He brought his bride to this country. He worked his way up. He purchased a plantation on the banks of the St. John's River in Florida following the cession of Florida by Spain to this country. He had a daughter Letitia, who was at Dungenness, the house of the widow of General Nathaniel Greene, on Cumberland Island outside of Savannah, where young Sam Humphreys had been sent by his father Joshua to inspect live-oak timbers for battleships. Later she became his bride. Thus it was that Letitia Atkinson and Samuel Humphreys became the parents of the last representative of the family that I shall mention, Andrew Atkinson Humphreys. You see the origin of his name. He was born in the year 1810 and died in the year 1883. You may notice the remarkable longevity of the various people I have referred to. I will be brief about General Humphreys. I could talk about him indefinitely. I think he had the strongest and handsomest face I ever saw on a soldier. His sword is on exhibition in yonder hall. He had, as you now observe, a mixture of blood which his forbears did not possess. They had a pure Welsh strain with some Norman. He had Norman, Welsh, Irish and Scotch—a pretty good mixture, and it asserted itself in his character. He was educated at the Germantown Academy, the old building which stands on School House Lane just below Green Street at the present time. He was caned there, was too spirited to submit to indignity, and would not go back to school, so he was sent to a boys' school at Nazareth under the tuition of the Moravians. From there he went to West Point and graduated as an officer, thirteenth in his class of thirty-five. He then became attached to the Army in various capacities as an engineer, served in the Florida Seminole War with distinction, and was in two battles in the Seminole War. But his great service, prior to the Civil War, was as an engineer, and his great achievement, which cannot be dwelt upon in too emphatic terms, was the exploration and mapping of the Valley of the Mississippi and the devising of means by which the destructive floods of the Mississippi and Missouri should not desolate that vast valley. When we think that the Valley of the Mississippi is as extensive as all Europe, cutting out Russia alone, and that it is the seat of future empire, using the word empire in the sense in which Bishop Berkley used it, as representing not imperial or political power but a field of authority embracing grandeur and strength—then can we realize the value of the work; he rescued that region from the devastation of floods and performed a service which was afterward carried out by the Eades jetties about the mouths of the Mississippi and the Gulf of Mexico. That work has been written of, spoken of, and translated into many languages; the engineers of the world have exhausted the vocabulary of praise upon it. Then came the Civil War. He commanded first in a subordinate position, but his great strength lay in his engineering capacity. He was a topographical engineer. He had an eye for topography, and could place troops in position and mark out lines of strategy. He closed the lines at the Battle of Malvern Hill in such a way as to prevent the retirement of the Army of the Potomac from the Peninsula from being a disastrous rout. He afterwards commanded the Second Division of the Third Corps under Sickels at the Battle of Gettysburg, and rescued that corps from disaster by the masterly way in which he changed front under fire. You remember that Sickels, by mistake, got so far out in the Peach Orchard, when the fighting of the second day took place, that there were more men killed on the second day than on the first and third combined. Sickels took up an advanced position. On the left was Little Round Top, on the right the Borough of Gettysburg, behind it Cemetery Ridge, the rear of Meade's Army guarded by Gregg's Cavalry to protect it from assault. The position of Sickels was so far in advance as to be in danger of being flanked and cut off by Longstreet's advance, which would have annihilated the whole Third Corps. Humphreys manoeuvred in such a way that under hot fire and flank attack he drew back, without breaking, the whole line until he brought it into contact with the right and left and closed up the gap. That was his great merit. His mind worked under fire with a precision that is indescribable. His personal gallantry was of the old-fashioned kind. Read the description of his charge on Maryes' Heights at the First Battle of Fredericksburg. Five divisions had attempted to carry that hill. A sixth division was called for. Humphreys led it in person. Shot through the hat, with two horses killed under him, he mounted a third, rallied and led his men, losing a larger percentage in forty minutes than the Light Brigade in an hour and a half. That charge, though unsuccessful, was one of the glorious achievements of the war. I have never talked to a soldier on either side, Confederate or Federal, without his telling me that Humphreys was the most remarkable scientific soldier the Army of the Potomac contained. The reason he did not reach the very top was that he had not the slightest trace of the politician about him. He was no newspaper soldier. He drove reporters absolutely out of the camp because they did not belong there, and he would not tolerate being questioned about plans. He could swear like a trooper, gentleman though he was, refined and exquisite in all his tastes; it is said the words blew out in such a way that reporters took their tickets from his camp straight back to Washington. But however choleric, his scientific mastery of himself and of his science was complete. After the Battle of Gettysburg he became chief-of-staff to General Meade. When Hancock was wounded in the Battle of the Wilderness, Humphreys commanded the Second Corps and clung so closely to Lee's retreating flank that Lee could not escape. He was like a wolf-hound clinging to the flank of a deer. His tirelessness enabled Sheridan to ride around Appomattox and head Lee off. Had there been a less tenacious pursuer, Lee might have escaped into the mountains near Lynchburg, Virginia, and guerilla warfare would have ensued. It was Humphreys who held Lee back, and it was through Humphreys' lines that the proposition was first made for Lee's surrender. After the war he became Chief of Engineers of the United States, and for thirteen years served in that capacity. One of his sons reached the rank of colonel and served creditably in the Civil War. He also served as a staff officer on his father's staff. He also served in the Indian Wars, during 1870, and later out in the far west. A second son served with great credit and fidelity in the artillery.

In conclusion, it gives me pleasure to say to this audience, that his only surviving child, a daughter, has been a generous benefactress of the Historical Society of Pennsylvania and has committed to its ownership the precious documents on which I have relied for this story. We have in our possession the originals, through the gift of Miss Humphreys, of the Humphreys' papers, and for that reason I have talked of the Humphreys Family.

DESCENT OF THE PROPERTY OF
MARY (POPPLETON) HURLEY PLEDGER MIDDLETON
OF SALEM COUNTY, NEW JERSEY

By Walter Lee Sheppard, Jr., F.A.S.G.

For those who are trying to work out a pedigree from South Jersey records for the first time, it is helpful to know that major information frequently is to be had from deeds, especially those of the colonial period. The type of record cited below is not found too often, but does occur in a satisfying number of cases, usually, however, with more dates given. The following is presented in summary form as just such an example, with supporting notations added to furnish some dates and substantiating data on most of the persons named.

August 12, 1746: Quit claim of John Nicholson of Salem County, New Jersey, and Sarah his wife to John Vining of Philadelphia, Province of Pennsylvania:

Henry Hurley of Salem County married one Mary Poppleton, spinster, of same, and had one daughter Sarah Hurley; said Henry Hurley died. Mary, his widow, married one Joseph Pledger of Mannington, Salem County, yeoman, who held two tracts, to wit, Bereton Fields and Hollybourne, by will and by purchase in fee simple, and by his will gave them to his wife Mary. After his death the widow Mary gave one of them, to wit, Hollybourne, to her daughter Sarah Hurley. Then the widow Mary Pledger married thirdly one Hugh Middleton and had a son John and a daughter Mary; and said Hugh by his last will and testament gave the above tracts, Bereton Fields and Hollybourne, to his son John. After Hugh's death, his son John also died under age, and his only sister Mary became vested with the property. This Mary Middleton married Benjamin Vining of Philadelphia, gentleman, and had two sons John and Benjamin Vining, and the son Benjamin dying soon after his father, these properties are now vested in John Vining as heir of his brother. Sarah Hurley married John Powell of Mannington, and had two daughters Mary and Sarah Powell. Mary Powell married James Mason and Sarah Powell married John Nicholson. Now for £50 and 100 acres of land said John Nicholson and Sarah his wife quit claim to John Vining the above mentioned tract, to wit, Hollybourne.[1]

The first above mentioned Henry Hurley, a weaver by trade, and Mary Poppleton, spinster, declared their intentions of marriage the first time before the Salem, New Jersey, Monthly Meeting of Friends on 30 1m (March) 1691, and were probably married within the next two

---

[1] The quit-claim deed, recorded Aug. 12, 1746, the same day it was executed, is entered at Trenton in New Jersey Deed Book X, 63.

months. The following year on August 17, 1692 he purchased a house and fourteen acres of land in Salem Town " at the corner of Bradway's street," from Jonathan Beere and Mary his wife. This property, except for " a lot of marsh in the townmarsh," Hurley assigned less than five months later to a carpenter, Richard Johnson.[2]

Hurley does not appear to have acquired any other real estate, and died intestate at Manneton Creek, Salem County. Letters of administration were granted to his widow Mary April 3, 1695. The inventory of his personal estate, amounting to £143,10,6 had been taken February 26, 1694/5.[3]

The widow Mary Hurley's second husband was JOSEPH PLEDGER of " Maninton Precinct, Salem County." They declared their first intentions of marriage before the Salem Meeting 30 10m (December) 1695, less than a year after Henry Hurley's death.

Joseph Pledger, born 4 6m 1672 according to Salem records, was a son of John Pledger, ship carpenter, and his wife Elizabeth of Portsmouth, County of Southampton, England. Salem records state that he " shipped himself aboard the shipp called the *Joseph and Benjamin*, master Mathew Paine, bound to Maryland," and arrived at West Jersey 13 1m 1674. After he had purchased land " from the Indians and seated himself before Fenwick's arrival, at Beritonfields, Township of New Salem,"[4] he arranged for the purchase of more land. On May 25, 1675, he was granted a patent for 3000 acres to be laid out in John Fenwick's projected colony in the province of New Cæsaria, or New Jersey.[5] His wife Elizabeth and son Joseph then shipped aboard the *Griffin*, Robert Griffin, master, bound for the Delaware, and according to Salem Meeting records " arrived in said river 23 9m at or near New Salem 1675."

With Pledger came Hipolite Lefevor of St. Martins-in-the-fields, Middlesex County, possibly with his wife Mary and family, who obtained a similar patent for 3000 acres on the same day as Pledger, after having purchased land from the Indians and having seated himself before Fen-

---

[2] Salem Deed Book 5, 213, 253, abstracted in " Calendar of Records in the Office of the Secretary of State, 1664-1703," *New Jersey Archives*, 1st Series, XXI, 599, 600, hereinafter cited as *N. J. Archives*, XXI. The assignment to Johnson was dated Jan. 3, 1692.

[3] Salem Will Book A, 154, abstract in " Calendar of Wills, 1670-1730, I," *New Jersey Archives*, 1st Series, XXIII, 250, hereinafter cited as *N. J. Archives*, XXIII.

[4] Salem Surveys, 1676, 45, abstract in *N. J. Archives*, XXI, 556: William Wade Hinshaw, *Encyclopedia of American Quaker Genealogy* (Ann Arbor, Mich., 1938), II, 37. On April 16, 1685 John Pledger of Bereton, Salem Tenth, gave a power of attorney to Steven Worlidge of Portsmouth, England, to enable the latter to sell Pledger's " land and houses in Bereton, County of Southampton." (Salem Surveys, 2, 20, abstract in *N. J. Archives*, XXI, 550.) It is obvious that the name of Pledger's tract in Salem was derived from that of his home in England.

[5] Salem, 1, 66, abstract in *N. J. Archives*, XXI, 561.

wick's arrival. Lefevor's plantation, adjacent to Pledger's, he called Hollybourne.[6]

Pledger and Lefevor subsequently acquired additional land adjoining these tracts, a portion of which on their western bounds, running " from the head of Great Mill Creeke N. W. downe the said Mill Creeke, the said Mill Creeke being the west side bounds of their said Plantacons called Holleborne and Bereton fields," they sold in 1678 to Walter, Francis and John Forrest of Burlington on which to build a grist mill.[7]

John Pledger died between October 17, the day on which he wrote his will, and November 24, 1694, when the inventory of his estate was taken. By his will, proved the following December 19, he left the home farm of Bereton Fields to his eldest son Joseph Pledger whom he named executor.[8] The younger son, John Pledger, born 27 9m (November) 1680, was to be looked after by five friends, one of whom, Joane Braithwaite, widow of William, was a sister of Hipolite Lefevor.

On November 14, 1689 Pledger had sold the Braithwaites, then of Braithwaite's Hall on Manneton Creek, 544 acres along the creek. Then in April, 1696, Lefevor sold his sister a part of his Hollybourne tract, comprising 200 acres on " the N. E. side of Hollybourne Creek," bounded on the west by John Pledger, Mihoppines Creek and Roger Carary, on the north by William Rumsey (to whom he had sold 400 acres in 1680), and on the east by the rest of Lefevor's land.[9]

Eight days after the sale to his sister Braithwaite, Lefevor, who had described himself as then of Packagomack, West Jersey, on May 5, 1696 had conveyed " the tract called Hollybourne," also comprising 200 acres,

---

[6] Salem, 1, 68, abstract in *N. J. Archives,* XXI, 561; Salem Surveys, 1676, 46, abstract in *N. J. Archives,* XXI, 557. Lefevor's family included his son Hipolite, Jr., who removed to New Castle about 1695 where he became an innholder, and his daughter Ann who married on Nov. 6, 1684 John Worlidge whom John Pledger called kinsman in 1687 when he sold him " 3 or 4 acres " on Alloways Creek " alias Mun Mouth River." (Salem Deeds 4, 54, abstract in *N. J. Archives,* XXI, 586.) A return dated June 12, 1676 of the survey of the land purchased by Pledger and Lefevor from the Indians, describes the land as being in the first half allottment of Alloways, " between Allowayes Creek, great swamp, Mill Creek, Fenwick's Creek and Maneton's Creek." Salem Surveys, 2, 12, abstract in *N. J. Archives,* XXI, 549.

[7] The warrant for survey of the new purchase, dated Nov. 2, 1676 and returned Nov. 12, 1676, described the land as being between " Mannatons and Allawayes Creeks, the Mill Creek and Fenwick's River." The deed to the Forrests was dated May 31, 1678. Salem Deeds, Liber B, 32, abstract in *N. J. Archives,* XXI, 566.

[8] Salem Wills, A, 129, abstract in *N. J. Archives,* XXIII, 368. The inventory included 3 Negro slaves, 7 silver spoons valued at £3,3, and a silver tankard valued at £5. The whole came to £477,7.

[9] Nov. 14, 1689, John Pledger to William Braithwaite: Salem Deeds, 5, 15, abstract in *N. J. Archives,* XXI, 591. The will of Joane Braithwaite, widow, names her " brother Lefevor." See Salem Wills, Liber 2, 120, abstract in *N. J. Archives,* XXIII, 56. April 27, 1696, Hipolite Lefevor to Widow Joane Braithwaite: Salem Deeds, 6, 44, abstract in *N. J. Archives,* XXI, 613. Sept. 25, 1680, Hipolite Lefevor of Packagomack, West Jersey and wife Mary to William Rumsey " part of the tract granted May 25, 1675 near Manhatton (Manneton) Creek ": Salem Deeds, 2, 15, abstract in *N. J. Archives,* XXI, 573.

to Joseph Pledger. This was bounded on the north by Hollybourne Creek and the land sold to Joane Braithwaite.[10]

Pledger lived to enjoy ownership of this property little more than a year, dying between July 1, when he wrote his will, and July 13, 1697 when the inventory of his personal property was taken. Styling himself of Manington Precinct, Salem County, he devised to his brother John his clothes and the effects—probably heirlooms—which he had received by the will of his father. To his wife Mary's daughter Sarah Hurley he stated he had given a bond of £40 to which he now added £20 more for a total of £60, to be received by her when she was of full age. His father had also left £10 to Joseph Nichols " if he behaved himself soberly and honestly." Now Joseph added £10 to this for a total of £20, also to be received when the lad came of age. To the Salem Monthly Meeting he left 40 shillings, and the rest of his real and personal estate to his wife Mary.[11]

A year after Joseph Pledger's death his widow Mary, then of Bereton Fields, by deed of gift dated June 30, 1698, made over to her minor daughter Sarah Hurley the 200-acre tract " called Hollybourne " which her husband had purchased from Hipolite Lefevor. The transfer was to become effective when Sarah arrived at the age of eighteen or married, the consideration to be a yearly payment of one ear of indian corn, if demanded.[12] With this conveyance the chain of title in Hollybourne to Mary's daughter Sarah was begun.

The twice widowed Mary (Poppleton) Hurley Pledger now married a third husband, HUGH MIDDLETON, High Sheriff of Salem County in 1698. He was a widower, having married, probably in January 1695, Mary Kenton, widow of William Kenton, who was formerly of Great Choptank River, Talbot County, Maryland, but of Salem County, West Jersey, at the time of his death early in 1694.[13] Mary Pledger and Hugh Middleton were married by 1703 when her brother-in-law John Pledger

---

10 Salem Deeds, 6, 26, abstract in *N. J. Archives*, XXI, 612.

11 Will of John Pledger: Salem Wills, A, 207, abstract in *N. J. Archives*, XXIII, 368. The will was recorded on July 20, 1697, a week after the inventory, which included the 3 Negro slaves his father had probably owned, and the silver tankard and spoons, now valued at £10,3, was taken. The total amount was £500,5,5.

12 Salem Deeds, 6, 237, abstract in *N. J. Archives*, XXI, 623.

13 Middleton was described as High Sheriff on May 10, 1698 when he sold to John Worlidge property which had belonged to Roger Milton. Middleton's wife Mary (Bradway) Kenton is established by the wills of her father Edward Bradway and his wife Mary. (Salem Wills, Liber A, 108, 193, abstracts in *N. J. Archives*, XXIII, 55, 56). See also Salem 6, 238, wherein William Kenton, Jr., exchanged with Middleton land in Maryland for the elder William Kenton's plantation in Salem County " bought of the father of John Worlidge," abstract of which is in *N. J. Archives*, XXI, 623.

sold them 214 acres along Salem and Mehoppines Creek.[14] The same year Middleton was commissioned a Justice of the Peace for Salem County, a commission which was renewed in 1707 on the same day he was appointed an " assistant " to the judges of the Pleas for the county.[15]

In his will written January 19, 1713/14 and proved exactly one month later, he made no mention of his wife Mary, she apparently having predeceased him, but left to their son John " the plantation whereon I live called Bereton Fields, containing 800 acres, and my negro Jack." To his daughter Mary Middleton he gave 240 acres on the north side of Holly-bourne Creek adjoining the land of John Pledger " of whom the land was originally bought," together with a moiety of a half-interest in a grist-mill which he held in partnership with John Van Meter. To his daughter-in-law (step-daughter) Sarah Hurley he left 200 acres on Alloways Creek, also called Monmouth River, adjoining land of William Willis. The residue of his estate he left to be divided equally between the before-mentioned three children. His " friends " Isaac Sharp and Bartholomew Wyat were named the executors, charged with the care and up-bringing of his son John and daughter Mary Middleton until they came of age or were married.[16]

From a comparison of the 800-acre bequest of the tract which he called Bereton Fields, and of the quit-claim deed of 1746, cited first above, it would appear that the original Bereton Fields and Hollybourne tracts were intended and included in the bequest, although he mentioned only the former by name. By this bequest, therefore, a second and conflicting title in Hollybourne was initiated by him when he left it to his son John Middleton. This son died soon after, according to the quit-claim deed, and the bequest became vested in his sister and heir MARY

---

14 April 30, 1703, John Pledger and wife Dorothy to Hugh Middleton: Salem Deeds, 7, 207, abstract in *N. J. Archives*, XXI, 638. Mary (Poppleton) Pledger Middleton was condemned by the Salem Monthly Meeting on 28 6m 1704 for marrying contrary to Friends' discipline.

15 " Abstracts of New Jersey Commissions, Civil and Military, From Liber AAA of Commissions in the Secretary of State's Office at Trenton," *Publications of the Genealogical Society of Pennsylvania*, VI, 183, 293; VII, 154, 155; X, 305.

16 Salem Wills, 1, 438, abstract in *N. J. Archives*, XXIII, 318. On Feb. 6, 1713/14, two weeks after Middleton's will was accepted for probate, one John Kellet, aged about 57 years, deposed " that he was at the house of Joseph Pledger in 1697 when the said Pledger was sick and died. Said Pledger, he says, was out of his mind all the time and not capable of making a will." There is no record of the instigator of this deposition; it might have been John Pledger who perhaps entertained hopes of breaking his brother's will with the idea of recovering by reversion Bereton fields, since Middleton could be considered as having only a life-tenancy in the tract, with no right to will it out of the Pledger family. If so, the recovery attempt was unsuccessful, for Middleton's will was duly probated on Feb. 19, 1713/14. The deposition was filed with the papers of Joseph Pledger's estate.

MIDDLETON who married BENJAMIN VINING, a widower whose first wife's Christian name was Ann.[17]

Born in 1685, Vining is said to have been the son of William and Mary Vining of Portsmouth, New Hampshire. He had been a member of the Pennsylvania Assembly for the city in 1716, was a Justice of the Peace from 1715 to 1717, and then removed to Salem County, although still owning considerable real estate in Philadelphia. He died September 1, 1735, aged 50 years, 7 months and 22 days, was buried near the chancel of St. John's Church in Salem, leaving two sons, John and Benjamin Vining, and his widow Mary with " a child in embro." [18]

By his will, dated August 20, 1734 and proved October 13, 1735, he left to his eldest son John Vining, grantee in the above first-mentioned quit-claim, Barrenton house and land of 300 acres where he then dwelt, being part of lands called the " sixth lott " as lately surveyed and beginning at the head of " Holiburn Creek, thence south by west to corner tree of old John Smith and John Pledger's, thence west to Mulhollow Creek, called Smith's Creek "; also that " fifth lot " called Petersfield of 1060 acres, excepting out of same, 300 acres formerly sold to William Willis, and 200 acres " since devised by Hugh Middleton to Sarah Hurley and her heirs." To his son Benjamin he devised the remainder of the Barrenton sixth lot, being the westernmost part of the late survey, containing 900 acres and beginning at the mouth of " Holiburn creek to Mulhollow Creek till it intersects Fenwick River," and other real estate, both in Salem and Philadelphia. The " child in embro " was to have a plantation on Mohoppony's Creek near Salem, together with the half of the grist mill, and real estate in Philadelphia. The residue of the whole estate he devised to his wife Mary upon condition that his " children may be piously educated in the Rubrick of the Church of England, and that my two sons may have a Grammar, Latin education and all be well taught to write well and learn Arithmetic." His wife and two sons were named executors; letters testamentary were granted only to Mary Vining, however, " the others being infants." She is reported to have married December

---

17 Philadelphia Deed Book G-2, 89: July 31, 1716 Benjamin Vining and Ann to Jeremiah Elfreth. The deed recites that on 15 10br (December) 1713 James Estaugh and Mary his wife had conveyed to Vining a messuage and lot on the east side of Second Street which Vining was now selling, *inter alia*, to Jeremiah Elfreth. The property, 32 feet north of Elfreth's Alley, became Jeremiah's home for the remainder of his life.

18 In the *Pennsylvania Gazette* for 19 4m (June) 1729, Vining offered for sale a house and lot in Chestnut Street, two lots in Front Street and three city lots " not fenced." He was then of Salem. Biographical details cited in the text are found in *Memorials of St. John's Church, Salem, N. J.*, Genealogical Notes, VII, 76, Collections of the Genealogical Society of Pennsylvania.

23, 1736 Nicholas Ridgely,[19] in 1746 Associate Judge of the Supreme Court of the three "lower counties on Delaware."

Mary (Middleton) Vining's half-sister SARAH HURLEY married JOHN POWELL. His parentage has not been ascertained, but he was probably a brother of the Jeremiah Powell of Alloways Creek who in his will directed his "cousin" Mary Mason to care for his daughter Elizabeth until she arrived at the age of eighteen. Jeremiah and John Powell in turn may have been the sons of an earlier Jeremiah Powell, a carpenter who purchased 500 acres on "MunMouth" River—Alloways Creek— from John Maddock in July, 1700 and died intestate the following December.[20]

John Powell, husband of Sarah Hurley, also died intestate in Salem County. Letters of administration on his estate were granted May 3, 1743 to James Mason and John Nicholson, "sons-in-law of said John Powell," of Elsenburrow, Salem County.[21]

JAMES MASON, reported 26 4m 1732 to Salem Meeting as married to MARY POWELL, daughter of John Powell, was probably the son James, born 11 6m 1709, of Thomas Mason of Mannington, Salem County, a ship carpenter who had married Elizabeth, the widow of Richard Tindall after the latter's death early in 1698. By this marriage Thomas Mason had acquired an interest in Tindall's property which included the home farm called Tindall's Bowery, in Manneton Precinct, and 500 acres at Virgin Spring.[22] When he died in the spring of 1729 his son James was still a minor. Letters testamentary were granted to Abel Nicholson and Samuel Wade on June 11, 1729.[23]

James Mason of Manington and wife Mary "late Mary Powell" on August 12, 1746 released for £50 their rights in the Hollybourne tract to John Vining, thereby extinguishing part of the claim in the tract which

---

[19] Abstract of will of Benjamin Vining in "Calendar of Wills, 1730-1750, II," in *N. J. Archives*, 1st Series, XXX, 506. The child "in embro" mentioned in Vining's will proved to be a daughter whom they named Mary. She subsequently married Rev. Charles Inglis, English missionary in Kent Co., Delaware where the Ridgelys settled in 1740. See *Memorials of St. John's Church, op. cit.*

[20] Will of Jeremiah Powell, Salem Wills, Liber 5, 32, abstract in *N. J. Archives*, XXX, 384. His will was dated 11 12m (February) 1743/4 and proved Apr. 3, 1745. Letters of administration were granted on estate of Jeremiah Powell, probably the carpenter, to his widow Elizabeth on Dec. 27, 1700, an inventory having been taken 14th of that month. Salem Wills, III, 62, abstract in *N. J. Archives*, XXIII, 373. The sale of land by John Maddock to this Jeremiah Powell is found in Salem Deeds, 7, 27, as noted in *N. J. Archives*, XXI, 626.

[21] West Jersey Wills, Liber 4, 371, abstract in *N. J. Archives*, XXX, 385, estate of John Powell. The inventory, totalling £1622,0,5, included bills, bonds and book debts amounting to £1156,6,5, and two mortgages on lands for £266.

[22] See Salem Deeds, 7, 3, 125, 185, abstracts in *N. J. Archives*, XXI, 625, 632 and 637.

[23] Will of Thomas Mason, abstract in *N. J. Archives*, XXIII, 309.

derived from Sarah Hurley.[24]   James Mason was survived by his widow Mary but no living children. In his will dated March 25, 1755 and proved September 1, 1755, he named various cousins, including Ann Nicholson, and the children of his sisters Mary Smith and Martha Wood. His widow was still living January 5, 1760 when she submitted an accounting as surviving executrix.[25]

The identity of JOHN NICHOLSON, grantor named in the first abovementioned quit-claim, who was reported on 29 10m (December) 1740 as married to SARAH POWELL, daughter of Sarah Hurley, has not been established definitely. It seems probable, however, that he was a grandson of the Samuel Nicholdson (sic) of Munmouth River, West Jersey, originally from Nottinghamshire, England, according to Salem records, on whose estate letters of administration were granted to his widow Anne June 12, 1685. From her will, dated 1 6m (August) 1693 and proved June 30, 1694, the names of their children are ascertained as Samuel, Joseph, Abell and Elizabeth Abbott.[26] They had also arrived on the *Griffin* in 1675.

The son Samuel Nicholson died also in 1694, and by his will apparently was unmarried. His brother Joseph moved to Gloucester County by 1696, and was of Cooper's Creek when he died in 1702.[27] The third son Abell Nicholson and his first wife Mary Tyler whom he married in 1694, remained in Salem County and were the parents of William, Samuel, John born 6 3m 1719 (who presumably was he who was reported on 29 10m 1740 as married to his first wife Sarah Powell, and on 26 8m 1754 as married to his second wife Hannah, widow of Joseph Darkin), Ann who married John Brick and Ruth who married Samuel Clement of Newton Township, Gloucester County. When Abell died in the spring of 1751 his lands at Elsonburgh included part of Samuel Carpenter's original 2000 acre tract which Abell had purchased in 1698 and 1703 from John Holme.[28]

Abell's presumed son John Nicholson and his wife Sarah Powell were

---

24 New Jersey Deed Book X, 65, recorded at Trenton.

25 Will of James Mason, West Jersey Wills, Liber 8, 240, abstract in " Calendar of Wills, 1751-1760, III," N. J. *Archives*, XXXII, 217.

26 Estate of Samuel Nicholdson, Salem Wills, Liber 2, 15; will of Anne Nicholson, Salem Wills, A, 120, both abstracted in N. J. *Archives*, XXIII, 339.

27 Salem Deeds, 6, 76, and Gloucester Deeds, 3, 219, 222, abstracted in N. J. *Archives*, XXI, 615, 671. Estates of Joseph and Samuel Nicholson, abstracted in N. J. *Archives*, XXIII, 340.

28 Abell Nicholson's wife Mary, with whom he declared intentions of marriage the first time 26 12m 1693, was a daughter of William Tyler of Alloways Creek. See Salem Wills, III, 93, abstract in N. J. *Archives*, XXIII, 474, also Salem Deeds, 5, 461, abstract in N. J. *Archives*, XXI, 609. For Abell's land bought of John Holme see Salem Deeds, 6, 222 and 7, 204, abstracts in N. J. *Archives*, XXI, 638; for his will abstract see N. J. *Archives*, XXXII, 235.

the grantors in the first above mentioned quit-claim, releasing their interest and rights in the tract called Hollybourne,—deeded by Sarah's grandmother to Sarah (Powell) Nicholson's mother Sarah (Hurley) Powell,—to Sarah (Powell) Nicholson's half-first cousin, John Vining.[29] By their quit-claim the first chain of title, established in 1698, was effectually extinguished, leaving the property vested in the heir who claimed under the second title, not set up until 1714.

It should be noted that a supposition of relationship between purchaser of a piece of property and the grantor many years later of the same property, with no intervening sale, is not always warranted. In the above cited case the land belonged to Mary Poppleton's second and childless husband; but those in whose possession the land is found are demonstrated to have been descendants of her first and third husbands.

The deed indicates that in the third generation there were no other descendants of Mary and her three husbands than those named in the recitation. The quit-claim of Mary (Vining) Inglis is not seen, though to clear her brother's title it should have been obtained. Why she is not named in the recitation does not appear.[30]

---

[29] John Vining is reported to have married Rachel Ridgely, kin to his step-father Nicholas Ridgely. Vining died Nov. 3, 1770, aged 46, and was buried next his father Benjamin in St. John's Church, Salem.

[30] The author is indebted to Hannah Benner Roach for the addition of much material, especially relating to the Vinings, and for the excellent and painstaking re-casting of this article to enhance its interest.

CAPTAIN JAMES IRVIN OF GERMANTOWN, PHILADELPHIA COUNTY, PENNSYLVANIA

By Marcia Moss Lewis

The following sketch of the Revolutionary service of Captain James Irvin of the Chestnut Hill militia company was also undertaken as a project in the first Course in Genealogical Methods. In the search for Irvin's antecedents, Mrs. Lewis explored data on Irvin-Irvine and Erwin families, the spelling of which names bore some 42 different variations. She covered the Cumberland County Irvine family of Revolutionary fame; the families of Samuel Evin Erwin, James and Thomas Erwin of Philadelphia County; of John Erwin of Wilmington, Delaware, of Arthur Erwin of Bucks County, and of Richard and David Irwin of Chester County and New Jersey without success. Her findings are contained in better than 200 pages of typed material. She also covered data on the families of Andrew, Valentine, George and Peter Smith of Germantown and the Northern Liberties in Philadelphia County for the parentage of James Irvin's wife. The material relating to these families is contained in some 35 typed pages. While the primary object of her search was not successful, as too often happens, she did locate pertinent data on James Irvin which follows here. Perhaps at some future time the identity of his parents will be discovered.

Many interesting facts have been discovered about James Irvin (Erwin-Irwin) of Germantown, Philadelphia County, Pennsylvania but a complete identification has not been made. The date and place of his birth and the names of his parents have not been established. The spelling of the name Irvin varies in the records, but on official documents his signature is James Irvin.[2]

When the " Flying Camp " was formed in 1776 James Irvin became a member of that Revolutionary military unit.[3] The barracks were in the Northern Liberties, and to a young man this gathering of troops for the defense of the Delaware must have been a thrilling adventure. There was much confusion and great excitement with strange men arriving each day from distant places.

---

[1] Hannah Benner Roach, " The Back Part of Germantown," *The Pennsylvania Genealogical Magazine*, XX, No. 2 (1956), 135.

[2] *Pennsylvania Archives*, 6th Series, I, 670, 925, 928-31. See his signature on Petition of the Officers of the Seventh Battalion of Philadelphia County Militia, reproduced herein (original on file in the papers of " Secretary of Supreme Executive Council, Lieutenancy of Philadelphia County, 1777-1784," Pennsylvania Historical and Museum Commission, Division of Public Records).

[3] United States Pension Records, Revolutionary War, File No. W-4704, Certificate No. 2191 (hereinafter U. S. Pension File), deposition of Frederick Axe, 23 August 1837; also *Pennsylvania Archives*, 2nd Series, XIII, 558, 559.

There were many delays in assembling the " Flying Camp " and there were many deserters, but after a proclamation by the Pennsylvania State Convention, offering a penalty of £3 for each deserter apprehended and a bounty of £3 to each loyal soldier, the situation improved.[4]   James Irvin went to Amboy, New Jersey, in one of the companies of Moore's Regiment [5] of the " Flying Camp."   While ovens and a slaughter house were being erected, each soldier was given a daily ration of:

> " 1 lb of flour or 1 lb of bread
> 1½ lbs of beef or 18 oz of pork
> 1 Qt. of beer." [6]

An important message from General George Washington was given the soldiers at Amboy: " His Excellency George Washington will consider any assistance he may receive at this time the greatest obligation, and such troops as turn out voluntarily in that service will have their names inrolled among the bravest of the Americans." [7]   There were several small encounters with the enemy near Amboy, New Jersey, and our soldiers prevented the British from obtaining supplies and important reinforcements.[8]

James Irvin became a First Lieutenant in Captain Matthias Gensell's Company of Moore's Regiment, Pennsylvania Line.   One of his soldiers, Frederick Axe, declared, " Whenever Capt. Ginsell was absent First Lieutenant James Irvin took command to the great satisfaction of all.   He was a brave and fearless officer and was greatly beloved by all of his men, and he served in every campaign that went out from Philadelphia." [9]

Lieutenant James Irvin and his men were with George Washington when the Hessians were captured at Trenton, New Jersey in December 1776.[10]   A month later, in 1777, he and his company fought in the battle at Princeton, New Jersey.

During the summer of 1777 the British invaded Pennsylvania, and James Irvin's company fought in the Battle of the Brandywine.   After

---

[4] J. Thomas Scharf and Thompson Westcott, *History of Philadelphia, 1609-1884* (Philadelphia, 1884), I, 331.

[5] U. S. Pension File, deposition of Frederick Axe, 23 August 1837.

[6] Journal of Captain Benjamin Loxley, *Collections of the Historical Society of Pennsylvania* (1853), 226.   Diary of Lieutenant James McMichael, *Pennsylvania Archives*, 2nd Series, XV, 196.

[7] Journal of Captain Benjamin Loxley, *Collections of the Historical Society of Pennsylvania* (1853), 230.

[8] *Ibid.*, 229, 235.

[9] U. S. Pension File, deposition of Frederick Axe, 23 August 1837.

[10] *Ibid.*, deposition of Margaret Irvin, 19 August 1837, which also gives the service at Brandywine and Germantown.

this decisive defeat they fought again early in October in the Battle of Germantown, where another contest was lost. Here the people were aroused to the real horrors of war: their homes, crops and cattle destroyed; the enemy commander General Howe occupied a house in Germantown.[11] About this time Lieutenant James Irvin was promoted to the rank of Captain in the Philadelphia County Militia.[12]

The records show that James Irvin was a resident of Germantown and paid taxes there in 1779[13] as a single man. He is the only Irvin (Erwin-Irwin) listed in the tax return for Germantown.

One of the most important victories in which Captain James Irvin participated occurred in 1779. His company under Colonel Beck assembled with General John Sullivan's forces to avenge the brutal Wyoming massacre by the six indian nations. They accomplished the difficult task of going up the Susquehanna in the summer when the river was very low. It was a magnificent undertaking to transport ammunition, men and supplies in this campaign. General Sullivan's army defeated the Six Nations and their Tory allies at the battle of Newtown. Then all of the Indian villages and crops were burned. The Indians fled to Canada, and the Six Nations alliance was destroyed forever.[14]

During the war years Captain James Irvin was in love with a Germantown girl, Margaret Smith. They probably delayed their marriage as he was away so often, fighting for his country. Although her parents have not been identified, she may have been the daughter of Peter Schmid and his wife Maria Elizabeth. They had a daughter Margareth born on 24 December 1761 and baptised on 11 April 1762 in the German Reformed Church of Germantown.[15]

Captain James Irvin and Margaret Smith were married on 11 May 1780 by their friend, the Reverend Michael Schlatter[16] of Barren Hill. The Reverend Mr. Schlatter was a loyal patriot, and his son Gerardus had been captain, when James served as a lieutenant, in the same company.[17]

---

11 John J. Macfarlane, *History of Early Chestnut Hill* (Philadelphia, 1927), 85; Edward W. Hocker, *Germantown 1683-1933* (Philadelphia, 1933), 107, 113.

12 U. S. Pension File, deposition of Margaret Irvin, 19 August, 1837.

13 *Pennsylvania Archives*, 3rd Series, XV, 42.

14 Wayland F. Dunaway, *History of Pennsylvania* (New York, 1950), 157, 158; *Pennsylvania Archives*, 2nd Series, XV, 233, 238, 243, 245, 246, 257, 261, 266, 268, quoting from journals of Lieutenant Erkuries Beatty and the Reverend William Rogers, D.D.

15 Records of German Reformed Congregation of Germantown, 1753-1856, II, 163 (transcript at the Genealogical Society of Pennsylvania).

16 U. S. Pension File.

17 *Ibid.*; Henry Harbaugh, *The Life and Times of the Reverend Michael Schlatter, 1716-1790* (Philadelphia, 1857); *The Pennsylvania Genealogical Magazine*, XX, No. 2 (1956), 132, 135.

Germantown Augst 11th 1780

To His Excellency the President & the Honourable
Executive Council of the State of Pennsylvania

The Humble Petition of the Officers of the
Seventh Battalion of Philadelphia County Militia

Most Humbly Sheweth

That Your Petitioners met this day ——
According to law, in order to form the Classes now
called, into a body to proceed on immediate service ——
But finding a general discontent prevailing on
account of that difference in the wages of the city
and County,) being one half(most humbly hope that
their Petition may be taken into Consideration and
such Addition granted to the county Militia as
may give that satisfaction, which may encourage
them to enter Chearfully into the service of their
Country by leaving their Families a sufficiency as not to
know the loss of their supporters and Your Petitioners
as in duty bound &c

Andrew Redheffer Capn
Daniel Beck Capt ——

Mattw Holgate Coll
John Bethell Major
Caleb Armitage Capt
Noe Townsend Capt
Jacob Hall Capt
John Lewring Capt
Peter Frailey Capt
James Irvin Capt

Petition of Officers of the Seventh Battalion, Philadelphia County
Militia, 11 August 1780, signed by James Irvin.

*From the original filed in the Division of Public Records, Pennsylvania Historical
and Museum Commission.*

For some time there had been much resentment in the Philadelphia County Militia occasioned by the small amount of pay received. After much discussion a petition of protest was made by the officers of the Militia: [18]

Germantown Aug[t] 11th 1780

To his Excellency the President & the Honorable
Executive Council of the state of Pennsylvania
The Humble Petition of the Officers of the
Seventh Battalion of Philadelphia County Militia

MOST HUMBLY SHEWETH

That Your Petitioners met today According to law, in order to form the Classes now called, into a body to proceed on immediate service But finding a general discontent prevailing on account of that difference in the wages of the city and County, being one half most humbly hope that their Petition may be taken into Consideration and such addition granted to the county Militia as may give that satisfaction, which may encourage them to enter Cheerfully into the service of their Country by leaving their families a sufficiency as not to know the loss of their support and Your Petitioners as in duty bound &. .

Andrew Redheffer Cap[n]
Daniel Beck Capt.

Matt[w] Holeget Coll
John Bethell Major
Caleb Armitage Cap[n]
Noe Townsend Cap[tn]
Jacob Hall Cp[t]
John Levering Cap[n]
Peter Frailey Cap[t]
James Irvin Capt[n]

This petition was rejected by the Council.

James Irvin and his family continued to live in Germantown,[19] but his name disappears from the records. After the war was over difficulties were endured by his family. The hardships of war possibly affected his health. The Irvins did not own a house but moved often from place to place, and were evidently never prosperous.[20]

There may have been several children born to James and Margaret Irvin but only two are known to have survived, a son, Andrew, and a daughter, Rebecca.[21] Rebecca was born 20 March 1793[22] just two years before her father Captain James Irvin's death in 1795.[23]

---

[18] Reproduced herein; see footnote 2.

[19] Tax list of 1782, see *Pennsylvania Archives*, 3rd Series XVI, 104.

[20] U. S. Pension File, deposition of Margaret Irvin.

[21] *Ibid.*; also depositions of Rebecca Higby, 13 November, 1847, and Joseph Fisher, November, 1847, and will of Margaret Irvin.

[22] Records of St. Michael's Evangelical Church, Germantown, Philadelphia, Part I, 816 (transcript at Genealogical Society of Pennsylvania).

[23] U. S. Pension File, depositions of Margaret Irvin, Andrew Irvin and Rebecca Higby.

After the death of her husband Margaret Irvin struggled valiantly to support her children. On 11 August 1805 her daughter Rebecca was baptized in St. Michael's Evangelical Church in Germantown.[22]

In 1825, Peter Hay, a member of the Pennsylvania State Legislature, assisted Margaret Irvin in presenting a petition for a state pension.[24] This petition was read in December, 1825, and laid on the table because she lacked evidence of her husband's commissions and discharge papers.[25] Later, in February, 1826, her petition was approved and she was granted a pension for his services as a private soldier in the Revolutionary War.[26]

There is no record that she received this state pension at this time. She kept trying to locate men who had served under her husband. On 19 January 1828 she obtained affidavits from Jacob Holgate, John Freeds and Paul Bishop, who declared they had served under Captain James Irvin.[27]

The Census of 1830 shows that Margaret Irvin resided in Green Court in the Northern Liberties in Philadelphia County, aged between seventy and eighty years.[28]

According to the State Treasurer's Pension Accounts, it was several years before the widow Margaret Irvin received her overdue state pension. Payments to her began after the Act of 4 May 1832 and continued until November, 1841. She received $40.00 annuity and $40.00 gratuity each year.[29]

An Act was passed in 1836 to give Federal pensions to widows of Revolutionary soldiers. Margaret Irvin was very old but she located several men who had known her husband. Frederick Axe, aged 79 years, Garret Rittenhouse and Henry Cress, all stated they had known Captain James Irvin of the Revolutionary Army.[30] His widow obtained a certified copy of the record of her marriage to James Irvin from her elderly friend Elizabeth Schlatter, daughter of the Reverend Michael Schlatter.[31]

---

[24] Ibid., deposition of Peter Hay, 15 July 1848.

[25] Journal of the House of Representatives of Pennsylvania, 1825-1826, I, 101 (report No. 50).

[26] Ibid., 456.

[27] U. S. Pension File.

[28] United States Census for 1830 (State of Pennsylvania, Philadelphia County, Northern Liberties, Ward 3, Schedule 75, p. 29), copy in microfilm box 157, part 1 at Historical Society of Pennsylvania. Green Court evidently opened off Green Street which ran from 358 North Front Street to Old York Road in the Northern Liberties (Philadelphia Directory for 1830, iv).

[29] State Treasurer of Pennsylvania, Pension Accounts, Vol. 10, 106, from Division of Public Records, Section 3, Act of 4 May 1832, P. L. 461.

[30] U. S. Pension File.

[31] Ibid.

Despite all the evidence which Margaret Irvin assembled, she never proved that her husband had served as an officer. Her United States pension was approved in 1838, and a private's services recognized, with a pension of $26.67 per annum.[32] This with her state pension provided for her, in her aged and infirm years, until her death on 29 October 1841. She was buried in the Ebenezer Methodist Church burial ground, Christian below Fourth Street, Philadelphia.[33]

The following is an abstract of Margaret Irvin's last will and testament: [34]

Philadelphia County.
Dated 28 October 1841   Proved 11 November 1841

" This is my last will and Testament I being of sound mind tho' week in body and for the love and affection I have for my children, Rebecca Higby and Andrew Erwin I give and bequeath all the moneys with Interest deposited in the Philadelphia Saving Fund in Walnut Street above third I further apoint my daughter Rebecca Higby Sole Exutrix to pay all bills incurred by my decease and then the balance to be equally devided in two parts Share and Share alike between Andrew Erwin and Rebecca Higby I further wish my Daughter Rebecca Higby to hold her share separate and apart from her said husband Charles Higby he to have no hold no right title or interest.

(signed)   her
Margaret X Erwin "
mark

Witnesses present at signing
Amos Palmer
John Beal Erwin
Mary Smith

Rebecca (Irvin) Higby, daughter of James and Margaret Irvin, was a milliner. Her husband, Charles Higby, was a carpenter. They did not own a house and moved about often, being listed at different business and residence addresses in Philadelphia City Directories. Rebecca's brother, Andrew Irvin, lived in Charlotte, North Carolina.[35]

In 1847 Rebecca (Irvin) Higby began to assemble proof that her father had been an officer during the Revolution. She obtained a certi-

---

[32] Ibid.

[33] Burial Records of the Philadelphia Board of Health, Vol. for Deaths, February 1, 1840-May 31, 1842, p. 180 (at the Genealogical Society of Pennsylvania). The records of Margaret Irvin's age vary, the 1830 Census listing her at between seventy and eighty years, her deposition in 1837 as aged 76, and the death record states her age as 84 years in 1841.

[34] Philadelphia Will Book 15, p. 229. The original Will, #202 of 1841, is missing from the records.

[35] U. S. Pension File, depositions of Rebecca Higby, 13 November 1847, and Joseph Fisher, November, 1847.

fied record of her parents' marriage from Mr. T. P. Chandler, a prominent attorney of Boston, Massachusetts: [36]

1780
May 11   JAMES IRVIN ⎫ of Germantown, Philadelphia
                       &   ⎬   County
            MARGARET SMITH ⎭ Adults.

I certify that the above is a true copy taken by me from an ancient book of marriage records, kept by Rev'd Michael Schlatter and now in the possession of my wife one of his descendants.

(signed)   T. P. Chandler [37]

Boston, Mass.
May 24, 1849.

She also sent copies of affidavits and proof from the Minutes of the Supreme Executive Council of the Commonwealth of Pennsylvania. All this successfully proved that James Irvin had been both a lieutenant and a captain in the Revolutionary War.

A certificate was issued by the United States Pension office on the 31st of October 1849 to be paid at the rate of $120.00 per annum to Rebecca Higby and her brother Andrew Irwin for the years between 4 March 1831 and 29 October 1841. [38]

At last James Irvin was officially proved an officer who had fought courageously for his country. The promise of Washington was fulfilled and the name of Captain James Irvin was enrolled as one of the bravest of American soldiers and officers.

---

[36] Harbaugh, p. 363.

[37] U. S. Pension File.

[38] *Ibid.*

GENEALOGICAL RECORDS OF THE CALLENDER, IRVINE AND DUNCAN FAMILIES

FROM *The Irvine Story*, BY NICHOLAS B. WAINWRIGHT

ARRANGED BY HANNAH BENNER ROACH

The Historical Society of Pennsylvania has four extensive collections of Irvine family papers, accessioned between 1887 and 1963: the General Irvine Papers, the G. A. Irvine Papers, the Newbold-Irvine Papers, and the Mrs. Caryl Roberts-Irvine Papers. These collections furnish the basic source material for Mr. Wainwright's account of the five generations of the family who owned land along the Brokenstraw Creek and the Allegheny River in Warren County, bordering the New York State line in northwest Pennsylvania.

Purporting to be no more than a distillation of the thousands of surviving manuscripts in the collections, Mr. Wainwright's 100-page booklet nevertheless succeeds in presenting a quite comprehensive picture of the development and decline of the property in Warren County, and the family, so far as it was concerned in it. He includes much carefully documented genealogical information, derived in large part from the Irvine Papers. Lack of an index, however, leaves the reader somewhat uncertain as to the numerous family relationships obtaining between the Irvines and the Callender and Duncan families.

To clarify these ramifications, the following skeletal arrangement is offered. As it is based *solely* on the records cited by Mr. Wainwright, it does not pretend to be a complete genealogical record. It is offered only as a guide to Mr. Wainwright's account, to which the page references, placed in parentheses in the arrangement, refer.

The Callender Family

CAPTAIN ROBERT CALLENDER, b. *ca.* 1726; d. 29 July 1776, *ae.* 50 years; m. 1st, MARY SCULL, d. 1765 (p. 12). *Issue* (p. 12):

 i. ANN CALLENDER, d. Philadelphia, 15 Oct. 1823 (p. 21, 23); m. 1770 (p. 11), GENERAL WILLIAM IRVINE, b. Ulster, Ireland, 3 Nov. 1741 (p. 2); d. Philadelphia, 29 July 1804 (p. 20, 23), of whom see below.
 ii. ELIZABETH CALLENDER, m. DR. JOHN ANDREWS of Philadelphia [1746-1813].
 iii. ISABELLA CALLENDER, m. WILLIAM NEILL of Baltimore.

Robert Callender m. 2nd, FRANCES GIBSON of Carlisle, Pa. *Issue* (p. 12):

 iv. ROBERT CALLENDER, JR., d. unm. 1802 in Pittsburgh.
 v. MARTHA CALLENDER, m. JUDGE THOMAS DUNCAN, son of Stephen and Ann Duncan, for whom see below.
 vi. CATHARINE CALLENDER, m. MR. NOLAND of Aldie, Va.
 vii. A Daughter, name not given, m. MR. THOMPSON of Carlisle.

The Irvine Family

GENERAL WILLIAM IRVINE (1741-1804), m. 1770, ANN CALLENDER (d. 1823), daughter of Capt. Robert Callender of Carlisle and his 1st wife, Mary Scull, for whom see above. *Issue:*

1. i. CALLENDER IRVINE, b. 24 Jan. 1775 (p. 12); d. Philadelphia, 9 Oct. 1841 (p. 52), of whom see below.
   ii. ANN IRVINE, b. 2 March 1778; d. 26 June 1831 (p. 12, n. 20).
   iii. MARY IRVINE, b. 1 Nov. 1780; d. 8 Nov. 1781 (p. 12, n. 20).
   iv. WILLIAM NEILL IRVINE, b. 1 Nov. 1782; d. Harrisburg, Pa., 26 Sept. 1854; m. JULIANA GALBRAITH of Carlisle (p. 13, n. 21). *Issue:* 1. DR. GALBRAITH A. IRVINE, b. *ca.* 1811 (p. 33, n. 83); d. Warren, Pa., Feb. 1867, *ae.* 56, leaving issue (p. 13, n. 21). 2. WILLIAM C. IRVINE, d. *ca.* 1855, leaving issue (p. 13, n. 21).
   v. ELIZABETH IRVINE, b. 3 Jan. 1786; d. 26 Aug. 1864; m. 29 Aug. 1805, DR. JAMES REYNOLDS, d. 1808. No issue (p. 13, n. 22).
   vi. MARY BULLEN IRVINE, b. 26 March 1788; d. 31 Jan. 1847; m. 4 Oct. 1805, CHARLES W. LEWIS. *Issue:* 1. WILLIAM IRVINE LEWIS, d. at the Alamo, 1836 (p. 13, n. 22).
   vii. ARMSTRONG IRVINE, d. unm. 1817 (p. 13, n. 23, p. 23).
   viii. REBEKAH ARMSTRONG DE ROSENTHAL IRVINE; m. CAPT. PETER SIMONS FAYSSOUX of Charleston, S. C. *Issue:* 11 children (p. 13).
   ix. JAMES IRVINE, b. 28 Oct. 1796; d. unm. Carlisle, Pa., 2 May 1848 (p. 13, n. 25).
   x. JOHN IRVINE, b. 28 Oct. 1796; d. unm. 1832 (p. 13, n. 25).
   xi. MARTHA IRVINE, b. 1799; d. inf. *ae.* 2 months (p. 13).

1. GENERAL CALLENDER IRVINE (1775-1841), son of General William Irvine and his wife Ann Callender, m. 22 Dec. 1801 (p. 18), PATIENCE ELLIOTT, b. ca. 1775; d. 11 Apr. 1852, ae. 77 (p. 57, n. 153). *Only issue:*

2. DR. WILLIAM ARMSTRONG IRVINE, b. Erie, Pa., 28 Sept. 1803 (p. 19); d. Philadelphia, 7 Sept. 1886 (p. 86); m. 14 Oct. 1833 (p. 37), SARAH JANE DUNCAN, b. Philadelphia, 14 July 1814 (p. 36); d. 29 June 1839 (p. 43), daughter of Dr. Stephen Duncan and his 2nd wife Margaret Ellis, for whom see below. *Issue:*

   i. MARGARET (Minnie) ELLIS IRVINE, b. 12 May 1835 (p. 38); d. 29 June 1925 (p. 88); m. Swarthmore, Pa., 10 Dec. 1857 (p. 87), THOMAS MONTGOMERY BIDDLE, b. 9 July 1829; d. Erie, Pa., 28 Jan. 1864 (p. 87, n. 206), son of William Macfunn and Julia (Montgomery) Biddle. Issue: 1. EMILY DUNCAN BIDDLE, b. Carlisle, Pa., 13 Apr. 1859 (p. 87); d. 1892 (p. 88); m. 23 Sept. 1886 (p. 88), SYDNEY AUGUSTUS STAUNTON, b. *ca.* 1850; d. 11 Jan. 1939 (p. 88). No issue. 2. LYDIA SPENCER BIDDLE, b. Philadelphia, 3 Nov. 1860 (p. 87); d. unm. 22 March 1932 (p. 88). 3. SARAH DUNCAN BIDDLE, b. Irvine, Pa., 17 May 1862 (p. 87); d. 7 June 1877, *ae.* 15 years (p. 87).
   ii. CALLENDER IRVINE, b. 22 Feb. 1838 (p. 38); d. 1850, *ae.* 12 years (p. 45).

3. iii. SARAH DUNCAN IRVINE, b. 19 May 1839 (p. 43); d. Irvine, Pa. 23 Sept. 1916 (p. 92), of whom see below.

3. SARAH DUNCAN IRVINE (1839-1916), daughter of General Callender Irvine and his wife Patience Elliott, m. Erie, Pa., 15 Oct. 1863 (p. 88), DR. THOMAS NEWBOLD, b. *ca.* 1829; d. *ca.* 1873-1874 (p. 91, n. 212), son of Michael and Esther (Lowndes) Newbold (p. 88, n. 210). *Issue* (p. 88, n. 211):

    i. ELIZABETH IRVINE NEWBOLD, b. 5 Sept. 1865; d. Philadelphia, 21 June 1929 (p. 96); m. Irvine, 14 Sept. 1889 (p. 91), EDWARD LOWBER WELSH, b. 28 Dec. 1866; d. 3 Jan. 1935 (p. 96, n. 224), son of John Lowber Welsh. *Issue:* 1. SARAH IRVINE WELSH, m. 1913, CARYL ROBERTS of Philadelphia (p. 97). 2. JOHN LOWBER WELSH, b. 6 June 1891; d. 6 March 1955 (p. 96, n. 224); m. 1921, CHARLOTTE LE MOINE DUNLOP of Virginia (p. 97).

    ii. MARY MIDDLETON NEWBOLD, b. Irvine, 10 Dec. 1866; d. 27 Dec. 1933 (p. 97).

    iii. MARGARET (Daisy) ELLIS IRVINE NEWBOLD, b. Irvine, 25 July 1868; d. 30 May 1955 (p. 97).

    iv. EMILY (Bonnie) DUNCAN NEWBOLD, b. Irvine, 2 Oct. 1869; d. 15 Dec. 1931 (p. 96).

    v. ESTHER LOWNDES NEWBOLD, b. Irvine, 22 May 1872; d. Irvine, 24 Apr. 1963 (p. 97).

The Duncan Family

STEPHEN DUNCAN, b. *ca.* 1729; d. 30 March 1794; m. ANN ———— b. 13 Dec. 1731; d. 19 Dec. 1794 (p. 34, n. 84). *Issue* (p. 34, n. 85):

    i. JUDGE THOMAS DUNCAN, m. MARTHA CALLENDER (p. 12, 34), for whom see above.

    ii. LUCY DUNCAN, m. JONATHAN WALKER.

    iii. ANN DUNCAN, m. SAMUEL MAHAN.

1. iv. JOHN DUNCAN, d. 1793 (p. 34), for whom see further.

    v. ROBERT DUNCAN.

    vi. JAMES DUNCAN.

    vii. STEPHEN DUNCAN, JR.

1. JOHN DUNCAN (d. 1793), son of Stephen and Ann Duncan, m. SARAH ELIZA POSTLETHWAITE, d. 16 Aug. 1849 (p. 44), daughter of Samuel and Matilda Postlethwaite (p. 34, n. 86), having m. 2nd, COLONEL EPHRAIM BLAINE, b. 1741; d. 1804 (p. 34, n. 88). *Issue* of John and Sarah Duncan (p. 34):

    i. MATILDA ROSE DUNCAN, d. Jan. 1848 (p. 44).

2. ii. DR. STEPHEN A. DUNCAN, b. ca. 1788; d. 29 Jan. 1867 in 80th year (p. 74, n. 186), for whom see below.

    iii. SAMUEL POSTLETHWAITE DUNCAN.

    iv. MARY ANN DUNCAN, m. 1808 (p. 36), DR. JAMES GUSTINE of Carlisle, d. *ca.* 1845 (p. 36, n. 97). *Issue* (p. 36, n. 97): 1. SAMUEL GUSTINE. 2. SARAH GUSTINE. 3. REBECCA GUSTINE. 4. MATILDA D. GUSTINE, m. Philadelphia, 17 Sept. 1839, CHARLES P. LEVERICH of New York. 5. MARGARET DUNCAN GUSTINE, m. HENRY LEVERICH of New York (p. 44).

v. AMELIA (Emily) DUNCAN, b. Carlisle, 26 Feb. 1793; d. unm. Irvine, 14 July 1866 (p. 74, n. 185).

2. DR. STEPHEN A. DUNCAN (1788-1867), son of John Duncan and his wife Sarah Eliza Postlethwaite, m. 1st, ———— (p. 36); m. 2nd, MARGARET ELLIS of Louisiana, d. *ca.* 1820 (p. 36). *Issue* (p. 36):

    i. JOHN ELLIS DUNCAN, b. 3 Aug. 1812; d. New Haven, Conn., 13 Sept. 1829 (p. 37).

    ii. SARAH JANE DUNCAN (1814-1839); m. DR. WILLIAM ARMSTRONG IRVINE (1803-1886), for whom see above.

Dr. Stephen A. Duncan m. 3rd, CATHARINE A. BINGAMAN of Natchez, by whom he had further *issue* (p. 36):

    iii. HENRY POSTLETHWAITE DUNCAN, b. Natchez, Aug. 1832; d. New York, 6 Dec. 1879; m. 5 Oct. 1847 (p. 36, n. 95), MARY SARGENT of Philadelphia.

    iv. MARIA DUNCAN, m. JULIUS J. PRINGLE of Charleston, S. C.

    v. SAMUEL P. DUNCAN.

    vi. CHARLOTTE B. DUNCAN.

    vii. STEPHEN DUNCAN, d. Philadelphia, 1833 *ae.* 3 years.

    viii. STEPHEN DUNCAN (2nd).

KING

THOMAS KING of Philadelphia, buried at Christ Church, March 1, 1726/7; married Oct. 31, 1703, Rebecca ———, who, by her will dated March 24, 1739/40, proved April 8, 1746, made her daughter Ann Topp the executor thereof. The children of Thomas and Rebecca King, several of whom were baptized at Christ Church, were:

   i. WILLIAM KING, b. Oct. 30, 1704; bu. Nov. 4, 1739.
   ii. THOMAS KING, b. Oct. 27, 1705; bu. Jan. 5, 1735/6; m. 6 May, 1732, Mary Davis.
   iii. MARY KING, b. Dec. 23, 1707.
   iv. JOHN KING, twin of above, bu. Dec. 16, 1709.
   v. SAMUEL KING, bu. July 22, 1717.
   vi. JOHN KING, bpt. Dec. 27, 1711; bu. July 17, 1735.
   vii. REBECCA KING, b. Dec. 29, 1712; m. Dec. 7, 1731, John Price.
   viii. ANN KING, b. Dec. 8, 1714; d. Nov. 13, 1789; m. (1) Feb. 21, 1734, Joseph Topp. Issue: 1. *Thomas Topp*, bpt. Christ Church, June 19, 1735. 2. *Ann Topp*, bpt. Feb. 28, 1737; d. unmarried, and by will of Nov. 23, 1789, proved Oct. 6, 1801, bequeathed estate to half-brothers, James and William Sharswood. Ann King Topp, m. (2), at Christ Church, April 30, 1747, George Sharswood,* whose will, executed June 3, 1776, was proved Sept. 24, 1783. Issue: 3. *George Sharswood*, b. March 24, 1747/8; died unmarried. 4. *James Sharswood*,† twin of above; d. Sept. 14, 1836. 5. *William Sharswood*, died unmarried.
   ix. SAMUEL KING, b. Sept. 27, 1718; d. 1754; m. Ann Evans.
   x. CHARLES KING, bpt. Aug. 2, 1720.
   xi. ELIZABETH KING, buried Aug. 27, 1721.

2. SAMUEL KING (Thomas), born at Philadelphia, Sept. 24, 1718; d. there in 1754; married Aug. 31, 1739, Ann Evans,‡ born in Pembrokeshire, Wales, March 25, 1720; died at Philadelphia, April 5, 1809. Children, order uncertain:

* George Sharswood, son of William Sharswood and grandson of George Sharswood of New London, Conn., was born at Cape May, New Jersey, where his father had for a time resided, Oct. 18, 1696. He came to Philadelphia as a boy of ten years and there spent the remainder of his life. His will of June 6, 1776; proved Sept. 22, 1783, named wife Ann, her daugher *Ann Topp*, and sons *James* and *William Sharswood*.

† James Sharswood, Revolutionary officer and eminent Philadelphian, married, April 2, 1775, Elizabeth, daughter of Joseph Bredin of Abington, Bucks Co., Penna., and was the grandfather of the late distinguished jurist of the Supreme Court of Pennsylvania, GEORGE SHARSWOOD, 1810-1883.

† Member of the Moravian Congregation in Philadelphia, as were her children.

    i.   ANN KING, b. Nov. 14, 1741.
   ii.   SAMUEL KING, b. July 27, 1745; d. March 28, 1795; married
         and had at least three children.
  iii.   JOHN KING, b. July 4, 1748.
3. iv.   JAMES KING, b. July 27, 1751; married Cornelia England.
    v.   SUSANNA KING, b. Nov. 26, 1754; d. March, 1759.
   vi.   SON, died young.
  vii.   SON, died young.
 viii.   DAUGHTER, died young.

3. JAMES [3] KING * (SAMUEL,[2] THOMAS [1]), born at Philadelphia, July
27, 1751; died there, December 31, 1832; married October 20, 1772, Cornelia England † of Lewes, Delaware. Is said to have had nine children,
four sons and five daughters, only four of whom were named in his will
of September 30, 1830, with codicil of March 21, 1831.

    i.   JAMES KING, m. Mary Rodney.‡ Issue: 1. *James King*, d. s. p.
         2. *Daniel Rodney King*, m. Katherine Wagner and had:
         Emily King; Mary Rodney King, wife of Samuel Vaughan
         Merrick; Catherine D. King, wife of Arthur Merriweather,
         who died 1897.
   ii.   CORNELIA KING, b. Dec. 29, 1761; d. July 19, 1851; bu. in St.
         James' Churchyard, Bristol, Penna.; m. (1) ——— Reynolds;
         m. (2) James Cooper, son of James and Sarah Erwin Cooper
         of Camden, New Jersey, who died Feb. 13, 1852. Issue: 1.
         Emily Cooper, d. y. 2. *Sarah Erwin Cooper*, m. Griffith
         Morgan Eldridge. 3. *Cornelia Cooper*, d. y. 4. *James King
         Cooper*, d. y. 5. *Erwin James Cooper*, m. Ellen Rowley Myers.
  iii.   JOSEPH KING.
  iv.   DANIEL KING, m. Eliza ———.

---

* The owner, or part owner, of the Brigantine *Cornelia*, 100 tons burden,
which was chartered Feb. 1, 1776, " to hire and let to freight " for a mission
between the Colonies and France. For a description of the charter " between
James King and Samuel Ward, Benjamin Franklin, Thomas McKean, Joseph
Hewes, Josiah Bartlett and Robert Morris, Esqrs., a Secret Committee appointed by the Honourable Continental Congress ", see *Pennsylvania Magazine of History*, vol. i, pp. 355-6.

† Her mother was Cornelia, daughter of Dr. Henry Fisher of Lewes, Delaware, who in his will of 8 Aug., 1748, named daughter Cornelia England.
The latter m. (2) John Adams of Sussex County, by whom she also had issue.

‡ Mary (Rodney) King, daughter of Hon. Daniel Rodney, 1764-1846, Governor of Delaware, by his wife Margaret Fisher, daughter of Major Henry
Fisher of Lewes.

King - Phillips - Hammond Family Records

THE FOLLOWING entries are extracted from family records submitted by George H. S. King of Fredericksburg, Virginia. Because of the interrelationship of these families, many similar entries appear in each of the four records. Such duplications have been omitted in the subjoined extracts. The earliest records appear to have been entered in *A Brief Concordance to The Holy Scriptures of the Old and New Testaments . . . by John Brown. Revised and Corrected. Philadelphia: Published by Mathew Carey, No. 118 Market Street. T. Kirk, Printer. 1803.* Pasted inside is what appears to be a bookplate; "This Bible / Is the Property / of George & Samuel King."

BIRTHS

Samuel King Was born September the 10th 1774.

Ann King Wife of Samuel Was born February 10th 1784
Long may they live and happy may they be,
In health, in wealth, in love, and in progeny.[1]

Mary Ann King daughter of Samuel & Ann Was born Monday the fourteenth of October at 2 O'Clock P. M. in the year of our Lord 1805.

John P. King was born Thursday the Eighteenth of June at 8 o'Clock A. M. in the year of our Lord 1807.

William S. King was born on Friday the Twenty Eight of December at 1 oclock in the morning in the year of our Lord 1810.

George P. King was born on Monday Morning at 1 (?) oclock the 29 of March — in the year of our Lord, 1813.

---

[1] This effusion is followed by an abbreviated record of their children which is omitted here. In its place is given a more detailed record which is written on a second page of births.

Louisa B. King was Born November 5 1815.

Amanda Rebecca King was born Monday the Fifteenth of June at 1 o'clock P. M. in the year of our Lord 1818.

Samuel King was born February 14th at 10 o.Clock A. M. in the year of our Lord 1821

Isreal Davis King was born February 4th 1824.

Benjamin Franklin King was born December 10th 1827.

(By) *Second Wife* (of Samuel King, Jr.)

Maggie Bell King was born March 8th 1860.

Lillia King was born August 27 1861.

Above two children of Samuel & Ann Elizabeth Chartters King

DEATHS

William King Departed this life May the third in the year of our Lord One thousand Seven hundred & Eighty Six.[2]

George King Departed this life December the fifth in the year of our Lord one thousand Seven hundred & Ninety Two.[3]

Catherine King Departed this life July the twenty first in the year of our Lord One thousand Eight hundred & four.

MARRIAGES

Samuel King & Ann his Wife were married the fourth day of October in the year of our LORD 1804.[4]

Nathan Browne Hammond & Mary Ann his Wife were married the twelth (*sic*) day of September in the Year of our LORD 1822.

John P. King and Catharine M. Dreisbach were married the 19th of February A D 1835.

[2] He was the eldest son of the immigrant George King, and was killed by the falling of a tree. For an extended and not entirely correct account of George King and his descendants, see Albert H. Gerberich, *The Brenneman History* (Scottdale, Pa., 1938), 763-770.

[3] George King, the immigrant, b. *ca.* 1731, m. Catharine Brenneman, b. *ca.* 1733, whose death entry follows that of George King. They lived in Willistown Twsp., Chester Co., where both died testate. They had nine children: William, Abraham, Catharine wife of John Trainer, Susanna wife of Daved Eakins, George, Sophia wife of Richard Pearce, Isaac, Joseph and Samuel King. Will of George King, Chester Co. Will Book 9, 81; will of Catharine King, Chester Co. Will Book 11, 47, Chester Co. Court House, West Chester, Pa.

[4] *Poulson's American Daily Advertiser* for 10 October 1804, carried the following: "Married: On Thursday evening the 4th inst., by the Rev. Mr. Jones, Mr. Samuel King to Miss Ann Phillips, both of the Great Valley, Chester County."

William S. King and Sarah Jane White were married the 15th of June A. D. 1837.

Philip R. Davis and Louisa B. King were married the 29th of November A. D. 1838.

George Phillips King and Susan Warren were married August 21th 1845.

Samuel King and Ann Eliza Adams were married August 29th 1844.

Ellis Adams and Amanda Rebecca King were married September 5th 1844.

Israel Davis King and Mary Ann E. Walters married Feby 7 1846.[5]

Samuel King and Ann Elizabeth Chartters married May 19 1859.

Dr. Wm. S. King and Virginia S. E. Evans married May 22 1867.

Geo. P. King and Anna Chancellor married March 25th 1868.

Benj: Franklin King and Minnie Banson married June 18 1868.

The second family record[6] was started by George P. King, son of Samuel King and his wife Ann Phillips. As it includes copies of entries in the earlier record, these have not been included in the following extracts.

BIRTHS

Elizabeth A. King daughter of Geo. P. and Susan King was born October 28th 1848.

William W. King son of Geo. P. and Susan King was born April 2nd 1854.

Naomi B. King was born Sept. 19th 1859; (*in another hand:*) was married to John James Payne of Fauquier County, Virginia, and died on 4th Feby: 1920.

Chancellor F. King was born 15th of may 1869.

George P. King Jr was born 20th of January 1871.

Melzie Samuel King was born 19th of September 1872.

Rufus H. King was born 21th day of September 1874.

DEATHS

Annastasia Chancellor, daughter, Rev. Melzi Sanford Chancellor and Lucy Fox Frazer, his wife, and Wife of Geo. P. King, Sr. died in Fredericksburg, Va. November 1st 1912.

[5] This date is given at 17 February in the Phillips Bible record and in *The Brenneman History*, cited in Note 2, 770.

[6] There is no fly-leaf to show the date the Bible was published.

Elisabeth A. King Died July 22nd 1849.

William W. King departed this life August 13th aged 3 years 4 months & 11 days.

Samuel King Died June 11th 1841 in the 67 year of his age.[7]

Mrs. Ann King wife of Samuel King died December 12th 1858 aged 75 years.[8]

George P. King died December the 3rd 1876.

Geo. Phillips King, Jr. departed this life June the 21st 1931 in the 60th year of his age.

Saml King, Jr. died in Filley, Nebraska Jan. 20, 1892, in the 71st year of his age.

Amanda R. King daughter of Samuel and Ann (Phillips) King and wife of Ellis Adams died at Fairmont, Ill. Sept. 1889.

Louisa B. King, daughter of Samuel King and wife of Philip R. Davis died near Waterloo, Kans. Feb. 15, 1891.

Mrs. Jane Bowen died 17th Aug. 1846 at the home of her son-in-law William Warren, Esq., in the City of Fredericksburg, Va.[9] She was the widow of Burkett Bowen. Their daughter Anne Bowen married on 16 December 1819 William Warren.

William Warren Senr departed this life Nov. 24, 1852, aged 59 years, 8 mos. 2 days.

Ann Bowen Warren departed this life 8th of July 1858 aged 61 years 7 months & 21 days.

The following extracts of Phillips family records are from a Bible reported to have been printed in New York in 1827 by Daniel D. Smith. It belonged to Mrs. Alice (Hammond) Stansbury of West Chester, Pa., and includes many King family entries, duplicates of those already given above, which have not been included here.

---

[7] Samuel King was of New London when he died testate. In his will he named as children John P., George P., Dr. William S., Mary Ann Hammond, Louisa B. David, Amanda R. King, Israel Davis King and Benjamin Franklin King. Chester Co. Will Book 18, 58. He is buried in Beulah Baptist Church Cemetery, near Russellville, Chester Co.

[8] Obituaries of Ann (Phillips) King appeared in Virginia, Maryland and Pennsylvania newspapers. *The American Republican and Chester County Democrat* said: "Deaths: On the morning of the 12th of the 12th month 1858, at the residence of her son, George P. King, in Fredericksburg, Virginia, ANN KING, relict of the late Samuel King, in the 75th year of her age, formerly of Chester County, Penna." She is buried in the family lot of her son George P. King, in the Fredericksburg Cemetery.

[9] This entry and the next three are all written in a modern hand.

BIRTHS

John Phillips was born y[e] 23[d] of 7th month — 1759.

Mary Phillips was born y[e] 26th of 10th m[o] — 1761

Sarah Phillips Daughter of John & Mary Phillips was born y[e] 9th of 12th m[o] 1780.

Joseph Phillips was born y[e] 26th of 10th m[o] 1782.

Ann Phillips was born y[e] 10th of 2[d] m[o] 1784.

John Phillips was born y[e] 12th of 7th month — 1788.

Mary Phillips was born y[e] 28th of 8th m[o] — 1790.

Priscilla Phillips was born y[e] 7th of 3[d] month 1793.

Deby Phillips was born y[e] 8th of 2[d] month — 1796.

Levi L Phillips was born y[e] 31st of 12th month 1798.

Sarah Phillips was born y[e] 22[d] of 2[d] month 1801.

MARRIAGES

John Phillips was intermaried (*sic*) with Mary Lewis y[e] 2[d] of 3[d] m[o] in the year — 1780.

Childrens Mariage (*sic*)

Joseph Phillips to Catharine Fahnestock 5th of 2[d] m[oth] 1807.

Ann Phillips to Samuel King 4th of October 1804.

John Phillips to Margaret Fox y[e] 8th month 20th 1807.

Rebecca Phillips to Sam[l] Lewis 18th of 10 month 1820.

Mary Phillips to Dan[l] J. Rhoads 28th 9 mo. 1810.

Priscilla Phillips to Sam[l] Brooke y[e] 8th of 4th month — 1813.

Deby Phillips to David Cope 11th of 1st month 1826.

Sarah Phillips to Adam Williamson y[e] 3[d] month 12th — 1823.

DEATHS

John Phillips deceased the 26th of the ninth month 1834 aged 75 years.[10]

Mary Phillips departed this life 4th Month 21st 1844 Aged 82 Years 5 months and 25 days.[11]

[10] John Phillips died testate in E. Whiteland Twsp., Chester Co. He bequeathed the farm he lived on, then in the tenancy of David Cope, to his wife Mary, as well as land in Tredyffrin. His executors, James Malin and David Cope, were to sell "the stores and dwelling houses at the cross roads," and the plantation partly in Whiteland and partly in Tredyffrin which was in the tenure of Benjamin Walton. Chester Co. Will Book 16, 612.

[11] Mary Phillips in her will divided her furniture between her daughter: bed, bedsteads, curtain, quilts, etc., a mahogany tea table, an "old clock," and a dining table. Money due her was to be divided between her sons. Jane Cope a granddaughter (?) attested to her handwriting when the will was proved 13 June 1844. Chester Co. Will Book S-18, 449.

Sarah Phillips Daughter of John & Mary Phillips deceas[d] 7th of 3[d] month — 1790.

Levi L Phillips deceas[d] 2[d] m[o] 25th in y[e] year 1814.

Priscilla Brooke wife of Samuel Brooke deceased the 29th of the 5th month 1834 Aged 41 years.

Mary Rhoads departed this life 6th month 13th June, 1839.

Rufus King Hammond died September 24th 1845 in the 22nd Year of his age.

Nathan B. Hammond died May 24th 1866 aged 67.[12]

Mary Ann Hammond, daughter of Saml. & Ann King died in Balto. Jan 17th 1888 in the 83[d] year of her age.

Joseph Phillips departed this life.

Annie Brown Atwood daughter of M. A. & N. B. Hammond died in Balto. Dec. 12th 1876.

Jane Cope departed this life.

The ensuing Hammond family records[13] are on supplemental pages in the Phillips Bible. Unlike the other records, they are all in the same handwriting.

Family Record

BIRTHS

Nathan B. Hammond was born on the 23 of April, in the year of Our Lord 1799.

Mary Ann King was born on the 14th of October in the year of our Lord 1805.

Catharine Elizabeth Hammond eldest child of Nathan B. and Mary Ann Hammond was born June 8th A. D. 1823.

Rufus King Hammond was born June 26, A. D. 1824.

Milton Hammond was born May[d] 3[d] A. D. 1826.

Ann E. Browne Hammond was born October 7th A. D. 1827.

James A. Hammond was born June 17th A. D. 1829.

John Wesley Hammond was born March 1st A. D. 1831.

Samuel King Hammond was born July 15th A. D. 1832.

William Browne Hammond was born April 19th 1836.

[12] Nathan B. Hammond was of Baltimore at the time of his marriage, but died at New London, Chester Co., according to the entry in the Hammond family record. That particular entry has not been extracted for this present record, because his death is entered here in the Phillips record. He and his wife are buried at Kelton Churchyard, near New London, according to George H. S. King. There is an extended eulogy of Mr. Hammond in the Hammond record, not included here.

[13] For additional records of this Hammond family, see *The Brenneman History*, 764, cited in Note 2.

Elisha Nathan Browne Hammond was born September 21st A. D. 1837.

Horace Nelson Hammond was born July 13th A. D. 1839.

MARRIAGES

Married in the 12th of September A. D. 1822 by the Rev. John Finley in the City of Baltimore Nathan B. Hammond to Mary Ann eldest daughter of Samuel and Ann King.

In happiness long may they live, And be through life contented, May Jesus Christ their Sins forgive, And die by all lamented. Married on the 19th of february 1835 John P. King, to Catharine M. Dreisbach.

Married on the 15th of Feb'Y 1852 Dr Milton Hammond to Mary Dungan.

Married on the 15th of April 1858 Dr Milton Hammond to Lizzie Hubbell.

Married the 23d of April 1861 by R. P. DuBois, William A. Atwood to Anne B. Hammond.

Married May 1st 1862, Samuel King Hammond to Hannah S. Kervey.

Married on the 21st of May 1863 at New London by R. P. DuBois Horace Nelson Hammond to Carrie S. Aldridge.

Married June 9th 1869 William B. Hammond, to Sophia C. Aldridge of and at Elkton Md. by Rev. J. Price, M. E. Minister.

Married in Phila at the Garard House, Nov 23d 1870 by the Rev. Joseph L. Evans, James Alexander Hammond to Mrs Amanda R. Hartman of West Chester, Pa.

DEATHS

Catharine Elizabeth Hammond Eldest child of Nathan B. and Mary Ann Hammond departed this life June 13th 1823 aged 5 days.

Elisha N. Browne Hammond departed this life, March 17th 1839 aged 17 months and 29 days.[14]

Departed this life March 30th 1802 James Hammond in the 32d year of his age.

Annie Hammond died 1812 aged 42 wife of James Hammond.

Departed this life october 8th 1854 Mrs. Mary Hammond wife of Dr Milton Hammond in the 22d year of age.

Departed this life, September 30th 1866 William A. Atwood in the (blank) of his age.

---

[14] The eulogy following this entry is omitted here.

Esther King

of Philadelphia and Bucks Counties and her Bowyer, Lynn and Elfreth Children

Dorothee Hughes Carousso

ESTHER KING is of more than average interest in genealogical research because of her multiple marriages. In an era when a man often outlived two or three or more wives, it is unusual to find a woman who outlived four husbands. Born in England about 1650, she came to Philadelphia at about the same time as William Penn, with her first husband, John Bowyer, by whom she had four surviving children. Her second marriage was to a man surnamed Lynn, by whom she had one son, Joseph Lynn. By her third husband, Josiah Elfreth, she had one son, Jeremiah Elfreth. Her fourth marriage was to Richard Willson of Bucks County. There appear to have been no children of this last marriage.

There is some evidence to support the speculation that Esther may have been related to Walter King, an original purchaser from William Penn, and a member of the Free Society of Traders. Letters of administration granted in Philadelphia on the estate of Benjamin King 3 2m 1689, to Esther Bowyer, "his sister and next of kin," establish her maiden name as King.[1] The evidence suggesting that she bore some relationship to Walter King is that most of the property in Pennsylvania acquired by her first husband, John Bowyer, was "taken up in the right of Walter King."

In his original grant from William Penn 26 July 1681, Walter King was described as being "of Haveyard in the Parish of Reinton," County Somerset, England.[2] A search of English records translates this location as being in Havyatt, Parish of Rayton, County Somerset. His original

---

[1] Philadelphia Administration Book A, 62, #121:1688, estate of Benjamin King. Unless otherwise stated, all wills, administrations and land records hereinafter cited are Philadelphia County records.

[2] Exemplification Book 8, 573: 26 July 1681, William Penn to Walter King.

purchase of land to be taken up in Pennsylvania was for a thousand acres, but these were laid out in several parcels in different locations.

Unlike many original purchasers, Walter King did come to live in Pennsylvania. He was a member of the Philadelphia Monthly Meeting of Friends.[3] He was also a member of the Pennsylvania Assembly in 1682/3.[4] In December 1687, he was a resident of Philadelphia County, but it seems that he returned to England shortly thereafter.[5] If he was, as supposed, related to Benjamin and Esther, he appears to have returned prior to Benjamin's death, since the administration of Benjamin's estate was to his sister as "next of kin."

In a letter of attorney dated 24 October 1694, and signed with his mark, King appointed Israel Hobbs, a Bristol carpenter, his attorney to collect several debts in Pennsylvania; King was then described as being "of ffayland in the County of Somerset." [6] Among English Friends' records for Bristol and Somerset appears the death record of one Walter King on 11 5m 1703, a resident of Fayland, Parish of Wraxall, and a member of the North Division Monthly Meeting.[7]

Judging from the date of birth of Esther's eldest child, John Bowyer, Jr., in 1671, her first marriage to JOHN BOWYER must have occurred about 1668 or 1669, presumably in England where her four surviving Bowyer children were probably born.

There is no indication that the Bowyers came to Philadelphia through any association with the Society of Friends, although succeeding gen-

---

3 On 1 5m 1684, Walter King and Dennis Rochford laid before the Philadelphia Monthly Meeting "a matter of difference depending between them touching payment for a servant" whom King had sold to Rochford. Original Philadelphia Monthly Meeting Minutes, examined at Friends' Record Department, 306 Arch St., Philadelphia.

4 "Votes and Proceedings of the House of Representatives of the Province of Pennsylvania," *Pennsylvania Archives*, 8th Series, I, 13. King was a representative for Philadelphia County at the first session which opened 12 1m 1682/3. The reader should bear in mind that until September 1752, the legal year in Pennsylvania began 25 March, called first month (1m) by Friends, although the historical year began 1 January, eleventh month (11m), according to Friends' reckoning. Dates between 1 January and 24 March were therefore double-dated, viz: 1 January (11m) 1682/3 to 24 March (24 1m) 1682/3, but 25 March was 25 1m 1683.

5 In August 1688, Walter King gave a letter of attorney to John Parsons and others, and by July 1689, was "late" of Philadelphia Co. By 25 1m 1690, he was of "Portburrie in the County of Somerset," England. See recitals in Deed Books E-1-5, 613: 13 10m 1687, Walter King to Francis Gamble; H-8, 357: 6 5m 1689, Benjamin Chambers to Rebecca Stanley; E-2-5, 258: 25 1m 1690, John Claypoole to John Parsons *et al.*

6 Deed Book E-2-5, 348: 24 Oct. 1694, Walter King to Israel Hobbs.

7 Digested Copy of the Registers of the Quarterly Meeting of Bristol and Somersetshire, Collections of the Genealogical Society of Pennsylvania (GSP), show the marriage at Bristol Meeting 6 7m 1663, of a Walter King and Margaret Prince, who, as the Widow Margaret King, resident of Bristol, was bur. at Portishead 9 2m 1704. A daughter Florence King, b. 18 Nov. 1667, appears in the registers of Bruton, Somersetshire. Esther Bowyer, b. *ca.* 1650, could not have been a daughter of Margaret (Prince) King, though Esther and her brother Benjamin might have been children of Walter King by a previous marriage.

erations of the family did become Friends. Other contemporary Bowyers came to Philadelphia at about the same time, but no conclusive evidence of any relationship has been found.[8]

John Bowyer, although an early settler in Philadelphia County, was
not one of William Penn's original purchasers. As previously stated, all
of his earliest land holdings were "in the right of Walter King" who was
an original purchaser. The earliest record of John Bowyer in Philadelphia is a warrant for a "city lott" to be located "between the front and
second streets att Skullkill," granted in the right of Walter King by a
warrant dated 11 8m 1683. The lot was surveyed a week later, south
of Walnut Street between the present Twenty-second Street (then
Schuylkill Front) and the present Twenty-first Street.[9] He obtained
a patent for the lot from the Commissioners of Property 30 5m 1687,
and two months later assigned it to Peter Sharbanow for £6.[10]

Another patent to John "boyer," dated 13 July 1687, was for a tract
of 200 acres "in the Manor of Springetsberry" and County of Philadelphia, adjoining land laid out for Edward Lane and the land "belonging to the German Town." As shown on the *Map of the Province of
Pennsylvania* charted by Thomas Holme, the location of this property
was in old Bristol Township, and extended from the east line of Germantown, now Stenton Avenue, to the present Cheltenham Avenue, in
the vicinity of Washington Lane. The land was granted by a warrant
from the Proprietor on 26 4m 1684; it was laid out by the Surveyor
General's order on 11 9m 1684, also "to John Boyer in right of Walter
King."[11]

On 5 June 1688, John Bowyer sold fifty acres of this land to Edward
Lane.[12] After John's death, his widow (then Esther Elfreth), with his
son John Bowyer, Jr., sold the remaining 150 acres to William Wilkins
of Philadelphia, for £31.[13]

---

[8] Among these were Hannah "Boyer" who appears as an adult in the Philadelphia Meeting minutes 5 8m
1685; Thomas Bowyer, on whose estate letters of administration were granted in Philadelphia 20 April 1708,
to Edward Lane, the widow Martha Bowyer having renounced. This Thomas Bowyer may have been a brother
of John Bowyer.

[9] See Warrants and Surveys of the Province of Pennsylvania, 1682-1759, III, 248, Municipal Archives,
Department of Records, City Hall, Philadelphia.

[10] Exemplification Book 1, 154: 30 5m 1687, Patent to John Boyer; Deed Book E-1-5, 594: 3 7m 1687,
John Boyer to Peter Sharbanow. He is not to be confused with the John Powyer, tanner of Wales, who,
although an original purchaser from Penn, did not come to Pennsylvania. Nor is John Bowyer to be confused with the Jan Boycar who was an early resident of Newcastle County.

[11] Exemplification Book 1, 170: 13 July 1687, Patent to John Boyer.

[12] Deed Book E-1-5, 594: 5 June 1688, John Bowyer to Edward Lane. Lane had come originally from
Bristol, and in 1708 administered Thomas Bowyer's estate. What, if any, was the relationship of these three
men?

[13] Deed Book E-4-7, 150: 16 Sept. 1695, Esther Elfreth and John Bowyer to William Wilkins.

On 15 9m 1684, John Bowyer, Sr., bought sixty acres of land in Shackamaxon from Gunner Rambo, which had been surveyed for Bowyer the month before out of land Peter Cock had granted Rambo, his son-in-law.[14] It fronted on Gunner's Creek or Run, earlier known as Tumanaromaning's Creek, which, having at that time a considerable flow, gave Bowyer easy access to the Delaware River less than a mile away. Its location, while northeast of the city proper, was advantageous since Bowyer was a shipwright by occupation. It has been said that ship-carpenters earned five and six shillings a day in wages, and on that pay could soon save money. "The ship carpenter, who laid by one day's wages a week could, in a month or two, be trading to the [West] Indies so as to give him £50 or £60 clear money at the end of a year, and that would buy him a farm, build him a house, or give him a share in some vessel on the stocks. In ten years he could become a capitalist, as many of his trade did so become." [15]

Here on Gunner's Creek, John and Esther Bowyer probably lived until his death four years later. Letters of administration on his estate were granted to his widow Esther on 29 6m 1688. The bond required, in the amount of £500, would indicate that his estate amounted to £250. It was underwritten by William Powell, a Philadelphia cooper, and William Royden of West New Jersey.[16] Three years later the estate still was not settled. In 1691 Esther presented a bill to the Commissioners "for work done by her Husband to the Proprietor's barge and boat, the sum of £5 7s. 6d., which was allowed." [17] The final payment was not made until 1693.[18]

Probably John Bowyer was a relatively young man at the time of his death since his wife survived him by twenty-two years and was married again three times before her own death in 1710.

Issue of Esther King by her 1st husband John Bowyer:

1. i. JOHN BOWYER, JR., b. 1671, probably in England; bur. 10 January 1732/3, in Christ Church Burial Ground, Philadelphia, of whom further.
2. ii. ESTHER BOWYER, b. *ca.* 1672, probably in England; d. between 27 November and 17 December 1749, in Bucks County, Pa., when her will was proved, of whom further.

---

14 Deed Book C-2-3, 194: 17 5m 1699, Gunner Rambo to John Bowyer.

15 J. Thomas Scharf and Thompson Westcott, *History of Philadelphia, 1609-1884* (Philadelphia, 1884), I, 152, hereinafter cited as Scharf and Westcott.

16 Administration Book A, 46, #71:1688, estate of John Bowyer.

17 "Minutes of the Board of Property," *Pennsylvania Archives,* 2nd Series, XIX, 79.

18 "William Penn's Account with Samuel Jennings, Receiver General, 1690-1693," *The Pennsylvania Magazine of History and Biography (PMHB),* XXXV (1911), 210.

iii. WILLIAM BOWYER, b. *ca.* 1674, probably in England; d. before 1750. Little is known of this son. The phrase in his mother's will in 1710, in which she left him a token five shillings "if he comes over here," indicates that he had probably returned to England. Her wording suggests that she did not seriously expect him to "come over here." [19] Another implication is contained in a Bucks County deed relating to the Willson-Clay property which named Jeremiah Elfreth in 1750 as "the only surviving child of Esther Willson." [20] From these sources, it would appear that William returned to England prior to 1710, and died before 1750.

3. iv. SARAH BOWYER, b. *ca.* 1680, probably in England; d. between 1711 and 1714, of whom further.

Esther's brief second marriage was to a husband surnamed Lynn, referred to only once as JOSEPH LYNN.[21] Since her only child of this second marriage bore the same name, it is not unlikely that the son was named after his father. Her marriage to Joseph Lynn must have taken place after 3 2m 1689, when the administration of the estate of her brother Benjamin was given to "Esther Bowyer."

By 25 March 1691, she was again a widow, when, as "Hester Lynn, Widdow," she leased from Thomas Tresse, a Philadelphia merchant, a piece of his bank lot between High (Market) and Mulberry (Arch) on Front Street, containing 17½ feet in width and extending 250 feet eastward into the river. The lease was for a term of fifty years, she paying yearly to Thomas Tresse "the sum of £1 12s. 1d. in good Merchantable winter wheat delivered at the dwelling house of said Thomas Tress att Philadelphia or in current silver money to bee paid att every half year." In addition, Esther was to build "a cartway under said Banck for the use of all people in the day tyme and likewise to make a Wharfe and staires in all respects according as the said Thomas Tress is obliged by virtue of his patent." Also, "what houses buildings wharfes and staires shall be erected upon the premises . . . said Hester Lynn doth promise will keep in repairs at her own charge." Among the witnesses to this lease was Josiah Elfreth who became Esther's third husband.[22]

Her eldest son, John Bowyer, Jr., also a shipwright, was about twenty when Esther leased this waterfront property in 1691. Possibly she ex-

---

[19] Will Book C, 199, #159:1710, will of Esther Willson.

[20] Recited in Bucks Co. Deed Book 9, 102: 24 March 1749/50, Rowland Powell *et al.* to Thomas Stanaland.

[21] See A Genealogy of the Evans Family Collected in the Years 1819, 1820 and 1821, by Samuel Morris Lynn of Philadelphia. Recopied by his daughter Lizzie T. Bonbright in 1888, GSP. Samuel Morris Lynn was a great-grandson of Esther King's son 4. Joseph Lynn. When he was collecting this family history, he may have had access to family Bible records, family letters, or had word-of-mouth knowledge of the family which is no longer available. Because of several discrepancies which occur in this work, possibly because of the various transcriptions, this source should be used with caution.

[22] Deed Book E-2-5, 208: 25 1m (March) 1691, Thomas Tresse to Esther Lynn.

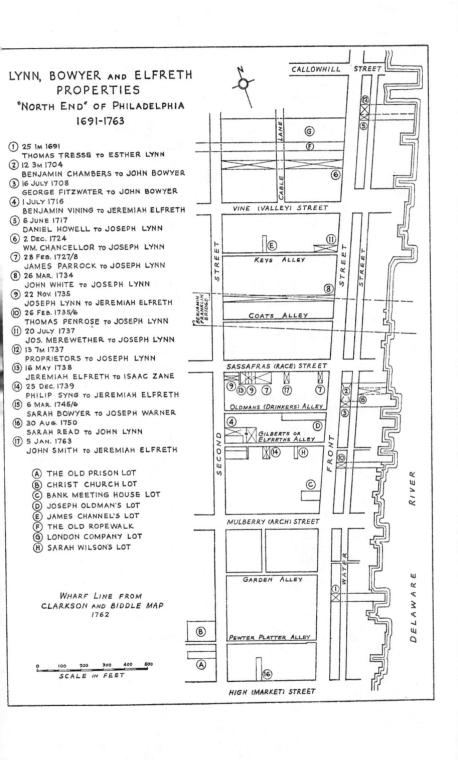

LYNN, BOWYER and ELFRETH PROPERTIES
"NORTH END" OF PHILADELPHIA
1691-1763

① 25 1m 1691
  THOMAS TRESSE to ESTHER LYNN
② 12 3m 1704
  BENJAMIN CHAMBERS to JOHN BOWYER
③ 16 JULY 1708
  GEORGE FITZWATER to JOHN BOWYER
④ 1 JULY 1716
  BENJAMIN VINING to JEREMIAH ELFRETH
⑤ 6 JUNE 1717
  DANIEL HOWELL to JOSEPH LYNN
⑥ 2 DEC. 1724
  WM. CHANCELLOR to JOSEPH LYNN
⑦ 28 FEB. 1727/8
  JAMES PARROCK to JOSEPH LYNN
⑧ 26 MAR. 1734
  JOHN WHITE to JOSEPH LYNN
⑨ 22 NOV. 1735
  JOSEPH LYNN to JEREMIAH ELFRETH
⑩ 26 FEB. 1735/6
  THOMAS PENROSE to JOSEPH LYNN
⑪ 20 JULY 1737
  JOS. MEREWETHER to JOSEPH LYNN
⑫ 13 7m 1737
  PROPRIETORS to JOSEPH LYNN
⑬ 16 MAY 1738
  JEREMIAH ELFRETH to ISAAC ZANE
⑭ 25 DEC. 1739
  PHILIP SYNG to JEREMIAH ELFRETH
⑮ 6 MAR. 1745/6
  SARAH BOWYER to JOSEPH WARNER
⑯ 30 AUG. 1750
  SARAH READ to JOHN LYNN
⑰ 5 JAN. 1763
  JOHN SMITH to JEREMIAH ELFRETH

Ⓐ THE OLD PRISON LOT
Ⓑ CHRIST CHURCH LOT
Ⓒ BANK MEETING HOUSE LOT
Ⓓ JOSEPH OLDMAN'S LOT
Ⓔ JAMES CHANNEL'S LOT
Ⓕ THE OLD ROPEWALK
Ⓖ LONDON COMPANY LOT
Ⓗ SARAH WILSON'S LOT

WHARF LINE FROM
CLARKSON AND BIDDLE MAP
1762

0 100 200 300 400 500
SCALE IN FEET

CALLOWHILL STREET

CABLE LANE

VINE (VALLEY) STREET

KEYS ALLEY

COATS ALLEY

BENJAMIN FRANKLIN BRIDGE

SASSAFRAS (RACE) STREET

OLDMANS (DRINKERS) ALLEY

GILBERTS OR ELFRETHS ALLEY

SECOND STREET

FRONT STREET

MULBERRY (ARCH) STREET

GARDEN ALLEY

WATER

DELAWARE RIVER

PEWTER PLATTER ALLEY

HIGH (MARKET) STREET

pected him to fulfill the terms of building the cartway (now Water Street), the required stone stairs from Front Street down to the river, as well as the wharf. Certainly less than three months after she leased the lot, Esther Lynn gave birth to her fifth known child, a posthumous son, Joseph Lynn.

The trade of ship-building played a significant part in the life of Esther King. Her first husband was a shipwright and, probably, her second. Two of her four sons, John Bowyer and Joseph Lynn, were shipwrights, as was her stepson, Henry Elfreth. Three of her grandsons, Joseph, John and Jeremiah Lynn, and the husbands of eight of her granddaughters, all were shipwrights: Jacob Williamson, Roger Brooke, Henry Dennis, Edward Austin, Philip Boyte, Joseph Warner, Samuel Bonham and Peter Bankson.[23]

Issue of Esther King by her 2nd husband Joseph Lynn:

4. v. JOSEPH LYNN, b. 14 June 1691; d. 12 8m 1742, in Philadelphia, of whom further.

Esther King's third marriage, this time to JOSIAH ELFRETH, was as brief as her second marriage, since by September 1693, when she was assessed as "Widow Elfrith," it is apparent that she had been widowed twice in little more than two years.[24] Josiah Elfreth had had an earlier marriage and a surviving son of that marriage, Henry Elfreth, the Philadelphia shipwright mentioned above. He was still under age in 1694 when his uncle Jeremiah Elfreth, Josiah's brother, died. Henry's mother, Josiah's first wife, is said, without supporting evidence, to have died in England before 1683.[25]

On 3 11m 1683/4, Josiah Elfreth obtained a warrant for six acres to be laid out in Philadelphia County.[26] On 2 8m 1684, he was issued a sec-

---

[23] Shipbuilding on the Delaware River in the early years of the province was a far more vital enterprise than is generally understood. Choice timber grew nearly to the river banks and in every shape and size necessary for keel and hull and masts. In 1690, Governor Daniel Coxe, then living in London, was having a "great ship" built at Burlington across the Delaware from Philadelphia, and was selling shares in it. It was described as being "of the burthen of One hundred and twentie tons or thereabouts," and was to be named the *Delaware Merchant*, for which see recital in Deed Book E-2-5, 168: 22 Dec. 1690, Charter party, Daniel Coxe *et al.* to Richard Morris. The weight of this intended vessel was three-fourths the size of the *Mayflower* of 180 tons. Considering the labor resources of the builders of the two different ships, the *Delaware Merchant*, though built seventy years or more later, was an ambitious project for Burlington in 1690.

[24] "The First Tax List for Philadelphia County," *PMHB*, VIII (1884), 85, 89, 105. This tax was assessed by virtue of an Act passed 15 May 1693; the list was not completed until 26 September 1693. The Widow "Elfrith's" property was rated at £50.

[25] Administration Book A, 182, #25:1694, estate of Jeremiah Elfreth. Henry Elfreth was a minor when letters were granted on this estate of his uncle Jeremiah Elfreth 1 April 1694, to Henry Flower. See the Elfreth Family Chart, Z51, 109, GSP, for the statement that Henry's mother, Josiah's first wife, died in England before 1683.

[26] "Old Rights," *Pennsylvania Archives*, 3rd Series, II, 699. No record has been found that Josiah ever took up this land.

126

ond warrant, this time for a city lot. It was surveyed the following week at the Center Square, 50 feet by 100 feet. Bounded north by William Dillwyn's lot, east by Market Square, south by a vacant lot and west by the Eighth Street from Schuylkill (now Fifteenth Street), it was patented to Elfreth on 2 6m 1687.[27] On 6 2m 1687, he had appointed David Lloyd his attorney to sell the lot to Christopher Sibthorpe, a Philadelphia brazier, for fifty shillings; the sale was not completed, however, until almost a year later.[28]

Josiah Elfreth already had interests in Salem County, West New Jersey, before he disposed of the Philadelphia property. On 21 August 1685, Edward Champnes signed an agreement of lease to "Josiah Elfreth of Allowayes, of 484 acres there near the grist mill, which said Josiah now inhabits." [29] Whether Josiah inhabited the 484 acres or the grist mill or both is not clear. A few months later, on 26 11m (January) 1685/6, he leased a second property in Salem County from Edward Bradway: "a plantation at Stow alias Unknown Creek." [30]

In 1691, Elfreth was in Philadelphia when he witnessed the lease between Thomas Tresse and Esther Lynn. Whether he was still a resident of Salem County at that time, or had moved back into Philadelphia remains undetermined. In either case, he did not buy any additional property in Philadelphia.

He does not appear to have been a member of any monthly meeting. No record has been found either in Philadelphia or in New Jersey of his death, nor of any settlement of his estate. He died before 15 September 1693, when Esther was first designated "Widdow Elfrith." [31]

Issue of Esther King by her 3rd husband Josiah Elfreth:

5. vi. JEREMIAH ELFRETH, b. *ca.* 1692; bur. 20 10m 1772, *ae.* 80 years, in Philadelphia, of whom further.

Esther King married her fourth husband, RICHARD WILLSON, some time between September 1695, and 7 5m 1699, when she was "now called

---

27 Exemplification Book 1, 168: 2 6m 1687, Patent to Josiah Elfreth.

28 Deed Book E-2-5, 7: 31 1m 1688, David Lloyd to Christopher Sypthorpe. Josiah Elfreth was listed as a renter of this property in 1689, for which see "The Blackwell Rent Roll, 1689," transcribed in *The Pennsylvania Genealogical Magazine* (PGM), XXIII, 89. The sale to Sibthorpe was not recorded until January 1689, shortly before Blackwell began compiling his rent roll, and apparently he was not aware of the transaction.

29 "Calendar of Records . . ," *New Jersey Archives,* 1st Series, XXI, 551.

30 *Ibid.,* 552. Stow Creek runs almost due south through Salem County to the Delaware River, nearly closing a triangle with the river and Alloways Creek to the north.

31 *PMHB,* VIII, 85, cited in Note 24 above.

Hester Willson." [32]   Scattered references to Richard Willson appear in Bucks County and Philadelphia County records; in the earliest of these he was a witness to the will of the governor's gardener, Ralph Smith of Bucks County, on 9 10m 1685.[33]

Willson's earliest business transaction in Bucks County was a purchase of land for which he gave a bond to Joseph English on 27 1m 1688, for the payment of £20. The condition of the obligation provided that Willson was to pay it off in "Wheat Indian Corn Beef and Pork delivered at ye house of William Biles of the said County of Bucks at or before the twenty fifth day of the first month next [then] ensuing . . . at the current price such goods pass at in the Market at Philadelphia at the time and day of payment . . . ." In the bond, Richard Willson described himself as a "Laborer," and signed it with his mark.[34] The day before, he had agreed to buy from Joseph English for £20 fifty acres of land, so the bond, in effect, was a mortgage. In this initial purchase, the land was described only as lying "in the County of Bucks," adjoining lands of Edmond Lovett and John Rowland. The deed was not acknowledged until 13 4m 1688, when it was "delivered unto Arthur Cook for use of Richard Willson." [35]

Later that same year he acquired an additional two acres from James Swafor (Swaffer) for 26 shillings. This may have been a watering area for stock, since in this deed Willson was called "husbandman," and the land was described as "being 8 rods front upon the Creek that runs between ye Island called Overton and the Main and 40 rods in length bounded by land of Lyonel Brittan and Daniel Gardiner." It was acknowledged 12 10m 1688, "by William Croasdale attorney to James Swafer delivered unto Richard Wilson [by] his attorney James Crosby [or Crosley]." [36]

[32] She is so-called in the memorandum appended to the deed recorded in Deed Book C-2-3, 194, cited in Note 14 above.

[33] "Abstracts of Early Bucks County Wills," *Publications of the Genealogical Society of Pennsylvania* (PGSP), I, 209. A contemporary Richard Wilson was a resident of Kent County (now in Delaware), but no relationship has been established between the two men. The Delaware Richard Wilson was a member of the Assembly from Kent County in 1686. *Pennsylvania Archives*, 8th Series, I, 78, cited in Note 4 above. Later, this Richard Wilson was a justice in that county. *Governor's Register, State of Delaware* (Wilmington, Del., 1926), I, 6, 7.

[34] Bucks Co. Deed Book 1, 159: 27 1m 1688, Bond, Richard Willson to Joseph English.

[35] Bucks Co. Deed Book 1, 170: 26 1m 1688, Joseph English to Richard Willson.

[36] Bucks Co. Deed Book 1, 190: 6 7m 1688, James Swafor to Richard Willson. The lands of Lionel Brittain and Daniel Gardiner, as shown on Thomas Holme's *Map of the Province of Pennsylvania*, were just above Penn's Manor of Pennsbury. Possibly Willson's was part of the same land which in early 1715, "William Blakey, of the County of Bucks, having formerly agreed with Sam'l Carpenter, by order of the other Commm'rs, for the Plantation on the Mann'r of Pensbury, where Richard Wilson in his life time Dwelt, to hold the same on Lease for the Term of 12 years from the 1st mo'th last, at the yearly Rent of £12 p. ann., and that the said William Shou'd be allowed the first years Rent to build on the said Plantation a good Logg House 24 foot long and 16 foot wide . . . ." *Pennsylvania Archives*, 2nd Series, XIX, 592.

In Esther's life this year of 1688 was the one in which her first husband, John Bowyer, died, leaving her a widow in her late thirties with four children all still under age. It is possible that Richard Willson may also have had a prior marriage and children of that marriage. However, if this is so, the children do not seem to have survived.[37]

References to Richard Willson's additional land transactions are found in Bucks County Court Records but not among recorded deeds. In open court he acknowledged the sale on 1 7m 1689, of his fifty acres to John Gibbs. Three months later, Gibbs acknowledged in court the sale to Willson of fifty acres on 10 10m 1689. The short interval between these two transactions suggests a short term mortgage rather than a sale, but it was not so noted in the acknowledgments, the last of which was not even made until "2 Wednesday of December 1693." [38]

By 10 9m 1690, Willson was considered a responsible member of the community when he was appointed an overseer of the highway "for ye lower pte of the river." The following year he was appointed overseer "from thence [the Governor's] below to Neshaminah." He was appointed constable of the same area on 14 7m 1692, was a member of the Grand Jury for Bucks County in 1696, and again in 1699.[39] In 1695, Francis "Rossell" of Bucks County, in his will had left to Willson "the rest of his personall estate and all lands not before disposed of to Samuel Carpenter." [40]

Willson acquired no additional property until 1706, when Sarah Dymock, widow of Tobias, sold two tracts of land totalling one hundred and fifty acres to him. These were contiguous, lying along the Delaware River in Bristol Township, just south of Pennsbury Manor. In depth from the river, the land extended northwest 320 perches, and had a frontage on the river of 75 perches. Sarah Dymock sold the property "with all ye houses, edifices, barns, stables, outhouses, gardens, meadows . . ." for £120 silver money.[41]

Richard Willson enjoyed his new plantation less than a year; letters of administration on his estate were granted in Philadelphia 12 November 1707, to Esther Willson of Bucks County, his widow.[42] Esther's

---

37 See recital in Bucks Co. Deed Book 4, 125: 18 March 1709, Isaac Atkinson to Willoughby Warder, Jr., wherein reference is made to Willson's only sister Ann Lenix, wife of William Lenix.

38 *Records of the Courts of Quarter Sessions and Common Pleas of Bucks County, 1684-1700* (Meadville, Pa., 1943), 108, 281.

39 *Ibid.*, 149, 158, 169, 266, 295, 306, 403.

40 *PGSP*, II, 21, will of Francis Rossell.

41 Bucks Co. Deed Book 3, 305: 17 Nov. 1706, Sarah Dimock to Richard Willson.

42 Philadelphia Administration Book B, 59, #21:1707, estate of Richard Willson.

fourth husband evidently was not a Friend; no mention of him appears in Friends Meeting records either in Philadelphia or Bucks County.

On 25 April 1708, Esther Willson purchased from John Large, tailor, for £45 a smaller plantation of one hundred acres lying a short way down river from her husband's plantation.[43] Apparently she lived on the smaller place with her daughter and son-in-law, Esther and John Clay, until her own death in 1710. Richard Willson's plantation of one hundred and fifty acres appears to have been divided: one-half to Esther, his widow (if he had left children, Esther's share would have been one-third); the other half to "William Lenix intermarried with Ann, ye only sister of said Richard Willson, being then living." William Lenix and Ann his wife, and their children, Richard Lenix and William Lenix, Jr., sold their rights in this property 13 May 1708, to Isaac Atkinson, a Bristol cordwainer. Esther made over her rights to Atkinson for £30 a month later.[44]

Esther witnessed the marriage of her youngest daughter, Sarah Bowyer, to Willoughby Warder, Jr. on 13 2m 1710, at the Philadelphia Meeting House.[45] Only four days later on 17 April, Esther had her will drawn up, being then "sick and weak in body." [46] She died in Philadelphia on 20 2m 1710, just one week after the wedding, and was probably buried in Friends' ground at the instance of her Quaker children.[47]

In her will Esther made provisions for all of her children. To her daughter Esther Clay she left her wearing apparel "with one chest of Drawers and one Iron Pott," and the interest of approximately £22. To her daughter Sarah Warder she left "my negro girl named Sarah and all my household goods not before given away." To her son John Bowyer, now well established in his own right, she left a token thirty shillings,

---

[43] Bucks Co. Deed Book 3, 418: 25 Apr. 1708, John Large to Esther Willson.

[44] The deed from Isaac Atkinson to Willoughby Warder, cited in Note 37 above, probably was actually made on 18 March 1709/10, and very likely was in the nature of a prenuptial arrangement, since it would then have been executed between the first declaration of marriage intentions by Sarah Bowyer and Willoughby Warder and their marriage on 13 April 1710. Esther Willson's sale of her rights in the plantation predated it, however, for which see Bucks Co. Deed Book 4, 9: 10 June 1708, Esther Willson to Isaac Atkinson. In this record it was recited that whereas "Richard Willson made no will but dyed intestate, ye said Esther became tenant in common during her life of one moyety" of the 150 acres.

[45] Marriage Records, Friends' Record Department, 306 Arch St., Philadelphia. Others of the family who were present at the marriage were Joseph Lynn and Jeremiah Elfreth, half-brothers of the bride, and her sister Esther Clay.

[46] The will of Esther Willson, cited in Note 19 above, was witnessed by John Hart and Lydia Warder, and proved 25 April 1710. John Sotcher of Bucks County and Henry Mallows of Philadelphia were her executors.

[47] The only mention in Friends' records of Esther King herself (other than as witness to a marriage, etc.) is the entry of her death in the Philadelphia Meeting records under "A Record of Deceased ffriends for ye year 1709/10." Her connection was solely through her children and grandchildren.

but his son Benjamin Bowyer was to have £3 15s., and a like sum was to be divided equally among John's other children. Her son William Bowyer was to have five shillings "if he comes over here." Her younger sons, Joseph Lynn and Jeremiah Elfreth, were each to have £37 10s. put out at interest until they were twenty-one years of age or married. To her stepson, Henry Elfreth, she bequeathed the money he owed her, plus £3 15s. which was to be divided amongst his children. As soon as her son-in-law John Clay had paid £30 of the £37 10s. he owed her "for ye Plantation I sould him," her executors were to convey it to him.

She requested that the residue of her estate be laid out in the purchase of land lately belonging to Jacob Janney "lying between Edward Ratcliff's land and Solomon Warder's land" with "assurance of the land to be made to Willoughby Warder and his wife Sarah." If the residue of her estate was not enough to purchase the land, such residue was to go to Sarah.

The following March, John Fisher of Bristol, weaver, and Mary his wife (late widow of Jacob Janney) sold 72½ acres lying between Edward Ratcliff's and Solomon Warder's lands to Willoughby Warder, Jr., for £33.[48]

1. JOHN BOWYER, JR., eldest child of Esther King and John Bowyer, was the only Bowyer son to remain in Philadelphia, and to follow in his father's footsteps as a shipwright. Born in 1671, presumably in England, he was only about eleven years old when the family migrated to Pennsylvania.

The first record of him in Philadelphia does not appear until nearly seven years after his father's death, when he was about twenty-four years of age. At that time, in September 1695, John and his mother, now Esther Elfreth, conveyed 150 acres of his father's Bristol Township property to William Wilkins.[49] Two years later on 9 February 1697, he witnessed the will of Giles Mora, widow of James Mora, and on 21 December 1701, the will of Henry Furnis, the sadler of Philadelphia.[50]

Married probably before 1705, John and his first wife, REBECCA, (surname unknown), were evidently members of Christ Church in Philadelphia, at that time Anglican, but now Protestant Episcopal. Although the congregation was founded in 1695, the church registers were not begun until 1709, hence no record is found of their marriage, nor of the baptisms of their children prior to 1710.

---

[48] Bucks Co. Deed Book 4, 162: 15 March 1711, John Fisher to Willoughby Warder, Jr.

[49] Deed Book E-4-7, 150, cited in Note 13 above.

[50] PGSP, III, 13, 249.

The land holdings of John Bowyer, Jr., were located both in and near the city. In 1699, Gunner Rambo and his wife Annita had confirmed to him the sixty acres his father had purchased from Rambo in 1684, as well as forty additional acres his mother, "now called Hester Wilson," had bought from Rambo, "all which the said Hester is willing should be made to her son John Bowyer." [51] Robert Turner, one of the most prominent Quaker merchants in town, held the land bordering the tract's east line. When John Bowyer's father was still alive, Turner, according to a deposition made by John Bowyer, Jr. in 1732, when he was "aged about sixty-one," did

. . . Ask and obtain leave as a Neighbourly kindness and upon Sufferance only of his Sd father, to set his fence upon the Lands then of the Sd John Bowyer the Elder in order to take in a Small Run of water for the benefit of the Sd Turners Cattle in the adjoining pasture on the Eastwardly Side of the Said Land which did not reach their dividing Line, but lay wholly within the Land of the Sd Bowyer. And that After ye decease of ye father of this Dep[t] he the Sd Robert Turner finding the Conveniency of that possession did treat with ye Mother of this Dep[t] and Endeavoured to persuade her to Sell a peice of the Sd Land as he remembers about six or Eight Acres, but that he this deponent being the proper and right heir and knowing that his sd Mother had no right to dispose Thereof always refusd and rejected the proposall; Yet notwithstanding the sd Robert Turner as he has Since heard and believes Did (on presumption As this Dep[t] supposes that he Might obtain the sd piece of Land which he so Earnestly desired) On or about the year 1691 take out a patent for his Adjoining Land and Caused to be included in ye sd patent about Eight Acres of the first mentioned Sixty acres of Land then of Right belonging to this Deponent on presumption as this Dep[t] supposes that he might also obtain a right wch he so Earnestly desired.

And this Deponent further Sayeth that he well know'g that he had never Alienated any part of the Aforementioned hundred Acres, And that the Sd Robert Turner had no legal or Equitable right to any part Thereof he this Deponent did afterwards About the Year One thousand seven hundred & nine sell and convey unto Samuel Carpenter [52] the whole hundred Acres of Land by the same Lines and bounds as the same Land was held by his father John Bowyer and his predecessor Gunner Rambo afsd paying no regard to the Unjust Intrusion made by said Robert Turner by incerting in his patent ye sd Eight Acres for which he never paid any consideration. [53]

In 1704, five years before he disposed of the Shackamaxon tract to Samuel Carpenter, John Bowyer, Jr. had bought a bank lot "and premises" in the city for £78 from Benjamin Chambers. The lot, 76½ feet

[51] Deed Book C-2-3, 194, cited in Note 14 above.

[52] Deed Book E-6-7, 106: 26 Nov. 1708, John Bowyer to Samuel Carpenter. Here Bowyer's memory appears to have been faulty as to the year in which he sold the property to Carpenter.

[53] The deposition is in Norris Estate 1700-1759, Logan Papers, XIII, 9, Historical Society of Pennsylvania (HSP). Samuel Carpenter sold the land to Isaac Norris and it was incorporated in Norris's Sepviva plantation, east of and adjacent to his Fairhill land. Draughts of the Bowyer tract as surveyed by Robert Longshore in 1684, and by Jacob Taylor when it was resurveyed in 1709 for Samuel Carpenter are also in the same volume of the Logan Papers, 7, 9-1/2. In Volume XIV, 38-1/2, of the Logan Papers, is a draught of the Sepviva land bordering the creek which shows the location of "Bowyer's ruins."

in breadth on the east side of Front Street between Mulberry and Sassafras (Race), lay between land formerly belonging to John Songhurst on the north, and the balance of land formerly belonging to the George Palmer heirs from whom Chambers had acquired 102 feet in all.[54]

Three years later in 1708, Bowyer bought for £55 from George Fitzwater the adjacent 25½ foot bank lot to the south which was the remaining portion of the original Palmer 102-foot lot.[55] Both properties extended 250 feet into the Delaware, and were subject to the same general conditions under which his mother had leased the Thomas Tresse lot back in 1691: a thirty-foot cartway was to be left open, a pair of stone steps was to be built down to a wharf.

Having acquired these properties in the city, Bowyer then disposed of his Shackamaxon land in 1709 to Carpenter, and apparently removed to the city where his first wife Rebecca died. She was buried from Christ Church 7 October 1711.[56]

Issue of 1. John Bowyer by his 1st wife Rebecca:

i. BENJAMIN BOWYER, b. before 1710, when he was mentioned in Esther Willson's will; bur. 24 November 1721, from Christ Church.

ii. THOMAS BOWYER, b. *ca.* 1705; d. after 1727, when he was named that year in his father's will. If he was the same Thomas "Boyer" who was buried from Christ Church 26 October 1738, then he lived to be at least thirty-three years old, and may have left survivors of whom no certain record has been found. If so, his would have been the only male line of descent from the first John Bowyer.

iii. MARY BOWYER, d. after 14 August 1727, when her father wrote his will; possibly the Mary Phillips bur. at Christ Church 29 May 1732; probably m. at Christ Church 9 August 1722, DAVID PHILLIPS. He may have been the David "Philip," labourer of Hilltown, Bucks County, whose will was written "about August 2, 1747," and proved in Philadelphia 10 November 1747. In it he devised to his "only son" William all his wearing apparel, a young gray mare and colt, his ax and grubbing hoe, and named his then wife Susanna executrix. This David Phillips was baptized as an adult 15 February 1729/30, at the Montgomery Baptist Church; his son William was baptized there the following 19 April 1730.[57] Known issue: 1. WILLIAM PHILLIPS (?), who, named only as "William, son of my daughter Mary," was devised £12 by his grandfather John Bowyer in 1727.

---

[54] Deed Book F-6, 292: 12 May 1704, Benjamin Chambers to John Bowyer; *ibid.*, 295: 31 Dec. 1727, George Palmer *et al.* to John Bowyer, is, in effect, Palmer's release of rights in the land to Bowyer, by Richard Hill, Palmer's attorney.

[55] Deed Book E-5-7, 41: 16 July 1708, George Fitzwater to John Bowyer. Fitzwater, son of Thomas Fitzwater and his 1st wife, was a step-brother of George Palmer, the father Thomas Fitzwater having married the widow Elizabeth Palmer, mother of George.

[56] Christ Church Burial Register, 17, Christ Church Archives, Philadelphia. Her name was entered as Rebecca "Boyear."

[57] Will Book H, 423, #207:1747, will of David Philip; Edward Mathews, *History of Montgomery Baptist Church in Montgomery Township, Montgomery County*, Pa. (Ambler, Pa., 1895), 10, 14. In this work David Phillips' death is entered as in December 1747, obviously in error.

iv. HANNAH BOWYER, bapt. 15 January 1710, at Christ Church; living in 1727, when her father left her £25 in his will. She was probably the Hannah Bowyer who attended the marriage of her half-sister, Sarah Bowyer, to Roger Brooke on 1 4m 1735, at the Philadelphia Meeting House. No further information.

After Rebecca's death in 1711, 1. John Bowyer married, about 1712, his second wife, SARAH HASTINGS, daughter of Joshua and Elizabeth Hastings.[58] By her, he had eight more children before his own death in 1732.

When he drew up his will 14 August 1727, nearly six years before his death, he was "indisposed." He was then about fifty-six. He bequeathed to his son Thomas £5; to his daughter Mary £4, and to her son William (presumably Phillips) £12; to his daughter Hannah £35. The difference in the amounts left to the two daughters suggests that Hannah may not have been married. These three were the surviving children of his first marriage to Rebecca. He then proceeded to divide in half the remainder of his estate, both real and personal: one half to his second wife, Sarah "in lieu of all her other rights;" the other half among his six surviving younger children plus the seventh child with which Sarah was then "enciente," naming them as John, Martha, Sarah, Elizabeth, Esther and Rebecca. The seventh, when she arrived, was Ruth.

His wife Sarah was appointed executrix of the will, with "my worthy friends and relations, James Parrock and Joseph Lynn, both of Philadelphia, shipwrights, and Jeremiah Elfreth of Philadelphia, smith," as trustees and advisers. Joseph Lynn and Jeremiah Elfreth were half-brothers of John Bowyer and of each other, and James Parrock was another relative and fellow shipwright. Witnesses to the will were his wife's brothers-in-law, Thomas Ashton and Robert Abbott, and the scriviner John Cadwalader; it was proved 3 March 1732/3.[59]

John Bowyer was buried in Christ Church Burial Ground at Fifth and Arch Streets in Philadelphia on 10 January 1732/3. His grave, in Section H, Plot LXIV, is to the right of the Fifth Street gate and directly adjoining the Fifth Street wall. His tombstone was simply inscribed:

---

[58] The recital in Deed Book G-10, 165: 12 Aug. 1727, John Bowyer *et al.* to James Serrel lists the other children of Joshua Hastings and wife Elizabeth as John Hastings (wife Hannah); Samuel Hastings (wife Mary); Mary, wife of Thomas Assheton, a Philadelphia shipwright; Elizabeth, wife of Robert Abbott. See also William Wade Hinshaw, *Encyclopedia of American Quaker Genealogy* (Ann Arbor, Mich., 1938), II, 441, cited hereinafter as Hinshaw.

[59] Will Book E, 220, #297:1732, will of John Bowyer. James Parrock had married at the house of Joshua Hastings on 27 9m 1698, his 1st wife Martha Hastings, probably a sister of Joshua. He was probably therefore an uncle-in-law of John Bowyer's wife, Sarah Hastings. Martha (Hastings) Parrock d. 27 2m 1702, and James Parrock married two more wives before his own death in 1755. His son James, who predeceased him in 9m 1731, was the husband of Priscilla Coats; their marriage in 1731 lasted only two months.

"In Memory of / JOHN BOWYER / who departed this life / January 1732 [*sic*] / Aged 62 Years." [60]

In 1733, Bowyer's executors sold the easternmost part of the south fifty feet of his bank lot — that part fronting the 30-foot cartway — to Samuel Hassel, a Philadelphia merchant, for £140. In 1746, thirteen years later, they sold to his son-in-law, Joseph Warner, for £300 thirty feet adjoining and north of Hassel's lot, which also fronted the cartway. [61] The land facing Front Street was retained until after Sarah Bowyer's death.

Unlike her mother-in-law, Sarah Bowyer did not remarry after her husband's death, but remained a widow for twenty-five years until her own death in 1757. In May of that year, she drew up her will. To her granddaughter Sarah "Williams," daughter of her late deceased daughter Martha, and to her own daughters Elizabeth Austin, Hester Boyte and Ruth Bonham, she devised each a one-sixth part of her estate. Another one-sixth she left to her "grandson Boyer," and to her "granddaughters Elizabeth Brooke and Sarah sisters of said Boyer," the children of her late deceased daughter Sarah Brooke, as tenants in common. The remaining one-sixth part was left to her granddaughter Sarah Warner, daughter of her late deceased daughter Rebecca, when she became eighteen or was married. Until then Sarah's father Joseph Warner was to receive the "benefit" of the sixth part and to maintain his daughter. If Sarah died under age or unmarried, he was to receive her share. She appointed as executrix her daughter Hester Boyte, and as executor her "esteemed friend Thomas Say of Philadelphia, Practitioner in Physick." The will, signed 4 May and probated the following 5 July 1757, was witnessed by Jeremiah Elfreth and John Parrock. She had died 25 6m (June) 1757. [62]

The following August her household goods were advertised to be sold, and in July 1758, it was announced that her real estate would be put up for sale. Her executors disposed of the land between Front Street and the cartway to various purchasers, among them Robert Waln, John Doyle, Ruth Webb and Mary Taggart. [63]

---

[60] Christ Church Burial Register, 17. See also, Edward L. Clark, *Records of Inscriptions on Tablets and Gravestones in Burial Grounds of Christ Church, Philadelphia* (Philadelphia, 1864), 307.

[61] Deed Book F-6, 289: 25 Aug. 1733, Sarah Bowyer *et al.* to Samuel Hassel; *ibid.*, D-56, 379: 6 March 1745/6, Sarah Bowyer *et al.* to Joseph Warner.

[62] Will Book K, 550, #340:1757, will of Sarah Bowyer; Death Records, Friends' Record Department, 306 Arch St., Philadelphia.

[63] For notices of the sale of her household goods and real estate see *Pennsylvania Gazette*, 4 Aug. 1757, 20 July 1758. The sale of some of the Front Street lots is recited in Deed Book D-12, 157: 1 Sept. 1758, Thomas Say *et al.* to Ruth Webb. Other sales have not been searched for this study.

Issue of 1. John Bowyer by his 2nd wife Sarah Hastings: [64]

v. WILLIAM BOWYER, b. *ca.* 1712; d. 31 5m 1713; bur. by Philadelphia Friends.

vi. JOHN BOWYER, b. *ca.* 1714; d. 23 10m 1728; bur. by Philadelphia Friends.

vii. MARTHA BOWYER, b. *ca.* 1716; d. 9 3m 1757, according to Philadelphia Friends' records; m. at Christ Church 28 December 1737, JACOB WILLIAMSON, who probably d. after 1770. Martha was disowned by Philadelphia Friends 29 1m 1742, for marrying out of unity, but when she died her death was recorded by Friends, perhaps through her mother's connection with the Society. Jacob Williamson was probably of Swedish parentage and the son of William Williamson who died in Bucks County in 1721, leaving a will in which he mentioned a son Jacob, among other children. [65] If Martha's husband was this son, he was the Jacob Williamson, shipwright of Northern Liberties, who, after his wife's death, sold for £600 to Edward Hill of Bensalem Township, Bucks County, the tract known as Dunk's Ferry in Bensalem which had belonged to his grandfather, Dunk Williams. In 1770, seven years later, he sold to Jeremiah Baker, 2nd husband of Jacob's deceased wife's sister Ruth, a lot on Queen (now Richmond) Street in Kensington. It was part of a lot he had purchased from Charles West in 1763, four months before he had sold the Dunk's Ferry land. [66] Known issue: 1. SARAH WILLIAMSON, named in her grandmother Sarah's will as "Sarah Williams;" perhaps was bur. at St. Peter's 13 September 1808; probably m. at Christ Church 25 March 1758, JONATHAN WELSH.

viii. SARAH BOWYER, b. *ca.* 1718; d. before 1757, as indicated in her mother's will; m. 10 4m 1735, at Philadelphia Meeting, ROGER BROOKE, a Philadelphia shipwright. After Sarah's death, a Roger Brooke, disowned by Friends 28 3m 1760, for joining another society, "left this City & went to Maryland." No further definitive information about him. [67] Issue: 1. ELIZABETH BROOKE, b. *ca.* 1736; living in 1757, when she was named in her grandmother Sarah Bowyer's will. 2. SARAH BROOKE, b. *ca.* 1737; living in 1757, when she was named in her grandmother Sarah Bowyer's will. 3. BOWYER BROOKE, b. *ca.* 1738; d. 18 3m 1815, *ae.* 77; m. 1st by New Jersey license dated 4 April 1761, [68] MARY BROWNE,

---

[64] Although Sarah (Hastings) Bowyer was of Quaker parentage and she remained a Friend, her husband John Bowyer belonged to the Anglican Christ Church in Philadelphia. Consequently records of their children are found in the records of both denominations. Hereinafter, unless otherwise noted, references to Friends' Meetings will indicate they are from the Philadelphia Monthly Meeting records and the dates given will be from those records. References to and dates from Christ Church will be found in the transcripts of that church's registers in GSP.

[65] See Abstracts of Bucks County Wills, 1685-1795, I, 26, GSP, for will of William Williamson, recorded in Bucks Co. Will Book I, 62.

[66] Bucks Co. Deed Book 11, 315: 1 June 1763, Jacob Williamson to Edward Hill; Philadelphia Deed Book I-8, 100: 15 Feb. 1770, Jacob Williamson to Jeremiah Baker.

[67] The Roger Brooke who "went to Maryland" in 1760 could have been either the husband or son of Sarah (Bowyer) Brooke. One Roger Brooke of Calvert Co., Md., left a will dated 6 January and proved 16 August 1776, in which he named a wife Mary, daughter Sarah, and brothers Basil and John Brooke. See James M. Magruder, Jr., *Maryland Colonial Abstracts, Wills, Accounts and Inventories, 1775-1777* (Annapolis, Md., 1936), I, 51. In 1790, another Roger Brooke in Frederick County, Md., had in his household 2 males over 16 beside himself, 2 males under 16, 2 females, and 19 slaves. *Heads of Families at the First Census of the United States . . . 1790 Maryland* (Baltimore, 1952), 62. What connection there was, if any, between these men bearing the same name has not been established.

[68] *New Jersey Archives*, 1st Series, XXII, 8, 52. For a corrected transcript of some New Jersey marriage licenses, see "New Jersey Marriage Licenses, 1727-1734, with Corrections to 1751," by Charles Carroll Gardner in *The Genealogical Magazine of New Jersey*, XVII-XXIII, *passim*.

daughter of Peter and Priscilla (Coats) Parrock Browne. Though both gave their place of residence as Gloucester when applying for their license, it was the Philadelphia Monthly Meeting which condemned Mary the same month for marrying contrary to Friends' discipline. She was deceased by 23 August 1767, when Bowyer Brooke m. 2nd at Christ Church, HANNAH REESE, b. *ca.* 1748; d. 9 12m 1814, *ae.* 66.[69] 4. ROGER BROOKE, who was not named in the will of his grandmother Sarah Bowyer in 1757, but was named in the will of his aunt, Ruth (Bowyer) Bonham Baker in 1805.[70]

ix. ELIZABETH BOWYER, b. *ca.* 1720; d. before 10 September 1759, when letters of administration on her estate, as Elizabeth "Ashton," were granted to her sister Esther Boyte; [71] m. by New Jersey license dated 27 September 1737, EDWARD AUSTIN, possibly he who was bapt. at Christ Church 28 November 1715, *ae.* 4 days, son of John and Mary Austin; deceased by 10 September 1759. On 26 1m 1742, Friends of the Philadelphia Meeting were directed to prepare a testimony against Elizabeth "Ashton (late Boyer)," for outgoing in marriage. Nine years later in 1751, the Philadelphia Meeting was informed "that the following persons had been dealt with, without any grounds to Expect their Reformation [among them] Edward Austin . . . ," presumably Elizabeth's husband, a shipwright by trade. The following year on 27 3m 1752, "A paper signed by Elizabeth Austin condemning her breach of Discipline in Marriage was read," which evidently reinstated her in the Society of Friends. As this was fifteen years after her marriage, it may be a clue to the approximate time of her husband's death, but no will or administration on his estate has been found in Philadelphia records. Known issue: 1. JOHN AUSTIN, b. *ca.* 1738; bapt. Christ Church 2 August 1741, *ae.* 3-6-0. 2. SAMUEL AUSTIN, b. *ca.* 1740; bapt. Christ Church 2 August 1741, *ae.* 19 months. 3. THOMAS AUSTIN, d. 25 4m 1749, according to Friends' records. 4. WILLIAM AUSTIN, d. 14 3m 1751, according to the same records.

x. ESTHER (HESTER) BOWYER, b. *ca.* 1722; d. after 1769; m. at Christ Church 2 April 1741, PHILIP BOYTE, a shipwright of Kensington; bur. at Christ

---

[69] Administration Book L, 237, #83:1815, estate of Bowyer Brooke, *c.t.a.* His will, dated 15 March 1815, named only two sons, Bowyer Brooke, Jr., and Reese Brooke, whose wife was Harriet. See also J. Bennett Hill and Margaret Howe Hill, "William Fisher, Early Philadelphia Quaker . . ," *PGM*, XXI, 264n. Well-named Bowyer, he carried the traditional family trade of ship-building into the fourth American generation. In 1776 and 1777, before the British occupation of Philadelphia, he built at least two guard boats for the State Navy Board, and furnished numerous galley sweeps and short oars for the Board. *Pennsylvania Archives*, 2nd Series, I, 93, 102, 119, 150, 158. When the city was reoccupied by the Americans in 1778, he was among those who proclaimed a traitor, but as he had taken the oath of allegiance in July of that year, he was discharged from the treason plea. *Ibid.*, 3rd Series, X, 522; 2nd Series, III, 25; 4th Series, III, 937. In the Grand Federal Procession of 1788, celebrating the ratification of the Federal Constitution, he and Warwick Hale, another shipwright, headed the contingent representing their trade, evidence that both were regarded highly by their fellow craftsmen.

For a time he was in partnership with John Wilson; the firm of Brooke & Wilson was listed in the 1785 Philadelphia *City Directory* as located on Water Street between Race and Vine. Their account book in the Manuscript Collections, HSP, contains a variety of interesting entries. Among their best known clients were Clement C. Biddle, for whom they built a boat in 1784; John Penn, who purchased two oars for 9s. in 1785; John Cadwalader, for whom they built a skiff the same year for £21 6s. 8d., and Stephen Girard, who had them build two yawls and a long-boat. Brooke's kinsman, Jeremiah Warder, was a regular customer with repairs to the Brig *Nancy*.

[70] The will of Ruth Baker names Roger Brooke's daughter Priscilla Wilson. See Will Book 1, 483, #439: 1806, will of Ruth Baker, for whom see the text below.

[71] Administration Book G, 175, #3:1759, estate of Elizabeth "Ashton."

*See Volume I of this work, p. 566.

Church 4 June 1753. A son of William and Lucy Boyte of Philadelphia, Philip had a reversionary right in a house and lot on the south side of Arch between Front and Second Streets in which his mother Lucy held a life estate. Both she and her second husband, Thomas Bowling, were deceased by 1762, nine years after Philip Boyte's death. In that year his widow, as Esther "Boyle," appealed to the Orphans Court for permission to sell her husband's reversionary right for the benefit of her two surviving children, Thomas and Esther Boyte, and to enable her to pay off the indebtedness of her husband's estate. Her petition granted, the property was sold to Ephraim Bonham,[72] the tenant in the house, who was a brother of her sister Ruth's husband, Samuel Bonham. In 1769, the Widow Boyte was assessed as Esther "Boyd" in the Northern Liberties; by 1780 the property was assessed as "Esther Boyd's estate," and was occupied by Richard Salter, a shipwright.[73] Issue, all bapt. at Christ Church: 1. SARAH BOYTE, b. 27 January 1742; bur. at Christ Church, 30 December 1744. 2. JOHN BOYTE, b. 26 September 1744; bur. at Christ Church, 23 July 1745. 3. THOMAS BOYTE, b. 15 February 1746; living in 1762 at the time of the Orphans Court proceedings. 4. ANN BOYTE, b. 20 July 1747; bur. at Christ Church 27 January 1747. 5. HESTER BOYTE, b. 17 January 1750; bur. at Christ Church 17 January 1773; m. at St. Paul's Anglican Church, Philadelphia, 30 November 1769, BENJAMIN GEORGE EYRE, b. 1 June 1747; d. 11 July 1789, bur. at Christ Church, son of George and Mary (Smith) Eyre of Burlington, N. J. Benjamin Eyre was a shipwright, first in Burlington where he was in business with his brothers Manuel and Jehu Eyre. By the time he m. in New York in 1774 his 2nd wife, MARY CHEESMAN, daughter of a New York shipbuilder, Benjamin had removed to Kensington where he was actively engaged in his trade until his last illness.[74]

xi. REBECCA BOWYER, b. ca. 1725; d. 29 6m 1752, bur. in Philadelphia as a Friend; m. at the Philadelphia Meeting 15 8m 1745, JOSEPH WARNER, b. ca. 1721; d. 4 2m 1796, ae. ca. 75, according to Northern District Monthly Meeting records.[75] Issue: 1. JOSEPH WARNER, d. 26 12m 1750. 2. REBECCA WARNER, d. 29 6m 1751. 3. SARAH WARNER, d. 10 9m 1757. When Joseph Warner m. 2nd at the Philadelphia Meeting 13 11m 1753, PRUDENCE WEST, daughter of Charles and Sarah (Parsons) West, he was identified as the son of George Warner, late of Kent County, Md., dec'd. A shipwright by trade, Warner had his "Boat Shead" and wharf on the "water lot" he purchased in 1746, the year after his first marriage, from John Bowyer's executors. This was only one of the properties he acquired during his life. Until 1780, he appears to have lived on the south side of Sassafras Street, between Front and Second; then he removed to a

---

[72] Orphans Court Book 6, 109: 12 June 1762. Joseph Lynn, Henry Dennis and a William Pearson audited Esther's accounts. For the sale of the Arch Street property, see Deed Book D-4, 134: 30 Oct. 1762, Esther "Boyle" et al. to Ephraim Bonham. The Bonham relationship is recited in New Jersey Deed Book A-L, 412: 6 Sept. 1754, Samuel Bonham to George Eyre, State House, Trenton, N. J.

[73] Pennsylvania Archives, 3rd Series, XIV, 120; XV, 469.

[74] The notice of his 2nd marriage to "Miss Cheesman" is from the Pennsylvania Packet, 14 Feb. 1774; his death was noted in the same paper, issue of 15 July 1789. Benjamin Eyre's will, dated 24 Apr. 1788, and proved 1 Aug. 1789, named his wife Mary and children Elizabeth, Ann, Harriett and Thomas, the latter the only known surviving child of his 1st wife Esther (Hester) Boyte. Will Book U, 329, #132:1789.

[75] Will Book X, 398, #11:1796, will of Joseph Warner, dated 23 Dec. 1788, and proved 12 Feb. 1796; letters testamentary were granted to Joseph and Charles Warner, his sons by his second wife.

plantation of about 90 acres in Roxborough Township, near the Wissahickon, which he had bought from William Morgan. When Warner died, he also owned three lots in the Northern Liberties, most of which he had acquired through his second marriage.[76]

xii. RUTH BOWYER, b. *ca.* 1727; d. by 3 May 1806, when her will was proved; m. 1st by New Jersey license dated 29 May 1747, SAMUEL BONHAM of Burlington; dec'd by 1758. Ruth was disowned by the Philadelphia Meeting 30 10m 1748, for marrying out of unity a non-Friend. Her husband was a shipwright by trade; they had removed to Kensington in the Northern Liberties by September 1754, when he and his wife Ruth sold to George Eyre of Burlington, property in the "Liberties" of Trenton, adjoining the Presbyterian Burying Ground of Trenton. The lots had been devised to Samuel Bonham and his brother Ephraim by their grandfather Enoch Anderson (otherwise Andrus or Andrews).[77] Only known issue: 1. CATHARINE BONHAM, bur. from Christ Church 2 January 1750/1. Ruth (Bowyer) Bonham m. 2nd at Christ Church 9 August 1758, JEREMIAH BAKER, a mariner in 1768, when he bought from Jacob Williamson a small lot on Queen Street in Kensington and when, two years later, also from Williamson, he bought a larger adjacent lot. By 1776, he had removed to the Sign of the Noah's Ark, "upper end of Front Street," and in 1780, with his wife Ruth, sold additional property on Queen Street which he had acquired. Probably the son of Jeremiah Baker of Salem County, New Jersey, when Ruth's husband died testate in November 1784, he described himself as an innholder and named Ruth executrix of his will.[78] In 1790, Ruth was living in the Northern Liberties with one slave, probably the same one to whom she devised $40 in her will. In 1805, "advanced in years," she drew up her testament, leaving bequests not only to her own relatives but to those of her late husband. To Bowyer Brooke, Jr., she left her silver tankard; to his brother Reese Brooke her silver watch and spice ball; to their father Bowyer Brooke, Sr., her sleeve buttons. To Priscilla Wilson, daughter of the latter's brother Roger Brooke, she left $100. After bequests to her husband's relatives, her residuary estate was to be divided equally among her own relatives: Bowyer Brooke, Jr. and his brother Reese, Thomas Eyre, son of Benjamin, and the unnamed two grandchildren of her niece Sarah

---

76 *Pennsylvania Archives*, 3rd Series, XIV, 199, 277; XV, 540; XVI, 29, 178, 650. According to Joseph Starne Miles and Rev. William H. Cooper, comps., *A Historical Sketch of Roxborough, Manayunk, Wissahickon* (Philadelphia, 1940), 41, Joseph Warner's Roxborough home was on the south side of School House Lane, between Vaux Avenue and Warden Drive; it was torn down about 1910. Warner devised the plantation to his son Charles by his 2nd wife Prudence, plus two lots in the Northern Liberties, £400 and his silver tankard. To his son Joseph, also by his 2nd wife Prudence, Joseph Warner left the house and lot where he had "formerly lived" on Sassafras, the "fraim" stable across on the north side of Sassafras, his water lot, wharf and boat shed, a lot in the Liberties, his eight-day clock and six silver table spoons. His wife Prudence was to have £40 yearly to be paid by his son Joseph during her widowhood.

77 For the sale to George Eyre see New Jersey Deed Book A-L, 412, cited in Note 72 above. For the will of Enoch Andrus, of Hunterdon Co., N. J., not included in the abstracts of wills published in *New Jersey Archives*, see New Jersey Will Book 4, 323, dated 2 Oct. 1741, and proved 8 Oct. 1741, State House, Trenton, N. J.

78 See Deed Book I-8, 100, cited in Note 66 above; recital in Deed Book I-7, 552: 30 Oct. 1770, Jeremiah Baker to Samuel Baker, and Deed Book D-7, 276: 27 May 1780, Jeremiah Baker to Daniel Ernst. For his location at the Noah's Ark, see *Evening Post*, 23 Jan. 1776. He was assessed from 1769 through 1783 in the Northern Liberties, for which see *Pennsylvania Archives*, 3rd Series, XIV, 120, 396, 659; XV, 356, 677; XVI, 509. For his will, written in 1776, see Will Book S, 505, #357:1784.

Welsh. Martha Douglas, and Hannah and Sarah Austin, the two daughters of William Austin, deceased, included among the residuary heirs, were possibly also her relatives. Executors of the will, proved 3 May 1806, were Bowyer Brooke, Sr. and Anthony James Morris.[79] She appears to have had no issue by her 2nd husband.

2. ESTHER BOWYER appears to have been the elder of the two daughters of John and Esther (King) Bowyer. Born about 1672, presumably in England, she married JOHN CLAY, a blacksmith of Falls Township, Bucks County, probably between 1695 and 1699, after her mother's removal to Bucks County.

John and Esther Clay lived with her mother on the 100-acre plantation in Bristol which Esther King had purchased in 1708, after the death of her fourth husband, Richard Willson. In her 1710 will, Esther King stated she had sold this plantation to John Clay, but this was probably a verbal agreement, and no conveyance had been made since he had not paid for it. Certainly no record of the transfer was entered in Bucks County deeds. In her will, Esther King further stipulated that, as soon as Clay had paid to her executors the balance of £30 which he still owed on the transaction, the executors were to convey the plantation to him. For whatever reason, that conveyance was never made. John Clay and his wife simply continued to live there on the plantation for the remainder of their lives without anyone contesting their right to do so. Presumably, their three daughters were born and reared there.

John Clay was not assessed in 1742 for the Bristol Township Poor Tax levied that year, although his three sons-in-law were. He died intestate six years later. In the letters of administration granted to his widow 27 December 1748, his occupation was given as "innkeeper."[80] From blacksmith in 1710, when Esther King died, to innkeeper in 1748, would indicate a decline in vigor due to old age. Probably he was in his late seventies since his wife was then aged about seventy-five. She died less than a year later, between 27 November, when her will was signed, and 17 December 1749, when it was probated.[81]

---

[79] For will of Ruth Baker, see Will Book 1, 483, cited in Note 70 above. The relationship to Ruth Baker of Martha Douglas and the Austin children remains uncertain. Martha Douglas may have been a daughter of Sarah "Williams" and Jonathan Welsh, mentioned in the text above, and the Martha Welsh who had married John Douglas at the Second Presbyterian Church 23 Aug. 1784. William Austin, whose two daughters, Hannah and Sarah, were remembered by Ruth Baker, possibly was a son of Edward Austin and Elizabeth Bowyer, Ruth's sister. Whether he was the William Austin, an attainted traitor, whose brother was Isaac Austin, also remains undetermined.

[80] The 1742 Bristol Township Poor Tax return is filed with Bucks Co. Quarter Sessions Court Records, GSP. The originals are in the Bucks Co. Court House, Doylestown, Pa. Bucks Co. Administration Book A, 22, estate of John Clay, cited in Index to Bucks County Administrations, GSP. A £50 bond was furnished by his son-in-law, Rowland Powell, and Edward Boulton.

[81] Bucks Co. Will Book 2, 171, will of Esther Clay, cited in Abstracts of Bucks County Wills, 1685-1795, I, 133, GSP.

She left twenty shillings to her daughter Mary Aspril and mentioned Mary's daughters, Sarah and Lydia. She left to her own two other daughters, Sarah Powell and Catherine Mountain, "and their children . . . all my right and claim to the Plantation whereon I now dwell."

In 1750, when they decided to sell the plantation, it was discovered that neither Esther Clay nor her children actually had any "right and claim" to it. Thus, forty years after Esther King's death, it was necessary to round up all of her heirs and secure their releases in order to vest the property legally in the Clay daughters. On 17 March 1750, twelve of Esther King's heirs joined with their spouses in releasing their rights in the plantation to the three Clay daughters and their surviving husbands. A week later they in turn sold it to Thomas Stanaland, Jr., of Bristol.[82]

Issue of 2. Esther Bowyer by her husband John Clay:

i. SARAH CLAY, d. after 1750, when she joined with her sisters in conveying the Bristol plantation to Thomas Stanaland, Jr.; m. ROWLAND POWELL presumably before 1742, when he was assessed for the Bristol Township Poor Tax that year. By 1750 he was a husbandman of the Northern Liberties, and perhaps the Rowland Powell of Philadelphia County who died before 21 April 1757, when his estate was administered by his son-in-law Michael Grover. However, Grover, who was of Lower Dublin Township, may have been a son-in-law through a prior marriage of Rowland Powell.[83] Powell and Sarah Clay had issue, according to the will of Esther (Bowyer) Clay: she named her daughters Sarah and Catharine, and mentioned "their children," but did not name them.

ii. MARY CLAY, d. after 1750, when she joined with her sisters in conveying the Bristol plantation as above stated; m. probably before 1742, the FRANCIS ASPRILL [84] who was assessed that year for the Bristol Township Poor Tax. Since he did not join in the 1750 deed, while both of Mary's brothers-in-law did, he was probably deceased by that year. Known issue: 1. SARAH ASPRILL, named in the will of her grandmother, Esther Clay. 2. MARY ASPRILL, named in the will of her grandmother, Esther Clay.

iii. CATHERINE CLAY, d. after 1750, when she also joined with her sisters in conveying the Bristol plantation; m. probably before 1742, JOSEPH MOUNTAIN who was assessed that year for the Bristol Poor Tax. A cooper by trade in Bristol, on 26 July 1749, as the "only son and heir at law of Richard Mountain, late

---

[82] Bucks Co. Deed Book 9, 102, cited in Note 20 above.

[83] See Administration Book G, 156, #71:1757, estate of Rowland Powell. One Rowland Powell was in Haverford Township as early as 1695. Whether he was the man who married Esther Clay has not been established. Michael Grover, in Lower Dublin by 1757, and still there in 1760 with wife Elizabeth, died testate there in 1802. In his will he named his son Powell Grover, his then wife Mary, daughters Martha Grover and Mary Roberts, grandson Grover Roberts, and Mary, Powell, Susannah, Elizabeth and Michael Grover, children of his son Michael Grover, the son of his prior wife Elizabeth Sherran. See Will Book 1, 1, #87:1802.

[84] The name Asprill is not a native Pennsylvania name. One Joseph Asprill (1742-1802) appears in New Castle Co., Delaware records; he allegedly was born and died in that place.

of the same place brewer, deceased," Joseph and his wife "Katherine" for £350 made over to Jonathan Thomas, an innholder of Burlington, all of Joseph's rights as heir at law of his grandfather, also named Richard Mountain, or as heir of his great-grandfather John Dallamane, to any property in the Parish of Andover in Hampshire or elsewhere in Great Britain.[85] In 1779, one Joseph Mountain was assessed in Turkeyfoot Township, Bedford (now Somerset) County on 200 acres, and in 1783 on 27 acres only; he was not included in the 1790 Census.[86] Probable issue: 1. JOSEPH MOUNTAIN, JR., m. 14 April 1772, ELIZABETH DRAKE, presumed living in Somerset County in 1828. 2. JOHN MOUNTAIN. 3. RICHARD MOUNTAIN. 4. MARTHA MOUNTAIN, m. *ca.* 1782, in Western Maryland, JAMES McPIKE.[87]

3. SARAH BOWYER, the younger of the two surviving daughters of Esther King and John Bowyer, was born about 1680, probably in England. She was only a small child at the time of her father's death and apparently was reared by the succession of Lynn, Elfreth and Willson stepfathers, her mother's later husbands.

She did not marry until 13 2m 1710, having announced first intentions at the Philadelphia Meeting 24 12m 1709/10, to WILLOUGHBY WARDER, JR., son of Willoughby Warder, Sr. of Bucks County. Four days after their marriage, Sarah's mother signed her will, and died on 20 April, only one week after the wedding.

The marriage was of brief duration. Sarah died prior to 1714, when her husband was condemned by the Falls Monthly Meeting on 3 10m 1714, for marrying contrary to discipline. The name of his second wife is unknown. Two years later the Falls Meeting noted in its minutes for 7 9m 1716, that Willoughby Warder, Jr. acknowledged having been overtaken with drink. Then, on 25 August 1720, at Christ Church in Philadelphia, he married his third wife, Mary Ellis, who survived him. He died in Makefield Township, Bucks County, between 5 March, when his will was written, and 31 March 1728, when it was proved. He devised £5 to his only son Jeremiah; it was the exact amount which had been bequeathed to Willoughby by his own father.[88]

---

85 Original deed, Joseph Mountain to Jonathan Thomas, Society Miscellaneous Collection, HSP.

86 *Pennsylvania Archives*, 3rd Series, XXII, 167, 251. The account of this Mountain family by Eugene Fairfield MacPike, in *PGSP*, X, 185-191, is in error in stating this Joseph Mountain was assessed in Cumberland County. Turkeyfoot Township is now in Somerset County, but in 1779 was in Bedford County. Somerset was not erected out of Bedford until 1795. Mr. MacPike felt that the Joseph Mountain of 1779 was a son of Joseph of Bucks County.

87 *PGSP*, X, 188, cited above. This account states that these Mountain children had a half-brother, George "Grinup." If so, it would indicate Catherine Clay married a second time. One George *Gwinup* was living in the Northern Liberties in 1790, having 1 male in his household and 4 females. Was this the same person? See *Heads of Families at the First Census . . . 1790 Pennsylvania* (Washington, D. C., 1908), 201, hereinafter cited as *1790 Pennsylvania Census*.

88 Bucks Co. Will Book 1, 119, will of Willoughby Warder, Jr., cited in Abstracts of Bucks County Wills, 1685-1795, I, 41.

Issue of 3. Sarah Bowyer by her husband Willoughby Warder, Jr.:

i. JEREMIAH WARDER, b. 1 January 1711; [89] bur. as a Friend 5 1m 1783, *ae.* 72; m. at the Philadelphia Meeting 13 2m 1736, MARY HEAD, b. *ca.* 1714; bur. 9 3m 1803, *ae.* 89, daughter of John Head, a joiner of Philadelphia. Possibly apprenticed to his grandfather Willoughby's cousin, "John Warder of Philadelphia, hatter," Jeremiah, also a hatter, was well established in Philadelphia by 1756. He lived in Third Street, opposite Church Alley, in the North Ward of the city. Between 1750 and 1771, he was part owner of at least four ships, and by the latter year had taken his sons into partnership and had expanded his business to include "East India and European Goods." [90] During the Revolution Jeremiah, like many of the Friends, was under suspicion of being sympathetic to the British. This suspicion may have been aggravated by the fact that his son John was an avowed Tory. However, John was in England, and "Jeremiah Warder and Sons" were permitted to carry on their business without serious consequences. Jeremiah's will, written 8 9m 1780, and proved 10 April 1783, named the seven surviving of his fourteen children.[91] Issue: 1. JOHN WARDER, b. 6 11m 1736/7; d. before 19 5m 1739. 2. LYDIA WARDER, b. 13 11m 1737/8; d. after 1780 and before 1788; m. at Philadelphia Meeting, 27 8m 1757, RICHARD PARKER, son of Richard Parker of Darby, Chester County; d. between 24 December 1771, when his will was written, and 10 February 1772 when it was proved.[92] 3. JOHN WARDER (2nd), b. 19 5m 1739; d. 15 5m 1740. 4. SARAH WARDER, b. 1 9m 1740; bur. 5 6m 1745. 5. MARY WARDER, b. probably 1741; d. 5 10m 1744. 6. JOSEPH WARDER, b. 25 3m 1742; d. before 1780; he was not mentioned in his father's will. 7. REBECCA WARDER, b. 11 2m 1743; d. intestate by 28 February 1805, when letters of administration on her estate were granted to her son Thomas Maybury; m. 8 12m 1766, THOMAS MAYBURY (Mayberry), son of Thomas and Sophia Maybury, b. *ca.* 1740; d. intestate in Pottstown, Pa., by 13 May 1797, when letters of administration on his estate were granted to his widow.[93] 8. JEREMIAH WARDER, JR., b. 13 5m 1744; d. 16 12m 1822, *ae.* 79; m. 1st at the Philadelphia Meeting 19 11m 1772, DEBORAH ROBERTS, dec'd. by

---

[89] See Robert C. Moon, *The Morris Family of Philadelphia* (Philadelphia, 1898), II, 398, for Jeremiah's birthdate.

[90] The relationship of John Warder, hatter, to Willoughby Warder, Sr., is established in the latter's will, for which see Will Book D, 424, #340:1725. For Jeremiah's location in Philadelphia, and notice of his importing business, see "Taxables in the City of Philadelphia, 1756," PGM, XXII, 37, and *Pennsylvania Gazette*, 11 July 1771. The ships of which he was part owner included the Snow *White Oak*, the *Philadelphia Packet*, the *London Packet* and the Ship *Lydia*. See "Ship Registers for the Port of Philadelphia, 1726-1775," PMHB, XXV (1901), 123; XXVI (1902), 394; XXVIII (1904), 223, 361.

[91] Will Book S, 247, #222:1783, will of Jeremiah Warder.

[92] Will Book P, 206, #133:1772, will of Richard Parker. His widow Lydia was deceased by 8 5m 1788, when their daughter Eleanor married John Foulke at the Philadelphia Meeting.

[93] Administration Book K, 198, #33:1805, estate of Rebecca Maybury. Her son William Maybury, ironmaster of Montgomery Co., was one of the sureties. Letters of administration on the estate of her husband Thomas Maybury were granted in Montgomery Co. to her and his brothers-in-law, John Warder and James Vaux. Another brother-in-law, Jeremiah Warder, Jr., and one of his own sons-in-law, Charles Jolly, furnished the bond of £2000. Montgomery Co. Administration Docket #14,351. Thomas Maybury "late of Pottstown," died siezed of some 895 acres, appraised at £4367, in Marlborough and Frederick Townships where his forges were, as well as land in Bucks County and elsewhere. See Montgomery Co. Orphans Court Book 1, 348, 350, 366, 371.

1780, daughter of Hugh and Mary Roberts; m. 2nd at Mt. Holly, New Jersey, 5 4m 1780, HANNAH MOORE. Jeremiah was disowned by the Philadelphia Meeting 31 10m 1799, for owning an armed vessel. 9. SARAH WARDER (2nd), b. 5 6m 1745; d. before 28 1m 1753. 10. MARY WARDER (2nd), b. 23 11m 1746; d. 30 5m 1746. 11. SUSANNA WARDER, b. 17 5m 1749; d. 20 10m 1812, *ae.* 63; m. at Philadelphia Meeting 9 1m 1777, JAMES VAUX, b. 1749; d. 6 10m 1842, *ae.* 93, son of George and Frances Vaux. 12. JOHN WARDER (3rd), b. 24 2m 1751; d. 7 5m 1828, *ae.* 77; m. in England ANN HEAD, b. 1758; d. 19 1m 1829, *ae.* 71, according to Northern District Monthly Meeting records. Attainted a Tory on 27 July 1780, he was in London as his father's agent at the time, and did not return to Philadelphia until 1786. He and his wife returned to England the following year, but came back to the city in 1788.[94] 13. SARAH WARDER (3rd), b. 28 1m 1753; m. 5 9m 1776, WILLIAM HUDSON MORRIS, b. 10 3m 1753; d. 14 9m 1807, son of Anthony Morris and his wife Elizabeth Hudson. 14. MARY WARDER (3rd), b. *ca.* 1754; d. after 1797; m. 25 2m 1773, CALEB EMLEN, b. 15 December 1744; d. between 26 February 1796, when his will was written, and 10 August 1797, when it was proved.[95]

4. JOSEPH LYNN, posthumous son of Esther King and her second husband, Joseph Lynn, was born in Philadelphia 14 June 1691. He was not quite nineteen when his mother died in 1710, and he may have been apprenticed to his half-brother, the shipwright John Bowyer, Jr., who was twenty years his senior. When he married MARTHA HILL [96] on 25 December 1712, he was six months past his twenty-first birthday.

Five years later on 27 May 1717, when he was almost twenty-six, the father of one son, and a full-fledged shipwright, he and his Elfreth half-brothers were admitted freemen of the city. Nine days later, he acquired title to his first property. This was a 25-foot bank and water lot at the "North end" of the city between Vine Street, the town's northern limit, and "the next public street north," later called Callowhill Street. Situated "beyond the Penny pott house" at Vine and on the east side of "the

---

[94] The minutes of Philadelphia Southern District Monthly Meeting noted that on 29 10m 1788, Ann Warder, wife of John, and two children, were received on a certificate from Devonshire House, London. For Ann's journal of her sojourn in Philadelphia, 1786-1788, see *PMHB*, XVII (1893), XVIII (1894), *passim.* For the proclamation against John Warder in 1780, see *Pennsylvania Archives*, 3rd Series, X, 537-539.

[95] The Philadelphia and, after 1772, the Northern and Southern District Monthly Meeting records, examined at Friends' Historical Library, Swarthmore, contain most of the vital records of the above-named children of Jeremiah and Mary Warder. Abstracts of these records are also in GSP. Moon's *Morris Family*, cited in Note 89 above, lists the issue of James Vaux and his wife Susannah Warder, as well as of William H. Morris and his wife Sarah Warder. Caleb Emlen's will, recorded in Will Book X, 613, #414:1797, names his wife and children.

[96] Joseph Lynn's birth date and those for his children are from "Notes and Queries," *PMHB*, XVII, 376. The wording of this record indicates it was taken from the family Bible record of 4. Joseph Lynn, since the exact hour of each birth is noted. Of special interest is the fact that the dates in these records are not in Old Style or Quaker dating; the months are named and the years single-dated. The surnames of Joseph's two wives are not given in the record. Their identity is from the Samuel Morris Lynn genealogy of the family, cited in Note 21 above.

Great Road or the front street of sd City" extended northwards, the lot may have been leased by Lynn prior to the time he bought it from Daniel Howell, a Whitemarsh yeoman.[97]

Agreeing to pay the arrears of quit rent due on it, Lynn obtained a patent for the lot the following year under the usual conditions. He was to "wharf out" into the river, and as it had been with his mother, build and maintain "one public pair of stone stairs ten feet wide" from Front Street down to the cartway to be opened between the street and the river, and from thence down to the Delaware. The wharf was to be known as Langston's Wharf, for Thomas Langston, the original owner of the lot.[98]

From below Vine up to Pegg's Run (now Willow Street) the bank was shallow, shelving down gradually to low water mark. At Vine Street, there was considerable erosion. In 1713, the grand jury had presented as a nuisance "the east end of Vine street, where Front street crosses it." In 1718 a gully, running down Vine (originally called Valley Street) and crossing Front Street, was presented as "not passable by coaches, wagons or carts, to the endangering of lives." Six years later, the bank at the end of Vine was again presented as "worn away to the middle of Front Street and very dangerous." [99]

Possibly it was the uncertain conditions at Vine at this time which decided Lynn to invest in land near home, rather than within the city proper and closer to the center of business. At any rate, that year of 1724 he bought for £100 two lots south of his bank lot, but on the west side of Front Street south of the old Willcox rope walk.[100] Cable Lane had been cut through midway between Front and Second Streets between Vine and Callowhill, and Joseph's 34-foot lots ran from Front to the lane, and from thence to Second Street.

Since by now his family included five living children, he felt impelled to continue adding to his estate for their future benefit. In 1728, he bought from James Parrock for £175 a house and lot on the south

<hr>

[97] *Minutes of the Common Council of Philadelphia, 1704 to 1776* (Philadelphia, 1847), 129, 131, 133. For his purchase see recital in Exemplification Book 2, 205: 20 June 1718, Patent to Joseph Lynn.

[98] The arrears of quit rent were settled for £3 15s. Lynn was henceforth to pay yearly two English silver shillings and sixpence "or value in coin current." See also *Pennsylvania Archives*, 2nd Series, XIX, 639-640.

[99] Scharf and Westcott, III, 2153, cited in Note 15 above. This area all has been filled in to accommodate Delaware Avenue and the docks, but vestiges of an old stone breakwater can still be seen on the bank west of Delaware Avenue north of Vine Street.

[100] Deed Book H-15, 433: 2 Dec. 1724, William Chancellor to Joseph Lynn. Chancellor, a sailmaker, was a son-in-law of Joseph Willcox, for notice of whose ropewalk see *Pennsylvania Archives*, 2nd Series, XIX, 210, 226.

side of Sassafras near Front Street, 137 feet of unimproved ground farther up Sassafras toward Second Street and another lot around the corner on the east side of Second.[101] Obviously his business was prosperous;
three years later it was still good enough to enable him to invest, with
four others, in the Philadelphia-built 50-ton Ship *Dragon*,[102] a vessel he
may very well have built.

During the thirties as he continued to prosper he acquired other city
property. In 1734, he bought for £560 a long, narrow 27-foot lot extending all the way from Front to Second about mid-way between Sassafras and Vine Streets. Two years later, he bought a 25-foot bank lot
from Thomas Penrose, another shipwright, for £180. It was on the opposite side of Front Street between Mulberry and Sassafras. In May of
the same year, he invested £100 in a copper mine tract of 50 acres up in
the back country in McCall's Manor (now Douglas Township, Montgomery County).[103]

These last acquisitions meant little, however, to Joseph Lynn's wife.
Just three months after his investment in the copper mine venture,
Martha Lynn died on 16 August 1736. She was buried from the Phila-
delphia Meeting the following day.

Issue of 4. *Joseph Lynn by his 1st wife Martha Hill:*

i. JOSEPH LYNN, b. 22 April 1716; d. testate in Cheltenham Township, Montgomery County, about November 1803, *ae.* 87; m. 1st at the Philadelphia Meeting 27 8m 1747, SARAH FAIRMAN, d. 15 12m 1756, daughter of Benjamin
   Fairman and his wife Susanna Field; m. 2nd SARAH HILL, probably the "Mrs.
   Linn" bur. at Christ Church 17 September 1827. At Joseph's death the newspapers noted that he had been for "many years a respectable shipbuilder of Kensington." The shipyard seems to have been moved to that location after 1750,
   when Joseph Lynn bought from the heirs of the Anthony Palmer estate for £725
   the latter's "Capitol Messuage" and a large tract of land on the northeast side of
   Hanover Street (now Columbia Avenue), extending to the Delaware River, as

---

101 Deed Book F-10, 122: 28 Feb. 1727, James Parrock to Joseph Lynn. In 1735, Lynn sold the Second Street lot to his half-brother, Jeremiah Elfreth, as well as the westernmost 51 feet of the Sassafras Street
property. See Deed Book G-2, 88: 22 Nov. 1735, Joseph Lynn to Jeremiah Elfreth.

102 "Ship Registers . . ," cited in Note 90 above, *PMHB* XXIII, 264. The other partners were Thomas
Leech, Jonathan Hood, William Chancellor and the master of the vessel, Charles Hargrave.

103 Deed Book H-15, 62: 26 March 1734, John White *et al.* to Joseph Lynn. The 27-foot lot, on which
was a brick messuage on Front Street and two wooden dwellings on Second, was originally John Day's lot;
the brick house may have been built by Day as early as 1685. For the bank lot, see Deed Book G-7, 273:
26 Feb. 1735/6, Thomas Penrose to Joseph Lynn. This property Lynn sold on ground rent to Stephen and
Simon Bazeley, for which see I-12, 299: 1 June 1737, Joseph Lynn to Stephen Bazelee, and recital in G-7,
279: 26 Feb. 1742, Simon Bazelee to Benjamin Shoemaker. For the copper mine investment, see Deed Book
F-9, 130: 6 May 1736, Bernhard Vanleer to Joseph Lynn. Vanleer, Jonathan Robinson and John Campbell
had leased the property for 99 years from George McCall 16 March 1735/6. This mining property is not
to be confused with the better known, but later copper mine near Audobon on the Perkiomen Creek.

well as meadow land at the causeway leading over Gunner's Run.[104]   In 1770, Joseph bought a farm in Cheltenham Township where he was regularly assessed after that on 83 acres and assorted livestock.   In 1790 in that township, he had 4 males over 16 in his household, including himself, 3 males under 16, and 5 females.[105]   Issue: 1. JOHN LYNN, d. 3 3m 1750.   2. SARAH LYNN, b. *ca.* 1754; d. 15 11m 1803, *ae.* 49, according to Northern District Monthly Meeting records; m. by the Mayor of Philadelphia 7 May 1801, GEORGE WILSON, d. 7 June 1820.[106]   3. FRANKLIN LYNN, m. by 1797, to one REBECCA, surname not known.[107]   4. JOSEPH LYNN.   5. JEREMIAH LYNN, probably d. by 22 May 1823, when letters of administration on his estate were granted Mary Lynn, possibly his wife.[108]   6. JOHN LYNN, living in 1802, when his father wrote his will. 7. ESTHER LYNN, said to have m. MICHAEL MYERS of Whitemarsh.[109]   8. BEN-JAMIN LYNN.   9. WILLIAM LYNN.   10. MARY LYNN, m. SAMUEL FELTY, probably b. 20 November 1774; d. 23 April 1854, *ae.* 79-5-30, son of Jacob and Ann Felty.[110]

---

104 Joseph Lynn's death, as noted in the 19 Nov. 1803, issue of *Poulson's American Daily Advertiser,* had occurred "lately."   His will, written 6 Oct. 1802, was not proved until 28 Apr. 1810.   In it, he left to his wife Sarah household goods and the income from his estate for life.   After her death, his daughter Sarah Wilson and son Franklin Lynn were each to have only 5 shillings since he already had provided for them. The rest of his estate was to be divided equally between his other children: Joseph, Jeremiah, John, Esther, Benjamin, William and Mary Lynn.   Executors were his wife and sons Joseph and John Lynn.   Witnesses were Benjamin Rowland and Jacob Miers.   See Montgomery Co. Will Book 3, 221, #3932:1810.   The Samuel Morris Lynn account of this family, cited in Note 21 above, states the widow Sarah Lynn died in 1827, "near a century old."   For the purchase of the Palmer property, see Deed Book G-12, 512: 1 Nov. 1750, Alexander Allaire to Joseph Lynn.   The property extended to the Delaware along the northeast side of the present Columbia Avenue (formerly Hanover) and encompasses the present Penn Treaty Park.   The "capitol" messuage probably was either the original Thomas Fairman mansion, or an alteration to it.

105 For the Cheltenham property, see recital in Montgomery Co. Deed Book 16, 344: 4 Apr. 1797, Joseph Lynn to Franklin Lynn; for his assessments, *Pennsylvania Archives,* 3rd Series, XIV, 319; XV, 18, 387; XVI, 116, 539.   *1790 Pennsylvania Census,* 156.   The Samuel Morris Lynn account, cited above, does not distinguish between the children of Joseph's first and second marriages, nor are many dates given.   One son, Benjamin, was also omitted.   In the account of Joseph's issue, given in the text, it seems probable that Sarah and Franklin were of the first marriage, the last seven named in his will being of the second marriage.

106 The notice of Sarah's marriage in "A Register of Marriages and Deaths, 1800-1801," *PMHB,* XXIII (1899), 241, states she was the "daughter of Joseph Lynn of the Northern Liberties."   The Samuel Morris Lynn account states she was George Wilson's 2nd wife.   When he died in 1820, he left five children: Mary, George, Susanna, Francis and Abigail Wilson, as recited in Philadelphia Deed Book JAH-14, 365: 28 Jan. 1870, Joseph E. Mitchell *et al.* to Dennis Kennedy.   This transaction concerned a house and lot, now 112 Elfreth's Alley, formerly Gilbert's Alley, which Sarah had purchased as a single woman in 1784.

107 The Samuel Morris Lynn account stated Franklin Lynn died in 1793.   But his father Joseph Lynn made over the Cheltenham farm to him in 1797, and two months later Franklin and his wife Rebecca, and Joseph and his wife Sarah, entered into a tripartite agreement with Benjamin Rowland, for which see Montgomery Co. Deed Books 10, 344: 4 Apr. 1797, and 10, 543: 15 June 1797.

108 For his probable death, see Administration Book M, 395, #116:1823.   The Samuel Morris Lynn account gives his death as occurring in 1826, however.

109 In 1790, one Jacob Miers, possibly the father of Michael, and living in Cheltenham Township, had 3 males over 16 in his family, including himself, and 4 females.   *1790 Pennsylvania Census,* 156.   He was probably the same person who witnessed the will of Esther's father, Joseph Lynn.

110 Jacob Felty, living in Cheltenham in 1790, had 3 males under 16, and 2 females in his household beside himself.   *Ibid.,* 155.   Samuel Felty's dates and parentage are given in the death record included in his original estate papers.   His wife Mary was then deceased, according to the same record.   See Montgomery Co. Will #2058:1854.   On 17 Jan. 1813, he was granted letters of administration on the estate of one Joseph "Linn" of Cheltenham.   Possibly this was his brother-in-law.

ii. JOHN LYNN, b. 17 September 1718; bur. in Philadelphia 17 2m 1802, ae. 83-3-17; m. 25 3m 1749, MARY COOPER, b. ca. 1730; bur. 25 4m 1792, ae. 62, daughter of William Cooper of Philadelphia. John Lynn started out as a shipwright like his father and brothers, but in 1750 purchased a house and lot on the south side of High Street between Front and Second for £1095, and some time thereafter became a shopkeeper. By 1780, he was assessed there, next door to the printer William Hall, as a "gentleman." He apparently retained a large portion of his share of his father's estate and, by leasing out the several tracts to tenants, received a substantial income in rents.[111] Issue: 1. MARTHA LYNN, b. 1750; d. testate 10 6m 1808, ae. 58; m. 1st at St. Michael and Zion Lutheran Church 8 April 1779, JOHN KEPPELE, b. ca. 1754; bur. 31 10m 1779, ae. 25, widower of her sister Deborah. When he died, he was lieutenant colonel of the First Battalion, Philadelphia city militia. She m. 2nd JOSEPH PARKER, who d. after 1808.[112] At the time of her first marriage, she was disowned by Friends 30 4m 1779, for marrying "her brother-in-law" contrary to discipline, but appears to have been reinstated before her death. 2. DEBORAH LYNN, b. 17 March 1752; bur. 24 11m 1776; m. 1st by New Jersey license dated 25 July 1772, JAMES LUKENS, b. ca. 1751; d. 6 3m 1776, ae. 23; m. 2nd 2 October 1776, JOHN KEPPELE, as above. She also was disowned for marrying contrary to discipline one not a Friend.[113] 3. JOSEPH LYNN, b. between 1754 and 1758; d. intestate 10 October 1800; m. at Providence, under auspices of the Chester Monthly Meeting, 17 6m 1784, ANN MORRIS, b. 1 8m 1760; d. testate 20 1m 1825, daughter of Jonathan and Alice Morris of Chester County.[114]

iii. ELIZABETH LYNN, b. 13 June 1720; d. after 1755; m. at the Philadelphia Meeting 24 7m 1742, ABRAHAM GRIFFITH, b. in Richland Township, Bucks County, 12 2m 1713; d. 25 October 1798, near Mt. Holly, New Jersey, son of Abraham Griffith and his wife Hannah Lester. Though Elizabeth had been left a plantation in Neshaminy of 130 acres by her father, the Griffiths lived first in Burlington, N. J. A miller by trade, Abraham was also a travelling Friend and appears to have moved around from place to place. From Burlington he moved back to Bucks County about 1748, then became a member of Abington Monthly Meeting where the births of their children were recorded. He was living in Norriton Township in 1774, and was in Upper Merion Township through 1790, when he had 1 male under 16 and 5 females in his family.[115] Issue: 1. JOSEPH

---

111 *Pennsylvania Archives*, 3rd Series, IX, 556: 30 Aug. 1750, Sarah Read to John Lynn; *ibid.*, XIV, 186, 260, 522; XV, 309, 595. For some of his tenants, see *ibid.*, XV, 331, 347, 582, 592. In 1772, John Lynn and his wife and her sister Deborah (Cooper) Lippincott petitioned the Orphans Court about legacies left by William Cooper in the custody of their brother Jacob Cooper. Mary was dealt with by the Philadelphia Meeting the same year for having "gone to law" against her brother Jacob over the same matter. Orphans Court Book 9, 312, entry under 8 June 1772; *PGSP*, XIV, 49.

112 At Martha's 2nd marriage, her father vested property for her use in the hands of Isaac Norris which she devised to her brother Joseph's children in her will, for which see Will Book 2, 308, #62:1808.

113 Christopher Marshall, the diarist, reported Deborah's 2nd marriage (to John Keppele) as having taken place "in the night at her father's house but unknown to him though he was in the house at the same time." See Diary of Christopher Marshall, Case 18, Marshall Papers, HSP, entry for 4 Oct. 1776.

114 Joseph and Ann Lynn were the parents of the family genealogist, Samuel Morris Lynn. For Ann's will see Will Book 8, 380, #19:1825. Letters of administration on her husband's estate had been granted to her 20 Oct. 1800, for which see Administration Book K, 56, #195:1800.

115 See Clarence V. Roberts, *Early Friends Families of Upper Bucks* (Philadelphia, 1921), 213-214, 216; Rosalie Fellows Bailey, "The Foos Family of Pennsylvania and Ohio," *PGM*, XVIII, 115.* *Pennsylvania Archives*, 3rd Series, XIV, 383; XV, 165, 554; XVI, 47, 219, 706; *1790 Pennsylvania Census*, 158.

*See Volume 1 of this work, p. 684.

GRIFFITH, b. 31 10m 1745; living in 1790; m. by license dated 3 January 1774, MARY THORNTON. 2. HANNAH GRIFFITH, b. 13 5m 1748; d. 1815 in Haverford; m. at St. Michael's Lutheran Church, Germantown, 30 April 1769, THOMAS BARTON, presumably living in Radnor Township, Delaware County, in 1790.[116] 3. MARTHA GRIFFITH, b. 23 11m 1750; d. 1750. 4. ABRAHAM GRIFFITH, b. 14 8m 1752. 5. SAMUEL GRIFFITH, b. 16 9m 1755.

iv. MARTHA LYNN, b. 29 May 1722; d. in Bucks County 7 12m 1774; m. at Philadelphia Meeting 14 3m 1751, HENRY DENNIS, son of John Dennis of Salem, New Jersey; d. probably in New York State after 1791. Henry Dennis was a widower when he married Martha Lynn. His first wife, Grace Bacon, whom he had married at Salem Monthly Meeting in 1741, had died in Philadelphia 27 1m 1749/50, leaving an infant daughter Rebecca who died unmarried 19 3m 1798, ae. 48. A ship-carpenter by trade, Dennis appears to have been a somewhat contentious man, at least in his dealings with his wife's relations. In 1759, before Joseph Lynn's city property was partitioned, Dennis and his brother-in-law Joseph Lynn, Jr. appeared before the Philadelphia Monthly Meeting "with a paper condemning their rash imprudent conduct . . . in quarreling." Again, early in 1761, he complained to the Meeting "against Jeremiah Lynn that a matter of Variance" subsisted between them. If these matters of variance had to do with his father-in-law's estate, Dennis's complaints appear to have borne fruit. In the following June, partition finally was made of the city lots and ground rents left by Joseph Lynn to his daughters. Martha and Henry received their lots: two on Second Street and one on Front Street; also, the ground rent issuing out of the bank lot which Lynn had purchased in 1736 and subsequently sold.

Henry Dennis promptly converted the legacy into cash and, in 1765, purchased a half-interest in the old Dewees' mill property on Wissahickon Creek at the upper end of Germantown Township. He held this only two years, then disposed of it.[117] In 1769, he was assessed in Mulberry Ward. In 1774, Martha, wife of Henry Dennis, obtained a certificate from the Philadelphia Meeting for herself and three children, Martha, John and Hannah, to Buckingham Monthly Meeting in Bucks County, where she died early in December of the same year. Henry appears to have returned to Philadelphia: in 1779, one Henry Dennis was assessed in Bristol Township, Philadelphia County. By 1791, he was referred to as being "of New York." [118] Issue: 1. JOHN DENNIS, d. in Philadelphia 13 12m 1756. 2. HENRY DENNIS, d. 20 8m 1757. 3. MARTHA DENNIS, b. ca. 1752; d. Solebury Township, Bucks County, 27 June 1824, ae. 72; m. at Buckingham Monthly Meeting 11 10m 1775, JAMES ARMITAGE, b. 27 1m 1749; d.

---

116 For Joseph Griffith, see *PGM*, XVIII, 115, cited above; *1790 Pennsylvania Census*, 70. For Thomas Barton, *ibid.*, 102.

117 See Deed Books H-15, 103: 30 June 1761, Peter Bankson *et al.* to Henry Dennis, for the Lynn properties, and H-15, 128: 6 Nov. 1761, Henry Dennis to Adam Hoops, for the sale. For the mill transactions, see Deed Books I-4, 1: 10 Jan. 1765, Silas Parvin to Henry Dennis, and I-4, 27: 9 Apr. 1767, Henry Dennis to Nathan Shepherd.

118 *Pennsylvania Archives*, 3rd Series, XIV, 201; XV, 12. See Extracts from Records of Buckingham Monthly Meeting Minutes, 1720-1803, Bu6F, 168, 223, 225, 253, GSP, for notices of this family. See also Births, Marriages and Deaths: Friends Monthly Meeting Records, Bucks County, Bu2F, 21, 37, 276-1/2, GSP, for additional notices, including Martha's death, and Henry's residence in New York in 1791. The *1790 New York Census*, 91, lists a Henry Dennis resident in Poughkeepsie, having 3 males over 16, 3 males under 16, and 2 females in his household, including himself.

*See Volume I of this work, p. 684.

6 7m 1816, in Solebury, son of Samuel and Elizabeth Armitage. 4. JOHN DEN-
NIS (2nd), in 1782 living in New York, having "married with a Woman not of
our Society by Assistance of an Hireling Minister," which he acknowledged in
1786 to the Buckingham Meeting. 5. HANNAH DENNIS, d. between 1792, when
a son Charles was born, and 1796, by which time her husband had m. a 2nd wife;
m. at Buckingham Meeting 11 5m 1791, OLIVER HAMPTON, b. *ca.* 1761; d. in
Solebury 13 October 1826, *ae.* 65, son of Benjamin Hampton.[119]

v. ESTHER LYNN, b. 19 February 1724; d. testate between 25 7m and 7 October
1795; m. 1st at Christ Church 11 October 1745, PETER BANKSON, b. 1710;
d. 10 9m 1766, *ae.* 56. Esther was condemned by the Philadelphia Meeting for
marrying out of unity, but may have made satisfactory acknowledgement; her
children's deaths were entered in Friends' records. Her husband, a non-com-
municant member of the Swedish Lutheran Church at Wicacoa (Gloria Dei, Old
Swedes'), was a grandson of Andrew Bengston and his wife Gertrude Rambo.
In 1754 he was reported in the Church Census made that year as understanding,
speaking, reading and writing English, which not all of the Swedish members of
the church could do.[120]   He was also a ship-carpenter and, having inherited
property in Passayunk, relinquished most of the rights he and his wife had in the
property devised to her by her father Joseph Lynn.   When Peter Bankson died in
1766, he and his family were living in the house on the west side of Front Street
near the old ropewalk above Vine, which was all they had kept of his wife's inheritance.   He left this to his wife, as well as the principal sum of £400 he had
lent to his brother-in-law, Henry Dennis, his silver tankard, bowl, four silver
table spoons, six silver tea spoons, sugar tongs, tea strainer, cream pot and salts,
and other household furnishings.   His wife was to have, in addition, two acres of
woodland, part of his Passayunk plantation, the balance of which he devised to
his daughter "Elionar."   Eleanor was to have additional pieces of silver: his pint
can, silver buttons, a pair of sugar tongs, two tablespoons, and a pair of gold
sleeve buttons.[121]   Issue (order uncertain): 1. MARTHA BANKSON, d. 3 8m 1745.
2. JOHN BANKSON, d. young 3 8m 1751. 3. JOSEPH BANKSON, d. young 13
8m 1751. 4. JACOB BANKSON, b. before 1754; d. 11 3m 1755. 5. ANDREW
BANKSON, d. young 6 7m 1759. 6. ELEANOR BANKSON, d. before 3 January
1790; m. at Christ Church 16 April 1777, JOHN RIGHTER, b. 26 January 1753;
d. testate in Roxborough Township 6 February 1790, *ae.* 37-0-10, bur. old Roxborough Burial Ground, son of Peter Righter.[122]

---

119 See transcripts of Buckingham and Falls Monthly Meeting Births and Deaths, Bu5F, 1, GSP, for
James Armitage's birth, and Births, Marriages and Deaths in Bucks County, Vol. II, Middletown, Richland,
Solebury and Wrightstown Monthly Meeting, 1680-1870, Bu4F, 412, for his death.   Martha Armitage's
death, and that of Oliver Hampton, are given in Deaths from Bucks County Intelligencer, Bu9A, GSP. It
should be noted that Samuel Morris Lynn's account is in error in stating that Martha Dennis married Thomas
Armitage, and Hannah Dennis married Joseph Hampton.

120 Transcript of Archivum Americanum: Upsal Documents Relating to the Swedish Churches on the
Delaware (1891), I, 493, HSP.   Peter, his wife who was "English," and their son Jacob are listed in the
census.

121 For Esther (Lynn) Bankson's share of the Lynn properties, see Deed Book I-7, 460: 30 June 1761,
Henry Dennis *et al.* to Peter Bankson.   For Bankson's will, see Will Book O, 26, #19:1766.

122 For the will of John Righter, ferryman, see Will Book U, 435, #175:1790.   For an extended account of him see Mildred Goshow, "A Study of the Righter-Reiter Families of Philadelphia County in the
Eighteenth Century," *PGM*, XXI, 29-30, 39. *

*See pp. 758-759, 768, this volume.

Esther (Lynn) Bankson m. 2nd at Christ Church 29 December 1767, JAMES CHANNEL, a widower. His first wife, Rebecca Keys, had died only the previous March, leaving him with a son Thomas and a daughter Rebecca. He was another shipwright and, after his marriage to Esther, they appear to have lived above Sassafras on the north side of Keys Alley, laid out from Front to Second along the south line of the lot Joseph Lynn purchased in 1737. Esther was disowned by Friends as a result of her second marriage to a non-Friend. By 1780, James Channel appears to have retired from active work since in that year, he was assessed, like John Lynn, as a "gentleman." But four years later, when he wrote his will, he still described himself as a shipwright, being then "advanced in years." It would appear he had been quite prosperous during his active years; he bequeathed to his wife Esther not only his silver watch and "all the Plate and Household Goods which she brought to me at our Marriage," but the principal sum of three bonds totalling £200 and a life tenure in the house in Keys Alley. To his daughter Rebecca, now married to George Pickering, he left a lot in Camden, New Jersey, and the principal sum of a £300 bond. If his son Thomas, "who went to sea and is supposed lost should be alive and return to Philadelphia," he was to have one half of the estate. The will was not proved until eleven years later on 5 February 1795. Esther, his widow, drew up her own will the following July, being then "sick and weak in Body." To her step-daughter Rebecca Pickering she left £10. To her brother Joseph Lynn she left a life estate in the lot between the east side of Cable Lane and Front Street which had been her share of her father's estate. To her niece Esther Lynn, Joseph's daughter, she left her silver pint bowl. The rest of her estate she devised to her only grandchild Esther Righter; if she died without heirs, the estate was to go to Esther Channel's "right heirs." The will was proved 7 October 1795, by her executors, her neighbor William Brooks, a sawsetter, and Thomas Norton, a merchant of the Northern Liberties.[123]

vi. SUSANNA LYNN, b. 20 September 1725; d. in infancy.
vii. SUSANNA LYNN (2nd), b. 18 December 1726; d. in infancy.
viii. SETH LYNN, b. 29 September 1727; d. 27 November 1727.

Less than a year after the death of his first wife Martha Hill, 4. Joseph Lynn married a widow as his second wife, by New Jersey license dated 26 May 1737. Born in 1707, SARAH (HUTCHINSON) NORWOOD [124] promptly presented Joseph with another son within a year of their marriage, and two more daughters within the next two years. In 1740, the year in which the last daughter was born, Joseph took a one-quarter share in the 40-ton Sloop *Joseph and Mary*,[125] and with Joseph Oldman, James Parrock and Jeremiah Elfreth, his half-brother, bought a large

123 See *Pennsylvania Packet*, 29 Oct. 1778, for the Channels' residence in Keys Alley. See also *Pennslyvania Archives*, 3rd Series, XV, 332, 628; XVI, 478, for his assessments in 1780-1782. For his will, see Will Book X, 182, #8:1790; for Esther's will, Will Book X, 345, #98:1795.

124 The marriage license, noted in *The Genealogical Magazine of New Jersey*, XVII, 47, cited in Note 68 above, states she was a widow. Her maiden name is given in Samuel Morris Lynn's account.

125 "Ship Registers . . ," PMHB, XXIV (1899), 108, cited in Note 90 above. The other owners of the ship were Joseph Rivers, Thomas Leech, Joseph Morris; the master of the ship was Andrew Hodge.

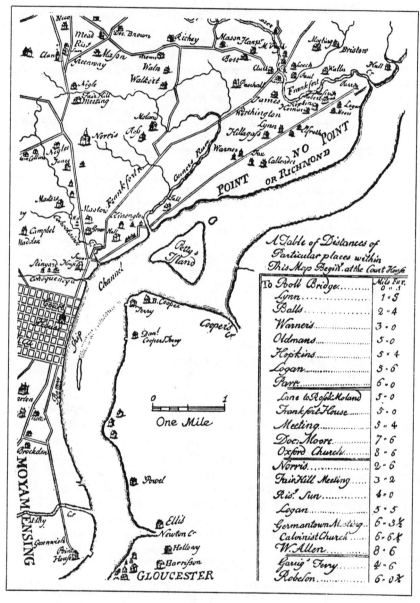

A Portion of A Map of Philadelphia and Parts Adjacent, N. Scull and G. Heap, *post* 1752.

tract of land at the mouth of the Frankford Creek in Shackamaxon, now called Point-no-Point.[126] Mariners and river-men had given this name to the land because of the changes in the appearance of the land at the mouth of the creek as it was approached from down-river. When first seen, it appeared to be a point jutting out into the river but, coming nearer, the point seemed to disappear. Then, on a closer approach, it seemed to jut out again, and so gave rise to the popular jingle,

> Point Look Out
> Point Look in
> Point no Point
> Point Agin.

Joseph Lynn had also added to his city holdings. Two months after his marriage he bought another Front Street lot, this one between Sassafras and Vine, at the northwest corner of Front Street and Keys Alley, laid out through to Second Street. The following September he had applied for and been granted "Liberty to Make up so much Ground beyond the North End of the City as may accomodate him to lay Timber & plank." In December, on his further application, the Proprietor, Thomas Penn, "was pleased to allow him the Priviledge of laying his Timber and Planks on the Ground opposite to his dwelling House and to extend Southward so far as the North line of the Lot called the London Companys untill the Propr'y should be pleased to give further Orders therein." [127]

In October 1742, some three months past his fifty-first birthday, Joseph Lynn, being sick and weak in body, drew up his will, having already decided on a division of his real estate among his children. To his three sons, Joseph, John and Jeremiah, he left 170 acres of the property at Point-no-Point. He had agreed with Samuel Parr to sell a portion of it to him, but as he had not yet conveyed it, his executors were to complete the bargain. To his recently married daughter Elizabeth Griffith, wife of Abraham, he left a plantation of 130 acres at Neshaminy, as well as a feather bed and furnishing, a chest of drawers, a table, looking glass and "other necessaries for housekeeping." His other two daughters by his first wife, Martha and Esther, were to have £18 a year paid to them by his wife until the youngest came of age. His eld-

---

126 Deed Book G-2, 274: 30 Apr. 1740, Samuel Holme to Joseph Lynn *et al*. Lynn and Joseph Oldman, brother of Jeremiah Elfreth's first wife, each were entitled to three-tenths of the whole tract, Parrock and Elfreth each two-tenths.

127 Deed Book H-15, 153: 20 July 1737, Joseph Merewether to Joseph Lynn. *Pennsylvania Archives*, 2nd Series, XIX, 93, 95-96. The family retained the original bank lot and the additional ground (in all, 65 feet) until 1775 when it was sold to Edward Shippen, Jr. for £1500. See Deed Book I-15, 83: 1 June 1775, Joseph, John and Jeremiah Lynn to Edward Shippen, Jr.

est son Joseph was to have his wearing apparell, his riding horse and a small silver tankard. John, the second son, was to have his silver bowl. Both were to have a feather bed and furnishings. Jeremiah, his son by his second wife, was to have his gold and silver buttons and buckles. The four children of his first wife were to have his four new silver spoons.

To his second wife Sarah, he devised his large silver tankard, seven old silver spoons, tongs, strainer and the rest of his silver; a mare and cow, his riding chair, and his Negro girl. Sarah was also to enjoy for her life the income of the two houses on Second Street on the lot he had purchased in 1734, now occupied by tenants; the income arising out of the bank lot between Mulberry and Sassafras Streets, which he had sold on ground rent in 1737 to Simon and Stephen Beezeley, and that issuing out of the one lot on the south side of Sassafras which he had sold on ground rent to John Price. After her death, these rents were to be divided among his daughters.

Having disposed of his personal estate, he next took thought for his business. The two sloops then on the stocks, the "large new Flat," and his three servants were to be sold, and the money arising from their sale applied to his debts. If this was not sufficient, then a lot in Bristol in Bucks County and one at Whitehill near Bordentown in West Jersey, were also to be sold. Out of the proceeds of these sales, his two sons Joseph and John were to take what was due them "for work and money I borrowed of them." Half of the amount was to be in cash, the other half in material. He appointed his wife and two eldest sons executors, and named his friend Thomas Leech to assist them. Seemingly as an afterthought, he devised £5 to his half-sister 2. Esther Clay.[128]

Two days later, on 12 October 1742, Joseph Lynn died at the age of fifty-one years, three months and twenty-eight days. His will was not proved until the following 4 November by the witnesses, his half-brother Jeremiah Elfreth, Samuel Hastings, and Christopher Marshall; Thomas Leech was the only one of the four who was a "juror," the others all affirmed, being Friends.

The executors' first act was to have the heretofore undivided Point-no-Point tract split up into appropriate shares. Then in July 1743, they sold 159 acres at the mouth of Frankford Creek to William Logan for £393 14s. and, a month later, 79 additional acres to Samuel Parr, as directed by Lynn in his will.[129]

---

128 Will Book G, 6, #3:1742, will of Joseph Lynn.

129 For the partition, see Deed Book G-2, 367: 12 Jan. 1742/3, Quadripartite partition; for the sale to Logan, D-59, 286: 8 July 1743, and to Samuel Parr, recital in D-2, 351: 25 Feb. 1779, William Parr to Richard Mason. It should be noted that not all of Joseph Lynn's real estate dealings have been included in this study, only those pertaining to his heirs remaining in his hands at his death.

No division of the city property could be made until after the widow Sarah Lynn's death, since she was entitled to the income during her life. She survived Joseph seventeen years, dying 4 June 1759, aged fifty-two years, eleven months and twenty-eight days. Her younger daughter Hannah died in January of the following year,[130] but it was not until 1761 that the ground rents and lots were parcelled out among Joseph's three surviving daughters, Martha Dennis, Hester Bankson, and their half-sister Sarah Lynn.

Issue of 4. Joseph Lynn by his 2nd wife Sarah (Hutchinson) Norwood:

ix. JEREMIAH LYNN, b. 22 February 1738; bur. 5 2m 1804, *ae.* 66, unmarried and without issue. After his mother's death, Jeremiah in 1760 disposed of his share of the Point-no-Point land to Abel James. His sister Hannah's share in the city property became vested in him and in his sister Sarah; after the initial partition, they made a separate division between them of their joint holdings. A shipwright by trade, he appears to have lived most of his adult life with his only surviving sister of the whole blood, Sarah, and her husband Benjamin Marshall.[131]

x. SARAH LYNN, b. 8 October 1739; d. 7 May 1797; m. at Philadelphia Meeting 22 10m 1761, BENJAMIN MARSHALL, b. 14 8m 1737; d. 29 January 1778, bur. at Plymouth Meeting Burial Ground, son of Christopher Marshall, the diarist, and his 1st wife, Sarah Thompson. Though he was a "tinn-plate worker" by trade, Benjamin Marshall appears to have participated with his brothers in the family business, a drug and colour shop: the Sign of the Golden Ball in Chestnut Street. When the British approached Philadelphia in 1777, Benjamin and his brothers and their families moved out of the city up into the country. During the winter, while nursing soldiers at Valley Forge and at his own home, he contracted a fever from which he died.[132] When his widow finally moved back to Philadelphia, her brother Jeremiah Lynn apparently took up residence with her. Issue: 1. ANN MARSHALL, b. 10 August 1762; d. young. 2. SARAH MARSHALL, b. 10 December 1763; d. 23 2m 1765, *ae.* 15 months. 3. HANNAH MARSHALL, b. 5 December 1765; m. at the Philadelphia Meeting 14 4m 1785, CASPAR WISTAR HAINES, b. 1762; d. 1801, son of Reuben Haines and his wife Margaret Wistar. 4. SARAH MARSHALL (2nd), b. 1767; bur. 2 11m 1775, *ae.* 8. 5. MARY MARSHALL, b. 22 July 1769; d. 17 3m 1770, *ae.* 8 months. 6. SUSANNA MARSHALL, b. 12 July 1771; bur. 27 7m 1772, *ae.* 1. 7. CHRISTOPHER MARSHALL, b. 10 May 1773; m. 1st at Philadelphia Meeting 9 10m 1800, MARY DORSEY, b. 12 8m 1772, daughter of Benedict and Sarah Dorsey; m. 2nd, PHOEBE

---

130 Both death dates and ages for Joseph and Sarah Lynn are given in the Samuel Morris Lynn account, cited in Note 21 above, as are those for Hannah, for which see text below.

131 See Deed Book I-6, 439: 7 May 1760, Jeremiah Lynn to Abel James, for the sale of the Point-no-Point property. See Deed Book H-15, 138: 14 Oct. 1761, Jeremiah Lynn to Sarah Lynn, for their mutual division. For his presumed residence with his sister, see the assessment lists, *Pennsylvania Archives*, 3rd Series, XIV, 183, 246; XV, 250, 744; XVI, 285, 787.

132 See "Correspondence of the Children of Christopher Marshall," PMHB, XVII, 366, 340-345, 346, for references to Benjamin's last illness and death.

SHOTWELL. 8. ESTHER MARSHALL, b. 22 November 1774; m. at High Street Meeting House 3 12m 1795, ABRAHAM GARRIGUES, b. 7 8m 1773, son of William and Mary Garrigues. 9. MARY MARSHALL (2nd), b. 17 July 1776; d. young. 10. ANN MARSHALL (2nd, twin of Mary?), b. July 1776; bur. 7 9m 1776, *ae.* 3 months. 11. BENJAMIN MARSHALL, b. 29 September 1777; m. at Philadelphia Meeting House 11 10m 1804, MARY CRUKSHANK, daughter of John and Mary Crukshank. 12. ANN MARSHALL (3rd), b. 18 June 1778; d. young.[133]

xi. HANNAH LYNN, b. 8 August 1741; d. testate unmarried and without issue in Philadelphia 11 January 1760, *ae.* 18-4-22. In her will, written ten days before her death when she was "very sick and weak," she bequeathed all her plate, lands and hereditaments to her brother Jeremiah and sister Sarah Lynn, to be shared by them equally. Sarah was also to have her Negro girl called "Bett." [134]

5. JEREMIAH ELFRETH, born about 1692, son of Esther King and her third husband, Josiah Elfreth, was only about a year old when his father died in 1693, at which time his half-brother Henry Elfreth, son of his father's first marriage, was at least thirteen years of age. Their uncle Jeremiah Elfreth died a year later, leaving to his "kinsman Jeremiah Elfreth, my brother Josiah Elfreth's son," twenty shillings, and the residue of his estate to his nephew Henry Elfreth.[135]

When Esther King moved to Bucks County after 1695, both Jeremiah and Henry Elfreth may have remained in Philadelphia, perhaps with their half-brother John Bowyer, Jr., by then of full age, and to whom Henry may have been apprenticed. Certainly when Henry married Sarah Gilbert, daughter of John Gilbert, at the Philadelphia Meeting 27 12m 1701/2, Jeremiah, though not more than ten years old, appears to have been Henry's only near relation present.

John Gilbert, Henry's father-in-law, had recently acquired three Front Street lots between Mulberry and Sassafras which extended all the way west to Second Street. He and Arthur Wells, his neighbor on the

---

[133] For the erroneous birth date, given as 18 June 1779, of this posthumous child, see "The Record of Some Residents in the Vicinity of the Middle Ferry . . ," *PGSP*, IX, 44. She is presumed to be the child mentioned by Charles Marshall in his letter of 29 Jan. 1778, to his father, for which see Note 132 above. Dates for the other children are from John W. Jordan, *Colonial Families of Philadelphia* (New York, 1911), II, 1025-1026, supplemented by records from Hinshaw, II, 355, 365, 432, 591, cited in Note 58 above. The Lynn family record, however, gives the birth of the 2nd child, Sarah Marshall, as 11 December 1762.

[134] The will of Hannah Lynn was proved 4 Feb. 1760, by her executors, Jeremiah and Sarah Lynn, and her "cousin" Christopher Marshall. Her sister Sarah did not marry Benjamin Marshall until 1761; whether Hannah was referring to Benjamin's brother, Christopher, or to his father, the diarist, has not been established. See Will Book L, 401, #255:1760, will of Hannah Lynn.

[135] Administration Book A, 182-182, #25:1693[/4], *c.t.a.* will of Jeremiah Elfreth, for abstract of which see *PGM*, XIX, 263. The account in this study of his nephew Jeremiah Elfreth and the latter's family is based on the researches of Hannah Benner Roach, historian of the Elfreth's Alley Association. The writer also wishes to acknowledge with sincere gratitude her generous counsel and practical assistance in the preparation of the entire study of Esther King and her children.

south, by 1702, had opened an alley from Front to Second Street between their respective properties for the accommodation of Wells's blacksmith shop and the boulting house Gilbert intended to build on the alley. At the northeast corner of the alley and Second Street, John Gilbert also erected a dwelling which he rented for a time to Henry and Sarah Elfreth. When Gilbert died in 1711, he left this corner property to their children, Caleb, John, Joshua, Elizabeth and Sarah Elfreth.[136]

Unlike his three half-brothers, John Bowyer, Joseph Lynn, and Henry Elfreth, who were shipwrights, Jeremiah Elfreth became a blacksmith, but to whom he was apprenticed remains unknown. Emulating his much-married mother Esther King, however, he was married five times in the course of his eighty years.

He was twenty-four when he married his first wife, SARAH OLD-MAN, daughter of Thomas Oldman and his wife Elizabeth Sykes. When Jeremiah and Sarah were married at the Philadelphia Meeting 12 4m 1716, none of Jeremiah's relations appear to have been present, but his bride's brothers and sisters, Thomas, Joseph, Ann and Mary Oldman, were all witnesses. A month later on 31 July 1716, Jeremiah acquired his first city property for £120 from Benjamin Vining.[137] This was a house and L-shaped piece of ground on the east side of Second Street and north side of the alley, then "commonly" called Gilbert's Alley, adjoining on the north and east the property at the corner of the alley which John Gilbert had devised to Henry Elfreth's children. Here, Jeremiah and his wife Sarah set up housekeeping; it remained Jeremiah's town dwelling all his life.

In 1720, four years after his marriage, Jeremiah leased from William Coats on a ground rent of £3 12s. four acres fronting a lane to be laid out in the Northern Liberties. The first payment of rent was not due until March 1722; Jeremiah was to "erect a good and sufficient inclosure or fence of Post and Rails of four Rails high" around the property within a year; if he failed to pay the rent, Coats could enter upon the messuage, barns, stables or other buildings "to be erected thereon," and distrain sufficient goods to satisfy the rent. That same year Jeremiah and his wife joined with her brothers and sisters in releasing their rights in her father's property to her brother Thomas Oldman, Jr.[138]

---

136 See the will of John Gilbert, Will Book C, 256, #225:1711.

137 Deed Book G-2, 89: 31 July 1716, Benjamin Vining to Jeremiah Elfreth.

138 Deed Book G-2, 92: 20 Aug. 1720, William Coats to Jeremiah Elfreth. The lane to be laid out through Coats' land was first called Hickory Lane, then Coats Street, and is now Fairmount Avenue. Elfreth's lot was at what would now be the northeast corner of Thirteenth Street. For the Oldman release, see Deed Book F-8, 271: 19 July 1720, Jeremiah Elfreth to Thomas Oldman et al.

Jeremiah's blacksmithing trade warranted his taking on apprentices of his own, but not all of them stayed for the full term of their indentures. In the spring of 1726, Thomas Davis, aged nineteen, ran away from Elfreth.[139]

Two years later Jeremiah's first marriage was abruptly terminated. Late in November 1728, his wife Sarah died, "having been the day before walking in her garden." As Thomas Chalkley, the noted "travelling Friend," set down in his journal, "She was a sober, young Woman, and her Death much lamented." [140]

Issue of 5. Jeremiah Elfreth by his 1st wife Sarah Oldman:

i. JOSIAH ELFRETH, d. 1 7m 1719.

ii. ELIZABETH ELFRETH, b. *ca.* 1719; d. in New Jersey 9 5m 1778, *ae.* 59-3-0; m. at Philadelphia Meeting 21 9m 1738, ISAAC ANDREWS, b. in New Jersey between 1712 and 1717, when his father died; d. in Deptford Township, Gloucester County, New Jersey, between 25 July 1775, when he wrote his will, and 14 February 1776, when the inventory of his estate was taken.[141] Son of Edward and Sarah Andrews of Little Egg Harbor, Isaac Andrews was a tanner by trade. His tannery and adjacent dwelling were in Haddonfield, but he also owned the plantation on Mantua Creek where he died, and which he left to his wife for her life, and then to his son Jeremiah Andrews. In addition, his own mother had left him a 50-acre tract near Little Egg Harbor, and his father-in-law Jeremiah Elfreth had left to his daughter, Elizabeth Andrews, three houses and lots on the south side of Sassafras between Front and Second Streets in Philadelphia. A year after Isaac's death, Elizabeth Andrews and her daughter Esther left Haddonfield and removed within the verge of Salem Monthly Meeting where she died the following year. Issue, as noted in Haddonfield Monthly Meeting records: [142] 1. SARAH ANDREWS, b. 25 6m 1739; m. at Haddonfield Meeting 23 11m 1758, JOHN MILLER, son of Ebenezer Miller of Greenwich, Cumberland County, New Jersey. 2. MARY ANDREWS, b. 25 4m 1741; d. 26 5m 1745, *ae.* 4. 3. JEREMIAH ANDREWS, b. 22 11m 1743/4; living in 1775 when his father wrote his will. 4. ELIZABETH ANDREWS, b. 23 5m 1747; d. 31 3m 1760, *ae. ca.* 13. 5. ISAAC ANDREWS, b. 21 9m 1749; probably d. in Evesham, New Jersey, 1m 1820.[143] 6. EDWARD ANDREWS, b. 8 10m 1751; d. 11 8m 1752. 7. LETITIA ANDREWS,

---

[139] *American Weekly Mercury,* 8 March 1725/6. Elfreth was not the only one of Esther King's sons to have problems with servants. Joseph Lynn's Irish servant, Arthur Fleming, ran away in 1730, and one of his sawyers, James Bond, absconded in 1738. See *ibid.,* 7 May 1730; *Pennsylvania Gazette,* 15 June 1738.

[140] *A Collection of the Works of Thomas Chalkley in Two Parts* (Philadelphia, MDCCXLIX), 219.

[141] "Abstract of Wills, V, 1771-1780," *New Jersey Archives,* 1st Series, XXXIV, 18, abstract of will of Isaac Andrews. The abstract of his mother's will is on the same page. For his father Edward's will, see *ibid.,* XXIII, 13.

[142] Abstract of Haddonfield Monthly Meeting Records, 1681-1828, 26, 88, 188, GSP. See Hinshaw, II, 20, 51, for Elizabeth Andrews' movements and death.

[143] "The Elfreth Necrology," *PGSP,* II, 172-174, gives an account of the Elfreth family. The death of one Isaac Andrews on page 174 of that account, presumably is that of Isaac, son of Isaac and Elizabeth Andrews.

b. 7 4m 1754; d. 8 4m 1760, *ae. ca.* 6.   8. HANNAH ANDREWS, b. 27 4m 1757;
d. 10 7m 1758.   9. EBENEZER ANDREWS, b. 13 5m 1761; dec'd by 1775 when
his father wrote his will.   10. ESTHER ANDREWS, b. 26 11m 1763; living in 1777
when she left Haddonfield with her mother.

iii. JEREMIAH ELFRETH, JR., b. 1723; d. 11 2m 1765, *ae.* 42; m. at Philadelphia
Meeting 27 8m 1752, HANNAH TROTTER, b. 1728; bur. 29 5m 1791, *ae.*
62, daughter of Joseph Trotter and his wife Dinah Shelton.   Jeremiah was a
gold- and silversmith by trade.   In 1760 Charles Stow, Jr. sold to him and his
wife Hannah a house and lot on the east side of Second Street south of Mulberry.
They lived there until Jeremiah's death when his widow Hannah went to live
with her father Joseph Trotter on Second Street south of High until his death in
1770.[144]   When her father-in-law Jeremiah Elfreth died in 1772, he left to her
two sons his Second Street homestead and part of the property fronting Gilbert's
Alley, permitting her to have the rents and profits therefrom after the death of
his own wife until his grandsons came of age.   Hannah's sons, both cabinet-
makers, partitioned the Second Street and Alley property in 1791.[145]   Josiah took
the Second Street homestead and the easternmost part of the Alley land still owned
by their grandfather at his death; Josiah took the store, which Jeremiah, Sr. had
built south of and next to the Second Street home, and the western part of the
Alley tract.   Issue: 1. JEREMIAH ELFRETH, b. in Philadelphia 2 9m 1754; d. in
Haddonfield, N. J., 12 3m 1825, *ae.* 71; m. in New Jersey in 1775, MARY (ROB-
ERTS) TAYLOR, b. 1751; d. 30 4m 1813, *ae.* 62, daughter of Jacob and Hannah
Roberts and widow of William Taylor.   2. JOSEPH ELFRETH, d. in infancy 11
7m 1758.   3. JOSIAH ELFRETH, b. 2 5m 1759; d. testate in Philadelphia, prob-
ably of yellow fever, 8 9m 1793, *ae.* 35; m. at the Northern District Meeting in
Philadelphia 12 4m 1785, RACHEL CATHRALL, b. 1759; d. 26 11m 1802, *ae.*
43, daughter of Isaac and Hannah Cathrall.

iv. SARAH ELFRETH, d. unmarried in Philadelphia 12 2m 1751.[146]

5. Jeremiah Elfreth's second wife, whom he married at the Philadelphia Meeting 8 5m 1731, was LETITIA (SWIFT) RICHARDSON. She
was an English woman who had arrived in Philadelphia about 1726,
bringing a certificate from Endfield Meeting in Middlesex County, England, and the same year had married, as his second wife, the silversmith,
Francis Richardson. He died 17 6m 1729, leaving her with a small son
John Richardson, and two nearly grown stepsons, Francis and Joseph
Richardson.[147]

Present at Jeremiah's second marriage were a number of his relations

---

144 Deed Book H-10, 543: 9 Apr. 1760, Charles Stow, Jr. to Jeremiah Elfreth and wife Hannah. *Pennsylvania Archives*, 3rd Series, XIV, 154.

145 Deed Book EF-22, 80: 27 5m 1791, Josiah Elfreth to Jeremiah Elfreth.

146 Her death record identifies her as a daughter of Jeremiah, but does not name her mother.

147 The "Elfreth Necrology," cited above, in error calls Letitia a daughter of John Swift. See "Early
Minutes of Philadelphia Monthly Meeting of Friends," PGSP, VIII, 78, for notice of "Lettice" Swift's certificate, and Harold E. Gillingham, "The Cost of Old Silver," PMHB, LIV (1930), 42-43, for an account
of Francis Richardson.

of the half blood: his eldest half-brother, 1. John Bowyer, who died two years later, and his wife Sarah; his next eldest half-brother, 4. Joseph Lynn; and John and Sarah Elfreth, two of the children of his deceased half-brother Henry Elfreth. None of the Richardson sons appear to have witnessed the marriage, but there was a cordial connection between the two families. Certainly Jeremiah Elfreth patronized young Joseph Richardson, a silversmith like his father Francis, ordering from him between 1731 and 1737 such items as silver buttons and tankards. Quite likely, he apprenticed his own son Jeremiah, Jr. to Joseph Richardson.

Letitia Elfreth died, without issue by Jeremiah, little more than two years later on 16 9m 1733. Barely a year later, on 12 10m 1734, 5. Jeremiah Elfreth married his third wife, ELIZABETH MASSEY, daughter of Samuel Massey and his wife Sarah Wight. Presumably they were Irish: the family had arrived from Cork in 1710.[148] At this wedding, Jeremiah's immediate family was represented by his son Jeremiah, Jr., his daughter Elizabeth Elfreth, his half-brother 4. Joseph Lynn, and Sarah Bowyer, widow of his half-brother 1. John Bowyer. This marriage was even briefer than his second, for Elizabeth (Massey) Elfreth died without issue 23 8m 1735.

A month after her death, 4. Joseph Lynn and his wife Martha sold to Jeremiah for £150 part of the property Joseph had bought in 1728. The sale included the westernmost 51 feet of land on the south side of Sassafras Street, and the lot around the corner on the east side of Second, south of Sassafras. Elfreth subdivided the Sassafras Street property into three lots, erected houses on them and, in 1738 sold the westernmost to Isaac Zane who had married Jeremiah's niece Sarah Elfreth, daughter of Henry.[149] His interest in acquiring additional real estate may have been sparked by his role as one of the tax assessors that year, a position to which he was elected annually from 1739 through 1745.[150]

In February 1737/8, following his first election as a tax assessor, Jeremiah applied to the Philadelphia Monthly Meeting for a certificate to Westbury Monthly Meeting on Long Island "on account of marriage."

---

[148] Hinshaw, II, 592. For the will of Elizabeth's father, Samuel Massey, a tallow-chandler, see Will Book D, 167, #196:1720.

[149] For the Lynn sale, see Deed Book G-2, 88, cited in Note 101 above. For the sale to Isaac Zane, see recital in Deed Book D-42, 164: 27 May 1760, Jeremiah Elfreth to James Hunter. For Jeremiah's sale for £90 of the Second Street lot in 1740, see Deed Book G-6, 505: 25 March 1740, Jeremiah Elfreth to Charles Williams.

[150] The *Pennsylvania Gazette* regularly noted election results early in each October. Jeremiah was an assessor for the city in 1737, then for the county from 1739 to 1745.

At that place, on 30 1m 1738, he married his fourth wife, RACHEL SEA-
MAN, daughter of Nathaniel and Rachel Seaman of Rhode Island. The
following June, Rachel Elfreth presented to the Philadelphia Meeting
her own certificate from Newberry Monthly Meeting in Rhode Island.
A year and ten months later, on 9 12m 1738/9, she died, apparently in
childbirth.

Issue of 5. Jeremiah Elfreth by his 4th wife Rachel Seaman:

v. RACHEL ELFRETH, d. in infancy 20 12m 1738/9, just eleven days after her
mother's death.

Undeterred by the death of four wives, 5. Jeremiah Elfreth was soon
casting about for a fifth. Having gone far afield for his last wife, he
now looked around Philadelphia again for a suitable mate.

The land on the south side of Gilbert's Alley toward Second Street
now belonged to Mary Wells, widow of Arthur Wells, the youngest son
of the man who, with John Gilbert, originally had opened the alley.
Arthur Wells, Jr., Mary's husband, had died in 1732, leaving her with
two small daughters, Rebecca and Katharine, and possessed not only of
100 feet of unimproved land on the alley but two houses around on Second Street south of the alley, one of brick and the other of wood. She
also owned two more houses on the east side of Front between High and
Chestnut Streets.[151]

Still interested in real estate, Jeremiah bought the easternmost 32 feet
of the Wells's alley ground in December 1739.[152] Six months later, on
5 4m 1740, he married the widow MARY WELLS at the Philadelphia Meeting. Born in 1700, she appears to have been of Dutch ancestry, and was
the daughter of Klass (Claes) Berends by his wife Catharine Claesson.
Her parents, who were Mennonites, had arrived in Philadelphia the year
of her birth from Hamburg, with a group of members of the Mennonite Church at Altona on the right bank of the Elbe, immediately west
of Hamburg.[153]

Less than two months before his fifth marriage, Elfreth, his half-

---

151 See Will Book E, 211, #287:1732, will of Arthur Wells, for description of these properties.

152 The sale to Elfreth of the ground on which the present 124 and 126 Elfreth's Alley houses stand,
is recited in Deed Book I-1, 233: 14 5m 1762, Jeremiah Elfreth to Isaac Cassel.

153 See recital in Deed Book G-1, 306: 23 Oct. 1718, Lodowick Christian Sprogell to Philip Christian
Zimmerman, for Mary Wells' parentage. Her mother, Catherine Claesson, had married Sprogell after the
death of her husband Claes Berendts. See also Samuel W. Pennypacker, *The Settlement of Germantown* . . .
(Philadelphia, 1899), 139, for their arrival; also John C. Wenger, *History of the Mennonites of the Fran-
conia Conference* (Telford, Pa., 1937), 88-89.

brother 4. Joseph Lynn, his first wife's brother Joseph Oldman, who lived around on Front Street, and James Parrock bought on shares the Point-no-Point land south of the mouth of Frankford Creek. In 1741, the following year, Elfreth bought additional acreage at the Point at sheriff's sale as agent for the others and on the same share-basis.[154]

In 1745, Elfreth acquired title to the bank lot Arthur Wells had owned and, in 1746, bought a 100-foot lot on the northeast side of Hanover Street in Kensington for £93. Anthony Palmer, who had acquired 191 acres here in 1731, between the road to Frankford and Gunner's Run, had laid out streets and was selling off large lots.[155] As shipwrights began moving farther away from the city in order to enlarge their yards, men associated with ship-building followed suit. Four years after Elfreth became a landowner here in Kensington, his Lynn nephews followed his example.

By 1762, Jeremiah Elfreth had erected houses on the lots on the south side of Gilbert's Alley and on his remaining lots on the south side of Sassafras Street between Front and Second, and was advertising them for sale. He found buyers for the alley properties, but none for the others, and so continued to rent them to tenants. He also sold, for £1500, a tract of 75 acres at Point-no-Point, by now called Richmond, which was part of his allotment of the entire tract. The next year he bought one more house and lot on Sassafras east of his other lots, paying £600 "proclamation money of New Jersey" for it. Later that year, being then about seventy years old, he apparently decided to retire from business, for he advertised "a parcel of smith's tools for sale: Anvils, Bellows, vizes, Beak-irons, sledges and sundry other items." [156]

Seven years later, on 23 2m 1770, when he was "weak in body and advanced in years," he drew up his will. To his fifth wife Mary, he left his best feather beds and furniture, best chest of drawers and seven leather bottom chairs. Also, "in lieu of Dower," she was to have that part, fronting Water Street, of the bank lot which had belonged to her first husband, the rents and profits of the two westernmost houses on

---

[154] See Deed Books G-2, 274, cited in Note 126 above, for the first Point-no-Point purchase, and recital in G-3, 382: 11 Jan. 1742/3, James Parrock to Robert Hopkins, for the sheriff's sale to Elfreth.

[155] For the bank lot, see Deed Book H-20, 129: 17 Dec. 1745, George Wilson to Jeremiah Elfreth; for the Kensington lot, Deed Book H-16, 158: 2 Apr. 1746, Anthony Palmer *et al.* to Jeremiah Elfreth. See Logan MSS, Large Miscellaneous, 71, 77, HSP, for maps of the Palmer tract and the lots laid out within it.

[156] *Pennsylvania Gazette,* 29 Apr. 1762, 14 Apr. 1763. For the sale of the alley properties, see Deed Books I-1, 233, cited in Note 152 above, and 1-1, 429: 17 5m 1762, Jeremiah Elfreth to Mary Smith. For the sale of the Point-no-Point land, see Deed Book I-3, 525: 17 July 1762, Jeremiah Elfreth to Thomas Bowlby; for Elfreth's last acquisition, Deed Book H-20, 127: 5 Jan. 1763, John Smith to Jeremiah Elfreth.

Sassafras, one of which he had been renting to his son-in-law Robert Dawson, and £200 Pennsylvania money to be paid her within six months of his own death.

To his daughter Elizabeth Andrews, he left the third house and lot on Sassafras which he had bought in 1763, and after his wife's death, the other two Sassafras Street properties. In addition, Elizabeth was to have a portion of the property on the alley "now commonly called Elfreth's alley," which was part of the original homestead ground, and half of the lot in the Northern Liberties on Hickory Lane which he had bought from William Coats. He left to his two grandsons, Jeremiah and Josiah Elfreth, the other half of the Hickory Lane lot, the homestead and the remaining adjoining lots on Elfreth's Alley, as well as the store next to the homestead on Second Street.

To his youngest child Esther Dawson, he left the other part of the bank lot formerly Arthur Wells' fronting Front Street, and also the Kensington property. Esther was to have £300 paid her within six months of his death, and after his wife's death, the rest of the bank lot. To his son-in-law Isaac Andrews and his Elfreth grandsons, he left his wearing apparel, and released both Isaac and the estate of his own son Jeremiah, Jr. from all debts. He appointed his sons-in-law and his brother-in-law, Barnaby Barnes, Mary's brother, executors. A year later he appears to have had second thoughts, and by a codicil dated 22 6m 1771, gave to his wife for her life the rents and profits of their home and the store and the rest of the lot "thereto belonging," which he had devised to his grandsons.[157]

He lived for another year, and was buried 20 10m 1772, aged eighty years. His widow Mary survived him only a few months; she died 22 3m 1773, aged seventy-three.

Issue of 5. Jeremiah Elfreth by his 5th wife Mary (Barnes) Wells:

vi. ESTHER ELFRETH, b. *ca.* 1742; d. 17 12m 1819, *ae.* 77; m. at Philadelphia Meeting 25 6m 1765, ROBERT DAWSON, b. *ca.* 1744; d. testate 8 4m 1819, *ae.* 75, according to Northern District Monthly Meeting records. Son of Robert Dawson who had arrived from London prior to 1738, the year he married Mary Warner at Christ Church, Robert Dawson, Jr. was a staymaker by trade. He and his wife Esther lived in one of his father-in-law's houses on Sassafras Street until after the death of Mary (Barnes) Elfreth. In 1773, Robert announced he had moved his shop "from next door to the Friends Meeting House in Second street to the house in Third a little above Arch and the fourth door from the Golden Swan." They probably lived over the shop. By 1785, his store was in Water Street, second door above the corner of Chestnut, in the

---

157 Will Book P, 340, #231:1772, will of Jeremiah Elfreth. The will was proved the day after his burial. Both his death and that of his wife are entered in Northern District Monthly Meeting records.

former premises of Arthur Wells, and he was selling dry goods. In 1790, he was back in the old neighborhood on the east side of Second Street, in the brick house Arthur Wells had built south of Elfreth's Alley. In his household were 2 males over 16, including himself, 5 females and one other free person, probably a servant or lodger.[158] When he died, he seems to have been quite prosperous, leaving to his wife a legacy of $3000, as well as plate, books, horse carriage and chair; and to his son Josiah $2000 and shares in the Schuylkill Navigation Company. To his daughter Rebecca, he left shares in the Water Loan of the city, and in the Insurance Company of North America, in addition to $800 in cash. His real estate was to be shared by his two surviving children after his wife's death.[159] Issue: 1. REBECCA DAWSON, b. 1770; d. 25 1m 1855, unmarried. 2. JOSIAH DAWSON, b. 1 9m 1772; d. 29 8m 1858, ae. nearly 86, unmarried. 3. ELIZABETH DAWSON, b. *ca.* 1776; d. 21 11m 1809, ae. 33, unmarried.

---

[158] Charles C. Dawson, *Collection of Family Records . . . and Other Memorials of Various Families and Individuals Bearing the Name Dawson . . .* (Albany, N. Y., 1874), 189. *Pennsylvania Archives,* 3rd Series, XIV, 200; *Pennsylvania Gazette,* 15 Sept. 1773; *Pennsylvania Packet,* 8 June 1785; *1790 Pennsylvania Census,* 220.

[159] Will Book 7, 10, #49:1819, will of Robert Dawson. He and his wife were members of Northern District Monthly Meeting in Philadelphia.

Lynn Family Record*

Joseph Lynn Senyore was born the 14th of June in the year of our Lord 1691.

Joseph Lynn Senyore was married the 25th of December in the year of our Lord 1712.

Joseph Lyn Juner was born the 22nd day of Aprell in the morning betwixt 8 or 9 of the clock in ye year of our Lord 1716.

John Lyn was born the 17th of September at half an hour after 11 at night in the year of our Lord 1718.

Elizabeth Lyn was born ye 13th of June at 26 minutes after 9 in the Morning in the year of our Lord 1720, and the Second day of the week.

Martha Lynn was born the 29th of May at 50 minutes after Eleven in the morning and in the year of our Lord 1722.

Esther Lyn was born the 19th of February at 35 minutes after one in the morning and in the year of our Lord 1724.

Susanah Lyn was born ye 20th of September between two and three in the morning and in the year of our Lord 1725.

The Second Susanah Lyn was born the 18th of December between two and three in the morning and in the year of our Lord 1726.

Seth Lyn was born the 29th of September 3/4 after eleven at night and dyed the 27th of November following.

Martha Lyn wife of ———— departed this Life 16th of August 1736 at 8 Oclock in the evening.

Joseph Lyn Senr was married to his Wife Sarah the 25th of May 1737.

---

* As transcribed in *The Pennsylvania Magazine of History and Biography,* XVII (1893), 376-377.**

**The Lynn Family Record has also been reprinted in *Genealogies of Pennsylvania Families: From The Pennsylvania Magazine of History and Biography* (Baltimore: Genealogical Publishing Co., Inc., 1981), 878-879, under the title "Lynn-Marshall."

Jeremiah Lyn was born the 22nd of February about 4 of the Clock in the morning in the year 1738.

Sarah Lyn was born the 8th of October about half an hour after 6 in the Evening in the year 1739.

Hannah Lynn was born the 8th of August about 4 of the Clock in the morning in the year 174—.

Joseph Lynn Senr departed this life October ye 12th 1742 aged 51 years and 3 month 28 days.

Sarah Lynn wife of Joseph Lynn departed this life ye 4th of June 1759 at 6 in the morning aged 52 years 11 months and 28 days.

Hannah Lynn departed this life y^e 11th of January 1760 aged 18 years 4 months and 22 days at half an hour after 3 afternoon and Sixth day of the week.

Sarah Marshall was born December 11th 1762.

MEMORIALS OF THE KNEASS FAMILY OF PHILADELPHIA.*

CONTRIBUTED BY MISS ANNA J. MAGEE.

JOHAN CHRISTIAN [1] KNEASS,† the first of his name in Pennsylvania, doubtless a native of the Palatinate, arrived at Philadelphia, on the ship *Richard and Mary* from Rotterdam, John Moore Commander, about 17 September, 1753,‡ on which day he took the required oath of allegiance to the Crown of Great Britain and the Province of Pennsylvania. He settled in Philadelphia and was a resident of Mulberry Ward until his death in 1801. In signing his name he invariably omitted the "Johan," which is believed to have been the Christian name of his father.

His wife Christina, who died or was buried, 30 July, 1803,‖ joined him, as early as 1785, in sundry conveyances of land, and both were members of St. Michael and Zion's Evangelical Lutheran Church, where their children were baptized. She

---

* Compiled by J. Granville Leach.

† Name indifferently written Kniess, Kneass, Niess.

‡ *Penna. Archives*, second series, vol. xvii, p. 390.

‖ Buried in Lutheran Cemetery. *Publications of The Genealogical Society*, vol. i, p. 239.

was the sister of one of the wives of William Englefried who also came to Philadelphia in the *Richard and John* in 1753, and whose will * of 3 December, 1781, left legacies to three of his children then living near Carlsruh in Baden, Durlach, Germany, and to "late wife's sister, Christine Kneass."

Children, born in Philadelphia:

    i.   WILHELM,[2] b. 1 Mar., bpt. 10 Mar., 1754; bu. St. Michael's and Zion's ground, 26 Feb., 1759.

2. ii.   CHRISTOPHER, b. 18 Jan., bpt. 1 Feb., 1756; d. 1793.

   iii.   CATHARINE, b. 10 June, bpt. 2 July, 1758; m., Old Swedes' Church, Phila., 19 Mar., 1775, John Specht.

   iv.   CHRISTINA BARBARA, b. 6 Feb., bapt. 17 Feb., 1760; d. y.

   v.   DOROTHEA, m. circa 1784, Jacob Ettwein, b. Bethlehem, Penna., 9 Aug., 1760; d. Philadelphia, 28 Sept., 1798, of yellow fever, son of the Moravian Bishop, John Ettwein.† His will of 1 Sept., 1798, named wife Dorothea, children John Godfrey, John Jacob, Maria Magdalena, and Daniel Kliest and made "wife Dorothea, brother-in-law Daniel Kliest and his wife my sister Maria Magdalena," executors.

   vi.   WILHELMINA, b. 3 Nov., bpt. 9 Dec., 1764; d. unmarried, 17 Dec., 1813.

   vii.   CHRISTINA, b. 26 Feb., bpt. 6 Mar., 1766; m. (1) 7 Dec., 1783,‡ John Henry Horn of Germantown, by whom she had, Hon. Henry Horn, member of Congress, 1831-1833.

   viii.   CHRISTIAN, b. 16 Dec., bpt. 30 Dec., 1770.

2. CHRISTOPHER [2] KNEASS (*Johan Christian* [1]), was born at Philadelphia, 18 January, 1756, and died there in 1793. On 30 June, 1777, he took the oath of allegiance to Pennsylvania, thus manifesting his sympathy with the cause of the colonies in the Revolutionary struggle. He removed to Lancaster, Pennsylvania, about the time of the occupation of Philadelphia by the British || and there remained until 1785 or 1786, when he returned to Philadelphia.

* *Philadelphia County Probate Records, Abstracts of*, 1682-1825, in Collections of The Genealogical Society of Pennsylvania.

† John Ettwein, a distinguished clergyman of the American Moravian Church, born Freudenstadt, Wurtemberg, Germany, 29 June, 1721; descended from Protestant Refugees of Savoy; united with the Moravians 1739; was consecrated Bishop in 1784, and stood at the head of his Church in Pennsylvania until his death, at Bethlehem, in 1802. His wife, Joannetta Maria Kymbel, was born at Hackenburg, Nassau, Germany in 1725, married in 1746, came to Pennsylvania 1754; died at Bethlehem, 1789.—*Pennsylvania Magazine of History and Biography*, vol. ii, p. 156, and other writings of John W. Jordan, LL.D., on the Moravians.

‡ St. Michael's Evangelical Lutheran Church, Germantown.—Copy of, in the Collections of The Genealogical Society of Pennsylvania.

|| September 19 [1777]—At one o'clock this morning news came to town

He married at Lancaster in 1779, Anna Justina Feltman, born at Lancaster, 16 July, 1764; died at Philadelphia, 10 January, 1843, daughter of John Feltman, Esq * by his wife Anna Margaret. Their three eldest children were born at Lancaster, and baptized in its Trinity Evangelical Lutheran Church; the three youngest were born at Philadelphia.

Children:

3. i. WILLIAM,[3] b. 25 Sept., 1780; d. 27 Aug., 1840.
4. ii. JOHN, b. 4 Jan., 1783; d. 15 Aug., 1849.
  iii. MICHAEL, b. 20 April, 1784; m. ANNA LOUISA FINTHER. Issue: 1. *Stewart*.[4] 2. *Mars*. 3. *Charles*. 4. *Ann*. 5. *Nelson*, composer of the music of the well-known song, "Ben Bolt." 6. *Alonzo*. 7. *Martha*.
5. iv. CHRISTIAN, b. 16 Dec., 1787; d. 15 Jan., 1845.
  v. JACOB.
  vi. FREDERICK FELTMAN, died unmarried.

3. WILLIAM [3] KNEASS (*Christopher,*[2] *Johan Christian* [1]), born at Lancaster, Pennsylvania, 25 September, 1780; died at Philadelphia, 27 August, 1840. Educated at Philadelphia, he became a copper and steel-plate engraver and an artist of much repute and merit. On 24 October, 1824, he was appointed engraver and die-sinker of the United States Mint, and while in this position superintended changes in the coinage, notably the gold coins of 1834 and 1838, and the silver coins of 1836-7-8, and 1840. Prior to this he, at one time, was a member of the firm of Kneass & Dellaker and at another of Kneass, Young & Company, and his engraving office on Fourth Street above Chestnut, was a meeting place

that General Howe's army was crossing the Schuylkill at Swedes' Ford, which set many people moving. Congress and other public bodies left before daylight.—*Diary of Jacob Hiltzheimer.*

Sept. 26. Well! here are ye English in earnest; about 2 or 3000 came in through Second street, without opposition or interruption—no plundering on ye one side or ye other.—*Journal of Elizabeth Drinker.*

* John Feltman was a prominent citizen of Lancaster where he held the office of Burgess from 1764 until his death in April, 1777. His son, Lieutenant William Feltman, was an officer of distinction in the Continental Army; was commissioned ensign in Tenth Pennsylvania Regiment, 4 Dec., 1776, and was promoted first lieutenant, 7 Nov., 1777. Under the rearrangement of the Line in 1781 he was transferred to the First Pennsylvania Regiment, and, with his command, participated in the Southern campaign, which included the siege of Yorktown and the surrender of Cornwallis. His Journal, covering his service from 26 May, 1781 to 25 Apr., 1782, was published by The Historical Society of Pennsylvania in 1853. It contains several mentions of letters to and from " sister Nancy Kneass " and " brother Kneass."

for the leading wits and men of letters of that day. During the War of 1812, he was one of the volunteer association of field engineers, who constructed fortifications on the western front of Philadelphia to ward off attacks, and, in 1815, at the February meeting of the American Philosophical Society, Colonel Jonathan Williams placed on deposit "A very large and elegant Military Map of the Vicinity of Phila., made from actual survey for the Committee of Defence of the City, by Messrs. Strickland, Brooke and Kneass." In 1813 he exhibited at the Academy, a fine aquatint of Strickland's sketch, "A View of Quebec." From that time to 1824 he engraved several pictures, and did good work on illustrated books." He was one of the first members of the Franklin Institute, indeed it was from his suggestion that the Institute had its origin.†
He was also an early member of the Academy of Natural Sciences,‡ the Musical Fund and Artists Fund Societies, and a member of the famous "Beef Steak Club," ‖ which numbered among its devotees Judge John K. Kane, William Strickland,§ John Struthers, Titian Peale and other equally known cotemporaries. Several of his verses, composed for special occasions and sung by the author, testified to his keen sense of humor and good-fellowship. At the exhibition of the Artists Fund Society in 1841, a portrait of Mr. Kneass, by Sully, was exhibited by his son, Samuel H. Kneass. A good engraving of him, hangs in the Assayers' office, United States Mint.**

* Scharf and Westcott's *History of Philadelphia*, p. 1057.

† *Fiftieth Anniversary of the Organization of the Franklin Institute*, 1824-1874, p. 13 *et seq.*

‡ Admitted May, 1814. Foundation of Society, 21 March, 1812.

‖ That the members of this ancient organization did not confine their menu to beef steak is evidenced by the diarist William Black of Virginia, who, during his stay in Philadelphia, in 1744, makes mention under date of Saturday, June 2d., of his visit " to the Tunn Tavern to Dine, having an Invitation the day before from the Governor who is a Member of the Clubb or certain Number of Gentlemen that Meet at this house every Saturday to Eat Beef-Steakes, and from that is Call'd the Beef-Stake Clubb; but when Dinner came there was more than twenty Dishes besides that of Stakes."—*Pennsylvania Magazine of History and Biography*, vol. i, p. 409.

§ WILLIAM STRICKLAND, 1789-1854, an architect without any superior in his own time in Philadelphia. With him was associated John Struthers, who came to Philadelphia, in 1816 from Glasgow, Scotland, where he and his father had been prominent architects and builders.

** *History of United States Mint* (1893), pp. 126-7.

He married 1st, 23 June, 1804, Mary Turner, daughter of William Honeyman,* by his wife Jane Davison, born 15 March, 1785; died 9 May, 1826. His second wife, Jane Kramer, died 3 October, 1854.

Children, by first marriage, all born at Philadelphia:

    i.   FULLERTON TULLY,[4] b. 14 March, 1805; admitted United States Military Academy, West Point, N. Y., 1820.

6. ii. SAMUEL HONEYMAN, b. 5 Nov., 1806; d. 15 Feb., 1858.

    iii. ANNA, b. 21 Jan., 1809; d. 3 April, 1811.

    iv. JANE HONEYMAN, twin of Anna, m. 24 Oct., 1835, JOHN L. McMULLIN, JR., of Philadelphia, and had issue.

    v. JOHN FELTMAN, b. 22 Dec., 1811; d. 17 April, 1831.

7. vi. STRICKLAND, b. 29 July, 1821; d. 14 Jan., 1884.

4. JOHN [3] KNEASS (*Christopher,*[2] *Johan Christian* [1]), born at Lancaster, Pennsylvania, 4 January, 1783; died at Philadelphia, 15 August, 1849. He was a prominent copper-plate printer and printed the notes of the United States Bank. Some years before his decease he retired from business, and is styled "gentleman" in the City Directories.

He married in 1804, Margaret, daughter of Major John Polhemus by his wife Susanna Hart, and granddaughter of the Hon. John Hart, a Signer of the Declaration of Independence. Mrs. Kneass was born at Hopewell, New Jersey, 9 February, 1783, and died at Philadelphia, April 21, 1854.

Children, born at Philadelphia:

    i. CAREY FELTMAN,[4] b. 5 Dec., 1804; d. Nov., 1852; m. (1) MARY ANN PROCTOR of Petersburg, Va., who died circa 1840; m. (2) 27 May, 1841, Emma McMichael. At the time of his decease Mr. Kneass was Inspector of Customs at Philadelphia. Issue: 1. *Margaret,*[5] b. 28 Dec., 1828; m. (1) Lafayette McDonald; m. (2) Samuel Goforth Page; had issue by both marriages. 2. *Lela Vultee,* b. 11 Aug., 1831; m. 12 June, 1852, William Wilson; had issue. 3. *Mary,* b. 23 Apr., 1837; d. 7 Aug., 1879; m. William Gal-

* William Honeyman, son of William Honeyman by his second wife Mary Wilson, born at Phila., 3 June, 1759; died there, 25 June, 1783. Commissioned 5 Feb., 1777, second lieutenant in the Second Pennsylvania Continental Line, commanded by Colonel John Philip De Haas, he was wounded at the battle of Iron Hill. In consequence of being disqualified for duty in the field he was transferred to the Invalid Corps, under Colonel Lewis Nicola, where he remained until 15 Dec., 1784. He married, 9 Nov., 1780, Jane Davison or Davisson. He left but two children, a son, Samuel Davison Honeyman, and a daughter, Mary Turner Honeyman, both of whom are named in his will, the latter becoming the wife of William Kneass, as named in the text. The elder William Honeyman, born in England, 2 Dec., 1711, died at Phila., 14 March, 1777; his children were baptized at Christ Church.

braith; no issue. 4. *Alexander*, b. 1842; 5. *Edmund Rich-ardson*, b. 23 June, 1845; married and had issue. 6. *Susan Moody*, b. 11 Sept., 1851; m. William H. Horton, and had issue.

ii. EDWARD POLHEMUS, b. 8 Aug., 1806; d. y.
iii. SUSAN MOODY, b. 26 Aug., 1808; d. y.
iv. EDWIN, b. 27 Feb., 1810; d. y.
v. WILLIAM STRICKLAND, b. 8 Jan., 1812; m. ANN WALKER. Issue:
1. *Joseph*.[5] 2. *Annc*. 3. *Catharine*. 4. *William*. 5. *Mary*.
vi. HANSON ALEXANDER, b. 6 March, 1713; married twice and had issue.
vii. ROBERT WATERLOO, b. 2 Nov., 1815; m. KATE CLARE. Issue:
James Thomas,[5] b. 22 Jan., 1858; m. 16 Apr., 1880, Mary Caroline Charlton, a great-great-granddaughter of Hon. John Hart, the "Signer."
viii. DALLAS ALEXANDER, b. 26 Sept., 1817; m. (1) 10 Sept., 1840, REBECCA WRAY HART, a great-granddaughter of Hon. John Hart, the "Signer." Mr. Kneass resided in Colorado in 1876.
ix. JAMES AKIN, b. 9 Nov., 1819; m. SARAH JANE JONES, who died at Philadelphia, 1 Nov., 1874. Issue: 1. *Lela Vultee*,[5] b. 21 Feb., 1852; d. 8 Apr., 1853. 2. *Mary Emma*, b. 25 May, 1854; d. 24 Feb., 1855. 3. *Mary Edna*, b. 6 Sept., 1856; d. 26 June, 1860. 4. *Grace Matilda*, b. 4 June, 1859; m. 6 June, 1882, David Even Camp. 5. *Ida Dunlap*, b. 28 Oct., 1860; m. 3 Feb., 1881, William Lewis Roth, and had issue. 6. Napoleon Bonaparte, b. 2 Feb., 1863.
x. CHRISTIAN, b. 20 Dec., 1821; died without issue.
xi. JOHN HART, b. 17 June, 1823; d. s. p. 1 April, 1846.
xii. ALFRED WEAVER, b. 25 May, 1826; m. 24 June, 1848, MARGARET CUNNINGHAM, dau. of William Cunningham. Issue:
1. *Amanda*,[5] b. 7 May, 1849; d. 1875; m. John Scully, and had issue: 2. *Virginia*, b. 1851; d. 1880; m. Joseph Hall; had issue. 3. *John*. 4. *Dallas A*. 5. *Sarah*, d. 1 June, 1862, "aged 15 mos., 29 days."

5. CHRISTIAN [3] KNEASS (*Christopher*,[2] *Johan Christian* [1]), born at Philadelphia, 16 December, 1787; died there, 15 January, 1845. His life was spent in his native city, where he was a prosperous merchant and manufacturer of saddlery hardware, his partner in business being his cousin, the Hon. Henry Horn, member of Congress in 1831-1833. During the War of 1812 he was in service in the Second Troop, Philadelphia Cavalry, commanded by Captain William Rawle, Jr.; * and in 1830 and 1831 he was a Common Councilman of Philadelphia, and an incorporator of the Girard National Bank in 1832. He was active in the counsels of the Democratic party, and the personal friend of President Jackson. It was upon his suggestion, it is said, that the first "Hickory Club" was formed to promote the election of that gentleman to the Presidency.

* *Pennsylvania Archives*, 2nd. ser., vol. xii. p. 386.

In 1844 Mr. Kneass was a Presidential Elector on the Democratic ticket.

He married, at Philadelphia, 14 May, 1810, Sarah Axford,* born at Trenton, New Jersey, 7 June, 1790; died at her residence on Arch Street above Thirteenth, 11 December, 1865. Mrs. Kneass was a granddaughter of Major John Polhemus † of the New Jersey Line in the Revolution, and a legatee named in his will, proved at Philadelphia, 5 June, 1834, of which Mr. Kneass was an executor, and a great-granddaughter of Hon. John Hart, of New Jersey, a Signer of the Declaration of Independence.

Children, all born in Philadelphia:

8. i.   CAROLINE AXFORD, b. 18 Sept., 1810; d. 8 Sept., 1886.
9. ii.   HORN RILEY, b. 10 Apr., 1813; d. 12 Dec., 1861.
   iii.   CHARLES AXFORD, b. 4 Oct., 1814; d. 24 July, 1815.
   iv.   SUSANNA POLHEMUS, b. 9 May, 1816; d. 14 April, 1817.
10. v.   NAPOLEON BONAPARTE, b. 17 April, 1818; d. 16 March, 1888.
   vi.   CORA MOODY, b. 21 Jan., 1820; d. 10 March, 1833.
   vii.   FREDERICK FELTMAN, b. 21 Jan., 1822; d. 21 Oct., 1854.
   viii.   FELTMAN HORACE EDWARD, b. 7 June, 1824; d. at New Orleans, 19 June, 1852; m. LEOCADIE GRASS of New Orleans.
   ix.   SARAH AXFORD, b. 10 June, 1826; d. 26 Jan., 1889; m. 3 Nov., 1853, SAMUEL SPARHAWK, b. Philadelphia, 25 Dec., 1823; d. there, 22 May, 1883. Issue: 1. *Helen Sparhawk,*[5] b. 17 Oct., 1854; d. 17 Sept., 1886. 2. *Samuel Sparhawk,* b. 16 Mar., 1856; d. 26 Dec., 1907; m. 9 Jan., 1894, Grace Emily Rafsnyder. 3. *Richard Dale Sparhawk,* b. 25 June, 1861; d. 21 Sept., 1913; m. 3 Nov., 1891, Mary E., dau. Robert Hume of Phila., who survived him; he was, for thirty-eight years preceding his decease, connected with the Mutual Life Insurance Company of New York; was a vice-president of the Philadelphia Association of Life Underwriters, a warden of the Church of the Atonement, and held membership in the Pennsylvania Society of the Order of Founders and Patriots of America and in the Pennsylvania Society of Sons of the Revolution. 4. *Horace Kneass Sparhawk,* b. 22 Dec., 1864; d. 6 July, 1866. 5. *Catharine Passmore Sparhawk,* b. 25 Sept., 1866. 6. *Edward Magee Sparhawk,* b. 10 Sept., 1868; m. Sept., 1898, Mary Howard of Denver, Colorado, and has issue. 7. *Louise Everly Sparhawk,* b. 21 June, 1870.
   x.   JACKSON CHRISTIAN, b. 30 June, 1828; d. 23 Oct., 1829.
   xi.   VIRGINIA SUSAN, b. 10 Oct., 1830.
   xii.   CORA MOODY, b. 3 Sept., 1833; d. 1909; m. 18 May, 1863, JOHN FREDERICK MAYO of New York. Issue: 1. *James Magee*[5] *Mayo,* b. 30 July, 1864; d. 17 June, 1865. 2. *Cora Evangeline Mayo,* b. 10 Mar., 1866. 3. *Lillian L. Mayo,* b. 20 Dec.,

* *Records of St. John's Evangelical Lutheran Church, Philadelphia,* Copy of, in Collections of The Genealogical Society of Pennsylvania.

† *Colonial and Revolutionary Families of Pennsylvania,* vol. i, p. 634.

1867. 4. *Carrie Madeleine Mayo*, b. 29 Sept., 1869; d. 1917. 5.
Jeannetta Olivia Mayo, b. 11 Nov., 1871; d. 13 Feb., 1873.
Helen Sparhawk Mayo, b. 25 Aug., 1873; d. 31 Aug., 1873.
7. *Marceleine Virginia Mayo*, b. 22 Aug., 1874; m. 27 June,
1894, Louis Clarence Bennett, of Brooklyn, New York.

6. SAMUEL [4] HONEYMAN KNEASS (*William*,[3] *Christopher*,[2]
Johan Christian [1]), was born at Philadelphia, 5 November,
1806, and died there 15 February, 1858. At an early age he
began the study of engineering in the offices of William Strickland, the most noted native architect of his time, who had
turned some of his attention to construction of railroads. In
1825 he went to England as assistant to Mr. Strickland, who
was commissioned, by the Pennsylvania Society for the Promotion of Internal Improvements, to examine into the canal
and railway system there, with a view to recommend methods
of construction for the proposed steam road from Philadelphia
to Columbia. Shortly after his return Mr. Kneass was appointed chief engineer of the North Western Railroad, and in
July, 1835, in conjunction with Mr. Strickland, he surveyed
and located a route for the Philadelphia and Delaware County
Railroad, which crossed the Schuylkill at or near Penrose, or
the old "Rope," Ferry. In April, 1836, he was appointed
chief engineer, and altered the road's approach to the city
by means of the present site of Gray's Ferry Bridge. In this
year the name of the road was changed to the Philadelphia,
Wilmington and Baltimore Railroad. He was also engaged in
the construction of the important waterways of the State,
principally that of the Delaware and Schuylkill Canal. In
1839 he again went to England on railroad business. On 26
April, 1849, he was appointed Principal City Surveyor, and
served as such until 9 May, 1853.

He married 14 March, 1837, Anna Arndt Lombaert of
Morrisville, Pennsylvania. Her portrait, by Sully, was
painted in 1839.

Children, born in Philadelphia:

i. CHARLES LOMBAERT,[5] b. 14 Dec., 1837; educated at Thomas
D. James' School, Phila., he entered the scientific department of Brown University in 1858, and engaged in the iron
business at Philadelphia the following year. At the outbreak of the Civil War he enlisted in April, 1861, as corporal in the "Washington Grays," and was commissioned 14

173

May, 1861, first lieutenant of the Eighteenth United States Infantry; joined his regiment at Columbus, Ohio, where he was made post-adjutant. In 1862, he was, for meritorious service, advanced to a captaincy and was killed at the head of his company at Murfreesboro, Tennessee, 31 December, 1862. Buried where he fell, his body was afterwards removed to Woodlands Cemetery, Philadelphia, and his name is inscribed on the monument, later erected in Washington Square, to the memory of the ''Washington Grays.'' He was unmarried.

ii. WILLIAM HARRIS, b. 18 June, ₋839; d. Boerne, Texas, 1 June, 1882; entered the scientific department of Brown University with his brother Charles in the Class of 1858; and afterward entered the Naval Academy, Annapolis, Md., but left to engage in civil engineering. He m. 15 July, 1863, AMELIA PRALL STRYKER, b. 23 Aug., 1839; d. Vevey, Switzerland, 10 Apr., 1878, daughter of Samuel Davis Stryker, by his wife Eliza Carr. Issue: *Samuel Stryker*,[6] b. Germantown, 16 Jan., 1865; was graduated Univ. of Penna., A. B. 1886; M. D. 1889; studied at Universities of Goettingen, Vienna and Paris, 1891-1892; is Associate, William Pepper Laboratory and Clinical Medicines, Univ. of Penna., member of University, Racquet, Union League and Pine Valley Golf clubs. 2. *Charles Lombaert*, d. y. 3. *David*, d. y.

iii. MARY HONEYMAN, b. 18 Jan., 1841; d. 18 Jan., 1900; m. 24 July, 1866, EDWARD RANDOLPH WOOD, ESQ., of Philadelphia. Mr. Wood was graduated, Haverford Coll. 1856; A. M. 1859; LL.B. Univ. of Penna., 1861; became identified with the business house of R. D. Wood & Co., and other large enterprises, but now, 1919, retired; many years vice-president of the Philadelphia Board of Trade, he was also chairman of the Correspondence Committee of the National Board of Trade, and, in 1912, was a delegate to the Republican National Convention of that year; he is a member of the Philadelphia and Art clubs, and was sometime president of the Penn Club. Issue: 1. *Juliana* [6] *Wood*, 2d., 2. *Marian H. Wood*. 3. *Charles Randolph Wood*, m. Margaret S. Voorhees, and has issue. 4. *Edward Randolph Wood, Jr.* Captain, U. S. A.

iv. SAMUEL HONEYMAN, b. 1844.

v. FRANKLIN.

7. STRICKLAND [4] KNEASS (*William*,[3] *Christopher*,[2] *Johan Christian* [1]), born at Philadelphia, 29 July, 1821; died there, 14 January, 1884. Educated chiefly at James P. Espy's Classical Academy of Philadelphia, he later entered the Rensselaer Institute at Troy, New York, from which he was graduated, civil engineer, in 1839, taking the highest honors. Soon after he was made assistant engineer and topographer on the State Survey for a railroad between Harrisburg and Pittsburgh. Subsequently he was employed by the British Commission in preparing the maps of the northeast boundary be-

tween the United States and the Provinces, and, by the Federal government, on the general map of the boundary-survey. In 1847 he was appointed by the Pennsylvania Railroad principal assistant engineer for the construction of its road across the Alleghenies, and, in connection with Mr. J. Edgar Thompson, laid out the well known " Horse-Shoe Curve," one of the most difficult engineering feats of the day. In 1855 he accepted the position of chief engineer and surveyor of the newly consolidated City of Philadelphia, to which he was re-elected three times, each for a term of five years. During his tenure of office, and under his direction, the Department of Surveys and Registry Bureau was organized and developed, and, under his surveys, an entire drainage system was provided for the city. Of the various bridges which during this period, came to span the Schuylkill River, those at Chestnut Street and at Callowhill Street were built from his designs.* He resigned this position, in 1872, to accept that of assistant to the president of the Pennsylvania Railroad, which he continued to fill until his death, at which time he was president of ten railroads associated with the Pennsylvania system, and was a director in forty-four companies.

In the Civil War he took a strong stand for the support of the Union; served as assistant engineer, with the rank of captain, in laying out fortifications in southern Pennsylvania, and was made chief engineer and major in the Home Guard. He also assisted in the preparation of topographical maps of the surroundings of Philadelphia with a view to the location of forts and other devices to protect the city from invasion.

One of the early members of the Union League he was, for many years, a director thereof, also a member of the American Philosophical Society, American Society of Civil Engineers, the Franklin Institute, the Engineers Club of Philadelphia, of which latter organization he was president in 1881, and an active member of the Old Seventh Presbyterian Church, and president of its Board of Trustees from 1872 until 1884.

He married, 17 August, 1853, Margaretta Sybilla Bryan, born 29 December, 1823, daughter of Hon. George Bryan, Auditor-General of Pennsylvania under Governors McKean,

* Scharf and Westcott's *History of Philadelphia*, vol. iii. p. 1749.

Snyder and Finley, and granddaughter of the Hon. George Bryan, president of the Supreme Executive Council of Pennsylvania in 1778.

Children, born at Philadelphia:

i. ANNA,[5] b. 4 Oct., 1854; d. 6 Feb., 1855.

ii. MARY BRYAN, b. 2 Nov., 1855; m. 30 Mar., 1880, ISAAC C. OGDEN; had issue.

iii. MARGIE BRYAN, b. 4 Dec., 1859; m. 20 Apr., 1882, J. RALSTON GRANT of Philadelphia; had issue.

iv. STRICKLAND LANDIS, b. 7 Jan., 1861; educated at Rugby Academy, Philadelphia, and Rensselaer Polytechnic Institute, Troy, N. Y., from which latter he was graduated civil engineer in 1880; has been connected with William Sellers & Company, Philadelphia, since 1883, and manager of injector department since 1895; awarded the John Scott Medal and premium by the Franklin Institute in 1900, for meritorious inventions; * contributor to engineering journals, and author of Practice and Theory of the Injector, a work which received commendation from the technical world; member of Franklin Institute, American Mechanical Engineers, American Railroad Master Mechanics' Assn., the University, Engineers, Philobiblon and Merion Cricket clubs, and the Penna. Socy. Sons of the Revolution. He m. 24 Oct., 1888, MARY STEWART EDWARDS, b. 15 May, 1864, dau. of Isaac C. and Charlotte (Brown) Edwards of Red Bank, N. J. Issue: 1. *Strickland* [6] *Kneass*, b. 10 July, 1889; Renss. Inst. '11; Lieutenant, U. S. A.; m. Martha Owsley. 2. *Edwards Kneass*, b. 7 Apr., 1891; Renss. Inst., '13; Lieutenant U. S. N. 3. *George Bryan Kneass*, b. 25 Oct., 1897; Univ. Pa., '18; Ensign U. S. N.

v. SAMUEL BRYAN, b. 15 Oct., 1862; m. 10 April, 1892, ANNIE WATSON BROWNLIE.

vi. HENRIETTA LOGAN, b. 3 Mar., 1869; m. 20 May, 1891, REV. STANLEY WHITE of Orange, N. J., b. 2 May, 1862; had issue.

8. CAROLINE [4] AXFORD KNEASS (*Christian,*[3] *Esq., Christopher,*[2] *Johan Christian* [1]), was born at Philadelphia, 18 September, 1810 and died at Bryn Mawr, Pennsylvania, 8 September, 1886. She was married, by the Rev. James Montgomery, D. D., rector of St. Stephen's Church, Philadelphia, 4 July, 1830, to James Magee, born at Philadelphia, 5 December, 1802; died there 3 November, 1878, eldest son of Michael †
and Francis (McAdoo) Magee.

* Who's Who in America, 1917-8.

† MICHAEL MAGEE, founder of the Magee family of Philadelphia, descended from sturdy Scotch covenanters who left Scotland for Ireland during the reign of the Stuarts. His immediate forebears were established at Rathmullen, in the extreme northern part of County Donegal, sometime before the middle of the eighteenth century, and here Michael Magee was born. In 1785 he was married, by the Rev. William Gamble, pastor of the Reformed

James Magee's first schooling was in the dames school of Mrs. Knox,* which he left to enter Dr. Walton's school for boys. At an early age he entered the pottery establishment of James Ronaldson and shortly afterward obtained a better position in the type-foundry of Messrs Binny and Ronaldson,† going later into the employ of Peter Dickson & Company, manufacturers of saddlery-hardware, etc. at Market and Decatur streets, Philadelphia, where he obtained a thorough

Church of Letterkenny, to Frances McAdoo of Rathmelton, in the same county. He came to Philadelphia in 1792 and immediately became book-keeper in the offices of Leedom & Lawrence, the well known iron founders, his wife and two children following prior to 1796. He died at Philadelphia, 31 Dec., 1804, his widow surviving until Dec., 1823. Their children were: *Frances, Lydia, Elizabeth, James* and *Michael*.

MICHAEL MAGEE, the youngest child, was born at Phila., 27 Feb., 1805; and died there 8 Oct., 1884. His business association as a member of the firm of James Magee & Co. began in 1830 and continued until 1 July, 1847 when a new firm was formed by Michael Magee and Napoleon B. Kneass, under the firm name of M. Magee & Co. in Philadelphia and Magee & Kneass in New Orleans, this partnership lasting until Jan. 1, 1865, when the firm was succeeded by Kneass & Mayo. In 1829 the Philadelphia office removed from No. 9, to 31 South Fourth street, remaining there until 1839, when it became established at 18 Decatur, now 24 to 26 Marshall street, and, at this location, Michael Magee continued until 1865, when he withdrew from active business life. During the Rebellion, the New Orleans house of Magee & Kneass occasioned Mr. Magee grave anxiety and much of his business and land interests in the Southern States were confiscated by the Confederate government. Deeply attached to farm life he was, at various times, the owner of several fine farms, the last was near Villa Nova, Montgomery county, on the old Gulph Road. He was a life member of the Penn. State Agricultural Society, the Penna. Horticultural Society and The Historical Society of Pennsylvania. He married 31 March, 1831, Catharine, daughter of George and Catharine (Wise) Horter of Gwynedd township, Montgomery county, Penna., whose ancestors had been prominently identified with the affairs of Germantown, before the middle of the eighteenth century. Their children were: 1. *George W.*, m. 28 Feb., 1855, Kate Widdowfield, and had issue. 2. *James Francis*, m. 1 Dec., 1859, Cynthia A. Jardin, and had issue. 3. *Michael S.*, d. y. 4. *Michael Horter*, d. 5 July, 1878. 5. *William Stewart*, m. 13 Nov., 1879, Eveline C. Frickie. For further particulars of this branch of the family, see *Colonial and Revolutionary Families of Pennsylvania*, vol. i, p. 578 *et seq.*

* A highly educated Irish lady and member of Dr. Wylie's Presbyterian church, who taught both boys and girls.

† Type founding was commenced in Philadelphia in 1796, by Andrew Binny and James Ronaldson, natives of Edinburgh in Scotland, where Binny had carried on the same business. After the retirement of Binny and Ronaldson, Richard Ronaldson continued the business and was in turn succeeded by Lawrence Johnson and George F. Smith. James Ronaldson was the first president of the Franklin Institute, 1824-1841; vice-president of the St. Andrew's Society of Philadelphia, 1829-30, and owned and laid out, in 1827, what is known as Ronaldson's Philadelphia Cemetery, as a burial place " for the interment of his friends and deceased human beings other than people of color."—For portrait and sketch of, see *Historical Catalogue of St. Andrew's Society.*

knowledge of this business. In 1824 he and a boyhood friend, George Taber, purchased the southern branch of Dickson & Company's trade at New Orleans, and organized the firm of Magee & Taber, with a manufacturing establishment at Fourth street near Market. So excellent were the products of the young firm that, within the first year of its operation, the attention of the Franklin Institute was attracted thereto and it received the first medal ever awarded for that branch of manufacture. At New Orleans, in 1824, there was but one firm in the saddlery-hardware business and this had the monopoly of the South-west trade, but the quality and style of the goods put forth by the new Philadelphia firm and shipped to New Orleans for sale, in its branch-house near Magazine and Canal streets, in that city, soon claimed recognition. Though remotely situated from the base of supplies and operated on a system of barter and long credits, the business grew rapidly and the profits were enormous to 1839 when competition decreased them. Meanwhile, Michael Magee, younger brother of the senior partner, entered the firm, which, in 1830, became James Magee & Co. in New Orleans and Magee, Taber & Co. in Philadelphia. So successful did the southern trade become that the brothers were led to invest largely in lands in the southern states, purchasing in 1841 over three thousand acres in Scott County, Mississippi,* and in, or about, 1846, over four thousand acres in Wilburger county, Texas.† On July 1, 1847, James Magee and George Taber retired from the business and a new firm was formed. Shortly before 1845, Mr. Magee had become interested in the projection of the Pennsylvania Railroad and used much effort to persuade Governor Shunk to sign the bill creating the charter of the corporation against the opposition of the Baltimore and Ohio Railroad. Indeed, so large was his vision and influence in the final attainment of the road that, he has been called "the father of the Pennsylvania Railroad." One of the incor-

---

* During the Civil War this land was confiscated by the Confederate government, but after 1866, the Federal government returned it to the rightful owners.

† In 1836 Texas revolted from Mexico and established a republic. Magee & Co., received large orders for saddles, etc. from the Lone Star State, and for part payment had land-claims in that State.

porators named in its charter, he was in its first directorate, and continued therein many years; he was also a director of the Harrisburg, Lancaster, Portsmouth and Mt. Joy Railroad, known as the Harrisburg Railroad; the founder of the Westmoreland Coal Company, its first president and member of its Board of Directors in continuous service from 1856 until his decease. In politics, he was first a Whig and subsequently a Republican and deeply deplored the course of his southern friends before and during the Civil War. After the war he gave much timely aid to Dr. Emanuel of Vicksburg, Mississipi, president of the Vicksburg & Meridan Railroad, in the rehabilitation of that company. He was a vestryman of St. Stephen's Episcopal Church from 1861 until his death in 1878. His portrait and that of his wife, by Sully, are in the possession of his only surviving daughter.

Children, all born in Philadelphia:

i. FANNIE SARAH [5] MAGEE, b. 11 July, 1832; d. at Atlantic City, N. J., 11 Aug., 1916; was the first president of the Woman's Auxiliary of St. Stephen's Church, a member of the Pennsylvania Society of Colonial Dames of America, the Philadelphia Chapter, Daughters of the American Revolution, the Sedgeley Club, the Associate Committee of Women to the Board of Trustees of the School of Industrial Art, the Academy of Fine Arts and other civic and social organizations, and was the author of an article on Major John Polhemus, in the *American Monthly Magazine*, September, 1896.

ii. CAROLINE LYDIA MAGEE, b. 20 Mar., 1836; d. 26 June, 1861.

iii. ELIZA JANE MAGEE, b. 10 Sept., 1837; d. 20 Apr., 1906; was a member of the Pennsylvania Society of the Colonial Dames of America and the Philadelphia Chapter, Daughters of the American Revolution.

iv. JAMES RONALDSON MAGEE, b. 18 Mar., 1839; d. unmarried, 3 Nov., 1914. His business life was centered in his father's large interests in the coal and iron industries of the State, particularly the Westmoreland Coal Company. He held membership in The Historical and Genealogical Societies of Pennsylvania, the Philadelphia Country and Union League clubs. With his sisters he united in establishing a memorial fund, in honor of their brother, Horace Magee, which should defray the expense attendant upon the Annual Church Service of the Pennsylvania Society Sons of the Revolution, in commemoration of General Washington's army going into winter quarters at Valley Forge, and insure the continuance of the service in the same style and beauty observed during their brother's life. Together with his brother and sisters he conferred many notable benefactions on St. Stephen's Church, and his last act of public benevolence was the endowment of the Library of the Philadelphia College of Physicians.

179

v. ANNA JUSTINA MAGEE, b. 21 Jan., 1843; is a member of the Acorn Club, the Pennsylvania Society Colonial Dames of America; the Philadelphia Chapter, Daughters of the American Revolution; the Associate Committee of Women to the Board of Trustees of the Pennsylvania School of Industrial Art, The Historical and Genealogical Societies of Pennsylvania and many civic and religious organizations. In 1917 she added to the memorials already bestowed by her family upon St. Stephen's Church, the present chancel with its reredos and furniture in memory of her eldest sister, and in 1918 she completed her first gift by an entire renovation of the church interior in keeping with the unique character of the chancel, thus making of the whole a filial tribute to her father.

vi. HORACE MAGEE, b. 29 Nov., 1845; d. unmarried, 4 Jan., 1912; was graduated at the University of Pennsylvania in the Class of 1865; studied law and was admitted to the Philadelphia bar, October 17, 1868, but never took up active practice, the large business interests of his father, as well as his own, engaging his attention. His principal energies were devoted to the organization and management of coal, iron and trolley systems. He was the organizer of Jeanette, Pennsylvania, which has grown to a town of more than ten thousand inhabitants; a director of the Kittanning Coal Company, the oldest director in point of service of the Westmoreland Coal Company, and a member of The Historical, Genealogical and Colonial societies of Pennsylvania, the Art, Philadelphia and Germantown Cricket clubs, and one of the most serviceable members of the Board of Managers of the Pennsylvania Society of Sons of the Revolution, in which organization he was deeply interested. He was zealous in the advancement of St. Stephen's Church, and a co-contributor to such of the Magee memorials in this church as antedated his decease.

vii. FRANK HAMILTON MAGEE, b. 20 Sept., 1854; d. unmarried, 2 Aug., 1904.

9. HORN RILEY [4] KNEASS (*Christian,*[3] *Esq., Christopher,*[2] *Johan Christian* [1]), born at Philadelphia, 10 April, 1813; died there 12 December, 1861; was graduated at the University of Pennsylvania in the Class of 1830; studied law under Hon. George Mifflin Dallas, afterwards vice-president of the United States, and was admitted to the Bar, 14 September, 1833.

He was the Solicitor for the District of Moyamensing from 1839 until 1842; for Philadelphia County in 1847 and 1848, and for the district of Penn Township from 1848 until 1850. During the latter year, the consolidation of the city of Philadelphia was perfected, and the office of District Attorney for the county created. He was nominated for this office by the Democratic party, and at the fall election of that year was returned as elected, and entered on the duties of the office, in which he was the first to serve. His election, however, was contested by his Whig opponent, William B. Reed, Esq., and resulted in the latter securing the place after Mr. Kneass has been in office about one year.

An eminent member of the Order of Odd Fellows, he held the position of Grand Master of the Order in Pennsylvania, and on 21 September, 1847, was installed Grand-Sire of the Grand Lodge of the United States. He was also a prominent member of the Masonic Order and Master of Washington Lodge, No. 59, F. & A. M., in 1843, and one of the founders of the Glenwood Cemetery Company.

The day following Mr. Kneass' death, a meeting of the Philadelphia bar was held, at which the Hon. George Sharswood presided, and these resolutions were adopted:

Resolved, That the Bar has heard with unfeigned regret of the death of their much esteemed brother, Horn R. Kneass, Esq.

Resolved, That the death of Mr. Kneass has removed from our midst one whose courtesy and kindness of manner, integrity and liberality of character, both professional and private, had won for him the sincere regard of all his brethren and the warm affection of those who knew him intimately.

He married, 10 December, 1839, Sarah Emerson Williamson, born at Wilmington, Delaware, 4 November, 1819; died at Baltimore, Maryland, 18 July, 1898; daughter of Hon. Nicholas Gilpin Williamson * of Wilmington, by his wife Sarah Emerson Loockerman.†

* Mr. Williamson (1777-1843) was postmaster of Wilmington, Delaware, under Presidents Monroe, John Quincy Adams, Jackson, Van Buren and Tyler, and was the second Mayor of Wilmington. His great-great-grandfather, Daniel Williamson (—— 1727), believed to have been a native of county Chester, England, came to Pennsylvania, in 1682, and settled in Chester County. Elected a member of the Provincial Assembly in 1708, he was five times re-elected. In 1685 he married, at Chester Meeting of Friends, Mary Smith by whom he had nine children, and died in 1727.

† Sarah Emerson Loockerman, daughter of Vincent Loockerman, Jr., by his second wife Mary Chew Knight, and grand-daughter of Hon. Vincent Loockerman (1722-1785), who served many years in the Assembly of the "Three Lower Counties," now Delaware, from 1752, and in 1784-88 was a member of the Council of Delaware. She was also a descendant of Col. Samuel Chew (1634-1677), a member of the Provincial Council of Maryland from 1669 until his death; Justice of the Provincial Courts, 1669; Keeper of the Great Seal, 1670; Secretary of the Province and Chancellor in 1675; Colonel, 1675.

hildren, all born at Philadelphia:

i.   NICHOLAS WILLIAMSON,[5] b. 21 Sept., 1840; d. Baltimore, Md.,
     26 Nov., 1896; was commissioned, 18 Sept., 1861, adjutant
     in Eighth Penna. Cavalry, promoted first lieutenant 12 Feb.,
     1862, and captain 15 Oct., 1862. After participation in
     many battles of the Civil War, he retired from the army to
     study medicine, in which he was graduated at Hahnemann
     Medical College, Philadelphia. Soon afterward he located
     in Baltimore where he continued in active practice until his
     death; was a frequent contributor to the current literature
     of his profession, and a member of the faculty of the
     Southern Homeopathic Medical College of Baltimore. He
     m. 7 Apr., 1874, LAURA PUNDERSON daughter of Ellsworth
     M. and Laura A. Punderson, of Baltimore. Issue, born at
     Baltimore: 1. *Harriet Punderson*,[6] b. 5 Dec., 1877. 2.
     Govert Loockerman, b. 3 Feb., 1882; d. 17 Apr., 1882. 3.
     Sallie Emerson, b. 12 Aug., 1883. 4. *Nicholas Robert*,
     b. 25 Jan., 1894.

ii. CHRISTIAN, b. 4 Mar., 1842; d. 1 June, 1891; educated largely
     at Muhlenberg College, he studied law in the office of his
     father and was so engaged, when, 19 Sept., 1861, he was
     commissioned second lieutenant in Company G, Eighth
     Penna. Cavalry, and was in active service at the front until
     17 March, 1862, when, by reason of impaired health, he
     resigned his commission, returned to his law studies, and
     was admitted to the bar, 4 March, 1863. Possessed of rare
     oratorical powers, he directed his attention to criminal law
     and made choice of the Court of Quarter Sessions as the
     field for his professional career; was First Assistant District
     Attorney of Philadelphia, under Col. William B. Mann.
     Upon his death a meeting of the bar was held, with Judge
     F. Amedee Bregy presiding. Prominent in public affairs,
     he was chairman of the Republican Executive Committee of
     Philadelphia, 1872-1877; a delegate to the convention that
     nominated James A. Garfield for the Presidency and was,
     in 1881, a member of the Legislature of Pennsylvania,
     serving on Judiciary general committee and as chairman
     of the Committee on Cities. By appointment of Governor
     Hartranft, in 1877, he was a member of the Municipal
     Commission to devise a plan for the government of Penn-
     sylvania cities. The report of this Commission is the basis
     of the present charter of Philadelphia, known as the
     ''Bullitt Bill.'' He was a member of Meade Post, No. 1,
     Grand Army of the Republic; of the Masonic Order and
     of the Union League. He m. 6 Feb., 1867, MARY PERRINE
     ALLISON, b. Philadelphia, 25 Feb., 1844, daughter and eld-
     est child of Hon. Joseph Allison, LL.D. Issue: 1. *Joseph
     Allison*,[6] b. 29 Oct., 1868; member of the Colonial Society
     of Pennsylvania and other organizations. It was due to
     his interest and co-operation that much of the data for
     this article was collected. 2. *William Perrine*, b. 22 Oct.,
     1869.

iii. HORN RILEY, b. 10 Feb., 1845; admitted to the Philadelphia
     bar, 11 Dec., 1869; served nine years as school director of
     the Eighth Ward, and as a member of the Board of Health
     for the city and county of Philadelphia; member of Com-
     mon Council 1873, 1874, 1899, and of the Union League.

He married Mrs. Camilla E. Whipple, granddaughter of the noted sculptor, Guiseppe Franzoni, who came to America in 1806, to adorn the new Capitol building at Washington, and a grand-niece of the late Cardinal Franzoni, who lost the papal throne through the veto of Austria.

iv. Robert Knight, b. 28 Apr., 1847, engaged in the practice of medicine in Baltimore; married, and is now deceased.

v. Juliette Bradford, m. 1 June, 1876, Louis Conrad Massey, Esq., b. Phila., 23 Aug., 1852, son of Lambert R. and Elizabeth (Conrad) Massey. He was graduated at the Univ. of Penna., Class '71, and admitted to the Philadelphia bar, 5 Dec., 1874; settled in the practice of law at Orlando, Florida, 1885; was appointed county commissioner, Orange County, Florida, 1887; commissioner to revise statutes of Florida 1889-92; commissioner on uniformity of state legislation since 1895; State Senator Nineteenth District, 1904-19; counsel for State Railroad Commission 1907-11; Grand Master of Masons, Florida, 1909-10; Chancellor, Episcopal Church, Southern Florida, since 1903; member Seminole Club, Jacksonville.

vi. Sarah Williamson, d. y.

10. Napoleon Bonaparte[4] Kneass (*Christian,[3] Esq., Christopher,[2] Johan Christian[1]*), born at Philadelphia, 17 April, 1818; died at Philadelphia, 16 March, 1888. He was appointed cadet at large to West Point Military Academy in 1832, by President Jackson, but left the Academy in 1835 to embark in mercantile pursuits at New Orleans, Louisiana. On 1 July, 1847, he entered into partnership in that city with Michael Magee, under the firm name of Magee, Kneass & Co. at New Orleans and M. Magee & Co. at Philadelphia, to trade as manufacturers and importers of saddlery and saddlery hardware, the New Orleans warehouse being at the Sign of the Golden Horsehead, No. 6 Magazine street, and the Philadelphia factory, 18 Decatur street. This connection continued until 1 January, 1865, when the New Orleans house, confiscated by the Confederate government during the Civil War, and restored in part after the war by the Federal government, was discontinued and the Philadelphia business reorganized as Kneass & Co.

At New Orleans, in 1845, he took an active part in the formation of the First Regiment of Louisiana Volunteers, the first strictly American regiment in that city, its leading purpose, aside from military duty, being to break up the custom of military parades on Sunday. He served as lieutenant, adjutant and captain in this regiment and assisted in raising troops to fill the Louisiana regiments called out for the Mexican War. A prominent member of the Odd Fellows, he held the position of Grand High Priest.

From 1850 he served some years as school director in Philadelphia, and, at the outbreak of the Civil War, organized in the Tenth Ward, three companies of Home Guard, many members of which later enlisted in volunteer regiments. When the various Home Guard companies were formed into a brigade, under General Pleasanton, he was tendered the command of one of the regiments, which he declined, but accepted that of major of the Gray Reserves, and later the lieutenant-colonelcy of that command. In 1862, when Pennsylvania was invaded by the Confederate Army, his regiment tendered its services for active duty, and went into the field as the Seventh Regiment, Pennsylvania Militia, with Mr. Kneass as colonel, and while in service he commanded for a short time the brigade of which his regiment was a part. Shortly after the regiment returned to Philadelphia he resigned his command owing to ill-health. The Gray Reserves later became the First Regiment, National Guard of Pennsylvania. A portrait of Colonel Kneass is in the First Regiment Armory.

He married, at New York City, 11 August, 1840, Caroline Amelia von Vultee, born at New York City, 4 September, 1821; died at Ridley Park, Pa., 24 July, 1900, daughter of Baron Frederick Louis von Vultee of Baden, by his wife Gertrude Wertheim of Hesse Cassel.

Children, the two eldest and seven youngest born at Philadelphia:

    i.   SARAH GERTRUDE,[5] b. 1 July, 1841; d. Jan., 1902; m. 20 Oct.,
         1864, JOHN SEXTON MILES, d. Jan., 1888. Issue: *John
         Kneass*[6] *Miles*, m. 12 May, 1888, Virginia Adele Corson,
         dau. of Stillwell F. Corson, and had issue.
    ii. CAROLINE PAMELA, b. 6 Aug., 1842; d. Dec. 9, 1918; m. 17
         Apr., 1865, John Head Brooks; d. July 16, 1904. Issue:
         1. *Caroline Amelia*[6] *Brooks*, b. 11 Feb., 1866. 2.
         Napoleon Bonaparte Kneass Brooks, b. 9 Feb., 1868; m.
         28 Nov., 1893, Maude, dau. John Waters. 3. *Eleanor D.
         Brooks*, b. 23 Apr., 1871; d. 9 Jan., 1876.
    iii. NAPOLEON BONAPARTE, b. New Orleans, 26 Dec., 1843; d.
         Phila., 3 Feb., 1898. Losing his sight from the effects of
         sun stroke at the age of seven, he nevertheless became
         eminent for his inventions, printing and authorship, in

connection with the blind. In 1867 he established *Kneass' Philadelphia Magazine for the Blind*, and for several years issued from his press more than was issued from the combined presses for the blind in the country. The author of several pieces of music, secular and sacred, he received premiums for his works from Franklin Institute, the Paris and the United States Centennial Expositions.

iv. JAMES MAGEE, b. New Orleans, 29 Apr., 1846; d. there, 7 Feb., 1849.

v. FLORENCE ADELE, b. New Orleans, 8 Jan., 1849; d. there, 31 March, 1850.

vi. PAULINE, b. 22 Sept., 1851.

vii. BLANCHE, b. 7 Feb., 1854; d. Phila., 17 June, 1855.

viii. LOUIS, b. 30 June, 1855; d. Phila., 1 July, 1855.

ix. PERCY VULTEE, b. 12 Sept., 1856; d. Phila., 17 Feb., 1892; m. 1 Sept., 1886, ELIZABETH M. SLOCUM, dau. of Alfred Marshall Slocum, M. D. Issue: 1. *Horace*,[6] b. Phila., 20 July, 1889; d. 29 July, 1889. 2. *Ethel Percy*, b. 10 July, 1891.

x. ELOISE, b. 20 Oct., 1858; d. y.

xi. CARL MAGEE, b. 22 Nov., 1860; m. (1) 25 Dec., 1888, MARY MOUNTFORT, dau. of Joseph Mountfort, Esq., of Denver Colorado; died Aug., 1904; m. (2) 1 June, 1910, Louise Lindauer, dau. of John Lindauer of Phila. For twenty-two years, 1892-1914, Mr. Kneass was Associate Editor of *The Ladies Home Journal*, and is now, 1919, a stock broker; is secretary of The Descendants of the Signers of the Declaration of Independence; member of the Pennsylvania Society Sons of the Revolution and one of its Color Guard; also member of the Manufacturers' Club of Philadelphia and the Philadelphia Country Club. In 1915 he was the compiler, with Wilfred Jordan, of a " CATALOGUE OF THE PORTRAITS AND OTHER WORKS OF ART IN INDEPENDENCE HALL, PHILADELPHIA. WITH A SHORT HISTORICAL SKETCH OF THE BUILDINGS COMPRISING THE STATE HOUSE ROW. '' This publication was issued by The Descendants of the Signers of the Declaration of Independence.

xii. LELA FREDERICKA VULTEE, b. 15 June, 1862; d. Phila., 9 Aug., 1871.

Nicholas Le Huray
Clock and Watch Maker of the Isle of Guernsey, of Philadelphia, and of Ogletown, Delaware

Contributed by LEWIS D. COOK, F.A.S.G., F.G.S.P.

To complement the brief biographical notice of Nicholas Le Huray by Henry C. Conrad in his "Old Delaware Clockmakers," published in the *Papers of the Delaware Historical Society*, Volume XX (1898), page 31, the following report is presented.

NICHOLAS LE HURAY, clock and watch maker, is so listed in Philadelphia city directories from 1828 to 1835, at 170 North Second Street. He removed in 1834 to Ogletown, Delaware, and was listed as a licensed preacher under the Reverend William K. Robison, pastor of the Welsh Tract Baptist Church in Kent County, Delaware, in the *Minutes of the Delaware Baptist Association,* at the meeting held from 6 through 8 June 1835, at that meeting house. He had held the same position previously in the New Market Street Baptist Church on Budd Street (now New Market Street) north of Poplar.[1] He died testate at his home at "Ogle Town, [New Castle County,] State of Delaware" on 8 February 1837, aged 65 years.[2]

His will, written at Ogletown 8 January 1834, and proved at New Castle 16 February 1837, begins, "Au Nom de Dieu soit, Amen, Nich' Le Huray, Sr., watch and clock maker, son of Nich' native of the parish of Torteval in the Island of Guernsey, but now residing in the State of Delaware," and directs, after debts are paid, that his farm situated in Ogletown, Christiana Hundred, Delaware, with all improvements thereon, be sold within one year after his death for the benefit of his wife and children. He devises to his wife Elizabeth the income from one-third of his personal and real estate, to be paid her annually during her lifetime, after her death the principal to be divided among their

---

[1] This congregation was established there in 1804, in the Northern Liberties of Philadelphia, by twenty members from the First Baptist Church of Philadelphia. J. Thomas Scharf and Thompson Westcott, *History of Philadelphia* . . . (Philadelphia, 1884), II, 1310.

[2] *Poulson's American Daily Advertiser,* issue of 13 Feb. 1837.

children as she pleases. The other two-thirds was to be divided equally between his children: Nicholas, Elizabeth, Sophia, Harriet, Charles, Emilia Caroline, and his granddaughter Julia Fries, daughter of his deceased daughter Julia, $150 to be deducted from the shares of Nicholas and Elizabeth as given them at their marriage. His one and one-quarter acre place three miles above Philadelphia on the Frankford turnpike at the corner of "Heart" Lane, with the stone house and two frame buildings thereon, was to be divided into four lots and sold within one year after his decease, and the proceeds divided as abovesaid. The stock of his store goods, viz: watches, chains, keys and jewelry, to be sold. To his son Charles he gave his watch and clock tools and cloths, watch materials and draws, and appointed his friend Jonathan Bee executor.[3]

Children of Nicholas Le Huray:[4]

i. NICHOLAS LE HURAY, Jr., b. *ca.* 1795; d. Philadelphia, intestate, 27 July 1846, aged 49 years. Buried in Laurel Hill Cemetery. Issue, among others: 1. ELEANORA LE HURAY, m. 19 February 1850, WILLIAM GRIFFITH. 2. GEORGE LE HURAY, in 1860 of Summit, New Jersey. 3. ELIZABETH LE HURAY, m. 28 June 1860, CHARLES SILVER. 4. ANNE ELIZABETH LE HURAY, d. August, 1828.

ii. ELIZABETH LE HURAY, b. *ca.* 1796; d. Philadelphia, 7 September 1843, in her 48th year. She married in or before 1822, ISHI HUNT CRAVEN, b. *ca.* 1791; d. 30 June 1860, in his 70th year in Germantown, Philadelphia. Buried in Ronaldson Cemetery, corner of Ninth and Bainbridge Streets, Philadelphia, without gravestone. His estate is not found in the Philadelphia probate records. Son of William Walling Craven of Oxford Township, Sussex County, New Jersey, and grandson of Thomas Craven (1708-1775), a schoolmaster,[5] Ishi Craven was a midshipman in the United States Navy during the first ten months of 1809, then resigned at New York after duty on the U.S. Brig *Siren.* He is listed in Philadelphia city directories of 1818-1830 as an accountant; in 1837 as a member of the firm of Otis and Craven, lumber merchants; 1839-1842 as a teller in the Schuylkill Bank; in 1854-1860 as a broker, member of the firm of I. Craven and Company, note and stock brokers. He was a charter member in 1820 of the Second Universalist Church of the Restoration, Philadelphia, as the register indicates. Issue: 1. ALFRED CRAVEN, d. Yorkville, S. Carolina, 1872; had a son Alfred Craven, Jr., and two daughters. 2. CAROLINE CRAVEN, m. THOMAS F. BRADY, and in 1860 resided in High Street, Germantown, Philadelphia.[6] 3. LOUISE HARRIET CRAVEN, d. unm. 6

---

3 New Castle County Will Book T, 290, will of Nicholas Le Huray.

4 As named in his will, and in death and marriage notices in *Poulson's American Daily Advertiser.*

5 See George N. McKenzie, ed., *Colonial Families of the United States of America* (Baltimore, 1914), IV, 104.

6 Caroline Craven and Thomas F. Brady had issue: 1. *Caroline Brady,* m. *Frank Higgins,* son of Dr. Frank Higgins of West Philadelphia. 2. *Thomas F. Brady, Jr.*

March 1869, aged 40 years; bur. Ronaldson Cemetery, Philadelphia. 4. Ishi Bullman Craven, b. Philadelphia, 31 October 1829; d. Brooklyn, New York, 13 December 1902; bur. Green-Wood Cemetery, Brooklyn. He m. 1st, in Chester, Pa., 23 August 1855, Mary Bunting Davis, b. 1 July 1836; d. Jersey City, New Jersey, 5 February 1863, dau. of David and Grace Ann Davis; bur. in Philadelphia. They had five children. Ishi B. Craven m. 2nd, in 1874, Emma Cecilia Harvey, b. Campobello, Maine; d. 9 October 1920; bur. Green-Wood Cemetery, Brooklyn. 5. Emma Matilda Craven, d. Omaha, Nebraska; m. Philadelphia, Benjamin Harris who d. September 1892; bur. Brooklyn, New York.[7] 6. Virginia Craven, d. unm. 1889; bur. Green-Wood Cemetery, Brooklyn. 7. Edmund (Edwin?) Craven, b. 1822; d. Philadelphia, 5 December 1831.

iii. SOPHIA LE HURAY, named in her father's will of 1834.

iv. JULIA LE HURAY, b. *ca.* 1808; d. 28 July 1828, in her 21st year;[8] m. JOHN FRIES, and had issue Julia Fries, named in the will abovesaid.

v. HARRIET LE HURAY, b. *ca.* 1811; d. 24 April 1837, in her 27th year; bur. from her brother Nicholas Le Huray's residence, "on the Frankford Road near the Hart Tavern," Northern Liberties, Philadelphia. She m. in Philadelphia, 20 April 1829, JOSEPH N. GOODRICH, the Rev. Elisha Cushman officiating. Issue: Four children.[9]

vi. CHARLES LE HURAY, b. *ca.* 1814; d. "in New Castle county, Delaware, near Newark," 8 June 1836, in his 23rd year.[10]

vii. EMILIA CAROLINE LE HURAY, named in her father's will.

---

[7] Emma Matilda Craven and Benjamin Harris had issue: 1. *Florence N. Harris*, b. 27 Nov. 1858; m. *Carl A. Jacobson*. 2. *Sarah Virginia Harris*, m. 1st, *Isaac N. Smith*, and 2nd, *Frank Leslie*. 3. *Emma Matilda Harris*, m. *George Tallman* and resided in Omaha, Nebraska.

[8] *Poulson's American Daily Advertiser*, issue of 30 July 1828.

[9] *Ibid.*, issues of 29 Apr. 1829, and 26 Apr. 1837.

[10] *Ibid.*, issue of 16 June 1836.

Ancestry and Children of Johann Jacob Lenz

and His Wife Anna Maria Löffler of Philadelphia, Pennsylvania

Walter Lee Sheppard, Jr., F.G.S.P., F.A.S.G.

JOHANN JACOB LENZ (variously Lentz and Lens), son of Hans Jacob, was born in Beutelsbach, Württemberg, 7 January 1727. In the local records he is referred to as "bachbecken" (baker on the brook) through the year 1758 (the year of the baptism of his eldest surviving son). After this date he appears either as "weingärtner" (vinedresser), or with both descriptions. He married four times, his first three wives each dying at or shortly after the birth of a child. His fourth wife, whom he married at Gross Hepach on 14 June 1757, was Anna Maria Löffler, daughter of Johann Melchior Löffler, born 17 May 1735 in Gross Hepach. She was the mother of his three surviving sons.[1]

In the autumn of 1769, the family obtained permission to emigrate to the New World, and an entry accordingly appears in the records of the parish of Beutelsbach, Deaconry of Schorndorf, in Württemberg, indicating that Jacob went "in the spring of 1769," and that his wife and children went to stay with his parents, then followed him in the fall. There is an entry showing that one Johann Jacob Lentz took the Oath of Allegiance at Philadelphia on 13 October 1769, as one of the immigrants who had arrived on the *Minerva*.[2] We have no positive evidence as to whether his wife and children actually came with him, or followed later, but they were certainly in Philadelphia in April of 1770, when his son Georg was born and baptized.

There is a record of the death on 20 December 1777 of one Jacob Lenz, born 6 April 1724 at Kirchweiler, "married about 27 years, had one child who died, aged 53 years, 8 months and 2 days.", in the records of St. Michael's and Zion Evangelical Lutheran Church, Philadelphia.[3] This is the only death record of a Jacob Lenz noted in the records of this church, where the couple were members, but he cannot be our man. Our Johann Jacob Lenz was certainly dead by 15 July 1778, when his widow Anna

Maria married as her second husband a man much younger than herself, Johann Christopher Keppler (also Kepler, Kepner), born about 1755/6, died about 1783, son of Bernhardt [3] (Andreas,[2] Johann Bernhardt [1]) Keppler and his wife Eva (Meyer), by whom she had a son who died in infancy, and a daughter Maria Elisabetha, who married Johann Adam Schoenneck, leaving descendants.

Anna Maria [4] appears in the census records as head of household, and in the city directories as a widow. She died 21 September 1818 and was buried the following day, aged "about 80 years, 4 months." [5] The Board of Health death record is more exact: "about 80 years, 4 months and 6 days," placing her birth at 15 May 1738, close enough to that in the Beutelsbach registers. She left a will signed "Mary Kebler," dated 5 April 1810, proved 14 October 1818, bequeathing her estate to her "daughter Maria Elizabeth Shinnick, except $100 which my son Jacob Lentz owes me from which my funeral expenses are to be paid, and the remainder to my children." The executor was her daughter; the witnesses, Gottlieb Klett and John Reachert.[6]

Children of Anna Maria Löffler and Johann Jacob Lenz: [7]

i. JOHANN JACOB LENZ, bapt. 23 July 1758; sponsors, Daniel Koch, citizen and farmer, absent, represented by —— Mayer; Mrs. Juliana Catherina Kaufman, widow, absent; Catharina, wife of Judge Johann Georg Mayer. A baker, he d. 10 May 1827, "aged 68 years, 9 months, 12 days." [8] He m. 1) 15 July 1788 LIELIA (actually, Lydia), widow of Dielman Kolb of Perkiomen, by whom he apparently had no surviving issue, and 2) 30 January 1800 SOPHIA SCHOENNECK,[9] daughter of Michael, by whom he had two daughters: ELISABETHA, b. ca. 1805, who m. William M. Taylor and left issue; and SOPHIA, b. ca. 1810, who d. unmarried.[10]

ii. GOTTLIEB LENZ, b. 1 April, bapt. 2 April 1761; sponsors, Daniel Koch, citizen and vinedresser; Mrs. Anna Maria, wife of Mr. Caspar Hammer; and Anna Catharina, wife of Johann Jacob Koch, vinedresser; d. 19 September 1761.

iii. GOTTLIEB (again) LENZ, bapt. 28 February 1763 or 1764 (both dates appear in the records); sponsors, same as immediately above; d. 25 July 1799. He m. 10 August 1787 ANNA KOCH (parents not identified) and had issue: ANNA MARIA, b. 10 January, bapt. 13 August 1788; sponsors, Jacob Lentz and Lielia (Lydia); GOTTLIEB, b. 4 October 1796, bapt. — August 1797; JOHANN JACOB, buried 12 May 1790, aged 2 months 16 days; JOHANN, b. 11 February, bapt. 2 July 1793; MARGARETHA, b. 4 November 1794, bapt. 2 August 1795.

iv. MARIA CATHARINA LENZ, bapt. 10 January 1767, sponsors: Mr. Christopher Friedrich Weinhardt, clerk of the court; Daniel Koch, vinedresser; Mrs. Anna Maria Hammer, schoolmaster's wife; and Anna Catharina, wife of Jacob Koch, vinedresser; d. 26 June 1768.

v. GEORG ADAM LENZ, b. 13 April, bapt. 28 April 1770; sponsors, Georg Adam Bub and wife Catharina. He was probably the George Lentz,[11] butcher, who in 1794 lived on Coates Street between St. John and 3rd, and from 1800 to 1813 at Coates and 4th. Administration was granted 30 August 1849 to widow HENRIETTA of George Lentz of Kensington, and this could well be the butcher, since in the inventory is a chopping block. If this indeed is the above Georg, then he would have to have been married three times. St. Michael's and Zion records the marriage 26 May 1792 of George Lentz to MARIA ANDRÄ, each living in Philadelphia, and the birth 11 March, baptism 8 April 1798, of GEORG, son of Georg Lentz and wife Anna Margaretha. The child here baptised could be the George Lentz, dealer, who died 24 October 1841, aged 43, and left a will dated May 1841, wife CHRISTIANN, and four minor children: JOHN, ELIZABETH, CATHARINE and WILLIAM.

Children of Anna Maria Löffler and Johann Christopher Keppler:

vi. MARIA ELISABETHA KEPPLER, b. *ca.* 1799, m. JOHANN ADAM SCHOENNECK.[12]

vii. JOHANN KEPPLER, b. 7 June, bapt. 7 Oct. 1782, St. John's Lutheran Church, Easton, Pa.;[13] sponsors, Christopher Bittenbender and Anna Elisabetha (Johann Christopher Keppler's brother in law and sister) and Johann Kepner (his brother). This child probably d. soon, since no further record is known.

The following ancestor table has been constructed from data supplied by Mr. Karl Friedrich von Frank, Schloss Senftenegg, Post Ferschnitz, Niederösterreich, Austria, who also supplied the parish records for the first four children named above. The number 1. is applied to any child of Jacob and Anna Maria (Löffler) Lenz. The father's number is always twice that of the child, and the mother's number is twice that plus one.

2. JOHANN JACOB LENZ, b. Beutelsbach 7 Jan. 1727, d. Philadelphia by 1778; to Pennsylvania 1769; m. 1) 6 Feb. 1753 Maria Magdalena b. 13 Mar. 1728, d. 18 Dec. 1753, dau. Johann and Anna Maria (Heckler) Koch, had a son Joh: Daniel, d.y.; m. 2) 16 July 1754 Maria Magdalena b. 4 May 1732, d. 23 June 1755, dau. Joh: Geo: and Anna Magdalena (Sieg) Danckwort, had a son Joh: Geo: prob. d.y.; m. 3) 27 Jan. 1756 Elisabetha b. 27 Dec. 1732, d. 27 Nov. 1756, dau. Bernhardt and Anna Magdalena Schmid, had a dau. Christina Magdalena, d.y.; m. 4) 14 June 1757 at Gross Heppach

3. ANNA MARIA LÖFFLER, b. Gross Heppach 17 May 1735, d. Phila. Pa. 21 Sept. 1818, to Pennsylvania 1769, m. 2) 15 July 1778, at Philadelphia, Johann Christopher Keppler, b. *ca.* 1755/6, d. *ca.* 1783; children: Maria Elisabetha, m. Joh. Adam Schoenneck; Johann, d.y.

4. HANS JACOB LENZ, "baker at the brook," b. Beutelsbach 5 Feb. 1690, d. ?. m. 1) Beutelsbach 14 Feb. 1719

5. ANNA CHRISTINA JETZLE (or JESSEL), b. Gross Heppach 20 May 1684, d. Beutelsbach 23 Nov. 1757.

6. JOHANN MELCHIOR LÖFFLER, "vinedresser," b. Gross Heppach 6 Jan. 1707, d. Gross Heppach 21 June 1778, m. 2) at Korb 13 Sept. 1757 Anna Catharina Heinrich, b. aft. 13 May 1729; m. 1) at Gross Heppach 26 Apr. 1729, as her 2nd husband,

7. ANNA CATHARINA MAHLER, b. Gross Heppach 12 Jan. 1696, d. 17 Mar. 1757. She had m. 1) 24 Aug. 1723 Joh: Ulrich Eihninger, d. 12 Sept. 1726.

8. JOH: GEORG LENZ, "baker by the brook," b. ?, d. ?, m. Beutelsbach 28 Oct. 1686
9. ANNA MARIA VETTERLIN, b. ?, d. Beutelsbach 8 June 1729.
10. JOSEPH JETZLE, ropemaker, b. Gross Heppach 8 Feb. 1633, d. Gross Heppach 1 May 1698, m. Gross Heppach 29 Apr. 1662
11. ANNA MARIA FRANK, b. ?, d. Gross Heppach 10 Mar. 1718, "aged 76 years."
12. THEODORUS FRIEDRICH LÖFFLER, citizen and vinedresser, b. Hohenasperg 15 May 1676, d. Gross Heppach 17 June 1751 m. 2) 24 Jan. 1736 Anna Barbara Werner d. 1752; m. 1) Gross Heppach 2 May 1699
13. ANNA MARIA JETZEL (or JESSEL) b. Gross Heppach, d. same 9 Feb. 1737 (dau. Joseph, 10 above).
14. JOHANN JACOB MAHLER, tailor & asst. judge of Gross Heppach, b. Blochingen 13 Sept. 1667, d. Gross Heppach 4 Dec. 1750, m. 2) Anna Catharina Böhler, m. 1) Gross Heppach 28 Oct. 1690
15. VERONICA MÜLLER, b. ?, d. Gross Heppach 11 Jan. 1708, aged 41 years 6 months.
16. GEORG LENZ, surgeon, m. 30 Nov. 1650
17. BARBARA KETTLER, dau. surgeon Jacob Kettler, bur. 28 Feb. 1676 aged 75, and wife Anna, bur. 12 Mar. 1665.
18. CASPAR VETTERLIN of Snaith.
19. ?
20. HANS JETZEL (JESSEL), ropemaker, b. ca. 1588 or 10 Apr. 1580, d. 16 Jan. 1667 aged 79, m. 10 Jan. 1636
21. CHRISTINA ———, widow of Friedrich Kübler.
22. CASPAR FRANK, vinedresser and member of town council, b. ca. 1609, d. Gross Heppach Jan. 1664 aged 54 years, m. 25 July 1640
23. MARIA ZIEGLER, dau. Leonhard Ziegler.
24. JOHANN GEORG LÖFFLER, baker and soldier, b. ?, d. in Hungary; served as a soldier in Hohenasperg, m.
25. ANNA SOPHIA SCHMID, dau. Joh: Schmid, "burger."
26. JOSEPH JETZEL (JESSEL), (same as no. 10); m.
27. ANNA MARIA FRANK (same as no. 11).
28. JOHANN GEORG MAHLER, burger and tailor, d. 1689, m.
29. ANNA RÜHL, b. in Blochingen, d. before 1698, dau. Hans Rühl, vinedresser.
30. JOHANN RUDOLPH MÜLLER, blacksmith of Gross Heppach, b. Switzerland, d. Gross Heppach 18 July 1692, m. (2nd husb.) 1657
31. MARGARETHA LUTZ (chambermaid), dau. Hans Jerg Lutz, "kramer in Gross Heppach," b. ca. 1640, d. Gross Heppach 23 Mar. 1711, aged 71 years; she m. 1) Hans Jerg Knaus.

NOTES

[1] "Who Was the Widow Anna Maria Lenz?", *National Genealogical Society Quarterly* (*NGSQ*), 49 (1961), 28-34. The evidences for Anna Maria and her husband Johann Jacob Lenz are quoted in this article, with sources cited. For the Kepler ancestry, see "Bernard Kepler (1673-1765) of Philadelphia," *NGSQ*, 61 (1973), 163-7.

[2] Ralph B. Strassburger and William J. Hinke, *Pennsylvania German Pioneers* (Norristown, 1934), List 276 C.

[3] Abstracts, photocopies and microfilms of the original records are in the Collections of the Genealogical Society of Pennsylvania.

[4] See note 1.

[5] Records of St. Michael's and Zion Church. It is suggested that Anna Maria deliberately lost three years in order to reduce the age difference between herself and her second husband.

[6] Philadelphia Will Book 6, p. 608.

[7] Certified transcripts of the parish registers have been supplied to the author by Mr. Karl Friedrich von Frank and are in his possession.

[8] See note 5 for this entry and for much of the subsequent information regarding this child and the other six children.

[9] See *The American Genealogist* (*TAG*), 17 (1940), 79-86; 19 (1942-43), 45, 176; *The Pennsylvania Genealogical Magazine,* XXII (1961), 133-43.[*]

[10] Will of Sophia Lentz, Jr., and probate material on George Lentz cited in *NGSQ,* 49 (1961), 34.

[11] *Idem.*

[12] See "The Family of Johann Adam Schoenneck," *TAG,* 50 (1974), 31-9.

[13] Abstracted for the author by Mrs. F. Spencer Roach from the original records.

[*]See pp. 837-848, this volume.

Ulrich Liebengut

DONALD J. MARTIN, JR.

with annotations by Hannah Benner Roach

ULRICH LEEBEGOOT,[1] aged 45, and his family which included Susanna Leebegoot, aged 36, Johan Pieter, aged 16, Adam, aged 13, Jacob, aged 10, and Anna and Maria, both aged 5, arrived at Philadelphia on the ship *Charming Betty* on 11 October 1733.[2] Extensive research in the parish registers of the Department of Bas-Rhin, France,[3] indicate that Ulrich Liebengut of the parish of Langensoultzbach, Bas-Rhin, is probably the immigrant.

In the registers[4] of that parish are recorded the following baptisms of the children of Ulrich Liebengut and his wife Anna Henni:

Hans Peter Liebengut baptized 12 July 1716
Hans Adam Liebengut baptized 6 January 1719
Hans Jacob Liebengut baptized 8 June 1721
Anna Margaretha Liebengut baptized 15 October 1723
Maria Catharina Liebengut baptized 4 July 1726
Albrecht Liebengut baptized 5 April 1729; died 14 April 1732

No mention of the family was found in the registers after the death of the child Albrecht in 1732.

---

[1] Leebegoot is a phonetic spelling of the surname Leibundgut. During the period of time he was born in Melchnau, Canton Bern, Switzerland, the surname was spelled *Lyb und Gut* in the parish registers of Melchnau. When reporting his name to the pastors who recorded his marriage and the baptisms of his children, he undoubtedly pronounced his name in the dialect peculiar to that parish or part of Canton Bern from which he had emigrated. To the pastors of Hungspach and Langensoultzbach, who probably were unfamiliar with the surname, it sounded like *Liebengut*, and so it was written. The surname underwent many alterations in spelling in colonial America. *Leibundgut* is the standard spelling today used in the district of Aarwangen, Canton Bern, Switzerland.

[2] William J. Hinke, ed., Pennsylvania German Pioneers (Norristown, Pa., 1934). I, 134, List 35-A.

[3] In the hope of finding the family, research was conducted in the parishes of Obermodern, Bischwiller, Climbach and Dauendorf, all in the Department of Bas-Rhin. The tombstone inscription of Adam Liebengut in the Falkner Swamp Reformed Church cemetery, Montgomery Co., Pa., records Adam's place of birth as "Elsass."

[4] The parish registers of Langensoultzbach, Bas-Rhin, France, are on microfilm at the Genealogical Society of the Church of Jesus Christ of Latter-day Saints, 50 East North Temple, Salt Lake City, Utah, 84150.

Ulrich Liebengut and Anna Henni were married 19 March 1715 in the parish of Hunspach, Bas-Rhin.[5] The entry of their marriage identifies Ulrich's birthplace as Melchnau, Canton Bern, Switzerland. His wife Anna is identified as the daughter of Michael Henni of the village of Homberg in the parish of Steffisburg, Canton Bern, Switzerland. Whether the passenger Susanna Leebegoot of the *Charming Betty* was actually Anna Henni, or a second wife, has not been determined.

Nicholas Scull surveyed a tract of land on 17 March 1737, for Ulrich Levengood in McCall's Manor. On 14 April 1742, pursuant to the division of George McCall's land among his heirs, both Ulrich and Peter Livingood were listed as having had land surveyed in that part of the manor "commonly called Douglass Mannor."[6] On this land Ulrich is presumed to have died; letters of administration were granted to his son Jacob Levergood of Philadelphia County 1 July 1751.[7]

His Sons

On 23 August 1748, Peter Liebgut's wife, aged 30 years, 8 months, had been buried in the New Hanover Lutheran Cemetery. Who she was has not been discovered, but his second wife was Christina Mohn to whom he was married by the pastor of the Falkner Swamp Reformed Church on 12 January 1749.[8]

Peter *Leavergood* was taxed in Douglas Township, Berks County, in 1758 and 1759, and died intestate there about 1767. He left his widow Christina and nine children: John, aged 18, Jacob, aged 17, Peter, aged 13, Daniel, aged 9, Adam, aged 2, Catharina, wife of John Becker, Anna Maria, aged 20, who by 1771 had married Henry Bitting, Christina, aged 15, who had married William Maberry by 1771, and Elizabeth, aged 7.[9]

[5] The parish registers of Hunsbach, Bas-Rhin, France, are on microfilm at the Genealogical Society, Salt Lake City.

[6] Nicholas Scull Note Book, Historical Society of Pennsylvania; Philadelphia Orphans Court Records, 14 April 1742.

[7] Philadelphia Administration Book F, 407, #42:1751, estate of Ulrich Levergood.

[8] "New Hanover Lutheran Church Records," *Pennsylvania German Society Proceedings and Addresses*, XX (1911), 433; *Pennsylvania Archives*, 2nd Series, VIII, (Harrisburg, 1878), 609. Data on the sons of Ulrich Liebengut has been collected and prepared for this paper by Hannah Benner Roach.

[9] Morton L. Montgomery, *History of Berks County in Pennsylvania*, (Phila., 1886), 968. Abstracts of Berks County Orphans Court Records, 63, 65, 88, Collections of the Genealogical Society of Pennsylvania (GSP). Peter *Lebengut* was naturalized 24 September 1762. See *Pennsylvania Archives*, 2nd Series, II (Harrisburg, 1890) 272, 273.

Adam Leavergood was also taxed in Douglas Township, Berks County, in 1759, but by 1769 he was living in New Hanover Township, Philadelphia County, where he died testate in early March 1804. His will, dated 16 February 1804 and proved 27 April 1804, named his wife Christina, sons Jacob, Mathias, John and Peter, daughter Elizabeth, wife of Charles Neiman, and mentioned the children of his daughter Catharine, the wife of Willian Kepner.[10]

Jacob Liebegut was married to Christina Brand 9 November 1748, by the pastor of the Falkner Swamp Reformed Church. By 1768 he had 200 acres in Douglas Township, Berks County, and died there testate in 1784. His will dated 6 December 1783, and proved 17 February 1784, named his wife Christina, sons Philip, Jacob and Peter, and John and Henry, the last two being under 21, and his daughter Catharine.[11] Jacob *Liebengut* and his wife Christina are both buried in the cemetery adjoining Zion Reformed Church, Hanover Street, Pottstown, Pa. The dates on the stone give his birth as 15 June 1721, and his death as 15 January 1784. Christina his wife was born in 1728 and died 12 August 1800. Many of his descendants are also buried in this cemetery.

No information about Ulrich Liebengut's daughters has been located.

---

[10] Adam Leibegut was naturalized at the same time as his brother Peter. *Ibid.*, 374. Both men took the sacrament on 19 September 1762. Adam's burial is entered in the transcript of the records of Falkner Swamp Reformed Church, 343, in *GSP*. His tombstone in the church's cemetery states that he lived with his wife in wedlock 60 years. Montgomery County Will Book 2, 385, will of Adam Liebenugh (*sic*).

[11] Jacob Liebegut also owned land in Philadelphia County and was of that county when he was naturalized in April 1761, having taken the sacrament the previous 22 March. *Pennsylvania Archives*, 2nd Series, II, 351, cited in note 9. He directed his executors to sell his land in New Hanover Township in his will. Berks Co. Will Book B, 40.

Dr. Donald J. Martin, Jr. has called to our attention the fact that his recent article "Ulrich Liebengut" *PGM*, XXIX, 253-255* had not been submitted to him for final approval and clearance. Due to recent changes in editorship and publication committee, the present editor was not aware of this oversight.

Dr. Martin also called to our attention that "the purpose of the article was to identify what is believed to be the correct European origin of the immigrant." He considers "publication of any more data on the descendants of Ulrich Liebengut to be premature until the research of all of the Liebengut families in colonial Pennsylvania has been completed."

---

*Pages 194-196, this volume.

THE McCLEAN FAMILY AND THE MASON-DIXON LINE

By ROBERT M. TORRENCE

Many articles concerning the early border disputes between Pennsylvania and Maryland explain why the Penns and the Calverts employed the English surveyors, Charles Mason and Jeremiah Dixon, to survey what is known as the Mason-Dixon Line. Some are more detailed than one recently published popular article [1] which describes the survey and displays excellent photographs of the carved stone markers but which gives the impression that Mason and Dixon accomplished this memorable work aided only by " wagons and tents, servants, axmen and laborers." It merely mentions that Colonel Alexander McClean, of Pennsylvania, and Joseph Neville, of Virginia, surveyed that part of the Line between Pennsylvania and West Virginia.

Earlier histories give space to these two men and more particularly to McClean's brother, Archibald McClean, who had preceded the English mathematicians on the survey and without whose assistance the project might have been delayed many years. Archibald McClean, an experienced Provincial surveyor, was engaged by Mason and Dixon soon after they arrived in Philadelphia on November 15, 1763, for he had been employed for three years by the Proprietaries on the southern boundary survey. In fact, Mason and Dixon were called in chiefly because of the slowness with which McClean and his colleagues worked and the two Englishmen repeatedly testified to the accuracy of the work of their predecessors. [2]

Archibald McClean, on July 4, 1760, was commissioned to make surveys for Thomas Penn, William Penn and Frederick, Lord Baltimore. [3] His surveying skills caused him to remove from his residence in Montgomery County, Pennsylvania, to Philadelphia County, where, on July 18, 1761 he received the commission of the Penn heirs to survey and adjust the peninsular and circular boundaries between the three lower counties and Maryland. [4] In company with John Lukens who also represented Pennsylvania, and Thomas Garnett, Jonathan Hall and John Frederick Augustus Priggs, representing Maryland, he established the " Middle Point," between Cape Henlopen and the Chesapeake, and located, in November and December, 1761, the well known " Arc of the Circle " around New Castle, Delaware and also the " Tangent Line through the Peninsula." [5] He is also said to have joined David Rittenhouse, of Pennsylvania, and Captain John Montresor, of the Royal Engineers, in the 1774 survey of the line between New York and Pennsylvania and to have entered the employ of Charles Carroll of Carrollton in order to establish the lines of his holding, " Carroll's Delight," then thought to lie in Maryland.[6]

As the leading surveyor working out of Philadelphia, Archibald McClean was the chief associate of Mason and Dixon. His brother Moses secured appointment as Commissary to the expedition and entertained Mason and Dixon overnight in his Montgomery County home,[7] but the association with the McClean family went further. As a York County historian records, " Six [?] of his brothers were also employed in assisting to establish the line from 1763 to June 4, 1766, when the party arrived as far west as the summit of ' Little Alleghany ' and were there stopped by troublesome Indians. On June 8, 1767, Mason, Dixon and Archibald McClean began to continue the survey from the top of the ' Little Alleghany,' accompanied by a delegation of friendly Indians as an escort, against the savages. On the 14th of June, they reached the top of the ' Great Alleghany,' where fourteen more friendly Indians joined them as interpreters. At this time, there were *thirty* assistant surveyors, fifteen ax-men and a number of Indians. They continued westward 240 miles from Delaware to ' Dunker Creek,' as marked on their map. This was thirty-six miles east of the western limit of the present Mason and Dixon line. The balance was run in 1782 and 1784." [8]

On November 27, 1764, while working with Mason and Dixon, Archibald McClean was commissioned Deputy Surveyor for Western York County, and removed his residence from Byberry, Philadelphia County, to York, Pennsylvania, in June, 1765.[9] Since none of the histories of the Mason-Dixon survey include biographical information concerning the surveying brothers who engaged in the work, this seems to be an appropriate place to do so.

Archibald McClean was the second of nine children of William McClean who was born in 1702 on the Isle of Mull, Scotland, emigrated to Ireland and from thence to Montgomery County (now in Adams County), Pennsylvania, where he died June 13, 1785,[10] having married at Londonderry, Ireland, February 20, 1733, Elizabeth Rule, daughter of a Presbyterian minister. The son, Archibald, was baptised at Abington Presbyterian Church, Montgomery County, June 27, 1736,[11] and died April 30, 1786,[12] being buried in the Old Marsh Creek Cemetery, now a part of the Gettysburg battlefield.

He followed his profession throughout his life. On February 21, 1781 he was appointed by the General Assembly of Pennsylvania a Co-

Commissioner, with John Lukens, to run and mark "a meridian line to the Ohio river," in connection with establishing the Pennsylvania and Virginia boundary. The work, for which McClean was paid only £2.4.9 specie, was done between September, 1781 and July, 1782 and a detachment of Westmoreland militia gave protection to the surveyors who were doing their survey in wartime. Lukens and McClean had the assistance of the latter's brother, Samuel; his brother Alexander was designated Alternate Commissioner.[13] Archibald McClean, in addition to his surveying accomplishments, became a member of the General Assembly of Pennsylvania. He served as Chairman of the first Committee of Safety for York County during the Revolution; he was Prothonotary, Register of Wills and Recorder of Deeds for the County from 1777-1786. His first official act was to record the Declaration of Independence, under his own signature, in the county records. While the Constitutional Congress held sessions in York, his residence was used as the Treasury Department.[14]

Colonel Alexander McClean, surveyor and younger brother of Archibald, was born at Abington, presumably on November 10, 1746, and died at Uniontown, Fayette County, Pennsylvania, December 7, 1834. After his work on the Mason-Dixon survey, he removed to Fayette County where, in 1772, he was made Deputy Surveyor for that county. In 1781 he was appointed by the Supreme Executive Council, as Chief Surveyor for the State of Pennsylvania; in 1782 he served as a member of the first Assembly and in 1783 was the Recorder and Presiding Justice of the Court of Common Pleas and Orphans Court.[15] When David Rittenhouse and Andrew Porter were appointed Commissioners to run the western boundary of Pennsylvania, Porter, on May 10, 1786, asked that Alexander McClean be his assistant. The appointment was made the same day and between June and October, 1786, McClean signed the official reports of progress with Porter. Their work was finished at Lake Erie.[16]

List of Children of William and Elizabeth (Rule) McClean: [17]

    i. William McClean, born December 26, 1733; died September 3, 1807, in Hamilton Ban Township, Adams County, Pa. He married December 6, 1757, Jane Witherow, born December 30, 1732; died July 23, 1785, and had issue: *a.* John McClean, *b.* Elizabeth McClean (married James Johnson), *c.* Margaret McClean (married Abraham Scott), *d.* William McClean, *e.* Rebecca McClean (married—Meredith), *f.* Mary McClean (married John Cox), *g.* Ann McClean (married Andrew Finley), *h.* Samuel McClean, *i.* Sarah McClean (married John Witherow), *j.* James McClean (married Margaret Reed), *k.* Jane McClean (married John Foster).

ii. Archibald McClean, mentioned above, married first, March 29, 1759, Ann (Annetje) Trump, by whom he had issue: *a.* Elizabeth McClean (married Thomas Clingan), *b.* Mary McClean (married Ensign Jacob Barnitz and was the mother of the Honorable Charles A. Barnitz), *c.* Levi McClean, *d.* Alexander McClean (married Margaret Lawrence). Archibald McClean married, second, March 11, 1777, Mary Leach Treat, of Abington, and had further issue: *e.* Esther Rule McClean (married Jacob Scudder), *f.* Rebecca Irwin McClean.

iii. (Major) Moses McClean, born January 10 and baptised March 26, 1738; surveyor and Commissary; married April 14, 1763, Sarah Charlesworth, and later resided in Chillicothe, Ohio. Issue: *a.* Archibald McClean.

iv. John McClean, born May 11 and baptised June 8, 1740; surveyor; removed to Washington County, Pa.

v. James McClean, born July 27 and baptised November 3, 1742; died September 14, 1825. He married April 6, 1773, Janet Hart, born in 1751; died January 6, 1815.

vi. Samuel McClean, born September 30, 1742; surveyor; married Margaret Porter and removed to Washington County, Pa.

vii. (Colonel) Alexander McClean, mentioned above, married October 26, 1775, at Uniontown, Pa., Sarah Holmes, born April 4, 1750; died March 26, 1832. Ten children.

viii. Elizabeth McClean, no information.

ix. Joseph McClean, born 1752; died 1776.

FOOTNOTES AND REFERENCES

[1] William Stump, " Mason-Dixon Line," illustrated with photographs by A. A. Bodine and A. L. Trussell and published in the magazine section, *The Baltimore Sun*, Sunday, December 2, 1956.

[2] *Report of the Secretary of Internal Affairs of the Commonwealth of Pennsylvania, Containing Reports of the Surveys and Resurveys of the Boundary Lines of the Commonwealth* (Harrisburg: 1887), p. xiii.

[3] John Gibson, ed., *History of York County, Pennsylvania* (Chicago: 1886).

[4] *Report of the Resurvey of the Maryland-Pennsylvania Boundary, Part of the Mason and Dixon Line* (Harrisburg: 1909), No. 335.

[5] The work of McClean and associates is described in scholarly detail in Thomas D. Cope, " When the Stars Interrupted the Running of a Meridian Line Northward Up the Delmarva Peninsula," *Proceedings of the American Philosophical Society*, Vol. 100, No. 6 (December, 1956), pp. 557-566. The same author has studied the Mason-Dixon survey (with no mention of the McCleans) in "Degrees Along the West Line, The Parallel Between Maryland and Pennsylvania," *Ibid.*, Vol. 93, No. 2 (May, 1949), pp. 127-133, and in numerous other articles.

[6] William Dunlap, *History of the New Netherlands, Province of New York, and State of New York, to the Adoption of the Federal Constitution* (New York: 1839-40), II, cxcix, mentions Rittenhouse only. In the British Museum is a plan, "A map of the province of New York, with part of Pennsylvania and New England, from an actual survey made by Captain Montresor, engineer, four sheets, 1775." *Dictionary of National Biography*, XXXVIII, 329.

[7] On February 13, 1765, Charles Mason recorded in his Journal, "Cross'd the River Schuylkill near the Swedes-ford and Lodg'd at Mr. McLane's Commissary for the Lines." The original Journal is in the National Archives; a photostat is at The American Philosophical Society.

[8] Gibson, pp. 395-396. See also *Pennsylvania Magazine of History and Biography* (hereinafter *PMHB*), XXXII, 495.

[9] Deposition of Archibald McClean dated December 8, 1789, in the suit of Digges Heirs vs. George Stevenson, No. 67, July Term, York County, Pa., C.P. 1780, filed as Blair MSS No. 22 at York County Historical Society. Gibson erroneously states that Archibald McClean located " in the Marsh Creek district of York County " in 1738 (*op. cit.*, p. 395), when he would have been two years old. He was living in Byberry on February 18, 1765. *PMHB*, LVIII, 207.

[10] William Henry Egle, M.D., ed., *Notes and Queries, Historical, Biographical and Genealogical, Relating Chiefly to Interior Pennsylvania* (Harrisburg: 1898), Annual Volume 1897, p. 223.

[11] *Records of Abington, Pa. Presbyterian Church, 1714-1864* (transcript at GSP), p. 25.

[12] *York County Deed Book* 00, p. 16. His will, dated October 5, 1785, was proved May 18, 1786. *York County Will Book* G, p. 105.

[13] *Report of the Secretary of Internal Affairs*, pp. 295-312. McClean's letters provide an interesting documentary account of the expedition.

[14] Gibson, pp. 123, 396.

[15] Franklin Ellis, ed., *History of Fayette County, Pennsylvania* (Philadelphia: 1882), p. 362.

[16] *Report of the Secretary of Internal Affairs*, pp. 378, 431.

[17] The dates of baptism here cited are from *Records of Abington, Pa. Presbyterian Church, 1714-1864*. The dates of birth, marriage and death are from Bible records in the possession of Helen H. Torrence, Baltimore, Md., great-great-great-great granddaughter of Archibald McClean.

JOHN McKNITT (ca. 1660-1714) AND SOME OF HIS KINSFOLK: ALEXANDERS — BREVARDS — DALES

By John Goodwin Herndon

In my study of the records of colonial Maryland and Delaware I have found the following variations in the spelling of the McKnitt name, indicative of many differences in pronunciation. I have not distinguished between the use of a capital K and a small k, nor between the placing of the c on the line with the other letters and its appearance in the familiar position above the line. The tabulation shows 1 Macknatt, 1 McNatt, or 2 with a short a; 4 Macknet, 18 Mac Knett, 1 Macnett, 5 McKnett, 2 McNett, or 30 with the short e; 1 with a long e, McNeet; 4 Macknit, 13 MacKnitt, 3 MaKnitt, 2 McKnit, 25 McKnitt, 1 McNit, 1 McNitt, or 49 with the short i; and 9 Mac Knite, 13 McKnight, 4 McKnite, 7 McNight, 2 McNite, or 35 with the long i sound. On the basis of these figures and with an unwarranted poetic license I have dared to write these fourteen lines. Call them a sonnet at peril to your soul !

A Guide to Pronunciation

Two people say he was lean, not fat,
Our worthy Scotch-Irish John MacKnatt;
Thirty assert he was firmly set,
Was Presbyterian John MacKnett;
One who speaks of him as grand to meet
Calls him honest, plain old John McNeet;
Forty-nine find him vigorous, fit,
Ocean-crossing, thrifty John McKnitt;
Yet thirty-five do def'nitely claim
John McKnight was his only name.
Fifty times and more we find it " Mac ",
But as for me, alas and alack,
The correct spelling I cannot say,
Since sixty-three omit the " a ";
Yet now, noting the dominant writ,
I'll just call him loyal John McKnitt.

John McKnitt, maternal grandfather of John McKnitt Alexander who was secretary of the Mecklenburg Convention of 1775, settled in Somerset County, Md., probably in 1684. He was accompanied by his first wife Jane, whom he had doubtless married in Northern Ireland a short time before sailing for America. Although her surname is not of record, I believe that she was an Alexander, probably sister to Samuel Alexander with whom John McKnitt was intimately associated in both Somerset and Cecil Counties.

It is uncertain whether the McKnitts landed at Philadelphia or New Castle-on-Delaware or at one of the Eastern Shore of Virginia ports of entry. What we do know is that they did not remain there, but located instead on the west side of the Pocomoke River on a tract called THE STRAND which, originally consisting of 1,000 acres, had been surveyed 7 March 1663 for Daniel Jenifer but patented in the name of Capt. Thomas Smith. At the time of John McKnitt's acquisition of his 88 acres thereof, the other owners were Thomas Carroll's orphans, 300 acres; Mark Gendron, 200 acres; Walter Lane, 200 acres; Thomas Layfield, 112 acres; and James Atkinson, 100 acres.[1] THE STRAND was in the Manokin neighborhood in which the Alexanders, Browns, Kings, Polks, Strawbridges, and Wallaces resided.[2] There he continued to live about 15 years during all of which time the Reverend Thomas Wilson was pastor of the Manokin Presbyterian Congregation.

To John and Jane McKnitt four children were born, their births being recorded thus in Somerset Court Liber IKL,[3] that veritable gold mine of information concerning many early families of Maryland's Eastern Shore:

> Robert Macknett ye son of John Mac Knett borne of Jane his wife at Manoakin the fourth day of June one Thousand Six hundred eighty and five.
>
> John Macknitt Son of John Macknitt, borne of Jane his wife ye 8th day of September one Thousand Six hundred eighty & seven.
>
> Katherine ye Daughter of John Macknitt borne of Jane his wife ye tenth day of August about eleven of ye Clock in ye forenoone annoq Dom one Thousand Six hundred eighty nine.
>
> Mary Macknitt Daughter of John Mac Knitt borne of Jane his wife at Manokin the twenty sixth day of February anno Domini One thousand Six hundred ninety and one [i.e. 1691/2].

---

[1] 9 *Rent Rolls* 61, being Volume I for Somerset and Dorchester Counties, in the Land Office at Annapolis, and *Somerset Rent Roll*, 53, in the Maryland Historical Society, Baltimore.

[2] Clayton Torrence: *Old Somerset on the Eastern Shore of Maryland*, 213, 232, 271, 364-5, 430, 468. Hereafter this book will be cited as *Old Somerset*.

[3] *opus cit.*, 169, 170, 171, 172, at Princess Anne.

After the accession of William and Mary to the Throne there was circulated among the citizens of Somerset County an Address of Loyalty, bearing date of 28 November 1689, which reads as follows: [4]

> To the King and Queen most Ex^t Maj^ty Wee your Majesty's subjects in the County of Somersett and Province of Maryland being refreshed and encouraged by your Majestys great and prosperous undertakings and by your late gracious letter to those of this province, do cast ourselves at your Majesty's feet humbly desiring and hopefully expecting the continuance of your Maj^tys care of us, as our Case or Circumstance doe or may require, in the confidence whereof wee resolve to continue (by the Grace of God) in the Profession and defence of the Protestant Religion and your Majesty's Title and interest against the French and other Paptists [*sic*] that oppose and trouble us in soe just and good a cause not doubting but your Majestys wisdom and clemency will afford unto us all needful suitable Aid and Protection for securing our Religion lives and liberty under Protestant Governors and Government, and enable us to defend ourselves against all Invaders. Thus praying for your Majestys long and happy Reigne over us, Wee know ourselves to bee (with due Reverence and sincerity) Your Majesty's Loyall Obedient and humble Servants.

Among the more the 200 signers were John McKnitt, William Alexander, Sr. and Jr., Adam Spence, John Deale (Dale), William Polk, John Pope, John Steel, Richard Woodcraft, John Porter, Robert Polk, John Strawbridge, Peter Dent, Nicholas Carpenter, Rev. Thomas Wilson, John West, Major Robert King, Richard Tull, and Edmund Howard—to mention a few who were business, church, or personal friends of John McKnitt or related to members of his family. The list of signers, which included many prominent members of the Church of England, some of whom are mentioned above, was, however, a sort of roster of heads of Presbyterian families.

Mary, fourth child of John and Jane McKnitt, was born, as already noted, 26 February 1691/2. Sometime within a year thereafter the mother died, for on 28 March 1693 John McKnitt married Jane Wallis (Wallace).[5] The officiating clergyman, whose name seems to have been incorrectly entered as " Mr. Burnett, minister of ye Gospel " (for Burnett is a name unknown in early Presbyterian or Church of England records), may well have been Reverend Thomas Barret who, in 1685, had been in correspondence with Reverend Francis Makemie, then in Somerset, concerning his Barret's moving to New England from his then location on the Ashley River, South Carolina.[6]

---

[4] VIII *Archives of Maryland* 139-142.

[5] *Somerset Court Liber IKL*, 173.

[6] *Old Somerset*, 535.

Next we read of the birth of John McKnitt's fifth child in these words: [7]

> Margaret McKnitt, Daughter of John McKnitt & born of Jane his wife at Monocan the 26th day of December anno Domini 1693.

The previous month Nicholas Carpenter had died. In his will he had named his friends Major Robert King and Capt. John King as executors. On 30 May 1694 the Somerset Court approved of their serving. John McKnitt was their surety.[8] This is the first reference to him as surety on any administration bond, but the fact that he later several times so qualified, both in Somerset and Cecil Counties, clearly indicates that he was a man of substance and integrity.

To John and Jane (Wallace) McKnitt there seem to have been born two other children, William and Jean or Jane. Proof is lacking on both of these assumptions. We find that William McKnett died in Dorchester County, which lies between Somerset and Cecil, in 1747.[9] It would be strange to find a stray McKnitt there. I place his birth year as about 1696. He left a widow Elizabeth and at least one child, a daughter named Ann. Mrs. Frances Alexander Butterworth, who in 1909 published *A Family of the House of Alexander,* expressed therein [10] her opinion that Andrew Alexander, born in 1697, whose wife was named Jean or Jane, had married a daughter of John McKnitt's. We may reasonably assume that this Jean or Jane was born about 1699. This Andrew Alexander purchased in 1745 from John McKnitt III land that had been part of John McKnitt, Sr.'s, Cecil County property.[11]

On 16 May 1698 William Wallace " of Manokin River, Somerset County, carpenter " made his will.[12] In it he mentioned his " cousin Jean Macknett." She was, of course, Jane (Wallace) McKnitt, whose husband was not only a witness to the will but also was surety for James Wallace when he in July 1698 qualified as administrator of his brother William's estate.[13] The testator also left property to " my two cousins John Bruard and John Wallace." The name Bruard is almost undeci-

---

[7] *Somerset Court Liber IKL,* 175.

[8] 15-C *Testamentary Proceedings* 47, Hall of Records, Annapolis.

[9] 27 *Accounts* 80-81, Hall of Records, Annapolis: "Representatives of William Macknett are this Accountant and one child Ann Macknett."

[10] *opus cit.,* 26.

[11] 6 *Cecil County Deeds* 480, at Elkton, dated 14 June 1745.

[12] 6 *Maryland Wills* 149, Hall of Records, Annapolis.

[13] 17 *Testamentary Proceedings* 187.

pherable and was undoubtedly intended to be Brevard.[14]

The same month the Prerogative Court had noted: [15]

> July 28th 1698, Came Major Whittington of Somersett County and . . .
> brought into the office the Inventory of the Estate of Amos Parsons late of ye said
> County appraised by Richard Tull and William Wallace to ye Value of 15£04:02d
> Sterl.—and Likewise the bond of John Macknitt of £30 8s with John Porter his se-
> curity for the said MacKnitt . . . Adm[ing] on the Effects of Amos Parsons deceased.

Then a curious error occurred in the Court's records. A minute was
written thus:[16]

> Amos Parsons, adm[r] of John MacKnitt, his Acct passed before ye Com[rs].
> November 15th 1698 and ordered to be recorded.

What was intended was, of course:

> John MacKnitt, adm[r] of Amos Parsons, decd., his Acct etc.

There was a suit in 1700 in Somerset entitled " The King agt. John
West." [17] In the report on that case there appears a note that the Court
ordered a payment of 387 pounds of tobacco to be made to John McKnitt
at the request of William Bladen, attorney for John West, or that the
Court had ordered such a payment to be made to John Contee's assigns
at John McKnitt's house. The odd use of the word " Ditto " on a certain line in that record makes uncertain which of these two readings is
correct. Either shows, however, that John McKnitt was still in Somerset.

The last reference to him in the records of that county during his lifetime was a minute adopted at the January 1701/2 term of court, which
is as follows: [18]

> John M[c]Nitt of Somerset Parish fined for concealing his son Robert M[c]Nitt
> from tithe list for 1701, said Robert being at that time 16 years old and upwards.

---

[14] *Somerset Wills EB-5,* 130, at Princess Anne. This will was badly abstracted, as
published, in II *Maryland Calendar of Wills* 155. The testator was Wallace not Wal-
lare; relationships mentioned in the will are, in some cases, omitted in the printed abstract.
The name of the cousin first listed was not Coverd, but, as stated, was probably intended
to be Brevard.

[15] 17 *Testamentary Proceedings* 179.

[16] *Ibid.,* 229.

[17] *Provincial Court Judgments WT-3,* 332a, Hall of Records, Annapolis.

[18] *Somerset Judicials* (1701-1702), 65.

It was about 3 years before this that Jane (Wallace) McKnitt had died. Her husband, thus left with the sole responsibility of the upbringing of his children whose ages ranged from 14 down to a year, removed to the northeastern end of Cecil County, Md., near the Pennsylvania line, probably at the suggestion of Matthew Wallace, who if not the younger children's grandfather, was certainly a close relative. But John McKnitt did not wait long before marrying again. He chose as his third wife Martha Dale, whose brother John had settled in Somerset before 1687 and whose brother James about 1699 " landed at Philadelphia, from there he went to the Head of Elk—he had a sister living there who was married to a gentleman by the name of McKnite." The Dales, we are told, " were from England; they were what were called Dissenters and were of the Presbyterian order." [19] To John and Martha (Dale) McKnitt were born two daughters Sarah about 1701 and Elizabeth about 1703 who married her first cousin John Dale, son of James. (See Dale Excurssu.)

The McKnitt home in Cecil County was on a tract called GLASGOW. There is substantial reason to believe that he and his family had lived there ever since his first coming from Somerset. He may even have been one of the fifteen " Irishmen " referred to in the grant to " Edwin O'Dwire and 15 Irishmen " in 1683 of the NEW MUNSTER tract out of which GLASGOW seems to have been carved by request of John McKnitt.[20] There seems to be no question that Matthew Wallace and his five Alexander associtaes were among that number. (See Alexander Excursus.) *
The patent to GLASGOW states that a warrant for its survey was granted to John McKnitt on 15 June 1713; that it contained 90 acres; that it adjoined on different sides three properties: BULLEN'S RANGE, a tract laid out for Samuel Alexander called SLIGO, and another called HIGH SPANIOLA; and that the annual rent was to be £o 3s. 7½d. The patent itself was not issued until 10 September 1716, about nine months after the death of the grantee, John McKnitt, Sr.[21]

In 1710 and 1711 he is known to have been surety on administration bonds in the case of three estates. The first such reference is found on a certification to the Prerogative Court at Annapolis 24 October 1710 from the Court of Cecil County; reading: [22]

---

[19] Printed copy of Adam Dale's letter to his grandson, E. W. Dale, dated 19 May 1851. (See Dale Excursus.)

[20] George Johnston: *History of Cecil County, Maryland,* 133-136; and Carl Ross McKenrick: " New Munster ", in XXXV *Maryland Historical Magazine* 147-159.

[21] 43 *Land Office Liber FF-7,* folios 75 and 76, and *Land Office Liber PL-4,* folio 131.

[22] 21 *Testamentary Proceedings* 294.

*Page 212, this volume.

William Williams, admr. of Ricd Tippit, his admstn bond in common forme with John Macknit and Andrew Wallace his securities in the sume of Twenty pounds Sterl dated the ii day of May 1710.

The second was returned from the Court of Cecil County to the Prerogative Court of April 1711, as follows:[23]

Francis Smith Admr of Thomas Yeoman his Admirs bond in Comon forme with Andrew Wallace and John Macknit his suretys in twenty pounds Sterl dated the 28th day of ffebry 17$\frac{10}{11}$

Also an Invty and an Account of the sd Yeoman Estate

The third, returned at the same time, goes thus: [23]

Andrew Wallace admr of John Dowing [Downing?] his Admt^{n} bond in Comon forme with Francis Smith & John Macknit his suretys in twenty pounds sterl dated the 28th day of ffeby 1710 [1710/11].

On 20 August 1714 " Thomas Stevenson of Bucks County Province of Pennsylvania, gentleman " executed a power of attorney " to his good friend John MacKnitt of Back Creek, Cecill County Province of Maryland " in connection with the disposal by Thomas Stevenson and his wife Sarah of his Cecil County holdings to a group whom he designated as " Matthew Wallace and Company." [24] The property involved was a tract of 1,050 acres on the " East Side of the main fresh of Elk River " which Stevenson had purchased 1 April 1714 from Robert Roberts, a glover, of Queen Anne County, Md., acres significantly designated as bounded by the lands of Daniel Pearce, Matthew Wallace, and David Alexander. The price paid by " Matthew Wallace and Company " was 172 10s. The grantees were named in the deed as " Matthew Wallace, yoeman, James Alexander, farmer, Arthur Alexander, farmer, David Alexander, farmer, James Alexander, weaver, and Joseph Alexander, tanner." (See Alexander Excursus.) The grantor had been elected in 1710 to the Pennsylvania Assembly, and continued to serve therein until his death; was a justice of the peace for Bucks County; had married Mrs. Sarah (Jenings) Pennington, daughter of Governor Samuel Jenings; had contributed to the building of a Dutch Presbyterian Church at Bensalem, Bucks County, although he and his family were Quakers; was owner of extensive real estate interests in Pennsylvania, Delaware, Maryland, and New Jersey; [25] but when or where he became acquainted with John Mc-

[23] *ibid.*, 342.

[24] 2 *Cecil County Deeds*, 280, 283, at Elkton.

[25] John R. Stevenson: *Thomas Stevenson, of London, England, and His Descendants,* 31-36.

Knitt has not been learned.

The recording on 22 November 1714 of the afore-mentioned power of attorney to John McKnitt brings us to the end of his life. He died sometime between that date and 24 December 1714 when his widow Martha and his son John, Jr., were appointed administrators of his estate.[26] At the April 1715 session of the Prerogative Court the following minute was adopted: [27]

> Martha Macknet and John Macknet, Admrs. of John Macknet, the Adminstn bond in Comon forme with Samuel Alexander & Adam Wallace their sureties in one hundred and fifty pounds Sterl. dated 24th day of January 17$\frac{14}{15}$ . . .
> which preceding bonds are ordered to be filed.

The inventory of the personal estate showed assets classified as follows: [28]

	£	s.	d.
Farm animals	20	0	0
Farm produce, etc.	40	13	8
Household furnishings	12	7	0
Plate, etc.	17	5	0
Notes and accounts	11	7	1
TOTAL	101	12	9

The notes and accounts were due from John Cochran, Samuel Alexander, John Gullett, and John Holthorn. The certificate reads: [28]

> Wee whose names are underwritten, appointed appraisers of the estate of John Macknett, Sr, late of Cecill County deceased have returned this inventory from under our hands and seals the 16th day of March 1715 1715/16.
> In the presence of   (signed) Francis Smith
> Adam Wallace   (signed) Oliver Wallace
> John Brevard

And finally we read that there was filed and ordered to be recorded [29]

> The Account of Jno. McKnitt Junr and Martha McKnitt, Administrators, etc., of John McKnitt Senr, late of Cecil County, deceased.

---

[26] 1 *Cecil County Bonds* 174, at Elkton.

[27] *Testamentary Proceedings* 425.

[28] 1 *Cecil County Inventories* 233-235, at Elkton.

[29] 1 *Cecil County Administration and Guardian Accounts and Distributions* 220, at Elkton.

Children of JOHN MCKNITT and his first wife JANE, possibly ALEXANDER:

1. ROBERT, b 4 June 1685 at Manokin, Somerset Co., Md.; still in Somerset, 1701; may be the Robert McKnight whose will, probated in New Castle County, Del., 7 April 1769, mentioned his wife Isabella, his sons Moses and ALEXANDER, and his grandchildren Isabella and William Nevins. If thus correctly identified, it follows that he had received his share of his father's property during his father's lifetime, and having removed outside the jurisdiction of the Maryland courts, his next younger brother qualified in his stead in 1714/15 as administrator of their father's estate.
2. JOHN, b 8 September 1687 in Somerset Co.; m Dorothy Wallace, who m 2ndly Robert Patton; died between 14 April 1733 and 13 June 1733; was a planter of Cecil Co.; left four children: Daniel, likely never to be " capable of maintaining himself "; John, who inherited his lands, and who died in 1747; Mary who m Adam Brevard, of Worcester Co., Md., and Hannah.
3. KATHERINE, b 10 August 1689 in Somerset Co.; m John Brevard. (See Brevard Excursus.)
4. MARY, b 26 February 1691/2 at Manokin, Somerset Co., m Thomas Powell, of Worcester County, Md.

Children of JOHN MCKNITT and his second wife JANE WALLACE:

5. MARGARET, b 26 December 1693 at Manokin; m James Alexander. (See Alexander Excursus.)
6. WILLIAM, b prob. ca 1696; died intestate 1747, Dorchester Co., leaving widow Elizabeth and daughter Ann. His personalty was appraised at 27 10s 0d.
7. JEAN (JANE), b prob. ca 1698, said to have m Andrew Alexander. (See Alexander Excursus.)

Children of JOHN MCKNITT and his third wife MARTHA DALE:

8. SARAH, b ca 1701 in Cecil Co., m 2 Feb. 1719/20 James Wallace.[30]
9. ELIZABETH, b ca 1703, in Cecil County; m her first cousin John Dale " Irish ". (See Dale Excursus.)

John McKnitt, Jr., was interested in two tracts. One was HISPANIOLA (frequently written HIGH SPANIOLA), originally surveyed 1 October 1678 for Nicholas Painter. It was on the east side of the Bohemia River and on the north side of Long Creek, contained 900 acres, and was assessed at £1 16s. annual rental (taxes).[31] In 1720 it was resurveyed for William

---

[30] *Records of St. Stephens Parish, Cecil County, 1687-1837*, p. 10, in the Md. Hist. Society, Balto., Md. " James Wallis and Sarah McKnight Spinster was married pr Mr. Richd Sewell by bans the 2nd day of febry Ao Do. 1719/20."

[31] 6 *Rent Rolls* 313, being Volume II for Kent and Cecil Counties, in the Land Office at Annapolis.

Richardson and found to contain 868 acres. The rent roll for Cecil County shows the following changes in its ownership.[32]

William Richardson	to John Macknett	150 acres	22 June 1723
William Richardson	to Saml Alexander	150 acres	30 Mch. 1724
Samuel Alexander	to Thos Stratton	150 acres	20 Mch. 1729
Thomas Stratton	to John Macknett	35 acres	29 Jany 1731
Thomas Stratton	to Robt Patton	150 acres	28 Aug. 1734

A note showed that this last transfer included a part of HISPANIOLA and BULLEN's RANGE. Consideration for the first of these sales was £33 15s. Robert Patton had married Dorothy, John McKnitt's widow, even before she qualified as executrix under his will. It would appear that John Mc-Knitt, Jr., died possessed of 185 acres of HISPANIOLA.

As to the second property we find in the Somerset records a deed, dated 2 September 1728, of which the following is an abstract: [33]

John Macknitt of Cecil Co., Md., and Dorothy, his wife, of the first part; Thos. Robins, of Somerset Co., of the second part; Francis Mercer, of Somerset County, of third part.

Ld. Baltimore by pat. June 10, 1666 granted Thos. Smith tract called THE STRAND west side Pocomoke River and sd. Smith alienated the same to Walter Taylor and John Remy, as by record in Secretary's office; and on Sep. 22, 1673 Remy conveyed to Henry Smith ½ of sd. tract being 500 acres, and Taylor sold to John Macknitt a part or parts of 500 acres, containing 133 acres and is now called GLAS-GOW, and said Macknitt hath lately contracted with sd. Robins to convey to him the said 133 acres—but no deeds having been made, said Macknitt now hereby conveys same to Francis Mercer.

(Signed) Jno ^{his} M_{mark} Macknit

(Signed) Dorothy McNitt

Dorothy wife of John McNight of Bohemia Manor, Cecil Co., acknowledges her dower in above land containing 133 acres on Pocomoke River which was formerly bought by John McNight—deceased—from Walter Taylor.

The reader will note that this gives a quite different account of the ownership of the tract called THE STRAND from that reported in the earlier part of this article. Most significant of all, however, is the reference to John McKnitt, Sr.'s, having called *this* tract GLASGOW, as he had also named his lands in Cecil County, a definite clue to the Scotch home of the subject of his sketch.

---

[32] *Ibid.*, 376.

[33] *Somerset Deeds Liber* 0-17, 96, at Princess Anne.

This is the last reference to John McKnitt, Sr., in the Somerset records, so far as the author of this article has been able to find; but still one remains in the Cecil records. It is, as previously noted, the mention of John McKnitt, Sr., in connection with the sale by John McKnitt III of 30 acres in Cecil County to Andrew Alexander 14 June 1745, described as " a property called GLASGOW formerly taken up by John McKnit late of sd County, grandfather to the abovesaid John McKnit on a branch of Bohemia Back Creek originally taken up by Nicholas Painter and called HIGH SPANIOLA . . . to John McKnits Plantation . . . to Long Creek." The deed was signed " John McKnitt." [34]

The fourth John was always John McKnight in the Cecil records. It is interesting to ask why, since the Scotch-Irish pronounced Hispaniola High Spaniola, they should not pronounce McKnitt McKnight. And here I leave the matter.

ALEXANDER *Excursus*

There is a well established tradition that seven Alexander brothers, Presbyterians from Scotland who had sojourned a while in the north of Ireland, probably at Raphoe, co. Donegal, and Sligo, co. Sligo, came to Cecil County, Maryland, before going on to Somerset. If we may judge from the circumstantial evidence remaining, then along with the brothers came two sisters: one, the wife of Matthew Wallace; the other Jane, who married John McKnitt.

In Somerset, at early dates, we find William, Andrew, Samuel, and John Alexander, and in Cecil County James, Francis, Joseph, and the afore-mentioned Samuel Alexander. I hazard a guess that they were sons of the Reverend James Alexander, of Raphoe, a member of Laggan Presbytery in 1680, whose ministerial brethren then in northern Ireland included David Brown, of Urney, William Traile, of Lifford, Thomas Wilson, of Killybegs, and William Liston, of Letterkenny, to mention a few. I name these because one David Brown became an important civic-minded Presbyterian leader in Somerset; because William Traile and Thomas Wilson soon joined Francis Makemie, " father of organized Presbyterianism in America ", in his labors in Somerset; and because William Alexander, Sr., of Somerset, had a grandson named for William Liston. At first in Somerset and later in Cecil, we find Matthew Wallace and John McKnitt.

[34] 6 *Cecil County Deeds* 480.

In *The Records of the General Synod of Ulster* [1] James Alexander and William Liston, of Raphoe, are noted as absent from the meetings in 1691, 1692, and 1694, after which Liston's name appears no more; but James Alexander, always absent from meetings of the Synod, sent excuses which were accepted, and finally his death on 17 November 1704 was minuted.[2] How early he became a member of Laggan Presbytery I do not know.

For convenience in identification let us assume that they were born in the following order and about the year named:

1. WILLIAM, 1646	4. JAMES, 1652	7. JOSEPH, 1660
2. ANDREW, 1648	5. FRANCIS, 1654	8. JOHN, 1662
3. ELIZABETH, 1650	6. SAMUEL, 1657	9. JANE, 1665

1. WILLIAM ALEXANDER, who was in Somerset about 1685, acquired HUNTING QUARTER (100 acres) in 1687,[3] and HOGG QUARTER (100 acres) at the head waters of Wicomoco Creek (at that time called river) and Manokin River was surveyed for him 25 April 1689.[4] In 1692 he was an assistant to the court in laying out the boundaries for the original parishes in Somerset, as was also his neighbor Matthew Wallace,[5] who was probably his brother-in-law. In September 1690 he witnessed a deed of gift from Reverend Thomas Wilson to his sons Ephraim and Thomas Wilson.[6] The date of his death is not of record, nor the name of his wife. One descendant of his [7] has said that her Christian name was Ann. She may have been a daughter of Reverend William Liston, of Letterkenny, for we find that the unusual name Liston was given to one of the grandsons of William Alexander. The only known child of this couple was William Alexander, Jr., whose dates were 1670-1735.[8] He married

---

[1] A copy of these records in three volumes is in the library of the Presbyterian Historical Society, Witherspoon Bldg., Philadelphia.

[2] *Opus cit.*, Vol. I, 96.

[3] *Somerset County Deed Liber 06*, p. 879.

[4] *9 Rent Rolls 156*, being Volume I for Somerset and Dorchester Counties, in the Land Office at Annapolis.

[5] *Old Somerset*, 153.

[6] *ibid*, 232.

[7] Mrs. Jane Zellner Gladney, Stamps, Ark., in VI *Compendium of American Genealogy* 248.

[8] In the *Somerset Judicials, 1725-1730*, he deposed in January 1725/6 that he was "aged about 56 years." His will was probated 1735, *Somerset Registry of Wills Liber E B* pp. 134, 137.

Catherine Wallace.[9]   One of his tracts was named RAPHOE.[10]

2. ANDREW ALEXANDER had two children whose births are recorded in Somerset Court Liber IKL, but the name of his wife is not entered. The children were Abigail, b 15 September 1677, and Elias, b 1679. Elias Alexander seems to have married his first cousin, Sophia, a daughter of his uncle, Joseph Alexander.

3. ELIZABETH ALEXANDER, as stated above, was probably the wife of Matthew Wallace, who figures so prominently in these notes.   He died between 1714 and 1716.

4. JAMES ALEXANDER was the person of that name called " weaver ", fifth listed of the Alexanders in the sale of land to " Matthew Wallace and Co." by Thomas Stevenson, of Bucks Co., Pa., through his attorney, John McKnitt, in 1714.[11]   He married Mary, daughter of John Steel.   In his will [12] he calls himself " James Alexander, carpenter, of New Minster, Cecil County."   He named as executors his wife Mary, his " father-in-law John Steel, yeoman, of New Castle County, Delaware ", and his " brother Francis Alexander of Cecil County, Maryland."   A witness was his brother Samuel Alexander.   The will of John Garner, of Cecil County, dated 7 March 1723/4, probated 22 October 1725,[13] contained a bequest of £40 to " the children of James Alexander by Mary Steel."   The eldest of these was Moses Alexander who was a witness to that will.   Another was David, and Arthur was probably another.   In their father's 1719 will mention by name is made of other sons named Joseph, John, and Francis the youngest.

5. FRANCIS ALEXANDER, mentioned in the will of his brother James as living in Cecil County in 1719, is not known to have had a family.

6. SAMUEL ALEXANDER, after settling on the Pocomoke about 1685, removed in 1723 to Cecil County.   That year he, John Brevard, and Peter Bouchelle were elders of the Broad Creek Presbyterian Congregation.[14]   On 13 June 1723 Richard Thompson deeded to Samuel Alexander and Peter Bouchelle " one acre of land for the use of the Presbyterian Congregation to erect [thereon] a meeting house " for which an annual rent of one ear of Indian corn was to be paid, if lawfully demanded.[15]   Himself patentee of SLIGO, he deeded 21 March 1723 to his son Martin the northern end thereof, adjoining ALEXANDRIA and BUL-

---

[9] *Somerset County Deed Liber 021*, p. 152.

[10] This was surveyed for him 20 May 1689.   It contained 200 acres " in the fork of the Southern most branches of the Rockiawakin."

[11] 2 *Cecil County* Deeds 280, 283, at Elkton.

[12] Abstracted *Calendar of Delaware Wills: New Castle County*, C-103.

[13] Baldwin: *Maryland Calendar of Wills* Vol. V p. 204.

[14] Frances Alexander Butterworth: *A Family of the House of Alexander* p. 12.

[15] Same reference as in footnote 14.

LEN'S RANGE. Witnesses were his sons Francis and Samuel Alexander, Jr.[16] The following year he gave a part of SLIGO and of ALEXANDRIA to his son Francis.[17] Witnesses were his son Samuel, Jr., and John, son of his brother James. Samuel Alexander, Sr., died testate, leaving a wife Mary, whose surname before her marriage is not of record, and the following children, certain of whom were mentioned in his will dated 29 March 1727 which was probated 14 June 18, 1733:

i.   James, b 1 January 1685 at Pocomoke;
ii. Martin, b 18 March 1687 at Annamessix; witness to the will of his father; died in Cecil County between 5 March 1750 and 1 August 1751; married Susannah Foster;
iii. Sarah, b 28 August 1690 at Pocomoke;
iv. Francis, b . . March 1693; donee mentioned above, 1724;
v.   Mary, b 1695, married, first, 1727 Thomas Craig; married, secondly, ... Lowery; mentioned 1750 in the will of her brother Martin;
vi. Andrew, b 1697, an extensive land owner; purchased GLASGOW in 1745 from John McKnitt III; said to have married Jean, daughter of John McKnitt and his wife Jane Wallace; and
vii. Samuel, b 1699 at Pocomoke, lived in Cecil Co., in 1724.

7. JOSEPH ALEXANDER is said by two students of the Alexander and McKnitt family records to have married Abigail McKnitt.[19] She was doubtless a sister of John McKnitt, Sr. (c. 1660-1714). In the Matthew Wallace and Company listing of Alexanders he is the last named, " Joseph Alexander, tanner." He is of especial interest to our story because he was the paternal grandfather of John McKnitt Alexander, secretary of the Mecklenburg Convention of May 1775. The reason given by Thomas Stevenson for conveying the NEW MUNSTER tract to Matthew Wallace and Company is stated in the original deed of 18 May 1714. Title was conveyed to them because these lands " had for some years past been improved and *possessed by them* and had been divided amongst themselves, each man according to his *holden* [holding] and that he the said Stevenson being minded to sell the tract of land, thought it most equitable, honest and right that they the said possessors thereof should have the first offer to buy or purchase each man his holden or division of ye same." [20] Another covenant provided that Stevenson would give

[16] *ibid*, 14.

[17] *ibid*, 15.

[18] *ibid*, 15.

[19] Mrs. Clarence W. Pettigrew, Pine Bluff, Ark., in V *Compendium of American Genealogy* 691, and W. S. Ray in his *The Mecklenburg Signers and Their Neighbors.*

[20] 2 *Cecil County Deeds* 280, quoted in George Johnston: *History of Cecil Co.* 126.

them each a better deed, if they demanded it within the next seven years. By a series of eight deeds, dated 15 August 1718, he conveyed his interest in 903 acres to Joseph, James, David, Arthur, Elijah (possibly Elias), and Mary Alexander, and by two others he transferred to John Gillespie and Matthew Wallace, Jr., their respective holdings.[21] One of these eight, to " Joseph Alexander and his son James Alexander, of Cecil County and in the Province of Maryland, tanner," provides that " whereas Joseph Alexander and James Alexander have by way of a swap restored unto Thomas Stevenson all and every lands with the apurtenancy thereof which they formerly bought of Thomas Stevenson, except 386 acres, the said Stevenson now conveys to Joseph Alexander . . . ", etc. George Johnston, in his *History of Cecil County,* wrote: [22]

> " The lands conveyed to the colony of Alexanders embraced the northeast part of the NEW MUNSTER tract and extended from a short distance north of Cowantown to the extreme northern boundary of NEW MUNSTER, which, as before stated, was about a mile north of the State line, as it was located by Mason and Dixon fifty years afterwards."

These lands were conveyed a few years later by " Joseph Alexander and James, his son, both of NEWMINSTER, Cecil County, Maryland " to " Joseph, John, and Francis Alexander, sons of James Alexander, carpenter, and to Mary Alexander, relict of James Alexander, 316 acres, being in NEWMUNSTER, aforesaid, and bought by James Alexander carpenter aforesaid, from one Thomas Stevenson and confirmed by the said Stevenson unto the children and relict of the said James Alexander, carpenter . . ." in conformity with " the last will of the aforesaid James Alexander, 18 December 1719." [23] (Thomas Stevenson had already turned over to James Alexander and his son Moses their appropriate " holdens ".)

When Joseph Alexander made his will 30 December 1726, he described himself as " tanner " and of NEW MINSTER in Cecil County. It was probated 9 March 1730.[24] Witnesses were Owen O'Donnel, Ann Taylor (the Widow Taylor), John Dale [" Irish "], and John McKnitt [Jr]. Joseph named his son James to be his executor; made bequests varying between 10 and 40 shillings to his son-in-law Elias Alexander, his daughters Sophia Alexander, Jane Muley, and Abigail Claphan, and his son Francis Alexander; and left to his son James the remainder of his estate.

---

[21] George Johnston: *History of Cecil Co.* 136, 137.

[22] *Opus cit.,* 137.

[23] 3 *Cecil Deeds* 282, at Elkton.

[24] *Cecil Wills* AA-1, p. 222.

8. JOHN ALEXANDER married Barbara ......, and while they lived in Somerset a daughter Esther was born in 1693 to them.

9. JANE ALEXANDER was mentioned in the account of John McKnitt, Sr., as possibly his first wife.[25]

Special note of James Alexander, son of Joseph, above, is important, for he was the father of John McKnitt Alexander, secretary of the Mecklenburg Convention of 1775. He served as one of His Lordship's Commissioners of Justice of Cecil County; was called James Alexander, esquire, when he with Andrew Steel and a relative Francis Alexander, elders of their respective churches, attended the meeting of Presbytery at Christiana Creek Church 13 September 1726.[26] He, John Brevard, and Robert Linton, all from "the head of Elk" neighborhood, attended Presbytery 31 October 1727.[27] His will,[28] dated 17 June 1772 and probated 31 May 1779, contained bequests to his wife Abigail; his grandsons George Alexander, James, son of Hezekiah Alexander, and Amos, son of Amos Alexander; his sons Amos, Ezekiel, and Hezekiah, Josiah and John McNit (sic) Alexander, and daughters Jemima Sharp, Elizabeth Sample, Abigail Bradley, and Margaret McCoy. Its most interesting provision was a grant to his son Ezekiel of

"all that tract of land lying on Long Creek in Mecklenburg County, North Carolina, together with all the improvements thereon, together with one year old horse colt and also ten Pounds in Money."

We have no way of knowing how long James Alexander remained in North Carolina, but that he was there as early as 1752 is of record.[29] He was twice married. As has already been noted,[30] his first wife was Margaret, daughter of John McKnitt, Sr. To them were born surviving children named Theophilus, Edith, and Keziah, in addition to Hezekiah, Jemima, Amos and John McKnitt Alexander who were mentioned in their father's will. He married secondly, about 1745, but the family name of his wife Abigail, who was the mother of the other children mentioned in his will, is not of record.

---

[25] F. A. Butterworth: *A Family of the House of Alexander*, p. 12.

[26] "Records of the Presbytery of Newcastle upon Delaware" in XV *Journal of the Presbyterian Historical Society*, p. 115.

[27] *Ibid*, 161.

[28] *Cecil Wills*, CC-3, p. 100.

[29] George W. Graham: *The Mecklenburg Declaration of Independence May 20, 1775 and The Lives of Its Signers*.

[30] *Supra.*

BREVARD *Excursus*

Wheeler, in his *History of North Carolina,* opens his account of the Brevard family in these words: [1]

> " The first of the name of whom anything is known was a French Huguenot. He left his native land on the revocation of the Edict of Nantes. Going to the northern part of Ireland among the Scotch-Irish he there formed acquaintance with a family of McKnitts. In company with them he set sail for American shores. One of the family was a young and blooming lassie. Brevard and herself discovered in each other kindred spirits, and a mutual attachment sprung up between them. They joined their fortunes, determined to share the hardships incident to a settlement in a new country, at that time filled with wild beasts and savages, and settled on the waters of the Elk River, Maryland. The issue of the marriage were five sons and a daughter: John, Robert, Zebulon, Benjamin, Adam, and Elizabeth."

Nearly 30 years later Wheeler prepared his *Reminiscences of North Carolina.* Therein the Brevard story begins thus: [2]

> " The first of the family, of whom much is known . . . was a Huguenot who fled from France on the revocation of the Edict of Nantes and settled among the Scotch-Irish in the North of Ireland. He came to Elk River, in Maryland, in company with the family of McKnitts, one of whom he subsequently married— issue John, Robert, Zebulon, Benjamin, Adam and Elizabeth."

A critical examination of the foregoing statements, in the light of researches into early Maryland records, clearly indicates certain inaccuracies therein. First of all, it needs to be pointed out that at the time of the revocation of the Edict of Nantes on 18 October 1685, John McKnitt and his wife Jane were already in Maryland, for their son Robert had been born there 4 June 1685.[3] Moreover, Katherine McKnitt, whom John Brevard married, was born in Maryland in 1689.[4] She was therefore no " young and blooming lassie " who, by her charms, won the heart of a young man on his trans-Atlantic crossing, as is clearly implied by the first account above quoted.

---

[1] *Opus cit.,* Vol II, 237.

[2] *Opus cit.,* 238.

[3] *Somerset Court Liber IKL,* 164.

[4] *Ibid.,* 171. Documentary proof of this marriage is lacking. If, however, John Brevard named a daughter of the McKnitt family of Cecil County, Md., as asserted, his wife must have been Katherine, since the husbands of the other daughters are known.

On the other hand, it is possible that the assertions about the "young and blooming lassie" apply to a girl of the Wallace clan, who may well have been the first wife of John Brevard. Support for the idea of such a union is found in the provision in the will of William Wallace,[5] dated 16 May 1698 and probated 15 June 1698 in Somerset County, Md., for a bequest transcribed as to the testator's "Cousin John Bruard", doubtless intended to be Brevard. Unless there was such a marriage, it is difficult to figure out how the Huguenot exile was a cousin of William Wallace, of Manokin River. Even then, he would have been merely a cousin-in-law.

That the children of John Brevard were by his second wife, Katherine McKnitt, rather than by his first one follows as a matter of biological probability. For the first wife, if a girl in 1685 with whom he fell in love and shortly thereafter married, would scarcely have had her first child about 1712, which is 27 years later. Katherine McKnitt was, moreover, of the right age for marriage about 1711, when she was in her twenty-second year.

Summarizing then from what we now know and combining it with Wheeler's statements, as modified by Graham's,[6] we might more safely assume the following to be approximately the correct story:

The first Brevard of whom we have record was a young Huguenot named Jean [John] who left his native France on the revocation of the Edict of Nantes and went to the North of Ireland where, among the Scotch-Irish, he became acquainted with certain members of the McKnitt family. Others of that family had already settled in Somerset County, Maryland. In company with some of their kinsfolk he sailed for America. Among these was a young and blooming lassie of the Wallace clan whom he discovered to be a kindred spirit. The mutual attachment which had sprung up between them ripened into love. In Maryland they were married. To them was born no surviving child, and she died, but just when or whether in Somerset or Cecil County we do not know.

He married secondly about 1711, Katherine McKnitt, whose father's home was in the Elk River neighborhood, in the northeastern corner of Cecil County, Maryland, bordering on Pennsylvania. Five sons and one daughter were the issue of this union, of whom John, Robert, and Zebulon, and their married sister Elizabeth and her husband migrated about 1747 to the Yadkin and Catawba county, and settled in what was subsequently Rowan County, and since Iredell County, North Carolina, while Adams and Benjamin remained in Maryland, Adam in Worcester County and Benjamin in Cecil.

The first reference to John Brevard in the Cecil County records so far discovered is dated 16 March 1715/6 when he witnessed the inventory

[5] *Somerset Wills Liber EB-5*, 130.

[6] George W. Graham: *The Mecklenburg Declaration of Independence May 20, 1775 and Lives of Its Signers*, 103.

of the estate of John McKnitt, Sr.,[7] who was his father-in-law. All subsequent ones deal with real estate matters.

The deed to his plantation was not recorded. He acquired it before 1724, probably much earlier, as it is mentioned as adjoining the second tract he subsequently purchased. The first recorded deed was dated 25 March 1721.[8] The grantor was Theophilus Jones, of Baltimore County, by his attorney Adam Wallace. The property conveyed was a tract called CHARLES CAMP which had been first surveyed 2 April 1685. On 12 December 1723 Martin Alexander sold to John Brevard a 16½ acre section of SLIGO which his father Samuel Alexander, Sr., had " made over to him " earlier that year. The deed, which was recorded 1 April 1724,[9] recited its boundaries thus:

> Beginning at a red oak marked with twelve notches standing on the South side of John Beuard his plantation and joining to the West end of John Beuard his tract of land called CHARLES CAMP, then running West and by South fourty-four perches to a red oak bush and thence North by West eighty-two perches to a hicare [i. e., hickory] Stake, thence thirty-one perches to a hicarie standing at the Northwest Corner of a tract of land called THE RANGE thence South and by East sixty-six perches to the Southwest Corner of THE RANGE thence East and by North thirteen perches to the Northwest Corner of CHARLES CAMP thence South and by East sixteen perches to the first Beginning.

The South side of John Beuard his plantation! The West end of John Beuard his tract! Beuard or Bevard gave way to Bervard, then to Bravard and Brevard. At about the same time—in October 1723—it is recorded [10] that John Breuard [sic] and John Glenn were witnesses to a transaction whereby James Wallace " of Cissel County . . . made over to Richard Wallace, of Somerset County . . . land at head of Rackawalkin River."

What ultimately happened to the lands possessed by John Brevard, Sr., cannot be proved from the records. He left no recorded Will, nor was there any administration on his estate noted in the Cecil County records. His son, John Brevard, Jr., " blacksmith ", in 1739 and 1741 purchased from William Foster and the latter's heirs two properties on " long Creek being a small creek running to Bohemia Back creek ", adjacent to the lands of Henry Ward's heirs and of Andrew Alexander, as well as the tract called CHARLES CAMP.[11]

---

[7] *Cecil Inventories*, Vol. I, 233-235.

[8] *Cecil Deeds Liber 3*, 361.

[9] *Cecil Deeds Liber 4*, 63.

[10] *Somerset Deeds Liber 021*, 125.

[11] *Cecil Deeds Liber 5*, 506 and *Liber 6*, 118.

John Brevard was active in Presbyterian affairs, not only in his local church but also in the meetings of the New Castle Presbytery and the General Synod. It has already been noted that he was an elder of the Broad Creek Presbyterian Church in 1723.[12] David Alexander and he were present as elders when the Presbytery met 9 August 1726 at Upper Elk Church.[13] On 31 October 1727 James Alexander, Robert Linton,[14] and he attended Presbytery at Octorara.[15] Andrew Wallace, Andrew Steel, and he were present at Presbytery 26 March 1728 when it met at the Head of Elk.[16] John Steel and he served similarly at Christiana Creek 10 June 1729.[17] John Brevard had likewise attended a meeting of the General Synod at Philadelphia 21 September 1726.[18]

The present writer has been unable to find any reference to John Brevard, Sr., subsequent to 10 June 1729. He therefore concludes that soon thereafter he died. If he was 20 years of age when he fled to Northern Ireland in 1685, then his dates could be said to be approximately and probably, or possibly if you prefer, " about 1665 to about 1730."

In this excursus no attempt has been made to distinguish between the spellings *Brevard* and *Bravard*, as found in the records of both Maryland and North Carolina. There was a tendency, however, for the descendants who remained in Maryland to adopt the *Bravard* form, and for the North Carolinians to spell their name *Brevard*.

Brief notes on the children of the original JOHN BREVARD, all of whom were born " near the Head of Elk " in Cecil County, Md., follow:

1. ADAM BREVARD, b ca. 1712, d Worcester Co., Md., where his Will,[19] dated 9 Nov 1782, was probated 15 July 1783. In addition to providing for his wife, chil-

---

[12] *Supra* 90.

[13] " Records of the Presbytery of New Castle upon Delaware ", in XV *Journal of the Presbyterian Historical Society* 113.

[14] The faithful service of Robert Linton to the Presbyterian Church is attested by his regular attendance upon the meetings of the General Synod of Ulster, as the Rev. John Wilson's elder from Ardmagh Presbytery and as Commissioner from Narrow-water, in June 1711, 1712, 1714, 1716, and 1717; then after his arrival in Maryland (or Delaware, or possibly Chester County, Pa.) upon the meetings of Presbytery, as an elder " of ye Congregation of Elk River ", in 1721, 1722, twice in 1723, 1725, twice in 1726 and 1727 each, and lastly in 1729, and in a like capacity at a meeting of the General Synod at Philadelphia 18 September 1728.

[15] XV *Jour. Pres. Hist. Soc.* 161

[16] *Ibid.*, 163.

[17] *Ibid.*, 184.

[18] *Records of the Presbyterian Church*, 82.

[19] *Worcester Wills Liber JW-4*, 510-511.

dren, and grandchildren, it set aside £15 as a gift toward the building of a meeting house for the Buckingham [Presbyterian] Congregation. He m ca 1733 Mary McKnitt, daughter of John McKnitt, Jr., and his wife Dorothy Wallace.[20]   Adam and Mary Brevard were listed as " kin " of John McKnitt, Jr., when the inventory of his estate was filed 8 Oct 1734.[21]   When the inventory of John McKnitt III was filed 7 July 1738, Mary Brevard, who was his sister, was listed as " kin." [22]   The family Bible, appraised at 3 shillings, was an item in that inventory.   Adam Brevard served as a private in the company of Capt. John Evens, of Somerset Co., in 1748.[23]

2. JOHN BREVARD, Jr., b ca. 1714, settled ca. 1747, Salisbury Dist., Iredell Co., N. C., d 1790, aged 75 years., m Jane McWhorter (1716-1800), daughter of Hugh McWhorter, of Pencader Hundred, New Castle Co., Del., whose will, dated 17 Feb 1749, was probated 6 March 1749.[24]   John and Jane Brevard had eight sons, all of whom had Revolutionary Service in N. C., and four daughters.[25]

3. BENJAMIN BREVARD lived all his life in Cecil Co., Md., where his Will, in which he mentions his children Joshua, Adam, Benjamin, Rachel, Rebecca, and Clarissa, was probated 27 March 1793.[26]

4. ELIZABETH BREVARD m ———, and located in N. C.

5. ROBERT BREVARD settled in Rowan Co., N. C., where several of his children were married.[27]

6. ZEBULON BREVARD, b 29 March 1724, m 7 March 1754 Ann Templeton, b Nov 1733; and had issue: Mary, 1755; David, 1757; Elizabeth, 1758; Jane, 1760; Sarah, 1762; Ann, 1766; Zebulon, 1769; James, 1771; Rhoda, 1773; and Thomas, 1775.[28]

---

[20] *Supra* 83.

[21] *Cecil County Administrations, etc.*, Vol. I, 334.

[22] *Cecil Inventories*, Vol. 3, 192.

[23] *Maryland Historical Magazine*, Vol. 6, 194.

[24] *Calendar of Delaware Wills: New Castle County*, 44.

[25] See Wheeler, Graham, or Ray, on Mecklenburg Families.

[26] *Cecil Wills Liber EE-5*, 306.

[27] His son John was sheriff of Rowan during the Revolution.

[28] Acklen: Bible Records and Marriage Bonds, 140-141.

DALE *Excursus*

The Dales were English Presbyterians who because of persecution left England and lived for several years near Londonderry, Ireland, whence certain of the family departed for America. John, James, and their sister Martha (who married John McKnitt, Sr.) settled in Maryland. The following notes are based on official records and a genealogical writing by Adam Dale hereinafter referred to.

JOHN DALE settled in Somerset County, Md., between 1683 and 1686. OAK HILL was surveyed for him 16 December 1686, a 200 acre tract near the head of the Pocomoke River. He later acquired from John Fletcher (almost certainly his father-in-law) another property called MORE HUSS in the St. Martin's River neighborhood, now Worcester County. John Dale signed the address of Loyalty to William and Mary heretofore mentioned. He and his wife Katherine were the parents of two children, Mary, born 30 November 1689, and Archibald, born 5 June 1691. John Dale died intestate between 5 May 1708 and 17 February 1708/9.

JAMES DALE sailed for Philadelphia before 1699; visited his sister Martha shortly after her marriage to John McKnitt in Cecil County, and continued to live there several years. On 4 February 1714 he bought a tract in Snow Hill, Somerset County (now Worcester), called JAMES PURCHASE. In 1720 there was surveyed for him a 200 acre property called CASTLE HILL near MORE HUSS. There he continued to live until his death in 1733. Of the children of James Dale only the name of the youngest, John, is known; but another son located in Philadelphia, and still another elsewhere in Pennsylvania.

JOHN DALE (son of James) who was born in Ireland about 1791 accompanied his father to America; lived with his Aunt Martha McKnitt's family until 1714; lived in the Snow Hill neighborhood, 1714-1733; sold in 1737 one half of CASTLE HILL (inherited from his father) to Adam Brevard, John's wife, Elizabeth (McKnitt) Dale, joining in the conveyance; purchased RED LANDS in 1738; was granted patent to BEAR QUARTER in 1747, and shortly thereafter received, jointly with John Dale " Inspector " (son of Archibald Dale), patent to RED LANDS ENLARGED; deeded to his son John Dale, Jr., and his son-in-law Elias Whaley his remaining interests in CASTLE HILL and BEAR QUARTER in 1754/5 and 1760, respectively; made his Will 24 January 1775, soon after the death of his wife Elizabeth. He died in

January 1778. His Will was probated 14 March 1778 in Worcester County Court. This John Dale was often called John Dale, Irish, or Senior, to distinguish him from John Dale, Inspector, or Junior. Through an error in transcription the Will of John Dale, *Irish,* has been listed in the records of Worcester County as that of John Dale, *Jr.* John Dale, Irish, and his wife Elizabeth McKnitt, who was his first cousin, had six children. These were John Dale who married Tabitha Milbourn; Martha Dale who married Elias Whaley; Sarah Dale who married Joseph Evans; Rhoda Dale who married Wheatley Hatfield; Thomas Dale who married Elizabeth Evans; and Ann Dale who married Robert Stevenson. In the records of this branch of the McKnitt connection that name was regularly spelled MacKnight of MacKnite. Both Adam Brevard and his son John Brevard were witnesses to the Will of John Dale, Irish.

THOMAS DALE (son of John Dale, Irish) was born 5 March 1744; married in Sussex County, Delaware, Elizabeth Evans, daughter of John Evans of NORTH PEATHERTON; served as an officer in the Revolution; was long an elder in Old Buckingham-by-the-Sea Presbyterian Church; had extensive land holdings both in Worcester County, Md., and Sussex County, Delaware; followed his son, Adam Dale, to Liberty, Smith County (now DeKalb), Tenn., where he died 6 January 1812. Thomas and Elizabeth (Evans) Dale had 5 sons and 5 daughters.

ADAM DALE (son of Thomas) was born 14 July 1768; served as a boy volunteer in the American forces in 1781, and as a captain during the War of 1812; married 24 February 1790 Polly Hall, daughter of William Jordan Hall, Esq., and his second wife, Sophia Woodcraft; founded Liberty, Tenn.; removed to Columbia, Tenn.; d 14 October 1851, Hazel Green, Alabama; and is buried in Rose Hill Cemetery, Columbia, Tennessee. A few months before his death he wrote a remarkably interesting and detailed letter to his eldest grandson, which was subsequently printed under the title, " Private History of the Dale Family." A photostatic copy of the original letter and a typewritten transcription of it were placed in the Library of the Daughters of the American Revolution in Constitution Hall, Washington, D. C., by the Honorable Robert Franklin Cole, a descendant of Adam and Polly (Hall) Dale, who has made a careful study of the Dale Family but his voluminous findings have not yet been published. In the library of the Historical Society of Pennsylvania there is a copy of Hale's *History of DeKalb County, Tennessee* in which there are some well written paragraphs concerning Adam Dale and a full-page picture of him.

Paul Marsh

BALDWIN MAULL

and

HELENE CARTER POTTER *

PAUL MARSH's origin is not yet known. He is listed by Monnette among "Those of New Amsterdam and New Jersey first appearing in Delaware" as "Captain Paul Marsh, 1676/7." [1] He is not mentioned elsewhere in Monnette's voluminous compendium of New Jersey colonial records and no reference to him has been found in New York or New Jersey Colonial records. There is a usual tradition of three brothers coming from England to America, one of whom settled in Sussex County, Delaware,[2] but there is no authentication of this tradition.[3] Two Paul Marsh marriages are recorded in London, and a Marsh family in Middlesex including a Paul and Peter is known at that time, but no connection has been established.[4]

Paul appeared in Maryland in 1664 and claimed 150 acres of land for transporting himself, Richard Crockett and Henry Hill in the same year. A tract of 150 acres on the east side of Bretton's Bay,[5] called "Marshe's Hope" was surveyed for Paul on 10 April 1665, and a warrant was issued dated 28 August 1665, "Returnable last of February next," and the land was patented to him 5 September 1666. In the survey he is described as "Captaine" and in the patent as "Gent."; no appellation is given in the warrant. The land was adjacent to land of William Thompson and William Wood, and later appeared in the possession of Henry Jarbo and John Heard.[6]

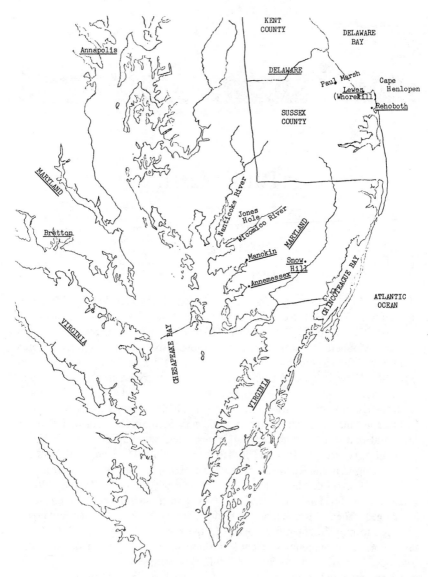

AREA OF PAUL MARSH'S ACTIVITY IN DELAWARE AND MARYLAND

Paul hired a servant (perhaps Richard Crockett or Henry Hill, who entered Maryland with him) to one Pope Alvey of Newtowne Hundred, St. Mary's County, in which the capital of Maryland was then located. Another servant of Alvey's died, blaming Alvey for her death. So Paul sued Alvey, asking security for the safe return of Paul's servant at the expiration of the servant's time. The suit was brought in the Provincial Court on 29 May 1665 but was continued until, on 4 January 1666, it was "compounded as by both partys confest &c." [7] In this interim Alvey was indicted for the theft of a cow, adjudged guilty and condemned to death, but granted respite — in effect a suspended sentence.[8] Paul was thus probably in St. Mary's, or near there, in 1665-6.

He probably then moved up to Ann Arundel County, where Annapolis is situated,[9] as he was described as being "of Ann Arundel" in August, 1668, when there was surveyed for him, according to a warrant dated 22 August 1668, not found, 1,000 acres of land on the south side of the Pocomoke River in Somerset County on the Eastern Shore,[10] "over against Ascomonoconson near the middle ground." [11] His rights were to be made good from 16 September 1668. The only abutting landowner mentioned in the patent (not issued until 1678) was Henry Bishop. While the survey was secured in 1668, we do not know that Paul actually settled the land. The rent roll spoke of it as "Poss^d bye Mathew Scarborough." It devolved into a tract called Vineyard, and became a part of Worcester County, which was carved out of Somerset County in 1742.[12]

Sometimes settlers named their plantations for a place from which they came. There is a place in Ireland in Tipperary County named Mardike, two miles northeast of Killemaule.[13] This fact could be an indication of Paul's origin — if he was the one to name the plantation.

Shortly thereafter, on 29 September 1668, one Daniell Curtis was charged with contempt by George Johnson, High Sheriff, who in the name of the Lord Proprietor had ordered Curtis to carry to "Captaine Marsh to Wiccocomoco" a sealed packet directed to the Lieutenant General of the province. The action was dismissed, though Curtis was required to pay court charges.[14] From this it appears that Paul had moved to the Eastern Shore, near Wiccocomoco and near the land recently surveyed for him and, as we have seen earlier, was already known as "Captaine." Then on 9 February 1669 Captain Paul Marsh was given Commission "to be Captain of Foot from Nantecoke to Manaokin." [15] Under a law adopted in 1661 a captain was authorized to enlist such men as he saw fit, and to train the militia.[16] It is interesting to speculate as to how, as a newcomer in Maryland in 1664, he had secured this rather important position of authority by 1668. Perhaps by force of character, perhaps by some friendship, perhaps because he had had previous military training or experience. His duties as captain would naturally make him known to a great part of the men of the area and no doubt helped him later in his political career. There is no record of appointment of a successor to Paul as captain for this particular area, although Capt. William Coulbourne of Somerset was to command a troop of horse to be raised in Somerset, 25 October 1673, and, as Colonel, commanded foot troops in Somerset and Dorchester in 1682.[17]

In 1670 Paul purchased land from James Jones and wife Sarah.[18] Jones had acquired 250 acres of land called "Jones Hole" by patent dated February 1663 on the basis of transporting 5 immigrants including Elizabeth Merideth (to become Paul's wife), and Jones had lately taken up another 400 acres "(the Pattent not yet come over)" called "Sunken Ground."[19] Out of this 650 acres he carved 200 acres called "Dunkirke"[20] for Paul Marsh and transferred it to him by deed dated 9 August 1670, witnessed 10 February 1675.[21] One of the boundaries was Johnson's Creek and another was "Marshe's Creek," suggesting that Paul might have been already settled there. Jones had received credit for 50 acres for bringing Elizabeth Merideth into Maryland and had been Trustee for her in Virginia. Very possibly Jones' grant to Paul related to Elizabeth's portion in Virginia and Jones' allotment on account of her entry into Maryland. It is interesting that another of the immigrants on whom was based James Jones' grant of Sunken Ground was one Hannah Marsh. The coincidence of names in the history of this tract is suggestive of some relationship to Paul.[22]

There is an interesting possibility suggested by use of the names Mardike and Dunkirke. In 1658 Cromwell sent a force of several thousand men to help the French capture Mardyck, a town on the east coast of France opposite Dover. This force later in the year helped Turenne to defeat a Spanish force and then to capture Dunkirk. This suggests that "Captaine" Marsh may well have seen service under Cromwell in these campaigns, and carried over to the naming of his new ventures a remembrance of the two engagements in which he had played a part, of which he was proud, and of which he would like to remind his neighbors. However, no record has been found of the English soldiers who served in France at that time.

Probably Paul's land-owning status helped to change his whole position in the community. As a matter of fact, the ownership in freehold of at least 50 acres, or a visible estate of £40 sterling, was a requisite for election to the Lower House in 1671.[23]

In that year, Paul was one of four delegates elected to the Lower House of Assembly of Maryland from Somerset County, with Ambrose Dixon,

Ambrose London and Roger Woolford. But only Marsh and Woolford took their seats. The Governor summoned only these two of the four elected, at the request of the Sheriff of the County made (as is stated) in order to save expense.[24] It is possible that Quaker connections of the other two created some difficulty. There are references to Paul as a deputy or delegate on 27 March, 19 April, 10 and 13 October 1671 and again on 12 February, 19 May and 12 and 13 June 1674.[25] All of these dates are comprised within a single term of office, as the session was prorogued from time to time. We do not know what part Paul played in any specific legislative matter since individual votes were not recorded and he is not listed as a member of any of the numerous committees named by the House for particular purposes.

On 3 June 1672 "Capt^a Paull Marsh" recorded his earmark for cattle.[26] From this we can assume that he was settled on one of his tracts of land in Maryland at this time, and running cattle on it. Registration of earmarks was required by Maryland law,[27] so it is possible that Paul had only recently become an owner of cattle.

In 1672 he had a specific commission of an interesting nature: [28]

Maryland ss^t

By his Excellency the Captain
General

These are to Empower and require you Captain Paul Marsh to raise and Muster such a Party of Men as shall be desired of you by Captain Thomas Iones Commander of the forces in Worcester County and with him the said Captain Iones to go unto the said Worcester County with your said Party of men and all Enemies that shall be shewed you by the said Captain Jones to encounter fight with Overcome and destroy or take Prisoners and them to secure and them to secure [sic] also to require you to press men Horses Provisions Ammunition and all other things necessary for this design & an Account of your Proceedings herein that you render unto me by all Opportunities and for your said Proceedings this shall be your sufficient warrant. Given under my hand and seal at Arms this Eleventh day of Iuly in the 41st year of the dominion of Cecelius &c^a. Annoq Doma 1672

To Captain Paul Marsh of   Cha: Calvert
Somerset County these

For the Lord Proprietarys   Locus Sigilli
Service

We do not know what actually occurred in the raid, but on 12 August 1672, Governor Lovelace of New York for the Duke of York sent a vigorously worded protest to the Governor of Maryland (sic) that Jones "who wth a Party as dissolute as himself took paines to ride to Y^e Whorekill,[29]

229

where in Derision and Contempt of the Duke's Authority bound ye Magistrates, and Inhabitants despitefully treated them, rifled and plundered them of their Goods; & when it was demanded by what Authority he Acted, answered in no other Language but a Cockt Pistoll to his Breast, wch if it had spoke, had forever silenced him." [30]

A deposition was made by Helmanus Wiltbanck (later a neighbor of Paul's), who was one of the victims of the raid, as to what took place:

"In the Year of our Lord 1671 in the Month of June Capt. Thomas Jones did come up in this place called Whoorekill wth 7 or 8 horsemen with force of Arms, and came to the House of Helmanius Wiltbank and tyed him, and rid to the rest of his Neighbours and tyed them and kept a Guard over them, and Plundered the Housing & carried the Goods away and left us.

"In the Month of September following came up the said Capt. Jones with a Troop of Horse with force of Armes and made forcible Entry in this Place, and called a Court of their own Men, and made us come to their Court and Demanded the Oath of Allegiance wherein we were not willing, whereupon the Court did Commit us to Prison and kept us untill the next Day without meat or Drink, and threatened to carry us for Maryland and confiscate our Estate, so that we were forced to take the Oath of Allegiance to be true to my Lord Baltimore, and so we remained untill the next Year. . . ." [31]

Correspondence and protests were exchanged at some length between the Governor of New York representing the Duke of York and the government of the Proprietor of Maryland.[32] In a private letter dated 2 June 1673 to Cecilius, Lord Baltimore, Governor Charles Calvert deprecates, in effect apologizes for, Jones' violent treatment of the settlers and tells that he caused their goods to be returned to them.[33]

Captain Thomas Jones, in charge of the raid, was a vigorous and well-known character on the scene in Maryland. He was an Indian Trader, captain, sheriff, collector, justice, secretary, etc., and involved in a number of lawsuits. His story is well told, and at length, in the Introduction to Volume LXV of the *Archives of Maryland*.

Although Paul Marsh was by the terms of his commission required to go with Captain Jones to Worcester County,[34] and to render an account of his proceedings "by all Opportunities," no record of any such account has been preserved and, indeed, there is no record of Marsh's actual participation in the raid. Did he fail to execute his commission to raise such party of men as desired by Captain Jones, and to go with Jones to Worcester County? Did Jones leave Captain Marsh or his company behind? There is a clear implication of his direct participation, however, in a letter of Governor Charles Calvert dated 2 June 1673, reporting to Cecilius, Lord Baltimore, on the raid. Speaking of Jones he says "I gave him a Commission to be a

Capt. for the said County of Worcester, and to leavy men &c, and to march up thither and take possession of that place for yor Lo^{pps} use, and Did associate with him one Capt Paul Marsh of Somerset County." [35]

If Paul was one of the raiders, it seems a little strange that he could return to Whorekill in a few years to live, secure a substantial land grant there, and live in amity with the families of the victims of the raids. As a result of a later raid in 1673, John Rhodes, Sr. was murdered by the Indians, yet Paul's grandson Peter Marsh married (second) Agnes Roades Field,[36] great granddaughter of the murdered man and granddaughter of his son John Roades, Jr., who supplied an affidavit as to his cruel losses.[37] Evidently Paul's part in the raid (if any) was not held against him by the Duke of York's representatives, since they appointed him, while still a relative newcomer at Whorekill, President of the Court there.[38]

We do not know when Paul married Elizabeth Meredith (Merideth, Merrideth), but we first learn of it in 1672. On 29 July 1656, Ellinor, widow of Phillip Merrydeth, deeded to Thomas Johnson [39] and James Jones as Trustees for her three daughters Elizabeth (later married Paul Marsh), Mary (later married Richard Hinman) [40] and Elynor (later married George Truitt or Trewett) [41] three hundred acres of land on Occahannock Creek in Northampton County [42] on the eastern shore of Virginia, together with 10 head of cattle, and each daughter was given a pot or kettle outright. The transfer of land was to be effective upon the mother's death, and the stock to remain in her possession until each girl reached 14.[43] This was probably a pre-marital settlement in anticipation of the widow's remarriage to George Johnson, which took place soon thereafter.[44] The land was originally patented to Nicholas Waddelow in 1649, payment to be made in 1656, and this payment date may also have had to do with the transfer by widow Merideth to her three girls in that year. It was not until 1672 that a patent was issued for this land to Elizabeth and Paul Marsh, Mary and Richard Hinman, and Elianor and George Trewett.[45]

Paul soon began to play a part in the life of what is now Sussex County, Delaware, a part of which was then claimed both by Lord Baltimore and by the Duke of York, i.e., land in the neighborhood of Horekill and to the south and west of there. There is no record of any landholding there on Paul's part at this time, but he must have had some interests there, as he was listed as lieutenant and president of the court at Horekill in November 1674, ranked first in the order of naming the justices, indicating seniority. When the Duke of York had reconquered this territory from the Dutch in 1664, the people of the territory were allowed to retain their justices, and this rule continued at least until 1676, when the Duke of York's Laws were adopted and corresponding Instructions sent to the South River (Delaware). Thus it seems likely that Paul was settled in this area before November 1674, and, as first-named in the list, was the oldest of the justices over whom he presided — Helmanus Wiltbanck, Alexander Molestede, John Kipshaven and Otto Wolgast. In one instance he was called "Lieut. and president of the Court." [46] He was one of those persons listed as present in the Horekill as a justice about 4 January 1675/6.[47]

Then we find the first reference to his landholding in Sussex. On 17 August 1676, Walter Wharton surveyed 600 acres for Paul but the survey was "long in his Possession" (Wharton's) and was returned with other surveys by Capt. Edm. Cantwell only on 18 November 1678, when it was "to bee certified as allowed now, the parties being in possession, or ready to goe upon the Land," by order of the Governor.[48] The land was "about three myles to the west of the Whorekill" (Lewes) called by the name of "Souldiers Resolves" and bordered on land of Helmanus Wiltbanck (an earlier settler) and Edward Southern, who also came to Sussex from Somerset.

Paul was again listed as a justice present in the Horekill on 19 March 1676/7, and as being absent from the court 11 June 1678.[49]

In the same year he was issued the patent for the 1,000 acres in Maryland surveyed for him on 27 August 1668, called "Mardike," in Somerset County on the south side of the Pocomoke River "over against Ascoumeneconson near the Middle Ground," neighboring Henry Bishop's land.[50] There is an extraordinary statement in this patent:

> . . . and whereas the said Paul Marsh hath informed us that through poverty he is Enforced to work in the ground, and not able to purchase rights for the said Land and humbly prayed our Letters pattent for the same No Know yees that we having taken into our consideration that the said Paul Marsh hath well and faithfully served our late father Cecilius of noble memory of our free grace and favour Do hereby give and grant unto him the said Paul Marsh. . . .

Presumably a "special warrant" was issued for this land.[51] No record of special warrants was kept at this time, but the patent itself was followed by a separate entry or item which perhaps constituted the "special warrant":

> Mr. Sec'y Calvert Whereas I have formerly ordered you to draw a pattent for One Thousand Acres for Paul Marsh called Mardike lying on the South side of Pocomoke River in Somersett County These are to order you to draw it up as single Rent and Given under my hand this 20th day of November 1678.
>
> Thomas Notley
>
> To the Honble William Calvert Esq. Princip
> Secy of Maryland

This land would have been in or near the presnt town of Snow Hill, Maryland.

The references to Paul's poverty and his services are intriguing. He had been in Maryland from 1664 to 1668 without making or keeping enough money (or tobacco) to allow him to take up the land in usual course, that is, to bring in new immigrants or purchase rights based on some one else bringing in new immigrants, and he evidently continued for 10 years thereafter, to 1678, without being able (or willing?) to do so. He had at some time performed services of value to Cecilius Calvert. We do not have any record of Paul's commission as captain until 1669, but he is referred to as "Captain" much earlier. Possibly his services as captain were the basis for the grant, or possibly some other services in Maryland or even before coming to Maryland. The reference to "our late father Cecilius," who died in 1675, show that the services were performed before 1675. Governor Charles Calvert's reference to him as "one Capt. Paul Marsh of Somerset County" in his letter dated 2 June 1673 to Cecilius, Lord Baltimore, does not suggest family familiarity with Paul.[52]

On 4 December 1678 Paul and his wife Elizabeth sold Mardike to William Stevens.[53] Good reason for him to get his patent for the land in order earlier in the year! Perhaps he still had his first piece of land "Dunkirke," but in any event he was preparing to go to, or more likely had already seated himself on, the 600 acre tract warranted to him in Sussex, as mentioned below. In this deed he signed his name as Paull, not Paul. This unusual spelling is found both in Maryland and in Delaware records — not in every case, but in so many cases that it must have been the way he regularly spelled his name.

Paul was not the only Somerset settler to look to Sussex land. By 1682 some forty-five persons are listed as having obtained from Lord Baltimore warrants for land located in what was thought by them to be a part of Maryland but later became a part of Sussex County, Delaware.[54] Edward Southern and John Rhoads and many other Somerset men, in addition to Paul Marsh, took up land near Horekill (now Lewes) in Sussex County.[55] We do not know what led them there — Lord Baltimore desired to put settlers on the disputed land and, subject to some uncertainty, they had a chance to get more or better land for themselves at lower cost within range of their friends and in many cases (as with Paul) not too far from the Maryland land which they continued to hold. They "ventured." But some defected and took their land there from the Duke of York. Governor Charles Calvert's great concern with the settlement of this disputed territory is expressed in letters to Cecelius, Lord Baltimore. Under date of 26 April 1672, he mentions that "the difference betwixt his Royal Highness, and yo͏ͬ Lo͏ᵖᵖ is not yett deter-mined, which wee are very Sorry for, because itt begetts a beleefe in Many th͏ᵗ yo͏ͬ Lo͏ᵖᵖ will hardly Recouer yo͏ͬ Right, And Causes many to take Land att the Hore Keele from the Gouernment of New Yorke. I am dayly perswading & Incouraginge persons to seat there in yo͏ͬ Lo͏ᵖᵖˢ Right, And some are already gone, And more I hope will Venture . . .",[56]

and under date of 2 June 1673 he refers to

"many psons here who have or Desire to seate and Inhabite there, and yet are unwilling to Remove their goods Servants and stocks untill they certainly know und͏ͬ whose Governm͏ᵗ they are like to be but howsomever in the meane time I shall Encourage all psons that I Can to seate there . . . on the 19th of June last I issued a proclamacon und͏ͬ yo͏ͬ Lo͏ᵖᵖˢ greate Seale declaring and affecting yo͏ͬ Lo͏ᵖᵖˢ Right to that place and Erected the same unto a County, and Called it by the name of Worcester County, assuring the then Inhabitants there that if they would take out Patents from yo͏ͬ Lo͏ᵖᵖ and take the oath of fidelity they should have all favor and proteccon . . ." [57]

Note that Paul's land in what is now Sussex County was "about three myles to the West of the Whorekill." Lord Baltimore felt that the land in this area was clearly his and, in order to get settlers on it, in 1669 he offered land in the area at less than usual rent, on condition that within four years of the date of grant the grantees bring in one person of English or Irish descent for every fifty acres to be granted.[58] So Paul was again, very probably, seeking to take up land without the immediate necessity of financing immigrants or finding funds for the purchase price.

In 1669 Maryland created the County of Durham to run north from the Horekill, and a new county to be named (later, in 1672, called Worcester County) to run south from the Horekill. Paul's property was west of the Horekill, and might have fitted into either of the proposed new counties, being neither to the north nor to the south of the Horekill, but no doubt at the time the line was drawn clearly enough in the minds of the inhabitants. Skirven (see note 54) lists 45 grants of land made by Maryland in the area that was later a part of Sussex, and there were many others. For example, John Avery (who also became a Judge in Sussex County) was granted land by the proprietors of Maryland "lying on the Seaboard side near Delaware Bay about four miles from the Whorekill on the east side of a bay called Rehoboth bay to be holden of the Manor of Worcester" on 6 August 1674. There is every probability that Paul Marsh originally had a similar grant from Maryland or had seated himself (and perhaps family) on a tract of land in expectation of securing such a grant, and finally had it from the Duke of York. On 15 January 1676/7 Paul was a witness to a survey for Cornelis Johnson of land near the land already surveyed for him.[59]

The next step in the development of Paul's Sussex land ownership came on 13 May 1679, as a result of Capt. Cantwell's certificate, when the Court examined and certified Paul Marsh "already seated" for 600 acres. After this, on 20 August 1679, a patent was granted to Paul for the 600 acres, called "Souldiers Resolves," together with 6 acres of marsh adjoining it, about 3 miles west of the Horekill, neighboring on land of "Hellmanus Willbanck" (a co-justice and earlier settler) and "Edward Southerin," another co-justice.[60]

Paul was still active in Maryland, as shown by the fact that he was a member of a jury dealing with an inquisition concerning land of David Williams, deceased 1 March 1678. His name was at the head of the list of jurors signing, which probably indicated that he was foreman of the jury.[61]

At this time Paul liquidated his wife's interest in Virginia. In 1680 Elizabeth and Paul Marsh sold their one-third of this property to Jonah Jackson, as did her sister Eleanor and George Trewett, while her sister Mary and Richard Hinman sold theirs to John Hameryn.[62]

On 8 March 1680/1, a survey for 600 acres of Sussex land called "Good Hope" was certified by Cornelius Verhoofe, surveyor, by virtue of a warrant (not found) from the Whorekill alias Deale Court, and on 14 February 1681, this survey was certified by a court at Deale (Lewes).[63] There may be some question whether this is the same parcel previously patented as "Souldiers Resolves" or a new parcel. The description of "Souldiers Resolves" showed four sides of equal length. It is highly unlikely that the bounds of the property could have conformed to this rigid pattern, as they ran along a stream and a beaver dam. It is suggested that the survey of "Good Hope" represents a corrected, confirming survey of the same property under a new name showing by plat the elongated irregular property as it lay, and that the action of the court is simply a certification of the survey and not stated as, or as leading to, a grant or patent, and there is no record of disposal by Paul or his estate of a second property.

On 13 December 1681, Paul was a juryman in an action on the case in Sussex County.[64] He was sued in January 1682 in the common matter of his dogs attacking his neighbor Michael Chambers' hogs in Paul's cornfield, but a nonsuit was entered and costs assessed against the plaintiff.[65]

He died by 1684, when letters of administration on his estate were granted to George Truitt of Somerset County, "being near related."[66] Paul's 600 acre tract of land in Sussex called "Good Hope" was sold to Anderson Parker and Matthew Spicer by deed dated 8 November 1704 of James, Philip, John and Peter Marsh.[67] Presumably these four were Paul's sons, and his wife Elizabeth was deceased. Then on 8 May 1706, James, Philip, John and Peter Marsh acknowledged in open court the transfer of this land.[68] On 10 November 1914, the following inscription was copied from the tombstone of Anderson Parker (died 1836) in the old Parker burying ground on the so-called Red Mill tract, outside of Lewes:

"This farm was purchased by Anderson Parker the elder from the heirs of Paul Marsh in 1704 and still remains in the Parker family."

This ends Paul's story, and the story of succeeding generations begins.

1. Paul Marsh had four sons, as noted above, presumably by his wife Elizabeth Meredith. All were stated to be "of Sussex County Annexed to the province of Pensilvania Plant[rs]" on 8 November 1704, when they deeded their father's land called "Good Hope" to Anderson Parker, Planter of Sussex County, and Matthew Spicer, Planter of Accomack County, Virginia.[69]

    i. James Marsh. He signed the deed by mark. There is no further record of James.

    ii. Philip Marsh. He also signed the deed by mark. In the 1743 Orphans Court proceedings in the estate of 2. Peter Marsh there is an item, "Bond & Interest Phil. Marsh due d[o]." Philip is shown as paying a debt due Richard Hinman's estate in 1745. Thus he was living in 1743 and 1745, but there is no further record of Philip.[70]

    iii. John Marsh. He signed the deed manually. He married Elizabeth, daughter of Henry Bowman, before 1721.[71] They had a daughter Comfort, who married by 1747 Daniel Brinkloe of Kent County, Delaware.[72] From a deed of 1754, it is clear that John had a granddaughter Elizabeth Pettyjohn, wife of Abraham, but it is not certain that she was a daughter of Comfort and Daniel Brinkloe.[73] John was dead by 7 May 1752, when letters of administration on his estate were granted to Robert Hall in Kent County, Delaware.[74] Evidently he had moved from Sussex County to the adjoining Kent County.

2. iv. Peter Marsh. He also signed the deed manually. He became the owner of several hundred acres of land in Sussex County and was designated "planter" in many of the deeds. He died between 27 November 1725, when his will was signed, and 1 January 1725/6, when it was probated.[75] No record of his wife has been found. He left children:

3. a. Peter Marsh, of whom further.
   b. Joseph Marsh, died by 1754.[76]
   c. James Marsh. He enlisted 12 or 22 August 1779 in the Delaware Regiment of Foot, which became the 1st Company, 2nd Battalion of a Regiment in the Southern Army. He served until 1780, when he was listed as "Sick Absent at Wilmington" (probably Delaware, rather than North Carolina) on 26 April, then "Missing in Action," undated, then "Joined the Enemy" before 1 August 1780.[77] There is no further record of James.
   d. Elizabeth Marsh. "Not being compos mentis therefore not capable," her brother Peter was appointed her guardian in 1743.[78]

2. Peter's lands, willed to his sons, were to remain in the hands of the executor until the sons arrived at the age of 20. Daughter Elizabeth received £20. Richard Hinman was executor and John Roades was one of the witnesses. Richard Hinman's daughter Naomi married John Roades, was widowed, and then married William Fassitt of "Worsister County, Maryland." She was executrix of her father's will, and she and her husband William Fassitt were eventually asked to account, in the matter of Peter's estate, still unsettled in 1743.[79]

3. Peter Marsh, called "yeoman" in a deed of 1735 [80] but later designated as "Gentleman," [81] was born about 1712, according to his tombstone. He married first Esther Purnell, born 21 August 1728, daughter of Thomas and Mary (Outten) Purnell of Worcester County, Maryland. They had children: [82]

   i. Joseph Marsh, b. 10 September 1747, d. bt. 5 March 1760 and 6 July 1769.
   ii. Peter Marsh, b. 25 February 1748/9. He m. 13 March 1776 Mary (Polly) Wilson, daughter of Rev. Matthew Wilson, pastor of the Presbyterian Church of Lewes, Indian River and Cool Spring, Delaware, from 1756 until his death in 1790. Mary, b. 11 June 1758, d. 19 October 1820, was buried 21 October 1820. Peter had died 19 July 1813, and his funeral was the following day. They had issue (Marsh):
   a. Esther Wilson, b. 15 February 1779, d. 14 September 1797, m. John Mustard, no issue.
   b. Joseph, b. 15 January 1781, d. 16 March 1832. A doctor, he married three times, had fourteen children.

c. Peter, b. 17 August 1783, d. unm. 13 June 1814.

d. Matthew, b. 8 September 1785, d. 25 October 1821. Married Comfort Bruce, issue.

e. Lydia, b. 12 July 1787, d. unm.

f. Margareta (called Peggy), b. 21 March 1799, d. 19 October 1833. Married John Rowland, no issue.

g. Sarah, b. 2 February 1792, d. unm. 27 June 1816.

h. Mary (Polly), b. 12 November 1794, d. 25 June 1795.

i. Mary (Polly), b. 24 April 1798, d. 6 October 1825. Married Thomas Perry, no issue.

iii. Mary Marsh, b. 17 December 1752, d. 16 October 1790. On 24 or 29 March 1768 she married John Maull of Lewes, Delaware, b. 9 October 1742, d. 9 January 1832. The Presbyterian record states that his funeral was the same day and that he was aged 90. For descendants, see Baldwin Maull, *John Maull (1714-1753) of Lewes, Delaware. A Genealogy of His Descendants in All Branches* (New York, 1941).

iv. Thomas Purnell Marsh, b. 21 December 1753, d. 3 March 1821 and buried 5 March. On 25 January 1776 he married Nancy Mackey, also a daughter of the Reverend Matthew Wilson, and evidently a widow. Her funeral was 29 June 1830. Her tombstone has no dates, merely the inscription "Aged 74." Thomas was a Ruling Elder at the time of his death. He was also in the Revolutionary War as Standard Bearer in Colonel David Hall's Battalion, appointed 16 September 1775.[83] They had issue, order uncertain (Marsh):

a. Henrietta, bapt. 1779.

b. George, bur. 23 November 1781.

c. Mary, b. 1787, d. 1859. Married William Cooper, issue.

d. Jane, b. 1789, d. unm. 1859.

e. James, bapt. 1792, d. 20 April 1869. Married Margaret Rhoades, issue.

f. Thomas Purnell, bapt. 1795. Unm.

g. John, b. 1795, d. 1872. Married Comfort Stockley, issue.

h. Nancy, b. 1798, d. unm. 1849.

i. Peter, b. 1802, d. unm. 1851.

j. Harriet, m. James Perry, issue.

k. Emily, bur. 6 August 1815. No issue.

l. Catherine, d. 1847. Married James Thompson, issue.

v. John Marsh, b. 19 May 1755, d. 11 August 1797. A doctor,

he married 27 or 29 February 1780 Susannah (Susan) Lewis, daughter of Wrexam and Sarah Lewis of Pilottown (part of Lewes). They had issue (Marsh):

    a. John, m. Lydia Stockley. They had issue.

    b. Matilda, m. Lewis Davenport. They had issue.

    c. Sydenham, married twice, and had issue by second wife, Eliza Richards.

  vi. Philip Marsh, b. 6 May 1757. After the settlement of his father's estate, no further record is found in Sussex County regarding Philip. He may be the man of that name in Worcester County, Maryland, who, 12 May 1797, married Polly Selby. A Philip Marsh witnessed the will of a Thomas Purnell of Worcester County in 1795. An undated will of a Philip Marsh there, with a bond dated 21 October 1817, may also be of this man. The sureties were Peter and Theodore Marsh, but no relationship was stated. A Philip is also listed in the 1800 census for Mattapony Hundred, Worcester County.[84]

Esther (Purnell) Marsh died 23 January 1759 and 3. Peter married, probably between 5 March and 4 May 1760,[85] Agnes (Roades) Field, widow of Nehemiah Field and sister of John Roades, first husband of Naomi Hinman. Agnes had had two sons by Nehemiah: Nehemiah and John Field. She and Peter Marsh had two daughters:

  vii. Hester Marsh, b. 26 November 1761, d. 8 December 1824, evidently unm. In 1778, she requested the Orphans Court of Sussex County that she, being over 14, be allowed to choose a guardian. The request was granted, and she chose John Maull, her half-sister's husband.[86]

  viii. Sarah Marsh, b. 4 February 1766, bapt. as Sally, 1768, d. 1821, evidently unm. John Maull was also appointed her guardian.[87]

3. Peter died 13 July 1769, aged 57 years according to his tombstone. He left a will dated 6 July 1769, from which we learn that his son Joseph had predeceased him.[88] On 5 March 1760 Peter had, by a Deed of Gift, given a slave to each of his children, including Joseph.[89] In his will, Peter confirmed the gifts, and gave to his three sons — Peter, Thomas Purnell and John — the slave "made over by a deed of gift to my son Jos. Marsh now deceased."

Peter's estate was large. He left one-third of all real and personal estate to his wife Agnes, including furniture, a negro, a horse, saddle and bridle, at her death to go to their two daughters. To each son he left about 500 acres of land, a negro, horse, bridle and saddle, oxen and various other items, except for Phillip (*sic*), to whom he left only the negro previously made over by deed of gift, and one English shilling. The two girls were willed money for schooling, a bed and furniture and other items. To son Peter he also left his "new large Bible." Also willed were gold sleeve buttons and silver shoe buckles. Agnes was named executrix, and the will was probated 19 August 1769.

Agnes died in 1777, and her funeral is recorded in the Presbyterian records on 4 December 1777. Her son John Field administered her estate.

Peter was a Vestryman of St. Peter's Episcopal Church in Lewes in 1747,[90] and the records of St. George's Chapel in Indian River Hundred show the births and baptisms of two of his children, Joseph and Peter.[91]

He had been an Ensign in the French and Indian Wars in the Regiment of Sussex County for the Southern District of Lewes and Rehoboth Hundred in 1756, and was an Ensign in the Militia Battalion for Sussex County in the Rehoboth District in 1758.[92]

NOTES

* The first part of this article, concerning Paul Marsh himself, is primarily by Mr. Maull while the second part, concerning later generations, is primarily by Mrs. Potter.

Special acknowledgment is made by Mr. Maull to Capt. Ross F. Collins of Annapolis, Md., for help in relation to unpublished Maryland records, and to Mr. Timothy F. Beard of the New York Public Library for many helpful suggestions.

[1] Orra E. Monnette, *First Settlers of Ye Plantations of Piscataway and Woodbridge, Olde East New Jersey, 1664-1714* (Los Angeles, 1930-35), 725.

[2] Sussex County, Delaware, is the southernmost of the three counties that comprise the state. It is bounded on the east by the Delaware River, Delaware Bay and the Atlantic Ocean, on the south and west by Maryland, and on the north by Kent County, Delaware. The southern part of the county, and a strip along the western border, were claimed by Lord Baltimore for Maryland. A settlement of this dispute was made in 1685, which in turn was subject to dispute along the western border until 1769. See Dudley Lunt, "The Bounds of Delaware," *Delaware History*, II (1947), 1-40.

[3] *Biographical and Genealogical History of the State of Delaware* (Chambersburg, Pa., 1899), 1197, 1382, and E. J. Marsh, *Genealogy of the Family of George Marsh . . .* (Leominster, Mass., 1887), iii-v. In some of these references, the name of the first settler is given as Peter Marsh. This article will show that Peter Marsh was not the original settler in Sussex County.

[4] Paul had a son, grandson and great-grandson named Peter, so that the concurrence of "Paul" and "Peter" in this English family offers what may be more than a coincidence. Note that both Peter and Paul were uncommon names in England at that time, at least among Puritans. See Donald Lines Jacobus, *Genealogy as Pastime and Profession* (New Haven, 1930), 24.

One James Marsh was a shipwright living at Wapping, now London. He had considerable property. He was buried 4 May 1615 at St. Mary Whitechapel, London, and his will was proved 20 May 1615. His wife Joan's will was proved 3 March 1620/1. They had several daughters and three sons — Peter, Paul and Julius.

Son Paul married at St. Mary Whitechapel *first* 26 February 1616/7 Susanna Bedoon and *second* 17 August 1621 Alice Wright. He was a shipwright, and was buried 29 April 1625, will proved 4 July 1625.

Son Peter was also a shipwright. He married by Bishop of London license 22 March 1611 Ellen Gibson. They had three daughters and one son James, baptized 31 August 1613. Peter's will was dated 29 June and proved 1 September 1632. Trace of James, son of Peter, has been lost; the possibility that he was the father of our Paul cannot be excluded.

For the above, see Register of St. Mary Whitechapel, London; Commissary Court of Lands Mss. 9171/23 f. 481 and Ms. 9171/24 ff. 440 and 478; PCC Rudd 41; PCC Audley 96; London marriages from the Genealogical Society of London, of which microfilm copies are available at the New York Public Library; and Noel Currer-Briggs, *Virginia Settlers and English Adventurers* (London, 1970), Vol. 3, pp. 545-6.

5 Britton's Bay in Maryland is presumably the bay on which the town of Britton is now located, on the north side of the Potomac River (the boundary between Maryland and Virginia), about 25 miles west of its entry into Chesapeake Bay, which is the southernmost point of Maryland on its western shore. Britton's Bay is and was then in St. Mary's County, in which was then located the then capital of Maryland, St. Mary's City, about 30 miles east of Britton's Bay.

6 Maryland Patents, Liber 8, f. 202; Liber 9, ff. 350-1; Liber 10, ff. 59-60; Rent Rolls, 7 & 8, ff. 32A & B and ff. 109, 109A. St. Mary's County original land records were destroyed in a court house fire in 1831. Both Richard Crockett and Henry Hill later appeared in Somerset County, where Paul Marsh settled (see Clayton Torrence, *Old Somerset on the Eastern Shore of Maryland* (Richmond, 1935), 443, 457. All subsequent references to this publication will give only the author's name and page number(s).), and both Richard Crockett and Paul Marsh purchased land from James Jones. Thus it appears that the three stayed together to some degree at least. See also Rent Rolls 9, f. 31.

7 *Archives of Maryland* (hereafter, *AM*), XLIX, 453, 455, 496, 546, 555.

8 *Ibid.,* 538-46.

9 Annapolis, in Ann Arundel County, became the capital of Maryland only in 1694.

10 Somerset County is the southernmost county of Maryland on its "Eastern Shore," bordered on the south by Accomack County, Virginia, on the east by the Atlantic Ocean, on the west by Chesapeake Bay, and on the north by the present Wicomico County, which at the time dealt with in this article was part of Somerset County. The mouth of the Pocomoke River is the boundary between Maryland and Virginia, and the town of Snow Hill lies on the middle reaches of the river.

11 Rent Rolls 9, ff. 112 A & B.

12 Patents 11, ff. 507-8; Patents 20, ff. 108-9; Patents LG#E, f. 657; Patents PT#2, ff. 235-6; Rent Rolls 9, ff. 112 & 269.

13 Bartholomew, *Survey Gazetteer of the British Isles, Seventh Edition* (Edinburgh, 1927).

14 *AM*, LIV, 724.

15 *Ibid.,* V, 61; Torrence, 395. Manokin River flows into Chesapeake Bay about 30 miles north of the Virginia border. About 10 miles farther north lies the mouth of the Wicomico River, and about 10 miles to the west of that lies the mouth of the Nanticoke River.

16 Newton D. Mereness, *Maryland as a Proprietary Province* (London, 1901), 282.

17 Torrence, 395.

18 Somerset County Land Records, 1665-1841, deed Liber 4, f. 319. James Jones had land for himself in Accomac, Virginia, near the Merideth land which he held in trust for Elizabeth Merideth and her sisters. He sold his own land in Virginia in 1659 and moved to Maryland by the early 1660's, and evidently Elizabeth went with him or followed him. He procured a number of properties, including the first "Jones Hole." Jones was a prominent man in Somerset, being one of the first magistrates there and continuing as such until his death in 1677. See Ralph T. Whitelaw, *Virginia's Eastern Shore* (Richmond, 1951), 498-9, 539. All subsequent references to this publication will give only the author's name and page number(s). Torrence, 329-30; Gust Skordas, *Early Settlers of Maryland* (Baltimore, 1968), 264, 314; Patents Liber 6, ff. 163-5.

19 Index Patents & Tracts Somerset B Ncs. 23-100; Patents Liber 6, ff. 163-5, and Liber 19, ff. 310 and 389-90. See also surveys of land called "Long Nose," next to land surveyed for Paul Marsh, dated 23 October 1672, and land called "Egypt," 31 October 1671 on warrant dated 25 October 1671, found in unpublished manuscript listing surveys, etc., presented by

Hampton L. Carson to the Historical Society of Pennsylvania. Other Jones citations concerning properties in Maryland: Patents Libers 12 f. 372, 13 f. 12, 17 ff. 196 and 400, 15 f. 397, 19 ff. 289, 310, 389, 439 and 428.

[20] There are seven places in England named Dunkirk or Dunkirke, in the counties of Gloucester, Nottingham, Norfolk, Wiltshire, Kent and Staffordshire. Again, some indication of Paul's origin may be found there. See Bartholomew, *op. cit.*

[21] The plantation called Jones Hole was on the west side of the Wicomico River about a mile above the present town of Whitehaven (Torrence, 94-5). Paul Marsh's tract "Dunkirke" adjoined.

[22] Skordas, *op. cit.,* 305.

[23] Mereness, *op. cit.,* 199.

[24] *AM,* II, 239, 311, 345, 422, 439, 440.

[25] *Idem.*

[26] *AM,* LIV, 760.

[27] John Leeds Bozman, *History of Maryland* (Baltimore, 1837), 359-60. See also Bernard Christian Steiner, *Maryland During the English Civil Wars* (Baltimore, 1907), 113.

[28] *AM,* V, 111.

[29] The Whorekill was located where is now the town of Lewes, in Sussex County, Delaware, on the western side of Delaware Bay, about two miles within Cape Henlopen. This Cape indicates the dividing line, on the Delaware side, between Delaware Bay and the Atlantic Ocean, and is opposite Cape May on the New Jersey side. It was also spelled Horekill, Hoerkill, Hoorekill, Hoornkill.

[30] See below, note 32.

[31] Leon deValinger, Jr., "The Burning of the Whorekill, 1673," *The Pennsylvania Magazine of History and Biography,* LXXIV (1950), 478-9. See also Torrence, 425, footnote, and John Goodwin Herndon, "Wiltbanck-Wiltbank of Sussex County, Delaware, and Philadelphia, Pennsylvania," *PGM,* XVIII (1950), 3-72. *

[32] *Pennsylvania Archives,* 2nd Series, VII, 749, 753, 755 and 761; *Minutes of the Executive Council of the Province of New York* (Albany, 1910), II, 679-83; "Calendar of Council Minutes, 1668-1783," *New York State Library Bulletin* 58 (March 1902), 16.

[33] *The Calvert Papers,* Maryland Historical Society Fund Publication No. 28 (Baltimore, 1889), 288-90.

[34] Lord Baltimore claimed the Whorekill and territory around it, and had purported to erect a Maryland county called Worcester, in which the Whorekill was included.

[35] As cited in note 33.

[36] Helene C. Potter, "Naomi Hinman of Lewes, Delaware, and Her Six Marriages . . .", *PGM,* XIX (1954), 243.

[37] deValinger, *op. cit.,* 482-3.

[38] See below, note 46.

[39] Elizabeth's Trustee, Thomas Johnson (who stayed in Virginia), was a prominent man in Accomack-Northampton. He was one of those who with Edmund Scarburgh attacked the Indians in 1651, and in 1652, as "Captain" Thomas Johnson, he was sufficiently engaged in the disturbances leading to the famous Northampton Protest — first cry for "no taxation without representation" in this country — to be heavily fined (Whitelaw, 31, 528-9). He had been sheriff of the county, one of the justices or commissioners, and a burgess for several terms. He had land on Muddy Creek with James Jones, and a part of it was sold to George Truitt (Whitelaw, 498-9). He was involved with the marriage of Sarah Smyth to John Hinman (Whitelaw, 444), helping her to make deeds of gift to her three children before her marriage. Thus, Thomas Johnson was not only Elizabeth Merideth's trustee, but in close contact with the families of both her brothers-in-law to be, Truitt and Hinman.

[40] The Hinmans were an early family in Accomack, Virginia. John Hinman is mentioned in the Accomack court record in 1635/6 and 1637/8 (Susie M. Ames, *County Court Records of Accomack-Northampton, Virginia, 1632-1640* (Washington, 1954), 47, 100). Sarah Hinman (widow of John Hinman and formerly of Thomas Smith) had land in 1646 with her son Richard Hinman (Whitelaw, 514). In 1660 Richard Hinman bought from Amy Waddelow (widow of Nicholas) land which descended to his son Richard when the father died later in

*See Volume III of this work, pp. 314-383.

the year (Whitelaw, 442-3). Son Richard had various land transactions throughout his years in Virginia, and in 1671 he and Mary (Merideth) Hinman, sister of Paul Marsh's wife Elizabeth, sold to John Hameryn her third of the 350 acres inherited by the three daughters (Whitelaw, 460, 474, 550, 598, etc.). Richard was then described as "of Accomack County." We do not know whether or not the Hinmans or the Truitts had been living on this property, which had been the Merideth home place. Thomas Hinman furnished a headright for John Wallop 17 November 1664 and Ja. Hinman for Mrs. Anne Toft 16 February 1665/6, but such headrights were often recorded long after the fact of entry (Stratton Nottingham, *Certificates and Rights, Accomack County, Virginia* (Onancock, Va., 1929), 13, 22). A Richard Hinman is listed among Accomack tithables in each year from 1669 to 1695, called "Senr" in 1692 (Stratton Nottingham, *Accomack Tithables, 1663-1695* (Onancock, Va., 1931), *passim*). A Richard Hinman was in Rehoboth in Sussex County on 30 June 1697 when he was a witness at a Roads wedding there, Richard Hinman became a neighbor of the Marshes there, and a Hinman married a Roades there *ca.* 1730 (C. H. B. Turner, *Some Records of Sussex County, Delaware* (Philadelphia, 1909), 26; Helene C. Potter, *op. cit.*, 243.). On 15 January 1713, Richard purchased 427 acres of land adjoining Marsh's land from John Roads, and at the same time Peter Marsh (Paul's son) purchased 200 of these acres (Shankland Survey Book, Sussex County, 1713-28, 1-2). This Richard was dead by 1719 (Whitelaw, 598). A Richard Hinman was executor of the will of Peter Marsh, dated 1725 (Sussex County, Reg. of Wills, Liber A, ff. 199-200).

41 George Truitt (Trewett, Trewitt, Truhett, etc.), husband of Ellynor Merideth, was of a family which had settled in Accomack. His father George died in 1670, his will dated 10 July and probated 16 October of that year, leaving land to sons Henry, James, George, John and Job, and mentioning daughters Jane, Dorothy, Susannah and Elizabeth. He had land at Onancock and at Muddy Creek, and thus the Truitt, Merideth and Johnson families were neighbors in Virginia. Sons Henry and George were left in charge of the father's estate (Stratton Nottingham, *Wills and Administrations, Accomack County, Virginia, 1663-1800* (Onancock, Va., 1931), 3). From the list of tithables we can deduce that Henry and George were the two elder sons and that Henry left Virginia (for Maryland) about 1676 and George about 1684, although they might have gone earlier and only sold their Virginia lands at about these dates. George Truitt and "Elianor" sold 450 acres on Muddy Creek in Virginia to Lt. Col. David Jenifer in 1685 (Whitelaw, 1111), and George purchased 600 acres in Somerset County, Maryland, in July 1689 (Torrence, 107). In Paul Marsh's administration papers dated 1684 in Sussex County, George is described as being of Somerset County, Maryland, indicating that he had moved from Accomack to Somerset by 1684, or a year earlier than his sale of land in Virginia, and five years earlier than his purchase of land in Maryland. George was named one of the overseers of the will of his stepfather-in-law, George Johnson of Muddy Creek, dated 10 December 1690 and probated 26 September 1692, even though Truitt had moved away and George's mother-in-law had died and Johnson had remarried someone named Mary (Nottingham, *Wills and Administrations, op. cit.*, 16).

George Truitt and his brother Henry were clearly Quakers. In Virginia, George was one of the six trustees (including George Johnson) who held title to the one acre site of the historic Guilford Quaker Meeting House. In Maryland, George and Henry entertained the celebrated Quaker preacher, Thomas Chalkley, near the head of Pocomoke in 1698. Another Quaker missionary, Thomas Story, visited George Truitt's residence and held meetings there for several years starting in 1699. George Truitt's house upon Pocomoke was named a Quaker meeting house in 1704, and George's will left an acre of land to the Quakers for a burying ground and meeting house in 1720/1 (Torrence, 85-111).

When in 1680 Paul and Elizabeth Marsh sold to Jonah Jackson their interest in the Virginia land that had come to Elizabeth from her mother, the Truitts did the same by separate deed (Whitelaw, 550).

42 Occahannock Creek is the western boundary between Accomack and Northampton Counties (as presently constituted) on the eastern shore of Virginia, and Thomas Johnson's and James Jones' lands were on the south side of the creek, a few miles from its entry into Chesapeake Bay. Eleanor Meredith's land was nearby (Whitelaw, maps). Occahannock Creek must have been a favored location — Edmund Scarburgh, Surveyor General of Virginia,

had his principal estate on the north bank of the Creek, and in 1655 this creek was chosen as the official port of that part of the Accomac-Northampton County, and the site of the church or meeting house, the Clerk's and Sheriff's offices, the prison and other public buildings (Whitelaw, 606).

43 Northampton County Deeds, Wills, No. 7, 8, 1665-8, 69-2407. There were two George Johnsons in Accomack, each a prominent Quaker. One went to Maryland, and his story is given at some length in Torrence, 316-9. The other stayed in Virginia, and was known as George Johnson of Muddy Creek (Whitelaw, 1206; Torrence, 507). It was he who married the widow Merideth. This George Johnson's land adjoining that of George Truitt, who married a Merideth daughter. Ellinor Merideth Johnson was alive in 1672, when she joined in a deed with her new husband George Johnson, but was dead by 1678, when George Johnson's wife was named as Mary (Whitelaw, 1206). George Johnson's house was recorded as a place for Quaker meetings, in 1692, after his death (Whitelaw, 1116).

44 Virginia Patents No. 2, 1693-51, p. 177. Warrant was 4, ff. 4 and 5. Virginia Patents Liber dated 28 April 1659. It is assumed by Whitelaw, 550, and stated in the daughters' deeds, that the transfer by Waddilow was to Philip Merideth rather than to his widow Ellinor. However, an Ellinor Merideth is recorded as entering Virginia without reference to her husband Phillip in a certificate dated 17 April 1665 issued to Robert Hutchinson, so that she may well have emigrated as a widow, and the patent might have been issuable to her husband while still in English residence. There is no record of a transfer from Waddilow either to Philip or to Ellinor Merideth. But a Philip Meredith aged 12 is listed as a passenger for Virginia in 1635 (John C. Hotten, *The Original Lists of Persons of Quality . . .* (London, 1874), 119).

45 Maryland Patents Book 6 430.

46 Paul's appointment is noted in C. H. B. Turner, *op. cit.*, 12, 14, 15, 29, and in John T. Scharf, *History of Delaware* (Philadelphia, 1888), 1211, but is not found in *Governor's Register, State of Delaware* (Wilmington, 1926).

47 C. H. B. Turner, *op. cit.*, 30.

48 *Duke of York Records* (Wilmington, 1903), 55.

49 C. H. B. Turner, *op. cit.*, 12, 15-16.

50 Maryland Patents 20, ff. 108-9 "now Worcester Co.". See also Rent Rolls 9 ff. 112A & B; Patent 2414, Somerset County; Patents LG#E, f. 657; Patents PT#2, f. 235. And at Maryland Historical Society is a note-book entitled, Somerset County Rent Roll 1707, listing under "Pognadenorton Hundred" a survey dated 27 August 1668 of Mordike for 1000 acres for Paul Marsh. Note that Paul Marsh's grandson Peter Marsh married Esther Purnell of Bogatenorton, where a former Quaker meeting was situated. There is still a Purnell Pond and Purnell Point on the shore of Chincoteague Bay on the Atlantic side of Maryland near Snow Hill, and a Truitt Landing between, as shown on the official map of Worcester (formerly Somerset) County, Maryland. This indicates a continuing relationship between the Marsh family and the neighborhood of Paul's former Maryland plantation.

51 "In addition to the foregoing 'common warrant', there was also the 'special warrant' issued or directed to be issued by Lord Baltimore himself with whatever conditions he might prescribe. Included in this category would be gifts, grants, orders, and so on." See Elizabeth Hartsook and Gust Skordas, *Land Office and Prerogative Court Records of Colonial Maryland* (Baltimore, 1968), 24.

52 *The Calvert Papers, op. cit.*, 283.

53 Somerset County (Md.) Land Records, Liber MA#3, f. 20.

54 Percy G. Skirven, "Durham County," *Maryland Historical Magazine*, XXV (1930), 157-67.

55 Torrence, 424-6, 443, 453-4, 457-8, and Carson manuscript, note 19.

56 *The Calvert Papers, op. cit.*, 253.

57 *Ibid.*, 283-4, 288.

58 Maryland Patents, Liber XVIII, f. 54. This policy continued for some time. See C. A. Weslager, *The English on the Delaware, 1610-1682* (New Brunswick, 1967), 199, 219-20.

[59] Edwin Jacquett Sellers, *Supplement to Genealogies* (Philadelphia, 1922), 65; *Duke of York Records, op. cit.,* 48.

[60] *Duke of York Records, op. cit.,* 54-55, 154; Scharf, *op. cit.,* 1202.

[61] *AM,* LI, 301-3.

[62] Whitelaw, 550.

[63] *Duke of York Records, op. cit.,* 66; N.Y. Colonial Mss. Indorsed Land Papers, Vol. 36, p. 76, item 4.

[64] C. H. B. Turner, *op. cit.,* 59.

[65] *Ibid.,* 86.

[66] *Ibid.,* 135; Public Archives Commission, Hall of Records, Dover, Del., Vol. M 2013, p. 37.

[67] Sussex County (Delaware) Deed Records, Liber F 6 ff. 24-5, Reel 733.

[68] Sussex County (Delaware) Deed Records, Liber A 1 f. 94, Reel 731. See also Sussex County Surveys, Land Warrants, Reel 2.

[69] See notes 67 and 68.

[70] Sussex County (Delaware) Orphans Court Records 1728-44, p. 145, and 1744-51, p. 13, Hall of Records, Dover, Del.

[71] Sussex County (Delaware) Deed Records, Liber F 6 f. 39.

[72] *Ibid.,* Liber H 8 f. 156.

[73] *Ibid.,* Liber I 9 f. 63.

[74] *Calendar of Kent County Delaware Probate Records 1680-1800,* Public Archives Commission (1944), 149.

[75] *Calendar of Sussex County Delaware Probate Records,* Public Archives Commission (1964), 35.

[76] Index to Sussex County Orphans Court Records, in Court House, Georgetown, Del. The records themselves for the period 1752-60 are lost.

[77] *Delaware Military Archives Revolutionary War,* Public Archives Commission (1919), 120, 459, 461-3, 1112, 1267.

[78] Sussex County Orphans Court Records 1728-44, Hall of Records, Dover, Del., 145.

[79] See note 36 above.

[80] Sussex County Deed Records, Liber G 7, f. 126, and other deeds.

[81] St. Peter's Church, Vestry Minutes of 1747, in Hall of Records, Dover, Del.

[82] Information on their six children and their offspring comes from the following sources, unless otherwise noted: The Marsh Bibles; inscriptions in Marsh Cemetery; St. George's Chapel Records in Hall of Records, Dover, Del.; and Baldwin Maull, *op. cit.,* 18. The Bibles are in the possession of Mr. and Mrs. Peter Marsh of Rehoboth, who represent several lines of descent from 3. Peter and Esther Marsh. Mr. Marsh is a great grandson of Matthew Marsh (1785-1821), son of Peter and Polly (Wilson) Marsh.

[83] *Delaware Military Archives Revolutionary War, op. cit.,* 1235.

[84] Records in Court House, Snow Hill, Md., and *Index to 1800 Federal Census of Worcester County Maryland,* compiled by Lowell M. Volkel and Timothy Q. Wilson.

[85] 5 March: the date Peter deeded a slave to each of his children (Liber I 9 f. 255); 4 May: the date Peter and Agnes deeded a lot in Lewes to *her* two sons, Nehemiah and John Field (Liber I 9, f. 256).

[86] Sussex County Orphans Court Book B, 66; birth and death dates are in the family Bible.

[87] *Idem.*

[88] Calendar of Sussex County, Delaware Probate Records, p. 84, and Archives, Vol. A86, 117.

[89] Sussex County (Delaware) Deed Records, Liber I 9, f. 255.

[90] Photostat in Hall of Records, Dover, Del.

[91] *Delaware Military Archives Revolutionary War, op. cit.,* 13, 15.

DAVID MEREDITH OF RADNOR, CHESTER COUNTY, AND OF PLYMOUTH, PHILADELPHIA COUNTY, PENNA. AND HIS STEP-CHILDREN SURNAMED MOORE

By Lewis D. Cook, F.A.S.G., F.G.S.P.

An unsuspecting reading of the words " David Meredith of ye parish of Llanbister in the county of Radnorshire, weaver, and Kathrine his wife with their five children namely Richard, Mary, John, Meredith, and Sarah," in the certificate of removal received and recorded by Radnor Monthly Meeting, Chester County, Penna., has provided the following two erroneous notices. That the first three listed children were in fact the emigrant David Meredith's stepchildren, surnamed Moore, is obvious from other relevant records cited hereinafter.

MERIDITH, DAVID, came from the parish of Llanbister, Radnorshire, Wales, in 1683 or 1684, and settled in Radnor township. . . . He was accompanied to this country by his wife Katharine and their five children—Richard, Mary, John, Meridith and Sarah. Katharine died in 1688 and in 1690 he was married to Mary Jones, a widow, of Upper Providence, as his second wife, by whom he probably had no children. . . . The time of his decease is not known; but from the circumstance of his name disappearing from the minutes of his meeting in 1695 (*sic*), it is supposed that it occurred about that period. He had sufferred imprisonment in Wales on account of his religious principles.—George B. Smith, *History of Delaware County, Penna.*, 1862, p 485.

DAVID MEREDITH, of the parish of Llanbister, county of Radnor, removed to Radnor, Penna., 1683. A Friend. Freeholder of 250 acres of land in Radnor, and elsewhere. Wife, Katherine. Children (surnamed Meredith): 1. Richard; 2. Mary; 3. John; 4. Meredith; 5. Sarah (born in Wales.)—Thomas A. Glenn, *Welsh Founders of Penna.*, 1911, vol. 1, 193.

DAVID MEREDITH, of the parish of Llanbister, in Radnorshire, Wales, weaver, purchased from Richard Davies of Welchpoole, in Montgomeryshire, gent., by Deed of 20 June 1682, a tract of 100 acres to be laid out in the Province of Pennsylvania. He was described as having been a member of the religious Society of Friends for the last twenty years and more in the certificate given him on 20th of 5th month (July) 1683 by Radnorshire Friends for his removal to Pennsylvania. He was probably the David Meredith of Radnorshire who, with one Richard Moore and eight other Friends, was fined in 1659 for " absence from the National Worship; " and the same two who were listed among 23 Friends committed to prison in 1664 " until they should take the oath of allegiance." [2]   It is impossible here to report definitely that David Meredith's wife KATHERINE MOORE, who arrived in Radnor Township, Chester County, Penna., with him, formerly a widow Moore as hereinafter appears, had been the widow of Richard Moore abovesaid.[3]

By Deed of 20 June 1682, Richard Davies of Welchpoole, Co. Montgomery, (Wales), Gent., conveyed to David Meredith of the parish of Llanbister, Co. Radnor, (Wales), weaver, for 2 Pounds sterling, and an annual quitrent of 1 shilling to be paid to William Penn, the Proprietary, a tract of 100 acres to be laid out in the Province of Pennsylvania. Recorded 16-12-1683/4 in *Phila. Deed Book C-1*, page 73, whence this abstract.

Radnor Shir. At or mens meeting ye 20th of ye 5th month 1683. Whereas or deare frind & brother David Meredith of ye parish of Llanbister in the affordsd. County, weaver, and Kathrine his wife with their five children namely Richard, Mary, John, Meredith, & Sarah, are disposed to remove themselves from their present dwelling to Pensilvania in America, These are therefore to certifie all whom whom it may concerne yt he is a man yt hath owned trueth these twenty years agoe & upwards; his life & conversation being well approved of, not only amongst frinds but alsoe amongst his neighboures & acquaintance, and soe have a good report. He was very loving to frinds and charitable amongst his neibours & soe leaves a good savour amongst us; & his dear wife doth own the same trueth & walkes accordingly thereunto; and we further certifie yt or sd frind David Meredith doth not transport himselfe & family to the place aforsd by reason of any dept or depts to any pson or psons wtsoever; neither by wrongful act by him, or any of his children, done or comitted agst any pson wtsoever; and soe we comitt him to the ptection of the almighty god of power; and to this testemony we put or names as followeth. Owen Humphrey, John Jarman, Daniel Lewis, Nathan Woodlife, David Griffith, John Lloyd, Edward Moore, Edward Jones, Richard Cooke, Roger Hughes, Jon Robert, Jon Watson, Rees ap Rees, Rich. Watkins, Thomas Parry.—*From the register of certificates, Radnor Monthly Meeting, Chester Co., Penna.*[4]

David Meredith and family must have arrived in Pennsylvania by 16th of 12th month (Feb.) 1683/4, the date of recording at Philadelphia his Deed abovementioned, just under seven months after the Radnorshire Friends signed the certificate for his removal to Pennsylvania. In the existing minutes of Radnor, Penna., Monthly Meeting, which begin with 10th of 2nd. month (Apr) 1684, David Meredith is first named in those of 14th of 11th month (Jan.) 1685/6, appointed to receive Friends quarterly collection in Radnor.*

Katherine Meredith the wife of David Meredith died, and was buried on 26th of 7th month (Sept.) 1688 in Friends burying place in Radnor.[6] David Meredith married secondly, on 21st of 3rd month (May) 1690, at the house of Thomas Minshall in Upper Providence Township, Chester

---

* Radnor Monthly Meeting for Friends business and discipline was composed of representatives from the local Preparative Meetings of Schuylkill, Merion, Haverford, Radnor, Newtown, and Plymouth.

County, Penna., by Friends ceremony, MARY JONES, of that township, widow. Evidently she predeceased him, as she is not named or mentioned in his Will of 28th of 10th month 1723.

Having purchased a tract of 980 acres in Plymouth Township, Philadelphia County, from Philip Price, which was confirmed to him by Deed of 4th March 1701/2, David Meredith and family removed from Radnor Township between 1704 and 1708 eastward and across Schuylkill River and settled thereon. The minutes of Gwynedd Monthly Meeting, [created in 1714 from Radnor Monthly Meeting, and composed of representatives from Plymouth and Gwynedd local Preparative Meetings], name David Meredith and John Shiers as the Overseers of Plymouth on 31st of 1st month 1719. The minutes of 31st of 11th month 1720 state that the Elders, "Robert Jones, John Humphrey, David Meredith, William Coulstone, and John Jacobs, are appointed to sit with our Ministers in their Meeting." David Meredith, aged about 90 years,[5] died at his home in Plymouth, a half mile eastward of the present borough of Norristown [7] and south of Germantown Pike, between 10th of 1st month (March) 1726/7 and 13th of 3rd month (May) 1727 following,—the date of probate of his Will.

Antenuptial agreement dated 24-2-1690 between David Meredith of Radnor, Chester Co., Penna., widower, and Mary Jones of Upper Providence Twp., said Co., widow, of the one part, and Thomas and Peter Jones of the other part, both of said Twp.[7]

Digest of Certificate of Marriage of David Meredith of Radnor Twp. in the Welsh Tract, Chester Co., Penna., widower, and Mary Jones of Upper Providence Twp., said Co., widow, on 21-3-1690 at the house of Thomas Minshall in said Co., signed by Witnesses: Thomas Jones, Peter Jones (*her sons*), Richard Moore (*his stepson*), Stephen Evans, Ann Powell, Phebe Taylor, Mary Taylor, Elizabeth Plott, Mary Moore (*his stepdaughter*), as next of kin, and others.—*Register of Radnor Mo. Mtg.*[6]

By Deed of 31-5-1694, David Meredith and wife Mary conveyed to Thomas Jones of Upper Providence Twp., Chester Co., Penna., in consideration of certain sums of money paid by said Jones to discharge the debts due by said Mary before her marriage to said David Meredith, 150 acres in said Twp. which had been conveyed to said Mary by Robert Robinson by his Deed of 3-4mo-1689. Agreement that if said Mary survives her husband David Meredith, she should enjoy the use of half the cleared land on said tract during her lifetime. Recorded in *Chester Co. Deed Book E-2*, page 316.

Roger Hughes acquired 250 acres by Deeds of 19 and 20 June 1682, and sold 125 acres thereof to David Meredith by Deed of 11 Sept 1691, who sold it to Richard Moore but not conveyed. The other moiety said Hughes sold to Thomas Parry, decd., who sold to Richard Moore but not conveyed, who is now possessed of the whole.—Minutes of the Welsh Purchasers, Board of Property of the Province of Penna., published in *Penna. Archives*, 3rd series, vol. 1, page 14.

David Meredith acquired 100 acres by Deeds of 19 and 20 June 1682 in his possession in Radnor. He also purchased of the Commissioners 250 acres, and paid the money to James Harrison. The whole 350 acres were laid out by virtue of two warrants, one from the Proprietor 19th of 1st mo. 1683, the other from the Commissioners, 17th of 3rd mo. 1687, and laid out 24th of said 3rd mo., and confirmed to him by Patent 26th 3rd mo. 1689. Of this he sold to Stephen Evans 150 acres by Deed dated 20th of 5th mo. 1691; the rest David Meredith holds.—Minutes, *ibid.*

By Deed of 4 March 1701/2 Francis Rawle of Phila. Co., mercht., and Elizabeth Fox, of Phila., widow of James Fox, confirmed to David Meredith of Radnor Twp., Chester Co., Penna., yeoman, for 5 shillings, the 980 acres tract in Plymouth Twp., Phila. Co., which they had conveyed to Philip Price by Deed of 6-8mo-1697 and said Price to said Meredith, being part of the 2500 acres which were granted to said Rawle and Fox by William Penn by Deed of lease and release dated 12 and 13 March 1685. Recorded 21 Aug. 1745 in *Phila. Deed Book G-6*, page 291, whence this abstract.

The Will of David Meredith of the Twp. of Plymouth, Phila. Co., Penna., dated 28th of 10th mo. 1723 and proved 13 May 1727, devises to my daughter Sarah's children, Edward Price, Mary Price, and Margaret Price, 30 Pds., viz. a bond on Thomas Ellis for 20 Pds. and a bond on John Shires for 10 Pds., to be equally divided among them, besides a bond of 29 Pds. which is in Rees Price's hand for Mary and Margaret, all to be put out to interest by ye executors and trustees or ye survivors of them till they are 21 years of age, but in case the children all die, it is to return to my son Meredith David's children; also I give to my son Meredith David all the rest of my estate both real and temporal, and do make him my son Meredith David my sole executor; lastly, I nominate Peter Jones, John Moore, David Jones, and Rees Preys to see this my last will and testament fulfilled. Witnesses: William Coulston, Thomas Ellis, John Rees.—Recorded in *Phila. Admin. Book C*, page 79, whence this abstract.

" Whereas Meredith David, the executor nominated in ye foregoing Will, died before ye probate of ye same testament was had, whereby ye right of admo. with ye Testament aforesaid annexed, became vested in Ellis Meredith, grandson and next of kin of ye said testator David Meredith, therefore admo. with ye testament annexed was granted to him ye sd. Ellis Meredith." Given under seal of office ye 13th day of May A.D. 1727.—*Ibid.*, page 80.

Children of David and Katherine (-Moore) Meredith:

2   i.   MEREDITH DAVID b 6-3mo-1675; d between 4 Feb. and 10 May 1727.
3   ii.   SARAH DAVID married 6-10mo-1705 REES PREES.

2. MEREDITH DAVID, born 6th of 3rd month (May) 1675 according to family record,* son of the emigrant David Meredith then of Radnorshire, Wales, died testate in Plymouth Township, Philadelphia County, Penna., between 4th of 12th month (Feb.) 1726/7 and 10 May 1727, the dates of his Will and its probate. Meredith David (as he was named in the Welsh system of patronymics instead of fixed surnames), of Rad-

---

* Record of the Meredith Family, copied 20 July 1884 by Sarah Pennell, wife of Joseph, is in the Gilbert Cope Collection of The Genealogical Society of Penna.

nor in the Welsh Tract, Chester County, Penna., " batchiller ", and
ELLIN ELLIS (PUGH) of said Tract, " Spinster ", were married on 22nd
of 11th month 1699/1700 at Radnor Meeting House, with David
Meredith (*his father*), Ellis Pugh (*her father*), Richard Moore (*his
stepbrother*), John Moore (*ditto*), Mary Meredith (*his stepmother*),
Sinai Pugh (*her mother*), and others signing the certificate as witnesses.[6]
The widow Ellin (Pugh) David died testate in Philadelphia County be-
tween 10th of 8th month 1733 and 3 January 1734.

The Will of Meredith David of Plymouth Twp., Phila. Co., Penna., dated 4-12mo-
1726/7 and proved 10 May 1727, names wife Ellin and children: David, Ellis, Richard,
John, Moses, Aaron, Sarah, Catherine, and Mary. Recorded in *Phila. Will Book E,* page
47, whence this abstract.

The Will of Ellin David of Phila. Co., Penna., widow, dated 10-8mo-1733 and
proved 3 Jan. 1734, names brother Job Pugh, children: Moses, Aaron, Mary, Sarah, and
Catherine; brother-in-law Ellis Roberts, *etc.* Recorded in *Phila. Will Book E,* page
279, whence this abstract.

Children of Meredith and Ellin (Pugh) David:

From the register and minutes of Gwynedd Monthly Meeting.

    i. DAVID MEREDITH b 9-9-1700; d unmar betw 10 March and 13 May
       1727.*

    ii. JOHN MEREDITH b 25-5-1703; d in 1727-28, unmar.

    iii. ELLIS MEREDITH b 6-12mo-1704; d unmar betw 20 June and 27 Sep.
       1728.ᵖ

---

* 12-11mo-1726/7: David Meredith the younger and Susanna Jones declared their intentions of marriage. It is expected that he produce a certificate of his clearness against next meeting.—*Minutes of Radnor Monthly Meeting, Chester Co., Penna.*

10-12mo-1726/7: David Meredith the younger and Susannah Jones declared their intentions of marriage the second time, and nothing appearing to obstruct, he producing a certificate from Gwynedd
Monthly Meeting which is ordered to be recorded, are left to their liberty.—*Ibid.*

Certificate dated "last day of 11th month 1726 " from Gwynedd Monthly Meeting to Radnor
Monthly Meeting for David Meredith to proceed in marriage with Susannah Jones belonging to your
meeting.[6]

9-1mo (March) 1726/7: " Account is brought that the marriage of David Meredith and Susannah
Jones is not accomplished, both families being sickley."—*Minutes, supra.*

The nuncupative Will of David Meredith of Plymouth Twp., Phila. Co., dated 10-1mo-1726/7 and
proved 13 May 1727, devises 40 Pounds to Susannah Jones. At the probate it was testified that " Whereas
David Meredith, deceased grandson of David Meredith also deced., in the time of his last sickness did make
the nuncupative Will above written but named no executors thereof, whereby ye right of admon. with the
said nuncupative Will annexed became vested in Ellis Meredith, next of kin to ye sd. David Meredith ye
grandson deced. Therefore Admon. with ye nunc. Will aforesd. annexed was granted to him ye sd. Ellis
Meredith."—Recorded in *Phila. Admin. Book C,* page 80.

ᵖ The Will of Ellis Meredith of Plymouth Twp., Phila. Co., dated 20-4-1728 and proved 27 Sept 1728,
names mother Ellin; brothers Moses, Aaron, and David; sisters Sarah, Katharine, Mary; uncle Job Pugh;
and appoints his mother Ellin Meredith execx., and Job Pugh, John Evans, Rowland Ellis, Cadwalader
Evans, Evan Evans, Thomas Ellis overseers. Witnesses: William Davis, Hugh Jones, Joseph Jones. Recorded in *Phila. Will Book E,* page 87, whence this abstract.

iv. RICHARD MEREDITH b 4-12mo-1706; d in 1727-28, unmar.

v. SARAH MEREDITH b 8-8-1708; mar in 4mo 1741 DANIEL WILLIAMS.

vi. MARY MEREDITH b 29-2-1711; d in infancy.

vii. KATHERINE MEREDITH b 22-9-1712; mar in 8mo 1733 MORDECAI YARNALL of Springfield Twp., Chester Co., Penna., who was b 11-7mo-1705, son of Francis and Hannah (Baker) Yarnall. He mar 2ndly 8-6mo-1745 Mary Roberts, and 3rdly 3 March 1768 Ann Maris, widow of Joseph Maris, and died 17 May 1772, a minister in the Society of Friends. See Yarnall Family in the *North American*, Phila., 9 March 1913.

viii. MOSES MEREDITH b 30-9-1714; mar 11-2mo-1739 at Middletown Meeting House, Chester Co., Penna., MARY PENNELL, dau of Joseph Pennell of Edgmont Twp., said Co.—*Register of Chester Mo. Mtg.*

ix. MARY MEREDITH b 30-9-1714, twin with Moses; mar 22-10-1738 at Gwynedd Meeting House, OWEN WILLIAMS, son of John Williams of Gwynedd Twp., Phila. Co., Penna.

x. AARON MEREDITH b 7-3mo-1716; mar in 12mo 1745/6 ELIZABETH EVANS.

3. SARAH DAVID, born in or shortly before 1683, daughter of the emigrant David Meredith, then of Radnorshire, Wales, came with her parents to Radnor Township, Chester County, Penna., and died between 1710 and 1718, first wife of REES PREES (PRICE) of Merion Township, Philadelphia County, Penna., whom she had married on 6th of 10th month (Dec.) 1705 at Radnor Meeting House. Rees Prees was born 11th of 11th month 1678 in Penllyn, Wales, and came to Merion Township abovesaid with his father Edward Rees and the latter's family in 1682. He died testate in Merion, and was buried 11th of 5th month (May) 1760 " aged about 84 years ", in Merion Friends burying place at the Meeting House. Rees Prees (Price) married secondly, on 9th of 10th month (Dec.) 1718 at Haverford Meeting House, ELIZABETH ELLIS, spinster. She died, and was buried on 5th of 12th month (Feb.) 1733/4 at Haverford Friends burying place. Rees Prees (Price) then married thirdly on 10th of 3rd month (May) 1737 at Haverford Meeting House, ANN (DAVIS) SCOTHORN, widow of Samuel Scothorn of Darby, Chester County, Penna., who had died there 13th of 1st month 1730/1.

By Deed of 19 Feb. 1738, Mordecai Yarnall of Chester Co., Penna., and wife Catherine, Owen Williams of Northwales, Phila. Co., and wife Mary, and Sarah Meredith of Plymouth Twp., said Co., spinster, released to Moses Meredith and Aaron Meredith, both of said Twp., yeomen, for 160 Pds., all their interest in the 862 acres there which were devised by David Meredith (*i.e.* Meredith David) to his four sons David, John, Ellis, and Richard, by his Will of May 1727. Recital that said sons John, David, and Richard died intestate and without issue, and that said son Ellis Meredith, surviving reversionary legatee, devised the tract to his brothers Moses and Aaron Meredith, parties hereto, they to pay to their sisters Catherine, Mary, and Sarah, parties hereto, the sum of 100 Pds. equally divided among them, by his Will of 20 June 1728. Recorded in *Phila. Deed Book G-6*, page 293, whence this abstract.

Digest of Certificate of Marriage of Rees Price of Merion Twp., Phila. Co., Penna., and Sarah Meredith of Radnor Twp., Chester Co., Penna., at Radnor Mtg. Hse. on 6-10mo-1705. Witnesses: Edward Prees (*his father*), David Meredith (*her father*), Meredith David (*her brother*), Richard Moore (*her stepbrother*), John Moore (*ditto*), Samuel Nicholas, Anthony Moore, John Moore, David Jones, Rebecca Moore, and 79 others.[6]

The Will of Reese Price of Merion Twp., Phila. Co., Penna., dated 29 Feb. 1760 and proved 12 May 1760, devises to wife Ann certain pieces of furniture, a horse and saddle, a cow, the brass kettle, the rents of 60 acres in Haverford, a negro wench " Sall ", the use of my desk, 50 Pds. and the interest of 60 Pds. annually, she to live with my son John Price; to eldest son Edward Price my large Bible; to each of my daughter Mary Harry's children (not named) 5 sh.; to each of my daughter Margaret Paschall's children (not named) 5 sh.; to son Ellis Price 10 Pds.; to son John Price two negro boys Tom and Wille, a horse, cart, plow, etc.; to daughter Jane my negro girl Daphne, certain pieces of furniture, and 100 Pds.; to daughter-in-law Mary Price, the wife of my son John Price, a mulatto wench; residue of estate to sons Ellis and John Price equally; and appoints sons Ellis Price and John Price and friend John Roberts, miller, execrs. Recorded in *Phila. Will Book L,* page 443, whence this abstract.

Children of Rees Price and 1st Wife Sarah David:

Names and dates from the register of Radnor Mo. Mtg.[6]

  i. MARY PRICE b 1-7mo-1706, who mar 12-10mo-1727 REES HARRY.
 ii. EDWARD PRICE b 14-11-1707/8; who was buried 3 June 1791 aged 84 in
     Merion Friends burying place.
iii. MARGARET PRICE b 28-3-1710; d intestate 6-12mo-1755 in Phila.[8] She
     mar 1st., out of Friends Mtg., BENJAMIN PASCHALL, who d intestate
     12-12mo-1744/5 in Phila. She mar 2nd. 19-5-1750 in Phila. Mtg. Hse.,
     as his 2nd. wife, WILLIAM MONTGOMERY of Phila., mercht.* Issue

* Administration upon the estate of Benjamin Paschall of Phila., lately deced., was granted 29 March 1745 to his widow Margaret Paschall.—*Phila. Admin. Book E,* page 60.

Digest of Certificate received by Phila. Mo. Mtg. of 27-2-1750 from Haverford (Radnor) Mo. Mtg., dated 10-2mo-1750: Margaret Paschall lived inoffensive until the breach she made in consumating marriage not in Friends way, which offence she has of late acknowledged in writing and was received by our Meeting, and as she has been a liver in the city from the time of her marriage, we refer her conduct for that time to your inspection, and we recommend her to your Christian care.—From transcript of *Certificates recorded by Phila. Mo. Mtg.,* in collections of The Genealogical Society of Penna.

Digest of Certificate of Marriage of William Montgomery of Phila., merchant, and Margaret Paschall of said city, widow, at Phila. Mtg. Hse. on 19-5-1750. Witnesses: John, Joseph, Mary, Mary, Elizabeth, Thomas, and Ann Paschall, Reese Price (*her father*), Ann Price (*her stepmother*), and 24 others.—Collections, *supra.*

Administration upon the estate of Margaret Montgomery deced., formerly Margaret Paschall, was granted 6 July 1756 to William Montgomery of Phila., her husband.—*Phila. Admin. Book G,* page 58.

By Deed of 25 July 1781, William Montgomery of Crosswicks, Burlington Co., N. J., Gent., and wife Mary, conveyed to William Clifton of the District of Southwark, Phila. Co., Penna., blacksmith. Recital that Mary Knowles of said District, widow, by Deed of 9 Nov. 1745 conveyed to Margaret Paschall, widow, a lot on the east side of Front St. there, 65 by 277 feet, and said Margaret Paschall afterwards intermarried with a certain William Montgomery of West N. J., and afterwards died intestate, leaving issue by her first husband three sons to wit John, Joseph, and Benjamin Paschall, and by her second husband the abovenamed William Montgomery, party hereto, and that afterwards the said Benjamin Paschall died under age and without issue, and the lot descended to the said John Paschall, Joseph Paschall, and William

by 1st. husband: (1) John Paschall; (2) Joseph Paschall; and (3) Benjamin Paschall who d a minor; and by 2nd husband: (4) William Montgomery.

Children of Rees Price and 2nd Wife Elizabeth Ellis: [6]

    iv. ELLIS PRICE b 14-7-1719.
    v. JOHN PRICE b 27-6-1721.
    vi. JANE PRICE b 6-9mo-1729.

THE STEPCHILDREN OF DAVID MEREDITH:

Children of N. N. and Katherine (   ) Moore:

1   i. RICHARD MOORE b *circa* 1674; d 1715.
2   ii. MARY MOORE b *circa* 1676; d 1762; mar ROBERT POUND.
3   iii. JOHN MOORE b *circa* 1678; d 1719.

1. RICHARD MOORE, elder son of the widow Katherine Moore, came with her and his stepfather David Meredith from the parish of Llanbister, in Radnorshire, South Wales, to Radnor Township, Chester County, Penna., and died there testate shortly before 16 October 1715. He married on 17th of 3rd month (May) 1701, by Friends ceremony at Radnor Meeting House, PHEBE (EVANS) PHILLIPS, widow of Phillip Phillips of Radnor, and daughter of Stephen Evans of same township, formerly of Radnorshire, South Wales, abovesaid.[5] She survived Richard Moore and married thirdly, 27th of 8th month 1715, at Radnor Meeting House, HOWELL JAMES of New Castle County, Delaware, widower, and survived him. She was living in 1748 in Radnor.

Richard Moore of Radnor in the Welsh Tract, Province of Penna., carpenter, and Phebe Phillips of the same place, widow, married at Randor Mtg. Hse. 17-3-1701, with witnesses signing: David Meredith (*his stepfather*), Stephen Evan (her father), John Moore (his brother), David Jones, Meredith David (his stepbrother), John Stephen (her brother), Sinai Pugh, James Moore, and others—*Digest of certificate recorded by Radnor Monthly Meeting.*[6]

Montgomery, and the said Joseph Paschall by Ded of 25 Sept. 1761 conveyed to William Montgomery, the father, his interest. And the said William Montgomery afterwards erected in the northwardly part of the lot a small brick messuage at his own cost and held the same with the whole lot during his life, but no Deed from the said John Paschall can be found, although there is strong presumption that he conveyed his interest to the said William Montgomery, the father. The said William Montgomery, by his Will of 24 Nov. 1769, devised the messuage and lot to his son, the said William Montgomery, party hereto. Recorded in *Phila. Deed Book D-6*, page 334, whence this abstract. The said Will was proved 20 Sept. 1771.

    Compare Price Family, in Thos. A. Glenn, *Merion in the Welsh Tract*, page 96, and Thos H. Montgomery, *History of the Family of Montgomery*, Phila. 1863, pages 103-104.

Phillip Phillip of Radnor, Chester Co., Penna., bachelor, and Phebe Evans of same place (referred to twice as " Phebe Stephens "), married at Radnor Mtg. Hse. 1st of 4mo 1693, with witnesses signnig: John Evans, David Meredith, Ellis Pugh, and others. —*Digest, supra.*

Phillip Phillips was buried 25-11-(Jan.)-1697 in Friends burying place in Radnor. —*Register of Radnor Mo. Mtg.*[6] His daughter Mary Phillips, born 3-1st mo-1694, married at Radnor Mtg. Hse 5-9mo-1719 David Morris of Marple Twp., Chester Co., Penna., son of David Morris.[6]

Howell James of New Castle Co., Del., widower, and Phebe Moore of Radnor, Chester Co., Penna., widow, married at Radnor Mtg. Hse. on 27-8-1715. Witnesses signing: Stephen Bevan, Jno Stephens, David Meredith, James James, and others. *Digest, supra.*[6]

Certificate dated 20-5-1683 for Stephen Evans of the parish of Llanbister, Radnorshire, Wales, wife Elizabeth and two children: John and Phebe, " disposed to remove themselves to Pensilvania in America ", given by Radnorshire Friends, received and recorded by Radnor Monthly Meeting, Chester Co., Penna.[6]

The verbal Will of Richard Moore of the township of Radnor in ye County of Chester, delivered or declared in the hearing of Steven Evans, David Harrey & Rees Thomas as followeth: First he declared that it was his will that all his depts and funeral expences should be payd & discharged. 2dly he declared his will was yt ye profits of his land and plantation be wholely towards the maintenant of his wife and children untill his son John attains the age of 21 years, and immediately after his will was that his son should possess himself of his sd land and plantation, excepting his mother's right during her natural life, upon condition his son should pay 15 pound to each of his sisters. 3dly It was his will that his children be at his wife's disposal. 4thly He named *his father David Meredith*, brother John Moore, his cosen John Moore, & his cosen David Jones, to be trustees & overseers for his wife & children. Philadelphia, Oct. 16, 1715: Personally appeared Rees Thomas and David Harry, two of the witnesses within named, and on solemn affirmation declared (*etc*), and administration was granted to Phebe Moore relict defuncti (*etc*).—*From photostatic copy of the original Will,* in collections of the Genealogical Society of Penna. The Will was recorded in *Phila. Will Book D,* page 38.

Bond of Howell James of New Castle Co., Del., yeoman, William Harry of Phila., innkeeper, and John Doe, bound to Peter Evans, Register Genl. for the Province of Penna., in the sum of 200 Pounds, dated 2 Nov. 1715, conditioned that if the said Phebe James late Phebe Moore, widow relict and adminx. of the nuncupative Will annexed of Richard Moore deced., makes Inventory and Appraisment of the estate of said deced. to be exhibited into the Register General's office at Phila. on or before 16 Nov. next.—*Digest of photostatic copy of the Bond,* in collections *supra.*

Inventory of the goods and chattels of Richard Moore late of Radnor, in Co. Chester, Penna., yeoman, deced. (no date), appraised by David Harry and Rees Thomas at a total 42-6-5.—*Ibid.*

Account of Phebe James now ye wife of Howell James of New Castle County upon Delaware, yeoman, adminx. of all and singular the goods & chattels of Richard Moore late of Radnor Twp., Co. of Chester, Penna., her late husband deced., dated 8 Nov. 1716, includes debts paid to Mary Phillips, Howell James, David Meredith, Owen Nicholas, Jno Pearsall, *etc.—Ibid.*

Release dated 30 Apr 1731: Henry Hartley of Upper Merion Twp., Phila. Co., Penna., and wife Phebe, daughter of Richard Moore late of Radnor, deced., releasing to John Moore, son and heir of said Richard Moore, all claim to the estate of said Richard Moore. Acknowledged 14 Apr 1753.—*Phila. Deed Book H-5,* 159.

Release dated 30 Apr 1731: Jonathan Morris of Marple Twp., Chester Co., Penna., and wife Catherine, daughter of Richard Moore of Radnor, deced., release to John Moore, son and heir of said Richard Moore, all claim to the estate of said Richard Moore. Acknowledged 14 Apr 1753.—*Ibid.,* page 160.

Release dated 6-2mo-1739: Joseph Pugh and wife Rebecca to John Moore, son and heir of Richard Moore and brother to the said Rebecca, releasing all claim to the estate of said Richard Moore, all late of Radnor Twp., Chester Co., Penna. Signatures attested 14 Apr 1753 by Henry Hartley of the city of Phila., mariner.—*Ibid.,* page 161.

Children of Richard and Phebe (Evans) Moore:

  i. PHEBE MOORE b 4-12mo-1701/2; married between 9-10mo-1725 and 13-11-1725/6 HENRY HARTLEY, who " was but lately come amongst Friends," and we " having made enquiry not only here but also with such Friends as knew him in his own Country, and also with his brother, find no objection."—*Minutes of Radnor Mo. Mtg.* This couple was living in Upper Merion, Phila., in 1731, and apparently he was the one of this name, of the city of Phila., a mariner, in 1753.

4 ii. JOHN MOORE b 24-9-1705; d 5-7mo-1750.

  iii. CATHERINE MOORE married 11-3mo-1726 at Radnor Mtg. Hse., JONA-THAN MORRIS of Marple Twp., Chester Co., Penna.[6]

  iv. REBECCA MOORE married 3-11mo-1733/4 at Radnor Mtg. Hse., JOSEPH PUGH, son of David Pugh of Radnor Twp., Chester Co., Penna.[6] They were living in Uwchlan, Chester Co., Penna., 1739.

2. MARY MOORE, born in 1676, daughter of the widow Katherine Moore, came with her and her stepfather David Meredith from the parish of Llanbister, in Radnorshire, South Wales, to Radnor Township, Chester County, Penna., and she died testate in Philadelphia 21st of 6th month (June) 1762 aged 86 years,[8] widow of ROBERT POUND of Philadelphia, butcher, who died there testate on 2nd of 4th month (June) 1710.[8] The minutes of Radnor Monthly Meeting for the years 1687-1692 and 1703-1711 being missing, the evidence of the marriage of this couple cannot be verified. But " Mary Pound " signed immediately after John Moore and Jane Moore in the near relatives column of the certificate of marriage of their daughter Jane Moore to Alexander Bane on 5th of 4th month 1713 at Merion Meeting House. And said John Moore of Blockley Township, Philadelphia County, Penna., in his Will

of 21 September 1719, devised "to my sister Mary Pound" twenty shillings.

The Will of Robert Pound of Phila., butcher, dated 19 May 1710 and proved 27 June 1710, names wife Mary execx. and devises to her and to sister Ann. Recorded in *Phila. Will Book C,* page 211, whence this abstract.

The Will of Mary Pound of Phila., widow, dated 16 April 1754 and proved 20 June 1762, with Codicil dated "about eight weeks" before probate, appoints Thomas Say of Phila., mercht., the execr. and guardian; devises estate to daughter Mary wife of Joseph Wood and to grandchildren Sarah, Elizabeth, Ann, Joseph, Robert, Thomas, and Josiah Wood, and to great-grandchild Mary Doyle. Recorded in *Phila. Will Book M,* page 317, whence this abstract.

Children of Robert and Mary (Moore) Pound:

From the Register of Philadelphia Monthly Meeting.[8]
- i. JOHN POUND, son of Robert, buried 24-5-1699.
- ii. SARAH POUND, daughter of Robert, buried 16-5-1702.
- iii. ANN POUND, daughter of Robert and Mary, died 14-4-1709.
- iv. CHRISTOPHER POUND, son of Robert and Mary, died 6-3-1705.
- v. ROBERT POUND, son of Robert and Mary, died 26-9-1721.
- vi. MARY POUND, married shortly before 29-7-1729, JOSEPH WOOD.

3. JOHN MOORE, younger son of the widow Katherine Moore, came with her and his stepfather David Meredith from the parish of Llanbister, in Radnorshire, South Wales, to Radnor Township, Chester County, Penna. By the 1st of 2nd month (April) 1702 he was a blacksmith by profession, resident in the adjacent Merion Township, Philadelphia County, on which date he acquired by Deed Poll from Hugh Roberts the 100 acres tract bounded by Indian and Mill Creeks in Blockley Township, said County, and moved thereon. John Moore died there testate two or three days before 2nd of 8th month (Oct.) 1719, on which date his remains were buried in Friends burying place at Merion Meeting House. The marriage of John Moore and JANE CUERTON in 1689 cannot be verified in the minutes of Radnor Monthly Meeting, as those for the years 1687-1692 are missing, and the certificate is not found on record in the register.[6] But her mother Margaret Cuerton and niece Sarah Cuerton signed in near relatives' column the marriage certificate of John and Jane Moore's daughter Jane Moore to Alexander Bane, dated 5th of 4th month 1713. Also, John and Jane Moore's son John Moore Jr. was declared, by Duck Creek Monthly Meeting of 11th of 7th month 1721 to be too near a relation to proceed in marriage with Elizabeth Cuerton, who was a niece of said Jane (Cuerton) Moore. JANE

CUERTON with her parents Richard and Margaret Cuerton came in the ship *Rebecca* from Liverpool, England, arrived at Philadelphia on 31st of 8th month (Oct.) 1685, and they settled in Merion Township, Philadelphia County, Penna.[9] She survived her husband John Moore and was still a resident of Blockley Township, Philadelphia County, on 25 September 1721, on which date she and their son James Moore conveyed the 100 acres homestead by Deed to David Jones. He conveyed it to the son James Moore by Deed of 19th of 8th month 1721.

The Will of John Moore of the township of Blockley, County of Phila., Penna., blacksmith, dated 21 Sept. 1719 and proved 4 Nov. 1719: 1st. All my debts etc. to be paid and discharged; Also " My dwelling house and plantation to be sold and my executors hereafter named are hereby impowered to make an unquestionable title in law to any person and his heirs forever that shall purchase the same "; Also, to wife Jane Moore one-third of all the estate after debts paid; Also, " Unto my dear mother the sum of ten pounds to be paid to her as she shall have need for the same towards her maintenance "; * Also, to my son Richard 5 Pds.; Also, to my daughter Jane 5 Pds.; Also, to my sister Mary Pound 20 shillings; the residue of my estate to my sons James, John, and Mordecai and my daughters Rose, Margaret, Mary, and Martha, equally divided, my son James to have two shares thereof and my daughter Rose 6 Pds. beside an equal share; Appoints wife Jane Moore and son James Moore execrs.; Desires friends David Jones, Thomas Jones, Edward Williams, and Robert Jones to be Trustees. Witnesses: David Jones, Sarah Cuerton, Edward Williams, Robert Jones.—*Digest from photostatic copy of the original Will,* in collections of The Genealogical Society of Penna. The Will was recorded in *Phila. Will Book D,* page 140.

The " Inventory of the goods, cattle, chattels, household-stuff, implements of husbandry and plantation of John Moore of Blockley in the County of Philadelphia, late deceased " was taken and appraised on 29th of 11th mo. (Jan.) 1719/20 by Edward Rees, Ed. Williams, and Robt. Jones, at 316-9-1, the list including a riding horse, 2 other horses, 2 mares, 1 colt, 8 swine, 6 cows, 4 heifers, 2 calves, 2 steers, 17 sheep, blacksmith tools, iron, and " old Bible and some other old books ", household furniture. —*Digest from photostatic copy of the original Inventory,* in collections *supra.*

By Deed of 25 Sept. 1721, Jane Moore, widow of John Moore of Blockley, Co. Phila., blacksmith, deced, and James Moore, son and heir of said John Moore, conveyed to David Jones of Blockley, for 100 Pds., the 100 acres tract there. Recital that the said John Moore possessed in his lifetime a tract in the City Liberties of Phila., bought of Hugh Roberts by Deed of 1st of 2nd month 1702, being 100 acres and 136 perches located on Mill Creek, and by his Will of 21 Sept. 1719 devised My dwelling house and plantation to be sold, and appointed his wife Jane Moore and his son James Moore execrs. Witnesses: Edward Williams, Robert Jones, Richard Moore, Robert Pound. Acknowledged 21 April 1785.—*Phila. Deed Book D-12,* 337.

Children of John and Jane (Cuerton) Moore:

Names and dates from the register of Radnor Monthly Meeting.[6]

      i. MARY MOORE buried 20-7-1690 in Merion Friends ground.

     ii. ROSE MOORE born 12-12-1693; living 1719, unmar.

    iii. JANE MOORE born 13-12-1693; married 5-4mo-1713 at Merion Meeting House, Phila. Co., Penna., ALEXANDER BANE of Goshen Twp., Chester Co., Penna.

5   iv. JAMES MOORE born 8-10mo-1695; was buried 13-3-1781.

     v. RICHARD MOORE born 22-12-1697.

6   vi. JOHN MOORE born   ; living 1722.

    vii. MORDECAI MOORE born 13-12-1702; living 1719.*

   viii. MARGARET MOORE born 1-10mo-1704; living 1719.

    ix. MARY MOORE born 24-2-1706; living 1719.

     x. MARTHA MOORE born 1-2mo-1708; buried 9-8mo-1719 in Merion Frds. grd.

4. JOHN MOORE, born 24th of 9th month (Nov.) 1705, only son of no. 1 Richard and Phebe (Evans-Phillips) Moore of Radnor Township, Chester County, Penna., died intestate in Philadelphia on 5th of 7th month 1750.[8] John Moore of Radnor and RACHEL COPPOCK, daughter of Jonathan Coppock deced. and wife Jane (Owen) Coppock of Springfield Township, Chester County, Penna., were married at Springfield Meeting House by Friends ceremony on 22nd of 7th month (Sept.) 1737,† and she, as Rachel Moore, requested Chester Monthly Meeting of 29th of 10th month 1744 for a certificate to Radnor Monthly Meeting. John Moore and wife Rachel requested Radnor Monthly Meeting of 12th of 6th month 1748 for a certificate to Philadelphia Monthly Meeting, and it was signed at the Meeting of 8th of 7th month next. The certificate was presented to Philadelphia Monthly Meeting of 27th of 11th month (Jan.) 1748/9 and it was recorded.[8] Jane (Coppock) Moore, who was 14 years her husband's junior, having been born 13th of 1st month (March) 1719, survived him, and she married secondly on 11 April 1754, according to the register of Christ Church, Philadelphia, DAVID REES. For this breach of Friends discipline she made acknowl-

---

* One Mordecai Moore produced his certificate from Radnor Mo. Mtg. at Chester Mo. Mtg. of 30-2-1728. But complaint of him was made at the Mo. Mtg. of 31-1-1729, by Chester Preparative Meeting, for having absconded from his creditors, and he was accordingly disowned by the Mo. Mtg. of 28-2-1729. No further account found.

† One John Moore belonging to Radnor Preparative Meeting requested Radnor Monthly Meeting of 14-9-1723 for a certificate in order to proceed in marriage with one belonging to Gwynedd Monthly Meeting, and it was brought accordingly to the Meeting of 12-10mo-1723 and signed. Subsequently, at Gwynedd Monthly Meeting of 31-10-1723 John Moore and Ann Jones declared their intentions of marriage, and he producing his certificate, they were permitted to proceed in marriage, which was reported to the Monthly Meeting of 28-11-1723 as having been orderly accomplished. The certificate of marriage is not found of record in the registers of Radnor or Gwynedd, and the parties remain unidentified here. If this bridegroom was the John Moore born 24-9-1705, this marriage at age of 18 was one previous to his marriage at age 32 in 1737. The matter is unresolved here.

edgment to Philadelphia Monthly Meeting of 29th of 4th month (April) 1757, which was accepted, and the Meeting of 27th of 5th month 1757 granted her, as "Rachel wife of David Reese", a certificate to Radnor Monthly Meeting, where it was duly received and recorded.[6] David and Rachel (Coppock-Moore) Rees were living in Radnor Township in 1766. Children of John Moore, if any there were, have escaped detection for this report.

By Deed of 11 Aug. 1733 John Moore and Phebe James, mother of said John and formerly wife of Richard Moore and now widow of Howell James, conveyed to Owen Nicholas a 50 acres tract in Radnor Twp., Chester Co., Penna., reciting that by agreement of Thomas Parry of 14 Feb. 1701/2 to convey 124 acres to Richard Moore who died before said conveyance was made, and said Thomas Parry by Deed of 29 Oct. 1715 conveyed to David Meredith, John Moore, David James, and John Moore of Radnor, the overseers of the Will of said Richard Moore deced., of the second part, and Howell and Phebe James and John Moore, son and heir of said Richard Moore, of the third part, to hold to said Phebe until the said John Moore, son and heir of Richard, arrived at age 21 years and then to his use. Recorded in *Delaware County Deed Book T-4*, page 558.

Certificate of marriage of John Moore, son of Richard Moore deced., of Radnor Twp., Chester Co., Penna., and Rachel Coppock, daughter of Jonathan Coppock deced., of Springfield Twp., said Co., on 22 Sept. 1737 at Springfield Meeting House, with witnesses signing: Phebe James (*his mother*), Robert Taylor (*her stepfather*), Mary Yarnall, Jonathan Morris (*his brother-in-law*), Catherine Morris (*his sister*), Henry Hartley (*his brother-in-law*), Phebe Hartley (*his sister*), and others.—*Digest of certificate recorded by Chester Monthly Meeting, Chester Co., Penna.*

Mortgage of 7 Apr. 1748: John Moore of Radnor, Chester Co., Penna., blacksmith, and wife Rachel and Phebe James of Radnor, mother of said John Moore, convey to Joseph Williams of Lower Merion Twp., Phila. Co., Penna., for 200 Pds., a messuage and 200 acres in Radnor. Mortgage satisfied 16 Nov. 1749.

Administration upon the estate of John Moore deced. was granted 13 Oct. 1750 to John Hughes of Phila., baker, the widow Rachel Moore having renounced her right.—*Phila. Admin. Book F*, page 334.

Mortgage of 23 Oct. 1766: David Rees of Radnor Twp., Chester Co., Penna., innholder, and wife Rachel, conveyed to Joseph Norris of Plymouth Twp., Phila. Co., yeoman, for 484 Pds., the John Moore tract of 200 acres in Radnor. Mortgage satisfied 30 Nov. 1769.—*Chester Co. Mortgage Book P*, page 43.

5. JAMES MOORE, eldest son of no. 3 John and Jane (Cuerton) Moore of Blockley Township, Philadelphia County, Penna., was born 8th of 10th month (Dec.) 1695, and he died there testate a day or two before 13th of 3rd month (March) 1781, on which day his remains were buried in Friends burying place at Merion Meeting House. He was married on 3rd of 9th month (Nov.) 1720, at Merion Meeting House, to SARAH THOMAS, who was born 16th of 11th month (Jan.) 1699/1700,

daughter of Abel Thomas and wife Elizabeth Humphreys of Merion Township, Philadelphia County. " Sarah the wife to James Moore " was buried on 29th of 2nd month (Feb.) 1760 in Merion Friends burying place abovesaid.[6] The paternal 100 acres homestead plantation on Mill Creek was conveyed to James Moore by Deed of 19th of 8th month (Oct.) 1721.

Abel Thomas and Elizabeth Humphreys were married 19-3-1693 in Merion Mtg. Hse., and they had issue: (1) Richard Thomas born 11-12mo-1693; (2) Sarah Thomas born 1-9mo-1697, who was buried 7-9mo-1698; (3) Sarah Thomas born 16-11-1699, who married 3-9-1720 James Moore; and (4) Elizabeth Thomas born 16-3-1702; according to the register of Radnor Mo. Mtg.[6] See also T. A. Glenn, *Merion in the Welsh Tract*, for Humphrey ancestry, but correcting the name " Thomas Abel " on page 250 to be Abel Thomas as abovesaid.

Certificate of marriage of James Moore, son of John Moore of Blockley Twp., Phila. Co., Penna., smith, deced., and Sarah Thomas, daughter of Abel Thomas of Merion, said Co., also smith, on 3-9mo-1720, with witnesses: Abel Thomas (her father), Eliza Thomas (her mother), Jane Moore (his mother), Richard Moore (his brother), Jno. Moore (his brother), Mordecai Moore (his brother), Richd. Thomas (her brother), Jno. Moore (his nephew), Alex. Bane (his brother-in-law), Rose Moore (his sister), Eliza Cuerton, and others.—*Digest from the register of Radnor Monthly Meeting.*

The Will of James Moore of Twp. of Blockley, Phila. Co., Penna., yeoman, " being far advanced in years and weak in body ", dated 30th Oct. 1780 and proved 17th March 1781, devises to son Abel my plantation whereon I now live, part of which is situate in Darby, Chester Co., during his natural life, and afterwards I devise all my land in Blockley aforesd. to my grandsons James and John Moore, their hers etc. in severalty forever, provided each of them, the said James and John Moore, within 12 months after the decease of my said son Abel pay unto my son Amos Moore, his heirs etc., 10 Pounds, unto my daughter Martha or her heirs 10 Pounds; and unto my daughter Mary or her heirs 10 Pounds in gold or silver, and after the decease of my said son Abel I give unto my grandson Abner Evans, his heirs etc., all my land in Darby Twp.; to Sarah Palmer my chest of drawers; to John Lambert 20 shillings; to Margaret Bennett 20 shillings; to said son Abel all the rest of the estate; and appoints son Abel sole execr. Witnesses: John Sellers, David Brooks, Samuel Gibson. Letters testamentary were granted 17 March 1781 to Abel Moore the execr. Recorded in *Phila. Will Book R*, page 391, whence this abstract.

Children of James and Sarah (Thomas) Moore:

Names and dates of births from the register of Radnor Monthly Meeting.

7   i. JOHN MOORE b 7-6mo-1722; d 19-7-1778.

8   ii. ABEL MOORE b 9-8mo-1723; d in 11mo-1784.

9   iii. AMOS MOORE b 11-8mo-1725; d 25-11-1815.

10   iv. MARTHA MOORE b 25-3-1728; mar 24 Dec 1747 SAMUEL CHAPMAN.

     v. ELIJAH MOORE b 26-9-1731; d before 1780.

     vi. MARY MOORE b 23-1-1732; living 1780; married one EVANS and had son Abner Evans living 1800.

6. JOHN MOORE, third son of no. 3 John and Jane (Cuerton) Moore of Blockley Township, Philadelphia County, Penna., born in 1699-1700, was named a devisee in his father's Will of September 1719, but final account of him after 1722 has escaped detection for this report. He transferred his membership from Radnor Monthly Meeting to Abington Monthly Meeting, Philadelphia County, Penna., by certificate dated 11th of 12th month (Feb.) 1719/20, and from Abington to Duck Creek Monthly Meeting, New Castle County, Delaware, by one of 31st of 5th month (July) 1721. At the Meeting of the last named on 11th of 7th month 1721, he and his first cousin ELIZABETH CUERTON, declared their intentions of marriage. She was born 11th of 7th month 1697, in Merion Township, Philadelphia County, Penna., daughter of William and Mary (Coborn) Cuerton, and she had removed within the verge of Duck Creek Monthly Meeting with her father, stepmother and family in 1715.[9] Friends discipline could not allow the marriage within such close degree of kinship, and the couple were married by a Justice of the Peace at her father's house in George's Creek. Accordingly, their names are not found further in the minutes and register of Duck Creek Monthly Meeting.

14-11-1719 at Haverford: John Moore having proposed for a certificate to this meeting, he intended removing towards Abington Meeting house, David Jones and Edward Williams are appointed to inspect into his clearness and conversation and to draw him a certificate in the behalf of the Monthly Meeting.—*Minutes of Radnor Mo. Mtg.*

11-12mo-1719 at Merion: The friends appointed to draw John Moore's certificate have brought it to this meeting, which was approved of and signed at the meeting by friends.—*Ibid.*

28-1-1720: John Moore produced a certificate from Merion (*sic*) Mo. Meeting which was read and accepted.—*Minutes of Abington Mo. Mtg.,* in collections Gen. Soc. Pa.

31-5-1721: A certificate was granted to John Moore in order to settle in ye verge of Duck Creek Mo. Meeting.—*Ibid.*

11-7mo-1721: John Moore, son of John Moore late of Blockley, County of Philadelphia, deceased, and Elizabeth Cureton, daughter of William Cureton of St. Georges Creek, published their intentions of marriage. But the nearness of the relationship between them and the smallness of this meeting, they are only permitted, and requested to appear at our next monthly meeting. And Joseph England is desired to make enquiry of ancient friends belonging to some other meeting, whether such marriage be allowed of.—*Minutes of Duck Creek Monthly Meeting, New Castle Co., Delaware,* in collections Gen. Soc. Pa.

22-8-1721: John Moore and Elizabeth Cureton who appeared at our last monthly meeting and signified their intentions of marriage with each other not appearing at this meeting, the aforesaid minute is discontinued.—*Ibid.*

19-1-1722: Information being given to this Meeting that William Cureton, a Friend belonging to Georges Creek Meeting, hath countenanced an indiscreet or disorderly marriage between his daughter Elizabeth and John Moore, this Meeting thinks it needful to stir up the minds of the Overseers of that Meeting that if anything be omitted in duly treating with the said Cureton concerning the said marriage, that they will be diligent in treating with him, and whereas the said William Cureton was appointed one of the Overseers of that Meeting, with John McCool, this Meeting appoints John Ashton to assist John McCool in the said affair and signify his answer or satisfaction given to our next monthly meeting.—*Ibid.*

18-4-1722: William Cureton brought to this meeting a written paper signifying his sorrow for his unadvisedly letting his daughter marry in his house by a Justice, but the Meeting being small and the paper being short in some things, it is left to the consideration of Friends.—*Ibid.*

7. JOHN MOORE, born 7th of 6th month (Aug.) 1722, eldest son of no. 5 James and Sarah (Thomas) Moore of Blockley Township, Philadelphia County, Penna., died 19th of 7th month (July) 1778, and was buried in Darby Friends Meeting burying place, Chester County, Penna. Merion Meeting, to which he belonged, requested Radnor Monthly Meeting of 29th of 2nd month (April) 1745 for a certificate for John Moore addressed to Darby Monthly Meeting in order for him to marry Rachel Poe, a " young woman ", and the certificate was read and signed at the Monthly Meeting of 10th of 3rd month 1745. Accordingly, John Moore of Blockley Township, Philadelphia County, and RACHEL POE of Darby Township, Chester County, were married on 26th of 4th month 1745, their certificate of marriage being recorded by said Darby Monthly Meeting. Rachel (Poe) Moore died 19th of 2nd month 1788, according to the register of said Monthly Meeting, and was buried in Friends burying ground in Darby. The estates of this John and Rachel Moore are not found of record in either Chester County or Philadelphia County probates.

Children of John and Rachel (Poe) Moore:

Names and dates of births from the register of Darby Mo. Mtg.

    i. HANNAH MORE b 4-3mo-1746; mar 20 Aug 1792 PATTENS SAVAGE, according to the register of Gloria Dei Ch., Phila. One Hannah Savage d 21-2-1826 aged 80, according to the register of Phila. Northern District Mo. Mtg.

11   ii. JAMES MOORE b 24-7-1747; d after 1822.

   iii. AMY MOORE b 6-3mo-1750; d 29-10-1821 in the Northern Liberties of the City of Phila., unmarried, aged 68 according to the register of Green

Street Monthly Meeting. She had been received by Phila. Northern District Monthly Meeting on certificate from Darby Monthly Meeting in Nov. 1812. Her elder sister Hannah Savage having renounced her right, Admin. on the estate of Amy Moore, singlewoman deced. intest. was granted 4 Feb. 1822 to Jonathan Roberts of the Northern Liberties, Collector of Taxes, who gave Bond of same date with James Moore of Blockley Twp., Phila. Co., farmer, and Richard Roe as securities.—*Phila. Admin. Book M*, page 311. The Adminr.'s Account, dated 12-7mo-1822, listed payments to William and Ruth Hamilton, Hannah Savage, Nathan Jones for the minor children of John Moore, by consent of James Moore, brother of the intestate, $75.00 each.—Digest of the original estate papers no. 35 for the year 1822 in office of the Register of Wills, Phila.

    iv. RUTH MOORE b 25-1-1752; mar WILLIAM HAMILTON and both were living in 1822. Ruth Moore was released by Darby Mo. Mtg. in 1788 for lack of unity.

12   v. JOHN MOORE b 6-8mo-1755; d 20-8-1817.

8. ABEL MOORE, born 9th of 8th month (Oct.) 1723, second son of no. 5 James and Sarah (Thomas) Moore of Blockley Township, Philadelphia County, Penna., died there testate two or three days before 15th of 11th month (Nov.) 1784, on which date his remains were buried Merion Friends burying place.[6] Abel Moore and HANNAH HIBBERD, birthright members of Friends, were married out of Meeting, on 21st January 1756 according to the register of Christ Church, Philadelphia, and he made acknowledgement of this infraction of Friends discipline to Radnor Monthly Meeting of 12th of 10th month 1756 which was accepted and his membership continued. Hannah (Hibberd) Moore likewise made acknowledgement, to Darby Monthly Meetings of 1st of 9th month and 1st of 12th month 1756, of her marriage by a priest. It was accepted by the Meeting of 2nd of 3rd month 1757, and a certificate for her addressed to Radnor Monthly Meeting was signed by Darby Monthly Meeting of 5th of 10th month 1757. Hannah (Hibberd) Moore was born 3rd of 4th month (June) 1733, daughter of Moses and Sarah (Bradshaw) Hibberd who resided within the verge of Darby Monthly Meeting. She survived her husband Abel Moore, and as his sole executrix and legatee conveyed his half of the paternal homestead in Blockley by her Deed of 14 April 1785 to (his nephews) James and John Moore of Darby Township, Chester County, Penna. She died testate in Blockley in 1801, without issue.

HIBBERD of Blockley Twp., Phila. Co., Penna. DANIEL HIBBERD came in 1682-83 as an employee ("servant") to obtain the 50 acres offered by William Penn to induce emigration to the Province of Penna. He married in 8th mo. 1697 RACHEL BONSALL, dau. of Richard and Mary Bonsall of Darby, Chester Co., Penna., and resided on a 100 acres tract across Cobbs Creek, in Blockley Twp., Phila. Co., Penna. He died there testate 24-2-1740. The Will of Daniel Hibberd of Phila. Co., dated 23 Apr 1740 and proved 10 May 1740, names wife Rachel, children Daniel (execr.), Moses, Aaron, and Mary (Davis), sons-in-law Thomas Hall, John Pearson, and George Sanders. —Recorded in *Phila. Will Book F,* page 193.   Children: (1) Mary Hibberd b 22-5-1698, married in 1718 John David of Radnor Twp., Chester Co., Penna.; (2) Aaron Hibberd b 1-2mo-1700, married Elizabeth ———; (3) Moses Hibberd b 14-2-1702, *q.v. postea;* (4) Phebe Hibberd b 28-12-1703; (5) Hannah Hibberd married in 1729 Thomas Hall of Phila.; (6) Martha Hibberd married by license of 19 March 1730 Joseph Lees of Darby; (7) Rachel Hibberd married by license of 30 July 1735 John Pearson of Darby. MOSES HIBBERD abovesaid, b 14-2-1702, d intestate in Darby Twp., Chester Co., Penna., 10-7mo-1762, and the admin. on his estate was granted 20 July 1762 to Sarah Hibberd, widow.   He married 10-7mo-1732 SARAH BRAD-SHAW, also of Darby, daughter of Thomas and Sarah (Levis) Bradshaw. She died 7-11mo-1777. Their children were: (1) Hannah Hibberd b 3-4mo-1733, married 21 Jan. 1756 Abel Moore of Blockley Twp., Phila. Co.; (2) John Hibberd b 6-10mo-1734 and d in 12mo-1734; (3) Mary Hibberd who married in 1758 John Palmer.—Cope mss and digest of the *Register of Darby Mo. Mtg.,* in collections of The Genealogical Society of Penna.

The Will of Abel Moore of Blockley Twp., Phila. Co., Penna., dated 22 July 1777 and proved 18 Nov. 1784, names wife Hannah Moore sole execx. and legatee. Witnesses: J. Sellers, Edwd. Williams, N. Sellers.   Recorded in *Phila. Will Book S,* page 502.

By Deed of 14 April 1785, Hannah Moore of Blockley Twp., Phila. Co., Penna., widow and sole legatee of Abel Moore late of same place, cooper, deced., who was the son, a grantee and also a devisee named in the Will of James Moore late of same place, yeoman, deced., conveyed to James Moore and John Moore of Darby Twp., Chester Co., Penna., wheelwrights, for 400 Pounds gold and silver money, the one-half of the plantation containing 100 acres on Indian and Mill Creeks in said Blockley Twp., same which William Penn by patent of 3 Dec. 1701 granted to Hugh Roberts, who by poll endorsed on the back of said patent on 1st of 2nd mo. 1702 granted same to John Moore, the father of the first-named James Moore, who devised by Will of 21 Sept. 1719 that the said premises be sold and appointed his wife Jane Moore and son the first named James Moore execrs. The said Jane Moore and James Moore by Deed of 25 Sept. 1721 conveyed said tract to David Jones of Blockley Twp., who by Deed of 19 of 8mo 1721 conveyed the same to the first named James Moore, and said James Moore by an agreement of 26 of 1st mo. Jan. 1756 with his son the said Abel Moore conveyed to him one-half the said plantation. And said James Moore died seized of the other half of the plantation and devised it by his Will of 30 Oct. 1780 to his son Abel Moore during his lifetime and afterwards to said James Moore's grandsons the said James and John Moore parties hereto. And said Abel Moore by Will of 22 July 1777 devised his estate in said plantation, on which he dwelt, and all other his estate, to his wife Hannah Moore, party hereto, who hereby conveys the like undivided half part of said plantation's buildings, improvements, etc. Acknowledged 16 April 1785 by said Hannah Moore before William Adcock Esq., one of the Justices of the Court of Common Pleas for the City and County of Phila., and recorded 4 May 1785 in *Phila. Deed Book D-12,* page 332, whence this abstract.

The Will of Hannah Moore of Blockley Twp., Phila. Co., Penna., dated 14 Jan. 1800 and proved 21 Oct. 1801, devises to my sister-in-law Martha Chapman 100 Pds., but if she dies before me, then to her son John Chapman; to Abner Evans 20 Pds.; to William Moore Senr. 75 Pds.; to Phebe Supple, daughter of John and Sarah Supple, 20 Pds.; to the four children of my niece Sarah Thomas, wife of John Thomas, namely Hannah, Mary, Susannah, and Johanna, 20 Pds. each; the residue of my estate to said Sarah Thomas wife of John Thomas, her heirs etc.; and appoints John Thomas of Blockley the execr. Witnesses: John Sellers, John Dunlap, Thomas Cummans. Recorded in *Phila. Will Book Y*, page 601, whence this abstract.

9. AMOS MOORE, born 11th of 8th month (Oct.) 1725, third son of no. 5 James and Sarah (Thomas) Moore of Blockley Township, Philadelphia County, Penna., died there 25th of 11th month (Nov.) 1815 and was buried in Darby Friends burying place.[10] He was married by Friends ceremony on 15th of 3rd month (May) 1751 to ELIZABETH SMITH, according to certificate recorded by Darby Monthly Meeting. She was born 19th of 5th month (July) 1725, daughter of William and Mary Smith of Darby Township, Chester County, Penna., and she died 22 July 1783.[11] The estate of Amos Moore is not found of record in either Philadelphia or Chester County probates.

Amos Moore requested Radnor Monthly Mtg. of 14-1-1750/51 for a certificate to Darby Mo. Mtg. in order to marry Elizabeth Smith.—*Minutes of Radnor Mo. Mtg.*

Amos Moore produced a certificate to Goshen Mo. Mtg., Chester Co., Penna., of 21-8-1751 from Radnor Mo. Mtg. for himself, and his wife Elizabeth produced one from Darby Mo. Mtg.—*Minutes of Goshen Mo. Mtg.*

Amos Moore and wife Elizabeth received certificate to Darby Mo. Mtg.—*Ibid.* of 17-8-1752.

Amos Moore and wife took certificate dated 3-1st mo-1753 from Darby Mo. Mtg. to Goshen Mo. Mtg., and also one dated 7-6mo-1758 to Radnor Mo. Mtg.—*Minutes of Darby Mo. Mtg.*

Children of Amos and Elizabeth (Smith) Moore:

The first 5 and the 7th names and dates of birth are from the register of Radnor Monthly Meeting;[6] other data are from bible record.[11]

  i. WILLIAM MOORE b 15-2-1752; married 15 Oct 1775 (*sic*) unknown; * had issue: (1) John Moore b 19 Feb 1775; (2) Samuel Moore b 27 Dec 1776; (3) Elizabeth Moore b 12 Jan 1779 and d 23 July 1783; (4) Ann Moore b 26 May 1781; (5) George Moore b 11 March 1783; and (6) James Moore b 27 Aug 1785.
  ii. ROSE MOORE b 17-2mo-1754; d young.
  iii. SAMUEL MOORE b 29-3-1756; " broke his leg with a cart and wheel Sept. 21, 1764, and died Oct. 5, 1764."

iv. SARAH MOORE b 16-3-1758; mar 17 Dec 1774 DAVID SHARPLESS,* according to the register of the German Reformed Church of Phila. (*Pa. Archives* 2nd series VIII, 716.), and not 16 Dec 1775 as in Bible record; and had issue: Elizabeth Sharpless b 5 Dec 1776, and Benjamin Sharpless b 26 Oct 1777, *q.v.* in Gilbert Cope, *Sharpless Family*, page 236.

v. JANE MOORE b 29-3-1760; buried 27-9-1762 in Friends burying place at Merion Mtg. Hse.

vi. ABEL MOORE b 27 Dec 1761; mar 24 Feb 1785 Mary Hastings.

vii. ROSE MOORE b 29-9-1762.

viii. MARY MOORE b 31 March 1764; d 13 March 1848; mar 5 Jan 1786 by John Pearson, J. P. of Chester Co., Penna., to JOB HELMS * of Darby, and had issue.[12]

SMITH of Darby, Chester County, Penna. WILLIAM SMITH came from Croxton, Leicestershire, England, to Darby in 1684.—*Penna. Mag. Hist. and Biogr.*, XXIV, 182. He died there testate 2-11mo-1727/8. His first wife, ELIZABETH SMITH, died 27-10-1702, according to the register of Darby Mo. Mtg. He married 2ndly in 10mo-1705 ELIZABETH PRITCHET, widow of Edward Pritchet of Darby; she died testate 13-12-1727/8. Issue by first wife: (1) Rose Smith b 14-12-1679/80, who mar 24-4-1701 John Bethell Jr.; (2) Sarah Smith b 10-10-1686, who mar 1st in 4mo-1706 her stepbrother Philip Pritchet, and 2ndly in 9mo-1713 David Thomas; (3) Elizabeth Smith b 17-1-1689/90, who mar 1st in 8mo-1707 William Bartram, and 2ndly in 9mo-1715 John Smith; (4) William Smith b 28-8-1691, who d 21-9-1736; (5) John Smith, twin with William; (6) Samuel Smith b 6-4mo-1695; (7) Mary Smith b 8-4mo-1697; and (8) Edward Smith b 7-10mo-1699. The Will of William Smith of Darby, dated 9 Apr 1726 and proved 8 Jan. 1727/8, devises to wife Elizabeth; her son Philip Prichard deced.; to son Edward the plantation purchased of Thomas Brasey, Jacob Simcock, and John Hallowell, during his lifetime and afterwards to his children; to son William 5 shillings, he having had his share; to daughter Rose Bethell 40 Pds.; to grandson Samuel Pritchard 20 Pds. at age 21; to daughters Elizabeth and Mary 40 Pds. each; to grandchildren William and Elizabeth Bartram, Ellen Fretwell, Francis, William, Joseph, and Elizabeth Bethell, William and Benjamin Pearson, Martha, William, and Sarah Smith, Samuel Pearson, Joice, Simon, John, and William Smith, 10 Pds. each when of age; to sons-in-law David Thomas, John Smith, and Enoch Pearson, 5 shillings each; and appoints son Edward Smith and Samuel Lewis Jr. the execrs.—Recorded in *Chester County Will Book A*, page 260, whence this abstract.

WILLIAM SMITH JR. b 28-8-1691, as abovesaid; d testate 21-9-1736 in Darby Twp. He mar in 1718 one MARY ———, who also d testate 13-3-1760. The Will of William Smith of Darby, dated 19 Nov 1736 and proved 21 Dec 1736, devises to son Samuel Smith my plantation in Darby when he is of age 21, with reversion to wife and my two daughters (not named); and appoints wife and friend John Davis the execrs.—

---

* This date of marriage, from the Helms-Moore bible record as transcribed (see note no. 11), is obviously a year late, and the marriage on 15 Oct. 1774 of one William Moor and Mary Crager, in the register of St. Paul's Church, Third Street below Walnut, Phila., probably applies here. Testimony against William Moore, son of Amos Moore, for his marriage out of Friends Meting was made at Radnor Monthly Meeting of 9-2mo-1781. The same against Sarah Sharpless was made at the Meeting of 14-8-1777. Mary Moore, daughter of Amos Moore, was granted a certificate to Drby Mo. Mtg. by Radnor Mo. Mtg. of 9-2mo-1781. Mary Helms, late Moore, was disowned by Darby Mo. Mtg. of 27-4-1786 for her marriage out of Meeting.

Chester Co. Will Book B, page 16. The Will of Mary Smith of Darby, dated 20 June 1759, with codicil dated 26 Feb 1760, and proved 25 Mar 1760, names grandchildren: Mary Davis, deceased daughter Rose's children: Nathan, Mary, Benjamin, Ann, and Joseph, when of age, grand-daughters Rachel Smith and Mary Smith the daughters of my son Samuel Smith; grand-daughter Rose Moore; daughter-in-law Elizabeth Smith; daughter Elizabeth wife of Amos Moore 100 Pds. and household goods; sons-in-law Lewis Davis and Amos Moore; and appoints son Samuel Smith and John Davis the execrs. William and Mary Smith Jr. had issue: (1) William Smith b 10-11mo-1719, who d 18-11-1722/3; (2) Rose Smith b 28-3-1722, d 17 Aug 1754, who mar Lewis Davis; (3) Elizabeth Smith b 19-5-1725, who mar 15-3-1751 Amos Moore; and (4) Samuel Smith b 19-8-1727.—*Register of Darby Mo. Mtg.*

10. MARTHA MOORE, born 25th of 3rd month (May) 1728, daughter of no. 5 James and Sarah (Thomas) Moore of Blockley Township, Philadelphia County, Penna., died testate in Philadelphia on 18th of 11th month (Nov.) 1815, aged 89 years, and was buried in Friends burying place in that city.[8] She married out of Friends Meeting, on 24 December 1747, according to the register of Christ Church, Philadelphia, SAMUEL CHAPMAN, and as Martha Chapman she made acknowledgement to Radnor Monthly Meeting of 11th of 2nd month (April) 1749 for that infraction of Friends discipline, and it was accepted. Samuel and Martha Chapman and their children, Sarah, James, Jane, and Ellin Chapman, took their certificate dated 12th of 4th month 1763 from Radnor Monthly Meeting to Philadelphia Monthly Meeting. " Sister-in-law Martha Chapman " was devised 100 Pounds in the Will of Hannah Moore, widow of Abel Moore, of Blockley Township, Philadelphia County, *q.v.,* dated 14 January 1800.

The Will of Martha Chapman, widow, of Philadelphia, dated 12 June 1813 and proved 28 Nov. 1815, names son John Chapman sole execr.; devises to grand-daughters Martha Chapman, Sarah Chapman, Ann Chapman, and Mary Roberts; to niece Martha Johnson Chapman, grandson John Chapman, and Elizabeth Thomas.—Recorded in *Phila. Will Book no. 6,* page 183, whence this abstract.

Children of Samuel and Martha (Moore) Chapman:

    i. Sarah Chapman
    ii. James Chapman
    iii. Jane Chapman b 1759; d 1-1-1765 aged 6 yrs., Phila.
    iv. Ellin Chapman b 1760; d 13-1-1765 aged 5 yrs., Phila.
    v. Jonathan Chapman d 20-6-1765 aged 2 mos., Phila.
    vi. John Chapman, named execr. of mother's Will of 12 June 1813; was received, with wife Mary, by Phila. Mo. Mtg. of 24-12-1812 on certificate from Phila. Northern Distr. Mo. Mtg. dated 22-12-1812.

11. JAMES MOORE, born 24th of 7th month (Sept.) 1747, elder son of no. 7 John and Rachel (Poe) Moore of Darby Township, Chester County, Penna., was named a grandson and co-devisee with brother John Moore in the Will of no. 5 James Moore of Blockley Township, Philadelphia County, dated 30 October 1780, of all lands in said Township. And by Deed of 14 April 1785, their paternal aunt Hannah Moore of Blockley Township, widow of no. 8 Abel Moore, conveyed to them as "James and John Moore of Darby Township, Chester County, wheelwrights," for 400 Pounds the other one-half interest in the said 100 acres homestead plantation of their grandfather James Moore. The two brothers moved to the homestead, having thus come into possession of the whole tract, and were living there in 1793. The first Federal Census, 1790, in the return for Blockley Township, listed James Moore as head of a family of 1 male over 16 years and 2 females. James Moore, a birthright member of Friends, was active in Darby Meeting, as is indicated by his appointment as Overseer of Youth on 3rd of 2nd month 1785, but he resigned that position a year later. He was called up before the Overseers in 1798 for not attending Meeting and for other behavior not in keeping with Friends discipline, and so was released from membership on 30th of 5th month 1799 for "lack of unity." He was the "James Moore of Blockley, farmer," who went security for Jonathan Roberts of Philadelphia as the administrator upon the estate of Amy Moore deceased intestate, in 1822, *q.v. supra*. The estate of James Moore is not found of record in Philadelphia County probates.

By Deed of 26 April 1793, James Moore, wheelwright, and John Moore, miller, both of Blockley Twp., Phila. Co., Penna., granted to Adam Rhoads of same place, yeoman, for 20 shillings, the privilege of taking water from Indian Creek for his meadow and mill for grinding bark, on the west side of said Creek and by a ditch then used for the purpose. Recorded in *Phila. Deed Book M.R.—18*, page 302, on 24 April 1818, whence this abstract.

12. JOHN MOORE, born 6th of 8th month (Aug.) 1755, younger son of no. 7 John and Rachel (Poe) Moore of Darby Township, Chester County, Penna., was named a grandson and co-devisee with brother James Moore, *supra*, in the Will of no. 5 James Moore of Blockley Township, Philadelphia County, Penna., dated 30 October 1780. John Moore was described in 1785 as a wheelwright of Darby Township, and in 1793 as a miller of Blockley Township, having inherited, with his brother James, the Moore homestead in the latter place and moved thereon. This John Moore died intestate on 20th of 8th month 1817, and was buried in Darby Friends Meeting burying place.[10] He had been released from

membership among Friends on 29th of 11th month 1798 for " lack of unit." His wife Ann Moore survived him.

Administration upon the estate of John Moore deceased intestate was granted 20 Sept. 1817 unto William Smith and Samuel Rhoads, with John Thomas of Blockley Twp., farmer, and Richard Roe, as securities.—*Phila. Admin. Book M, page 48.*

Petition of William Smith, one of the adminrs. of the estate of John Moore deced., that said John Moore lately died intestate, leaving a widow Ann Moore and issue six children, all minors under the age of 21 years; that petitioner, with Samuel Rhoads, took out Letters of Admin. on the estate of said deced., and have made settlement of the admin. accounts in the Register's office for the City and County of Phila., of which copy is here exhibited, by which it appears that the personal property of said deced. is greatly insufficient for the payment of his debts and the maintenance and education of his said minor children; that the said deced. died intestate seized in fee of a certain tract of land water rights on which are erected a grist and saw mill and two log tenements, situated in Blockley Township, Phila. Co., adjoining lands of Samuel Rhoads, Thomas Goodwin, James Moore, Cobb Creek, and Joseph Rhoads, containing 50 acres. Requests the Court to order the sale of said premises. So Ordered.—From the Minutes of the Phila. Orphans Court, December 1817 term, in *Docket no. 26, page 312.*

Report of sale of real estate of John Moore, deced., by Court Order: That the adminrs. did on 26 Jan. last expose the tenements, mills, etc. to public sale on the premises, and sold them to William Carter of Blockley Twp., farmer, for $146.00 an acre, he being the highest bidder. Confirmed by the Court.—*Ibid.,* 20 Feb. 1818 Session, in *Docket no. 27, page 10.*

On petition of Ann Moore, widow of John Moore deced., Nathan Jones was appointed guardian of the persons and estates of Rachel, George, Elijah, and Ruth Moore, minor children under the age of 14 years, of said John Moore. And on petition of John and James Moore, minor children above the age 14 years, of said John Moore deced., Samuel Goucher was appointed guardian of their persons and estates.—*Ibid.,* 17 April 1818 Session, in *Docket no. 27, page 44.*

Children of John and Ann (   ) Moore:

    i. JOHN MOORE b before 1804; d intestate in Blockley Twp., Phila. Co., Penna., and admin. on his estate was granted 21 Aug 1821 to Nathan Jones, Esq., of said Blockley.—*Phila. Admin. Book M, page 286.*

    ii. JAMES MOORE b before 1804; d intestate in Blockley Twp., Phila. Co., Penna., and admin. on his estate was granted 21 Aug 1821, same as in the above.—*Ibid.*

    iii. RACHEL MOORE b after 1804.

    iv. GEORGE MOORE b after 1804.

    v. ELIJAH MOORE b after 1804.

    vi. RUTH MOORE b after 1804.

ANTHONY MOORE of Philadelphia, locksmith, died there intestate and was buried in Friends burying place on the " last day of 11th month " (Jan.) 1688.[8] He appears to have been an uncle to the three children of the widow Katherine Moore, nos. 1, 2, and 3, *supra*, as his daughter Margaret (Moore) Nicholas of Phila., in her Will of 27 April 1743, devised *inter al.* to her " cousin Mary Pound ", evidently referring to no. 2 Mary (Moore) Pound also of Philadelphia. And his son Anthony Moore, daughter Rebeckah Moore, and son-in-law Samuel Nicholas signed in the near relatives' column the certificate of marriage of the widow Katherine Moore's daughter Sarah Meredith at Radnor Meeting House on 6th of 10th month 1705, as also did John Moore. Likewise, his daughter Margaret (Moore) Nicholas signed the certificate of marriage of no. 1 John Moore's daughter Jane Moore at Merion Meeting House on 5th of 4th month 1713. Anthony Moore's widow JANE MOORE died 24th of 12th month (Feb.) 1711/12, and was buried in Philadelphia Friends burying place.[8]

Anthony Moore received a Warrant for a City Lot on 3-11mo-1683.—Minutes of The Board of Property, Prov. of Penna., published in *Penna. Archives,* 3rd series, II, page 747.

Jane Moore, widow, requests to take upon a rent three squares in the town of Philadelphia for 21 years at the usual rent of thirty years. It was granted provided she bring security to pay the rent for that time and to leave it in good condition &c.— *Ibid.* of 18-4-1692, *Penna. Archives,* 2nd series, XIX, page 88.

Children of Anthony and Jane (   ) Moore:

Names and dates from the register of Phila. Monthly Meeting.[8]

> i. ANTHONY MOORE d 28-2-1760 testate; mar one Mary who d 12-5-1753; had issue: (1) Rebecca Moore buried 21-10-1722; (2) Anthony Moore; (3) John Moore; (4) Jane Moore: (5) Rebecca Moore, and (6) Mary Moore, all named in his Will of 19 April 1754.
>
> ii. MARGARET MOORE d 11-3mo-1743 testate in Phila.; married SAMUEL NICHOLAS who d testate 19-4-1709; had issue: (1) Martha Nicholas mar one Roberts; (2) Mary Nicholas mar Owen Evans of Gwynedd, Phila. Co.; (3) John Nicholas of Phila., carpenter; and (4) Anthony Nicholas of Phila., mercht. as see *Phila. Deed Book I-12,* page 477.
>
> iii. JOHN MOORE d 29-7-1700.
>
> iv. MARY MOORE d 15-4-1714.
>
> v. REBECKAH MOORE mar 24-8-1709 EDWARD CADWALADER of Merion, Phila. Co., son of Cadawalader Jones.
>
> vi. JANE MOORE d 3-8mo-1699.
>
> vii. KATHERINE MOORE buried 25-9-1694.

References:

[1] Fuller biographical notices of David Meredith, in which only the last two named children, Meredith and Sarah, are properly assigned to him, and without any mention of his three stepchildren Moore, appear in Ellwood Roberts, *Plymouth Meeting*, 1900, pages 27 et seq., and in *The Friend*, (1856), vol XXIX, page 148.

[2] Joseph Besse, *Sufferrings of the People Called Quakers*, London, 1753, vol. II, pages 742-743, 750, and 751.

[3] The names of David Meredith and Moore are not found in the Radnorshire Monthy Meeting, Wales, items of marriage, birth, and death, incorporated into the *Register of the General Meeting of Herefordshire, Worcestershire, and Wales, 1657-1725*, a digest of which is in the collections of The Genealogical Society of Penna. In Ellwood Roberts, *Plymouth Meeting*, (Norristown, Pa., 1900), page 54, is mention, but unfortunately not a transcript, of a Deed of 1679 from one John ap Meredith to David Meredith, conveying property in the parish of Llandoghy in Radnorshire, Wales, which Deed was brought to Plymouth by the grantee, and was in possession of Mr. Lewis Aaron of Rochelle Ave., Wissahickon, Phila., in 1900.

[4] Transcript in collections of The Genealogical Society of Penna. This certificate for removal was one of four from "Radnorshire", all of same date 20-5-1683. The other three were in behalf of: (2) John Jarman of the parish of Llangerig, County Montgomery, and wife Margaret with their children Elizabeth and Sarah; (3) Stephen Evans of the parish of Llanbister, Radnorshire, wife Elizabeth and children John and Phebe; and (4) David James, wife Margaret and his daughter Mary "who have for several years past inhabited amongst us," in the parishes of Llandegley and Glascum, Radnorshire, and having arrived in the Province of Pennsylvania in the 8th month 1682, require a certificate from us.—*Register of Radnor Monthly Meeting, Chester Co., Pa.*

[5] *The Journal of Thomas Chalkley*, 1749, page 182: "1726. In the Fourth Month I left my Family and went back in the Woods as far as Oley. . . . I called to see my old Friend *David Meredith*, who being about 89 years of Age, I thought it probable I might not have another Opportunity of seeing him. He met me with Gladness, and told me it was their Meeting day; so that I stay'd and was much comforted and tendered by the Power of Christ; after which I came home that night."

[6] Transcript of the *Register of Radnor Monthly Meeting* is in collections of The Genealogical Society of Penna.

[7] See photograph of house of David Meredith, with biographical notice of him, in Ellwood Roberts', *Plymouth Meeting*, 1900.

[8] Digest of the Minutes and Registers of Philadelphia Monthly Meeting, published in Hinshaw, *Encycl. American Quaker Genealogy*, II.

[9] L. D. Cook, Cuerton of Merion Township, Phila. County, Penna., published in *The American Genealogist*, XXVII, 225 and 228.

[10] Gilbert Cope, *Sharpless Family*, 1887, page 237; Hannah Davis' Record of Deaths in Delaware Co., Penna., of which a copy is in collections of The Genealogical Society of Penna.; Graveyard records of Darby Meeting, Mrs. Samuel M. Flaherty, Recorder, of Lansdowne, Pa.

[11] Helms-Moore Bible Records, shelf no. Ph-42.8, pages 89-91, in collections *supra*.

[12] Charles Major's notes, including copy of records of Moore-Helms-Pyewell from a Bible published 1739, in mss collections, Hist. Soc. Penna.

271

THE STEPCHILDREN OF DAVID MEREDITH

Revision of statements in this *Magazine*, XIX*

The following edition of the account under this title is found necessary by the discovery of a Deed of 1704 which was not recorded until 1756 in the Philadelphia registry, and which proves that John Moore of Radnor and John Moore of Merion, treated as one in my preceding account, were in fact two individuals. Proper apologies are offered to our readers. Since the three children surnamed Moore are named before the two surnamed David, in the certificate for David and Katharine Meredith's removal, quoted on page 218, and one of the latter is of record as born in 1675, it is assumed here that the Moores were older. But no evidence has been found to show that David Meredith's two children were by his wife, the former widow Katherine Moore; he may have been a widower likewise at the time of their marriage.—*L. D. Cook*

For page 224: *Children of N. N. and Katherine (   ) Moore:*

1   i. RICHARD MOORE d 1715.
     ii. MARY MOORE buried 20-7mo (Sept.)-1690 in Friends burial ground in Radnor,[6] unmarried.
     iii. JOHN MOORE named as brother in the Will of Richard Moore in 1715; estate not found in Chester County probates; left widow and children living in 1723.*

* A men's committee of four, "or as many of them as can, are desired to speak with and advise John Moore's widow and children and others that are removed from amongst us and that was accounted of us or was married amongst us, with respect to their conduct and conversation, who had no certificates to other meetings."—*Minutes of Radnor Monthly Meeting* of 8-6mo-1723. The John Moore who "lately dyed intestate," administration upon whose estate was granted 7 Jan. 1715/16 to Robert Ellis by the Philadelphia Register of Wills etc. (*Admin. Book B*, page 125), has not been identified here.

For page 266: *Change text to begin:*

2. MARY MOORE, born in 1676, daughter of James Moore of Philadelphia, *q.v. postea,* died testate in Philadelphia 21st of 6th month (June) 1762 aged 86 years, widow of Robert Pound (*etc.*)

For page 227: *Change text to begin:*

3. JOHN MOORE, son of James Moore of Philadelphia, blacksmith, *q.v. postea.*

For page 228: *insert this item of evidence:*

By Deed of 25 Dec. 1704, John Moore of the Welsh Tract, County of Philadelphia, blacksmith, son and heir of James Moore, deceased, Griffith Owen of Philadelphia, Practitioner in Physick, and Rowland Ellis of said Welsh Tract, Gent., conveyed to Cadwalader Watkin of Merion in said Welsh Tract, yeoman. Recital that the Commissioners of Property under William Penn sold 100 acres to said James Moore in his lifetime, with warrant for survey thereof dated 6-5mo-1692 of 100 acres in the Welsh Tract, and it was surveyed, bounded east by Henry Pugh, south by land now of Peter

---

*For pp. 224, 266 (read 226), 227, 228, 229, 230, and 241 see pp. 253, 255, 256, 257, 258, 259, and 270, this volume.

Jones, west by Thomas David, and north by Thomas Johns, which said 100 acres the said James Moore sold to Hugh John, who sold his right therein to Robert John, who by his Will gave the same to William John, who sold his right therein to the said Griffith Owen and Rowland Ellis. To clear the title, no regular conveyance having been made to divest the said John Moore of his legal right in said land, this Indenture witnesses that the said John Moore, at the direction of the said Griffith Owen and Rowland Ellis, parties hereto, as well as for the consideration of 20 Pounds Pennsylvania money paid to said Owen and Ellis by said Cadwalader Watkin, they acquit etc. to him, as also for 5 shillings paid to said John Moore by said Watkin, he the said John Moore grants etc. to him all the said 100 acres, under the yearly Quit Rent accruing to the Proprietor William Penn, and will defend his title against all persons claiming from the said James Moore. Recorded 14 February 1756 in *Phila. Deed Book H-7*, page 56, whence this abstract.

For page 229: line 3: i. MARY MOORE *to be deleted.*

For page 230: *insert:*

JAMES MOORE OF PHILADELPHIA

JAMES MOORE, a blacksmith employed in the construction or repair of the Proprietor William Penn's Mill in Philadelphia County in or before 1692, died before 25 December 1704, as was recited in a Deed of that date given by his son John Moore, but his estate is not found in the probate records of that County, and his name does not appear in the minutes or registers of Philadelphia Monthly Meeting. The name of his wife, who evidently survived him and was mentioned in his son's Will of 21 September 1719, has not been recovered for this report. One James Moore, possibly the subject hereof, signed as a witness the certificate of marriage of John Roberts of Wayne, Philadelphia County, and Elizabeth Owen, late of Ridley Township, Chester County, at Haverford Meeting House of Friends on 2-11mo-1692. James Moore received a warrant for the survey of his City Lot dated 17-4mo-1684; one for his 100 acre tract dated 11-6mo-1685,—*Penna. Archives* 3rd series, II, p. 752; and one for his 100 acre tract in the Welsh Tract in Merion Township dated 6-5mo-1692.

The Proprietary, by his Warrant dated 17-4-1684, granted to James Moore of Philada., blacksmith, a lott at the Center of 50 foot in breadth, which was taken up and built on; the said James Moore by Deed dated 7-10mo-1693 granted the said lott and house to Richard Worthin, who by Deed to be drawn and dated granted the same to Elizabeth Price, who desires a Patent. Granted, the Deed being produced. Minutes of the Commissioners of Property, Philadelphia, of 5-8mo-1702, in *Penna. Arch.* 2 XIX, 328.

The Proprietor being indebted to James Moore, the said James Moore requests he may purchase 100 acres in the Welsh tract at the price of five pounds, he engaging to pay what it amounts to above the debt in money; it was granted.—Minutes of 30-4-1692, in *Ibid.*, 89.

James Moore having purchased 100 acres of land for 5 Pounds did this day satisfy the Commissioners for the said 5 Pounds in manner following, viz: 2 Pounds 19 shillings 8 pence being due to him for work done to the Proprietor's Mill and 2 Pounds 1 shilling 6 pence paid in cash unto Capt. Markham in part of the balance of Oliver Dunkly's account.—*Ibid.* of 12-9mo-1692, p. 92.

Children of James and N. N. Moore:

2   ii. MARY MOORE d 1762; married ROBERT POUND, *see revisions for page 226, supra.*

3   i. JOHN MOORE d 1719, *see revisions for page 227, supra.*

For page 241, line 1: *Change text to be:*

He appears to have been a brother to the James Moore of Philadelphia, blacksmith, and uncle to the latter's two children, nos. 2 and 3 above, now properly identified, as his daughter Margaret (Moore) Nicholas of Philadelphia, in her Will of 27 April 1743 devised *inter al.* to her " cousin Mary Pound," evidently referring to no. 2 Mary (Moore) Pound, *supra.*

ROBERT MIDDLETON, OF MARYLAND, AND SOME OF HIS DESCENDANTS

By John Goodwin Herndon, Ph.D, F.A.S.G., F.G.S.P.

#1. ROBERT MIDDLETON [1] was transported into Maryland, along with Benjamin Arnold and Thomas Thornton, by Benjamin Rozer, of Charles County, Md., prior to 16 February 1671,[2] but the place of his birth has not yet been established. He was born *circa* 1651, for in a deposition he filed in August 1681 he gave his age as "about thirty years." [3] He married *circa* 1672 MARY WHEELER, daughter of Major John Wheeler, of Charles County. She was born 22 March 1658, and died *post* 6 May 1708. Robert Middleton died *ante* 5 April 1708, in Prince Georges County, Md.

From the time of his arrival in Charles County when he was about 20 years of age until his death in that part of Charles County that had become Prince Georges County he was active in advancing both his own and his county's interests, in real estate development, and in military, civil, and church affairs.

Law Suits

He early brought suit against one Richard Boughton, who, however, did not appear when on 10 March 1673/4 the case was scheduled for trial.[4] The Court thereupon adopted the following minute: [5]

Robert Middleton peticons the Court for an attachmt agt the Est of Richd Boughton for the Sume of eight hundred pounds of tob[acco]: he proveing his debt in Court, it was granted him.

---

[1] The late Hugh C. Middleton, who was long a student of early Middleton records, was a great-great-great-grandson of this Robert Middleton. Writing from Augusta, Ga., 16 September 1924, to Mrs. Hannah Milnor (Robinson) Ljungstedt, he expressed the opinion that this Robert Middleton was one of the sons of Anthony Middleton who was, he said, of Charles City, Va., in 1623, and that said Anthony was a son of Thomas Middleton who married in England, in the late sixteenth century, a daughter of Dedrick Anthony. He gave many supporting arguments but, in that letter, no proof. [File Case: Genealogical Society of Pennsylvania].

[2] *Early Settlers in Maryland*, II: 411.

[3] *Maryland Archives*, XV: 403.

[4] *Ibid.*, LX: 526.

[5] *Ibid.*, LX: 549.

Later that same year he was successful in his suit against one Jacob Leah [6] and soon there started another contest, this against one Henry Bennett, which Middleton won 8 January 1677/8.[6a]

He was defendant in suits brought by Kenelm Cheseldyne,[6b] executor of John Jones, 14 August 1678, and by Thomas Hussey,[6c] 10 June 1678, and by John Contie [7] begun at the April 1705 term for Prince Georges County Court and continued for three years. On 9 August 1687 Robert Middleton, by C. Lomax his attorney, sued Richard Clouden in a plea of trespass.[7a] These cases all seem to be without genealogical significance.

Land Grants, Surveys, Certificates, Patents, and Sales

ROBERT MIDDLETON had extensive land interests in Charles and Prince Georges Counties. The regular procedure to obtain rent-roll title to land in Maryland was for an applicant to request the Lord Proprietor that a survey be made of the land desired. If favorably considered, a survey was made, and thereafter on the payment of the first annual rent (at the rate of a shilling for each 25 acres) a patent was issued. But if the applicant wished to transfer his right in the land to another person immediately, a certificate would be issued to him and the patent issued to the person he designated. Below are listed all the real estate transactions to which ROBERT MIDDLETON was a party, except a few concerning which there is doubt whether it was Robert Sr. or Robert Jr. who was the interested party. They are not included herein. On 14 July 1679 *Wickham* a tract of 112 acres at the " easternmost [end] of Panguaya Manor " was conveyed for him.[8] On 18 July 1692 (or 1693) Robert Middleton, planter, and Mary his wife, both *signed* a deed of conveyance to John Clements, " tayler," the consideration being 8,000 pounds of tobacco.[9]

In 1683 *Hard Shift*, 160 acres, in Charles County, was patented to Robert Middleton.[10] This property was located on the south side of

---

6 *Maryland Archives*, LX: 574.

6a *Charles County Land Records*, G-1: 79.

6b *Ibid.*, H-1: 26.

6c *Ibid.*, H-1: 158.

7 *Provincial Court Judgments*, TB-2:88, TL-3:578, PL-1:91, 250 and PL-2:43.

7a *Charles County Land Records*, O-1:5.

8 *Charles County Rent Rolls*, 2:88.

9 *Charles County Deed Records*, S-1:127.

10 *Land Office Records*, CB-3: 238.

Goose Bay. On 13 March 1688 Robert Middleton, " tayler ", and Mary his wife, sold this tract to Philip Lynes, merchant, of St. Marys County for 2250 pounds of tobacco. Robert signed, but then Mary made her mark.[11]

In 1686 *Saturday's Work*, 500 acres in Piscataway Hundred, was patented to Robert Middleton.[12] On 12 March 1688 he sold this tract " on the north side of the Maine Run of Kisconto Creek " to Robert Doyne, Gent., also of Charles County, for 10,000 pounds of tobacco. Witnesses were Humphrey Warren, John Courts, and Cleborne Lomax. The following day " Robt. Middleton & Mary his wife . . . acknowledged ye within written Indenture to be their act & deed. . . ." [13] This valuable tract is situated about 12 miles below Washington on the Oxon Hill Road over Anacostia Bridge and adjoins the estate where Sumner Welles, former Under Secretary of State of the United States has his home.

On 22 March 1687 the following entry was made: [14]

By virtue of a Warrant for 2000 acres [we have] granted unto William Hutchison dated 7th of this instant and by assignment to WM. MIDDLETON, *son to ROBERT MIDDLETON* for 123 acres *Godfather's Guift* on Eastern Branch of the Potomac about 4 miles of the Riding Place of the Eastern Branch.

And later it was " possessed by Robert Middleton." [15]

On 5 July 1687 *Apple Hill,* a 552-acre tract " in the woods above Piscataway " was surveyed for John Wheeler and Robert Middleton and patented to them 12 June 1688.[16] Later Major John Wheeler transferred his interest in this real estate to William Hutchison. Then on 8 January 1699 " William Hutchison and Sarah his wife, Robert Middleton and Mary his wife, all of Prince Georges County " sold to Francis Marbury, also of Prince Georges County, this tract for 20,000 pounds of tobacco. This deed was witnessed by Richard Edelin and Hickford Lemon.[17]

On 27 March 1688 *Apple Dore* 607 acres, was surveyed for Robert Middleton and Henry Boteler, 367 acres to Middleton and 240 to Boteler. The next day *Middleton's Lott,* 96 acres, " on the north side of the main fresh of the Piscataway " was surveyed for Robert Middleton and pat-

---

11 *Charles County Deeds Records, PH-1:* 97.

12 *Land Office Records,* 22: 227 and *NS-B:* 432.

13 *Charles County Deeds Records, P-1:* 99.

14 *Land Office Records,* 22: 379.

15 *Rent Rolls of Piscataway Hundred, Prince Georges County:* 148.

16 *Prince Georges County Rent Rolls,* I: 96.

17 *Prince Georges County Deed Records,* A: 295.

ented to him 12 June 1688.[18]   Then came a shift in locale for next *Carrick Fergus*, 181 acres, in Charles County, was surveyed and the certificate issued to Robert Middleton who assigned to Robert Doyne his rights therein and the patent was issued to the latter.[19]   That same year 1688 *The Garden*, 160 acres, and *Sangwar*, 350 acres, were certified to Robert Middleton, who assigned his rights therein to Wm. Hutchison.[20]   Two years later, 15 June 1690 *Mount Pleasant*, 164 acres, was surveyed for Robert Middleton and patented to him 10 November 1695.[21]   This tract was situated on Long Point and Piney Branch of Mattawoman Branch and was assigned by Middleton to William Hutchison.[22]   Finally mention should be made of *Middleton's Kindness*, owned by John Clement and Elizabeth his wife, which they conveyed to Thomas and Elizabeth Plunkett, and which the latter couple conveyed to Robert Middleton 14 January 1695.

His wife: Mary Wheeler

Documentary evidence of the identity of Robert Middleton's wife is found in the following quotation from part of a deed of gift from Major John Wheeler to Robert and Mary Middleton: [23]

This Indenture ye thirtieth day of Ja:y in ye tenth yeare of Dominion of ye Right Honble Charles L Baltimore Ld Proprietor of the Province of Maryland etc and in ye yeare of Lord one thousand six hundred eighty & foure Between Jno Wheeler of Charles County in ye province of Maryland gent of ye one part & Robert Middleton & Mary his wife of ye aforesaid County & province of ye other part Witnesseth ye sd Jno Wheeler for and in consideration of ye fatherly love and naturall affection which he hath and beareth towards his naturall borned daughter Mary the wife of the aforesd Robt Middleton as also for divers other good causes & considerations him hereunto more especially moving hath given granted and confirmed and by these . . . all that tract called Wheeler's Hope [in Charles County] on a fresh run which runneth into Piscattaway Creek, laid out for 365 acres. . . .

Mary Wheeler, daughter of Major John Wheeler and his wife Mary, was born 22 March 1658.[24]   The date of her death is not known to be of record.

---

18 *Prince Georges County Rent Rolls*, I: 96.

19 *Land Office Records* 22: 373 and NS-B: 570.

20 *Ibid.*, 22: 374.

21 *Patents*, CC-4: 78, and *Rent Rolls of Piscataway Hundred*: 139.

22 Recorded 28 June 1693, *Charles County Deed Records*, S-1: 126.

23 *Charles County Deeds Records*, L-1: 52.

24 *Maryland Archives*, LX: 117.

John Wheeler came to Maryland about 1659, was captain of the Charles County Militia, 1676, and its major, 1689, and was Justice of the County Court in 1685.[24a]

John Wheeler gave his age as 21 years in a deposition dated 22 January 1652.[25] On 26 October 1658 he was about 25 years of age.[26] As Major John Wheeler he deposed on 22 October 1691 that he was 61 years old.[27]

Mary his wife gave her age as 40 years in court on 9 March 1669/70.[28] As she was recorded as Major John Wheeler's widow as the August 1694 court, he had died before that date, but the date of her death is not of record. His Will dated 11 November 1693, was probated 9 January 1694/5.[29] By its terms he left bequests or legacies to his 5 sons, but none to his daughters, Mary, Winifred, and Sarah. One of the properties he mentioned was *Middleton's Lot*, 96 acres *which he devised to his son Francis Wheeler*. Sarah Wheeler was the wife of William Hutchison, and doubtless William Hutchison was godfather to William Middleton, son of Robert and Mary (Wheeler) Middleton.

His Military Record

An Act of Assembly of November 1678 directed the Treasurer of the Eastern Shore of Maryland to pay ROBERT MIDDLETON as reimbursement of his expenses incurred in his services against the Nanticoke Indians.[30] What his rank was it not stated.

At the request of Captain Randolph Brandt, dated 20 June 1681, ROBERT MIDDLETON was that day commissioned cornet [second lieutenant in a troop of cavalry.][31]

An Act of Assembly of August-September 1681 awarded to ROBERT MIDDLETON, as reimbursement of expenses incurred by him " for the public good," 4,500 pounds of tobacco for one account, 1,575 pounds for another, and 1,050 pounds of tobacco for still a third account.[32]

24a This is the record of John Wheeler as noted by the Society of Colonial Wars in the State of Maryland in its 1940 publication, *Genealogies of the Members and Record of Ancestors*: 389.

25 *Maryland Archives*, X: 226, but whether 1651/2 or 1652/3 was intended does not appear.

26 *Charles County Land Records*, A: 25.

27 *Ibid.*, R-1: 275.

28 *Ibid.*, 3D-1: 150, and *Maryland Archives*, LX: 254 (apparently in February 1668/9).

29 *Maryland Wills*, 7: 70.

30 *Maryland Archives*, VII: 100.

31 *Ibid.*, XV: 382, 385.

32 *Maryland Archives*, VI: 212, 219.

Raphael Semmes [33] in his *Captains and Mariners of Early Maryland* wrote:

During the same year [1681] Captain Randolph Brandt, a Commander of mounted troops in Charles County found that he needed new commissions for himself and some of his officers. He asked the Governor to send " one for myself, if with your Lordship's good likeing, one for my lieutenant George Godfrey, one for Robert Middleton, Cornett, as Mr. Henry Hawkins has sollicited to be excused his wife being lately dead, and one for a Quarter Master if approved by your Lordship." The commissions were issued as Brandt had solicited.

His Testimony in the Fendall Affair

In " The Tryall of Capt. Josias Fendall at a Provincial Court holden for the Right Hon[ble] the Lord Prop[r] at St. Johns the 15th day of November Anno 1681 " Fendall was accused of attempting to " raise a mutiny and sedition against the person of the said Prop[rieta]ary." [34] The accused was given the right to " except " or " except to " [35] any proposed juror and he did so in the case of each who, in answer to the question, " What is your religion? ", answered, " Catholic " or " Roman Catholic." One of the evidences,[36] William Boyden, claimed that Robert Middleton had told him in the presence of several other persons that Capt. Fendall was going to call the Lord Proprietary to account and that it was high time to do so. Later William Taylor, another evidence, made a quite similar statement. Soon thereafter when Robert Middleton was called the following interchange took place: [36a]

Attorney General: Robert Middleton, what can you say? Let the Court and the Jury hear you.

Middleton: I upon oath do say that what has been declared by Boyden and Taylor that I should report that Capt Fendall was gone to call my Lord to an account and that it was high time to do so is altogether thereto untrue.

Court: If you are Evidence for the Lord Proprietary, you are not then for the prisoner. Speak to the business—what you know in behalf of his Lordship against the prisoner at the Bar.

Middleton: I have nothing to say against him.

---

[33] He received an A.B. degree from Princeton, an LL.B., from Harvard Law School, and a Ph.D. from The John Hopkins University. His book was published by the Johns Hopkins Press, Baltimore, 1937.

[34] *Maryland Archives*, V: 312-328 and XVII: 31.

[35] The present-day equivalent term is " to challenge."

[36] The regularly used term in Maryland. The synonym usually employed elsewhere is " witness ", " evidence " ordinarily meaning " that which is legally presented to a competent tribunal as a means of ascertaining the truth of any alleged matter of fact under investigtion before it." But in the expression " He turned State's evidence " we mean he became a witness for the state.

[36a] For record of the trial see *Maryland Archives*, V: 312-328, and XVII: 31.

After hearing several other persons' testimony the Jury brought in the following amazingly wishy-washy verdict:

We find Josias Fendall guilty of speaking severall seditious words without fórce or practice and, if the hon^ble Court think him guilty of the breach of the Act of Assembly, we do or else not.

Those were hard times indeed, for on the morrow Capt. Fendall was sentenced to pay 40,000 pounds of tobacco for a fine, to be kept in jail at his own costs until the fine should be paid, and on its payment to be forever banished from the Province. One of the judges then added that the sentence had been " mitigated with all the Moderation possible." Then the Secretary of the Court, William Calvert, announced:

The sentence is as favourable as could be expected. The Law of our Province would have allowed boaring (sic) of the Tongue, Cropping of One or both ears and other corporall punishments but wee have forbourne that and taken this less shamefull way of punishm^t.

His Civil Appointments: (1) Boundary Commissioner

In the autunm of 1679 ROBERT MIDDLETON served as a member of a commission of twelve men appointed to settle the boundaries of the property of certain persons in Charles County.[37] His refusal to sign the ward is interesting because of the reference therein to Col. Benjamin Rozer who had brought him into Maryland. The dates mentioned are 18 September, 10 October, and 7 November 1679.

His Civil Appointments: (2) Probate Assignments

On Saturday 9 January 1685/6 ROBERT MIDDLETON and Thomas Wheeler were sureties on the bond of Major John Wheeler [their father-in-law and father, respectively] as administrator of the estate of John Probart, deceased.[38]

On Die Mercur[39] 4 April 1688 Justice John Wheeler of Charles County made return that he had sworn [James] Thompson administrator of the estate of Andrew Clarke, deceased, and Wm. Hutchison and Robert Middleton appraisers of the estate.[40]

---

37 Maryland Archives, LI: 308-311.

38 Testamentary Proceedings, 13: 276.

39 In early Maryland records days of the week were often recorded with their Latin names whose full forms were dies followed by Solis or Dominica, Lunae, Martis, Veneris, Mercurii, Jovis, and Saturni.

40 Testamentary Proceedings, 14: 62.

On 7 May 1702 ROBERT MIDDLETON and Francis Wheeler filed their account as appraisers of the goods and chattels of John Marshall of Prince Georges County.[41]

On 7 July 1705 ROBERT MIDDLETON and Francis Marbury filed their first report as appraisers of the " goods and chattels of Mr. Jno. Hawkins of Piscattaway in Prince Georges County, deceased, at his plantacon in Piscattaway." [42]

On 1 May 1706 ROBERT MIDDLETON and John Reymond, appraisers of the estate of John Baldwin, late of Prince Georges County, filed their inventory of his goods and chattels, which on 1 October 1706 " was ordered to be entered on the records of the Prerogative Court." [43]

His Civil Appointments: (3) *Other Court Assignments and Appearances*

ROBERT MIDDLETON was a juror at the November 1680 and August 1698 terms of the Provincial Court,[44] and a witness in numerous other causes heard between September 1692 and September 1707.[45] He was, as has already been noted, also mentioned by William Boyden and William Taylor, of Charles County, in their deposition dated 4 October 1681 concerning the Fendall affair.[46]

On 10 September 1689 he demanded 200 pounds of tobacco as the price of one wolf head.[47]

At the November term of court in 1704 he recorded the mark for his cattle.[48]

He was on the bond of [his son] John Middleton when the latter was licensed 19 December 1704 to keep an ordinary.[49]

His Civil Appointments: (4) *Coroner of Prince Georges County*

ROBERT MIDDLETON was commissioned one of the two coroners for Prince Georges County 15 May 1696.[50] Later that year he signed, as

---

[41] *Prince Georges County Inventories*, BB: 40.

[42] *Ibid.*, BB: 79.

[43] *Ibid.*, BB: 93.

[44] *Provincial Court Judgments*, WC: 258 and IL: 59.

[45] *Ibid.*, DSC: 159, TB-2: 213, 236, TL-3: 578, 579, PL-1: 156 and PL-2: 7, 11.

[46] *Maryland Archives*, XVII: 31.

[47] *Charles County Land Records*, P-1: 187.

[48] *Prince Georges County Land Records*, C: 171.

[49] *Ibid.*, B: 338.

[50] *Maryland Archives*, XX: 546.

Coroner for that County [51] the Address of Loyalty to their "Dread Soveraign (sic) William III" on receipt "of the news Arriv'd here of the horrible intended conspiracy agt his Royall p^rson." [52] On 14 June 1697 he was again elected coroner. On that day an attachment of contempt against Thomas Greenfield, administrator of Richard Charlett, deceased, was issued by the Prerogative Court returnable the first day of September 1697 "directed to Mr. Robert Middleton, Coroner of Prince Georges County." [53] At the November 1704 term of Court he took again the required oath as coroner. [54] He was still so serving when at the September 1706 term of Court the case of Thomas Greenfield, administrator of Richard Charlett, against Elizabeth Bigger, administrator of James Bigger, was heard. [55]

His Religious Affiliation

In the Fendall affair ROBERT MIDDLETON had avoided being drawn into the religious conflict of his times by either defending Fendall or attaching any blame to the acts of the Lord Proprietary. But his position as a Protestant is beyond question. In the first place, he was one of the 79 signers [56] of the "Address of the Inhabitants of Charles County to their most Excellent Majesties King William and Queen Mary", dated 28 November 1689, whose subtitle was "The humble Address of the Gentlemen, Merchants, Planters, Freeholders, and Freemen Their Majesties *Protestant* [57] Subjects in Charles County in the Province of Maryland." Its concluding sentence was:

We daily pray the Divine Providence to protect your Majesties against all your Ennemies, that you may be a lasting and strong sanctuary for the Protestant Interest and at last Crowned with the just reward of your glorious undertakings in the possession of an Immortal and Eternal Diadem.

---

51 *Ibid.*, XX: 425.

52 *Ibid.*, XX: 538.

53 *Testamentary Proceedings*, 17: 6.

54 *Prince Georges County Land Records*, B: 335.

55 *Provincial Court Judgments*, PL-1: 17.

56 Among the signers were William Hutchison and Robert Middleton, their names next to each other's; but the former was printed in the transcribed copy as Hutchinson and the latter as Edward instead of Robert. There was no Edward Middleton resident in Charles County, Md., as that date. This document appears in *Maryland Archives*, VIII: 137-138.

57 Italics not in the printed copy in the *Archives*, cited.

His Church Offices

ROBERT MIDDLETON, as one of the Wardens of St. John's Church, was present at a Vestry held at Broad Creek for Piscataway Parish, 26 August 1704 and attended all Vestry meetings thereafter through 9 April 1705, on which date the following entries were made in the *Register of St. John's or Piscataway Parish, Prince Georges County:* [58]

There was elected and chosen Mr. William Tannehill and Mr. Robert Middleton to be vestrymen in the roome of Mr. Thomas Addison and Mr. James Beall.
There was elected Thomas Gallon and Daniel Connell to be church wardens in the Roome of Robert Middleton and James Green for the ensuing year.

Then it was noted that on 25 March 1706

Robert Middleton [was] present as vestryman & took the required oaths.

He continued to attend Vestry meetings with great regularity. At one of these it must have given him high satisfaction to be present, when on 13 April 1707 his eldest son, John Middleton, who was also present, was elected to the Vestry " and took the oath of abjuration and the others by law apptd."

ROBERT MIDDLETON was last in attendance as vestryman 10 May 1707. Then among the entries of the Vestry " held at Broad Creek for Piscataway Parish April 5, 1708 being Easter Monday was this one:

This day likewise was Mr. [John] Langham chosen in the room of Mr. Robert Middleton late deceased.

His Death

ROBERT MIDDLETON died intestate, probably late in March or early in April 1708. The second official record (the Church record being the first official record) of his decease is found in a bond dated 6 May 1708, " being the seventh year of Her Majesty's Reign ", described thus: [59]

Robert Middleton, of Prince Georges County; Mary Middleton [widow] administratrix John Middleton [eldest son] administrator; Thomas Middleton [second son] surety; Edward Willett, witness, and William Middleton [youngest son], witness.

---

[58] *Opus cit.,* 12, 13, 15, 16, 17, and 18 for all references to Robert Middleton.

[59] Box 2, Folder 20, Prince Georges County Bonds.

Under date of 16 June 1708 the following entry appears in the records of the Prerogative Court: [60]

The following proceedings returned from Prince Georges Co:
. . . Mary Middleton and John Middleton adms to Robert Middleton, their administrators bond in comon form, with Thomas Middleton their surety in one hundred and forty pounds sterling, dated the sixth of May 1708.

Children of Robert and Mary (Wheeler) Middleton

   i.   JOHN MIDDLETON (b prob. *ca.* 1673), administrator of his father's estate 1708; vestryman of St. Johns (Piscataway) Church 1707-1709, 1728-31; heir to *Wheeler's Hope,* 1709; patentee of *Refuse* 1713, *The Mistake* 1714, *Maiden Bowers* and *Nothing Worth* 1726; captain in Colonial forces, 1728-1731; gave power of attorney to his brother Thomas, 1734, when he was called " late of Prince Georges County "; constable of Piscattaway Hundred 1719; was taxed 1753 on *Nothing Worth* which in 1754 was taxed to *his heirs;* m MARY ———, and had issue, a dau., CHARITY MIDDLETON who m WILLIAM LUCKETT.

   ii.   THOMAS MIDDLETON (b 1674: d 1744, Prince Georges Co., Md.) m 1st PENELOPE, daughter of WILLIAM and MARY HATTON, and had *issue:* HATTON, THOMAS, MARY (wife of WM. HAWKINS), PENELOPE, SARAH, ELIZABETH, ELINOR, and SUSANNAH MIDDLETON: m 2ndly ALICE, widow of THOMAS SMALLWOOD; m 3dly SUSANNAH, widow of GEORGE BRETT. THOMAS MIDDLETON was patentee of *Long Point.*

   iii.   JAMES MIDDLETON (d testate 1769, Charles Co.) m SARAH daughter of JOHN SMITH, of Jordan, Calvert Co., Gent., and had issue: SMITH, JAMES, and IGNATIUS MIDDLETON, and daughters ANN (who m 1st THOMAS JENKINS, and 2ndly CHARLES BEAVIN), MARY (who m ——— HAWKINS), SARAH (who m EDWARD JENKINS), CHARITY (who m ——— DAVIS), and MARTHA (m MARMADUKE SEMMES).

   iv.   ROBERT MIDDLETON (b *ca.* 1681/2 — d *ca.* 1749) m ELIZABETH, daughter of the above mentioned JOHN SMITH, and seems to have had a son WILLIAM MIDDLETON who apparently died young.

2. v.   WILLIAM MIDDLETON, whose line will be continued in the next issue of this *Magazine.*

---

[60] *Testamentary Proceedings,* 21: 25.

ROBERT MIDDLETON, OF MARYLAND, AND SOME OF HIS DESCENDANTS

By JOHN GOODWIN HERNDON, PH.D., F.A.S.G., F.G.S.P.

2. WILLIAM MIDDLETON [son of Robert and Mary (Wheeler) Middleton] was born in 1685, apparently between 5 July and 19 October, according to depositions he made in 1730,[1] 1743,[2] and 1747,[3] or about May-July 1683, according to others he made toward the end of his long life when he may have unintentionally added two years to his age.[4] He died in his native Charles County in the Province of Maryland between 15 May 1769, the date of his Will,[5] and 15 November 1769, the date of its probate. He was married twice.

His First Wife

His first wife, whom he married between 10 July 1710 and 14 July 1712, as will more fully appear in the various family notes which follow,[6] was ELIZABETH TEARES, widow of John Keech, and daughter of HUGH and RUTH (HOLLAND) TEARES. She was born about 1689, and died between 1748 and 1758. She was the mother of all his children.

His Second Wife

His second wife was named HENRIETTA,[7] but her surname has not been learned. They were married between 1748 and 1758, and she was named by him as his executrix in his Will. The date of her death has not been ascertained.

---

[1] On 19 October 1730 he gave his age as 45 years. 5 *Chancery Record* IR#2: 453.

[2] On 4 July 1743 he gave his age as 57 years. 8 *Chancery Record* IR#5: 329.

[3] On 7 May 1747, when he was described as William Middleton, of Charles County, Gent., he gave his age as 61 years. *Ibid*: 293.

[4] He gave his age as 82 years on 1 July 1765; as 83 on 25 April 1767, and as 85 on 17 June 1768. See "Charles County Depositions" at Maryland Historical Society, as also in *Charles County Deed Books* 57 N: 768 and 60 A-3: 190, at Annapolis.

[5] 37 Maryland Wills 393, at Hall of Records, Annapolis.

[6] *Infra* 166-173.

[7] Her name is actually written *Heniretta* and *Heneritta* in the deeds and in the Will, in which the compiler of this account has found it, spellings which he believes to be scribal errors.

His Designations

In the Deeds to which WILLIAM MIDDLETON was a party he was usually called Gentleman, but occasionally other designations were used: Planter,[8] Merchant,[9] Mr.,[10] and Esquire.[11] On hundreds of records of the Charles County Court of the years 1739-1748 he is referred to as " one of His Lordship's Justices of the Peace for this County."

His Public Offices

The period of service of WILLIAM MIDDLETON as a Member of the Lower House of the Maryland Assembly, representing Charles County, was continuous from the session which began 11 July 1732 through the one that started 26 May 1741.[12] Then after an interval of several years he was again elected to that Body and served therein, as shown by the following entry: [13]

Mr. WILLIAM MIDDLETON a member elected for Charles County in the Room of Mr. JOHN COURTS deceased took the oaths etc. 30 May 1748.

WILLIAM MIDDLETON served as one of the Justices for Charles County for nearly ten years. His first and last commissions were dated 18 October 1739 and 22 October 1747, respectively.[14] His service was continuous from 1739 until at least as late as 9 August 1748.[15]

Deeds to His Children

A Deed dated 9 March 1735/6 and recorded 30 March 1736,[16] recites that WILLIAM MIDDLETON " for the natural love and affection he beareth unto his daughter ELEANOR TYLER, wife of BENJAMIN TYLER" conveyed to her one moiety of that part of *His Lordship's Favour*, situate between the lands of James Keech and John Abernethy, deceased, which he, William Middleton, had bought of Thomas and James Abernethy.

---

8 For example, from Richard Beale, 25 December 1724, and from James Keech, 7 July 1730. *Charles County Deed Book* L-2: 185 and M-2: 231.

9 For example, to James Griffen, 14 March 1743, and to John Wheatley and John Estep, 9 January 1744/5, *ibid* X-2: 108 and Z-2: 24.

10 *Testamentary Proceedings* #40: 19, citing order dated 14 September 1732.

11 From Stephen Delancy and Co., dated 13 October 1737. *Charles County Deed Book* O-2: 207-208.

12 *Archives of Maryland*, vol. #37: 445; vol. #39: 54, 151, 220, and 439; vol. #40: 39, 122, 169, 280, and 518; and vol. #42: 83 and 192.

13 *Ibid.*, vol. #46: 27.

14 *Commission Records, 1726-1788*: 49, 55, 61, 62, 66, 68, 70, 71, 76, and 80, in the Hall of Records, Annapolis.

15 *Charles County Deed Book* #69: 1.

16 *Ibid.*, O-2: 120.

In an unindexed Bill of Sale it is recorded that on 16 February 1743/4 Peter White, a carpenter, sold a negro man named Tomacoe to WILLIAM MIDDLETON who then endorsed it, as follows: [17]

I hereby assign the within Bill of Sale unto my son SAMUEL MIDDLETON his heirs and assigns.

At the same time another Bill of Sale to William Middleton was recorded. It was from William Bryan who sold for £11 15s. 5d. a negro boy named George. This Bill of Sale was likewise assigned to SAMUEL MIDDLETON.

By a Deed dated 5 August 1748 [18] WILLIAM MIDDLETON Sr. conveyed

to HOLLAND MIDDLETON, WILLIAM MIDDLETON, Jr., and ROBERT MIDDLETON, for £10 current money of Maryland and also the natural love and affection which I have unto my sons HOLLAND, WILLIAM and ROBERT

certain tracts which he describes, Holland Middleton to have his portion at the southernmost corner, William Jr. to have his at the northernmost corner, and Robert to receive the southwestern part. He then effected a redistribution of a previous transaction by providing that the land formerly belonging to Robert, containing 110 acres, was to go to William Jr., who was also to receive the tract known as *Griffen's Seat*. The endorsement on this Deed is of especial interest because of its wording:

WILLIAM MIDDLETON, Sr., acknowledged this land to be the right of inheritance of HOLLAND MIDDLETON, WILLIAM MIDDLETON, Jr., and ROBERT MIDDLETON.

By a Deed dated 6 May 1749, recorded 31 May 1749,[19] WILLIAM MIDDLETON Jr. sold to Hugh Mitchell, also of Charles County, the above-mentioned 110 acres, described as " of manor land called *Zachia Manor* ", subject to a life interest therein of himself, called William Middleton, Jr., party to these presents, Robert Middleton, and Hugh Middleton, *sons of* WILLIAM MIDDLETON, Sr., of Charles County.

This completes the thus-far-discovered documentary evidence of the names of the children of William Middleton, Sr., viz., Eleanor, Samuel, Holland, William, Jr., Robert, and Hugh.

Certain Interfamily Transactions

The following are merely samples of the many types of interfamily transaction in which WILLIAM MIDDLETON, Senior, figured, in addition

---

17 *Ibid.*, Z-2: 23.

18 *Ibid.*, Z-2: 287.

19 *Ibid.*, Z-2: 343.

to the deeds of gift already cited. Among other things they show how closely tied he was to the entire group of the early Middletons. Religious differences did not affect his fraternal feelings, for his brothers James and Robert had married into the Catholic family of John Smith, of *Jordan,* Gentleman, while his other brothers, John and Thomas, and their children were ardent Church of England adherents. His own famliy affiliations were also Protestant. Chronologically arranged, these transactions show him as:

(1) principal creditor of John Smith, Gent., when the latter's estate was being inventoried; [20]

(2) co-security with Henry Holland Hawkins [21] on the bond of Richard Tubman (also a family connection), administrator of the estate of Eleanor Philpott (also a family connection); [22]

(3) witness to a Deed from Richard Beale to John Diggs, Gent., which recites that Richard Beale was a son of John Beale by Eleanor Bayne,[23] daughter of Walter Beane (Bayne);

(4) evidence,[24] as was also his brother Robert Middleton, in a case heard 19 October 1730; [25]

(5) beneficiary under the Will of his friend Robert Roberson [or Robinson], dated 7 July 1733 and proved 2 October 1734, which was witnessed by James Keech,[26] Elizabeth Middleton [probably wife of William], and William Luckett [husband of Charity, only daughter of John Middleton, William's brother];

(6) joint purchaser [27] with his brother James Middleton of a part of *His Lordship's Favour* from John Abernethy's heirs, which James Keech had sold to John Abernethy. At the same time, 13 March 1734/5, they purchased a part of *Jordan,* formerly sold by Robert Middleton and Elizabeth, his wife, who were brother and sister-in-law of William Middleton;

(7) surety on the bond of Mary Gardiner (administratrix of Joseph Gardiner) who subsequently was married to James Keech as his second

---

20 *Charles County Inventories, 1667-1717*: 419-421 (1716).

21 His mother and Elizabeth (Teares) Middleton's mother were sisters.

22 *Testamentary Proceedings* #16: 144, 20 April 1723.

23 Widow successively of John Stone and Hugh Teares. Deed dated 19 September 1723.

24 That is, he testified. See this *Magazine*, vol. xix: 96, footnote 36, for a fuller explanation.

25 *Chancery Record* IR #2: 453.

26 He was a brother to John Keech, whose widow married William Middleton. James Keech's first wife was Ruth Hawkins, first cousin to Elizabeth (Teares) Middleton.

27 *Charles County Deed Book* O-2: 77.

wife. An appraiser of that estate was Samuel Middleton, William's son; [28]

(8) co-security with his brother James on the bond of their brother Thomas Middleton, who was administrator with *his* wife Alice, then administratrix of the estate of her deceased former husband Thomas Smallwood, the bond being dated 7 May 1735; [29] and

(9) administrator of his brother Thomas Middleton's estate. His bond was dated 28 January 1744/5.[30] His sureties were James Keech and James Griffen.

His Real Estate

The first appearance of the name of this WILLIAM MIDDLETON on any Maryland record is dated 20 March 1687 when a tract of 183 acres lying near Broad Creek in what is now Prince Georges County was surveyed for him. Called *Dalkeith*, it was patented to him 12 June 1688.[31] Two days after the first entry another was made, reciting that out of the 2,000 acres granted to William Hutchison, he had assigned 183 acres " to WILLIAM MIDDLETON, son of Robert Middleton " and called *Godfather's Guift*.[32] On 18 June 1719 William Middleton and Elizabeth, his wife, for £20 10 shillings and " divers other good causes and considerations them hereunto moving " deeded *God Father's Gift* to Benjamin Belt, of Prince Georges County.[33]

At various dates WILLIAM MIDDLETON owned, either by patent, resurvey, purchase, or devise, all or part of *Ye Meadows*, 400 acres, (1720); *Longpoint* (1730); *Three Brothers*, 250 acres, (1734); *Mudd's Rest*, 200 acres, (1737); *His Lordship's Favour*, 324 acres, (1738); *Griffen's Seat*, 254 acres, (1740); *Middleton's Rich Thicket*, 100 acres, (1742); *Middleton's Hope*, (1742); *Addition to May Day*, 120 acres, (1744); *Thompson Town*, 100 acres, (1747); and *Partner's Purchase*, 126 acres, (1748). In addition to what has already been said about cer-

---

[28] *Testamentary Proceedings* #29: 478; *Inventories* #20: 313, and *Accounts* #16: 41, dated, respectively, 4 December 1734, 19 February 1734/5, and 15 February 1737/8.

[29] *Testamentary Proceedings* #30: 55.

[30] *Ibid.*, #31: 559.

[31] *Prince Georges County Rent Roll*, vol. i: 96.

[32] *Ibid.*, vol. i: 96, and *Land Office Liber* #22: 379. Since this gift or assignment was made by William Hutchison to William Middleton when the latter was a baby, we must conclude that William Hutchison was his godfather. The compiler of this record is of the opinion that William Hutchison's wife Sarah was sister to Robert Middleton; but he has not found documentary proof of that assumption.

[33] *Prince Georges County Deed Book* E: 786 (at Annapolis). What the " other good causes " were can only be surmised. The compiler of this record has found that a son of Benjamin Belt was named Middleton Belt. It seems likely therefore that either Benjamin Belt or his wife was also of Middleton lineage.

tain of his real estate transactions, some genealogical gleanings may be obtained from deeds involving some of the above-listed properties. For example, WILLIAM MIDDLETON conveyed to Jno. Boswell for £22 " for and during the Natural Life of Samuel, Robert, and Hugh Middleton all that tract of Manor Land called *Middleton's Hope* that lyeth on the West Side of Samsons Branch . . . said to contain one hundred acres, be it more or less. . . ." [34] Again, SAMUEL MIDDLETON [son of William] conveyed to his brother ROBERT MIDDLETON " for 20,000 pounds of tobacco and for other good causes and considerations him hereunto moving " 83 acres of the tract called *Three Brothers* as " a good true indefeasable Estate of Inheritance of fee simple ", and acknowledged the land " to be the Right and Inheritance of Robert Middleton, his heirs and assigns forever." [35] And finally, there was the indenture dated 30 August 1758 between " WILLIAM MIDDLETON, of Charles County in the Province afs[d], Gentl. and Samuel Hanson, of the same County and Province, Gentl." whereby the former " in full possession and . . . firmly seized in his Demesne of an Indefeasable estate of Inheritance in fee simple in the before bargained land and premises [*Middleton's Rich Thicket*] " sells the same to the latter who " after the decease of the said William Middleton and Heneritta [*sic*] his wife " shall have, hold, occupy, possess and peaceably enjoy the same.[36]

His Last Will and Testament

The following is a copy of the Will of WILLIAM MIDDLETON and a record of its being presented for probate: [37]

In the Name of God Amen. I William Middleton of Charles County Maryland being sick and weak but of sound and disposing mind and memory do make this my last will and testament in manner and forme following.

First I desire that all my just debts be paid by my executrix herein after mentioned.

Secondly I give and bequeath to my grandsons Isaac and Hugh Middleton all my wearing apparel to be equally divided between them except a druget coat breeches and hatt which said coat breeches and hatt I give and bequeath to my son Robert Middleton provided he makes application for them in ten months after my decease otherwise to my grandson William Morris Middleton.

Thirdly I give and bequeath to my wife Heniretta all the remaining part of my personal estate to her, her heirs and assigns forever.

Lastly I do appoint my wife executrix of this my will and testament hereby annuling all other wills by me heretofore made.

---

34 *Charles County Deed Liber* O-2: 516.

35 *Ibid.,* Z-2: 292.

36 *Ibid.,* G-3: 257-259.

37 *Maryland Wills,* vol. 37: 393, at Annapolis.

In witness whereof I do hereunto affix my hand and seal this fifteenth day of May 1769 Anno Dom.

Signed sealed and declared
by the said William Middleton
to be his Last Will and   /s/ WILLIAM MIDDLETON (seal)
Testament in the presence of
us witnesses thereunto requested

Thos. Thornton
Sam. Hanson
Geo. Lee

15th. November 1769 Samuel Hanson swears to will before deputy commissary of Charles Co. Maryland.

Children of William and Elizabeth (Teares) Middleton:

i. ELEANOR MIDDLETON, who was married to BENJAMIN TYLER as early as 9 March 1735/6; settled in Virginia.

ii. SAMUEL MIDDLETON, died intestate,[38] somewhat *ante* 28 June 1764; married ELIZABETH WARD, died testate, Charles Co., Md., w.d. 1 July 1783, w.p. 12 September 1784;[39] and had issue, Horatio Middleton, Ann (Middleton) Douglas, and Samuel Ward Middleton.

iii. HOLLAND MIDDLETON, in South Carolina when by deed[40] of 2 February 1767 he conveyed to Elizabeth (Ward) Middleton, of Charles Co., Md., widow of Samuel Middleton, all Holland's rights in a part of *Wheeler's Purchase*, of which Samuel Middleton died possessed; married by October 1740 SARAH ———; he died, testate, Hancock Co., Ga., 1795/6, leaving wife named MARY ——— and children named Susannah (Middleton) Berry, Sarah (Middleton) Dickinson, Zachariah Middleton, Robert Middleton, John Middleton, Benjamin Middleton, Mary Middleton, and possibly others.[41]

3 iv. WILLIAM MIDDLETON, Jr., whose line is continued below.

v. ROBERT MIDDLETON, who married ANNE ———, and was witness to a deed in Prince William County, Va., 27 April 1761;[41] and removed to Georgia where he lived in 1769 and 1770.

vi. HUGH TEARE MIDDLETON, born *ca.* 1730,[41] died intestate, 30 November 1803 at his home "Locust Dale", Edgefield Co., S. C., married four times and had three sets of children, the names of two of his wives being mentioned in the administration of his estate, LUCY WILLIAMS (3rd wife) and AGATHA GARRETT (4th wife). His children were Hugh Middleton who predeceased him and whose wife was born Mildred Martin; John Middleton; Martha (Middleton) Tennent, Sarah (Middleton) Quarles; Elizabeth Middleton who later married Alexander Speer; Mary Middleton; and Philadelphia Adelia Middleton who later married Andrew Calhoun Hamilton.

[38] *Inventories*, vol. 84: 228-232.

[39] *Charles County Wills*, B-1: 393-394.

[40] *Charles County Deed Book* O-3: 149.

[41] As shown in the Middleton papers, Semmes Collection, Maryland Historical Society, in notes contributed by the late Hugh Calhoun Middleton who died at Augusta, Ga., in June 1946, and is buried at Clark Hill, South Carolina, 21 miles northwest of Augusta.

3. WILLIAM MIDDLETON [son of William and Elizabeth (Teares) Middleton] lived most of his life in Charles County, Md., where he was born, probably about 1718. About 1740 or earlier he married MARY COGHILL, daughter of William and Anne (Smallwood) Coghill. They made their home on the tract that WILLIAM MIDDLETON, Sr., had received by devise under the Will of Robert Robertson, and which WILLIAM MIDDLETON, Jr., sold 6 May 1749 to Hugh Mitchell, subject to the life interest therein of himself and two of his brothers " these three being sons of WILLIAM MIDDLETON, Sr., of Charles County, Maryland." [1] Whether they had lived a while earlier in Prince Georges County we do not know but one John Stewart, of that County, confessed judgment to WILLIAM MIDDLETON, Jr., for 847 pounds of tobacco 25 July 1745 which Middleton caused to be recorded 25 August 1748.[2] He was a witness in the Essex County, Va., Court to a deed between certain of the Coghills, as will more fully appear in subsequent pages,[3] a fact that strongly suggests that he was living there at that date, 21 November 1752. In any event all other items known concerning him are found in the records of his native county. His wife MARY came into Court and consented to the sale of the 38 acres of the tract called *Griffen's Seat* which her husband WILLIAM owned and which he was conveying to George Maxwell by Deed dated 15 August 1753.[4]

Just before this sale WILLIAM MIDDLETON, Jr., had been " admitted to keep an ordinary at Charlestown " by the August 1753 Court of Charles County. He gave bond in the sum of £40 with Matthew Stone and Walter Maddox as his sureties. He paid the required fee, called a " fine ", of £3 10 shillings.[5] That is the last mention of his name until his death late in 1755.

On 1 January 1756 William Garnett, who had been appointed WILLIAM MIDDLETON's administrator, furnished bond for £200 with Hugh Mitchell and Daniel of St. Thomas Jenifer, his sureties.[6] The administrator swore to the inventory " of the estate of William Middleton, late of Charles County," on 15 June 1756. The appraisal had been made 12 March 1756 by John Hanson and John Theobald in the sum of £53 6s.

1 *Charles County Deed Book* Z-2: 343.

2 *Prince Georges County Deed Book* BB-2: 491.

3 *Infra* 173-176.

4 *Charles County Deed Book* A-3, Part 2: 123.

5 *Charles County Land Book* E-3: 221.

6 *Testamentary Proceedings*, vol. 36: 278.

$6\frac{1}{2}$d. Daniel of St. Thomas Jenifer and Samuel Cannon were listed as creditors and Samuel and Robert Middleton as kin.[7]

There has been preserved no record of the distribution of his estate. Doubtless his widow MARY was entitled to one-third of the net distributable amount and his sons ISAAC and HUGH MIDDLETON, mentioned in the Will of their grandfather WILLIAM, Sr., to two-thirds.

Children of William and Mary (Coghill) Middleton:

4　i. ISAAC SMALLWOOD MIDDLETON, whose line is continued below.
5　ii. HUGH MIDDLETON, whose line is continued below.

4. ISAAC SMALLWOOD MIDDLETON [son of William and Mary (Coghill) Middleton] was born about 1741 in Charles County, Md., and died probably in 1788 or 1789 in Fairfax County, Va. About 1766 he married ELEANOR, whose family name has not been discovered, nor has the date of her birth or death.

He was first mentioned in the Charles County records in the Will of his maternal uncle SMALLWOOD COGHILL, dated 23 July 1759, wherein the testator called him " cousin." [1]　Secondly he was named in the Will of his grandfather WILLIAM MIDDLETON, dated 15 May 1769, already cited.[2]

On 11 February 1771 ISAAC SMALLWOOD MIDDLETON sold for £270 to Henry Hardy, Jr., of Prince Georges County, a tract containing 290 acres, *called Gardeners Meadows Resurveyed*, ELEANOR MIDDLETON consenting to the sale of this property of her husband's.[3]

---

[7] *Inventory Book* #60: 696. This expression " Kin " or " Next of Kin " is used in Maryland frequently to record the name of some relatives, but not necessarily the closest kin. Samuel and Robert Middleton were, however, in this case, brothers to the deceased intestate. The John Hanson who was an appraiser in this case was later President of the Continental Congress, and Daniel of St. Thomas Jenifer listed as a creditor of William Middleton, Jr., was later a member of the Continental Congress.

[1] *Md. Historical Magazine*, vol xxii (1927), p. 156.

[2] *Supra* 146.

[3] *Prince Georges County Land Book* #19 (AA-2): 220-221. *Gardeners Meadows*, a tract of 1037 acres, was assigned by Charles Digges, of Charles Co., to Luke Gardiner, and patented to the latter 30 September 1717. It passed to Ignatius Gardiner who conveyed it, or a part of it, in 1732 to George Hardy; and in 1750 it was resurveyed for John Wynn, Jr., in accordance with an order dated 25 August 1749. The new patent called the property *Gardeners Meadows Resurveyed* and included 315 acres of the original survey which passed to John Wynn, Jr. He conveyed 290 acres of these 315 to Smallwood Coghill 9 October 1753. He died possessed of them, and provided in his Will that on the death of his wife Keziah Coghill, the land should become the property of ISAAC SMALLWOOD MIDDLETON, to whom there should be immediately transferred one slave. On 26 June 1761 Keziah Coghill, executrix of Smallwood Coghill, was shown indebted to the decedent's estate in the sum of £1272 5s. 11½d. John Wynn, of Prince Georges Co., and Henry Acton, of Charles Co., were her sureties. To the decedent's " cousin " ISAAC SMALLWOOD MIDDLETON was transferred a negro girl named Vick, valued at £40. The residue of the personal property went to the widow, Keziah Coghill. On her death title to the 290 acres was vested in ISAAC SMALLWOOD MIDDLETON who conveyed them, as stated, to Henry Hardy, Jr.

On 12 August 1771 he and his brother HUGH MIDDLETON signed a note for £10 7s. 2d., payable to Samuel Hanson. As the note was not paid when due, Samuel Hanson instituted a suit 4 January 1773 against these brothers " late of Charles County, planters "; and at the trial Peter Griffen came into Court as " pledge for the said HUGH and ISAAC ", and Baker Johnson appeared as their attorney. The Court found for Samuel Hanson, but he agreed to take " common money " and to release the defendants from " the payment of any penalty of interest on principal or costs." [4]

ISAAC SMALLWOOD MIDDLETON was recorded as S. Isaac Middleton in the 1775-1778 census of Port Tobacco, Upper Hundred, Charles County, taken by Samuel Smallwood, constable.[5]

During the Revolution he served as First Lieutenant in Capt. Smallwood's Company, in the 26th Battalion of Charles County Militia, being commissioned 9 May 1778.[6] In the same year he subscribed the Oath of Fidelity.[7]

In 1784 or early in 1785 he and his family settled in Fairfax County, Va., where numerous of his relatives had preceded him. In the 1785 tax list ISAAC MIDDLETON was charged with the ownership of 4 slaves, 2 horses, and 1 cow and a year later with 4 slaves, 1 horse, and 3 cattle. On 16 March 1787 he accounted for his son William (sometimes called William, Jr., to distinguish from an older relative of the same name who lived nearby), who had then reached his sixteenth year. On 24 March 1787 he accounted for both his son William (then 17) and his son Samuel, who then was 16. Since we have been unable to find any mention of this ISAAC SMALLWOOD MIDDLETON in any Virginia or Maryland record after this date, we conclude that he died in Fairfax County, Va., where his children continued to live for several years, and we fix the date of his death as prior to the tax listing of March 1789.

Children of Isaac Smallwood Middleton and His Wife Eleanor—

    i.   WILLIAM MIDDLETON, born between 25 March 1767 and 19 March 1768, Charles Co., Md., became Commissioner of the Revenue for Fairfax Co., Va., by 1803 and served until at least 1808; assumed responsibility as head of his father's family in 1789 by accounting to the tax authorities for his younger brothers as they reached 16 years of age and also for his brother Samuel the year before Samuel became 21.

4 *Charles County Deed Book U-3*: 699.

5 Gaius M. Brumbaugh, *Maryland Records*, vol. i: 303.

6 *Archives of Maryland*, vol. xxi: 72; also Hodge, *Unpublished Records*, vol. i: 40 and vol. ii: 239.

7 *Calendar of Maryland State Papers #5*: Item 24: 16; also Hodge *Unpublished Records*, vol. v: 65.

ii. daughter (?)

6 iii. SAMUEL MIDDLETON, whose line is continued.

iv. SMALLWOOD COGHILL MIDDLETON, born bet. 23 March 1772 and 19 March 1773, Charles County, Md., resided in Fairfax Co., Va., most of the time from 1785 to 1800, signed a recommendation [8] for a Fairfax County miller, dated 4-10-1796; settled in Loudoun Co., Va., in 1801, where he purchased a lot on the outskirts of Leesburg on 5 January 1804 from John Drish and Eleanor,[9] and then mortgaged it 14 October 1805 to William Elliott, of Loudoun Co. CASSANDRA MIDDLETON, wife of the grantor, signed with a mark.[10] He later in life arranged 24 July 1832 for the digging of a grave for his wife, aged 60 years, in the burial section owned by his brother James Middleton in the Congressional Cemetery.[11]

v. ISAAC SMALLWOOD MIDDLETON, born between 20 March 1773 and 19 March 1774 in Charles Co., Md., lived for a while in Fairfax Co., Va., where his oldest brother William Middleton accounted for him in 1790 as living with him and having become 16 years of age; by 1822 was listed in the Washington City Directory as a carpenter, employed at the Navy Yard, and living at the southwest corner of Sixth and G Streets, S.E. His wife, ANNE, died in Washington 29 March 1825, survived by her husband and nine of their children.[12] She was buried two days later in the Congressional Cemetery, where on 1 November 1824 their 5-year-old daughter Elizabeth Jane had also been buried.[13] By 1827 he had become "superintendent of public works at the Navy Yard near Pensacola, Florida."[14] There he and his children lived for many years.

vi. Daughter (?)

7 vii. JAMES MIDDLETON, whose line is continued.

viii. ELECTIUS MIDDLETON, found in the records of Alexandria, Va., and known to have been associated with his brother James in Methodist Church interests in Washington, D. C.[15] His wife was ANN PARSONS, a daughter of James Parsons who had died *ante* 22 July 1799.[16] They are known to have had at least two sons and two daughters.

---

[8] *William and Mary Quarterly*, First Series, vol. 27: 247.

[9] *Loudoun County (Va.) Deed Book* 2-D: 383.

[10] *Ibid.*, 2-f: 429.

[11] "The Washington Parish Burial Ground, 1820-1839: 50", in the DAR Library, Washington, D. C.

[12] *National Intelligencer*, issue of 7 April 1825, noted in *National Genealogical Society Quarterly*, vol. 40: 22.

[13] *Congressional Cemetery Records*, typescript, vol. 1: 17, 19, in the DAR Library, Washington, D. C.

[14] *House of Representatives List of Private Claims, 1834-1842*, vol. ii: 476.

[15] *Columbia Historical Society Publication*, vol. 8: 74-75.

[16] *Alexandria County Deed Book* M: 116-127.

5. HUGH MIDDLETON [son of William and Mary (Coghill) Middleton] was mentioned in the Will of his grandfather WILLIAM MIDDLETON, Sr., and was associated with his brother ISAAC SMALLWOOD MIDDLETON as a defendant in a suit brought by Samuel Hanson, as has been noted. He also removed from Charles Co., Md., to Fairfax County, Va., where he lived for several years. He was there during the later years of the Revolution, as is known from the following item in the records of the February term 1782 of the Fairfax County Court: [1]

> The STATE OF VIRGINIA
> To HUGH MIDDLETON for 4000^w. Hay 5/- £10:0:0

In others words, Hugh Middleton contributed 4,000 pounds of hay for use by the Quartermaster-General in charge of supplies for the Army, and these were appraised as worth 5 shillings for each 100 lbs., or a total of £10.

His name appears on the Personal Property Tax Lists of Fairfax County for the years 1783 and 1784, owing 2 slaves, 4 horses, and 7 cattle in 1783 and 4 slaves, 3 horses, and 4 cattle in 1784. In the latter year he accounted for a son, but did not name him.

HUGH MIDDLETON was plaintiff on a writ of replevin against William Bird 25 November 1786.[2] William Bird was a vestryman, along with General George Washington, of the Pohick Church. A suit that HUGH MIDDLETON had brought against Thomas Wear was dismissed in 1786.[3]

Some time between then and 1790 HUGH MIDDLETON had gone to the Evitts Creek District of Western Maryland.[4] He settled there, in Allegany County, about three miles east of Cumberland. Toward the end of his life, there was patented to him by the State of Maryland, in 1840, a tract of 42 acres called *Addition to Head Spring*.[5]

Child of Hugh and Rachel (———) Middleton:

i.   IGNATIUS MIDDLETON was born 10 December 1772, according to an entry in the Records of St. Johns, Broad Creek Church, but the family name of Rachel, his mother, is not given. He helped to found the Methodist Church in Allegany County, Md., and his son David Middleton helped to found a Methodist Church in Coshocton Co., Ohio.[6] David Middleton married Sarah Lewman. Their daughter

---

1 *Fairfax County Booklet*, item 10 on page 11, Archives, Richmond, Va.

2 *Fairfax County Court Order Book, 1783-1788*: 313.

3 *Ibid.*, 242.

4 *First Census of the United States—Maryland: Heads of Families, 1790*.

5 From records of the Land Office in Annapolis.

6 From letter dated 18 April 1949 from Louis T. Payne, 135 South Grand Avenue, Los Angeles 12, Calif., to John G. Herndon.

Ann Middleton married Thomas Collier. They had a daughter Margaret Ellen Collier who married James Payne. Their son Albert Ceely Payne married Mary Ladusky Hutchins. Their son, Louis T. Payne was born 5 April 1885 in Dayton, Ohio.[7]

Child of Hugh and Lurenna (————) *Middleton:* [8]

    ii.   JOEL MIDDLETON (b on Warrior Mountain, Allegany Co., Md.) m ELIZABETH THORNBURG, and had

        (1) William Middleton of Elk Garden, W. Va.;

        (2) Benjamin Franklin Middleton (b 19 February 1843), m twice, and had issue by each marriage;

        (3) John Middleton, of Cumberland Co., Md.;

        (4) Francis Elizabeth Middleton m Lawrence Dolan;

        (5) Jennie Middleton m Michael C. S. Twigg;

        (6) Emeline Middleton m Jacob Harden of Cumberland; and

        (7) Thomas Middleton, of Spring Gap, Md.

6. SAMUEL MIDDLETON [son of Isaac Smallwood Middleton and his wife Eleanor] was born between 15 April and 11 May 1771, Charles County, Md.; married twice; and died 20 March 1817, Rockville, Maryland.

On the tax list of 24 March 1788, the first prepared in Fairfax County, Va., after SAMUEL MIDDLETON had reached 16 years of age, his brother William accounted for him. After absence in 1789 and 1790 he returned to live with his brother William who again accounted for him 14 April 1791, when he was 19. There is a tradition that when he was 17 he rode on his horse to near Louisville, Ky., and remained there at least a year or two; but there has been found absolutely nothing to support this claim. It seems likely that he has been confused with his son Thomas Jefferson Middleton who did ride out to Kentucky and did settle there.

When the tax list of 11 May 1792 was prepared, SAMUEL MIDDLETON was taxed directly for the first time. In his remaining years in Virginia he gradually added to his "wealth", being taxed in 1793 on his ownership of one slave and five horses. A year later he had another horse, and in 1796 another slave. He was taxed there 4 July 1796 for the last time. A few months later he married ANN O'NEALE, daughter of William and Sarah (Young) O'Neale, of Montgomery County, Md., and seems to have settled there soon thereafter, if not immediately. Some of the O'Neales had lived near the Middletons in Fairfax County a few years earlier. Among these were ANN O'NEALE's uncle Charles O'Neale and his family. It is probable that SAMUEL MIDDLETON first met his future bride at her uncle's home.

---

[7] From letter dated 6 March 1949 from Louis T. Payne to J. G. Herndon.

[8] Hist. of Allegany Co., Md., vol. i: 624-626.

On 23 July 1803 WILLIAM O'NEALE conveyed to SAMUEL MIDDLE-
TON four lots in the town of Rockville.[1] These the latter transferred
20 August 1804 to Jesse Leach.[2] Not only were these lots given to
SAMUEL MIDDLETON—the consideration was purely nominal, five shillings—but at approximately the same time WILLIAM O'NEALE, by a series of transactions, transferred to SAMUEL MIDDLETON and to WILLIAM
O'NEALE, Jr., a substantial number of slaves. As there was a large
family interest in the in the holdings of WILLIAM O'NEALE, it was only
natural that sooner or later there should be instituted a suit in chancery,
which is referred to in the notes on the O'NEALE family which follow.[3]

 ANN (O'NEALE) MIDDLETON was buried 7 July 1807 in the
Churchyard of Prince Georges Episcopal Church, Rockville.[4] She was
the mother of the first five children of SAMUEL MIDDLETON.

He married, secondly, in Montgomery County, Md., 4 May 1809
ANN CULVER [5] who died 6 September 1831.[6] She was the mother of
SAMUEL MIDDLETON's last four children.

At a meeting of the Vestry of Prince Georges Church on a Saturday
in April 1815 the following decisions were reached: [7]

The Vestry then appointed John C. Redman and SAMUEL MIDDLETON Church
Wardens and likewise agree to put about subscriptions immediately for the purpose of
raising a sum of money to erect a new church in the town of Rockville.

On 27 May 1815 SAMUEL MIDDLETON qualified as a Church Warden, a
part of his oath being: [8]

I do swear that I do not hold myself bound in allegiance to the King of Great
Britain and that I will be faithful and bear true allegiance to the State of Maryland.

On 11 May 1816 Redman and Middleton were reappointed Church
Wardens for the ensuing year.[9]

On 17 September 1816 the Montgomery County Court appointed
SAMUEL MIDDLETON guardian to his two sons, THOMAS JEFFERSON
MIDDLETON and BENJAMIN FRANKLIN MIDDLETON, then under 14

---

1 *Montgomery Extract Deed Book M-4*: 342, in the Land Office, Annapolis.

2 *Montgomery County Deed Book L*: 414, in the Court House at Rockville.

3 *Infra* 177-178.

4 Gaius M. Brumbaugh; *Maryland Records*, vol. i.: 571.

5 *Montgomery County Marriage Register*.

6 " Rock Creek Church Records " in DAR Library, Washington, D. C.

7 *Records of Prince Georges Parish, Rock Creek*, Frederick County, 1726-1829: 193. Of course,
after the establishment of Montgomery County, this church was no longer in Frederick County.

8 *Ibid.*, 194 and 260.

9 *Ibid.*, 196.

years of age. He, being in Court, accepted the appointment and gave bond with approved security.[10]

The Court on 5 November 1816 appointed Isaac and Camden Riley to view and report the annual value of the real estate belonging to the children of SAMUEL MIDDLETON which descended to them from their maternal grandfather, WILLIAM O'NEALE, deceased, in right of their mother. Their report, dated 12 March 1817, appraised the property at an annual rental of $100, and listed the following buildings: Frame dwelling, 28' x 16'; log kitchen, 16' x 12'; smoke house, 12' x12'; log quarter, 16' x 16'; log stable, 20' x 14'; log house, 23' x 28' (thatched with fodder); and tenement log house, 18' x 16'.[11]

SAMUEL MIDDLETON died intestate 20 March 1817.[12] On 13 May 1817 letters of administration on his estate were issued to his brother-in-law William Culver, after Samuel's widow, ANN (CULVER) MIDDLETON had renounced appointment as administratrix.[13] The inventory was filed 17 June 1817 and a report of sales totaling $4,383.89 was presented 9 September 1817.[14] The first account was passed 19 January 1819 and the final one 10 December 1822. Of the net estate of $1222.50½, the widow was allowed $407.52 and each of the children who was living at the death of SAMUEL MIDDLETON was allotted $101.88.[15]

Children of Samuel Middleton and His First Wife Ann O'Neale:

8 i. ELIZABETH MIDDLETON whose line is continued.

 ii. WILLIAM O'NEALE MIDDLETON (1799-1820); on his death William Culver was appointed administrator of his estate, but on his death Francis Valdenar was appointed *admin. de bonis non* of Wm. O'N. Middleton, and distributed $123.76 to the step-mother of the deceased and $30.94 to each of the eight other children of his father.

 iii. MATILDA MIDDLETON, b 3 September 1800, d 26 June 1890, m 10 December 1818 ISAAC RILEY, b August 1774, d 5 July 1850, and had issue:

  (1) Amos Riley, lived in California;

  (2) Van Buren Riley, lived in St. Joseph, Mo.;

  (3) Sarah Riley m Edward Viers, lived near Rockville;

  (4) Martha Riley m Samuel Magruder, of Rockville;

  (5) Fanny Riley m Frank Mace; and

  (6) Josephine Riley (b 1841; d 29 July 1933) m John W. Keys, of Rockville.

---

[10] *Orphans Court Minutes, Jan. 1811-Oct. 1816:* 179.

[11] *Montgomery County Orphans Court Book* K: 54.

[12] "Rock Creek Church Records," in DAR Library, Washington, D. C.

[13] *Orphans Court Minutes, 1821-1824:* 261-262.

[14] *Ibid., Liber* K: 424-426, 286-288.

[15] *Ibid., Liber* P: 69.

9 iv. THOMAS JEFFERSON MIDDLETON, whose line is continued.
10 v. BENJAMIN FRANKLIN MIDDLETON, whose line is continued.

Children of Samuel Middleton and His Second Wife Ann Culver:

vi. SAMUEL CALEB MIDDLETON, b 16 March 1810; d 26 September 1828.

vii. HENRY CLAY MIDDLETON, b 17 July 1812; died 1858 or 1859.

viii. REUBEN MIDDLETON, b 27 January 1814, and baptized 7 October 1814 in Rock Creek Church; an attorney, member of the firm of Hughes and Company, lived in Hyattsville, Md.; m in Prince Georges County 22 July 1843 MARY ELLEN HYATT, and had issue:

(1) Nellie Middleton; and

(2) Catherine Hyatt Middleton married 22 May 1866 Lemuel Clark, and lived at Hyattsville, Md.

ix. CAROLINE MIDDLETON, b *ca* 1816, m 13 Feb 1838 BENJAMIN BEALL, and had issue:

(1) Clarence Beall, who died unm., 1920;

(2) Elizabeth Beall m De Ford Webb;

(3) Eugene Reuben Beall.

BENJAMIN BEALL married, secondly, Susan A. ———.

7. JAMES MIDDLETON [son of Isaac S. and Esther Middleton] was born 1 April 1777 in Fairfax County, Va., and died 27 June 1860 at the home of his son Lemuel J. Middleton in Washington, D. C. His family Bible [1] states that his wife was HANNAH JOHNSON (born 20 July 1779, Fauquier County, Va.), daughter of Tunis Johnson, of Fauquier County; but oddly omits the date of their marriage, which was probably solemnized in 1800. Late in her life she was baptized 20 July 1841, when her age was recorded as 63 years, by Rev. K. John Stewart, rector of Rock Creek Episcopal Church, in which church her son Erasmus Johnson Middleton was an active member. She died 31 May 1842, and was buried in Congressional Cemetery, her age then being given as 62 years, 1 month, and 20 days. Her mother had been buried there 23 July 1822; but the cemetery entry does not list her name, merely designating her as " James Middleton's mother in law, aged 90 years ". In the family Bible JAMES MIDDLETON is described as " son of Isaac Middleton, of Maryland, formerly of England." Isaac was " of Maryland " all right, but the phrase " formerly of England " is, of course, incorrect, except as it might be understood to mean that the family was " formerly of England."

---

[1] The records of this distinguished Washington City family are preserved in the DAR Library in Martha A. Benn's 1930 typescript entitled, " A Few Notes on Various Branches of the Middleton Family ", and in the DAR collection of family Bible records.

JAMES MIDDLETON was a house carpenter by trade. He and his brother ELECTIUS MIDDLETON were proprietors of one of the better known carpenter shops in the early days of Washington, D. C., and it seems likely that they were employed in connection with the construction of the White House. JAMES MIDDLETON was a member of the seven-man committee which in 1800 arranged for the renting of pews in St. Andrews Presbyterian Church, the first of that denomination in the emerging Capital City.[1] In an address on " Early Methodism in the District "[2] there was this reference to him and his brother Electius:

On account of the large increase of the congregation the society moved from Greenleaf's Point to another location. The place of worship now chosen by the Methodists, while more commodious than the one they were leaving, was certainly not more elegant. On New Jersey Avenue, south of D Street, there stood, at the beginning of the last century, a building that had served for years as a tobacco house for the Carrolls of Duddington Manor. . . . It had an interesting history. Before it became a Methodist meeting-house, it was used for the same purpose by the Protestant Episcopalians. . . . It served the double purpose of church and school house. . . . After it ceased to be used as a church, the tobacco house became a carpenter's shop conducted by James and Electius Middleton. It stood until 1817, when it was destroyed by fire through an accident occurring while a workman was boiling glue. . . . The first trustees . . . [of the new church] formally dedicated to the worship of God in November 1811 . . . [included] Electius Middleton [and eight others].

JAMES MIDDLETON was listed in the Washington directories of 1822, 1827, 1830, and 1834. In the first of these, his place of business is shown as on the west side of New Jersey Avenue, between K and L Streets. Next it was at the Union at Greenleaf's Wharf. In 1830 he lived with his son Erasmus on 6th Street, S. E., between D and E Streets. Four years later he was shown as a house carpenter on the west side of 12th Street, between E Street and Pennsylvania Avenue.

For a while JAMES MIDDLETON and his wife lived in Loudoun County, Va. They were residents there in 1809 when they conveyed certain real estate to George Coryell, of Alexandria, D. C. [now Va.], but by 1816 they had returned to Washington City.[3]

Children of James and Hannah (Johnson) Middleton:

    i.   NORAH MIDDLETON, b 10 September 1801; confirmed 29 May 1837 by Bishop Wm. Stone, in Rock Creek Episcopal Church, d unm. 7 April 1841.

---

[1] W. B. Bryan, " The Beginnings of the Presbyterian Church in the District of Columbia ", in *Records of the Columbia Historical Society,* vol. 8, pp. 43-66, esp., p. 55.

[2] Rev. Dr. W. M. Ferguson's address, in the same publication, pp. 67-77, esp. pp. 74-75.

[3] *Alexandria County Deed Books* Z: 373 and D-2: 324-327, in Alexandria, Virginia, Courthouse.

11	ii.	ERASMUS JOHNSON MIDDLETON, whose line is continued.
12	iii.	DANIEL WESLEY MIDDLETON, whose line is continued.
13	iv.	LEMUEL JAMES MIDDLETON, whose line is continued.
	v.	HORACE MADISON MIDDLETON, b 27 May 1809, Loudoun County, Va., d unm. 7 May 1838.

8. ELIZABETH MIDDLETON [daughter of Samuel and Ann (O'Neale) Middleton] was born 18 October 1797,[1] Rockville, Md., died 27 June 1876, Washington, D. C., and was buried in Glenwood Cemetery there. She was the second wife of her husband, WILLIAM BIRCKHEAD.[2] They were married 3 March 1814 by the Reverend Samuel Martin, rector of the Rock Creek Episcopal Church.

WILLIAM BIRCKHEAD was born in Ann Arundel County, Md., in 1780. He was a cabinet maker by trade. He married, first, in Montgomery County, Md., 14 March 1811 MARY CULVER who died about a year later. He served from 19 August 1814 to 8 October 1814 as a corporal in Capt. Benjamin Burch's company of District of Columbia militia; was wounded during the battle of Bladensburg; and honorably discharged at Washington. His widow's pension application papers show that he died 5 September 1832 in Washington. Her bounty-land application, designated as M 55-160, Wt. 43031, was presented by her brother Benjamin Franklin Middleton and her brother-in-law Edward Birckhead.

Children of William and Elizabeth (Middleton) Birckhead:

	i.	ELIZA ANN BIRCKHEAD (b 5 February 1815; d August 1887, Washington, D. C.) m GEORGE GORDON, as his second wife, and had issue, 4 sons and 4 daughters, among whose descendants were Judge Peyton Gordon (1870-1946), associate justice of the Supreme Court of the District of Columbia, and Rear Admiral Malcolm Gordon Slarrow, also of Washington.

---

[1] A photostatic copy of the birth records of herself and her children is in the collections of the Genealogical Society of Pennsylvania.

[2] In the File Case in the DAR Library, Continental Hall, Washington, D. C., there is a " Report on the Birckhead Family of Maryland " which shows that Christopher Birckhead and his wife Joan Day had a son Nehemiah; that that Nehemiah Birckhead (d 1720) married first Elizabeth Hope, and had a son Nehemiah Birckhead; that that Nehemiah Birckhead (b 17 August 1683, d 1744) m in 1706 Sarah Hutchins [daughter of Francis and Sarah (Billingsley) Hutchins], whose older sister Margaret married six years later Nehemiah's father as her second husband and his second wife; that Nehemiah and Sarah (Hutchins) Birckhead had a son John Birckhead who married " the sixth day of the 12th month 1745 " Christian Harris, daughter of Joseph and Ann Harris, of Calvert Co.; that John and Christian (Harris) Birckhead had three sons, the eldest of whom was Nehemiah Birckhead born " the 29th of the 10th month called December 1746 "; that that Nehemiah Birckhead who served during the American Revolution as a private in Capt. Richard Chew's Company, Col. John Weems' Battalion, married during or about 1769 Anne Harrison, one of the daughters of William and Mary (Freeland) Harrison, of Calvert County; that Nehemiah and Anne (Harrison) Birckhead had 8 children, the sixth of whom was William Birckhead who married first Mary Culver and secondly Elizabeth Middleton.

ii. WILLIAM NEHEMIAH BIRCKHEAD (b 23 August 1816) m JANE BIRCH, of Staten Island; a printer by trade; settled in California; had a daughter Jennie Birckhead who m ———— Farless.

iii. MARY ELIZABETH BIRCKHEAD (b 27 October 1819; d 14 October 1820).

iv. ANGELINA MATILDA BIRCKHEAD (b 17 December 1822; d unm February 1907).

v. ISABELLA SARAH BIRCKHEAD (also b 17 December 1822; d unm August 1892).

vi. MIDDLETON BIRCKHEAD (b 22 January 1824; d early in 1911, Washington, D. C.) m twice; no issue.

vii. MARY ELIZABETH BIRCKHEAD (b 18 January 1826), m her first cousin SAMUEL CALEB MIDDLETON, son of Thomas Jefferson Middleton.

viii. FRANKLIN MIDDLETON BIRCKHEAD (b 26 August 1828; d unm 25 July 1875, Washington, D. C.).

ix. OLIVER H. BIRCKHEAD (b 12 October 1830; d unm 18 March 1872).

9. THOMAS JEFFERSON MIDDLETON [son of Samuel and Ann (O'Neale) Middleton] was born either 4 October 1803 or 4 December 1804, Rockville, Md., and died 26 February 1885 near Bridgeport, Cedar Run Precinct, Franklin County, Ky. He married in Bourbon County, Ky., 21 February 1827 MARY ANN LEACH (b 20 March 1803 or 22 March 1802, Montgomery County, Md.), daughter of Judge Jesse Leach and his first wife Mary, daughter of Michael and Mary (Willett) Letton.[1]

Children of Thomas Jefferson Middleton and His Wife Mary Ann Leach:

14 i. SAMUEL CALEB MIDDLETON, whose line is continued.

ii. OSCAR MIDDLETON, b 26 September 1830; d in Virginia City, Nevada.

iii. MARY T. MIDDLETON, b 22 May 1832, m ———— FINNEY; born, lived, and died in Kentucky.

iv. JESSE RIGGS MIDDLETON, b 27 June 1834, served under Genl. John C. Breckinridge, and was killed in action during the battle of Murphreesboro, Tenn., 2 January 1863.

v. REUBEN FRANKLIN MIDDLETON, b 27 March 1836, a Baptist minister.

vi. ANN ELIZA MIDDLETON, b 29 August 1844; d 8 March 1869; m JOHN SANDERS, and had issue.

---

[1] For a detailed account of the life and family of THOMAS JEFFERSON MIDDLETON see " Thomas Jefferson Middleton, of Maryland and Kentucky: Reminiscences and Two Letters ", published in *The Register of the Kentucky Historical Society*, vol. 50: pp. 340-346. In that account there are two slight errors which are here called to the reader's attention. The last word in the first footnote should have been *any*, not *many*, and in footnote #21 *Adam* Riley should have been *Isaac* Riley.

10. BENJAMIN FRANKLIN MIDDLETON [son of Samuel and Ann (O'Neale) Middleton] was born in 1807. He married 8 December 1834 ELIZABETH CONNELLY, whose death occurred shortly before 27 January 1853 when she was buried in Congressional Cemetery. At the time of his marriage he was established as a merchant whose place of business was on the south side of Pennsylvania Avenue, Washington, D. C., between 4½ and 6th Streets, N. W. Later he was in business there with his brother-in-law BENJAMIN BEALL, transacting business as "Middleton and Beall", wholesale and retail grocers. In addition to the children named below, he and his wife had three others whose burials (but not their given names) are noted in the Records of the Congressional Cemetery under dates of 2 July 1847, 1 July 1848, and 9 November 1859. BENJAMIN FRANKLIN MIDDLETON's Will [1] was probated 21 February 1863.

Children of Benjamin Franklin Middleton and His Wife Elizabeth Connelly:

   i.   ALPHEUS MIDDLETON, formed a partnership with Horatio Browning and transacted business as "Browning and Middleton"; married JENNIE DUVALL, daughter of Washington Duvall. Alpheus Middleton was buried in Oak Hill Cemetery, Georgetown, D. C.

   ii.   MARIAN MIDDLETON m JOHN HYATT, and had:
       (1) Helen Hyatt, m ——— McCeney, and had Houston McCeney.
       (2) Belle Hyatt; and
       (3) Houston Hyatt.

   iii.   HELEN MIDDLETON m J. BUCHANAN HOUSTON, president of the Pacific Mail Company.

   iv.   JESSE MIDDLETON, d unm.

11. ERASMUS JOHNSON MIDDLETON [son of James and Hannah (Johnson) Middleton] was born 28 July 1803, Washington, D. C., and died there 9 November 1882. His first wife, SOPHIA WESTON HOWARD (b 16 November 1808; d 23 June 1834), daughter of Thomas and Ann Howard, and he were married by the Reverend Mr. Wilson, a Methodist minister, 27 April 1826. He and his second wife, Mrs. ELLEN (ROSS) NOBLE, were married 17 April 1842 by Rev. W. A. Harris, rector of Rock Creek Church. She was a daughter of Richard Ross, of Washington.

ERASMUS J. MIDDLETON was clerk of the Circuit Court, with offices in City Hall, Washington, as early as 1853 and probably as early as 1834. The Washington City Directory for 1863 says that he was clerk of the District Court. The next year he is " deputy clerk, Supreme Court of

---

[1] Montgomery County, Md., Will Book JWS-1: 133, in which Alpheus Middleton, John Hyatt, and J. Buchanan Houston were named executors.

the D. C.". In later years he was designated either as clerk or assistant clerk of that court. His home was the beautiful estate called " Sidney ", which after his death was sold to the Roman Catholic Church which established on it what is now the Catholic University of America.

In the History of the Rock Creek Episcopal Church [1] the following is one of the many references to the Middletons:

In 1870 it was decided to use the unproductive ground for a larger churchyard, a charter was taken out and the result may be seen. Dr. Buck [Rev. Charles E. Buck, the rector] was most ably assisted in this undertaking by Mr. ERASMUS J. MIDDLE-TON, Jr., in fact he often said it could never have been accomplished without Mr. Middleton. . . . Mr. Middleton's grandfather, Mr. Richard Ross, was a vestryman about 1830, his uncle Mr. Richard L. Ross about 1850, his father Mr. ERASMUS J. MID-DLETON many years, and he himself was faithful vestryman, Sunday School Superintendent and teacher.

The MIDDLETON window [was] given by the Sunday School and Mr. Middleton's mother.

The MIDDLETONS owned "Sydney" now the Roman Catholic University.

Children of Erasmus Johnson Middleton and His First Wife Sophia Weston Howard:

   i.   JAMES HOWARD MIDDLETON, b 20 June 1827, d 8 June 1848, Saltillo, Mexico.

   ii.   MARY VIRGINIA MIDDLETON, b 22 February 1829.

   iii.   THOMAS HOWARD MIDDLETON, b 8 March 1831, buried in Congressional Cemetery, in the burial section of his grandfather James Middleton, 9 July 1832.

   iv.   SOPHIA WESTON MIDDLETON, b 21 April 1833, d 2 August 1833, and buried the next day in the above-mentioned ground.

Children of Erasmus Johnson Middleton and His Second Wife Ellen Ross:

   v.   ERASMUS JOHNSON MIDDLETON, Jr., b 29 November 1844; d 17 February 1881.

   vi.   RICHARD ROSS MIDDLETON, b 19 March 1846; d 18 February 1849.

   vii.   ELIZABETH MIDDLETON, b 8 January 1848; d 16 November 1848.

   viii.   ELLEN MIDDLETON, b 4 November 1849; d 13 July 1850.

12. DANIEL WESLEY MIDDLETON [son of James and Hannah (Johnson) Middleton] was born 1 May 1805, in Washington, D. C., and died there 28 April 1880. His funeral service was held in the Chamber of the Supreme Court of the United States, at the request of that Court on whose staff he had served 58 years, the last 33 as its clerk. When he died, he was said to have had a personal acquaintance with more of the great lawyers of the United States than any person then living. It is un-

---

[1] Copied from "Rock Creek Church Records", typescript, in "Genealogical Records Committee DC DAR; vol. 16", DAR Library, Washington, D. C.

fortunate for us that in none of the tributes paid him [1] is there any mention of his family. How many children he had we do not know, nor the date of the death of his wife. He married in Washington 31 May 1836 HENRIETTA VAN DYKE. His home was at 568 New Jersey Avenue, N. W. He was a vestryman of Trinity Episcopal Church for many years.

Among his children were:

i. HORACE P. MIDDLETON, a physician who during 1865 was attached to the Medical Headquarters of the Army in Washington; and

ii. DANIEL WESLEY MIDDLETON, Jr., who in 1865 was a clerk with Riggs and Co., and who in 1869 and 1870 was receiving teller with that banking firm; and who the following year established the firm of Middleton and Co., bankers and brokers, 601 Fifteenth Street, N. W., his partner being his cousin Samuel Eliot Middleton.

13. LEMUEL JAMES MIDDLETON [son of James and Hannah (Johnson) Middleton] was born 8 April 1807, Washington, D. C., and died there 12 June 1875. In 1834 and again in 1853 he was a clerk in the Post Office Department; but in 1846 he was a grocer with his store at 9th and Pennsylvania Avenue. During the Civil War he was an ice dealer with place of business at 303 F Street. In 1865 he formed a partnership with William M. Russell. They soon changed the name of their business to "Washington and Georgetown Ice Company", and located at Tenth Street Wharf. He married 16 September 1829 CATHERINE MARY ELIOT (b 24 October 1807; d 16 December 1888).

Children of Lemuel James Middleton and His Wife Catherine Mary Eliot:

i. ELIZABETH GREENLEAF MIDDLETON, b 6 January 1831; d 19 November 1832.

ii. JOHNSON VAN DYKE MIDDLETON, (b 15 December 1834; d 29 January 1907), appointed assistant surgeon, U. S. A., 1861, was assigned to the Office of the Medical Director by 1863, and retired as Deputy Surgeon General; m 1st 8 March 1859 HELEN ELIZABETH BURR (b June 1833; d 16 November 1863); m secondly 13 June 1865 MARGARET HAINES THOMPSON (d March 1910); no issue.

iii. LEMUEL JAMES MIDDLETON, Jr., b 1 December 1836; d 27 March 1838.

iv. CATHERINE MARY MIDDLETON (b 23 April 1839; d 1 November 1922) married 24 June 1858 Capt. ALEXANDER HENDERSON, U. S. N., who died 12 January 1901. He had purchased "Woodley" from his brother-in-law Frank Eliot Middleton. The Hendersons had five children.

---

[1] These were collected and published. Copies are in The Historical Society of Pennsylvania and The Library of The U. S. Supreme Court.

v. SAMUEL ELIOT MIDDLETON (b 7 July 1841; d 13 March 1903, St. Paul, Minnesota) m 8 August 1861 SOPHIA WASHINGTON (b 20 May 1839; d 11 August 1872), daughter of Richard Conway Washington and his wife Sophia May Roberts, and had issue, a son, Richard Washington Middleton, b 2 September 1862. Samuel Eliot Middleton was employed as a clerk in the Treasury Department in 1864 and 1865; by 1868 he had become cashier of the Treasury; and by 1870 he had formed a partnership with his cousin D. Wesley Middleton, Jr., under the name Middleton and Company, and located at 601 Fifteenth Street, N. W.

vi. HANNAH JOHNSON MIDDLETON (b 7 October 1843; d 6 January 1923) m 3 October 1865 Capt. HENRY L. HOWISON, U. S. N., who retired 10 October 1899 as commander-in-chief, South Atlantic Fleet, having been commissioned Rear Admiral 30 September 1898. He d.s.p., 31 December 1914. For the details of his distinguished career, see *Who Was Who*, vol. i: 597.

15 vii. FRANK ELIOT MIDDLETON, whose line is continued.

viii. NORA MIDDLETON (b 10 February 1848; d 21 May 1875) m 16 October 1872 Dr. AUGUSTUS A. DeLOFFRE, U. S. A. (d 4 September 1899).

16 ix. WILLIAM ELIOT MIDDLETON, whose line is continued.

14. SAMUEL CALEB MIDDLETON [son of Thomas J. and Mary Ann (Leach) Middleton] was born 28 June 1828 near Midway, Ky., and died 13 April 1892, Washington, D. C., and buried in Glenwood Cemetery, Washington. On 15 April 1855 he married in Washington, D. C., his first cousin MARY ELIZABETH BIRCKHEAD (b 18 January 1826, that city; d there 1 August 1913). They were early members of the Methodist Chapel on M Street, between 9th and 10th, which in 1869 became the Mt. Vernon Place Methodist Church. There their children were baptized in their infancy. After coming to Washington, Mr. Middleton was long employed by William I. Mitchell, whose carpet business was established at 813 Market Place, just off Pennsylvania Avenue. From 1870 until their deaths, Mr. and Mrs. Middleton lived at 948 L Street, N. W.

Children of Samuel Caleb Middleton and His Wife Mary Elizabeth Birckhead:

i. HENRY OSCAR MIDDLETON (b 26 May 1856; d 8 June 1925) m STELLA TOWNSEND (living 1953, Los Angeles), and had issue, a daughter Edith who m Henry Boesche. They have no issue.

ii. MARY ISABEL MIDDLETON (b 11 October 1859; d 21 March 1936, Boston, Mass.) m ca. 1883 WILLIAM H. BUTLER, as his second wife. She had no issue. By his first wife he left a daughter May who married Fred Behrens. They also died without issue.

iii.   JEFFERSON MIDDLETON (b 2 April 1862, Washington, D. C.; d 3 April 1953, Suburban Hospital, Bethesda, Md., his residence being at the home of his son, Frederic A. Middleton, 4717 Ellicott Street, Washington, D. C., N. W.), served in the Geological Survey and Bureau of Mines from 1884 until his retirement in 1932; was Grand Chancellor of the Knights of Pythias, of the District of Columbia in 1906; member of the Association of the Oldest Inhabitants of the District of Columbia and of the Sons of the American Revolution; author of certain Government publications on ceramics; was married 31 October 1888 by the Rev. Dr. William Alvin Bartlett, pastor of the New York Avenue Presbyterian Church, to EVA BELLE CAULDWELL (b 19 May 1867, Washington, D. C.; d 29 November 1930, Ardmore, Pa.), daughter of Andrew and Mary Sutliff (McGay) Cauldwell, of Washington, D. C., and had issue:

    (a) George Elmer Middleton (b 12 January 1890, Washington, D. C.) m in Chicago, Ill., 19 August 1915 Esther Anne Engelhorn, and has issue.

    (b) Grace Cordelia Middleton (b 15 February 1893, Washington, D. C.) m in Washington, D. C., 7 April 1915 John Goodwin Herndon, and has issue.

    (c) Isabel Middleton (b 20 August 1896, Washington, D. C.) m there 8 December 1918 Felix Muskett Morley, and has issue.

    (d) Frederic Andrew Middleton (b 21 March 1903, Washington, D. C.) m there 14 April 1933 Helen Splain Kelley, and has issue.

iv.   ROSE FLORENCE MIDDLETON (b 2 April 1862, twin of Jefferson Middleton) died 10 September 1863. She and her twin brother were buried in graves in the same family plot in Glenwood Cemetery, Washington, D. C., nearly ninety years apart.

15. FRANK ELIOT MIDDLETON [son of Lemuel James Middleton and his wife Catherine Mary Eliot] was born 10 August 1845, and died 28 February 1923. He married 6 September 1870 ELLA KING CLARK (b 9 March 1853), daughter of John F. Clark, of Maryland. Like his brothers before him, he began his career with a clerkship during the Civil War. By 1869, however, he was " on his way up " with the First National Bank of Washington. During the next two years he was receiving teller there. His advancement continued and his financial position likewise.

On 25 October 1877 he purchased " Woodley." Concerning " Woodley " the following was written by Wm. Bogardus Bryan, in his *A History of the National Capital:* [1]

[By 1794 Mr. Forrest] sold to his brother-in-law Philip Barton Key 250 acres of the Rosedale tract which Mr. Key named Woodley. Mr. Key, who practised law in the

---

[1] *Opus cit.* (1914), pp. 413-414.

District up to the year 1806, when he transferred his business in the District to his nephew Francis Scott Key, built a house on the south side of Woodley Road, still standing, and between 30th and 31st streets, where he lived, except during the summer, until his death in the year 1817.

Francis Scott Key's name is etched on a window pane in its front hall. Presidents Van Buren, Tyler, Buchanan, and Cleveland spent certain summers during their terms as our Chief Executive in residence at "Woodley." Colonel Edward M. House, as President Wilson's personal representative, held pre-war conferences there with foreign diplomats. President Polk's distinguished Secretary of the Treasury, Robert J. Walker, owned "Woodley", but sold it in 1865 to W. S. Huntington, as trustee. After 12 years the Huntingtons sold it to FRANK ELIOT MIDDLETON; and he sold it, 17 years later, to his brother-in-law Alexander Henderson, who then held the rank of commodore in the U. S. Navy. In 1929 Secretary of State Henry L. Stimson purchased it.

Children of Frank Eliot Middleton and His Wife Ella King Clark:

    i.   FRANK ELIOT MIDDLETON, Jr. (b 13 November 1877) m 2 June 1913 Mrs. GERTRUDE ALDER NEWMAN; issue, one daughter.

    ii.   SOPHIE BELLE MIDDLETON (b 27 August 1879), lived at 3511 Lowell Street, N. W., Washington, D. C., in 1935.

    iii.   JOHN CLARK MIDDLETON (b 5 October 1883) m 5 October 1909 MARGARET COYNE; issue, two daughters.

16. WILLIAM ELIOT MIDDLETON [son of Lemuel James Middleton and his wife Mary Catherine Eliot] was born 23 May 1851, and died 12 June 1912. He married 15 November 1877 ANNA WHITWELL (d 7 January 1926), and had issue:

    i.   WILLIAM WHITWELL MIDDLETON (b 27 January 1881) m 12 June 1906 KATE MUNSON, of Virginia.

    ii.   HARRY MIDDLETON (b 2 October 1882) m LOUISE LAMB.

    iii.   NEWTON MIDDLETON (b January 1885) m 12 October 1909 FLORENCE SHARPE.

    iv.   FREDERICK ELIOT MIDDLETON (b 27 July 1892) m 29 January 1916 Mrs. REBECCA SIMMS, of Baltimore. He was, according to one contributor of Middleton data, president in 1935 of the Washington D. C. Real Estate Board; but another gave the name of that official as Frank E. Middleton.

HUGH TEARES OF MARYLAND

Notes on Hugh Teares, of Charles County, Maryland

The first reference to HUGH TEARES which we have found in the Charles County records recites that he, as administrator of the estate of Nicholas Skidmore, of Charles County, deceased, furnished bond for £60, dated 26 January 1694/5, with Henry Hawkins as his surety.[1]

On 2 September 1699 a tract called *Our Lordship's Favour*, supposed to contain 1,000 acres, was surveyed for him, " Beginning at a Bounded Red Oak and Corner Tree of Notley Rosier's Land ", but at a later date its possessors were listed as Joseph Lancaster, 603 acres; Samuel Hawkins, 250 acres; James Keech, 250 acres; and Robert Brent, 33 acres.[2] The poor job of estimating the acreage or of surveying it caused an entry to be made in the record, reading, " 136 acres more than the survey." A resurvey was ordered. The patent to *Our Lordship's Favour* was issued, however, to Major Boarman who deeded this tract to HUGH TEARES.[3]

Within five months of the original survey HUGH TEARES had died. The following is a rather full abstract of his Will[4] which was dated 23 January 1699/1700 and proved in Court 20 February 1699/1700 by three of the witnesses to his Will, *viz.*, Thomas Smoot, William Deere, and Eliz*. Dutton:

In the Name of God Amen. I HUGH TEARES of " Nangemy ", Charles County, Province of Maryland, Gent., being of perfect health of body and mind do hereby revoke all former Wills and Testaments by me heretofore made and declare this to be my last Will and Testament.

I bequeath my body to the earth to be decently interred and my soul to Almighty God, hoping for a Joyfull Resurrection in and through the merits of his dear Son Christ my Redeemer.

I give and bequeath to my dearly beloved wife ELINOR TEARES one moiety at *Sinah*, to her and her heirs forever;

I give the other moiety to my dear child ELIZ^A. TEARES and to her heirs forever; but if the aforesaid ELINOR TEARES should dye without issue to her body, the whole to descend to ELIZABETH TEARES and to her heirs forever. If ELIZ^A. TEARES shall dye without issue, then the whole shall descend to ELINOR TEARES aforesaid; but if both ELINOR and ELIZ^A. TEARES shall dye without issue, I will and bequeath 300 acres to ANN BAYNE, Jr., and EBSWORTH BAYNE, another 300 acres to HENRY and RUTH HAWKINS, another 300 acres to ELLENOR and ELIZABETH STONE, and 100 acres to CHARLES and EDWARD PHILPOT, Jr.

---

1 *Testamentary Proceedings* #15-C: 167.

2 *Charles County Rent Roll* #1: 40.

3 *Charles County Deed Book* M-2: 309.

4 *Maryland Will Book* #11: 204-208.

I further give and bequeath to ELIZ^A. TEARES aforesaid all my DECEASED WIFE's wearing apparel and rings, together with the bed I usually lay upon when at home, with one pair of HOLLAND sheets and one diaper tablecloth and half a dozen diaper napkins, and a pair of HOLLAND sheets which I have with Mr. [HENRY] HAWKINS.

And my further will and desire is that ELIZABETH TEARES, aforesaid, do live with her Aunt ELIZ^A. HAWKINS, and whatever legacies I have bequeathed to her be delivered unto the aforesaid ELIZ^A. HAWKINS for the use of my said daughter ELIZABETH TEARES: one mare known by EDWARD PHILPOT that I formerly gave unto her to be delivered to the aforesaid Aunt ELIZABETH HAWKINS, for the use of ELIZ^A. TEARES, and also one man servant, having at least five years to serve and being in perfect health of body and under twenty-five years of age, to be delivered to ELIZ^A. TEARES when she shall arrive at the age of Sixteen years or at the date of her marriage, by my wife ELINOR TEARES, my executrix.

I name my friends Capt. JOHN BAYNE, Major JAMES SMALLWOOD, and Mr. JOHN HAWKINS as assistants to my executrix.

In the records of the Prerogative Court of Maryland three entries concern HUGH TEARES. The first, dated 3 May 1702, reads as follows:[5]

The Will of HUGH TEARES of Charles County, naming ELLINOR TEARES exec. was proved by three persons.

The second, dated 12 May 1702, recites that JNO. and ELLINOR BEALE, administrators of HUGH TEARES, furnished bond, dated 8 December 1701, in the sum of £378, with W. STONE as their surety.[6] The third, dated 7 July 1702, states that on 27 February 1699 [i.e., 1699/1700] the estate of HUGH TEARES was appraised at £189 8s. 11d., by JOHN CAGE and Jos. FENDALL.[7]

Elsewhere [8] it is also noted:

That the Inventory of Mr. HUGH TEARES, late of Charles County, was appraised 23 February 1699 for 189/7/11 but that JOHN CAGE one of the appraisers died before signing [it].

The fact that HUGH TEARES was styled " Mr." and " Gentleman " shows his standing in the Charles County neighborhood where he lived; but what office, if any, he held has not been ascertained.

He is known to have married twice. His first wife was RUTH HOLLAND whose sister ELIZABETH was the second wife of HENRY HAWKINS. The mention of " HOLLAND sheets which I have with Mr. HAWKINS " in the Will of HUGH TEARES is interesting and important. They were not Dutch sheets, but were family linen. The father of RUTH and

---

[5] *Testamentary Proceedings* 19 A: 75.

[6] *Ibid.*, 78.

[7] *Ibid.*, 85.

[8] *Inventories and Account Book* #21: 262.

ELIZABETH HOLLAND was probably named HENRY HOLLAND, and he may have been, as one student of family records claimed,[10] a grandson of PHILEMON HOLLAND (1552-1637) who was called " translator-general in his age."

NOTES ON ELLINOR BAYNE, OF CHARLES COUNTY, MARYLAND

How long HUGH TEARES remained a widower we do not know, but concerning his second wife we have a great deal of information. She was born about 1667, named ELLINOR BAYNE,[11] youngest daughter of WALTER BEANE (BAYNE) who died testate in 1670 and his wife ELLINOR BAYNE who died testate in 1701. When 17 years of age she was married, in 1684, to JOHN STONE, a son of Governor WILLIAM STONE. JOHN STONE died about July 1698, testate, and provided in his Will that his wife ELLINOR should have administration on that part of his estate which would pass to her and her children. These were ELLINOR, ELIZABETH, and WALTER STONE. She was married to HUGH TEARES just about one month when he died in the early part of 1699/1700. Somewhat before 8 December 1701 she had been married to her third husband, JOHN BEALE, for on that date they were designated by the Charles County Court as administrators of HUGH TEARES' estate. She and JOHN BEALE had one son RICHARD BEALE, born in 1705. She died *ante* 1717. In an Act for the Relief of JOHN BEALE, Gentleman, and RICHARD BEALE, a minor, introduced in the Maryland Assembly in 1717 some details of her family relationships are recorded.[12]

NOTES ON ELIZABETH (HOLLAND) [WINE] HAWKINS, OF CHARLES COUNTY, MARYLAND

Let us now return to consider further data concerning blood relatives of ELIZABETH (TEARES) MIDDLETON, the first wife of WILLIAM MIDDLETON. Her mother, for example, is identified in the following recital: [13]

Know all men by these presents that I Henry Wine of Pitchley in ye County of Northamptonshire doe by these presents exchange a parcell of land left to me by my father

---

[10] Hugh C. Middleton; notes in Genealogical File, Genealogical Society of Pennsylvania.

[11] See especially *Provincial Judgments* #21: 516; but also the Wills of Walter Beane, Elinor Bayne, and John Stone in *Maryland Wills*, vol. i: 386, vol. xi: 298, and vol. vi: 153; as well as deeds from " Richard Beale, son of John Beale by Eleanor Bean (Bayne), daughter of Walter Bean (Bayne) " to John Diggs and from Richard Beale, planter, of Essex County, Va., to John Ebernathy, Innkeeper, of a part of *His Lordship's Favour* recorded in *Chas. Co. Deed Book* L-2: 117 and 380. William Middleton was a witness to each of these two Deeds, dated 19 September 1723 and 14 August 1727, respectively.

[12] *Archives of Maryland*, vol. xxxviii: 256.

[13] *Charles County Deed Book* P-1: 78.

Francis Wine in Maryland in Wiccocomico River near ye head there of the quantity of ninety acres of ground commonly called by ye name of *Burton* something below William Marshalls with my mother Mistress Elizabeth Hawkins wch [she] is free to dispose of at her own pleasure and I am content, [and I] do by these presents forever quit any title or claime whatsoever to ye above menconed ninety Acres of Land commonly called *Burton*. In witness whereof I have hereunto set my hand and seale this fifth day of October 1688 in ye fourth yeare of ye Reign of our Sovereign Lord James ye Second of England Scotland France & Ireland King defender of ye faith etc.
Witness
  Nicholas Colborne
  Priscillya Bradley

/s/ HENRY WINE (Seal)

The above Mrs. Elizabeth Hawkins came here and freely acknowledged in open Court all her right title and interest in ye above menconed land [and conveyed it] unto her sister Ruth Tears wife of Hugh Tears and to ye heirs of her [Ruth's] body lawfully begotten.

This June Court Annoq Domi 1689 /s/ Rd: Boughton Clerke

ELIZABETH (TEARES) MIDDLETON is called *kinswoman* in the Will of her aunt, Mrs. ELIZABETH (HOLLAND) [WINE] HAWKINS, of which the following is a full abstract:

In the Name of God Amen: I, ELIZABETH HAWKINS, of Charles County, Maryland, widow, being sick and weak of body but of sound memory, do make this my last Will.

Imprimis To my three grandchildren, Francis Wine, Elizabeth Wine, and Mary Wine, son and daughters of Henry Wine, late of the Kingdom of Great Britain, deceased: £10 sterling in lieu of all claims any of them may have.

Item To my daughter Elizabeth Lewis, wife of ———— Lewis, of Great Britain aforesaid: 5 shillings.

Item To my granddaughter Elizabeth Keech: one set of calico curtains and counterpane, three cane chairs, one table, one side saddle, one cow and calf, and one breeding mare, being in Zachia [Manor], with all her future increase; and my negress Elly and her increase, except that her first female child is to go to my granddaughter Martha Keech.

Item To my granddaughter Martha Keech: One featherbed, the next to the best that I commonly lie upon, and its furniture; three cane chairs, one table, two pair of sheets, one pair of pillow cases, half a dozen napkins, one table cloth, one cow and calf, a breeding mare being in Zachia [Manor] with all her increase, and my negro Peter. If either granddaughter die before arriving at the age of sixteen years or without issue, the negroes with their increase are to return to my son Henry Holland Hawkins.

Item To my grandson Henry Holland Hawkins, son of Henry Holland Hawkins aforesaid: my negro Jack, the featherbed I commonly lie on with its furniture, one table, one looking glass, one diaper tablecloth, and seven diaper napkins.

Item To my granddaughter Elizabeth Hawkins: 500 acres, called *Jamaica*, lying in Prince Georges County, also a featherbed and furniture, table cloth, and seven diaper napkins, and my negress Pegg.

Item To my grandson John Hawkins: my negro Jimmy.

Item To Richard Tubman, son of the Reverend Richard Tubman, decreased: one servant lad not under five years to serve.

Item To my kinswoman Elizabeth Middleton, wife of William Middleton: I give and bequeathe all the best of my wearing apparel.

Item To my son Henry Holland Hawkins: my negro Congo and my negress Betty with all her future increase, for life; then afterwards to be equally divided amongst his children. To him I give also the remaining part of my estate which, after his death, is to be divided equally amongst his children. But if my son die before any of his children arrive at the age of 21 years, then all the estate bequeathed to him is to be put and remain in the hands of Michael and John Martin or the survivor of them for the use of my said son's children, when they arrive at age or marry.

Lastly I appoint my son Henry Holland Hawkins to be my whole and sole executor.

In witness whereof I have hereunto set my hand and seal 12 June 1716.

Signed, sealed, published, and delivered

in presence of

Matthew Stone   her

William Howard   ELIZABETH (x) HAWKINS (seal)

                                 mark

On 14 June 1717 the above Will was proved in common form by the oath of Matthew Stone, one of the witnesses, before A. Contee, D.C.

NOTES ON FRANCIS WYNE, OF CHARLES COUNTY, MARYLAND

FRANCIS WYNE is first mentioned in the Maryland records in the following items in *Land Office Patent Series* Liber 4: 584 as follows:

5th October   WILLIAM MARSHALL Enters rights as followeth Vizt. for Nicholas
[1660]   Grosse his transportation into this province in Anno 1651 and one other right by assignment from Humphrey Warren, and one other right by assignment from WALTER BEANE which assignments are as followeth:

I do assign Mary Bennett to serve WILLIAM MARSHALL from the tenth day of December 1660 the full and just term of seven years according to the Conditions of the Indenture. Witness my hand this 20th Day of february 1660.

Wittness FRANCIS WYNE   /s/ HUMPHREY WARREN

I WALTER BEANE do assign and sett over my whole right Title and Interest of my Servant FRANCIS WYNE unto WILLIAM MARSHALL or his assigns. Witness my hand 29th September 1660.

Testes:

John Hatch   WALTER BEANE /his mark

James Walker

Mem.^m No warrant hath as yet been issued for the above rights.

Other entries relating to FRANCIS WYNE are found in Charles County Court Procedings in *Archives of Maryland,* vol. liii:

He was named as defendant in a suit at a court held 25 September 1661; witness on a power of attorney, dated 8 July 1662, from THOMAS STONE to EDMUND LINDSEY; called a " cooper " in an apprenticeship contract with THOMAS MARIS,

3 October 1662; a " cooper " also in assignment of a patent from WILLIAM COD-
WELL, 12 May 1663. In a deposition, apparently dated 30 April 1664, but at latest
5 April 1665, he gave his age as " thirty years or thereabouts." On 25 April 1665
FRANCIS WINE " Cooper " sells to HENRY HAWKINS for 10,000 pounds of
tobacco and caske 700 acres on the north side of the Potomac River and the west of
the main fresh of the Wicomoco.

In those Proceedings as reported in *Archives of Maryland,* vol. lx,
FRANCIS WYNE is mentioned in connection with two transactions:

The deed from ELIZA. EMANSON to FRANCIS WYNE, dated 16 June 1671 was
printed, and at a Court held 8 August 1671

> ELIZA. EMANSON came & acknowledged to FRANCIS WINE a parcell of land
> *Glovers poynt* in Nangemy Creeke as by Convey: hereafter recorded may appeare.

At a Court 10 September 1672

> FRANCIS WYNE entreth this ensuing marke of a mare given to his daughter,
> vizt, one flower delence on *his* (sic) buttock.

He seems to have continued to prosper, for on 2 March 1679/80 this
entry was made in *Land Office Patent Liber WC#2:* 100-101:

> Came FRANCIS WYNE of Charles County and prod. rights to Three hundred
> acres of Land for transporting George Goodman Willm Harbinger Francis Herman
> Elizabeth Ealor and Mary Gubins into this province to inhabit
> Warr^t. then granted to FRANCIS WYNE of Charles County for three hundred
> and fifty acres of land three hundred acres thereof are as aforegoing—fifty acres more
> due for transporting Jn°. Curtis into this province to inhabit.

FRANCIS WYNE was twice married. By his first wife whose name is
not of record he had a son JOHN WYNE, named in his Will. Sometime
before 1672 FRANCIS married ELIZABETH HOLLAND, for on 10 September 1672 he caused to be entered the mark on the mare he had given to
his daughter. She was mentioned in his Will and in her Mother's Will.
In the latter she was designated as ELIZABETH LEWIS of Great Britain.

When WILLIAM MARSHALL made his Will 22 April 1673, he designated FRANCIS WYNE, whom he called *brother,* one of his executors.
When FRANCIS WYNE made his Will 14 November 1681, he owned two
properties in Northamptonshire which he devised equally to his son
HENRY WYNE, then of London, and his daughter ELIZABETH; and nine
tracts in Charles County, Maryland, totaling 1134 acres, which he left
to his son JOHN WYNE. To ELIZABETH (HOLLAND) WYNE was left
the residuary estate, real and personal, and she was named executrix.
FRANCIS WYNE's Will was proved 6 March 1682 and recorded in *Maryland Will Book,* vol. ii: 173.

Notes on Henry Hawkins, of Charles County, Maryland

Henry Hawkins, of Charles County, in his Will dated 18 October 1698 and proved 12 May 1699, recorded in *Maryland Will Book 6*: 310, named his wife Elizabeth (who was the widow of Francis Wyne) and his six children. Of these two were by his first wife. They were Henry Hawkins and Ellinor (Hawkins) Tubman. The others were children of his second wife and were John Hawkins, Henry Holland Hawkins (so named to distinguish him from his half brothers, Henry Hawkins and Henry Wine), Ruth Hawkins and Mary Hawkins. Henry Holland Hawkins became " whole and sole executor " under his mother's Will. Ruth Hawkins became the first wife of James Keech, Gent., and had daughters named Martha and Elizabeth Keech, mentioned in the Will of their grandmother Elizabeth Hawkins already cited.

Henry and Eleanor Hawkins were early settlers. They and their son John were in Charles County by 25 April 1665, when Henry Hawkins purchased 700 acres there, as recorded in *Charles County Deed Book B-1*: 231-232.

Notes on the Keech Family of Charles County, Maryland

John Courts, of Charles County, Maryland, died testate between 1697 and 1702, and named in his Will his daughter Elizabeth, wife of James Keech.

Capt. James Keech, of St. Marys County, died testate in 1708, and named in his Will his children, James, John, Courts, and Margaret Keech, and his wife Elizabeth Keech. The last named died testate between 1718 ad 1730, and named in her Will her son Courts Keech.

With the sons James and John Keech we are directly concerned. James married, as his first wife, Ruth Hawkins, daughter of Henry Hawkins and Elizabeth Holland, and by her had issue, two daughters Martha and Elizabeth Keech, named in the Will of their grandmother already cited. The second wife of James Keech was Mary Gardiner. John Keech was the first husband of Elizabeth Teares whose second husband was William Middleton.

As an illustration of the confusion one may encounter in examining old records we cite these entries made in *Testamentary Proceedings*, vol. xxii: 98, 136, the first two at the Court of April 1712 and the last at the Court of July 1712:

At the request of Mrs. ELIZA. KEECH, executrix of JAMES KEECH, deceased, late of St. Mary's County, ordered that no further citation issue against her until further order. . . .

Commission issued to Mr. Joseph Manning, Deputy Commissary of Charles County, to pass the account of WILLIAM MIDDLETON *et ux.*, admrs of JOHN KEECH, decd., on their petition for the same.

The proceedings returned from Charles Co., by Mr. Joseph Manning Deputy Commissary are as follows, *viz*—

the account of WILLIAM MIDDLETON and ELIZ^A. his wife, administrators of JOHN KEECH, decd.

Other items of interest in the settlement of the estate of JOHN KEECH, first husband of ELIZABETH TEARES, are as follows:

At a Court held 10 July 1710 one of the proceedings from Charles County reads as follows:

ELIZ^A. KEECH adm of JOHN KEECH

Her administration bond in common form with HENRY HAWKINS her surety in £100 sterling dated 12 May 1710.

At a Court held April 1711

JOHN KEECH's inventory mentioned as having been reported by Joseph Manning Deputy Commissary for Charles County as filed.

NOTES ON THE COGHILL FAMILY OF VIRGINIA AND MARYLAND

Introduction

WILLIAM MIDDLETON was one of the witnesses to two indentures recorded in the Essex County, Va., Court 21 November 1752, both dated 8 May 1752. The first of these [1] is between

SMALLWOOD COGHILL of the Province of Maryland, eldest son and heir of WILLIAM COGHILL, late of said Province deceased, who was the eldest son and heir of JAMES COGHILL, late of Sitterburn Parish in Rappahannock County in the Colony of Virginia deceased, of the one part

and

FREDERICK COGHILL the younger of Essex County, in the said Colony of Virginia, of the other part

and recites that

Whereas the aforesaid JAMES COGHILL was in his life time and at his death seized in his demesme as of fee of and in one tract or parcel of land . . . in the freshes of Rappahannock on the south side of the river and now in the countys of Caroline and Essex containing by estimation and according to the patent for the same 1050 acres and also . . . of another tract of land . . . in the Parish of Sitterburn (now St. Anne) and County of Essex . . . on the branches of Occupation Creek . . . 600 acres . . . which JAMES COGHILL by his Will 5th October 1684 did devise to his wife MARY COGHILL for and during her natural life and did devise to his eldest son WILLIAM COGHILL 225 acres and to his son JAMES COGHILL 225 acres and to his son DAVID 200 acres and to his son FREDERICK 200 acres, and the child unborn at the date of the Will 200 acres, and of the other tract of 600 acres to his daughters MARGARET and MARY . . . and

Whereas MARY, the widow of the said JAMES COGHILL, and his sons WILLIAM, JAMES, DAVID, and the child unborn at the date of the said will, and also his daughters MARGARET and MARY, have since died, whereby the rights in fee to the said two tracts of land have descended and come to the said SMALLWOOD COGHILL, as eldest son and heir of WILLIAM COGHILL, eldest son and heir of JAMES COGHILL, except such parts as have been sold by WILLIAM and JAMES COGHILL, and except the part devised to FREDERICK COGHILL their brother, the reversion in fee simple expectant on the death of FREDERICK COGHILL being also descended and come to the said SMALLWOOD COGHILL, by which he, the said SMALLWOOD, conveys to FREDERICK COGHILL, Jr. (the son of FREDERICK above named), all his interest in the tracts mentioned and also the parcel devised to FREDERICK COGHILL, Sr. [father to FREDERICK Junr.].

1. JAMES COGHILL, founder of the family in America, is first mentioned in the records of Virginia when on 24 March 1664/5 he received a patent to 246 acres in Rappahannock County on the south side of the Rappahannock river.[2] This tract was on Lucas Creek, and it was granted him for transporting five persons to Virginia. He assigned this land to Thomas Kirk 4 August 1666.[3] The following year he received a patent to 1050 acres beginning about a mile from Port Tobacco Creek in the same County for transporting 21 persons to Virginia, and another patent for 600 acres for transporting 12 persons. He was a planter who bought and sold other lands. Deeds dated 16 October 1665 and 11 October 1667 were signed by JAMES COGHILL and his first wife ALICE. Deeds signed by him with no wife joining were dated 9 November and 18 December 1667, thus revealing that ALICE had died between 11 October and 9 November 1667. He and his second wife MARY signed a deed dated 17 May 1673, thus showing that they were married between 18 December 1667 and that date. His Will, dated 5 October 1684, was proved 1 September 1685 in the Rappahannock County Court. His widow subsequently married a Mr. DUCKSBURY, by whom she had a son George, mentioned in her Will, dated 21 April 1715 and proved 5 November 1715.

2. WILLIAM COGHILL [son of JAMES and ALICE COGHILL] was born probably about 1666 in Rappahannock County, Va. On 26 March 1689, however, he and his first wife, then living in Charles County, Md., executed a deed for the conveyance of his Rappahannock County lands, recorded in the court records of Essex County, Va. He married again,

---

1 *Essex County Deed Book* #26: 157-161, in the Archives, Virginia State Library, Richmond. The first part of this long quotation was copied by the compiler of this record, JGH, but the last paragraph is copied from the abstract found in J. H. Coghill: *The Family of Coghill*: 101.

2 N. M. Nugent: *Pioneers and Cavaliers*: 523.

3 For this and the other information in this paragraph JGH acknowledges his indebtedness to J. H. Coghill, *The Family of Coghill*: 95 *et seq.*

about 1719, ANNE SMALLWOOD. She was a daughter of JAMES SMALL-WOOD (b October 1668; d 1723) and his wife MARY (BOYDEN) GRIF-FIN, daughter of JOHN BOYDEN;[4] and a granddaughter of Col. JAMES SMALLWOOD and his wife, HESTER.[5] WILLIAM COGHILL's Will was dated 24 April 1729 and probated 4 June 1729.[6] He left to his son SMALLWOOD COGHILL 70 acres near Broad Creek and certain personalty to be turned over to him when he reached 16 years of age; and to his daughters MARY and LYDIA he gave certain personalty to be theirs on their 16th birthday or the day of their marriage; and to his wife ANNE he gave the residue of his personalty, named her his executrix, and provided that in the event of her death Mrs. MARY SMALLWOOD should have the care of his children.

ANNE COGHILL made her Will 20 November 1729 and it was probated 18 March 1730 in Charles County, Md.[6] It is genealogically valuable, because it mentions other relationships. She bequeathed to her son SMALLWOOD COGHILL certain personalty, but provided that he was not to sell it before he was 21 without the consent of her mother MARY SMALLWOOD or his uncle MATTHEW SMALLWOOD, and stated that SMALLWOOD and her daughters MARY and LYDIA were then under 16 and that the girls should not receive their share of the personalty she was giving them until they were 16 or married. She named her mother MARY SMALLWOOD to be her executrix.

Children of William and Anne (Smallwood) Coghill:
3   i. SMALLWOOD COGHILL m KEZIAH —.
4 ii. MARY COGHILL m WILLIAM MIDDLETON, Jr.
5 iii. LYDIA COGHILL, no further information.

3. SMALLWOOD COGHILL [son of William and Anne (Smallwood) Coghill] was one of the " sundry inhabitants of Prince Georges County " who on 16 October 1742 petitioned the Governor and the Maryland Assembly to divide the County " from the mouth of Rock Creek south to a bridge near Kennedy Farril's and east to the Patuxent River and along the river to Baltimore and Anne Arundel Counties." [7] He was a warden of Broad Creek Church in 1759. His Will, dated 23 July 1759 and probated in Charles County 27 August 1759, left a slave named Vick to his " cousin " ISAAC SMALLWOOD MIDDLETON, and provided that on the

---

[4] Md. Hist. Magazine, vol. xxii: 156.

[5] *Ibid.*, vol. xxii: 147.

[6] *Ibid.*, vol. xxii: 156.

[7] *Calendar of Maryland State Papers, No. 1, The Black Books*; item 454.

death of KEZIAH, the testator's wife, the tract called *Gardener's Meadows* should "fall to my cousin ISAAC SMALLWOOD MIDDLETON. Of course, the relationship of SMALLWOOD COGHILL to ISAAC SMALLWOOD MIDDLETON was that of uncle to nephew, but in the middle of the eighteenth century and earlier, the word *cousin* was often used to include *nephew*. Witnesses to the Will were John Wynn of Prince Georges County [whose second wife was Ann, widow of the John Smallwood who died in 1765, and daughter of Ralph Marlow, and oddly enough John Winn (Wynn)'s mother was also named Ann Smallwood, being daughter of William Smallwood who died in 1706], Henry Acton, of Charles County, and William Marlow. Mention has already been made of the way in which *Gardener's Meadows* passed from SMALLWOOD COGHILL to ISAAC SMALLWOOD MIDDLETON.

On 26 June 1761 there was the final accounting of the personalty belonging to the estate which, in addition to the legacy of "one Negro Girl named Vick" valued at £40, to the testator's "cousin" ISAAC SMALLWOOD MIDDLETON, amounted to £1272 5s. 11½d. Disbursements totaling £37 13s. 10d. were allowed, while the residue, £1234 12s. 1½d., was retained by the Accountant executrix KEZIAH COGHILL. The inventory was signed by MARY MIDDLETON and JOHN SMALLWOOD who were, respectively, the testator's sister and uncle, and called his next of kin.

4. MARY COGHILL [daughter of WILLIAM and ANNE (SMALLWOOD) COGHILL] received under the Will of William Bally, of Prince Georges County, dated 22 March 1724/5 and proved 26 March 1726, 270 acres on Muddy Hole, Stafford County, Va., adjoining the lands of Richard West. From 1730 to 1742 this tract was in Prince William County, and thereafter in Fairfax County, Va. General George Washington, in his diary, refers many times to Muddy Hole, for he had to ride through it on his way to Pohick Church. It is of interest to note that in the Fairfax County tax list of 1782 the name of Sybil West immediately precedes that of HUGH MIDDLETON, brother of ISAAC SMALLWOOD MIDDLETON. When MARY disposed of this land has not been ascertained. The marriage of WILLIAM MIDDLETON and MARY COGHILL took place about 1740.

NOTES ON THE O'NEALE AND BALL FAMILIES
OF MARYLAND

THOMAS BALL, "taylor", of Prince Georges County, Md., "in good sound mind but weake in body" made his Will "December ye third 1748 "[1] and probated 4 April 1749,[2] by which he left:

To LAURENCE O'NEALE part of a tract called *Token of Love*, containing 197 acres; but if Laurence should die before he reaches 21 years of age, then the land should "fall" to WILLIAM O'NEALE, Jr; and if they should both die under age, the land should fall to their father to do with as he pleases;

To SUSANNAH EVANS [Ewens] one mourning gold ring;

To ELEANOR O'NEALE one wedding gold ring; and

To ARDEN EVANS [Ewens], whom he designated executor, all his movables, wearing apparel, and ready money.

Taking this Will and that of WILLIAM O'NEALE, SR., into consideration, there is no doubt that THOMAS BALL had two daughters: Susannah who was married to Arden Evans [Ewens] and Eleanor married to William O'Neale, Sr. When THOMAS BALL wrote his Will, all of western Maryland was in Prince Georges County. Frederick County, though erected in June 1748, first functioned 10 December 1748. Upon the creation of Montgomery County, the tract *Token of Love*, which is just below Rockville, was included in the new County.

In the Maryland records the surname O'NEALE is found in many counties with various spellings. Because the various members of the family seem to have invariably *written* it themselves O'NEALE, that spelling is used throughout this article.

1. WILLIAM O'NEALE was among the residents of Prince Georges County who, somewhat before 11 May 1744, petitioned the Maryland Assembly to divide that county into two counties.[3] He made his Will 2 December 1759 and it was proved 17 December 1759,[4] and therein:

referred to himself as a planter, infirm in body but of sound mind and memory;

bequeathed personalty to his wife ELEANOR and his ten children all of whom he named;

named two of his tracts *Wheel of Fortune* and *Come by Chance*;

stated that a patent for a third tract containing 50 acres had been applied for;

directed that the two named tracts be divided into four parts, his sons WILLIAM, JOHN, HENRY, and DAVID to choose their parts serially by seniority; and

---

[1] One copyist says "November 3d."

[2] One copyist says "24 April 1749." The Will was recorded in 26 *Md. Wills*, Hall of Records, Annapolis, and in *Frederick County Will Book A-1*: 18, Courthouse, Frederick, Md.

[3] *Archives of Maryland*, vol. xlii: 459, 472; and *Calendar of Maryland State Papers—The Black Books*—Item 461.

[4] 31 *Maryland Wills* 132-133, Hall of Records, Annapolis; and *Frederick County Wills Liber A-1*: 135, Courthouse, Frederick, Md.

gave to his eldest son LAURENCE [who had already been provided with land by the Will of his grandfather Thomas Ball] a horse.

Children of William O'Neale and His Wife Eleanor Ball:

    i. LAURENCE O'NEALE (b 1738), sheriff of Frederick Co., 1774; member, House of Delegates, from Montgomery Co.; judge, Orphans Court, Montgomery Co., 1790-92; married HENRIETTA NEILL (daughter of Charles Neill), of Montgomery Co.; and had issue, possibly among others, Henry, John, Mary Ann, and Eleanor O'Neale. [Eleanor m Francis Jamison.]

    ii. JOANNA O'NEALE (b *ca.* 1740) was married to WILLIAM LODGE, and had, probably among others, a daughter Elizabeth.

    iii. ANN O'NEALE (b *ca.* 1742), mentioned in her father's Will.

2   iv. WILLIAM O'NEALE, whose line is continued.

    v. MARY O'NEALE (b *ca.* 1746), said to have died in 1820, aged [5] " about 70 ", buried in Rock Creek Parish, wife of EVAN JONES, and to have left issue.

    vi.-x. ELEANOR, ELIZABETH, JOHN, HENRY (b 1755), and DAVID O'NEALE, all mentioned in the Will of their father.

2. WILLIAM O'NEALE, called " Jr." in Thomas Ball's Will, was a petit juror in 1774 in Frederick Co., in the case of *Proprietary v. Wm. Vermillion* [6] and in an early case in Montgomery Co.,[7] and was one of the first two persons appointed to a guardianship in that county. He served in the Montgomery Co. militia during the Revolution [8] and subscribed the oath of fidelity and allegiance in that county.[9] He was twice married, first about 1766, his wife being SARAH YOUNG (*ca.* 1742-*ante* 1806), daughter of William and Eleanor Young, of Prince Georges Co. She was the mother of his three children. His second wife and he were married in 1806, she being SARAH (BEALL) ADAMS (1743-1814), daughter of Robert Beall who died about 1788 in Montgomery Co., and widow of Benjamin Adams, to whom she had been married about 1768. WILLIAM O'NEALE paid for pew 31 in Prince Georges Parish Church, Rock Creek.[10] He died 13 February 1812.

His widow, SARAH (BEALL) O'NEALE, made her Will two weeks later.[11] It was probated 5 November 1814. Therein she called herself

---

[5] According to a letter dated 23 February 1948 from Mrs. Martha Sprigg Poole, 4340 Verplanck Place, Washington 16, D. C., to JGH.

[6] *Calendar of Maryland State Papers—The Black Books—*Item 1511.

[7] Sharf's *History of Maryland*, vol. i: 659.

[8] *Index to the Maryland Militia in the Revolution*, 99, 114, DAR Library, Washington, D. C.

[9] The name William O'Neale appears both in the list of subscribers reported by the Worshipful Joseph Wilson 19 January 1778 and in the Prince Georges Parish list of 9 March 1778. Brumbaugh and Hedges: *Revolutionary Records of Maryland*, Part I, p 5 (21), and 279.

[10] See its *Vestry Records*, 226, his death being also noted.

[11] Dated 27 February 1812, recorded in *Montgomery County Wills*, Liber #1: 35.

" widow and relict of WILLIAM O'NEALE " and appointed " Alexander Adams my son and my son-in-law Richard West executors " and to them left all her property " to be equally divided between them."

On 26 February SARAH O'NEALE, widow of WILLIAM O'NEALE, SR., renounced appointment as his administratrix, and WILLIAM O'NEALE, JR., was instead appointed administrator, his surety bond being fixed in the sum of $10,000.00.[12]

On 21 June 1813 WILLIAM O'NEALE, JR., brought a suit in chancery " to divide the lands of WILLIAM O'NEALE, SR., who died intestate " [13] and on the same day John Wade and Ann his wife brought another suit to divide the land of Thomas West, whose wife had been Eleanor O'Neale. As a result of these suits we have the names of the children and all or most of the grandchildren of William O'Neale, Sr., as well as the names of his tracts owned at the date of his death 13 February 1812, which were *Exchange, New Exchange Enlarged, Piney Grove, Pig Pen, Wheel of Fortune, The Risque, Spital Fields, Adamson's Choice, Hard Bargain, Allison's Discontent, Smock Alley, Constant Friendship, Thompson's Adventure, Cleared Marsh, I Am Content,* and *Pleasant Mountains.*

In the first of the suits above mentioned it is recited that WILLIAM O'NEALE, SR., left " three children, to wit: William O'Neale, Jr.; Eleanor West, widow of Thomas West; and Ann Middleton, wife of Samuel Middleton, [Ann] who is since dead, leaving William O'Neale Middleton, Thomas Jefferson Middleton, Benjamin Franklin Middleton, Elizabeth Middleton, and Matilda Middleton, all under 21."

The matter was not then settled, for William O'Neale and his sister Eleanor West filed a petition 5 August 1825 in another chancery proceeding [14] then pending, which shows that " their father Wm. O'Neale of Montgomery County died possessed of 180 acres, being part of *Resurvey on Wheel of Fortune, Partnership,* and *Hard Bargain,* intestate some years ago, leaving them of full age, as also SAMUEL MIDDLETON, the husband of ANN, daughter of the said WM. O'NEALE, deceased, who died sometime previous to her father's decease, SAMUEL MIDDLETON since died, leaving as his heirs living: Elizabeth Burkit [Birckhead], Matilda, since married to Isaac Riley, and Thomas J. Middleton and Benja. F. Middleton, both minors."

Children of William O'Neale and His First Wife Sarah Young:

    i. WILLIAM O'NEALE (b 1769) m his first cousin ELIZABETH LODGE, daughter of William and Joanna (O'Neale) Lodge, and had Ann,

[12] *Montgomery County Wills,* Liber H: 39, 55.

[13] *Montgomery County Record for 1807-1816:* 543, Rockville, Md.

[14] Chancery Papers #3888, Land Office, Annapolis, involving division of land under the Will of William O'Neale, who died testate in Frederick County, December 1759, as result of suit by William Lodge, assignee of Henry O'Neale, in the partition of tract named *Wheel of Fortune.*

wife of Samuel Spates, Elizabeth West, Mary Jones, Joanna Peddicord, Sarah Nichols, Catherine O'Neale, and Eleanor O'Neale.

   ii. ELEANOR O'NEALE m THOMAS WEST (d *ante* 21 June 1813), and had Ann, wife of John Wade; Sarah, wife of Evans Jones; William O'Neale West; and the following who were minors in 1813: Emmaline E. West, Julius West, Richard West, Thomas West, Erasmus West, Henry West, and Eliza C. West.

  iii. ANN O'NEALE m SAMUEL MIDDLETON, as his first wife. For their descendants, see pages 155-156, 158-160, 163-164.*

The following is a list of most of the Middleton estate settlements up to 1919 recorded in the Office of the Register of Wills, U. S. Court House, John Marshall Place, Washington, D. C., which was obtained after the preceding article had been completed. Full names, where known, are used in this list, even though only initials may have appeared on the original. Details as to the books in which records of particular settlements are to be found are on file among the Middleton papers in the Collections of the Genealogical Society of Pennsylvania. The numbers opposite certain names correspond to the numbers assigned to them in the text. Those without such cross references have not been identified by the compiler of this record.

ALPHEUS MIDDLETON #10-i	Administration		31 Jan.	1908
BENJAMIN FRANKLIN MIDDLETON #10	Probate of Will		21 Feb.	1863
CATHERINE MARY [ELIOT] MIDDLETON	Will	dated	19 July	1886
wife of #13		proved	19 Oct.	1900
EDWARD MIDDLETON	Will	dated	2 Dec.	1871
		proved	8 June	1883
ELECTIUS MIDDLETON #4-viii	Administration		17 Apr.	1815
ELLEN ROSS MIDDLETON, wife of #11	Will	dated	7 Apr.	1898
	Codicil		22 May	1903
	Will-codicil	filed	20 Apr.	1904
		proved	2 July	1904
ERASMUS JOHNSON MIDDLETON, Jr. #11-v	Will	dated	6 Dec.	1878
		filed	28 Feb.	1881
FRANCIS G. MIDDLETON	Will	dated	18 Aug.	1882
		filed	30 Mch.	1885
		proved	4 Apr.	1885
HARRIET E. MIDDLETON	Will	dated	28 Feb.	1900
		filed	18 Apr.	1900
		proved	18 May	1900
JESSE MIDDLETON #10-iv	Administration		29 May	1914
J. BENJAMIN MIDDLETON	Will	dated	20 Nov.	1902
		filed	11 Apr.	1919
JOHN H. MIDDLETON	Administration		24 Apr.	1891
JOHN W. MIDDLETON	Will	dated	19 Oct.	1889
		filed	3 Feb.	1892
JOHNSON VAN DYKE MIDDLETON #13-ii	Will	dated	8 Oct.	1892
		filed	25 Mch.	1907
MARGARET HAINES [THOMPSON] MIDDLETON	Will	dated	28 Apr.	1909
wife of #13-ii	Codicil		4 Jan.	1910
	Will-codicil	filed	10 May	1910
RICHARD MIDDLETON	Will	dated	20 Oct.	1883
		filed	25 May	1886
		proved	7 July	1886
SAMUEL CALEB MIDDLETON #14	Will	dated	10 Apr.	1892
		filed	28 May	1892
		proved	28 May	1892
THOMAS JEFFERSON MIDDLETON #9	Petition for Letter of Administration		8 May	1885
	Grant of Letter		29 May	1885
	Bond of $4000 furnished		————	

---

*For pp. 155-156, 158-160, and 163-164 see pp. 300-301, 303-305, and 308-309, this volume.

MOLENAAB—MILLER CHART

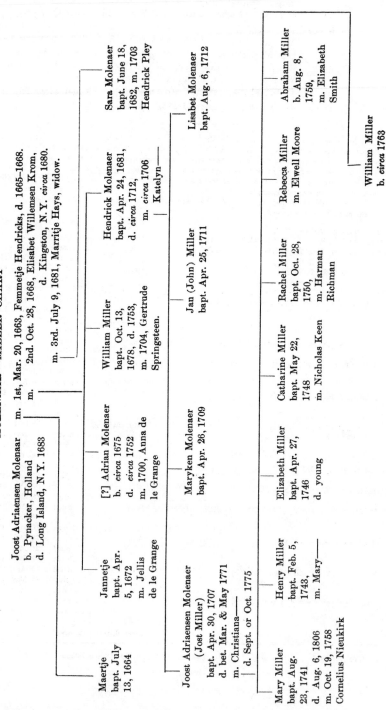

Joost Adriaensen Molenaar   m. 1st, Mar. 20, 1663, Femmetje Hendricks, d. 1665–1668.
b. Pynacker, Holland   m. 2nd. Oct. 28, 1668, Elisabet Willemsen Krom,
d. Long Island, N.Y. 1683   d. Kingston, N.Y. circa 1680.
                           m. 3rd. July 9, 1681, Marritje Hays, widow.

Maertje
bapt. July
13, 1664

Jannetje
bapt. Apr.
5, 1672
m. Jellis
de le Grange

[?] Adrian Molenaer
b. circa 1675
d. circa 1752
m. 1700, Anna de
le Grange

Sara Molenaer
bapt. June 18,
1682, m. 1703
Hendrick Pley

Hendrick Molenaer
bapt. Apr. 24, 1681,
d. circa 1712,
m. circa 1706
Katelyn

William Miller
bapt. Oct. 13,
1678, d. 1753,
m. 1704, Gertrude
Springsteen.

Maryken Molenaer
bapt. Apr. 26, 1709

Lisabet Molenaer
bapt. Aug. 6, 1712

Jan (John) Miller
bapt. Apr. 25, 1711

Joost Adriaensen Molenaer
(Jost Miller)
bapt. Apr. 30, 1707
d. bet. Mar. & May 1771
m. Christiana——
d. Sept. or Oct. 1775

Abraham Miller
b. Aug. 8,
1759,
m. Elizabeth
Smith

Rebecca Miller
m. Elwell Moore

Rachel Miller
bapt. Oct. 28,
1750,
m. Harman
Richman

Catharine Miller
bapt. May 22,
1748
m. Nicholas Keen

Elizabeth Miller
bapt. Apr. 27,
1746
d. young

Henry Miller
bapt. Feb. 5,
1743,
m. Mary——

Mary Miller
bapt. Aug.
23, 1741
d. Aug. 6, 1806
m. Oct. 19, 1758
Cornelius Nieukirk

William Miller
b. circa 1763

ANCESTRY OF JOST MILLER OF SALEM
COUNTY, NEW JERSEY.

By Bertha Edwards McGeehan.

The ancestry of Jost Miller of Salem County, New Jersey, 1707-1771, father of Mary Miller, wife of Colonel Cornelius Nieukirk,* has long been the subject of genealogical speculation. Much of the difficulty arose from the fact that his surname was originally Molenaar, Molenaer, which, in course of time, became anglicized as Miller. His first American ancestor, on the paternal line, was Joost Adriaensen, whose son, Hendrick, became the father of Jost Miller.

Joost Adriaensen was a miller from Holland who some time after his arrival in this country, assumed the surname Molenaer, a variant of the Dutch Mollinaar which described his occupation. He came from Pynacker, Province of South Holland, about three miles from Delft, in December, 1659, on the Ship *Faith*,† and settled in Wiltwyck, now Kingston, Ulster County, New York.

On April 30, 1658, Joost Adriaensen and Company entered a petition for leave to build a saw and grist mill at Turtle Falls on South River. Permission to build was granted May 6, of the same year.‡ The date of the petition is in conflict with the date of his arrival on the *Faith* and it may be that the petition was presented preparatory to his coming.

He apparently prospered, as, on May 8, 1677, he received a grant from the Court at Kingston for six acres of land over the Mill Kill. In September of the same year he purchased a house and lot in Kingston from Jans Borhans; § and on October 8, following, was taxed one bushel of wheat for "a

---

* *Publications of The Genealogical Society of Pennsylvania, Special Number*, March, 1934, p. 51. (Page 443, this volume.)

† O'Callahan, *Documentary History of New York*, Volume III, p. 55.

‡ *Calendar of New York Historical Manuscripts*, Dutch, 1630-1664, p. 196.

§ *Calendar Land Papers*, New York, 1643-1843, pp. 15, 17.

County House & a Certaine Lott for a Pasture beyond the Mill Dam or Creek, Lott No. 3 Containing about 6 acres." *

His standing among his fellow townsmen is evidenced by his appointment, June 10, 1672, one of the two Commissioners of Kingston;† and, as Joost Ariaens he was local militiaman in 1665; Schepen ‡ in 1665, 1668, 1672 and 1674, and deacon in 1667. §

Joost Adriaensen was married three times and had issue by each marriage. He married first in the Dutch Church at Kingston, March 20, 1663 Femmetje Hendricks, of Meppelen.‖ In the record he is described as young man of Pynacker. Femmetje also came in the ship *Faith*, in 1659. Possibly their romance was the outcome of the voyage.

On June 7, 1663, three months after their marriage, the Indians rose against the settlers. Some were killed, many wounded, a few captured. Femmetje was among those carried off, but was soon ransomed.

A year later their child Maertje was born. Sometime later Femmetje returned to Holland, taking the child with her and no further record of them has been found here. They were still in Holland, September 2, 1665, when the "worthy Joost Adriaensen Vermeulen ¶ of Pynacker" appeared before the Secretary of Wiltwick to make the following disposition of his estate: "six schepels of Wheat to the poor of Wiltwyck"; to his wife Femmetje Hendricks and their daughter Maertje "possession of estate gained and acquired here by him", and of "all such estate as he has in the old country, or might inherit." His brothers-in-law, Albert Jansen Van Steenburgh and Roeloff Hendricks were made executors, "they to send any balance to his lawful wife and child in the old

---

* *The New York Genealogical and Biographical Record*, Volume II, p. 146.

† *Calendar of Council Minutes*, New York, p. 16.

‡ The duties of a Schepen were of a judicial character. In civil cases his judgment was final where the amount involved was small. In matters of more importance an appeal from his decision could be taken. He had authority also to pronounce judgment in all criminal cases, but his judgments were subject to certain rights of appeal.

§ *The Holland Society Year Book*, 1897, p. 118.

‖ Hoes, *Baptismal and Marriage Registers of the Old Dutch Church of Kingston*, New York, p. 500.

¶ Of the Mill.

328

country." The will was written in Dutch, his wife, Femmetje, called by her maiden name, a custom many years retained by the Dutch, was appointed executor of his property in Holland, and his signature thereto was Joost Adryaens.*

Three years later, October 28, 1668, he and Elisabet Willemsen Krom were married at the Kingston Dutch Church. † In the record she is called a young maiden from Pynacker; he, from Opynen, "widower of Femmetje Hendricks." The names of the two towns were doubtless transposed in the marriage entry, as all other references to him state he came "from Pynacker." Possibly Elisabet was from Opynen, a town a few miles from Theil in the Province of Gelderland, Holland.

Elisabet Krom, second wife of Joost, died either before, or soon after, April 24, 1681, the date of baptism of their youngest child, Hendrick.

Shortly thereafter, having adopted Molenaer as a surname, Joost Adriaenszen Molenaer, widower of Lysbeth Croning (Krom), married, thirdly, in New York Dutch Church, July 9, 1681, Marritje (Mary) Hays, daughter of Jacob and Christina (Cappoens) Hays, and widow of Philip Lieuw.‡ By this union there was one child, Sara, baptized in Kingston, at the home of Jan Joosten, June 18, 1682. Joost Adriaens Molenaer was then living on a farm of fifty acres, which he owned, in Bushwick, Long Island. He and his wife joined the Dutch Church of New York City, May 30, 1683.§

On July 27, following, he made a second will and died at his home in Bushwick before October 17, 1683, the date of its probate at Fort James.‖ Under it his wife, Maria Hays was constituted "sole heiress" of his estate. His administrator, Jan Joosten, filed petition August 14, 1684, asking payment for accommodations, etc. furnished by the decedent to the Court of Sessions in 1681; and on April 23, 1685, as administrator of estate of Joost Adriens, late of Boswick [Bushwick],

---

* Anjou, *Ulster County Probate Records*, American Record Series, Volume I, p. 29.

† *Kingston Dutch Church Records, op. cit.*, p. 503.

‡ *New York Dutch Church Record of Marriages*, 1639-1801, p. 49; *The New York Genealogical and Biographical Record*, Volume LXV, pp. 314-16.

§ *New York Genealogical and Biographical Record*, Volume LIX, p. 69.

‖ Fernow, *Calendar of Wills on file and recorded in the Office of the Clerk of Appeals, of the County Clerk at Albany, and of the Secretary*

he agreed to arbitration regarding some land in Hurley, Ulster County, called Wasmaker's land "sold to Derrick Shepmoes by Joost Adriaens in his life time."

His widow, Maria Hays, married Captain Peter Praa of Newtown and had a somewhat distinguished progeny.

Child of Joost Adriaesen Molenaer and Femmetje Hendricks:

    i. MAERTJE[2], baptized July 13, 1664; was living in Holland, September 2, 1665; probably died young.

Children of Joost Adriaensen Molenaer and Elisabet Willemsen Krom:

    i. JANNETJE[2], baptized April 5, 1672; married *circa* 1690, Jellis de le Grange; had four children, all of whom married.
    ii. ?ADRIAN, born *circa* 1675, probably in Kingston; married May 19, 1700, Annetje de la Grange, sister of Jellis de le Grange; removed to Somerset County, New Jersey and was executor of Hendrick Molenaer's will. Having no issue he and wife, by their respective wills, bequeathed all property to Annetje's nephews and nieces. There seems little doubt that Adrian belongs in the list of children; nevertheless the question mark is used.
    iii. WILLEM, baptized October 13, 1678; married, under license of October 18, 1704, Gertrude Springsteen; removed to Newtown, Long Island, where he died May 11, 1753; by his will of February 24, 1752 his entire estate was devised to his wife. As early as 1704 he had Anglicized his name and was William Miller on marriage license and will. Some of his descendants are, 1937, living in New York.
2. iv. HENDRICK, baptized April 24, 1681; married Katelyn ———.

Child of Joost Adriensen Molenaer and Maria Hays:

    i. SARAH, baptized 18 June, 1682; married 1703, Hendrick Pley.

2. HENDRICK MOLENAER, youngest child of Joost Adriaensen and Elisabet Willemsen Krom, was baptized in Kingston on April 24, 1681, and died in Somerset County, New Jersey, about 1712. The first knowledge of him in New Jersey is the record of the baptism of his son, Joost Adriaensen Molenaer, in 1707, in the First Reformed Church of Raritan.

Many Dutch settlers left New York and became resident in New Jersey, among them being the families of Nieukirk, Van Gelder, de le Grange, DuBois and Krom. Jan Joosten, a

---

of State . . . 1626-1836, p. 2; *New York Historical Society Collections, Abstracts of Wills,* 1665-1707, p. 69; *Ulster County Probate Records,* Volume I, p. 30; *Calendar of New York Historical Manuscripts English,* p. 111.

sponsor at the baptisms of four of Joost Adriaensen Molenaer's children and administrator of his estate, purchased land in Somerset County and lived there for a time. His family took the surname Van Meter. Adrian and Hendrick Molenaer may have accompanied him when he left New York for New Jersey.

On November 16, 1709, Hendrick Molenaer, yeoman, of Somerset County, purchased from John Van Meter, a tract on the South Branch of the Raritan River, "now in the peaceable possession and enjoyment of the said grantee." The quantity of acreage is not given. The consideration was "a competent sum of good and lawful money." This property had been purchased by Jan Joosten (Van Meter) in 1700. In this deed Hendrick is called "Hendry Miller." *

It is quite possible that Hendrick died before November 7, 1712, as the deed from Van Meter was acknowledged on that date by one of the subscribing witnesses. He made his will January 26, of that year; signed it Hendrick Mulnenaere, stated he was "sick and weak of body." The Van Meter tract he willed to his two sons, "Yost Ariency and John," and to "his beloved wife Cateline" the sole use and benefit of his estate, real and personal, to be disposed of to the best advantage for bringing up their children. He appointed Adrian Molenaer, doubtless his brother, and Isaac Bodine, both of Somerset County, his executors.†

There seems to have been some difficulty in administering the will. On March 4, 1718, Adrian Molenaer and Isaac Bodine renounced their right to act as executors and Adrian wrote to the Surrogate:

> Mr. J. Barclay, Let no administration be granted on the estate of Hendrick Mulliner, till the other executor, Isaac Bodine have notice thereof and let good security be taken if administration be granted for the due administration of the said Estate. Ari Molenaer.

On June 9, 1719, the Court appointed Isaac Van Meter administrator, and John and Henry Van Meter became his bondsmen in the sum of £300. All were yeomen of Salem County, New Jersey. The inventory showed assets valued at £139. It described the decedent as "Henry Miller of East

---

* *New Jersey Deeds*, Secretary of State's Office, Trenton, Liber C2, f. 20.

† *New Jersey Archives, Abstracts of Wills*, Volume I, pp. 332-333.

Division of N. J. of Sumersett Co. upon Rariton River deceased."

Henry Molenaer or Miller, married about 1705/6, Katelyn, or Catalyn . . ., who survived him and married before 1722, Isaac Van Meter, who had lived in Somerset County before removing to Salem County. Whether she married him before he became the administrator of the estate of her deceased husband, Hendrick, in 1719, is not known, but they were married by 1722.

Transcripts of two authenticated documents are here submitted as evidence of her marriage to Isaac Van Meter:

> 1731—I do Intrust father and Brother Joost Arianse Muliner To Act and do for me and in my behalf in afare of our Estate this from under my hand twenty Eight Day of October. John Miller.

The endorsement upon this paper reads:

> Novr 1st, 1731, This day I Joos Arian Muller have * * * ed and agreed and Concluded that my father in law Isaac Lemetra should be discharged of all Engagements and have a Quietus and according I have prayed Michl Kearney Surr. off Eastern Division to Give and Grant unto the said Isaac Lemetra a Quietus and full discharge out of the office and I do hereby oblidge myself My heirs Ex^{rs} and admrs to save the said Kearney and office harmless witness my hand the day & year above said. Joost Arianse Mulier.*

Joost Adriaensen, the eldest son, still kept to the Dutch spelling of his name, but Jan had adopted the English, John Miller. In designating Isaac Lemetra [Van Meter] "father-in-law", Joost meant step-father; John called him "father."

As before stated, the marriage of Katelyn Molenaer, widow, and Isaac Van Meter had taken place before 1722, when the baptism of Sarah, a child of Isaac's, on 2nd month 23, of that year, is recorded in the First Presbyterian Church of Philadelphia.† On 6th month 12, 1724, four families of Pilesgrove, New Jersey, had their children baptised. Among these children was Abraham,‡ a son of "Isaac and Cataline Ver

---

* *New Jersey Archives, Abstracts of Wills*, Volume 2, p. 351.

† *Records of First Presbyterian Church, Philadelphia*, p. 28. Transcript of, in Collections of The Genealogical Society of Pennsylvania.

‡ *Ibid.*, p. 33.

Meeter". These baptisms were also entered in the Records of the First Presbyterian Church in Philadelphia. There being no Presbyterian Church in Salem County at that time, parents usually awaited the visitation of clergy, that their children could have the rite of baptism.

The children of Katelyn or Catherine (. . .) Molenaer Van Meter, by her first husband, lived with her and their stepfather Isaac in Salem County. In 1725 Catharine Van Meter and her son "Joost Adriansen Mulinaer" witnessed the will of Andrew Hoffman of Pilesgrove.*

Soon after this date Catharine died. Isaac Van Meter married again and later moved to Virginia, where he died. In 1758 the records show that part of his property, a negro man and girl, valued at £50, were in the possession of Jost Miller of Salem County.†

Children of Henry Molenaer, or Miller, and Katelyn . . .‡

    3. i. JOOST 3 ADRIAENSEN, baptized April 30, 1707.
      ii. MARYKEN, baptized April 26, 1709.
      iii. JAN, baptized April 25, 1711.
      iv. LISEBET, baptized August 6, 1712.

3. JOOST 3 ADRIAENSEN MOLENAER (*Henry* 2, *Joost* 1), was born in Somerville, Somerset County, New Jersey about 1706/7, and died at Mannington, Salem County, in 1771.

He left Somerville with his mother, brother and sisters to live in Salem County. He was married, before 1741, to Christiana, surname unknown. The Presbyterians then had a Church in Pittsgrove. On April 30, 1741, the Church Covenant was signed by forty-nine members, "Jost" Miller and John Miller being among its signatories.

In 1744 Joost Adriaensen Molenaer signed his name Jost Miller as bondsman on the estate of Cornelius Nieukirk, of Salem County.§ A comparison of the signatures of Jost Miller on the will of Andrew Hoffman in 1725;|| on his release to his stepfather in 1731, and on the bond of 1744, show them to have been written by the same hand and establishes the fact that Jost Miller, of Salem County, was son of Hendrick and

---

* *New Jersey Archives, Abstracts of Wills*, Volume I, p. 232.

† *Ibid.*, Volume III, p. 337.

‡ *Somerset County New Jersey Quarterly*, Volume II, pp. 44, 45, 139, 140.

§ *New Jersey Archives, Abstracts of Wills*, Volume II, p. 355.

|| *Ibid.*, Volume I, p. 232.

Katelyn Molenaer, of Somerset and Salem Counties, and grandson of Joost Adriaensen of Kingston, New York.

Jost Miller purchased from John Hart in 1766, five tracts of land, 677½ acres in all, for £2,400; * in 1770 he and wife Christiana sold 500 acres which he had purchased from the executors of the estate of Isaac Van Meter, his step-father.†

On March 26, 1771, Jost Miller, of Mannington Township, Salem County, made his will and died soon thereafter. He gave to his wife, Christiana, the plantation on which they lived, for the term of five years, so that she might educate their younger children. It was then to be sold and the money divided among his seven children. His personal estate was valued at £1,027. 5. 2, according to an inventory made May 3 following.‡ Christiana, the widow and Charles Elliott, as executors, sold on February 26, 1772, 250 acres of the land which Jost had purchased from John Hart in 1766.§

Christiana lived less than five years after her husband's decease. On September 28, 1775, she made her will, which was proved May 23, 1776.‖ By it she devised to each of her three sons, Henry, Abraham and William, one third of her land in Alloways Creek Township, called Round Island; with £40 extra for schooling for William, who was then about twelve years of age. Her daughters were to receive her wearing apparel, and her daughter Rachel, a negro girl, in consideration of her loss when "my house" was burned. Her sons, Henry and Abraham, were named executors, but Henry died soon after his mother and Abraham became sole executor.

On May 28, 1776, the children of Jost Miller executed a Power of Attorney to Charles Elliott, the surviving executor of their father's will, authorizing him to sell the decedent's real estate. It is recited in the Power of Attorney that Christiana, Jost's widow, had died within the five years of his death; that his son Henry was dead and that his widow Mary had been appointed administratrix of his estate; and that the then living children of Jost Miller were: Mary, wife of Cornelius Nieukirk; Catharine, wife of Nicholas Keen; Rachel,

* *New Jersey Deeds*, Secretary of State's Office, Trenton, Liber A, f. 471.

† Salem County, New Jersey, *Deed Book* H, f. 175.

‡ *New Jersey Archives, Abstracts of Wills*, Volume V, p. 349.

§ *Salem County Deeds*, Liber I, f. 698.

‖ *New Jersey Archives, Abstracts of Wills*, Volume V, p. 347.

wife of Harman Richman; Rebecca, wife of Elwell Moore; Abraham, and William, a minor.*

Children of Jost Miller and Christiana:

i.   MARY,[4] baptized August 23, 1741; married Cornelius Nieukirk.
ii. HENRY, baptized February 5, 1743; married Mary ————.
iii. ELIZABETH, baptized April 27, 1746; died young.
iv. CATHARINE, baptized May 22, 1748; married Nicholas Keen.†
v.   RACHEL, baptized October 28, 1750; married Harman Richman.
vi. REBECCA, married Elwell Moore.
vii. ABRAHAM, born August 8, 1759; married Elizabeth Smith.
viii. WILLIAM, born *circa* 1763.

Mary, Henry, Elizabeth, Catharine and Rachel were baptized in the Pilesgrove Presbyterian Church.‡ The record of Abraham's birth is in the Friends' Meeting Records at Salem.§

Mary Miller, eldest child of Jost and Christiana Miller, married Cornelius Nieukirk, October 19, 1758, who became a Captain in the Revolutionary War, and following that war, was made Lieutenant Colonel by joint-act of the New Jersey Legislature. Mrs. Nieukirk died August 6, 1806, in her 67th year.||

* *New Jersey Deeds*, Secretary of State's Office, Trenton, New Jersey, Liber A1, p. 468.

† *The Descendants of Jöran Kyn of New Sweden*, pp. 68, 166.

‡ *Records of Pilesgrove or Pittsgrove Presbyterian Church, New Jersey*, pp. 15, 21, 25, 29, 33.

§ Salem, New Jersey, *Friends Monthly Meeting Records*, Volume I, p. 289.

|| An account of their descendants and his ancestors is given in the *Society's Publications, Special Number*, March, 1934.

Mintzer Family Notes

THE appended Bible record is taken from two pages removed from an old Bible found in Haverford, Pa.[1] Most of the record appears to be in one very legible but unknown handwriting.

John Mintzer, whose name heads the record, was the son of Adam Mintzer, a carter in the Northern Liberties of Philadelphia, and his wife Rosanna, and the grandson of Mark Mintzer, also a carter of the same place, and his wife Sarah.

MARCUS MUENZER (MINTZER) is reported to have married 12 October 1742, SARAH ELIZABETH BRAUN, a member of the Moravian Church, who was born in October 1717, in Württemberg, and came to Pennsylvania in October 1738. As MARK MINSER of Philadelphia, he was naturalized in the fall of 1740, so he must have been in the province since at least 1733.[2]

The Philadelphia Moravian Church register for 1766 lists only one child for them: Sarah Muenzer, born 20 August 1748. But there were other children, for Mark in his will, dated 10 November 1781, and proved 21 January 1782, named as his children Barbara, Adam, Joseph, William, Englebert, Margaret, Sarah Lampater, a deceased son David and a deceased daughter Mary Seiler. His widow Sarah Mintzer, whose will was dated 8 January and proved the following 22 September 1796, named only her "undutiful son Joseph," to whom she left 25 cents, her daughters Barbery Wilkison and Margaretha Kurtz wife of George Kurtz, grandchildren Betsy and Peggy Kurtz, and Betsy and Anna Barbara Wilkison.[3]

The marriage registers of St. Michael's and Zion Evangelical Lutheran Church of Philadelphia show the marriages of some of the children

---

[1] The record was contributed by Effie M. Shaw, 2217 Oakwood Lane, Richmond, Va. 23228, in May 1972. No title page was included.

[2] See "Register of Members and Their Children Belonging to the Moravian Congregation in Philadelphia, in 1766," in William Henry Egle, *Notes and Queries Historical, Biographical and Genealogical . . . ,* Annual Volume, 1896, 214. *Pennsylvania Archives,* 2nd Series, II (1876), 351.

[3] Philadelphia Will Book D, 65, #70:1782, will of Mark Mintzer. Other legatees named in his will were his grandchildren Mark and David Mintzer, children of his deceased son David, and Jacob, Mathias, Henry, Emmanuel, Margaret and Elizabeth Seiler, children of his deceased daughter Mary Seiler. Philadelphia Will Book Y, 490, #321:1796, will of Sarah Mintzer, "widow of Marcus."

of Mark Mintzer. On 6 January 1761, JOHANNES THOMAS BISSHANS and ANNA MARGRETHA MUENTZER were married. On 11 November 1766, JOHN LAMPATER married SARAH MUENTZER. ADAM MUENTZER and ROSINA REIS were married on 16 July 1767. MARIA BISSANS, widow, married, as her second husband, GEORGE KURTZ, on 26 October 1773.[4]

No marriage has been found for ENGLEBERT MUENTZER, but he was married by 1781 when he and his wife MARY were sponsors, at St. Joseph's Roman Catholic Church in Philadelphia, at the baptism of Mary Dauber, daughter of Sebastian and Mary Dauber. The baptismal registers of that church show that Englebert, a Protestant, and his wife Mary, had three children baptised there: Joseph in 1782, Anna Mary in 1783, and William in 1785. As *Ingleburd Minser*, he was listed as an innkeeper in the Northern Liberties in 1781. By 1790 he had moved up to Douglas Township in Montgomery County.[5]

ADAM MINSER (MINTZER), son of Mark, survived his father only three years. In his will, dated 4 March 1784, and proved 11 March 1785, he named his wife ROSANNA, and mentioned children without naming them. His widow Rosanna, however, in her will dated 10 March and proved the following 31 August 1818, named her two sons John and Adam, and two daughters, Elizabeth and Mary.[6] She had died on 13 July 1818, aged 70 years, 8 months and 24 days, and was buried in the graveyard of St. Michael's and Zion Lutheran Church. Here also were buried four of her children: *Catharine Minser*, who died 5 October 1812, aged 41 years, 2 days. *Mary Minser*, wife of *James McClaskey*, had died 5 May 1820, aged 44 years, 3 months, 13 days. *George Minser* died 13 September 1812, aged 33 years. *Margaret Minser* died 20 October 1789, aged 7 years, 9 months and 27 days. The eldest daughter, *Elizabeth Muentzer*, born 12 October and baptized the

---

4 *Pennsylvania Archives*, 2nd Series, IX, 312, 328, 331, 353. See also Burials, 1745-1771, St. Michael's and Zion Church, 356-7, in Collections of the Genealogical Society of Pennsylvania (GSP), for an extended burial notice of Joh: Thomas Bisans, first husband of Anna Margretha, daughter of Marcus Müntzer. He was b. 2 August 1731, and d. 17 October 1771. *Joseph Muntzer*, perhaps the "undutiful son," mentioned in the will of Sarah Mintzer, m. at the German Reformed Church, 27 July 1797, *Elizabeth Fischbach.* See *Pennsylvania Archives*, 2nd Series, VIII, 699.

5 *Records of the American Catholic Historical Society*, IV (1893), 42, 54, 67, 169. *Pennsylvania Archives*, 3rd Series, XVI, 73. *Heads of Families at the First Census . . . 1790: Pennsylvania* (Washington, D.C., 1908), 160. In the published assessment lists in the *Pennsylvania Archives*, the family surname is variously given as *Menser, Minser* and *Mintzer*.

6 Philadelphia Will Book T, 148, #92:1785, will of *Adam Minser.* A witness to his will was John Lampater who had married Adam's sister Sarah. Philadelphia Will Book 6, 596, #97:1818, will of *Rosanna Mintzer.* Witnesses to her will were Jonathan Carmalt, Jr., James and Caleb Carmalt. In 1817 she was listed in the *Directories* as living at 246 N. Second Street.

following 13 November 1768, at St. Michael's and Zion Church, had married at the same place on 1 January 1792, *Jacob Luter.* [7]

In the Philadelphia City *Directories,* the address of JOHN MENTZER, son of Adam and Rosanna, was 315 North Third Street from 1802 until his death. First listed as a carter, the last two years of his life he was called a shopkeeper. In his will, dated 7 July and proved the following 3 September 1819, he named his wife Deborah, and his children as Jacob Mentzer, his youngest son William Mentzer, his daughter Rosanna Stimble, wife of George, and daughters Sarah Bruner and Eliza Mentzer.[8]

His widow DEBORAH MENTZER continued to live at 315 North Third Street until 1837. After her son-in-law George Stimble died, she was listed first as a storekeeper and then as a grocer. In 1837 she was at 148 Tammany, and in 1840, the year before her death, she was listed at 148 St. John Street. She, too, was buried in St. Michael's and Zion churchyard.

GEORGE S. STIMBLE, who married ROSANNA MINTZER, daughter of John and Deborah, first appeared in 1816 in Philadelphia *Directories* as a grocer living at 315 North Third Street with his wife's parents. From 1820 until his death in 1822, he was listed there as an accountant. No obituary has been found for him, but one for Rosannah, his wife, appeared in the 2 December 1819 issue of *Poulson's American Daily Advertiser*:

Died on Tuesday evening, MRS. ROSANNAH STIMBLE, consort of George S. Stimble, aged 23 years, and eight days, of a pulmonary consumption which she bore with calm resignation and Christian fortitude. This amiable woman was a kind and affectionate companion, a vigilant mother, a kind and sincere friend, and a devout Christian, in performing the various duties assigned to her important station in society. She endeared herself to a large connection of relatives and friends, to whom her death would be an inseparable loss, did not her Christian virtues leave this consoling reflection — That

> Her immortal soul has taken flight
> To joyful scenes of pure delight
> There with God to dwell above
> In endless pleasure, peace and love.

The friends and relatives of the above are particularly invited to attend her funeral this afternoon at two o'clock from the residence of her mother, No. 315 North Third Street.[9]

[7] St. Michael's and Zion Gravestone Inscriptions, GSP. St. Michael's and Zion Baptisms, 1759-1771, 455, GSP. *Pennsylvania Archives,* 2nd Series, IX, 407.

[8] Philadelphia Will Book 7, 55, #97:1819, will of John Mintzer. It was witnessed by Caleb and James Carmalt, who had witnessed his mother's will the year before.

[9] She was buried in the churchyard of St. John's P. E. Church, Northern Liberties, erected on land adjoining the Coats' family burial ground.

Mintzer-Stimble Bible Record

Births

John Mintzer born October 14th 1770
Deborah Mintzer born February 24th 1772
Issue:
John Mintzer born July 28th 1795
Rosanna Mintzer born November 22nd 1796
Sarah Mintzer born February 25th 1799
John Mintzer born October 30th 1801
Elizabeth Mintzer born November 7th 1802
Jacob S. Mintzer born March 29th 1805
William C. Mintzer born August 15th 1809

George S. Stimble born February 17th 1794
Rosanna Stimble born November 22nd 1796
Issue:
John M. Stimble born April 7th 1815 [10]
Deborah M. Stimble born June 24th 1816
Elizabeth S. Stimble born February 16th 1818

Marriages

John Mintzer and Deborah Cox Married June 22nd 1793 [11]
George S. Stimble and Rosanna Mintzer Married August 22nd 1813

Deaths

John Mintzer Died August 6th 1819
Rosannah Stimble Died November 30th 1819
George S. Stimble Died April 13th 1822
Sarah Bruner Died August [blank] 1821
William C. Mintzer Died July 7th 1830
Elizabeth Stimble Died November 3rd 1831
John M. Stimble Died July 14th 1816
Elizabeth S. Stimble Died July 15th 1819
Deborah Mintzer Died Suddenly on the Eavning of the 22th of October 1841 at 9 Oclock [12]
Jacob S. Mintzer died on the evening of Octo 21st 1867 at a quarter before twelve Oclock

[10] John Mintzer Stimble was baptized 17 September 1815, according to the records of St. John's P. E. Church, Northern Liberties, in GSP.

[11] Their marriage is entered in the register of St. Michael's and Zion Lutheran Church, wherein it is given as 20 June 1793. On 13 October 1796, John's brother *Adam Mintzer* and *Sarah Migdoll* were married in the same church. *Pennsylvania Archives*, 2nd Series, IX, 409, 419.

[12] In the 1850 Philadelphia *Directory*, Jacob S. Mintzer was listed as living at 315 N. 3d Street, apparently the old family home. He was Treasurer of the District of Northern Liberties. The Mayor of the District was William Wilkinson, attorney and counsellor-at-law at 158 Coates Street.

Note: For a variant account of the Mintzer Family, see *Bulletin of the Historical Society of Montgomery County, Pa.*, Volume XIII (No. 2, Spring 1962), noted by the Editor after this account had gone to press.

MOUNTAIN, DRAKE, AND MACPIKE FAMILIES.

The English surname Mountain seems to have been derived from the French Montaigne. The famous French essayist, Michel de Montaigne, obtained his title from the chateau where he was born, 28 February, 1533.* The family-name was Eyquem. There were Eyquems, or Ayquems, who were Sieurs de Lesparre, in France, before 1152, but there appears to be no connection between them and the progenitors of the essayist.†
The latter's grandfather bought the chateau of Montaigne, not far from the city of Bordeaux, where some of the family resided. Here must be left the early family in France, with these **few clues for the benefit** of those who may later pursue the quest.

It seems evident that other members of the family of Montaigne, in France, probably Huguenots, migrated early to England, and that some of their descendants eventually found their way to the American colonies.

Among the early State Papers of Her Majesty's Record Office at London is one entitled: "Promise of certain Walloons and French to emigrate to Virginea." The date affixed is 1621, which from the context and notes seems correct. "Such as offer themselfs to goe into Virginea numbered two hundred and twenty-seven including fifty-five men, forty-one women, one hundred and twenty-nine children and two servants." The signatures, indistinctly written, are headed by that of Mounsier de la Montagne, medical student, marrying man, and Mounsier de la Montagne, apothecary and surgeon, marrying man. Hotten's Lists of Emigrants to America, 1600-1700,‡ give the names of the signatories.

These Lists also include the name of Jo. Mountain, aged twenty, as having embarked from Gravesend, 3 April, 1635,§ to be transported to St. Christopher's, and that of John Mountain who left Barbadoes for Antigua in the sloop *True Friendship*, 7 October, 1679.§

The first of the name to settle in the American colonies was Jean de la Montaigne, or Johannes de la Montagne as he was best known. According to O'Callaghan, he was born in 1592; was a Huguenot physician, of varied acquirements, and came to New Netherlands in 1637. In 1638 was appointed one of the council under Kieft; 1641 was appointed by Kieft to command an expedition consisting of fifty men in two yachts to Fort Good Hope, now Hartford, on the Connecticut River, to maintain the Dutch rights there against the encroachments of the English; 1643 saved the life of Director Kieft, attacked by Maryn Adriaensen, and the same year was sent to Staten Island with three companies to put down the

---

* *Encyclopedia Britannica*, eleventh edition, vol. xviii, page 748, where reference is given to the elaborate researches of M. Malvézin, in his "Michel de Montaigne, son origin et sa famille," 1875.

† *Ibid.*

‡ New York, 1874, p. 20.

§ *Ibid.*, pp. 50, 191.

Indians; 1644 headed an expedition against the Indians of Long Island, where one hundred and twenty savages were killed; 1645 accompanied Kieft on his first voyage to Fort Orange, to secure the friendship of the Mohawks, on which occasion he conducted an analysis of the war paint of the natives, and discovered gold therein, to the great comfort of Kieft; 1647 was retained in the council of Stuyvesant; 1648 was dispatched to the South river to secure the Dutch acquisitions there. In 1652, it having been determined to establish a school in the city tavern, he was for the time appointed schoolmaster; 1653 he was in the enjoyment of an income of nearly four hundred dollars a month from his public offices; 1656, on the retirement of De Decker, he was appointed Clerk of the Courts and vice-director at Fort Orange, now Albany, which offices he appears to have filled successfully. In 1664 he surrendered the fort to the English and swore allegiance to the new dynasty.*

Another account gives his birth as of 1596 and states that, at the age of twenty-four, as a refugee from Saintonge, France, he entered the University of Leyden, Holland, remaining there seventeen years, part of the time as a professor. He and his wife arrived in New Amsterdam in 1637.† He married before coming to New Netherlands, Rachel Monjour, who accompanied him, and on the voyage, off the island of Madeira, gave birth to a daughter, Maria, 26 January, 1637, who became the wife of Jacobus Kip.‡ His second wife was Agnietie Gillis, widow, whom he married 18 August, 1647. By both marriages there were children, some of whose baptisms are to be found on the records of the Dutch Church of New York. One daughter was captured by the Indians and held prisoner for a time.§ Many descendants of this early settler have held, with considerable pertinacity, to the original form of the name. There are indications that some of these may have settled in New Jersey and eastern Pennsylvania.‖

There are several references to Edward and Joseph Montayne in the *Indexes to New Jersey Wills and Administrations, 1705-1804,* and to a Joseph Montayne, and the surname MONTANYE, in the volumes of the *Somerset County Historical Quarterly.*¶ Abram, Edward, Edward, Jr. and Joseph Montayne served in the New Jersey militia during the Revolution from Essex, Morris and Somerset counties.**

In the colonial and later records of New Jersey and Pennsylvania the name Mountain occurs with some frequency. John Mountain is in a "list of Servants †† imported by Benjamin Clarke, Senr., and Benjamin

* *History of New Netherlands,* ii, 21; *Documents relating to the Colonial History of New York.*

† Manuscript notes from Dr. Howard Mountain, Confluence, Pennsylvania (1927).

‡ *New York Genealogical and Biographical Record,* vol. viii, pp. 68, 125.

§ *Ibid.,* Dr. Howard Mountain.

‖ *New York Gen. and Biog. Record,* vol. iii, p. 47; *Chronicle of the Yerkes Family,* by J. Granville Leach.

¶ Plainfield, New Jersey, 1912-1919.

** STRYKER'S *Jerseymen in the Revolution,* p. 692.

†† The term "servant" or "laborer," as applied to emigrants in colonial times, must not be misunderstood.

Clarke, Junr., 1683/4, August 14, 1685.''* The New Jersey marriage licenses mention one John Mounten, of Salem county, and Mary Muckehenny, of Sussex county, under date of March 23, 1757.

David Elder Mountain was in the Cumberland County, Pennsylvania, Militia in 1780, and George Mountain in Philadelphia Militia in 1781.

A James Mountain of Virginia appears in a list of ''Personal Names in HENNING'S *Statutes.*†

In the published reports of the First Census of the United States, 1790, is found a Hugh Mountain in Franklin county, Pennsylvania, and a Jonathan Mountain, Simsbury town, Hartford county, Connecticut.

The Parish Register of Christ Church, Middlesex county, Virginia,‡ shows entry of the marriage of John Mountain and Elizabeth Jones, December 26, 1800.

One Richard Mountain married Mary Paulin at Falls Monthly Meeting of Friends, September, 1711. His name appears some years later on the civil records of Bucks county, Pennsylvania.

Roger Mountain, born in Ireland, aged 27, barber, enlisted August 6, 1746, in Captain John Diemer's Company, Provincial Service, recruited by authority of Proclamation of Governor George Thomas, June 9, 1746; went into winter quarters at Albany, New York; discharged October 21, 1747, the late intended expedition against Canada having been laid aside. A James McPick, or McPike, was in the same regiment.§

Leaving these scattered notes, which may be useful to a future student of the subject, attention will now be given to a more connected narrative. In a deed, dated March 24, 1749, recorded August 23, 1753, at Doylestown,‖ Pennsylvania, the contracting parties are thus described:

''Rowland Powell of Northern Liberties, of the city of Philadelphia, husbandman, and Sarah, his wife; Mary Asprell, and Joseph Mountain of Bristol, in the county of Bucks, Cooper, and Catharine, his wife; the said Sarah, Mary and Catharine being the daughters of John Clay and Esther, his wife, which said Esther was a daughter of Esther Wilson, late of said city, deceased, of the one part, and Thomas Standaland, Junr., of Bristol township, Bucks county, of the other part.'' The deed was signed by Joseph Mountain and Catharine Mountain.

The will of Esther Clay, relict of John Clay of Bristol, Bucks county, blacksmith, dated November 27, 1749, probated December 17, 1749,¶ mentions daughter Mary Aspril, and her daughters Mary, Sarah and Lydia; daughters Sarah and Catharine and their children; John Hall and Samuel Bunting, Junr., ex'rs. Witnesses: Thos. Stanaland and Thos. Stanaland, Junr. and Darby Brannyn.**

The Joseph Mountain and Catharine Clay, his wife, who signed the deed,

* *New Jersey Archives,* First Series, vol. xxi, p. 84.

† Compiled by J. J. Casey, in 1896, vol. i, p. 86.

‡ Published by the National Society of the Colonial Dames of America, Richmond, 1897.

§ *Pennsylvania Archives,* Fifth Series, vol. i, pp. 7, 15.

‖ Bucks County Deed Book No. 9, page 102.

¶ Bucks County, Will Book No. 1, page 171.

** The author is much indebted to Mr. Warren S. Ely, Librarian of the Bucks County Historical Society, for data herein presented.

dated March 24, 1749, previously mentioned, were unquestionably identical with the Joseph Mountain of Bucks county, cooper, and Katherine, his wife, who were parties to an indenture made July 25, 1749.* This Joseph Mountain was therein described as "only son and heir-at-law of Richard Mountain, late of the same place, brewer, deceased, but heretofore of the parish of Andover, in the county of Hampshire, England,† who was eldest son and heir-at-law of Richard Mountain, late of same place, and his wife who was the only daughter and child of John Dallamano, late of Andover." An investigation of the title followed Joseph Mountain's transfer of the Andover property, by which it was shown that John Dellamano died in 1672. It was further shown that his son-in-law, Richard Mountain, by his will of January 5, 1701, gave Andover land to his eldest son Richard, should he return to Andover within seven years of his, the testator's, decease, otherwise said land should revert to sons Joseph and Benjamin, who were sons of a second wife Ann, who was also bequeathed lands, as was his daughter, Ann Gray.

It has been thought that the Joseph Mountain of Bucks county who signed the indenture of July 25, 1749, was identical with the Joseph Mountain who, in 1779, was taxed for land in Turkeyfoot township, Cumberland county, now Somerset county, Pennsylvania. But this is unlikely since the former's wife was Katherine, or Catharine, whereas the latter's wife was Elizabeth Drake, as will presently be shown. Joseph Mountain of Bucks County was, in all probability, at least twenty-five years of age in 1749 when he and his wife Katherine signed the Indenture, while Joseph Mountain of Cumberland County married, 14 April, 1772, Elizabeth Drake, by whom he had seven children, the youngest born in 1785. It is, however, quite possible that the former Joseph was the father of the latter.

Here it seems proper to insert a tradition dictated about 1868 by John Mountain McPike (1795-1876) and preserved in writing, as follows:

"J. Mountain, from New Jersey—English, about 1554.‡ Children: Joseph, John, Richard, Martha; also half-brother George Grinup. Joseph Mountain married Miss E. Drake; one child, Joanna. Martha Mountain married Captain James M'Pike." §

Whether or not John Mountain or his brother, Richard, ever married and had issue, is not stated. The name Richard is significant.

The reference to New Jersey as the former place of residence is rather confusing, because the tradition preserved by the Mountains now living

* Notes contributed by Mr. Ogden D. Wilkinson of Philadelphia to *The Pennsylvania Magazine of History and Biography*, vol. xxx, pp. 381-382. Mr. Wilkinson has since sent the author interesting material and suggestions.

† Among published marriage licenses for Hampshire, England, are the following:
1709, Samuel Mountain, Stockbridge, and Mary Sutton, Andover.
1716, John Mountain, Romsey, and Sarah Shipton, Andover.
1726, Benjamin Mountain, Andover, and Eliz. Penton, Winchester.
1726, Joseph Mountain, Andover, and Anne Spearing, Winchester.
1736, John Mountain, Andover, and Jane Elcombe.
1774, Robert Mountain, Winchester, and Elizabeth Leader.
There are doubtless wills of Mountains recorded at Winchester, Hampshire.

‡ 1654? Cf. *Pennsylvania Magazine of History and Biography*, xxx, p. 251.

§ Circa 1782, in Western Maryland.

in Somerset county, Pennsylvania, is that their ancestors came from Bucks county. Nevertheless, the relationship is very clear, as will soon appear. The "J. Mountain, from New Jersey" may, or may not, have been identical with the Joseph Mountain of Bucks county, living in 1749, *et seq.*, bue he must have been the father of the Joseph Mountain of Cumberland county, later Somerset county, Pennsylvania, who married, 14 April, 1772, Elizabeth Drake and had seven children. The process of reasoning for this conclusion here follows:

Three original letters, written in 1821, 1823 and 1828, signed by Elizabeth Mountaine, are now in the possession of the Misses Eleanor and Mary Sleeth, of Rushville Indiana, who are great-granddaughters of Captain James McPike and Martha Mountain, his wife. These letters are each addressed to the writer's "Dear Nephew" (i. e. nephew-in-law), Joseph McPike, Newport, Kentucky. The earliest letter, dated February 14, 1821 (bearing on the outside the postmaster's endorsement: "Smythfield, Pa., February 15") reads, in part:

"Catty and David live with me and Joanna . . . . Hannah Mountaine and her father and mother are well. Joseph Mount[ain] and family, and Jonathan are all well. . . . . I must not forget brother James, for him . . . . . . and me [are] both traveling to the grave as fast as time can roll around. . . . . Give my love to brother George Grinup And sister Grinup and all the family."

The foregoing letter mentions some new towns or villages near Smythfield: "one on big yough; Smithfield has 18 houses; Petersburg lyes joining our land."

The writer's reference to her aged "brother James" means James McPike [*] (born *circa* 1751) whose wife, born Martha Mountain, was a sister of the Joseph Mountain who, according to the tradition, married a Miss E. Drake. The latter certainly seems to have been identical with the Elizabeth Mountain, writer of the three letters.

The second letter, dated May the 5, 1823, with an outside endorsement: "Smythfield, S. C., Pa., May 6," reads, in part:

"We are all enjoying a tollerable degree of health at present . . . . . looking for you and your companion; try and bring her or cousin patsee with you. . . . . Hannah Mountaine is at her father's and is very unhealthy, and has been for a long time. Three of her children live with me. Joseph is married and lives on one part of this place. . . . ."

The name "patsee" refers to Martha McPike, youngest daughter of James McPike and Martha, his wife.

The third letter, dated 10th March, 1828, at Petersburg, Somerset County [Penna.] says:

". . . . . . I and all the rest of the family are well, ... you will please give my love to your Father and Brothers and Sisters and all inquiring friends. . . . . . Joanna Mountaine is living with me and two of John Mountaine's children, that is, Catharine and David. Jonathan is out in State of Ohio a-learning the waggon-making trade with his cousin Oliver Drake. . . . . . ."

The relevancy of the foregoing extracts from letters signed by Eliza-

[*] *Pennsylvania Magazine of History and Biography*, vol. xlii, pp. 90-91 (January, 1918).

beth Mountaine will become clear when considered in connection with the genealogical records which follow, by the courtesy of Dr. Howard Mountain of Confluence, Pennsylvania. His great-grandfather, Joseph Mountain, was the first of the family to move into Cumberland, now Somerset County. Land there was bought from the Indians in 1768, and in 1769 the first permanent settlers arrived. The oldest settlement is known as the Turkeyfoot Region, where the first settlers are said to have been Drakes. The first Mountain settled near Petersburg, now called Addison post-office. He was the Joseph Mountain who married, April 14, 1772, Elizabeth Drake, and had issue:

     i. ELIZABETH, born May 1, 1773.
2. ii. JOHN, born October 5, 1774.
    iii. CATHARINE, born December 2, 1776.
    iv. AGNES, born February 8, 1779.
    v. JOANNA, born February 8, 1781.
    vi. JOSEPH, born March 17, 1784.*
    vii. DAVID, born October 24, 1785.

The eldest daughter, Elizabeth, was named after her mother. Is it not probable that the second daughter, Catharine, was named after her paternal grandmother? If speculation may be further allowed, it would seem quite possible that the eldest son, John, may have been named after his paternal grandfather? The fourth daughter, Joanna, was certainly identical with her namesake mentioned in letters of her mother, Elizabeth Mountaine, partly before quoted. It is true that the tradition dictated about 1868 mentions only one child, Joanna, but, owing to the lapse of time, the existence of other children may have been forgotten. This may be easily explained since, as shown in Elizabeth Mountaine's letters (1821-1828), Joanna was the only child still living with her. The others, if then living, had undoubtedly departed from the family hearth † to establish homes of their own. In fact, the letters contain some internal evidence of this. The writer's grandson, Joseph, had married and settled upon a part of the home-place near Petersburg.

2. John Mountain, eldest son of Joseph and Elizabeth (Drake) Mountain, was born October 5, 1774. He married Hannah Drake, born August 4, 1775, daughter of Oliver ‡ and Frankey (Skinner) Drake; resided at Petersburg, and had issue:

* A tombstone to the memory of Joseph Mountain gave his age at time of death, in 1804, as twenty years.

† Mountain deeds of record in the Land Office at Cumberland, Allegheny County, Maryland:
Mountain, Elizabeth, and Joseph, to Wm. Thistle, Book C, page 590 (1803).
Mountain, Aaron and Mary, to Michael Kenard, Book 41, page 630 (1874).

‡ Oliver Drake, son of David Drake, born in New Jersey, January 25, 1745; married 22 August, 1770, Frankey Skinner. He settled at Draketown, Somerset County, Pennsylvania, and built the first grist mill in that section. His children were: 1. *Ann*, born March 8, 1771. 2. *Hannah*, born August 4, 1775; married John Mountain, q. v. 3. *Jonathan*, born September 15, 1777; married July 11, 1813, Sarah Tannin; settled at Draketown and continued his father's business. 4. *Lydia*, born March 8, 1780.
In a later generation there was an Oliver Drake, who went to Ohio and engaged in wagon-making, as mentioned in Elizabeth Mountain's letter before quoted. He was probably a son of the Jonathan Drake born September 15, 1777.—From Dr. Howard Mountain, who long ago copied his records from a family Bible, since lost.

i. JOSEPH, born March 31, 1798.
ii. CATHARINE, born January 31, 1800.
iii. FRANCES, born February 28, 1802.
iv. DAVID, born December 4, 1804.
3. v. JONATHAN, born October 24, 1806.

The children, Catharine and David, were of course identical with the Catharine ("Catty") and David, children of John Mountain and Hannah, his wife, mentioned in Elizabeth Mountaine's letters.

3. Jonathan Mountain, youngest son of John and Hannah (Drake) Mountain, born October 24, 1806; married Elizabeth Pringey, and had issue:

i. WILLIAM R.
ii. JOSEPH P.
iii. HARRISON H.
iv. WALTER S.
v. NOBLE W.
vi. LEVI
vii. ROSS
viii. MARTHA
ix. NEWLON
x. HOWARD
xi. MARY J.

Of these, only two, Ross and Howard, are now living (1928). There are, however, numerous descendants of that generation.

—Eugene Fairfield MacPike

THE MULLICA FAMILY OF NEW SWEDEN.

Charles J. Werner in his little book *Eric Mullica and His Descendants, A Swedish Pioneer in New Jersey* (New Gretna, N. J., C. J. Werner, 1930) gives much information about this early settler on the Delaware, but nothing about his family antecedents. The writer of this article, endeavoring to trace back his family lineage (the Mulkey family is supposed to be descended from the Mullicas), has discovered some additional facts which may be added as a postscript to Mr. Werner's book.

Eric Mullica, sometimes called Eric Palsson, Eric the son of Pal, was not the first of his family to settle in America. His father was a Paul Malich, mentioned once in a passing reference by Amandus Johnson in his exhaustive study of the Swedish colony.* This Malich was usually called Paul Joranson (Jonsson, or in the anglicized form of Johnson). Joranson, hired in the province of Jamtland as a farm hand, came to America with the fourth Swedish expedition in 1641.† (Actually he was neither Swedish nor Finnish, since the reference already mentioned spoke of him as " Paul Malich, the little Pole "; he was apparently then from the region known as Little Poland.)‡ Joranson is mentioned several times in the Swedish records. In 1654-1655 a census of the colony named him as residing on the Schuylkill.§ Shortly afterwards he returned to Sweden to seek his long over-due pay.‖ Some time following the Dutch conquest of New Sweden Joranson removed with a group of his fellow colonists to the English proprietary colony of Maryland. He was made a denizen of Maryland in 1660, included in a group of former residents of New Sweden.¶ In a claim, entered on April 29, 1661, Johnson requested land of the Maryland authorities for transporting himself, his wife Aquetta, his sons Hendrick and Andreas, and his daughters Margaretta, Annakin, and Christen into the colony.**

---

* *The Swedish Settlements on the Delaware, 1638-1664* (University of Pennsylvania, D. Appleton & Company, Agents, New York, 1911), II, 547.

† *Ibid.*, I, 151-155; II, 711.

‡ See the forthcoming article by the writer, *The Malecki Family, Early Polish Pioneers in America,* to be published in the *Annals of the Polish Roman Catholic Union.*

§ Johnson, *Swedish Settlements on the Delaware,* II, 711, 717.

‖ *Ibid.*, II, 619. A Pawel Jonsson was paid at this time.

¶ *Proceedings of the Council of Maryland, 1635-1667,* in *Archives of Maryland* (Baltimore: Maryland Historical Society, 1885), II, 430.

** Liber No. 4, folio 552, in the Land Commissioner's Office of the State of Maryland; information sent to the writer by Arthur Trader.

Then there is found as of the same date and entered on the same page in the records, another claim which serves to reveal the family identity of Paul Johnson. A certain Bertrell Hynderson presented a claim for the transportation of himself, Sindricke Hinderson, Andreas Mullika, and John Jorgenson. Johnson apparently died a few years after his removal to Maryland for we learn that the Rev. Lars Lock, pastor for the Swedish settlers, drew up a deed of division between Paul Jon's widow and her children, dated at Tranhook (Crane Hook) on April 14, 1664.* Unfortunately this document, which was available to the historian Acrelius, cannot be located today.

Of the two sons of Paul Joranson Malich mentioned above, nothing is known of Hendrick; no mention has been found of him under his family name or under the name of Paulson, but it is possible he may have called himself Johnson. Andreas is mentioned many times. In 1682 the Maryland colonial legislature passed an act naturalizing several persons of Swedish names, including "Andrew Paulson als Mullock." † He was a resident of Cecil County, which bordered the Swedish settlement along the Delaware River.

Little need be said here about Eric Palsson Mullica since the main facts about him have long been known.‡ We have only circumstantial evidence as to his parentage but this seems sufficient. He was born in Mora Parish, Helsingland, Sweden, in April, 1636. He married Ingabor Helm, daughter of the prominent Captain Israel Helm. Eric and Ingabor Mullica had the following children: Andrew, Olof (Wolle, William), Eric, John, Anna, Helena, Catharine, and Stephen.§ Some time between 1693 and 1698 this family, including only the younger children, removed from the Tacony Creek region near Philadelphia and settled on Little Egg Harbor in eastern New Jersey near the mouth of the stream since known as Mullica River. Eric Mullica was dead by 1704 since the Rev. Andreas Sandel visiting at Little Egg Harbor in that year made note of the fact that his wife was then a widow.‖

Eric Mullica may have had other brothers besides Andrew. In 1678 an Oele Paulson appearing before the New Castle Court made mention

---

* Israel Acrelius, *A History of New Sweden,* translated from the Swedish, with introduction and notes, by William M. Reynolds (Philadelphia: The Historical Society of Pennsylvania, 1874), p. 177.

† *Proceedings and Acts of the General Assembly of Maryland,* in *Archives of Maryland,* VII (1889), 487, 489, 676, 577.

‡ In addition to the book by Charles Werner, see also a short article by Lewis D. Cook, "Early Swedes and Finns of New Jersey in Public Office," in *The Genealogical Magazine of New Jersey* (Newark: The Genealogical Society of New Jersey), XIII, no. 2 (April, 1938), p. 25.

§ "Extracts from the Parish Records of Gloria Dei Church, Philadelphia," in *The Pennsylvania Magazine of History and Biography* (Philadelphia: The Historical Society of Pennsylvania, 1878), II, 225, 226.

‖ "Extracts from the Journal of Rev. Andreas Sandel, Pastor of Gloria Dei Swedish Lutheran Church, Philadelphia, 1702-1719," in *The Pennsylvania Magazine of History and Biography,* XXX, 295, 296.

of a brother Renk * (probably Eric, but possibly Henrick). There was a John Paulson who may have belonged to the same family; the evidence in support of this relationship is fragmentary and inconclusive.

The writer believes that there were other members of the Mullica family in America. Peter Kalm, a Finnish-Swedish scientist who visited America in 1749-1750, in writing of his travels set down the following item: "Erich Rannelson had an old paper about his family and its immigration which read as follows: ' Erich Mulleen aged 46 years, from Helsingland in Swedland, arrived in Dellaware River in the ship Orn the 26th day of May, 1652 (actually 1654). His wife Ingeri Philips aged 36 years from Wermland in Swedland, arrived in Dellaware River in the ship Mercurius, March 1654 (1656). This family as follows, listed a daughter Anna, 16 years; a son Andreas, 14; Olle, 11; Erich, 9; Johan, 7; a daughter Eleanora, 4; and Catharina, 1 year old.' " † It should be noted that this Erich Mulleen was from Helsingland, the same section where Eric Mullica, the son of Paul Joranson Malich, was born. The writer believes that Erich Mulleen and Paul Joranson Malich were brothers. There was an Eric Joranson on the Gyllene Haj, the ship scheduled to leave with the Orn late in 1653. The Haj became unseaworthy and had to delay its sailing several months while its sister ship went on alone.‡ Joranson may have transferred from the Haj to the Orn when the former was held up. Concerning this branch of the family, there is no information available. Mention might be made of the large family by the name of Rannels, or Runnels, living in the neighborhood of Mullica Hill, New Jersey. The evidence at hand indicates that this family was related to the Mullicas.—Floyd Mulkey,

WILLIAM MURDOCH (1705-1761), OF PHILADELPHIA, AND HIS DESCENDANTS: MURDOCH, BEALE, SWEERS, TINGEY, KELLY, WINGATE, CRAVEN, DU-LANY, CROSBY, AND DUFFIELD

BY LEWIS D. COOK, B.Sc.

The genealogy of this family which has produced many officers of the United States Navy has not been described accurately or comprehensively in its single published notice.[1] The following account of the first three generations in all seven lines of descent incorporates essential documentary evidences contemporary with the subjects, so that compiler's deductions and predications are made apparent.

1. WILLIAM MURDOCH, born in 1705, came from Armagh[2] in the Province of Ulster, Ireland, to Philadelphia between 1735 and 1737. In the latter year he had a child baptised in Christ Church there, and acquired two adjacent 20-foot properties on the north side of Chestnut Street between Front and Second Streets.[2a] He died testate in Philadelphia, and was buried 27 September 1761 in Christ Church burial ground,[3] SE corner of Fifth and Arch Streets, with gravestone marker inscribed:[4]

> In Memory of
> WILLIAM MURDOCH
> who died Sept 26th 1761
> Aged 56 years

His wife, whom he married before emigration, was Mary HAMMOND according to family records;[2] she died 25 August 1770, aged 55 years,[2] and was buried same day in said ground.[3]

William Murdoch's Real Estate

By Deed of 2 October 1752 Joseph Shippen of the city of Philadelphia, merchant, and wife Mary, conveyed to William Murdoch of said city, taylor, for 90 Pounds, a lot on the west side of Front Street continued southward beyond said city, 18 feet 6 inches frontage on said street and 70 feet depth, bounded east by said street, south by Isaac Bollings, west by other ground of said Shippen, and north by William Branson, together with the brick messuage now thereon erected by the said William Murdoch, and all other buildings, kitchen, improvements. Recorded 2 July 1792 in *Philadelphia Deed Book D-36*, p. 143.

By seven-parts Deed of 13 May 1780 Mary Beale of the Island of Santa Cruz in parts beyond the sea, widow, by John Beale her eldest son and attorney, Ann Murdoch of the city of Philadelphia, widow of Thomas Murdoch decd., Cornelius Sweers of said city, gentleman, and wife Hannah, John Murdoch of said city, silversmith, and wife Sarah,

---

[1] All footnotes are at the end of this article, beginning on page 61.*

*Page 372, this volume.

Thomas Tingey of said city, mariner, and wife Margaret, Sarah Murdoch of said city, spinster, and Samuel Murdoch of said city, merchant. Recital that William Murdoch, late of said city, deceased, owned divers messuages and lots of ground in the district of Southwark, County Philadelphia, and by his Will of 24 September 1761 devised all his estate to his children equally, and died leaving issue a son William and the said Mary Beale, Samuel Murdoch, Thomas Murdoch, Hannah Sweers, John Murdoch, Margaret Tingey, and Sarah Murdoch, and that the son William Murdoch and wife Jane by their Deed of 26 July 1763 conveyed his one-eighth part to said Samuel Murdoch, and that the said Thomas Murdoch by his Will of 9 October 1722 devised one-third of his real estate to his wife the said Ann Murdoch party hereto, and the rest between his nephew Thomas Murdoch and niece Sarah Sweers who are infants between 11 and 12 years old, and afterwards said testator died. The said devisees desiring partition of said messuage agreed on sale at public auction and to divide the proceeds thereof, and the messuage was exposed to sale at public auction at the London Coffee House in Philadelphia on 29 April last and was struck off to said Samuel Murdoch at 24,150 Pounds current money of Penna. This Indenture conveys messuage and lot on west side of Front Street in the District of Southwark, County Phila., 18 feet 6 inches frontage on said street by 74 feet depth, bounded south by Isaac Belling, north by William Branson. Recorded 2 July 1792 in *Philadelphia Deed Book D-35*, p. 246.

By another Deed of 13 May 1780 the same seven grantors, with recital as above, conveyed to Peter Day of the District of Southwark, County Philadelphia, mariner, highest bidder at 12,000 Pounds at public auction of the property held at the London Coffee House in Philadelphia on 29 April last, the messuage and lot at NW corner of Almond and Front Streets in said Southwark, having 13 feet frontage on Front Street, and 54 feet on Almond Street, bounded North by a messuage and lot intended to be conveyed to James Elliott. Recorded 8 May 1780 in *Philadelphia Deed Book D-2*, p. 219.

By a third Deed of 13 May 1780 the same seven grantors, with recital same as above, conveyed to James Elliott of said city two contiguous messuages and lots on the West side of Front Street in the District of Southwark, County Philadelphia, one containing 12 feet frontage on Front Street and the other 15 feet frontage on said street, by 54 feet depth, bounded South by the messuage and lot intended to be conveyed to Peter Day (see above) and North by one sometime of Daniel Harrison. Recorded in *Philadelphia Deed Book D-2*, p. 297.

By Deed of 24 February 1780, the same seven grantors, with same recital and addition that said William Murdoch the father in his lifetime owned two messuages and lots on the North side of Chestnut Street in the city of Philadelphia, between Front and Second Streets, containing 40 feet frontage on Chestnut Street by 20 feet depth, and that John Vining Esq after Murdoch's death claimed them and began an action of Trespass and Ejectment for recovery thereof, and that said Murdoch heirs by advice of their counsel purchased the property from said Vining and it was conveyed by his executors to William and Samuel Murdoch by Deed of 15 August 1771 in Trust for all the devisees of said Murdoch deceased, whereby it came into possession of the grantors hereof, and that the said devisees desiring partition, the property was exposed to sale at public auction at the London Coffee House in Philadelphia on 29 January last, and said Samuel Murdoch was highest bidder at 13,900 Pounds current money of Pennsylvania, and that he is sensible that the price is below the real value of the premises, and offered to pay to his said brothers and sisters for their shares thereof 20,000 Pounds for the whole,

" which generous offer they thankfully accepted.", and by this Indenture convey to him their shares. Recorded 13 April 1782 in *Philadelphia Deed Book D-4*, 233.

The Will of William Murdoch

In the Name of God, amen. I, William Murdoch of the City of Philadelphia, Taylor, being weak in body but blessed by God of sound and well disposing mind and memory, do make this my last Will and Testament in manner following, that is to say:

I give and devise unto my beloved wife Mary for and during her Natural Life all that my messuage and lot of ground wherein I now live, Also all my Household goods Chattles and Moveables to her own use. All the Residue of my Estate I give and devise unto all and every of my Children part and share alike, to be equally divided between them, also the House and Lot wherein I now dwell after my wife's decease I devise unto all my Children part and share alike, their several and respective heirs and assigns forever, to be equally divided between them. And I nominate and appoint my said Wife Mary and my two sons William and Samuel to be the Executors of this my last Will and Testament. In Witness whereof I have hereunto set my hand and seal the twenty fourth day of September in the year of our Lord one thousand seven hundred and sixty one. (signed) William Murdoch (his mark). Signed sealed published & declared for and as his last Will and Testament in the presence of us: William MacClenachan,[5] Richd Farmar, Jno Reily. Philada. Novr. 3d 1761:—Then personally appeared Richard Farmar and John Reily two of the witnesses to the foregoing Will and on Oath did declare that they saw and heard Wm Murdoch the Testator therein named sign seal publish and declare the same Will for and as his last Will and Testament and that at the doing thereof he was of sound mind memory and understanding to the best of their knowledge. *Coram* William Plumsted Register General.

Be it Remembered that on the 3d November 1761 the Last Will and Testament of William Murdoch in due form of Law was proved and probate or Letters Testamentary were granted to Mary Murdoch, Samuel Murdoch and William Murdoch Executors in the sd Will named, being duly sworn well and truly to administer the deceas'd's Estate & bring an Inventory thereof into the Reg. Gen'l's office at Philada. at or before the 3d of Decr. next and render a true acct when required. Given under the seal of the sd. office *p* William Plumsted Reg. Genl. (Recorded in *Phila. Will Book M*, p. 212.)

Children of William and Mary (Hammond) Murdoch [2]

(The first two were born before their parents' arrival in Phila.; the other nine were baptised successively in Christ Church there.)

     i.   *John Murdoch* b about 1733; bur 4 July 1737 NS.[3]

2. ii. *Mary Murdoch* b 27 May 1735; mar George BEALE.

   iii. *Susannah Murdoch* b 5 Aug 1737; bur 19 Jan 1745.

3. iv. *William Murdoch* b 7 July 1739; d after 1767.

4. v. *Samuel Murdoch* b 7 Oct. 1741; d. 13 July 1803.

5. vi. *Thomas Murdoch* b 2 Mar 1744; d. 9 Aug 1779.

6. vii. *Hannah Murdoch* b 16 Jan 1746; mar Cornelius SWEERS.

7. viii. *John Murdoch* b 8 July 1748; d 1786.

8. ix. *Margaret Murdoch* b 26 July 1750; mar Thomas TINGEY.

   x. *Sarah Murdoch* b 12 Feb 1752; d 14 July 1780 unmar.

   xi. *James Murdoch* b 27 Nov 1753; bur 5 Oct 1756.[3]

SECOND GENERATION

2. MARY MURDOCH, eldest daughter and second of the eleven children of William and Mary Murdoch, was born 27 May 1735 (New Style) and came with her parents from Ireland or England in 1735-37 to Philadelphia, where she married 2 March 1756 George BEALE, according to the register of Christ Church.[3] They settled in the Island of Saint Croix (Santa Cruz) in the Danish West Indies (now the Virgin Islands, U.S.A.), where he " had two of the finest plantations on the island ".[2] George Beale died before 4 February 1780, the date of the deed in which " Mary Beale of the Island of Santa Cruz, widow, by John Beale her eldest son and attorney ", joined the other heirs and devisees of her father William Murdoch of Philadelphia, deceased, in conveying some of his real estate. She returned to that city by 10 December 1782, on which date Archibald McCall of Philadelphia, merchant, and wife Judith, conveyed by deed to " Mary Beale of said city, widow ", for 1100 pounds specie, a messuage and lot 20 feet wide extending from the west side of Water Street through to the east side of Front Street, " on the bank ".[5a] Mary (Murdoch) Beale died, at some date in 1803-04, testate.

The Will of Mary Beale of the District of Southwark, County Philadelphia, widow, dated 5 April 1796 and proved 15 October 1804, devises to granddaughters Mary Kelly and Eleanor Kelly her messuage and lot purchased from Archibald McCall, situated " in from the street on the bank, between Water and Front Streets in the said city, also all plate marked with my initials MB and all household furniture," with reversion to the survivor in case of death of either unmarried or without issue, or to grandson John Kelly in case of death of both unmarried or without issue, or to son-in-law John Kelly their father in case of death of all three grandchildren, except he marry again, in which event the same to be sold for benefit of said granddaughters and the plate divided between them equally. Appoints son-in-law John Kelly and [brother-in-law] Thomas Tingey executors. By Codicil of 3 September 1803 devises 100 dollars to said son-in-law John Kelly. Recorded in *Phila. Will Book no. 1* p 248.

Children of George and Mary (Murdoch) Beale: [6]

10. i. John Beale b 27 Dec 1756;[2] of Phila. 1780.
11. ii. George Beale.
12. iii. Mary Beale d before 1796; mar John KELLY.
    iv. Thomas Beale.

3. WILLIAM MURDOCH, eldest son and fourth of the eleven children of William and Mary Murdoch of Philadelphia, was born there 7 July 1739 and baptised in Christ Church 26 July 1739. William Murdoch and Jane BROOKS were married 31 January 1763, according to the register of St. Paul's Church, Philadelphia, with license of same date. She was

one of the four children of George Brooks of Philadelphia, " Painter and Glazier ", who died there intestate in 1760. In 1767 William Murdoch and wife were living in Greenwich Township, Cumberland County, N.J., but final record of them has not been discovered. His estate is not found on record in Cumberland County probates or in those of Philadelphia. Their only known child Thomas Brooks Murdoch is discovered by the devise to " Nephew Thomas Brooks Murdoch ", in the Will of William's brother Thomas Murdoch of Philadelphia, dated 9 October 1772.

By Deed of 26 July 1763 William Murdoch of the city of Philadelphia, " Hatter ", and wife Jane, conveyed to his brother Samuel Murdoch of same place " Merchant ", for 187 pounds 10 shillings, grantor's eighth part in the estate of their father " William Murdoch late of the city of Philadelphia aforesaid Taylor deceased ", and it was recorded 2 July 1792 in *Deed Book D-36*, p 140.

By Deed of 4 May 1765 William Murdoch of the city of Philadelphia, " Hatter ", and wife Jane, conveyed to William Faries of same city " Painter ", for 35 pounds, a 15 feet 9 inches by 24 feet lot there which said Jane received in the division of the real estate of her father George Brooks late of said city " Glazier ", deceased, and this Deed was recorded 28 August 1772 in *Deed Book I-10*, p. 542.

By Deed of 27 May 1767 William Murdoch of Greenwich Township, Cumberland County, N. J., " Hatter ", and wife Jane, conveyed to Margaret Trotter of the city of Philadelphia, widow, for 450 pounds, a messuage and 13 by 25 feet lot on the north side of Chestnut Street there, reciting that it was part of the estate of " George Brooks, father of the above named Jane Murdoch, Painter and Glazier of the said city ", who died intestate leaving a widow and four children unto whom his real estate descended, and that partition thereof was made 20 June 1760 by the Orphans Court. Deed recorded in *Deed Book I-2*, p 368.

Child of William and Jane (Brooks) Murdoch:

13. i. Thomas Brooks Murdoch b 1763-1769.

4. SAMUEL MURDOCH, second son and fifth of the eleven children of William and Mary Murdoch of Philadelphia, was born there 7 October 1741 and baptised in Christ Church 19 October 1741. He died 13 July 1803 testate, and was buried 14 July 1803 in Christ Church burying ground, SE Cor 5th and Arch Streets.[3]

Samuel Murdoch and Ann LEWIS were married 8 September 1774, according to the register of St. Paul's Church, 3rd Street below Walnut, Philadelphia, with license of 1st September 1774.[6a] The bride was born 26th of 12th month 1753, youngest of the twelve children of Robert and Mary (Pyle) Lewis of Kennet Township, Chester County, Penna., who removed to Philadelpiha in 1758,[7] birthright members of the Society of Friends. Ann (Lewis) Murdoch died 6-9mo-1779 age 26.[8]

The Federal Census of 1790 lists Samuel Murdoch as grocer, with store on east side of Front Street and west side of Water Street, in the Southern District of Philadelphia.

The Will of Samuel Murdoch of Philadelphia, Merchant, dated 8 July 1803 and proved 23 and 29 August 1803, leaves sister Sarah Sweers an annuity of 40 pounds and requests son Robert Murdoch to care for her for "the great care she has taken of me during my sickness"; devises to said son Robert the remainder of estate excepting 80 dollars to Sarah Maltby "for her services during my stay in her house", to nephew Samuel Murdoch my gold watch and wearing apparel; to Thomas Tingey a portion "coming to me of 600 acres of land on Sleepy Creek, New Jersey"; and appoints Thomas Tingey, Joseph Lownes, and John Large executors, "until the return of my son Robert Murdoch, and on his arrival do request that he be invested with the sole executorship", and "In case it should please God to take my son Robert Murdoch before he returns, all the property of his I give to Margaret Tingey, wife of Capt. Tingey, and her daughters Margaret, Hannah, and Sarah Tingey." Recorded in *Philadelphia Will Book no. 1*, p. 127.

Children of Samuel and Ann (Lewis) Murdoch:

    i. Mary Murdoch buried 8-8mo-1776 age 1 yr in Phila Frds b. gr.

    ii. Phebe Murdoch buried 31-7mo-1778 aged 2 yrs in same.[8]

14. ii. Robert Murdoch d 17 Dec 1817 aged 39 yrs.

5. THOMAS MURDOCH, third son and sixth of the eleven children of William and Mary Murdoch of Philadelphia, was born there 2 March 1744 NS and baptised 18 March 1744 "aged 19 days" in Christ Church. He died 9 August 1779 "at 5 o'clock in the morning, opposite Wilmington, Del., in the river Delaware, returning from Martinico, W.I.",[2] and was buried 10 August 1779 as "Captain Thomas Murdoch" in Christ Church burial ground,[3] SE cor 5th and Arch Streets, Philadelphia, with gravestone inscribed: "*In Memory of | Thomas Murdoch | died August 9th 1779 | aged 34 years*".[4] He was evidently the one of this name who appears as Master of the brigantine *Nancy* of 30 tons in 1769 and 1770, of sloop *Chance* of 35 tons in 1772, and of brigantine *Fancy* of 40 tons in 1773.[9]

Thomas Murdoch and Ann STERRAT were married 14 September 1768, according to the register of St. Paul's Church, 3rd Street below Walnut, Philadelphia, with license of same date.[9a] The Will of Thomas Murdoch of Philadelphia, dated 9 October 1772 and proved 18 February 1780, names wife Ann, brother Samuel Murdoch, nephew Thomas Brooks Murdoch, and niece Sarah Sweers. Recorded in *Philadelphia Will Book Q*, p 260.

Child of Thomas and Ann (Sterrat) Murdoch:

    i. Mary Murdoch buried 7 Aug 1773 in Christ Ch bur grd.[3]

6. HANNAH MURDOCH, third daughter and seventh of eleven children of William and Mary Murdoch of Philadelphia, was born there 16 January 1746 and baptised in Christ Church 28 January 1746. As Mrs. Hannah Sweers she died 19 June 1810 aged 63 years,[10] and was buried in Christ Church burial ground, SE Cor 5th and Arch Streets.[3] In the Federal Census of 1790, Hannah Swires, boarding house, east side of Front Street, 2 males over 16, 3 males under 16, 3 females, and 1 slave, is so listed, Philadelphia, Southern District and in the Philadelphia Directory for 1791, " Hannah Swires, boarding house, 71 So. Front Street."

Cornelius SWEERS and Hannah Murdoch were married 26 April 1770,[11] with license of 24th.[12] He took the oath of Allegiance to Pennsylvania on 27 June 1777 in Philadelphia.[13] On 25 February 1777 he had been appointed Clerk of the Philadelphia Navy Board.[14] Later he was commissioned Deputy Commissary General of Military Stores of the Continental Army, but was charged with malconduct, and by Resolution of Congress of 1 August 1778 was confined in Philadelphia gaol for trial.[15] Convicted and sentenced to the pillory, Cornelius Sweers wrote a petition for mercy to the Supreme Executive Council of Penna., dated 21 April 1779.[16] His estate is not found in Philadelphia probates, and the date of death between 1780 and 1790 and place of burial have not been recovered for this account. As " Cornelius Sweers of the city of Philadelphia, Gentleman ", he joined the other heirs of William Murdoch in conveying real estate by Deeds of 24 February 1780 and 13 May 1780, cited above.

Children of Cornelius and Hannah (Murdoch) Sweers: [2]

 i.   Sarah Sweers b 22 Feb 1771; d 31 July 1854 in Bklyn NY; mar 17 Aug 1796 Charles MALTBY.[17]
 ii. Samuel Sweers b 6 July 1772; d 9 Nov 1773; bur in Christ Ch bur grd Phila.[3]
 iii. Mary Sweers b 9 Dec 1774; d 29 July 1775; bur same.
 iv. William Sweers b 26 Nov 1775; d 7 Nov 1776; bur same.
 v.   Mary Sweers b 24 Nov 1776; d 25 Nov 1783; bur same.

7. JOHN MURDOCH, fourth son and eighth of the eleven children of William and Mary Murdoch of Philadelphia, was born there 8 July 1748 and baptised in Christ Church 21 July 1748. He died in Woodbury, N.J., in 1786 intestate, and his wife Sarah Murdoch died there in 1796 also intestate. John Murdoch, goldsmith, Front Street between Walnut and Spruce Streets, was so listed in the Philadelphia Directory for 1785.

John Murdoch and Sarah WHITALL " both of Philadelphia " were married 11 July 1772 " at the house of Elijah Weed, at the corner of Arch & Fourth Streets " by the Rev. William Rogers, pastor of the First Baptist

Church of that city,[18] with a license of same date. The bride was a daughter of James and Ann (Cooper) Whitall,[19] of Red Bank, Deptford Township, Gloucester County, N.J., a birthright member of the Religious Society of Friends. Sarah Murdoch appeared at the Women Friends Monthly Meeting at Haddonfield, N.J., of 14-6mo-1773 with her written admission of infraction of the discipline in her marriage out of Meeting to one not a member, and the Meeting of 13-9mo-1773 accepted it and restored her to membership. Sarah Murdoch requested of the Monthly Meeting of 12-9mo-1774 a certificate to Philadelphia. Her request was granted, and she presented the certificate to the Women's Meeting of the Southern District of Philadelphia of 22-2mo-1775, and as " Sarah wife of John Murdoch " she was received as a member.[20] They removed in 1785 to Woodbury.

Administration upon the estate of John Murdoch, silversmith, late of Woodbury, Deptford Township, Gloucester County, N.J., deceased intestate, was granted to [his widow] Sarah Murdoch, who gave Bond dated 31 October 1786, with (her brother) John S. Whitall as fellowbondsman.[21] Administration upon the estate of Sarah Murdoch, late of Gloucester County, deceased, intestate, was granted to Dr. Benjamin Whitall Jr., who gave bond dated 28 December 1796, and administration *de bonis non* was granted to [her son] James Murdoch of said County, who gave bond dated 27 November 1797, said Dr. Benjamin Whitall being then deceased.[21]

Children of John and Sarah (Whitall) Murdoch: [2]

15. i.   James W. Murdoch d 1833-34; mar Maria Kelly.
16. ii. John Murdoch d 6 June 1829; mar Louise Ramundeau.
    iii. Joseph Murdoch d in Sep 1802.
    iv. Hannah Murdoch d 20 July 1797.
17. v.   Samuel Murdoch d after 1822; mar Mary Black.
    vi. William Murdoch d in Jan 1799.[22]

8. MARGARET MURDOCH, fourth daughter and ninth of the eleven children of William and Mary Murdoch of Philadelphia, was born there 26 July 1750 and baptised in Christ Church 8 August 1750. " THOMAS and MARGARET TINGEY (were) married on Easter Sunday evening the 30th March 1777 by the reverend Cecil Wray Goodchild, minister of the English Episcopal Church in the island of St. Croix." [29] The register of St. John's Church, Christiansted, St. Croix, West Indies, also contains record of this marriage, with the pertinent detail that it was celebrated " At the house of Mr. Beale ", who was the bride's brother-in-law and her host at the time.

1750 Sep 11: Born in London, son of a clergyman.[23]

1771 July 31: Appointed to command fort and garrison at Pitts Harbour, Chateau Bay, Labrador, by Capt the Hon John Byron, Commander-in-Chief of His Majesty's vessels employed about the Island of New Foundland.[24]

1777 Mar 30: Married in St Croix, Danish West Indies, Margaret Murdoch of Philadelphia.[2]

1778 Jan 19: Daughter Ann Tingey born in St Croix.[2]

1778 Apr 10 to Nov 16: Commander of merchant brig *Lady Clausen* on voyage from Bass End Harbour, St Croix, to Gottenburg, Denmark, and return.[25]

1779 Sep 26: Son Thomas Tingey born in Philadelphia.[2]

1780 Feb 24: Thomas Tingey of Philadelphia, " mariner ", and wife Margaret, cograntors of Murdoch real estate by Deed.

1781 June 1: Daughter Mary Tingey born in St Croix.[2]

1782 Sep 27: Daughter Margaret Gay Tingey born in St Croix.[2]

1783 Nov 19: Daughter Hannah Tingey born in Philadelphia.[2]

1785 Aug 24: Daughter Phebe Tingey buried in Philadelphia.[3]

1786   : Commander of merchant ship *Pallas* of Philadelphia.

1786 June 27: Son Thomas Tingey buried in Philadelphia.[3]

1788 July 2: In St. Croix, letter to Richard Vaux *re* sale of goods there.[26]

1788 Aug. 16: In St. Croix, letter to John Wilcocks *re* same; expresses Hope to receive my family; left optional with Mrs. Tingey to come or wait till I had leisure to return." [26]

1789 Mar 23: An officer of merchant ship *Harmony*, Capt Willett, off Cape of Good Hope; left ship at Calcutta, India.[26]

1789 Dec 15 to 18 Jan 1790: At Calcutta, India; letters *re* merchant trading and shipping to John Fitzsimmons, Stephen Ward, Daniel Tyson, Richard Vaux, William Porteous, Samuel Wilcox, David Cay, and Thomas Willing Francis.[26]

1790 Federal Census, Southern District of City of Philadelphia; south side of Union Street; Capt Thomas Tingey, mariner, 1-2-4, 1 slave.

1790 Jan 22: Having accepted commission from Graham, Mowbray & Co., to take command of ship which they had purchased in England, he sailed as supercargo from Bengal in ship *La Maria*, Capt Antonio Morelett, bound for Ostend; anchored at Madras 3 Feb to 13 Feb; shipwrecked on shore at Table Bay, Cape of Good Hope 12 April.[26]

1790 Apr 29: Sailed from Cape of Good Hope as supercargo in Dutch ship bound for Amsterdam; arrived 29 July in London.[26]

1790 Aug 23: Embarked at Deal, England, as supercargo in ship *Goliath*, bound for New York; arrived 1 Dec in Phila.[26]

1791 *Philadelphia Directory* lists " Tingey, Thomas, sea captain, 16 Union Street." (Now DeLancey Street.   LDC)

1791 Jan 22: In command of ship *Barings*, for the owners Willing Morris & Swanwick of Philadelphia, departure from Delaware Bay prevented by ice; bound for India.[26]

1791 Nov 14 to Dec 18: with ship *Baring* at Calcutta, India.[26]

1792 Jan 3: Sailed in ship *Baring* from Calcutta, bound for England, *via* Ostend; Jan 15 at Madras; Mar 16 at Cape of Good Hope; June 6 to July 17 at London; arrives with ship *Baring* at Philadelphia, *via* Ostende, Sep 18.[26]

1792-93: In a list of "over one hundred prominent citizens of the City," subscribers to the building fund: Thomas Tingey. (T. W. Balch, *The Philadelphia Assemblies*, 97-99.)

1793 Jan: Left Philadelphia by stagecoach on business trip to Brown & Francis at Providence, R. I., and made engagement there to command their ship *GW* (?George Washington) on voyage to Bengal, India, in succeeding Oct or Nov.[26]

1793 Jan to June 15: In Philadelphia.[26]

1794 *Philadelphia Directory* lists "Tingey, Thomas, sea captain, 121 South Third Street." (By Deed of 27 March 1793 Thomas Franklin of Philadelphia, gentleman, conveyed to Thomas Tingey of said city, mariner, a brick messuage and lot 19½ by 100 feet, on east side of Third Street between Walnut and Spruce Streets, bounded North by late Francis Ferris and South by Samuel Lobdell, as is recited in a Deed of 24 Oct 1796 in which Thomas Tingey of Philadelphia, mariner, and wife Margaret, conveyed same property to Matthew Randall of same place, merchant, for 3000 Pounds. *Philadelphia Deed Book D-62 p 85.*)

1794   : Thomas Tingey, a Private in the First Company of Third Regiment of Philadelphia City Militia, under command of Lieut Col Samuel McClean. (*Penn Archives* 6th ser V, 508.)

1795 May 4: Sailed from Philadelphia in command of merchant ship *Ganges*, launched there April 4, on voyage to Madeira, Bengal, and Madras, India, with crew of 26 including his nephews James Murdoch 3rd officer, John Murdoch clerk, and William Murdoch ordinary seaman, returning to home port Philadelphia on 17 May 1796.[25]

1796 Oct 24: Thomas Tingey of Philadelphia, "mariner", and wife Margaret convey to Matthew Randall their house on east side of Third Street, between Walnut and Spruce, by deed.

1796 Nov 30: Daniel Clarkson of South Brunswick Twp, Middlesex County, N. J., conveys to Thomas Tingey of same place, "Gentleman", for 3,667 Pounds, a 330 acre plantation there in Mapletown, on Heathcote Brook, (south of the village of Kingston and east of Princeton). Tingey and wife mortgaged the property to grantor on same date for $7000, and by deed of 28 April 1800 reconveyed it to him.[27]

1797 Feb 6: His letter from Kingston to daughter Margaret G. Tingey at "Mrs. Capron's Boarding School, New Market Ward, Philadelphia", mentions family's visit at Capt. Truxtun's residence in Perth Amboy, N. J.[28]

1798 Sept 3: Commission as Captain in U. S. Navy, and orders to command USS *Ganges* were contained in letter from Benjamin Stoddert, Secretary of the Navy, addressed to "Capt Thomas Tingey, Princeton", dated 16 Sep; accepted in letter by Tingey at "Kingston, 17th September 1798". (Official Letter Book)

1799 March 25: On board ship *Ganges* in Hampton Roads, bound for West Indies, states his letter to daughters Margaret and Hannah at Kingston, N. J.[28] USS *Ganges*, 504 tons, purchased by U. S. Navy in 1798, fitted with 24 guns; sold in 1801. For action in War with France, see Appleton's *Cyclopedia of American Biography* VI, 122; *Dict Amer Biogr* XVIII.

1800 *Philadelphia Directory*, under "American Navy", lists: Sloop of War *Ganges*, 24 guns, Capt Thomas Tingey, Lieutenants James Burnes, Henry Kenyon, Allen M'Kenzie, Purser Robert Lewis, Surgeon's Mate Daniel Hughes.

1800 Jan 22: Capt Thomas Tingey USN of Kingston, N. J., appointed superintendent of the new Navy Yard at Washington DC. Letter of same date from Secretary Stoddert to William Marbury, naval agent for District of Columbia, says: " Capt Thomas Tingey, of the Navy, an officer of great merit in our service, has been ordered to Washington with a view to superintend the building of the 74-gun ship, and to aid in the arrangement of the navy-yard, the improvements of which he will also superintend. . . . Captain Tingey being a man of understanding and *having seen the navy-yards of England*, will be able to direct the layings of that in Washington to greatest advantage." (Hidden, *History of the Washington Navy Yard*, published in Senate Documents, 1st session of 51st Congress, 1890)

1800 Feb: At Georgetown, Potomac, (Washington DC); letter to daughters at Kingston, N. J., " I hope you went to the Assembly you mention to be instituted at Trenton. It will always be extremely satisfactory to me to hear of your enjoyment of the pleasures of society in large mixed assemblies sometimes, as well as more frequent small social parties; both have their uses, & may be made profitable in unbending and enlarging the amiable qualities of youthful minds, fitting them for casual & transient social intercourse, as well as for imbibing valuable permanent friendly attachments, assists much in correcting the ' Mauvaise honte ' which is however frequently the result of an amiable & becoming diffidence. In this correction it is nevertheless equally essential to avoid the levity of the giddy & thoughtless as the haughty reserve of the prude or the sullen silence of the melancholy,—the first too frequently progresses to licentiousness, while the two latter have a tendency to promote malignancy in the mind, and under it prone to envious sarcasm, cousin german to, or nearly approximating, slander! that most detestable quality of Youth or Age of either Sex." [28]

1800 May 16: Returned with wife to Washington from Kingston, N. J., by this date and took lodgings, after which they were guests of Mr. & Mrs. Law and of Mr. & Mrs. Beale in Georgetown.[28] ("Captain Thomas Tingey and Mrs. Tingey, who lived in a two-story frame house at the northwest corner of 11th and G Streets, SE, according to the Centinel of Liberty of 6 April 1801 "—W. B. Bryan, *Hist of Natl Capital*, 381.)

1804 Nov 23: recommissioned Captain USN., and appointed Commandant of Washington Navy Yard and Navy Agent. (*Dict Amer Biog* 1936)

1807 Occupied the newly-built Commandant's Houses in Navy Yard, designed by B. H. Latrobe, Architect and Surveyor of the public buildings of the U.S. at Washington. House escaped destruction in the burning of the Yard in 1814 and serves its original function 1947.

1814 Aug 24: Order from Secretary of the Navy to Commandant Tingey directing the ships, stores, etc., at the Navy Yard to be destroyed at the approach of the invading British, and in the evening he executed same by firing, and to escape capture retired by boat across the Potomac river to Alexandria where he wrote report to Secretary on 27th. (Original report in files of Naval Records and Library of Navy Dept. See also there the Booth-Tingey communications, published in *Americana* I, 7-27)

1829 Feb 23: Commodore Thomas Tingey, USN, died in Commandant's House at Washington DC Navy Yard; aged 79 years, intestate.

Niles' Register, Baltimore, 14 March 1829:

Died, at the navy yard, Washington, aged 79 years, commodore Thomas Tingey, commandant of the yard and for 28 years a resident there, in that capacity. He was among the oldest officers of the navy, and much esteemed for his public and private character./Naval General Order:/As a mark of respect to the memory of commodore Thomas Tingey, late of the United States' navy, who died this morning at 10 o'clock, the flags of the navy yards, stations and vessels of the United States' navy are to be hoisted half mast, and thirteen minute guns fired at noon on the day after receipt of this order. Officers of the navy and marine corps are to wear crape for thirty days./ Navy Department, Feb. 23d, 1829.

Gravestone inscription, Washington (Congressional) Cemetery:

SACRED
to the memory
of
Commodore THOMAS TINGEY
of the U.S.Navy who departed this life the 23rd February 1829 aged 79 years.
Also of his wives
MARGARET, who departed this life the 25th April 1807 aged 57 years.
ANN BLADEN, who departed this life April 1814, aged 29 years.

and grand daughters
TINGEY ANNA WINGATE
who departed this life
20th August 1910 aged 11 months 27 days

ANN MARY CRAVEN
who departed this life
26th Sept. 1827 aged 21 years
11 months & 6 days.
Blessed are the dead who die in the Lord

His first wife Margaret (Murdoch) Tingey, having died in Washington, D. C., 25 April 1807, aged 57 years, as abovesaid, Commodore Thomas Tingey married, secondly, 9 December 1812 in Christ Church in that city Ann Bladen DULANY, who died 28 April 1814, aged 29 years, and was likewise buried. He married, thirdly, 19 May 1817, apparently in Ringoes, Hunterdon County, N. J., Ann Evelina CRAVEN, the Rev Mr. Kirkpatrick, minister of the Presbyterian Churches of East Amwell Township, said County, officiating (*County Clerk's Marriage Records*). She was born 26 March 1787 there, and died, testate, 28 July 1861 in Lambertville, said County, and was buried in Goat Hill Cemetery there, with gravestone marker, daughter of Dr. Gershom Craven and wife Rebecca (Quick) Craven of " Willow Hill ", Ringoes, and thus a sister of Tingey's son-in-law Tunis Craven, USN. See her obituary in Appendix.

Division of Tingey Real Estate

By Indenture of 15 June 1837, Archibald Henderson of Washington DC, Thomas T. Craven, Alfred W. Craven, Tunis A.M. Craven, and Charles E. Craven, heirs-at-law of Hannah T. Craven deceased wife of Tunis Craven, and Daniel F. Dulany and wife Sarah A.T. Dulany of Fairfax County, Va., conveyed to Margaret G.T. Wingate of Maine for $5.00 the lots nos. 11, 12, 13, 14, 15, 19, 20, 21 in Square no 974 and lot no. 6 in Square no. 902, containing 53, 413 square feet and assessed at $745.00. Recital that Commodore Thomas Tingey late of Washington DC died intestate in 1829 in possession of real estate there, to wit:—lots nos. 6, 7, 8, 9, 10 in Square no. 902; lot no. 10 in

Square no. 878; lots nos. 5, 6, 7, 8, and 22, 23, 24 in Square no. 973; and lots nos. 8 to 24 inclusive in Square no. 974, leaving as sole heirs-at-law three daughters Hannah T. Craven since deceased wife of said Tunis T. Craven, Margaret G. T. Wingate wife of Joseph F. Wingate, and Sarah A. T. Dulany wife of Daniel F. Dulany, and that after death of said Thomas Tingey the said Tunis Craven and Joseph F. Wingate by their deeds dated 16 March 1829 and recorded conveyed their rights in said property to said Archibald Henderson in Trust for disposition by their wives, and all parties interested in the division of said real estate have agreed that said Margaret G.T. Wingate shall have and possess the lots as first abovesaid, that Tunis Craven shall have lots nos. 5, 6, 7, 8, 22, 23, 24 in Square no. 973 and nos. 7, 8, 9, 10 in Square no. 902, containing 52,766 square feet and assessed at $629.00, and that said Sarah A. T. Dulany shall have lots nos. 8, 9, 10, 16, 17, 18, 22, 23, 24 in Square no. 974 and no. 10 in Square no. 878, containing 53,950 square feet and assessed at $780.00.

Will of the Widow of Thomas Tingey

The Will of Ann E. Tingey of Lambertville, N. J., dated 27 March 1860 and proved 2 September 1861, devises to " Sydney Sewall, grand daughter of my departed husband, all the silverware that belonged to him *viz* Tea pot, sugar bowl, 12 tea spoons, 10 table spoons, and soup ladle; " orders executors to sell her house and lot where she lives in Lambertville, also her stock, shares and stock in Washington, D. C., Bank, in Brooklyn Savings Bank, and in Boston and Providence Railroad Company; devises the bond for $450.00 held against Thomas Craven, USN., to his daughter Eveline Craven; to Elizabeth Kirkpatrick daughter of Dr. Jacob Kirkpatrick $100.00; to sister Catharine Craven sufficient income for her support; residue of estate to be divided equally between Isaac and Rebecca Craven children of brother Thomas Craven, Helen and Martha Crabb daughters of Thomas Crabb, Hannah T. Craven wife of Revd Elijah Craven, Annie Seabrooks daughter of Thomas Seabrooks, Alfred Barber son of Johnson Barber, Margaret Dulany and Julia Wingate grandchildren of my deceased husband Thomas Tingey; and appoints Charles O. Holcombe, Alfred Barber, and James D. Stryker the executors.

Children of Thomas and Margaret (Murdoch) Tingey: [29]

 i. Ann Tingey b 19 Jan 1778 in St Croix; bap 4 Mar 1778 St. John's Ch Christiansted; d 2 Sep 1778.

 ii. Thomas Tingey b 26 Oct 1779 in Phila.; bap 22 Dec 1779 Christ Ch; d 23 Dec 1779; bur Christ Ch.[3]

 iii. Mary Tingey b 1 June 1781 in St Croix; bap 15 Sep 1781 St. John's Ch Christiansted; d 1781.

18. iv. Margaret Gay Tingey b 27 Sep 1782 in St Croix; bap 10 Nov 1782 in St John's Ch Christiansted; mar 29 Nov 1808 Joseph Ferdinand WINGATE.

19. v. Hannah Tingey b 19 Nov 1783 in Phila.; bap 6 Dec 1783 Christ Ch; mar 25 Sep 1803 Tunis CRAVEN.

 vi. Phebe Tingey b   1785; bur 24 Aug 1785 in Christ Church burial ground, Phila.[3]

 vii. Thomas Tingey b 7 Feb 1786; bur 27 June 1786 *ditto*.[3]

 viii. Thomas Tyson Tingey b ——; bur 25 July 1790 *ditto*.[3]

20. ix. Sarah Ann Tingey b 19 Aug 1791 in Phila.; mar 1 April 1811 Daniel French DULANY.

10. JOHN BEALE, eldest son of George and Mary (Murdoch) Beale of the Island of St Croix, Danish West Indies (now Virgin Islands of the U.S. of A.), born there 27 December 1756, " Was sent to England to be educated; inherited the family estate ",[2] but of him no final account has been obtained for this record. As her " Eldest son and attorney ", John Beale represented Mary (Murdoch) Beale, widow, of St Croix, in conveying her share of her father's real estate in Philadelphia by the seven-part Deeds of 1780. He is not named or mentioned in her Will of 5 April 1796, Philadelphia.

11. GEORGE BEALE, born about 1758, second son of George and Mary (Murdoch) Beale of St Croix, DWI, " was educated in France ".[2] George Beale " Sr.", aged about 65 years, formerly of Norfolk, Va., died 9 December 1823 at the residence of his son in Washington, DC, as noticed in the *National Intelligencer* of next day.[30a] He married first Mary DIXON, who died before 1816, daughter of Thomas and Mary (Tucker) Dixon of Elizabeth County, Va.[30] In 1810 George Beale established a cut-nail factory in Washington and imported coal from Richmond for retail trade, having settled in the federal city in 1809, coming there from Norfolk, Va.[28] He married *secondly* 4 December 1817, with a Prince George County, Md., license of 2 September,[31] Elizabeth (Lane) BOWIE, widow of Captain Eversfield Bowie of said County who had died in March 1815 in Washington, DC, and was buried in Rock Creek Churchyard.[32] She was born 10 August 1780, daughter of Captain Lane and his wife Barbara (Brook) Lane.[32]

Children of George Beale and 1st wife Mary Dixon: [33]

21. i.   Robert Beale b 1790; mar Eliza Jane Forbes.
22. ii.   George Beale b   1792; d 5 Apr 1835.
23. iii. Catharine Ann Beale mar 20 Oct 1826 John Peirce CROSBY.
      iv. Ellen Beale.
      v.   Maria Beale.
      vi. John Beale.

Children of George Beale and 2nd wife Elizabeth (Lane) Bowie:

      vii. a child d young.
24. viii. Elizabeth Ann Beale b 1818; mar Cdr William D. PORTER USN.

12. MARY BEALE, daughter of George Beale and Mary Murdoch of the Island of St. Croix, Virgin Islands of the United States, apparently died before the date of her mother's Will of 5 April 1796, having mar-

ried before 1788 Captain JOHN KELLY who died testate 12 January 1821, in 81st year, at his home, no 81 Penn Street, District of Southwark, County of Philadelphia, Penna., and was buried in St. Mary's R.C. Churchyard on 4th Street below Locust in the City of Philadelphia.[34] The Federal Census of 1790 lists John Kelly, grocer, with store on west side of Swanson Street in Southwark Town, Philadelphia County, and the Philadelphia Directory of 1821 lists John Kelly, grocer, 20 Swanson Street, and 79 Penn Street. In 1788 Capt. John Kelly paid rental of £1 2s. 6d., for pew no. 4 in St. Mary's Church.

The Will of Capt. John Kelly of Southwark, Philadelphia County, Penna., Grocer, dated 11 January 1821 and proved 23 February 1821, devises to son John the messuage and lot where I now dwell, on the east side of Penn and west side of Water Streets, between Cedar and Almond Streets, all household goods, furniture, plate, and silver, the house to be rented "until my son returns"; orders stock of goods and liquors in his store and cellar, all fixtures etc to be sold and the proceeds, with the residuary estate, to be put out at interest for daughter Maria Murdoch, and at her death to all her children and to Mary Duffield; and appoints Joseph Snyder, blacksmith, and Thomas Brown Sr., stove merchant, the executors. Also directs that "In case my son should depart this life before he returns to this country" that said house be included in the residuary estate, and devises to said son books, charts, and nautical instruments. Recorded in *Philadelphia Will Book no. 7*, page 261.

By Deed of (*blank*) 1837, "John Kelly of the Navy of the U.S. of A.," Maria N. Murdoch of Kingsessing Twp., Philadelphia County, Penna., widow, Ellen D. Murdoch, John J. Murdoch, and William A. Murdoch, of same place, children of said Maria N. Murdoch, and Mary Kelly Duffield of New York, heirs and devisees of John Kelly late of Southwark, County Philadelphia, deceased, discharge Thomas Brown and Joseph Snyder, executors of said Kelly. (*Phila. Deed Book* SHF-19, page 615)

By Deed of 15 Feb 1840 the Sheriff of Philadelphia conveyed to Charles Stokes of Philadelphia, gent., the highest bidder at a public sale held at the Merchants' Exchange on 6 Jan., the messuage and lot on the bank between Front and Water Streets in said city, which Archibald McCall and wife by Deed of 10 Dec 1782 conveyed to Mary Beale, reciting that said grantee by her Will of 5 April 1796 devised the property to Maria Murdoch, then Maria Kelly, and to Eleanor Kelly, and that said Maria Kelly married James W. Murdoch and said Eleanor Kelly married John Duffield and died intestate leaving issue 3 children: Charles E. Duffield, Mary Duffield late of Phila., and James Duffield late of NYC, and that their father John Duffield is also since deceased. Recites further that Sheriff seized this property of James W. Murdoch and wife Maria in her right and of Charles E. Duffield, Mary Duffield, and James M. Duffield, in execution of judgment obtained against them by said Charles Stokes, executor of the estate of Mary Stokes decd., in an action for debt of $1807.20 and cost of $25.25. Recorded in *Phila. Deed Book GS-11*, 439. By Deed of 9 March 1840 said Charles Stokes conveyed same property to William E. Stevenson. *Deed Book GS-11*, 444.

Children of Capt. John and Mary (Beale) Kelly:

    i. Maria Nesbit Kelly mar 29 Nov 1807 Capt. James W. MURDOCH, no. 10.

25. ii. Eleanor Kelly mar 16 May 1805 John DUFFIELD.

26. iii. John Kelly, Commodore USN, d 5 Feb 1863, in 68th yr.

13. THOMAS BROOKS MURDOCH, born 1763-1772, son of William and Jane (Brooks) Murdoch of Philadelphia and of Greenwich Township, Cumberland County, N.J., is supposed here to be identical with the Thomas Murdoch of Philadelphia, who is listed in Philadelphia Directories of 1810 to 1839 or later as a bookbinder, who served in the War of 1812 as an officer in Artillery volunteers, and who had wife Elizabeth and four sons, including James Edward Murdoch, the actor, lecturer, and manager (See *Dictionary of American Biography*, XIII, 341.) But the estate of Thomas Murdoch is not found in Philadelphia probates, and other than the baptism of two children in Christ Church, no further records have been found. Thomas Murdoch, bookbinder, and Elizabeth KEEL, daughter of Baltus Keel or Keely, were married 23 Jany 1808, the Rev. Mr. Helfenstein of First Reformed Church, Phila., officiating.

Children of Thomas and Elizabeth (Keely) Murdoch:

i. Susannah Elizabeth Murdoch b 27 Sep 1808, bap 26 July 1809 in Christ Church, Phila.

ii. James Edward Murdoch b 25 Jan 1811, bap 6 Sept 1811, Christ Church, Phila.; d 19 May 1893 in Cincinnati, Ohio; mar 23 Aug 1831 Eliza M. Middlecott, *per* register of St. Andrew's Church, Phila., daughter of a London silversmith.

iii. Three sons, of whom no information for this account.

14. ROBERT MURDOCH born in 1778, only son of Samuel and Ann (Lewis) Murdoch of Philadelphia, died there 17 December 1817 aged 39 years, intestate, and was buried next day in Christ Church burial ground, SE Cor 5th and Arch Streets.[35] Robert Murdoch and Emily BRIDGES, daughter of the late Robert Bridges of Philadelphia, were married 20 December 1808, by Bishop William White, the Rector of Christ Church, Philadelphia.[3] Mrs. Emily Murdoch, of Front Street near South, aged 29 years, died 10 November 1817,[35] and was buried on the 12th in said burial ground.[3]

Administration on the estate of Robert Murdoch deceased was granted 23 December 1817 to David Lewis and Lawrence Lewis, with Anthony Stocker and George Lewis, both of the city of Philadelphia, merchants, as securities (*Phila. Administration Book M*, p 66).

By deed of 1 August 1834, Harriet B. Murdoch, Ann L. Murdoch, Emily M. Murdoch, and Robert B. Murdoch, children and heirs of Robert and Emily Murdoch, formerly Emily Bridges, one of the daughters of Robert Bridges, late of the city of Philadelphia, deceased, convey to Mary Bridges of said city, spinster, for $1.00 the one-fifth part of two ground rents. (*Phila. Deed Book GS-34*, p 331)

Jemima Bridges petitioned the Philadelphia Orphans Court of 20 February 1818 that Robert Murdoch died leaving issue Harriet Bridges Murdoch, Ann Lewis Murdoch, Emily Mary Murdoch, Robert Bridges Murdoch, and Phebe Pemberton Murdoch, all minors under age 14, and the Court appointed her their guardian. (*Phila. Orphans Court Docket no 27*, p 3). On 20 March 1829 Mary Bridges was appointed guardian of Robert Murdoch's children (*Idem no. 31*, p. 443).

Children of Robert and Emily (Bridges) Murdoch: [36]

i. Harriet Bridges Murdoch b 5 Oct 1809.

ii. Ann Lewis Murdoch b 28 July 1811.

iii. Emily Mary Murdoch b 28 Mar 1813.

iv. Robert Bridges Murdoch b 25 Mar 1815; " went to Columbus, Georgia, where he married and has children: Harriet, Anne Lewis, and Emily Murdoch ".[2]

v. Phebe Pemberton Murdoch d 3 Dec 1819 aged 2 yrs 6 mos.

15. JAMES WHITALL MURDOCH, born after 1772 and died 1833-34, son of John and Sarah (Whitall) Murdoch of Philadelphia and of Woodbury, N.J., is last listed, in the Philadelphia City Directory of 1833, as " Sea captain, 5 North 13th Street ", but his estate is not found in the Philadelphia probates and the exact date and place of his death has not been recovered here. Capt James W. Murdoch and Maria N., daughter of the late Capt John KELLY, were married on 29 November 1807,[37] being first cousins once removed. In 1837 his widow Maria N. Murdoch and children Ellen D., John J., and William A. Murdoch, were living in Paschallville, Kingsessing Township, Philadelphia County.[38] Further record of his widow has not been found for this account. One James Murdoch was commissioned Lieut USN 15 Nov 1799 and discharged 14 Apr 1804 (Callahan, *Officers of the U.S. Navy*), and James W. Murdoch, Lieut 9 Aug 1804, was out of service 25 June 1806.

Children of Capt. James W. and Maria N. (Kelly) Murdoch: [2]

i. Ellen Duffield Murdoch married William CURRY; no issue.

ii. John Joseph Murdoch married ———— in St. Louis, Mo.; widow and children lived near Philadelphia.

iii. William A. Murdoch, a farmer, of Darby Township, Delaware Co., Penna., 1844, and of Kingsessing Township, Philadelphia County, 1848; mar Hannah Smith, daughter of Elizabeth (Paschall) Smith; his estate not found in Philadelphia probates; had two daughters, one of whom married.[2]

16. JOHN MURDOCH, born in Philadelphia, son of no. 7 John and Sarah (Whitall) Murdoch of that city and of Woodbury, N.J., died 6 June 1829 in Havana, Cuba, a senior partner of the house of Murdoch, Storey & Co. of that city, and after nearly 30 years residence there.[39] He married Louise RAMUNDEAU of Havana.[1]

Children of John and Louise (Ramundeau) Murdoch: [40]

i. Margaretta Gimball Murdoch b 13 Jan 1806; mar the Rev Clement F. JONES of Md., 13 Oct 1831 in Trinity Church, Boston, Mass.[37]

ii. James Murdoch b 17 Apr 1807; d 15 June 1883 unmar in Boston, Mass; a master mariner.

iii. Charles Tracy Murdoch b 5 Jan 1809; d 25 Nov 1853 Cambridge, Mass; grad Harvard 1828; mar Elizabeth Fosdick; no issue.

iv. Joseph Murdoch b 4 July 1810; d 27 Apr 1884 Boston, Mass; insurance broker there; mar Caroline Dorcas Smith; no issue.

v. John Murdoch b 5 Feb 1813; d 16 May 1871 Pepperell, Mass; mar Elizabeth Smith 3 Oct 1850 Roxbury, Mass; 6 children.

vi. William Murdoch b 23 Apr 1814; d 1882 (?); a planter in Cuba.

vii. Louisa Murdoch b 13 Jan 1817; d 1887 (?); mar —— KING and res Baltimore, Md.

17. SAMUEL MURDOCH died after 1817, in which year the Philadelphia City Directory lists him as " Sea-captain, 24 Union Street "; was a son of John and Sarah (Whitall) Murdoch of Philadelphia and of Woodbury, N.J. He married 10 May 1815 in Burlington County, N.J.,[41] Mary BLACK, who was born 27 April 1786 in Springfield Township, said County, daughter of John and Lydia Black. She died 14 January 1886 aged 99 years and 9 months in Mt Holly, said County, and was buried there, having been baptised 10 April 1871.[42]

Children of Samuel and Mary (Black) Murdoch: [2]

i. Emma Murdoch

ii. Mary Murdoch

iii. Anna Whitall Murdoch b 9 Aug 1822; bapt 4 Mar 1859 in St. Peter's Church, Phila., with sponsors Mary C. K. Smith and F. M. R. St. Felix.

18. MARGARET GAY TINGEY, born 27 September in the Island of St Croix, Danish West Indies,[29] and baptised 10 November 1782 in St John's Church, Christiansted, there, eldest of the three surviving children of Capt Thomas and Margaret (Murdoch) Tingey, of St. Croix and of Philadelphia, died 19 June 1862 in Oldtown, Maine, and was buried there with gravestone marker. She married 29 November 1808 in Washington, D.C., the Rev. Andrew T. McCormick, rector of Christ Church, officiating, (See certificate in Appendix), Joseph Ferdinand WINGATE who was born 29 June 1786 at Hallowell, Mass., and died 15 May 1864 at South Windsor, Maine, son of Joshua and Hannah (Carr) Wingate. He represented Maine in the U.S. Congress 1827-31.

Children of Joseph Ferdinand and Margaret Gay (Tingey) Wingate: [42a]

i. Tingeyanna Margaretta Wingate b 23 Aug 1809 at Roxbury, Mass; d 20 Aug 1810 aged 12 mos 27 days; bur in Tingey plot in Washington (Congressional) Cemetery.

ii. Virginia Ann Nesbit Wingate b 29 Jan 1811 at Washington; d 30 Apr 1837 at Hallowell, Mass; mar as his 1st wife her 1st cousin Thomas Tingey CRAVEN USN., *q.v.*

iii. Julia Nesbit Wingate b 19 Nov 1812 at Hallowell; d in Home for Aged in Bangor, Maine, unmar; bur Oldtown.

iv. Sydney Ellen Wingate b 10 Mar 1815 at Bath, Maine; d 26 Mar 1887 at Oldtown, Maine; mar 8 Aug 1837 at South Windsor, Maine, George Popham SEWELL, b 24 Apr 1811 at Georgetown, Maine, who d 30 Dec 1881 at Oldtown, son of Joseph and Hannah (Shaw) Sewall of Farmingham, Mass.; 6 children. (Chas. N. Sinnett, *Sewell Genealogy*, 42)

v. Henry Wingate b 15 Mar 1817 in Maine; d 4 May 1854 at Lexington, Mass, aged 37 years and 2 months; Lieut USN 8 Sep 1841; mar Frances Martha Skinner who d 15 Sep 1849 aged 32 at Lexington, dau of (? Wm H) Skinner of Charlestown, Mass; had issue: Margaret Wingate 1844- ca 1907 unmar, lived in family of cousin Alfred W. Craven in NYC as a teacher and chaperone; Henry Tingey Wingate d 13 Apr 1849 aged 3-10-0; Frances Wingate ca 1846-92 unm.

vi. Margaretta Wingate d aged 3 or 4 years; bur Oldtown, Maine.

19. HANNAH TINGEY born 19 November 1783 in Philadelphia, baptised 3 December 1783 in Christ Church there, daughter of Captain Thomas Tingey and wife Margaret Murdoch Tingey, died 4 May 1835 at the Mansion House (hotel) in Hicks Street, Brooklyn, N.Y., where she resided during the duty of husband Tunis Craven at the nearby New York Navy Yard, and was buried in the Craven lot in Greenwood Cemetery, Brooklyn. She married 25 September 1803 at Washington, D.C. (the Rev A. T. McCormick, rector of Christ Church officiating), Tunis CRAVEN,[43] a coal merchant of Alexandria, Va., Purser USN 1812, Storekeeper and Clerk of the Portsmouth N.H. Navy Yard 1813-29 and at New York Navy Yard in Brooklyn 1830-43, who was born 1 August 1781 at Ringoes in Amwell Township, Hunterdon County, N.J., and died 19 July 1866 at the home of his son Alfred W. Craven in West 19th Street, New York City; buried in Greenwood Cemetery; son of Dr. Gershom Craven (A.B. Princeton 1765) and wife Rebecca (Quick) Craven, of " Willow Hill ", Ringoes, abovesaid.

Children of Tunis and Hannah (Tingey) Craven:

i. Margaretta Tingey Craven b 24 Mar 1804 at Wash., DC; d 25 June 1828 at New Brunswick, NJ; bur in Greenwood Cem Bklyn NY; mar Francis SANDER-

SON, Lieut. USN, b 15 Nov 1801, who d 23 Aug 1831 at Balto. Md.; son of Thomas Francis and Margaret (Schley) Sanderson, of Lancaster, Penna.; and had issue.[43a]

ii. Anna Maria Craven b 10 Oct. 1805 at Wash., DC.; d there 26 Sep. 1807; bur in Tingey plot in Congressional Cem.

iii. Thomas Tingey Craven, Rear Admiral USN, b 30 Dec. 1808 in Wash DC Navy Yard; d 23 Aug. 1887 at Charlestown, Mass., Navy Yard; bur. at Geneva, NY, and reinterred 1928 in Arlington National Cem.; mar 1st his first cousin Virginia Ann Nesbit Wingate *above*; mar 2nd 21 Apr 1840 (? at West Point NY) Emily Truxtun Henderson who was b at Georgetown DC and d 28 Nov. 1883 at Staunton, Va., aged 65, and was bur. at Geneva, NY, and reinterred in Arlington National Cem; dau of Thomas Henderson, Surgeon USA, and wife Anna Maria Truxtun, dau of Commodore Thomas Truxtun USN, and had issue.[43b]   (See *Dictionary of American Biography*)

iv. Alfred Wingate Craven b 29 Oct 1810 at Wash DC; d 29 Mar 1879 at Cheswick, England; bur in Greenwood Cem Byln, NY; grad Columbia 1829; mar 1840 Maria Schermerhorn, b 8 July 1813, who d 4 Oct 1864; bur in Greenwood Cem; dau of John and Lucretia (Lefferts) Schermerhorn of NYC; and had issue.[43c]   (See *Appleton's Cycl Amer Biog; Natl Cycl Amer Biog.*)

v. Tunis Augustus Macdonough Craven, Capt USN; b 11 Jan 1813 in Portsmouth, NH, Navy Yard; d 5 Aug 1864 in command of monitor *Tecumseh* in Battle of Mobile Bay, Alabama; mar 1st 16 Apr 1838 at "Linden Hill", Flushing, L.I., Mary Carter who was b 1 Apr 1816 and d 14 Feb 1843 in Brooklyn NY; bur Greenwood Cem there; dau of Robert and Jane (Foster) Carter of Brooklyn and of "Linden Hill", Flushing; and had issue.[43d]   (See *Dict Amer Biogr; Appleton; etc.*) T.A.M. Craven mar 2nd 4 June 1844 in Balto., Marie Louise Stevenson, b 23 May 1817 there, who d 27 Apr 1905 NYC, dau of George Pitt and Elisabeth (Goodwin) Stevenson, and had issue.[43d]

vi. Charles Edmiston Craven b 13 May 1817 at the house of grandfather Com Thomas Tingey in Wash Navy Yard; d 24 Jan 1839 unmar; bur Greenwood Cem Bklyn NY.

20. SARAH ANN TINGEY, born 19 August 1791 in Philadelphia; died 20 September 1861 at Warrenton, Va.; daughter of Captain Thomas and Margaret (Murdoch) Tingey; mar 1st April 1811 at Washington DC (the Rev A. T. McCormick, rector of Christ Ch officiating) Daniel French DULANY, Sr., son of Col Benjamin Tasker and Elizabeth (French) Dulany, and resided at " Oak Mount ", Fairfax County, Virginia; and had issue: [44] (*order uncertain*)

i. Daniel French Dulany b 6 Jan 1812 at Shuters Hill, Fairfax Co Va; Lieut USN; mar Sarah Gantt and had issue: French Dulany, and Nannie Dulany who mar John Peyton de Butts.

ii. Mary Dulany b 14 Mar 1813; d 30 Nov 1856 at " Oakmont "; mar 7 May 1833 Spencer Mottrom BALL, b 24 Feb 1801, who d 21 Apr 1859, son of Dr. Mottrom and Martha Corbin (Turberville) Ball, of Fairfax County Va. and had issue.[45]

iii. Nancy Dulany mar Dr John HUNTER of Wash DC and had issue: John Chapman Hunter who mar Emma Briscoe, and Lucy Mason Hunter.[46] Dr John Hunter mar 2nd Mary Brooke, of Md.

iv. Sarah Ellen Dulany mar Maj John N. CHICHESTER, of Alexandria Va.

v. James Heath Dulany, Capt, *dsp.*

vi. Margaret Dulany unmar,

vii. William Heath (or Herbert?) Dulany.

viii. Winnie Tingey Dulany.

ix. Upton Heath Dulany.

FOURTH GENERATION

21. ROBERT BEALE, born in 1790; married Eliza Jane Forbes. Administration upon the estate of one Robert Beale deceased intestate was granted 14 November 1866 to Mary D. Beale by the Probate Judge of Washington, D.C.

Child of Robert and Eliza Jane (Forbes) Beale:

i. James Shields Beale MD 1844-84, mar 1873 Fanny S. Marbury.[47]

22. GEORGE BEALE JR., born in 1792, died 5 April 1835 intestate, Washington, D.C.,[48] second son of George Beale Sr and his first wife Mary Dixon Beale. He was appointed a Purser USN 24 July 1813.[49] He served with Commodore Macdonough in the Battle of Lake Champlain 11 September 1814, and on 10 February 1820 was awarded a silver medal for gallantry there by the Congress.[50] George Beale married 14 May 1819 in Philadelphia Emily TRUXTUN,[51] who was born 30 September 1798 in Perth Amboy, N.J., tenth of the twelve children of Commodore Thomas Truxtun USN and wife Mary Fundran (or Van Drill or Vaudreill?) Truxtun of Philadelphia. Administration upon the estate of George Beale deceased was granted 18 April 1835 to his widow Emily Beale.[52]

Children of George and Emily (Truxtun) Beale: [50] (all born in Washington, D.C.)

i. Truxtun Dixon Beale b 17 Jan 1820; d 22 Dec 1870 Wash DC; mar 8 Oct 1844 Mary Anna Tillinghast, b 28 May 1826, who d 14 Sept 1918 in Phila. and was buried in St. James-the-Less Church yard, Phila.[53]

ii. Mary Elizabeth Beale b ————; d ————; mar William READ, b 24 Apr 1823 New Castle, Del, who d 29 Apr 1884 Montgomery Co., Md.[53a]

iii. Edward Fitzgerald Beale b 4 Feb 1822; d 22 Apr 1893; mar 27 June 1849 Mary Engle Edwards, of Chester, Pa.[54]

iv. George Nancrede Beale b 14 Nov 1829; d ————; mar 2 June 1851 Elizabeth Brown Wheeler of Wash, DC.[54a]

v. Emily Truxtun Beale b 7 Sep 1832; d 6 Nov 1880 at West Point; mar 18 Sep 1855 Junius Brutus WHEELER, Col USA, who d 15 July 1886.[54b]

23. CATHERINE ANN BEALE, daughter of no. 11 George Beale and his first wife Mary Dixon Beale of Washington, DC, was married 26 May 1820 to John Peirce CROSBY, who was born 17 December 1795 and died 10 October 1828, son of Peirce and Christiana (Richards) Crosby of Crosby's Mills, near Chester, Penna.[55]

Children of John Peirce and Catharine (Beale) Crosby: [55]

  i. Mary John Crosby mar 1st Nathaniel Davis CROSBY; mar 2nd James J. MILLER of Lexington, Ky.

  ii. Peirce Crosby, b 16 Jan 1824; d 15 June 1899; Rear Adml USN; mar 1st 16 Oct 1850 Matilda Boyer of Lexington Va who d 1853; mar 2nd in Mar 1861 Julia Wells who d 1866; mar 3rd 15 Feb 1870 Miriam Gratz who d 1878; mar 4th 24 June 1880 Louise Audenried.[56]

  iii. Ann Cornelia Crosby mar Charles William RABORG of Chester, Penna., who d 23 Dec 1859, and had issue.[55]

  iv. Christiana Crosby mar Walter W. QUEEN, rear Adml USN, who was b 6 Oct 1824 Wash DC and d there 24 Oct 1893.[57]

24. ELIZABETH ANN BEALE born in 1818, daughter of no. 11 George Beale and his second wife Elizabeth (Lane-Bowie) Beale, married William David PORTER, Commodore USN, born 10 March 1809 in New Orleans, who died 1st May 1864 in New York City, son of David Porter USN and wife Evelina (Anderson) Porter.[58]

Children of William David and Elizabeth Ann (Beale) Porter: [59]

  i. William David Porter mar Mary GILLAM of Va.

  ii. Edna Dixon Porter mar John D. IMBODEN, General CSA.

  iii. Mohena Tuscarora Porter.

25. ELEANOR KELLY, born in November 1789, died 19 February 1812 aged 22 years and 3 months,[60] and was buried in the Third Presbyterian Churchyard, 4th and Pine Streets, Philadelphia, with gravestone marker.[61] John DUFFIELD and Miss Eleanor Kelly were married 15 May 1805, the Rev Philip Milledoler of said church officiating.[61] The Philadelphia Directory for 1812 lists John Duffield, merchant, 12 Chestnut Street, and Murdoch and Duffield, merchants, 99 So. Front Street. John Duffield died at Washington, DC., 21 November 1821, " late of the firm of Murdoch & Duffield, Merchants, of Philadelphia ",[62] and was buried in the churchyard abovesaid, with gravestone marker.[61] By Deed of 29 November 1814 Robert Murdoch and John Duffield of the city of Philadelphia, merchants and co-partners under the firm name of Murdoch and Duffield, were released from all claims by their creditors. *Deed Book IC-32,* 453. The estate of John Duffield is not found in Philadelphia probates.

Children of John and Eleanor (Kelly) Duffield: [61]

i. Charles Edward Duffield b 27 May 1806.

ii. Mary Kelly Duffield b 8 Mar 1808; mar John SKILLMAN.

iii. James Murdoch Duffield b 31 Oct 1809; mar in Brooklyn, N.Y., 1st Jan 1831 Margaret A. Prince.

26. JOHN KELLY born in 1796, only son of Capt John and Mary (Beale) Kelly of Philadelphia, died 5 February 1863 in his 68th year, at the home of his son near Hatboro, Montgomery County, Pa.[63] John Kelly was commissioned Midshipman USN 1 Feb 1814; Lieut 13 Jan 1825; Commander 8 Sept 1841; Capt 14 Sept 1855; and was a Commodore on the retired list 16 July 1862.[64]

Children of John and Margaretta (Hopkins) Kelly: [2]

i. Ellen D. Kelly d 10 Dec 1832 in 8th yr.[65]

ii. Mary Elizabeth Kelly mar 1 May 1848 Thomas SMITH,[66] *dsp.*

iii. Ellen Margaretta Kelly mar Henry C. DAVIS of Phila; *dsp.*

iv. John Hopkins Kelly mar 1st Rebecca ———; 2nd ———.[67]

FOOTNOTES

[1] Jos. B. Murdock, *Murdock Genealogy*, 1925, p 215.

[2] See transcript of family records in appendix hereto, in which dates are stated as being *New Style*, the revision by addition of 11 days to *Old Style*, effective in 1752.

[2a] Taxables of Chestnut Ward of Philadelphia, 1754, published in *Penna Mag Hist & Biogr* XIV, include William Murdock. Between the then city limits of South and Arch Streets, and from Front to Second Streets, were Walnut, Chestnut, and High Wards.

[3] Register of Christ Church, Phila. Baptisms and Burials 1709-60 are published in *Penna Mag Hist & Biogr* XVII, 109 and V, 463; Marriages in *Penna Archives* 2d series VIII.

[4] E. S. Clark, *Inscriptions in the Burial-Grounds of Christ Church, Phila.*, published 1864, p 297.

[5] William Murdoch and William Murdoch Jr., were among the 94 signatories to the agreement of 24 June 1760 for raising money for the purchase of a lot for a church building since known as St. Paul's Church, 225 South 3rd Street, Philadelphia (N. S. Barratt, *Hist Old St Paul's Ch*, 29 and 32). The rector, the Rev. William McClenachan, was one of the witnesses to William Murdoch's Will.

[5a] Recorded 10 March 1840 in *Phila. Deed Book GS-11*, p 438.

[6] George Beale, born about 1734, who married 1756 Mary Murdoch in Philadelphia, as above, could not have been son of John Beale of Richmond County, Virginia, as stated in *Abr Comp Amer Geneal* II, 191, as the latter died 1767 naming six daughters and no son in his Will. See Beale pedigree in *Va. Mag Hist & Biogr* XXXII, 51. The baptisms of the children of this George and Mary (Murdoch) Beale are not found in the register of Christ Church, Phila., nor in that of St John's, Christiansted, Island of St Croix.

[6a] *Penna. Archives* 2nd series IX, 457 and II, 214.

[7] Robert Lewis b 21-1-1714, son of Ellis Lewis and wife Elizabeth of Kennet Twp., Chester Co., Penna., member of Provincial Assembly, mar 23-3-1733 at Concord Meeting, Chester Co., Mary Pyle dau of William Pyle of Thornbury Twp., said Co., and removed to Philadelphia with certificate of 11-5-1757 from Wilmington Mo. Mtg. which was recd by Phila Mo. Mtg. of 26-5-1758. Robert Lewis, merchant of Phila. by Will of 2 Mar 1786 and proved 18 Sep 1790 devised to children Nathaniel, Phebe Pemberton, Robert, and William Lewis, and to grandchildren Mary Green, Hester Eddy, David Lewis, Phoebe Lewis, and Robert Lewis the children of son Ellis Lewis decd, Robert Lewis son of son Nathaniel Lewis, Eli and Sarah Canby, and Robert Murdoch. Robert and Mary (Pyle) Lewis had issue: Ellis Lewis b 15-5-1734; Eli Lewis b 3-6-1735; Elizabeth Lewis b 7-10-1736 who mar 26-7-1753 Thomas Canby Jr. of Wilmington, Dela.; Phoebe Lewis b 24-11-1737/8 who mar 1st 7-9-1758 Samuel Morton and 2nd 12-7-1775 James Pemberton of Phila; Mary Lewis b 24-5-1739 who mar 12-3-1761 William Bettle of Phila; Robert Lewis b 1-2-1741; William Lewis b 26-11-1742/3; Nathaniel Lewis b 26-8-1744; Lydia Lewis b 5-12-1745/6; William Lewis 2d b 8-9-1747; Joshua Lewis b 29-10-1749; and Ann Lewis b 26-12-1753 who mar 8 Sep 1774 Samuel Murdoch. Robert Lewis Senr was buried 13-4-1790 aged 77 yrs in Friends burial grd Phila; his wife Mary Lewis was bur 26-6-1782 aged 68 yrs likewise. (Records of Phila. Southern District Mo. Mtg; Minutes of Phila. Mo. Mtg. publ in Hinshaw, *Encycl Amer Quaker Genealog* II, 580; Lewis genealogy publ in *Colonial Families of Philadelphia* 1911. p 1065.)

[8] Records of Southern Distr Phila Mo. Mtg.

[9] Ship Registers 1762-76, publ in *Penna Archives* 2d ser II, 652 etc.

[9a] *Penna Archives* 2d ser IX, 452, and II, 214.

[10] Records of Philadelphia Board of Health; in Genealog Soc Pa.

[11] Register of St. Michael's & Zion Lutheran Church, Phila., published in *Penna. Archives* 2nd series IX, 340.

[12] Marriage License Index, published *Idem* 2nd series II, 214.

[13] Oath of Allegiance to State of Penna 1776-94, publ *Idem* III, 11.

[14] *Penna Archives* 2nd series I, p 83.

[15] *Idem* 1st series VI, 413, 672. *Journals of the American Congress* 1774-88, publ 1823, vol II, 597, 610, 627; III, 1, 2, 6, 31, 32, 192.

[16] Petition of C. Sweers is in ms. collections of Hist Soc Pa.

[17] See Dorothy Maltby Verrill, *Maltby-Maltbie Family* (1916) p 133, for this line continued.

[18] Register of Rev Wm Rogers, publ in *Penna Mag Hist & Biogr* IX, 105; Register of First Baptist Church of Philadelphia, publ in *Penna Archives* 2d series VIII, 762; Marriage Licenses publ in *Idem* II, 214.

[19] James Whitall, b 4-9mo-1717 OS, d 29-9-1808 NS in Woodbury, Gloucester Co., N.J., son of Job and Jane (Siddon) Whitall of same Deptford Twp.; mar 23-9-1739 Ann Cooper, b 23-4-1716, who d 22-9-1797, dau of John and Ann Cooper; and had issue: James Whitall Jr b 22-12-1741/2, d 18-2-1796; Job Whitall b 27-1-1743, d 11-9mo-1797; Benjamin Whitall d 1797; Zathu Whitall rem to Phila.; Hannah Whitall mar Joseph Matlack; John S. Whitall; and Sarah Whitall mar John Murdoch of Phila. (Asa Matlack's Notes, in Collections of Genealogical Society of Pennsylvania; Records of Haddonfield and Woodbury Monthly Meeting.)

[20] From the original Minutes of Haddonfield and Southern District Philadelphia Monthly Meetings, now deposited at 302 Arch St., Phila. Sarah Murdoch witnessed the marriage certificate of her brother John S. Whitall at Woodbury Meeting 16-5-1788.

[21] Abstracts of Wills etc publ in *N. J. Archives* XXXVI, 166 and XXXVIII, 262.

[22] Names of children and dates are from family records (See Appendix) which state also that the son " William Murdoch was killed on board the ship *Criterion,* Capt Weeks, of which he was first officer, in an engagement with a French privateer in the Bay of Bengal, on his passage from Calcutta to Philadelphia in January 1799."

[23] In a letter dated Bath, Maine, 23 Aug 1807, Margaret Gay (Tingey) Wingate to her father Capt. Thomas Tingey at Washington, says: Mrs. Vaughn " Was not a little gratified, she said, to hear you were born in London, I in St Croix, (she) having passed many happy years in both places ". Statement that " Commodore Tingey's father was an Episcopal minister " is found in writing of a grand daughter Sydney Ellen (Wingate) Sewall (1815-87), but the facts have not been here determined by search in England. In a letter dated Phila. 7 Jan 1793, Tingey thanked one Joseph Collins for " Kind intentions relative to payment of what is due to my sister from the estate of the late Robt. Smith. I have had her son these 6 years, who is now advancing fast to manhood," and in one dated 10 an 1793 to Josh. Hadfield, Tingey mentioned addressee's " Accommodation of my relatives in Liverpool. I have requested my sister Mrs. Susanna White, no. 1 Knight Street, Liverpool, to wait for your orders on the subject. I hope to recover for her a small sum many years due to her in No. Carolina." [See Footnote 26] In *Thurston Genealogies* (1892), page 646, it is stated that one Robert Thurston died as Captain of English merchant ship in the West Indies trade, having married Susanna Tingey, sister of Capt Thomas Tingey [above said], and that upon the widow's remarriage, Tingey brought the children, Robert and Susanna Thurston, to this country. Compare letter above.

[24] Original written appointment is in possession of Miss Helena Palmer, Forrest Hills, L. I., 1947; photostat copy in that of compiler.

[25] Log Book is in possession of James W. Sewall, Oldtown, Me.

[26] Tingey Letter-Book 1788-1793, containing 87 business letters, presented to compiler by said Mr. Sewall in 1931.

[27] *Middlesex County, N. J., Deed Books no. 2,* pp 40, 99, 250; *no. 6,* p 288; *Mortgage Book no. 5,* p 28.

[28] Letters of Tingey Family 1797-1825, in possession of James W. Sewall, Oldtown, Maine, copied by compiler, 1931.

[29] Names of children and dates of births are from record written in parents' bible, *The Christian's New & Complete Family Bible,* printed for C. Cooke, no 17 Paternoster-Row, London (no date), in possession of James W. Sewall, Oldtown, Maine, 1931 (*see Appendix hereto*). But in the register of St John's Church, Christiansted, St Croix, the birth dates are: Ann 9 Feb 1778, Mary 11 Aug 1781, Margaret Gay in Oct 1782. The portrait in oils of Commodore Thomas Tingey USN is now, 1947, in possession of Sidney G. DeKay of NYC, a descendant of Hannah Tingey Craven, and is ascribed by his elder brother Eckford Craven DeKay to the painter Trumbull, which contradicts its inclusion in Fielding O. Lewis' published catalogue of the works of Gilbert Stuart. The *copy* of

this portrait, which was made for Rear-Adml Thomas T. Craven, USN., (1808-87), is now in possession of the latter's grandson Vice-Adml Thomas T. Craven, USN, and is mentioned by Lewis abovesaid. One of the St. Memin pastel portraits of Tingey is in possession of James W. Sewall of Oldtown, Maine, and another in that of Frederick B. Craven USN. A reproduction of the small medallion portrait of Tingey appears published in the *St.-Memin Collection of Portraits* by Elias Dexter, New York, 1861, as no. 396., as also that of his son-in-law Tunis Craven. Commodore Tingey's Navy dress uniform was presented by his great-great-grandson Lt Col Sidney Gilder de Kay to the N.Y. Historical Society, whose *Annual Report* of 1933 carries a photograph of it opposite page 20. The surname *Tingey* is pronounced with a short " i " and a soft " g ".

[30] " The wife of George Beale, of Washington, D. C., was Mary Dixon of Virginia. Her sister Elizabeth was the wife and widow of Major William Anderson, of Chester."—from J. H. Martin, *History of Chester, Penna.*, p. 213. For Major Wm Anderson see *Biogr Direct Amer Congress*. Thomas Dixon and wife Sarah (Tucker) Dixon were the parents of Dr. Anthony Tucker Dixon, of the Amercian Revolution, and of Mary Dixon who married George Beale.—from *Tyler's Quart Hist & Geneal Mag* X, 44. The Will of Thomas Dixon, dated 11 June 1773 and proved 27 Jan 1774, devises estate to wife Sarah, with reversion to son Anthony Tucker Dixon; orders plantation bought of Thomas Hawkins to be sold, and at death of wife the slaves to be divided " among all my children " except Rosea Bryan; appoints executors his wife, Col Cary Seldon, and William Roscow Curle.—from *Abstracts of Wills of Elizabeth City County, Va., 1610-1800*, p. 134.

[30a] *Natl Geneal Soc Quarterly* XXXV, 23.

[31] *New Eng Hist Genealog Reg* LXXIII.

[32] W. W. Bowie, *The Bowies and Their Kindred*, 1899, pp 115-116.

[33] The present account corrects that published in F.M.M.Beal, *Colonial Families of the U.S., Bell-Beale-Beal-Bale*, 1931, p. 234, which ascribes this George Beale Jr as son of one John Beale of vicinity of Buchanan, Botetcourt County, Va., and names his first wife as Betty Lewis daughter of Genl Andrew Lewis.

[34] *Poulson's Daily American Advertiser*, Phila.; records of burials of Philadelphia Board of Health (in Genealog. Soc. Pa.).

[35] *Poulson's Daily American Advertiser*, Phila.; Burial Register of Christ Church; Burial Register of Phila. Board of Health.

[36] The first four children were baptised 16 May 1821, per Register of St. Peter's Church, 3rd and Pine Streets, Phila., with these names and dates of births.

[37] *Poulson's Daily American Advertiser*, Phila.

[38] Paschallville, a one-time village now in 40th Ward of City of Philadelphia, which was built about Cobb's Creek and along Darby Road, northeast of the Blue Bell Tavern, at 73rd Street. It was named for the Paschall family, early residents of Kingsessing Township (Joseph Jackson, *Encyclopedia of Philadelphia* IV, 966). This corrects the statement in Joseph Murdock's *Murdock Genealogy* (1925) that this James Murdoch lived in " Paschalville, N. J."

[39] Death notice in *Poulson's Daily American Advertiser*, Phila.; also in *Woodbury (NJ) Village Herald*.

[40] All born in Havana and educated in New England. See continued in Jos Murdock, *Murdock Genealogy*, published 1925, pp 215 etc.

[41] Burlington County Clerk's Marriage Records.

[42] Register of St. Andrew's Church, Mt. Holly, N. J.

[42a] Names, dates and places of birth from family records.

[43] Craven Armorial. Letter written by Tunis Craven in 1838 is sealed in black wax impressed with his die: Over an oval ring laterally, containing his initials TC, a crest: On a chapeau turned up, a griffin *passant*, wings addorsed. Letter is in possession of James E. Sewall, Oldtown, Maine, 1931.

[43a] Issue: 1-Hannah Tingey Sanderson b 26 Nov 1827 Bkln, d 5 Apr 1863 Newark NJ, mar 24 Mar 1852 Bkln the Rev Elijah Richardson Craven DD, who was b 28 Mar 1824 Wash DC and d 5 Jan 1908 Phila, son of Elijah R. and Sarah E. (Landreth) Craven, as his first wife. See biographical notice of him in *Proc NJ Hist Soc,* new series, I, 103. *LDC*

[43b] Issue: by 1st wife: 1-Thomas Tingey Craven Jr d after 1851; 2-Virginia Craven d about age 25 unmar. Issue by 2nd wife: 2-Anna Truxtun Craven b 19 Feb 1841 Bkln, d in May 1915, mar 9 June 1864 at Trinity Church, Geneva, NY, Frederick Griswold Barnard of Mendon, NY, b 14 Feb 1840, who d 31 Mar 1920; 2-Alfred Wingate Craven d infancy; 3-Charles Henderson Craven b 30 Nov 1843 at Fort Preble, Portland, Me., d 1 Mar 1898 Wash DC, Lieut Cdr USN, mar 1874 Mary Folger; 4-Henry Smith Craven b 14 Oct 1845 Bound Brook, NJ, d 7 Dec 1 1889 at USN Hospital, Bkln NY, mar Eugenia, dau of Martin von Klinkofstrom the Russian Consul at S. Francisco, and she d 1930 at Forrest hills, LI; 5-Alfred Craven b 16 Sept 1846 Bound Brook, NJ, d 30 Sept 1926 Pleasantville NY, mar 1871 Nina Florence Browne, dau of Ross Browne of S. Francisco. (See *Encycl Amer Biogr* XXXIII.); 6-Emily Henderson Craven b 4 Jan 1848 Stanton, Va., d 17 July 1927 at Bellefonte, Pa., mar 4 Jan 1869 at Mare Isld Navy Yard, Edgar Clarence Merriman, USN, b 24 July 1840 Bradford, NY, who d 11 Dec 1894 Yonkers, NY; 7-Mary Craven d infancy; 8-Evelyn Tingey Craven b 12 Aug 1851 New London, Ct, mar in May 1872 at Vallejo, Cal, John M. Gregory of Suisun, Nevada; 9-Maria Forrest Craven *alias* Ida b 14 July 1855 Stanton, Va., mar 21 Apr 1881 at Geneva, NY, Frank Warren Hackett, b 11 Apr 1841 Portsmouth NH, who d 10 Aug 1926 there, Asst Secy USN; 10-Macdonough Craven b 9 Nov 1848 Annapolis Md, d 10 Feb 1919, mar 15 Sept 1896 at Rockhurst, Spuyten Duyvil-on-Hudson, Caroline Lesley, b 3 Oct 1862. *LDC*

[43c] Issue: 1-Charles Edmiston Craven b 20 Sep 1841, d 13 July 1847; 2-Minna Craven b 14 Dec 1843, d 11 Apr 1927 NYC, mar 14 Mar 1870 NYC Sidney Brooks DeKay, b 7 Mar 1844, who d 30 Aug 1890 Staten Island NY, Major USA; 3-Alice Craven b 5 Dec 1847 NYC, d 18 May 1927 Bar Harbor, Me, mar 25 Sep 1877 Aulick Palmer, Lt USN, Consul at Dresden, US Marshall of Wash DC. *LDC*

[43d] Issue: by 1st wife: 1-Mary Augusta Craven b 3 Apr 1839 Bkln, d 20 July 1923 Bound Brook NJ, mar 6 May 1863 NYC Charles Waesche Thomae, b 25 Aug 1834 Balto Md, who d 22 Apr 1906 Bound Brook NJ; 2-Augustus Carter Craven b 5 Sep 1840, d 19 Mar 1863 Bound Brook NJ, unmar., 2nd Lieut 4th Art; 3-Robert Craven b 7 Feb 1843 Bkln NY, d 18 Apr 1927 Phila, mar 17 May 1865 NYC Cora Cochran, b 14 Nov 1842, who d 4 Feb 1919 in Phila. By 2nd wife: 4-Louis Stevenson Craven b 12 June 1845 Bkln, d 10 Mar 1888 S. Diego, Cal, 5-Ellin Travers Craven b ———, d 8 Jan 1940 NYC, mar 12 Apr 1893 NYC, Frank Learned, b 6 May 1854 in Pittsfield, Mass, who d 4 Sep 1910; 3-Alfred Edmiston Craven b 18 May 1855 Bound Brook, d 11

Mar 1898 Asheville NC, mar Matilda MacDonald, of So. Bound Brook, NJ, who d 14 Oct 1921 Haddonfield, NJ. *LDC*

[44] *Penna Mag Hist & Biogr* III, 1; Ms Pedigrees (Dulany) no. 2077, pp 193 et seq, in *Collections of Genealog Soc Pa; Americans of Royal Descent.*

[45] *Colonial Families of the U.S.*, II, 46; *Va Mag Hist & Biogr* XXXXIII, 430; Hayden, *Virginia Genealogies*, 1931.

[46] *William & Mary College Quarterly* X, 136.

[47] *Abridged Comp Amer Geneal* II, 191.

[48] Death notice, *Poulson's Daily Amer Advr*, Phila, 7 Apr 1835.

[49] Hammersly, *Officers of the U.S.Navy*, 1901.

[50] Maria S. Beale Chance, *Family of Edward F. Beale*, 1943.

[51] Rt Rev Wm White, Bishop of Penna., rector of Christ Ch, Phila, officiating, *per* register of said Church. See TRUXTUN in *Dict Amer Biogr.*

[52] Administration no. 5384 OS, Register of Wills, Wash DC.

[53] She was daughter of Joseph Leonard and Rebecca (Power-Air) Tillinghast of Providence RI, and had issue: 1-Charles Willing Beale 1845-1932; 2-Emily Power Beale 1848-1936, mar Horace Binney Hare of Phila; 3-Constance Rebecca Beale 1852-9 Jan 1937 unmar, of Phila; 4-Edward Fitzgerald Beale b 31 Mar 1853 Wash DC, d 17 Oct 1947 ae 95 at Strafford, Penna., mar 18 Apr 1877 Maria Litchfield Lewis of Phila, b 21 June 1856, who d 1928, and had issue: Maria Scott Beale b 7 Feb 1878 in Phila, who mar 14 Oct 1903 Burton Chance MD; Leonard Tillinghast Beale b 28 May 1881, who mar 9 Dec 1911 Anna Lewis; Emily Power Beale b 20 Dec 1885, who mar 20 June 1908 Arthur Morton Wilson; Helena Rutgers Beale b 27 Mar 1888, who mar 18 Oct 1911 Samuel A. Crozer Jr.; and Hope Truxtun Beale b 7 Apr 1896, who mar 1st Oliver Eaton Cromwell, 2nd John Quigley, and 3rd John Bromley. (*Samuel Carpenter and Descendants*, 1912, p 193.)

[53a] 1st Lieut USA, son of Hon George Read 3rd and wife Louisa Ridgeley Dorsey Read of New Castle, Del., and had issue: 1-George Read mar Alice Dickson or Dixon, 2-William Thompson Read, 3-Emily Truxtun Read mar Gen Mancil Clay Goodrell, 4-Mary Anna Read mar J. Bates, 5-Gertrude Parker Read mar Paul Randolph, 6-Blair Beale Read or F. P. Blair Read, 7-Edith Ross Read mar Elber Howe Brodhead. (from H. P. Read, *Rossiana*, 1908, pp 272 and 294.)

[54] J. H. Martin, *History of Chester, Pa.*, 264; *Dict Amer Biogr*, 1929. She was daughter of Congressman Samuel Edwards and wife Mary (Engle) of Chester, Pa, and had issue: 1-Mary Beale b 1852, d 26 June 1925, who mar 11 Feb 1877 G. Bakhmeteff; 2-Emily S. Beale b 1854, who mar John R. McLean of Wash DC and had son Edward Beale McLean who purchased in 1911 the famous *Hope* diamond for his wife Evelyn (Walsh) McLean who d 26 Apr 1947; 3-Truxtun Beale b 6 Mar 1856, who mar 1st Harriet S. Blaine and 2nd Marie Ogle (see *Natl Cycl Amer Biogr*). *LDC*

[54a] Born 14 Dec 1832 in Wash DC, daughter of John Hill and Mary Elizabeth (Brown) Wheeler, and had issue: 1-Elizabeth Beale b 6 Nov 1852, who mar 1st one Stuyvesant and 2nd Capt Davis Porter Heap; 2-Thomas Truxtun Beale b 16 Aug 1854, d in June 1861; 3-John Wheeler Beale b 26 Aug 1856, who mar 13 Dec 1877 Kathrine Carroll; 4-Violet Blair Beale b in June 1862, who mar 2 Feb 1881 George C. Bloomer. (from *History of the Wheeler Family in America*, 1914, p. 274.)

[54b] Born 21 Feb 1830 in Murfreesboro, N.C., son of John and Sarah I. (Clifton) Wheeler, and had.issue: 1-Emily Beale Wheeler b 5 Sept 1857; 2-Sarah Clifton Wheeler

b 27 Nov 1860, d 4 May 1901, who mar 6 July 1881 Lieut James G. Warren; 3-Mary Eliza Beale b 4 Jan 1861, who mar 25 May 1892 George Ker; 4-Gertrude Wheeler b 21 Jan 1867, who mar 18 Aug 1887 Thomas M. Vance; 5-Julia Wheeler b 8 Apr 1869; 6-Amy Wheeler b 19 Feb 1871; 7-John Wheeler b 19 May 1872, d 3 Sept 1872; and 8-William Mackall Wheeler b 22 June 1874. Surgeon USN, who mar 21 Feb 1907 Laura Forbes Denby. (from *History of the Wheeler Family in America*, 1914, p 261. See Heitman, *Register of the U.S.Army 1789-1903*, p 1024)

[55] J. H. Martin, *History of Chester, Penna.*, p. 213; *National Genealogical Society Quarterly* XXIX, 127.

[56] *Dictionary Amer Biogr.*

[57] Lamb, *Biogr Dictionary of the U.S.*

[58] Appleton, *Cylcl Amer Biogr.*; Martin *supra* p 252.

[59] W. W. Bowie, *The Bowies and Their Kindred*, 1899, p 116.

[60] Death records of Phila. Board of Health (*Collects. Gen Soc Pa*).

[61] Register and Gravestone Inscriptions, Third Presb Ch of Phila.

[62] Obituary notice in *Poulson's Daily American Advertiser*, Phila. Family records add that " Charles Duffield married a lady of Phila." and had one son who died unmarried. Mary Duffield married John Skillman and had: Catharine Newberry Skillman who married Henry M. Curtis of N.Y., and had son Henry Skillman Curtis; and Ellen Maria Skillman died unmarried adult; and two children who died in infancy. James Murdoch Duffield married Margaretta Prince of Brooklyn and had Anna Duffield, Emma Duffield who married Thomas Pope and had son Richard Pope in the P.E. ministry; Rosalie Duffield married Samuel Osborne and had Samuel Duffield Osborne; Alice Maud Osborne who married George W. Dow; and that said James Murdoch Duffield married 2nd Miss Brainard and had three sons and a daughter who live in Connecticut.

[63] Obituary notice in *The Public Ledger*, Phila., of 7 Feb 1863.

[64] Callahan, *Register of U.S.Navy Officers*, p 309.

[65] " At the house of her father, John Kelly, Schuylkill 8th St., between Walnut and George "—*Poulson's Daily Am Adv.*, Phila.

[66] The Rev R. B. Loxley officiating, in Montgomery Co., Penna., per Thompson Westcott's Notes in collections Genealog Soc Pa.

[67] John H. Kelly had by 1st marriage son Charles Ernest Kelly who mar 7 Nov 1878 at 1309 Walnut St., Phila., Elizabeth Buffington Smith (*reg of S. Peter's Ch*), and had John Barry Kelly, Charles Ernest Kelly Jr., Rudolph Kelly, and Wilson Smith Kelly; and by 2nd marriage: George Kelly, Benjamin Loxley Kelly, Thomas Smith Kelly, and Mary Kelly, according to family records.

APPENDICES

MURDOCH FAMILY RECORDS. An extensive but informal outline of Murdoch descendants made about 1872, incorporating data " from the St. Felix family Bible " whose existence now escapes discovery, begins as follows. Apparently it was compiled by Miss Victorine Reynaud St. Felix of Brooklyn, N.Y., a descendant of no. 6 Hannah (Murdoch) Sweers. A copy made about 1905 by Mrs. Charles W. Thomae (1839-1923) of New York City and of Bound Brook, N.J., a descendant of no. 8 Margaret (Murdoch)

Tingey, is here quoted by the present compiler. A similar copy which was enclosed in an undated letter from Miss St. Felix abovesaid to Miss Sydney Margaret Sewall (1842-1917) of Oldtown, Maine, is in possession of her nephew, James Wingate Sewall.

Our Ancestors who came to Philadelphia, Penna., were William Murdoch of Armagh, Ireland, and his wife Mary Hammond, an English heiress whose half-sister was maid-of-honor to the Queen of England. They were married in Europe, and I think that their eldest child was born there. Do not know the date of marriage.

Their children were:

Mary Murdoch born May 27th 1735.
Susannah Murdoch born August 5th 17.—[*The rest of the date was cut off when the Bible was rebound.*]
William Murdoch born July 7th 1739.
Samuel Murdoch born October 7th 1741.
Thomas Murdoch born March 2d 1744.
Hannah Murdoch born January 16th 1746.
John Murdoch born July 8th 1748.
Margaret Murdoch born July 26th 1750.
Sarah Murdoch born February 12th 1752.
James Murdoch born November 27th 1754.

All the above are New Style

Mary Murdoch departed this life August 25th 1770 aged 55 years. Thomas Murdoch departed this life August 9th 1779 at 5 o'clock in the morning opposite Wilmington Del. in the river Delaware returning from Martinico, W.I.

1st Child: Mary Murdoch married March 2d 1756 John (*sic*) Beale a planter of Santa Cruz, who had two of the finest plantations on the Island. John Beale born December 27th 1756 was sent to England to be educated; inherited the family estate. George Beale was educated in France; married Emily Truxton daughter of Commodore Truxton U.S.N. The Beales of Washington are their descendants. Mary Beale married Capt. John Kelly; settled in Philadelphia. Their children: Maria N. Kelly married James Murdoch; Elenor Kelly married John Duffield of Phila.; John Kelly, Com. U.S.N. married Margaretta Hopkins.

4th Child: Samuel Murdoch married Miss Lewis of Phila., Pa. Robert Murdoch, only child, married Emily Bridges.

6th Child: Hannah Murdoch and Cornelius Sweers were married Thursday evening April 26th 1770. [Children were:] Sarah Sweers born February 22d 1771; Samuel Sweers born July 6th 1772, died Nov. 9th 1773; Mary Sweers born December 9th 1774, died July 29th 1775; William Sweers born November 26th 1775, died Nov. 7th 1776; Mary Sweers born November 24th 1776; died Nov. 25th 1783. Sarah Sweers and Charles Maltby of Norwich, Engl., son of George Maltby, merchant, were married August 17th 1796.

7th Child: John Murdoch married Sarah Whitall of N.J. Children: James Murdoch married Maria Nesbit Kelly; John Murdoch married a Lady of Cuba; Joseph Murdoch died Sept. 1802 of consumption; Hannah Murdoch died July 20th 1797; Samuel Murdoch married Mary Black (*of*) Mt. Holly, N.J.; William Murdoch killed on board the ship Criterion, Capt. Weeks, (of which he was the first officer), in an engagement with a French privateer in the Bay of Bengal, on his passage from Calcutta to Philadelphia in January 1799; Joseph Murdoch died Sept. 1802, consumption.

8th Child: Margaret Murdoch married Thomas Tingey, U.S.N. There were nine children; those that lived were: Margaretta Gay Tingey married Joseph Wingate, Maine; Hannah Tingey married Tunis Craven, N.J.; Sarah Tingey married Daniel Dulany. (*End quote*)

*   *   *   *   *

The record of births of the children of William and Mary Murdoch in *New Style* dates in the section just above compare with the following items from the register of Christ Church, Philadelphia, in *Old Style* dates, which have the primary value of having been entered at the time of actual baptisms:

1737 Sept 7: Susannah daughter of William & Mary Murdoch, aged 2 weeks.

1739 July 15: William, son of William & Mary Murdoch, aged 3 weeks.

1741 Oct 19: Samuel, son of William & Mary Murdoch, aged 5 weeks.

1743/4 Mar 7: Thomas, son of William and Mary Murdoch, aged 19 days.

1745/6 Jan 28: Hannah, daughter of William and Mary Murdoch, born 5 Jan 1745 (*sic*).

1748 Sept 21: John, son of William and Mary Murdoch, born 27 June 1748.

1750 Aug 8: Margaret, daughter of William and Mary Murdoch, born 15 July 1750.

1751/2 Feb 27: Sarah, daughter of William and Mary Murdoch, born 1 Feb 1752.

1753 Dec 20: James, son of William and Mary Murdoch, born 27 Nov 1753.

UNIDENTIFIED MURDOCK-MURDOCH OF PHILADELPHIA.

ROBERT MURDOCH married 7 March 1781 Mary Christina Shoemaker, according to the register of Gloria Dei (Swedes') Church, in the District of Southwark, County Philadelphia, and had a daughter Margaretha Murdock, born 12 October 1793, who was baptised 3 November 1793 in First Reformed Church of Philadelphia. Christina Murdock aged 40, was buried 2 October 1797; James Murdoch aged 40 was buried 8 October 1797, and Elisabeth Murdoch aged 10-4-6 was buried 2 December 1802, according to the register of said church. On petition of Ann Murdock to Philadelphia Orphans Court of 20 March 1810, her daughter Ann Murdock a minor under 14 years was placed under guardianship of Jesse Shoemaker. And on petition of said Ann Murdock to the Court of 19 August 1814 Elizabeth Murdock, a minor under 14, was placed under her guardianship, her late guardian Jesse Shoemaker being deceased.

WILLIAM MURDOCH, a vestryman of Christ Church 1810-23, born in 1768, died 29 December 1836 aged 68 years in Philadelphia and was buried in Christ Church burial ground on 30th. Elizabeth wife of William Murdoch was buried 8 April 1789 in St Peter's Churchyard, Philadelphia, possible first wife of this William Murdoch. William Murdoch married (2ndly in that case) Mary ———— who was born 6 March 1778 and baptised 24 March 1802 with daughter in Christ Church, Philadelphia. She died 20 July 1839 aged 62 years at Downingtown, Penna., and was buried in said Christ Church cemetery. Administration upon the estate of William Murdock deceased was granted 3 January 1837 to (his son-in-law) James Casey of no. 35 No. Water Street, said city of Philadelphia. Mary Dolley Murdoch, born 17 December 1801, daughter of said William and Mary Murdoch or Murdock, was baptised 24 March 1802, and she married 24 November 1822 said James Casey, *per* Christ Church register.

380

JOHN MURDOCH, blacksmith of Kensington, Philadelphia, in 1805 etc., married 18 November 1792 Elizabeth Reynolds, according to the register of St. Paul's Church, in that city. She was one of the children of John Reynolds Sr late of Kensington, in the Northern Liberties of the city of Philadelphia, deceased, as recited in a Deed of 26 September 1805, recorded in *Deed Book MR-19*, p 522.

JOHN MURDOCH, listed in Philadelphia Directories of 1790 *etc* as Barber, Hairdresser, Perfumer, 59 Walnut Street; born in 1750, died 4 April 1816 aged 66 years and was buried 6 April in St Paul's Churchyard in said city. He married 5 January 1778 Hannah Jorden, according to the register of said church, and she was buried likewise, on 16 October 1801. Their children, all baptised on same date 18 July 1793 in said church, were: William Murdoch born 25 November 1778 (possibly identical with the William Thompson Murdoch eldest son of John, who was buried 25 September 1801 according to obituary notice in Poulson's Phila. newspaper); Jonathan Murdoch born 20 November 1781, who died 2 February 1811 a " Doctor " according to obituary notice in Poulson's; John Murdoch born 15 September 1783; Mary Murdoch born 15 July 1785, who died 17 July 1787 according to gravestone in St Paul's Chyd.; Ann Murdoch born 23 August 1787, who died 11 March 1811, having married 17 November 1808 Robert Sewell; Charles Anderson Murdoch born 9 April 1789; George Davis Murdoch born 15 April 1791; and Samuel Wright Davis Murdoch born 21 January 1793.

* * * * *

RECORDS OF THE FAMILY OF THOMAS TINGEY, USN.

COLLECTED BY LEWIS D. COOK, PHILADELPHIA, 1930.

From *The Christian's New & Complete Family Bible,* printed for C. Cooke, no 17 Paternoster-Row, London (no date), in possession of a descendant, James W. Sewall, Old-town, Maine, 1930:

Thomas and Margaret Tingey—married on Easter Sunday evening the 30th March 1777 by the reverend Cecil Wray Goodchild, minister of the English Episcopal Church in the island of St. Croix.

1st child—Ann, born Monday 19th Jany, 1778 & died the 2d Sept. same year, in St. Croix.

2d child—Thomas, born in Philadelphia, 26th October 1779; died 23d Dec. same year.

3d child—Mary, born in St. Croix, 1st June 1781; died ——— same year.

4th child—Margaret Gay, born in St. Croix the 27th September 1782.

5th child—Hannah, born in Philadelphia the 19th November 1783.*

6th child—Phebe, born in Philadelphia ——— & died ———*

7th child—Thomas, born Feby 7th 178- & died ———*

8th child—Thomas Tyson, b——— & died ———*

9th child—Sarah Ann, born in Philadelphia the 19th August 1791.

Margaret Murdoch born July 27, 1750.

* * * * *

* From the *Registers of Christ Church, Philadelphia:*

Baptism: 22 Dec 1779: Thomas, son of Thomas & Margaret Tingey, born 26 October 1779.

6 Dec 1783: Hanna, daughter of John & Martha Tingey (*sic*), born 19 Nov. 1783.

Burial: 24 Aug 1785: Child of Capt Tingys; buried in Christ Ch. Cem.
             27 June 1786: Child of Capt Tingey; buried in Christ Ch. Cem.
             25 July 1790: Thomas, son of Thomas Tingee, buried *ditto.*

From the *Register of St John's Church, Christiansted, St Croix, Danish West Indies,*
now Virgin Islands of the U.S. of America.

Marriage: Thomas Tingey & Margaret Murdoch, at Mr Beale's (by virtue of a
             licence) March 30, 1777.   Cecil Wray Goodchild, Minister.

Baptism: 4 March 1778: Ann, daughter of Thomas and Margaret Tingey, born 9
             Feb 1778.

             15 Sept 1781: Mary, daughter of Thomas and Margaret Tingey, born 11
             Aug 1781.

             10 Nov 1782: Margaret Gay, daughter of Thomas and Margaret Tingey,
             born — Oct 1782.

*   *   *   *   *

Inscription on gravestone in Washington (Congressional) Cemetery, Washington,
D.C., sites nos. 1-2-3-4-5 in Range 57, as copied in July 1930:

Sacred | to the memory | of | Commodore Thomas Tingey | of the U.S. Navy who
departed this life | the 23rd February 1829 aged 79 years. | Also of his wives | Mar-
garet, who departed this life | the 25th April 1807 aged 57 years | Ann Bladen, who
departed this life | April 1814, aged 29 years. | and grand daughters | Tingey Anna
Wingate | who departed this life | 20th August 1810 aged 11 months | and 27 days |
Ann Mary Craven | who departed this life | 26th Sept. 1827 aged 21 years | 11
months and 6 days | Blessed are the dead who die in the Lord.

*   *   *   *   *

Register of Christ Church, 620 G Street SE, Washington D.C.:

Captain Thomas Tingey and Ann B. Dulany were married in Christ Church, Washington Parish, December 9th 1812 by the Reverend A. T. McCormick.

Daniel Dulany and Sarah Tingey were married in Christ Church, Washington Parish,
April 1st 1811, by the Reverend A. T. McCormick.

*   *   *   *   *

Pennsylvania Archives 6th Series V, 508:

Return of the First Company of the Third Regiment of the Militia of the City of
Philadelphia, commanded by Lieut. Colonel Commandant Samuel McClean, 1794:
(List of Privates includes name of Thomas Tingey.)

*   *   *   *   *

Obituary Notice clipping:

Died in this place, 28th ult.,* Mrs. Ann E. Tingey, widow of Commodore Tingey,
U.S.N., in the 75th year of her age.   God, in his sovereign wisdom, has removed to
a brighter world one who possessed, in an unusual degree, the esteem and affection of
all who knew her.   Her life was marked by deeds of benevolence, and many here and
elsewhere have had impressive evidence of her deep sympathy for the poor and needy.
Her self-denying spirit, her unceasing interest in the welfare of those around her, her
unobtrusive piety, and her winning exercise of all the attributes of the highest type
of noble womanhood, were an impressive commentary on those excellencies which

382

are the loveliest adornment of her sex. The closing months of her life were marked by intense bodily suffering which she bore with Christian fortitude. She has left us; but the memory of her deeds will long survive her mortal existence, and her Christian example will long yield fruits to be matured only in that other world whither all the living are hastening. * Lambertville, N.J., July 1861. *LDC*

Marriage Certificate, in possession of a descendant, James W. Sewall, Oldtown, Maine, 1930:

To all whom it may concern. I hereby certify | that on the 29th day of November in the year of | our Lord 1808, I solemnized according to Law the | rites of Marriage between Joseph Wingate and | Margaret G. Tingey—and I further certify that | during the said Margaret's residence for several years in this city, she has been a regular attendant | on my minstry, and warmly attached to the | discipline and doctrines of our holy & apostolic | Church, and tho' I am not absolutely certain that she | was a communicant, yet I have no hesitation | in saying she would have been cordially received | by me as a worthy participator in that holy | rite. Nay more, were she now a resident in | this place, and I Rector of Christ Church, from | the knowledge I have of her amiable manners & | goodness of heart, I would not hesitate a moment | to admit her as an acceptable & worthy guest | at the table of our Lord. | Andw T. McCormick | late Rector of Christ Church | City of Washington | Feby 3, 1824.

Family Records in possession of James W. Sewall abovesaid:

Joseph Ferdinand Wingate and Margaret Gay Tingey married at Washington City, D.C., by Rev. Mr. McCormick Nov. 29th 1808.

(Children) 1. Tingeyanna Margaretta, first daughter, born at Roxbury, Mass., Aug. 27, 1809; died at Washington City Aug 24, 1810.
2. Virginia Ann Nesbitt, born at Washn. City Jany 29, 1811.
3. Julia Nesbitt born Nov. 19, 1812, at Hallowell.
4. Sydney Ellen born March 10, 1815, at Bath.

Sarah Ann Tingey married Daniel French Dulany at Washington by Revd. Mr. McCormick April 4, 1811.
(Children) 1. Daniel French Dulany born 6 Jan 1812 at Shuters' Hill; 2. Mary Little Dulany born 1813 at Shuters' Hill.

Hannah Tingey married to Tunis Craven at Washington by Revd. Mr. McCormick September 25, 1803.
(Children) 1. Margaretta Tingey Craven born at Alexandria 6 Sept. 1804; 2. Ann Mary Craven born at Alexandria 10 Oct. 1806; 3. Thomas Tingey Craven born at Washington 30 Dec. 1808; 4. Alfred Wingate Craven born at Washington 20 Oct 1810; 5. Tunis Augustus Craven born at Portsmouth 11 Jan. 1813.

Mrs. Margaret Tingey died April 25, 1807 aged 57 years. Thomas Tingey remarried, Nancy Dulany, at Washington by Revd. Mr. McCormick. A daughter born in March 1812. Mrs. Ann Tingey died April 28th 1814 aged 32. Sarah Ann Tingey Dulany Sept. 20 ———.

(*Obituary notice* clipping). Deceased—Mrs. Sarah A. T. Dulany, aged 70 years, widow of the late Daniel F. Dulany, Sr., of Oak Mount, Fairfax County, Va., and daughter of the late Commodore Thomas Tingey of the United States Navy, died at Warrenton, Va., on the 20th ult.

By Deed of 24 Oct. 1796, THOMAS TINGEY of Philadelphia, mariner, and wife Margaret, conveyed to Matthew Randall of Philadelphia, merchant, for 3,000 Pounds, a brick messuage and lot on the East side of Third Street, between Walnut and Spruce Streets, 19½ by 100 feet, bounded North by the lot of late Francis Ferris and South by Samuel Lobdell, being same which Thomas Franklin of Philadelphia, gentleman, conveyed to said Thomas Tingey by Deed of 27 March 1793. Recorded in *Philadelphia Deed Book D-62*, p 85.

Philadelphia City Directories:

1791—Thomas Tingey, mariner, no. 16 Union Street.

1790—Thomas Tingey, mariner, South side of Union Street.*

   * Fourth name on the Census List of the Street, taken this same year. Union Street is now DeLancey Street, from Front to Fourth Streets. LDC

From the Rev. H. M. Pigott, rector of *St. John's Church, Christiansted, Virgin Islands, U.S.,* 15 February 1930:

The register gives no information as to the parents of Capt. Thomas Tingey and of Margaret Murdoch. The marriage entry, as you probably know, mentions that the marriage took place at the house of Mr. Beale, by virtue of a licence.

By Deed of 30 November 1796 David Clarkson of South Brunswick Twp., Middlesex County, N.J., Gentleman, conveyed to THOMAS TINGEY of same place, gentleman, for 3,667 Pounds, a plantation in said township which said Clarkson purchased from Thomas Vandike now deceased, by Deed of 14 November 1777, in which it is described as " All that plantation and farm on which the said Thomas Vandike dwelleth, lying and being in Mapletown, consisting of seven lots of land and meadows, . . . which said Vandike purchased from John Smith by Deed of 25 April 1749, Beginning on the road in Mapletown, in the line of said Vandike and Smith, thence along said line to the rear of their lots 88 chains and 80 links; thence South by West 5 chains and 65 links to part of the land which Matthias Vandike purchased of John Smith by Deed of 26 April 1749; thence along said Matthias Vandike's line North 69 degrees West 65 chains and 15 links to a corner of Matthias Vandike's land; thence along his line South 31 degrees West 5 chains and 42 links to the line of Matthias Vandike's old plantation; thence along his old line West North West to the aforesaid road; thence along said road to the place of beginning. Containing 65 acres. Lot no. 2: 130 acres; no. 3: 63½ acres; no. 4: 12 acres; no. 5   ; no. 6: 25 acres; no. 7 58½ acres; being bounded North by Heathcotes Brook, West by Samuel Moore's lot (no. 6), East by Aaron Longstreet Jr., South by land bought of William Hollingshead called no. 5. "The whole of the seven lots or plantation, containing 427 acres and one-half and 14 rods or perches of land. And also that other lot or tract adjoining the above, containing three acres. Excepting out of the above 8 lots a parcel sold by said David Clarkson to George K. Jackson, containing 100 and ¾ acres. With all messuages, houses, barns, stables, buildings, fences, etc. Recorded in *Middlesex County Deed Book no. 2,* p 40.

By Deed of 28 April 1800, THOMAS TINGEY of South Brunswick Township, Middlesex County, N.J., and wife Margaret, conveyed to David Clarkson the plantation which said Clarkson formerly purchased of Thomas Vandike now deceased, and heretofore sold to said Thomas Tingey by Deed of 30 November 1796 *(supra)*. Recorded in *Middlesex County Deed Book no. 2,* p 250.

See also: Elias Combs and wife to Thomas Tingey, 1797, recorded in Book no. 2, p 99; and Thomas Tingey to John Gulick, 1806, in Book no. 2, p 288; also Mortgage given by Thomas Tingey to said David Clarkson for $7500 on land in Mapletown, recorded 19 December 1796 in *Book no. 5 of Mortgages*, page 28.

Inscriptions from Gravestones in Oldtown, Maine, copied 1930:

Margaret G. Tingey, wife of Joseph F. Wingate, June 19, 1862.

James Bradbury, son of George P. & Sydney E. Sewall, died August 30, 1851, age 2 years.

Sydney Ellen Wingate March 10, 1815; March 26, 1887.

Joseph Sewall August 22, 1854; Jan 16, 1887.

George P. Sewall April 24, 1811; Dec. 30, 1881.

Sydney Margaret Sewall April 25, 1842; June 14, 1917.

James Wingate Sewall Nov. 11, 1852; May 25, 1905.

George Tingey Sewall July 19, 1844; October 31, 1909.

Hannah Virginia Sewall, daughter of George Popham & Sydney (Wingate) Sewall, July 27, 1846; Dec. 19, 1918.

*   *   *   *   *

Note: Mr. James W. Sewall Jr. informed me in Sept. 1930 at his home in Oldtown that Julia Wingate, sister of the above Sydney Ellen (Wingate) Sewall, died in a home for the aged, in Bangor, Maine, and was buried in this cemetery in Oldtown but without gravestone marker, and that she had lived with her sister in Oldtown previous to the Home.   L.D.Cook

*   *   *   *   *

OLD NIEUWKIRK HOUSE AT HURLEY, ULSTER COUNTY, NEW YORK

In possession of the family, 1933

The
van Nieuwkirk, Nieukirk, Newkirk Family

ILLUSTRATIONS *

*See pp. 386, 419, and 442, this volume.

NOTE

To avoid any mischance in the indexing of Dutch names we have retained the original index to this article as well as the original pagination. Thus, the name index to the "Van Nieuwkirk, Nieukirk, Newkirk" article appears on pp. 477-497, instead of at the back of the volume.

FOREWORD

NOT always are the fruits of labor enjoyed by those who give time, energy and material means to the furtherance of altruistic projects. In a very real sense is this true of Dr. Adamson Bentley Newkirk and Thomas Jefferson Newkirk, whose long-continued, unselfish efforts toward a complete history of the Newkirk family make every member of it their debtor.

After the death of these co-laborers, the collective family records became the property of The Genealogical Society of Pennsylvania, through the courtesy of Dr. Newkirk's widow. In accordance with her desire the earlier portion of the genealogical data, assembled and collated by her husband, is published in this second SPECIAL NUMBER of the Society's PUBLICATIONS.

Space does not permit inclusion of all branches of the family to the present day, since this is intended not as a complete genealogical history, but the foundation for one. It is of interest to know, however, that the gathered source material, in forty-eight bound folio volumes, is embraced in the Collections of the Society and available to those who seek further information regarding this early Holland-American family.

While too much appreciation cannot be given Dr. Newkirk and those associated with him, the result of their combined effort as herein presented is due, in large measure, to the interest and generous assistance of M. Atherton Leach, Editor of the Society's Publications.

P. F. N.

ERRATA*

Page 48.

Correction and addition, line twenty-three: Cumberland County Marriage Records, Book A, in County Clerk's Office, Bridgeton, New Jersey, gives marriage, or license, date of Garrett Newkirk and Catherine Elwell, as of *November 4, 1802.* Their daughter, Caroline E. Newkirk, married *Isaac Robinson Smith* of Philadelphia, son of Walter and Elizabeth (Robinson) Smith of Marsh Creek, York County, Pennsylvania, and had issue. Among the latter, Elizabeth R. Smith married Colonel A. Loudon Snowden of Philadelphia, United States Minister to Greece, Roumania and Servia; also to Spain.

Line 28: Samuel Newkirk, born January 12, 1788; married Rachel Newkirk, born March 4, 1787, daughter of Matthew and Catherine (Burroughs) Nieukirk, *vide* page 52; line 37. ED.

ERRATA*

Page 67.

Correction, line twenty-two: should read William Brooks Nieukirk married *Mary F. Glaspey*, not Glasbey.

Page 69, line five: Cumberland County Marriage Records, Book B, County Clerk's Office, Bridgeton, New Jersey, gives marriage, or license, date of William Brooks Nieukirk and *Mary G. Glaspey* as of *June 25, 1867.* ED.

---

*For pp. 48, 67, and 69 see pp. 439, 459, and 461, this volume.

SOME DESCENDANTS OF GERRET CORNELISSE AND MATTHEUS CORNELISSE VAN NIEUWKIRK.

FROM THE MANUSCRIPT * OF THE LATE

ADAMSON BENTLEY NEWKIRK, M.D. OF LOS ANGELES, CALIFORNIA,

In the Collections of The Genealogical Society of Pennsylvania.

FIRST GENERATION

The name Newkirk is not common in the United States; yet aside from the members of the family to be traced in the following pages, there are others found throughout the country.

The list of Palatines remaining in New York in 1710 contained the entry: ''Johan Henrick Newkirk, 36; Anna Maria, 33; Johannes, 11; John Henrick, dead.'' The descendants of this family mainly resided in Orange and Ulster Counties, New York; but are to be found in many parts of the United States and Canada. Johannes, or John, son of John Henry or Johan Henrick, had eleven children, became fairly wealthy for his time and died, according to the probate of his will, at Wallkill in 1777.

In 1738 a German named Hendrick Nikerick † arrived at Philadelphia and settled in Berks County, Pennsylvania. His descendants are numerous. Those remaining about Reading, Pennsylvania, assumed the name Newkirk, while those in Washington County, Maryland, took that of Niekirk. Descendants of the latter are to be found at Republic, Ohio, or as having migrated therefrom.

There have been Newkirk arrivals from Holland in recent years, with the prefix van; others without it. Also a number

---

* Dr. Newkirk's alignment of families has been adhered to throughout this compilation; his spellings of proper names usually so. Families not herein carried forward will, in many instances, be found more fully treated of in the *Collections* which bear his name in The Genealogical Society of Pennsylvania.

† Hendrick Nikerick, aged thirty-two in ship *Nancy*, William Wallace, master, qualified September 20, 1738. — *Pennsylvania Archives, Second Series*, vol. xvii, 164.

(1)

of Germans named Newkerchen, who have adopted the form Newkirk.

This brief explanation will suffice to show that all New-kirks found in the United States are not traceable to the same progenitor.

CORNELISSE[1] VAN NIEUWKIRK, some time resident of Slichtenhorst in Gelderland, Holland, was the father of two sons who sailed on the Dutch ship *Moesman* for New Netherland, 25 April, 1659. A diligent search for further information concerning him has not yet been productive.

Children, the youngest born in Slichtenhorst:

2. i. GERRET[2] CORNELISSE, married Chieltje Slecht.
3. ii. MATTHEUS CORNELISSE, married (1) Anna Lubi; (2) Catryna Paulus.

---

* Slichtenhorst, a small district south of the city of Nijkerk, where many of the estates, or farms, belonged originally to the Adelijk Juffrouwen-Stift (convent for ladies of noble birth), at Hoch-Elten, Germany, near the Dutch frontier.

An article in *The New York Genealogical and Biographical Record,* for January, 1934, by Richard Schermerhorn, Jr. entitled: REPRESENTATIVE PIONEER SETTLERS OF NEW NETHERLAND AND THEIR ORIGINAL HOME PLACES, gives five settlers as from Nykerck, Gelderland; one from Nieuenkerk, Zeeland, and one from Niewkerk, Rhine Province. Among the best known settlers from Nykerck (Nijkerk) was Brant Aertz van Schlichtenhorst whose name derived from the district about five miles to the southward. — *Cf. An Armory of American Families of Dutch Descent,* by William J. Hoffman, M. E., in the foregoing publication, July, 1933, pp. 244, *et seq.*

Another article in the same publication for April, 1932, NOTES ON OLD DUTCH-AMERICAN FAMILIES, by William J. Hoffman, M. E., draws attention to the inestimable value of the Dutch patronomic to students of Dutch genealogy, and calls for careful reading.—ED.

SECOND GENERATION

2. GERRET [2] CORNELISSE VAN NIEUWKIRK (*Cornelisse* [1]). The passenger list * of the *Moesman*, 25 April, 1659, contained the entry: "Gerrit Corn. van Niew-Kerk,* and Wife and boy and sucking child." The boy was his brother Mattheus, aged about twelve years. Following a custom, somewhat common in Holland families after arrival in New Netherland, the brothers were more or less known as Gerret (or Gerrit) Cornelisse and Mattheus Cornelisse. The children of the elder brother, Gerret, appear in official records of Ulster County and those of the Kingston Dutch Church as van Nieukirk and Nieuwkirck, or Nieuwkerck, without the van prefix. Those of the younger brother, Mattheus, adhered to the prefix and are on official and church records of Bergen County, New Jersey, as van Nieuwkirk or van Nieuwkerck. The descendants of both later changed the surname spelling and, in the fourth generation, Newkirk became the prevailing form. Some branches of the family continued the spelling NIEUKIRK to the present day and these, it would appear, all descend from Gerret Cornelisse's grandson, Cornelius Nieukirk, who so wrote his surname, and who moved to Salem County, New Jersey, about the year 1718.

Gerret Nieuwkirk promptly secured a home lot at Midwout, Long Island, which he sold after a few years. Bergen's *Early Settlers of King's County, New York* † gives the following brief account of this transaction:

> Van Nukerk, Gerrit Cornelisse, probably from Nykerk, a town in Gelderland, or Nieuwerkerk, a town in Zeeland, sold March 10, 1665, to Arent Evertse, molenaer (miller), a farm on the east side of the road in Flatbush of 18ª morgens, abutting on Corlaer's Flats, as per page 20 of Liber D, Flatbush records.

On April 24, 1666, Gerret and his wife became members of the Dutch Church at Bergen. Their son Jan was baptized in New York, September 8, 1666, but the parents may have been residents of Bergen at the time. The next record found of them is at the baptism of their daughter Gerretje, at Kingston,

---

* O'Callahan, *Documentary History of New York*, iii, 35.

† 351. *Cf.* Gerret Cornelise van Duyn, 331-2.

(3)

New York, March 12, 1669. About this time the father purchased a farmstead in the Hurley Patent, in Ulster County. In 1670, he is listed in Captain Henry Pawling's Company of Foot Militia, as from Hurley, at the Rendezvous of April 5th of that year,* and on May 26, 1677, was one of the witnesses to the deed from the Indians to Louis Du Bois and Associates for the Paltz Patent.† The next public record of him would appear to be of June 9, 1695, when he, his wife and brother Mattheus were witnesses at a baptism ‡ in the old Dutch Church of Kingston.

His will, executed February 3, 1686, probated March 4, 1695/6, styled him of Hurley. The document is conclusive as to the seniority of the three sons and two daughters named. There may have been other children who predeceased him, as had the nursing child, the *Moesman* passenger.

He married in Holland, Chieltje (Cornelia) Cornelissen Slecht,§ to whom was bequeathed his entire estate with reversion, at her decease, to their five children equally. She was deceased before June 30, 1702.

Children of Gerret Cornelisse and Chieltje (Slecht) Niewkirk, or Nieuwkerk:

  i. CHILD ³, name unknown, born in Holland; died after April, 1659.
4. ii. CORNELIS GERRETSE, married Jannetje Jansz Kunst.
5. iii. ARIE GERRETSE, born Flatbush, L. I.; married Lysbeth Lambertse.
  iv. JAN GERRETSE, baptized New York Dutch Church, September 8, 1666; married at Kingston, July 23, 1687, Titjen Deckers and was a sponsor at the baptism of his niece, Neeltje, daughter of Jacob and Gerretje (Nieuwkirk) Du Bois, May 27, 1716. This is an early instance on the Kingston Church Records where the family name appears as Nieuwkirk.
6. v. NEELTJE GERRETSE, born *circa* 1667; married (1) Peter Crispell; (2) Johannes Schepmoes.
7. vi. GERRETJE GERRETSE, bapt. Kingston, March 12, 1669; married (1) Barent Kunst; (2) Jacob Du Bois.

3. MATTHEUS² CORNELISSE VAN NIEUWKIRK (*Cornelisse¹*), born at Slichtenhorst in Gelderland, accompanied his brother Gerret Cornelisse to New Netherland in the ship *Moesman*, in 1659. He settled at Bergen, New Jersey, and there died May 12, 1705.

---

* *Report of the State Historian, State of New York, Colonial Series*, vol. i, 379.

† *Documents Pertaining to the Colonial History of New York*, xiii, 507.

‡ Mattheus, son of Pieter Lambertse Brink and Geertruyt Mattheusen, grandson of Mattheus Cornelisse and great-nephew of Gerret Cornelisse.

§ Name variously spelled Slecht, Slegt, Sleght.

He married first, December 14, 1670,* Anna, daughter of Jacob Lubi by his wife Geertruyt Leons. The banns were published at the Bergen Reformed Church, November 27, preceding, and the ceremony was performed before the Court at Bergen. His wife died at Bergen, December 20, 1685, and he married, second, Catryna Paulus. The entry of this marriage from the Bergen Church records reads:

> Matheus Cornelisse van Nieuwkerck, wid. of Anna Lubi, born at Slechtenhorst in Gelderland, and Catryna Paulus, from Bergen, New Jersey, both living in Bergen, married August 15, at Bergen, by the Voorleezer [Reinier] Van Giesen, in the presence of the Court at Bergen in the church, Banns having been published 5 July, 1686.†

Catryna van Nieuwkirk long survived her husband. Her will, dated at Bergen September 30, 1731, was not probated until May 7, 1764.‡ She made bequests to her surviving children, Peter the eldest, Gerret, Paulus, Cornelius and Jannetje, but made no mention of step-children.

Children of Mattheus Cornelisse and Anna (Lubi) van Nieuwkirk, born at Bergen, New Jersey:

8.   i. GEERTRUYT[3], married Peter Lambertse Brink.
    ii. GERRETJE, bapt. June 23, 1673; married Aelt Juriaensen, both described as of Bergen; had certificate to and were married at New York, by Dominie Selyns, July 6, 1695. The groom was the son of Juriaen Thomassen van Ripen, and his wife Reyckje Harmens Coerten.§ Issue: *Annetje Juriaensen*[4], bapt. Bergen, May 1, 1696.
    iii. JACOMYNTJE, bapt. April 2, 1678; married April 20, 1701, Jacob Symonsen Van Winkle, born August 9, 1678, son of Symon Jacobs and Annetje Ariaense (Sip) Van Winkle.¶ Issue, born Bergen County: 1. *Waling*[4] *Van Winkle*. 2. *Jacob Van Winkle*. 3. *Simeon Van Winkle*, m. Geertruydt Van der Houex, and had thirteen children, born in Bergen County: i. ANNATJE[5], born March 16, 1729. ii. SARAH, born August 29, 1731. iii. JOHANNES, born December 6, 1733. iv. MICHAEL, born April 6, 1736. v. SIMEON. vi. ELEANOR. vii. CATHARINE, bapt. June 17, 1739. viii. MARIANUS, bapt. June 5, 1741. ix. CHARITY. x. GEERTRUYDT. xi. JOHANNES, bapt. November 7, 1749. xii. BENJAMIN, born December 6, 1756. xiii. HANNAH.
    iv. CORNELIS, born March 11, 1680; died June 7, 1691.
    v. JACOB,‖ born November 21, 1682; married April 27, 1707, Sara

---

* *New Jersey Archives, First Series*, xxii, 576.

† *New Jersey Archives*, vol. xxii, 576.

‡ *Ibid.*, vol. xxxiii, 453.

§ *New York Genealogical and Biographical Record*, vol. lvi (1925), 268.

¶ *Ibid.*, 251.

‖ He appears to have called himself Jacob Matthuesen.

Cornelis of North Haarlem. Issue: 1. *Antie* [4] *Newkirk*, bapt. at Hackensack, New Jersey, February 29, 1708; married, May 30, 1747, Johannes Bikelo. 2. *Jacomyntje Newkirk*, married Abraham, son of Johannes and Helena (Spier) Van Winkle. Children: i. GEERTRUYT [5] VAN WINKLE, born February 15, 1747. ii. JACOB VAN WINKLE, born January 9, 1750. iii. SIMEON VAN WINKLE, born December 22, 1755. iv. HELENA VAN WINKLE, born February 28, 1758.

Children of Mattheus Cornelisse and Catryna (Paulus) van Nieuwkirk, born at Bergen:

    i. JANNETJE [3], born July 8, 1687; died May 15, 1691.
    ii. TRYNTJE, bapt. December 17, 1688; died February 16, 1689.
    iii. JAN, born April 20, 1690; died January 17, 1691.
    iv. JANNETJE, born May 17, 1691; married April 21, 1733, Gerrit Didericks of Bergen, born September 17, 1695, son of Wander and Aaltje (Gerrits) Didericks.* Issue: 1. *Aaltje* [4] *Didericks*, born Schraalenburgh, New Jersey, June 6, 1736; married, December 7, 1752, Jacob Brinkerhoff.† Issue all born in Bergen County: i. JANNETTE [5] BRINKERHOFF, born November 15, 1753; died young. ii. JANNETTE BRINKERHOFF, born January 1, 1755. iii. HENDRICK BRINKERHOFF, born August 17, 1756. iv. GERRIT BRINKERHOFF, born April 4, 1762. v. ELIZABETH BRINKERHOFF, born June 23, 1765.
    v. PETER, born August 26, 1694; married June 12, 1726, Tryntje Dirckje. They were at Belleville, New Jersey, from 1732 to 1756, perhaps later. Issue: 1. *Tryntje* [4] *Newkirk*, bapt. at Belleville, June 16, 1732; married Jacob Garrabrant.‡ Child: MARITIE [5] GARRABRANT, bapt. Second River Church, July 11, 1756.
9.   vi. GERRET, married Catryntje Kuypers.
10. vii. PAULUS, married Helena Spier.
    viii. CORNELIS, born September 13, 1703; married, October 18, 1749, Lea Maris, widow of Abraham Cammega.|| They resided at Schraalenburgh. No children.

---

* *New Jersey Archives, First Series*, vol. xxii, 576, 560.

† Brinkerhoff, Blinkerhof. *Ibid.*, 476.

‡ Garrabrantz, Gerrebrantse.

§ *Cf. New Jersey Archives*, vol. xxii, 508, 494.

|| Kammega, Kammigaa.

THIRD GENERATION

4. CORNELIS [3] GERRETSE VAN NIEUWKIRK (*Gerretse,*[2] *Cornelisse*[1]) was born, probably, on Long Island, *circa* 1662. In 1686-1687 he was a private in the Kingston Troop of Horse under Captain Hendrickus Beekman.*

He died at Hurley, Ulster County, New York, between February 7 and March 4, 1695/6, the dates of the execution and probate of his will, which provided that his wife should have the children, whom he named, taught reading and writing, and permit them to acquire a profession, or trade. Under his father's will he had received considerable real estate which he materially increased.

The entry of his marriage, on the Kingston records, reads: "Cornelis Gerritz, j. m., born in N. Jorck [New York] and resid. in Horley [Hurley], and Jannetie Jansz Kunst, j. d., born in Kingston, and resid. in Horley. First publication of Banns, 5 Oct. 1683." Date of marriage not given.

His wife, Jannetje Kunst, baptized at Kingston Church, February 24, 1664, survived him and, as late as August 2, 1729, is described in a quit-claim deed as Jannetje Newkirk, widow of Cornelis Newkirk, late of Hurley.† She was the daughter of Jan Barentsen Kunst ‡ and his second wife,

---

* *Report of the State Historian of New York, Colonial Series,* vol. ii, 448.

† *New York Genealogical and Biographical Record,* vol. xvi, 27-8.

‡ Jan Barentsen Kunst, son of Barent Kunst of Holland, came to America on the *Guilded Beaver* in May, 1658, from Alckmaer, twenty miles from Amsterdam, Holland. He located in Beverwyck, Albany County, New York, and married Jennette Ariens, by whom he had one child, a daughter, Hillitje Jans Kunst, who married Nicholas Roosevelt. These latter were the ancestors of Theodore Roosevelt and Franklin D. Roosevelt, presidents of the United States. His first wife having died, Jan Barentsen Kunst, on April 29, 1663, married Jacomyntje Cornelis Slecht, daughter of Cornelis Barentsen Slecht, and by her had two children: *Jannetje Kunst,* above named, and *Barent Kunst,* who married Gerretje Gerretse Niewkirk, *q. v.,* and died within a year after his marriage, leaving a widow and an only child, Jacomyntje. After the death of Jan Barentsen Kunst, his widow married at Kingston, after October 27, 1668, Gerret Focken, a young man from Friesland, Holland, by whom she had: *Tryntje Focken,* who married Solomon Du Bois, and *Hillitje Focken,* who married Gerret Wynkoop. Again a widow, Jacomyntje married a third time, November 24, 1672, Jan Elting, and had five children: *Aaltje, Roeloff, Cornelis, Geertje* and *William.*

(7)

Jacomyntje   Slecht,   daughter   of   Cornelius   Barentsen
Slecht.*

---

* Cornelis Barentsen Slecht of Woerden, near Leyden, Holland, father
of Jacomyntje (Slecht) Kunst and grandfather of Jannetje Kunst,
wife of Cornelis Gerretse Nieuwkirk, was in New Netherland as early
as 1652. In 1653 his wife, Tryntje Tysen Bos, was a licensed midwife
for Esopus. He was a miller and magistrate, prominent in civil affairs
of Esopus and in those of the church.

Most people in the then inhabited portions of Ulster County were Hollanders and recognized the laws of their native country as proper for their
observance in the new. At the beginning little law was needed, for
generally each respected the rights of others; contracts were promptly
complied with, and little disorder prevailed. But, as the small neighboring communities of Kingston and Hurley increased in population, a form
of local government became necessary.

On May 16, 1661, knowledge came to Peter Stuyvesant, Director General of New Netherland, that Esopus, which had been inhabited for six
or seven years, was without government. He, therefore, immediately
erected the locality into a village and granted it a charter under the
name Wiltwick, which was afterwards changed to Kingston. The charter
so granted provided punishment for offences, and required the enforce-
ment of the laws of the fatherland. To this end a board of Schepens
was created, it being in effect a court, with additional powers to look
after the county business generally. The first Schepens appointed were
Albert Heymans Roosa, Cornelius Barentsen Slecht and Evert Pels, with
Roeloff Swartwout as Schout (Sheriff). All these were native Hollanders.

At the burning of Hurley by the Indians, June 7, 1663, Cornelis
Barentsen Slecht and son Hendrick were officially reported as present,
but in the official list of captives no mention of the name of any member
of this family is found. A few years before, however, a son of Mr.
Slecht had been captured by the Indians, made to run the gauntlet and
then burned at the stake.

In the Spring of 1664 the English assumed control of New Netherland. The Dutch, traditionally loyal to their fatherland, and indomitable
in spirit, resisted this so far as in their power. Nevertheless, an English
garrison was at once established at Wiltwick under the command of
Captain Daniel Brodhead. This created an unfortunate situation, and
disorder, fighting and rioting ensued. On April 28, 1667, a petition,
signed by a large number of the inhabitants, was forwarded to the Governor, reciting that ''upon the 4th day of Feb. last, upon the doleful cry
and lamentation of the children of Cornelis Barentsen Slegt, that their
father was miserably beaten and wounded by Capt. Brodhead,'' they had
repaired to his house and ascertained that the complaint was true. This
was soon followed by another petition which recited ''That Cornelis
Barentsen Slegt is beaten in his own house by his soldier George Porter,
and after this by the other soldiers, and forced to prison, and at his
imprisonment used very hard . . . and his arms by force taken out of
his house which still do remain by said Capt. Brodhead.''

If these petitions served no further purpose, they gave the Governor

Children of Cornelis Gerretse and Jannetje (Kunst) Nieuwkirk, all but the last baptized † at Kingston:

11.   i. GERRIT⁴, married Grietje, or Marguerite Ten Eyck.
12.   ii. JAN, married Janneke Van Brestede.
13.   iii. ADRIAN, married Aaltjen Bogaard, Bogaert, or Bogart.
14.   iv. BARENT, married Rebecca Van Buntschooten.

the information which he needed, namely to locate the causes of the
clashes, and the leading characters therein. Some of the causes seem of
little consequence now, but then they were large factors. As an instance:
Tjerck Classen De Witt was beaten by Capt. Brodhead and cast into
prison. He afterwards testified before a commission, that the reason the
Captain beat him was because he "would keep Christmas Day on the day
customary with the Dutch and not on the day according to the English
observation." Captain Brodhead admitted all this to be true, but insisted that the offence was a sufficient justification for the treatment
administered.

Matters went from bad to worse, and on April 16, 1667, the Governor
appointed a commission to investigate the troubles. This was a mere
formality since the findings had already been prepared. There was to be
no jury and but few admitted to the hearing. It was, therefore, easy
for the commission to decide that a state of rebellion and insurrection
existed, and that the four principal instigators were Antoni d'Elba,
Albert Heymans Roosa,ᵃ Arent Albertson and Cornelis Barentsen Slecht.
These gentlemen were taken to New York for sentence, and Roosa was
banished for life from the government; the others for shorter terms out
of Esopus, Albany and New York. These sentences were soon modified,
and the accused permitted to return to their homes, but the spirit of
resistance was neither modified nor crushed.

Captain Brodhead was finally suspended, and died July 14, 1667, leaving a widow and three sons, Daniel, Charles and Richard, all of whom
became prominent and highly respected citizens, and whose descendants
espoused the cause of American Independence with a fealty and devotion
equal to any engaged in that great cause.

The children of Cornelis Barentsen Slecht and his wife Trintje Tysen
Bos, were: 1. *Jacomyntje Slecht*, who, as elsewhere stated, was three
times married, with issue by each marriage. 2. *Hendrick Slecht*, who
married Elsje Barens, August 1, 1666, and had children. 3. *Annetie
Slecht*, wife of Cornelius Hoogeboom, who left no issue. 4. *Mattys
Slecht*, who married Mary Magdaleen Crispell. 5. *Pietronella Slecht*, who
married Jochem Hendrick Schoonmaker, August 16, 1679.

† *Baptismal and Marriage Registers of the Old Dutch Church of
Kingston, New York*. Transcribed and edited by Roswell Randall Hoes,
Chaplain U. S. N., New York, 1891.

ᵃ Albert Heymans Roosa, agriculturist from Gelderland, with wife and
eight children emigrated to New Netherland on the ship *Spotted Cow* in
April, 1660.—O 'Callahan, *Documentary History of New York*, iii, 36.

15. v. GILLES or GIELETJEN, married Jacobus Swartwout.
  vi. JACOMYNTJE, bapt. June 8, 1694; married (1), September 28, 1715, Hendrick Kip, baptized July 7, 1688. In his will of December 12, 1751, probated December 14, 1754, he bequeathed property to his wife, with remainder to Cornelius Newkirk, eldest son of Gerret, and to cousin Cornelius Newkirk, son of Jan. On August 25, 1755,* his widow married Captain Peter Du Bois. Issue: *Jannetjen* [5] *Kip*, bapt. September 23, 1716; deceased, unmarried, before December 12, 1751.
16. vii. CORNELIUS, married Rachel Ten Eyck.

5. ARIE [3] NIEUWKIRK (*Gerretse*,[2] *Cornelisse*[1]), or, as he was more commonly known, Arien Gerritsen, was born at Midwout, Long Island, *circa* 1661. He resided for a time at Hurley but was later at Saugerties, and was prominent in the early military and civil affairs of Ulster County; was Justice of the Peace in 1699, and Judge of the Ulster County Probate Courts before 1725.

He married, after October 17, 1686, Lysbet Lambertse Brink, born at Hurley, baptized February 14, 1666, daughter of Lambert Huybertse Brink and his wife Hendricke Cornelisse, natives of Wageningen, Gelderland, Holland.†

Children of Arie Gerritsen and Lysbet Lambertse (Brink) Nieuwkirk, baptized at Kingston Dutch Church: ‡

    i. GHILJE [4], baptized January 29, 1688.
17. ii. JAN, married Dorothea Douw.
18. iii. HENDERIKJE, married Cornelius Wynkoop.
19. iv. GERRET, married Anna Vischer.
20.   v. ARIAANTJE, married Jacobus Elmendorf.
21. vi. LEA, married Jacob Rutsen.
22. vii. RACHEL, married Jan Cornelius Bogart.
23. viii. CORNELIUS, married Dina Hoogteeling.

6. NEELTJE [3] GERRETSE NIEUWKIRK (*Gerretse*,[2] *Cornelisse*[1]), born probably at Bergen, *circa* 1667; died at Hurley, *circa* 1706. She married, first, Peter Crispell,§ baptized at Kingston, December 21, 1664, died *circa* 1695, son of Anthony and

---

* KIP FAMILY IN AMERICA, Montclair, New Jersey, 1928, by Frederic Ellsworth Kip.

† *Cf.* THE BRINK FAMILY, by Benjamin Meyer Brink, in *Olde Ulster*, vol. ii, 120.

‡ Dr. Newkirk takes exception to the statement in *Ulster County New York, Probate Records*, by Gustave Anjou, Ph.D. (*American Record Series*, New York, 1906, volume 1, pp. 169, 184) that "Arie Gerritsen van Neukerk" had a son Coenradt.

§ *Cf.* THE CRISPELL FAMILY OF ULSTER COUNTY, NEW YORK, by Thomas G. Evans, in *The New York Genealogical and Biographical Record*, xxi, 83, *et seq.*

Maria (Blanshan *) Crispell. She married, second, February 18, 1697, Johannes Schepmoes, baptized at Kingston, April 7, 1672, son of Dirck Jansen Schepmoes and wife Maria Willems.

---

* Matthew Blanshan (Blanchan, Blancsan, Blansjan) and wife, Magdalena Jorisse, parents of Maria (Blanshan) Crispell, were natives of Artois, French Flanders, residing at Mannheim, Germany. On April 22, 1660, the Dutch ship *Guilded Otter* sailed for America with a mixed passenger list from Holland, Germany and France, many of whom were soldiers. In the list is "Matthew Blanchan, from Artois; agriculturist, wife and three children", also "Anthony Krupel (Crispell) from Artois, Agriculturist, and wife." All went first to what is now Kingston, but soon located at Hurley.

On June 7, 1663, Hurley and part of Kingston were burned by Indians, many inhabitants killed and many women and children carried away captives. The family of Matthew Blanshan suffered heavily; his two younger children, Elizabeth and Matthew, Jr., his daughter Catharine, wife of Louis Du Bois, and her three children, Abraham, Isaac and Jacob, and his daughter Maria, wife of Anthony Crispell, and her daughter Mary Magdalena, were among the captives. The distress of the community was great. Within three months, however, the captives were all restored. Some had been ransomed or exchanged, while others were rescued by Captain Martin Cregier in a sudden attack upon the savages, who, in their excitement, did not take time to murder the captives.

Many traditions are still extant as to the treatment of the captives by the Indians. The one that, when attacked, the Indians had placed Catharine Du Bois upon a pile of wood preparatory to burning her, and that she delayed their purpose by singing hymns to them until the moment of the attack, is not improbable, and is consistent with Indian character, their purpose being probably not to burn, but to frighten her. The captives reported that they had not been subjected to any greater hardships than the Indians themselves had been compelled to undergo.

Matthew Blanshan made two wills. In the first, dated July 17, 1665, he mentions his wife Magdalena Jorisse as "lawful wife who shall possess the whole estate here in America as long as she remain a widow"; also "all the land in Artois, where I was born, and in Armentiers and other places", she to keep the "three children, Magdalena, Elizabeth and Matthew, until they reach their majority or marry." She was then, to act toward them as she treated the two married daughters, Catharine and Maria. In his second will, dated August 22, 1671, he mentions his wife but directs that certain property be divided among his children, Catharine, Maria, Magdalena, Elizabeth and Matthew. He, no doubt, died at Hurley, in 1688, and from the fragmentary records extant, he appears to have been a man of prominence. Of his five children: Catharine, married Louis Du Bois; Maria, married Anthony Crispell; Magdalena, married Jan Mattys Jansen [Van Keuren]; Elizabeth, married Peter Cornelisse Louw, and Matthew, Jr., married Margaret Claes Van Schoonhoven.

Children of Peter and Neeltje Gerretse (Nieuwkirk) Crispell:

    i. ANTHONY [4] CRISPELL, bapt. April 17, 1692; married September 11, 1719, Lea Roosa, daughter of Heyman Aldertse Roosa and wife Anna Margaret Roosevelt. His will, dated Hurley, Ulster County, March 9, 1767, probated August 16, 1771, mentioned sons Johannes and Cornelius, and daughter Neeltje, wife of Dirck Roosa.

    ii. ARIANTJE CRISPELL, born June 30, 1694; married March 10, 1712, Andries Ten Eyck, son of Matthew Ten Eyck * and wife Jenneke Roosa. He and his wife located in Somerset County, New Jersey, and were members of the First Reformed Church of Raritan as early as August 9, 1713. When the Readington Church was formed they became members of it and their son Matthew, was the first child baptized in the new church. Andreas Ten Eyck was a brother of Rachel Ten Eyck, wife of Cornelius Nieukirk, who settled in Salem County, New Jersey. Issue: 1. *Neeltje* [5] *Ten Eyck*, bapt. October 15, 1717. 2. *Matthew Ten Eyck*, bapt. February 21, 1720. 3. *Jannetje Ten Eyck*, bapt. May 20, 1722. 4. *Petrus Ten Eyck*, bapt. February 21, 1725. 5. *Andries Ten Eyck*, bapt. March 19, 1727. 6. *Johannes Ten Eyck*, bapt. September 9, 1732. 7. *Abraham Ten Eyck*, bapt. December 21, 1735. 8. *Adrientje Ten Eyck*, bapt. May 27, 1739. 9. *Marytje Ten Eyck*, married Jaques Vanderbeck.

    iii. JOHANNES CRISPELL, bapt. October 27, 1695; married December 15, 1725, Anna Margaret Roosa, daughter of Aldert Roosa and wife Aagje Krom. Issue: 1. *Petrus* [5] *Crispell*, bapt. November 26, 1727; died young. 2. *Albert Crispell*, bapt. November 10, 1728; died young. 3. *Rachel Crispell*, bapt. October 1, 1732; married December 11, 1756, Petrus Roosa; had issue. 4. *Arriantje Crispell*, bapt. August 25, 1734, married April 26, 1758, Abraham Elmendorf; had issue. 5. *Petrus Crispell*, bapt. September 19, 1736; married November 10, 1762, Gerretje, daughter of Garret Du Bois and wife Margaret Elmendorf; had issue. 6. *Elizabeth Crispell*, bapt. February 24, 1738; married Cornelius J. Elmendorf. 7. *Lea Crispell*, bapt. December 14, 1740. 8. *Albert Crispell*, bapt. February 13, 1743. 9. *Johannes Crispell*, bapt. April 21, 1745; married Rebecca Roosa. His will, dated May 29, 1809, probated November 6, 1810, described him of Shawangunk, and mentioned sons Anthony and John and their sisters.

Child of Johannes and Neeltje Gerretse (Nieuwkirk) Schepmoes:

    i. MARIA [4] SCHEPMOES, bapt. May 1, 1698; married May 26, 1720, Simon Van Wagenen, son of Gerret Aartsen Van Wagenen † and wife Clarissa Evertse Pells. She died in 1734 and her husband re-married. Issue: 1. *Clara* [5] *Van Wagenen*, bapt. May 14, 1721; married December, 1743, Hendrick Krom; had issue, baptized at Kingston. 2. *Johannes Van Wagenen*, bapt. November 18, 1722; married (1) August 2, 1748, Elizabeth Burhans, a widowed daughter of Barent Burhans; married

---

* *Cf.* THE TEN EYCK FAMILY in New York, in *The New York Genealogical and Biographical Record*, vol. lxiii, 163.

† *Vide,* VAN WAGENEN FAMILY, *The New York Genealogical and Biographical Record*, vol. x, p. 81.

(2) in 1760, Helena Kittle; had issue by both marriages. 3. *Gerret Aartsen Van Wagenen*, bapt. March 24, 1724; married Annatje Bosch [Busch]; resided in Ulster County; had issue. 4. *Neeltje Van Wagenen*, bapt. November 6, 1726; married Henrich Bosch; had issue. 5. *Jacob Van Wagenen*, bapt. July 7, 1728. 6. *Maria Van Wagenen*, bapt. December 21, 1729; married November 23, 1751, Abraham Krom of Ulster County, and had issue. 7. *Annatje Van Wagenen*, bapt. February 20, 1732; married Jonas Schmidt of Ulster County, and had issue. 8. *Sarah Van Wagenen*, bapt. March 24, 1734; married March 26, 1759, Henrich Schmidt, and had issue.

7. GERRETJE[3] GERRETSE NIEUWKIRK (*Gerretse,*[2] *Cornelisse*[1]), was baptized at Kingston, March 12, 1669, and died at Hurley after April 3, 1739. She married first, Barent Kuntz, baptized at Kingston, January 30, 1667, son of Jan Barentsen Kunst and wife Jacomyntje Slecht, and brother of Jannette Kunst, wife of Cornelis Gerretse Nieuwkirk, who died about a year after marriage. She married second, Jacob Du Bois, a widower, third son of Louis * Du Bois and wife Catharine

---

* The earliest comprehensive record of Louis Du Bois begins with that of his marriage at Mannheim, Germany, whither he had gone to escape persecution because of his religion. Translated it reads:

"Louis Du Bois, son of the late Chretian Du Bois, of Wikres, near La Basse, on the one side, and Catharine Blanshan, daughter of Matthew Blanshan, citizen of Mannheim, on the other side, were married in the French Church at Mannheim the 10th Oct., 1655."

The little Hamlet of Wikres contained about three hundred inhabitants devoted to agriculture, and is in the Province of Artois, French Flanders. Here Louis Du Bois was born October 21, 1626. The family was then a very ancient one, and is referred to in the archives and books of heraldry "as one of the most ancient and noble of the realm." How long he had been at Mannheim is unknown; he was twenty-nine years old at his marriage, and was probably about ten years older than his wife.

In New Netherland, to which he emigrated in 1660, he was farmer, merchant, magistrate and leading citizen, and is found to have been in the forefront of every undertaking. In 1677 he organized the movement which resulted in the purchase of about forty thousand acres of land from the Indians, known as the New Paltz Patent. The Village of New Paltz was laid out, and on the principal street a number of substantial stone residences built, several of which are still standing. A church was organized with Louis Du Bois the first elder.

For a time, he and his associates, all of whom were Frenchmen, resided at New Paltz, but he later returned to Kingston and spent the remainder of his life with the Dutch settlers of Kingston and Hurley. He left a large family, all named in his will; his widow married Jean Cottin, the schoolmaster. — *Cf.* DU BOIS FAMILY OF ULSTER COUNTY, by H. O. Collins, in *The New York Genealogical and Biographical Record*, vols. xxvii, xxviii.

Blanshan, one of the captives of the Indians at the burning of Hurley.

Jacob Du Bois, baptized October 9, 1661, was a farmer at Hurley, where he died in 1745, leaving a will dated April 3, 1739, probated June 7, 1745, which mentioned wife Gerretje, to whom a number of bequests were made, with life interest in landed estate and remainder to children. By his first wife, Elizabeth Vernooy, whom he married March 8, 1689, he had one child, Magdalena Du Bois, baptized May 25, 1690, named in his will. She married first, Garret Roosa; second, October 20, 1718, Peter Van Nest, and with him settled in Monmouth County, New Jersey; had issue.

Child of Barent and Gerretje (Nieuwkirk) Kuntz:

 i. JACOMYNTJE [4] KUNST, born in Hurley; married at Kingston, June 26, 1713, Henry Pawling,* who died at New Providence, Philadelphia, later Montgomery County, Pennsylvania, August 30, 1739, aged fifty years, youngest son of Henry Pawling of Ulster County, New York, and wife Neeltje Roosa. He and his brother, John Pawling, removed from Ulster County and settled some ten miles from Norristown, Pennsylvania, where he and his family were members of St. James' Church, Perkiomen. Issue: 1. *Henry* [5] *Pawling*, bapt. June 27, 1714, in Ulster County; will proved Montgomery County, Pennsylvania, November 3, 1792; married about 1740, his cousin Eleanor, daughter of John Pawling and wife Aagje De Witt, born February 27, 1715. 2. *Sara Pawling*, bapt. July 8, 1716. 3. *Elizabeth Pawling*, bapt. March 22, 1719. 4. *Barent Pawling*, married Elizabeth, daughter of Josiah James; was in Berks County, Pennsylvania, in 1766, and probably had issue. 5. *Levi Pawling*, a Colonel in the Revolutionary war, and Judge in Ulster County; married at Kingston, October 12, 1749, Helena Burhans, bapt. May 14, 1732, daughter of William Burhans and his wife Gerritje Ten Eyck, widow of Gerret Newkirk; had issue. 6. *John Pawling*, bapt. December 27, 1732; married May 23, 1755, Neeltje Van Keuren, daughter of Thomas and Mary (Pawling) Van Keuren. 7. *Elinor Pawling*, married, before April 22, 1746, James Morgan.

Children of Jacob and Gerretje (Nieuwkirk) Du Bois; all born in Ulster County:

 i. BARENT [4] DU BOIS, bapt. May 3, 1693; died at Pittsgrove, Salem County, New Jersey, January 22, 1749, leaving a will which made bequests to all his children. He married April 23, 1715, Jacomyntje, born October 30, 1693, daughter of Solomon Du Bois and wife, Tryntje Focken, *q. v.* His family Bible is in the possession of the Salem County Historical Society, from which source the present

---

* *Cf.* LINEAGE OF THE PAWLING FAMILY, by Mrs. J. Frank Kitts, printed in *Olde Ulster*, vol. i, pp. 339 *et seq.*; PAWLING FAMILY OF NEW YORK AND PENNSYLVANIA, in *Publications of The Genealogical Society of Pennsylvania*, vii, 1-25. (Pages 526-550, this volume.)

record was taken. Issue, the first three born in Ulster County, the remainder in Salem County: 1. *Catherine*[5] *Du Bois*, born September 10, 1716; married Jacob Elwell and resided in Salem County; had issue. 2. *Jacob Du Bois*, born February 9, 1719; died Salem County, September 28, 1794; married Yonica, daughter of Cornelius Nieukirk; had issue, *q. v.* 3. *Solomon Du Bois*, born September 6, 1721; died unmarried, 1756. 4. *David Du Bois*, born November 18, 1724; died October 12, 1801; married Elizabeth, daughter of Cornelius Nieukirk; had issue, *q. v.* 5. *Jonathan Du Bois*, born December 3, 1727; died December 15, 1772; was a clergyman of the Reformed Dutch Church and one of the first trustees of Rutgers College; married Helena, daughter of Nicholas Wynkoop and wife, Ann Kuyper. 6. *Isaac Du Bois*, born January 2, 1731. 7. *Gerret Du Bois*, born April 16, 1734; married Luraney Ogden. 8. *Abraham Du Bois*, born November 16, 1738; married December 1, 1761, Elizabeth Preston.

ii. LOUIS [4] DU BOIS, born in Ulster County, January 6, 1695; died at Pittsgrove, Salem County, New Jersey, in 1784; married June 21, 1720, Margaret, daughter of Matthys Jansen and wife Aaltje Elmendorf, bapt. Kingston, June 4, 1699. At the date of his will, February 12, 1784, his sons Jacob and Matthew were deceased, as was also his wife. Issue, all born in Salem County: 1. *Jacob*[5] *Du Bois*, born April 18, 1721, called "little Jacob" to distinguish him from his cousin Jacob, son of Barent, *q. v.*; was a clergyman and died in Salem County, May 1, 1768; married May 9, 1750, Mary Allegar, born January 6, 1721; had eight children. 2. *Matthew Du Bois*, married Jacomyntje, daughter of Cornelius Nieukirk, *q. v.* 3. *Anna Du Bois*, born February, 1724; married at Philadelphia, November 24, 1750, Rev. David Marinus, had three children: JOHN [6] MARINUS, GARRET W. MARINUS, BENJAMIN MARINUS. 4. *Gerretje Du Bois*, born August 18, 1726; died unmarried. 5. *John Du Bois*, born February 21, 1728; died unmarried, July 26, 1746. 6. *Elizabeth Du Bois*, born April 10, 1730; married Garret, son of Cornelius Nieukirk, *q. v.* 7. *Cornelius Du Bois*, born February 26, 1732; died in Salem County; estate divided among his nine children December 3, 1795; married Margaret . . . . 8. *Peter Du Bois*, born April 10, 1734; died 1795; married Amy Greenman. In 1775 he volunteered in the Salem County, New Jersey, militia, and was lieutenant under his cousin, Captain Jacob Du Bois, when there were seven of the name serving in his Company; later promoted to a Captaincy; had seven children. 9. *Joseph Du Bois*, born April 16, 1737; died in Salem County; married Sarah, daughter of Cornelius Nieukirk. Issue: *q. v.* 10. *Benjamin Du Bois*, born August 17, 1739; died at Freehold, New Jersey, August 21, 1827; was pastor of the Freehold Dutch Reformed Church for more than sixty years and an earnest advocate of American Independence; married October 15, 1765, Phermertje (Phebe) Denise, born July 7, 1744, died June 7, 1839, daughter of Teunis Denise and wife Femmynte Danielse Hendriekse; ten children born at Freehold. 11. *Samuel Du Bois*, born May 7, 1741; died Salem County, June 8, 1811; married 1777, Upham, daughter of Francis and Ann Thompson; three children.

iii. GIELTJIE DU BOIS, bapt. May 13, 1697; died young.

iv. GERRET DU BOIS, bapt. March 20, 1700; died young.

v. ISAAC DU BOIS, bapt. February 1, 1702; lived at Greenkill, Ulster County, where he owned and operated a mill; died before September 21, 1773, date of probate of will. He married (1) August 5, 1731, Neeltje Roosa, bapt. April 5, 1713, daughter of Aldert and Aagje (Krom) Roosa. He married (2) October 5, 1760, Jannette Roosa. Issue by first wife, all born in Ulster County: 1. *Jacob* [5] *Du Bois*, bapt. January 14, 1733; married September 26, 1754, Rebecca Van Wagenen; had two children. 2. *Rachel Du Bois*, bapt. January 2, 1737; died August 24, 1803; married December 17, 1757, Andries de Witt, bapt. March 3, 1728; died June 9, 1806; had three children. 3. *Sarah Du Bois*, bapt. February 4, 1739; married December 16, 1763, Tobias Van Buren, bapt. August 9, 1741, son of Cornelius Van Buren and Sarah Hoogteeling; five children. 4. *Peter Du Bois*, bapt. February 22, 1741; died young. 5. *Jannetjen Du Bois*, bapt. September 30, 1744; married William Eltinge, Jr.; had six children. 6. *Johannes Du Bois*, bapt. October 12, 1746; married Elizabeth Jansen; three children. 7. *Peter Du Bois*, bapt. July 27, 1753; not mentioned in father's will; probably died unmarried.

vi. GERRET [4] DU BOIS, bapt. February 13, 1704; died at Marbletown, New York; married at Marbletown, July 18, 1730 Margaret Elmendorf, bapt. June 20, 1708, daughter of Coenradt and Blandina (Kierstede) Elmendorf. With his brothers, Jacob and Barent, Gerret Du Bois went to Salem County, New Jersey, and, with his wife Margaret, was among those who, in 1742, organized the Presbyterian Church at Pittsgrove. Shortly thereafter they returned to Marbletown. Issue, the first five born in Salem County; 1. *Blandina* [5] *Du Bois*, born 1732; died Ulster County, November 4, 1765; married December 20, 1754, Charles De Witt, born 1727; died August 27, 1787, son of Johannes and Mary (Brodhead) De Witt; he was one of the prominent men of Ulster County, a member of the Provincial Congress, Continental Congress and State Assembly; five children. 2. *Coenradt Du Bois*, born Salem County *circa* 1735; married Maria De Lamater, bapt. June 22, 1740, daughter of Martin and Elizabeth (Nottingham) De Lamater; eleven children. 3. *Gerretje Du Bois*, married November 10, 1762 Petrus Crispell, bapt. September 19, 1736, son of Johannes and Anna Margaret (Roosa) Crispell; had issue. 4. *Margurite De Bois*, probably died unmarried. 5. *Sarah Du Bois*, bapt. Salem County, July 4, 1742; married December 22, 1775, Petrus P. Crispell, bapt. October 3, 1743, son of Peter and Lea (Roosa) Crispell; four children. 6. *Catharine Du Bois*, bapt. Ulster County, April 14, 1745; probably died young. 7. *Janneke Du Bois*, bapt. May 8, 1748; married July 5, 1776, Thomas Jansen, son of Hendricus and Maria (Cantine) Jansen. His will probated November 11, 1808, mentions wife Jenneke and four children. 8. *Tobias Du Bois*, bapt. March 31, 1751; married Mary, daughter of Isaac Smith of Ulster County and had five, perhaps eight children.

vii. CATHARINE DU BOIS, bapt. March 24, 1706; married February 12, 1724, Petrus Smedes, bapt. Kingston, December 7, 1701, son of Benjamin and Magdalena (Louw) Smedes. He was a miller at Greenkill; will probated October 13, 1783. Issue born in Ulster County: 1. *Benjamin* [5] *Smedes*, bapt. July 4, 1725; died before 1783; married November 22, 1754, Rachel Decker; six children. 2. *Gerretje Smedes*, bapt. January 1, 1727; married December 21, 1751, Jacob Ten Broeck, bapt. Kingston, May 3, 1724. His will probated October 28, 1793 named wife, Gerretje, and four children. 3. *Magdalena Smedes*, bapt. August 25, 1728; died prior to October 5, 1765; married, as first wife, May 19, 1749, Jonathan Elmendorf. He was Colonel Jonathan, son of Coenradt and Blandina

(Kiersted) Elmendorf, born December 14, 1723; died 17 January, 1798; had four children. 4. *Jacob Smedes*, bapt. December 3, 1732; will probated February 21, 1798; married Maria Decker who survived him as did their three children; resided in Montgomery precinct, Ulster County. 5. *Catharine Smedes*, bapt. June 29, 1735; married (1) March 20, 1755, Charles Hardenbergh, bapt. January 7, 1733, son of Johannes Hardenbergh and wife, Maria Le Fevre; had two children; married (2) July 10, 1761, Abraham Helm; three children. 6. *Sarah Smedes*, bapt. December 11, 1737; married, as second wife, December 13, 1760, Dirck Wynkoop, born October 15, 1732, son of Evert and Ariantje (Schepmoes) Wynkoop. Judge Wynkoop's will, probated February 28, 1797, named his wife Sarah, son Peter and four daughters of last marriage. 7. *Peter Smedes*, bapt. May 25, 1740; married November 27, 1767, Elsie Hasbrouck, bapt. June 4, 1742, daughter of Daniel and Wyntie (Deyo) Hasbrouck. His will probated March 15, 1805, named wife Elsie and four of their ten children. 8. *Elizabeth Smedes*, bapt. May 23, 1742; died young. 9. *Elizabeth Smedes*, bapt. November 11, 1744; died at Saugerties, New York; married May 20, 1767, Lucas Kiersted, M.D., born February 20, 1743; his will of October 24, 1821, probated October 18, 1826, made bequests to wife Elizabeth and to their six daughters, one of whom had deceased, leaving issue. 10. *Jacomyntje Smedes*, bapt. July 28, 1747; married June 17, 1768, Jacob Blanshan, bapt. January 11, 1747, son of Matthew and Annatjen (Frere) Blanshan of Ulster County; three children. 11. *Johannes Smedes*, bapt. June 3, 1750, probably died before date of father's will.

viii. REBECCA [4] DU BOIS, bapt. October 31, 1708; married September 15, 1726, Petrus Bogardus, bapt. December 3, 1699, son of Evert and Tjaetjen (Hoffman) Bogardus.* His will, dated June 4, 1767, probated September 25, 1775, disposed of considerable real estate; mentioned share in estate of Anneke Jans; wife Rebecca, and six of their eight children: 1. *Gerritje* [5] *Bogardus*, bapt. February 18, 1728; unmarried at date of father's will. 2. *Evert Bogardus*, born 1732. 3. *Tjaetjen Bogardus*, bapt. December 22, 1734; died unmarried before June 4, 1767. 4. *Maria Bogardus*, bapt. July 25, 1736; married Benjamin Low. 5. *Jacob Bogardus*, bapt. August 17, 1740; executor of father's will. 6. *Petrus Bogardus*, bapt. December 25, 1742; died young. 7. *Petrus Bogardus*, bapt. January 1, 1749. 8. *Catharine Bogardus*, bapt. December 16, 1753; married Coenradt Cornelius Elmendorf.

ix. JOHANNES DU BOIS, bapt. November 10, 1710; resided at Hurley; married December 11, 1736, Judike [5] Wynkoop, bapt. August 31, 1712, daughter of Cornelius and Hendrikje (Nieuwkirk) Wynkoop, and grand-daughter of Arie and Lysbet Lambertse (Brink) Nieuwkirk (No. 5). Issue, all born in Ulster County: 1. *Catharine* [5] *Du Bois*, bapt. September 25, 1737; married November 24, 1764, Abraham Hermanse; five children. 2. *Jacob Du Bois*, bapt. May 27, 1739; died young. 3. *Jacob Du Bois*, bapt. July 27, 1740. 4. *Cornelius Du Bois*, bapt. January 30, 1743; died June 24, 1829; married February 18, 1769, Geertje Van Vleet, born September 4, 1737; died May 24, 1819; four children born in Ulster County. 5. *Johannes Du Bois* (twin), bapt. January 30, 1743. 6. *Jacomyntje Du Bois*, bapt. December 2, 1744; died young.

---

* Evert Bogardus was eldest son of Pieter Bogardus and wife, Wyntje Cornelis Bosch, and grandson of Rev. Everardus Bogardus and his second wife, Anneke Jans.

7. *Hendrica Du Bois*, bapt. December 28, 1746; married Jacob Newkirk, bapt. August 26, 1744, son of Cornelius Newkirk and Neeltjen Du Bois; four children, *q. v.* 8. *Petrus Du Bois*, born March 28, 1749; died April 2, 1830; married December 23, 1779, Ariantje Newkirk, born January 31, 1749; died August 25, 1805, daughter of Cornelius and Dina (Hoogteeling) Newkirk; four children, none of whom left issue. 9. *Johannes Du Bois*, bapt. August 4, 1757; afterwards known as *John Jeremiah Du Bois*; died Ulster County, April 7, 1832; married (1) Rachel LeFevre; issue, one daughter, Neeltje Du Bois; married (2) Annatje Bevier, born May 12, 1764, daughter of Jacob and Ann (Verney) Bevier; four children. 10. *Abraham Du Bois*, bapt. February 17, 1754. 11. *Jacomyntje Du Bois*, bapt. June 13, 1756.

x. Sarah [4] Du Bois, bapt. December 20, 1713; married June 21, 1734, Conrad Elmendorf, bapt. October 10, 1710, son of Coenradt and Blandina (Kersted) Elmendorf. Issue bapt. Ulster County: 1. *Tobias [5] Elmendorf*, bapt. May 25, 1735; was living at Cobuskill, Scholarie County, April 18, 1806. 2. *Jacob Elmendorf*, bapt. June 19, 1737; married November 13, 1773, Leah Bloomandal, was living in Hurley in 1806. 3. *Coenrad Elmendorf*, bapt. June 15, 1740; died young. 4. *Sarah Elmendorf*, bapt. January 16, 1742; married November 16, 1771, Johannes P. Dumond; living at Hurley in 1806, and then a widow; five children. 5. *Coenrad Elmendorf*, bapt. February 2, 1746; married Annatje, daughter of Benjamin and Anna (Swart) Slecht; two children. 6. *Petrus Elmendorf*, bapt. October 2, 1748; married April 14, 1776, Anna Du Mond; five children. 7. *Jonathan Elmendorf*, bapt. July 21, 1751; married November 29, 1789, Margaret Felton; seven children. 8. *Geertje Elmendorf*, bapt. July 29, 1753; married Abram Louw Valkenburg of Valkenburg; he made his will September 8, 1825; probated November 24, 1826, under which his beneficiaries were: children Abraham, Catharine and Sarah; grand-sons Abraham van Valkenburg, Jr., Abraham Valkenburg Seaman, and Abraham Valkenburg Britt.

xi. Neeltje Du Bois, bapt. May 27, 1716; married September 9, 1737, Cornelius Newkirk, bapt. Kingston, May 1, 1715, son of Gerret and Gerritje, or Marguerite (Ten Eyck) Newkirk, *q. v.*, No. 11. His will executed December 12, 1781, probated February 14, 1783 made bequests to nine of his children.

8. Geertruyt[3] van Nieuwkirk (*Mattheus*,[2] *Cornelisse*[1]), born probably at Bergen, East Jersey, September 18, 1671; married Peter Lambertse Brink; baptized at Kingston, June 26, 1670; son of Lambert Huybertse Brink and his wife Hendricke Cornelisse, and brother of Elizabeth who married Arie Nieuwkirk, No. 5.

Children, baptized in Ulster County:

i. Hendrick [4] Brink, bapt. April 23, 1693.
ii. Mattheus Brink, bapt. June 9, 1695; married Abigail Bell; resided Deer Park, Orange County, New York. Issue: 1. *Petrus [5] Brink*, bapt. May 29, 1739. 2. *Jan Brink*, bapt. June 7, 1741; died young. 3. *Jacobus Brink*, bapt. October 3, 1742. 4. *Samuel Brink*, bapt. January 6, 1745. 5. *Jan Brink*, bapt. July 5, 1747. 6. *Jacobus Brink* (twin), bapt. July 5, 1747.

---

* *Cf.* The Brink Family, in *Olde Ulster*, vol. ii, 120, *et seq.*

7. *Elizabeth Brink*, bapt. January 3, 1748; died young. 8. *Geertje Brink*, bapt. May 13, 1750. 9. *Mary Brink*, bapt. March 27, 1752. 10. *Hester Brink*, bapt. February 24, 1754. 11. *Gerret Brink*, bapt. April 14, 1756. 12. *Elizabeth Brink*, bapt. January 28, 1759.

iii. CORNELIUS [4] BRINK, bapt. July 25, 1697; married December 14, 1724, Maria Cool (Cole); lived at Deerpark. Issue: the first two baptized at Kingston, remainder at Deerpark: 1. *Petrus [5] Brink*, bapt. May 21, 1727. 2. *Elizabeth Brink*, bapt. November 5, 1732. 3. *Maria Brink*, bapt. November 1, 1738. 4. *Hermanus Brink*, bapt. July 5, 1741. 5. *Leonard Cole Brink*, bapt. January 6, 1745. 6. *Johannes Brink*, bapt. April 19, 1747.

iv. LAMBERT BRINK, bapt. November 26, 1699; died young.

v. LAMBERTUS BRINK, bapt. January 15, 1702; married January 17, 1727, Rachel Van Garden; resided at Rochester and Deerpark (Mamakaking), New York. Issue: 1. *Catherine [5] Brink*, bapt. October 6, 1728. 2. *Peter Brink*. 3. *Matthew Brink*. 4. *Cornelius Brink*. 5. *Jenneke Brink*, bapt. November 1, 1738. 6. *Arie Brink*, bapt. June 17, 1740. 7. *Daniel Brink*, bapt. March 11, 1742.

vi. ANTJE BRINK, bapt. April 2, 1704; married William Moore; settled in Walpeck, Sussex County, New Jersey. Issue: 1. *Johannes [5] Moore*, bapt. Walpeck, July 4, 1733.

vii. LYSBET BRINK, bapt. August 11, 1706; married Johannes Kuyckendall; resided at Walpeck. Issue: 1. *Johannes [5] Kuyckendall*, bapt. Walpeck, July 18, 1741.

viii. GERRET BRINK, bapt. September 18, 1709; married Maria Titsort; removed from Deerpark, Orange County, to Walpeck, New Jersey. Issue: 1. *Petrus [5] Brink*, bapt. June 18, 1734. 2. *Geertje Brink*, bapt. August 23, 1737. 3. *Maria Brink*, bapt. May 29, 1739. 4. *Stephanus Brink*, bapt. May 31, 1741. 5. *Lydia Brink*, bapt. May 3, 1743. 6. *Hester Brink*, bapt. January 13, 1745. 7. *Gerret Brink*, bapt. March 8, 1747. 8. *Janneke Brink*, bapt. May 6, 1750.

ix. JOHANNES BRINK, bapt. May 11, 1712; married Lena Cole; removed to Walpeck. Issue, first two baptized at Deerpark: 1. *Maria [5] Brink*, bapt. November 1, 1738. 2. *Johannes Brink*, bapt. May 31, 1741. 3. *Lisabeth Brink*, bapt. April 24, 1744. 4. *Helena Brink*, bapt. May 24, 1746. 5. *Johannes Brink*, bapt. July 12, 1747. 6. *Geertje Brink*, bapt. December 25, 1748. 7. *Benjamin Brink*, bapt. December 10, 1752.

x. HELENA BRINK, bapt. November 7, 1714; married Hugh Pugh; resided in Walpeck. Issue, first and last baptized at Walpeck, the others at Deerpark: 1. *John [5] Pugh*, bapt. May 19, 1736. 2. *Margaret Pugh*, bapt. May 30, 1738. 3. *Peter Pugh*, bapt. June 17, 1740. 4. *Isaac Pugh*, bapt. October 17, 1743. 5. *Hugh Pugh*, bapt. August, 1746.

9. GERRET[3] VAN NIEUWKIRK (*Mattheus[2], Cornelisse[1]*), born at Bergen, East Jersey, November 18, 1696; died there April 23, 1785. The entry of his marriage reads: "1730. September 5, Garret Mattheusen Van Nieuwkerk, young man, born and living at Bergen, and Catryntje Kuypers, young woman, born and living at Ahasemus." She was a daughter of Hendrick Kuyper * of Bergen County and died September 14, 1751.

---

* *New Jersey Archives*, xxxiii, 237.

Children of Gerret and Catryntje (Kuyper) van Nieuwkirk, born in Bergen County:

i. MATTHEW 4, born March 3, 1734; died July 10, 1811; married
Catlyntje Toers, born September 30, 1739, daughter of Arent
and Annatje (Spier) Toers, also of Bergen County. Issue:
1. *Garret 5 Newkirk,* born April 9, 1766. 2. *Aaron Newkirk,*
born October 22, 1768; died April 1, 1849; married Jennetje
Vreeland. Their daughter, CATHARINE 6 NEWKIRK, born in
Bergen County, May 15, 1807; removed with her husband,
Cornelius M. Vreeland, to Lisbon, Illinois, where she died
January 10, 1892, and he July 17, 1877; the descendants of
their eight children are to be found in the West. 3. *Hendrick
Newkirk,* born June 22, 1771; died unmarried.
ii. JANNETTE, born May 5, 1737; died unmarried, October 4, 1779.
iii. HENDRICK, born April 4, 1741; died July 8, 1795; married
September 10, 1779, Janneke Vreeland, born December 1, 1758,
who, on May 26, 1798, married (2) Joseph Van Winkle.
Issue, born in Bergen County: 1. *Garret 5 H. Newkirk,* born
January 8, 1781; died unmarried October 21, 1860. 2. *George
Newkirk,* born November 25, 1783; died August 19, 1861;
married February 9, 1805, Sarah, daughter of George Van
Derhoff; six children. 3. *Catryntje Newkirk,* born September
7, 1791; died July 25, 1848; married Hartman Van Wagenen;
four children.
iv. CATHARINA, named in will of grandfather, Hendrick Kuyper,
September 16, 1754.

10. PAULUS³ VAN NIEUWKIRK (*Mattheus², Cornelisse¹*), born
at Bergen, August 20, 1699; died probably at Schraalenburgh,
New Jersey, February 5, 1763; married, June 18, 1728, Helena
Spier, who died April 6, 1801; daughter of Barent Hendrickse
Spier.

Children of Paulus and Helena (Spier) van Nieuwkirk,
born in New Jersey: *

i. CATRINA 4, born May 10, 1729; died unmarried September
18, 1759.
ii. CATLYNTJE, born May 7, 1723; probably died young.
iii. MATTHEW P., born Belleville, April 30, 1735; died November
12, 1818; married, before February 16, 1766, Geertje Kogh,
who died February 27, 1828. He is frequently mentioned in
Bergen Dutch Church records. Issue: 1. *John 5 M. Newkirk,*
born May 18, 1781; died Bergen County, March 1870;
married February 1, 1806, his cousin, Maritje, daughter of
Jacob and Fitje (Hennion) Newkirk, q. v. born July 13,
1782, died September 4, 1852; had four children.
iv. BARENT, born April 24, 1737; married April 6, 1765, Antje,
daughter of Arent and Annatje (Spier) Toers. Issue: 1.
Lena 5 Newkirk, bapt. New York City, January 13, 1767.
2. *Arent Newkirk,* born September 1, 1768. 3. *Annatje
Newkirk,* bapt. July 1, 1770. 4. *Matthew Newkirk,* bapt.
May 24, 1772. 5. *Barent Newkirk,* bapt. May 8, 1774. 6.
Catherine Newkirk, died May 27, 1814; married first, February 1, 1795, Elihu Baldwin; married second, August 15, 1801,
Ebenezer Bassett. 7. *Jannetje Newkirk,* born November 15,
1777; died September 17, 1779.

---

* *The New York Genealogical and Biographical Record,* lv, 322, 324, 326.

v. JANNETJE [4], bapt. May 26, 1740; died October 4, 1779; married Jan Van Geisen. Issue, born at Passaic, New Jersey: 1. *Rachel* [5] *Van Giesen*, born October 1, 1770. 2. *Paulus Van Geisen*, born March 16, 1773. 3. *Johannes Van Geisen*, born July 23, 1775.

vi. JACOB, born November 22, 1743; died June 9, 1818; married February 13, 1769,[*] Fitje Hennion, born April 20, 1744; died January 23, 1808. Issue: 1. *Maritje* [5] *Newkirk*, born July 18, 1770; died August 1, 1776. 2. *Paulus Newkirk*, born November 25, 1772; died young.[†] 3. *Paulus Newkirk*, born April 13, 1776; died August 27, 1776. 4. *Jacob Newkirk*, born April 28, 1778; died December 5, 1796. 5. *Garret J. Newkirk*, born July 21, 1780; died Bergen County August 22, 1818; married February 22, 1806, Rachel, daughter of George Shepherd, she born September 6, 1784; died January 16, 1861; had six children. 6. *Maritje Newkirk*, born July 13, 1782; died September 24, 1852; married February 1, 1806, *John M. Newkirk*, son of Matthew P. and Geertie (Kogh) Newkirk, *q. v.*; four children. 7. *John J. Newkirk*, born October 23, 1786; died August 15, 1860; married May 14, 1814, Gertrude Collard, born June 15, 1788; died January 23, 1858, daughter of John Collard; five children.

vii. JOHANNES, born October 9, 1746; died September 29, 1749.

viii. RACHEL, born Schraalenburgh, March 11, 1751; married Dirck Van Hooten; both became members of the Dutch Church of Patterson, New Jersey. Issue, born at Patterson: 1. *Antje* [5] *Van Hooten*, born February 10, 1776. 2. *Helmigh Van Hooten*, born March 19, 1778. 3. *Catalyntje Van Hooten*, born October 6, 1781.

---

[*] *The New York Genealogical and Biographical Record*, lv, 327-8.

[†] Another daughter, Lena Newkirk, died July 25, 1776.

11. GERRIT[4] NEWKIRK (*Cornelis*[3], *Gerretse*[2], *Cornelisse*[1]), baptized at the Dutch Church of Kingston, July 28, 1684; died at Hurley, Ulster County in 1724; married Gerritje, or Marguerite, Ten Eyck, baptized February 10, 1689, daughter of Mathys and Jenneken (Roosa) Ten Eyck.

The will of Gerrit Newkirk, executed July 25, 1724, was probated September 3, 1724.* His legatees were wife and five children, with provision for expected child. His signature was Gerrit Newkirk. After his decease, his widow married June 22, 1731, William Burhans, by whom she had one child, Helena Burhans, baptized May 14, 1732; married October 12, 1749, Levi, son of Henry and Jacomyntje (Kunst) Pawling, *q. v.* Levi Pawling was a Colonel in the Revolution, Judge of Ulster County Courts and generally esteemed.

Children of Gerrit and Gerritje, or Marguerite (Ten Eyck) Newkirk, all born in Ulster County:

  i. CORNELIUS [5], bapt. September 28, 1711; died young.
 ii. JANNETJEN, bapt. October 12, 1712; married January 15, 1730, Garret Elmendorf, bapt. January 26, 1696, son of Coenrad and Arriantje (Van der Berg) Elmendorf. Issue: 1. *Conrad* [6] *Elmendorf*, bapt. August 14, 1734. 2. *Garret Elmendorf*, bapt. March 14, 1736; died young. 3. *Margrietje Elmendorf*, bapt. April 3, 1737. 4. *Garret Elmendorf*, bapt. January 16, 1743.
iii. CORNELIUS, bapt. May 1, 1715; died, Ulster County, before February 14, 1783, the date of probate of his will which made bequests to wife Neeltjen and nine of his children. He married September 9, 1737, Neeltjen Du Bois, daughter of Jacob and Gerretje (Newkirk) Du Bois, q. v., who, bapt. May 27, 1716, survived her husband. Issue, born in Ulster County: 1. *Catharine* [6] *Newkirk*, bapt. February 26, 1738; married October 26, 1765, John E. De Witt, bapt. September 19, 1733, son of Egbert and Mary (Nottingham) De Witt; four children. 2. *Garret C. Newkirk*, bapt. September 23, 1739; married December 8, 1764, Leah, daughter of Cornelius and Dina (Hoogteeling) Newkirk, *q. v.*, bapt. April 29, 1744; five children. 3. *Margrietjen Newkirk*, bapt. October 24, 1742; named in father's will. 4. *Jacob Newkirk*, bapt. August 26, 1744; married Hendrica, daughter of Johannes and Judike (Wynkoop) Du Bois; four children all of whom died unmarried. 5. *Jannetjen Newkirk*, bapt. October 12, 1746; died young. 6. *Matthew Newkirk*, bapt. April 2, 1749; married December 9, 1774, Cornelia, daughter of Samuel and Sarah (Le Fever) Bevier; no issue. 7. *Jannetjen Newkirk*,

---

* *Ulster County Probate Records, American Record Series A*, by Gustave Anjou, vol. ii, p. 110.

(22)

bapt. August 5, 1750; married Richard Brodhead; five children. 8. *Benjamin* 6 *Newkirk*, bapt. October 15, 1752; married September 7, 1774, Margaret Brodhead; six children. 9. *Isaac Newkirk*, bapt. April 7, 1754; married Anna Jane Brodhead; ten children, all born in Ulster County. 10. *Jacomyntje Newkirk*, bapt. June 8, 1755; died young. 11. *Jacomyntje Newkirk*, bapt. October 29, 1758; married January 24, 1778, Henry Brodhead; had issue.

iv. MATTHEW 5, bapt. January 13, 1717; married November 8, 1740, Annetje Kool, bapt. September 20, 1713, daughter of Jacob and Sarah (Legg) Kool, who predeceased her husband. He served in the Foot Company of Militia at Hurley, under command of Captain Cornelius Wynkoop in 1738.* His will of June 1, 1789, probated March 28, 1791, mentioned sons Garret and Jacobus, daughter Margaret, grandson Matthew Oliver and ten slaves. He resided at Marbletown. Issue: 1. *Garret* 6 *Newkirk*, bapt. October 16, 1740. 2. *Jenneke Newkirk*, bapt. November 4, 1746. 3. *Benjamin Newkirk*, bapt. February 14, 1748; not named in father's will. 4. *Catharine Newkirk*, bapt. August 5, 1750. 5. *Margaretta Newkirk*, bapt. June 6, 1755; married February 15, 1778, Dr. James Oliver of Marbletown, New York. 6. *Jacobus Newkirk*, bapt. March 5, 1758; was living June 1, 1789.

v. BENJAMIN, bapt. October 30, 1720; served in Captain Cornelius Wynkoop's militia Company of Foot at Hurley, in 1738.†

vi. COENRADT, bapt. May 14, 1722; died at Hurley, January 25, 1805; married May 13, 1747, Ann De Witt, bapt. March 23, 1725; died October 12, 1805, daughter of Johannes and Mary (Brodhead) De Witt. His will of April 26, 1796,‡ bequeathed ''all lands which I own in the great Patent in Lot 3, which was by the last will of Charles Brodhead devised unto my well beloved wife.'' Issue: 1. *Andrew* 6 *Newkirk*, bapt. April 3, 1748. 2. *Benjamin Newkirk*, bapt. August 26, 1750; died unmarried. 3. *Johannes Newkirk*, bapt. November 3, 1751. 4. *Charles Newkirk*, bapt. April 22, 1753. 5. *Margaret Newkirk*, bapt. August 24, 1754; died unmarried January 28, 1839. 6. *Mary Newkirk*, named in her father's will. 7. *Gerretje Newkirk*, bapt. March 5, 1758. 8. *Anne Newkirk*, bapt. November 22, 1759. ix. *Jannette Newkirk*, bapt. June 20, 1762; died unmarried November 10, 1872. x. *Blandina Newkirk*, bapt. May 20, 1764. xi. *Coenradt Newkirk*, bapt. June 5, 1766; living 26 April, 1796. xii. *Andries Newkirk*.

vii. GERRETJEN, bapt. November 22, 1724; married November 12, 1743, Abraham Van Keuren, born September 23, 1711; died October 12, 1776, son of Tjerck Matthysen and Marytje (Ten Eyck) Van Keuren. Issue born in Ulster County: 1. *Garret* 6 *Van Keuren*, bapt. November 9, 1746. 2. *Margaret Van Keuren*, bapt. January 28, 1750; died young. 3. *Abraham Van Keuren*, bapt. February 16, 1752. 4. *Margaret Van Keuren*, bapt. February 9, 1755. 5. *Marietje Van Keuren*, bapt. December 12, 1756. 6. *Tjerck Van Keuren*, bapt. July 13, 1760. 7. *Martin van Keuren*, bapt. October 26, 1762. 8. *Levi Van Keuren*, bapt. December 6, 1767.

---

* *Second Annual Report of State Historian of New York, Colonial Series,* vol. i, p. 610.

† *Ibid.*, vol. i, p. 610.

‡ *Ulster County Probate Records, American Record Series A,* vol. i, 168-9.

12. JAN⁴ NEWKIRK (*Cornelis³, Gerretse², Cornelisse¹*), baptized November 29, 1685; married in New York Dutch Church, November 6, 1708, Jenneke Van Brestede. She was baptized September 12, 1683, daughter of Andries and Annetje (Van Borsum) Brestede.* It is probable that most of their married life was spent in Dutchess County. Their children were baptized in New York, and at the baptism of the two eldest, Nicholas Roosevelt † and wife Hillitje were sponsors.

Children of Jan and Janneke (Brestede) Newkirk:

 i. CORNELIUS⁵, bapt. March 19, 1710; died young.
 ii. ANNATJE (twin), bapt. March 19, 1710; married (1), July, 1727, William Miller; married (2), April 6, 1733, John J. Dobbs; married (3), ———— Cutler. Issue: 1. *John⁶ Miller*, bapt. July 3, 1728. 2. *John Dobbs*, bapt. January 15, 1734. 3. *Anna Dobbs*, bapt. October 13, 1736. 4. *Jenneke Dobbs*, bapt. November 26, 1738. 5. *Isaac Dobbs*, bapt. April 17, 1743.
 iii. ANDRIES, bapt. January 23, 1712; probably died without issue before November 13, 1763.
 iv. CORNELIUS (twin), bapt. January 23, 1712; died young.
 v. JANNETJE, bapt. February 21, 1714; married (1), Jan Hermance; (2), Jacobus Van Etten. Issue, the first two bapt. in Ulster County, the others in Dutchess County: 1. *Jan Hermance⁶*, bapt. January 24, 1738. 2. *Abraham Hermance*, bapt. April 14, 1740. 3. *Jacomyntje Hermance*, bapt. May 8, 1743. 4. *Goozen Hermance*, bapt. December 15, 1745. 5. *Jacob Hermance*. 6. *Jenneke Van Etten*, bapt. September 14, 1754.
 vii. ENGELTJE, bapt. April 8, 1716; married Isaac Ryckman, resided in New York City. Issue: 1. *Johannes⁶ Ryckman*, bapt. January 4, 1741; died young. 2. *Isaac Ryckman*, bapt. April 17, 1743. 3. *Johannes Ryckman*, bapt. November 9, 1746.
 viii. CORNELIA, bapt. January 14, 1719; married (1), October 20, 1738, Philipus Hoff, born in Dutchess County, but resided in Ulster County; married (2), October 14, 1748, Cornelius Van Keuren, widower of Kezia Hoogteeling. Issue: 1. *Catharine⁶ Hoff*, bapt. October 7, 1739. 2. *John Hoff*, bapt. September 6, 1741. 3. *Andries Hoff*, bapt. July 31, 1743. 4. *Cornelius Van Keuren*, bapt. January 14, 1750. 5. *Thomas Van Keuren*, bapt. July 12, 1752.
 ix. JACOMYNTJE, bapt. March 14, 1722; died young.
 x. CORNELIUS, bapt. May 8, 1723; married May 17, 1749, Maria Cooper; located at Fishkill, Dutchess County. His will of November 13, 1763, gave certain bequests to each of his four sisters, Annatje Cutler, Janneke Van Etten, Engeltje Ryckman and Cornelia Van Keuren, and to his nephew Abraham, son

---

* *New York Genealogical and Biographical Record*, vol. xxvii, p. 103.

† As elsewhere noted, Nicholas Roosevelt married Hillitje Kunst, daughter of Jan Barentsen Kunst, by his first wife Jannetje Ariens. Cornelis Gerretse Newkirk and his sister Gerretje Gerretse Newkirk married respectively Jannetje Jans Kunst and Barent Kunst, the only children of Jan Barentsen Kunst by his second wife, Jacomyntje Cornelis Slecht.

of Jan Hermance. A legacy left him by his uncle Hendrick Kip, to be received after the death of his aunt Jacomyntje, wife of Peter Du Bois, was, with the remainder of his estate, to go to wife Maria.

xi. JACOMYNTJE, bapt. June 21, 1727, probably deceased at date of her brother's will.

13. ADRIAN⁴ NEWKIRK (*Cornelis³, Gerretse², Cornelisse¹*), baptized February 27, 1687; married April 27, 1711, Aaltjen, daughter of Hendrick and Jennette (Martens) Bogaard of Marbletown. He was a prominent citizen of Ulster County.

Children of Adrian and Aaltjen (Bogaard) Newkirk, all baptized in Ulster County:

i. JANNETJEN⁵, bapt. March 15, 1713; married September 14, 1731, Johannes Burhans, bapt. February 18, 1709; died 1804, son of Johannes and Margriet (Legg) Burhans. Issue all born in Ulster County: 1. *Johannes⁶ Burhans*, bapt. November 18, 1733; died young. 2. *Hendricus Burhans*, bapt. January 25, 1735. 3. *Saartje Burhans*. 4. *Aaltjen Burhans*, bapt. September 9, 1739. 5. *Johannes Burhans*, bapt. June 7, 1742. 6. *Margriet Burhans*, bapt. September 7, 1744. 7. *Cornelius Burhans*, bapt. August 15, 1746. 8. *Hendricus Burhans*, bapt. August 1, 1748. 9. *Helena Burhans*, bapt. October 18, 1750. 10. *Jannetje Burnhans*, bapt. January 28, 1753. 11. *Jacomyntje Burhans*, bapt. December 27, 1755.

ii. ZARA (Sarah), bapt. October 16, 1715; died June 19, 1788; married September 30, 1737, John William Meyer, born West Camp, New York, February 13, 1714; died September 12, 1794, son of Christian and Ann Geertruyd (Theunyes) Meyer whose parents came to New York with the Palatinate emigration; resided at Saugerties. Issue born in Ulster County: 1. *Christian⁶ Meyer*, bapt. October 24, 1738; died young. 2. *Christian Meyer*, bapt. August 24, 1739. 3. *Aaltjen Meyer*, bapt. March 11, 1741. 4. *Hendricus Meyer*, bapt. December 26, 1742. 5. *Maria Meyer*, bapt. November 2, 1743. 6. *Johannes Meyer*, bapt. February 19, 1746. 7. *Petrus Meyer*, bapt. June 25, 1750. 8. *Tobias Meyer*, bapt. December 26, 1751. 9. *Leah Meyer*, bapt. January 2, 1754. 10. *Benjamin Meyer*, bapt. November 11, 1755. 11. *Samuel Meyer*, bapt. February 6, 1757.

iii. CORNELIUS, bapt. July 14, 1717; died young.

iv. HENDRICUS, bapt. September 3, 1722.

v. CORNELIUS, bapt. February 28, 1725; married May 28, 1752, Lea Van Etten; resided in Ulster County. Issue: 1. *Arie⁶ Newkirk*, bapt. February 16, 1753. 2. *Jacobus Newkirk*, bapt. February 27, 1755. 3. *Catharine Newkirk*, bapt. August 14, 1757. 4. *Johannes Newkirk*, bapt. April 7, 1760. 5. *Maria Newkirk*, bapt. February 7, 1763. 6. *Petrus Newkirk*, bapt. October 6, 1765. 7. *Benjamin Newkirk*, bapt. February 4, 1776; married Catharine Van Keuren.

vi. RACHEL, bapt. January 21, 1728; married May 15, 1748, Hezekiah Du Bois, baptized February 25, 1727, son of Hezekiah and Ann (Person) Du Bois. Resided at Saugerties. Issue: 1. *Maria⁶ Du Bois*, bapt. September 12, 1756. 2. *Hendricus Du Bois*, bapt. April 24, 1765. 3. *Aleda Du Bois*, bapt. April 19, 1763.

vii. JACOMYNTJE, bapt. May 18, 1729; married November 22, 1749, Johannes Van Etten, bapt. December 26, 1721, son of Jacobus and Catharine (Kool) Van Etten. His will, dated at

Shawangunk May 11, 1802; probated October 22, 1803, mentioned his wife Jacomyntje and children. Issue: 1. *Jacobus* [6] *Van Etten*, bapt. October 8, 1750; died after May 11, 1802. 2. *Catharine Van Etten*, bapt. January 15, 1758; married Wilhelmus Row. 3. *Maria Van Etten*, bapt. August 9, 1774; married Elias Van Etten.

viii. GERRET [5], bapt. November 25, 1732; married Cornelia Wells, bapt. May 29, 1737, daughter of Samuel and Marytjen (Oosterhout) Wells; resided at Saugerties. Issue: 1. *Aaltjen* [6] *Newkirk*, baptized December 28, 1758. 2. *Samuel Newkirk*, bapt. June 4, 1760. 3. *Trintje Newkirk*, bapt. December 11, 1763. 4. *Marytje Newkirk*, baptized May 12, 1765; died young. 5. *Hendricus Newkirk*, bapt. August 17, 1767. 6. *Margrietje Newkirk*, bapt. September 17, 1769. 7. *Petrus Newkirk*, bapt. January 13, 1772. 8. *Johannes Newkirk*, bapt. June 30, 1774. 9. *Annatje Newkirk*, bapt. February 4, 1776.

14. BARENT [4] NEWKIRK (*Cornelis* [3], *Gerretse* [2], *Cornelisse* [1]), baptized at Kingston, Ulster County, October 13, 1689; died near Martinsburg, Berkeley County, Virginia, in 1765. He was a millwright, carpenter and farmer at Kingston, from which he removed to Virginia about 1732, acquiring by purchase from his brother-in-law, John Hood, in September, 1737, a tract of five hundred and thirty-five acres. On this he built a mill * and large house, some portions of which are still standing, and by thrift acquired a competence. In the records of Orange, Frederick and Berkeley counties, Virginia, the name Barent became Barnet and Barnabas. He married, May 23, 1713, Rebecca van Buntschooten,† baptized at Kingston, January 28, 1692, daughter of Teunis Elias and Gerretje (Gerrets) van Buntschoten,‡ who was named in her husband's will of February 18, 1765.

Children of Barent and Rebecca (van Buntschooten) Newkirk, the five eldest baptized at Kingston Dutch Church.

i. GERRETJEN [5], bapt. April 14, 1714; married ———— Hoagland, named in her father's will.

ii. CORNELIUS, bapt. August 12, 1716; married twice; was deceased at the time of his father's will, leaving eldest son *Barent* [6] *Newkirk*; descendants of, reside in Indiana.

iii. TEUNIS, bapt. July 13, 1718; married Mary ————. By deed of August 2, 1769, he and wife Mary conveyed one hundred and six acres of land willed to him by his father, to his cousin John Hood. In 1773, Teunis, Barnet and Peter Newkirk were in Bedford County, Pennsylvania. In 1783 Teunis

* August 7, 1759. — Permission granted to Barnet Newkirk and John Hoogland to build a mill on Tulisse Run.—*Court Orders Frederick County, Virginia.*

† Van Buntschoten, van Benschoten, Bunschotten. Rachel van Buntschooten, sister of Rebecca wife of Barent Nieuwkirk married Jan Hoed, October 27, 1718.—*Kingston Dutch Church Records.*

was in Westmorland County, and, in 1787 in Fayette County, Pennsylvania, where he was a small land holder; later he removed to Fairfield County, Ohio, where he died. Issue: *Christopher* 6 *Cornelius Newkirk*; descendants of, in Indiana.

 iv. HENRY, bapt. January 1, 1721; resided for a time in Berkely County, where he was appointed constable in 1746. A Court record at Winchester, Virginia, dated August 4, 1752 states that ''on motion of Peter Newkirk, Henry Newkirk, John Hoagland, Jacobus Hoagland and Teunis Hood are added to the list of tithables.'' He later settled in Westmoreland County, Pennsylvania, and later still in Fairfield County, Ohio; descendants of, in Indiana and Kentucky.

 v. ELIAS, bapt. October 21, 1722; married and located near Louisville, Kentucky; descendants of, in Ohio and Kentucky.

24. vi. ABRAHAM, married Kezia Shipman.

 vii. TOBIAS, born *circa* 1723; married Penelope Brosard; lived and died in Duplin County, North Carolina, where he was an extensive farmer and slave holder as were his descendants. Issue: 1. *Henry* 6 *Newkirk*, born Duplin County, January 10, 1750; married and had issue. 2. *Abraham Newkirk*, born June 15, 1754. 3. *Rachel Newkirk*.

 viii. JEMIMA, named in her father's will; married ―――― Hoagland.

25. ix. PETER, married Cornelia Sousley.

15. GILLES 4, or GIELETJEN NEWKIRK (*Cornelis* 3, *Gerretse* 2, *Cornelisse* 1), baptized November 5, 1691; died after June 13, 1749; married October 5, 1714, Jacobus Swartwout,* born February 13, 1692; died April 5, 1749; son of Thomas and Lysbeth (Gardenier) Swartwout. He resided at Fishkill; his will of December 4, 1744, made bequests to wife and his nine children.

Children of Jacobus and Gilles (Newkirk) Swartwout; the first three baptized at Kingston, the remainder born in Dutchess County, New York:

 i. THOMAS 5 SWARTWOUT, born October 2, 1715; married Mary Garsling. Issue, the four eldest born at Fishkill, the two youngest at Rombouts: 1. *Elizabeth* 6 *Swartwout*, bapt. December 19, 1751. 2. *Jacobus Swartwout*, bapt. November 3, 1754. 3. *William Swartwout*, bapt. November 3, 1754. 4. *Thomas Swartwout*, bapt. May 15, 1757. 5. *Mary Swartwout*, bapt. September 23, 1759. 6. *Samuel Swartwout*, bapt. February 18, 1763.

 ii. ELIZABETH SWARTWOUT, bapt. May 26, 1717; married Jacob DePeyster of Fishkill.

 iii. JANNETJEN SWARTWOUT, bapt. October 11, 1719; married Maes (Moses) Ostrander. Issue, born at Fishkill: 1. *Jacobus* 6 *Ostrander*, born May 23, 1740. 2. *Cornelius Ostrander*, born July 22, 1742. 3. *Thomas Ostrander*, born April 26, 1745.

 iv. CORNELIUS SWARTWOUT, born January 21, 1722; married June 19, 1746, Elizabeth, daughter of Henry and Catharine Ter Bos, or Ter Bosch. Issue, born at Fishkill: 1. *Jacobus* 6 *Swartwout*,

---

* *Vide* SWARTWOUT FAMILY in *New York Genealogical and Biographical Record*, vol. vii, p. 46.

born 1747. 2. *Henry Swartwout,* born 1749. 3. *Cornelius Swartwout,* born December 24, 1751. 4. *Catharine Swartwout,* born June 25, 1758. 5. *Elizabeth Swartwout,* born October 16, 1759. 6. *Simon Swartwout,* born December 19, 1761. 7. *Maria Swartwout,* born August 19, 1764.

 v. RUDOLPHUS [5] SWARTWOUT, born May 6, 1724; married (1), October 1, 1749, Gerardina, daughter of Abraham and Femmetje Remsen [Vanderbeek] Brinkerhoff; married (2) October 14, 1762, Sarah Polhemus, who died March 5, 1820, aged ninety-four years, two months, twelve days. His will of March 10, 1777 was probated February 10, 1783. Issue born at Rombouts: 1. *Aeltje* [6] *Swartwout,* born 1750; married Cornelius Adriance. 2. *Elizabeth Swartwout,* born 1753; married Francis Hasbrouck. 3. *Gieletjen Swartwout,* bapt. May 7, 1757; married Theodorus Adriance. 4. *Jacobus Swartwout,* bapt. December 4, 1758; named in father's will. 5. *Johannes Swartwout,* born 1763; named in father's will.

 vi. SAMUEL SWARTWOUT, bapt. January 23, 1726; married April 16, 1749, Phebe, daughter of John Pudney of Rombouts. Issue born at Rombouts: 1. *Jacobus* [6] *Swartwout,* born 1750. 2. *Johannes Swartwout,* bapt. February 15, 1753. 3. *Gieletjen Swartwout,* bapt. December 28, 1757. 4. *Phebe Swartwout,* bapt. June 1, 1760. 5. *Elizabeth Swartwout,* bapt. July 20, 1762. 6. *Jacomyntje Swartwout,* bapt. August 10, 1765. 7. *Jannette Swartwout,* bapt. August 12, 1767. 8. *Thomas Swartwout.*

 vii. JACOMYNTJE SWARTWOUT, born October 14, 1728; married September 19, 1748. Hendricus Rosecrans, Jr. Issue: 1. *Gieletje* [6] *Rosecrans.* 2. *Cornelius Rosecrans,* bapt. Rombouts, March 15, 1760. 3. *Derrick Rosecrans,* born at Fishkill. 4. *Jannette Rosecrans,* bapt. Fishkill, July 15, 1762. 5. *Maria Rosecrans,* bapt. February 16, 1764. 6. ——— *Rosecrans,* bapt. Hopewell, New York, April 11, 1768.

 viii. CATHARINE SWARTWOUT, bapt. September 3, 1732; married Joseph Dorland. Issue: 1. *Jacobus* [6] *Dorland,* born Hopewell, New York, December 21, 1758.

 ix. JACOBUS SWARTWOUT, bapt. November 5, 1734, married March 9, 1760, Aeltje Brinkerhoff, born September 23, 1740, daughter of Isaac and Sarah (Rapelje) Brinkerhoff. He was a Colonel in the Revolution; resided at Fishkill, and there made his will October 23, 1823, which was probated February 19, 1827. Issue: 1. *Sarah* [6] *Swartwout,* born December 23, 1760. 2. *Derrick Swartwout,* born August 21, 1762; removed to Rockland County, New York. 3. *Gieletjen Swartwout,* born October 7, 1764; married Peter Waldron; had issue. 4. *Isaac Swartwout,* born December 21, 1767; resided at Fishkill. 5. *Jacobus Swartwout,* born June 26, 1770; named in father's will. 6. *Aeltje Swartwout,* bapt. January 1, 1773; died young. 7. *Aeltje Swartwout,* born November 30, 1773; married John Slecht (Slegt), and had issue. 8. *John Swartwout,* born January 11, 1782; not named in father's will.

16. CORNELIUS [4] NIEUKIRK (*Cornelis,*[3] *Gerretse,*[2] *Cornelisse*[1]), wrote his surname Nieukirk, and this form has been followed by many of his descendants. He was baptized at Kingston, August 30, 1696, and died at Pilesgrove, as it was then known, later Pittsgrove, Salem County, New Jersey, August 17, 1744.

In 1715 he was listed as a soldier in Captain Johannes Schepmoes' Hurley Company of Foot, Ulster County Regiment, New

THE PRESBYTERIAN CHURCH OF PITTSGROVE AT DARETOWN,
NEW JERSEY, BUILT 1767.

From *1864-1906 Almanac and Year Book, First National Bank of
Woodstown, New Jersey.*

The *History of the Presbyterian Church of Pittsgrove in Salem
County, New Jersey*, by Rev. Allen H. Brown and Rev. John Ewing,
states that: April 30, 1741, has been generally accepted as the date of
organization of this ancient church. The *History of the Presbyterian
Church in America*, by Richard Webster, page 349, also makes the statement that ''a church covenant at Pilesgrove, or Pittsgrove, was signed
April 30, 1741.'' The manuscript records of the Presbyterian Congregation of Pittsgrove contains the following: ''The Church Records of
the Presbyterian Congregation at Pilesgrove, begun April 30th day. In
the year of our Lord 1741. By the Revd. David Evans The first gospel
Pastor there.'' The Church Covenant follows soon after on same page.
It is signed by four Van Meters, and then by Cornelius Nieukirk, Rachel
his wife, Abraham Nieukirk (their son) etc. A brief history called, *The
Presbyterian Church of Pittsgrove, at Daretown, New Jersey*, printed in
the *1864-1906 Almanac and Year Book First National Bank Woodstown,
N. J.* page 11, fixes the date of the church building—''According to the
date on the keystone over the doorway, this church, which is still standing, and an engraving of which appears in this Almanac, was built in
1767.''

York Militia, under the command of Colonel Jacob Rutsen.* The date of his removal to Pilesgrove is not well defined. It is of record, however, that he purchased three hundred and eighty acres of land on Morris River in Salem County, May 23, 1718. As he was a millwright he may not have located there until some years later, probably not until his marriage in 1721. His children were all born in Salem County though two were baptized at Kingston. The eldest, Abraham, was born June 8, 1722, which in a measure, fixes the date of removal as before that date. In his new home he was a foremost citizen and died leaving a good estate, as is attested by the inventory thereof, on file in the office of the Secretary of State at Trenton, New Jersey. Letters of administration were granted to his widow, Rachel, and son Abraham, November 8, 1744.

When, on April 30, 1741, the Presbyterian Church of Pittsgrove was organized he, his wife and his son, Abraham, signed the Church Covenant as constituent members and continued their membership until death, when both husband and wife were buried side by side in its old Churchyard, where their gravestones bear these inscriptions:

Here lieth the body / of / Cornelius Nieukirk / one of the first and chief promoters / of the Gospel in this place; / who died August 17, 1774, / aged 48 years.

O always think that die you must
By faith and love make sure of Christ,
Live just and Godly every day,
So death to youll be peace and joy.
Farewell

In Memory / of Rachel Nieukirk, / whose maiden name was Ten Eyck, / wife of Cornelius Nieukirk, of Pittsgrove / who departed this life / August 13, 1771 / Aged 71 years, ten months and two weeks / Being dead yet speaketh.

My numerous progeny attend
If Happiness you mean to find
Tis not in Honour Health or Gold
Or all the Pleasures of your World
Tis faith in Christ tis Love supreme
To thy good God; and Love to Man,
To obey Persevere and resign
This! this is happiness divine!
In Life in Death Eternity!
Vain all, all life is Vanity.

---

* *Report of State Historian, State of New York, Colonial Series,* vol. i, p. 560.

Cornelius Nieukirk was married March 17, 1721, by Domine Petrus Vas of Kingston, to Rachel Ten Eyck, baptized at Kingston, November 5, 1699, by Domine Johannes Petrus Nucella of that Church, daughter of Mathys Ten Eyck of Hurley and his wife, Jannetje Roosa. Rachael Nieukirk executed her will at Pittsgrove, July 5, 1762, naming therein as legatees: sons Abraham, Matthew, Garret and Cornelius; daughters: Yonica Du Bois, Elizabeth Du Bois, Catherine Garrison, Jacomyntje Du Bois and Sarah Du Bois; grandchildren: Rachel Du Bois, Sen.; Rachel, daughter of Matthew Du Bois, and Rachel, daughter of Cornelius Nieukirk. Her daughter, Mary, is un-mentioned; son Matthew Nieukirk and Jacob Du Bois, are appointed executors.

Children of Cornelius and Rachel (Ten Eyck) * Nieukirk, born in Salem County:

26. i. ABRAHAM[5], married (1) Ann Richman; (2) Sarah S. Van Meter.

ii. MATTHEW, born September 17, 1724; died unmarried April 17, 1797; buried in Daretown churchyard. His will, of record in the office of the Secretary of State * at Trenton, has been of large value in determining the various relationships of his family. He is probably the Revolutionary waggon master in New Jersey Militia, without date of service.

27. iii. GARRET, married Elizabeth Du Bois.

iv. YONIKA, born August 6, 1728; married June 3, 1747, Jacob Du Bois, born February 19, 1719; died September 28, 1794; son of Barent Du Bois, *q. v.* Jacob Du Bois was captain of the Pittsgrove Minute Men of Salem County, 20 September, 1775. The Muster Roll of his Company is the earliest known list of Salem County soldiers in the Revolution and contains the names of seven of the Du Bois family, as well as others mentioned in this compilation. It appears in full on pages 32-3 following. He was also a member of the Salem County Committee of Correspondence which met at Salem January 7, 1775. Issue all born in Salem County: 1. *Rachel[6] Du Bois,* born September 21, 1749; died October 15, 1811; married May 3, 1768, John Hayman Krom, born March 20, 1741; son of John and Elizabeth (Hayman) Krom; died of small pox December 1776, while serving as a Revolutionary soldier, had four children. 2. *Catherine Du Bois,* born October 15, 1751; married Joel Garrison, who died in Salem County, *circa* 1798, leaving six children. 3. *Sarah Du Bois,* born September 23, 1754; married John Du Bois, born August 12, 1752, son of Rev. Jacob Du Bois and wife Mary Allegar, who died intestate, leaving six children, among whom his estate was divided in 1802. 4. *Jonathan Du Bois,* born October 2, 1757; died, unmarried, February 21, 1838. 5. *David Du Bois,* born September 19, 1761; died in May, 1837; married first, Elizabeth Burroughs, daughter of Joseph F. and Eleanor (Du Bois)

---

* *Cf.* THE TEN EYCK FAMILY IN NEW YORK. By Henry Waterman George, in *The New York Genealogical and Biographical Record,* vol. lxiii, pp. 157, *et seq.*

Burroughs, who died September 23, 1803; married second, April 23, 1804, Freelove Whitaker, born March 29, 1778; died January 1, 1842, daughter of Ambrose and Rachel (Leake) Whitaker; had eight children, two by first, six by second marriage. 6. *Lydia Du Bois*, twin, born September 19, 1761; died February 29, 1848; married Andrew Du Bois. Issue: 1. REBECCA DU BOIS, born July 1, 1781.

v. JACOMYNTJE [5], born June 9, 1731; married May 21, 1751, Matthew Du Bois, born May 8, 1722; died Salem County, 1773; will dated March 25, 1773; proved April 22, following; son of Louis and Margaret (Jansen) Du Bois, *q. v.* Issue, born in Salem County: 1. *Sarah* [6] *Du Bois*, born February 24, 1753. 2. *Lewis Du Bois*, born December 25, 1755; married December 22, 1777, Rebecca Craig; his estate in Salem County was divided in December, 1823, among his children: SAMUEL [7] DU BOIS, SARAH DICKINSON, REBECCA DU BOIS, ELIZABETH NICHOLAS, and the heirs of his son, JOHN DU BOIS, deceased, who had married Sarah Newkirk, born May 29, 1786, daughter of Jacob Newkirk. 3. *Anna Du Bois*, born August 23, 1757. 4. *Rachel Du Bois*, born November 24, 1759. 5. *Cornelius Du Bois*, born January 2, 1762. 6. *Matthew Du Bois*, born September 5, 1765; probably died young. 7. *Benjamin Du Bois*, born December 30, 1767.

28. vi. CORNELIUS, married Mary Miller.

vii. ELIZABETH, born May 8, 1735; died January 12, 1802; married David Du Bois, son of Barent and Jacomyntje (Du Bois) Du Bois, *q. v.*, born November 18, 1724; died November 12, 1801; a Revolutionary soldier. Both husband and wife are buried in the Daretown churchyard. Issue, born in Salem County: 1. *Rebecca* [6] *Du Bois*, born May 20, 1753; died December 4, 1822; married John Burroughs, who died June 1, 1823, in seventy-first year. 2. *Eleanor Du Bois*, born January 18, 1755; died December 4, 1822, married Joseph F. Burroughs, who died February 8, 1797, aged forty-one years; four children. 3. *Anna Du Bois*, born December 6, 1756; married Joseph Haywood; had issue. 4. *Isaac Du Bois*, born October 20, 1758; died in 1822; estate divided in 1823; married Elizabeth, daughter of Benjamin Burroughs. Issue, living in 1823: JAMES [7] DU BOIS; ABRAHAM DU BOIS; DAVID DU BOIS, born June 14, 1791, married Ruth Swing; CORNELIUS DU BOIS; ISAAC DU BOIS; REBECCA DU BOIS, born May 8, 1786; married November 12, 1807, Joseph Newkirk; MICHAL DU BOIS, born April 20, 1789, married Cornelius M. Newkirk, *q. v.*; RACHEL DU BOIS. 5. *Barnet Du Bois*, born September 7, 1760; married Ruth, daughter of Nathaniel Diament; his will of January 22, 1803; probated March, 1804 mentioned wife Ruth and sons, CHARLES [7] DU BOIS and DAVID DU BOIS. 6. *Leah Du Bois*, born April 8, 1762; married ―― Burroughs; named in her father's will March 5, 1791. 7. *Jacob Du Bois*, born December 7, 1763; died January 2, 1844; married Mary Moore, who died November, 1850; located at Norway, Herkimer County, New York, where both died; seven children. 8. *Rachel Du Bois*, born October 22, 1765; died July, 1801; married Uriah Rose, son of Ezekiel and Elizabeth (Newkirk) Rose, *q. v.* 9. *Catherine Du Bois*, born March 19, 1767; died October 9, 1852; married David Whitaker, born October 17, 1767; died July 29, 1807, son of Ambrose and Ruth (Harris) Whitaker; after the death of her husband, by whom she had six children, Catherine Whitaker, with her three youngest children, located a few miles south of Onward, Cass County, Indiana, where she and they died and are buried in the Thomas Cemetery. 10. *Garret Du Bois*, born March 18, 1770; died

August 7, 1839. 11. *Solomon Du Bois*, born March 26, 1774; died July 17, 1801; buried in Daretown Churchyard; married Lydia Heward, born March 3, 1778, daughter of Joseph and Elizabeth Heward; Mrs. Du Bois married second, John Clark, and died May 12, 1809; one son: SOLOMON 7 DU BOIS, born February 6, 1802, survived. 12. *Mary* 6 *Du Bois*, born January 18, 1776; married Lewis Whitaker, born October 15, 1770; died October 1, 1828, son of Ambrose and Rachel (Leake) Whitaker.

viii. CATHERINE 5, born November 5, 1737; married William Garrison.

ix. MARY, born August 19, 1740; married Aaron Brown of Daretown, born August 1, 1737. Issue: 1. *Matthew* 6 *Brown*, born January 29, 1764. 2. *Levi Brown*, born May 23, 1766. 3. *Sarah Brown*, born August 19, 1770. 4. *William Brown*, born June 26, 1775.

x. SARAH, born April 25, 1742; died January 28, 1813; married first, Joseph Du Bois, son of Louis and Margaret (Jansen) Du Bois, *q. v.*; by this marriage an only child, *Benjamin* 6 *Du Bois*, died in his non-age. She married second, April 20, 1782, Judge Henry Wynkoop of Doylestown, Pennsylvania. Issue: 1. *Susannah* 6 *Wynkoop*, born Doylestown, April 11, 1784; died March 2, 1849; married October 13, 1808, John Lefferts, born in 1779; died January 14, 1859, son of Arthur and Adriana (Van Arsdale) Lefferts; they resided at Lodi, Seneca County, New York where their eight children were born: SARAH 7 W. LEFFERTS, born August 19, 1809. ELIZABETH V. LEFFERTS, born February 20, 1811. HENRY WYNKOOP LEFFERTS, born February 16, 1813. EDWARD V. LEFFERTS, born September 8, 1815. JAMES L. LEFFERTS, born April 27, 1818. READING BEATTY LEFFERTS, born March 10, 1822. MARY HELEN WYNKOOP LEFFERTS, born February 2, 1825; WORTH LEFFERTS, born February 25, 1828.

MUSTER ROLL OF MINUTE MEN OF PITTSGROVE, SALEM COUNTY, NEW JERSEY.*

"We the Subscribers Do Voluntarily Enlist ourselves in the Company of Captain Jacob Dubois in the Township of Pitts Grove in the County of Salem under the Command of Colonel Samuel Dick and Do promise to Obey our Officers in such service as they shall appoint us Agreeable to the Rules and Orders of the Province".

Peter DuBois, 1st Lieu.
Abram DuBois, 2d Lieut.
William Conckling, Ensign

Serjants	st.
Joel Garrison	1
Benjn. Vanmeter	2
Elias Craig	3
James Stratton	4

---

* *Vide* Frank H. Stewart, *Salem County in the Revolution*, p. 8; letters to, and later Muster Rolls, pp. 16, 17, 19, show continuous service for Jacob Du Bois and many of his Company.

Jacob Vanmeter	Benjamin Hughs
Benjm. Burroughs	Henry Johnson
Ezekiel Rose	Ezekiel White
Elijah Johnston	Reuben Langly
William Murphy	Willm Crum
Isaac Dubois	Cornelius Woolsey
Joseph Thompson	Isaac Newkirk
James Murphy	John Crum
Robert Tullis, Jr.	Jacob Steelman
Francis Tullis	Joseph Abbott
George Waggoner	Abdon Abbott
Philip Titus	John Burroughs
John Burroughs	Isreal Elwell
James Burroughs	Aaron Brown
Gidion Tullis	Samuel Dubois
Jacob Tullis	John Dindlespike
John Nealy	Alexr Steel
William Nealy	David Weeks
Joseph Nealy	James Johnson
Samuel Swing	John Dubois
John Miller	Benjamin Dubois
George Fauver	Wilm Thompson
Henry Huet	Co Niewkirk, Jr.
John Craig, Jr.	Wm. McClung
Thomas Rose	John Ricker
Robert Patterson	Joseph Jones
Cornelius DuBois	Alexr Jones
Isaac Vanmeter	Moses Nickles
John Johnson	Cornelius Burroughs

Pitts Grove 20th Sept. 1775

A true Copy from the Original by Jacob Dubois Captn.

17. Jan [4] Newkirk (*Arie* [3], *Gérretse* [2], *Cornelisse* [1]), baptized at Kingston, August 24, 1690; married Dorothea Douw, baptized at Albany Dutch Church, March 23, 1701, daughter of Hendrick Douw * and his wife, Neeltye Myndertse, and located at Hurley.

Children of Jan and Dorothea (Douw) Newkirk, baptized at Kingston:

    i. Adrian [5], bapt. June 12, 1720; married first, November 7, 1741, Marretjen Rutsen, bapt. September 9, 1722, daughter of Jacob and Lea (Nieuwkirk) Rutsen; married second, October 27, 1765, Tryntje Louw, bapt. April 2, 1727, widow of Philip Bevier and daughter of Petrus Matthew Louw and wife, Catharine Du Bois. Issue, the first four baptized in Kingston Dutch Church: 1. *Lea* [6] *Newkirk*, bapt. January 23, 1743; married Zachariah Hoffman; resided at Shawangunk. 2. *Henricus Newkirk*, bapt. July 29, 1744. 3. *Dorothea Newkirk*, bapt. October 27, 1745; married, as third wife, July 24, 1769, Nathaniel Cantine. 4. *Elizabeth Newkirk*, bapt. December 13, 1747. 5. *Jacob Rutsen Newkirk*, bapt. April 1, 1750; married Annatje Person. One Jacob Newkirk was commissioned, March 23, 1778, Lieutenant-Colonel, Second or South

* Munsell, *Collections on the History of Albany*, vol. iv, 118.

End Regiment, Ulster County, New York under Colonel James Clinton.* 6. *Myndert Newkirk,* bapt. September 2, 1753. 7. *Jan Newkirk,* bapt. January 1, 1755. 8. *Catharine Newkirk,* bapt. January 25, 1761. 9. *Johannes Newkirk,* bapt. July 1, 1764. 10. *Elias Newkirk,* bapt. September 14, 1766. 11. *Philip Newkirk,* bapt. September 14, 1766, twin of Elias. 12. *Gerret Newkirk,* bapt. November 13, 1768; married and had issue; descendants living in Missouri and Illinois in 1870. 13. *Daniel Newkirk,* bapt. May 10, 1772.

ii. HENDRICUS, bapt. November 12, 1721.

iii. ELIZABETH, bapt. March 24, 1723; married October 4, 1741, Peter van Bergen, born 1721, son of Martin van Bergen and wife Catrina Meyer of Albany. No issue.

iv. GERRET, bapt. December 20, 1724; married Elizabeth van Bergen; had issue; soldier, in Captain William McGinniss' Company, Ulster County Militia, in 1755.†

v. MEYNDERT, bapt. April 17, 1726.

vi. NEELTJE, bapt. April 27, 1728.

18. HENDRIKA [4] NEWKIRK (*Arie* [3], *Gerretse* [2], *Cornelisse* [1]), baptized at Kingston, November 11, 1692; married December 14, 1711, Cornelius Wynkoop, son of Major Johannes Wynkoop and his wife, Judith Bloodgood; resided at Hurley. By will of September 19, 1739, proved April 3, 1747,‡ Cornelius Wynkoop devised his estate to wife Hendrika and his ten surviving children.

Children of Cornelius and Hendrika (Newkirk) Wynkoop:

i. JUDIK [5] WYNKOOP, bapt. August 31, 1712; married December 11, 1736, Johannes Du Bois, bapt. November 10, 1710; resided at Hurley, *q. v.*

ii. ELIZABETH WYNKOOP, bapt. January 9, 1715; married December 15, 1739, Philippus Du Mond,§ bapt. September 28, 1707, son of Walran Dumond and wife Catrina Ter Bosch. Issue: 1. *Catrina* [6] *Du Mond,* bapt. November 9, 1740. 2. *Maria Du Mond,* bapt. May 9, 1742. 3. *Johannes Du Mond,* bapt. January 22, 1744. 4. *Hendrika Du Mond,* bapt. December 29, 1745. 5. *Annatjen Du Mond,* bapt. June 12, 1748. 6. *Hendrika Du Mond,* bapt. October 28, 1750. 7. *Elizabeth Du Mond,* bapt. June 2, 1754. 8. *Cornelis Du Mond,* bapt. June 19, 1757.

iii. CORNELIA WYNKOOP, bapt. March 17, 1717; married July 4, 1741, Jan Van Dusen, Jr. of Hurley, who died after December 16, 1754.|| Issue: 1. *Hendrika* [6] *Van Dusen,* bapt. May 23, 1742; died young. 2. *Hendrika Van Dusen,* bapt. September 2,

---

* Fernow, *Documents Relating to the Colonial History of the State of New York,* vol. xv (*State Archives, The Revolution,* vol. i, 299, 543).

† *Second Annual Report of State Historian of the State of New York Colonial Series,* vol. i, p. 720.

‡ *Ulster County Probate Records. American Record Series,* vol. ii, 138, 139.

§ Dumont, Du Mon, Du Mond, Du Mont.

|| *Ulster County Probate Records,* vol. i, p. 136.

1744. 3 *Johannes Van Dusen*, bapt. May 19, 1746. 4. *Catharine Van Dusen*, bapt. March 11, 1750.

iv. JOHANNES [5] WYNKOOP, bapt. August 15, 1719; named in his father's will.

v. CATHARINE WYNKOOP, bapt. February 18, 1722; married June 20, 1747, Lucas Elmendorf, bapt. May 4, 1718, son of Coenradt Elmendorf and wife Blandena Kierstede. No issue.

vi. LEA WYNKOOP, bapt. May 31, 1724; died young.

vii. ADRIAN WYNKOOP, bapt. August 21, 1826; died in August, 1795; married October 25, 1754, Catharine Louw; served as Mayor in New York forces in the Revolution. No issue.

viii. LEA WYNKOOP, bapt. January 27, 1728; named in father's will.

ix. CORNELIUS C. WYNKOOP, bapt. November 5, 1732; married April 24, 1760, Maria Catherine Ruhl; was a lawyer and practiced in New York City. Issue, the first seven baptized in New York: 1. *John [6] C. Wynkoop*, bapt. January 21, 1761. 2. *Maria Wynkoop*, bapt. July 4, 1762. 3. *Catharina Wynkoop*, bapt. November 20, 1763. 4. *George Pieterson Wynkoop*, bapt. July 17, 1765. 5. *Anna Sabina Wynkoop*, bapt. July 13, 1766. 6. *Elizabeth Wynkoop*, bapt. December 3, 1769. 7. *Cornelius Wynkoop*, bapt. May 24, 1772. 8. *Henrietta Wynkoop*, bapt. March 23, 1775. 9. *Augustus Wynkoop*, bapt. September 10, 1777.

x. PETRUS WYNKOOP, bapt. November 15, 1734; married Janneke Hardenburg, daughter of Jacobus Hardenburg and wife, Trintje Elting. Issue bapt. Ulster County: 1. *Cornelius [6] Wynkoop*, bapt. June 11, 1775. 2. *Janneke Wynkoop*, bapt. September 22, 1776. 3. *Petrus Wynkoop*, bapt. January 25, 1779.

xi. MARIA WYNKOOP, bapt. November 15, 1734; named in father's will.

19. GERRET [4] NEWKIRK (*Arie* [3], *Gerretse* [2], *Cornelisse* [1]), baptized at Kingston, May 30, 1697; married at Albany, New York, October 19, 1718, Anna Vischer, baptized September 6, 1696, daughter of Johannes Vischer and wife, Elizabeth Nottingham.

Children of Gerret and Ann (Vischer) Newkirk the first baptized at Albany, the remainder at Kingston:

i. ELIZABETH [5], bapt. November 1, 1719; married October 31, 1738, Isaac Wimple,* bapt. August 28, 1715, son of Johannes and Ariantje (Swits) Wimple; resided in Albany County. Issue: 1. *Arriantje [6] Wimple*, born 1740. 2. *Catalina Wimple*, born 1742. 3. *Annatje Wimple*, bapt. March 27, 1747. 4. *Johannes Wimple*, born May, 1749.

ii. ARY, bapt. August 6, 1721.

iii. JOHANNES, bapt. January 12, 1724; married January 9, 1759, Rachel Clute of Schenectady, who survived him. Resided for some years at Schenectady but later in Montgomery County, New York where he executed his will January 15, 1793; probated October 2, 1806.† Issue, the first four baptized at Schenectady: 1. *Garret [6] L. Newkirk*, bapt. February 4, 1760;

---

* WIMPLE GENEALOGY in *The New York Genealogical and Biographical Record*, xxxv, 195.

† *Montgomery County Probate Records*, Liber 1, p. 353.

named in father's will, as were William, John and Annatje. 2. *Tanneke Newkirk*, bapt. May 4, 1762. 3. *William Newkirk*, bapt. February 3, 1765. 4. *John Newkirk*, bapt. September 10, 1767. 5. *Arie Gerretsen Newkirk*, bapt. June 12, 1773. 6. *Annatje Newkirk*, bapt. July 29, 1776.

   iv. ANNA [5], bapt. January 23, 1726; was witness to a baptism at Albany in 1755.

   v. GARRET CORNELIUS, bapt. January 12, 1729; married Nellie Quackenbos; resided for a time at Schenectady and later in Montgomery County. His will of July 6, 1808; proved January 7, 1822,* named children *Garret* [6], *William, Cornelius, Mary,* and grand-children, Cornelius [7], Margaret and Mary, children of son Cornelius. His wife was already deceased. Issue, the first four born in Schenectady: 1. *Garret* [6] *C. Newkirk*, born January, 1760. 2. *Abraham Newkirk*, bapt. October 31, 1762. 3. *William C. Nieukirk*, born 1764. 4. *Johannes Newkirk*, bapt. October 17, 1767. 5. *Cornelius Newkirk*, born 1769. 6. *John Newkirk*, bapt. July 2, 1772. 7. *Maria (Mary) Newkirk*, bapt. December 18, 1775.

   vi. JACOB, bapt. September 10, 1732; married Peterje Philipps; lived in Montgomery County. Issue, baptized at Schenectady: 1. *Annatje* [6] *Newkirk*, bapt. August 23, 1763. 2. *Sarah Newkirk*, bapt. October 25, 1765.

   vii. WILLIAM, bapt. October 12, 1735.

20. ARIAANTJE[4] NEWKIRK (*Arie*[3], *Gerretse*[2], *Cornelisse*[1]), born November 19, 1699; died after July 8, 1776; married December 1, 1722, Jacobus Elmendorph, baptized June 3, 1694, son of Coenradt Elmendorph † and his wife, Ariantje Gerrits Van den Berg. His will, made at Kingston, July 8, 1776, probated November 3, 1792,‡ devised his estate to wife and surviving children and grand children: sons Coenradt, Jacobus, Cornelius, Arian; eldest daughter Arientje, wife of Abraham Slecht; daughter Margaret, wife of Egbert Dumond and grand children Jan Slecht, Elizabeth Slecht, wife of Oke Suydam and Margaret and Ariantje Slecht; the children of deceased daughter Elizabeth.

Children of Jacobus and Arientje (Newkirk) Elmendorph, name changed to Elmendorf, baptized at Kingston:

   i. ELIZABETH [5] ELMENDORF, bapt. May 26, 1723; died prior to September 16, 1758; married May 9, 1746, Johannes Slecht,§ born October 18, 1719, son of Jan Slecht and wife Elizabeth Smedes; who married second, Gerritje Van Bunschooten by whom he had two children. Issue by his first marriage: 1. *Elizabeth* [6] *Slecht*, married Oke Suydam. 2. *Ariantje* [6] *Slecht*,

---

* *Ibid.*, Liber 3, p. 278.

† THE ELMENDORF FAMILY. By George H. Van Wagenen. *New York Genealogical and Biographical Record*, vol. xx, p. 101, *et seq.*

‡ *Ulster County Probate Records, American Record Series*, vol. ii, pp. 100, 101.

§ Name variously written, Slecht, Sleght, Slegt.

bapt. April 16, 1740. 3. *Jan*, or *Johannes Slecht*, bapt. January 13, 1752. 4. *Margaret Slecht*, bapt. September 8, 1752.

ii. ARIANTJE[5] ELMENDORF, bapt. December 6, 1724; married December 14, 1751 Abraham Slecht, brother of Johannes Slecht. Issue: 1. *Jacobus*[6] *Slecht*, bapt. April 20, 1753. 2. *Abraham Slecht*, bapt. July 27, 1755. 3. *Arriantje Slecht*, bapt. October 16, 1757. 4. *Jan Slecht*, bapt. June 1, 1760. 5. *Elizabeth Slecht*, bapt. August 15, 1762.

iii. COENRAD JACOBUS ELMENDORF, bapt. November 27, 1726; married November 17, 1756, Catrina Hardenbergh, bapt. September 7, 1729, daughter of Gerardus Hardenbergh and Janneke Elmendorf. Issue: 1. *Coenrad*[6] *Edmundus Elmendorf*, bapt. October 5, 1763. 2. *Jacobus C. Elmendorf*, bapt. April 13, 1772. 3. *Antje Elmendorf*, bapt. April 30, 1775.

iv. ARIAAN GERRITSE ELMENDORF, bapt. December 29, 1728; died unmarried, after July 8, 1776.

v. MARGARET ELMENDORF, bapt. at Kingston, *circa* 1732, record lost; married March 9, 1760 Egbert Du Mont, son of John Du Mont and wife, Rachel Schoonmaker, who practiced law at Kingston. No issue.

vi. GERRET ELMENDORF, bapt. May 5, 1734; not named in father's will.

vii. JACOBUS ELMENDORF, bapt. July 18, 1736; married Elizabeth Sammons and died after January 11, 1795. Issue, baptized at Kingston: 1. *Jacobus*[6] *Elmendorf*, bapt. February 18, 1771. 2. *Elizabeth Elmendorf*, bapt. August 1, 1772. 3. *Jacobus Elmendorff*, bapt. November 22, 1774. 4. *Arriantje Elmendorff*, bapt. January 5, 1777. 5. *Cornelius Elmendorf*, bapt. December 2, 1778; died young. 6. *Maria Elmendorf*, bapt. March 5, 1780; died young. 7. *Carlintje Elmendorf*, bapt. April 6, 1783. 8. *Sarah Elmendorf*, bapt. November 6, 1785. 9. *Cornelius Elmendorf*, bapt. April 8, 1787. 10. *Maria Elmendorf*, bapt. January 11, 1795.

viii. CORNELIUS ELMENDORF, bapt. December 17, 1738; died after November 13, 1792.

ix. PETRUS ELMENDORF, bapt. February 18, 1742; died before July 8, 1776.

21. LEA[4] NEWKIRK (*Arie*[3], *Gerretse*[1], *Cornelisse*[2]), baptized August 9, 1702; married December 9, 1720 Jacob Rutsen, Jr., son of Jacob Rutsen and wife, Marretjen Hansen.

Children of Jacob and Lea (Niewkirk) Rutsen, baptized at Kingston:

i. MARRETJEN [5] RUTSEN, bapt. September 9, 1722; married Adrian Newkirk, *q. v.*

ii. ELIZABETH RUTSEN, bapt. November 15, 1724; married Abraham Roosa who died intestate, at Shawangunk, in 1788. Issue: 1. *Aldert*[6] *Roosa*, bapt. April 7, 1745. 2. *Leah*[6] *Roosa*, bapt. April 12, 1747. 3. *Jacob Roosa*, bapt. December 31, 1749. 4. *Isaac Roosa*, bapt. April 21, 1751. 5. *Rebecca Roosa*, bapt. March 18, 1755. 6. *Sarah Roosa*, bapt. January 22, 1757.

iii. CATHERINE RUTSEN, bapt. September 3, 1729.

iv. ZARA, or SARAH, RUTSEN, bapt. September 21, 1729; married January 20, 1756, as second wife, Nathaniel Cantine of Marbletown, baptized October 25, 1724, son of Peter Cantine and wife Elizabeth Blanshan. Sarah (Rutsen) Cantine died before May 20, 1765, when Nathaniel Cantine married Dorothy Newkirk, bapt. October 27, 1745, daughter of Adrian Newkirk, *q. v.* and wife Marretjen Rutsen. Issue, born at Marbletown: 1. *Leah* ⁶ *Cantine,* bapt. May 15, 1758. 2. *Elizabeth Cantine,* born April 20, 1762.

v. ANNATJEN RUTSEN, bapt. November 25, 1732; married January 26, 1752, Johannes Crispell. They resided at Shawangunk. Issue: 1. *Catharine* ⁶ *Crispell,* born August 25, 1754. 2. *Arriantje Crispell,* born August 31, 1758. 3. *Marretjen Crispell,* born March 8, 1761. 4. *Anthony Crispell,* born March 17, 1765. 5. *Sarah Crispell,* born May 29, 1768.

22. RACHEL⁴ NEWKIRK (*Arie³, Gerretse², Cornelisse¹*), baptized April 9, 1704; married Jan Cornelius Bogert, baptized at Hackensack, New Jersey, March 30, 1702, son of Cornelius Bogert and his wife, Willemtje van Voorhees.

Children of Jan Cornelius and Rachel (Newkirk) Bogert, the first, and the last four baptized at Hackensack, New Jersey:

i. CORNELIUS ⁵ BOGERT, bapt. August 1, 1736; married Sietsye Demarest; resided in Bergen County, New Jersey. Issue born there: 1. *Jacob* ⁶ *Bogert,* bapt. June 20, 1762. 2. *John Bogert,* bapt. March 4, 1764; died young. 3. *Marya Bogert,* bapt. September 10, 1769. 4. *Cornelius Bogert,* bapt. August 20, 1770. 5. *Airy Bogert,* bapt. May 16, 1773; died young. 6. *Lideya Bogert,* bapt. April 21, 1776. 7. *Bregy Dowder Bogert,* bapt. February 7, 1779. 8. *Jan Bogert,* bapt. April 15, 1781. 9. *Albert Bogert,* twin, April 15, 1781. 10. *Petrus Bogert,* bapt. May 17, 1783. 11. *Christentje Bogert,* bapt. June 23, 1786. 12. *Airy Bogert,* bapt. July 27, 1788.

ii. WILLEMTJE BOGERT, bapt. at Schaarlenburgh, April 15, 1739; married Jacobus Peek, son of Jacob Peek and wife Sarah Demarest; resided in Bergen County. Issue: 1. *Jacobus* ⁶ *Peek,* bapt. May 6, 1758. 2. *Rachel Peek,* bapt. March 24, 1762. 3. *Jan. Peek,* bapt. July 7, 1765. 4. *Samuel Peek,* bapt. March 31, 1768. 5. *Sarah Peek,* bapt. March 13, 1770. 6. *Cornelius Peek,* bapt. November 16, 1774. 7. *David Peek,* bapt. August 30, 1778. 8. *Margrietta Peek,* bapt. March 16, 1783.

iii. JACOB BOGERT, bapt. November 8, 1741; died young.

iv. SARAH BOGERT, bapt. June 3, 1744; married Isaac Roos (Rose); resided in Bergen County. Issue: 1. *Jonathan* ⁶ *Roos (Rose),* bapt. March 15, 1788. 2. *Sietsye Roos (Rose),* bapt. November 13, 1790.

v. ANTJEN BOGERT, bapt. December 26, 1746.

vi. JACOB BOGERT, bapt. November 8, 1741; married Margriette ———; resided in Bergen County. Issue: 1. *Lea* ⁶ *Bogert,* bapt. January 20, 1781. 2. *Sarah Bogert,* bapt. December 9, 1784. 3. *Cornelius Bogert,* bapt. November 20, 1785.

vii. RACHEL BOGERT, bapt. September 2, 1753; married Jacob Dumont; resided in Bergen County. Issue: 1. *Johannes* ⁶ *Dumont,* bapt. December 16, 1791. 2. *Jacob Dumont,* bapt. March 10, 1794.

23. CORNELIUS ⁴ NEWKIRK (*Arie ³, Gerretse ², Cornelisse ¹*), baptized at Kingston, November 12, 1710; died in February, 1788; married October 29, 1731 Dina Hoogteeling, baptized May 7, 1710, who died after September 15, 1787, daughter of Philip Hoogteeling and wife, Jennette Roosa. In 1738 he

was a trooper under command of Captain Johannes Ten Broeck, Ulster County Militia.* He resided at Hurley, where he made his will, September 15, 1787. On this instrument, which disposed of a good estate, the findings of the Supreme Court of New York, in *2 Gaines, 345*, were: that Cornelius Newkirk died testate in February, 1788, having two sons, Philip and Cornelius and four daughters, Jannet, wife of Benjamin Roosa, Leah, wife of Garret C. Newkirk, Henderika, wife of Cornelius Du Mond; Ariantje, wife of Petrus Du Bois, and his grandson Petrus, the son of Ary Newkirk, a deceased son, who was an infant; and that in 1793, his son Philip Newkirk departed this life having as heirs his children Cornelius P., Elizabeth and Maria who died in infancy.

Children of Cornelius and Dina (Hoogteeling) Newkirk, baptized at Kingston:

 i. ELIZABETH 5, bapt. October 1, 1732; died unmarried.
 ii. JANNETJE, bapt. October 20, 1734; married November 18, 1759, Benjamin Roosa of Hurley. Issue: 1. *Elizabeth 6 Roosa*, bapt. November 9, 1760. 2. *Leah Roosa*, bapt. December 25, 1765.
 iii. ARIE, or ARY, bapt. September 11, 1737; died in infancy.
 iv. PHILIP, bapt. April 13, 1740; married Jannetje Roosa, bapt. August 17, 1746, daughter of Heyman Roosa and wife, Jannetje Frear. His will of July 29, 1793, names wife Jannetje and children Cornelius P., Mary and Elizabeth. Issue, born in Hurley: 1. *Jannetjen 6 Newkirk*, bapt. March 23, 1775; died young. 2. *Dina Newkirk*, bapt. June 30, 1776; died young. 3. *Cornelius P. Newkirk*, bapt. February 1, 1778; survived his father. 4. *Maria Newkirk*, bapt. October 5, 1781; died young. 5. *Elizabeth Newkirk*, bapt. June 10, 1787.
 v. ARIE, bapt. October 3, 1742; died before September 15, 1787; married November 18, 1768, Maria Crispell, bapt. February 24, 1751, daughter of Peter Crispell and wife, Lea Roosa. Resided at Hurley. Issue: 1. *Cornelius 6 Newkirk*, bapt. June 1, 1771; died young. 2. *Petrus Newkirk*, bapt. August 13, 1775.
 vi. LEAH, bapt. April 29, 1744; married December 8, 1764, Garret C. Newkirk, bapt. September 23, 1739, son of Cornelius Newkirk and wife, Neeltje Du Bois, q. v. Issue: 1. *Diana 6 Newkirk*, bapt. October 20, 1765. 2. *Neeltje Newkirk*, bapt. March 26, 1769. 3. *Cornelius Newkirk*, bapt. March 3, 1773. 4. *Elizabeth Newkirk*, bapt. July 28, 1776; died young. 5. *Elizabeth Newkirk*, bapt. August 30, 1783.
 vii. HENDERIKA, bapt. March 9, 1746; married October 30, 1785, Cornelius Dumont of Hurley.
 viii. ARIANTJE, born January 31, 1749; died August 25, 1805; married December 23, 1779, Petrus Du Bois, born March 28, 1749; died April 2, 1830, son of Johannes Du Bois and wife, Judike Wynkoop. Issue: 1. *Judike 6 Du Bois*, born March 18, 1784; died unmarried August 1, 1845. 2. *Petrus Du Bois*, bapt. October 1, 1786; died unmarried. 3. *Dina Du Bois*, born February 2, 1789; died unmarried. 4. *John P. Du Bois*, born December 4, 1791; died unmarried July 21, 1854.

---

* *Second Annual Report of State Historian of the State of New York, Colonial Series*, vol. i, p. 610.

ix. CORNELIUS C., bapt. October 15, 1752; married January 12, 1779, Sarah Kierstede, bapt. September 2, 1759; died April 29, 1818, daughter of Christoffel Kierstede and wife, Catharine de Meier. Resided at Hurley; his will of June 18, 1832, mentions sons Cornelius, Christopher, Philip, and William deceased and the four children of deceased daughter Catharine, late wife of Ten Eyck De Witt. At the outbreak of the Revolution he was commissioned, October 25, 1775, Cornet of Kingston Company of Horse, commissioned lieutenant June 16, 1778, and captain October 23, 1779. This company was attached to the First, or Northern Regiment, Ulster County, New York Militia.* Issue: 1. *Cornelius 6 Newkirk,* bapt. November 26, 1780. 2. *Christopher Newkirk,* born November 24, 1782. 3. *William Newkirk,* bapt. August 3, 1788; died before June 18, 1832. 4. *Philip Newkirk,* born January 4, 1791. 5. *Catharine Newkirk,* born November 24, 1793; deceased before June 18, 1832; married Ten Eyck De Witt; had four children.

* Fernow, *op. cit. State Archives, The Revolution,* vol. i, p. 298.

24. ABRAHAM [5] NEWKIRK (*Barent* [4], *Cornelis* [3], *Gerretse* [2], *Cornelisse* [1]), born, probably, in Ulster County, New York, October 19, 1724; died *circa* 1790, in Washington County, Pennsylvania, near what is now the town of Bentleyville. He accompanied his father to Virginia and lived in Berkeley County, until about 1770, when he and his family removed to Pennsylvania. He married in Virginia, *circa* 1749, Keziah Shipman, daughter of Tunis Shipman, who died in Washington County and is buried with her husband on the Warner farms, overlooking Bentleyville. Later Newkirks are buried in the old Newkirk Churchyard and in that of Pigeon Creek.

Children of Abraham and Keziah (Shipman) Newkirk, all born in Berkeley County, Virginia:

> i. TUNIS [6], born July 20, 1750; died near Lancaster, Fairfield County, Ohio, May 1, 1823. Beginning with 1780, he made purchases of various tracts of land in Berkeley County, among them the homestead of his grand-father, Barent Newkirk. He married, first, *circa* 1779, Margaret Miles, born April 13, 1759; died June 11, 1798, daughter of George Miles a prominent member of the military organizations of the county and a citizen of some prominence. He married, second, April 9, 1801, Susannah Hay, born in Berkeley County, July 6, 1781; died in Fairfield County, Ohio, July 4, 1842; daughter of William Hay, a great uncle of Hon. John Hay, one time Secretary of State for the United States. Issue, nine by first and five by second marriage, the ten eldest born in Berkeley County: 1. *George* [7] *Newkirk*, born March 12, 1780; died *circa*, 1822; married September 2, 1802, Mary Mason, born 8-10-1781; died 2-10-1857; lived on the old Newkirk farm about ten miles north of Martinsburg, West Virginia, at what was known as Little Georgetown; had three children, through one of whom, a son, JAMES [8] MASON NEWKIRK, was continued in that vicinity. 2. *Henry Newkirk*, born October 10, 1781; died March 21, 1800. 3. *John Newkirk*, born August 25, 1783; died July 1, 1787. 4. *Anna Newkirk*, born January 25, 1786; died July 1, 1787. 5. *James Newkirk*, born December 11, 1788; died 1817; married January 10, 1815, Mary Porterfield; lived at Little Georgetown; two daughters. 6. *Joseph Newkirk*, born January 18, 1791; married first, August 8, 1816, Eveline Kemp, born 1798; died August 24, 1823; married second, in 1824, Frances Stuart, who died June 17, 1871; he located at Big Prairie, Ohio, where he died March 5, 1869, and is buried in the Newkirk burying ground at that place; had fourteen children. 7. *Reuben Newkirk*, born March 5, 1795; died unmarried, October 7, 1819. 8. *Isaac Newkirk*, born June 5, 1795; died in Berkeley County, Virginia, August 29, 1873; married first, September 29, 1836, at Indianapolis, Indiana, Ellen Foote; married second, October 24, 1844, at Berkeley County, Ellen

(41)

Ellis Seibert; four children. 9. *Infant Newkirk*, born August 28, 1797, died soon. 10. *Anna Newkirk*, born November 3, 1802; died near Perryville, Ohio, May 23, 1882; married at Lancaster, Ohio, March 26, 1818, John Comer, who died February 25, 1872; twelve children. 11. *Jeptha Newkirk*, born in Fairfield County, May 11, 1807; married July 25, 1830, Nancy Ann Michaels, born August 14, 1806; died April 9, 1880; he died July 14, 1881, in Fairfield County, Ohio, of which, some years previously, he had been elected County Treasurer; nine children. 12. *John W. Newkirk*, born January 22, 1813, married March 3, 1836, Julia Ann Stansberry; lived in Fairfield County, where he died December 26, 1864; seven children. 13. *Virginia Newkirk*, born October 17, 1817; married February 4, 1835, John Lamb; died at Reading, Michigan, April 16, 1902; resided Fairfield County; nine children. 14. *Jane Perty Newkirk*, born January 5, 1821; died Hillsdale, Michigan, February 22, 1889; married October 25, 1844, Daniel Lincoln Pratt, born Plainfield, Massachusetts, June 24, 1820; died Hillsdale, November 7, 1902, a successful lawyer who served many years as Judge of the Circuit Court; nine children.

ii. DRUSILLA [6], died young.

iii. ISAAC, born 1754; married Rhoda Carroll; settled in Washington County, Pennsylvania. Both he and his wife are buried in the Pigeon Creek churchyard, Bentleyville, where gravestones record their deaths, his, on January 31, 1823, aged sixty-nine years; hers, on February 18, 1825, aged sixty years. He served in the Revolution with Pennsylvania troops from Washington County,* and in 1782, accompanied Captain William Crawford in the ill-fated expedition against the Wyandot and Delaware Indians on the Muskingum; was a purchaser of lands at Big Prairie, Ohio, on which some of his children later settled. On February 27, 1786, he took out a warrant for 300 acres of land in Washington County, on Pigeon Creek, called *Agricultura*; there being two claimants for the land, title was not definitely settled in Isaac Newkirk until November 3, 1807. Issue, born in Washington County: 1. *John [7] Newkirk*, born August 7, 1786; married Christena Clouse; located at Big Prairie, Wayne County; served as Justice of the Peace and in other official capacities, died October 2, 1827, his wife having died September 17, preceding; seven children. 2. *Henry Newkirk*, born September 25, 1789; died Big Prairie, August 21, 1847; married March 19, 1818, Jane Hart, daughter of David and Sarah Hart, she born January 26, 1801; died February 21, 1854, and, with most of her family is buried in the Newkirk Cemetery at Big Prairie; seven children.† 3. *Reuben Newkirk*, born February 29, 1792; married March 1, 1817, Margaret Leyda, born October 20, 1793; died August 19, 1855; settled in Wayne County, Ohio, in 1817, where he died August 19, 1855; five children. 4. *Tunis Newkirk*, born November 26, 1794; married, first, January 7, 1820, Jane Rainey; married second, October 20, 1840, Amanda F. Niblick; lived at Bentleyville, where he died October 7, 1866; thirteen children. 5. *Jane Newkirk*, born April 13, 1795; died November 14, 1840; married in February, 1810, John Springer, who died January 11, 1869; resided at Bentleyville where she and her husband are

---

* *Pennsylvania Archives*, vol. iv, 415, 722.

† One of these, Narcissa N. Newkirk, married, June 20, 1860, Benjamin Douglas, author of *History of Wayne County, Ohio*.

buried; eight children. 6. *George W. Newkirk*, born January 18, 1797; died June 5, 1846; married Mary Bennett, born March 11, 1797; died March 28, 1879; resided at Bentleyville. 7. *Cyrus Newkirk*, born May 5, 1799; died November 17, 1850; married November 29, 1825, Sarah A. Alexander, born March 28, 1803; died May 19, 1893; lived at Bentleyville; nine children.* 8. *Lousianna Newkirk*, born November 5, 1803; died January 27, 1868; married *circa* 1823, George Leyda, born November 24, 1794; died March 17, 1864; lived in Washington County, Pennsylvania; three children. 9. *Luzarby Newkirk*, born May 27, 1806; died September 16, 1864; married John Rainey, born November 5, 1799; died September 29, 1882; lived at Big Prairie, Ohio; both buried in Newkirk Cemetery; seven children. 10. *Susannah Newkirk*, born February 18, 1807; died February 18, 1830; married James Leyda, born July 17, 1801; died March 27, 1800; lived at Big Prairie; buried in Newkirk Cemetery; one child, died young.

    iv. ELIZABETH [6], married ———— Hall or Hull; lived in Washington County, Pennsylvania.

    v. SOPHIA, born 1761; died in Mercer County, Pennsylvania, March 17, 1854, aged ninety-three years; married, first, John Knox, by whom she had one son, *James [7] Knox*; married, second, James Rice, with whom she removed to Mercer County. Issue: 2. *Hannah [7] Rice*, born January 22, 1800. 3. *William Rice*, born December 1, 1802. 3. *Keziah Rice*, born August 7, 1805. 4. *Robert Rice*, born May 9, 1808.

29.   vi. ABRAHAM, married (1) Margaret Knox; (2) Marcia Stewart.

    vii. HENRY, born February 2, 1768; died in Beaver County, Pennsylvania, near Darlington, December 13, 1853, where he is buried; married, March 1, 1791, Rebecca Davis, born in Maryland, March 25, 1771; died Beaver County, *circa* 1830. He settled first in Washington County, Pennsylvania where he held a certificate for 400 acres on Pigeon Creek, called *The Legacy*, surveyed to him February 25, 1786, and which adjoined his brother Isaac's lands, *Agricultura*. He later conveyed *The Legacy* to his brother Abraham, and removed after 1812 to Beaver County. Issue all born in Washington County: 1. *Catherine [7] Newkirk*, born February 17, 1792; married James Swasic, lived at Mandfield, Ohio; had issue. 2. *John Forest Newkirk*, born July 22, 1794; married Elizabeth McBride, born March 6, 1794; died April 26, 1868; resided in Beaver County, Pennsylvania, where he died May 5, 1857; nine children. 3. *Rhoda Newkirk*, born October 26, 1796; married James Ludlow; may have removed to Indiana. 4. *Bathsheba Newkirk*, born September 6, 1799; died June 2, 1845; married Matthew Dillon, born January 19, 1795; died 31 May, 1854; resided in Beaver County near Darlington; six children. 5. *Keziah Newkirk*, born April 3, 1802; died February 17, 1872, married 6 December, 1825 Matthew Welsh, born January 5, 1794; died December 29, 1864; resided in Beaver County; five children. 6. *Shipman Newkirk*, born October 17, 1804; married in 1827, Jane Thompson, born December 16, 1804; died September 3, 1869; removed from Washington County, Pennsylvania to Beaver County in the same State about 1835, and, sometime after the birth of his youngest child in 1852 to Brooklyn, Iowa, where he died, March 10, 1889; twelve chil-

---

* Clyde C. Newkirk of Boston, journalist and caricaturist, better known as Newton Newkirk, born at Bentleyville, Pennsylvania, August 20, 1870, is a son of Joseph Alexander Newkirk, and grandson of Cyrus Newkirk and wife Sarah A. Alexander.

dren. 7. *Phebe Newkirk*, born April 29, 1808; died March 8, 1891; married April 26, 1827, Robert Douthitt, born in Beaver County, September 19, 1802; died there February 11, 1891; five children. 8. *Louisarba Newkirk*, born May 14, 1810; died *circa* 1835; married Alexander Heights; lived in Beaver County; two children; only son died unmarried, February 12, 1862. 9. *Louisiana Newkirk*, born October 11, 1812; died March 12, 1900; married May 19, 1830, William Hunt, born June 21, 1801; died August 5, 1851; lived for a time in Lawrence County, Pennsylvania, but subsequent to 1851 in Beaver County.

viii. REUBEN 6, born *circa* 1769; married in Berkeley County, Virginia, September 24, 1797, Mary Kemp; for some years he was a merchant at Shepherdsville, Virginia, but about 1803 he joined his brother, Teunis Newkirk, in Fairfield County, Ohio, where he died April 29, 1855, and is buried at Lewis Center. Issue, the two eldest born in Virginia, the others in Ohio: 1. *Delilah 7 Newkirk*, born August 11, 1798; married Andrew Ramsay; resided in Fairfield County, where their eight children were born. 2. *Cyrus Newkirk*, born May 27, 1800; married in 1819, Catherine Wildermuth; lived in Fairfield County, Ohio, Mt. Pleasant, Iowa, and Richland Center, Wisconsin; nine children born in Fairfield County. 3. *Zelu Newkirk*, born October 27, 1804; married first, December 26, 1819 Asa Phelps; second, April 18, 1841, Horatio Evans widower of her sister Permelia (Newkirk) Evans; lived until 1847 in Fairfield County; later removed to Marshall, Illinois, where she died April 28, 1861; six children, four by first, two by second marriage. 4. *Permelia Newkirk*, born December 23, 1805; married August 11, 1822, Horatio Evans; lived in Fairfield County; six children. 5. *Shipman Newkirk*, born June 18, 1807; married January 21, 1830, Elizabeth Rice; lived in Fairfield County, where he died October 11, 1852; his widow removed to Logan County, Illinois, where she died; seven children. 6. *Missouri Newkirk*, born October 17, 1809; married October 12, 1826, William Henry Cooper of Fairfield; she died November 26, 1856; two children. 7. *Henry Newkirk*, born January 14, 1812, married first, November 18, 1832, Elizabeth Hempy, who died in Fairfield County, April 2, 1844, aged 31 years, 6 months; he married second, Mary Ann Barfield and moved to Henry County, Iowa; later to Richland County, Wisconsin, where he died November 23, 1881; eleven children. 8. *Anna Newkirk*, born March 13, 1814; married May 15, 1831, David C. Wildermuth; lived in Richland County, Wisconsin, where she died January 2, 1907, and he, April 6, 1890; ten children. 9. *John C. Newkirk*, born March 14, 1817; married in Fairfield County, October 20, 1836, Sarah Walters; removed in 1847 to Delaware County, Ohio, where he died December 24, 1881; four children. 10. *Olivia Newkirk*, born October 20, 1820; married October 31, 1836 Peter Bolenbaugh, born March 6, 1816; died in Kosciusko County, Indiana, March 6, 1887; she died there December 17, 1900; nine children.

25. PETER 5 NEWKIRK (*Barent 4*, *Cornelis 3*, *Gerretse 2*, *Cornelisse 1*), born *circa* 1727, probably in Virginia; died intestate in Bullitt County, Kentucky, in 1804; appraisers being appointed at the September term of Court, in that year to evaluate his estate. The date of his settlement in Bullitt County is uncertain, but probably before 1796. With wife Cornelia

he conveyed, by deed of September 19, 1771, to Jacob Hoofman one hundred and six acres of land on the bank of the Potomac, in Orange County, Virginia, devised to him by his father, Barent Newkirk. He married Cornelia Sousley, who died in Bullitt County, *circa* 1805, and had nine children, doubtless born in Virginia.

Children of Peter and Cornelia (Sousley) Newkirk, order uncertain:

i. PETER [6], born *circa* 1765; "died December 6, 1833, aged sixty-eight years"; married January 2, 1792, Mary daughter of Thomas Stafford of Jefferson County, Kentucky. His will of December 4, 1833 probated February 3, 1834 named wife, Mary, and the children which follow. Issue: 1. *Thomas [7] S. Newkirk*, died before 1852, without issue. 2. *Pearson Newkirk*, died before 1852, without issue. 3. *Cassandra Newkirk*, married September 24, 1813, Samuel Applegate. 4. *William Newkirk*, married September 21, 1816, Sarah Applegate. 5. *Mary Newkirk*, married June 25, 1820, Levy Asher. 6. *Linea Newkirk*, married March 24, 1824, Robert Scott. 7. *Elizabeth Newkirk*, married June 4, 1829, John Kelly. 8. *Enoch Boone Newkirk*, married November 27, 1831, Frances Kelly. 9. *Kesiah Newkirk*, married March 11, 1834, Jonathan Brentlinger. 10. *Jemima Newkirk*, married December 18, 1834, Henry Bates. Mary (Stafford) Newkirk survived her husband, and in her will of October 2, 1848, proved May 9, 1849, named as beneficiaries: granddaughters, Mary Coston; Ellen, only daughter of William and Sarah Newkirk; Martha Ann, daughter of Robert and Linia Scott; Franky, daughter of John and Elizabeth Kelly; Martha Ann Young, only daughter of Enoch Boone and Frances Newkirk; Mary Katherine, only daughter of Henry and Jemima Bates; also Susannah, daughter of Jonathan and Kezia Brentlinger. Remainder of estate was devised to her son Thomas S. Newkirk.

ii. BENJAMIN, of Jefferson County, Kentucky, 1796, and of Lawrence County, Indiana, in 1807; may have married three times: (1) Mary Hawkins; (2) Alsey Sparks; 3. Elizabeth ———; had issue.

iii. RICHARD, had land in Bullitt County, 1805; later in Indiana.

iv. TOBIAS, married and had issue. Family tradition is responsible for the statement that he was "eldest son" and killed by the Indians in Kentucky. Issue: 1. *Peter [7] Newkirk*, born April, 1783. 2. *Henry Newkirk*. Both sons had descendants.

v. ISAAC, living in Lawrence County, Indiana, in 1841; had wife, Elizabeth Hall.

vi. TEUNIS, of Bullitt County, Kentucky in 1786, and as late as 1833; married Catharine Drake; descendants in Missouri.

vii. CHARLES, of Bullitt County, in 1828; had wife Camilla ———.

viii. WILLIAM, of Bullitt County; made his will September 13, 1840; proved November 9, 1840; named wife Rebecca; sons, *Asa H. Newkirk; Clifton H. Newkirk; Charles C. Newkirk; John H. Newkirk*; daughters *Louisa Hall Newkirk; Elizabeth Gentry, Mary Ann Hough*, wife of Austin Hough. In 1853 John H. Newkirk was of Jefferson County; Samuel C. Gentry and wife, Elizabeth, were of Henderson County; the others of Bullitt County, Kentucky.

ix. LOUISA, had land in Bullitt County, October 22, 1808.

26. Abraham [5] Nieukirk, (*Cornelius* [4], *Cornelis* [3], *Gerretse* [2], *Cornelisse* [1]), born in Salem County, New Jersey, June 8, 1722; died there in June, 1765. With his parents he was one of the organizers of the Pittsgrove, now Daretown, Presbyterian Church and is buried in its graveyard. He married first, December 23, 1745, Ann Richman; second June 23, 1762, Sarah S. Van Meter, who survived him and married William Robinson, 16 March, 1767. His descendants usually spelled their surname, Newkirk.

Children of Abraham and Ann (Richman) Nieukirk, born in Salem County:

i. Elizabeth [6], born November 3, 1746; died Salem County, December 9, 1794; married February 22, 1768, Ezekiel Rose, son of John and Mary Rose of Salem County, born December 9, 1794; was a Revolutionary soldier in Captain Jacob Du Bois' Company of Salem County militia. After the death of his wife, Elizabeth Newkirk, he married a widow, Charlotte Moore, by whom he had two daughters, and died in Union County, Indiana, December 5, 1824. Issue by first marriage: 1. *Uriah* [7] *Rose*, born January 18, 1770; died Union County, Indiana, October 18, 1839; married first, Rachel Du Bois, born October 22, 1765; died January 12, 1802, daughter of David Du Bois and wife, Elizabeth Newkirk, *q. v.*; married second, April 9, 1804, Tamson Garrison; four children by first marriage, ten by second: Elizabeth [8] Rose, born August 4, 1794; married John Sleesman; lived in Cincinnati, Ohio and had five children. Mary Rose, born September 9, 1796; married Ephraim Dunlap, lived in Cincinnati; four children. Anna Rose, born May 8, 1798; drowned in the Ohio River, in 1816. Ezekiel Rose, born September 11, 1800; died in Union County, Indiana, May 12, 1884; married February 5, 1830, Hannah Colson, born Salem County, June 12, 1807; died July 2, 1886; removed to Union County before July, 1831; nine children. 2. *Isaac Rose*, born January 29, 1771; died in young manhood. 3. *John Rose*, born August 28, 1774; was a school teacher and author of a small arithmetic text-book; married first, Ann Richman; second, Elizabeth (Rose) Harker, daughter of Abraham and Catherine (Robinson) Rose, born April 6, 1798; three children by first marriage born at Bridgeton, New Jersey; one by second marriage, born at Cincinnati: Fannie [8] Hampton Rose, born January 23, 1822; Joseph Mayhew Rose, born May 8, 1824; Martha Newell Rose, born November 30, 1827; Sarah Rebecca Rose, born March 22, 1838.

ii. Mary, born August 3, 1748; married January 2, 1772, William Thompson.

iii. Rebecca, born March 17, 1750; married Uriah Mayhew, born July 27, 1746; died in 1803; resided in Cumberland County, New Jersey. Issue, born in Cumberland County: 1. *Anna* [7] *Mayhew*. 2. *Elizabeth Mayhew*. 3. *Polly Mayhew*, married and had issue. 4. *Abraham Mayhew*, born May 16, 1788; died November 21, 1863. 5. *Israel Mayhew*. 6. *Ezekiel Mayhew*, married and had issue. 7. *Hannah Mayhew*. 8. *Thomas Mayhew*, married and had issue. 9. *Isaac Mayhew*, married and had issue.

iv. ISAAC [6], born November 29, 1753; died Salem County, June 2, 1802; married Ann Curry, born May 5, 1753; was revolutionary soldier in Captain Jacob Du Bois' Company, Salem County Minute Men, under enlistment of September 20, 1775.* Issue born in Salem County: 1. *Elizabeth* [7] *Newkirk*, born February 17, 1776. 2. *Abraham Newkirk*, born June 17, 1777. 3. *Martha Newkirk*, born December 9, 1778. 4. *Sarah Newkirk*, born October 18, 1780. 5. *Robinson Newkirk*, born August 29, 1782. 6. *William Newkirk*, born April 29, 1784. 7. *Isaac Newkirk*, born September 9, 1785. 8. *Jacob Newkirk*, both December 6, 1788. 9. *Rebecca Newkirk*, born September 10, 1789. 10. *Benjamin Newkirk*, born September 20, 1791. 11. *Ann Newkirk*, born June 6, 1793. 12. *Mary Newkirk*, born January 6, 1797.

v. JACOB, born April 27, 1763; died Salem County, November 19, 1826; married first, ———— Whitaker, daughter of David and Catherine Whitaker, who died in child-birth; married second, Phebe Thompson, born June 13, 1766, daughter of John and Mary Thompson. Issue, born in Salem County: 1. *Catherine* [7] *Newkirk*, born January 17, 1783. 2. *Sarah Newkirk*, born May 29, 1786. 3. *John Newkirk*, born March 2, 1789. 4. *William Newkirk*, born July 21, 1791. 5. *Mary Newkirk*, born September 26, 1793. 6. *Rebecca Newkirk*, born November 11, 1795. 7. *Abraham Newkirk*, born April 19, 1798. 8. *Isaac Newkirk*, born July 27, 1801. 9. *Jacob Newkirk*, born September 11, 1803. 10. *Phebe Newkirk*, born December 22, 1805; died young. 11. *Thompson Newkirk*, born April 14, 1806. 12. *Victor M. Newkirk*, born September 3, 1811.

vi. ANN, born November 28, 1764; died in Union County, Indiana, December 31, 1854; married Josiah Du Bois, born July 18, 1762, son of Rev. Jacob and Mary (Allegar) Du Bois. He died in Salem County, after which his widow Ann, and most of their children located in Fairfield, Franklin County, Indiana, where she died December 31, 1854. Issue, born in Salem County: 1. *Sarah* [7] *Du Boisi*, born May 8, 1788. 2. *Mary Du Bois*, born December 16, 1790. 3. *Abraham Du Bois*, born January 9, 1792. 4. *Ann Du Bois*, born August 1, 1793. 5. *Abigail Du Bois*, born May 15, 1795. 6. *Rebecca Du Bois*, born March 6, 1796; died in Franklin County, Indiana, February 4, 1880; married William S. Rose, born Salem County, New Jersey, November 25, 1791; died Franklin County, February 1, 1876; ten children. 7. *Elizabeth Du Bois*, born April 16, 1804. 8. *Phebe Du Bois*, born May 8, 1807. 9. *Josiah Du Bois*, died young. 10. *Eleazer Du Bois*, died young.

27. GARRET [5] NIEUKIRK (*Cornelius* [4], *Cornelis* [3], *Gerretse* [2], *Cornelisse* [1]), was born in Pilesgrove, later Pittsgrove, Salem County, New Jersey, March 23, 1726, and died there September 9, 1786, leaving a will, executed a month previous to his decease, which mentions all his children. Like many of his family and neighbors he was faithful to the Revolutionary cause and served for a time in the Commissary General's Department.

---

* *Muster Roll of Minute Men of Pittsgrove, Salem County, New Jersey,* this volume, page 33.

He married May 16, 1753, Elizabeth Du Bois, born April 10, 1730; died January 6, 1785, daughter of Louis Du Bois and wife, Margaret Jansen and grand daughter of Jacob and Gerretje (Nieuwkirk) Du Bois, q. v. Both husband and wife are buried in the old Churchyard at Daretown. Their homestead, a spacious mansion at Pittsgrove, withstood, substantially unchanged, the ravages of time for more than a century.

Children of Garret and Elizabeth (Du Bois) Nieukirk, born at Pittsgrove:

i. ELIZABETH [6], born May 1, 1754; married August 8, 1774 Robert Patterson.

ii. CORNELIUS, born November 24, 1756; died Pittsgrove, Salem County, November 16, 1823; married March 19, 1776, Abigail Hanna, born March 3, 1757; died November 20, 1802. He enlisted as private in Captain Jacob Du Bois Company of Minute Men, September 10, 1775, and his name appears in subsequent muster-rolls. Issue, born in Salem County usually wrote their surname, Newkirk: 1. *Ann* [7] *Newkirk*, born October 24, 1777; married William Wallace. 2. *Elizabeth Newkirk*, born August 8, 1779; married Constant Woodman. 3. *Margaret Newkirk*, born August 25, 1781; married Hosbel Shull. 4. *Garrett Newkirk*, born August 10, 1783; married December 4, 1803, Catherine Elwell; five children, three of whom died young; of the others, CAROLINE [8] E. NEWKIRK, married Isaac Smith of Philadelphia; MARGARET S. NEWKIRK, married Samuel Hibler of Philadelphia. 5. *Mary H. Newkirk*, born November 24, 1786; married John M. Taber. 6. *Samuel Newkirk*, born January 12, 1788; died 1823; married and had issue; his son, Matthew [8] Newkirk, merchant of Newark, Ohio, was Ruling Elder in the Presbyterian Church of that place. 7. *Sarah Newkirk*, born June 25, 1791. 8. *Matthew Newkirk*, born May 31, 1794; died in Philadelphia May 31, 1868, on his seventy-fourth birthday. He began mercantile life in Philadelphia in 1810; enlisted for service in the War of 1812, First Company Washington Guards, First Brigade, First Division, Pennsylvania Militia; engaged in business in 1821, under the firm named of Newkirk & Heberton, at 95 Market Street and by assiduity and prudence retired with a competence in 1839,* and was thereby able to generally devote himself to public, charitable and religious affairs. He was a director in the United States Bank; first president of the Philadelphia, Wilmington and Baltimore Railroad, now part of the Pennsylvania system and in testimony of his fruitful and wise administration of the latter † a marble monument was erected on the line of the road at Gray's Ferry, on the west bank of the Schuylkill River below Philadelphia. Long connected with the Little Schuylkill Navigation Company,

---

* His residence at the southwest corner of Thirteenth and Arch Streets, built in 1836, is claimed to have been the first private house in which gas was introduced throughout.

† To the construction of the whole line of the Philadelphia, Wilmington and Baltimore Railroad Mr. Newkirk lent his best energies. The present system of baggage checking is said to owe its *original suggestion* to him, and he was partly responsible for the origination of express service.

he devoted himself to the development of the resources of the land in Schuylkill County and to the advancement of the social and religious life of the colliers at Tamaqua. Mainly through his exertions in 1854, funds for the re-operation of the Cambria Iron Company at Johnstown, Pennsylvania were secured and its future assured. He was a member of the Committee of Philadelphia Select Council to erect Girard College; a contributor of money and real estate to the establishment of Fairmount Park; for thirty-four years an active Trustee of the College of New Jersey, now Princeton; president of the Female Medical College of Philadelphia; a large contributor to Lafayette College, and to the State Polytechnic College, of which latter he was for a time the president. He was aso president of Pennsylvania State Temperance Society; an Elder of the Central Presbyterian Church of Philadelphia and a Trustee of The General Assembly of the Presbyterian Church from 1833 until his death, and treasurer thereof from 1838 to 1850. On May 1, 1817, he married Jane Reese Stroud who died in 1819, without issue; he married second, July 2, 1821, Margaret Heberton, daughter of George Heberton, Esq., of Philadelphia, who was the mother of all his children and who died November 28, 1841. In July, 1846, he married Hetty M., daughter of Edward Smith of Philadelphia, who survived him. Issue: four children who died young and the following: 1. GEORGE 8 HEBERTON NEWKIRK, died September 22, 1861. 2. MARY JANE NEWKIRK, married William Henry Oliver of New York; died October 31, 1861. 3. WILLIAM HENRY NEWKIRK, died March 11, 1864. 4. MATTHEW NEWKIRK, JR., a clergyman of the Presbyterian Church, settled in Philadelphia, and author of *A Memorial of Matthew Newkirk* *

ix. *Hannah Newkirk*, born February 17, 1798; married June 6, 1816 Peter Du Bois, born July 24, 1789; died March 14, 1876; son of Thomas and Sarah (Foster) Du Bois.

iii. JOHN 6, born July 18, 1759; married Susanna Hurst; Revolutionary soldier, in Captain Cornelius Nieukirk's Company; died Pittsgrove; will dated February 23, 1784; proved June 2, 1784, named wife and infant children. Issue: 1. *Mary 7 Newkirk*, died young. 2. *John Newkirk*, died unmarried.

iv. MARGARET, born February 17, 1762; married Jesse Rambo. Issue: *Catherine 7 Rambo.*

v. SARAH, born June 1, 1765; died December 7, 1828; married David Vanmeter, born July 17, 1761; died November 25, 1816. Issue: 1. *Amy 7 Vanmeter*, born February 16, 1785; 2. *Elizabeth Vanmeter*, born July 16, 1788. 3. *Ephraim Vanmeter*, born May 16, 1791. 4. *Rebecca Vanmeter*, born May 8, 1796; married Benjamin Newkirk. 5. *Margaret Vanmeter*, born June 4, 1801.

vi. MATTHEW, born March 22, 1769; died January 7, 1820; married first, Mary, daughter of Benjamin and Bathsheba (Dunlap) Van Meter, who died July 7, 1802; married second, March 5, 1803, Rebecca Mayhew, who died September 11, 1809, aged twenty-five years; married third, Elizabeth, daughter of Jonathan Foster. Issue, born in Salem County, four by first marriage, three by third: 1. *Elizabeth 7 Newkirk*, born September 9, 1789; married ——— Essinger; removed to Pennsylvania; had issue. 2. *Bathsheba Newkirk*, born November 25, 1792; died June, 1861; married Judge Jeremiah Stull, born November 6, 1791; died October

* *A Memorial of Matthew Newkirk.* Prepared by his only surviving son, Matthew Newkirk, Jr. Printed for Private Circulation, 8vo., p. 122, por. Philadelphia, 1869.

19, 1854, son of John and Mary Stull; both buried at Centerton, New Jersey; four children, born in Salem County. 3. *Ann* [7] *Newkirk*, born March 7, 1795; died March 16, 1831; married first, Henry Van Meter; married second, James S. Caruthers, born March 20, 1782; died January 17, 1840; one child by first marriage; six by second, all born in Salem County. 4. *Sarah Newkirk*, born May 14, 1800; married November 3, 1821, Nicholas Olmstead; eight children born in Salem County. 5. *Matthew Newkirk*, born March 8, 1814; died Newark, Ohio, December 22, 1887; married at Cincinnati, March 2, 1837, Nancy Miller, St.Clair; six children, of whom three died young. 6. *Nathaniel Reeve Newkirk*, born July 22, 1817; was a physician at Bridgeton, New Jersey, where he died November 11, 1866; married December 5, 1856, Martha Reeve Bacon, born January 29, 1826; died July 22, 1909; daughter of John and Ann (Hall) Bacon of Salem County; six children, born in Cumberland County: ELIZABETH [8] THOMPSON NEWKIRK, born September 25, 1857; died young. JOHN BACON NEWKIRK, born March 6, 1859; married December 1, 1915, Mary Chapman Borton of Moorestown, New Jersey; no issue. MATTHEW NEWKIRK, born July 16, 1860; died young. ANNA BACON NEWKIRK, born January 7, 1862; died young. HORATIO WOOD NEWKIRK, born February 4, 1863; died young. ISAAC ROBERTS NEWKIRK, born March 22, 1865; resides in Philadelphia; married March 12, 1899, Mary Louisa Maris, born April 11, 1866; died October 14, 1924. Issue: i. *Louisa* [9] *Maris Newkirk*, born January 23, 1901; married December 12, 1929, William Hill Steeble of Chestnut Hill, Philadelphia. ii. *Martha Bacon Newkirk*, born January 23, 1904. 7. *Mary* [7] *Elizabeth Newkirk*, born August 26, 1819; died unmarried July 6, 1884.

28. CORNELIUS [5] NIEUKIRK (*Cornelius* [4], *Cornelis* [3], *Gerretse* [2], *Cornelisse* [1]), born in Pilesgrove, now Pittsgrove, Salem County, New Jersey, September 2, 1783, and died there, November 8, 1795. He was buried in the Presbyterian Church yard at Daretown, where repose his parents and many of his kinsfolk, and where the inscription on his gravestone reads:

Here lie the Remains / of Colonel / Cornelius Nieukirk. / Who departed this Life / November 8th 1795 / in the 61 year of his age. / He filled the various offices / of Life with general esteem. /

My Wife my Friends and Children dear
Reflect on me without a tear:
But when you think of my cold Grave,
Remember him who dy'd to save,
Attend the means which God hath giv'n
To pardon Sin and give you Heav'n.

Hoc-momento Eternitas pependit.

A good citizen and ardent patriot he was in service in the Revolution as Captain, Second Regiment, Salem County, New Jersey Militia, prior to December 13, 1776; was with other militia troops at Mt. Holly at the time of the Battle of Princeton; served at Gloucester under Colonel Benjamin Holme,

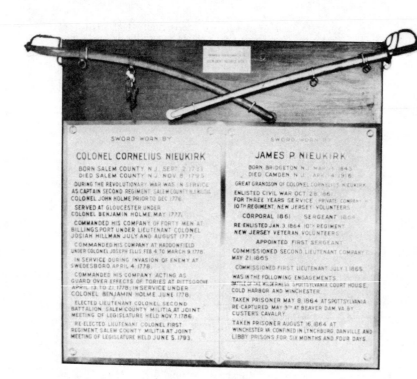

REVOLUTIONARY AND CIVIL WAR SWORDS

Presented by descendants of respective owners to The Historical
Society of Salem County, New Jersey

May 1777; commanded his Company of forty men at Billingsport, under Lieut. Col. Josiah Hillman, July and August 1777, and probably saw General Washington when he visited the fortification, August 1, of that year; in service October 1777; the Class Rolls of his Company, dated October 25, are given on succeeding pages, as is the pay-roll of his Company at Haddonfield; commanded his Company at Haddonfield under Colonel Jacob Ellis, February 4, to March 9, 1778; in service March 18, 1778; and during invasion of enemy at Swedesboro, April 4, 1778; commanded his Company which acted as guard over effects of Tories at Pittsgrove, April 13 to 21, 1778; in service June, 1778; and in July, 1778.* Without doubt he saw later service. His military sword, worn during the Revolution, and that of his great-grandson, James P. Nieukirk of the Civil War, have been presented to the Salem County Historical Society. See photographic reproduction on opposite page.

Records in the Adjutant General's Office at Trenton show that he was commissioned Lieutenant-Colonel of Second Battalion of Salem County Militia, November 7, 1786; commissioned Lieutenant-Colonel of First Salem Regiment, June 5, 1793, and resigned as Lieutenant-Colonel of Fourth Salem Regiment of Militia, November 6, 1794.†

Colonel Cornelius Nieukirk and his brother, Matthew, were signatories to the Salem County petition of 1787, favoring the ratification of the Federal Constitution by the State of New Jersey.

His will of October 16, 1795; probated June 17, 1796 disposed of a considerable estate. He married October 19, 1758, Mary, daughter of Joast ‡ and Christiana Miller of Salem County, who is buried beside her husband in the Daretown Presbyterian Churchyard. Her gravestone bears the inscription: In / memory of / Mary widow / of Col. Cornelius Nieukirk / who departed this life / August 6th, 1806 / In the 67th year of her age.

---

* *Salem County in the Revolution*, by Frank H. Stewart.

† Letter from Adjutant General R. Heber Breintnall, under date of July 23, 1906, to Adamson B. Newkirk of Los Angeles, California.

‡ Joast Miller, died in 1771, leaving wife Christiana, and children Henry, Mary, Catherine, Rachel, Rebecca, Abraham and William.—*New Jersey Archives*, vol. xxxiv, p. 349.

Children of Colonel Cornelius and Mary (Miller) Nieukirk, all born at Pittsgrove:

    i. GARRET [6], named first in his father's will; probably not eldest child; is thought to have married Catherine Elwell of Pittsgrove, December 4, 1802.

    ii. RACHEL, born August 4, 1759, married first, October 24, 1778, William Elwell, who died April 14, 1788; leaving son, *Samuel*[7] *Elwell*, named in will of his grandfather, Colonel Cornelius Nieukirk in 1795. Rachel (Nieukirk) Elwell married second, before October 16, 1795, Levi Elwell, whose will, dated November 11, 1807, probated the following year, names the children which follow and wife Rachel. Issue: *Isaac*[7] *Elwell*, married in Salem County, April 6, 1811, Elizabeth Rose. 2. *Joast Elwell*. 3. *Matthew Elwell*. 4. *Dorothy Elwell*. 5. *Elizabeth Elwell* married March 19, 1822, David Du Bois; lived in Franklin County, Ohio.

    iii. JOAST, born 6 March, 1761; died August 22, 1825; married Sarah Ayers, born January 9, 1762; died November 1, 1821. Revolutionary soldier: private in Captain Cornelius Nieukirk's Company, October 20, 1777 to March 9, 1778; was commissioned Lieutenant in Salem County Militia under date of May 20, 1800. Issue, born at Pittsgrove: 1. *Jacob*[7] *Newkirk*, born December 13, 1781. 2. *Joseph Newkirk*, born August 20, 1783. 3. *Susannah Newkirk*, born September 13, 1785. 4. *Rebecca Newkirk*, born June 14, 1788; died unmarried, October 28, 1813. 5. *Sarah Newkirk*, born March 30, 1790. 6. *Cornelius M. Newkirk*, born June 26, 1792; died May 4, 1874; married February 11, 1815, Michal Du Bois, born April 20, 1789; died June 30, 1864; daughter of Isaac and Elizabeth (Burroughs) Du Bois, *q. v.* 7. *Mary Newkirk*, born May 1, 1793; died June 9, 1794.

    iv. MATTHEW, born February 7, 1764 *; died September 27, 1823; Commissioned Second Lieutenant in Salem County Militia, October 11, 1799, and promoted to First Lieutenant, September 13, 1800; married December 18, 1785, Catherine Burroughs, born November 26, 1767; died April 28, 1828. Issue, born in Salem County: 1. *Rachel*[7] *Newkirk*, born March 4, 1787. 2. *Hannah Newkirk*, born August 22, 1789. 3. *Christiana Newkirk*, born August 17, 1791. 4. *Benjamin Newkirk*, born December, 1794.

    v. CHRISTIANA, born January 21, 1765; † died January 1, 1833, buried in Daretown Churchyard; married April 16, 1809, William Lippincott; who pre-deceased her.

    vi. ABRAHAM, born June 4, 1768; died in Muskingum County, Ohio, in 1843; married October 5, 1807, Grace Loper, daughter of William and Elizabeth Loper. After the death of Abraham Newkirk his widow and family located near Mt. Carmel, Illinois. Issue, born in Salem County: 1. *William*[7] *Newkirk*, born August 21, 1809; died near Mt. Carmel, June 4, 1877; was a physician; married March 11, 1832, Sarah Crooks in Muskingum County, where his five children were born. 2. *Hugh Newkirk*, born May 25, 1813; died near Mt. Carmel, June 6, 1848; married Theresa Herr and had five children. 3. *Zachariah Newkirk*, born June 15, 1816; died near Mt. Carmel, November 6, 1863; married first, Covilla Heggens;

---

* Another date given as February 28, 1763.

† Another date, January 22, 1764.

second, Eliza Ann Greathouse. Issue, two children by first, seven by second marriage, all born in Wabash County, Illinois.

vii. REBECCA 6, born August 3, 1771; died August 23, 1779.

viii. ANDREW, born August 2, 1773; died January 2, 1850; married May 3, 1795, Tryphenia Fish, born April 11, 1776; died September 10, 1848. Issue, all born in Salem County: 1. *William 7 Nieukirk*, born January 29, 1797; died November 4, 1874; married first, March 20, 1824, Christianna Hitchner, who died October 11, 1851; second, Rebecca Fisher. No issue. 2. *Enoch Nieukirk*, born June 21, 1799; died in Salem County; married first, April 5, 1823, Lydia Hutchinson, born July 2, 1798; died February 3, 1828; married second, April 12, 1833, Susannah Ayars, born September 11, 1797; died October 26, 1851, daughter of John C. Ayars and wife Mary Sparks; married third, March 25, 1852, Ann Abbott, born September 24, 1816; died April 3, 1902, daughter of Joel and Susan Abbott; six children two by first marriage, one by second, three by third. 3. *Lydia Nieukirk*, born October 11, 1801; died January 28, 1802. 4. *John Nieukirk*, born December 26, 1802; died September 28, 1882, in Salem County; married first, Sarah Ann Elwell, born August 17, 1805; died February, 1857; married second, Hannah Moore; two daughters by first marriage. 5. *Rebecca Nieukirk*, born June 3, 1805; died unmarried, December 29, 1874. 6. *Edmund Nieukirk*, born September 23, 1807; died October 12, 1885; married October 11, 1834, Lydia Elwell, born February 13, 1816; died February 6, 1871; of their five children, a son, WILLIAM 8 NIEUKIRK, born March 19, 1839 alone survived; he married Hannah J. Cassiday; lived in Salem County; raised a large family, and died June 28, 1898. 7. *Eliza Nieukirk*, born August 11, 1812; died unmarried April 20, 1832. 8. *Israel F. Nieukirk*, born August 13, 1815; died May 22, 1847; married Temperance Anderson; one child: ANDREW A. NEWKIRK, born December 9, 1835; died unmarried March 1, 1883.

30. ix. CORNELIUS, married Mary Reed.

x. ELIZABETH, born March 21, 1777; married November 8, 1796, John Cade; they located in Gloucester County, New Jersey, where he died in 1850. No issue.

xi. BENJAMIN, born October 4, 1780; died November 15, 1827; married November 14, 1806, Elizabeth Elwell, born October 15, 1783; died September 7, 1867; both buried in iron-fenced enclosure in Daretown Presbyterian Churchyard. No issue.

xii. MARY, born January 1, 1783; died June 8, 1786.

xiii. JOHN, born August 28, 1785; died unmarried July 8, 1806.

COLONEL NIEUKIRK'S PITTSGROVE MILITIA CLASS ROLLS.

"Class Rolls of Capt. Cornelius Nieukirk's Company, Salem County Foot Militia, October 20, 1777."

Cornelius Nieukirk, Capt.
David Sithen, 1st Lieut.
Abraham Elwell, 2nd Lieut.
Joel Alderman, Ensign

CLASS 1

William Richman, Sergeant

Benj. Shores	Edward Hughes
John Reed, Sr.	John Nelson, Sr.
John Murphy	James Garrat
John Simmons	John Nixon
William Hampton	

CLASS 2

William Aarons, Corporal

Isaac Richman	Neh. Richman
Abraham Elwell, Jr.	Samuel Goslin
William Loper	

CLASS 3

Thomas Harding, Sergeant

Benj. Brown	Wm. Gentry
William Elwell	Enoch Moore
Thomas Harris	Wm. Alderman
Samuel Elwell	Chris. Van Zant

CLASS 4

Abraham Nelson	Thomas Elwell
Samuel Mayhew	Richard Graham
F'k Dindlesbecks	Henry Richman
Joshua Lacy	Alexander Elwell

CLASS 5

John Combs, Sergeant

John Reed, Jr.	John Nelson
James Stratton	Isaac Garrison
Joseph Johnson	William Shird
Joshua Clark	Joseph Nelson
John Richman	

CLASS 6

James Odair	William Coon
David Mayhew	Henry Pawlin
John Cindle	Moses Doty
Thos. Pearson	John Mayhew
John Rutter	Obadiah Crothers
(or Butler)	

CLASS 7

Robert Patterson	Uriah Biggs
Jonathan Elwell	Benj. Harding
Garret Aarons	John Jordan
Jesse Rambo	Daniel Goolder

CLASS 8

Robert Ayres, Corporal

Joseph Nelson	John McCalshinder
Frederick Garrison	(Mac Altioner)
Cornelius Trimnel	Samuel Nelson
Moses Richman	David Nelson
Michael Money	Davis Nelson
Ananias Clark	Joast Nieukirk
Thomas Sparks	George Nixon
Hugh McGuire	Calvin Gamble
James McGuire	Thomas Hewitt
Peter Bateman	William Pounder
David Moore	Amariah Elwell
John Johnson	Robert Wible
Andrew Lock	Judah Foster
John Keen	James Stratton
	Daniel Nelson

For some reason, probably because they were not ordered out, or were absent at the time, the following names are crossed off the various classes: *

---

* Courtesy of Frank H. Stewart, *Salem County in the Revolution.*

CLASS 2

Hugh Cowperthwait
John Garman
Joshua Combs

Thos. Hutchinson
Samuel Mayhew
Joseph Casson

CLASS 3

Joseph Garrison

John Hewitt

CLASS 4

David Cake, Corporal

Abraham Graham

David Sayre

CLASS 5

Moses Atkinson

Amariah Elwell

Joseph Cindle

CLASS 6

John Hutchinson

CLASS 7

Asa Pownder

William Smith

James Murphy

CLASS 8

Jonathan Thurston
Daniel Nelson
Cornelius Austin

John Garrison
Thomas Poarch
Artis Seagrave

Ananias Nelson

PAY ROLL AND AMMUNITION DISTRIBUTION.

A pay roll of Capt. Cornelius Nieukirk's Company of Foot Militia in Col. Benj. Holme's Battalion for the County of Salem under ye command of Col. Joseph Ellis in Haddonfield, March ye 7th, 1778.

Cornelius Nieukirk, Captain
David Sithen, Lieut.
Joel Alderman, Ensign
Solomon Smith, Sergeant
Isaac Garrison, Sergeant
George Dixon, Sergeant
Robert Ayres, Sergeant
Thomas Parker, Corporal
Adam Louderback, Corporal
John Dunlap, Corporal
Daniel Jarman, Corporal
Walter Harris, Drummer
Even Elwell, Fifer

PRIVATES

Garret Aarons
Uriah Biggs
Joseph Bateman
Ridgway Cook
Peter Danford
Jonathan Elwell
James English
Jacob Elwell
John Ford
Ezekiel Garrison
William Graham
Calvin Gamble

Richard McCaney
Israel Moore
Daniel Murphy
George Martin
Charles McHenry
David Nelson
Joast Nieukirk
Jacob Nelson
Davis Nelson
Asa Pownder
Jesse Rambo
Moses Richman

Benjamin Harding
Conrod Hires
John Jordan
Azariah Jarman
Jackonias Lloyd
Math. Lowderback
Giles Loverin
John Linsey
Michael Money
Samuel Mayhew
John McCoy

Jacob Richey
James Sims
Jacob Sayres
John Stull
Joseph Straughn
William Smith
Jeremiah Sutton
Lewis Thompson
Adam Woldrick
Benj. Weatherby
Thomas Adams

Nearly all of the above soldiers enlisted on February 4, 1778. Eight of them enlisted between that date and February 15th. They were discharged March 9th, 1778. Jacob Elwell and William Smith left.

Account of ammunition given out, Haddonfield, Feby. ye 6, 1778, to companies of:

Capt. Nieukirk
Capt. Haywood
Capt. Dickinson
Capt. Sparks
Capt. Kelley

CAPTAIN NIEUKIRK'S COMPANY

Cornelius Nieukirk—5 cartridges
David Sithin, 1st Lieut.
Abraham Elwell, 2nd Lieut.
Joel Alderman, Ensign—5 cartridges
Robert Patterson—5 cartridges
Jona   n Elwell—5 cartridges
A   Pou...er—5 cartridges
W:'''am Smith—5 cartridges
Evin Elwell, Fifer
Walter Harris, Drummer
Uriah Biggs—5 cartridges
Benjamin Harding—5 cartridges
John Jorden—5 cartridges and a gun
Thomas Mason—5 cartridges
Robert Ayres, Corporal—5 cartridges
Samuel Nelson
David Nelson—5 cartridges
Davis Nelson—5 cartridges
Joost Nieukirk—5 cartridges
Michael Money—a gun *

---

* Courtesy of Frank H. Stewart, *Salem County in the Revolution.*

SIXTH GENERATION

29. ABRAHAM [6] NEWKIRK (*Abraham* [5], *Barent* [4], *Cornelis* [3], *Gerretse* [2], *Cornelisse*) was born in Berkeley County, Virginia, March 10, 1764. With his father and others of his family he left Virginia and located in Washington County, Pennsylvania. Here in 1786, he purchased from his cousin, Henry Newkirk, a tract of land containing 413 acres, adjoining the town of Bentleyville, known as *The Legacy,* and this was the birthplace of all his children.

On March 28, 1816, he sold all his holdings in this tract and on April 15, 1817, purchased a farm of 110 acres on Brush Creek, Adams County, Ohio, a few miles west of Dunkinsville, on which he continued to reside until his death October 5, 1840. He donated a church lot and burying ground on one corner of his land, which is now known as Hull Church, and with his wife, Margaret, he is here buried, as are some of his children and descendants.

He married first in 1785, Margaret Knox, who died July 8, 1823, and second, Marcia Stewart who survived him.

Children of Abraham and Margaret (Knox) Newkirk:

    i. HANNAH [7], born May 6, 1787; died September 18, 1864; married as second wife John Hull, born November 17, 1782; died November 22, 1865; lived at Dunkinsville, Ohio, and both were buried in Hull Churchyard. Issue, the first six born in Washington County, Pennsylvania, the last two at Dunkinsville: 1. *Newkirk* [8] *Hull,* born November 24, 1806; died September 21, 1884; married Miriam Freeland; lived at Dunkinsville; no issue. 2. *Abraham Hull,* born August 3, 1809; died December 3, 1868; married May 15, 1830, Eliza Gilpin; lived near Dunkinsville; nine children. 3. *Cyrus Hull,* born October 6, 1811; died in Grant County, Indiana, November, 1894; married Anna Jones; five children. 4. *Josiah Hull,* born August 6, 1813; died in Adams County, Ohio, October 6, 1875; married in 1835, Charlotte Jones, born September 19, 1816; died February 17, 1874; buried in Hull Churchyard; five children. 5. *Lorinda Hull,* born November 12, 1815; married December 9, 1834, John Kees; lived in Adams County, Ohio, and Brown County, Illinois; five children. 6. *Margaret Hull,* born January 10, 1817; died August 11, 1863; married Andrew Mahaffy; lived in Adams County, Ohio, and Brown County, Illinois. 7. *Orpha Hull,* born November 26, 1819; died Brown County, June 15, 1888; married August 17, 1840, Arthur Smith, born Adams County, Ohio, January 3, 1817; died November 15, 1885, in Brown County, Illinois; seven children. 8. *George Washington Hull,* born January 3, 1823; died Ashland, Kentucky, April 13, 1893; married Frances Dale Russell, born Stouts, Ohio, June 14, 1817; died August 4, 1886; one daughter.

(57)

31. ii. HENRY [7], married Hannah Bentley.

   iii. ANNA, born June 1, 1792; married John B. Clary; lived in Cass County, Indiana, and died there August 29, 1839. Issue, the first, born in Darke County, Ohio, the remainder in Rush County, Indiana: 1. *Isaac* [8] *N. Clary*, born January 28, 1819; married December 7, 1843, Rebecca Remley; lived in Cass County, where he died October 5, 1899; nine children. 2. *Margaret Clary*, born August 17, 1820; married William Michael; lived and died at Logansport, Indiana; two children. 3. *John C. Clary*, born September 18, 1826; married first, 8 October, 1847, Susannah Foy, who died February 24, 1863; married second, 14 July, 1863, Narcissa W. Dunham; she died March 17, 1898, and he married third, Susannah Ballenger; lived at Logansport, of his nine children four died young. 4. *Rachel A. Clary*, born January 18, 1826; married in September, 1846, Thornley Michael; lived in Cass County and there died, March 6, 1905; five children. 5. *William D. Clary*, born May 12, 1828; married December 2, 1852, Elizabeth J. Worl; was living at Lucerne, Indiana, in 1877, with wife and nine children.

   iv. ORPHA, born July 15, 1794; married John Dunkin; moved to Memphis, Missouri, and there died in October, 1851. Issue, born in Adams County, Ohio: 1. *Harkless* [8] *Dunkin*, born May 9, 1816; married Lydia Matthews; lived at Dunkinsville, Ohio where she died October 19, 1877; five children. 2. *Henry Dunkin*, born January 8, 1818; married Virginia Sproule; lived in Dunkinsville; later in Memphis, and in Lee County, Iowa, where he died May 6, 1882; eight children, the youngest born in Lee County. 3. *Margaret Dunkin*, born August 1, 1820; married William Wittenmeyer; lived at Dunkinsville; buried with her three children at Jacksonburg, Ohio. 4. *John Dunkin*, born April 30, 1825; married first, September 7, 1847, Esther Jones; second October 30, 1858, Elizabeth Hilt; died at Browing, Missouri, February 15, 1884; ten children. 5. *Sarah J. Dunkin*, born August 20, 1832; married first March 5, 1851, Dr. George William Mason, born July 16, 1824; died at Tipton, Missouri, April 10, 1865; she married second, September 15, 1868, Rev. E. J. Keplinger, who died November 17, 1898; she lived the latter part of her life at Pueblo, California, and died there July 2, 1911; two children survived infancy. 6. *Joshua Dunkin*, born October 5, 1835; married November 16, 1853, his cousin Anna Fear, born December 21, 1833, *q. v.* who survived him; he died at Powersville, Missouri; eight children, three died young.

   v. NANCY, born October 3, 1796; married June 10, 1819, Dr. Peter Fear, born September 29, 1795; died June 7, 1855; lived in Adams County, Ohio, where she died October 24, 1850. Issue: 1. *Maria* [8] *Fear*, born February 22, 1820; married September 23, 1837, Charles Thurman, born February 22, 1812; died in 1890; resided in Adams County; nine children. 2. *Margaret Fear*, born August 2, 1822; married George William Phillips, born February 16, 1818; died at West Union, Ohio, March 15, 1874; she died March 4, 1882, at Bahalia, Ohio; seven children. 3. *Francis Fear*, born December 11, 1824; married first, at Winchester, Ohio, January 29, 1851 Mary Ellen Sparks; married second, October 31, 1865, Martha Rawlings; he died at Waverly, Kansas, April 28, 1902; nine children, seven by first marriage, two by second. 4. *Orpha Fear*, born February 11, 1827; married Samuel Mahaffey; removed to a North Western State. 5. *Cyrus Fear*, born September 26, 1829; died young. 6. *John F. Fear*, born October 7, 1831; died young. 7. *Anna Fear*, born December 21, 1833; married her cousin Joshua

Dunkin, *q. v.* 8. *Matilda Fear*, born January 6, 1836; married May 27, 1857, Samuel H. Beard, lived at West Union, Ohio; six children. 9. *William Fear*, born March 18, 1838; died young.

vi. JOHN [7], born March 17, 1799; married Sarah Walmsley, moved with his father to Adams County, Ohio; located later in Rush County, Indiana, and in 1855 in Tipton County, Indiana, where he died. Issue, born in Rush County: 1. *Elizabeth* [8] *Newkirk*, born May 30, 1825; married first, October 31, 1839, Wesley P. David; married second, August 24, 1874, James Morris, and died March 30, 1895; lived in Rush County; of her ten children, surnamed David, five died young, or unmarried. 2. *Emily A. Newkirk*, born October 1, 1827; married December 21, 1844, John P. Simmonds, and died in Tipton County, June 3, 1870; six children. 3. *Leah Newkirk*, born May 6, 1831; married Thomas Cochran; lived in Tipton County, and there died August 8, 1905; eight children. 4. *James Ross Newkirk*, born March 5, 1832; married March 19, 1856, Melissa A. Hasket; died after birth of youngest child, June 22, 1877; lived near Tipton, Indiana; ten children. 5. *Margaret A. Newkirk*, born June 3, 1837; married February 17, 1859, John Wesley Tichenor; lived in Tipton County; five children. 6. *Christopher C. Newkirk*, born September 24, 1838; married first, November 2, 1865, Sarah Walmsley; married second, March, 1872, Susan C. Eiler; lived in Tipton County, and there died February 10, 1904; three children, two by first marriage. 7. *John W. Newkirk*, born April 5, 1840; killed in the Civil War, 1862. 8. *Jonathan H. Newkirk*, born March 2, 1843; married October 6, 1867, Nancy A. Moody; lived at Frankton, Tipton County; two of his three children died young. 9. *Holliday S. Newkirk*, born January 25, 1847; married July 3, 1869, Frances Houchins; resided at Mapleton, Iowa; four children.

vii. KEZIAH, born August 8, 1801; died February, 1884; married Amos Dunkin; lived in Adams County, Ohio. Issue: 1. *Abraham* [8] *Dunkin*, born September 26, 1824; died Bentonville, Ohio, April 23, 1898; married February 3, 1853, Martha Ann Downing; eight children. 2. *Hercules Dunkin*, born April 11, 1826; married Damaris Sample; lived at Bentonville, there died; five children. 3. *Sarah Dunkin*, born March 11, 1828; married first, March, 1849, Benjamin F. Howell; second, December 28, 1858, John Lawill, lived at Cherry Fork, Ohio; two children, surname Howell. 4. *Emma Dunkin*, born April 11, 1830; married ———— Myers; lived at Bentonville; died without issue, August 6, 1855. 5. *Jane Dunkin*, born February 7, 1832; married December 31, 1854, George H. Darling, born at West Liberty, West Virginia, May 7, 1833; lived at West Union, Ohio, where he died January 10, 1895, and she March 30, 1901; five children. 6. *Margaret Dunkin*, born April 24, 1834; married first, in March, 1859, Marcus Hawk, who died October 29, 1884; married second, George Roush; lived at Russell, Brown County, Ohio; four children, surname Hawk. 7. *Reason Dunkin*, born July 31, 1836; married in 1857, Frances Lawill; died without issue at his home, near Bentonville, Adams County.

viii. SHIPMAN, born April 25, 1805; married Mary Bayless; born June 5, 1808; died March 5, 1873, daughter of Daniel Bayless * lived in Rush County, Indiana; died August

---

* *Vide Genealogy and History of the Newkirk, Hamilton and Bayless Families.* By Thomas J. Newkirk, Evanston, Illinois, 1916, sm. quarto, 88 pp. por.

31, 1874. Issue: 1. *Daniel* [8] *Bayless Newkirk*, born January 1, 1825; married August 3, 1845, Polly Hamilton, born January 1, 1829; lived in Madison County, Indiana, until 1869; appointed Justice of the Peace, November 1, 1855; was Captain of Company M, Second Regiment, 11th Military District of Indiana, under commission of July 18, 1854; removed to Rush County, where he died December 3, 1903; and his widow April 29, 1911; six children; one of whom was THOMAS [9] JEFFERSON NEWKIRK, Esq., born in Madison County, Indiana, October 30, 1854; died at Daytona, Florida, December 27, 1919; lawyer, and author of the *Genealogy and History of the Newkirk, Hamilton, and Bayless Families*, and collaborator with Dr. Adamson Bentley Newkirk in an enlarged history of the Newkirk family and affiliates; a tireless worker and of more than usual ability. 2. *Mary Newkirk*, born June 12, 1829; married February 14, 1850, Joseph Kiser; lived at Sexton, Indiana; she died November 16, 1912; eight children of whom three died young. 3. *Sarah J. Newkirk*, born December 11, 1830; married July 3, 1845 Aaron Walker, lived in Rush County she died, 1848; one surviving daughter. **4.** *William Riley Newkirk*, born January 1, 1837; married first, August 20, 1855; Polly Ann Cross; married second, October 21, 1875, Rebecca Daugherty; lived in Rush County; three children. 5. *Malinda J. Newkirk*, born August 14, 1840; died December, 1920; married November 14, 1861, Joseph M. Bell; lived at Rushville, Rush County; six children. 6. *Margaret A. Newkirk*, born July 21, 1845; married February 1, 1866, George W. Hendrix, born in North Carolina, May 15, 1837; lived in Rush County, where she died December, 1913; five children. 7. *George Marshall Newkirk*, born August 11, 1850,* married first, Melinda J. Cross; married second, April 27, 1881, Malissa Fry; lived in Rush County; died July 22, 1899; six children, two by first marriage.

ix. WILLIAM [7], born August 1, 1806; married Rebecca Storer; lived at Belfast, Highland County, Ohio, where he died, April 19, 1887. Issue: 1. *Abraham* [8] *Newkirk*, born November 7, 1827; married first, November 10, 1853, Martha Ann Lovett; second, February 14, 1867, Eliza Ann Grimes; eight children, five by first marriage, born Highland County. 2. *Macy S. Newkirk*, born April 3, 1833; married September 30, 1847, John Williamson; lived at Ripley, Oklahoma; eleven children.

x. CYRUS, born May 16, 1810; married Cassa Ann Phillips, born in Virginia, November 6, 1814, daughter of William Phillips; lived in Adams County, Ohio until the Spring of 1854, when with his wife and children he removed to Grant County, Indiana; died October 2, 1855. Issue: 1. *Abraham* [8] *Newkirk*, born August 17, 1834; married December 27, 1867, Rebecca J. Gray, born Randolph County, Indiana, May 12, 1849; lived in Grant County, where he died July 11, 1871; two children. 2. *William Newkirk*, born May 1, 1836; married first, November 6, 1861, Sarah S. Nesbit, who died September 17, 1900; married second, Anna Nesbit; lived in Grant County, and there died June 10, 1907; three children survived infancy. 3. *Margaret J. Newkirk*, born February 1, 1839; married June 9, 1861, Hercules S. Kilgore; lived at Swayzee, Grant County; six children. 4. *George Newkirk*, born November 5, 1842; married first January 9, 1867, Martha Ann Floyd; she died March 30, 1874, aged twenty-seven years; married second, July 18, 1875, Virginia Frances (Fellows) Kingery; of his five children but one survived: MAUDE [9] NEWKIRK, born

---

* Another record gives 1849 as year of birth.

April 21, 1879, married November 24, 1902, Thomas Carey Devaney; lives at Eugene, Oregon. In August, 1862, George Newkirk enlisted in Co. H. 101 Indiana Volunteers of the Federal Army and served his Country until June 21, 1865, when he was honorably discharged, having participated in many of the noted battles * of the Civil War; his Company became part of the Third Division of the 14th Army Corps of the Army of the Cumberland, and of its service he has left a most graphic account; † he resided in Monroe Township, Howard County, Indiana and was twice elected County Commissioner by large Republican majorities, serving from 1888 to 1894; was a prominent Mason, joining that Order in 1865 and passed through the various degrees.‡ 5. *Mary A. Newkirk*, born November 27, 1844; married April 16, 1864, Hamilton Bishop, born July 4, 1839; died September 23, 1909; she died July 28, 1908; resided in Howard County; seven children. 6. *Sarah K. Newkirk*, born September 10, 1846; died young. 7. *John Francis Newkirk*, born March 2, 1850; married March 29, 1877, Margaret Jane Warwick; lived at Swazey, Indiana; three children. 8. *Emma Elizabeth Ellen Newkirk*, born August 8, 1852; married October 5, 1870, John Wesley Bishop, residence Russiaville, Indiana; six children. 9. *Louisa Adaline Newkirk*, born October 7, 1854; married January 14, 1875, Milton Stout; residence Russiaville; four children.

xi. EMILY [7], born June 10, 1813; married first Charles Osman; married second Abraham Hawk. Issue: Two daughters by first marriage who died in early life.

30. CORNELIUS [6] NIEUKIRK (Colonel Cornelius [5], Cornelius [4], *Cornelis* [3], *Gerretse* [2], *Cornelisse* [1]), born in Pittsgrove, Salem County, New Jersey, September 13, 1775; was a farmer and died March 9, 1826. He married August 14, 1797, Mary Reed, born April 29, 1779; died September 23, 1823.

Children of Cornelius and Mary (Reed) Nieukirk, born in Pilesgrove:

i. JAMES [7] E. NIEUKIRK, born May 23, 1798; died October 15, 1878; married first, Maria Vansant; second, Sarah Thomas. Issue born in Salem County: 1. *Reed* [8] *Newkirk*, born December 21, 1821. 2. *Mary A. Newkirk*, born October 23, 1824. 3. *Emily Newkirk*, born May 9, 1827. 4. *Sarah E. Newkirk*, born April

---

* Including Utoy Creek, Jonesboro, Hartsville, Milton, Hoover's Gap, Tullahoma, Chickamauga, Chattanooga, Missionary Ridge, Graysville, Ringgold, Tunnel Hill, Rocky Face Ridge, Adairsville, Dalton, Resaca, Ackworth, Cassville, New Hope Church, Pickett's Mills, Culp Farm, Big Shanty, Lost Mountain, Pine Mountain, Marietta, Kenasaw Mountain, Smyrna, Peach Tree Creek, Atlanta, Chattahoochee River, Ezra Church, Murfreesboro, Allatoona, "The March to the Sea", Savannah, Sister's Ferry, "Through the Carolinas" and on to Washington, where he took part in the Grand Review of 1865.

† Copy of, in Newkirk Collection of The Genealogical Society of Pennsylvania.

‡ *Biographical Sketch of George Newkirk*, printed at Georgetown, Indiana, n. d., 12mo., 4 pp., por.

12, 1829; died in Delaware; married Joseph Smith, lived in West Philadelphia, had one son, GEORGE 9 W. SMITH. 5. *Julia A. Newkirk*, born October 21, 1833; married William D. Mullin; resided in Delaware City; had sons; surnamed Mullin, JAMES,9 WILLIAM and HARRY. 6. *Firman A. Newkirk*, born April 15, 1837; resided at Edgemore, Delaware; married March 19, 1862, Anna Maria Jarrell; had three children: ALEXANDER 9 JARRELL NEWKIRK, born July 30, 1864; ELIZABETH NEWKIRK, born May 29, 1866; ALFRED C. NEWKIRK, born July 19, 1872. 7. *William A. Newkirk*, born July 4, 1840; died in Delaware; married Eliza Groose; had four children: WILLIAM 9 NEWKIRK, FRANK NEWKIRK, LIDE NEWKIRK, JULIA NEWKIRK. 8. *James E. Newkirk*, born June 20, 1844; married March 18, 1869, Sarah E. Hynson; of the ten children, born in Baltimore, five survived childhood: JAMES 9 E. NEWKIRK, born May 20, 1871; CLARA V. NEWKIRK, born September, 1874; FLORENCE MAY NEWKIRK, born February 3, 1878; MARY E. NEWKIRK, born July 31, 1884; ALICE V. NEWKIRK, born March 8, 1888.

ii. EMILY 7 NIEUKIRK, born May 23, 1800; died in Salem County, March 6, 1876; married February 1, 1821, William Conklyn, Jun., born March 21, 1797; died August 6, 1868. Issue, born at Deerfield, New Jersey: 1. *George 8 Whitefield Conklyn*, born May 18, 1822. 2. *Charles Pitman Conklyn*, born September 1, 1823; died unmarried February 7, 1851. 3. *Mary Reed Conklyn*, born October 9, 1825; married William S. Harker; resided at Deerfield; four children. 4. *Elizabeth Newkirk Conklyn*, born July 18, 1828; married George W. Cake; resided at Bridgeton, New Jersey; seven children. 5. *Martha A. Conklyn*, born September 25, 1832; married Charles Fithian Boone; died at Woodstown, New Jersey; four sons. 6. *Caroline Conklyn*, born August 31, 1834; married November 8, 1851, Charles Loveland Frazer; resided at Bridgeton; two children.

iii. ALEXANDER NIEUKIRK, born August 23, 1802; died December 29, 1823.

iv. FURMAN NIEUKIRK, born November 25, 1805; died June 28, 1806.

v. REED NIEUKIRK, born June 5, 1810; married March 22, 1834, Jane S. Young, born January 13, 1815; died September 28, 1872. Issue: 1. *Tamson 8 Brickett Newkirk*, born December 19, 1834; married March 11, 1855, Isaac A. Smith; resided at Salem; had three children to survive infancy. 2. *Thomas A. Newkirk*, born February 23, 1837; died at Salem, July 17, 1912; married February 5, 1861, Kate Dunham; four children, born in Salem County: PRESTON 9 S. NEWKIRK, married Belle Shephard; FANNIE S. NEWKIRK, married George W. Fowler; FRANK H. NEWKIRK, born March 9, 1873; died January 21, 1888; HOWARD B. NEWKIRK, married Jane Westcott Murphy. 3. *John Young Newkirk*, born July 7, 1843; married May 15, 1872, Ella Spence Shaw; resided in Salem County; had seven children. 4. *Aaron H. Newkirk*, born November 16, 1849; married Sally Jenkins; resided at Salem; three children. 5. *Isaac Smith Newkirk*, born September 10, 1855; married April 14, 1884, Sally B. Ray; resided at Salem; six children.

vi. FURMAN NIEUKIRK, born December 8, 1813; died September 8, 1825.

32. vii. LAMBERT NIEUKIRK, married Ann Mitchell.
33. viii. ELBERT NIEUKIRK, married Hannah Brooks.

31. HENRY [7] NEWKIRK (*Abraham* [6], *Abraham* [5], *Barent* [4], *Cornelis* [3], *Garretse* [2], *Cornelisse* [1]), born near Bentleyville, Washington County, Pennsylvania, December 25, 1789; married February 20, 1816, Hannah Bentley, born November 27, 1792, daughter of Benjamin and Mary (Baldwin) Bentley * of Sharon, Pennsylvania.

Shortly after marriage he removed from his birthplace to Brown County, Ohio, formed from Adams County in 1817. Here in 1819, in conjunction with Allen Woods, he purchased and platted the town of Georgetown, the County seat. He died October 24, 1821 and is buried in the old Cemetery of the town. His widow married William Shepperd and died in Georgetown, May 5, 1856.

Children of Henry and Hannah (Bentley) Newkirk, born at Georgetown:

    i. LORINDA [8], born June 7, 1817; married July 19, 1837, Dr. James Sidwell, born September 6, 1814; died October 7, 1866. Of their seven children, but one, *Nathan* [9] *Henry Sidwell*, M. D. lived to maturity. He, born October 18, 1840; died June 15, 1883, at Wilmington, Ohio, married and had nine children.

    ii. ADAMSON BENTLEY, born March 12, 1819; was graduated from the Starling Medical College of Columbus, Ohio, March 1, 1849, and practiced medicine the balance of his life in Jamestown, Zenia, and Freesburg, Ohio; Memphis, Tennessee; Manteno and Chicago, Illinois, and Falls City, Nebraska. During the Civil War he was agent of the United States Government, and during President Grant's term of office, he was Internal Revenue Collector for the 8th District of Tennessee located at Memphis. He died at Falls City, December 18, 1883, from injuries received by a fall when making a professional call at night. He married September 4, 1844, Lucy Mary Taliaferro Barker, born in Bracken County, Kentucky, August 18, 1826; died in Chicago, December 18, 1882, daughter of William Musgrave and Jane Champ (Buckner) Barker. Issue: 1. *Laura* [9] *Matilda Newkirk*, born Jamestown, Ohio, July 24, 1847; died Los Angeles, August 30, 1930; married June 15, 1871, Henry Jacob Shepherd, born Marion, Ohio, September 29, 1842; died Raleigh, Tennessee, October 15, 1871; married second, January 1, 1879, Andrew Kinkaid Shepherd,† born Ripley, Ohio, November

---

* For information on the ancestry and family of Benjamin Bentley, *vide* THE BENTLEY FAMILY WITH GENEALOGICAL RECORDS. *The Tribe of Benjamin.* By General Roeliff Brinkerhoff, 1897.

† A second cousin of Henry Jacob Shepherd and half brother of William Shepherd, who married Hannah (Bentley) Newkirk, widow of Henry Newkirk.

(63)

18, 1820; died San Diego, California, March 21, 1905; two
children by second marriage: LUCY [10] ETHEL SHEPHERD;
ADAMSON CLARE SHEPHERD. 2. *William Henry Newkirk*,
born Jamestown, Ohio, December 3, 1849; died January 26,
1850. 3. *Clara Barker Newkirk*, born near Feesburg, Ohio,
May 9, 1851; resided at Los Angeles. 4. *John Naylor Newkirk*,
born Chicago, September 17, 1854; died at San Diego, June
30, 1928; postmaster, San Diego, two terms, held other public
offices; married May 24, 1882, Alice Parker, born May 27,
1857; died October 15, 1922, daughter of Albert Parker and
niece of Senator Cullum of Illinois; two daughters: JULIET [10]
CULLUM NEWKIRK; LUCY BARKER NEWKIRK. 5. *Adamson
Bentley Newkirk*, Jr., born Hyde Park, Chicago, March 12,
1858; was graduated from Rush Medical College of Chicago,
February 24, 1860; after which he engaged in the practice
of his profession at Falls City, Nebraska. In November,
1889, he removed to Los Angeles, where he was eminently
successful as a physician and surgeon until shortly before
his death; was President of San Pedro Cancer Sanitarium
for a number of years, specializing in radium treatment. He
died May 12, 1927, when the Los Angeles Commandery No.
9, Knights Templar, of which he was an honored member,
took charge of his funeral service. In addition to his arduous
calling, Dr. Newkirk had long been engaged in collecting
genealogical data of the male and female descendants of
Cornelisse Van Nieuwkirk of Slichtenhorst, Holland, whose
two sons, Gerret and Mattheus, came to New Netherland on
the ship *Moesman* in 1659. By great assiduity, and in
collaboration with Thomas J. Newkirk * of Evanston, Illinois,
he accumulated a vast amount of family source material
which, tabulated and bound in 47 folio manuscript volumes,
now form the Collection bearing his name in The Genealogical Society of Pennsylvania. He married at Falls City, June
7, 1887, Eva May Ingram, born at Highland, Iowa, July 20,
1860; died Los Angeles; daughter of Rev. J. W. Ingram and
wife, Julia Hicks. It is owing to Mrs. Newkirk's interest in
carrying out her husband's wishes that his collection has its
present depository; in appreciation of her action the Society's
Board of Directors elected her to honorary membership; a son,
WILLIAM [10] BENTLEY NEWKIRK of Falls City survives. 6. *Jane
Champ Newkirk*, born Manteno, Illinois, December 31, 1860;
married at Falls City, February 16, 1889, Charles Edward
Smith; together they attended the International Sunday
School Convention held in Jerusalem, Palestine, in April 1904;
later they had charge of the American School of Archaeology,
and made their home in Jerusalem until 1910, when they
returned to America; Mr. Smith died at Boyle Heights,
Los Angeles, September 11, 1917; Mrs. Smith is, 1933, a resi-
dent of Los Angeles; one son, died in infancy. 7. *Joseph
Thornton Newkirk*, born Chicago, January 25, 1864; died in
Los Angeles, January 18, 1925; married at Los Angeles,
January 6, 1897, Mrs. Elizabeth Auer; no issue. 8. *Malvina
Ann Newkirk*, born Raleigh, Tennessee, August 20, 1867;
resides at Los Angeles.

iii. CYRUS [8], born Brown County, Ohio, March 12, 1821; married
December 3, 1849, Rebecca Isaminger, born Franklin Furnace,
Ohio, June 29, 1828. He first devoted his attention to the
iron industries of Ohio, superintended the building of the
Buckeye and Vinton Furnaces, was General Manager of the

* Thomas J. Newkirk, author of *Genealogy and History of the Newkirk, Hamilton and Bayless Families*, q. v.

Buckeye Furnace in 1852-53, and General Manager of the Vinton Furnace 1854-57. He moved to Sedalia, Missouri, where he was President of its First National Bank, Treasurer and a Director of Sedalia, Kansas City & Southern Railroad, 1879; a Director in Kansas City & Southern Lumber Company (mill and plant at Sedgwic, Arkansas); President of Board of Trade of Sedalia, 1888; shortly after this he went to Los Angeles and there died December 16, 1902; his widow died June 7, 1907. Issue: 1. *Mary* [9] *Eliza Newkirk*, born Buckeye Furnace, November 18, 1852; resides, 1933, at Los Angeles; married November 3, 1875, Samuel Scarlet Woodward, born Shelby, Ohio, December 6, 1833; died June 17, 1911; one son LEIGH [10] N. WOODWARD. 2. *Emma Jane Newkirk*, born Vinton Furnace, November 15, 1855; resides 1933, at Corona, California; married at Sedalia, November 29, 1881, Edward Augustus Phillips, born Pennington, New Jersey, March 31, 1835; died at Ocean Park, California, October 12, 1909; four sons were born in Kansas City: NEWKIRK [10] READING PHILLIPS, now deceased; GRANT KENNEDY PHILLIPS; EDWARD AUGUSTUS PHILLIPS; JOHN HOWELL PHILLIPS. 3. *Ida Belle Newkirk*, born McArthur, Ohio, August 4, 1861; married, Sedalia, November 23, 1892; Elmer Satley; residence Monessen, Pennsylvania; one daughter, DOROTHY [10] SATLEY. 4. *Lucy Markley Newkirk*, born Georgetown, Ohio, June 26, 1862; died at Redlands, California, December 28, 1912; married October 8, 1884, George M. Galbreath, three children. 5. *Corrie Alice Newkirk*, born Sedalia, August 12, 1867; married at Sedalia, June 3, 1891, William Minton Jones; resides at Sedalia; two children.

32. LAMBERT [7] NIEUKIRK (*Cornelius* [6], *Colonel Cornelius* [5], *Cornelius* [4], *Cornelis* [3], *Gerretse* [2], *Cornelisse* [1]), was born in Pittsgrove, Salem County, New Jersey, November 26, 1815, and there died. He married September 23, 1836, Ann Mitchell.

Children of Lambert and Ann (Mitchell) Nieukirk, all born in Salem County and all used Newkirk as their surname:

i. GEORGE [8] M. NEWKIRK, born December 18, 1837; died March 2, 1900; married December 8, 1860, Anna E. Seagrave. Issue, born in Salem County: 1. *Sarah* [9] *Ann Newkirk*, born October 21, 1862; married March 22, 1881, John F. Foster; residence Collingswood, New Jersey; nine children, surname Foster. 2. *Nettie Newkirk*, born March 26, 1866; married February 15, 1886, John T. Wykoff; residence Sewell, New Jersey; four children, surname Wykoff. 3. *James Sinnickson Newkirk*, born January 6, 1868; married August 24, 1907, Catherine Bittner; residence, Camden, New Jersey; three children, surname Newkirk. 4. *Lena S. Newkirk*, born April, 1870; married June 27, 1889, Howard C. Norcross; residence Haddonfield, New Jersey; three children, surname Norcross. 5. *Georgeanna Newkirk*, born July 8, 1878; married August 19, 1899, Job Kay Stratton; residence Haddonfield; two children, surname Stratton. 6. *Clara Newkirk*, born September 11, 1880; married September 27, 1899, Robert Harris Stafford, residence Haddonfield; one son, surname Stafford.
ii. JOSEPH H. NEWKIRK, born December 14, 1839; married March 8, 1865, Mary E. Dilks. Issue, born in Cumberland County, New Jersey: 1. *Ann* [9] *Newkirk*, born July 18, 1866; married

February 12, 1887, Edward Harris, residence Quinton, New Jersey; two children, surname Harris. 2. *John P. Newkirk,* born October 9, 1867; married October 17, 1894, Lotta Welch, residence Bridgeton, five children. 3. *Elbert Newkirk,* born October 13, 1869; married March 13, 1894, Emma C. Lawrence, residence Bridgeton, four children. 4. *Mollie Newkirk,* born December 20, 1871; died in Salem County; married December, 1895, Samuel H. Shimp; four children. 5. *Emma R. Newkirk,* born September 24, 1873; married John D. Mitchell; residence Shiloh, New Jersey; six children. 7. *Frank Newkirk,* born August 20, 1875; married December 21, 1898, Hannah M. Rasinger; residence Bridgeton; seven children. 8. *Richard A. Newkirk,* born April 10, 1877; married August 18, 1902, Henrietta Johnson Loper; residence Greenwich, New Jersey. 9. *Eva H. Newkirk,* born November 16, 1878; married March 8, 1905, George Padgett; residence Harmersville, New Jersey. 10. *Jennie C. Newkirk,* born November 4, 1884.

iii. JOHN 8 P. NEWKIRK, born August 17, 1843; died April 10, 1864.

iv. MARY NEWKIRK, born June 3, 1884; married July 13, 1867, John Holladay; residence, Hancock's Bridge, New Jersey. Issue, born in Salem County: 1. *William 9 Holladay,* born and died November 8, 1868. 2. *Rachel Holladay,* born May 25, 1870; married ———— Nittinger; residence Salem, New Jersey; nine children. 3. *Caroline E. Holladay,* born February 10, 1874; married December 14, 1891, H. Lindley Smith; residence Greenwich; ten children. 4. *Lambert Holladay,* born February 8, 1876; married December 3, 1901, Elizabeth C. Daniels; residence Pennsgrove, New Jersey; seven children, three of whom died in infancy. 5. *Samuel Holladay,* born December 5, 1880; married June 21, 1898, Emily Sheppard; residence Greenwich; six children. 6. *George Holladay,* born September 18, 1884; married Mary Welch; residence Philadelphia. 7. *Lillie F. Holladay,* born July 13, 1887; * married March 28, 1905 Henry Warren Pancoast; residence Hancock's Bridge; two children. 8. *Anna Holladay,* born February 27, 1888. 9. *Mary Holladay,* born October 18, 1891. 10. *John Holladay,* born April 7, 1894.

v. SAMUEL C. NEWKIRK, born November 12, 1846; died in Salem County; married Phebe P. Hannah. Issue, born in Salem County: 1. *Edward 9 F. Newkirk,* born June 18, 1867. 2. *Jennie Newkirk,* born December 14, 1869.

vi. CAROLINE E. NEWKIRK, born July 26, 1851; married December 10, 1870, Richard Sayre; residence Atlantic City, New Jersey. Issue: 1. *Ephraim 9 Lambert Sayre,* born March 23, 1872; died young. 2. *Evaline Sherron Sayre,* born June 24, 1874; married October 4, 1898, Daniel C. Reynolds; residence Atlantic City. 3. *Albert S. Sayre,* born April 23, 1877; married July 22, 1900, Bertha Conover; residence Atlantic City. 4. *Howard L. Sayre,* born October 5, 1880; married February 2, 1904, Lillian Conover; residence Atlantic City. 5. *Milton W. Sayre,* born May 16, 1883; married September 3, 1903, Florence Goodyear; residence Atlantic City. 6. *Edith A. Sayre,* born July 13, 1889; married November 12, 1911 Eugene B. Parker; residence Atlantic City.

vii. QUINTON K. NEWKIRK, born January 19, 1856; married March 7, 1883, Lydia Ridgway; residence Greenwich. Issue: 1. *Anna 9 Ridgway Newkirk,* born May 1, 1884; died January 12, 1904. 2. *William Powell Newkirk,* born December 25, 1885. 3. *Mary Harris Newkirk,* born August 30, 1889.

viii. CHARLES R. NEWKIRK, born January 14, 1858; married Sallie B.

---

* August 5, 1886 is also given as date of birth.

Farnkoff; residence Woodstown, New Jersey. Issue, born at Woodstown: 1. *Susan* 9 *A. Newkirk*, born March 26, 1879. 2. *Henry Newkirk*, born July 7, 1882; died young. 3. *Ann Newkirk*, born September 14, 1885; died young. 4. *Maggie Newkirk*, born June 5, 1887; died young. 5. *Charles Newkirk*, born July 22, 1888; died young. 6. *Benjamin Newkirk*, born August 22, 1889; died young. 7. *Malinda Newkirk*, born September 13, 1890. 8. *Anna May Newkirk*, born August 3, 1892; died young. 9. *Florence Newkirk*, born December 31, 1897. 10. *John Newkirk*, born August 28, 1898; died young.

ix. LAMBERT 8 NEWKIRK, born October 14, 1860; married Sarah Elwell.

33. ELBERT 7 NIEUKIRK (*Cornelius* 6, *Colonel Cornelius* 5, *Cornelius* 4, *Cornelis* 3, *Gerretse* 2, *Cornelisse* 1), born at Pittsgrove, Salem County, New Jersey, September 23, 1818; died in Cumberland County, New Jersey, June 10, 1893. He married March 11, 1841, Hannah Brooks, born June 23, 1820; died September 26, 1890; daughter of John Brooks, Philadelphia, born February 1, 1785; died in 1833, and his wife, Margaret Low, born March 31, 1789; died December 25, 1875.

Children of Elbert and Hannah (Brooks) Nieukirk, born in Cumberland County:

34. i. WILLIAM 8 BROOKS NIEUKIRK, married Mary F Glasbey.
    ii. JOHN BROOKS NIEUKIRK, born February 17, 1843; died April 20, 1920; served in the war to maintain the Union, in Company H, 24th Regiment, New Jersey Volunteers; married May 28, 1864, Mary Ann Ireland, born October 18, 1845; died May 23, 1932; resided in Bridgeton. Issue: 1. *Margaret* 9 *Kendall Nieukirk*, born December 5, 1864; died October 8, 1932; married December 1, 1886, Charles H. Kienzle, born February 13, 1865; residence Bridgeton; two children: EDWARD 10 F. KIENZLE born September 14, 1887; died April 19, 1915; married May 29, 1908, Verna Emily Long, born April 11, 1891; residence Bridgeton; two children. MARGARET C. KIENZLE, born May 22, 1891; married April 12, 1913, Edwin A. McGraw, born October 1, 1888; two children. 2. *Hannah B. Nieukirk*, born November 4, 1866; married September 30, 1890, Franklin J. Lore, born June 18, 1867; residence Bridgeton; two children: FRANKLIN 10 J. LORE, Jr., born August 24, 1891; married July 5, 1916, Mildred Hunt, born May 27, 1893; two children. HARRY T. LORE, born January 3, 1894; married February 28, 1918, Pearl Leiser, born November 10, 1898. 3. *Elizabeth Nieukirk*, born February 10, 1869; married February 20, 1895, William L. Naglee born January 26, 1869; residence Pleasantville, New Jersey; had issue: HELEN 10 H. NAGLEE, born June 14, 1896; married June 6, 1917, George W. Reed, born February 22, 1897. 4. *Mary Ann Nieukirk*, born December 28, 1870; died July 20, 1872.
35. iii. JAMES P. NIEUKIRK, married Rachel Rice Ford.
    iv. ADELINE BROOKS NIEUKIRK, born June 14, 1846; died May 18, 1893; married January 3, 1864, Joseph L. Mulford, born September 24, 1844; died July 5, 1912, served in the United States Navy during the Civil War; son of David P. Mulford and his wife Phebe Sutton. Issue, born in Cumberland County: 1. *Henry* 9 *Kendall Mulford*, born October 10, 1866; married November 12, 1890, Lillian Bell Ware, born June 23, 1867; residence Phila-

delphia. Five children: MARION [10] RAY MULFORD, born February 17, 1892; died January 18, 1919; married April 30, 1918, Colonel Robert Edes Kimball, no issue. HENRY KENDALL MULFORD, Jr., born December 11, 1893; married September 14, 1918, Jeannette Sheaffer; issue: *Elizabeth* [11] *Sheaffer Mulford*, born May 1, 1920. ESTHER STEWART MULFORD, born March 6, 1895; died June 23, 1932; married October 3, 1917, Arthur Leon Meyer and has two children: *Marion* [11] *Mulford Meyer*, born March 20, 1921; *Suzanne Meyer*, born June 18, 1923. LILLIAN WARE MULFORD, born February 12, 1902; married June 18, 1925, Henry Harold Fehr, born March 18, 1900. 2. *Ray Ford Mulford*, born June 24, 1886; died February 8, 1889.

v. MARY [8] REED NIEUKIRK, born December 6, 1852; died December 18, 1914; married March 23, 1869, Joseph Atwood Fisler, born October 23, 1843; died May 10, 1913; resided at Clayton, New Jersey. Issue, born at Clayton: 1. *Elbert* [9] *Nieukirk Fisler*, born October 24, 1870; married August 6, 1890, Nellie Hewitt Herring, born April 30, 1875; residence Clayton; six children: JOSEPH [10] MULFORD FISLER, born February 5, 1892; married February 13, 1915. Selina P. Ladd, born December 4, 1890; issue: *Joseph* [11] *Mulford Fisler*, Jr., born August 8, 1917. LUBERTA [10] FISLER, born October 20, 1894; died January 18, 1933; married first, October 14, 1917, Lawrence Brown Ford, born June 26, 1897; died July 11, 1921; married second, January, 1, 1926, Robert E. Moore, born February 3, 1899; issue by first marriage: *Mildred* [11] *Ford*, born January 19, 1921. ELBERT [10] NIEUKIRK FISLER, Jr., born June 24, 1896; DENNIS [10] HAYS FISLER, born April 3, 1899; married April 24, 1922, Doris Sutliff, born March 24, 1898; has issue: *Ruth* [11] *Fisler*, born January 23, 1923. RUSSELL [10] C. FISLER, born June 11, 1902; LESLIE [10] CRANOR FISLER, born March 20, 1904. 2. *Euphemia* [9] *Fisler*, born June 21, 1872; died December 14, 1888. 3. *Florence* [9] *Fisler*, born April 10, 1874; married May 14, 1902, James Preston Potter, born July 28, 1874; died May 21, 1926; residence Clayton; one child died an infant. 4. *Warren* [9] *Fisler*, born February 9, 1881.

34. WILLIAM [8] BROOKS NIEUKIRK (*Elbert* [7], *Cornelius* [6], *Colonel Cornelius* [5], *Cornelius* [4], *Cornelis* [3], *Gerretse* [2], *Cornelisse* [1]), born Cumberland County, New Jersey, December 6, 1841; died June 21, 1918, served in the United States Navy during the Civil War. He married January 21, 1867, Mary F. Glaspey, born June 17, 1839; died May 29, 1924.

Children of William Brooks and Mary F. (Glaspey) Nieukirk, born in Cumberland County:

> i. WILLIAM [9] GLASPEY NIEUKIRK, born February 21, 1869; married June 20, 1896, Alna Pratts; born June 21, 1874; residence Bridgeton. Seven children: 1. *Ruth* [10] *Woodruff Nieukirk*, born March 20, 1897; married November 11, 1920, Hewitt A. Cole born March 9, 1893; four children: ROY [11] B. COLE, born May 25, 1921; DOROTHY [11] M. COLE, born April 13, 1923; HELEN D. COLE, born November 17, 1925; HARRY [11] A. COLE, born June 27, 1927. 2. *Lucy* [10] *Pratts Nieukirk*, born March 2, 1899; married January 1, 1920, Oscar T. Brown; born October 10, 1883. Issue: FRANCIS [11] E. BROWN, born December 5, 1921. JEAN [11] E. BROWN, born July 26, 1925. 3. *Mary Emma Nieukirk*, born July 11, 1901; married February 10, 1923, William S. Davis, born December 22, 1894. Issue: ARTHUR [11] S. DAVIS, born September 16, 1925. 4. *Grace* [10] *B. Nieukirk*, born June 23, 1903. 5. *Edith* [10] *Mulford Nieukirk*, born July 15, 1905. 6. *Alna* [10] *Francis Nieukirk*, born July 19, 1908. 7. *William Thomas Nieukirk* [10], born May 15, 1910.
>
> ii. ELBERT NIEUKIRK, born June 7, 1874; unmarried; resides near Bridgeton.

35. JAMES [8] POLK NIEUKIRK (*Elbert* [7], *Cornelius* [6], *Colonel Cornelius* [5], *Cornelius* [4], *Cornelis* [3], *Gerretse* [2] *Cornelisse* [1]), born Bridgeton, New Jersey, March 16, 1845; died Camden, New Jersey, April 4, 1916. When sixteen years of age, inspired to assist in perpetuating the Union, he, one morning on his way to school, hid his books under a fence and disappeared. When found by his parents at Beverly, New Jersey, he had enlisted on October 28, 1861 for three years' service in Company H, 10th Regiment New Jersey Volunteers, and before the close of the year became a Corporal. He reenlisted January 3, 1864 in the 10th Regiment, New Jersey Veteran Volunteers, and was made 1st Sergeant. On May 21, 1865, he was commissioned Second Lieutenant Company C, 10th Regiment, and on July 1, of the same year, First Lieutenant, Company C, and was honorably discharged at the close of the War, July 1865. His regiment was part of Sedgwick's

(69)

6th Army Corps, and with it he participated in the battles of the Wilderness, Spottsylvania, Cold Harbor and Winchester, Virginia. He was taken prisoner May 8, 1864, at Spottsylvania, and recaptured by Custer's Cavalry May 9, at Beaver Dam; was again taken prisoner August 16, 1864, at Winchester, and spent six months and four days in the Confederate prisons at Lynchburg, Danville and Libby. He married January 2, 1867, Rachel Rice Ford, born April 7, 1850; died May 23, 1927, daughter of Philip Ford * of Cape May County and Camden, New Jersey, and his wife Abigail Buck Sheppard. Mrs. Nieukirk was a descendant, in the ninth generation, of John Howland, the *Mayflower* passenger of 1620.

Children of James Polk and Rachel Rice (Ford) Nieukirk, born in Camden, New Jersey, the first and fifth excepted:

> i. MATTIE 9 FORD NIEUKIRK, born Clayton, New Jersey, October 1, 1867; died January 29, 1912; married December 4, 1888, Raymond Rodgers Blydenburgh, born November 9, 1865. Issue: 1. *Helen* 10 *Blydenburgh*, born September 1, 1892; died young. 2. *Raymond Rodgers Blydenburgh, Jr.*, born Camden, April 4, 1894; married first, November 27, 1915, Adelaide M. S. Reynolds, born December 9, 1896; died October 19, 1919; married second, December 7, 1920, Ruth E. Moore, born February 20, 1896. Issue by first marriage, a daughter, ADELAIDE 11 C. BLYDENBURG, born September 25, 1916; by second marriage: RAYMOND 11 RODGERS BLYDENBURGH, 3rd., born October 17, 1921. MARGARET 11 JEAN BLYDENBURGH, born February 5, 1927.

---

* Philip Ford (born May 5, 1823; died January 2, 1884; son of Charles Ford of Cape May County, born January 23, 1798; died November 12, 1855) was grandson of Philip Ford, M. D. of Cape May County, born October 14, 1768; died October 29, 1820, who married Hannah Hughes, born at Cape May, September 23, 1776. Of this marriage there were five children: *Charles Ford*, before mentioned, *Philip Ford, Eleanor Ford, Hannah Ford* and *Elizabeth Ford*. Dr. Ford was one of the Committee appointed by the New Jersey Medical Society November 9, 1819, to organize a District Medical Society for the County of Cape May. Hannah (Hughes) Ford married second, March 11, 1824, Lewis Corson, also of Cape May. She was the grand-daughter of Ellis Hughes (1708-1752) of Cape May, who married Hannah Whillden (c 1719-1739), granddaughter of Joseph Whillden and Hannah Gorham who married c 1683, and removed from Plymouth County, Massachusetts, to Cape May. By this marriage they became the progenitors of all those in Cape May, who later claim Mayflower descent from Hannah, daughter of Captain John Gorham and grand-daughter of John Howland.—*The Rise, Minutes, and Proceedings, of the New Jersey Medical Society, Established July 23, 1766*, p. 186; *Mayflower Index*, Compiled and edited for the General Society of Mayflower Descendants by William Alexander McAuslan, Historian General, 1932.

ii. PHILIP [9] FORD NIEUKIRK, born April 18, 1870; married June 19, 1895, Mabel Van Gilder, born May 14, 1874, daughter of Aaron Van Gilder and his wife, Emma McDowéll of Camden; resides at Riverton, New Jersey. Issue: 1. *Ray* [10] *Ford Nieukirk*, born at Camden, July 19, 1896; married June 19, 1920, Francis Edward Fanning, born April 5, 1898; son of Francis Joseph Fanning and his wife Grace Lloyd of Maplewood, New Jersey; reside at West Orange, New Jersey; two children: PHILIP [11] FORD NIEUKIRK FANNING, born Philadelphia, January 28, 1924; GRACE LLOYD FANNING, born Newark, January 28, 1927.

iii. CHARLES ELBERT NIEUKIRK, born July 1, 1873; unmarried; resides at Camden.

iv. JAMES LEWIS NIEUKIRK, born April 29, 1876; died February 28, 1924; married September 1, 1916, Alice Hall Hendrickson, born January 23, 1883. Issue: *James* [10] *Polk Nieukirk*, 2nd., born June 27, 1919.

v. ADDIE MULFORD NIEUKIRK, born July 14, 1879; married October 22, 1902, Leon Geoffrey Buckwalter, born January 28, 1880; died April 20, 1928; resides in Merchantville, New Jersey. Issue: 1. *James* [10] *Nieukirk Buckwalter*, born May 2, 1907; married April 19, 1932, in Boston, Massachusetts, Elizabeth Vaughan; born Sommerville, Massachusetts, November 11, 1907, daughter of Frank Mendell Vaughan, M. D., and his wife Josephine Plummer. 2. *John Buckwalter*, born April 29, 1911; died young. 3. *Helen Louise Buckwalter*, born August 22, 1915.

vi. RAYMOND BLYDENBURGH NIEUKIRK, born December 8, 1881; married December 29, 1910, Josephine Rose, born September 25, 1881; enlisted May 25, 1898, for service in the Spanish American War; private in Company M, Third New Jersey Volunteer Infantry; mustered out February 11, 1899, following which he enlisted, early in 1900, in the National Guard of New Jersey as private in Company M, same regiment, and was Brigade Color Serjeant 1901-1908; resides in Toronto, Canada. Issue: 1. *Margaret* [10] *Rose Nieukirk*, born Atlanta, Georgia, September 30, 1911. 2. *Philip Ford Nieukirk*, 2nd., born Camden, April 24, 1913.

vii. EDMUND HEWITT NIEUKIRK, born February 22, 1885; married June 26, 1913, Bessie May Galloway, born July 11, 1890; resides in California.

APPENDIX

ADDRESS DELIVERED BEFORE THE NEWKIRK FAMILY REUNION AT
KOKOMO, HOWARD COUNTY, INDIANA, BY THOMAS
JEFFERSON NEWKIRK, IN 1914

THE NEWKIRK FAMILY is an ancient one and, like most
other families of Teutonic origin, the name has undergone
many changes on its long journey to its more usual, present
way of spelling with seven letters.

The first authentic record of any member of this family is
found in the histories of the Lower Rhine regions of Germany;
there being towns named Neukirchen in both the counties
of Grevenbroech and Moers.

The name of Adolphus de Nieukirchen is mentioned in a
document of the Monastery of Gehrden as early as 1153.
From 1337 to 1350, many of the Newkirks were property
owners in their native places in Germany. The name generally appears as Neukirchen and, by this name, there are
many German arrivals in this country, even to the present day.
In 1599, mention is made of Gottfried Neukirch and shortly
before of Arnold Heinrich Neukirk, professor of Theology.

One writer on Heraldry has contributed the following to the
family lore:

VAN NEUKIRCHEN, called NYVENHEIM

The continuous line of this old family of Julich begins
with Johan von Neukirchen, Lord of Neuraidt in Oelen,
who married, in 1403, Anna van Nyvenheim, heiress of
Gerode.

From Julich the family went to the Lower Rhine, acquired many hereditary offices in the course of time; much
wealth and furnished a number of Knights and Com-
manders to the German Order. One branch removed to
the Netherlands, while the other remained in the Rhine
region.

Walter Godfried van Neukirchen, called Nyvenheim, in
the thirteenth generation of the continuous genealogie,
Lord of Drieberg, Kessel, Mook and Musschenberg, was,
by his wife, Elbertina van Tengnagel van Gillikum, whom
he married in 1703, the ancestor of the present branch of
the family living in France.

(73)

Thus it is seen that the family of ancient origin had spread to three countries: Germany, Holland and France, many centuries ago.

The branch of the family to which those here present trace their lineage located in Holland; but the date has not yet been ascertained. It is the belief of the writer of this paper, however, that the family had lived in Holland for at least many hundred years before the American progenitor sailed to New Netherland.

Naturally, this causes some inquiry concerning the country of their ancestors, and it may be truthfully answered that history records no more heroic events than those brought out in the revolt of the Netherlands, which resulted in the establishment of the Dutch Republic.

Ridpath, the historian, says of it:

> Never in all the world did man have such a battle with nature as in Holland. The eloquent Taine in describing the situation says: 'As you coast the North Sea from the Scheldt to Jutland, you will mark in the first place that the characteristic feature is the want of slope. In Holland the soil is but a sediment of mud; here and there only does the earth cover it with a crust of mire, shallow and brittle, the mere alluvium of the river, which the river seems ever ready to destroy. Thick mists hover above, being fed by ceaseless exhalations. They hazily turn their violet flanks, grow black, suddenly descend in heavy showers: the vapor like a furnace-smoke, crawls forever on the horizen. Thus watered, the plants multiply; in the angle between Jutland and the continent, in a fat, muddy soil, the verdure is as fresh as that of England. Immense forests covered the land even after the eleventh century. The sap of humid country, thick and potent, circulates in man as in the plants and by its respiration, its nutrition, the sensations and habits which it generates, affect his faculties and his frame.'
>
> How Holland diked back the sea is known to all the world. Year after year, generation after generation, this sturdy and indomitable people fought back the hostile and ever aggressive deep until at last, far off in that bleak north-western horizon, the figure of man, standing complaisant on the long mole of earth which his own industry had raised, was seen between the North Sea and the sky. The Dutch Minerva planted a garden where the surly Neptune had lately set his trident.

Such then is some idea of the country of this family's ancestors. If, as Taine says, the sap of the country had affected the faculties and frames of the Hollanders, it had but made them strong in intellect and rugged in frame.

In religion the Hollanders were Protestants; they had without any reservation, accepted the doctrines of Luther, as Germany had done. But they were not to enjoy the freedom of their religion without a struggle. Holland was under the rule of Spain, which was Catholic; and the rulers of the Catholic world were determined to destroy the protestant religion by convicting and executing its followers upon the charge of being heretics. To that end a court of church inquiry was established. To this the Protestants applied the name of the " Council of Blood."

Long years of prosecution of the Protestants followed. Those who would not embrace the Catholic faith were robbed of their property first, and of their lives afterwards. During these turbulent times the only concession the bigoted officials who pretended to rule Holland ever made to their wretched subjects, was instead of being burned alive they should be hanged. Hordes of Spanish soldiers, clad in the menacing trappings of war, herded these unarmed and helpless people in groups; would frequently hang scores of them at a time to the boughs of a single tree, in the presence of those last in order of death. In spite of this, the people who survived maintained their faith, and by their courage and heroism, threw off the yoke that oppressed them and took their place among the nations of the earth.

The Newkirk ancestors were from the low, or coast country, of Holland. They spoke the pure Dutch language. In their native country they were agriculturalists, manufacturers and merchants. By the industry and thrift of its people, Holland had surpassed, in, or about, 1573, all other countries of northern Europe. For more than a century her ships carried the commerce of the world; her manufacturers and artisans furnished very much of it.

Early in the seventeenth century, the people of Holland turned their attention to the New World. They literally came in swarms. Soon New Netherland was established in practically all that country which is now included in the boundaries of the State of New York. They brought with them little property. Their greatest possession was religion, which to them meant everything. They were strictly honest and good citizens. To this day how often is it said that this or that man came from good old Knickerbocker stock. That only means he was a descendant of the early Holland emigrants.

When the Transvaal was established in South Africa by the Hollanders, some of the Newkirk family located in that country. The discovery of the first diamond, resulting in the location of the great Kimberly diamond mines, the greatest wealth-producing mines in the entire world's history, was made by a member of this family, a Native Hollander—Shaulk Van Newkirk.

The foregoing gives some account of the origin of the family; some idea of the country in which it lived; something of its personalities and religion. The progenitor to whom those of the family in this country trace their ancestry was Gerret Cornelisen Van Nieuwkerck. Accompanied by his wife, child and brother, he arrived April 25, 1659, more than two hundred and fifty-five years ago.

He came on the Holland ship *Moesman* with many of his countrymen. His wife's maiden name was Chieltje Cornelissen Slecht (Charlotte in English). They spoke nothing but the Dutch language; had need for no other since everyone spoke Dutch. Gerret was a son of Cornelius van Nieuwkercke and is believed to have been born at Slichtenhorst, Gelderland, Holland.

In his native country he was a farmer, and immediately upon his arrival made application for land at Flatbush, Long Island. He was granted eighteen morgens, or thirty-six acres. There he resided until he sold it, 10 March, 1665. It is not known what was paid for this land, but it is now in the heart of the City of Brooklyn. Newkirk Street, which runs through or by it, is the only thing left to show that Gerret ever inhabited this territory.

This article will attempt to trace and follow the family history from the arrival of Gerret to the present. Family history is entertaining to those interested. Before proceeding, however, some may desire to know of the family genealogy, now in preparation. The work was commenced more than twenty-five years ago by Dr. A. B. Newkirk, a talented and well educated member of the family. Located on one side of the continent, whereas the field of operation is practically on the other, he was compelled to carry on the work almost entirely by correspondence. Indifference of members of the family made the work slow, but he succeeded to a remarkable degree.

Some years ago, the writer of this paper examined a large family genealogy and was impressed with the magnitude of that work. Upon inquiry it was learned that one of the compilers had devoted half his life to it, besides a considerable expenditure of money to complete the material. The Newkirk family genealogy would probably contain twice as many names as that if published in full.

The writer then resolved to assist Dr. Newkirk in the work, and has since searched records in more than half the court houses in a vast strip of country stretching from the Rocky Mountains to the Atlantic Ocean. Hundreds of members of the family were visited in the quest for information. Numerous cemeteries, public and private burying grounds were visited in the gathering of history from speechless marble. Even the repose of the dead was only secure when it was remembered that:

> Gray has noted the waste of breath,
> In addressing the dull cold ear of death.

During all these years both Dr. Newkirk and his co-worker have vigorously prosecuted the work by correspondence, by searching published archives, histories and genealogies; devoting all time possible.

Now a few words as to the spelling of the name by the emigrant ancestor. The passenger list of the *Moesman* gives it van Niew-kirk; the official records of Ulster County and those of the Kingston Dutch Church as van Nieuwkerck, Niewkirk. The prefix " van " was soon dropped as were several letters in the surname. In a short time the name was generally spelled as now, Newkirk; with the exception of Cornelius Nieukirk of Salem County, New Jersey. Some of his descendants continue this spelling; many of them, however, use the common spelling—Newkirk.

After selling his land at Flatbush, Gerret is next found at Hurley, Ulster County, New York, where he spent the remainder of his days. He had five children: Arien, generally called Arie, Jan, Neeltje, Gerretje and Cornelis. They all married and had large families.

Arie married Elizabeth Lambertse of Kingston, New York. They had three sons and five daughters, all of them located in New York.

John, called Jan in Dutch, married Titjen Deckers.

Neeltje married Peter Crispell, a prominent man of his day. They had two sons and one daughter; the sons and their descendants becoming prominent. After the death of Peter Crispel, Neeltje married Johannes Schepmoes, by whom she had one daughter.

Gerretje married, first, Barent Kunst and had one daughter. She married, second, Jacob DuBois. They had six sons and six daughters. Their descendants were numerous and some prominent.

This brings the line to the son of Gerret, from whom most of the family here descend,—Cornelis Gerretse Van Newkirk, who married September 16, 1683, Jennetje Jans Kunst. Her sister, Hillitje Jansz Kunst, married Nicholas Roosevelt, head of the family from which Theodore Roosevelt, Ex-President of the United States, descended.

Cornelis Gerritse Van Newkirk had seven children: five sons and two daughters. In order of birth they were: Gerrit, Jan, Adrian, Barent, Gilles, Jacomyntje and Cornelius.

They all married in Ulster County, New York, and remained there, with the exception of Cornelius and Barent. Cornelius married Rachel Ten Eyck and located at Pittsgrove, Salem County, New Jersey. He had four sons and five daughters. Four of his daughters married men named DuBois. Two of the sons of Cornelius and two of his sons-in-law were soldiers in the Revolutionary War.

There are many descendants of Cornelius Nieukirk in Salem County, New Jersey. The early settlers there established a Presbyterian Church at what is now Daretown, New Jersey. Cornelius Newkirk and his son, Abraham, became members at the organization in 1741. A large plot of ground was provided for a cemetery where many of the Newkirks are buried.

There is another beautiful country church called Friendship, about five miles from Daretown, where many Newkirks are buried. This church owns fifty acres of land with a nice residence for a parsonage—all a gift from Joseph Newkirk.

Abraham Newkirk, one of the sons of Cornelius, died early in life, leaving two sons and four daughters. Many of their descendants located in the west. The late William Newkirk of Connersville and Jacob Newkirk, who located in Union County, Indiana, as well as the Newkirks in and about Peoria, Illinois, were of this line. There are many people in Union County named Rose, Elwell, Husted, DuBois, and others, who are descendants of this Abraham Newkirk.

Those who read the *Indianapolis News* no doubt frequently read syndicate articles written by a very clever writer, signed Ida Husted Harper—that is her correct name, and she is a descendant of this Abraham Newkirk.

Barent Newkirk, son of Cornelis Gerritse, is the one from whom most of you attending this reunion are descended. He was baptized October 13, 1689, married May 23, 1713, Rebecca Van Buntschooten. They both resided at Kingston. Her family were prominent Hollanders. Some distinguished themselves in the professions.

He moved from Hurley, or Kingston, sometime after his brother, Cornelius, had located in Salem County, New Jersey. He was in Virginia about 1737, when, in September of that year, he bought a large farm in Berkeley County, about ten miles north of the present City of Martinsburg, at the foot of the North Mountain. There is a very old church and burying ground there, but no monument to the grave of Barent, who died in 1765.

He had nine children — two daughters, Gerretjen and Jemima, both of whom married men named Hoagland, and seven sons: Cornelius, Tunis, Henry, Elias, Tobias, Peter and Abraham.

Cornelius died before the death of his father, leaving a son, Barent, generally called Barney, some of whose descendants live in Switzerland County, Indiana.

Tunis died in Fairfield County, Ohio. He had a son, Cornelius, who located first in Estell County, Kentucky and later in Crawford County, Indiana, where many of his descendants still reside.

Henry resided for a time in Berkely County, Virginia, then in Westmoreland County, Pennsylvania and still later in Fairfield County, Ohio, where he died. Some of his descendants located in Marion County, Indiana and others in Kentucky.

Elias had eight children, some of whose descendants live in Indiana County, Ohio, and in Kentucky.

Tobias, son of Barnet, lived and died in Duplin County, North Carolina. He had but three children, Abraham, Henry and Rachel. Abraham was a Revolutionary soldier. He had a large family, most of whom became prominent in the affairs of the day. Many of his descendants were extensive property holders and owned many slaves. In the Civil War they lost all their belongings. But the old Dutch spirit would not die, and they are now fast coming back to their own. When their slaves were emancipated, like other slaves, they took the name of their masters. As a result, hundreds of negroes in North Carolina are named Newkirk.

Peter Newkirk, son of Barent, married Cornelia Sousley and lived in Bullitt County, Kentucky. He had a number of children. Among them, Tobias, who was killed by the Indians about 1790, had two sons, Henry and Peter. Their descendants are in Alabama, Arkansas and Missouri. Peter's son, Peter, located in Jefferson County, Kentucky. Another son, Tunis, located in Moniteau County, Missouri, while four of his sons, William, Benjamin, Isaac and Richard, located in Lawrence County, Indiana, where many of their descendants reside.

This includes all of Barent's children, except his son Abraham, the ancestor of a large proportion of those here present.

Abraham married Kezia Shipman. He was born in 1724 and died in Washington County, Pennsylvania, about 1790. He had three daughters and five sons: Tunis, Isaac, Abraham, Henry and Reuben.

Isaac married Rhoda Carroll who was of the family of Carrolls to which Charles Carroll of Carrollton, signer of the Declaration of Independence, belonged. Isaac was a Revolutionary soldier and Indian fighter. He was with Captain Crawford in the ill-fated expedition against the Indians of the Sandusky Country, but escaped the massacre. On his return home he passed through what is now Big Prairie, Wayne County, Ohio. He was so pleased with the fine land he saw there, that when the Government opened it for sale, he purchased one thousand acres and sent four of his children— John, Henry, Reuben and his daughter, Luzarby, who had married John Rainey—to live on this land. They cleared it, built nice homes on it, as well as a church and school house. They and their descendants are mostly buried in the beautiful Newkirk Cemetery near this church. Many descendants of Isaac remain in Wayne County, Ohio. The other children of Isaac remained in Washington County, Pennsylvania. At

Bentleyville, in that county, there is an old brick church called the Newkirk Church, in which many Newkirks are buried.

Tunis, son of Abraham, was married twice. He lived in Berkeley County, Virginia; was a large land owner, holding much of the land which had been owned by his grandfather Barent. His wife, whose maiden name was Margaret Miles, died in 1798. They had nine children. Tunis deeded the Virginia land to his children by his first wife. Many of their descendants still live in Berkeley County, West Virginia, and own some of the land originally that of their ancestor Barent. He married, second, Susannah Hay and located in Fairfield County, Ohio. He had five children by his second wife. The descendants of Tunis are very numerous, residing in various places in Ohio and elsewhere.

Henry Newkirk, son of Abraham, located in Beaver County, Pennsylvania, where many of his descendants still reside. One of his sons, Shipman, located at Brooklyn, Iowa, and many of his descendants live about that place.

Reuben Newkirk, son of Abraham, located in Fairfield County, Ohio. His descendants have scattered to various states; one grandson, William Newkirk, residing (1914), in Indianapolis.

Abraham Newkirk, the son of Abraham, who so many here are proud to call ancestor, was born March 10, 1764; married first, Margaret Knox; resided in Washington County, Pennsylvania. He owned a large farm there, which he sold in 1816 and located at Dunkinsville, Ohio, where his death occurred October 5, 1840. He and his wife are buried in the burying ground of the old Hull Church, near Dunkinsville. The ground upon which this church and burying ground are located was donated by Abraham. He had eleven children, as follows:

1. Hannah, who married John Hull. They had eight children, the descendants of whom largely reside in Adams County, Ohio.

2. Henry, who married Hannah Bentley. He owned the land and plotted Georgetown, the County seat of Brown County, Ohio. He died October 21, 1821, in his thirty-second year. He had three children: Lorinda, Adamson Bentley and Cyrus. This Adamson Bentley Newkirk was the father of the

gentleman who made it possible to save the family history from becoming lost, Dr. A. B. Newkirk, of Los Angeles.

3. Anna Newkirk, who married John B. Clary. They located in Cass County, Indiana, where she died eighty-five years ago. They had five children. Their descendants reside mostly in Cass County. Many attend the reunion.

4. Orpha Newkirk, who married John Dunkin. They had six children and located at Memphis, Missouri, where she died in October, 1851. Most of their descendants are living in Union County, Missouri.

5. Nancy Newkirk, who married Dr. Peter Fear. They lived in Adams County, Ohio and had nine children; two of whom are still living. Dr. Carey N. Fear, a successful physician at Waverly, Kansas, is a grandson.

6. John Newkirk, married Sarah Walmsley. They had nine children and located in Tipton County, Indiana. One son Jonathan, resides at Frankton, Indiana, while another, Holliday S. resides at Mapleton, Iowa.

7. Keziah Newkirk, married Amos Dunkin, had seven children and resided in Adams County, Ohio, where their descendants still reside.

8. Shipman Newkirk, grandfather of the author of this article, located in Rush County, Indiana, where nearly all his descendants reside. He married Mary Bayless. They had seven children, one of whom, Malinda J. Bell, was living in 1914.

9. William Newkirk, married Rebecca Storer and located at Bellfast, Highland County, Ohio. He had but two children; both were living in 1914, — Abraham, at Bellfast, Ohio, and Macy Williamson, at Snyder, Oklahoma.

10. Cyrus Newkirk, married Cassa Ann Philipps and located in Grant County, Indiana, where he died October 2, 1855. They had nine children, of whom Margaret J. Kilgore, Emma Elizabeth Bishop and Louisa A. Stout, three of the daughters, and George and John F., two of the sons, were still living in 1914. Of these, George is the genial president of the Newkirk Family Association and can speak for himself. The children of Cyrus lived in Grand and Howard Counties, Indiana.

11. Emily Newkirk, married Charles Osman. They had two daughters who died quite young.

Thus, briefly, and in a general manner, the outline of the Newkirk family history has been given, but how little the outline tells. It must be realized, when it is stated that the descendants of Gerret Cornelisse Van Nieuwkerck, living and dead, exceed, in numbers, the entire population of this county.

Generally speaking, the Newkirks, in the male line, have been, like their ancestors in Holland, farmers, merchants and manufacturers. Few have entered the professions.

The family challenges comparison with any other in the points of intelligence, integrity and good citizenship. It is doubted if any other family in the country can produce a membership with as large a percentage of home owners.

The family furnished many Revolutionary soldiers; many for the War of 1812. To the Civil War, New York, New Jersey, Pennsylvania, Ohio, Indiana, Illinois and other northern states sent scores of the family to battle for the Union cause; while West Virginia, North Carolina, Missouri, Alabama, Kentucky and Arkansas sent scores to the Southern colors.

INDEX

A

Aarons, Garret, 54, 55
  William, 54
Abbott, Abdon, 33
  Ann, 53
  Joel, 53
  Joseph, 33
  Susan, 53
Adams, Thomas, 56
Adriance, Aeltje, 28
  Cornelius, 28
  Gilletjen, 28
  Theodorus, 28
Albertson, Arent, 9
Alderman, Joel, 53, 55, 56
  Wm., 54
Alexander, Sarah A., 43
Allegar, Mary, 15, 30, 47
Anderson, Temperance, 53
Anjou, Gustave, 10, 22
Applegate, Cassandra, 45
  Samuel, 45
  Sarah, 45
Ariens, Jannetje, Jennette, 7, 24
Asher, Levy, 45
  Mary, 45
Atkinson, Moses, 55
Auer, Elizabeth, 64
Austin, Cornelius, 55
Ayars, Ayers, Ayres,
  John C., 53
  Mary, 53
  Robert, 54, 55, 56
  Sarah, 52
  Susannah, 53

B

Bacon, Ann, 50
  Martha Reeve, 50
  John, 50
Baldwin, Catharine, 20
  Elihu, 20
  Mary, 63
Ballenger, Susannah, 58
Barens, Elsje, 9
Barfield, Mary Ann, 44
Barker, Jane Champ, 63
  Lucy Mary Taliaferro, 63
  William Musgrave, 63
Bassett, Catharine, 20
  Ebenezer, 20
Bateman, Joseph, 55
  Peter, 54

Bates, Henry, 45
  Jemima, 45
  Mary Catharine, 45
Bayless, Bayliss, 59, 60, 64
  Daniel, 59
  Mary, 59, 82
Beard, Matilda, 59
  Samuel H., 59
Beekman, Hendrickus, 7
Bell, Abigail, 18
  Joseph M., 60
  Malinda J., 60, 82
Bennett, Mary, 43
Bentley, Benjamin, 63
  Hannah, 58, 63, 81
  Mary, 63
Bevier, Ann, 18
  Annatje, 18
  Cornelia, 22
  Jacob, 18
  Philip, 33
  Samuel, 22
  Sarah, 22
  Tryntje, 33
Biggs, Uriah, 54, 55, 56
Bikelo, Antie, 6
  Johannes, 6
Bishop, Emma Elizabeth, 82
  Emma Elizabeth Ellen, 61
  Hamilton, 61
  John Wesley, 61
  Mary A., 61
Bittner, Catherine, 65
Blanchan, Blancsan, Blanshan,
  Blansjan
  Annetjen, 17
  Catharine, 11, 13, 14
  Elizabeth, 11, 37
  Jacob, 17
  Jacomyntje, 17
  Magdalena, 11
  Margaret, 11
  Maria, 11
  Matthew, 11, 13, 17
Bloodgood, Judith, 34
Bloomandal, Leah, 18
Blydenburgh, Adelaide C., 70
  Adelaide, M. S., 70
  Helen, 70
  Margaret Jean, 70
  Mattie Ford, 70
  Raymond Rodgers, 70
  Ruth E., 70

(85)

477

Newkirk, Nieukirk, Fannie S., 62
  Fitje, 20, 21
  Florence, 67
  Florence May, 62
  Frances, 41, 45, 59
  Frank, 62, 66
  Frank H., 62
  Furman, 62
  Furman A., 62
  Garret, 6, 15, 20, 23, 26, 30,
    31, 36, 39, 47, 48, 52
  Garret Cornelius, 22, 36, 39
  Garret H., 20
  Garret J., 21
  Garret L., 35
  Garret Mattheusen, 19, 20
  Geertje, 20, 21
  Geertruyt, Gertrude, 4, 5, 18, 21
  George, 20, 41, 60, 61, 82
  George Heberton, 49
  George M., 65
  George Marshall, 60
  George W., 43
  Georgeanna, 65
  Gerret, Gerretse, Gerrit, 3, 5,
    6, 7, 9, 10, 14, 18, 19, 20, 22,
    24, 25, 26, 27, 28, 33, 34, 35,
    36, 37, 38, 41, 44, 46, 47, 50,
    57, 61, 63, 64, 65, 67, 69, 76,
    77, 78
  Gerret Cornelisse, 1, 2, 3, 4,
    7, 76, 82
  Gerretje, Gerritje, Gerretjen,
    3, 4, 5, 7, 13, 14, 18, 22, 23,
    48, 77, 78, 79
  Ghilje [Chiltje?], 10
  Gilles [Gieletjen, 10, 27, 78
  Gottfried, 73
  Grace, 52
  Grace B., 69
  Grietje (Marguerite), 9, 14,
    18, 22
  Hannah, 49, 52, 53, 57, 58, 62,
    63, 67, 81
  Hannah B., 67
  Hannah J., 53
  Hannah N., 66
  Helena, 6, 20
  Henderikje, Hendrica, Hen-
    drika, Hendrikje, 10, 17, 18,
    22, 34, 39, 40
  Hendrick, Hendricus, Henricus,
    1, 20, 25, 26, 33, 34
  Henrietta Johnson, 66
  Henry, 27, 41, 42, 43, 44, 45,
    57, 58, 63, 67, 79, 80, 81
  Hetty M., 49
  Holliday S., 59, 82
  Horatio Wood, 50
  Howard B., 62
  Hugh, 52
  Ida Belle, 65

Newkirk, Nieukirk, Isaac, 23, 33,
    41, 42, 43, 45, 47, 80
  Isaac Roberts, 50
  Isaac Smith, 62
  Israel F., 53
  Jacob, Jacobus, 5, 18, 20, 21,
    22, 23, 25, 31, 33, 36, 47,
    52, 79
  Jacob Rutsen, 33
  Jacomyntje, 5, 6, 7, 8, 10, 15,
    23, 24, 25, 31, 78
  James, 41
  James E., 61, 62
  James Lewis, 71
  James Mason, 41
  James Polk, 51, 67, 69, 70, 71
  James Ross, 59
  James Sinnickson, 65
  Jan, Jan Gerretse, 3, 4, 6, 9,
    10, 24, 33, 34, 78
  Jane, 42, 43
  Jane Champ, 64
  Jane Perty, 42
  Jane Reese, 49
  Jane S., 62
  Jane Westcott, 62
  Janneke, Jannet, Jannetje,
    Jannetje Jansz, Jannetjen,
    Jannette, Jenneke, 4, 5, 6,
    7, 8, 9, 13, 20, 21, 23, 24,
    25, 39, 40
  Jemima, 27, 45, 79
  Jennie, 66
  Jennie C., 66
  Jeptha, 42
  Joast, Joost, 52, 54, 55, 56
  Johan Henrick, 1
  Johannes, 1, 21, 23, 25, 26, 34,
    35, 36
  John, 36, 37, 41, 42, 47, 49, 53,
    59, 67, 73, 78, 82
  John Bacon, 50
  John Brooks, 67
  John C., 44
  John F., 82
  John Forest, 43
  John Francis, 61
  John H., 45
  John Henrick, 1
  John Henry, 1
  John J., 21
  John M., 20, 21
  John Naylor, 64
  John P., 66
  John W., 42, 59
  John Young, 62
  Jonathan, 82
  Jonathan H., 59
  Joost, see Joast
  Joseph, 31, 41, 52, 78
  Joseph Alexander, 43
  Joseph H., 65

Peek, Cornelius, 38
   David, 38
   Jacob, 38
   Jacobus, 38
   Jan, 38
   Margrietta, 38
   Rachel, 38
   Samuel, 38
   Sarah, 38
   Willemtje, 38
Pells, Pels, Clarissa Evertse, 12
   Evert, 8
Person, Ann, 25
Petson, Annatje, 33
Phelps, Asa, 44
   Zelu, 44
Phillips, Cassa Ann, 60, 82
   Edward Augustus, 65
   Emma Jane, 65
   George, 58
   Grant Kennedy, 65
   John Howell, 65
   Margaret, 58
   Newkirk Reading, 65
   Peterje, 36
   William, 60
Plummer, Josephine, 71
Poarch, Thomas, 55
Polhemus, Sarah, 28
Porter, George, 8
Porterfield, Mary, 41
Potter, Florence, 68
   James Preston, 68
Pounder, Pownder, Asa, 55, 56
   William, 54
Pratt, Daniel Lincoln, 42
   Jane Perty, 42
Pratts, Alna, 69
Preston, Elizabeth, 15
Pudney, John, 28
   Phebe, 28
Pugh, Helena, 19
   Hugh, 19
   Isaac, 19
   John, 19
   Margaret, 19
   Peter, 19

Q

Quackenbos, Nellie, 36

R

Rainey, Jane, 42
   John, 43, 80
   Luzarby, 43, 80
Rambo, Catharine, 49
   Jesse, 49, 54, 55
   Margaret, 49
Ramsey, Andrew, 44
   Delilah, 44
Rapelje, Sarah, 28
Rasinger, Hannah M., 66
Rawlings, Martha, 58

Ray, Sally B., 62
Reed, George W., 67
   Helen H., 67
   John, 53, 54
   Mary, 53, 61
Remley, Rebecca, 58
Reynolds, Adelaide M. S., 70
   Daniel C., 66
   Evaline Sherron, 66
Rice, Elizabeth, 44
   Hannah, 43
   James, 43
   Keziah, 43
   Robert, 43
   Sophia, 43
   William, 43
Richey, Jacob, 56
Richman, Ann, 30, 46
   Henry, 54
   Isaac, 54
   John, 54
   Moses, 54, 55
   Neh, 54
   William, 53
Ricker, John, 33
Ridgway, Lydia, 66
Robinson, Catharine, 46
   Elizabeth, 48
   Sarah S., 46
   William, 46
Roos, see Rose
Roosa, Aagje, 12, 16
   Abraham, 37
   Albert, 38
   Albert Heymans, 8, 9
   Aldert, 12, 16, 37
   Anna Margaret, 12, 16
   Benjamin, 39, 40
   Dirck, 12
   Elizabeth, 37, 39
   Garret, 14
   Heyman, 39
   Heyman Aldertse, 12
   Isaac, 37
   Jacob, 37
   Jannetje, Jannette, Jenneke,
      Jenneken, Jennette, 12, 16,
      22, 28, 30, 38, 39
   Lea, Leah, 12, 16, 37, 39
   Magdalena, 14
   Neeltje, 12, 14, 16
   Petrus, 12
   Rachel, 12
   Rebecca, 12, 37
   Sarah, 37
Roosevelt, Anna Margaret, 12
   Franklin D., 7
   Hillitje, 7, 24, 78
   Nicholas, 7, 24, 78
   Theodore, 7, 78
Rose, Roos, Abraham, 46
   Ann, 46
   Anna, 46
   Catharine, 46

104

ADDITIONS

VAN NIEUWKIRK, NIEUKIRK, NEWKIRK: A GENEALOGICAL SURVEY. A search was recently undertaken to ascertain whether the ancestry of the van Nieuwkerk family could be determined in Holland.

It was known that to New Netherland there came in 1659, Gerrit Cornelisse from Nykerk; his wife, Chieltje Cornelisse, "a nursing child," and a boy twelve years old, the latter in all probability, Mattheus Cornelisse, Gerrit's brother.*

When Mattheus Cornelisse married in 1670 in New Netherland, he was designated as a young man or bachelor, from Slichtenhorst, near Nykerk.

The progenitor having been designated in the passenger list as "from Nykerk," it was logical to first consult the church records of that city. These proved to be very incomplete, especially for the years 1655-1659, the period in which, in all probability, the marriage of Gerrit Cornelisse to Chieltje Cornelisse had taken place. This marriage however, could not be found in the available records. The search might have been stopped here, as the searcher also did not find the baptism of a child of these parents in the baptismal registers of Nykerk. However, it was continued since other clues might be found.

One entry which might possibly apply, was the baptism at Nykerkon, July 11, 1658, of *Disje*, abbreviation for Matthys, Thys, Thysje, Thiesje, Disje, the Dutch form for Mattheus. It was a child of *Gerrit Cornellisen* and *Aeltien Gerrits*. (*Inventory* 1138.) Other children of this couple do not appear in the baptismal records of Nykerk, neither does the marriage of Gerrit Cornelis and Aeltien Gerrits appear in the marriage records which, as has already been noted, are very incomplete.

If this Gerrit Cornelissen, with another wife, should be the settler in New Netherland, then the child Disje, would be designated as "a nursing child."

The next step was to ascertain if a boy, Mattheus, with a father, Cornelis, was baptized in Nykerk at a time that his age was approximately twelve years in 1659. The villagers of Slichtenhorst had to go to nearby Nykerk to have their children baptized. Mattheus was born in Slichtenhorst, according to his marriage entry in New Netherland.

The only child baptized at Nykerk which could be considered, was one *Deuws*, a son of Cornelis Aertzen and Geertien Beerents, baptized at Nykerk, December 4, 1642 (*Inventory* 1136). Deuws is a variant of Deus, Dewus, Teuws, Tewus, Tewis or Mattheus. Although there

---

* THE VAN NIEUWKIRK, NIEUKIRK, NEWKIRK FAMILY. SOME DESCENDANTS OF GERRET CORNELISSE AND MATTHEUS CORNELISSE VAN NIEUWKERK. From the manuscripts of the late Adamson Bentley Newkirk, M.D. of Los Angeles, California now in the Collections of The Genealogical Society of Pennsylvania.—*Publications, Special Number*, March, 1934.**

**Pages 386-497, this volume.

is a difference of about four years, discrepancies of this kind occur constantly in all records.

Then came an effort to find if more children of Cornelis Aertzen and Geertien Beerents had been baptized at Nykerk. The following three were found there:

i.   Geertien, baptized March 5, 1637.

ii. Geertien, baptized August 26, 1638.

iii. Jan, baptized March 28, 1641.

In the first baptismal entry the mother is recorded as Geertien *Jans*, but this in all probability is a mistake, as such a couple do not appear in the Nykerk registers. The mother is also designated as Geertien Brants, instead of Beerents. This is her real patronymic for as will be shown, her father was Brandt Berntz (Beerents) and she is named, as was customary, sometimes as Brandts and sometimes as Berents, the patronymic of her father, by which he was known and by her used as a surname. This was quite common in those days as may be verified in my van Cortlandt article, printed in a recent number of *The New York Genealogical and Biographical Record*. As will be realized, a search in the older records is very difficult and only an experienced Dutch genealogist is able to make the correct deductions.

Again, the baptismal registers failed to show the baptism of Gerrit Cornelisse, for the records between 1628 and 1634 are missing. It is to be noted, however, that Gerrit Cornelisse in America named his oldest daughter Geertruy (Geertien), possibly after her grandmother Geertien Brandts.? The marriage of Cornelis Aertsz and Geertien Brandts was also not to be found in the Nykerk records, as the marriages from 1620 to 1634 are missing.

Before trying to trace the ancestry of Cornelis Aertsz, a search was made for the baptism of his wife, Geertien Brandts, and it is found that Geertgen was baptized at Nykerk, July 13, 1617, as the daughter of Brandt Bernts and Jantgen Cornelis (*Inventory* 1135, *folio* 71-vo.).

The marriage of the parents was found, *Inventory* 1135, *folio* 124-vo., Anno Domini 1605, 2nd March: Brandt Berndtz, Berndt Elbertz soon op *Slichtenhorst* and Jannichgen Cornelis, Cornelis Rotgers dochters op Nautenha, a farm under *Slichtenhorst*.

Although not so stated in the previous entry, Brandt Berntsz was a widower when he married Jannichgen Cornelis for, on March 1, 1599, the marriage register of Nykerk contains the following (*Inventory* 1135, *folio* 116): Brandolph Berntz, Bernt Elbertz soon op Slichtenhorst and Gertrudt Niclas. Ante aliquot anno tempore Everhardi Suarii coram Ecclia solemniter proclamati sed hoc die demum solemniter consociati.

This means that the banns of this marriage had been proclaimed some years previous, at the time of Reverend Everhardus Swaer, but the marriage was solemnized at present. Reverend Swaer had been a priest, before he became converted to the Protestant religion, hence undoubtedly this belated entry.

Gerrit Jansen
b. abt. 1550 lived at Arokemehen near Nykerk

Aerdt Gerrits b. abt. 1575 at Arokemehen according to
his marriage entry, that is if he is the same
as the Aerdt Gerrits who marries Aertgen Stephens
which is not absolutely proved

mar. 1st, prior to 1601, Elbertgen Wolters
mar. 2nd at Putten (banns at Nykerk Jan./Feb.1608)1608 Aertgen Stephens
dau. of Stephen Jansz. and born at Putten.

Cornelis Aerdts
bapt. Nykerk Sept. 24,1601, d. Nykerk Jan.31,1647

| Wolter Aerdts ba. Nykerk 1603 | Gerrit Aerdts ba. Nykerk Jan. 8,1609 | Jan Aerdts ba. Nykerk Mar.4,1610 | Aerdt Aerdts ba. Nykerk Nov.10,1611 |

Aug.14

Geertgen Brandts
bapt. Nykerk July 13,1617 possibly born at
Slichtenhorst, for she was the dau. of
Brandolph (Brant) Berntz, Bernt Elbertsz,
at Slichtenhorst, and of Jannichgen Cornelisdr.,
Cornelis Rotgertsdr. "op Nautenha" under
Slichtenhorst.
Cornelis Aerdts owned property in Arokemehen.

Gerrit Cornelisse
b. abt. 1629/33

mar.
Aeltien Gerrits

| Geertien Cornelisse ba. Nykerk Mar.5,1637 | Geertien Cornelisse ba. Nykerk Aug.26,1638 | Jan Cornelisse ba.Nykerk Mar.28,1641 | Deuws Cornelisse (Mattheus) bapt. Nykerk Dec. 4,1642 |

Disje (nickname for Mattheus)
bapt.Nykerk Jul. 11, 1658

Possibly the Gerrit Cornelisse who came with his wife, a nursing child
and a brother Mattheus Cornelisse abt 12 years old came in 1659
from Nykerk to America. His wife appearing in the American records
is Chieltje Cornelisse.

The complete list of the children of Brandt Berntsz are by his first marriage to Gertrudt Niclas:

i.   Altghen, November 21, 1594.
ii.   Reiner, May 27, 1596.
iii. Claes, March 12, 1598.
iv.   Evertgen, October 6, 1600.   All
v.   Renger, April 8, 1602.   these

By his second wife, Jannetgen Cornelis: children

vi.   Gryt, October 22, 1609.   baptized
vii. Bernt, September 3, 1607.   at Nykerk
viii. Geert, November 1, 1612.
ix.   Reimer, December 8, 1614.
x.   *Geertgen*, July 13, 1617 [wife of Cornelis Aertsz].
xi.   Brant, October 15, 1620.

After this, it was important to find the parents of Cornelis Aertsz.

There was baptized at Nykerk on September 24, 1601, Cornelis, son of Aerdt Gerrits and Elberts Wolters. This same couple had another child, Wolter, baptized August 14, 1603.

In all probability the same Aerdt Gerrits married between January 21, and February 21, 1609, a second time. (*Inventory* 1135, *folio* 126):

Aerdt Gerritz, Gerrit Janssens soon, te Arck (Arck short for Arckemehen, a district near Nykerk, also sometimes called Mehen) and Aertghen Stephens, Stephen Janssens dochter te Putten, town near Nykerk. In Putten copulati.

The following children were baptized at Nykerk, of these parents:

i.   Gerrit, January 8, 1609.
ii.   Jan, March 4, 1610.
iii. Aerdt, November 10, 1611.

The baptismal and marriage registers did not give any further data.

The "Book of the dead" of Nykerk disclosed: 31 January, 1647, Cornelis Aertss in de Mehen (Arckemehen); 23 December, 1654, Gerritgen Brandts; 3 October, 1646, Een kindt van Cornelis Aerts.

The search was now continued in the "Verpondingskohieren" or tithe registers of Nykerk, in which are enumerated those who paid tithes on property.

These of 1650 exist. In this was entered, on *folio* 166, that Cornelis Aerts' zuster (sister) was the owner of a farm and one and a half morgen, three acres, which her sister rented. The same entry occurs in the 1651 register.

In the 1650 register for the district of Arckemehen, or Erck, is entered: *folio* 143, Cornelis Aerts (should read heirs of Cornelis Aerts, an omission often found in these records), rents three and a half morgen; *folio* 153, vo., Cornelis Aerts weduwe owner of the Plascampie, (name of farm or land), two morgen; *folio* 162, vo.; Kill Ariss and the widow of Cornelis Aerts have the "kleymen Papencampken (name of farm), near the dike 7/4 morgen.

I have shown the foregoing on a separate pedigree page which will give a more comprehensive idea of that which has been found. The absolute proof of the ancestry of the American settler is not there. The circumstantial evidence points, however, to the fact that this may be so; that the findings set forth is the possible solution, and affords a working basis for further investigation.

WILLIAM J. HOFFMAN, New York.

James Nixon and Thomas Milhous

RAYMOND M. BELL, F.A.S.G.

and

FRANK R. BAIRD

TWO of Richard Milhous Nixon's great-great-great-great-grandfathers lived within nine miles of each other for a number of years. Both men were coopers (barrel-makers).

JAMES NIXON first appears in Brandywine Hundred, New Castle County, now in the State of Delaware, on 3 April 1731, when he bought a one hundred acre farm three miles north of the present city of Wilmington. The deed lists him as a cooper.[1] He probably was a native of Ireland and probably a Presbyterian. He may have attended the Lower Brandywine Presbyterian Church, founded in 1720.

THOMAS MILHOUS first appears in New Garden Township, Chester County, Pennsylvania, on 28 12m (February) 1729/30, when he presented his Irish certificate of removal to the New Garden Monthly Meeting of Friends.[2] He had come from Timahoe, County Kildare, and, along with his wife and children, brought with him a servant girl, Ann Cunningham, aged sixteen.[3] Thomas Milhous settled on a two hundred acre farm in Steyning Manor, three miles south of Kennett Square, and eleven miles northwest of the site of Wilmington, just inside the Pennsylvania line. His deed for the farm, dated 21 October 1738, lists him as a cooper.[4]

Thomas Milhous moved to Pikeland Township, Chester County, in 1744[5] and died there in 1770. His will, written 25 February 1765, and probated 12 May 1770, devised to his three eldest sons, John, James, and Thomas,

---

[1] Nixon's purchase of land in 1731 from Joseph and Mary Cox is recited in New Castle County Deed Book Z-II, 49: 2 April 1803, George Nixon to William Young.

[2] Abstracts of Records of New Garden Monthly Meeting, 1718-1768, I, 146, in Collections of the Genealogical Society of Pennsylvania (GSP). See also Albert Cook Myers, *Immigration of the Irish Quakers into Pennsylvania 1682-1750. . . .* (Baltimore, Md., 1969), 355. The certificate from Dublin Monthly Meeting was dated 29 5m (July) 1729.

[3] Ann Cunningham's certificate, included in that of her aunt of the same name, and dated the same day as Thomas Milhous's, was received at Philadelphia Monthly Meeting 26 10m (December) 1729. See Myers, *Irish Quakers,* 293, cited in Note 2.

[4] Chester County Deed Book S, 315: 21 October 1738, William Penn [brother and heir of Springett Penn, who was a grandson of William Penn, the Founder] and James Logan to Thomas Millhouse.

[5] He received a certificate of removal to Goshen Monthly Meeting 28 5m (July) 1744. See Abstracts of New Garden Monthly Meeting, I, 295, cited in Note 2.

"five shillings each they having received their shares heretofore." His wife Sarah was to have "my best feather bed and furniture thereunto belonging as also her saddle and bridle and bay mare called Jennie," and "a riding chair with harness also one third of my estate." To his son Robert and daughter Sarah Parker he left "one third of my estate to be divided equally." To his youngest son William he left "the remaining third part of my estate." [6] This youngest son William went to eastern Ohio in 1805.[7]

James Nixon died in Brandywine Hundred in 1775. His will, written 16 May 1773, and probated 26 June 1775, devised to his wife Mary sixty pounds in cash "besides the third of the benefit of the place where I now live and bed and bedding and furniture for one room." To his three married daughters he left £45; to his daughter Jean £60 in cash "now in the hands of the Revd. Mr. Smith of Pequea, besides a horse and saddle and bed." To his eldest son George he left "the plantation where John Reily formerly lived," 106 acres, and £70 in cash. To his son James, Jr., he devised "the plantation whereon I now live containing one hundred acres," and his Negro man Ned and Negro woman Nance. The oldest son George Nixon moved to western Pennsylvania in 1803.[8]

William Milhous's grandson, Joshua V. Milhous, went to eastern Indiana in 1854; George Nixon's grandson, George Nixon III, went to central Ohio in 1853. Frank Nixon, the latter's grandson, went to California in 1907, where he met and married Joshua Milhous's granddaughter, Hannah Milhous, who had gone to California in 1897. Their son, Richard Milhous Nixon, was born in California in 1913.

Did the two coopers, Thomas Milhous and James Nixon, ever meet?

[6] Abstracts of Chester County Wills, 1758-1777, II, 365, will of Thomas Milhous, GSP.

[7] William Wade Hinshaw, *Encyclopedia of American Quaker Genealogy. Ohio* (Ann Arbor, Mich., 1946), IV, 154. His certificate from Uwchlan Meeting, Chester County, to Concord Meeting, Belmont County, Ohio, was dated 5 9m (September) 1805, and was received 24 12m (December) 1805.

[8] Washington County Deed Book 1-S, 214: 18 October 1803, Henry Woods to George Nixon.

The Family of Thomas Ollive

of Wellingborough, Northamptonshire
and of Burlington County, West Jersey*

Research by
JANE W. T. BREY

D URING the seventeenth century, England was beset with political, economic and religious problems. A regicide, the civil war, the plague and great fire of London all contributed to the economic hardships experienced throughout England. Religious dissension, particularly among the Protestant majority, gave rise to various sects and the eventual persecution of those who did not conform to the Established church.

It was also a period during which England was expanding her empire by the establishment of colonies in the New World and inadvertently was providing a safety valve for the mounting tide of dissatisfaction in the Old World. To these new colonies were drawn groups of dissident sects, members of which hoped by their migration to better themselves and to live according to their own lights, unfettered by regulations imposed on them by an indifferent government.

Among these dissenters were the followers of the Quaker George Fox. Fined and imprisoned year after year for their refusal to pay tithes or

* This study was undertaken in order to correct certain inaccuracies, in the author's *Quaker Saga*, published in 1967, made concerning the wives of Isaac Marriot, John Woolston and Thomas Ollive, and their relationship to each other, which appeared on pages 267, 375, 377 of that work.

take oaths, the Quakers looked with growing interest on the newly opened lands acquired by England from the Dutch under the Treaty of Westminster in 1674. In particular the land on the east bank of the Delaware River, when it was offered for sale on shares to adventuring investors, was of special interest to men of both small and large means.

Included among these investors were two Quakers, Thomas Ollive, a haberdasher of some substance, of Wellingborough in Northamptonshire, and Daniel Wills, a "practicioner in chymistry," of the town of Northampton, both of whom had been fined and imprisoned at various times in Northampton Gaol. They joined with other purchasers from the south of England to form what became known as the London Company. In like manner Quakers from Yorkshire formed the Yorkshire Company. Jointly these companies engaged to establish settlements on the Delaware for the benefit of their Quaker investors.

Deeds of lease and release, dated 22 and 23 January 1676/7, executed by William Penn, Gawen Lawrie, Nicholas Lucas and Edward Billinge, conveyed to Thomas Ollive and Daniel Wills jointly one share or propriety of land to be laid out in the new colony. On the same day the same grantors conveyed a second share to Ollive, Wills, and William Biddle of London.[1] A month later on 26 February 1676/7, Ollive and Wills sold about a third of a share to six underpurchasers in various fractional amounts. The largest single underpurchaser was John Woolston, also of Northamptonshire, who had been in Northampton gaol with Ollive, and who bought one-eighth of a share from Ollive.[2]

Having disposed of what property they had in England, and subscribed their names to a mutual covenant of "Concessions and Agreements," dated 3 March 1676/7, outlining in detail regulations for the proposed settlement,[3] Thomas Ollive, Daniel Wills and John Woolston travelled to London where they loaded their household goods on board the ship engaged for the voyage, the *Kent*, Gregory Marlow, master.

[1] "Calendar of Records . . . ," *New Jersey Archives*, 1st Series, XXI, 441. It should be remembered that in England until September, 1752, double dating between 1 January and 25 March was in effect, in order to distinguish between the legal and historical year. Not all writers of legal documents, however, were careful to follow this usage, so that in many cases the reader must take careful note of the context and the chronology of events to establish the precise date.

[2] The other purchasers were Robert Powell, clothier, and Thomas Eves, packer, both of London, John Roberts, yeoman of Overston, Northants., Richard Parks, ironmonger, of Hook Norton, Oxon., and Thomas Harding, boxmaker, of London. See *ibid.*, 397, 424, 464, 467, 478, 479.

[3] See Samuel Smith, *The History of the Colony of Nova-Casesaria or New Jersey . . . to the year 1721* (Spartansburg, S. C., 1966 reprint), Appendix II, 521, 538. John Woolston did not sign the version printed here, but may have signed the copy kept in England. The original of the printed version obviously must have been signed after it was sent over, for many of the names subscribed to it were of men who were inhabitants of the area before the *Kent* sailed from England.

With well over 200 passengers on board, the vessel sailed from London in April, 1677.[4]

Their first landfall was in August, 1677, at Sandy Hook in the New York government. Here they presented their credentials to the authorities, and here the first commission for magistrates for the east bank of the Delaware was granted to Thomas Ollive, whose name headed the list, Daniel Wills, and seven others.[5] All but three Yorkshire proprietors represented the London purchasers. When they resumed their voyage and arrived finally in the Delaware, it was these commissioners or magistrates who purchased land from the Indians and selected the site of the first settlement, now called Burlington. For a time, however, at least one colonist, John Woolston, referred to it as "Thomas Ollive's Town" on the Delaware.[6]

Although much has been written about this Thomas Ollive [7] and his public service in West Jersey between 1677 and 1692, there has been much confusion and uncertainty as to his origin and relationship to several other early West Jersey settlers, notably the Woolstons, Jenings, Marriots, Lippincotts and Wills. Certain members of these families were all remembered in Ollive's will, a verbatim copy of which follows:

Thomas Ollive's will [8]

The 8th day of the 9th month [November] 1692, I Thomas Olive of willingborough in the county of burlington in west new Jersey, being weake in body but of perfect memmory & rememberance praised be god doe make and ordaine this my last will & Testament in manner & form following

first I committ my soul into the hands of Almighty god my creator & my body to be buryed in Christian buryall

Item — I give to An the wife of samuell Jenings the sum of five pounds

Item — I give to Joyce the wife of Isiak Marriot the sum of five pounds

Item — I give to John Woolston Junior the sum of five pounds

Item — I give to my Brother benjamin olive of London the sum of five pounds

---

4 Goods were loaded on the *Kent* consigned to West Jersey between 19 March and 31 March, according to Walter Lee Sheppard, Jr. and Marion Balderston, "Early Shipping to the Jersey Shore of the Delaware," *Passengers and Ships Prior to 1684* (Baltimore, Pa., 1970), 139-141.

5 *New Jersey Archives*, 1st Series, I, 291.

6 See *ibid.*, XXI, 400, 23 December 1680, John Woolston to Thomas Potts "for ⅛ of a lot in Burlington, called Thomas Ollive's Town."

7 This surname appears in contemporary documents under various spellings: Oelife, Olave, Olife, Olive, Olliff, Olliffe, Ollive, Olyff, etc. Not all members of the same family spelled it identically, and scribes seem to have been unable to decide upon a consistent spelling in the same document. The usual modern form is "Olive," but Thomas himself signed his will as Thomas "Ollive."

8 The following transcript is made from a xerox copy of the original, filed in Unrecorded Wills, Volume 3, 231-238, furnished by the Archives and History Bureau, New Jersey State Library, Trenton. The will, an abstract of which is in *New Jersey Archives*, 1st Series, XXIII, 346, was admitted to probate 24 December 1692.

Item — I give to my sister Sarah Gurney if liveing the sum of forty shillings

Item — I give to my sister Martha the sum of forty shillings

Item — I give to my cozen Thomas Olive the sum of twenty shillings

All which sums to be paid within two years after my decease if legally demanded

Item — I give unto the children of freedom lippingcot the sum of five pounds to be eaqually divided amongst them & to be paid when they shall come to the age of eighteen years

Item — I give unto Mary my wife al my plantation being about 800 acres of land with the house & houses thereupon erected as also the mills meadows & all other appertinencies thereunto belonging as also all my goods & chattels bils bonds & wrighteings whatsoever with the reversion of my propriety of land. To sum up all in short I give her all my estate both real & personal to her & her heires for ever upon condition that shee shall pay all my debts & legacies. And doe make her Joyntly with her father Daniel wills & brother John wils executors of this my last will & testament revoaking all other wills & testaments

In wittnesse whereof I have hereunto set my hand & seal the day & year above written

Signed & sealed in the presence of us

Jaimes delaplaine
Daniel Leeds
Edward Lancaster

/s/ Tho: Ollive

In this will Thomas Ollive noted only five specific relatives: his brother Benjamin Olive of London, his two sisters Sarah Gurney and Martha [Olive], his "cozen" Thomas Olive, and his own wife Mary, daughter of Daniel Wills, whom he had married in his own home under the care of Burlington Monthly Meeting on 8 5m (July) 1691,[9] when she was just twenty-one years of age. A new search, in English Quaker and Anglican church records, for the identification of the other legatees has now resolved some, if not all, of the uncertainties concerning Thomas Ollive's own identity and his relationships to the others.

His place of nativity, as now established, was in Buckinghamshire where the marriage of his father Thomas Oliffe was entered in the register of the parish church of St. James [10] at Bierton, a village one-and-a-

[9] Transcript of Records of Burlington and Mt. Holly Monthly Meeting, 1678-1872, 18, in Collections of the Genealogical Society of Pennsylvania (GSP).

[10] This church stands near the south end of the village of Bierton (anciently Barton, Burton, Berton) and is conspicuous from the hills bordering the vale of Aylesbury. The building is cruciform with a square tower at the juncture of the nave, aisles and chancel. In the upper story are four mullioned windows with pointed arches, and against that on the north side is the dial of a clock. Anciently the Manor of Bierton was appendant to Aylesbury as a chapel of ease. George Lipscomb, *County History of Buckinghamshire, England* (London, 1847), 97. In 1969 the church's unpublished registers for 1628-1635, 1635-1645, and 1645-1700, were searched for the author by Miss Cicely Baker, through the courtesy of the vicar, the Reverend R. A. R. Henesey-Law. At that time the registers were in the care of the Buckinghamshire Archeological Society in the muniment room of the Buckinghamshire County Museum in Aylesbury.

half miles northeast of the county town of Aylesbury:

1630   4 November Thomas Oliffe and Ann Hopkins alias Jones married

The baptisms and burials of some of their children were also entered in the church registers:

1631   6 November John son of Thomas Oliffe baptized
1634/5   24 February Mary daughter of Thomas Oliffe baptized
1635   14 June Francis son of Thomas Oliffe baptized
1635/6   24 February Mary daughter of Thomas Oliffe buried
1636   14 June Francis son of Thomas Oliffe buried
1636/7   1 February *Thomas* son of Thomas Olife baptized
1638/9   19 February Mary Oliffe buried
1639/40   18 March Henry son of Thomas Oliffe baptized
1642   21 November Sarah daughter of Thomas Oliffe baptized
1643/4   3 January [*name faded, possibly Martha*] daughter of Thomas Olif baptized

The mother of these children, Ann Hopkins, alias Jones, wife of Thomas Oliffe, Sr., appears to have died about 1645, whereupon the father took a second wife, Elizabeth,[11] to whom the following children were born, according to St. James's register:

1646   5 July Ann daughter of Thomas & Elizabeth Oliffe baptized
1647   22 November Hannah daughter of Thomas & Elizabeth Oliffe baptized, born 14 November
1649   24 June Richard son of Thomas & Elizabeth Oliffe baptized; buried 26 June
1651   16 October *Benjamin* son of Thomas & Elizabeth Oliffe baptized

The Quarterly Meeting records of London and Middlesex [12] provide further information on this youngest son of Thomas Oliffe, Sr.:

1680   2 7m [Sept.] Benjamin Olive, dyer of Old St., Middlesex, son of Thomas Olive of Barton [Bierton], Bucks., and Elizabeth Meakins, daughter of John and Margaret Meakins, married at Waltham Abbey, Essex

The births and deaths of their family are entered in the same Quarterly Meeting records:

1681   22 3m [May] John son of Benjamin Olive, Cripplegate Parish, Peel Meeting, born
1682/3   10 12m [Feb.] Thomas son of Benjamin Olive & Elizabeth, Cripplegate Parish, Peel Meeting, born

11 According to Miss Baker, the old registers were written in a very confused manner and difficult to search, but she found no burial entry for Ann Oliffe, and no marriage for Thomas and Elizabeth. The inference is that he probably married her in another parish, the records of which also have not been published.

12 See Digest of Marriages, Births and Burials, Quarterly Meeting of London and Middlesex, GSP, for the following entries.

1685   18 10m [Dec.] Elizabeth daughter of Benjamin Olive & Elizabeth, Inks
        Green, Chinkford Parish, Essex, Tottenham Meeting, born
1686   23 9m [Nov.] Margrett daughter of Benjamin Olive & Elizabeth, Totten-
        ham Meeting, born
1687/8 22 1m [March] Benjamin son of Benjamin & Elizabeth Olive, Chingford
        Parish, Tottenham Meeting, born
1688/9 21 1m [March] John son of Benjamin Olive of Hall End, Essex, died of
        a consumption, aged 8
1690   30 8m [Oct.] John son of Benjamin Olive, Chingford Parish, Essex, Tot-
        tenham Meeting, born
1692   19 9m [Nov.] Joseph son of Benjamin Olive, Dyer, Walthamstow Parish,
        Essex, Ratcliff & Barking Meeting, born
1695/6 4 11m [Jan.] Ann daughter of Benjamin Olive, Citizen & Dyer, London,
        Cripplegate Parish, Peel Meeting, born
1698   20 4m [June] Jonathan son of Benjamin Olive, Old St., Peel Meeting,
        died, aged 2 weeks
1702   7 7m [Sept.] Nathaniel son of Benjamin Olive, Edmonton Parish, Peel
        Meeting, died, aged 3 months
1711   30 5m [July] John son of Benjamin Olive, dyer, died of a fever, age 21,
        Cripplegate Parish, Peel Meeting
1713   20 7m [Sept.] Benjamin Olive, Sr., Olave Parish, Cripplegate, London,
        Dyer, died of convulsion, aged 62 years [13]
1717   19 2m [Apr.] Elizabeth Olive, widow, St. Giles Parish, Cripplegate, Lon-
        don, died of Consumption, aged 57 years; buried 23 2m 1717, Bun-
        hillfields, Peel Meeting

The marriage and age at death of Benjamin Olive, citizen and dyer
of London, thus provide indisputable proof of the parentage of his half-
brother, Thomas Ollive, the emigrant to West Jersey. Both were the
sons of Thomas Oliffe, Sr., of Bierton, Buckinghamshire.

Contemporaneous with the elder Oliffe, was another Oliffe family [14]
in Bierton, according to the registers of St. James's church at Bierton:

1628   14 May Richard Olive and Joan Greene married

Their first child, however, was baptized in the parish church of
Aston Abbots,[15] a village some three miles north of Bierton:

[13] It is evident from these records that Benjamin Olive moved around from place to place as his occupation of dyer warranted. From Cripplegate Parish he had moved to Chinkford Parish in Essex by 1685;
by 1692 he was in Walthamstow Parish; by 1696 was back in London in Cripplegate Parish and had
become a Citizen of London and member of the Dyers' Guild. By 1702 he was up in Edmonton Parish,
and then was back in London by 1711.

[14] The registers of St. James, as transcribed by Miss Baker, also include the family of a Roger Olife
of Bierton whose children were baptized between 1636 and 1641; the children of a Francis Oliffe who
were baptized between 1661 and 1668, and the children of a Henry Oliffe whose children were baptized
between 1665 and 1678. The above Roger Olife was obviously a contemporary of Thomas and Richard
Oliffe, while Francis and Henry may have been the emigrant Thomas Ollive's elder and younger brother.

[15] "Aston Abbots, 1559-1837," *Buckinghamshire Baptisms, Marriages and Burials* (London, 1912),
I, 17.

1628/9   14 March William son of Richard and Jone Olliff baptized

But baptism and burials of later children were entered in St. James's register:

1631   2 October Mary daughter of Richard Oliffe baptized
1635   15 September Francis son of Richard Oliffe baptized
1635   1 November Ann daughter of Richard Oliffe baptized
1640   10 August John son of Richard Oliffe baptized
1642   12 September William son of Richard Oliffe buried
1643   23 May John son of Richard Oliffe buried
1647   22 May Jone Oliffe buried

The last entry above may have been transcribed incorrectly, for among the marriages in the registers of the parish church at Stone, a few miles southwest of Aylesbury, is the entry of a second marriage for Richard:

1646   28 September Richard Olife and Joyce Fenner married [16]

Baptisms and burials of their children were entered in St. James's register at Bierton:

1650   7 October Elizabeth daughter of Richard & Joyce Oliffe baptized
1651   6 October *Thomas* son of Richard & Joyce Oliffe baptized
1651/2   7 February Elizabeth daughter of Richard & Joyce Oliffe buried
1655   19 August John son of grazier Olliffe baptized [17]
1655/6   5 March Richard son of Richard Ollife grazier baptized, born 18 February, buried 24 March
1657   28 April *Joyce* daughter of Richard Ollife grazier baptized, born 10 April
1659   2 November *Anne* daughter of Richard Ollife & wife baptized
1661   14 April Richard Oliffe buried

The last entry above appears to be the burial of the father of the above children. In the light of later evidence, he is believed to have been the brother of Thomas Oliffe, Sr., (the father of Thomas Ollive, the emigrant to West Jersey), and was in all probability the latter's uncle.

A year after Richard Oliffe's burial, his widow was married again at the Stone parish church where she had first been married:

1662   15 May, Robart Gurny and Joyce Olife [18]

[16] "Marriages at Stone, 1538 to 1812," *Buckinghamshire Parish Registers* (London, 1907), III, 47.
[17] An entry in the register of St. James of the birth and baptism on 6 and 27 June 1655, of Margaret, daughter of Richard Ollife and wife "that dwells in the Mercer's rents," would seem to indicate another Richard who was not "grazier Ollife."
[18] "Marriages at Stone," 48, cited in Note 16.

Sometime during the next ten years, Joyce Gurny's [19] children, Thomas, Joyce and Anne Oliffe, joined the Upperside Monthly Meeting of Friends at Aylesbury. In 1672 the first of them came under the notice of the Meeting. That year Samuel Jenings, salesman of Aylesbury, and Anne Oliffe of the same place, declared their intentions of marriage before the Meeting. Consent to their union was granted by the Meeting 4 10m (December) 1672, which directed that "Samuel (before ye consummation of their intended Marriage) should endeavour to give al reasonable satisfaction to Anne Olive's Grandfather and Grandmother, concerning a provision of future maintenance to be made for said Ann in case she should survive ye s^d Samuel." This apparently was accomplished to the satisfaction of the Meeting, for they were married under the care of the Meeting 7 11m (January) 1672/3.[20]

The next Oliffe to come under the Meeting's notice was Anne's brother, Thomas Oliffe of Aylesbury. On 4 10m (December) 1678, he was granted permission to marry Dorothy Doyly of Adderbury, Oxon., by the Upperside Monthly Meeting of Buckinghamshire. They were married on 17 12m (February) 1678/9, at H. Horn's house under the care of Banbury Monthly Meeting.[21]

Before that year was over, Samuel Jenings, Thomas's brother-in-law, had become the father of two children: William Jenings, born 18 9m (November) 1675, and Sarah Jenings, born 10 2m (April) 1679. Samuel was also entertaining thoughts of emigrating to the New World,

[19] At the time of the Episcopal Visitation in Buckinghamshire in October and November 1662, one Robert Gurny and his wife, having been cited "for not coming to church to heare the sermon nor divine service," were excommunicated as they had not appeared after public proclamation was made. No definite proof has been found so far that this couple were indeed Robart Gurny and his wife Joyce. *Episcopal Visitation Book for the Archdeaconry of Buckingham, 1662*, Buckinghamshire Record Society (1947), VII, 48.

[20] *Minute Book of the Monthly Meeting of the Society of Friends for the Upperside of Buckinghamshire, 1669-1690*, Records Branch of the Buckinghamshire Archeological Society (1937), I, 19. See also "Marriages" entered in the Digested Copy of the Registers of the Quarterly Meeting of Buckinghamshire, 1658-1725, GSP. Although Anne was not baptized until 1659, probably she was the eldest child of Richard and Joyce Ollife, born perhaps about 1648, unless she was the Ann, baptized in 1635, daughter of Richard's first wife Jone. No death record for either girl has been found in the registers of St. James. The modern spelling of Anne's husband's surname is "Jennings," even though in seventeenth and eighteenth century documents the accepted form was "Jenings." His direction, by the Meeting, to clear his intended marriage with Anne's grandparents implies that both her parents were then deceased.

[21] *Minute Book, Upperside Monthly Meeting*, 51, 65, cited above. See also Digested Copy of the Registers of the Quarterly Meeting of Berkshire and Oxfordshire, and of Buckinghamshire, in GSP, for the births and burials of their children: Thomas, b. 6 10m (December) 1679; Anne, b. 2 8m (October) 1681; Dorothy, b. 24 10m (December) 1683; Joyce, b. 25 6m (August) 1685; Doily, b. 21 5m (July) 1688; Dorothy (2nd), b. 29 3m (May) 1690. Their father, Thomas Olliffe of "Ailsbury," who had been imprisoned for 30 months "for not receiving the Sacrament," was discharged from his confinement in 1686, according to Joseph Besse, *A Collection of the Sufferings of the People Called Quakers* (London, 1753), I, 83, hereinafter cited as Besse, *Sufferings*.

having purchased in September, 1678, a one-quarter share of a propriety in the new province of West Jersey, from George Hutcheson, one of the original proprietors.[22]

By 26 3m (May) 1680, Jenings' thoughts of emigrating had crystallized, for on that date Upperside Monthly Meeting, held at the house of Thomas Ellwood in Coleshill, Amersham, Hertfordshire, granted Jenings a certificate of removal:

> Whereas Samuel Jenings late of Alisbury in ye County of Bucks Salesman, hath signified unto us yt he hath an intention (if ye Lord permit) to transport himself with his Wife & Children unto ye Plantation of West-new-Jersey in America, & hath desired a Testimonial from this Meeting, for ye satisfaction of friends there or elsewhere, unto whom he may be outwardly unknown. We therefore . . . hereby certify al whom it may concern, yt ye said Samuel & Anne his Wife, having lived in these parts for many years, have walked conscientiously & honestly amongst us . . . according to ye best of our knowledge & observation of them . . . .

Among those signing the certificate was Thomas Olliffe of Aylesbury, brother of Jenings' wife Anne. It is also apparent that Samuel and his family had already removed themselves to London preparatory to taking shipping for the voyage, as evidenced by a further notice in the same minutes:

> Rowland Foster of Wiccomb complaining to this Meeting, yt Joyce Olliffe formerly of Alisbury, having for some time entertained him in ye way of a Sutor in order to Marriage, is lately removed to London, in order to transport herself beyond ye Seas, to his great trouble & dissatisfaction; The Meeting desired T. Ellwood to speak with the said Joyce at London, & acquaint her, That it is ye Judgmt of this Meeting, yt she ought (before her departure) to endeavour to give ye said Rowland satisfaction in this case, & yt if he shal desire to have ye business heard by some Friends of London, to be chosen indifferently by him & herself, she ought not to refuse it.

Obviously she had decided — perhaps at the last minute — to join her sister and family, and so had left Aylesbury without obtaining the requisite certificate of clearness. Two months later Thomas Ellwood reported back to the Meeting that "he had delivered their Message to Joyce Olliffe, who received it very kindly; & yt afterwards, Rowland Foster & she discoursing together, did wholly end ye Controversy yt had been between them each of them solemnly releasing ye other by a writing under their hands."[23]

22 New Jersey Archives, 1st Series, XXI, 394, cited in Note 1: 16, 17 September 1678, George Hutcheson to Samuel Jenings. The births of the Jenings' children are entered in the Digested Copy of the Registers of the Quarterly Meeting of Buckinghamshire, GSP.

23 Minute Book, Upperside Monthly Meeting, 82-84, cited in Note 20.

With this problem settled, the Jenings were free to depart, according to Jenings' account [24] written in the New World to Friends in England on 17 October 1680: "Dear Friends, This may give you an account of mine and my families safe arrival in New-Jersey, with all the rest that came with us . . . . about sixe weeks since, we arrived in Delaware river . . . ." Probably by the ship which had carried them over, Joyce Ollife [25] wrote back to Upperside Meeting for the neglected certificate; on 2 1m (March) 1680/1, Thomas Ollife acquainted the Meeting

that his Sister Joyce Ollife (who ye last summer went from England to live in New Jersey in America) hath by letter desired him to move this Meeting for a Certificate on her behalf. The Meeting in order thereunto desired John Archdale, Nicholas Noy & William Kidder to make inquiry concerning her clearness, & to speak particularly with Rowland Foster.

The following April William Kidder reported back to the Meeting that he had spoken with Rowland Foster concerning Joyce, and that "said Rowland did leave ye matter wholly to Friends of this Meeting to do therein as they should think fit." Whereupon the Meeting issued the requisite certificate, which, however, contained certain conditions:

. . . These are therefore to certify al whom it may concern, that upon inquiry made concerning her, we find that, there having formerly been some affection tending to Marriage between ye said Joyce Olliffe & one Rowland Foster of Wiccomb in this County, wch afterwards upon more serious thoughts through a dissatisfaction on her part, was wholly laid aside, ye said Rowland Foster, by a Writing under his hand bearing date ye second day of ye 4th mo: 1680 did acquit her & leave her perfectly free, with this proviso, yt she ye said Joyce Olliffe should keep herself free from ingaging in Marriage to Isaac Marriot for ye space of one year. And, unless there be some affection tending to Marriage between her & ye said Isaac Marriott (wch we have no certain knowledge of) we do not know, nor have ground to suppose yt she is under any engagement to or entanglement with any person in England, but we do look upon her to be clear & free as aforesaid, so far as we have been able to inform ourselves . . . .[26]

Communications being what they were, Upperside Monthly Meeting apparently was unaware that Isaac Marriot, whom Joyce obviously had met while in London the previous summer awaiting transportation to West Jersey, had already come to an understanding with her. The

[24] Smith, *History of the Colony of Nova-Caesaria* . . . , 124, cited in Note 3. The letter was directed to "William Penn, Edward Byllinge or Gawen Lawrie." They may have sailed on the *Content* of London, reported variously to have arrived in the Delaware in September or October, 1680. See "The Philadelphia and Bucks County Registers of Arrivals," *Passengers and Ships Prior to 1684*, 172, cited in Note 4.

[25] Joyce Ollife was one of the witnesses at the marriage in Burlington on 14 8m (October) 1680, of Freedom Lippincot and Mary Custin, for which see the text below, and Book of Births, Deaths, Marriages, 1677-1777, Burlington Monthly Meeting, on deposit at Friends Archives, 3rd and Arch Streets, Philadelphia.

[26] *Minute Book, Upperside Monthly Meeting*, 92-94, cited in Note 20.

minutes of Peel Meeting in London, under date of 26 11m (January) 1680/1,[27] noted that

Izack marriot of Holbourn Joyner, the sone of Richard Marrit of Wappingham in Northampton Shyer husbandman deceased, did propose to take to Wiff Joyce Ollives the Sister of Samuell Jenings Wiff, & now in new Jersey & doth desyer A certificate by consent of this meeting to the 2 weekes meeting wch was consented unto by the meeting & John Edge & Tho: Zachary ar desyrd to get a Certificate & present him to the 2 Weeks meeting.

The certificate was duly issued to Isaac under date of 7 12m (February) 1680/1, and by the following September he was in Burlington, having concluded arrangements for his marriage to Joyce Olliffe by virtue of a pre-marital agreement: [28]

Isaac Marriott By one Bond dated Sept. 3^d 1681, bound in ffowre Hundred pounds of Lawfull English money to Sam^ll Jennings & Thomas Oliffe—now in England, as ffee ffees for Joyce Olliffe, with Condition in Consideration of a Marriage intended betweene ye said Isaac & Joyce, That if (after ye said intermarriage) The said Isaac shall depart this life before ye said Joyce, Then ye said Isaac shall give & bequeath Two Hundred pounds sterling of his Estate to ye said Joyce, her Exec^rs & Assignes; And if ye said Joyce shall depart this life before ye said Isaac & leave no Issue of her body then liveing; That then ye said Joyce shall have liberty before her decease, by her will, to dispose of what Legacyes shee shall please, not exceeding in ye whole one Hundred pounds sterling; which will ye said Isaac thereby Covenants to perform. But if ye said Joyce shall die before ye said Isaac & leave Issue of her body then liveing, Then ye said Isaac, his Exec^rs, Adm^rs or Assignes, shall pay to ye abovesaid Sam^ll Jennings & Thomas Olliffe, their Exec^rs or Assignes, Two Hundred pounds Sterling for the use & benefit of each child or children then liveing, at such tyme as ye said Sam^ll Jennings & Thomas Olliffe, their Exec^rs or Assignes, shall see it needfull to take such child or children into their own Tuition; Sealed and delivered to Sam^ll Jennings to ye uses abovesd before John Butcher, Thomas Walters & Thos. Revell.

Four days later on 7 7m (September) 1681, Joyce Ollive married Isaac Marriott, late of Holborn, at the house of Thomas Gardiner in Burlington. Witnesses included Thomas Ollive, of West Jersey, and Samuel and Anne Jenings.[29]

Now, if the premise is valid that Thomas Oliffe, Sr., and Richard Olliffe, both of Bierton, Buckinghamshire, were brothers who had children baptized in St. James's parish church, then those children were first cousins to each other. That being so, it is clear why Thomas Ollive of

27 Gilbert Cope, "Notes from Friends Records in England," *Publications of the Genealogical Society of Pennsylvania* (PGSP), III, 229.

28 Transcript of Records of Burlington and Mt. Holly Monthly Meeting, 1678-1872, 237; "Burlington Court Records," in John F. Stillwell, *Historical and Genealogical Miscellany* (New York, 1906), II, 4. The author is indebted to Mr. George Ely Russell for this reference.

29 Transcript of Records of Burlington and Mt. Holly Monthly Meeting, 1678-1872, 5, GSP.

West Jersey, son of Thomas Oliffe, Sr., of Bierton, remembered in his will children of his uncle, Richard Ollife: Anne, wife of Samuel Jenings, and Joyce, wife of Isaac Marriott. He felt there was no need to identify them as cousins since they were both in West Jersey when his will was written. He also remembered their indisputable brother Thomas of Aylesbury, but identified him only as his "cozen Thomas Olive," because he was in England and not in West Jersey.

But what of John Woolston, Jr., also remembered in Thomas's West Jersey will? What, if any, was Woolston's relationship to the testator Thomas, to Anne Jenings and her sister Joyce Marriot and their brother Thomas Oliffe of Aylesbury? In order to establish his identity, it is necessary to go back in time and pick up the thread of the emigrant Thomas Ollive's life.

As already noted, he was baptized in Bierton at St. James's church 1 February 1636/7, son of Thomas Olife, Sr., and his wife Ann. The next recovered record places the younger Thomas Ollive in the market town of Wellingborough, Northamptonshire, about ten miles northeast of the English county town of Northampton. When or why young Ollive removed there remains unknown; he may have been sent there as apprentice to a haberdasher, the calling he followed until his removal to West Jersey. It is claimed that he was converted to Quakerism about 1654 or 1655 by William Dewsbury when he visited that area, and that in 1657 Thomas Ollive with others was fined "under the Name of Sabbath-breakers, for no other cause than travelling to their religious Meetings on the First-day of the Week." [30] Be that as it may, whatever the time of his conversion, by 1666 he was a sufferer for his convictions.

On 20 3m (May) 1666, Thomas Ollive, now aged 29, was at a meeting at the house of John Mackerness in Findon (Finedon), a village about three miles northeast of Wellingborough. A constable appeared at the meeting "with a Rabble of Assistants" bearing a warrant to arrest those attending the meeting. When it was over the constable and his assistants "dragged" about forty of those present to a neighboring alehouse where they were detained all night. Next morning they were put in a cart and waggon and conveyed to Ealson where Justice Yelver-

<hr>

[30] Besse, *Sufferings*, I, 530, cited in Note 21. See also *The Friend*, XXVII (1854), 228, 236, 237. The Thomas Olive who was fined in 1657 might have been the Thomas Olive, Gent., late of Holdenby, for whom a precept was issued to the sheriff to appear with others before the justices at Northampton Castle after Easter to answer "divers felonies," for which see *Quarter Sessions Records of the County of Northampton, 1630, 1657-8*, Northamptonshire Record Society (1824), I. The emigrant Thomas Ollive would have been only 20 years of age at that time, and certainly not dignified by the name of "gent." which was a term used to signify a man of material substance.

ton and another justice fined them each forty shillings. Since they refused to pay the fine, they were sent to the county gaol for six weeks. Among those so gaoled were Thomas Ollive, John Nottingham and Judith Ollive, all from Wellingborough, and a John Woolston from "Attleborough" (now known as Irthlingborough), a few miles north of Wellingborough.[31]

While Thomas Ollive was confined in Northampton Gaol he wrote his first religious tract which he called "A Signification from Israel's God to English rulers and inhabitants." To this he added a postscript to the effect that it was written "the 3rd of 5th month 1666 where I am a prisoner with near 80 more of the people of the Lord, who, at this day suffer for the testimony of a pure conscience, waiting for the Lord to plead our cause and clear out innocency in the face of our enemies." [32]

There has been a persistent tradition that Thomas Ollive had a wife Judith, and a woman of that name was among those imprisoned in Northampton Gaol at the same time as Thomas. If she was his wife, he did not mention her in his postscript, and no marriage record for him has been found in either Anglican or Quaker records. Another persistent tradition is that in these early years Thomas Ollive married into the Woolston family, and that one of Thomas's sisters married John Woolston. In the hope that a search in the unpublished parish registers of Irthlingborough, where John Woolston lived, might clarify these Ollive-Woolston traditions, the registers were examined in August 1969, and again in 1970.[33]

From these examinations it is apparent that the Woolston family was one of long standing in the neighborhood, the name appearing as early as 25 May 1562, when a Robert Sibley married an Elizabeth Wolson. Thirty years later in the register is the marriage on 27 November 1592, of Geffery Wolson and Alice Drage, and the baptisms and burials of their children:

1592   11 October Jhon Woolson son of Gefferie Wolson baptized [34]
1593   20 April Jhon Wolson buried

---

31 Besse, *Sufferings*, 1, 534, cited above.

32 Four years later, Ollive again suffered for his principles, as reported in a letter of 23 4m (June) 1670. It appears that "the wicked Ruler's Agents came & streined from Thomas Ollive 60 pds. worth of good cloth at one time," probably because he had refused to pay tithes. Besse, *Sufferings*, I, 536.

33 They were first searched for the author by the courtesy of the Reverend Canon J. K. King, The Rectory, Irthlingborough, Northants; later a further search was made for Mrs. D. Warren, of 1 Chestnut Road, Yardley Gobion, near Towcaster, Northants., at the request of the author.

34 The proximity of the date of baptism of this child, and the date of marriage, poses the question as to whether the father was the same person who married Alice Drage. Perhaps errors in transcription were made.

1594	30 March Alice Wolson daughter of Geffery Wolson baptized
1596	16 May Jnon Wolson son of Geffery Wolson baptized
1598/9	28 January William Wilson [*sic*] son of Jeffery Wylson baptized
1601	28 December Gefferie Wolson son of Gefferie Wolson baptized
1604	26 May Thomas Wolson son of Gefferie Wolston baptized
1607	20 June Simon Wolston son of Jefferie Wolston baptized
1609/10	17 February Thomas Wolston buried

Search in the registers also brought to light the marriage on 29 January 1628/9, of John Wolston (presumably baptized 16 May 1596, inasmuch as no other John Wolston of the period appeared in the register) and Anne Reeve. The baptisms of their children in the same registers were also found:

1629	6 December *William Wolston* son of John baptized
1631	18 December Thomas Wolston son of John and Anne baptized
1633	22 December *John Wolston* son of John and Anne baptized
1635/6	6 March Alice Wolson daughter of John and Agnes baptized [35]
1638/9	10 February Geffery Wolstone son of John and Agnes baptized
1641	21 April Elizabeth Wolston daughter of John and Agnes baptized
1642/3	10 March Agnes Wolstone wife of John Wolstone buried
1665	22 September John Wolston buried

This last John Wolston could not have been the man imprisoned with Thomas Ollive in Northampton Gaol in 1666, but his son John, baptized 22 December 1633, could have been Ollive's fellow prisoner. While there is no record of that John Wolston in the Northampton Friends' records of the meeting at Wellingborough, those records do include the marriage of William Woolston, his presumed elder brother, who was baptized 6 December 1629. He was of "Artillonyberry" when he married 2 10m (December) 1659, Susanna Nottingham. The births of their children were also entered in the Meeting records:

1660	30 6m (August) Ann daughter of William and Susanna Woolston
1662/3	6 1m (March) *John* son of William and Susanna Woolston of Artellingberry
1663/4	6 12m (February) Thomas son of William and Susanna Woolston of Irelinborow [36]

[35] Here the mother's name is given as Agnes which, according to Mrs. Warren, at the time was interchangeable with Anne, as Wilson and Wolson appear for Wolston or Woolston. The parish register does include the baptism on 12 June 1601, of Agnes Reeve, daughter of Richard Reeve and wife Amy Broughton, who were married 6 November 1598. No death for an Anne Wolston was noted in the register.

[36] Friends records for Wellingborough show that Thomas Woolston and Alice Worms, both of "Arteingborrow," were married 18 10m (December) 1695, and had the births of their children entered in the records, one of whom was Jeofry, b. 26 4m (June) 1699. It seems evident that this Thomas was the son of William Woolston and his wife Susanna Nottingham. See Digested Copy of the Registers of the Quarterly Meeting of Friends of Northamptonshire, GSP.

1666	1 6m (August) Samuel son of William and Susanna Woolston of Irtellingborow
1668/9	17 11m (January) Mary daughter of William and Susanna Woolston of Artellborough
1672	7 8m (October) Susanna [37] daughter of William and Susanna Woolston of Artellingberry

Although this William Woolston had his childrens' births entered in the Wellingborough Friends Meeting records, his own death was entered in the register of the parish church at Wellingborough: "1685 27 November, William Woolston of Irthlingborough buried." His will, dated 23 October 1685, at Irthlingborough, and proved in Northamptonshire 8 December 1685, named his son Thomas executor. He left to his wife (unnamed) ten pounds, "the house formerly Sharps in Irthlingborough, land known as Kelleson's" and household goods. He named his "brother Jeffery Woolston of Queenhithe, London," and left to his "eldest son *John Woolston in America* the sum of ten pounds to be paid to him within three years after my decease." His younger sons Sam and William were to receive ten pounds when they reached the age of fourteen, and a further sum of thirty pounds at twenty-one years of age. He also named his daughters Ann, Mary and Susanna. He further noted that "whereas some of my children have had legacies given them by the will of their grandfather Nottingham, and some others, such legacies are included in legacies left by my will." [38]

The parentage of John Woolston, Jr., legatee under the will of the emigrant Thomas Ollive, is thus established by his father's will. He was the son of William Woolston and Susanna Nottingham, and the nephew of John Woolston, emigrant to West Jersey in 1677, who was his father's brother. Moreover, it appears that he also was related to Thomas Ollive, for on 1 4m (June) 1685, Thomas Ollive of Northampton River, West Jersey, made over to John Woolston, Jr., "of yᵉ north branch of Rankokus Creek . . . for yᵉ naturall love which he hath to yᵉ said *John Woolston his Nephew*," a tract of 100 acres within the Second

---

[37] The marriage of Susanna Woolston is entered in the Wellingborough parish church register, searched for Mrs. Warren: "1698 September 6, danyel man, Smith, & Susan Woolstone, Quakers, married in their own way." The deaths of Daniel Man and his wife Susan, who both died (or were buried) on the same day, were entered in Wellingborough Friends records as having taken place on 15 3m (May) 1713, while the Wellingborough parish register included the burial of one child: "1701 October 23, A son of Danyel Man, Smith."

[38] Northants Archdeaconry Wills, J, 306, 3rd Series, will of William Woolston, searched for Mrs. Warren.

Tenth adjoining 200 acres where John, Jr., was "seated." [39]

To establish the identities of John Nottingham who was in North-ampton Gaol with Thomas Ollive in 1666, and Susanna Nottingham who married William Woolston in 1659, the unpublished registers of the Anglican church at Wellingborough were searched in the spring of 1970. The first pertinent entry proved to be the marriage record of a Thomas Nottingham and Mary Hills on 24 April 1624. Baptisms from 1624 to 1628 are missing in the register, a page evidently having been torn out. But later pages revealed the following Nottingham baptisms and burials:

1628/9	8 February Mary daughter of Thomas Nottingham baptized
1631	11 April Mary daughter of Thomas Nottingham baptized
1634/5	24 January Susanna daughter of Thomas Nottingham baptized
1636/7	9 February Hannah daughter of Thomas Nottingham baptized
1639	*Judith* daughter of Thomas Nottingham baptized
1641/2	13 February John son of Thomas Nottingham baptized
1642	20 December Mary daughter of Thomas Nottingham buried
1644	24 April Mary daughter of Thomas Nottingham baptized
1644	29 October Mary daughter of Thomas Nottingham buried

The death (or burial) of Thomas Nottingham, father of the above children, was entered in Wellingborough Friends records as having occurred on 2 11m (January) 1670/1. As a yeoman of Welling-borough, Thomas Nottingham in his will, dated 19 December 1670, and proved 28 February 170/1, mentioned his wife Mary, his son (-in-law) William Powers and Elizabeth his wife (presumably the eldest daughter born perhaps about 1626), their sons Thomas and Sam Powers, and his own sons Sam and John Nottingham. He left legacies "to every Daughter," without naming them individually. He devised other lega-cies to his "Daughter Potter's children," to his "Daughter Palmer's children and Sam Palmer her husband," to his *Daughter Woolston's* children," and to his "*Daughter Ann Custance*, lately deceased, her

[39] West Jersey Deeds, Liber B, Part 1, 91, a xerox copy of which was supplied by the Archives and History Bureau, New Jersey State Library. The abstract of the record in *New Jersey Archives*, 1st Series, XXI, 410, omits the phrase "his Nephew." John Woolston, Jr. had come over in 1677 with his uncle, John, Sr., Thomas Ollive and Daniel Wills, according to the account written in 1715 by Daniel Wills, Jr., and printed in George DeCou, *Burlington, A Provincial Capital* . . . , (Philadelphia, 1945), 30. He married in Burlington public court 6 10m (December) 1683, Lettice Newbold, b. 14 October 1659, daughter of Michael and Ann Newbold, originally from Sheffield Park, Yorkshire. "Marriages, 1665-1800," *New Jersey Archives*, 1st Series, XXII, lxxvi.

children, except Hannah, the wife of John Hansell." He named his wife Mary and son John Nottingham executors.[40]

"Daughter Woolston" named in this will undoubtedly was Susanna Nottingham, wife of William Woolston, and the son John [41] the man who was in Northampton Gaol in 1666 with Thomas Ollive, John Woolston, Sr. (son of John and Anne), and Judith Ollive. It therefore seems more than likely that Judith was Thomas Ollive's wife, and was included in her father's will under the bequest to "every Daughter," but having no children, was not specifically identified. If this premise is valid, then John Woolston, Jr., son of Judith's sister Susanna Nottingham and William Woolston, was Judith's nephew, and a nephew by marriage of Thomas Ollive of West Jersey. On that assumption, the often repeated but undocumented claim of a supposed marriage of Thomas Ollive to a sister of John Woolston, Sr., variously named as Judith or Elizabeth Woolston,[42] is no longer reasonable.

That there was a further bond of relationship between the Woolstons and Thomas Ollive has been put forth in a number of unsubstantiated claims. One of these is that John Woolston, Sr., had married a sister of Thomas Ollive before his emigration, and that her death in England was perhaps a reason for his decision to emigrate. That claim says she was Ann Ollive whose son John Woolston, Jr., came with his father to West Jersey in 1677.[43] The last part of that statement is demonstrably false, in light of the identification of John Jr. as the son of William Woolston, noted above. And while it is a fact that Thomas Ollive did have a half-sister Ann, baptized at St. James's parish church in Bierton, 5 July 1646, there is no further reference in the parish

---

[40] Northants Archdeaconry Wills, L, 135, 3rd Series, will of Thomas Nottingham, searched for Mrs. Warren. John Nottingham was surety for Elizabeth Powers, widow and sole executor of the estate of William Powers, when administration was granted 22 November 1676. *Administrations of the Archdeaconry of Northampton, 1546-1676* (London, n.d.), 84, estate of William Powers.

[41] John Nottingham had previously been arrested on 6 September 1663, when he was taken at a meeting in Bugbrook with others "for refusing the Oath." Then in July, 1666, soon after his release from Nottingham Gaol, he was again arrested and though sentenced to transportation, it being his third offence, he was kept imprisoned until 1672. Besse, *Sufferings*, I, 533, 535, 537. After his release he married on 12 10m (December) 1672, Mary Ashby of Bugbrook, under the care of Wellingborough Friends Meeting. Their childrens' births and deaths were all entered in that Meeting's records. Significantly their first child, Judith, b. 29 1m (March) 1674, who d. 12 2m (April) following, was followed later by a second Judith, b. 26 4m (June) 1685; the name Judith is found only in the Nottingham family and never in any Woolston family record so far examined.

[42] See for example, "The Genealogical Record of John Wills (New Jersey 1660-1746/7)," *National Genealogical Society Quarterly*, XLII (1954), 65, n.9; William Bacon Evans, "Additional Information on Thomas Ollive, 1692," the original of which is in Haverford College Library, Haverford, Pa., and a photocopy in Friends House, London.

[43] Arthur E. Bye, *History of the Bye Family and Some Allied Families* (Easton, Pa., 1956), 318-319, Note A.

registers either to her or to her sister Hannah, born 14 November 1647, and neither of them are mentioned in Ollive's 1692 will. John Woolston, Sr. could have married either of these girls, possibly after he got out of Northampton Gaol.[44] He did marry Hannah Cooper, daughter of William and Margaret Cooper of Pine Poynte, under the care of Burlington Monthly Meeting on 7 8m (October) 1681, and in his will, written 12 3m (May) 1698, spoke of his "now wife Hanah."[45] Such phrasing often indicated a prior wife, but neither English Friends records, nor Anglican parish register so far searched have provided proof of a first marriage for him.

While John Woolston, Sr., was not a legatee under the will of Thomas Ollive, the children of Freedom Lippincott were. Freedom was the son of Richard and Abigail Lippincott who appear to have come from Devonshire originally, whence they emigrated early to New England, perhaps in the late 1630s. Finding the climate there not to their taste, especially in religious matters, they returned to Plymouth in the late 1640s where Freedom, their fourth son, was born about 1655. In 1660 they once more emigrated, this time to Rhode Island, and from there made their way with others to Shrewbury in East Jersey.[46]

In 1676 Richard Lippincott purchased from John Fenwick 1000 acres of land in Salem, West Jersey, on "Chohanzich R. and Wee-hatt-quack Cr." Three years later in May, 1679, Richard and his wife Abigall, now of "New Shrowsbury," planter, divided his 1000 acres between his five sons, giving each 200 acres.[47]

On 2 7m (September) 1680, sixteen months later, "Freedom Lipingcott of Shrewsbury and Mary "Costoms" of Burlington proposed their intentions of marriage before the Burlington Monthly Meeting held at John Woolston's house in Burlington. They passed meeting the fol-

---

[44] Often in the early days of Quakerism record keeping among the Friends was apt to be quietly centered in the personal hands of one Friend until such time as monthly meetings were formed around structured meeting houses. Thus many early vital record of Friends do not exist, particularly if the events normally recorded occurred when religious dissent was considered illegal, and Anglican clergy were helping English justices to persecute dissenters.

[45] Transcript of Records of Burlington and Mt. Holly Monthly Meeting, 1678-1872, 7, GSP; will of John Woolston: Unrecorded Wills, Volume 4, 221, xerox copy from Bureau of Archives and History, New Jersey State Library, Trenton. See also abstract in *New Jersey Archives*, 1st Series, XXIII, 517.

[46] See James S. Lippincott, *The Lippincotts in England and America* (Philadelphia, 1892), 43, for a record of their children from which their parents' wanderings can be deduced, and Abstract of Marriages and a Copy of the Record of Births and Deaths of the Members of Shrewsbury Monthly Meeting of Friends, 130, 131, in GSP. The original record from which that copy was made was badly torn, so that birth years for the younger children are uncertain.

[47] *New Jersey Archives*, XXI, 565, 567. At first also called "Shrewsbury Neck on Cohanzye," New Shrewsbury apparently was so designated because of the numbers from Shrewsbury in East Jersey who took up land there.

lowing 6 October, and eight days later were married at Burlington. The unpublished marriage record is of special interest: [48]

Burlington ye 14th of ye 8th m^o 1680

These are to Certifie whome it may conserne that Freedome Lippingcott of Shrewsbury & Mary *Custin* of Burlington hath Declared their Intentions of Marriage at two severall Monthly Meetings heare & after ye Consideration & Consent of friends & Relations they were Joyned in Marriage at a Publique Meeting in Burlington ye Day and yeare above written; in ye presence of us

Tho: Ollive	Tho: Ellis
Remembrance Lippincott	John Pallcoast
Tho: Palmer	John Sterks
John Woolston	Jude Ollive
Samuel Jenings	Ann Jenings
Wm Peachee	Joyce Ollive
Tho: Gardiner	Ann Peachee
Daniel Wills	Ann Tucker
Walter Pumphrey	Frances Bucker
Robert Stacy	Annall Eves

The surname of the bride, given in the above record, is not the same as that given in the extant Minute Book, which is a fair copy of the original record. Genealogical records of the Lippincott family have said her surname was Curtis, but personal observation of the original recorded certificate proves that to be incorrect. What actually was her surname, and who were her relations, if any, who gave their consent and witnessed this marriage?

Remembrance Lippincott was Freedom's eldest brother. A connection between Thomas Ollive, John Woolston, Ann Jenings and her sister Joyce Ollive, who married Isaac Marriot the next year, has already been demonstrated. Where did Mary Custin fit into this group?

It will be recalled that Thomas Nottingham in his 1670 will, left legacies to the children of his daughter "Ann Custance, lately deceased." This Ann was a sister of Susanna Nottingham Woolston who was John Woolston, Jr.'s mother, and therefore a sister-in-law of John Woolston, Sr. who witnessed the marriage. If the first syllable of "Custance" is pronounced as in "just," and if consideration is taken of the vagaries of seventeenth century phonetic spelling, then "Custin" could have been the way the clerk heard it when he omitted the last sibillant. If

[48] This marriage record is taken from the original Burlington Monthly Meeting Book of Births, Deaths and Marriages, cited in Note 25, whereas the entry in the copy of the Minute Book is apparently the source from which William W. Hinshaw took his information for his entry in his *Encyclopedia of American Quaker Genealogy* (Ann Arbor, Mich., 1938), II, 238, wherein her name is given as Mary Customs.

Mary Custin was a daughter of Ann Custance, she was then a niece by marriage of John Woolston, Sr., and a true first cousin of John Woolston, Jr.

Also one other name subscribed to the marriage record of Mary Custin is of particular interest: that of Jude Ollive. This is only the second time that her name is coupled in surviving records with Thomas Ollive, John Woolston, Sr., and members of the Nottingham family. No positive contemporary proof has been found to date that she was Thomas Ollive's wife, but there is little doubt that she came with him to West Jersey in 1677 as a member of "his family." As "Judy Olive" she was one of the women who witnessed the birth at Burlington on 1 10m (December) 1677, of Ann Wills, daughter of Daniel and Mary, who had arrived on the *Kent* with Thomas Ollive.[49]

Again as "Jude Olive" she was present at the birth on 1 3m (May) 1678, of Joseph Peachee, son of William and Ann, and as "Judy Olive," at the birth on 21 12m (February) 1678/9, of John, son of Thomas and Hannah Eves. Later that year as "Judeth Olive" she was present when Mary, daughter of Thomas and Suzanah Budd, was born on 2 7m (September) 1679.[50]

Three years after the marriage in 1680 of Freedom Lippincott and Mary Custin, "Judeth" Olive was present at the "birthing" on 25 7m (September) 1683, of Hannah, daughter of John and Sarah Roberts. The next year she was present at the birth on 20 5m (July) 1684, of Samuel, son of Thomas and Anna Eves; was a witness at the marriage of Henry Ballinger and Mary Harding on 4 9m (November) 1684, and six weeks later at the birth of Samuel, son of Freedom and Mary [Custin] Lipincott on 24 10m (December). On 29 8m (October) 1686, she was present at the birth of Benjamin, son of Thomas and Ann Eves, and two months later on 28 10m (December), at the birth of Thomas, son of Freedom and Mary [Custin] Lipincott. Significantly, she was not present on 22 6m (July) 1689, when their daughter Judith, Lippincott was born.[51]

Judith Ollive's death is not noted in Friends records, and she has not been found a party to any deeds of conveyance which Thomas Ollive

---

[49] See "Seventeenth Century Birth Records in the Delaware Valley," *The Pennsylvania Genealogical Magazine* (PGM), XXVII (1971), 84. Who else comprised his family is uncertain. One known servant was Ann Burcham who married William Satterthwaite, shoemaker, on the last day of 12m (February) 1685/6. Transcript of Records of Burlington and Mt. Holly Monthly Meeting, 1678-1872, 12, GSP.

[50] *PGM*, XXVII, 84.

[51] *Ibid.*, 86-88. A second daughter Mary Lippincott was b. 29 7m (September) 1691, who was also a legatee under the will of Thomas Ollive. *Ibid.*, 90.

executed between the time of his arrival and his own death.[52]   It was not until the early part of the nineteenth century, when Asa Matlack (1783-1851) copied genealogical notes which had been entered in a small volume by John Wills (1660-1747), son of Doctor Daniel Wills (Thomas Ollive's co-passenger on the *Kent*), and brother of Ollive's young wife Mary Wills, that Judith's death date came to light.   The entry, as copied by Matlack, reads:

Judy Olive, Died on ye 4 an hour before day of 9 month [November] and was buried on the 6 day of same month 1688.[53]

In this entry she was not identified as the wife of Thomas Ollive, although other wives were identified in the record of burials Matlack copied.   Perhaps John Wills, who knew Judith, thought her too well known to need special identification when he made the original entry.   Matlack, however, did identify her in another one of his books of miscellaneous notes.   He wrote that "Thomas Olive came to this country with wife Judy," and again that "After Thomas Ollive's wife Judy deceased in 1688 he married in 4 month 1691 to Mary Wills daughter of Daniel and Mary." [54]

If, as Matlack claimed, Judy was Thomas's wife, then she was also the aunt of Mary "Custin" Lippincott who named her third child Judith, born less than a year after the elder Judith's death.   And if that assumption is valid, then Thomas Ollive's legacies to his first wife's niece's children are fully explained.

[52] Her irregular and infrequent appearance at "birthings" and marriages perhaps might be attributed to such poor health that for months at a time she did not appear in public.   It seems strange, however, that she never joined with Thomas Ollive, assuming she was his wife, in the conveying of land.

[53] See "Miscellaneous Notes" in Matlack's Historical Notes of Old Coles Church with a copy of the Church Register, 1766-1830, 219, copy in GSP.

[54] *Ibid.*, (Book 6), 723; 226.   Matlack in this entry gives Thomas Ollive's death as 3 9m (November) 1692, which obviously is incorrect since his will was plainly dated 8 9m 1692.

SOME ACCOUNT OF THE PAWLING FAMILY OF NEW YORK AND PENNSYLVANIA.

CONTRIBUTED BY JOSIAH GRANVILLE LEACH.

HENRY PAWLING, a gallant young Englishman of means, education, and enterprise, came to America in 1664, in the military expedition sent out by the Duke of York and Albany to secure the patent accorded to him in that year, by his royal brother, King Charles II. The patent covered all the territory from Maine to the Delaware River, and measures were at once taken for the reduction of the Dutch. The expedition, under Sir Richard Nicolls, a colonel in the English army, sailed from Portsmouth, England, 18 May, 1664, and arrived at New Netherlands in August. By September,[*] New Amsterdam and Fort Orange had surrendered, and the whole territory came under the control of the Duke of York and his agent and governor, Colonel Nicolls,[†] and its name changed to that of New York. One of the earliest acts of the new government was the establishment of a garrison for protection

---

[*] New Netherland surrendered to the English, 29 Aug., 1664.—*New York Calendar of Council Minutes.*

[†] See "Biography of Richard Nicolls," in the *New York Genealogical and Biographical Record,* vol. xv, p. 103.

against the Indians at Esopus,* later Kingston, Ulster County, and the promotion of settlements in this district. Lands were promised to the "soldiers and all other persons who had come over into these parts with Colonel Nicolls," and Mr Pawling was appointed, 9 November, 1668, to lay out lands at Esopus Creek to induce the former to become settlers.† The garrison, of which Henry Pawling was a member and probably an officer, was maintained until the autumn of 1669, when, all fear of Indian depredations having ceased, the troops were withdrawn from service.‡ On 9 September of this year Sir Francis Lovelace, having succeeded Colonel Nicolls as governor,‖ appointed seven leading men of the Province a commission to "regulate affairs at Esopus and the New Dorpes," with Mr. Pawling as one of the commissioners. This body sat as a Special Court, at Esopus, from September 17th. to 29th., inclusive, during which time it located sites for the villages of Hurley and Marbletown, heard grievances, made redress, passed ordinances for the general betterment and government of the locality and appointed officers to carry out the same.§ Among the latter, "Mr Pawling was Voted to be ye Officer to whom ye Indyans should repaire for Redress of Injuryes in Kingston,** Hurley †† and Marbletown." This appointment was due, doubtless, to the fact that, while at the garrison, he had be-

* Esopus, or "Sopus," as known to the early Dutch, included Kingston and the country south of the Rondout. The Esopus Indians who inhabited the region were of Algonquin stock, allied to the Mohegan and other river tribes.

† Brodhead's History of the State of New York, vol. ii, p. 656.

‡ New York State Library Bulletin 58, Calendar of Council Minutes, 1668—1783, p. 10.

‖ Governor Nicolls was in service in an official capacity as late as 21 August, 1668. The earliest record of Sir Francis Lovelace as governor bears date 23 May, 1668; while "Instructions for the well regulating of ye Militia and other officers at Albany," were signed by both governors in August, 1668.

§ Report of State Historian of New York, Colonial Series, vol. i, pp. 264-269 ; Minutes of the Executive Council of the Province of New York, vol. i, pp. 256-282.

** Kingston, so named in compliment to Governor Lovelace's maternal seat at Kingston Lisle, near Wantage in Berkshire.

†† So called from Hurley House, originally a monastery known as Lady Place, in a wooded valley near Maidenhead, on the Thames, in Berkshire. The manor came into possession of the Lovelace family in the sixteenth century and the house was built by Sir Richard Lovelace, whose son became Baron Lovelace of Hurley. In the vault beneath the house frequent meetings were held during the reign of James II., and, according to an inscription on its walls, several consultations for calling in the Prince of Orange were there held.

come acquainted with the Indian tongue and displayed marked ability to deal with this people. So acceptably did he meet the demands of the complex position that the Governor and Council, on 27 January, 1673, voted that, he "be thanked for his vigilance concerning the Esopus Indians." *

By another appointment of Governor Lovelace, he was again commissioner of a Special Court, held at the Town Hall in Kingston, from 30 March to 11 April, 1670, "for setting out the Boundaries of Kingston, Hurley, and Marbleton, and for Regulating the affairs of these places and yᵉ parts adjacent," Captain Dudley Lovelace, brother of the Governor, being President of the Court.† The Court Minutes of April 11th "bear the signatures of the gentlemen justices, of which none is in a more elegant hand than that of Henry Pawling." ‡

On Easter Monday, 4 April of this year, he was made Captain, with instructions "to raise and exercise the inhabitants of Hurley and Marbleton according to the discipline of war, proclamation of this fact being forthwith made by beat of drum publiquely in the Towne of Kingston." He was, further, "appointed to be present at the Rendezvous at Marbleton Tomorrow yᵉ 5th of April." That he kept the appointment the following testifies:

"Tuesday April 5th, 1670.—This day Capt Pawlings ffoot Company appeared at Rendevouse where they were musterd & exercised in their arms. The President also caused all the Laws relating to the Military Affaires to be read before them, and then marched them with fflying colours to the Towne of Hurley and there dismissed them. The Colours were Lodg with a Guard at the Town Hall in Kingston, where the Souldiers were commanded to appeare next day in Court to draw their lots." ‖

One day later, 6 April, he and his lieutenant, Christopher Beresford, received grants of land in Marbletown,‖ and on the 7th, "Captain Pawling" was made "Viewer for measuring and laying out of the Home Lots and Streets of Hurley and Marbleton," and for the determining of the fencing of these

* New York State Library Bulletin 58, Calendar of Council Minutes, p. 18.

† Minutes of the Executive Council of the Province of New York, vol. i, pp. 256-282.

‡ Ibid., Fac-simile of last page Court proceedings, with signatures facing p. 286.

‖ Report of State Historian of New York, Colonial Series, vol. i, pp. 290, 291, 295, 379.

lots and lands. He was also chosen to supervise the building of a bridge * at Marbletown, in which latter service he was to be assisted by "Captain Thomas Chambers,† Surveyor General of his Ma'ties High-ways."

Twelve days thereafter his commission as Captain was signed by Governor Lovelace, a draft of which is of record in the Colonial Archives and reads:

"To Henry Pawling Capt'a . . . . . By Vertue of ye Commission & authority unto mee given (by H's Royall Highness I do constitute & appoint) you Henry Pawling & you are hereby constituted & appointed to bee Capt of the foot comp'y listed & to be listed in the Townes of Marbleton & Hurley & Wyltwyck at Esopus. You are to take into y'r charge & care the s'd comp'a as Capt'a thereof & duly to exercise both yer inferior offic'ers & souldy'ers in Armes & to use y'er best care skill & endeavor to keepe them in good orders & discipline, hereby requiring all inferior officers & souldy'ers under yer charge to—likewise to observe & follow such orders & directions as you shall from time to time receive from mee & other your superior officers according to the discipline of warre.

"Given under my hand & seale this 18th day of Apr in ye 22th yeare of his Ma'ties Reigne Annoq Domini 1670."

On the back of the draft is an endorsement by Governor Lovelace, which reads in part as follows: "Whereas, Mr. Henry Pawling came over a soldier with my predecessor Colonel Richard Nicolls" . . . . ‡

Without doubt, Captain Pawling continued to exercise his military office, in connection with his civil one, as a court of appeals in Indian affairs, until that unexpected event, the reoccupation of New York by the Dutch in 1673. The occupation lasted only until July, 1674, when a treaty of peace restored it to English rule, and Sir Edmund Andross was sent over as governor, in whose first administration, or that of the previous Dutch interim, Captain Pawling would seem to have had no place. There was a quick succession of gubernatorial incumbents in New York, which at that time numbered about

---

* Report of State Historian of New York, Colonial Series, vol. i, pp. 290, 291, 295, 379.

† Captain Thomas Chambers, the hero of Fort Wiltwyck in the Indian raid of 1663, and the original patentee of the manorial grant of Fox Hall, which was invested, by Governor Dongan in 1686, with power to hold Court Leet and Court Baron.

‡ Report of State Historian of New York, Colonial Series, vol. i, p. 379.

40,000 inhabitants, and politics and religious bias, as in England, went hand in hand. The "Anglican Andross" was replaced by the "Papist Governor" Thomas Dongan, who, in turn, gave way for a second Andross régime in the person of his agent, Lieutenant-Governor Francis Nicholson.

The division of the colony into counties was one of the earliest of Governor Dongan's administrative acts, and Ulster County, so called from the Duke of York's Irish title, was established under that of 1 November, 1683. Two years later Captain Pawling was appointed by the governor its High Sheriff,* a position of dignity and responsibility which marked the measure of the man, and in which, for four years, he gave unqualified satisfaction. In February, 1689, he responded to a call for assistance in the war then pending against the French and Indians, and marched with a detachment of volunteers to Albany, where he arrived on the 13th of that month.† At Albany, he was a member of the Convention, composed of prominent military and civil officers, which assembled on the 15th for the consideration of measures defensive and offensive, Peter Schuyler, Mayor of Albany, being president. Schenectady had been burned by the savages; diverse of its inhabitants were in captivity; immediate action was necessary, and, on the 21st, among other resolutions,

"Itt was Proposed to yt gentn of Sopus to levy 50 men out of there County for our assistance to lye in Garrison here, who Replyed that they would use all Endevors to Perswade there People for a Supply, but by there unhappy Revolutions and Distractions Some adhering to ye first majestracy oyres to there new leaders They cannot Execute yt Power & Command as is Requisite on such occasions People being under no Regulation. Resolved to write to ye Civill & Military officers of Sopus for ye assistance of 50 men to lye in Garrison here to Defend there Majes King William & queen Mary's Interest in these Parts." ‡

The "unhappy Revolutions and Distractions," alluded to by the gentlemen from Esopus, were, largely, those engendered by the supporters of the quondam Lieutenant-Governor Leisler,

* New York Civil List, p. 45.

† " Capt. Garten, Capt. Paling, Capt. Buckman, Capt. Matthys, with thirty men came from Sopus."—O'Callaghan's *Documentary History of the State of New York, vol. ii, p. 88.*

‡ Ibid., pp. 41-2.

and it would appear that, Captain Pawling and his associates did not desire to commit themselves or their constituency to the Leislerian policy of the hour. No record evidence is at hand to show him, at any time, a supporter of the first real republican ruler to attain to power in the new world, or, to have been an accessory to the death of the only political martyr to stain with his blood the soil of New York.

An interesting sidelight on the character of the subject of this sketch, and his vision of men and means is to be found in the circumstance of his being, in 1666, while still in garrison service, so large a purchaser at the sale of Dr. Gysbert van Imbrock's library at Esopus. This was a remarkable sale of books for the time and place, and, it is perhaps equally remarkable that the titles thereof, together with the names of the purchasers and the prices paid, have been so largely preserved. Three hundred and sixty-eight books, at a cost of 130 gulden, were bought by Mr. Pawling, many of a religious nature, others school books. *Exquisite Proofs of Human Misery*, Megapolensis' *Short Way*, Borstius' *Succinct Ideas*, a *French Catechism*, *Stories of David*, and a *Gardiner's Book* are a few of the suggestive titles of his acquisition.*

Eleven years thereafter, 1676, as a signatory to the petition "for a minister to preach both Inglish and Dutche, wch. will bee most fitting for this place, it being in its Minority," the man again stands out in the open, large, liberal, kindly.

His worldly goods and acres increased with his years. In addition to his first grants in the uplands of Marbletown, where he continued to reside, he secured by petition, in or about 1677, some twenty acres at Hurley, adjoining the Washmaker's lands, and also another tract at "Cuxing,"† on the west of Redoubt Kills‡ with a piece of woodland, together with forty additional acres at Marbletown. Shortly before his decease he purchased ten thousand acres known as Pawling's Purchase, on the east side of the Hudson River in Dutchess County, near Crum Elbow, a portion of which is now the pleasant village of Staatsburgh. The description of

---

* American Record Series A., Ulster County Wills, vol. i, pp. 24-5.

† Koxing Creek, a tributary of Rondout Creek.

‡ Redoubt Kills, i. e. Rondout Creek.

its survey,* for Jacob Regniers by Angus Graham, Surveyor General, 5 April, 1704, includes the patent of four thousand acres granted to the widow Pawling and her children,† 11 May, 1696. The present town of Pawling‡ in Dutchess County, through which runs the Harlem division of the New York Central Railroad, links the memory of this pioneer, together with that of his son, Ensign Albert Pawling, for whom it was so named, to the intimate association of to-day's activities. In 1778 a considerable detachment of American troops were stationed at Pawling, and for a time General Washington had his headquarters there.

The connection, if any, between Captain Henry Pawling of Ulster County and the Henry Pawling, said to have been of Padbury in Buckinghamshire, one of William Penn's supporters in his proposed Holy Experiment, the founding and settling of Pennsylvania, and a purchaser in 1681 of one thousand acres of Penn's fair lands along the Neshaminy, with two lots in his "dream city of Philadelphia," has not been ascertained. That they were not identical, as was suggested in Mrs. J. Frank Kitts' valuable article, the "Lineage of the Pawling Family,"‖ or, in the "Annals of Phoenixville," by the late Honble Samuel W. Pennypacker, is conclusive from the fact that, on the 10th 1st month, 1696/7, "Henry Pawling acknowledged in open Court of Bucks County, Pennsylvania," one year after the death of Captain Pawling, "a deed of 480 acres of land in fee, dated 4 December, 1689, acknowledged and declared by said Henry Pawlin grantor to Richard Burgess grantee, and the seal of the said deed being imperfect and broken, the said Pawlin did and new make the said seal." The lands of this "first purchaser" of Penn adjoined those of William Paxson, also of Buckinghamshire, in England, and

* New York Calendar of Land Papers, i, p. 146.

† Tjerck DeWitt and Anne his wife, by deed of 1 Nov., 1736, conveyed to son, Henry DeWitt, their estate right in and to a certain patent of 11 May, 1696, by which 4000 acres were granted to the children of Neeltje Pawling, widow of Henry Pawling, to wit: Jane, Wyntje, John, Albert, Anne, Henry and Mary, of which, said Anne is Anne DeWitt, party to these presents.— Dutchess County Deeds, Liber i, ff. 285-87.

‡ Pawling Precinct was formed from Beekman Precinct, 31 Dec., 1768. The latter embraced the land granted to Col. Henry Beekman, whose daughter, Catharine, became the wife of Ensign Albert Pawling.

‖ Published in Old Ulster, vol. i, pp. 339 et seq.

there were sundry land transactions between the two of record in Bucks County, to which Henry Pawlin came with the early settlers. Certain it is that he was there as early as September, 1687, and there remained until as late as 12 September, 1705, at which time he was serving on the Grand Jury.*

Captain Pawling closed his active, eventful and honorable life, at his seat in Marbletown, prior to 25 March, 1695, the date of probate of his will,† which had been executed 21 January, 1691. His entire estate was left to his wife, subject to the payment of his debts, with remainder at her decease to his children.

He married, on or about, 3 November, 1676,‡ Neeltje Roosa, daughter of Captain Albert Heymans Roosa‖ by his wife Wyntje Ariens of Marbletown. She survived her husband and was living as late as 27 October, 1745, when she was a legatee under the will of her son, Ensign Albert Pawling.

Children, born, doubtless, at Marbletown:

1. i. JANE, m. John Cock of Marbletown, banns, 27 Oct., 1706.
   ii. WYNTIE, bapt. 20 July, 1679; m. as second wife, in 1698, Captain Richard Brodhead, son of Captain Daniel Broadhead by his wife Ann Tye.
2. iii. JOHN, m. (1) Aagje De Witt; (2) Ephia.
   iv. JAMES, bapt. 25 November, 1683; died young.
   v. ALBERT, bapt. 29 March, 1685; d. in 1745; m. 26 November, 1726, Catharine, daughter of Colonel Henry Beekman, and widow of Captain John Rutsen. He was an ensign in Marbletown, Ulster County, militia, 7 October, 1717, and represented Ulster County in the New York Assembly, 1726-1737. He had no issue.
   vi. ANNE, bapt. 19 June, 1687; d. before 1739; m. 18 January, 1708, Captain Tjerck De Witt, son of Captain Andries De Witt, bapt. 12 January, 1683; d. at Kingston, 30 August, 1762.
3. vii. HENRY, m. Jacomyntje Kunst.
   viii. MARY, bapt. 30 October, 1692; § m. Thomas Van Keuren.

* Minute Book Common Pleas and Quarter Sessions Courts, Bucks County, Pennsylvania, 1684-1730.

† See full copy of will, in Albert Schock Pawling's Pawling Genealogy, pp. 13-14.

‡ It is uncertain whether this is the date of the marriage, or that of the first publication of banns. probably the latter.

‖ Albert Heymans Roosa came to New Netherland from Herwynen in Gelderland in the *Spotted Cow*, 15 April, 1660, with wife Wyntje Allard, or Arians, and eight children aged respectively 17, 15, 14, 9, 8, 7, 4 and 2 years. He settled in the Esopus district at Wyltwyck, now Kingston, where he was one of the first magistrates, and, in 1673, captain of the militia of Marbletown and Hurley. He died at Hurley, 27 Feby., 1679.

§ " After her father's death."—*Kingston Registers.*

2. JOHN [2] PAWLING (Captain Henry [1]), born, probably, at Marbletown, Ulster County, New York; was baptized at Hurley, 2 October, 1681, and died in Perkiomen Township, Philadelphia, later Montgomery County, Pennsylvania, in June, 1733.

The larger part of his life was spent in the community of his birth, in the cultivation and improvement of his lands and the enlargement of his flocks and herds. Rugged and typical, industrious and sincere, he and several succeeding generations of his family clung to the soil, which rewarded his and their intelligence and discrimination with much more than a competence. Imperfect and meager are the memoranda of those early Marbletown days, but sufficient to show that, to such institutions as the emergencies of the time demanded and established, John Pawling gave his aid, with a predilection to military rather than civil affairs. As one of "the freeholders and inhabitants of Ulster County," he was a signer * to the petition and address of the Protestants of New York to King William III, dated 30 December, 1701, setting forth their loyalty to his majesty during the Leisler troubles.† In June, 1709, he was recommended for lieutenant in the Ulster County militia, under Captain Wessels Ten Broeck, raised for the proposed expedition against Canada, and in such capacity took part in the ill-fated campaign against that place, June to September, 1711.‡

It was about this time that his attention, together with that of his friend and neighbor Isaac Du Bois, was attracted to the fertile lands of Pennsylvania, where, on 26 March, 1709, a return of survey of 625 acres, for John Pawlin, was made to the office of the Proprietary. This tract along the Perkiomen in Van Bebber, later Perkiomen Township, then in Philadelphia County, purchased jointly and held in common by the two friends, was not divided until some years after both had left it forever. On 10 September, 1713, he, then described as "John Pawling of Marbletown in Ulster County in the Province of New York," purchased of James Shattick, of Phila-

* Of the 687 individual signers to this State paper only 61 made their mark.

† New York Colonial Documents, vol. iv, pp. 933-941.

‡ Report of the State Historian of New York, Colonial Series, vol. i, pp. 434, 441.

534

delphia County, five hundred acres "beginning at a black oak at a corner of T. Padget's land and in the line of land belonging to the Free Society of Traders." That he somewhat promptly removed thereto is evidenced from a deed of 22 September, 5th George, [1719], by which he, at that time of Philadelphia, Pennsylvania, conveyed certain lands in Kingston to Gerrard Van Wagenen of the latter place. Aagje his wife was a party to the deed which was witnessed by Edward Farmer, Henry Pawling and Daniel Brodhead.* To these purchases in this picturesque region he made additions, notably a four hundred and fifty acre tract, also on the Perkiomen, with the edifices, tenements and mills, which, about 1730, he bought of Hans Jost Heijt.† On these broad acres, in addition to agricultural pursuits, he operated grist mills, and attained much material wealth and standing in his new environment, and Pawling's Mills became, says a local antiquarian, a well-known landmark in the surrounding country, as did Pawling's Ford, near where the Perkiomen empties its waters into the Schuylkill. In 1747, the mansion house and mills, situated directly within the two branches of the Perkiomen, devised by John Pawling to his eldest son, Henry Pawling, were sold by him to Peter Pennypacker, who added fulling mills to the grist mills already in operation some twenty or more years, and the place thereafter was known as Pennypacker's Mills. Under its new name it was made historic from being the camping ground of Washington's army before and after the Battle of Germantown, the old house being the headquarters of the commander-in-chief after the Battle of Brandywine.‡

During the Indian troubles of 1728 the settlers along the Schuylkill became alarmed at the news that the Flathead Indians, the Catawbas, had entered the Province with the inten-

* Ulster County Deeds, Liber Cle., f. 5.

† See also "The Pawlings on the Perkiomen," in *The Perkiomen Region,* edited by the late Henry S. Dotterer, vol. ii, p. 57 et seq.

‡ It was then that Washington moved his army of eight thousand Continentals and two thousand militia to the head of the Skippack road at Pennypacker's Mills and fixed his headquarters in the house then owned by Samuel Pennypacker, 1746-1826. In the year 1900, forty acres of the original tract and the mansion house were acquired by the late Honᵇˡᵉ Samuel W. Pennypacker, who restored the house and in it spent his last years and days.

tion of striking at the local Indians and settlers.* There were various petitions for means and measures of defence, and on 10 May in this year, Mr. Pawling was among those who petitioned for protection to the inhabitants of Falkner Swamp and Goshenhoppen against the common foe. Some disturbance was occasioned by the mistakes and misunderstandings of the white inhabitants, and the government, foreseeing trouble, commissioned John Pawling, Marcus Huling and Mordecai Lincoln † to assemble the colonists and put them in a position of defence. The work for which the Commission was appointed ‡ was undoubtedly well accomplished, since both John Pawling and Mordecai Lincoln were made justices of the peace and of the Courts of Philadelphia County, 5 March, 1732, and re-commissioned 3 December of the following year. The former was holding this position at the time of his decease.

His will, executed 5 May, 1733, proved 5 June following,‖ described him as of "Bebber's township, gentleman," provided for the extension of the family burial ground § on the east side of the Perkiomen, "where divers of my family" are buried, and made extensive bequests to his children, with provision for wife Ephia. The eldest son, Henry, was given the Jost Heijt tract of four hundred and fifty acres, and the younger sons, John and Joseph, the home plantation and an equal division of the undivided Pawling-Dubois tract, all of which was to be occupied by the eldest son until the younger ones had severally attained the age of twenty-one years.

He married 1st., at Kingston, Ulster County, New York, 23 August, 1712, Aagje, daughter of Tjerck Classen De Witt,**

* Keith's " Chronicles of Pennsylvania from the English Revolution to the Peace of Aix-la-Chapelle, 1688-1748."

† Great-great-grand father of him who was, perhaps, America's greatest American, Abraham Lincoln.

‡ Pennsylvania Archives, Second Series, vol. ix, pp. 705-6.

‖ Recorded Philadelphia Will Book E, p. 243.

§ " Whereas, there is a burying place upon the Land that I have bequeathed to my son *Joseph*, where divers of my family and others are buried. It is my will that there shall be a quarter of an acre of Land laid out commodious thereto, the wᵏ I do hereby give and bequeath for a burying ground from the day of my Decease thenceforward and forever."

** The surname De Witt is of unusual antiquity and eminence in the Low Countries, few more so. The first of this name in New Netherlands, Tjerck

one of the early magistrates of that county; baptized at Kingston, 14 January, 1684; died after 1725, and is, doubtless, one of those alluded to in her husband's will as interred in the family burying ground. The date of his second marriage, or the surname of "wife Ephia," who survived him, has not been ascertained.

Children,* the four eldest born, probably, at Marbletown:

4. i. HENRY,[3] bapt. 1 Nov., 1713; d. 1763.
   ii. ELEANOR, b. 22 Feby., 1715; m. her cousin, Henry Pawling.
   iii. HANNAH, living 5 May, 1733; died before 9 Sept., 1746.
   iv. DEBORAH, m. Christopher Ziegler.
   v. REBECCA, m. Captain Abraham De Haven.
5. vi. JOHN, b. 28 Aug., 1722; d. 23 Oct., 1789.
6. vii. JOSEPH, b. 1724; d. in May, 1797.

3. HENRY [2] PAWLING (Captain Henry [1]), born, doubtless, at Marbletown, Ulster County, New York, in 1689; died in Lower Providence Township, Philadelphia, now Montgomery County, in 1739.

Little or nothing is known of his life in Ulster County save

Claessen De Witt," "van Grootholdt en Zunderlandt," probably Saterland, a district in Westphalia on the southern border of East Friesland, was married in the Dutch Reformed Church of New Amsterdam, 24 Apr., 1656, to "Barbara Andriessen van Amsterdam." After a time he settled at Wiltwyck (Kingston), where he died 17 Feby., 1700. Many of his descendants in both male and female lines have been distinguished as scientists, statesmen, in the learned professions and military life. Through his eldest son, *Capt. Andries De Witt*, he was great-grandfather of *Col. Charles De Witt*, 1727-1788, prominent in Ulster Co. throughout the political events which preceded and accompanied the Revolution; of *Mary De Witt* 1737-1795, who married Gen. James Clinton and was the mother of *De Witt Clinton*, 1769-1828, leading Federalist, liberal patron of the sciences, literature and art, and a really great governor of New York, 1817-1828; of *Thomas De Witt*, 1741-1809, Major in Third New York Regiment in the Revolution, whose eldest son, *Jacob H. De Witt*, was Adjutant in the War of 1812, later Colonel and Member of Congress 1819-1821; and great-great-great-grandfather of *Peter De Witt*, widely known lawyer of New York City, during the earlier part of the last century. *Simeon De Witt*, a member of Washington's military staff and, for more than fifty years, Surveyor-General of New York, also descended through the eldest son of the worthy pioneer.—See De Witt Family of Ulster County, New York, by Thomas Gried Evans, in the *New York Genealogical and Biographical Record*, vols. 17, 18, 22.

* By deed of 9 September, 1746, such of his children as were then living: Henry Pawling, John Pawling and Elizabeth his wife, Joseph Pawling and Elizabeth his wife, Henry Pawling of or near Schuykill and Eleanor his wife, Abraham De Haven and Rebecca his wife and Christopher Zeigler and Deborah his wife, conveyed to the heirs of Isaac Dubois deceased, their interest in certain lands purchased in common by their deceased father and the said Isaac Dubois. In the body of the instrument the elder John Pawling is styled "Captain John Pawling."—*Philadelphia County Deed Book G No. 12, p. 731.*

that, in 1715, he served in Captain William Nottingham's Marbletown Company of Foot, Colonel Jacob Rutsen's Ulster County Regiment of militia.* By 22 September, 1719, his removal to Pennsylvania had been accomplished. This, without doubt, was simultaneous with that of his elder brother. He settled in Lower Providence Township, on a plantation of five hundred acres at the confluence of the Schuylkill and Perkiomen, opposite what later became the almost sacred hills of Valley Forge. To the early settlers this region was known as the fat land of the Egypt District, and the analogy is close between these fair lands, so regularly inundated by the spring freshets and encrusted with the rich alluvial soil brought down by the upper river, and those in the East enriched by the annual life-bearing overflow of the Nile. His choice for a home and farm-stead could scarcely have been excelled. Robert Sutcliff, the English diarist, said of it in 1804:† "I am convinced that it is one of the most beautiful and healthful situations I have known either in England or America." Just prior to the Revolution, a portion of this estate was purchased by James Vaux of Croyden, near London, England, the ancestor of the present Philadelphia family of his surname, and for many years was known as "Vaux Hall." ‡ Here Henry Pawling devoted himself to agriculture and reaped a competence. The inventory of his real and personal estate includes: eight slaves, eight horses, twenty-five cattle, thirty-one sheep and fourteen pigs.

From an early date the Pawlings were prominently identified ‖ with the Episcopal church of St. James, Perkiomen. At the first recorded meeting of its vestry, 2 October, 1737,

* Report of New York State Historian, Colonial Series, vol. i, p. 561.

† "Colonial Homes of Philadelphia and its Neighborhood," by Harold Donaldson Eberlein and Horace Mather Lippincott, pp. 189-198.

‡ In 1804, Vaux Hall went into the prossession of William Bakewell, who re-named it "Fatlands." Subsequently it passed by purchase into the hands of descendants of Samuel Wetherill, the able leader of the Fighting Quakers. One of these, as an act of pious patriotism, gave the use of the private burial ground at "Fatlands" for the re-interment of those who had been buried in the Free Quakers' Graveyard on the west side of Fifth Street below Locust Street, Philadelphia, and whose remains it became necessary, in Nov. 1905, to remove. The tombstone inscriptions of this ground will be found in the *Publications of The Genealogical Society of Pennsylvania*, vol. iii, pp. 135-38.

‖ *Pennsylvania Magazine of History*, vol. xix, pp. 87-95.

Henry Pawling is present as a vestryman, and at that of June, 1738, as church warden.* In its grounds he was buried, and there a granite stone still plainly records: "In Memory of / Henry Pawling / who Died August the / 30th 1739. Aged 50 Years."

He married, 26 June, 1713, Jacomyntje,† daughter of Cornelis Borents Kunst by his wife Jacomyntje Slecht of Hurley, who survived him, and, with son Henry, administered on his estate, 10 October, 1739.

Children,‡ the first three baptized at Kingston:

7. i. HENRY,[3] bapt. 27 June, 1714.
   ii. SARAH, bapt. 8 July, 1716; survived her father.
   iii. ELIZABETH, bapt. 22 March, 1719; survived her father.
   iv. BARNEY, was living in 1791; m. before 12 Dec., 1754, Elizabeth, only surviving child of Josiah James of Phila. Co. In 1766 he was a warrantee of lands in Berks Co., Penna. He was probably the father of *Josiah*,[4] *Isaac* and *John*, enrolled in Philadelphia Co. for service during the Revolution; of *Rebecca*, who m. David Schryver of New York, and *Elizabeth*, who m. Owen Glancy.‖
8. v. LEVI, m. Helena Burhans.
   vi. ELEANOR, m. before 22 Apr., 1746, James Morgan.
9. vii. JOHN, b. 27 Dec., 1732.

4. HENRY [3] PAWLING (Lieutenant John,[2] Captain Henry [1]), baptized at Kingston, New York, 1 November, 1713; died in Cumberland County, Pennsylvania, in or about April, 1763.

He had not reached his majority when his father's death brought upon him, not only the responsibility of the education of his younger brothers, but the administration of their considerable landed estate as well as that of his own, a total aggregation of twelve hundred acres. In "A List of the Names of the Inhabitants of the County of Philadelphia, with

* The church was, in 1738, broken into and robbed of a pulpit cloth and cushion of plush purple fringed with black silk, also a pewter communion service and baptismal basin. A reward of five pounds was offered by the wardens, William Moore and Henry Pawling.—*Pennsylvania Gazette.*

† 2 April, 1729, Henry Pawling and wife Jacomyntje "of Philadelphia in Pennsylvania" were signatories to quit-claim deed to land in Dutchess Co., N. Y., Dutchess Co. Deeds.

‡ An un-recorded deed of 22 Apr., 1746, from Levi Pawling of Marbletown, N. Y. to James Morgan of Philadelphia Co., Pa., recites that, Henry Pawling died intestate leaving eldest son Henry, dau. Sarah, dau. Elizabeth, son Barney, son Levi (the grantee), son John, and dau. Eleanor married to James Morgan, the said grantee.

‖ For descendants of Owen Glancy and Elizabeth Pawling, see Jones Family, by Mrs. Ellen M. Beale; also Rodman Family, by the late Charles Henry Jones Esq.

the quantity of Land they respectively hold therein, according to the uncertaine Returns of the Constables Anno Dom: 1734," his name appears, with the foregoing acreage, as the largest landholder in "Parkiomen and Skippak Township," indeed, the largest in the County.*

His father's will suggests his trustworthiness; his advertisement in the *Pennsylvania Gazette* his progressiveness. It reads:

"December 12, 1735. There has been ever since March last, about the plantation of Henry Pawlin, junior in Perkiomen, a flea-bitten mare branded S. T. upon the near Shoulder, with a reddish Spot upon her Flank and a Bell about her Neck. She is about 13 hands high, and has now a young Colt with her. Whoever owns her is desired to come and fetch her and pay the charges.   HENRY PAWLIN JR."

The qualities mentioned, together with the landed estate which he controlled afforded him a recognized position in the county, and, in 1748, on or about 4 August, he was appointed Captain in the Associated Regiment of Philadelphia County, commanded by Colonel Edward Jones.†

Between 1741 and 1745 he received from the Proprietary four warrants for lands then in Lancaster, later in Antrim Township, Cumberland County, one containing seven hundred and forty-five acres, and another one hundred and twenty-one acres. This acquisition was, doubtless, the compelling cause of his disposal of the four hundred and fifty acre tract, received under his father's will, known as Pawling's Mills, to Peter Pennypacker, and his removal westward to what then was practically the frontier, where he died.

His will of 31 December, 1762, proved 19 April, 1763,‡ named but two children, a son Henry, and daughter Ellinor still in her minority. His only other legatees were: "the sons of my brother-in-law, Henry Pawling of Philadelphia."

He was, probably, twice married.‖ His wife, at the execution of his will, was Mary, daughter of Nicholas Hickes of Cumberland County, whom he had married prior to 6 Sep-

* *Publications of The Genealogical Society of Pennsylvania*, vol. i, p. 180.
† Pennsylvania Archives, second series, vol. ii, p. 504.
‡ Cumberland County Wills, Liber A, f. 106.
‖ See *Pennsylvania Gazette*, July, 1742.

tember, 1749, and whom he made the executrix of his estate,* The date of her death has not been ascertained.

Children:

i. HENRY,[4] b. circa 1748; received from John Penn a patent for his father's Cumberland County lands, dated 31 Oct., 1769; served in the County militia during the Revolution, and was a delegate to the Convention of Associated Battalions held at Lancaster, 4 July, 1776, to choose Brigadier Generals to command the Provincial forces. In 1783 he was a candidate for the Legislature. He was living in Kentucky in 1791 with the rank of Colonel. He died intestate in February, 1794.[†] His heir at law was an only sister Eleanor, then the wife of Dr. Johnston. His widow, Sarah m. Benjamin Price.

ii. ELEANOR, m. Dr. Robert Johnston, a distinguished surgeon in the Pennsylvania Line during the Revolution. It was at his house, in Franklin County, that Washington stopped to dine when on his way to quell the Whiskey Insurrection. It was also at his house, that the death occurred of the eminent Revolutionary surgeon, Dr. Barnabas Binney, ancestor of the Binney family of Philadelphia.[‡]

5. JOHN [3] PAWLING (Lieutenant John,[2] Captain Henry [1]), born on the Perkiomen, Philadelphia, later Montgomery County, Pennsylvania, 28 August, 1722; died there, 23 October, 1789.

Towards the close of the so-called War of the Austrian Succession he was, in 1748, commissioned ensign in the Provincial forces, Captain Abraham De Haven's Company of the Philadelphia County Associated Regiment of Foot.[||]

In the census of 1756 for Skippack and Perkiomen, he is listed as farmer with three children under twenty-one, four hundred acres, two negroes, two horses, two mares, fourteen sheep and twenty horned cattle; in that of 1776, he had four hundred and seventy acres, four negroes, four horses and four horned cattle. At the execution of his will, 12 October, 1789,[§] he was also the owner of a house and lot in Philadelphia.[¶]

* Egle's "Notes and Queries," fourth series, vol. i, p. 216; also will of Nicholas Hickes in Abstracts of Cumberland County Wills, COLLECTIONS OF THE GENEALOGICAL SOCIETY OF PENNSYLVANIA.

† 4 Yeates, p. 526, Pennsylvania Supreme Court Reports.

‡ *Pennsylvania Magazine of History and Biography*, vol. 24, p. 47.

Pennsylvania Archives, second series, vol. ii, p. 504.

§ Philadelphia County Wills.

¶ "On the west side of Second Street opposite the New Market, bounded eastward with Second Street, southward with ground of Edward Shippen, westward with a four foot alley and leading into Lombard Street." The income of this was to be applied " to the use of daughter Rebecca Lynch."

He was chosen a vestryman of St. James', Perkiomen, 26 April, 1749, and continued as such, under yearly re-elections, until 1760. After this, he was more or less identified with the Rev. Henry Melchoir Muhlenberg's Congregation at Trapp, in the adjoining township of Providence, drawn thereto doubtless by the eloquence of the "Patriarch of the Lutheran Church in America." It is to him that Dr. Muhlenberg refers in his Journal under, "Wednesday, March 12, 1777 : Mr John Pawling sent word that his married daughter had died and was to be buried in our churchyard tomorrow and requested my services." Some years previous to this, one of his younger daughters, and one or more of his negro dependants, had been baptized by the good Doctor, and, something more than a decade later, he and his wife were buried in the God's Acre adjoining the Trappe Church, one of the historic churches of the Commonwealth. The ledger stone over their graves reads: "In Memory of / John Pawling / who Departed this Life / October the 23d 1789 / Aged 67 years 1 month / and 25 Days. / Elizabeth Pawling, / wife of John Pawling / Born May 16, 1723 / Died Dec. 9, 1791.

His wife, Elizabeth, was the daughter of Herman DeHaven by his wife Annica Updengraf.

Children, all born on the Perkiomen :

    i.   ANN,[4] buried 13 March, 1777; m. Jacob Pennypacker; had issue.
    ii. DEBORAH, m. William Twaddell; had issue.
    iii. HANNAH, m. John Hiester, 1745-1821, colonel in the Revolution and major-general after the war; represented Chester County in the State Senate 1802-06, and was member of Congress, 1807-09. Ex-Governor Guy of Wisconsin descends from this line.
    iv. REBECCA, m. 13 April, 1786, Michael Lynch.
    v.   RACHEL, b. 13 July, 1765; bapt. 31 March, 1766; m. 7 April, 1784, George Reiff of Lower Salford Township. The late Major George G. Groff, M. D., Ph. D., of Bucknell University, is a descendant of this marriage.

6. JOSEPH [3] PAWLING (Lieutenant John,[2] Captain Henry [1]), born on the Perkiomen, Philadelphia, later Montgomery County, Pennsylvania, in or about 1724; died there in May, 1797.

Under his father's will he had an estate of nearly four hundred acres along the Perkiomen — one-half of the home plantation and one-half of his father's portion of the undivided Dubois tract, the middle of the creek being the division line between his and his brother John's farmstead. According to the Perkiomen–Skippack census of 1756, he then had four hundred acres, four children, one slave, &c. In 1776, he was taxed for three hundred acres, two negroes, four horses, six cattle. To his patrimonial estate he made some additions, one, in 1774, of one hundred and fifteen acres which he subsequently conveyed to his son Benjamin,* and for years preceding his decease was counted as of large means and standing in his community. He lived in "the times which tried men's souls," and he passed the ordeal to the full satisfaction of a man's most scrutinizing critics, his neighbors.

His early religious affiliations appear to have been, mainly, with the Evangelical Lutheran Augustus Church of New Providence, commonly called the Old Trappe Church. There several of his children were baptized by Dr. Muhlenberg, and there he was one of the largest contributors to the support of Dr. Muhlenberg, and there, too, he probably remained until after the death of this well-beloved pastor of his people. During the Revolution and immediately following, largely through the activity of the Pawling family, St. James' Perkiomen, so the minutes of the vestry attest,† took strong measures to meet the new condition of public sentiment, and Mr. Slator Clay, receiving deaconate orders, was placed in charge. At the meeting of the congregation and vestry, 22 April, 1788, to provide for Mr. Clay's continuance, Joseph Pawling was elected vestryman, and continued to serve in this office, or as trustee or church-warden, until 4 April, 1793, when he was succeeded by his son Benjamin, who had first been elected vestryman, 17 May, 1776.‡ Mr. Pawling was one of the largest contributors to the support of the Rev. Mr. Clay, as he had been to that of Dr. Muhlenberg, and in the allotment of pews, 20 December, 1788, he was assigned pew No. 2, his cousin, Judge Henry Pawling, having the first pew.

His will of 12 January, 1797, proved 29 May following,‖

* Montgomery County Deeds, Liber i, f. 266.

† Copy of Vestry Minutes, 2 Act., [1737] to 28 March, 1799, in possession of The Historical Society of Pennsylvania.

‡ "Benjamin Pawling of Perkiomen."

‖ Recorded Montgomery County Will Book 2, p. 2.

543

provided for wife, Elizabeth, and the children hereinafter given. The inventory of his personalty included four slaves: Phillis, Peter, Anthony Mix and Pegg, valued at $205. Two hundred and forty-nine acres of his land was appraised at £2929.

He married, before 9 September, 1746, Elizabeth ———, who, with her husband, is interred in the family burying ground, to which he, having received it under his father's will, made by his own a considerable addition,* and which, under the trust therein established, is still in a good state of preservation, as are the tombstones of Mrs. Pawling and her son Benjamin.

Children, all born in Perkiomen Township:

> i. RACHEL,[4] d. 11 Oct., 1828; m. 10 Oct., 1771, Lewis Trucken-miller † of Skippack, Revolutionary soldier, Pennsylvania militia, 1778; d. Oct., 1826.‡ Issue: 1. *John* [5] *T. Miller.* 2. *Hannah T. Miller,* m. Solomon Grimley. 3. *William T. Miller.* 4. *Elizabeth T. Miller,* m. Adam Hatfield, Captain in Fifty-first Regiment, Penna. Militia in War of 1812, who died at Philadelphia, 8 Jan., 1846, in his sixty-sixth year; buried in Trappe churchyard. These latter were the parents of Dr. Nathan L. Hatfield, b. 2 Aug., 1804; d. 29 Aug., 1887, an eminent physician, and president of the Philadelphia Board of Health 1846-47, and father of the late Walter Hatfield, a prominent iron-master of Phila., the late Dr. Nathan Hatfield, surgeon to the Philadelphia Hospital, and of Major Henry Reed Hatfield, a member of the Board of Managers of The Genealogical Society of Pennsylvania.
>
> ii. BENJAMIN, b. 25 Dec., 1750; bapt. 25 Aug., 1751; d. 9 Oct., 1800; m. Rebecca, dau. of Samuel and Rebecca Lane, b. 28 Feb., 1756; d. 19 Sept., 1830; Revolutionary soldier, 2d lieut., Capt. William Bull's Company, First Battalion, Phila. Co. militia, in 1778. Issue: 1. *Elizabeth,*[5] b. Feb., 1777; m. 20 Feb., 1803, Edward Vanderslice. 2. *Joseph,* married and had three sons, BENJAMIN, CURTIS, and ALBERT, who settled in Wabash, Indiana. 3. *Sarah,* m. 8 June, 1806, Evan Rees. 4. *Samuel Lane,* went to Union Co., Penna. 5. *Rebecca,* m. ——— Millon. 6. *Mary,* m. Benjamin Davis. 7. *Harriet,* m.

* " Two acres for a family burying ground to run from the lower end of said burying ground to a small run of the Northeast bank thence along said bank up the run so as to take in two acres of land, as [there] is some dead already buried there, and to[o] for the family or as many of them as choose to bury their dead there. which said two acres of land I give and devise to my sons Benjamin and Joseph their heirs etc. in trust for the use of a burying ground."

† According to his signature. His children and grand-children however divided the surname, using the letter T, as a prefix to Miller.

‡ By deed of April, 1829, the heirs of Lewis Truckenmiller joined in conveying land bequeathed to his wife Rachel by her father, Joseph Pawling. The deed recites that, the said Rachel had deceased leaving the following children: John T. Miller, Hannah T. Grimley, William T. Miller and Elizabeth T. Hatfield.—Montgomery County Deed Book 45, p. 129.

544

John S. Davis. 8. *Eleanor*, d. unmarried. 10. *Benjamin*, was
living in Iowa in 1871.
iii. JOSEPH, b. 28 Aug., 1753; d. 23 Oct., 1840; m. (1) 29 Sept.,
1783, Susannah Lukens; m. (2) 5 Nov., 1793, Mary Shannon,
b. 20 Mar., 1766; d. 8 Mar., 1839. Mr. Pawling served in the
Pennsylvania militia during the Revolution. About 1794 he
removed to Snyder Co., Penna., and later to Salem, Union Co.,
where he died. Many of his descendants still reside in this
vicinity. Issue by first marriage: 1. *John*,[5] settled in Kentucky. Issue by second marriage: 2. *Samuel*, b. 9 Feb., 1794;
d. 23 Nov., 1874; m. 24 Jan., 1815, Elizabeth Woodling, and
had issue.* 3. *Joseph*, b. 23 Sept., 1797; d. 6 Oct., 1846; m.
14 Feb., 1826, Margaret Rebecca Ritzman, and had issue. 4.
Nathan, b. 28 Feb., 1808; removed to Knox Co., Ill., and had
issue. 5. *Elizabeth*, m. Ezekiel Davis. 6. *Maria Teresa*, m.
Samuel Stetler, resided at Bloomsburg, Penna. 7. *Hannah*,
m. Jacob Woodling. 8. *Susannah*, m. Christian Houtz, resided
in Utah.
iv. MARIA ELIZABETH, b. 5 Oct., 1756; bapt. 5 Jan., 1757; m. William Shannon.
v. HANNAH, bapt. 9 Aug., 1761; m. John De Haven.
vi. ANNA, b. 6 June; bapt. 9 Aug., 1762; m. 9 Oct., 1788, Jonathan Jones.

7. HENRY [3] PAWLING (Henry,[2] Captain Henry [1]), baptized
at Kingston, New York, 27 June, 1714; died in Providence
Township, Montgomery County, Pennsylvania, in November,
1792.

He succeeded to his father's estate on the Schuylkill and
rose to prominence in local and Provincial affairs. From 25
May, 1752, he was for some years justice of the peace and of
the Courts of Common Pleas for Philadelphia County, and
served as a member of the Provincial Assembly from that
county in 1751, and from 1764 consecutively until the outbreak of the Revolution.† In 1761 he was appointed commissioner for improving the navigation of the Schuylkill
River, in which position he was, in 1773, succeeded by his son
John Pawling, Jr. He was also appointed in 1761 to take
charge of a building operation and the preparation of a plant-
ing ground for the friendly Indians at Wyoming. In the
assessment list of Perkiomen Township for 1776, he appears
as Henry Pawling, Esq[r]., with two hundred and ninety acres,
two negroes, four horses and eleven cows.

* From this line descends Albert Schock Pawling of Lewisburg, Penna.,
Compiler of the PAWLING GENEALOGY, 1905.

† Oct. 1, 1770. Went to the State House to give my vote for Joseph Fox,
Michael Hillegas, *Henry Pawling*, Thomas Livezey, Thomas Mifflin, George
Gray, Samuel Miles and Edward Pennington for Assemblymen.—Diary of
Jacob Hiltzheimer, p. 22.

The example of the father in his connection with St. James' Church, Perkiomen, was followed by the son, who, elected church warden 4 April, 1743, continued to serve as such, or as a vestryman, until his decease. Measured by the Minutes of the Vestry, Mr. Pawling was, during all this period, its most active parishioner. By his will, he left a legacy of ten pounds towards the enclosure of its churchyard with a stone wall. His sons Henry, John and Nathan were also vestrymen.

Judge Pawling's will of 18 November, 1781, proved 3 November, 1792, provided that, his lands in the Schuylkill River, called "Catfish Island," should be sold; that his son Henry should have the remainder of his tract in Providence Township, with mansion house and between two and three hundred acres; that daughter, Catharine Stalford, should receive two hundred and seventy-five acres of land in Lucerne County and all silver plate; and that his interest in lands on Wyalusing Creek in Northumberland County should, after paying an incumbrance of £250 to daughter Rachel Bartholomew, be vested in his grandson, Levi Pawling. The instrument further provided a competence for all his children, either in lands or money, and legacies to his brother, Barney Pawling and cousin-nephew, Colonel Henry Pawling of Kentucky. James Vaux, his neighbor, was constituted one of his executors.

He married, about 1740, his cousin Eleanor, daughter of Lieutenant John Pawling by his wife Aagje De Witt, born, probably, at Marbletown, 22 February, 1715, and died before the execution of her husband's will.

Children, born, probably, in Lower Providence Township:

    i.   RACHEL,[4] b. 1742; d. 1794; m. Col. Edward Bartholomew, of Philadelphia.

    ii.   JOHN, b. 17 May, 1744; will proved 24 June, 1815; m. 9 Sept., 1771, Elizabeth, only daughter of Rees Morgan of Lancaster County, by his wife Margaret Edwards. On Assessment List of Providence Township, 1776, for two hundred acres, &c. Issue: 1. *Margaret*,[5] m. 25 Mar., 1792, Robert Adolf Farmer. 2. *Henry*, living at the making of his grandfather's will, but not at that of his father's. 3. *Eleanor*, b. 1 Aug., 1775; d. 16 June, 1855; m. 2 July, 1795, John Cornman, M. D., of Phila., who d. 23 Apr., 1813. 4. *Elizabeth*. 5. *John Morgan*, b. 1 Dec., 1783; d. 26 Nov., 1838; m. 1 Feb., 1811, Rebecca Prather. 6. *Rachel*, d. unmarried at Greencastle, Penna., 20 June, 1861. 7. *Fanny*.

   iii.   HENRY, b. 25 Sept., 1746; d. 23 Oct., 1822; buried at St. James', Perkiomen; m. 11 Dec., 1769, Rebecca, dau. of William Bull.

He was Captain in Col. Robert Lewis' Battalion of the Flying Camp in 1776.* In 1784 he was appointed one of the Commissioners for the new county of Montgomery and was also one of its first Associate Judges. Issue: 1. *Levi*,[5] b. 1770; d. 1845; m. 17 Oct., 1804, Elizabeth, dau. of Maj. Gen. Joseph Hiester, Governor of Pennsylvania, who died at Norristown, 27 July, 1826. Distinguished as a lawyer and Federalist, he filled many positions of trust in his town and county, and was Member of Congress 1817-19.† He had three sons and four daughters: JOSEPH [6] HIESTER PAWLING, 1806-1847. HENRY DEWITT PAWLING, M. D., 1810-1892, the well-known physician of King of Prussia, Pa.; m. Anna D., dau. of Levi Bull of West Chester. JAMES MUHLENBERG PAWLING, ESQ., 1811-1838; m. Lydia Wood. ELIZABETH PAWLING, m.‡ Hon. Thomas Ross of Doylestown, Pa., eminent lawyer and Congressman, 1849-53. ELLEN PAWLING, m. Henry Freedley, Esq., of Norristown. REBECCA PAWLING, m., as second wife, Henry Freedley, Esq. MARY PAWLING, m. Sylvester N. Rich, Esq., of Philadelphia. 2. *Henry*, named in his father's will, 5 July, 1817. 3. *William*, of Pawling's Bridge, d. 1835, leaving three sons: HENRY [6] PAWLING, THOMAS PAWLING, ALBERT PAWLING. 4. *Eleanor*, m. 28 Feb., 1799, James Milnor, Esq., of Philadelphia, Member of Congress, 1811-1813, who, abandoning the law, entered the ministry of the Episcopal Church; was Doctor of Divinity and rector of St. George's, New York, 1816-1844.

iv. BENJAMIN, m. after 1776, Susanna Ballinger. Revolutionary soldier in 1778; named in father's will; said to have removed to Canada.

v. NATHAN, b. 1750; d. unmarried 27 March, 1795; Revolutionary soldier; Cornet of the Montgomery County Troop of Horse, in 1786; Lieutenant of Light Dragoons, commanded by Capt. James Morris, in 1792; High Sheriff of Montgomery County; buried at St. James', Perkiomen.

vi. JESSE, named in his father's will; officer in British army; removed to Canada.

vii. WILLIAM, d. about August, 1845.

viii. CATHARINE, m. Joseph Stalford; removed to Luzerne Co., Pa. Their son, *John Pawling Stalford*, b. Perkiomen, 20 Oct., 1788; d. Wyalusing, Bradford Co., Pa., 27 Jan., 1863; was the father of John Bradford Stalford, now, or late, the president of the Bank of Wyalusing.

8. LEVI [3] PAWLING (Henry,[2] Captain Henry [1]), born in Lower Providence Township, Philadelphia County, Pennsylvania, circa 1722; died at Marbletown, Ulster County, New York, in March, 1782.

Inheriting the considerable estate of his uncle, Albert Pawling, Esq., at Marbletown, his removal thereto had been accom-

* Pennsylvania Associators and Militia, vol. i. p. 558.

† In this connection see also AUGE'S MEN OF MONTGOMERY COUNTY," pp. 252 et seq.

‡ Of the issue of this marriage; Hon. Henry Pawling Ross, was President Judge of Mont. County Courts, and George Ross, Esq., was a well-known lawyer at Doylestown and a member of the Contitutional Convention.

plished before 22 April, 1746. At this time he, described as of that place, was party to a conveyance of land on the Schuylkill and Perkiomen to his brother-in-law, James Morgan. After this, his life was identified with Ulster County and the Provincial affairs of New York, where he achieved a large measure of distinction in the field of politics and military service.

On 17 September, 1761, he was appointed one of a Commission to hold a meeting with the Delaware Indians relative to the renewal of a treaty of peace. He was a member of the Provincial Convention which met at New York, 20 April, 1775, to elect delegates to represent the Province in the Continental Congress; a member of the Fourth Provincial Congress and Representative Convention, 1776-77, and also a member of the second Council of Safety which continued in session from 8 October, 1777, to 7 January, 1778, and was succeeded by the Legislative Convention. An early justice of the peace, he was appointed by an ordinance of the Provincial Convention, 8 May, 1777, first Judge of the Ulster County Courts. He was also State Senator from Kingston district, 1777 to 1782. During the Revolution he was Colonel commanding the Third Regiment, Ulster County Militia, under commission of 28 October, 1775.

His will of February, 1782, was proved 19 March following. It named wife "Halana" and children Albert, Henry, Levi and Margaret.

He married at Kingston, 12 October, 1749, Helena, daughter of William Burhans by his wife Gretje Ten Eyck.

Children, born at Marbletown:

    i.   ALBERT,[4] bpt. 22 Apr., 1754; d. Troy, N. Y., 10 Nov., 1837; m. (1) 28 Apr., 1782, Gretje Ten Eyck, b. 21 Nov., 1756; d. 23 May, 1789; m. (2) Eunice, dau. of Col. Joshua Porter, and widow of Joshua Stanton. In the Revolution, he became successively cornet of Light Horse, lieutenant Third Regiment, Continental Line, brigade-major on staff of Gen. Clinton, lieutenant-colonel commanding an Ulster Co. regiment, and, he is said to have been a colonel on Washington's staff. He was, in 1791, the first High Sheriff of the newly erected Rensselaer County, and became one of the founders of and the first president of the village of Troy, 1802-1816, and its first mayor 1816-1820, after its incorporation as a city. He served on many important committees and, in 1824, was chairman of the committee to provide for the reception of General Lafayette.

   ii.   HENRY, b. 22 April, 1752; d. 29 June, 1836; m. 12 March, 1782, Anna, dau. of Rev. John W. Brown, who died at Hagaman's

Mills, Montgomery Co., N. Y., 29 Dec., 1828; m. (2) Mrs. Sela Wells. A Revolutionary soldier, he became Captain in the Second Regiment, New York Continental Line. Upon the fall of Forts Clinton and Montgomery, he was captured and confined for months in the prison ship *Archer*, and later on the *Myrtle*. His military Journal, now or late in the possession of Sutherland DeWitt, Esq., vividly describes the hardships on the former ship. The war ended, he settled in Montgomery Co., where he was Captain of Light Infantry in 1786, and which he represented in the State Legislature of 1798-9. He was also town-clerk of Amsterdam in 1798. His descendants are to be found in Montgomery and Steuben Counties, to the latter of which he removed shortly before his death.

iii. WILLIAM, bpt. 3 July, 1757; d. unmarried, before his father.

iv. LEVI, b. 12 Oct., 1759; m. 16 Oct., 1787, Jane, dau. of Alexander and Jane (Armour) Wilson.

v. MARGARET, bpt. 1 July, 1764; m. Levi Deyo, son of Peter Deyo, by his wife Elizabeth Helm.

9. JOHN [3] PAWLING (Henry,[2] Captain Henry[1]), born in Lower Providence Township, Philadelphia County, Pennsylvania, 27 December, 1732; died at Rhinebeck, Dutchess County, New York, 30 December, 1819, and is buried in the graveyard of the old Dutch Reformed Church of that place.

He settled in that part of Rhinebeck Precinct known as Staatsburgh, which included the land purchased from the widow Pawling and her children, by Dr. Samuel Staats. Here, in 1761, he built a stone house on the post road on land originally part of that patented to his paternal grandmother.* Occupied with the peaceful pursuits of husbandry, he nevertheless followed the military traditions of his family and attained the rank of major in the Provincial forces. His captaincy in the Crown Point Expedition is thus noted in the Book of Military Appointments, etc., in 1759-60: "April 28, 1759. John Pawling Capt. For Dutchess County gave Capt Pawling his Comm'n & Qualified him, d[elivere]d him his 2 Lt Comm'n and Warr't on the Treasurer."† He is called Major Pawling in the Muster Roll of men raised in ye County of Dutchess and passed for Capt. Peter Harris's Company, May ye 1: 1760." The fact of the latter title is further evidenced by a bond, bearing date 3 November, 1767, between

* May 19, 1729. Description of the boundaries of a patent granted to Neeltje Pawling, in Dutchess beginning at a river side and running eastward, by the side of a fresh meadow called Mansakin and a small creek called Nancapaconmak and following said southerly and southeasterly as it runs to Hudson's River by the Crum Elbow called by the Indian name Eaquorsinck containing within the said bounds 4000 acres.—New York Calendar of Land Papers, p. 194.

† Report of the State Historian of New York Colonial Series, vol. ii, pp. 515, 520, 557.

"Major John Pawling of Staatsburgh, Dutchess County, Levi Pawling Esq. of Marbletown, Ulster County, and Johannes Cramer of Oswego, Beekman's Precinct, New York."[*] In the struggle between the Colonies and the mother country, Major Pawling espoused the cause of the former and served it with fidelity.

He married, first, at Kingston, 23 May, 1754,[†] his cousin Neeltje, daughter of Thomas Van Keuren by his wife Mary Pawling; second, 15 April, 1770, Marietje, daughter of Jacob Van Deusen by his wife Alida Ostrander.

Children of first marriage:

i. HENRY,[4] b. 30 Nov., 1755; d. Johnstown, N. Y., in 1825; m. Elizabeth ———. Revolutionary soldier.
ii. CORNELIUS, b. 22 Jan., 1758. Revolutionary soldier.
iii. JOHN, b. 24 Oct., 1760. Revolutionary soldier.
iv. MARY, bpt. 11 Nov., 1764; m. ——— Kane.

Children of second marriage:

v. LEVI, b. 29 Jan., 1771; d. Staatsburgh, 12 Feb., 1858; m. (1) Gertrude T., dau. of Harman Jansen Knickerbocker; m. (2) 18 May, 1816, Hannah, dau. of Stephen Griffing by his wife Elizabeth Uhl. Among the children of the latter marriage: Gertrude,[5] b. 25 Apr., 1822; m. David Wallace of Hyde Park, N. Y., and had: 1. JOHN 'ALVA WALLACE, m. Emeline Coyle; these latter were the parents of Katharine, wife of John Frank Kitts, author of *The Lineage of the Pawling Family*. 2. MARY CAROLINE WALLACE, m. John B. Roach, the late eminent shipbuilder of Chester, Penna., who was survived by five children: William Macpherson Roach and John Roach of Chester, Penna.; Mrs. Charles E. Schuyler of New York, since deceased; Mrs. George Forbes of Baltimore, widow of Frederick Farwell Long, M. D., and Emeline, wife of the Hon. William Cameron Sproul, State Senator of Penna., and president of Union League, Philadelphia.
vi. ELEANOR, b. 11 Mar., 1772; d. Rhinebeck, 11 Sept., 1862; m. Capt. Peter Brown.
vii. RACHEL, b. 13 Feb., 1774; d. Staatsburgh, 22 Nov., 1850; m. Christopher Hughes.
viii. ALIDA, m. Peter Ostrom.
ix. CATHARINE, b. 11 May, 1778; d. young.
x. JESSE, b. 2 Mar., 1780; m. 14 Oct., 1804, Leah, dau. of William Radcliff. He was commissioned second lieutenant, Dutchess Co. Artillery Company, 1814.
xi. JACOMYNTIE, b. 25 May, 1782; m. 18 Dec., 1803, Wait Jaques.
xii. ELIZABETH, b. 5 Aug., 1784; d. 27 Sept., 1872; m. 5 June, 1803, William P. Stoutenburgh.
xiii. REBECCA, b. 4 Apr., 1785; d. 13 June, 1832; m. Frederick Streit Uhl.
xiv. JACOB, b. 4 Mar., 1787; d. Watertown, N. Y., 23 Mar., 1877; m. 27 Feb., 1822, Martha, dau. of Capt. Isaac Russell.
xv. CATHARINE, b. 28 Dec., 1789; m. (1) Jacob Conklin; (2) John Coyle.

[*] Dutchess County Deeds, Liber 5, f. 208.   [†] First publication of banns.

The Family of William Penn

A Collated Record*

WITH the approach, in 1968, of the two hundred and fiftieth anniversary of the death of William Penn, the Founder of Pennsylvania, the time is appropriate for a capsulization within these pages of the basic genealogical information which has been recovered on his ancestry and descendants. New information uncovered in recent years, which adds to or corrects certain aspects of the family history, has appeared in various publications over the years. The aim of the present study, therefore, is to present in one record an up-to-date collation of this new material and the still valid genealogical data.

In only a minor sense is this study the result of original research since the greater part of it has been taken from the work of others. It incorporates a brief mention of pertinent material drawn from the English researches of Brigadier Oliver F. G. Hogg, a descendant of William Penn. In his monograph, *Further Light on the Ancestry of William Penn,* published by the Society of Genealogists in London in 1964, he has extended the Founder's ancestry one generation farther back in the sixteenth century, and has uncovered new data on the generations immediately preceding the Founder himself.

Specific items relating to the Founder's relatives and progeny which have been uncovered by Francis James Dallett, a Fellow of the Genealogical Society of Pennsylvania presently residing in England, are included in brief, extracted, with his permission, from his "Further Gleanings" which are presented separately in full in other pages of this issue. His findings supplement the "Genealogical Gleanings, Contributory to a History of the Family of Penn," by the late J. Henry Lea of Fairhaven,

---

* Collected and arranged by the Editor.

Massachusetts, which appeared in *The Pennsylvania Magazine of History and Biography* in Volumes XIV (1890), XVI (1892), XVII (1893),* and in *The New England Historic and Genealogical Register,* Volume 54 (1900). They also supply various records missing from the late Howard M. Jenkins' *The Family of William Penn, Founder of Pennsylvania: Ancestry and Descendants* (Philadelphia and London, 1899), which first appeared serially in *The Pennsylvania Magazine* in Volume XX (1896) through Volume XXII (1898). These sources, with the addition of the recent findings of genealogical import by Henry J. Cadbury, which have appeared in the same publication, provide the basic framework for the present study.

For the benefit of those unfamiliar with the Founder's progeny, it should be noted that he was twice married and was the father of sixteen children. However, by his first wife, Gulielma Maria Springett, only his eldest surviving son, William Penn, Jr., has known descendants living today. They stem from the latter's granddaughter, Christiana Gulielma Penn who married Peter Gaskell. An account of their progeny appears in a separate paper in this issue. By the Founder's second wife, Hannah Callowhill, only their second son, Thomas Penn, has descendants living. They stem from Thomas's youngest daughter, Sophia Margaretta Juliana Penn who married William Stuart, Archbishop of Armagh. As Brigadier Hogg, of this branch of the family, has compiled an extended account of their progeny, the present record is limited to a brief account of their children and grandchildren. If possible, his complete record will appear in full in a subsequent issue of this *Magazine.* All of the other children of the Founder either died unmarried, had no issue or, leaving issue, were the progenitors of lines which so far as is known became extinct within one or two generations. Thus, none of his living descendants bear the single surname of Penn, since they all stem from female lines.

In his monograph on William Penn's ancestry, Brigadier Hogg has established beyond question that JOHN PENNE of Minety, then in the county of Gloucester and hundred of Crowthorne and Minety, is the Founder's earliest proven progenitor. Minety, which takes its name from "mint stream," in the sixteenth century administratively belonged to Gloucestershire, but physically was completely surrounded by Wiltshire.[1] The first Subsidy Roll recording the surname of Penn in the

---

[1] Minety lies about seven miles due south of Cirencester in Gloucester, four or five miles northeast of Malmesbury in Wiltshire, and eight or nine miles west of Swindown, the nearest industrial town, also in Wiltshire. Brigadier Hogg notes (p. 15), in the monograph cited in the text, that through shifts in population from country to town, Minety has become a small Wiltshire village with a population of about 705.

*J. Henry Lea's article on the Penn family is reprinted in *Genealogies of Pennsylvania Families: From The Pennsylvania Magazine of History and Biography* (Baltimore: Genealogical Publishing Co., Inc., 1981), 546-631.

hundreds of Minety and Cirencester is that of 14-15 Henry VIII. It shows that in 1522, John Penne of Minety paid a tax of six shillings eight pence on his chattels. A quarter of a century later in 1550, the Subsidy Roll of 3 Edward VI shows that he paid six shillings tax on movable goods worth six pounds. After that his name no longer appears on the rolls, and he is presumed to have died shortly thereafter.[2]

During his lifetime, however, his undoubted son 1. WILLIAM PENNE of Minety, was also listed. On the Gloucester Lay Subsidy Rolls of 36 and 37 Henry VIII he was assessed thirteen shillings in 1544-46.[3] Then on 5 February 1547/8, one Richard Andrewes of Hales, in Gloucestershire, granted to "William Penne, yoman" of Minety, a messuage, about forty acres of land in Minety, and the moiety of a croft, as well as one acre, three roods of land in the tenure of one John Rydeler. In addition to this holding, he was taxed six shillings on personalty worth six pounds on the Subsidy Roll of 2-3 Edward VI for 1548-1550. Ten years later the roll of 2 Elizabeth I listed him as being taxed in 1560 on goods now worth eight pounds. By 1594, on the next extant roll for Minety of 35-37 Elizabeth I, the name of Penn is missing, bearing out his death 12 March 1591/2.[4] He was buried before the altar in Minety Church where a monumental stone, no longer extant, recorded his death.

In his will, dated 1 May 1590, and proved 21 April 1592, he called himself "Willm Penne of Myntie in the County of Glouc, yeoman." To the children of his deceased son 2. William Penn, whom he named as Giles, William, Maria, Sara and Susanna Penn, he bequeathed twenty pounds apiece when they came of age, or at the time of their marriage. To Margaret Penn, widow of his son William Penn, he left an annuity of ten pounds so long as she "keep herself sole and chaste and unmarried." If she married again or led an unchaste life, she was to receive twenty pounds, "a good Bed with all manner of Furniture thereunto belonging and so she quietly [was then] to depart." As heir and sole executor he named his grandson George Penn, eldest son of his deceased son William; he was to receive, after debts and legacies were paid, the residue of his estate, "moveable and unmoveable." As overseers he named Robert George of Cirencester, Richard Lawrence of Withington, Glos., and Francis Bradshaw of Wokely, Wilts., with power to see that all his testamentary instructions were carried out. To his daughter Ann Greene and her daughter Elizabeth Greene he gave each a heifer. To Richard

2 Hogg, *Further Light*, 12, 42.

3 J. Henry Lea, "Genealogical Gleanings . . . ," *The New England Historic and Genealogical Register* (*NEHGR*), 54 (1900), 326. Brigadier Hogg does not include this item in his account. A pedigree chart preceding Mr. Lea's record of the Penn family begins with William Penne of Minety.

4 Hogg, *Further Light*, 12, 42.

Bidle he gave one cow, to his daughter Katherine Bidle a heifer, to William Mallibroke a yearling heifer, and to Alice Thermor his "old white mare." Witnesses to the will included Francis Bradshaw, William Taylor, and Richard Munden.[5]

Issue of 1. William Penne of Minety:

2. i. WILLIAM PENN of Malmesbury, d. *ca.* 1588, of whom further.

   ii. ANN GREENE, living in 1590; m. one GREENE, possibly Marmaduke Greene of Ballincham, as suggested by J. Henry Lea in his pedigree chart of the Penn family. Known issue: 1. ELIZABETH GREENE, living and named in her grandfather's will in 1590. Mr. Lea suggests that Robert Green, apprenticed 13 April 1602, to Giles Penn of Bristol, draper, was also a son. He also notes a Marmaduke Green who d. abroad unmarried, administration on whose estate was granted 3 October 1623, to his sister Ann Sympson.[6]

2. WILLIAM PENN, son of William Penne of Minety and grandson of John Penne of the same place, was apprenticed as a law-clerk to the counsellor-at-law, Christopher George of Bawnton, near Cirencester, eventually becoming his chief clerk. He was married by 1570 to MARGARET RASTALL, daughter of John Rastall, Alderman of Gloucester, and his wife Anne George, a sister of the above Christopher.

William and Margaret Penn apparently settled in Malmesbury, four or five miles southwest of Minety. In the Malmesbury Subsidy Rolls of 1570-71, 13 Elizabeth I, William was taxed six shillings on his movable goods, and was taxed there again ten years later. According to Brigadier Hogg, he was not listed in the Subsidy Roll for 1586-87, but in the 1587 Lay Subsidy Roll for Malmesbury borough in the Public Record Office is the entry for "Willms Pene goods iij li--viij d," as cited by Mr. Lea.[7] It is apparent, however, that William Penn was deceased by 1588, and that in 1590 his widow and six children were living in Minety with the elder William Penne.

Issue of 2. William Penn of Malmesbury and his wife Margaret Rastall:

   i. GEORGE PENN, b. perhaps *ca.* 1571; d. intestate in Brinkworth, Wiltshire, and was bur. at Minety 5 11m 1632; m. probably before 1600, ELIZABETH, who survived him, and was administratrix of his estate.[8] He proved his grandfather's will in 1592, and as his heir was taxed on the Minety property at least through 1604, as shown on the Subsidy Rolls of 40 Elizabeth I

[5] A transcript of the will is in *ibid.*, 37-39, and also in J. Henry Lea, "Genealogical Gleanings . . . ," *The Pennsylvania Magazine of History and Biography* (PMHB), XIV (1890), 57-61. *

[6] *NEHGR*, 54, 325

[7] *PMHB*, XIV, 291. This last entry is not cited by Brigadier Hogg.

[8] The record of letters of administration on the estate of "George Penn late of Brinkworth, co. Wilts, decd," is in the Prerogative Court of Canterbury, 1631-33, fo. 138b, as cited in *PMHB*, XIV, 178, and noted on Mr. Lea's pedigree chart. *

*For pp. 57-61, 291, and 178 see *Genealogies of Pennsylvania Families: From The Pennsylvania Magazine of History and Biography*, pp. 553-557, 592, and 578.

(1598-98), 42 Elizabeth I (1599-1600), and 1 James I (1603-1604). He was a churchwarden in Minety in 1608, but by 1621 had removed to Brinkworth, a few miles south of Minety and east of Malmesbury, where he became one of the "Preservators, Keepers and Officers of the forest of Braydon." Letters of administration on his estate were granted Elizabeth Penn, his relict, 15 December 1632. Known issue: 1. WILLIAM PENN, d. testate ca. April, 1676, at Kinsale, Ireland. Sometimes termed Ensign, by 1667 he was Clerk of the Cheque at Kinsale, and on corresponding terms with his cousin Admiral Sir William Penn who mentioned him in his 1669 will.[9]

Other issue [10] of George Penn possibly include: (2.) ELIZABETH PENN, m. at St. Thomas, Bristol, 18 September 1620, GEORGE JONES of Grittenham, Wilts., when he wrote his will 20 February 1629, in which he named his presumed father-in-law, George Penn, as overseer. The will was proved 7 October 1629. (3.) MARGERY PENN, spinster of Brinkworth, m. at Brinkworth by license 17 October 1622, JOHN SHERER. (4.) SUSANNA PENN, spinster of Brinkworth, m. at Brinkworth by license 2 August 1633, RICHARD CUSSE, mercer of Wotton Bassett, Wilts. (5.) ELEANOR PENN, bapt. at Cirencester 27 October 1611; m. by license 12 May 1635, EDWARD KEENE, b. ca. 1608, yeoman of Blackbourton, Oxon. At the time of marriage she was aged 24, and he aged 27. She was called cousin in Admiral Penn's will. (6.) CHRISTIAN PENN, d. intestate as Christian Tucke of Charlton, Wilts., before 1630/31, when letters of administration on her estate were granted to George Penn.

3. ii. GILES PENN, b. ca. 1573; dec'd by 25 February 1656, of whom further.
   iii. WILLIAM PENN, apprenticed as "Willus Penne," son of William "de Myntye . . . defunct," 6 August 1596, to John Aldworth, merchant of Bristol; admitted as "marchaunt" to the Liberties of Bristol 5 June 1607; dec'd by August 1628; m. before 1610 to MARGERY, who survived her husband and was living in 1628. Brigadier Hogg establishes that William Penn was in business with his elder brother Giles in Bristol; by 1618 they had suffered severe financial losses "to their utter ruin," and were hoping for employment abroad, as suggested by some of their creditors, in order to pay their debts and recover their estates. Known issue: 1. CATHERINE PENN, bapt. at St. Mary Redcliffe, Bristol, 23 December 1610. 2. MARTHA PENN, bur. at St. Mary Redcliffe 12 August 1628, as daughter of Margery Penn, widow.
   iv. MARIA PENN, named in her grandfather's 1590 will.

---

[9] M. Jackson Crispin, "Captain William Crispin," *PMHB*, LIII (1929), 122-124, *adds some slight information on "Ensign Penn" to that furnished by Brigadier Hogg. His will is entered in Cork and Ross Wills, 1676. A copy of a pedigree chart of 37 pages, from the Virginia State Library, reported to be a record of his descendants, but without documentation, is in the Collections of the Genealogical Society of Pennsylvania.

[10] The list of possible daughters of George Penn of Brinkworth in the text above follows neither Mr. Lea nor Brigadier Hogg in all respects, but is the present arranger's own list, based on an evaluation of the evidence they presented. Mr. Lea listed Elizabeth, Eleanor and Christian as George's daughters, but considered Susanna, who m. Richard Cusse, a daughter of William of Malmesbury and sister of George. In view of her residence at Brinkworth when she married, that contention seems unlikely. Margery, who m. John Sherer, if a daughter of George, was perhaps named for her aunt, wife of George's brother William. Certainly Eleanor, bapt. at Cirencester, who m. Edward Keene, and was called "cousin" by Admiral Penn, was more likely George's daughter than a niece, as suggested by Brigadier Hogg (p. 27). Her marriage allegation is given by Mr. Lea in *PMHB*, XVI (1892), 336, taken from the Diocesan Registry, Sarum, Wilts.*

*For pp. 122-124 and 336 see *Genealogies of Pennsylvania Families: From The Pennsylvania Magazine of History and Biography*, pp. 212-214 and 604.

v. SARA PENN, named in her grandfather's 1590 will.

vi. SUSANNA PENN, named in her grandfather's 1590 will.

3. GILES PENN, son of William Penn, the law clerk of Malmesbury, and his wife Margaret Rastall, was born perhaps about 1573. Brigadier Hogg suggests that he may have been named for Giles, Lord Chandos who, in 1573, became lord of the manor of Minety. He was apprenticed, as "*Egidius Penne, filius Willi Penne nup. de Myntie . . . defunct,*" to the linen draper, John Horte of Bristol, and Juliane his wife, on 1 May 1593, a year after his grandfather's will was offered for probate. It was as "Gylles Penne, draper," that he was admitted to the "Liberties" of Bristol on 3 April 1600, "because he was Prentice of Mr. John Horte, Alderman, Deceased." [11] The following 5 November 1600, he married at St. Mary Redcliffe, Bristol, JOAN GILBEART (Gilbert), of a family originally from Yorkshire.

From draper Giles Penn progressed to merchant with his younger brother William, and by 1618 had been overtaken with financial losses. In 1630 records show that he was travelling between England and the Barbary Coast, importing and selling assorted goods. Styled Captain Penn in 1631, he was in London in 1636, and the following year, when he was appointed resident consul for Charles I at Sallee (Salé in Morocco), he was described as "a man well-experienced in the language and custom of the said country." He was deceased, probably overseas, by 1656, when a new consul was appointed at Sallee.[12]

Issue of 3. Giles Penn and his wife Joan Gilbeart:

i. GEORGE PENN, bapt. at St. Mary Port, Bristol, 1 October 1602; d. in England, July-August 1664; m. in Antwerp a Spanish lady and settled at San Lucar, having followed his father's profession and prospered. In 1643, he was arrested by the officers of the Inquisition and imprisoned in Seville for three years until under torture he abjured the Protestant faith. His property had been siezed, his wife divorced from him (she was a Roman Catholic), and he was expelled from Spain. No known issue.[13]

ii. GILES PENN, bapt. at St. Nicholas, Bristol, 4 October 1603; probably died in infancy.

iii. HENRY PENN, bapt. at Christ Church, Bristol, 26 January 1604; d. unmarried beyond the sea, with administration on his estate granted to his father George on 7 June 1632.[14]

(iv.) ELIZABETH PENN, said to have been a sister of the Admiral, b. perhaps *ca.* 1605; d. in Boston, Mass., 1640; m. before 1621 in London, WILLIAM

---

[11] The apprenticeship and citizenship records cited in the text above are from *NEHGR*, 54, 326-327.

[12] For a more extended account of Giles Penn's activities, see Hogg, *Further Light*, 27-31.

[13] George Penn's baptism is in *NEHGR*, 54, 328, his death in Jenkins, *The Family of William Penn*, 17, cited in the text, and quoted from Pepys' *Diary*. Brigadier Hogg elaborates (p. 31-32) the details of his life more extensively than Jenkins.

[14] Henry Penn's dates are given on Mr. Lea's pedigree chart.

HAMMOND, d. in London before 1634. With her son and daughters she came to Boston on the ship *Griffin,* arriving 16 September 1634, in company with the Rev. Mr. Lothrop. Issue: 1. BENJAMIN HAMMOND, b. in London 1621; d. in Rochester in 1703, *ae.* 82; m. in Sandwich in 1650, MARY VINCENT, b. in England in 1633. 2. ELIZABETH HAMMOND. 3. MARTHA HAMMOND. 4. RACHEL HAMMOND.[15]

v. RACHEL PENN, "daughter of Gyles Penn," bapt. at St. Mary Redcliffe, Bristol, 24 February 1607; m. by license 26 October 1630, at St. Gregory by St. Paul, London, RALPH BRADSHAW, b. *ca.* 1611, son of Lawrence Bradshaw and his wife Sarah Hinchman; his will was probated 31 January 1667/8. Issue: 1. ROBERT BRADSHAW, d. without issue. 2. WILLIAM BRADSHAW, d. in infancy. 3. James Bradshaw, b. *ca.* 1646; d. 1691 in New Castle on the Delaware River; m. MARY, who survived him. 4. JOHN BRADSHAW, b. *ca.* 1651. 5. REBECCA BRADSHAW, d. *ca.* 1664-1665; m. at St. Dunstan's, Stepney, Middlesex, 28 September 1652, as his first wife, WILLIAM CRISPIN, bapt. 3 October 1627; d. beyond the sea en route to Pennsylvania 1681/2. Letters of administration on his estate were granted in Ireland 7 July 1682. His cousin William Penn, the Founder, had intended him to be Chief Justice in the new province. 6. SARAH BRADSHAW, d. in infancy. 7. MARY BRADSHAW, d. in infancy. 8. ANNE BRADSHAW. 9. FRANCES BRADSHAW, m. after 1664, WILLIAM ASSHETON, attorney-at-law, coroner of Lancashire, and a Deputy Herald of Arms. They were the progenitors of the Philadelphia Assheton (Ashton, etc.) family.[16]

vi. ELEANOR PENN, bapt. at St. Mary Redcliffe, Bristol, 26 May 1610; bur. there 24 November 1612.

vii. A Daughter, name unknown, who possibly married WILLIAM MARKHAM of Ollerton, Notts. Issue, called nephews by Admiral Penn: 1. WILLIAM MARKHAM, b. perhaps *ca.* 1635; d. testate in Philadelphia 12 4m (June) 1704; m. 1st, according to the entry in Pepys' *Diary* of 5 August 1666, ANN (NAN) WRIGHT; m. 2nd, *ca.* January 1683/4, MRS. JOANNA JOBSON, widow of Capt. Eben Jobson; she was living in New York in 1726. William Markham preceded his cousin, the Founder, to Philadelphia, as Deputy Governor of Pennsylvania.[17] 2. GEORGE MARKHAM.

---

15 This record of a possible daughter of Giles Penn is included in Jenkins, 253, but was first published in *NEGHR,* 30 (1876), 29, and was part of an extended family record. The pertinent part of the record was reported to have been from an account first made in 1700 by Benjamin Hammond's son John. There were many Hammond families in London; a search of the published church records has failed to substantiate the record, but inasmuch as the family appears to have been dissenters, there probably would be no church entries referring to them.

16 Rachel (Penn) Bradshaw's family data is extracted from Francis James Dallett, "Further Gleanings," published in the present issue of this *Magazine,* to which the reader is referred.

17 William Markham's origins are suggested in *The Dictionary of American Biography.* The seal he is said to have used was that of the Markhams of Sedgebrooke, Notts. from which the Ollerton branch descended: Azure on a chief Or, a demi-lion rampant issu. In John F. Watson, *Annals of Philadelphia . . . ,* (Philadelphia, 1927), III, 85, Markham's age was said to have been twenty-one when he was commissioned Deputy Governor by William Penn in 1681. It hardly seems likely that his cousin would have intrusted the initiation of his government to so young a man. In Watson, I, 23, it is also stated that Markham was aged fifty-four when he died in 1694! The correct death date is given in Edward Armstrong, ed., *Correspondence Between William Penn and James Logan . . . ,* (Philadelphia, 1870), II, 294, 307. His will, dated 13 December 1703, and proved 3 July 1704, is recorded in Philadelphia Will Book B, 364, #137:1704. He reported his second marriage to William Penn in a letter dated 27 March 1684, Markham to Penn, Society Autograph Collection, Historical Society of Pennsylvania (HSP).

viii. ANN PENN, bapt. at St. Thomas, Bristol, 21 January 1618; bur. at St. Mary Redcliffe, Bristol, 23 February 1651, apparently unmarried.

4.   ix. WILLIAM PENN, the Admiral, bapt. at St. Thomas, Bristol, 23 April 1621; d. testate at Wanstead, Essex, 16 September 1670; bur. at St. Mary Redcliffe, Bristol, 3 October 1670, of whom further.

The life of 4. WILLIAM PENN, youngest child of Giles Penn and his wife Joan Gilbeart, is stated succinctly on the monument erected to his memory by his widow and son in the church of St. Mary Redcliffe.[18] Trained for the sea service under his father with whom he served as a lad on numerous mercantile voyages, the monument states he became a lieutenant in the Royal Navy, and in 1642 (at the age of twenty-one) was appointed a captain. The following year on 6 January 1643/4, at the church of St. Martin, Ludgate, London, he married a young widow, MARGARET (JASPER) VAN DER SCHUREN, daughter of Johann Jasper, a merchant of Rotterdam and Ballycase, County Clare, Ireland, and widow of Nicasius Van der Schuren of Kilconry, parish of Kilrush, County Clare.[19] They established a household in London on Tower Hill in the parish of St. Catherine.

In 1645, when he was twenty-three, he was appointed Rear Admiral; in 1647, Vice Admiral of Ireland; in 1650, Admiral of the "Streights;" in 1652, Vice Admiral of England. In 1653, at the age of thirty-two, he was a general in "the first Dutch Warres;" and on 4 December 1654, by order of Cromwell, was granted lands in County Cork in Ireland "in consideration of the great losses sustained by General Penn and his wife by the rebellion in Ireland." Upon the Restoration he was knighted by Charles II on 9 June 1660, made Admiral of the Navy, Governor of the town and fort of Kinsale and, in 1664, was chosen Captain Commander under the king in the successful fight against the Dutch. In 1669, he retired from active affairs to Wanstead in Essex, where he died testate 16 September 1670, aged forty-nine years and four months. He was interred "In Led" in St. Mary Redcliffe the following 3 October.[20]

In his will, dated 4 April 1669, and proved in London 6 October 1670, he devised £300 and all his jewels not otherwise bequeathed to his wife Dame Margaret Penn, as well as the life use of half of his plate and household goods, coaches, coach-horses and mares, and cows. During his

---

18 The best transcript of the inscription on the Admiral's monument is in Hogg, *Further Light*, 33. The transcripts given by Jenkins in *PMHB*, XX, 15, and in *The Family of William Penn*, vary considerably in form, but only slightly in wording.

19 Their marriage record is extracted from Mr. Dallett's "Further Gleanings" in this issue, to which the reader is referred.

20 His burial date has uniformly been given as 30 September 1670, but the register of St. Mary Redcliffe indicates otherwise, for which see *PMHB*, XIV, 296. Possibly a funeral service was held at Wanstead on the thirtieth, after which the funeral cortege proceeded to Bristol for interrment. *

*For p. 296 see *Genealogies of Pennsylvania Families: From The Pennsylvania Magazine of History and Biography*, p. 597.

minority his younger son Richard was to have £120 yearly out of the personal estate for his maintenance and, when he came of age, £4000 sterling, with the Admiral's favorite diamond ring, all his swords, guns and pistols. To his granddaughter, Margaret Lowther, he left £100, to his nephews, James Bradshaw and William Markham, and to his cousin William Penn, son of George Penn "late of the forest of Braydon, deceased," each ten pounds. To his nephews, John Bradshaw and George Markham, he left five pounds apiece, and to his cousin "Elianore" Keene six pounds, to be paid her yearly in quarterly installments. His servant, William Bradshaw, was to have forty shillings for a ring; his servant, John Whrenn, five pounds, and the poor of the parishes of Redcliffe and St. Thomas in Bristol, each twenty pounds.

To his eldest son William Penn, whom he named sole executor, he left his gold chain and medal, the other half of his plate and household goods, directing him to provide out of the personal estate suitable mourning for Dame Margaret, for his son Richard, for his daughter Margaret and her husband Anthony Lowther, for Dr. Whister and his wife, and for such servants as Dame Margaret should nominate. Sir William Coventry, of the parish of St. Martin in the Fields, was to act as mediator in the event of any differences between Dame Margaret and his son William. Witnesses were R. Langhorn, John Radford, and William Markham, probably the nephew.[21]

Dame Margaret Penn survived her husband twelve years, dying a year after her son obtained his charter for Pennsylvania from King Charles. Letters of administration on the estate of Margaret Penn, late of "Waltham Stow," Essex, were granted 13 March 1681/2, to her son, the Founder of Pennsylvania.[22]

Issue of 4. Admiral Sir William Penn and his wife Margaret (Jasper) Van der Schuren:

5.   i. WILLIAM PENN, the Founder, b. in London 14 October 1644; d. at Ruscombe, Berks., 30 5m (July) 1718, bur. at Jordans Friends' Meeting ground near Chalfont, Bucks., of whom further.

   ii. MARGARET PENN, b. *ca.* 1645; d. 5 December 1718, *ae.* 73,[23] bur. at Wal-

---

[21] A transcript of his will is given in Hogg, *Further Light*, 39-41, and an abstract of it in *PMHB*, XIV, 171.

[22] Cited in *ibid.*, 180, from Administration Act Book, fo. 31, Prerogative Court of Canterbury. *

[23] In Mr. Dallett's "Further Gleanings" in this issue, her death date is given as 5 December 1719, but in a letter of Hannah Penn, dated 9 3m (May) 1720, she is reported to have died five months after her brother William, the Founder. It seems evident that the transcript of the monumental inscription which Mr. Dallett quotes is in error. For the letter, see Jenkins, *The Family of William Penn*, 116, or *PMHB*, XXI (1897), 17. The list of their children, however, is extracted from Mr. Dallett's transcript, to which the reader is referred; their birth dates are mainly conjectural. See also Henry J. Cadbury, "Intercepted Correspondence of William Penn, 1670," *PMHB*, LXX (1946), 362n.

*Page 623, this volume.

thamstow, Essex; m. at Clapham, Surrey, by license 14 February 1666/7, ANTHONY LOWTHER, b. *ca.* 1640; d. 27 January 1692, *ae.* 52, bur. at Walthamstow in the church of St. Mary the Virgin, son of Robert Lowther of Maske, Yorkshire. Anthony Lowther was M.P. for Appleby in 1678 and 1679. Issue: 1. MARGARET LOWTHER, b. 8 February 1667/8; d. *ca.* 1719-1720; m. BENJAMIN POOLE, Esq.[24]   2. WILLIAM LOWTHER, d. *ca.* 1669, *ae.* 6 months, bur. at Walthamstow.   3. ELIZABETH LOWTHER, b. *ca.* July 1670; prob. d. before 1681.   4. ROBERT LOWTHER, b. *ca.* 1672; d. *ca.* 1693, "a Gent. of great hopes and learning;" bur. at Walthamstow.   5. WILLIAM LOWTHER (2nd), b. *ca.* 1674, created Baronet in 1697; d. in April 1704; m. Catherine Preston, daughter of Thomas Preston of Holker, Lanc.   6. ANN CHARLOTTE LOWTHER, b. *ca.* 1676; d. after 1681, in childhood.   7. ANTHONY LOWTHER, JR., b. *ca.* 1678; d. *ae.* 1 year and 8 months, bur. at Walthamstow.   8. JOHN LOWTHER, b. *ca.* 1680; m. by 1720, and living in 1731.[25]   9. ANTHONY LOWTHER (2nd), b. *ca.* 1682; d. *ca.* 1702, *ae.* 20 years, bur. at Walthamstow.

iii. RICHARD PENN, b. *ca.* 1648.   Described by Samuel Pepys in 1664/5, as "a notable stout, witty boy," he probably was destined for sea-service by his father, and was in Italy in 1670, but d. testate unmarried and was bur. at Walthamstow 9 April 1673.   In his will, dated 4 April 1673, and proved 11 April following, he devised £10 to the poor of Walthamstow where he directed he was to be buried; left £40 yearly to his mother for her life; £50 to his sister Margaret Lowther and £30 to her husband, as well as two guns and a pair of pistols to be selected by his brother William; to his sister-in-law Gulielma Maria Penn £50 "in token of love," and £10 to his servant George Haman.   He named his mother executrix.[26]

5. WILLIAM PENN, eldest son of 4. Admiral Sir William Penn, and his wife Margaret (Jasper) Van der Schuren, was baptized at Allhallows Church, Barking, London, on 23 October 1644.   Since his numerous biographers have covered the varied aspects of his life *in extenso,* this present record includes only basic vital statistics and is restricted to brief references to his residence in Pennsylvania.

---

[24] In John Burke and John Bernard Burke, eds., *A Genealogical and Heraldic History of the Extinct and Dormant Baronetcies of England, Ireland and Scotland* (London, 1841), 419, Benjamin Poole is stated to have d. in January 1656, son of James Poole, Esq. of Poole, Cheshire, by his wife Mary, sister of Sir Edward Mostyn. The death date is an obvious impossibility, but the further note that Benjamin, "by his wife Margaret, daughter of Anthony Lowther, esq. of Cleveland," had a daughter and heir who m. John Nichol, esq. of Minchendon, Middlesex, is corroborated by the recital in *Pennsylvania Archives,* 3rd Series, I, 34, in which the daughter's name is given as Margaret, and states that the Nichols were living in 1731. Margaret (Lowther) Poole's death is noted in the 1720 letter from Hannah Penn, cited above.

[25] John Lowther, his elder sisters Margaret and Ann Charlotte, and his elder brother William (2nd), were granted lands by William Penn in 1681, to be laid out in Pennsylvania. Their sale in 1731 is recited in *Pennsylvania Archives,* 3rd Series, I, 34. John's marriage is noted in the 1720 letter from Hannah Penn, cited above.

*

[26] An abstract of Richard's will is in *PMHB,* XIV, 173. When Richard was in Italy in the 1670's, he was described as "my cousin Richard Penn," in a letter to Admiral Penn from Captain William Poole (later Sir William Poole?). The connection with the family of Benjamin Poole is unknown, as is the exact relationship of Sir Richard Rooth, another commander in the English navy, who also appears to have had some relationship to Admiral Penn, according to allusions in Granville Penn's *Memorials,* as cited by Jenkins in *The Family of William Penn,* 25n.

*For p. 173 see *Genealogies of Pennsylvania Families: From The Pennsylvania Magazine of History and Biography,* p. 573.

He entered Christ Church College, Oxford, as a "gentleman commoner," 26 October 1660, but remained less than two years. It was during this period, as he recalled twenty years later, that he "had an opening of joy, as to these parts" — culminating in his charter from the king and the founding of Pennsylvania. He married first, at King's Chorleywood, parish of Rickmansworth, Herts., 4 2m (April) 1672, GULIELMA MARIA SPRINGETT. Born "a few weeks after the death of her father," Sir William Springett, who had died 3 February 1643/4, she is named on his mural monument in the church at Ringmer, Sussex, as "Gulielma Maria Posthuma Springett." Her mother was Sir William Springett's first wife, Mary, only daughter of Sir John Proude.[27]

Penn was in his thirty-seventh year when he received the charter for Pennsylvania in March, 1681. He was just past his thirty-eighth birthday when, having left his pregnant wife and small children in England, he landed at New Castle on the Delaware River in October, 1682. He remained in his province of Pennsylvania until mid-August, 1684, when he returned to England on the Ketch *Endeavour*.

During the next ten years he suffered imprisonment, the temporary loss of his government, and the loss of his wife Gulielma Maria, who died 23 12m (February) 1693/4, six months before Pennsylvania was restored to him. She was buried at Jordans, aged fifty years. Heretofore the number of their children has been thought to be seven. It is now known that they had eight. Of these only three lived beyond infancy.

Issue of 5. William Penn, the Founder,
by his 1st wife Gulielma Maria Springett:

i. GULIELMA MARIA PENN, b. at Rickmansworth, Herts., 23 11m (January) 1672/3; d. 17 1m (March) 1672/3, bur. at Jordans.

ii. WILLIAM PENN, b. at Rickmansworth, 28 11m (January) 1673/4; d. 15 3m (May) 1674, bur. at Jordans.

iii. MARIA MARGARET PENN (twin), b. at Rickmansworth, 28 11m 1673/4; d. 24 12m (February) 1674/5.

iv. SPRINGETT PENN, b. at Walthamstow, Essex, 25 11m (January) 1675/6; d. at Lewes, Sussex, 10 2m (April) 1696.

v. LETITIA PENN, b. at Warminghurst, Sussex, 6 1m (March) 1678/9; d. testate and was bur. at Jordans 6 April 1746; m. at Horsham, Sussex, 20 August 1702, WILLIAM AUBREY, son of William and Elizabeth Aubrey; bur. at Jordans 23 May 1731. No issue. She came to Philadelphia with her father and stepmother in 1699, and returned with them in 1701. In her will, dated at Christ Church, Spitalfields, 20 July 1744, she left to her nephew 9. William Penn, son of her brother 6. William Penn, a silver cup and salver, silver teakettle and other items. She left bequests to her great-nieces and grand-nephew: £50 to Mary Margaretta Fell, £40 to Gulielma

[27] For the inscription see, M. Atherton Leach, "Gulielma Maria Springett, First Wife of William Penn," *PMHB*, LVII (1933), 103.

Maria Frances Fell, and £40 to Robert Edward Fell. To her nephew 9. William Penn, she devised all her American estate for life, and then to his daughter Christiana Gulielma Penn, who later m. Peter Gaskell. To the poor women of Devonshire House Friends' Meeting in Bishopsgate Street, London, she left £50, and named her nephew 9. William and his daughter Christiana Gulielma her residuary legatees.

6. vi. WILLIAM PENN, Jr., b. at Warminghurst, 14 1m (March) 1680/1; reported to have d. in Belgium 23 June 1720, of whom further.

vii. A Daughter, unnamed, b. at Warminghurst, 1m (March) 1682/3, while her father was in Pennsylvania; d. in infancy.[28]

viii. GULIELMA MARIA PENN (2nd), b. at Warminghurst, 17 9m (November) 1685; d. at Hammersmith, Middlesex, 20 9m 1689, bur. at Jordans.

Just over two years after the death of his first wife, 5. William Penn married secondly at Bristol on 5 1m (March) 1695/6, HANNAH CALLOWHILL, born 11 12m (February) 1670/1,[29] daughter of Thomas Callowhill, linen draper of Bristol, and his wife Hannah Hollister. Three years later on 3 September 1699, accompanied by his second wife and daughter Letitia, Penn sailed on the *Canterbury* for Pennsylvania, arriving at Philadelphia the following 3 December. 6. William Penn, Jr., the only surviving son of the first marriage, remained in England, having been married only the previous January. The Founder's stay in Pennsylvania on this second and last visit was only slightly longer than his first; he had stayed twenty-two months the first time, twenty-three months the second time. He and his wife and daughter left on the *Dolmahoy* 3 November 1701, arriving in England early in December of the same year.

For a time the Penns lived at Bristol, although Penn occasionally took lodgings in London when he had business there, or a house in the suburbs. From 1710 until his death, the family home was at Ruscombe in Berkshire near Twyford and about six miles from Reading. It was at London, however, that Penn suffered his first stroke early in 1712, and then a second one at Bristol the following October. A third stroke in February, 1712/13, at Ruscombe, so shattered his physical strength and disabled his mental powers that he never recovered. He died testate at Ruscombe 30 July 1718, aged seventy-four years, and was buried at Jordans the following 5 August.

---

[28] See Henry J. Cadbury, "Another Child to William and Gulielma Penn," *PMHB*, LXXIV (1950), 111. It should be noted that Mr. Cadbury has translated the dates from Friends' reckoning to modern reckoning. See also Marion Balderston, ed., *James Claypoole's Letter Book* . . . 1681-1684, (1967), 198, 203. Mrs. Balderston has pointed out that although Penn himself wrote "Worminghurst" as he heard it pronounced, the place then, as now, is properly spelled "Warminghurst."

[29] See Henry J. Cadbury, "Hannah Callowhill and Penn's Second Marriage," *PMHB*, LXXXI (1957), 77, which corrects earlier accounts of her birth.

In his will, written at London when he was recovering from his first stroke, he noted that since his eldest son 6. William was amply provided for by a settlement of "his Mothers and my ffathers Estate," he was devising the government of his province to English trustees, but neglected to specify the nature of the trust. To other trustees, of which his wife, his father-in-law Thomas Callowhill, and his sister Margaret Lowther were three, he left all his lands in Pennsylvania and America, with power to sell so much as would be sufficient to pay his debts. They were then to convey to his daughter Letitia Aubrey, and to the three children of his son, 6. William — Gulielma Maria, Springett, and William Penn, 3rd, or their heirs — each 10,000 acres to be laid out in Pennsylvania. The rest of his lands were to be conveyed by the trustees to and among the children of his second marriage. All his personal estate and arrears of rent due him he left to his wife Hannah for the benefit of herself and her children. Out of the rents she was to have £300 yearly for life. He hoped at least some of his children would settle "in America where I leave them so good an Interest to be for their Inheritance from Generacon to Generacon. . . ." A codicil, dated 27 3m (May) 1712, in which he affirmed these provisions to have been his will and desire, was witnessed, among others, by Eliz: Penn and Tho: Penn, believed to have been Negro servants.[30]

Penn's will was offered for probate by his widow Hannah, whom he had named sole executrix, at Doctors' Commons 4 November 1718. A fortnight later she executed a "deed poll of appointment" in which she assigned half of Pennsylvania and the Lower Counties of Delaware to her eldest son John, and divided the other half of those lands among her three younger sons, Thomas, Richard and Dennis Penn. After the death in 1720 of the Founder's eldest son, 6. William Penn, Jr., Springett Penn, the latter's eldest son, attempted to claim the Proprietary right to the government of Pennsylvania as heir-at-law by right of primogeniture. As a result, on 23 October 1721, Hannah Penn began a suit in the Court of Exchequer to establish the validity of her husband's will and the bequests in it, but died before it was settled. She had survived her husband eight years, dying 20 10m (December) 1726, aged fifty-six, and was buried at Jordans.

The suit was settled finally on 4 July 1727, in favor of the younger branch of the family, barring the elder branch from the government and limiting it to the specific bequests in the Founder's will. On 5 July following, a family deed sextipartite confirmed the deed poll of assignment made in 1718, except for certain parts no longer valid. It was agreed

---

[30] A transcript of Penn's will is in *PMHB*, XIV, 174-176. *

*See *Genealogies of Pennsylvania Families: From The Pennsylvania Magazine of History and Biography.* pp. 574-576.

that a cash settlement and annuity was to be set up for Margaret Freame, Hannah's only surviving daughter, which was to be paid by John Penn, the eldest son. He was to retain the life interest in half of the Pennsylvania and Delaware lands, but since Dennis Penn had died, the other half was to be vested for life in Thomas and Richard Penn as tenants in common.[31] The three surviving sons were thereby confirmed as joint proprietors of the Province of Pennsylvania.

Issue of 5. William Penn, the Founder, by his 2nd wife Hannah Callowhill:

ix. A Child, unnamed, b. or d. 1697.[32]

x. JOHN PENN, the American, b. at Philadelphia 29 11m (January) 1699/1700; d. testate and unmarried at Hitcham, Bucks., 25 October 1746, bur. at Jordans. He was apprenticed 17 August 1715, to Brice Webb, draper of Bristol and, until the duties of the Proprietorship devolved on him, may have followed that business. Holding a one-half interest under the sextipartite deed, he was chief Proprietor, and in September, 1734, came to Pennsylvania with his sister Margaret and her son, young Thomas Freame, Jr., to join his brother Thomas. John appears to have left much of the proprietary business to him, and remained in Philadelphia only a year, returning to England in September, 1735, to attend litigation over the Maryland boundary. In his will, dated 20 October 1746, he left his share of the Manor of Perkasie in Bucks County, of Liberty Land and of High Street lots to his nephew John, son of his brother Richard, to whom he devised his half of the New Jersey property. To his brother Thomas he left his half of the Pennsylvania and Delaware land, as well as "the Franchise of Gov[t]" for life, with remainder entailed on Thomas' sons in succession, then to his brother Richard and his sons in succession. In default of male heirs, the "remainder" was to go to Thomas' heirs.[33]

7. xi. THOMAS PENN, b. at Bristol 9 1m (March) 1701/2; d. at London 21 March 1775, of whom further.

xii. HANNAH MARGARITTA PENN, b. at Bristol 30 5m (July) 1703; d. at Bristol by 1m (March) 1707/8.

xiii. MARGARET PENN, b. at Bristol 7 9m (November) 1704; bur. at Jordans 12 February 1750/51; m. at London 6 5m (July) 1727, THOMAS FREAME, citizen and grocer of London, son of Robert Freame and his wife Alice Vice; d. *ca.* March, 1741. He came to Philadelphia, probably with his brother-in-law Thomas Penn, in 1732, and was joined by his wife and young son in 1734, when they arrived with John Penn, the American. At the outbreak of the War of Jenkins' Ear, he "turned soldier," and was cap-

---

[31] See William Brooke Rawle, "The General Title of the Penn Family to Pennsylvania," *PMHB*, XXIII (1899), 64-68, 224-226, and "The Breviate," *Pennsylvania Archives*, 2nd Series, XVI, 439-444. The complicated entailment established over the years by the Penn family has been reduced to its barest elements for the present record, since in the main it is only of general interest from a genealogical point of view. Not having legal training, the present compiler begs the reader's indulgence for any errors which may be detected!

[32] This child is noted by Mr. Cadbury in *PMHB*, LXXXI, 79. As he points out, Penn had eight children by his first wife, and eight by his second, not seven by each as has hitherto been uniformly believed.

[33] *PMHB*, XXIII, 237-240, which recites John Penn's will.

tain of a company in Colonel Gooch's Regiment, stationed at Chester in July, 1740. Sailing with the regiment that fall, he participated in the abortive attack on Cartagena in Spanish South America. After being "at the Siege of all the fortifications and in particular at Boccha Chico Castle" where he behaved gallantly, he was excused from further duty during the siege. A few days later he was siezed with a fever and died within 24 hours, apparently in March, 1741. His will was proved in Philadelphia 10 July following, and in London 4 September 1744. Margaret Freame and her children returned to England with Thomas Penn in the fall of 1741, arriving in November of that year. Issue: 1. THOMAS FREAME, JR., b. *ca.* 1730; bur. at Jordans 2 6m (August) 1746. 2. PHILADELPHIA HANNAH FREAME, b. in Philadelphia 1740-1741; d. in London without surviving issue 14 April 1825, bur. at Stoke Poges; m. 8 May 1770, THOMAS DAWSON, Baron Dartrey, later Viscount Cremorne of Castle Dawson, County Monaghan, Ireland; d. 1813.[34]

8. xiv. RICHARD PENN, b. at Bristol 17 11m (January) 1705/6; d. testate 4 February 1771, of whom further.

xv. DENNIS PENN, b. at Ealing, Essex, 26 12m (February) 1706/7; d. unmarried 6 11m (January) 1722/3, bur. at Jordans.

xvi. HANNAH PENN, b. in Ludgate Parish, London, 5 7m (September) 1708; d. at Kensington, 24 11m (January) 1708/9, bur. at Tring, Herts.

6. WILLIAM PENN, JR., sixth child of the Founder by his first wife, Gulielma Maria Springett, was born at Warminghurst 14 1m (March) 1680/1, ten days after his father's grant from Charles II. He was not quite eighteen when he married at Bristol, according to Friends' ceremony, on 12 11m (January) 1698/9, MARY JONES, born 11 11m (January) 1676/7, daughter of Charles Jones, Jr. of Bristol, and his wife Martha Wathers. As a marriage settlement, William Penn, Sr. apparently made over to young William the Irish estate of Shanagarry in Cork, entailing it on his male heirs. In 1666, the estate reputedly was worth £1000 a year. On his mother's death in 1694, Warminghurst in Sussex had become his by inheritance from her, and on young William's marriage, he and his wife appear to have taken up residence there, his father and stepmother moving to Bristol.

William Penn, Jr. came to Philadelphia without his wife, arriving 2 February 1703/4, with John Evans, commissioned Lieutenant Governor by the Founder. His stay was not a success and was brief. After disposing of some of the Pennsylvania land given him by his father, he was back in England by mid-January, 1704/5. He and his wife lived at

---

[34] Biographical data on Thomas Freame, amplifying what little was known to Mr. Jenkins, comes from several sources. His presence at Chester in 1740 is from *Pennsylvania Gazette*, 24 July 1740; his war service and death is in Richard Hockley to John Wragg, 15 June 1741, as quoted in *PMHB*, XXVII (1903), 422-423; an abstract of his will is in Lothrop Withington, "Pennsylvania Gleanings in England," *PMHB*, XXXIV (1910), 191. The death of his daughter, Lady Cremorne, is extracted from Mr. Dallett's "Further Gleanings" in this issue, to which the reader is referred for more details.

Warminghurst until it was sold in 1707, then apparently rented properties until his father's death in 1718. He unsuccessfully essayed a political career in seeking a seat in Parliament, and appears to have left the upbringing and expenses of his children to his stepmother. In 1719, he made an unsuccessful attempt to get the Pennsylvania Assembly to acknowledge his claim as chief Proprietor and heir-at-law. Irresponsible and unstable, he apparently died in Liége, Belgium 23 June 1720, reputedly of a consumption. His widow Mary Jones was buried at Jordans 5 10m (December) 1733.

Issue of 6. *William Penn, Jr. and his wife Mary Jones:*

i. GULIELMA MARIA PENN, b. at Warminghurst 10 9m (November) 1699; d. probably in London, 17 11m (January) 1739/40, bur. 22 January 1739/40, at St. Margaret's Church, Westminster; m. 1st, at St. Mary Magdalen Church, Fish Street, London, 14 February 1720,[35] AUBREY THOMAS, b. in Pennsylvania 30 11m (January) 1694, son of Rees and Martha Thomas; d. before 1724. Issue: 1. WILLIAM PENN THOMAS, d. unmarried *ca.* 1742. She m. 2nd, CHARLES FELL, d. at Windsor 1 October 1748, son of Charles Fell; administration on his estate was granted in London 17 October 1748, to his son Robert. Issue: 2. MARY MARGARETTA FELL, bapt. 23 August 1724; dec'd by 1769; m. JOHN BARRON of Leeds, Yorkshire who, in 1774 was of Philadelphia.[36] 3. GULIELMA MARIA FRANCES FELL, bapt. 10 August 1725; living in Shrewsbury, County Salop, in March, 1769; m. by 26 May 1750, JOHN NEWCOMB of Leir, Glos.; dec'd by March, 1769. 4. ROBERT EDWARD FELL, bapt. 29 November 1726; d. testate in Bordentown, N. J., in November, 1786.[37] Both Robert Fell and John Barron came to Philadelphia about 1769 to take up and sell holdings which had descended to Gulielma Maria (Penn) Fell under the will of her grandfather.

ii. SPRINGETT PENN, b. at Warminghurst 10 12m (February) 1700/1; said to have d. in Dublin, Ireland, either 30 December 1730, or 8 February 1731, unmarried and without issue. By his father's death he considered himself heir-at-law of the American estates of his grandfather and of the Proprietorship, and unsuccessfully challenged both the will and the apportionment made by his stepmother Hannah Penn, as noted previously.

9. iii. WILLIAM PENN, 3rd, b. at Warminghurst 21 1m (March) 1702/3; d. at Shanagarry, Ireland, 6 12m (February) 1746/7, of whom further.

7. THOMAS PENN was born at Bristol 9 1m (March) 1701/2, the eleventh child of the Founder and the third of his second wife, Hannah Callowhill. He was apprenticed in 1716 to Michael Russell, a mercer in White Hart Court, Gracechurch Street, London, under whose tutelage he

---

[35] The marriage is extracted from Mr. Dallett's "Further Gleanings," cited above.

[36] He may be the John Barron who died intestate in Philadelphia 3 November 1794, and was buried at St. Peter's P. E. Church, as noted in the registers of Christ Church, Philadelphia. The will of a John Barron, Jr., proved 26 November 1804, in Philadelphia, names his mother as Martha Johnston.

[37] The administration on the estate of Charles Fell, and will of Robert Edward Fell, are extracted from Mr. Dallett's "Further Gleanings," to which the reader is referred.

no doubt acquired his aptitude for business. Under the sextipartite deed of 5 July 1727, Thomas was vested in a life interest in one quarter of the Pennsylvania property. In September, 1731, he was a party to a further settlement. Under this agreement, 9. William Penn, 3rd, Letitia Aubrey, and Charles Fell and his wife, Gulielma Maria Penn, agreed to relinquish their claims in the province and government to John, Thomas and Richard Penn for £5500 payable to William, 3rd, now heir of the eldest branch of the family. Excepted and reserved to William was "the Palace of Pennsbury" with 4000 acres contiguous to it; the individual 10,000-acre tracts devised to Letitia Aubrey, and to William, 3rd, and Gulielma Maria under the will of the Founder, and any other lands deeded, granted or patented to them by the Founder. Richard's one-quarter share, however, was to be held in trust by John and Thomas, apparently because of some disapproval of his recent marriage. The following May of 1732, the descent of the Pennsylvania property was established between the three brothers. In the event of the death of any one of them, his share was to go to his eldest son in tail male with remainder to his second, third and other sons successively.[38]

With these matters settled, Thomas, accompanied by his brother-in-law Thomas Freame, sailed for Pennsylvania, arriving at Chester 11 August 1732. During his nine-year stay in Philadelphia, Thomas had a small house built on the Springettsberry Manor lands adjoining the city, near the present Twentieth and Hamilton Streets, and embellished the grounds with a great variety of plants and trees. His elder brother John, and his sister Margaret Freame and her young son joined him, arriving 19 September 1734. John remained only a year, but Margaret Freame stayed until the news of her husband's death in the late spring of 1741. She and her brother Thomas then returned to England, arriving at Plymouth late the following November.

On the death of John Penn, the American, in 1746, his half-interest was left to Thomas who thus became the principal Proprietor by virtue of holding a three-quarters right. With the improvement of his financial situation, by 1747 he was established in a town house in New Street, Spring Gardens, near Charing Cross, which continued to be his town residence until his death. In 1750, Thomas and Richard mutually agreed to an alteration in such of the provisions of the May, 1732, settlement as were no longer applicable, and in August, 1751, eight days before Thomas's marriage, the entailment of the Proprietary estate was re-established in a marriage settlement. The estate was to descend in tail male to his eldest son by his prospective bride, with remainder to suc-

---

[38] Recited in *PMHB*, XXIII, 233-236. Annuities for the widows were also settled.

cessive sons. Failing that, to first and successive sons by any other wife of Thomas, then in tail male to his brother Richard Penn, then to his nephew John Penn, son of Richard; then to the nephew John's eldest son and every other son successively; then to Richard, second son of Richard and Thomas's nephew, and to his sons in order of birth. If these all failed, as it did in 1869, the property was to descend to Thomas's heirs "in tail general." [39]

At the Church of St. George, Hanover Square, London, on 22 August 1751, Thomas Penn married LADY JULIANA FERMOR, born in 1729, daughter of Thomas, Earl of Pomfret. They entertained some thoughts of coming to Pennsylvania the following year, but the birth of their first child in 1752 prevented it, and they never came to the province.

In 1760, Thomas Penn acquired the country estate of Stoke Poges in Buckinghamshire which he made his principal home. About 1771, he suffered a stroke of palsy from which he never fully recovered. He died on 21 March 1775, in London where he had gone in failing health to spend the winter. His widow survived him twenty-six years, dying at Ham, Surrey, 20 November 1801, in her seventy-third year. Both are buried in the church at Stoke Poges.

Issue of 7. Thomas Penn and his wife Lady Juliana Fermor:

i. WILLIAM PENN, b. 21 June 1752; d. 14 February 1753, *ae*. 7 months, bur. at Penn, Bucks.

ii. JULIANA PENN, b. 19 May 1753; d. 23 April 1772, bur. at Stoke Poges; m. 23 May 1771, WILLIAM BAKER of Bayfordbury, Herts. Issue: 1. JULIANA BAKER, b. *ca*. 1772; d. 11 September 1849, at Gunters Grove, Stoke Courcy, Somerset; m. 18 January 1803, JOHN FAWSET HERBERT RAWLINS. They had no issue.

iii. THOMAS PENN, JR., b. 17 July 1754; d. 5 September 1757, bur. at Penn.

iv. WILLIAM PENN (2nd), b. 22 July 1756; d. 24 April 1760, bur. at Penn.

v. LOUISA HANNAH PENN (twin), b. 22 July 1756; d. 10 June 1766, bur. at Penn.

vi. JOHN PENN, called "the Younger," b. in London 23 February 1760, bapt. 21 March 1760, at St. Martin's in the Fields; d. unmarried at Stoke Park 21 June 1834, bur. at Stoke Park. He was still a minor when he succeeded to the Pennsylvania property and Stoke Poges upon the death of his father. Entering Clare Hall, Cambridge, as a nobleman by virtue of his mother's position, he received his M.A. in 1779, the year the Pennsylvania Assembly on 29 November divested the Penn family of its Proprietorship and title to the land, except for their private holdings. In recompense the Assembly agreed to a settlement of £130,000, payable in annual installments not to exceed £15,000, to the heirs of Thomas and Richard Penn.

In 1783, John Penn came to Pennsylvania to look after the family's remaining property. The next year he bought 15 acres on the west bank of

---

39 *Ibid.*, 333-338. The marriage settlement itself is in HSP.

the Schuylkill, and began the erection of Solitude, now within the grounds of the Zoological Society. In the city he lived at the northeast corner of Sixth and Chestnut Streets.[40] After his return to England in 1788, Parliament voted the family an annual pension of £4000, in recompense for their losses in America. Stoke Poges being in sad repair, he demolished part of it, and erected a new home which he called Stoke Park. In the ensuing years he participated in politics in a gentlemanly way: was Sheriff of Bucks in 1798, was in Parliament in 1802, was made governor of the Island of Portland in Dorset in 1805, and about 1815, erected Portland Castle in that place. In 1811, the year Cambridge awarded him the degree of LL.D., the College of Arms sent him a pedigree on vellum under the common seal of the College, "shewing and certifying Mr. Penn's descent from The Blood Royal of England." The charge was £13 16s. 8d.[41]

vii. GRANVILLE PENN, b. in London 9 December 1761; d. at Stoke, 28 September 1844, bur. at Stoke Park. He matriculated from Magdalen College, Oxford, 11 November 1780, but took no degree, and became an assistant clerk in the war department. In the years following his Oxford schooling, he appears to have formed an irregular attachment with an unknown woman, by whom he had issue: WILLIAM GRANVILLE, b. ca. 1785; d. January 1864, in Bath, ae. 79, bur. at Stoke Park. He lived in Ceylon from 1805 to 1821; m. and had several daughters and one son, WILLIAM TURNOUR GRANVILLE, Lieutenant of the 8th Regiment of Foot in 1842, who retired as a captain about 1850 or 1851. William Granville appears to have been an intimate friend of his halfbrother Granville John Penn.[42]

On 24 June 1791, GRANVILLE PENN m. ISABELLA FORBES, b. 1771; d. 1847, bur. at Stoke Park, eldest daughter of General Gordon Forbes and his wife Mary Sullivan of Cork. They settled in London, but when his elder brother John Penn, the Younger, died in 1834, Granville Penn inherited Stoke Park and Portland Castle. In 1838, the College of Arms granted him an "Augmentation to the Armorial Ensigns used by his Family," permitting him and "the other descendants of his Grandfather the said William Penn," to "henceforth bear and use the Armorial Ensigns following, that is to say, A Fess charged with three Plates, and, on a Canton of honourable Augmentation, a Crown, representing the Royal Crown of King Charles the Second, and, for the Crest, A Demi-Lion, gorged with a Collar charged with three Plates, and above, An Escroll, thereon the Word 'Pennsylvania.'" Signed by Queen Victoria, the grant was accompanied by a painting in full color showing the augmentation on the achievement of arms.[43]

---

[40] Owned by Justice John Lawrence, the house had recently been vacated by Robert R. Livingston, first Secretary for Foreign Affairs under the Confederation. It was a relatively new dwelling, having been built by Lawrence after he acquired the ground in 1771. The site of the house is now within the bounds of Independence State Mall.

[41] A letter from Sir Isaac Heard, Garter, dated 27 June 1811, advising him the pedigree had been sent, is in Case 41, Penn Papers, HSP. The pedigree itself is not among the papers.

[42] The Dictionary of National Biography calls Granville Penn's son "Colonel" Granville, apparently confusing him with the grandson, Captain William Turnour Granville. See also Nicholas B. Wainwright, "The Penn Collection," PMHB, LXXXVII (1963), 413-414.

[43] The grant was dated 31 July 1838, and recorded in the College of Arms 7 August 1838. The total cost to Granville Penn was £123 15s. 6d. The bill, the grant and the illustration of the arms are in Case 41, Penn Papers, HSP.

Issue by Isabella Forbes: 1. SOPHIA PENN, b. 1793; d. without issue, 1827; m. 1818, SIR WILLIAM MAYNARD GOMM, who eventually purchased the Penn mansion in New Street. He m. 2nd, Elizabeth, daughter of Robbert Kerr, but died childless. 2. LOUISA EMILY PENN, b. 1795; d. unmarried 27 May 1841, bur. at Stoke Poges. 3. ISABELLA MARY PENN (twin?), b. 1795; d. unmarried 28 January 1856, bur. at Stoke Poges. 4. HENRIETTA ANN PENN, b. 1797; d. unmarried 13 June 1855, bur. at Stoke Poges. 5. JOHN WILLIAM PENN, d. in childhood; bur. at Stoke Poges 18 December 1802. 6. WILLIAM PENN, b. ca. 1800; d. unmarried at Brighton, 7 January 1848, bur. at Stoke Poges. Matriculating at Christ Church, Oxford, 5 June 1818, ae. 18 years, he received his B.A. in 1833, and M.A. in 1837, at which time he was of Semoure Hall, Norfolk. In 1844, he was a barrister-at-law of Lincoln's Inn. 7. JULIANA MARGARET PENN, d. in infancy; bur. at Stoke Poges, 21 March 1804. 8. GRANVILLE JOHN PENN, b. November 1802; d. unmarried intestate 29 March 1867, bur. at Stoke Poges. He studied at Christ Church College and received his M.A. there, then became a barrister-at-law. Inheriting Stoke Park and Portland Castle on the death of his father in 1844, he found he was unable to maintain Stoke financially, and it was sold in 1848, after the death of his mother. He eventually settled at Portland Castle. He visited Pennsylvania twice, in 1852 and in 1857. 9. THOMAS GORDON PENN, b. 1803; d. of unsound mind unmarried 10 September 1869, bur. at Stoke Poges. He studied at Christ Church College, receiving his M.A., then took holy orders in the Anglican Church. When the entailed Proprietary estate fell to him upon the death of his brother Granville John Penn, it was held in Chancery until his death since he was judged incapable of managing it. As the last male Penn, the estates then passed to the heirs of his aunt, Sophia, wife of Archbishop William Stuart, for whom see below.[44]

10. viii. SOPHIA MARGARETTA JULIANA PENN, b. 25 December 1764; d. 29 April 1847, of whom further.

8. RICHARD PENN, fourteenth child of the Founder and sixth of Hannah Callowhill, was born at Bristol 17 11m (January) 1705/6, at the house of his grandfather, Thomas Callowhill. He was apprenticed to business in London, and married there by license dated 26 October 1728, apparently in St. Saviour's Church, Southwark, HANNAH LARDNER, born about 1709, daughter of Dr. John Lardner, deceased, late of Gracechurch Street, London.[45] Apparently because of the marriage, the following January, 1729, Richard's one-quarter interest in the American estates was vested in his brothers John and Thomas Penn in trust for Richard. And although nominally he was one of the three joint Proprietors, he was the only one of them who never came to America, even after his brother John left him his half of what remained of the Founder's

44 For the dispersion of the Penn memorabilia and papers, see PMHB, LXXXVII, 406-419, cited in Note 42.

45 Their marriage allegation is extracted from Mr. Dallett's "Further Gleanings" in this issue, to which the reader is directed.

East and West Jersey property, and named Richard his sole executor of that part of his estate.

Richard and his wife had their principal residence at Stanwell, Middlesex, a suburb of London, but in his will, written 21 March 1750, he said he was then possessed "of a house called Batavia House, in the parish of Sunbury, in the County of Middlesex," and in a codicil he left a house in Cavendish Square to his wife. He had also devised in his will all his "private & particular rights to any Manors Tracts Lands Tenem^{ts} or Hered^{ts}" and his proprietary rights in New Jersey and arrears of rents to his American executors, Lynford Lardner, his wife's brother, and Richard Peters, in trust to sell, collect and remit the proceeds to his English executors. By his last codicil he made his son Richard residuary legatee and devised the New Jersey land in fee to him, John, the elder son, having been left the one-quarter right in the Province. He died 4 February 1771, and was buried at Stoke Church where he directed a family vault was to be erected. His widow Hannah survived him fourteen years, dying at Laleham, Middlesex, according to *The Gentleman's Magazine,* 20 April 1785.

Issue of 8. *Richard Penn and his wife Hannah Lardner:*

i. JOHN PENN, called the Elder, b. 14 July 1729; d. testate 9 February 1795, *ae.* 66 years, bur. at Christ Church, Philadelphia; m. 1st, *ca.* 1747, probably GRACE COX, d. 17 March 1760, daughter of James Cox; m. 2nd, at Christ Church, Philadelphia, 31 May 1766, ANN ALLEN, d. in Upper George Street, London, 4 July 1830, daughter of Chief Justice William Allen of Philadelphia. No issue by either wife. John Penn's first marriage at the age of eighteen was disapproved of by his uncle Thomas Penn, and he was sent to the Continent with a tutor to oversee his studies abroad. After Thomas's marriage in 1751, John agreed to come to Pennsylvania, and arrived in Philadelphia 1 December 1752.[46] During his stay he was a member of the Provincial Council and one of the commissioners attending the Albany Conference in 1754. He returned to England in the late autumn of 1755.

Three years after the death of his first wife, his uncle Thomas Penn and his father Richard commissioned him Lieutenant Governor of the Province, and he returned to Philadelphia, arriving on the *Pennsylvania Packet* 29 October 1763, with his brother Richard Penn.[47] Upon the death of their father Richard in 1771, his one-fourth interest in the Proprietary estate became vested in John as the eldest son, and he returned to England with his American wife. Sailing on the Ship *Brittania* 5 May, they arrived in England 4 June 1771.[48] Two years later they were back in Philadelphia, having come from New York, where they landed, and were met at Bristol on 29

---

[46] See the item in the *Pennsylvania Gazette,* 7 December 1752, reporting his arrival.

[47] *Ibid.,* 3 November 1763; *Minutes of the Provincial Council of Pennsylvania . . . ,* (Harrisburg, 1852), IX, 71.

[48] *Pennsylvania Journal,* 9 May, 1 August 1771.

August 1773, by "a great number of Gentlemen and ladies who accompanied them to town." [49]   Once more commissioned Lieutenant Governor in place of his brother Richard, he acquired the property in the upper part of Blockley Township on the west side of the Schuylkill which became known as Lansdowne.

When the British approached Philadelphia in the fall of 1777, John Penn and his wife were taken into military custody and sent to the Union Iron Works in New Jersey under parole until the British evacuated the city. Hoping to prevent confiscation of his whole property, he had taken the oath of allegiance to the Commonwealth and the United States by 15 July 1778,[50] but the following year the family was divested of its Proprietorship and the land, with the exception of their private estates, by Act of Assembly.   In the ensuing years he was occupied in the management of the private estates not sequestered by the Commonwealth, and in achieving the settlement of indemnity of £130,000 granted the family.   In 1787, he and his brother Richard came to an agreement resulting from the "so great alteration in the affairs and estate of the Proprietary family."   Out of the share John would receive, Richard, as younger brother was to have one-third, John retaining two-thirds.[51]   In the spring of 1788, John Penn and his wife went back to England, leasing Lansdowne to William Bingham, who occupied it until 1792, when once more the Penns returned to Philadelphia [52] where John died in 1795.   By his will, probated in Philadelphia 18 February 1795, he left his one-quarter right to the Manor of Springettsberry in Philadelphia County to his brother Richard for life, with remainder to Richard's son William in tail male, then to Richard's second son Richard, Jr. in tail male, with residue to his wife Ann (Allen) Penn.

ii. HANNAH PENN, b. *ca.* 1731; d. testate at Cavendish Square, London, bur. at Stoke Poges 2 October 1791; m. 19 July 1774, JAMES CLAYTON, late of Sunbury, Middlesex; bur. at Stoke Poges 23 January 1790. No issue. By her will, proved 21 October 1791, Hannah (Penn) Clayton left her estates to her brothers John and Richard Penn, and to Richard's children.

iii. RICHARD PENN, b. *ca.* 1736; d. testate at his house in Richmond, 27 May 1811, in his 76th year; m. at Christ Church, Philadelphia, 21 May 1772, MARY MASTERS, b. 3 March 1756, daughter of William Masters and his wife Mary Lawrence; d. 16 August 1829, *ae.* 73 years, at the house of her younger son Richard, Jr., in Great George Street, London.   Richard Penn first came to Philadelphia in 1763 with his elder brother John, as noted above, and remained until October, 1768, when he returned to England.   When John went to England in 1771, on the death of their father, Richard was sent over as Lieutenant Governor during his brother's absence, arriving 16 October 1771.[53]   On his brother's resuming the governorship in 1773,

---

[49] *Pennsylvania Gazette*, 1 September 1773.

[50] Recited in "The Diary of James Allen," *PMHB*, IX (1885), 440.

[51] Recited in *PMHB*, XXIII, 354-355.

[52] *Pennsylvania Packet*, 30 April 1788; Margaret L. Brown, "Mr. and Mrs. William Bingham of Philadelphia," *PMHB*, LXI (1937), 305. John Penn, the Elder, spent more time in America than any other member of the Penn family. He was in the province thirty of his sixty-six years.

[53] *Pennsylvania Gazette*, 17 October 1771.

there was considerable coolness between them for a time, heightened by a dispute between them over the interpretation of provisions in their father's will. The dispute was settled in 1774, when Richard released to John the fourth part of his father's lands devised him for life. The following year he purchased the property in the Northern Liberties, known as Peel Hall, where Girard College now stands.[54]

That same year Richard and his wife carried the "Olive Branch" petition of the Continental Congress for presentation to the King. They remained in England during the Revolution, and Richard was elected to the House of Commons early in 1784, for the borough of Appleby, Westmoreland. He was still representing it when he and his wife came back to Philadelphia, having arrived at New York on the *Speedy Packet* 17 September 1786,[55] to join his brother in pressing their claims to Pennsylvania property. After the agreement of 1787, noted before, relating to the portions of income he and his brother John would receive from the sale of lands, Richard went back to England where he continued to represent various constituencies in Parliament. From 1796 to 1802, he sat for the city of Lancaster. In 1807, he paid another visit to Philadelphia with members of his family, residing on Chestnut Street between Eighth and Ninth, but stayed only about a year. He appears to have been the most popular and well-liked member of the Penn family to visit Philadelphia since the death of his grandfather, the Founder.[56]

Issue: 1. WILLIAM PENN, b. 23 June 1776; d. in Nelson Square, Southwark, London, 17 September 1845, bur. at St. Mary Redcliffe, Bristol; m. by Dr. James Abercrombie of Christ Church, Philadelphia, 7 August 1807, CATHARINE JULIA (or JULIANA CATHARINE) BALABREGA, b. 13 March 1785, bapt. at Christ Church, daughter of Jacob and Mary Balabrega; d. after 1812. No known issue. William Penn was entered at St. John's College, Oxford, but took no degree, though he had remarkable abilities and was an excellent classical scholar. He came to Philadelphia with his father in 1807, and remained until at least 1812, living in various parts of the State. On his father's death in 1811, his Uncle John's life-interest in the fourth part of the general estate, and the one-third part of the sales of their private estate were vested in him, but his extravagance and lack of restraint brought him into debt, and after his return to England he appears to have spent much of the remainder of his life in or about the debtors' prison in London. 2. HANNAH PENN, d. unmarried at Richmond, Surrey, 16 July 1856. She

---

[54] On Richard Penn's marriage in 1772, his wife was given by her mother the house and lot on the south side of Market Street between Fifth and Sixth, the site of which is now within the bounds of the first block of Independence State Mall. After it burned in 1780, it was sold to Robert Morris. The Penns occupied it as their town house until they left for England in 1775. Peel Hall was sold in 1779, by their attorney, Tench Francis, to Owen Biddle for £9387 in inflated Pennsylvania currency, as recited in Henry D. Biddle, "Owen Biddle," *PMHB*, XVI, 316-317. Richard's quarrel with his brother John was settled by the agreement of 17 May 1774, cited in *ibid.*, XXIII, 353-354.

[55] *Independent Gazette*, 23 September 1786. His presence in Philadelphia was noted by Jacob Hiltzheimer in his entry for 14 October 1786, for which see *PMHB*, XVI, 171.

[56] After his brother John's death in 1795, Richard Penn, by his attornies in Philadelphia, instituted a suit against his brother's executors over the division of payment coming to Richard from sales of Pennsylvania land under the 1787 agreement. A decision, handed down by the Pennsylvania Supreme Court in 1800, was for the defendants, John's executors, for which see *PMHB*, XXIII, 355.

had accompanied her father and brother to Philadelphia in 1807. 3. RICH-ARD PENN, b. *ca.* 1784; d. unmarried at his house in Richmond, Surrey, 21 April 1863, *ae.* 79 years. For many years he was in the Colonial Department of the English government, and was elected a Fellow of the Royal Society in 1824. Upon the death of his brother William in 1845, the life use of his grandfather Richard's fourth of the Pennsylvania rights were vested in him, but on his own death in 1863 without issue, the right passed to his second cousin, Granville John Penn, in accordance with the limitations of the family entail. 4. MARY PENN, b. 11 April 1785; d. 26 March 1863; m. 1821, as his second wife, SAMUEL PAYNTER who d. 24 July 1844. Of Richmond, he was a J.P. for Surrey and Middlesex, and was High Sheriff of Surrey in 1838. No issue. 5. A Daughter, unnamed, d. 17 June 1790, presumably in infancy.

    iv. WILLIAM PENN, b. *ca.* August 1747; d. 4 February 1760, *ae.* 12 years, 8 months, bur. at Penn Church, Bucks.

9. WILLIAM PENN, 3rd, grandson of the Founder, was born at Warminghurst 21 1m (March) 1702/3, the youngest child of 6. William Penn, Jr., and his wife Mary Jones, and was only seventeen when his father died in 1720. By the death of his elder, unmarried brother Springett Penn, in 1730/1, he inherited the remaining estates settled upon his father by the Founder, including the Irish property of Shanagarry in Cork, and The Rocks in Surrey, presumed to have been part of the estate of his grandmother, Gulielma Maria (Springett) Penn. As noted previously in the account of 7. Thomas Penn, in 1731 William released for £5500 the claim, instituted by his brother Springett, to the general right of the elder branch of the family in the soil and government of Pennsylvania, to the younger branch, represented by his uncles John, Thomas and Richard Penn.[57]

On 7 10m (December) 1732, William married by Friends' ceremony at Wandsworth, Surrey, CHRISTIAN FORBES, born about 1715, daughter of Alexander Forbes and his wife Jane Barclay. The marriage was lamentably brief, however, for she died, following the birth of her first and only child, on 1 November 1733, and was buried at Jordans on the seventh of the month.

Issue of 9. William Penn, 3rd, by his 1st wife Christian Forbes:

    i. CHRISTIANA GULIELMA PENN, b. 22 October 1733; d. in London 24 March 1803, *ae.* 69 years, at her home in Thornhaughstreet; m. in London 14 August 1761, PETER GASKELL of Bath, b. *ca.* 1730; d. in Bath in January, 1785. From her great-aunt Letitia Aubrey, she inherited lots in Philadelphia, and land in the Manor of Mount Joy in Upper Merion Township, and in Fagg's Manor. Neither she nor her husband ever came to Philadelphia, but one of her sons did, settling in Delaware County. An extended account

[57] *Ibid.,* 229-231.

of him, and of Christiana's other issue and their progeny follows in "The Penn-Gaskell Family," in the present issue of this *Magazine*.

Three years after the death of Christian Forbes, 9. William Penn, 3rd, married again. At St. Paul's Cathedral, William Penn, then of Withyan, Sussex, widower, by license dated 7 November 1736, was united in marriage with ANN VAUX, of the parish of St. Diones, Backchurch, London, and daughter of Isaac Vaux of London. They removed to Ireland and in 1738 were living in Ballyphechane in the South Liberties of Cork.

The marriage was not a success, however, for by 1742 she had left him and returned to England and William, then living in Dublin, had instituted a suit for divorce in Doctors' Commons. In April, 1746, he was back in Cork, concerned about the inventory of his aunt Letitia Aubrey's goods and the provisions of her will under which his thirteen-year-old daughter, Christiana Gulielma, was residuary legatee. Less than a year later he himself was dead, dying at Shanagarry of a dropsy 6 February 1746/7. In his will, dated 17 10m (December) 1743, he appointed his uncles John and Thomas Penn guardians of his two children during the minority of his son Springett. When he came of age he was to become executor. To his wife, who apparently had blocked the divorce proceedings, he left one shilling on the advice of counsel since she had "eloped" from him and thereby forfeited her dower rights and thirds.

Issue of 9. William Penn, 3rd, by his 2nd wife Ann Vaux:

ii. SPRINGETT PENN, b. at Cork, Ireland, 1 1m (March) 1738/9; d. of consumption testate, unmarried and without issue at Dublin, in November, 1766. Until he came of age, Springett was under the supervision of his great-uncle Thomas Penn, but subsequently appears to have been under the influence of his mother. In his will, dated 21 December 1762, he left her all that part of the Penn estates in Ireland and America coming to him from his father. In February, 1767, three months after Springett's death, his mother married, as his third wife, Alexander Durdin, a Dublin attorney. She died testate the following 13 April 1767. In the interval between her second marriage and death, she had drawn her own will in which she devised to Durdin all the estate left her by her son. As a result of her bequest, a long-drawn-out lawsuit followed between Durdin and Christiana Gulielma (Penn) Gaskell, Springett's half-sister, as she tried to establish her claim to her father's property. The suit in Chancery did not terminate until 1800, at which time the Shanagarry estate was divided between the heirs-at-law of Peter Gaskell and Alexander Durdin.

10. SOPHIA MARGARETTA JULIANA PENN, eighth child of 7. Thomas Penn and his wife, Lady Juliana Fermor, was born 25 December 1764. She married 3 May 1796, WILLIAM STUART, born in March, 1755, youngest son of John, third Earl of Bute. Destined for the church, he studied

at St. John's College, Cambridge, received his M.A. in 1774, obtained a Fellowship, and later received the vicarage of Luton, Bedfordshire, which he held for fourteen years. Taking the degree of D.D. in 1789, four years later he became Canon of Windsor, then Bishop of St. David's, and in 1800 was made Archbishop of Armagh, primate of all Ireland.

Said to have been a man with "a strong taste for humor, and strong feelings of indignation," he died in London 6 May 1822, after the inadvertent consumption of a dose of laudanum and camphorated spirits. His widow survived him twenty-five years, dying 29 April 1847. She was buried at Luton, Bedfordshire, in the Stuart family vault. Because their descendant, Brigadier Oliver F. G. Hogg, has compiled an extended record of all their descendants, a condensed account of only their children and grandchildren is given here.

Issue of 10. Sophia Margaretta Juliana Penn and her husband William Stuart:

i. MARY JULIANA STUART, b. 3 April 1797; d. 10 July 1866; m. 28 February 1815, THOMAS KNOX, Viscount Northland, afterwards 2nd Earl of Ranfurly of Dungannon Park, County Tyrone, Ireland; d. 26 April 1840. Issue:[58] 1. THOMAS KNOX, 3rd Earl, b. 13 November 1816; d. 20 May 1858, leaving issue; m. 10 October 1848, HARRIET RIMINGTON, d. 16 March 1891, daughter of James Rimington of Broomhead Hall, Yorkshire. Their second son, Sir Uchter John Mark Knox, 5th Earl and Governor of New Zealand, visited Philadelphia in 1904.[59] His daughter, Lady Constance Harriet Stuart Knox, who m. Major Evelyn Milnes Gaskell, visited Philadelphia in 1933, and subsequently was made an honorary member of the Genealogical Society of Pennsylvania. 2. MARY STUART KNOX, d. 14 May 1903, leaving issue; m. 20 September 1854, JOHN PAGE READE of Sutton, Suffolk; d. 28 September 1880. 3. LOUISA JULIANA KNOX, d. 31 March 1896, leaving issue; m. 14 August 1839, HENRY ALEXANDER of Forkhill, Armagh; d. 1 December 1877. The Major Dudley Alexander who accompanied the 5th Earl of Ranfurly to Philadelphia in 1904 as his private secretary, appears to have been their son. 4. ELIZABETH HENRIETTA KNOX, d. unmarried 28 January 1909. 5. JULIANA CAROLINE FRANCES KNOX, d. 11 December 1906, leaving issue; m. 15 October 1862, GENERAL SIR EDWARD FORESTIER-WALKER, K.C.B.; d. 27 July 1881. 6. WILLIAM STUART KNOX, b. 11 March 1826; d. 15 February 1900, leaving issue; m. 26 August 1856, GEORGINA ROOPER, d. 4 November 1926, daughter of John Bonfoy Rooper of Abbots Ripton,

---

[58] Mary Juliana Stuart's birth and death dates are taken from the account in the *London Illustrated News* of July, 1866, as given in the *Penn-Logan Correspondence*, I, xxxiv, cited in Note 17. This account also gives the death of her husband Thomas Knox as in April 1840, rather than 21 March 1858, as given in *Burke's Genealogical and Heraldic History of the Peerage, Baronetage and Knightage* (London, 1897), under "Ranfurly," which was followed by Mr. Jenkins. Since birth dates for daughters are not given in *Burke's Peerage*, the order of births for Mary Juliana Stuart's children is purely conjectural. Some death dates have been taken from the 1959 edition of the *Peerage*, edited by L. G. Pine. Others are from *A Genealogical and Heraldic History of the Landed Gentry of Great Britain and Ireland* (London, 1898), and from the 1938 edition of the *Peerage*.

[59] See *PMHB*, XXVIII (1904), 510.

Hunts. A member of Parliament for Dungannon, 1851-1874, he was a major in the 51st Foot and Honorary Colonel of Mid-Ulster Artillery. 7. FLORA SOPHIA ANNE PENN KNOX, d. unmarried 27 February 1905. 8. GRANVILLE HENRY JOHN KNOX, b. 1 August 1829; drowned in the River Tamar in southwestern England 18 August 1845. 9. ADELAIDE HENRIETTA LOUISA HORTENSE KNOX, d. 28 August 1911, leaving issue; m. 26 September 1850, JOSEPH GOFF of Hale Park, Hants.; d. 26 December 1872.

ii. WILLIAM STUART of Tempsford Hall, Beds., and Aldenham Abbey, Herts., b. 31 October 1798; d. 7 July 1874; m. 1st, 8 August 1821, HENRIETTA MARIA SARAH POLE, d. 26 July 1853, eldest daughter of Admiral Sir Charles Morice Pole, Bt. William Stuart was educated at St. John's College, Cambridge, receiving his M.A. in 1820. A member of Parliament for Armagh from 1820 to 1826, he sat for Bedfordshire from 1830 to 1834, and in 1846 was high sheriff of that county. On the death of the Rev. Thomas Gordon Penn in 1869, he became the "tenant in tail general" of all the remaining property entailed in Pennsylvania by John, Thomas and Richard Penn. The following year by indentures of 5 August and 2 September 1870, he "barred the entail," and on 11 November 1870, confirmed all Penn conveyances previously made in Pennsylvania.[60] In 1965, their descendant, Dr. Rosalind Esme Pole Stuart, was in Philadelphia, and in October of that year attended the dedication at Harrisburg of the William Penn Memorial Museum and Archives Building.

Issue of William Stuart:[61] 1. MARY POLE STUART, d. 25 January 1852, leaving issue; m. 1 August 1843, JONATHAN RASHLEIGH of Menabilly, Cornwall; d. 12 April 1905. 2. HENRIETTA POLE STUART, d. 13 February 1887, leaving issue; m. 4 September 1845, REGINALD THISTLETHWAYTE COCKS. 3. WILLIAM STUART, b. in London at the house of his grandmother, widow of Archbishop Stuart, in Hill Street, 7 March 1825; d. 21 December 1893, leaving issue; m. 13 September 1859, KATHERINE NICHOLSON, d. 16 October 1881, eldest daughter of John Armytage Nicholson of Balrath, County Meath, Ireland. 4. CHARLES POLE STUART of Sandymount House, Woburn Sands, Beds., barrister-at-law, b. 7 May 1826; d. 26 August 1896, leaving issue; m. 20 March 1860, ANNE SMYTH, d. 19 October 1918, eldest daughter of Robert Smyth of Gaybrook, County West Meath, Ireland. 5. CLARENCE ESME STUART, M.A. Cambridge, b. 29 May 1827; d. without issue 8 January 1903; m. 16 April 1853, CATHERINE CUNINGHAME; d. 10 March 1901, daughter of the late Colonel Cuninghame of Caddell and Thornton, County Ayr, Scotland. 6. LOUISA POLE STUART, d. 5 January 1858, leaving issue; m. 3 August 1852, the Reverend OLIVER MATTHEW RIDLEY; d. 10 January 1907.

---

[60] To bar the entail he had granted all the Pennsylvania estate to William Levi Bull in trust to reconvey it to him in fee simple, "clear and discharged of and from all limitations, conditions, covenants and restrictions" previously entered into and agreed upon by his ancestors. In 1874, Stuart's widow released any dower right which she might be thought to have in the estate.

[61] The order of their births is conjectural, based on data from Sir Bernard Burke, *A Genealogical and Heraldic History of the Landed Gentry* of Great Britain and Ireland (London, 1898), and from *Burke's Peerage* for 1915, under "Bute," from which death dates have been taken.

William Stuart, following the death of his first wife Henrietta, m. 2nd, 31 August 1854, Georgina Adelaide Forestier-Walker, daughter of General Forestier-Walker, who survived him. She m. 2nd, 15 December 1875, the 9th Earl of Seafield.

iii. LOUISA STUART, b. *ca.* 1801; d. unmarried 20 December 1823, *ae.* 22 years.[62]
iv. HENRY STUART, b. 1804; d. unmarried 26 October 1854.

---

[62] The death date for Louisa is given on the memorial tablet erected to the memory of her father, as quoted in the *Penn-Logan Correspondence,* I, xxxiii, and varies from the account in Jenkins, *The Family of William Penn,* 193. The former account says she was buried in the family vault at Sutton, whereas Mr. Jenkins states the vault was at Luton. He gives her date of death as 29 September 1823.

The Penn-Gaskell Family

Addenda to the Family of Penn

HANNAH BENNER ROACH, F.G.S.P., F.A.S.G.

D ESCENDANTS of William Penn, Founder of Pennsylvania, survive today, but only through female lines. By his first wife, Gulielma Maria Springett, one child only left progeny. This was William Penn, Jr. whose granddaughter is the ancestress of the Penn-Gaskell family.

The standard genealogical account of the Penn family is the late Howard M. Jenkins' long-out-of-print *The Family of William Penn*, published in 1899. In it the Penn-Gaskell line, representing the senior branch of the family, stemming from the Founder's first marriage, received less attention than the junior branch, descendants of Penn's second marriage. Through the researches in England of Francis James Dallett, and an examination of Philadelphia records, it is now possible to extend the account of the senior branch given by Mr. Jenkins, and to clothe it with more substance than he provided.

All descendants of the Penn-Gaskell branch, whether in England or in America, issue from the marriage of the Founder's grandson, William Penn, 3rd, and his first wife Christian Forbes, through their daughter CHRISTIANA GULIELMA PENN, born 22 October 1733, and her husband, PETER GASKELL, born about 1731, sometime of Bath, Somerset, England. On 13 August 1761, the London office of the Vicar General of the Archbishop of Canterbury issued a marriage allegation as follows:

Appeared personally Peter Gaskell of the parish of Saint Pancras in the County of Middlesex and made Oath that he is a Batchelor of the age of thirty years and upwards and that he intends to intermarry with Christiana Gulielma Penn of the Parish of Sunninghill in the County of Berks, aged upwards of twenty-six years . . . and prayed a License for them to be Married in either of the aforesaid parish Churches. /s/ Peter Gaskell [1]

The ceremony was performed 14 August 1761, in the Church of St. Pancras, Middlesex, by the Reverend William Nicolls, in the presence of

---

[1] Vicar General's Marriage Allegations, Lambeth Palace Library, London, located and furnished by Mr. Dallett, as are all English records unless otherwise noted.

Thomas Hicklin and Mary Talbot, both of whom signed the register with the bridal pair.[2]

The Gaskells settled in Bath from which place, in 1773, they initiated steps to recover lands in Pennsylvania which had descended to Christiana Gulielma. For the purpose of "Docking, Barring and Cutting of all estates Tail and remainders in Tail and reversions of all lots and lands in or near the City of Philadelphia and Liberties thereof or elsewhere," they empowered Abel Evans and Joseph Reed in Philadelphia to commence an amicable action. Joseph Reed was to sue forth against Abel Evans one or more "writs of entry sur Disseisin en le post" so that a good and perfect common recovery with double vouchers might be had for the use of the Gaskells.[3]

Two years later in 1775, by their attorney Joseph Galloway, the Gaskells agreed to a partition of city lots originally assigned to Christiana's grandfather William Penn, Jr., by his father, the Founder. The division was made with John and Thomas Hurst, Charles Hurst, their attorney, John Barron, and Israel Morris, who were or represented the issue of Christiana's aunt, Gulielma Maria (Penn) Fell.[4] Then in 1778, in the midst of the Revolution, having authorized Charles Hurst to locate and have surveyed "at his own charge and expense," some 36,000 acres of land which they claimed under warrants issued by the Founder to his son William, to his daughter Letitia Aubrey, and to his granddaughter Gulielma Maria Penn, the Gaskells assigned to Hurst better than half of the surveyed lands.[5]

Peter Gaskell's death was reported in *The Bath Chronicle,* issue of 27 January 1785, as examined by Mr. Dallett in the Bath Reference Library: "Last week died Peter Gaskill, esq., in Westgate-Buildings." His will, dated 20 December 1783, and proved 5 February 1785, by his executors, is on record in the Prerogative Court of Canterbury, Register Ducarel, folio 78, an abstracts of which follows:

---

[2] P.90/PAN.1/50, Greater London Record Office, County Hall, London, S.E.1.

[3] Philadelphia Deed Book D-22, 68: 26 June 1773, Peter Gaskell to Abel Evans and Joseph Reed. The deed was not recorded until 3 September 1788.

[4] Philadelphia Deed Book I-14, 484: 29 May 1775, Deed of Partition between Peter Gaskell and John Hurst *et al.* The land, 204 feet in breadth, extended along the north side of South Street from Delaware Second Street to the Schuylkill. It included not only the lot of William Penn, Jr., but also the lot originally assigned to the Lowthers. There were 35 lots marked off within the area, as shown on the draft appended to the deed. Of these, 22 went to the Gaskells. Possibly it was this partition which occasioned the suit for damages brought by Hurst and Barron, as mentioned by Howard M. Jenkins, *The Family of William Penn, Founder of Pennsylvania, Ancestry and Descendants* (Philadelphia, 1899), 242. In 1782 and 1783, Peter Gaskell's estate was assessed at £6730 for property in the south part of Dock Ward, Philadelphia, and at £600 for property in North Ward. *Pennsylvania Archives,* 3rd Series, XVI, 320, 436, 737.

[5] Philadelphia Deed Book D-17, 351: 30 May 1778, Peter Gaskell, "surgeon," of Bath to Charles Hurst. This deed, sealed in London in June, 1783, was recorded in Philadelphia 27 December 1786.

The will of Peter Gaskell, of the City of Bath in the County of Somerset, Gentleman. . . . In consequence of being kept out of the rents of my estate, I have contracted debts in Bath and vicinity to Tobias Salmon, Simon Draper, the Reverend Richard Graves, Rector of Claverton, Robert Noak Brewer and others. . . . Rents due in Ireland. . . . Suit between Springett Penn and myself in the Court of Chancery.[6] Personal estate I shall be entitled to on the death of my father Peter Gaskell, of Bollington near Macclesfield, in the County of Chester. . . . Loving wife Christianna Gulielma Gaskell and Tobias Salmon to be joint executors. . . . /s/ Peter Gaskell

Witnesses:
Ed. Vernon Goodall, William Goodall
N.B. The names of my father's executors are John Gaskell of Rainow, Gentleman, and William Wardle of Macclesfield, Button Merchant.

Peter Gaskell, Sr., mentioned in his son's will, died shortly before the son. His will, dated 10 March and proved the following 6 November 1784, was recorded in the Probate Records of Lancashire in the jurisdiction of the Consistory Court of the Bishop of Chester, at the Lancashire Record Office, Preston. In abstract it reads:

Will of Peter Gaskell, of Bollington Cross in the County of Chester, yeoman. . . . My brother John. . . . Tenement in Disley called Cock Knowle. . . . My servant, Sarah Dale. . . . My only son and heir Peter, and Peter's second son Peter, and his younger children, Alexander, William and Jane. . . . John Gaskell of Ingersley in Rainow and Thomas Wardle of Macclesfield, button manufacturer, to be executors. . . . /s/ Peter Gaskell

Peter Gaskell, husband of Christiana Gulielma Penn, is thus shown to have been the son of a country gentleman-cum-yeoman having a link with Macclesfield, as suggested by Jenkins in his account of the family; the adjacent villages of Bollington and Rainow, both in Cheshire, are two miles north of Macclesfield. But what connection Peter's family had with the Gaskells of Lancashire and Buckinghamshire has not yet been established.[7]

According to Mr. Dallett, Westgate Buildings, the Georgian terrace of houses in Bath where Peter and Christiana Gulielma (Penn) Gaskell lived, still stands. In Claverton village, outside Bath, just below the American Museum in Britain on Claverton Down, remains Claverton Old Rectory, the home of Gaskell's principal creditor, the Reverend

---

[6] Springett Penn was Christiana Gulielma Gaskell's half-brother, issue of her father's second marriage to Ann Vaux. He died in 1766 without issue. The Chancery suit, carried on by Ann Vaux's second husband, Alexander Durdin, was over the descent of the estates originally settled on William Penn, Jr., the Irish portion of which was chiefly in contest.

[7] Mr. Dallett suggests that the elder Peter Gaskell was perhaps a son of John Gaskell of Rainow, gent., bur. 3 June 1768, at Adlington, Cheshire. John Parsons Earwaker, *East Cheshire: Past and Present* (London, 1877), I, 217. The posterity of Peter Gaskell's uncle John Gaskell of Ingersley in Rainow, gentleman, acquired Ingersley Hall in the nineteenth century. John Upton Gaskell still lived there in 1882, and was also then proprietor of Tower Hill, "an old house here, formerly belonging to the Savage and the Brocklehurst family, from whom it passed by descent to the Gaskells." Thomas Helsby, ed., *The History of the County Palatine and City of Chester*, by George Ormerod (London, 1882), III, 771.

Richard Graves; it would have been very familiar to the Gaskells' young son Peter who went to Pennsylvania after his father's death.

In the Administration Act Book of the Prerogative Court of Canterbury for November, 1803, are recorded letters of administration granted 25 November 1803, on the estate of young Peter's mother, Christiana Gulielma Gaskell, late of the Parish of St. Giles in the Fields, Middlesex, widow, to Thomas Penn Gaskell, her eldest child. She had died at her house in Thornhaugh Street, London, 24 March 1803, aged sixty-nine.

Issue of Peter Gaskell and his wife Christiana Gulielma Penn:[8]

    i. THOMAS PENN GASKELL, b. *ca.* 1762; d. at his house in Fitzwilliam Square, Dublin, Ireland, 19 October 1823, *ae.* 61 years; m. 1794, MISS WARD, daughter of John Ward and his wife Jane Vesey, heretofore described as a daughter of the Dowager Countess of Glandore. Mr. Dallett reports that following the death of John Ward, Jane (Vesey) Ward m. 1 November 1777, William Crosbie, Earl of Glandore, of Glandore, County Cork, and Viscount Crosbie of Ardfert, County Kerry, by whom she had no further issue and, dying in September, 1787, was bur. at Ardfert.[9] Thomas Penn Gaskell and his wife had issue an only son who died in infancy. The Shanagarry estate, which Thomas inherited from his mother, thus fell to his brother 1. Peter in America.

1. ii. PETER GASKELL, b. *ca.* 1764; d. in Pennsylvania 16 July 1831, in his 68th year, of whom further.

    iii. ALEXANDER FORBES PENN GASKELL, d. unmarried after 1816, when he was writing to his brother Peter in Radnor, from Gray's Inn, London, according to letters in the Penn-Gaskell-Hall correspondence in the Historical Society of Pennsylvania. He was somewhat aggrieved that his brother had not accepted the offer made earlier by Alexander to house two of Peter Gaskell's young sons in England to train them as clerks in an "English profession" as opposed to an "American business." [10]

2. iv. WILLIAM PENN GASKELL, b. *ca.* 1769; d. in England, 17 November 1842, *ae.* 73 years, of whom further.

    v. JANE GASKELL, b. *ca.* 1772; d. in England, testate and unmarried, 19 May 1844, aged 72 years, according to her death notice in *The Gentleman's Magazine,* July 1844, page 103, and in which she was described as "a lineal descendant of William Penn and Robert Barclay." Her residence was given as New Ormond Street in the parish of St. Andrew Holborn above Bars, Middlesex, London, in her will dated 27 April 1837, and proved 1 June 1844, by her nephew William Penn Gaskell, her executor, on record in the Prerogative Court of Canterbury, No. 460 of 1844. In the will she directed that she was to be

---

8 Genealogical data in the following pages is based on the information given in Jenkins, cited in Note 4, except when otherwise noted.

9 *The Complete Peerage* (London, 1926), V, 659. In John W. Jordan, *Colonial and Revolutionary Families of Pennsylvania* (New York and Chicago, 1911), I, 13, the wife of Thomas Penn Gaskell is identified as "Lady Diana Sackville, daughter of the Dowager Countess of Glandore."

10 The letter in the Penn-Gaskell-Hall Correspondence, Gratz Collection, Historical Society of Pennsylvania (HSP), was examined by Mrs. Robert I. Cummin for Mr. Dallett in April, 1967, as per a letter from her.

buried in the parish in which she happened to be residing at the time of her death, "not to be buried in a vault" and that her funeral "be conducted in the simplest manner."

To her "Dear brother William Penn Gaskell of Cheltenham in the County of Gloucester Esquire," she devised "our dear Mother's picture" and other goods. To his wife Elizabeth Gaskell, silver, etc. To Caroline Phillips, then living with her, as a testimony for service, she left an annuity of £40 for life and £10 for mourning, also various household effects including "silver marked P.G." To her nephew William Penn Gaskell, son of her brother William, her Bible; to Saint John's Chapel, Bedford Row, £19; the leasehold house in New Bond Street in the occupation of Mrs. Owen, and held under lease of the City of London, and all residue after payment of legacies, she left to her nephew William, he and John Freeman of Bishopsgate Street in London to be executors. The will was witnessed by Wm. Tooke, 39 Bedford Row, and W. Hallowes, his clerk. A codicil dated 23 March 1844, revoked bequests of silver and china to Elizabeth Gaskell, widow of her "late dear brother William Penn Gaskell," deceased, leaving them to Mary Gaskell, wife of her "dear nephew" William Penn Gaskell, and to his daughter Jane Gaskell. The codicil was witnessed by Tooke and by Elizabeth Remmie, 20 Ormond Street.

1. Peter Gaskell, born about 1764, second son of Peter Gaskell and his wife Christiana Gulielma Penn, first appears in Philadelphia records in 1786, when he was assessed as a single man in North Ward, lodging with the Widow Sarah Clark.[11] The dwelling appears to have been on the east side of North Fourth Street, about five doors above Market Street, and near the Friends' burying ground.

Although he was a comparative stranger in town, as a landowner and resident he was liable for militia duty; in 1786 and 1787, at least, he was enrolled in Captain Charles Syng's 5th Company of the Third Battalion commanded by Colonel John Shee.[12] Peter may also have been involved in the efforts of his mother's attornies to establish her claim to Philadelphia property contested by her father's other heirs. In 1789, Thomas Clifford and Miers Fisher, her attornies, applied to the Pennsylvania Supreme Executive Council to set a time for hearing "the objection of the Attorney General" to receiving "a declaration in ejectment, on her demise, to try her title to three equal fourth parts of divers lots of ground" in the city, extending from the west side of Delaware Fourth Street to the Schuylkill, 102 feet in breadth. The hearing was held 11 August 1789, but was rejected "unanimously" the following 8 September.[13]

Peter was still lodging with the Widow Clark in 1790, but was not

11 Philadelphia Assessment Lists, North Ward, Municipal Archives, Department of Records, City Hall, Philadelphia.

12 Pennsylvania Archives, 6th Series, III, 1073, 1074, 1081.

13 Minutes of the Supreme Executive Council of Pennsylvania . . . (Harrisburg, 1863), XVI, 108, 130, 153.

enumerated individually. She was listed as having four males over sixteen years of age in her household, and four females including herself.[14] He remained with her until 1793, when the yellow fever epidemic drove him out of town. That year, on 5 December 1793, he married at St. James' Episcopal Church, Perkiomen, at Evansburg in Lower Providence Township, Montgomery County, ELIZABETH EDWARDS. Born about 1773, she is said to have been the daughter of Nathan Edwards of Radnor.[15]

They lived in Montgomery County in Upper Merion Township for several years where, in 1795 Peter Gaskell signed a petition, with thirty-five residents of the county, for the erection of a bridge over Perkiomen Creek.[16] But a year later, when he bought the property he called Ashwood in Radnor Township, Delaware County, he was described as "Peter Gaskell of Radnor, yeoman," and in 1798 was taxed in Radnor for his "saw'd logd weather boarded" two-story house. It was then described as being 45 by 19 feet, had 27 windows, with a smoke house which was 10 by 8 feet.[17] The property fronted on Spring Mill Road and extended east to the Lower Merion Township line. Ashwood, much enlarged by later Penn-Gaskells and their successors, still stands on what is now called Ashwood Road in Villanova, and is the home of G. Clinton Jones, IV.

In 1806, three years after their mother's death, Peter's brothers and sister in England released their claim to a lot on the west side of Delaware Second Street "opposite the New Market and between Cedar and Lombard Streets." Bounded on the south by "ground claimed by Charles Hurst," the consideration money was $266.66. Similar deeds for other lots may have been executed but were not recorded.[18]

When Peter was sixty years old, and after he had succeeded to the Irish property of Shanagarry upon the death of his eldest brother Thomas

[14] *Heads of Families at the First Census of the United States . . . 1790, Pennsylvania* (Washington, D. C., 1908), 222. Peter Gaskell was assessed regularly at Sarah Clark's in North Ward from 1786 to 1792, after which his name disappeared from the Philadelphia assessment lists.

[15] Jenkins, 244. Her parentage, however, is open to question, for no evidence has been found to establish it. The only Nathan Edwards located to date died in Middletown Twp., Delaware Co., in 1785, before their marriage, listed in *Pennsylvania Archives*, 2nd Series (Harrisburg, 1880), 171.

[16] Peter Gaskell was assessed in U. Merion Twp. on 136 acres of land and dwelling, 2 horses and 2 cattle, from 1793, when he was a single man, through 1795, and was described as a farmer. Original tax duplicates, Montgomery County Historical Society, Norristown, Pa. The petition for the bridge is in the *Bulletin of the Montgomery County Historical Society*, X (1956), 123.

[17] Delaware County Deed Book C, 285: 10 May 1796, John Bewley to Peter Gaskell. United States Direct Tax, 1798, Microfilm Roll 7, National Archives, Washington, D. C. An illustrated historical and architectural survey of Ashwood (north of Lancaster Pike and Spring Mill Road), prepared without benefit of the 1798 Direct Tax record, is in Historic American Building Surveys, U. S. Department of the Interior, File PA-194. These records were examined by Mr. Dallett.

[18] Philadelphia Deed Book GWR-31, 88: 7 June 1806, Thomas Penn Gaskell *et al.* to Peter Gaskell. The Philadelphia deed indices were examined only up to 1850.

Penn Gaskell, he assumed the additional surname of Penn "by royal license" 31 May 1824, "in compliance with the testamentary injunction of his brother." Neither his elder nor younger brothers used the hyphenated form since they both bore Penn as a Christian name and went by the double name, Penn Gaskell. Peter, however, and his descendants thenceforth used the hyphenated name (now extinct in his line), as his younger brother William's descendants have done in England in recent years, according to Mr. Dallett. It is of interest to note that the name invariably is indexed as Gaskell in Philadelphia public records.

Mr. Dallett points out that Peter Penn-Gaskell, as he now called himself, was something of an amateur artist and probably the first person to paint in Radnor. A portrait by him of his neighbor, George Fisher Curwen of Walnut Hill in Lower Merion, belongs to Miss Elinor Ewing Curwen of Villanova, Pa. Peter's interest in art probably accounts for the portraits Thomas Sully painted about 1829 or 1830, of Peter and his wife Elizabeth, of their eldest surviving son Thomas, of their youngest son Isaac, and of their daughter Jane, following the death of the fourth son, Alexander Forbes Penn-Gaskell. Some of these portraits now hang in the entrance hall of the Historical Society of Pennsylvania, others in Lemon Hill in Fairmount Park.

Three months after the death of his fourth son, Peter Penn-Gaskell "the elder," then residing in the city, purchased for $4500 a three-story brick messuage and lot on the south side of Mulberry (Arch) Street, just west of Delaware Twelfth Street.[19] The property was purchased for his third son, married four years earlier, who was listed in 1829 at that address as "P. P. Gaskell, Jr."

Peter Penn-Gaskell, Sr. died in Radnor 16 July 1831, in his sixty-eighth year, and was buried in the Lower Merion Baptist churchyard. His widow Elizabeth died testate three years later on 19 July 1834, in her sixty-second year, and was buried beside her husband. In her will she left three thousand dollars for the erection of monuments over the remains of her husband, herself and their children. In the course of time large flat marble tablets were placed upon the graves with appropriate inscriptions, some portions of which are badly eroded.[20]

---

19 Philadelphia Deed Book GWR-37, 30: 8 December 1829, Isaac Collins to Peter Penn-Gaskell. The lot, 46 feet west of the corner of Twelfth Street, was 24 feet wide and extended 173 feet to Sheaff Street, now presumably Ludlow.

20 In 1938, the late Edward M. Hocker copied all inscriptions then in the churchyard, including the Penn-Gaskell stones. They were difficult to read then, and have not improved with time. Occasionally he mistook "threes" for "fives:" Christiana Gulielma Hall, daughter of Peter and Elizabeth Penn-Gaskell, d. in 1830, *not* 1850, and her parents d. in 1831 and 1834, *not* 1851 and 1854. However, Jane, their daughter, whom Jenkins said d. in 1852, aged 24 years, Mr. Hocker correctly transcribed as "1832, in her 24th year." The ages quoted by Jenkins do not correspond to the inscriptions; he may have gotten these from the church burial record. In the record given in this present text, they are corrected to read as given on the tombstones.

Issue of 1. Peter Penn-Gaskell and his wife Elizabeth Edwards:

 i. WILLIAM PENN-GASKELL, b. *ca.* 1794; d. unmarried 12 October 1817, in his 24th year, bur. L. Merion Baptist churchyard.

 ii. THOMAS PENN-GASKELL, b. *ca.* 1795; d. in L. Merion Township, 18 October 1846, in his 52nd year, bur. 20 October following "in his vault at St. John's R. C. Church, Thirteenth Street above Chestnut, Philadelphia;" m. by the Right Reverend Bishop White, of Christ P. E. Church, 22 December 1825, MARY McCLENACHAN, daughter of George McClenachan and his wife Mary Morris;[21] d. 21 December 1867, in L. Merion Township and was bur. 24 December following in the vault in St. John's Church. Thomas Penn-Gaskell, as the eldest surviving son, succeeded to the entailed Shanagarry estate on the death of his father Peter in 1831. According to John F. Watson, when Thomas visited the property "he was received with all the pomp and circumstances of Lordship, which a numerous tribe of tenants and mansion house menials could confer."[22] His widow, Mary Penn-Gaskell, entertained Granville John Penn, her husband's cousin, in January 1852, at her home, Penn Cottage, located on a 73-acre tract east of the Ashwood tract in Lower Merion.[23]

 iii. ELIZA PENN-GASKELL, b. *ca.* 1799; d. testate unmarried at Ashwood, where she had lived all her life, 23 November 1865, in her 67th year, bur. at L. Merion Baptist churchyard. In her will she made elaborate provision for preserving the ownership of Ashwood in the family, but by 1888 the last part of it had been sold.

3. iv. PETER PENN-GASKELL, JR., b. 3 April 1800; d. in Philadelphia testate 6 April 1866, of whom further.

 v. ALEXANDER FORBES PENN-GASKELL, b. *ca.* 1803; d. at Ashwood unmarried, 8 September 1829, in his 27th year, bur. at L. Merion Baptist churchyard.

4. vi. CHRISTIANA GULIELMA PENN-GASKELL, b. *ca.* 1807; d. 20 March 1830, in her 24th year, of whom further.

 vii. JANE PENN-GASKELL, b. *ca.* 1809; d. unmarried 7 July 1832, in her 24th year, bur. at L. Merion Baptist churchyard. The portrait of her by Sully, painted in 1829 "for Mr. Hall," apparently was commissioned by her brother-in-law, rather than by her father.

 viii. ISAAC PENN-GASKELL, b. *ca.* 1811; d. unmarried 24 October 1842, in his 32nd year, bur. L. Merion Baptist churchyard. He had received the degree of M.D. from the University of Pennsylvania in 1834. He left a will dated 23 October 1842, which was probated 16 May 1843, by his eldest brother Thomas, to whom letters of administration had previously been granted, though "his belief of the mental incapacity" of Isaac "to make a will remains unaltered."[24]

---

[21] George McClenachan (1769-1833, son of Blair and Ann McClenachan) and Mary Morris, his wife (d. 1849 in her 74th year, daughter of Jacob and Meribah Morris) are interred, with many other members of her family, in the L. Merion Baptist churchyard near the Penn-Gaskell lot.

[22] John F. Watson, *Annals of Philadelphia and Pennsylvania . . .* (Philadelphia, 1927), I, 126.

[23] For an account of the entertainment, see *The Pennsylvania Magazine of History and Biography* (*PMHB*), XXIV (1900), 231. The size of the Penn Cottage tract is in Edward H. Browning, *Welsh Settlement of Pennsylvania* (Philadelphia, 1912), 485.

[24] Jenkins, 246.

2. WILLIAM PENN GASKELL, born about 1769, fourth child of Peter Gaskell of Bath and his wife Christiana Gulielma Penn, remained in England and was the progenitor of the English branch of the Penn Gaskell family. A landed proprietor of Burnham, Bucks, when his first child was born, by 1835 he had retired to Cheltenham where he died seven years later. Described as a surgeon in 1806 when he released with his brothers and sister their rights in the lot in Philadelphia to Peter Gaskell, he married before 1808, ELIZABETH, surname not known, who survived him. According to Mr. Dallett, the notice of his death in 1842 appeared in *The Gentleman's Magazine* for January 1843, page 106:

"Nov. 17. At Cheltenham, aged 73, William Penn Gaskell, esq. lineally descended, through his mother, from William Penn, the founder and original proprietor of Pennsylvania, and [from] Sir William Springett, who was killed at the siege of Banbury."

An abstract of his will, dated 24 July 1835, and proved at London 7 December 1842, reads:

Will of William Penn Gaskell of Cheltenham in the County of Gloucester. . . . All real estate in England, Ireland, America or elsewhere to my dear son William Penn Gaskell. Also £13,000 at 3 percent to be his at my decease. To my dear wife Elizabeth Gaskell all household goods. To my dear wife also £1000 in the 3½ percent standing in my name and her name which I consider hers already. To dear wife for her life the interest of £5000 in the 3½ percent and at her death to my son William Penn Gaskell. Also any money left me by the late — Cotton, Esquire, or his wife, to my wife. Gold watch to my son. Gold reading glass to my dear sister Jane Gaskell. Son William Penn Gaskell and my wife Elizabeth Gaskell to be executors . . . .   /s/ William Penn Gaskell

The will was witnessed by Thomas Gilling, William Wakefield, and Harriet Marden, Spinster, and was proved on the oath of "William Penn Gaskell Esquire the son to whom Administration was granted, power reserved of making grant to the widow, the other Executor." [25]

Issue of 2. William Penn Gaskell and his wife Elizabeth:

5.   i. WILLIAM PENN GASKELL, JR., b. 20 February 1808; d. in England 27 December 1881, of whom further.

    ii. ELIZABETH PENN GASKELL, d. unmarried between 2 August 1830, when she was corresponding with her cousin Eliza in Pennsylvania, daughter of 1. Peter Penn-Gaskell, and 24 July 1835, when her father wrote his will without naming her.[26]

3. PETER PENN-GASKELL, JR., born 3 April 1800, was the fourth child and third son of Peter Penn-Gaskell, Sr. and his wife Elizabeth Ed-

25 His death certificate, located by Mr. Dallett, is filed at the General Register Office, Somerset House, Strand, London, W.C.2, where his will is No. 815 of 1842. All information on this English Penn Gaskell line has been supplied by Mr. Dallett.

26 Penn-Gaskell-Hall Correspondence, Gratz Collection, HSP, cited in Note 10.

wards. Undoubtedly he was one of the sons his English uncle, Alexander Forbes Penn Gaskell, had offered to train as a law clerk in 1816. But Peter was probably apprenticed to some Philadelphia merchant instead, for by 1824 he had been in co-partnership with the merchant Thomas Earle for at least a year. On the first of March of that year, Thomas Earle and Peter Penn-Gaskell, as agents or commission merchants having become indebted to "divers persons" through unfortunate business ventures, assigned all their real, personal or mixed estate to Howell Hopkins. He was charged with their conversion into funds and the distribution of the monies arising out of the sale to their creditors, the largest of which was the Farmers and Mechanics Bank. After the creditors were satisfied, the estate was to be reconveyed to Earle and Penn-Gaskell.[27]

This apparently was only a temporary setback, for less than a year later Peter Penn-Gaskell was married by the rector of Christ Church on 15 February 1825, to LOUISA ADELAIDE HEATH, born 2 October 1805, daughter of Charles P. Heath. In 1829, they were living in the house on Mulberry Street above Twelfth which Peter's father had purchased. Here they lived until 1835, when Peter purchased for $12,500 a three-story brick house and lot on the north side of Chestnut between Schuylkill Sixth (Seventeenth) Street and Schuylkill Seventh (Sixteenth) Street. A year later he bought another house and lot further up Chestnut Street for $3500, nearer the corner of Schuylkill Sixth.[28] Since this was a smaller property, the three-story house was the one they occupied, listed in the City Directory in 1855 as 523 Chestnut, and in 1861, when the house-numbering system in Philadelphia was stabilized, as 1613 Chestnut Street. Four years later, when he wrote his will, he was of 1613 Chestnut Street, "and of Shanagarry, County Cork," which he had inherited on the death of his elder brother Thomas in 1846. In his will he devised Shanagarry to his eldest son William, and in the event of his death without male heirs, to his own younger son Peter.[29]

Peter Penn-Gaskell, Jr. died in Philadelphia 3 April 1866, and was buried the following 7 April in Laurel Hill Cemetery in Section G, Lot 168, which he had purchased in 1847. His widow Louisa Adelaide was in London, residing at Eastbourne Terrace, Hyde Park — possibly visiting her husband's relatives — when she wrote her will 29 June 1869.

---

27 Philadelphia Deed Book GWR-2, 135: 1 March 1824, Thomas Earle and Peter Penn-Gaskell to Howell Hopkins. The amount to be paid the bank was $117.32, "being 45 percent of the amount of debt owing."

28 Philadelphia Deed Book AM-67, 575: 19 September 1835, Charles H. White to Peter Penn-Gaskell. This first property, formerly owned by Simon Gratz, was 22 feet wide and extended north 158 feet to Ranstead Street, then called Linden. The second lot was 18 feet by 158 feet. Deed Book SHF-4, 646: 7 October 1836, William A. Rhodes to Peter Penn-Gaskell. Its subsequent history has not been traced.

29 Philadelphia Will Book 57, 304, #207: 1866. The will of Peter Penn-Gaskell, dated 26 April 1865, was proved 10 April 1866, by his wife Louisa and son Peter Penn-Gaskell, 3rd.

Portraits of herself, her husband's father, and her deceased daughter Gulielma she left initially to her daughter Mary Penn-Gaskell Coates, and all other paintings, books, her large Bible, and the residue of her silver plate to her son Peter Penn-Gaskell, 3rd. Three codicils, dated 22 July 1870, 7 November 1873, and 27 March 1877, in which she named grandsons Harold Coates, Penn-Gaskell Skillern, Granville Quinn, and her own son "Willie" Penn-Gaskell, were added before her death 7 February 1878. In the last codicil she left her one-third share of the house at 1613 Chestnut Street to her son Peter Penn-Gaskell, 3rd, "now living in London." She was buried in the lot in Laurel Hill Cemetery beside her husband and those children who had predeceased her.[30] The monument now standing on the lot bears the Penn shield: a crescent in chief, on a fess three plates, and is surmounted by a cross dexter, the figure of Justice sinister. The motto is so badly eroded it is difficult to decipher.

Issue of 3. Peter Penn-Gaskell, Jr. and his wife Louisa Adelaide Heath:

6.   i. ELIZABETH PENN-GASKELL, b. 19 December 1825; d. in Tennessee 23 October 1866, of whom further.

ii. LOUISA PENN-GASKELL, b. 15 August 1827; d. 28 March 1848, bur. in the family lot in Laurel Hill; m. at St. Stephen's P. E. Church, Philadelphia, 15 May 1845, WILLIAM GERALD FITZGERALD, of New York. Only issue: WILLIAM PENN-GASKELL FITZGERALD, b. 8 February 1847; d. 4 July 1847, bur. in the Penn-Gaskell lot in Laurel Hill.

iii. MARY GULIELMA PENN-GASKELL, b. 3 August 1829; d. 21 June 1830. Her remains were bur. in Laurel Hill 25 October 1847, nine days after her father purchased the lot. Her first burial place remains unknown.

iv. GULIELMA PENN-GASKELL, b. 29 May 1831; d. 25 October 1850, bur. in the family lot at Laurel Hill.

v. HETTY PENN-GASKELL, b. 29 January 1833; d. 23 October 1847, bur. in the family lot in Laurel Hill.

vi. MARY PENN-GASKELL, b. 12 September 1834; d. testate in Delaware County, Pa., 22 August 1877, bur. from the residence of her mother, 4058 Chestnut Street, Philadelphia, in the family plot in Laurel Hill;[31] m. 22 March 1865, DR. ISAAC T. COATES of Chester, Pa., who d. 23 June 1883. Issue: 1. PETER PENN-GASKELL COATES, b. 26 February 1866; bur. 26 January 1869, *ae.* 2-11-0, in the Penn-Gaskell lot in Laurel Hill. 2. HAROLD PENN-GASKELL COATES, b. *ca.* 1870; m. FLORENCE JARVIS, said to be of Philadelphia. He was listed in the City Directory of 1891 at 711 and 3701 Walnut Street, but

---

[30] Philadelphia Will Book 92, 552, #544: 1878, will of Louisa Penn-Gaskell. Her birth and marriage dates are from the Penn-Gaskell-Skillern Bible records in the Collections of the Genealogical Society of Pennsylvania. Her death date is from the inscription on the marble obelisk, now the only stone standing on the Penn-Gaskell lot in Laurel Hill. Unless otherwise noted, all dates in the accounts of her issue are taken from the Bible record, the interment records of Laurel Hill, or from the obelisk.

[31] Mary P. G. Coates' death notice is in the *Philadelphia Inquirer* for Friday, 24 August 1877. In her will, on record in Delaware County Will Book G, 58, she left her interest in 1613 Chestnut Street, Philadelphia, to her son Harold Coates.

was not listed before or thereafter. That year he conveyed the interest his mother had left him in the house at 1613 Chestnut Street. At an undisclosed later date he was living at 4100 Spruce Street, Philadelphia, when he asked for an estimate from Laurel Hill Cemetery for maintaining the family lot.[32] According to Mr. Dallett, Dr. Penn G. Skillern thought they lived in Virginia and had issue, of whom nothing is known. 3. CHARLES MORTON COATES, b. October 1872; bur. 20 May 1873, *ae.* 7 mos., in the Laurel Hill lot.

vii. WILLIAM PENN-GASKELL, b. 9 July 1836; d. unmarried 6 December 1865, bur. in the family lot at Laurel Hill. He served with credit in the Union Army, and was discharged as a captain on a surgeon's certificate 5 July 1864. An obituary in a New Orleans newspaper, dated 13 January 1866, stated he died of consumption "in the bosom of his family."

viii. JANE PENN-GASKELL, b. 4 July 1839; d. 1 November 1863, bur. in the family lot at Laurel Hill; m. 15 October 1862, WASHINGTON IRVING, said to have been a nephew of the author. He may have been the man who was paymaster, U.S.N., 1 June 1861, and who was wholly retired 11 February 1870.[33] No issue.

ix. EMILY PENN-GASKELL, b. 27 January 1842; d. 17 February 1869, bur. in the family lot at Laurel Hill; m. 13 January 1864, JOHN PAUL QUINN, U.S.N.; d. 6 June 1869. He was assistant surgeon, 9 May 1861, and surgeon, 30 October 1864.[34] Issue: 1. HAMILTON QUINN, b. and d. September 1865, *ae.* 42 hrs., bur. in the family lot at Laurel Hill. 2. GRANVILLE PENN QUINN, b. 6 January 1868; d. Washington, D. C., bur. in the family lot in Laurel Hill, 24 May 1892, *ae.* 24. A week before his death he made over his rights in 1613 Chestnut Street to Delia E. Quinn for $5000. She has not been identified, nor has the B. C. Quinn who witnessed the conveyance.[35]

7. x. PETER PENN-GASKELL, 3rd, b. 24 October 1843; d. *ca.* 1905, of whom further.

4. CHRISTIANA GULIELMA PENN-GASKELL, born about 1807, sixth child of Peter Penn-Gaskell and his wife Elizabeth Edwards, was married in Philadelphia by the rector of Christ Church on 2 January 1827, to WILLIAM HALL, born about 1799 or 1800, whose middle name is variously given as Von Swartzbrick or Swabric. He is reported to have been born at Wavertree, Lancashire, son of Richard Hall, a Liverpool merchant, who sent the young man to Philadelphia to manage a branch office.[36]

Their marriage was of short duration, for Christiana died in her twenty-fourth year on 29 March 1830, following the birth of her sec-

---

[32] According to the records of Laurel Hill Cemetery, a lien of $90 remains against the lot for maintenance from 1 May 1912, to 1 May 1920. In Philadelphia Deed Book TG-48, 491: 10 August 1891, Harold P. G. Coates to Rush Kersey Morton, Harold's wife's name was given as Florence J. Coates.

[33] Edward W. Callahan, ed., *List of Officers of the Navy of the United States and of the Marine Corps from 1775 to 1900* . . . (New York, 1901), 290.

[34] *Ibid.,* 450.

[35] Philadelphia Deed Book TG-202, 61: 17 May 1892, Granville P. Quinn to Delia E. Quinn.

[36] Jordan, 16, cited in Note 9.

ond child. Her husband survived her thirty-two years, dying 26 September 1862, in his sixty-third year. Both are buried at Lower Merion Baptist churchyard.

Issue of 4. Christiana Gulielma Penn-Gaskell and her husband William S. Hall:

i. WILLIAM PENN-GASKELL HALL, b. 26 November 1827; d. in Camden, N. J., 2 May 1862, bur. L. Merion Baptist churchyard. From 1842-1844 he was a member of the class of 1846 of the College, University of Pennsylvania, and from 1844-1846 a student in the Medical Department. He was "Devoted to literary and scientific study; and spent most of his time in foreign travel." A member of the Historical Society of Pennsylvania, he was also the author of a number of poems published in the *Bizarre* and in newspapers.[37]

8. ii. PETER PENN-GASKELL HALL, b. 16 March 1830; d. 1 February 1905, of whom further.

5. WILLIAM PENN GASKELL, JR. was born in England at Burnham, Bucks, 20 February 1808,[38] eldest child and only son of 2. William Penn Gaskell, Sr. and his wife Elizabeth. He was admitted pensioner at Corpus Christi College, Cambridge, 4 July 1826; matriculated at Michaelmas, 1827; Scholar, 1829, and received his B.A. in 1831.[39] He was the author of *An address to the operative classes, being the substance of a lecture explanatory . . . of the nature and objects of the Cheltenham Mechanics' Institution,* published at Cheltenham in 1835, a copy of which is in the British Museum.

About 1840, he married by common law, with ceremony following by license on 27 June 1842, at St. John's Church, Paddington, by the Reverend J. Symons, rector of Radnage, Berks., to MARY HOBBS, born at Sandhurst about 1815, daughter of John Hobbs of Sandhurst, Gloucester.[40] They lived in Paddington, Middlesex, for a number of years: in 1841, at No. 5 Bayswater Terrace; in 1842, at No. 17 Porchester Terrace; in 1845, at No. 32 Eastbourne Terrace. From 1847 to 1855, at least, they were at Great Marlow, Bucks, where William's property was at Lane End, and where they were listed in the 1851 Census. He was then farming thirty-six acres and employing three laborers and four house servants. By 1865, they had moved to Ealing, Middlesex, where they died.

---

37 *Biographical Catalogue of the Matriculates of the College, University of Pennsylvania . . . 1749-1893* (Philadelphia, 1894), 152.

38 Jenkins, 243, gives his precise date of birth. Mr. Dallett reports that the year is corroborated by the 1851 Census, in which his age was then 43 years, and the place of birth as Burnham. H.O. 107/1719/2/1. Public Record Office, London. Data on him and his family has been supplied by Mr. Dallett.

39 J. A. Venn, *Alumni Cantabrigienses, Part II,* III, 22.

40 Their marriage certificate is filed at Somerset House. In the 1851 Census, Mary Penn Gaskell was aged 36 years.

William Penn Gaskell died testate 27 December 1881, having drawn his will 16 February 1877. Then of No. 1 Craven Terrace, Ealing, he left to his "dear wife Mary the house, garden and blacksmith shop at Sandhurst" as her claim to dower. All personal and other estate he left in trust to his three eldest sons, William Penn Gaskell, Thomas Penn Gaskell, and Alexander Barclay Penn Gaskell, for the benefit of his ten children, all named. The three sons were to act as trustees and were appointed executors. The will was proved at London 13 February 1882, by "William Penn Gaskell of 10 New Broad Street, London, Accountant, Thomas Penn Gaskell of 8 Victoria Chambers, Westminster, Civil Engineer, and Alexander Barclay Penn Gaskell of 1 King's Bench Walk Temple, London." The personal estate amounted to £22,911 17s. 7d.[41]

His widow Mary survived him less than three years, dying testate 8 August 1884, at Shangarry, Hamilton Road, Ealing, Middlesex. Her will was proved 12 February 1885, by their three eldest sons.[42]

Issue of 5. William Penn Gaskell and his wife Mary Hobbs:[43]

i. WILLIAM PENN GASKELL, 3rd., b. *ca.* 1840; d. testate 30 March 1886, at No. 40 Castletown Road, West Kensington, Middlesex.[44] An accountant, he left his property to his four sisters.

ii. THOMAS PENN GASKELL, b. 12 April 1841, at Bayswater, Middlesex; d. testate at Bayswater 3 May 1928; m. 12 March 1878, at the parish church of Mansfield, Notts., ADA WALLIS, b. *ca.* 1854, daughter of Henry Bell Wallis; d. after 1928.[45] Thomas Penn Gaskell was a civil engineer of London, and in 1886 lived at Grange Bank, Brighton Rd., Sutton, Surrey. He was the author of five books, all to be found in the British Museum: *Railways: Their Financial Position and Prospects* (London, 1874); *Free Trade, a Failure from the First* (London, 1903); *Protection Paves the Path of Prosperity* (London, 1913); *The Coming Great Depression in Trade* (London, 1914); and *The Curse of Cobdenism* (London, 1919). By his will, dated 14 June 1921, when he was living at 22 Fitz George Ave., Kensington, he left the copyright of his books to his wife and included the following direction: "I suggest to my trustees that the portrait of Guilelmina [Christiana Gulielma] Penn, the grand-

---

[41] William Penn Gaskell's death date is from his will, No. 108 of 1882, Somerset House.

[42] Mary Penn Gaskell's death date is from the probate of her will, No. 122 of 1885, Prerogative Court of Canterbury, Somerset House.

[43] All the children, except Jane, received Penn as a Christian name; all of them later adopted it as part of a double surname. In the next generation, William Penn-Gaskell, b. 1883, added the hyphen.

[44] The date of his death is in the probate of his will, No. 707 of 1886, Somerset House. Dated 26 February 1882, it was proved 28 August 1886, by his brothers Thomas and George. One Charles Wilfred Gaskell, admitted pensioner, aged 22, at Jesus College, Cambridge, in October, 1894, son of W. P. Gaskell, Esq., was born at Fulmer, Bucks, and matriculated at the same college in Michaelmas, 1894. It is suggested by Venn, *Alumni Cantabrigienses, Part II*, III, 22, that his father was William Penn Gaskell. As the only one of the name possible to have been his father, he, however, appears to have been unmarried and, like all his brothers, used the double surname Penn Gaskell.

[45] His birth certificate and their marriage certificate are at Somerset House. Ada Wallis' age at marriage was 24 years.

daughter [great-granddaughter] of William Penn shall on the death of my wife remain in my family as an heirloom and I make this suggestion without imposing any trust on them." [46] Issue: 1. WALLIS WILLIAM PENN GASKELL, some time of 204 Bishopsgate, London; killed in action in World War I, 26 May 1915, with administration granted to his father 20 December 1915.[47] 2. ADA PHYLLIS PENN GASKELL, living in 1945. Her portrait was hung in the Royal Academy Exhibition of 1911. She was named in the wills of her aunt Elizabeth Penn Gaskell and of her uncle George Edward Penn Gaskell. One HAROLD EDWARD PENN GASKELL, called nephew in the will of George Edward Penn Gaskell in 1945, at that time married to WINIFRED and father of *Gulielma Penn Gaskell,* wife of *Murdoch McLennan,* may have been a son of Thomas Penn Gaskell.

iii. JANE GASKELL, b. *ca.* 1843, at Paddington; d. testate unmarried, 19 December 1923, at No. 92 Earls Court Square, Middlesex.[48]

iv. ALEXANDER BARCLAY PENN GASKELL, b. 19 March 1845, at Paddington; d. testate 30 August 1930, at No. 31 Edith Rd., West Kensington, Middlesex; m. at St. John's Church, Notting Hill, Middlesex, 9 October 1880, MIRIAM DA COSTA, b. *ca.* 1847; d. testate at No. 31 Edith Rd., 18 February 1927, daughter of Isaac Gomes Da Costa, late of 62 Ladbroke Grove, Notting Hill, dec'd.[49] A barrister-at-law, in 1882 Alexander B. Penn Gaskell had offices at No. 1 King's Bench Walk, Temple, London. Issue: 1. LESLIE DA COSTA PENN GASKELL, Lieutenant in Norfolk Regiment and temporary Major, R.F.C., d. 4 February 1916, at Royal Flying Corps Hospital, 37 Dorset Square, Middlesex.[50] 2. WILLIAM PENN-GASKELL, b. 4 April 1883, at Fulham, Middlesex; living in 1963 at Gardiners Ground, Beaulieu, Hampshire; m. 26 June 1919, at All Saints Church, Poole, Dorset, IRIS ELEANOR BURGOYNE (NEDHAM) DEANE, widow, daughter of Capt. Charles Sewell Nedham. Commissioned in the 2nd Hampshire Regiment 3 September 1904, he became Major on the Reserve of Officers 17 December 1919. He returned to the colours, joining the Royal Tank Corps, became Major 8 August 1923, and retired 17 December 1926.[51] It was he who used the hyphen in his name, as does his son.[52]

---

[46] His will, proved by his widow and brother George 4 March 1929, is No. 513 of 1929, at Somerset House.

[47] Probate No. 2110 of 1915, Somerset House.

[48] In the 1851 Census her age was 8 years. The date of her death and residence are from the probate of her will, No. 2358 of 1925. Dated 7 February 1923, it was proved by her sister Elizabeth as executrix on 28 December 1925.

[49] Enrolled as a student of the Inner Temple 13 November 1865, Alexander Penn Gaskell was called to the Bar 6 June 1868. Joseph Foster, *Men-at-the-Bar* (London, 1885), 172. His birth certificate and their marriage certificate are at Somerset House. She was aged 33 years when married. Death dates are from the probate of their wills, also at Somerset House. His, No. 2407 of 1930, was dated 30 July 1924, when he was then retired, and was proved 4 December 1930 by his second son. Hers, No. 1448 of 1927, was proved 16 July 1927, by her husband.

[50] His death date is from the administration of his estate at Somerset House, granted 25 January 1919 to his father.

[51] His birth certificate is at Somerset House. Other information is from *The Army List.*

[52] Their son, *Leslie de Nedham Penn-Gaskell,* Lieutenant-Commander, R.N., in 1963 served on H.M.S. *Sea Eagle* at Londonderry, Northern Ireland, in the Supply Branch. He m. *Joyce Jessup* and had issue: *Nigel William Penn-Gaskell,* b. 10 May 1963, according to a birth announcement in *The London Times.*

v. GULIELMA MARIA PENN GASKELL, b. 6 February 1847, at Great Marlow, Bucks; d. after 1882; m. 10 November 1877, at Christ Church, Ealing, Middlesex, EDWARD BOWEN, b. *ca.* 1851, son of John Bowen, dec'd.; probably d. between 1922 and 1924.[53] Edward Bowen was a Licentiate of the Royal College of Physicians, Edinburgh, and a Licentiate in Midwifery and Member of the Royal College of Surgeons in 1876. As a surgeon, at the time of his marriage he was of St. Luke's Parish, Lower Norwood, Surrey. Attached to Guy's Hospital, London, he lived for some time at Rushmere, Ritherdon Rd., Upper Tooting, London, S.W. Known issue:[54] 1. JOHN ALEXANDER BARCLAY PENN BOWEN, b. 25 November 1882; living in 1945; m. FRANCES STELLA, surname unknown, living in 1945. John A. B. Penn Bowen was commissioned 23 July 1901, promoted Major, Royal Army, 1 October 1917; retired 15 March 1922, and had been in the Royal Engineers in India.[55] In 1937 he was living at 32 Elgin Crescent, London, W.11. He and his wife were named in the 1945 will of his uncle George Penn Gaskell, who also mentioned their son John Ivor Erskine Penn Bowen, living in 1966, at Colchester, Essex, and had a daughter, Mrs. Peter Gregory. 2. PETER BOWEN, mentioned in the 1945 will of George Penn Gaskell with "all his sons and daughters." 3. GULIELMA MARIA PENN BOWEN, unmarried in 1945, and named in the same will. 4. JANET PENN BOWEN, unmarried in 1945, when named in the same will. A Mrs. Hilda Penn Deane, named as a niece in the 1945 wills of Elizabeth Penn Gaskell and her brother George, together with her son of an earlier marriage, Edward Stephen Patrick Dorman, was probably a daughter of this family.

vi. ELIZABETH PENN GASKELL, b. *ca.* 1849, at Great Marlow, Bucks; d. testate unmarried 28 May 1947, at No. 14 Bedford Ave., Bexhill-on-Sea, Sussex.[56]

vii. MARY PENN GASKELL, b. in 1851, at Great Marlow, Bucks; d. unmarried 22 March 1885, at Shangarry, Hamilton Rd., Ealing, Middlesex.[57]

viii. FREDERICK OCTAVIUS PENN GASKELL, b. 2 November 1852, at Lane End, Great Marlow, Bucks; d. 25 March 1890, at Johannesburg, South Africa.[58]

ix. ALFRED PENN GASKELL, d. testate unmarried 17 November 1922, at No. 17 Melville Rd., Brighton, Sussex.[59]

x. GEORGE EDWARD PENN GASKELL, b. *ca.* 1857; d. testate 12 June 1946, at Chalfont and Gerrards Cross Hospital, Bucks; m. ELEANOR CHAR-

---

[53] Her birth certificate and their marriage certificate are at Somerset House. Edward Bowen was aged 26 years when married. Data on his background is from listings in *The Medical Directory* of 1922 and of other years; his name was gone from the listings in 1924.

[54] Possibly an incomplete record. The order of their births is not known.

[55] Information from *The Army List*.

[56] In the 1851 Census she was aged 2 years. Her death date is from the probate of her will at Somerset House. Dated 1 August 1945, it was proved 25 March 1948, by her nephews John Alexander Barclay Penn Bowen and William Penn-Gaskell.

[57] In the 1851 Census her age was given as "under 2 months." Her death date is given in the continued administration of her estate, 28 December 1925, to her brother George, at Somerset House.

[58] His birth certificate is at Somerset House; his death date in the continued administration of his estate, 28 December 1925, to his brother George, also at Somerset House.

[59] His death date is in the probate of his will (a joint probate with that of his sister Jane), No. 2358 of 1925, at Somerset House. His will, dated 5 November 1918, named his sisters Jane and Elizabeth; the latter proved the will 28 December 1925.

LOTTE (LINDSAY?), who d. testate 8 May 1937, at No. 14 Mapesbury Rd., Cricklewood, Middlesex.[60] The only one of his father's ten children mentioned by Howard M. Jenkins in 1899, George Penn Gaskell matriculated at Lincoln College, Oxford, 18 October 1877, aged 20; Scholar, 1877-1881; B.A. 1881.[61] He was a barrister-at-law of Lincoln's Inn in 1884, but practised as a solicitor. In 1898, he was living at No. 12 Nicoll Rd., Willesden, S.W., London. He retired to The Orchards at Chalfont St. Peter, Bucks, a house close to several former homes of his ancestors, and was living there when he wrote his will. No surviving issue.

6. ELIZABETH PENN-GASKELL, born 19 December 1825, eldest child of Peter Penn-Gaskell, Jr. and his wife Louisa Adelaide Heath, married 26 July 1855, SAMUEL RUFF SKILLERN, born 16 March 1834, at Huntsville, Alabama. According to the present Dr. Penn-Gaskell Skillern, Samuel R. Skillern was "a nephew of the famous international beauty and wit, Madame Claude Le Verte, of Mobile."

Samuel Skillern had graduated from the Medical School of the University of Pennsylvania, receiving his M.D. in 1854,[62] the year before his marriage. Apparently the young couple lived in the South for a time: they were in Columbia, South Carolina, when their first child was born. During the Civil War, however, he served as surgeon with the rank of major and was in charge of Satterlee General Hospital, near what is now Forty-fourth and Baltimore Avenue.[63] In 1865, the year the war ended, they were living at Thirty-fifth and Hamilton Avenue, according to the City Directory.

Elizabeth Penn-Gaskell Skillern died testate the following year, however, at Pulaski, Tennessee, on 23 October 1866. Exactly five months before she had drawn her will in Philadelphia. In it she devised to her own issue, in equal shares, the income of her share of £10,000 her father Peter Penn-Gaskell, Jr. had directed in his will was to be raised out of the Shanagarry estate in Ireland for the use and benefit of his married daughters.[64] She was buried 3 November 1866, in her father's lot at Laurel Hill Cemetery.

Her husband continued to practice in Philadelphia; in 1880 he was living at 3416 Baring Street, and later at 3509 Baring Street. He married secondly, Sarah Ross, daughter of William H. Ross, former governor

---

60 Their death dates are from the probates of their wills in Somerset House. His, dated 25 October 1945, and proved 10 October 1946, named many members of his family and mentioned "my late wife's brother Bertram Alexander Lindsay," suggesting her maiden name. It was witnessed by his farm manager and farm secretary. His wife's will, dated 27 March 1937, was proved 7 October 1937.

61 Joseph Foster, *Alumni Oxonienses*, Later Series, II, 513.

62 *General Alumni Catalogue of the University of Pennsylvania* (1922), 528.

63 Data from his obituary in the Philadelphia *Public Ledger*, Friday, 18 February 1921, page 5, column 2.

64 Will of Elizabeth Penn-Gaskell Skillern recorded in Philadelphia Will Book 59, 402, #100: 1866.

of Delaware. She died about 1911, leaving issue, Dr. Samuel R. Skillern, Jr., Dr. Ross H. Skillern, and Claude L. V. Skillern. Dr. Samuel Skillern, Sr., died at the home of his son, Ross, in Ardmore, Pa., 17 February 1921, aged eighty-seven.[65]

Issue of 6. Elizabeth Penn-Gaskell
and her husband Samuel Ruff Skillern:[66]

9.　i. PETER PENN-GASKELL SKILLERN, b. 28 April 1856, at Columbia, S. C.; d. 25 July 1931, of whom further.

　ii. IRVING H. SKILLERN, b. 24 April 1858; d. 1 October 1858, *ae.* 5 mos. 6 days.

　iii. LOUISE FITZGERALD SKILLERN, b. 17 May 1859; bur. at Laurel Hill in the Penn-Gaskell lot, 11 March 1862.

7. PETER PENN-GASKELL, 3rd, born 24 October 1843, youngest child of Peter Penn-Gaskell, Jr. and his wife Louisa Adelaide Heath, was their only son to have issue and carry on the Penn-Gaskell name in the American branch of the family.

Educated at Heidelberg University, he returned to America at the outbreak of the Civil War, and at the age of nineteen was commissioned second lieutenant in the First Regiment New Jersey Cavalry on 7 April 1862. Promoted to first lieutenant the following 7 November, he was made captain 23 October 1863, but resigned 3 February 1864, to become major in the Second Louisiana Cavalry in which he served until 7 September 1864. His elder brother William dying in 1865, on the death of his father Peter Penn-Gaskell, Jr. in 1866, Peter, 3rd, succeeded to the Shanagarry estates in Ireland. He was admitted by "Dispensation" to Lodge No. 51, Free and Accepted Masons of Pennsylvania, on 24 May 1866, but resigned 23 April 1868,[67] and removed to England.

He married in England on 6 July 1869, MARY KATHLEEN STUBBS, daughter of Charles Edward Stubbs of Sussex Square, Hyde Park, London. They visited Philadelphia, probably in 1876, the Centennial Year, and, when in 1877 an engraving of his ancestor, William Penn, the Founder, was presented to Peter by the Historical Society of Pennsylvania, he became a subscriber to the Society's Publication Fund.[68] He is reported to have died in 1905; when his widow, Mary Kathleen Gaskell, died 13 November 1915, she was living at 50 Castle Hill Avenue, Folke-

---

[65] From Dr. Skillern's obituary, cited above.

[66] The names and dates of these children are from the Penn-Gaskell-Skillern Bible record cited in Note 30. Of them, Louise is the only one who appears to have been buried at Laurel Hill.

[67] In Jordan, 16, cited in Note 9, there is a somewhat fuller account of Peter Penn-Gaskell, 3rd, than that given in Jenkins, 249. *Memoirs of Lodge No. 51, F. & A. M. of Pennsylvania* (Philadelphia, 1941), 443, gives his Masonic membership.

[68] *PMHB*, I (1877), frontispiece, 509, and Archives of The Historical Society of Pennsylvania. Watson, *Annals*, III, 98.

stone, Kent. Her will was proved at Dublin by her son, Captain William Penn-Gaskell, and sealed at London 29 March 1916.[69]

Issue of 7. Peter Penn-Gaskell, 3rd, and his wife Mary Kathleen Stubbs:

    i. WILLIAM PENN-GASKELL of Shanagarry, County Cork, d. testate 12 October 1916, in action in France. A captain in H.M. 18th Service Battalion, Manchester Regiment, probate of his will was granted at Cork to William Bennett Barrington, solicitor, and Henry Foster Longfield, land agent, and sealed at London 30 March 1917.

    ii. PERCY CHARLES PENN-GASKELL, of Redbrook House, Hythe, Kent, d. testate 26 February 1937, at Bevan House, Folkestone, Kent. When he wrote his will he was of Elinligh Court, Stelling, Kent, and was retired as a major in H.M. Army. Probate was granted at London on 7 May 1937, to Nina Irving Baber, wife of Philip Baber, and to Ernest Harold Wainwright, solicitor. Mrs. Baber, then of 9 Bush Lane, London, and Wainwright, the solicitor, he named trustees for his daughter Patricia Penn-Gaskell until she reached the age of 30 or was married. Having succeeded to the Irish estates, he left them in trust for his daughter. He named his sister Winifred Penn-Gaskell, and mentioned his and her "combined collections of pewter." He also established a trust for his godson Peter Baber, and desired that when he became aged 25, or upon the testator's death, he assume the surname of Penn-Gaskell, but without any legal obligation to do so. The will was witnessed by M. A. Semple, clerk to Messrs Kingsfords, Solicitors, Canterbury. Major Percy Penn-Gaskell m. after 1911, an actress, but she was not named or mentioned in his will. Issue: 1. PATRICIA PENN-GASKELL, b. after 1911; in 1951, as Mrs. Patricia Fox, she lived at 38 Grenville Place, Brighton, Sussex.

    iii. WINIFRED ETHEL PENN-GASKELL, of Scobitor, Widecome-in-the-Moor, Devon, when she wrote her will 22 July 1937, was unmarried. She appointed the National Provincial Bank, Ltd., 66 Trafalgar Square, London, W.C. 2, and Mrs. Ivy Gatliff of Colley House, Tedbury St. Mary, Exeter, as executors. To Mrs. Gatliff she left the portrait of her great-grandfather "Tat Tito;" to the Torquay Corporation her pewter collection and portrait of the Earl of Peterborough by Michael Dahl. To her niece, Patricia Penn-Gaskell, daughter of her late brother, Major Percy Charles Penn-Gaskell, she left personal effects, and legacies to friends. The will was witnessed by clerks at Messrs Kitsons, Solicitors, Torquay.[70]

8. PETER PENN-GASKELL HALL, born 16 March 1830, second and younger son of Christiana Gulielma Penn-Gaskell and her husband William S. Hall, was tutored abroad, attended Princeton College, studied law and was admitted to the bar of Philadelphia. Commissioned second lieutenant 31 May 1861, in the Twenty-sixth Pennsylvania Volunteers, he was advanced to first lieutenant 25 August following, and four months

---

[69] From the Probate Index of the Prerogative Court of Canterbury, Somerset House, comes all information on her will and those of her children, and is supplied by Mr Dallett.

[70] Data on Mrs. Patricia Fox, who was or is an actress also, and on the will of her aunt Winifred Penn Gaskell, is from a letter to Mr. Dallett by Laurence Easterbrook of Kitsons, Easterbrook & Co., Torquay, Devon, dated 28 September 1966.

later on 24 December 1861, married ANNIE M. MIXSELL, born about 1841, daughter of Philip Mixsell of Easton, and his wife Sarah Deihle.[71]

He participated in the Peninsula Campaign of 1862, and on 6 November 1863, was commissioned major and appointed paymaster of Volunteers, which office he held until 15 November 1865. At the end of the war he entered the regular army and was appointed paymaster with the same rank 17 January 1867. He served until 2 July 1891, when he retired after more than twenty years' service. He was brevetted lieutenant-colonel for meritorious service.

His first wife Annie died at Vicksburg, Mississippi, 14 February 1869, and was buried at Lower Merion Baptist churchyard.

Issue of 8. Peter Penn-Gaskell Hall by his 1st wife Annie M. Mixsell:

    i. CHRISTIANA GULIELMA PENN-GASKELL HALL, b. at Ashwood, 19 April 1863; d. testate unmarried at Fox Street and Abbottsford Ave., Philadelphia, 25 June 1938; bur. at L. Merion Baptist churchyard. In her will, dated 30 June 1905, five months after the death of her father, and proved 25 June 1938, by her half-brother, Peter Penn-Gaskell Hall, Jr., she left him all family portraits — presumably those exhibited at the Academy of Fine Arts' Historical Portrait Exhibition in 1887-1888 — for his life. He was to decide which member of the family was best fitted to have them after his decease, and in no case were they to be divided, but to descend as a whole. In default of his decision, they were to go to the city of Philadelphia as a permanent part of the collection then in Memorial Hall, or to such other public art gallery as might be established in Fairmount Park. The whole were to be designated as presented by herself "in memory of the Penn-Gaskell family, descended from William Penn in the ninth generation." [72]

    ii. ELIZA HALL, b. at Baltimore, Md., 1 February 1865; d. *ca.* 1917, at 906 Spruce St., Philadelphia; m. 1 July 1892, HENRY J. HANCOCK, d. *ca.* 1906, son of George W. Hancock and his wife Elizabeth James A member of the Philadelphia Bar, the Hancocks lived at the Lincoln Apartments, 1222 Locust Street, with his office first at 403 Girard Building, and later in the Real Estate Trust Building. After her husband's death, Eliza made her home with her half-brother Peter Penn-Gaskell Hall, Jr. until he moved elsewhere, at which time the property on Spruce Street appears to have been turned over to her. From about 1915 until her death she was the only one listed at that address in the City Directories. Issue: 1. Jean Barclay Penn-Gaskell Hancock, d. unmarried; bur. in St. David's churchyard, Radnor, Pa.

    iii. EDWARD SWARBRIC HALL, b. at Ashwood, 1867; d. at Vicksburg, Miss., January, 1869; bur. at L. Merion Baptist churchyard.[73]

---

71 Jordan, 20, which amplifies the account in Jenkins.

72 Will of Christiana Penn-Gaskell Hall recorded in Philadelphia Will Book PS-128, 346, #2651: 1938. In the Penn-Gaskell-Hall Correspondence, cited in Note 26, there are numerous letters written in 1899, by "Gulie," as she signed herself, to her father describing the European tour she and her sisters were making. In the light of the cost of such a tour today, the amount of money her father sent for their expenses is of some interest.

73 His name is so spelled on the stone in the churchyard.

iv. ANNIE M. HALL, b. at Vicksburg, Miss., January, 1869; d. at Holly Springs, Miss., May, 1869, bur. at L. Merion Baptist churchyard.

In November 1871, some two and a half years after the death of his first wife Annie, 8. PETER PENN-GASKELL HALL married AMELIA MIXSELL, at San Antonio, Texas. She was apparently deceased by 1899, when the daughters were touring Europe. Her husband took up residence at 906 Spruce Street after his retirement from the Army, and lived there until his death, occupying his time with his memberships in the Historical Society, Society of Colonial Wars, the Colonial Society, of which he was president, the Philadelphia Club, and other organizations.[74] He died 1 February 1905, and was buried at Lower Merion Baptist churchyard.

Issue of 8. Peter Penn-Gaskell Hall by his 2nd wife Amelia Mixsell:

v. WILLIAM PENN-GASKELL HALL, b. at San Antonio, Texas, 16 January 1873; d. 27 July 1927, bur. at L. Merion Baptist churchyard; m. at St. Luke's P. E. Church, Philadelphia, 8 December 1904, CAROLINE HARE DAVIS, b. 20 July 1876; d. 2 September 1942, daughter of Sussex Delaware Davis, Esq. and his wife Mary Fleming Hare, bur. at L. Merion Baptist churchyard. Educated at private schools, he was listed as a civil engineer before his marriage while he was living at 906 Spruce Street with his brother Peter. After his marriage he was listed at 1118 Spruce Street until 1910, and was associated with his brothers in the Hall Gas Engine Company which they established in 1905. A member of the Racquet Club, Colonial Society, Society of Colonial Wars, etc., he probably died at his place in Chester County, Leventhorpe. Issue:[75] 1. MARY FLEMING HARE HALL, b. at 1118 Spruce Street, 31 December 1905; m. and has issue. 2. WILLIAM LEVENTHORPE PENN-GASKELL HALL, b. at Atlantic City, N. J., 9 October 1908; m. and has issue.

vi. PETER PENN-GASKELL HALL, JR., b. at New York City, 14 March 1875; d. testate unmarried at Hahnemann Hospital, Philadelphia, 26 April 1962, bur. at L. Merion Baptist churchyard, where his name is inscribed on the stone of his grandmother. An engineer by profession, with his brothers he established the Hall Gas Engine Works in 1905, and was president of the company for some years. From about 1915 through 1925 he was listed at 2833 Pratt Bldg., in which latter year he was listed as president of the Hall Planetary Thread Milling Machine Co., and was living with his sister at Fox and Abbottsford Avenue. At his death he was living at the Parkway House, 22nd and the Parkway, and had a summer place at Kentmore Park, Kennedyville, Md. He left his estate to his nephew, William Penn-Gaskell Hall, Jr., and named the Second National Bank of Philadelphia executor.[76]

vii. AMELIA HALL, b. at New York City, 9 February 1877; dec'd; m. by Arch-

---

[74] Jordan, 20.

[75] *Ibid.*, 22.

[76] Peter Penn-Gaskell Hall's will is #1570: 1962, examined on microfilm, City Hall.

bishop Ryan at the Cathedral of SS. Peter and Paul, Philadelphia, 10 December 1902, RICHARD PHILIP McGRANN of Grandview, Lancaster County; dec'd. Issue: BERNARD PENN-GASKELL McGRANN, b. at Grandview 20 November 1903; m. SARAH H. (KEOWN) STEVENSON.[77]

viii. PHILIP PENN-GASKELL HALL, b. at Ashwood, 10 September 1878; dec'd; m. at Wilmington, Del., 21 December 1901, MARY ELOISE FULTON; dec'd. Educated at the Forsythe School, Philadelphia, as a machinist he was associated with his brothers in the Hall Gas Engine Works and was secretary of the company for a number of years. Between 1905 and 1930 he was listed at various addresses in the city, but apparently lived, or had his permanent residence, in New London Township, Chester County. Known issue: 1. MARY ELOISE HALL, b. at 906 Spruce Street, 4 October 1902. 2. AMELIA HALL, b. at 906 Spruce Street, 27 November 1905.[78]

9. PETER PENN-GASKELL SKILLERN, born 28 April 1856, at Columbia, South Carolina, eldest and only surviving son of Elizabeth Penn-Gaskell and her husband, Samuel Ruff Skillern, was educated at Rugby Academy, Philadelphia, Phillips Andover Academy, and Pennsylvania Military Academy. He was graduated from the Medical School of the University of Pennsylvania in 1877, and was in practice in 1890, at 427 South Broad Street. Five years later he was located at 241 South Thirteenth Street, where he lived and practiced until his death. By 1890 he had dropped the Christian name of Peter and thenceforth was known as Dr. Penn-Gaskell Skillern.

At the church of St. James the Less in Philadelphia, he married first, on 7 October 1878, ANNA DORSEY, born 17 October 1861, at 2121 Delancey Place, daughter of Robert Ralston Dorsey, M.D., of Philadelphia. She died 8 October 1900, at 241 South Thirteenth Street, and was buried in the churchyard of St. James the Less. Penn-Gaskell Skillern married secondly, after 1900, THEODOSIA HARTMAN, born 19 February 1860, and died 23 June 1935, without issue. Her husband had predeceased her, dying testate 25 July 1931.[79] Both are buried at St. James the Less.

Issue of 9. Penn-Gaskell Skillern and his 1st wife Anna Dorsey:

i. VIOLET PENN-GASKELL SKILLERN, b. 13 November 1879, in Philadelphia; d. 20 May 1948, bur. at St. James the Less. The Bible from which many of the dates in this present record have been taken, was in her possession when photostats were made for the Genealogical Society of Pennsylvania.

ii. PETER PENN-GASKELL SKILLERN, JR., b. at Philadelphia 26 March 1882;

---

[77] Jordan, 21; *General Alumni Catalogue*, cited in Note 62.

[78] Jordan, 21.

[79] The will of Dr. Peter Penn-Gaskell Skillern is recorded in Philadelphia Will Book 564, 42, #2720: 1931. Dated at Sharon Hill, Pa., 9 October 1921, it was proved 5 August 1931, by his widow to whom he left his estate. Data on him and his family is largely from information supplied Mr. Dallett in 1961 by his son, Dr. Penn G. Skillern of South Bend, Indiana.

living in 1961 at South Bend, Indiana; m. at Kjoge, Denmark, 1 October 1918, LISA MARGRETA VALENTINER, daughter of Julius Valentiner of Kjoge; living in 1961. Like his father, he dropped the Christian name of Peter and went by the hyphenated Penn-Gaskell. He was educated at William Penn Charter School, Philadelphia, and was graduated from the Medical School of the University of Pennsylvania, M.D., in 1903. He was a member of Phi Delta Theta, Phi Alpha Sigma, the class bowling team, and in 1903 received the Medical Society prize in bandaging. A surgeon, he was later associate professor of surgery in the Graduate School. Twice commended for devotion to service in World War I, he was a lieutenant in the Marine Corps, U.S.N.R.F. in the transport service. A member of the University and Aesculapian Clubs, in 1922 he was at 1523 Locust Street, but had removed to South Bend, Indiana by 1924.

Issue: 1. PENN-GASKELL SKILLERN, M.D., b. 26 July 1920, in Philadelphia; living in East Cleveland, Ohio, in 1961; m. at Cleveland 4 April 1959, NORA BETTY MORRIS, b. in Mattingley, Hampshire, England, 15 December 1930, daughter of Frederick George Morris of Crowthorne. They have no issue. 2. ANNA LISA SKILLERN, b. in Philadelphia 16 September 1922; m. at New Orleans, La., CARL TASSO SMITH, b. at Angola, Ind., 18 April 1919. He is a graduate of Louisiana State University, and has three daughters and two sons, all b. at New Orleans.[80] 3. SCOTT DORSEY SKILLERN, M.D., b. at South Bend, 17 May 1924; m. at Gary, Indiana, 9 March 1957, JOYCE McCULLOUGH, b. at Gary, 22 May 1931, daughter of William Elmer McCullough. Scott Dorsey Skillern graduated from the University of Pennsylvania in 1951, and in 1961 was of South Bend, Indiana.[81]

---

[80] The children are: 1. *Lisa Suzanne Smith*, b. 13 September 1948. 2. *Richard Mark Smith*, b. 31 October 1950. 3. *Christine Smith*, b. 10 December 1952. 4. *Carl Tasso Smith, Jr.*, b. 15 February 1955. 5. *Nancy Smith*, b. 31 December 1956.

[81] In 1961, they had one daughter: *Dorsey Skillern*, b. 1 June 1958, at South Bend.

601

Penn-Gaskell Halls
of the Twentieth Century

HANNAH BENNER ROACH, F.G.S.P., F.A.S.G.

D ATA pertaining to the Penn-Gaskell Hall descendants of William
Penn — issue of 8. Peter Penn-Gaskell Hall by his second wife,
Amelia Mixsell — was presented in the last issue (No. 2, 117-118) of
this *Magazine* as part of "The Penn-Gaskell Family: Addenda to the
Family of Penn." * That data was limited to the information available
in published works and public records. Through the interest expressed
by various members of this branch of the family (the only one still closely
associated with the Philadelphia area) and their generous cooperation,
it is now possible to expand and amend that record, as well as previous
published accounts, and to include all the twentieth-century members
omitted heretofore.

Of particular interest are the birth and death records entered in the
Bible of Peter Gaskell and his wife Elizabeth Edwards, here published
for the first time:[1]

Births

Peter Gaskell born May 19, 1764 ⎱ and in May 1826 will be 62 yrs of age
⎰ Married Anno Domini 1793 [2]
Eliza Gaskell born Jany 31, 1773 ⎰ and E.G. will be then about 8 yrs & 4 months less
Thomas Penn Gaskell died 19th day of November 1823 about 2½ years before I shall be
62 yrs of age [3]

[Children of Peter Gaskell and Elizabeth Edwards:]

William Penn Gaskell born Sunday 29th June 1794

---

[1] The Bible descended to 8. Peter Penn-Gaskell Hall and is now held by his grandson, William Penn-
Gaskell Hall, Jr., of Berwyn, with whose kind permission the record is now published. The title page in part
reads: "The Holy Bible Containing the Old and New Testament, together with the Apocrypha. . . . Printed
and Published by Mathew Carey, No. 122 Market Street, Philadelphia, 1808." The entries occur between the
end of the Old Testament and the beginning of the Apocrypha. There are no marriage entries.

[2] Their marriage certificate, also in the possession of Mr. Hall, reads: "This is to Certify all whom it may
concern That Peter Gaskell and Elizabeth Edwards were joined together in Holy Matrimony this 5th day of
November in the Year of our Lord 1793, by me Slator Clay, Rector of the United Churches of St. Davids
Radner [sic] &c." The Rev. Clay's charge included also St. James' Episcopal Church, Perkiomen, where the
marriage is entered incorrectly as taking place on 5 December, and St. Peter's Episcopal Church, Great Valley,
E. Whiteland Twp., Chester Co.

[3] From the wording of the above entries, it would seem that Peter Gaskell may have entered them in the
Bible early in 1826, perhaps transferring them from some older record.

*Pages 579-601, this volume.

Thomas Penn Gaskell born Wednesday January 6th 1796
Eliza Gaskell born Wednesday February 28th 1798
Peter Gaskell Junr born Thursday April 3d 1800
Alexander Forbes Gaskell born Monday Septembr 20th 1802
Christiana Gaskell born Monday May 27th 1805
Jane Gaskell born Tuesday December 13 1808
Isaac Gaskell born Wednesday Jany 9th 1811

[Children of Christiana Gaskell and her husband William S. Hall:]

William Penn Gaskell Hall born November 26th 1827
Peter Penn Gaskell Hall born Tuesday March 16th 1830

[Children of Peter Penn Gaskell Hall by his 1st wife Annie M. Mixsell:]

Christiana Gulielma Hall born Sunday April 19th 1863 [entry in a new hand.] *at Ashwood, Penna* [added in a different hand]
Eliza Penn Gaskell Hall born February 1st 1865 *Baltimore* [added as above]
Edward Swabric Hall born Wednesday January 9th 1867 [entry in a new hand.] *at Ashwood, Penna* [added in another hand]
Annie Maude Mixsell Hall born *Vicksburg, Miss.* 1869 [added as above]

[Children of Peter Penn Gaskell Hall by his 2nd wife Amelia Mixsell:]

Wm Penn Gaskell Hall born Jany 15th 1873 *at San Antonio, Texas* [added in a new hand]
Peter Penn Gaskell Hall born March 14th 1875
Amelia Penn Gaskell Hall born Jany 8th 1877
Philip Penn Gaskell Hall born Sept. 24th 1878

[Child of Eliza Hall and Henry J. Hancock:]

Jean Barclay Penn Gaskell Hancock born March 24th 1893 at 2023 Delancey St. Phila. [entered in a new hand]

Deaths [4]

William Penn Gaskell departed this Life Sunday 12th October 1817 in the 24th Year of His Age
Alexander Forbes Penn-Gaskell departed this life on tuesday the 8th of September 1829 in the 27th year of his age
Christiana Gulielma Hall departed this life on monday the 29th day of March 1830 in the 24th year of her age
Peter Penn-Gaskell departed this life on Saturday at four o'clock the 16th day of July 1831 aged 67 years and two months
Jane Penn-Gaskell departed this life Saturday 7th July 1832 in the 24th year of her age
Elizabeth Penn Gaskell departed this life Saturday the 19th day of July 1834 in the 62 year of her age
Docr Isaac Penn-Gaskell departed this life Monday the 24th day of October A.D. 1842 in the 31st year of his age

Peter Penn-Gaskell Hall (Colonel U.S.A.) died Wednesday Feb. 1st 1905 at 4:30 A.M. in the 75th year of his age

---

4 The death records are in several different handwritings.

William Penn Gaskell Hall departed this life Friday the 2nd day of May 1862 in the 35th year of his age

Eliza Penn Gaskell departed this life thursday November 1865 [sic] in the 67th year of her age

Annie M. Hall departed this life Feby 14th 1868 [sic] aged 28

Edward Swabric Hall departed this life 1869

Annie M. M. Hall departed this life 1869 [this and the previous two entries in the same hand]

Annie M. Hall died in 1869 Feb. 14th at Vicksburg, Miss. [this entry in a different hand]

[*Between the Apocrypha and the New Testament:*]

Elizabeth Edwards departed this life Tuesday October 26th 1819 [5]

Supplementing these records, it may now be added that a year and a half after the death in 1869 of his first wife, Annie Maude Mixsell, 8. PETER PENN-GASKELL HALL (born 16 March 1830, of the above record) married his second wife, her sister AMELIA MIXSELL, born 13 November 1847, daughter of Philip Mixsell of Easton.[6] The ceremony was performed in San Antonio, Texas, on 13 September 1871, by the rector of St. Mark's Protestant Episcopal Church, the Reverend W. R. Richardson.[7] She died in East Bradford Township, Chester County, on 27 October 1925, aged seventy-eight, and was buried the following 30 October in the Lower Merion Baptist Churchyard. She had survived her husband twenty years.

Their eldest child, (v.) WILLIAM PENN-GASKELL HALL, was born at San Antonio, Texas, on 15 (not 16) January 1873, according to the Bible record, and died at his home in Willistown Township, Chester County, 27 July 1927.[8] He had married at St. Luke's Protestant Episcopal Church, Philadelphia, on 8 October 1904 (not 8 December as previously reported), CAROLINE HARE DAVIS. Born at Cape May, New Jersey, 20 July 1876, daughter of Sussex Delaware Davis, she died at Pennsylvania Hospital, Philadelphia, 2 September 1942.[9] Both she and her husband are buried at Lower Merion Baptist Churchyard.

[5] Was she the mother of Peter Gaskell's wife?

[6] Amelia Mixsell's birth date is noted on a manuscript pedigree chart of the descendants of Giles Penn through his son, Admiral Sir William Penn, in the Albert Cooke Myers Collection, Chester County Historical Society, West Chester, Pa.

[7] The marriage is recorded in Bexar Co., Texas, Marriages, Vol. E, 388, #3950-1/2, San Antonio, Texas.

[8] His death certificate in error states he was born 16 Jan. 1874, and died 29 July 1927, aged 53-6-13. The account in the West Chester *Daily Local News* of his death is also in error, giving his age as 56. The numbers assigned the descendants of 8. Peter Penn-Gaskell Hall who were included in the last issue of this *Magazine* have been maintained in the present account of those descendants as reference aids to interested readers, but are included in parentheses in this present record.

[9] For an account of her marriage, see the Philadelphia *Public Ledger*, Sunday, 9 October 1904; for her obituary, see *The Philadelphia Inquirer*, Friday, 4 September 1942.

Their eldest child, (1.) MARY FLEEMING PENN-GASKELL HALL, was born at 1118 Spruce Street, Philadelphia, on 30 (not 31) December 1905.[10] She was married in the garden of Leventhorpe, her father's place in Willistown Township, by the rector of St. Luke's Episcopal Church, Philadelphia, on 8 June 1927, to COURTLAND YARDLEY WHITE, III. He was born at Philadelphia on 2 July 1902, son of Dr. Courtland Y. White, Jr., M.D., and his wife Emily Heroy Sherwood. The marriage was dissolved in 1946, and Mr. White died at Philadelphia on 25 January 1950.[11] Mrs. White, a member of the Colonial Dames of America, Chapter II, Philadelphia, resides in Haverford.

*Issue of (1.) Mary Fleeming Penn-Gaskell Hall
and her husband Courtland Yardley White, III:*

i. COURTLAND YARDLEY WHITE, IV, b. at Philadelphia 15 April 1928. A graduate of Episcopal Academy, 1947, during the Korean War he served in the U. S. Army as private, 1st Class. He graduated from Haverford College in 1956, and m. at the Episcopal Cathedral Church of St. Mark, Minneapolis, Minn., on 7 September 1957, SUSAN SWAIN OPSTAD, b. in Minneapolis 24 February 1936, daughter of Raymond Eugene Opstad and his wife Helen Evelyn Swain of Minneapolis. A descendant of John Howland of the Mayflower Compact, she was graduated from Bryn Mawr College, 1958, *cum laude,* and received her M.A. in Political Science from the University of Minnesota. Mr. White is doing graduate work at that university where he teaches the Humanities. His wife, while doing further graduate work there, is a teaching associate in the Department of Political Science. Issue: 1. COURTLAND Y. WHITE, V, b. at Minneapolis, 2 March 1964.[12]

ii. GULIELMA PENN-GASKELL WHITE, b. at Philadelphia 16 April 1930; m. at Philadelphia by Magistrate Nathan N. Beifel on 4 May 1956, DR. MAX KROOK, b. at Standarton, South Africa. Gulielma graduated from Radcliffe College, 1952, and received her M.A. in Elementary Education from Harvard University, 1964. She has taught remedial reading in the Boston Institute of Reading, and currently is teaching and tutoring as a volunteer in Roxbury and in the Arlington Public School. Her husband received his doctorate from Cambridge University, England, and is now Professor of Astrophysics and Applied Mathematics at Harvard. They reside in Arlington, Massachusetts. No issue.

The second child of (v.) William Penn-Gaskell Hall, Sr., and his wife Caroline Hare Davis, is (2.) WILLIAM LEVENTHORPE PENN-GASKELL HALL, JR., born in Atlantic City, New Jersey, 9 October 1908.

[10] This corrects her birth date and full name, as confirmed by her birth certificate, on record at the Bureau of Vital Statistics, City Hall Annex, Philadelphia.

[11] His death notice is in *The Philadelphia Inquirer,* 26 January 1950. He married 2nd, Helen Schloss, and had issue by her twin children: Peter Sherwood White and Kate Elizabeth White.

[12] As per his birth certificate on file in the Division of Public Health, Section of Vital Statistics, Minneapolis.

He graduated from St. Paul's School, Concord, New Hampshire, in 1927, and received a B.S. in Engineering from Massachusetts Institute of Technology, 1931/32. Until the advent of World War II, he participated in national and international figure-skating competitions. Stationed at Ft. Monroe, Virginia, in 1943, when he held the rank of first lieutenant, he was commanding officer of the 3rd Training Battery, Coast Artillery School Detachment, was a member of the school's staff and faculty, and on the Coast Artillery Board. His active service during the war extended from 1942 to 1946; in 1960 he graduated from the U.S. Army Command and General Staff School, Ft. Leavenworth, Kansas, and was retired as lieutenant colonel, U.S. Army Reserves, after twenty-seven years of service. He has been associated with E. I. du Pont de Nemours & Company, Wilmington, Delaware, since 1935, where he is an engineer in the Engineering Research Division.

He married first, at Christ Church, Philadelphia, 19 September 1936, ANNAH COLKET McKAIG, born at Radnor, Pennsylvania, 26 March 1917, daughter of Edward S. McKaig and his wife Annah Colket French. The marriage was dissolved in 1958.[13]

Issue of (2.) William Leventhorpe Penn-Gaskell Hall
by his 1st wife Annah Colket McKaig:

i. JOANNAH COLKET HALL, b. at Bryn Mawr, Pa., 23 September 1941; bapt. at St. Martin's P. E. Church, Radnor. She attended the Shipley School and graduated from the Stoneleigh Prospect Hill School and from Bennett College, making her debut in 1959 at a dance at the Radnor Hunt Club. She m. at Old St. David's P. E. Church (Radnor), 16 February 1963, CHARLES MARSHALL GLASS, son of Mr. and Mrs. Sydney W. Glass of Grange Farm, West Chester, Pa.[14] They were divorced without issue in 1965.

On 2 May 1959, (2.) William Penn-Gaskell Hall married secondly, at the Neshaminy-Warwick Presbyterian Church, Hartsville, Bucks County, OLIVE ELIZABETH THOMAS, born in Warren, Pennsylvania, daughter of Mr. and Mrs. Clair Stanley Thomas of Warren. A graduate nurse anesthetist of Jefferson Medical College, Philadelphia, during World War II she was a member of the group at that institution who pioneered applications of spinal anesthesia. Mr. and Mrs. Hall reside in Willistown Township, Chester County.[15]

---

[13] Annah Colket Hall married 2nd, at Towson, Md., 7 July 1959, Dr. John D. Gadd, from whom she was divorced without further issue.

[14] For an account of their marriage, see the Philadelphia *Evening Bulletin*, 17 February 1963. The engagement was announced in the West Chester *Daily Local News* 15 December 1962.

[15] Originally called Leventhorpe, for a time their residence was known as Happy Valley Farm, then Rebel Fox Farm, and is now known as Little Ashwood.

*Issue of (2.) William Leventhorpe Penn-Gaskell Hall
by his 2nd wife Olive Elizabeth Thomas:*

ii. CHRISTIANA ELIZABETH PENN-GASKELL HALL, b. at Bryn Mawr, Pa., 2 November 1960.

iii. PETER THOMAS PENN-GASKELL HALL, b. at Bryn Mawr, Pa., 9 January 1965.

The second son of 8. Peter Penn-Gaskell Hall by his second wife Amelia Mixsell was (vi.) PETER PENN-GASKELL HALL, JR. Born in New York City 14 March 1875, he died unmarried without issue in Philadelphia 26 April 1962, as reported in the last issue of this *Magazine* (p. 117). A member of the Franklin Institute, he was awarded their Edward Longstreth Medal in 1936 for "the encouragement of invention." He also was a member of the American Society of Mechanical Engineers, and of the American Ordinance Association. He had retired from business in 1956.[16]

His sister, (vii.) AMELIA PENN-GASKELL HALL, third child of 8. Peter Penn-Gaskell and his second wife Amelia Mixsell, was also born in New York City on 8 January 1877. She married in Philadelphia at the Cathedral of SS Peter and Paul, on 10 December 1902, RICHARD PHILIP MACGRANN, heretofore incorrectly given as *McGrann*. He was born at Grandview, Manheim Township, Lancaster County, 13 October 1875, son of Bernard J. and Mary Francis MacGrann. He attended St. Mary's Academy in Lancaster, Mercersburg Academy, and was graduated from Princeton in 1896. A horse show exhibitor for a number of years, at the time of his death on 24 July 1935, he was of Killishandra Farms, East Lampeter Township, Lancaster County. His widow survived him twelve years and was buried 30 April 1947, in the cemetery of the Church of the Good Samaritan, Paoli, where he is also interred.[17]

*Issue of (vii.) Amelia Hall and her
husband Richard Philip MacGrann:*

i. BERNARD PENN-GASKELL MacGRANN, b. at Grandview 20 November 1903, graduated from Princeton, 1924, and from the University of Pennsylvania Law School, 1928; m. at Holy Trinity P. E. Church, Philadelphia, 24 March 1960, MRS. SARAH H. (KEOWN) STEVENSON, b. 7 December 1896, daughter of William John Keown and his wife Martha Foster Kelder. Mr. MacGrann has been associated with the Franklin Institute since 1958, and is on the staff of the Director of Membership's Committee. No issue.

---

[16] For his obituary see *The Philadelphia Inquirer*, 27 April 1962.

[17] Data on Mr. MacGrann is from his obituary in the *Coatesville Record*, 25 July 1935, examined at the Chester County Historical Society. In it, his name is given as *McGrann*. The church records only give the date of burial of Mrs. MacGrann. She had died 26 April.

The youngest child and third son of 8. Peter Penn-Gaskell Hall and his second wife Amelia Mixsell, was (viii.) PHILIP PENN-GASKELL HALL, born 24 September 1878, at Ashwood, the family's residence in Radnor Township. He married in Wilmington, Delaware, on 21 December 1901, MIRIAM ELOISE FULTON.[18] Born at 2108 Fitzwater Street, Philadelphia, she was the daughter of John Clifton Fulton and his wife Mary Elizabeth Allison. At the time of her death 21 June 1954, in Crozer Hospital, Upland, the Hall's Philadelphia residence was 4921 Wissahickon Avenue.[19] Philip Hall, who survived his wife, died at 4039 Chestnut Street, Philadelphia, 15 November 1961. Both are buried at Mt. Moriah Cemetery.

They had three children, the eldest of whom is (1.) MIRIAM ELOISE PENN-GASKELL HALL, born at the home of her Fulton grandparents, 4 October 1902.[20] She married at Hagerstown, Maryland, 31 December 1925, HAROLD SEARLES SAVIDGE of Danville, Pennsylvania. Born there 20 December 1894, he died there 23 August 1960, and is buried at Rush Church, Danville. Mrs. Savidge resides in Hatboro, Pennsylvania.

Issue of (1.) Miriam Eloise Penn-Gaskell Hall
and her husband Harold Searles Savidge:

i. ROBERT FULTON SAVIDGE, b. at Philadelphia 21 March 1927; m. at the Church of the Immaculate Conception, Philadelphia, 11 April 1953, MARY CAROL HOFFER, b. at Philadelphia 30 December 1929, daughter of Norman E. and Winifred M. Hoffer. Robert Savidge served in the Korean War as staff sergeant, U. S. Army, 1948-1951. As a photogrammetrist, he uses aerial photography in cartographic engineering. The Savidges' residence is North Hills, Pennsylvania. Issue: 1. MARY BETH SAVIDGE, b. at Chestnut Hill, Philadelphia, 27 May 1954. 2. KATHLEEN ALLISON SAVIDGE, b. at Chestnut Hill, 21 March 1957. 3. MARK SAVIDGE, b. at Chestnut Hill, 30 June 1959; d. 2 July 1959. 4. AMY COURTNEY SAVIDGE, b. at Philadelphia, 1 November 1962. 5. ROBIN CAROL SAVIDGE, b. at Chestnut Hill, 6 March 1968.

The second child of (viii.) Philip Penn-Gaskell Hall and his wife Miriam Eloise Fulton, is (2.) AMY PENN-GASKELL HALL, born at 3916 Pine Street, 27 November 1905. She married at Elkton, Maryland, 3 January 1923, FRANCIS PELZER LYNAH, born in Charleston, South Carolina, 6 February 1899, son of Arthur A. Lynah and his wife Eliza DeSaussure Pelzer. Mr. Lynah, who served in the U.S. Coast Guard Reserve from August, 1939, to March, 1946, is now retired. Their residence is Wayne, Pennsylvania.

---

[18] Heretofore her name has been given incorrectly as *Mary* Eloise Fulton.

[19] For her obituary see *The Philadelphia Inquirer*, 22 June 1954.

[20] Her birth certificate, on file in Philadelphia Municipal Archives, Birth Registrations, Book 2 of 1902, 247, in error gives her father's name as Frank Hall.

i. FRANCIS PELZER LYNAH, JR., b. in Charleston, S. C., 7 April 1924; attended Admiral Farragut Academy; received a B.S. in Mechanical Engineering from Swarthmore College; M.S. in Physics from Drexel Institute of Technology. During World War II, he served as a Naval aviator with rank of lieutenant, junior grade, from March, 1943, to November, 1945. At the Swarthmore Presbyterian Church on 23 August 1947,[21] he m. ELAINE ALDEN KITE, b. in Ridley Park, Pa., 5 February 1927, daughter of William Stanley Kite and his wife Miriam Lovett Eggleston, a descendant of John Alden. Their residence is Newtown Square, Pa. Issue: 1. FRANCIS PELZER LYNAH, III, b. in Bryn Mawr, Pa., 3 December 1951. 2. STEPHEN KITE LYNAH, b. in Milwaukee, Wis., 26 August 1955.

The third and youngest child of (viii.) Philip Penn-Gaskell Hall and his wife Miriam Eloise Fulton, is (3.) PHILIP PENN-GASKELL HALL, JR., born at New London, Chester County, 20 September 1912.[22] A star athlete at Friends' Central School, he attended Temple and Villanova University.

In 1934, the Associate Committee of Women of the Genealogical Society of Pennsylvania initiated the project of obtaining a place in the Hall of Fame for the Founder of Pennsylvania. As a result of their enthusiasm and correspondence, a bust of William Penn by the sculptor, A. Stirling Calder, was unveiled by young Philip Penn-Gaskell Hall 28 May 1936, in the Hall of Fame at the University Heights Campus of New York University.[23] Two years later on 14 September 1938, he was the first of the Penn descendants to accept from the Conard-Pyle Company, proprietors of the Star Rose Gardens at West Grove, Chester County, one red rose as payment of the annual quit rent laid down by his ancestor, William Penn, 3rd, in 1742.

This pleasant ceremony has its roots in a deed of lease and release executed 24, 25 September 1731, wherein John, Thomas and Richard Penn confirmed to William Penn, 3rd, grandson of the Founder, 5000 acres of unlocated land in the Province. In 1742, William Penn, 3rd, conveyed the right to the still unlocated land to William Allen (later Chief Justice of the Province), subject to an annual quit rent of one red rose forever

---

[21] An account of their marriage is in *The Philadelphia Inquirer*, 24 August 1947.

[22] The family record in John W. Jordan, *Colonial and Revolutionary Families of Pennsylvania* (New York and Chicago, 1911), I, 21, from which data was extracted for the account in the last issue of this *Magazine*, does not include his name as Mr. Jordan's work was published before he was born.

[23] See the account in *The Philadelphia Inquirer*, 29 May 1936, and the reports of the Associate Committee of Women in *Publications of the Genealogical Society of Pennsylvania*, XII (No. 3, 1935), 312; XIII (Nos. 1-2, 1936), 165.

"if demanded." [24]   Allen had the land surveyed and in 1748 conveyed fifty-three acres of it to one Samuel Cross.   One hundred and eighty years later this tract (now in Penn Township, Chester County) was acquired by the Conard-Pyle Company, along with the old tavern building which had been erected on it at the intersection of the roads leading to West Grove and New London.   In the restoration of the inn, henceforth known as the Red Rose Inn, an investigation of the title to the land revealed the old quit rent laid on the property.   The Conard-Pyle Company elected to pay the quit rent, and for ten years it was accepted in appropriate ceremonies by the president of the Chester County Historical Society as representative of the Proprietary.   In September, 1938, Philip Penn-Gaskell Hall, Jr. was the first Penn descendant to accept the rent. Since then it has been received by various members of the Hall family.[25]

On 10 November 1935, Philip Penn-Gaskell Hall, Jr., married at Philadelphia, HORTENSIA LUISA MEDRANO, born at Philadelphia, daughter of Higinio Julio Medrano, Cuban Consul at Philadelphia, and his wife Amelia Luis Iraola.   During World War II, Mr. Hall was associated with a shipbuilding company engaged in building cargo vessels for the U.S. Navy, and has remained with the same concern.   His residence is Moylan-Rose Valley, Pennsylvania.

Issue of (3.) Philip Penn-Gaskell Hall, Jr.
and his wife Hortensia Luisa Medrano:

i. AMY PENN-GASKELL HALL, b. at Ridley Park, Pa., 24 October 1941. A graduate of Mater Misericordiae Academy, Merion, Pa., and of West Chester State College, in 1947 she was the recipient of the quit rent from the Conard-Pyle Company.   Her engagement to CHRISTOPHER PAUL SCHRODE, b. at Philadelphia 23 June 1940, son of Dr. Paul F. Schrode of Wynnewood, and the late Mrs. Claude Rains of Sandwich, N. H., was announced 14 December 1967.   They have chosen 15 June for their marriage.   Mr. Schrode, a graduate of West Chester State College, has been serving with the U.S. Army Intelligence in Baltimore.

ii. MIRIAM PENN-GASKELL HALL, b. at Philadelphia 18 April 1949, is attending Rosemont College.   On 23 November 1953, she set off the so-called "atomic blast," at the site of the old Chinese Wall along Market Street in Philadelphia, which marked the start of ground-breaking for Penn Center,[26] and is the most recent Penn descendant to accept the quit rent of one red rose from the Conard-Pyle Company.

---

[24] In 1772 a similar rent of one red rose was laid on land in Manheim Twp., Lancaster Co., by Henry William Stiegel when he gave land in the township for the use of a Lutheran congregation.

[25] These have included Mrs. Francis P. Lynah, Sr., and her son F. Pelzer Lynah in 1939, and Joannah Colket Hall in 1950 and 1951.   A transcript of the deed to William Allen, and numerous clippings and programs describing the presentation ceremonies are in the Albert Cooke Myers Collection, Chester County Historical Society.

[26] An account of the ceremony is in *The Philadelphia Inquirer*, 25 November 1953.

Penn-Gaskell Notes

JOHN INSLEY CODDINGTON, F.A.S.G., F.G.S.P.

THE following items are offered as supplements to the article on "The Penn-Gaskell Family: Addenda to the Family of Penn," which appeared in the Number 2 (1967) issue of Volume XXV of this Magazine.* **

On pages 114-115 of that issue is an account of the family of the youngest child of 3. Peter Penn-Gaskell, Jr.: 7. Peter Penn-Gaskell, 3rd (1843-*ca.* 1905), and his wife Mary Kathleen Stubbs. The daughter of this couple, MISS WINIFRED ETHEL PENN-GASKELL, was a great friend of my mother, Elizabeth (Magevney) Coddington (17 September 1873 - 30 December 1914), and of my half-sister, Elizabeth (Coddington) Coddington (21 April 1883 - 3 August 1968).

My sister had a "Birthday Book," in which many of her friends inscribed their birthdays, usually, one regrets to say, omitting the years. In this book are listed the birthdays of Miss Penn-Gaskell, of her mother, Mrs. Mary Kathleen (Stubbs) Penn-Gaskell, and of the latter's mother, Dona Manuela R. C. de Stubbs, who was born in Bolivia on "2 June." She married Charles Edward Stubbs, a mining engineer in Bolivia and Peru, and their daughter Mary Kathleen Stubbs was born in Lima on "16 November."

As stated in "The Penn-Gaskell Family," Peter Penn-Gaskell, 3rd, and Mary Kathleen Stubbs were married in England on 6 July 1869. William Penn-Gaskell of Shanagarry, County Cork, was their oldest child, and was born about 1870. WINIFRED ETHEL PENN-GASKELL was their second (not third) child, and she stated her date of birth fully in the Birthday Book, as "20 September 1873." I also remember that she once remarked to me that she was "just three days younger than" my mother.

Miss Penn-Gaskell died in Ashburton Hospital, Ashburton, Devonshire, 6 November 1949, aged 76. Her executor was Mr. S. W. Smith of the Trustee Branch of the National Provincial Bank, Ltd., of Exeter, Devonshire. Mr. Smith has died since 1949.

Miss Penn-Gaskell's brother, Percy Charles Penn-Gaskell, a Major in World War I, was the third and youngest of his parents' children. His only child, Patricia Maud Penn-Gaskell, was in 1967 Mrs. Patricia Maud Fox; her address was in care of the Westminster Bank, Ltd., Kensington

---

*Pages 579-601, this volume.
**Pages 596-597, this volume.

611

Branch, 115 Old Brompton Road, London, S.W. 7. Mrs. Fox does not answer genealogical inquiries.

The eldest sister of 7. Peter Penn-Gaskell, 3rd, was 6. ELIZABETH PENN-GASKELL (1825-1866), who married DR. SAMUEL RUFF SKILLERN (1834-1921). On page 113, lines 13-15, of "The Penn-Gaskell Family," it is stated that according to the present Dr. Penn-Gaskell Skillern, Samuel R. Skillern was "a nephew of the famous international beauty and wit, Madame Claude Le Verte, of Mobile." *There may be a confusion of generations here. Dr. Claude Le Vert (with no final "e" to his name), of Mobile, Ala., married Ann Lea Metcalf, and both of them died before 1840. Whether or not Mrs. Ann Lea (Metcalf) Le Vert was "a famous international beauty and wit" is doubtful, but her daughter-in-law certainly *was* just such a lady.

A son of Dr. Claude and Ann Lea (Metcalf) Le Vert was Henry Strachey Le Vert, M.D., born in King William County, Virginia, 25 December 1804, and died at Mobile 16 March 1864. He married at Mobile, 14 February 1836, Octavia Celestia Walton. She was born at Augusta, Ga., 10 August 1811, and died at Augusta, 13 March 1877, daughter of George Walton (1787-1863) and his wife Sarah Minge Walker (1793-1861), and granddaughter of George Walton (1749-1804), Signer of the Declaration of Independence from Georgia. Mrs. Octavia Celestia (Walton) Le Vert had no French ancestors, but she gave herself great airs as "Madame Le Vert," spoke French fluently, and presided over a celebrated *salon* in Mobile, where she was indeed renowned for her beauty and wit. She and her husband had five children, three of whom died in childhood. Of the two surviving daughters, one was a spinster, and only the youngest, Cornelia Henrietta Le Vert (1846-1876) married. Her husband was Lawrence Augustus Rigail Reab of Augusta, Ga., to whom she was married on 16 December 1868.

In view of the foregoing, it would appear that Dr. Samuel R. Skillern's relationship to Madame Le Vert is more likely to have been one of cousinship, than that of nephew and aunt.

---

*Page 595, this volume.

Penn-Gaskell Addenda

Francis James Dallett, f.g.s.p., f.a.s.g.

A BRIEF account of Mary Penn-Gaskell, born 12 September 1834, daughter of Peter Penn-Gaskell, Jr., and his wife Louisa Adelaide Heath, appeared in this *Magazine* in Volume XXV (1967), 107.* She married 22 March 1865, Dr. Isaac T. Coates, and died testate 22 August 1877. The following information can now be added to the previous account.

Isaac Taylor Coates, son of Moses and Lydia (Taylor) Coates, and grandson of Moses Coates, founder of Coatesville, Pa., was born 17 March 1834, in Coatesville. He graduated from the Medical School of the University of Pennsylvania, M.D., 1859. Coates entered the United States Navy as Acting Assistant Surgeon, 1861, and served aboard the U.S.S. *Bienville* and other vessels during the Civil War. He resigned in 1865, the year of his marriage, and the same year became Assistant Surgeon, 77th Pennsylvania Infantry. Subsequently he was attached to the Seventh Regiment, U.S. Cavalry, under General Custer. Later he practiced his profession in Reno, Nevada, and in the southwestern states. He died 23 June 1883, in Socarro, New Mexico. He was the author of a *Centennial Oration on Chester* (Pa.).

All the above information was supplied in 1906 by his relation, Joseph R. T. Coates, of Chester, Pa., to the General Alumni Society of the University of Pennsylvania, and is in the biographical folder of Isaac Taylor Coates in the University of Pennsylvania Archives.[1]

In October 1906, Dr. Coates's only surviving child, Harold Penn-Gaskell Coates, then employed by the Electric Light Company of St. Louis, Mo., advised the University of Pennsylvania Alumni Society of the date of death of his father, as above, and that his mother, Mary (Penn-Gaskell) Coates, had died 22 August 1877, at Philadelphia (not in Delaware County). In 1906 a genealogy of the Moses Coates family was published, and it is possible that Harold Penn-Gaskell Coates supplied the information of his own family which appeared therein. This

---

[1] See also Howard A. Kelly and Walter L. Burrage, *Dictionary of American Medical Biography* (New York, 1928), I, 238.

*Page 589, this volume.

record states that he married on 2 July 1891, FLORENCE ELIZABETH JARVIS, who was born in Philadelphia, and that they had two daughters: ROSALEEN JARVIS PENN-GASKELL COATES, born 14 March 189-[*sic*], and LUCRETIA YALE MORTON COATES, born 20 November 1902.[2] Perhaps a St. Louis genealogist could furnish the later history of this branch of the Penn-Gaskell family as represented by Harold Penn-Gaskell Coates and his daughters.

According to the alumni records in the Princeton University Archives, PETER PENN-GASKELL HALL, born 16 March 1830, son of Christiana Gulielma Penn-Gaskell and her husband William S. Hall, and a first cousin of Dr. Isaac Coates's wife Mary Penn-Gaskell, was a non-graduate member of the Class of 1849 of the College of New Jersey — since 1896 known as Princeton University. He entered the sophomore class in 1846, was dismissed on 5 March 1847, for refusing to withdraw his name from a petition, was restored by action of the faculty on 22 March 1847, but was withdrawn from the College by his father on 29 March 1847.[3]

Additional information on the Skillern branch of the Penn-Gaskell family is included in the recently published *The Ancestry and Posterity of Matthew Clarkson (1661-1702)*, a work reviewed in this issue of this *Magazine*.

---

2 Truman Coates, M.D., comp., *A Genealogy of Moses and Susanna Coates who settled in Pennsylvania in 1717, and Their Descendants,* 113, 123.

3 See "The Penn-Gaskell Family," in Volume XXV (1967), 115, of this *Magazine* for further details of his life. (Page 597, this volume.)

Penn-Gaskell Bible Record

HANNAH BENNER ROACH, F.G.S.P., F.A.S.G.

THE original and a photostatic copy of the following Bible record are in the Collections of the Genealogical Society of Pennsylvania. When the original record was given to the Society [1] no title page was included, but a comparison of the original sheets with other Bible records in the Society's collections which have similarly decorated borders, indicates that the pages came from *The New Testament of our Lord and Saviour Jesus Christ Translated out of the Original Greek . . .* which was printed in Philadelphia by Kimble and Sharpless, perhaps in 1826.

This *New Testament* apparently belonged to Peter Penn-Gaskell, Jr. (son of Peter Penn-Gaskell and his wife Elizabeth Edwards), whose marriage to Louisa Adelaide Heath is the first entry in the record. For further data on this family the reader is referred to "The Penn-Gaskell Family" in Volume XXV (No. 2, 1967) and to "Penn-Gaskell Addenda" in Volume XXVII (No. 4, 1972) of this *Magazine.*[*]

Family Record

Marriages

Peter Penn-Gaskell born April 3rd A.D. 1800 [and] Louisa Adelaide Penn-Gaskell born October 2nd A.D. 1805 Married Feby 15th 1825.

William Gerald Fitz'Gerald and Louisa Penn-Gaskell Married May 15th 1845.

Samuel R. Skillern and Elizabeth Penn Gaskell Married July 26th 1855.

Washington Irving and Jennie Penn-Gaskell Married Oct. 15th 1862

J. Paul Quinn and Emily Penn-Gaskell Married January 13th 1864.[2]

Isaac T. Coates and Mary Penn-Gaskell Married March 22nd 1865.

Penn-Gaskell Skillern and Nannie Dorsey Married October 7 1878.

Births [3]

Elizabeth Penn-Gaskell, born Decr 19th A.D. 1825.

Louisa Penn-Gaskell, born August 15th 1827.

Mary Gulielma Penn-Gaskell, born August 3rd 1829.

Gulielma Penn-Gaskell, born May 29th 1831.

---

*See pp. 579-601 and 613-614, this volume.

Hetty Penn-Gaskell, born January 29th 1833.

Mary Penn-Gaskell, born September 12th 1834.

William Penn-Gaskell, born July 9th 1836.

Jane Penn-Gaskell born July 4th 1839.

Emily Penn-Gaskell born January 27th 1842.

Peter Penn-Gaskell Jun[r]. born October 24th 1843

Penn-Gaskell Skillern born April 28th 1856 [4]

Irby H. Skillern born April 24th 1858 died Oct 1 - 1858 aged 5 mos- 6 days

Louise Fitz-Gerald Skillern born May 17th 1859.

Peter Penn-Gaskell Coates born February 26th 1866.

Granville Penn Quinn born January 6th 1868.

Deaths [5]

Mary Gulielma Penn-Gaskell Died June 21st 1830

Hetty Penn-Gaskell Died October 23rd 1847

Louisa Fitz'Gerald Died March 28th 1848

Gulielma Penn-Gaskell Died October 25th 1850

Jennie Penn-Gaskell Irving Died Nov. 1st 1863

William Penn-Gaskell Died Dec. 6th 1865.

Peter Penn Gaskell Died April 3rd 1866

Elizabeth Penn-Gaskell Skillern died at Pulaski - Tenn. Oct. 23 - 1866. her husband Samuel Ruff Skillern born March 16, 1834 at Huntsville - Alabama died Feb 17 - 1921 at Ardmore Pa.

Emily Penn-Gaskell Quinn Died Feb[y] 17th 1869

Mary Penn-Gaskell Coates Died August 22nd, 1877

Penn-Gaskell Skillern died July 25 - 1931

NOTES

[1] The donor was Miss Violet Penn-Gaskell Skillern, daughter of Peter Penn-Gaskell Skillern and his first wife Anna (Nannie) Dorsey of the Bible record.

[2] At the top of this page of marriages is pasted a newspaper notice which reads: "Quinn — Penn-Gaskell, — On Wednesday, the 13th inst., by the Rev. Dr. Ducachet, Dr. John Paul Quinn, United States Navy, and Emily, youngest daughter of P. Penn-Gaskell, Esq." In pencil is added the year: 1864, and the month: Jan.

[3] The first ten birth entries all appear to be in the same handwriting.

[4] Preceding the births of the three Skillern children is the penciled notation that they were the children of Elizabeth Penn-Gaskell and Samuel Ruff Skillern.

[5] At the top of the page of Deaths is written in ink "Section G. N°. 168. Lauril Hill Cemitary," and in pencil "Clearfield St. & Ridge Avenue." which is where the family is interred.

A Penn-Gaskell Hall Marriage
of 1852
Addendum to the Family of Penn

FRANCIS JAMES DALLETT, F.G.S.P., F.A.S.G.

The Penn-Gaskell family of Philadelphia had a parochial connection with St. Stephen's Protestant Episcopal Church in that city in the nineteenth century which was more extensive than has been realized by genealogists of the William Penn posterity. The marriage of one member of the family at St. Stephen's in 1845 was mentioned by Hannah Benner Roach in her "The Penn-Gaskell Family, Addenda to the Family of Penn," *PGM* XXV, 2 (1967), 97-119, an article to which the present writer was a major contributor. *

The union of Louisa Penn-Gaskell (one of the ten children of Peter Penn-Gaskell, Jr., and his wife Louisa Adelaide Heath) to William Gerald Fitzgerald, of New York, 15 May 1845,[1] was, however, but one of six family weddings at St. Stephen's. Louisa's sisters, Elizabeth, Mary, Jennie (Jane) and Emily also married in the church, as recorded in the registers.[2]

Yet another family wedding took place at St. Stephen's. Of more interest than the others because it introduces a formerly unknown bride to the family history, this previously unnoticed ceremony was that which on 28 August 1852 united the Penn-Gaskell sisters' first cousin Peter Penn-Gaskell Hall with Adelaide Gougenheim, as the latter name is spelled in the record.[3] Thus the "first" and "second" wives of Peter Penn-Gaskell Hall (1830-1905), the sisters Annie M. Mixsell and Amelia Mixsell, appear to have been actually his second and third wives.

Who was Adelaide Gougenheim? No notice of her wedding appeared in the Philadelphia newspapers.[4] The Philadelphia Board of Health's register of deaths in Philadelphia prior to 1860 does not include an Adelaide Hall. She was not interred in the family plot in the Lower Merion Baptist Churchyard. Were the Halls divorced and the name of the first wife dropped from family records?

Unfortunately, little is known of Peter Hall's movements in his younger years. At the time of the 1852 marriage, Hall was twenty-two years old, and his brief career at Princeton long behind him. He had entered the College of New Jersey as a Sophomore 13 August 1846, joined the Cliosophic Society that year, but left Princeton in March 1847.[5]

Peter Penn-Gaskell Hall is not listed as a householder in the Philadelphia directories of this period and, except for the knowledge that he read law during part of

*Pages 579-601, this volume.

it, details of his life and career are obscure until his admission to the Philadelphia bar 4 November 1858.[6]

The Philadelphia Directory for 1852 lists no one of the name Gougenheim. One Gugenheim (later spelled Guggenheim), "trader," appears.[7] Although it is possible that Peter Penn-Gaskell Hall chose his first wife from a modest *milieu* and married her in his own church, it is also probable that Adelaide Gougenheim belonged to another family whose surname was, correctly, Gougenheim, as the rector of St. Stephen's appears to have been accurate speller of the names he entered in his register.

NOTES

[1] Roach, *op. cit.*, 107. Further details of the family appear in a second article by Mrs. Roach, "Penn-Gaskell Halls of the Twentieth Century," *PGM*, XXV, 3 (1968), 174-182. *

[2] Record of St. Stephen's Church, Philadelphia, transcribed copy, Collections of the Genealogical Society of Pennsylvania, Ph28E. See also Index to Parish Register, St. Stephen's, by Thos. H. Montgomery, September 1880, 58, also in the Society's Collections, Ph28.1E.

[3] Record, *ibid.*, 83; Index, *ibid.*, 47.

[4] Search was made in *The Public Ledger, The Evening Bulletin* and *The North American.*

[5] Non-graduate student file, Princeton University Archives.

[6] John Hill Martin, *Martin's Bench and Bar of Philadelphia* (Philadelphia, 1883), 274.

[7] Simon Guggenheim lived in Culvert Street, above 4th, a small thoroughfare which ran from 3rd Street to Old York Road, north of Beaver Street. This man may have been a brother of Meyer Guggenheim who emigrated from Langnau, Switzerland, in 1848, and settled in Roxborough Township (Gatenby Williams, *William Guggenheim* (New York, 1934), 14). There was no daughter Adelaide in the family of Meyer; Simon arrived too late to be included in the 1850 census. Deaths of other persons of the name, but always spelled Guggenheim, are found in the Death Records of the Philadelphia Board of Health, GSP Collections Ph29A:37 and 38.

*Pages 602-610, this volume.

Further Penn Gleanings

Collected by

FRANCIS JAMES DALLETT, F.G.S.P., F.A.S.G.

SUPPLEMENTING the "Gleanings" of the late J. Henry Lea of Massachusetts, published many years ago in *The Pennsyvania Magazine of History and Biography*[*] and in the *New England Historic and Genealogical Register*, and the recent researches of Brigadier Oliver F. G. Hogg, presented in his *Further Light on the Ancestry of William Penn*, the following miscellaneous records relating to English Penns and to the family of William Penn, Founder of Pennsylvania, provide additional light on hitherto obscure aspects and on various members of the Penn family.

1539 — Thomas Penne, described as sub-prior of Bradenstoke Priory at its dissolution in 1539, signed the original document of surrender as Thomas Pen, "superior." The Thomas Penne who was accused of heresy in 1551 was, in fact, vicar of Mickleton, Gloucestershire, suspended for simony and later restored.[1] It is highly possible that the Thomas Penns were one, the same man who became a parish priest after secularization, and married. It is possible that he was a relation, even a brother, of William Penn (d. 1592) of Minety, and thus arose, quite honestly, a tradition of a secularized monk in the ancestry of the Minety Penns, later to be confused with a similar legend connected with the Penns of Penn. This is, of course, speculation.

1590 — In the will of William Penn of Minety, dated 1 May 1590, he named as one of his overseers, Francis Bradshaw, gentleman of Wokely (Wokesy, an old variant of Oaksey, Wilts.). Seven years later on 27 August 1597 (40 Elizabeth I), Francis Bradshaw and John Warneford, gentleman, were enfeoffed by John Stumpe in the latter's premises in Malmesbury, Wilts., the former Abbey House.[2] Stumpe, originally a

---

[1] See O. F. G. Hogg, *Further Light on the Ancestry of William Penn* (London, 1964), published by The Society of Genealogists, 6, 9, 11, 23, for a discussion of the sub-prior Thomas Penne, and of the man accused of heresy. In this study, Brigadier Hogg, a distinguished military historian and genealogist, deals with legend versus fact in the ancestry of William Penn, the Quaker and Founder. He explodes finally the myth that Penn's family were connected with the Penns of Penn, sums up existing evidence, and presents new facts relative to the true Wiltshire origins of the Pennsylvania Penns. See also *Bristol and Gloucestershire Archeological Society Proceeedings* (BGASP), LX, 122, 126, 128, for details regarding the suspension of the vicar of Mickleton, and the religious difficulties of a Joan Pen of Stoneham, Glos., of the same period.

[2] *Wiltshire Notes and Queries*, VIII, 453. For a transcript of the will of William Penne of Minety see *The Pennsylvania Magazine of History and Biography* (PMHB), XIV (1890), 57-61. [**]

[*] See *Genealogies of Pennsylvania Families: From The Pennsylvania Magazine of History and Biography* (Baltimore: Genealogical Publishing Co., Inc., 1981), 546-631.

[**] *Ibid.*, 553-557.

clothier of North Nibley, Glos., had obtained the site of Malmesbury Abbey at its suppression and built Abbey House. Stumpe's brother, Sir James Stumpe, Kt. (d. 1563),[3] was leasor of the manor of Rodbourne, Wilts., where many Penns lived. Thus Francis Bradshaw, Penn's overseer, came into possession of Malmesbury Abbey with a John Warneford. In 1546, an earlier John Warneford was recognized as holding the manors and 200 messuages and cottages at Bromham, Bremhill, Stanley, Rowden, Whitley, Shaw, Whaddon and elsewhere in Wiltshire, of Thomas Seymour, Kt., and Andrew Baynton, Esq., who in that year quit claimed these manors to Warneford and to Anthony Pen.[4] This suggests the possibility of a Penn-Warneford-Bradshaw kinship which may be the origin of a supposed Penn of Minety connection with Malmesbury Abbey.[5]

1611 — Penns of Rodbourne, not listed by Mr. Lea or Brigadier Hogg, include Jane Penn of Hillmarton, d. *ca.* 1611, and a Thomas Penn of Alderton, d. *ca.* 1615. The inventory and bond on the estate of Jane Penn, and the will of Thomas Penn are in the Archdeaconry Court of Wilts. The probate documents, however, shed no light on any connection with the Penns of Minety.

1620 — The published marriages of Brinkworth show the marriage of John Sherer [6] to Agnes Lewen on 24 June 1620, and of John Sherer, probably the same man and a widower, to Margery Pen on 17 October 1622.

1630 — Rachel Penn, baptized 24 February 1607, daughter of Giles and Joan (Gilbert) Penn, married by license 26 October 1630, at the Church of St. Gregory by St. Paul, London, Randall (otherwise Ralph) Bradshaw.[7] The 1664-5 Visitation of Lancashire gives the pedigree of "Bradshaw of Pendleton" [8] and shows that Laurence Bradshaw of Hope, in the parish of Eccles, Lancashire, married Sarah Hinchman of Andover, Southampton, and had four sons and three daughters. The eldest son, the gentleman who entered his pedigree at the Visitation, was "Raphe Bradshaw, of Pendelton, co. Lancaster, aet 53 an. 16 March 1664, mar-

---

3 *BGASP,* XXXVIII, 174. Sir James Stumpe's will is in the Prerogative Court of Canterbury, Register Chayre, folio 23, at Somerset House, London.

4 Calendar of Feet of Fines for Wiltshire, C.P. 25 (2) 324, at the Public Record Office, London. Unfortunately, the document gives no details about Anthony Pen.

5 Hogg, *Further Light,* 10 *et seq.*

6 His name is printed in error as *Shere* in Hogg, 26. Also in error on the same page is the Penn-Cusse marriage date. It is 1633, not 1663.

7 Transcript of the register at The Society of Genealogists, London, Mss. Mx13.

8 Arms: Argent, two bendlets between as many martlets, sable, a cinquefoil in the fess point, gules; crest: In front of an oak tree, a stag statant, proper. See F. R. Haines, ed., *The Visitation of the County Palatine of Lancaster, made in the year 1664-5, by Sir William Dugdale, Knight,* Chetham Society Publications, 84 (Manchester, 1872), Part I, 53.

ried Rachell, dau. of Giles Pen, a merchant in Bristol." The will of Raphe Bradshaw of Pendleton, gent., is missing in the Lancashire probate records of the Consistory Court of the Bishop of Chester, but probate of the will was granted 31 January 1667/8, to Nathan Leech and Ralph Bradshaw. The children of Raphe Bradshaw and Rachel Penn, as listed in the Visitation pedigree, but not in the order of birth, were:

    i. Robert Bradshaw, a merchant, ob. s.p.
    ii. William Bradshaw, died an infant.
    iii. James Bradshaw, now a merchant, at sea, aet 18 an. 16 March 1664.
    iv. John Bradshaw, aet 13.
    v. Rebecca Bradshaw, wife of William Crispin merchant of London.
    vi. Sarah Bradshaw, died young.
    vii. Mary Bradshaw, died young.
    viii. Anne Bradshaw.
    ix. Frances Bradshaw.

The eldest daughter, Rebecca Bradshaw (d. *ca.* 1664-5), married at St. Dunstan's, Stepney, Middlesex, as his first wife, William Crispin, baptized 3 October 1627, at Holy Trinity, Hull, Yorkshire; died "transmarinus" 1681/2, letters of administration on his estate being granted 7 July 1682, in Ireland to John Suxberry and John Watts.[9]

The youngest daughter, Frances Bradshaw, married after 1664, William Assheton (Asheton, Ashton), an attorney-at-law, a coroner of Lancashire and a Deputy Herald at Arms. As progenitors of the Philadelphia Asshetons, they had issue: Robert Assheton (1670-1727), who came to Pennsylvania; Frances Assheton, baptized at Salford 15 March 1675; Mary Assheton, baptized at Salford 6 May 1680; and Rachel Assheton.[10]

James and John Bradshaw, sons of Ralph and Rachel (Penn) Bradshaw, were named in the will of their uncle, Admiral Penn. James Bradshaw, born about 1646, the "merchant at sea" listed in the Visitation pedigree, followed his first cousin William Penn to Pennsylvania and from him obtained the post of Surveyor of New Castle County. He died about 1691, for on 28 1m (March) 1691, the Commissioners of Property in Philadelphia ordered the profits of the place of Surveyor continued to

---

[9] Captain Crispin was appointed a commissioner for settling the colony of Pennsylvania, and was to have been chief justice. There is no evidence to support the long-held contention he was also to have been surveyor general. According to the Eccles Parish registers, Ralph Bradshaw "of ye Pole," father of Rebecca, was bur. 30 Oct. 1667, his daughter Sarah, 28 July 1635. See M. Jackson Crispin, "Captain William Crispin," *PMHB*, LIII (1929), 97, 104, 126, 130, 321n. for vital records; and M. Jackson Crispin, "The Crispins of Kingston-on-Hull," *Publications o f the Genealogical Society of Pennsylvania*, X (1928), 105 *et seq.* The marriage record is in Thomas Colyer-Fergusson, ed., *The Marriage Registers of St. Dunstan's, Stepney, in the County of Middlesex*, II (Canterbury, 1899), 83. The relationship of Rebecca (Bradshaw) Crispin to William Penn has long been known despite such erroneous statements as in Mabel Richmond Brailsford, *The Making of William Penn* (London, 1930), 13, which makes Captain Crispin husband of a hypothetical maternal aunt of Penn, Anne Jasper.

[10] Charles P. Keith, *The Provincial Councillors of Pennsylvania . . .* (Philadelphia, 1883), 282; *PMHB*, LIII, 295n.

*See *Genealogies of Pennsylvania Families: From The Pennsylvania Magazine of History and Biography*. 183, 189, 216, 220, and 272.
**See Volume I of this work, pp. 373-390.

his widow, Mary Bradshaw.[11] He was one of the very few first settlers of Penn's colony whose name was actually entered in a Visitation pedigree.

1643/4 — The marriage of Captain (later Admiral) William Penn and Margaret Van der Schuren, widow, took place at the church of St. Martin Ludgate, London, on 6 January 1643/4, and was "by Mr. Dyke, Lecturer then: witness Mr. Roche churchwarden then." [12] She was the daughter of John Jasper of Rotterdam and Ballycase, County Clare, Ireland (where he was naturalized), and the widow of Nicasius Van der Schuren of Kilconry, parish of Kilrush, County Clare.

1666 — On 12 February 1666/7, the Faculty Office of the Archbishop of Canterbury issued a marriage license to Anthony Lowther, aged 24, and Margaret Pen, aged 15, daughter of Sir William Pen. The marriage took place 14 February 1666/7, at Clapham, Surrey. At that time Admiral Penn had a country house at Clapham. He subsequently moved to Clay Street, Walthamstow, Essex, and the Lowthers to a house called Sweetacre or Swetsacre, on Church hill in the same parish.[13]

1670 — In the British Museum is the manuscript work book of the Herald-painter who painted the monument to Admiral Sir William Penn in St. Mary Redcliffe Church, Bristol. The artist, who seems to have been in the best employment for funerals of the nobility and gentry in the reign of Charles II, records: Worke don for the funall of Right / honll: Sr: Will: Penn Interd at / Bristow: / ars of Buckinghamshire. / ffor a great Atchievement / ffor 2 pennons / ffor 10: Buck Esctons [buckram escutcheons] / ffor a Standard of England.[14] Accompanying sketches gave the full armorial achievment and a second plain coat, each bearing the arms of Penn of Bucks.

1692 — Inscription on a monument on the south wall, above the gallery, of the parish church of Walthamstow, Essex, as given in *St.*

---

11 *Pennsylvania Archives*, 3rd Series, XIX, 66.

12 The registers of St. Martin Ludgate are at Guildhall Library, London, Ms. 10,212 and 10,213. While the register shows the marriage as taking place 6 June 1643, the entry is not in original sequence and was reconstituted by the certificate of Richard Roche on 2 July 1652, as reference to the original shows. Roche evidently wrote June in error for January, confirmed by the entry for 6 January 1661/2, in Pepys' *Diary*. This corrects the error in M. Atherton Leach, "Gulielma Maria Springett, First Wife of William Penn," *PMHB*, LVII (1933), 99, and the error in O. F. G. Hogg, "Pedigree of Penn of Co. Wilts and of Bristol," *The Wiltshire Archeological and Natural History Magazine*, LX, 130, which fixes the place of marriage at St. Mary Redcliffe, Bristol.

13 Index to registers of Clapham, Society of Genealogists, London, correcting the pedigree by Hogg, cited above, which states the Lowthers were married in London. See also George F. Bosworth, *Some Chapters in the History of Walthamstow*, Walthamstow Antiquarian Society, Publication No. 22 (1929), 19, and Howard M. Jenkins, *The Family of William Penn* (Philadelphia, 1899), 255, first published in *PMHB*, XXII (1898), 327.

14 Add. Mss. 26,683, f.51b, British Museum. The inscription on the monument is in Jenkins, 18-19, and in Hogg, 33-34, which also contains a definitive statement on the usurpation of the arms displayed on the monument.

Mary the Virgin, Walthamstow. Inscriptions in the Church and Church-yard, Walthamstow Antiquarian Society, Publication No. 23, (1930), 19: Near this place lyeth the body of AN / THONY LOWER [Low-ther] / of Maske in Clieve / land in the County of York, Esqr, descen / ded from the antient family of the Low / thers of Lowther Hall in the County / of Westmoreland, Baro^ts He died 27 / day of January 1692. Aged 52 years. / He married Margaret daughter of S^r / William Penn, Knight, by whom he had / issue six sons and three daughters, vid^t / Margaret, William, Elizabeth, Robert, / William, Anne Charlotte, Anthony, / John, and Anthony, of which the follow / ing five lye here buried, Margaret mar / ried to Benjamin Poole Esqr / William aged / 6 months, Robert (a Gen^t of great / hopes and learning) died in the twenty / second year of his age, very much lamen / ted, Anthony aged one year and eight / months, and Anthony aged twenty years. / Here also lyes the body of MARGARET wife to / the above said Anthony Lower [*sic*] / Esqr who / died the 5th day of Decem^br 1719 aged 73 years.

(Arms: In a lozenge: Or, six annulets, three, two and one, sable [Lowther]; impaling Argent, on a fess sable, three plates, in chief a lion passant gules [Penn].) [15]

The difference of the lion passant in the Penn arms as impaled by Anthony Lowther should be noted. The arms are now placed in error over the Mores monument in the north aisle of the church and the Mores arms are over the Lowther monument. The inscription corrects previous accounts of the Lowther children as being not four in number, but nine, and the date of Margaret Lowther's death and her age, which has not previously appeared.

1720 — On 14 February 1720, at the Church of St. Mary Magdalen Old Fish Street, London, Aubrey Thomas of the parish of St. Michael Cornhill, and "William Mary" Penn, of the parish of St. Andrew Holborn, were married.[16] The bride was Gulielma Maria Penn, born 10 9m 1699, daughter of William Penn, Jr., and his wife Mary Jones, and the first granddaughter of William Penn, the Founder, to marry. She married secondly, Charles Fell.

1728 — The Vicar General's Marriage Allegation Bond of 26 October 1728 states that: Appeared personally Hannah Lardner of the Parish of Woodford in the County of Essex aged above nineteen years & a Spinster and alledged that she intendeth (with the Consent of Frances

---

[15] There is no probate for Margaret Lowther in 1719 or 1720 in the Prerogative Court of Canterbury. It is of interest to note that the Penn arms described above are identical with those described by Mr. Lea in his "Genealogical Gleanings," *PMHB*, XIV (1898), 51, as belonging to the Penns of Worcestershire, being "the same as those borne by the Founder differenced by 'in cheife a lyon passant gules.'" In the time of Cromwell they were in the church window at Churchill, near Stourbridge. *

[16] Transcript of the register is at The Society of Genealogists, London, Mss. Mx13.

*See *Genealogies of Pennsylvania Families: From The Pennsylvania Magazine of History and Biography*, 547.

Lardner her Sister and Guardian lawfully assigned her Parents being both dead) to marry with Richard Penn of St. Dionish Barkchurch London aged above two & twenty years and a Batchelor. Prayed License for them to be Married in the parish Church of St. Saviours Southwark in the County of Surry. /s/ Hannah Lardner.[17]

1748 — In the Administration Act Book of the Prerogative Court of Canterbury, at Somerset House, for October 1748, is the following: On the Seventeenth day [October 1748] Admon of the Goods Chattels and Credits of Charles Fell late of the Parish of St. Margaret Westminster in the County of Middx Widower decd was granted to Robert Edward Fell the natural and lawfull son of the said decd being first sworn duly to adster.

1751 — On 22 August 1751, the marriage was solemnized at the Church of St. George, Hanover Square, London, of "Thomas Penn, of St. Martin in the Fields, Esq. B. & the Hon. Juliana Fermor, of St. James, Westm[r] S. Special License." [18]

1786 — *The Army List* for this year carries, for the last time, the name of Robert Edward Fell, Lieutenant Colonel, 79th Regiment of Foot, original commission 25 May 1772.[19]

1787 — Abstract of the will of Robert Edward Fell in the Prerogative Court of Canterbury, Major 66: The will of Robert Edward Fell of Hamlet of Clitha in the parish of Lanarth in the County of Monmouth, Esquire: To nephew, William Hawkins Newcomb, £5000. Executor to pay to the Trustees of the marriage settlement of my niece, Philadelphia Brookholding, with Thomas Brookholding of the City of Worcester, the £500 I have secured to them. From affection I have for said Niece and her husband, I devise to my Friend Pryce Owen of Shrewsbury in the County of Salop, Esquire, over such sum as I am engaged to pay, the further sum of £500 upon trust, the yearly interest to go to Thomas Brookholding and his assigns for life; at his death the principal to go to my said niece Philadelphia Brookholding, if living, or to Thomas if she predeceases him; they may have the principal while living if required. To Thomas Brookholding upon trust, £1000, the interest to be paid to my Sister, Gulielma Maria Frances Newcomb, or her assigns for life and at death interest of £500 to niece Gulielma Maria Newcomb in-

[17] Faculty Office Allegation Series, Lambeth Palace Library, London. It was most unusual for the prospective *bride* to apply for the license. Hannah evidently was taking no chances.

[18] John H. Chapman, ed., *The Register Book of Marriages Belonging to the Parish of St. George, Hanover Square, in the County of Middlesex,* Harleian Society, Vol. XI (London, 1886), I, 46. The marriage of Thomas Penn's daughter Sophia Margaret, to the Hon. and Right Rev. William Stuart took place in the same church 3 May 1796. *Ibid.,* 147.

[19] To Jenkins' account of his activities (p. 271), may be added that he became a member of the Society of the Sons of St. George at Philadelphia, 23 January 1773.

dependent of any husband, with principal at her death to nephew William Hawkins Newcomb. Remaining £500 on trust for niece Susanna
Margaretta Crompton, wife of Richard Crompton, Gentleman, for life,
independent of her husband, and at death principal to be divided amongst
any child or children then living when they attain the age of 21. If she
dies without issue, principal to Thomas Brookholding and William Hawkins Newcomb. To Thomas Brookholding, my Gold watch, chain and
seals; to niece, Philadelphia Brookholding, my diamond shirt pin, sleeve
buttons set with garnetts, and all my laced ruffles. To nephew, William
Hawkins Newcomb, my sword and pistols. To servant Thomas Dur-
man, if in my service at my decease, shooting and fishing tackle, and £10
for mourning. Servant Ann Lokier, if in my service at my decease, my
small silver tea pot or Argyle and £10 for mourning. Servant Ann Jenkins, if in my service at my decease, two silver table spoons and 5 guineas
for mourning. To Richard Crompton, husband of my niece Susanna
Margaretta Crompton, £100 he owes me secured in the name of Richard
Benbow. Niece Gulielma Maria Frances Newcomb £20. Residue of
estate to be equally divided between Thomas Brookholding and William
Hawkins Newcomb. Thomas Brookholding to be sole Executor. Dated
24 March 1784. /s/ Robert Edwd. Fell [*seal*]
Witnesses: Samuel Morgan, Ann Morgan, Benjn. Esner
Proved at London 22 February 1787 by Thomas Brookholding, sole ex-
ecutor. "Testator was formerly of the Hamlet of Clitho in the Parish
of Lanarth in the County of Monmouth but at Borden Town in the
State of New Jersey in North America deceased & died in Novr. last." [20]

1825 — Philadelphia Hannah Freame (*c.* 1740-1825), daughter of
Margaret Penn and Thomas Freame, and granddaughter of William Penn,
the Founder, by his second wife Hannah Callowhill, married on 8 May
1770, Thomas Dawson, Baron Dawtrey and Viscount Cremorne. For
their issue, Thomas Dawson, d. 9 October 1787, and Juliana Frances Anne
Dawson, d. 8 June 1789, and for an extended biographical account of
Lord and Lady Cremorne, see Thomas Faulkner, *An Historical and Topographical Description of Chelsea and Its Environs* (Chelsea, 1829), I,
65-72. In this work is recorded Lady Cremorne's death in Stanhope
Street, Mayfair, on 14 April 1825, her burial at Stoke Poges churchyard,
attended by the Royal Princesses, and a list of her pictures, chiefly Old
Masters, sold at auction on 6 June 1827, by her executor, Granville Penn.
Opposite page 70 is a lithographic view of Chelsea Farm, the Cremorne's

---

20 This corrects the inaccurate version of the will in Jenkins (p. 141), and adds the name of Susanna
Margaretta Newcomb's husband, Richard Crompton, of which he was not aware. The present compiler has
notes on the Brookholding family subsequent to 1787, which will be published later. There is a possibility
that Penn descendants in this line are extant.

country house in Chelsea on the Thames. More information about their establishment there — the house, later called Cremorne House, was enlarged by the architect James Wyatt — and additional views are in Alfred Beaver, *Memorials of Old Chelsea* (London, 1892), 158-159. Beaver points out that Lady Cremorne, whose Christian name was the name of her American birthplace, was a particular friend of Queen Charlotte and is "celebrated in the *Percy Anecdotes* as the best mistress of a household that ever lived." The will of the Right Honorable Philadelphia Hannah, Viscountess Cremorne, was proved in June 1826, in the Prerogative Court of Canterbury, Swabey, 317, but adds nothing new to the knowledge of the Penn family. Granville Penn's family were the principal heirs. The present day Dartrey Road and Cremorne Road preserve the family name in Chelsea.

Miscellanea

The ancestry of William Penn in the direct male line has been developed by Brigadier Hogg to John Penne of Minety and the early years of the sixteenth century. The genealogy of the founder's great-great grandmother, Anne George, wife of John Rastall, Alderman of Gloucester, has been established in Major Thorne George, *Pedigrees and History of the Families of George and Gorges* (Folkestone, Kent, 1903). Here her ancestry is correctly traced in unbroken sequence to 1310 when the George family acquired the Gloucestershire manor of Baunton (held by the family until 1707). In the same work, her ancestry is tentatively extended to the Norman Conquest, but includes an entirely fanciful link with the celebrated Gorges family. See Oswald Barron, "Georgics," *The Ancestor*, IX (April, 1904), and Raymond Gorges, *The Story of a Family Through Eleven Centuries . . . being a History of the Family of Gorges* (Boston, 1944).

At an undisclosed date prior to 1702, William Penn "Sent over into this Province one Martha Durant, a Relation of his own, with her husband, John Durant, and Children." By 1702, the husband was dead and Martha, "being now in a great Strait and having an opportunity of entring upon a Way for a Livelyhood," presented to the Board of Property a "Certificate Under the Propr'y's hand" for 600 acres of land Penn had granted the Durants. In 1712, when Martha again appeared before the Board, she was "wholly destitute of all manner of Support," and "must of necessity perish for want, or come upon the Publick, unless the Proprietor . . . shall think fitt to relieve and assist her . . . adding that her Cousin, R. Assheton, was willing to advance Something for her if the Proprietor would do the Same." The Board then ordered "that R. Assheton be Treated with, and as she is desirous to keep a small Shop for Drams and Hucksters ware, that five pounds be immediately advanced to her . . . ," as noted in *Pennsylvania Archives*, 2nd Series, XIX, 283, 351, 541. It seems probable that Martha's relationship to Penn and to Robert Assheton was derived from Rachel Penn (wife of Ralph Bradshaw) who was the Founder's aunt and Assheton's grandmother.

The Queen's Warrant

VICTORIA, by the Grace of God, of the United Kingdom of Great Britain and Ireland Queen Defender of the Faith &c To Our Right Trusty and Right Entirely Beloved Cousin and Councillor Bernard Edward Duke of Norfolk Earl Marshal and Our Hereditary Marshal of England, Greeting: Whereas Our Trusty and Well beloved Granville Penn, of Stoke Park in Our County of Buckingham Esquire, only surviving Son and Heir of Thomas Penn, late of the same place Esquire deceased (by the Lady Juliana, his Wife, Daughter of Thomas Earl of Pomfret), and Grandson and Heir Male of William Penn Esquire, sometime Proprietor and First Settler of the Province of Pennsylvania in North America, hath by his Petition humbly represented unto Us, that Our Royal Predecessor King Charles the Second, by His Royal Charter under the Great Seal of England, granted to William Penn Esquire, the Petitioner's said late Grandfather, his Heirs and Assigns (in reward and memorial of the eminent Services rendered to the Crown, at the period of the Royal Restoration, by his late Father, Sir William Penn, Vice Admiral of England), all that Tract of Land in North America, called the Province or State of Pennsylvania, with the Royalties, Franchises, and other Hereditaments and Premises in the said Charter mentioned: That the Heirs and Descendants of the said Grantee, Proprietaries of the said Province, having been, by an Act of the State of Pennsylvania, in 1779, divested of the Charter Rights so derived to their Family, an Act entitled "An Act for settling and securing a certain Annuity for the use of the Heirs and Descendants of the late William Penn Esquire," in consideration of the meritorious Services of the said William Penn, and of the great extent of the losses sustained by his Heirs and Descendants, was passed, unanimously, by both Houses of Parliament and received the Royal Assent on the 9th of June 1790: That, with a view to commemorate the aforesaid Royal Grant, and, at the same time, the compensatory Grant generously awarded by Parliament in lieu thereof, the Petitioner is desirous of bearing an honourable Augmentation to the Armorial Ensigns used by his Family, and of obtaining our Sanction for that purpose; and therefore most humbly prays Our Royal License and Authority, that he and the other Descendants of his Grandfather the said William Penn, according to the Limitations of the abovementioned Royal Charter, may bear and use certain honourable Armorial Augmentations accordingly: And We being graciously pleased to approve thereof; Know Ye that We, of our Princely Grace and special Favor, have given and granted, and by these Presents do give and grant unto the said Granville Penn Our Royal Licence and Permission that he, and the other Descendants of his Grandfather the said William Penn, may henceforth bear and use the Armorial Ensigns following, that is to say, A Fess charged with three Plates, and, on a Canton of honourable Augmentation, a Crown, representing the Royal Crown of King Charles the Second, and, for the Crest, A Demi-Lion, gorged with a Collar charged with three Plates, and, above, An Escroll, thereon the Word "Pennsylvania," as in the Painting hereunto annexed; Provided the said Armorial Distinctions be first duly exemplified according to the Laws of Arms and recorded in the Heralds Office, otherwise this Our Licence and Permission to be void and of none Effect: Our Will and Pleasure, therefore, is, that you, Bernard-Edward Duke of Norfolk Earl Marshal, to whom the Cognizance of Matters of this Nature doth properly belong, do require and command, that this Our Concession, and especial Mark of Our Royal Favor, be registered in Our College of Arms; to the end that Our Officers of Arms and all others upon occasion may take full Notice and have Knowledge thereof. And for so doing this shall be your Warrant. Given at our Court at Saint James's the thirty first day of July 1838 in the second year of Our Reign.

By Her Majesty's Command

/s/   Russell

Granville Penn Esqre — Licence that he and the other Descendants of his Grandfather William Penn Esqre may bear certain honourable Armorial Distinctions. Recorded in the College of Arms London pursuant to a Warrant from the Earl Marshall of England this seventh day of August 1838.

/s/   Chas. Geo. Young
York Herald & Register *

* Case 41, Penn Papers, Historical Society of Pennsylvania.

THE ARMORIAL ENSIGNS GRANTED THE PENN FAMILY
BY QUEEN VICTORIA

From the Drawing in the Historical Society of Pennsylvania

The Stuart Branch
of the Family of Penn

BRIGADIER OLIVER F. G. HOGG, C.B.E.

F.S.A., F.R.HIST.S., F.S.G.

DESCENDANTS of William Penn in the Penn-Gaskell line have been associated with Philadelphia life since 1785. Representatives of the English Stuarts, the other eventual co-heirs of the Founder, while nearly all living in England, have also been familiar here because of their retention of important Penn heirlooms, as well as remnants of Proprietary rights. Mrs. Frederick Robert Wynne of Church Crookham, Hampshire, (No. 33 of the following record) by law the "heir-general" of the Penn family, has deposited the final nucleus of the family archives with the Bedfordshire Record Office. Her younger sister, Dr. Rosalind Esme Pole Stuart of Folkestone, Kent, still holds certain Philadelphia quit-rents which have descended to her through generations of her Penn ancestors. In addition, various Stuarts, Knoxes, Milnes-Gaskells, Hoggs, Wilbrahams, and other descendants of the Stuart branch have visited in Pennsylvania officially and privately for three-quarters of a century.

The usual policy of this *Magazine,* in presenting the genealogical record of a man's descendants, is to omit data on his living progeny. But William Penn belongs to history as the Founder of Pennsylvania, and some of his descendants were actively concerned with and involved in the history of Pennsylvania's colonial development. Although none of the Stuart or Penn-Gaskell descendants have been actively involved in Pennsylvania's later history, they are none-the-less extensions of Penn himself, continuous links between the past and the future. Their collected records, added to those of their Penn progenitors, therefore enlarge the overall picture of the Founder. All of these records furnish prime evidence of the manner in which each generation of the family, during a period of four hundred years, adjusted to changing circumstances, and indicate the degree to which the infusion of new blood during that same period has reinforced or diluted basic characteristics.

Published genealogical data on the nineteenth-century members of the Stuart line has been limited to the 1896-1899 account in *The Family of William Penn* by the late Howard M. Jenkins, and to the brief recapitulation presented in this *Magazine* in 1967 (Volume XXV, No. 2, 93-96),* intentionally kept short in the knowledge that a more extended account of the Stuart branch would be forthcoming. In this year of the two hundred and fiftieth anniversary of the Founder's death, it is only appropriate that Brigadier Hogg's researches, by augmenting the earlier accounts, have now brought this branch of the Penn family into the twentieth century.[1] — *Editor.*

Sophia Margaret Penn, granddaughter of William Penn, the Founder of Pennsylvania, was the daughter of his son Thomas Penn, Chief Proprietor of Pennsylvania, and the latter's wife, Lady Juliana Fermor. Known also as Sophia Margaretta and Sophia Margaret Juliana Penn, she was born 25 December 1764. At the Church of St. George, Hanover Square, Middlesex, she married on 3 May 1796, The Honorable and Most Reverend William Stuart, D.D., later Archbishop of Armagh and Primate of All Ireland. He was born in March, 1755, the fourth son of John, 3rd Earl of Bute, Knight of the Garter and Prime Minister under King George III. William Stuart was educated at Winchester and at St. John's College, Cambridge, of which he was M.A. in 1774, and D.D. in 1789. After ordination, he was vicar of Luton, Bedfordshire for fourteen years until he became Canon of Windsor in 1793. Later appointed to the See of St. David's, Stuart became Archbishop of Armagh in 1800.

After their marriage, Archbishop Stuart and his wife lived at Luton Hoo, Bedfordshire, and at 36 Hill Street, London (the Stuart lease of the latter residence only running out about twenty-five years ago). The Archbishop died at his London house on 6 May 1822, in tragic circum-

---

[1] Brigadier Hogg's record is essentially a basic outline of the Stuart branch of the family and, beyond listing honors and civil or military service, makes no pretension to being a comprehensive biographical record of individual members of the family. Its great value lies in the collation for the first time, in a concise framework, of data on the family in such sources as *Burke's Peerage* and other related works which are not everywhere readily available to researchers on this side of the Atlantic. (This, and all subsequent footnotes, have been supplied by the Editor.)

*Pages 575-578, this volume.

stances, told in detail in Howard M. Jenkins, *The Family of William Penn*, 191-192. Briefly, during his last illness his wife was his devoted nurse. Unfortunately, she poured out some medicine for him from the wrong bottle which had been handed to her. It was laudanum and the poison killed him. While dying from its effects, he managed to scrawl this little note of comfort to his wife: "I could not have lived long, my dear love, at all events." This occurrence was instrumental in securing passage in England of the law that poisons must be sold in bottles of distinctive shape and usually of dark blue, green or brown color.

Sophia Margaret (Penn) Stuart died 29 April 1847, and was buried in the Stuart family vault at Luton.

Issue of Sophia Margaret Penn and her husband The Honorable and Most Reverend William Stuart, D.D.:

1.   i. MARY JULIANA STUART, b. 3 April 1797; d. 11 July 1866,[2] of whom further.
2.   ii. WILLIAM STUART, b. 31 October 1798; d. 7 July 1874, of whom further.
    iii. HENRY STUART, b. 5 April 1804; d. unmarried 26 October 1854. He was sometime member of Parliament for Bedfordshire.
    iv. LOUISA STUART, d. unmarried 29 September 1823,[3] and was bur. at Luton.

1. MARY JULIANA STUART, first child and elder daughter of Sophia Margaret Penn and her husband The Honorable and Most Reverend William Stuart, D.D., was born 3 April 1797. She married 28 February 1815, THOMAS KNOX, Viscount Northland, who, succeeding his father, became Thomas, 2nd Earl of Ranfurly, of Northland House, Dungannon, County Tyrone, Ireland. The 2nd Earl of Ranfurly was born 19 April 1786, and died 21 March 1858.[4] His widow survived him and died 11 July 1866.

Issue of 1. Mary Juliana Stuart and her husband Thomas Knox, 2nd Earl of Ranfurly:

    i. LADY SOPHIA DIANA KNOX, b. 18 December 1815; d. 28 December 1815.
3.   ii. THOMAS KNOX, 3rd Earl of Ranfurly, b. 13 November 1816; d. 20 May 1858, of whom further.
4.   iii. LADY MARY STUART KNOX, b. 21 July 1818; d. 14 May 1903, of whom further.
5.   iv. LADY LOUISA JULIANA KNOX, b. 9 February 1820; d. 31 March 1896, of whom further.

---

[2] In the last issue of this *Magazine*, p. 94, Mary Juliana Stuart's death date is given as 10 July 1866. *

[3] As reported in Edward Armstrong, ed., *Correspondence Between William Penn and James Logan* . . . (Philadelphia, 1870), I, xxxiii, Louisa Stuart's age and death date on the memorial tablet erected to the memory of her father was 20 December 1823, aged 22 years. However, Francis James Dallett reports that in Cobb's *History of Luton Church*, 323, the date is given as 20 September 1828, aged 22 years.

[4] The 2nd Earl's death was incorrectly given as 26 April 1840, in the last issue of this *Magazine*, p. 94. That date was the date on which his father died and of his succession to the title.

*Page 576, this volume.

v. Lady ELIZABETH HENRIETTA KNOX, b. 5 April 1822; d. unmarried 28 January 1909.

vi. Lady JULIANA CAROLINE FRANCES KNOX, b. 18 February 1825; d. 11 December 1906; m. 15 October 1862, as his 2nd wife, General Sir EDWARD FORESTIER WALKER, Knight Commander of the Bath, of the Manor House, Bushey, Herts., who d. 27 July 1881. No issue.

6. vii. The Honorable WILLIAM STUART KNOX, b. 11 March 1826; d. 15 February 1900, of whom further.

viii. Lady FLORA SOPHIA ANNE KNOX, b. 2 August 1827; d. unmarried 27 February 1905.

ix. The Honorable GRANVILLE HENRY JOHN KNOX, b. 1 August 1829; d. 18 August 1845.

7. x. Lady ADELAIDE HENRIETTA LOUISA HORTENSE KNOX, b. 23 May 1833; d. 28 August 1911,[5] of whom further.

2. WILLIAM STUART, eldest son of Sophia Margaret Penn and her husband, The Honorable and Most Reverend William Stuart, D.D., was born 31 October 1798. He was educated at St. John's College, Cambridge; M.A. 1820. William Stuart was commissioned justice of the peace and deputy lieutenant for Bedfordshire, and was member of Parliament for Armagh, 1820-1826, and for Bedfordshire, 1830-1834. His seats were Aldenham Abbey, Hertford, and Tempsford Hall, Bedford.[6]

He married first, on 8 August 1821, HENRIETTA MARIA SOPHIA POLE, daughter of Admiral Sir Charles Morrice Pole, Baronet, Knight Commander of the Bath. She died 26 July 1853, and he married secondly, 31 August 1854, GEORGINA ADELAIDE FORESTIER WALKER, daughter of General Sir Edward Forestier Walker, who subsequently married Stuart's niece, Lady Juliana Caroline Frances Knox, as his second wife, and as noted above. William Stuart's children were all by his first wife. He died 7 July 1874.

Issue of 2. William Stuart and his 1st wife Henrietta Maria Sophia Pole:

8. i. MARY POLE STUART, b. 3 September 1822; d. 25 January 1852, of whom further.

ii. HENRIETTA POLE STUART, b. 10 February 1824; d. 13 February 1881; m. 4 September 1845, REGINALD THISTLETHWAYTE COCKS, b. 6 October 1816, second son of Thomas Cocks of London. He matriculated 15 May 1834, at Christ Church, Oxford. Issue: 1. AGNITA HENRIETTA COCKS, b. 21 October 1846; d. unmarried 15 September 1938. 2. MARY COCKS. 3. AMABEL MARGARETTA COCKS, b. 27 November 1849; d. 1891; m. 15 December 1874, WILLIAM NEWCOME NICHOLSON, b. 22 May 1833,

---

[5] The death date of Lady Goff is from the probate of her will #1816 of 1911, Principal Registry, Somerset House, London, as confirmed by Mr. Dallett.

[6] On the death in 1869 of the Rev. Thomas Gordon Penn, unmarried and without issue, William Stuart became the "tenant in tail general" to all the remaining property which John, Thomas and Richard Penn had entailed in Pennsylvania.

fourth son of John Armytage Nicholson of Balrath-Burry, County Meath, Ireland. No known issue.

9.   iii. WILLIAM STUART, b. 7 March 1825; d. 21 December 1893, of whom further.
10.   iv. CHARLES POLE STUART, b. 7 May 1826; d. 26 August 1896, of whom further.
     v. CLARENCE ESME STUART, b. 29 May 1827; d. 8 January 1903; m. 16 April 1863, CATHERINE CUNINGHAME, d. 10 March 1901, daughter of Colonel John Cuninghame of Cadell Thornton, Ayr, Scotland. No issue.
    vi. LOUISA POLE STUART, b. in August, 1828; d. 7 January 1858; m. 3 August 1852, as his 1st wife, the REVEREND OLIVER MATTHEW RIDLEY, b. 12 May 1824; d. 10 January 1907. Issue: 1. THE REVEREND OLIVER STUART RIDLEY, b. 8 June 1853; d. unmarried 13 April 1935. 2. HENRY NICHOLSON RIDLEY, b. 10 December 1855; d. 24 October 1956. A Fellow of the Royal Society, he m. in 1941, LILY ELIZA DORAN, daughter of Charles Doran. No issue. 3. THE REVEREND CHARLES WILLIAM RIDLEY, b. 28 December 1856; d. 23 May 1905; m. in 1885, JESSIE DOWDALL, daughter of Thomas Dowdall. No issue. 4. FANNY LOUISA POLE RIDLEY, d. unmarried 22 August 1935. 5. MARY LOUISA RIDLEY, d. 23 March 1935; m. 14 February 1912, LIEUTENANT COLONEL JOHN PERCY GRAVES, Royal Guernsey Artillery, d. 13 February 1916.

3. THOMAS KNOX, 3rd Earl of Ranfurly, eldest son of Thomas Knox, 2nd Earl of Ranfurly, and his wife 1. Mary Juliana Stuart, was born 13 November 1816. He married 10 October 1848, HARRIET RIMINGTON, daughter of James Rimington of Broomhead Hall, Yorkshire. She died 16 March 1891, having survived her husband who died 20 May 1858.

Issue of 3. Thomas Knox, 3rd Earl of Ranfurly,
and his wife Harriet Rimington:

    i. THOMAS GRANVILLE HENRY STUART KNOX, 4th Earl of Ranfurly, b. 28 July 1849; d. unmarried on a shooting expedition in Abyssinia on 10 May 1875. He was a captain in the Grenadier Guards.
    ii. Lady AGNES HENRIETTA SARAH KNOX, b. 19 March 1851; d. 29 December 1921; m. 1 December 1870, NUGENT MURRAY WHITMORE DANIELL, of the Bengal Civil Service, who d. 8 August 1908. No issue.
11.   iii. UCHTER JOHN MARK KNOX, 5th Earl of Ranfurly, b. 14 August 1856; d. 1 October 1933, of whom further.

4. LADY MARY STUART KNOX, second daughter of Thomas Knox, 2nd Earl of Ranfurly, and his wife 1. Mary Juliana Stuart, was born 21 July 1818. She married 20 September 1854, as his second wife, JOHN PAGE READE of Crowe Hall, Suffolk, who was born in 1806 and died 28 March 1880. She died 14 May 1903.

Issue of 4. Lady Mary Stuart Knox and her husband John Page Reade:
    i. EVELYNE HELEN REVELL READE, d. unmarried 24 March 1909.

ii. HUBERT GRANVILLE REVELL READE, b. 28 March 1857; d. unmarried 13 October 1938. He was educated at Eton.

12. iii. RAYMOND NATHANIEL NORTHLAND REVELL READE, b. 16 February 1861, in London; d. 18 October 1943, of whom further.

5. LADY LOUISA JULIANA KNOX, third daughter of Thomas Knox, 2nd Earl of Ranfurly, and his wife 1. Mary Juliana Stuart, was born 9 February 1820. She married 14 August 1839, HENRY ALEXANDER of Forkhill, Armagh, Ireland, who was born 16 February 1803. A barrister-at-law and deputy lieutenant and high sheriff for Armagh in 1856, he died 1 December 1877. His widow died 31 March 1896.

Issue of 5. Lady Louisa Juliana Knox and her husband Henry Alexander:

i. A Daughter, still born, 21 July 1840.

ii. BLANCHE CATHERINE SOPHIA ANNE ALEXANDER, b. 10 December 1841; d. 16 June 1878; m. 4 September 1877, the REVEREND FREDERICK ANTHONY HAMMOND of Lauriston House, Dover, Kent, who d. 1907, son of Colonel Hammond of Lauriston House. No issue.

iii. ALICE MARY JULIANA ALEXANDER, b. 17 August 1843; d. unmarried 13 February 1921.

13. iv. CONSTANCE HENRIETTA GEORGINA ALEXANDER, b. 23 April 1845; d. 16 October 1927, of whom further.

14. v. EMILY LOUISA JANE ALEXANDER, b. 19 August 1850; d. 23 August 1900, of whom further.

vi. GRANVILLE HENRY JACKSON ALEXANDER, b. 26 June 1852; d. 3 September 1930; m. 25 February 1880, DAISY MATTHEWS, d. 20 September 1937, youngest daughter of M. Matthews of San Francisco. Her husband inherited the family estates at Forkhill, Armagh, was deputy lieutenant and justice of the peace for that county, and its high sheriff in 1883. He was commissioned a lieutenant of the 83rd Regiment, and captain of the 3rd Battalion, Royal Irish Fusiliers. No issue.

vii. HENRY NATHANIEL ALEXANDER, b. 7 June 1854; d. 28 January 1923; m. 6 November 1883, MARY STUART ERSKINE, d. 13 May 1928, daughter of Claude Erskine. Henry Alexander joined the Indian Civil Service and was Inspector General of Prisons, Bombay. Issue: 1. CONSTANCE MARY ALEXANDER, b. 2 June 1885; d. unmarried 5 December 1956.

viii. CLAUDE HENRY ALEXANDER, b. 31 May 1856; d. 19 March 1915. A major in the Wiltshire Regiment, he m. 1 October 1896, IRENE CHRISTINE TEMPLIN, d. 25 November 1958, daughter of Colonel William Templin of Lennox Place, Brighton, Sussex. Issue: 1. DOROTHY ALICE ALEXANDER, b. 8 October 1897. Unmarried. 2. ROSEMARY IRENE ALEXANDER, b. 18 December 1900; m. 1 October 1942, as his 2nd wife, COUNT GASTON DRU, who d. 11 August 1945, son of Colonel Dru. No issue. 3. NANCY STUART ALEXANDER, b. 11 September 1902; m. 16 September 1950, as his 2nd wife, REAR ADMIRAL RICHARD ROY WALLACE, Commander of the Order of the British Empire, b. 14 December 1895; d. 24 January 1963. No issue.

ix. RONALD HENRY ALEXANDER, b. 15 August 1858; d. unmarried 2 August 1936, having served in World War I.

15. x. FREDERICK HENRY THOMAS ALEXANDER, b. 30 November 1860; d. 26 September 1921, of whom further.

xi. DUDLEY HENRY BLAYNEY ALEXANDER, b. 13 January 1863; d. unmarried 20 July 1931. Educated at Marlborough, he was adjutant of the 3rd Volunteer Battalion, Bedfordshire Regiment, 1894-1897; private secretary to the Governor General of New Zealand (Earl of Ranfurly), 1897-1904;[7] major of the West Yorkshire Regiment. Received Companion, Order of St. Michael and St. George, 1904. General Staff officer (III), 1914-1919, during World War I. Knight of Grace, Order of St. John of Jerusalem.

16. xii. EDITH ELLEN ALEXANDER, b. 1864; d. 27 May 1892, of whom further.

6. THE HONORABLE WILLIAM STUART KNOX, second son of Thomas Knox, 2nd Earl of Ranfurly, and his wife 1. Mary Juliana Stuart, was born 11 March 1826. He was a major in the 51st Regiment of Foot; honorary colonel of the Mid-Ulster Artillery; deputy lieutenant and justice of the peace for County Tyrone, Ireland, and member of Parliament for Dungannon in 1851-1874. He married 26 August 1856, GEORGINA ROOPER, born in 1832, daughter of John Bonfoy Rooper of Abbots Ripton, Huntingdon. She died 4 November 1926, her husband having predeceased her 15 February 1900.

Issue of 6. Colonel The Honorable William Stuart Knox and his wife Georgina Rooper:

i. VIOLET MARY KNOX, b. 2 March 1864; d. unmarried 23 December 1928.

ii. FLORENCE MAY KNOX, b. 22 July 1865; d. 11 February 1943; m. 14 November 1889, ALBERT GEORGE SHAW, colonel of the late Queen's Royal West Surrey Regiment, of Hurst Grange, Twyford, Bucks. Issue: 1. DOROTHY SHAW, b. 1891; m. December, 1920, MAJOR CHARLES PASKE, 23rd Indian Cavalry, who d. in November, 1953. 2. EILEEN SHAW, b. 1894; m. 10 October 1928, LIEUTENANT WALTER COWAN, Royal Artillery.

17. iii. THOMAS GRANVILLE KNOX, b. 22 March 1868; d. 15 January 1947, of whom further.

7. LADY ADELAIDE HENRIETTA LOUISA HORTENSE KNOX, youngest daughter of Thomas Knox, 2nd Earl of Ranfurly, and his wife 1. Mary Juliana Stuart, was born 23 May 1833. She married 26 September 1850, JOSEPH GOFF, M.A., of Barton Grange, Hertfordshire, who was born 28 October 1817, and died 25 December 1872. In her widowhood, Lady Adelaide Goff lived at Hale Park, Hampshire; she died 28 August 1911.

---

[7] With his cousin, 11. Uchter John Mark Knox, 5th Earl of Ranfurly, then Governor of New Zealand, Major Alexander visited Philadelphia on 17 August 1904, and examined Penn manuscripts and relics at the Historical Society of Pennsylvania.

Issue of 7. Lady Adelaide Henrietta Louisa Hortense Knox and her husband Joseph Goff:

i. JOSEPH GRANVILLE STUART GOFF, b. 7 June 1851; d. unmarried 24 September 1881. He was a lieutenant in the 43rd Regiment, and a justice of the peace.

ii. ADA MARY GOFF, b. 1853; d. unmarried 22 April 1932.

iii. GERALD LIONEL JOSEPH GOFF, b. 8 March 1855; killed in action at Magersfontein, S. Africa, 11 December 1899. Educated at Eton, he was commissioned justice of the peace for Hampshire and Wiltshire. Lieutenant Colonel, 1st Battalion, Argyll and Sutherland Highlanders, he served in the Zulu War, 1879 (medal and clasp), in the Transvaal, 1881, and in the South African War, 1899. He married, as her 1st husband, 23 May 1894, ELLEN MARY CHARLOTTE DUNDAS who d. 23 May 1927, third daughter of Sir Robert Dundas of Arniston, first Baronet. No issue.

iv. BERTRAM LYULPH JOSEPH GOFF, b. 12 July 1857; d. 25 May 1911. He was educated at Eton and was a captain in the Highland Light Infantry and Royal Garrison Regiment. He m. 2 July 1902, HELEN MARIA MACLEOD, eldest daughter of Captain Norman A. Macleod of Orbost, Invernessshire. No issue.

v. CECIL WILLIE TREVOR THOMAS GOFF, b. 26 March 1860; d. unmarried 4 August 1907. He was a major in the East Lancashire Regiment, and Companion of the Distinguished Service Order.

vi. ALGERNON HAMILTON STANNUS GOFF, b. 14 April 1863; d. 20 June 1936. He was educated at Winchester and at the Royal Military Academy, Woolwich. A major in the Royal Field Artillery, he served in South Africa in 1900, and in World War I. Companion, Order of St. Michael and St. George, 1915. Major Goff purchased Standerwick Court, Somerset, in 1919, and sold his father's seat, Hale Park, which he had inherited, in 1920. He m. 24 February 1906, EMILY DORA GREENHILL-GARDYNE, d. 17 September 1915, fifth daughter of Lieutenant Colonel Charles Greenhill-Gardyne. No issue.

18. vii. GWENDOLINE JANE ELIZA GOFF, b. 1869; d. 5 September 1951, of whom further.

8. MARY POLE STUART, eldest child of 2. William Stuart and his wife Henrietta Maria Sophia Pole, was born 3 September 1822. She married 1 August 1843, as his first wife, JONATHAN RASHLEIGH of Menabilly, Cornwall, of Fenitor Court, Devonshire, and of Lissadrone, County Mayo, Ireland. Born 7 January 1820, he was deputy lieutenant and justice of the peace for Cornwall, high sheriff of the same county in 1877, and justice of the peace for Middlesex and Westminster. He died 12 April 1905, his wife Mary Pole (Stuart) Rashleigh having died 25 January 1852.

Issue of 8. Mary Pole Stuart and her husband Jonathan Rashleigh:

19. i. CAROLINE MARY STUART RASHLEIGH, d. 3 January 1880, of whom further.

ii. JONATHAN RASHLEIGH, b. 26 May 1845; d. 8 December 1872; m. 1 November 1870, MARY FRANCIS LABOUCHERE, d. February 1874, daughter of John Labouchere of Broom Hall, Surrey. Jonathan Rashleigh was educated at Harrow. Dying in his father's lifetime, his only son became the heir to Menabilly and all the estates of the family. Issue: 1. JOHN COSMO STUART RASHLEIGH, b. 2 July 1872; d. 8 January 1961. He was educated at Eton and Trinity College, Cambridge; M.A. in 1897, and M.D. in 1904. Justice of the peace for Cornwall, 1912, and for Devon, 1911, high sheriff of Cornwall in 1908, he was lord of many manors but sold Menabilly. He m. 1st, in 1898, GERTRUDE DANIELS, daughter of Henry Daniels; 2nd, 29 August 1921, ELIZABETH EVANS, daughter of William Evans of Cleveland, Yorkshire. She was justice of the peace for Devon in 1937. No issue by either marriage.

iii. ALICE HENRIETTA RASHLEIGH, b. 16 April 1848; d. unmarried in April, 1934.

iv. MARY ANNA RASHLEIGH, d. unmarried 5 August 1905.

20. v. EVELYN WILLIAM RASHLEIGH, b. 6 January 1850; d. 29 April 1926, of whom further.

9. WILLIAM STUART, eldest son of 2. William Stuart and his wife Henrietta Maria Sophia Pole, was born in London, at the house of his grandmother, on 7 March 1825. He inherited and later sold his father's seat, Aldenham Abbey. Called to the Bar at the Inner Temple in 1851, he was justice of the peace for Hertfordshire; justice of the peace and deputy lieutenant and high sheriff for Bedfordshire in 1875; justice of the peace for Huntingdon, member of Parliament for Bedford in 1854-1857, and 1859-1868, and honorary colonel, 3rd Battalion, Bedfordshire Regiment.

He married 13 September 1859, KATHERINE NICHOLSON, eldest daughter of John Armytage Nicholson of Balrath-Burry, County Meath. She died 16 October 1881, and he died 21 December 1893.

Issue of 9. William Stuart and his wife Katherine Nicholson:[8]

i. WILLIAM DUGALD STUART, b. at Southsea, Portsmouth, 18 October 1860; d. 2 April 1922; m. 11 July 1895, MILLICENT HELEN OLIVIA BULKELEY HUGHES, d. 2 February 1933, daughter of Captain G. W. Bulkeley Hughes. Educated at Eton, William Dugald Stuart was commissioned as a second lieutenant in the King's Royal Rifle Corps, promoted to lieutenant 1 July 1881, and to captain 13 November 1889. He served with the Manipore expedition in Burma in 1891 against the Dacoits (medal and clasp), and subsequently against the Chins and Lushais in Upper Burma. He continued to serve in India until 1893, when he was placed on the Reserve of Officers. He was a justice of the peace and honorary lieutenant colonel of the 3rd Battalion of the Bedfordshire Regiment, after having served

---

[8] The birthplaces of their children are given by Mr. Jenkins in "The Family of William Penn," *The Pennsylvania Magazine of History and Biography* (PMHB), XXI (1897), 443.

in it as a major. He saw service in World War I as temporary major of the 14th Battalion, King's Royal Rifle Corps. Major Stuart inherited and lived at Tempsford Hall, Beds., which was burnt down in 1898 but rebuilt, and is now a clinic. During the fire the portion of the elm tree under which William Penn signed the treaty with Indians was badly charred. Pieces of it were afterwards distributed to members of the family. Issue: 1. WILLIAM ESME MONTAGUE STUART, b. 22 December 1895; killed in action in World War I, 7 October 1916.

ii. MARY CHARLOTTE FLORENCE STUART, b. at Kempstone, Beds., 2 May 1863; d. unmarried 31 January 1918. She lived in London.

iii. HENRY ESME STUART, b. at Kempstone, Beds., 15 July 1865; d. 21 August 1905; m. 16 December 1899, EMILY CORNWALL, who d. 28 May 1922, daughter of James Cornwall. Issue: 1. MARGARET ESME SYLVIA STUART, b. 17 November 1902; m. in 1928, JAMES LYLE. 2. WINIFRED HILDA MURIEL STUART, b. 17 November 1902; m. LAWRENCE DESJARDINS. 3. DOROTHY FRANCES IRMA STUART, b. 28 June 1904; m. 11 June 1930, CLIFFORD FRANK BUTCHER, and has issue.

iv. ELIZABETH FRANCES SYBIL STUART, b. at Kempstone, Beds., 20 May 1867; d. unmarried 15 November 1931. She lived at Farleigh Hungerford, near Bath, Somerset.

10. CHARLES POLE STUART, second son of 2. William Stuart and his wife Henrietta Maria Sophia Pole, was born 7 May 1826. A barrister-at-law and justice of the peace for Bedfordshire, he lived at Sandy Mount, Woburn Sands, Bedford. He married 20 March 1860, ANNE SMYTH, born 18 June 1833, eldest daughter of Robert Smyth of Gaybrook, County Westmeath, Ireland. Her husband predeceased her, dying 26 August 1896. She died 19 October 1918.

Issue of 10. Charles Pole Stuart and his wife Anne Smyth:

i. ROBERT ALEXANDER STUART, b. 5 July 1862; d. 30 March 1899, drowned in the *Stella* disaster; m. 6 January 1897, NINA EDITH MARGARET STOKER, b. 1 November 1876; d. 30 January 1963, daughter of the Reverend H. E. Stoker. Issue: 1. ENID FRANCES ANNE STUART, b. 28 November 1897.

21. ii. REGINALD POLE STUART, b. 22 July 1863; d. 20 April 1934, of whom further.

iii. CHARLES DUDLEY STUART, b. 26 October 1864; d. unmarried 13 March 1917.

iv. MAUD FRANCES STUART, d. unmarried 11 March 1889.

v. CONSTANCE MARY STUART, b. 11 July 1866; d. unmarried 1 March 1938. She was a Sister of Mercy, Church of England.

vi. JAMES FRANCIS STUART, b. 16 November 1867; d. 5 July 1876.

vii. RALPH ESME STUART, b. 9 April 1869; d. 27 October 1927. He was a major in the Royal Artillery. He m. 1st, 30 April 1907, BEATRICE KITCHEN, who d. 28 August 1913, daughter of John Kitchen of Scarborough, Yorks., and m. 2nd, 25 February 1919, ELIZABETH THOMPSON, d.

July, 1962, daughter of Samuel Thompson of Muckamore Abbey, County Antrim, Ireland. No issue.

viii. FLORENCE AMABEL STUART, b. 1 November 1870; d. unmarried 4 May 1938. She was also a Sister of Mercy, Church of England.

ix. GRACE HENRIETTA STUART, b. 30 June 1872; d. unmarried 1 June 1955.

x. FREDERICK CLARENCE STUART, b. 5 August 1873; d. 12 October 1879.

xi. KATHERINE EVELYN STUART, b. 18 April 1877; d. 3 May 1887.

11. UCHTER JOHN MARK KNOX, 5th Earl of Ranfurly, and second son of 3. Thomas Knox, 3rd Earl of Ranfurly, and his wife Harriet Rimington, was born 14 August 1856. He was a Privy Councillor, Knight of the Grand Cross of St. Michael and St. George, Knight of the Grand Cross of St. John, and Officer of the Legion of Honor.

A Lord in Waiting from 1895-1897, the 5th Earl of Ranfurly served as Governor General of New Zealand, 1897-1904.[9] He was sworn of the Privy Council of Ireland, 23 August 1905, and of the Privy Council of Northern Ireland, 27 November 1923. From 1915-1919, during World War I he was Director of the Ambulance Corps.

He married 10 February 1880, the HONORABLE CONSTANCE ELIZABETH CAULFEILD, born 30 November 1858, only child of James Alfred Caulfeild, 7th Viscount Charlemont, Companion of the Bath. She died 25 July 1932, and her husband, the 5th Earl, the following year on 1 October 1933.

Issue of 11. Uchter John Mark Knox, 5th Earl of Ranfurly, and his wife the Honorable Constance Elizabeth Caulfeild:

i. LADY ANNETTE AGNES KNOX, b. 21 November 1880; d. 11 July 1886.

22. ii. THOMAS UCHTER CAULFEILD KNOX, Viscount Northland, b. 13 June 1882; d. 1 February 1915, of whom further.

23. iii. LADY CONSTANCE HARRIET STUART KNOX, b. 21 April 1885; d. 29 April 1964, of whom further.

iv. LADY EILEEN MAUD JULIANA KNOX, b. 3 May 1891; m. 1st, 24 November 1914, MAJOR CHARLES LORRAINE CARLOS CLARKE, Royal Bucks Hussars, son of Charles Carlos Clarke. Issue: 1. CHARLES THOMAS ALEXANDER CLARKE, b. in 1915. 2. DIANA CLARKE, b. in 1917; d. without issue 29 December 1949; m. FULKE WALWYN of Saxon House, Lambourne, Berks. Lady Eileen's 1st marriage was dissolved in 1934, and she m. 2nd, 3 August 1935, PETER STANLEY CHAPPELL, only son of Thomas Stanley Chappell of Moreton House, Moreton Morrell, Warwickshire. There is no issue of this marriage.

12. RAYMOND NATHANIEL NORTHLAND REVELL READE, second son of 4. Lady Mary Stuart Knox and her husband John Page Reade, was

---

9 See Note 7 above for mention of his visit to Philadelphia in 1904. For a notice of Penn portraits and memorabilia at his seat, Dungannon Park, County Tyrone, Ireland, see W. M. Conway, "Portraits of Some of the Descendants of William Penn, and Memorials of Him in the Possession of the Earl of Ranfurly," *PMHB*, VIII (1884), 353-362.

born in London 16 February 1861. He was educated at Eton and at the Royal Military School, Sandhurst. Gazetted to the 85th King's Light Infantry in 1880, he served in the Afghan War that year (medal); in the Ashanti Expedition in 1895 (star); the Anam Expedition, Nigeria in 1898 (medal and clasp), and in the South African War (medal and four clasps). He was instituted Companion of the Bath in 1908.

During World War I he was in active service, receiving the British war and victory medals and was made Companion of the Order of St. Michael and St. George in 1918. That year he served on the Inter-allied Military Mission in Greece, and was made Commander of the Greek Order of King George I. Subsequently Commandant of the Royal Military College, Canada, serving in many staff appointments and commanding Divisions, Revell Reade retired as a major general in 1920.

He married 9 June 1894, ROSE FRANCES (SPENCER) GREENWAY, widow of Captain Greenway, and daughter of Colonel Almeric George Spencer. Major General Reade died 18 October 1943.

Issue of 12. Raymond Nathaniel Northland Revell Reade and his wife Rose Frances (Spencer) Greenway:

24.   i. MARY SPENCER REVELL READE, b. 7 August 1897, of whom further.

13. CONSTANCE HENRIETTA GEORGINA ALEXANDER, third daughter of 5. Lady Louisa Juliana Knox and her husband Henry Alexander, was born 23 April 1845. On 3 October 1867, she married COLONEL GREGORY COLQUHOUN GRANT, born in 1835, son of Colquhoun Grant of Kirchirdy, Morayshire, Scotland. Colonel Grant served in the Indian Army and died in 1902. His widow survived him twenty-five years, dying 16 October 1927.

Issue of 13. Constance Henrietta Georgina Alexander and her husband Gregory Colquhoun Grant:

25.   i. STUART COLQUHOUN GRANT, b. 7 February 1873; d. 26 August 1946, of whom further.

     ii. ALAN COLQUHOUN GRANT, b. 1 July 1874; d. unmarried 27 March 1924. He was chief of police at Port Said.

     iii. ROSE VERE GRANT, b. 19 November 1875; d. 3 April 1941; m. 22 July 1909, MAJOR JACK DAVY, b. 1866; d. 24 January 1927. No issue.

14. EMILY LOUISA JANE ALEXANDER, fourth daughter of 5. Lady Louisa Juliana Knox and her husband Henry Alexander, was born 19 August 1850. She married 25 March 1874, ARTHUR MELVILL HOGG, born 20 August 1845. The fourth son of Charles Hogg of Eastwick Park, Surrey, his father was sheriff of Calcutta in 1848, and secretary of

the Bank of Bengal, 1847-1851.   Arthur Melvill Hogg was colonel of the 6th Bombay Cavalry and died 21 November 1901.   His wife had died 23 August 1900.

Issue of 14. Emily Louisa Jane Alexander and her husband Arthur Melvill Hogg:

  i. CONRAD CHARLES HENRY HOGG, b. 4 August 1875; d. unmarried 20 May 1950. He was educated at Bedford and at the Royal Military Academy, Woolwich. Colonel, late Royal Engineers, he served in the South African War, 1900-1902, in World War I, and in the 3rd Afghan War, 1919. He was instituted Companion of the Order of St. Michael and St. George, and Chevalier of the Legion of Honor. He retired from the Army in 1925.

26. ii. PHILIP GRANVILLE HARDINGE HOGG, b. 21 December 1878; d. 17 April 1951, of whom further.

27. iii. BARBARA LOUISA GRANT HOGG, b. 22 May 1881; d. 13 March 1963, of whom further.

  iv. MAUD EDITH HAMMOND HOGG, b. 17 March 1885; d. 4 May 1890.

  v. OLIVER FREDERICK GILLILAN HOGG, b. 22 December 1887, was educated at Bedford and at the Royal Military Academy, Woolwich. Commissioned in the Royal Artillery in 1907, he has held many technical staff appointments and served in both World Wars, retiring as a brigadier in 1946. He holds the Mons Star and Victory medal, the Commander of the Order of the British Empire (1943), and the Order of Polonia Restituta, 3rd class. He is a Fellow of the Society of Antiquaries, of the Royal Historical Society, of the Society of Genealogists and is the compiler of this record. He is also a Fellow of the Royal Society of Arts and of the Royal Geographical Society, and is a Leverhulme Research Fellow.

  He m. 11 February 1919, ELLA HAROLD HALLAM, b. 20 June 1895, elder daughter of Arthur Harold Hallam of Shanghai. Issue: 1. NIUL UCHTRED ALEXANDER HOGG, b. 5 January 1922. Educated at the Royal Navy College, Dartmouth, he entered the Royal Navy in 1939, and served in World War II, being severely injured and invalided out of service. B.A. and M.A., Exeter College, Oxford. He is a barrister-at-law and Assistant Registrar, Her Majesty's Land Registry. He m. 1st, 5 September 1946, JANE HUDDLESTON HUDDLESTON, b. 1 October 1926, daughter of Edward Huddleston. The marriage was dissolved in 1951, and he m. 2nd, 5 February 1966, DORIS FAITH (LISHMAN) HARRYMAN, b. 24 August 1913, daughter of Alfred Lishman and widow of Albert Leslie Harryman. No issue.

15. FREDERICK HENRY THOMAS ALEXANDER, fifth son of 5. Lady Louisa Juliana Knox and her husband Henry Alexander, was born 30 November 1860.   He was a captain in the Leicestershire Regiment and in the Army Pay Corps.   On 7 June 1899, he married BLANCHE BANCROFT, daughter of Lieutenant Colonel W. C. Bancroft of Knellwood, Farnborough, Sussex.   Captain Alexander died 26 September 1921, and his widow 25 November 1931.

Issue of 15. Frederick Henry Thomas Alexander and his wife
Blanche Bancroft:

i. ELIZABETH MAUD ALEXANDER, b. 22 July 1902; d. in October, 1959; m. 12 April 1928, KENNETH EVERS-SWINDELL. Issue: 1. PENELOPE ANN EVERS-SWINDELL, b. 8 December 1930. 2. A Daughter, name unknown.

ii. FREDA ALICE ALEXANDER, b. 1904; d. 25 March 1905.

16. EDITH ELLEN ALEXANDER, youngest daughter of 5. Lady Louisa Juliana Knox and her husband Henry Alexander, was born in 1864. She married 15 August 1891, as his first wife, COLONEL HENRY HERBERT SOUTHEY of the 7th Bombay Lancers, who died 30 October 1926. She had died 27 May 1892.

Issue of 16. Edith Ellen Alexander and her
husband Henry Herbert Southey:

28.　i. EDITH SOUTHEY, b. in 1892; d. 26 June 1955, of whom further.

17. THOMAS GRANVILLE KNOX, only son of 6. Colonel The Honorable William Stuart and his wife Georgina Rooper, was born 22 March 1868. Captain in the 3rd Battalion, Royal West Surrey Regiment, he was also deputy lieutenant and justice of the peace for County Tyrone, Ireland. On 24 February 1897, he married the HONORABLE HARRIET GEORGINA LUCIA AGAR-ELLIS, daughter of Leopold Agar-Ellis, 5th Viscount Clifden. She died 4 July 1928; her husband surviving her, died 15 January 1947.

Issue of 17. Thomas Granville Knox and his wife
the Honorable Harriet Georgina Lucia Agar-Ellis:

i. CONSTANCE GEORGINA KNOX, b. 1898; m. 6 October 1919, DR. HENRY BRAUND, member of the Royal College of Surgeons, who d. 11 April 1954. Issue: 1. A Child, sex unknown, b. July, 1920.

18. GWENDOLINE JANE ELIZA GOFF, youngest child of 7. Lady Adelaide Henrietta Louisa Hortense Knox and her husband Joseph Goff, was born in 1879. She married 12 June 1894, EDWARD SIDNEY WILBRAHAM, born 21 August 1869, second son of Colonel Thomas Wilbraham. In 1936 she succeeded her brother, Algernon Knox, at Standerwick Court, Somerset, and disposed of her interest in the property to her younger son Thomas Wilbraham in 1946. Her husband died 20 December 1939, and she on 5 September 1951.

Issue of 18. Gwendoline Jane Eliza Goff
and her husband Edward Sidney Wilbraham:

29.　i. EDWARD JACK WILBRAHAM, b. 18 November 1895, of whom further.

ii. THOMAS ROGER WILBRAHAM, b. 11 March 1907; d. 14 February 1966; m. 18 December 1945, IRIS JANET HILL, youngest daughter of T. Sarsfield Hill of Calcutta, India. Thomas Wilbraham was educated at Eton, and was a major in the Rifle Brigade. He lived at Standerwick Court until he sold it, and at Woolverton Grange, Somerset. Issue: 1. ANN WILBRAHAM, b. 30 October 1946.

19. CAROLINE MARY STUART RASHLEIGH was the eldest daughter of 8. Mary Pole Stuart and her husband Jonathan Rashleigh. She married 21 November 1867, MAJOR CHARLES POORE LONG who was born in 1834, second son of William Long of Hurt's Hall, Suffolk. He was educated at Harrow and served in the 14th Regiment of Foot. He died 2 November 1871, and his widow 3 January 1880.

Issue of 19. Caroline Mary Stuart Rashleigh
and her husband Charles Poore Long:

    i. MARY ELEANOR LONG, d. 1933; m. April, 1892, JOHN MARTIN LONGE, d. 5 January 1933, second son of the Reverend John Longe, Rector of Sternfield, Suffolk. No issue.

30. ii. WILLIAM EVELYN LONG, b. 10 February 1871; d. 22 January 1944, of whom further.

20. EVELYN WILLIAM RASHLEIGH, youngest child of 8. Mary Pole Stuart and her husband Jonathan Rashleigh, was born 6 January 1850. He married 29 April 1879, JANE ELIZABETH ONLEY, daughter of Onley Savill Onley of Stisted Hall, Essex. Evelyn Rashleigh died 29 April 1926, and his widow on 13 October 1947.

Issue of 20. Evelyn William Rashleigh and his wife Jane Elizabeth Onley:

    i. JONATHAN ONLEY RASHLEIGH, b. 2 June 1880; d. 7 December 1880.

31. ii. WILLIAM STUART RASHLEIGH, b. 17 June 1882, of whom further.

32. iii. JANE HENRIETTA RASHLEIGH, b. 1887, of whom further.

21. REGINALD POLE STUART, second son of 10. Charles Pole Stuart and his wife Anne Smyth, was born 22 July 1863. He was lieutenant colonel of the South Staffordshire Regiment. He married 29 June 1895, HESTER MYBURGH, daughter of Gerhard Myburgh, Consul General of the Netherlands in South Africa. Lieutenant Colonel Stuart died 20 April 1934,[10] and his widow on 30 March 1940.

Issue of 21. Reginald Pole Stuart and his wife Hester Myburgh:

33. i. KATHLEEN ANNE POLE STUART, b. 20 August 1899, of whom further.

---

[10] On the death in 1922 of William Dugald Stuart, son of 9. William Stuart, it is presumed that the title of *Proprietary de jure* passed to his cousin 21. Reginald Pole Stuart. William Dugald Stuart's elder son, William Esme Montague Stuart, who would have succeeded to the title, had died in 1916, unmarried and without issue, and his younger son, Henry Esme Stuart, had predeceased his father in 1905 without male issue.

ii. ROSALIND ESME POLE STUART, b. 28 October 1900. A Ph.D., London
   University, she is unmarried.[11]

22. THOMAS UCHTER CAULFEILD KNOX, Viscount Northland, only
son of 11. Uchter John Mark Knox, 5th Earl of Ranfurly, and his wife
the Honorable Constance Caulfeild, was born 13 June 1882. A captain
in the Coldstream Guards, he was aide-de-camp to the Governor General of New Zealand (his father), 1903-1904, having served in the South
African War (medal and two clasps). He was a Knight of Grace of
the Order of St. John of Jerusalem.

He married 12 June 1912, HILDA SUSAN ELLEN COOPER, younger
daughter of Sir Daniel Cooper, 2nd Baronet, and was killed in action at
Cuinchy in World War I, 1 February 1915.

*Issue of 22. Thomas Uchter Caulfeild Knox, Viscount Northland,
and his wife Hilda Susan Ellen Cooper:*

   i. THOMAS DANIEL KNOX, 6th Earl of Ranfurly, b. 29 May 1913; m. 17
      January 1939, HERMIONE POYNTZ LLEWELLYN, eldest daughter of
      Griffith Robert Poyntz Llewellyn of Llanvapley Court, Abergavenny, Mon-
      mouth. She is Commander of the Order of St. John of Jerusalem. The 6th
      Earl was educated at Eton and Trinity College, Cambridge, M.A. He was
      aide-de-camp to the Governor General of Australia, 1936-1938, and served
      in World War II, being taken prisoner. A Knight of Grace of the Order
      of St. John of Jerusalem, he was Governor and Commander-in-Chief of the
      Bahamas, 1953-1956. He was instituted Knight Commander of the Order
      of St. Michael and St. George. Issue: 1. LADY CAROLINE KNOX, b. 11 De-
      cember 1948.

   ii. THE HONORABLE EDWARD PAUL UCHTER KNOX, b. 23 May 1914; d.
       unmarried 11 December 1935.

23. LADY CONSTANCE HARRIET STUART KNOX, second daughter of
11. Uchter John Mark Knox, 5th Earl of Ranfurly, and his wife the
Honorable Constance Elizabeth Caulfeild, was born 21 April 1885. She
was Woman of the Bedchamber of her Majesty Queen Mary, 1937-1953,
and Lady-in-Waiting to H.R.H. the Duchess of Kent from 1953 until
her death. She was made Commander of the Royal Victorian Order in
1953, and Dame of Justice of the Order of St. John of Jerusalem.[12]

Lady Constance Knox married 7 November 1905, MAJOR EVELYN
MILNES-GASKELL, born 19 October 1877, eldest son of the Right Honorable Charles George Milnes-Gaskell of Thornes House, Yorkshire, and

---

[11] On 13 October 1965, when she participated in the dedication at Harrisburg of the William Penn
Memorial Museum and Archives Building, she was described as the *Proprietary de jure,* apparently in error.
She does hold, however, certain Philadelphia quit rents which have descended to her from her Penn ancestors.

[12] When she visited Philadelphia in January, 1934, a reception in her honor was given at the Historical
Society of Pennsylvania, for a notice of which see *The Philadelphia Inquirer,* Sunday, 28 January 1934.

Wenlock Abbey, Salop. He was educated at Eton and Trinity College, Cambridge, M.A. 1899. Major in the Queen's Own Yorkshire Dragoons, he was deputy lieutenant and justice of the peace for Yorkshire. He died 14 September 1931, and Lady Constance Milnes-Gaskell on 29 April 1964.

Issue of 23. *Lady Constance Harriet Stuart Knox and her husband Evelyn Milnes-Gaskell:*

i. MARY JULIANA MILNES-GASKELL, b. 2 July 1906; m. 12 July 1934, LEWIS MOTLEY, younger son of Major Lewis Motley of Spen Hill, Far Headingly, near Leeds, Yorkshire. Issue: 1. CHRISTOPHER STEVEN MOTLEY, b. 7 December 1935. 2. MICHAEL JOHN MOTLEY, b. 21 October 1937. 3. TIMOTHY BROOKE MOTLEY, b. 22 December 1941. 4. CHARLES OSBURN MOTLEY, b. 15 December 1943.

ii. CHARLES THOMAS MILNES-GASKELL, b. 5 November 1908; d. 5 November 1943, killed in an aeroplane accident while on active service in World War II. Educated at Eton and the Royal Military College, Sandhurst, he was lieutenant colonel of the Coldstream Guards. He m. 12 November 1936, LADY ETHEL PATRICIA HARE, elder daughter of Richard Granville Hare, 4th Earl of Listowel. Issue: 1. JAMES MILNES-GASKELL, b. 13 November 1937. 2. ANDREW MILNES-GASKELL, b. 20 November 1939. 3. TOM MILNES-GASKELL, b. 2 March 1942.

24. MARY SPENCER REVELL READE, only child of 12. Raymond Nathaniel Northland Revell Reade and his wife Rose Frances Spencer, was born 7 August 1897. She was commissioned justice of the peace (1937), and Commander of the Order of the British Empire (1953). On 1 January 1918, she married SIR FERGUS GRAHAM, 5th Baronet, of Netherby, Cumberland. Born 10 March 1893, he was educated at Eton and Christchurch College, Oxford, B.A. 1914; M.A. 1920. Commissioned captain in the Irish Guards, he served in World War I and was severely wounded.

He was member of Parliament for North Cumberland, 1926-1935; private secretary to the Minister of Pensions, 1933-1935, and to the Postmaster General, 1935. Member of Parliament for Darlington, 1951-1959, he is justice of the peace and deputy lieutenant for Cumberland, and Knight Commander of the British Empire.

Issue of 24. *Mary Spencer Revell Reade and her husband Captain Sir Fergus Graham, 5th Baronet:*

i. CHARLES SPENCER RICHARD GRAHAM, b. 16 July 1919; m. 5 February 1944, SUSAN SURTEES, only daughter of Major Robert Lambton Surtees, Officer of the Order of the British Empire, of Redworth Cottage, Littlestone-on-Sea, Kent. A major in the Scots Guards, Charles Graham served in World War II, and in Malaya, 1949-1950. He was high sheriff of Cumberland in 1955. Issue: 1. JAMES FERGUS SURTEES GRAHAM, b. 29 July 1946. 2.

MALISE CHARLES RICHARD GRAHAM, b. 19 September 1948. 3. SUSANNAH ANNE MARY GRAHAM, b. 8 May 1951.

    ii. CYNTHIA MARY GRAHAM, b. 13 November 1923; d. 13 January 1927.

25. STUART COLQUHOUN GRANT, eldest son of 13. Constance Henrietta Georgina Alexander and her husband Colonel Gregory Colquhoun Grant, was born 7 February 1873. He served in the Army in the South African War, 1900-1902, and in World War I, 1914-1915 (Star and Victory Medal). He received the Order of the British Empire in 1919, and the Territorial Decoration. He married 24 January 1906, GRACE POTTER, daughter of Frederick Potter of New York. He died 26 August 1946.

Issue of 25. Stuart Colquhoun Grant and his wife Grace Potter:

34.   i. PAMELA GRANT, b. 23 December 1906, of whom further.

26. PHILIP GRANVILLE HARDINGE HOGG, second son of 14. Emily Louisa Jane Alexander, and her husband Arthur Melvill Hogg, was born 21 December 1878. Educated at Bedford and at the Royal Military Academy, Woolwich, he was a lieutenant colonel in the Royal Engineers, serving in South Africa from 1900-1902, and in World War I. He was a Companion of the Distinguished Service Order. He married 29 July 1905, GERALDINE PETLEY, born 10 October 1883, daughter of Captain E. W. Petley, R.N. Lieutenant Colonel Hogg died 17 April 1951.

Issue of 26. Philip Granville Hardinge Hogg
and his wife Geraldine Petley:

35.   i. CECILY IRENE BARBARA HOGG, b. 14 June 1906, of whom further.
    ii. GRANVILLE ALEXANDER HOGG, b. 28 September 1907; d. 18 March 1961; m. 1st, a Russian lady who d. January, 1967. The marriage was dissolved and he m. 2nd, 30 March 1957, BARBARA HARGREAVES. No issue.
36.   iii. PEGGY PATRICIA O'NEILL HOGG, b. 10 October 1911, of whom further.

27. BARBARA LOUISA GRANT HOGG, eldest daughter of 14. Emily Louisa Jane Alexander and her husband Arthur Melvill Hogg, was born 22 May 1881. She married 11 January 1908, ARTHUR ANDERSON MCNEIGHT, born 9 July 1880. A colonel in the Indian Medical Service, he died 14 August 1966, his wife having predeceased him on 13 March 1963.

Issue of 27. Barbara Louisa Grant Hogg and
her husband Arthur Anderson McNeight:

    i. OLIVE MAUREEN MCNEIGHT, b. 10 November 1912; d. 8 September 1961; m. 17 October 1939, GEORGE KENNETH DONALD, d. 1 October 1961, second son of Sir John Donald, Knight Commander of the Order of the

Indian Empire, Companion of the Order of the Star of India. Issue: 1. JEAN MAUREEN DONALD, b. 22 February 1944; m. at Battle Church, 29 July 1967, JOHN PETER FITZGERALD, younger son of Maurice Corbin Fitzgerald of the Bungalow, Avenue House, Belsize Park Gardens, London, N. W. 3. 2. HEATHER LYNNE DONALD, b. 19 March 1946.

28. EDITH SOUTHEY, only child of 16. Edith Ellen Alexander and her husband Henry Herbert Southey, was born in 1892. She married 29 April 1916, LIEUTENANT COMMANDER EUSTACE HALLIFAX of the Royal Naval Air Service, son of Admiral Hallifax. She died 26 June 1955.

Issue of 28. Edith Southey and her husband Eustace Hallifax:

i. PETER JOHN DE COURCY HALLIFAX, b. 9 March 1917; m. 19 December 1953, in Blenheim, New Zealand, HELEN SCOTT JOHNSTONE, b. 15 January 1924. Issue: 1. CHARLOTTE VANESSA JANE HALLIFAX, b. 4 January 1955. 2. RICHARD GRANVILLE DE COURCY HALLIFAX, b. 30 September 1957.

ii. MICHAEL EUSTACE HALLIFAX, b. 18 September 1919; m. 11 December 1942, ELIZABETH HOWARTH, daughter of Frederick Howarth. Issue: 1. GUY STUART HALLIFAX, b. 16 October 1949. 2. CLIVE ALEXANDER HALLIFAX, b. 13 October 1951.

iii. PAMELA EDITH HALLIFAX, b. 30 June 1922; m. 15 May 1945, MICHAEL ROLAND LEAHY, b. 15 September 1919. A major in the Royal Artillery, he is a Member of the Order of the British Empire and holds the Military Cross. He retired from the Army in 1958. Issue: 1. CHRISTOPHER MICHAEL LEAHY, b. 8 March 1947. 2. ANTHONY JOHN HALLIFAX LEAHY, b. 24 March 1949. 3. JONATHAN EDMUND LEAHY, b. 22 September 1950. 4. PHILIPPA SARAH LEAHY, b. 14 June 1953.

29. EDWARD JACK WILBRAHAM, elder son of 18. Gwendoline Jane Eliza Goff and her husband Edward Sidney Wilbraham, was born 18 November 1895. Educated at Eton, he is a major in the Rifle Brigade, and holds the Military Cross. He married at the Church of St. Martin's-in-the-Fields, Chestnut Hill, Philadelphia, 24 September 1927, EVELYN MARTIN, elder daughter of Carl Neidhard Martin of Llewellyn Farm, Bryn Mawr, Pennsylvania, and his wife Aline S. Taylor.[13]

Issue of 29. Edward Jack Wilbraham and his wife Evelyn Martin:

i. ELIZABETH JOAN WILBRAHAM, b. 12 August 1928; m. 24 September 1949, CAPTAIN GEOFFREY ERNOL SPARROW, Rifle Brigade (Military Cross), only son of Lieutenant Colonel W. G. K. S. Sparrow of Birtles Old Hall, Chelford, Cheshire. Issue: 1. GEOFFREY RANDALL JOHN SPARROW, b. 14 August 1951. 2. JUSTIN MAURICE ANDREW SPARROW, b. 12 June 1953. 3. PIERS CHRISTOPHER MARTIN SPARROW, b. 15 March 1958.

[13] For an account of their wedding, see *The Philadelphia Inquirer*, Sunday, 25 September 1927. According to that account, the newly married couple expected to take up residence at 7 Cheltenham Terrace, London.

ii. MARTIN JOHN WILBRAHAM, b. 4 June 1931; m. 1 December 1964, the HONORABLE CATHERINE MARY SIDNEY, b. 20 October 1942, second daughter of William Philip Sidney, 1st Viscount De L'Isle and 6th Baron De L'Isle and Dudley. Issue: 1. ALEXANDER JOHN WILBRAHAM, b. 22 October 1965.

30. WILLIAM EVELYN LONG, son of 19. Caroline Mary Stuart Rashleigh and her husband Charles Poore Long, was born 10 February 1871. He was educated at Eton and at Trinity Hall, Cambridge. He inherited and lived at Hurt's Hall, Suffolk, was justice of the peace for that county and its high sheriff in 1914. He married 22 February 1898, MURIEL HESTER WENTWORTH, youngest daughter of Thomas Frederick Charles Vernor Wentworth of Wentworth Castle, Yorkshire. He died 22 January 1944.

Issue of 30. William Evelyn Long and his wife Muriel Hester Wentworth:

i. WILLIAM GEORGE LONG, b. 28 March 1899. Educated at Eton and at Trinity College, Cambridge, he served in both World Wars and lives at Hurt's Hall.
ii. ALINE HESTER LONG, b. 25 January 1906; m. 27 June 1928, MAJOR HUGH FRANCIS TRAVERS ALDOUS, Royal Engineers, b. 30 September 1900, second son of Hugh Graham Aldous of Gedding Hall, Bury St. Edmunds, Suffolk. The marriage was dissolved in 1938. Issue: 1. EVELYN FRANCES ALDOUS, b. 26 March 1930; d. 24 June 1930. 2. JUDITH ALINE ALDOUS, b. 5 November 1934. 3. HUGH WILLIAM ALDOUS, b. 21 December 1935.
iii. MOYRA EVELYN LONG, b. 18 June 1908; d. 11 May 1923.
iv. LOUISA LONG, b. 12 November 1909; m. 22 January 1938, CAPTAIN ALAN WALMESLEY, Royal Welsh Fusiliers, who holds the Military Cross. No issue.

31. WILLIAM STUART RASHLEIGH, second son of 20. Evelyn William Rashleigh and his wife Jane Elizabeth Onley, was born 17 June 1882. He is an associate member of the Institute of Civil Engineering, and a justice of the peace for Cornwall. He married 2 September 1913, DOROTHY FRANCES HOWELL, daughter of Francis Butler Howell of Lostwithiel, Cornwall.

Issue of 31. William Stuart Rashleigh and his wife
Dorothy Frances Howell:

i. JONATHAN RASHLEIGH, b. 9 July 1914; d. September, 1914.
ii. GWENDOLINE OENONE RASHLEIGH, b. 4 July 1915; m. ARTHUR FORBES JOHNSON, Royal Air Force (Distinguished Flying Cross), and has issue.
iii. DAPHNE RASHLEIGH, b. 10 June 1916; m. 23 August 1946, MAJOR

ARTHUR HENRY REDE BUCKLEY, Royal Marines (Officer of the Order of the British Empire), and has issue.

iv. MORWENNA RASHLEIGH, b. 14 May 1917; m. 16 December 1940, LIEUTENANT PETER CROOME, Royal Navy, and has issue.

v. WILLIAM FRANCIS RASHLEIGH, b. 4 January 1920; drowned at Fowey, Cornwall, 25 June 1926.

vi. JENNIFER MARY RASHLEIGH, b. 21 March 1921; m. 1st, 29 September 1939, SQUADRON LEADER MICHAEL LAWSON-SMITH. Issue: 1. ANTHONY MICHAEL LAWSON-SMITH, b. 23 December 1940. The marriage was dissolved in 1947, and she m. 2nd, 26 January 1948, PETER CARELTON RASHLEIGH, son of Dr. Hugh George Rashleigh, and has further issue: 2. HUGH CARLETON RASHLEIGH, b. 4 March 1950.

vii. PHILIP STUART RASHLEIGH, b. 15 November 1924.

viii. HONOR RASHLEIGH, b. 18 August 1927.

32. JANE HENRIETTA RASHLEIGH, youngest daughter of 20. Evelyn William Rashleigh and his wife Jane Elizabeth Onley, was born in 1887. She married 8 August 1914, HARRY RASHLEIGH, born 22 May 1880, third son of Sir Colman Battie Rashleigh, 3rd Baronet. Harry Rashleigh served in both World Wars and was a justice of the peace for Cornwall. He died 26 April 1950.

Issue of 32. Jane Henrietta Rashleigh and her husband Harry Rashleigh:

i. ELIZABETH RASHLEIGH, b. 18 May 1915.

ii. MARY VIVIEN RASHLEIGH, b. 9 September 1917; m. 23 January 1941, COMMANDER PHILIP JOSEPH KIDD, Royal Navy, second son of Hugh Kidd of Weybourne Holt, Norfolk, and has issue.

iii. SIR HARRY EVELYN BATTIE RASHLEIGH, 5th Baronet, b. 17 May 1923; m. 8 June 1954, HONORA ELIZABETH SNEYD, only daughter of George Stuart Sneyd of The Watch House, Downderry, Cornwall. Sir Harry Rashleigh was educated at Wellington. Issue: 1. SUSANNA JANE RASHLEIGH, b. 19 April 1955. 2. FRANCES ELIZABETH RASHLEIGH, b. 12 July 1956. 3. RICHARD HARRY RASHLEIGH, b. 8 July 1958.

iv. PETER RASHLEIGH, b. 21 September 1924; m. 4 December 1949, LOLA EDWARDS, of New South Wales, Australia. Issue: 1. MARGARET ANNE RASHLEIGH, b. 16 May 1950. 2. EDWARD HARRY RASHLEIGH, b. 28 November 1952; d. January, 1953. 3. BETTINE JANE RASHLEIGH, b. 11 October 1954. 4. JIM OWEN RASHLEIGH, b. 2 April 1956.

33. KATHLEEN ANNE POLE STUART, elder daughter of 21. Reginald Pole Stuart and his wife Hester Myburgh, was born 20 August 1899. The heir-general of the Stuart family, she married 7 July 1926, FREDERICK ROBERT WYNNE, Group Captain, Royal Air Force, born in 1895, son of Frederick Edward Wynne. He served in World War I, 1915-1917, with the South Wales Borderers in Mesopotamia; from 1917-1919

with the Royal Air Force in Egypt, Palestine and Syria; wing commander, 1937; group captain, 1940; retired in 1945. He was made Member of the British Empire, 1922.

Issue of 33. Kathleen Anne Pole Stuart and her husband Frederick Robert Wynne:

i. LUCY ELIZABETH ANNE WYNNE, b. 17 May 1930; m. 14 January 1961, ALAN TURNER.

ii. FREDERICK OWEN STUART WYNNE, b. 17 June 1933; m. 6 September 1955, SUSAN SHEILA BUSHELL, daughter of Jack Reginald Bushell (Distinguished Flying Medal). Issue: 1. OWEN CHRISTOPHER WYNNE, b. 30 August 1959.

iii. ALTHEA KATHLEEN WYNNE, b. 6 October 1936; m. 1 September 1961, PHILIP DRESMAN. Issue: 1. RUTH KATHLEEN DRESMAN, b. 11 December 1962. 2. REBECCA DRESMAN, b. 31 January 1963. 3. JAMES BARNABAS DRESMAN, b. 5 March 1966.

34. PAMELA GRANT, only child of 25. Stuart Colquhoun Grant and his wife Grace Potter, was born 23 December 1906. She married first, 9 April 1930, COLONEL GORDON CALTHROP THORNE, Companion of the Distinguished Service Order. He died 3 March 1942, and she married secondly, 1 August 1945, KENT GALBRAITH COLWELL. Her present residence is Morristown, New Jersey. There is no issue of the second marriage.

Issue of 34. Pamela Grant and her 1st husband Gordon Calthrop Thorne:

i. JENNIFER CLARE THORNE, b. 22 September 1931; m. 14 September 1957, MALCOLM SCULLY HAYDEN. Issue: 1. CHRISTOPHER SCULLY HAYDEN, b. 20 October 1963. 2. ELIZABETH GRACE HAYDEN, b. 28 January 1965.

ii. FREDERICK GORDON POTTER THORNE, b. 18 July 1935; m. 8 November 1957, SUSAN WHITTLESEY, daughter of Robert Taylor Whittlesey. Issue: 1. GORDON POTTER THORNE, b. 11 October 1959. 2. DAVID WHITTLESEY THORNE, b. 12 October 1960. 3. STUART KIMBALL THORNE, b. 14 March 1962.

35. CECILY IRENE BARBARA HOGG, elder daughter of 26. Philip Granville Hardinge Hogg and his wife Geraldine Petley, was born 14 June 1906. She married 5 February 1931, ROBERT B. WOODS, lieutenant-colonel in the Royal Artillery, born 13 May 1900, son of Ernest Woods of Liphook, Hampshire.

Issue of 35. Cecily Irene Barbara Hogg and her husband Robert B. Woods:

i. FAITH WOODS, b. 30 March 1934; m. 19 June 1954, DAVID KENNETH

TIPPETT, born in 1927, son of Colonel Tippett. Issue: 1. Louisa Clare Tippett, b. 19 July 1956. 2. Piers Robert David Tippett, b. 14 September 1957.

36. Peggy Patricia O'Neill Hogg, younger daughter of 26. Philip Granville Hardinge Hogg and his wife Geraldine Petley, was born 10 October 1911. She married 7 December 1932, as his first wife, Douglas Creyke Maurice of Manton Grange, Marlborough, Wiltshire. The marriage was dissolved.

Issue of 36. Peggy Patricia O'Neill Hogg
and her husband Douglas Creyke Maurice:

i. TESSA O'NEILL MAURICE, b. 1 August 1934; m. 25 June 1955, DAVID KINGSLEY OLIPHANT, son of Lieutenant Colonel K. I. P. Oliphant of Fittleton, Netheravon, Wiltshire. Issue: 1. Bruce Kingsley Oliphant, b. 3 April 1957. 2. Anthony David Oliphant, b. 24 October 1958. 3. James Robert Oliphant, b. 20 May 1962.

Margaret, Marchioness of Carnarvon

Contributed by
Francis James Dallett, f.g.s.p., f.a.s.g.

Margaret Penn, daughter of Admiral Sir William Penn, married Anthony Lowther, and had among other issue a daughter Margaret (b. 1667/8-1719/20), who married Benjamin Poole, as noted in the last issue of this *Magazine*, page 78. The Pooles had issue a daughter Margaret who married 1st, John Keck, and 2nd, John Nicol (Nichol) of Minchenden House, Southgate, Middlesex. They in turn had issue an only daughter and heir, Margaret Nicol, b. *ca.* 1736, who, "with £150,000," married 22 March 1753, at the Church of St. George, Hanover Square, London, James Brydges, b. 16 December 1731, Duke of Chandos and Marquess of Carnarvon, Earl of Carnarvon and Viscount Milton, Baron Chandos of Sudeley, *de jure* Lord Kinloss and a Baronet. He was member of Parliament for Winchester and Radnorshire, and Lord Steward of the Household from 1783 until his death at Tunbridge Wells, Kent, 29 September 1789. He was buried the following 10 October at Whitchurch, Middlesex. His wife Margaret Nicol had died without issue at Southgate 14, and was buried, as the Marchioness of Carnarvon, 29 August 1768 at Whitchurch, Middlesex. Administration on her estate was granted in the Prerogative Court of Canterbury 8 September 1768. She attained the highest rank of any descendant of Admiral Sir William Penn. (*The Complete Peerage* [London, 1913], III, 132-133.)

Corrigenda[*]

Brigadier Hogg notes that several errors inadvertently appeared in his account of the Stuart branch of the Penn family which appeared in the last issue of this *Magazine*:

Page 156, 21 lines from the bottom: The death of Daisy Matthews was 20 September 1939, *not* 20 September 1937.

Page 157, line 6: Dudley Henry Blayney Alexander died 30 July 1931, *not* 20 July 1931.

Page 160, lines 9, 11 and 18: Read *Kempston* for Kempstone.

Page 163, 3 lines from the bottom: Read *Lieutenant-General* W. C. Bancroft, *not* Lieutenant Colonel.

Page 164, 8 lines from the bottom: Edward Sidney Wilbraham was born 12 August 1860, *not* 21 August 1869.

Page 172, 11 lines from the bottom: Gordon Potter Thorne was born 11 October 1958, *not* 11 October 1959.

Brigadier Hogg also points out that until the Statute of Westminster, defining the status of dominions, came into force in 1930, the Dominions of the British Empire did not have complete independence, and that the King's representative in colonial territories was a governor, not a governor-general. Since Lord Ranfurly served in New Zealand between 1897-1904, before the enactment of the Statute, he was only the Governor, *not* the Governor General, as incorrectly stated on page 157, line 18, page 161, line 14, and on page 166, line 6.

Mr. Dallett notes that according to *Pennsylvania Archives*, 2nd Series, XIX, 410, there was a fifth child, John, born to William and Frances (Bradshaw) Assheton, who was deceased by 27 10m 1703, and who was omitted in the account of that family in the No. 2 issue of Volume XXV, 122, of this *Magazine*.

---

*For pp. 122, 156, 157, 160, 161, 163, 164, 166, and 172 see pp. 621, 635, 636, 639, 640, 642, 643, 645, and 651, this volume.

Notes on William Penn's Relatives

Hannah Benner Roach, F.G.S.P., F.A.S.G.

WILLIAM PENN, "son of George Penn late of the fforest of Brayden in the County of Wilts gent Deceased," was bequeathed £10 in the 1670 will of Admiral Sir William Penn.[1] He was the Admiral's first cousin, son of the Admiral's uncle George Penn who was a brother of Giles Penn, the Admiral's father.

William Penn, son of George, died testate in Ireland in 1676. His will appears to have been lost when the Public Record Office in Dublin was burned in 1922. But among the Albert Cook Myers Papers on deposit in the Chester County Historical Society at West Chester, Pa., fortunately is a short abstract of the will, made by Mr. Myers before the first World War. His abstract[2] follows:

> Will of William Penn of Kingsalle, Co. Cork, Ireland, "taken Sicke in Boddey" [dated] 27 April 1676 . . . "to Amey Penne my dafter" £20 "and on Bed" & [furniture?] & 2 plates to be paid within 3 months of her day of marriage. To Margret Penn, "my dafter £20 & 1 Bed & 2 pewter plates" 3 months before marriage. "To James Penne my son" £10 "To William Penn my son" £50 "which is due mee from the Treasury office in London ffor Sallery & £60 more due from the office of Ordinance wch was disbursed by mee ffor his Maties youse ffor [*illegible*] rest at Kinsalle." To s^{d} W P "2 shuts of clothes" & "my Buffe Dublett" & "all such money as is due to mee from William Penn Esqr" & "a Buffe Bellt wth silver Buckels & one Sworde & on Scarffe of sillke with gould & silver" [illegible] & "2 pair of sillke stockings" & "my silver watch" 2 fowling pieces a case of small pistols, "on cloke & a longe coate & on hatte" etc. Rest of goods to "Joane Penn my wiffe" [my] extrx.
>
> Witt: Will: Bishop   /s/ Wm Penn
> Probated 21 July 1676

This will adds a new dimension to the Founder William Penn's relatives, but Mr. Myers found only one other item. In the Public Record Office in Dublin, among the Marriage License Bonds for the Diocese of

---

[1] For a full transcript of the Admiral's will see Brigadier Oliver F. G. Hogg, "Further Light on the Ancestry of William Penn," published by the Society of Genealogists in London in 1964. An abstract is in J. Henry Lea, "Genealogical Gleanings, Contributory to a History of the Family of Penn," in *The Pennsylvania Magazine of History and Biography*, XIV (1890), 171. *

[2] Portions of this abstract are not legible, and his use of quotation marks is erratic, but is presented in the text above as he wrote it; see Albert Cook Myers Collection, XLIX, 136.

*See *Genealogies of Pennsylvania Families: From The Pennsylvania Magazine of History and Biography* (Baltimore: Genealogical Publishing Co., Inc., 1981), 571.

Cork and Ross, he noted the entry: Amy Penn and Richard Clarkson, 1681.

Admiral Sir William Penn also bequeathed money to other relatives, among them his nephew William Markham, to whom he left £10 sterling, his nephew George Markham, to whom he devised £5 sterling, and to his "Cosin Elianore Keene The yearly summe of six pounds sterling to be paid unto her yearly during her life . . . by quarterly payments." Among the Penn Papers at the Historical Society of Pennsylvania, is a Cash Book kept by William Penn's steward, Philip Ford, which lists itemized expenses of his employer during the years 1672 to 1680. Among the items in this book are entries of payments made in accordance with the Admiral's will, and of miscellaneous payments to other relatives:

6 9m [Nov.] 1672 To Cash pd will Markeham in full a legacy left his son Geo: [3] per S^r W P £5
7 3m [May] 1673 To Cash pd Eliz: Jones [4] per order £1
22 3m 1673 To Cash pd will Markham per ord^r 10s.
20 4m [June] 1673 To Cash pd will Markeham in p^t R Penns acc^t £2 10s.
16 7m [Sept.] 1673 To Cash pd will Markeham in full £2 10s.
9 11m [Jan.] 1678[/9] To Cash pd will Browne in full £3 due Elliner Keene [5]
7 12m [Feb.] 1678/9 To Cash pd Rich Vicridge on Ellin^r Keenes Acct £4
11 7m [Sept.] 1679 To Cash pd thy Cousen [6] Markham £6
17 11m [Jan.] 1679/80 To Cash pd Richard Vickeridge for Widdow Keene £8

Little is known of George Markham, legatee under the will of the Admiral, and brother of William Markham who became Penn's lieutenant governor in America. There is a distinct possibility, however, that George may have come over in 1699 when the Proprietor, accompanied by his new secretary, James Logan, arrived in Philadelphia for his second visit. Immediately after their arrival, Logan opened a Cash Book of the Proprietor's expenses and moneys received. In this Cash Book, now at the American Philosophical Society in Philadelphia, are entries showing payments to George Markham:

[3] This entry provides indisputable proof of the father of George and his brother William Markham. An earlier item, among the Admiral's papers in the Penn Manuscripts, Private Correspondence, I, 7, in the Historical Society of Pennsylvania (HSP), also refers to the elder William Markham: 1668 July 22 paid Wm Markham £50.

[4] It is probable that Elizabeth Jones was the sister of William Penn of Kinsale, and widow of George Jones of Grittenham, Wilts. See *The Pennsylvania Genealogical Magazine* (PGM), XXV, (1967), 73. (Page 555, this volume.)

[5] She was the Admiral's "Cosin" who had married Edward Keene in 1635, and like Elizabeth Jones, was a first cousin once removed of the Founder.

[6] Undoubtedly this was the Founder's own first cousin, later his deputy governor in Pennsylvania.

22   4m [June] 1700   By Geo: Markham Exp[s] on y[e] Barge &c 14s.
24   4m 1700   By Geo: Markham for his voy: to Pennsb[y] 12s.
16   5m [July] 1700   To G. Markham laid out on y[e] Barge 6s. 6d.
 3 10m [Dec.] 1700   By Boatswain Markham in p[t] £5
12 11m [Jan.] 1700/01   By Boatswain Markham £5

No further entries in his name appear in the Cash Book, and no other record of him in Pennsylvania has been found; it is probable that he left the province.

Another "relation" of the Proprietor was Martha Durant who was also a "cousin" of Robert Assheton. To supplement the brief account of her, given in this *Magazine* in Volume XXV (1967), 127, may now be added the following information.*

It seems that after the death of her husband, John Durant, which apparently occurred prior to March 1702,[7] she promptly married a man named Joyce or Joice who was deceased by December 1712.[8] She herself was dead by 4 9m (November) 1713, for James Logan on that date made the following entry in his account book: [9]

The Prop[rs] prop[r] Acc[t] D[r] to Cash £1.8.4 paid towards y[e] funeral charges of his Kinswoman Martha Joyce (formerly Durant) Viz: Given her daughter Martha to buy sundries 6/3; p[d] Geo: Painter for 3 Gallons of wine at 3/9 & 6[d] of Sugar at 7[d] is 14/9. paid the woman that laid her out and attended the funeral & for ale 7/4, in all £1.8.4.

[7] "Minutes of the Board of Property," *Pennsylvania Archives*, 2nd Series, XIX, 283.

[8] A survey of land in Charlestown Twp., Chester Co., for "M. Durant als Joice," was returned into the Surveyor General's office 12 11m (Jan.) 1702/3, for which see Taylor Papers, IX, 1870, 1871, in HSP; *Pennsylvania Archives*, 2nd Series, XIX, 541.

[9] Pennsylvania Journal, 1712-1732, Penn Manuscripts, HSP.

*Page 626, this volume.

THE PERKINS FAMILY, A SKETCH OF INTER-COLONIAL MIGRATION.

CONTRIBUTED BY THE LATE MISS EMILY RITCHIE PERKINS.*

IT is not the purpose of this article to speculate upon the degree of relationship between the early colonists of the Perkins name in New England. It has been supposed, and frequently stated in print, that John Perkins of Ipswich, Massachusetts, Abraham and Isaac Perkins of Hampton, New Hampshire, were brothers, and cousins of the Rev. William Perkins of Topsfield, Massachusetts, and all remotely related to that famous non-conformist divine, Rev. William Perkins, who, living in the reign of Elizabeth, 1558-1603, was a fellow of Christ's College, Cambridge, and an author of much repute among the early fathers of New England. Somewhat recent investigation has, however, shown that, the three first named colonists were not brothers, though the latter two doubtless were, and cousins of the former.

REV. WILLIAM PERKINS of Topsfield, son of William Perkins, merchant taylor of London, by his wife Katherine, and grandson of George Perkins of Abbots Salford, Warwickshire, was born in London, 25 August, 1607, from which port he sailed for New England in the William and Francis, 9 March, 1632. The earliest mention of him in Massachusetts, is in March, 1633, when, with the eminent John Winthrop, Jr., the before named John Perkins and ten others, he assisted in the settlement of Ipswich. His father was a patron of Harvard Col-

* The manuscript, unfinished at her decease 16 June, 1918, was completed by another hand.

Miss Perkins, a life-member of this Society, was an artist of real ability, a talented poetess and playwright; an amateur actress of distinction and created the leading role in her successful drama, "The Changeling," the elfish story of mystical Irish lore which led to the founding of the Plays and Players' Club of Philadelphia, in the spring of 1911. She was a charter member of the Plastic Club, an active member of the Huntington Valley and New Century clubs and of the Society of Mayflower Descendants in Pennsylvania.

lege which led to the son having a considerable grant of land at Roxbury in 1641. He removed to Weymouth in 1643, which he represented in the General Assembly or Court of the Colony in 1644, and was captain of the military company in 1645, having been a member of the Ancient and Honorable Artillery Company of Boston from 1638. From 1650 to 1655, he preached at Gloucester, and later at Topsfield, where he spent the last years of his useful life, dying there 21 May, 1682, aged seventy-five years. He was, says one writer, probably the most accomplished among the early settlers of Topsfield. A scholar, a man of business, farmer, clergyman, soldier and legislator, he bore himself in each of these relations with ability and prudence.*

He married, at Roxbury, 30 August, 1636, Elizabeth Wootten, by whom he had ten children, nine of whom survived and made good alliances. Many of his descendants were distinguished. His grandson, the Rev. Daniel ³ Perkins, 1697-1782, Harvard, 1717, son of Captain Tobijah ² and Sarah (Denison) Perkins died at Bridgewater, Massachusetts, in the eighty-sixth year of his age and the sixty-second of his ministry in that place, which was ''not long only, but peaceful and efficacious; '' some of his descendants settled in Canada, the Mohawk Valley, New York and Charleston, South Carolina. Another grandchild, Elizabeth ³ Perkins, 1700-1768, daughter of John ² and Anne (Hutchinson) Perkins, married the Rev. Nathaniel Sparhawk of Lynnfield, Massachusetts; her son Rev. Edward Perkins Sparhawk was graduated at Harvard, 1753; another son, John ⁴ Sparhawk,†

* See *New England Historical and Genealogical Register*, vol. xxxviii, p. 320; vol. x, p. 210.

† The eldest child, Eliza ⁵ Sparhawk, married Hon. Joel Jones, Presiding Judge of the District Court of the City and County of Philadelphia, and Mayor of Philadelphia, 1849. Among their children were, the late Rev. John Sparhawk Jones, the eminent Presbyterian divine, and the late Samuel Huntington Jones, Esq., of the Philadelphia bar.

His eldest son, Thomas ⁵ Sparhawk, served in the War of 1812, in Capt. Condy Raguet's Co. of Washington Guards, Fourth Detachment of Penna. Militia, in the service of U. S. 13 May, 1813 to 18 July, 1814; was fifth sergeant in same company, commanded by Captain Thomas Franklin Pleasants, in the second campaign—First Regiment Volunteer Infantry, under Colonel Clement C. Biddle, attached to the Advanced Light Brigade, Brigadier-General Thomas Cadwalader, stationed at Camp Dupont, 20 Aug., 1814, to Jan. 3, 1815. *John ⁶ Sparhawk*, his son, was one of the organizers of the Y. M. C. A. of

M. D. removed to Philadelphia, about 1750, where he became a merchant and a signer of the Non-Importation Resolutions of 1765, and where his descendants have occupied prominent positions to the present time.

ABRAHAM PERKINS OF HAMPTON, NEW HAMPSHIRE.

ABRAHAM PERKINS, recognized as one of the historic founders of New Hampshire, 1638, was admitted freeman at the Hampton settlement, 13 May, 1640. In the preceding January the town granted him eighty acres of land, and in 1646 three shares in the Commons. He was possessed of a good education, was an excellent penman, town marshal in 1654, selectman some years between 1650 and 1683, and much employed in town business.* He died 31 August, 1683, aged about seventy-two years. His wife Mary, born *circa* 1618, died at Hampton, 29 May, 1706, is believed to have been a daughter of Humphrey Wise of Ipswich, Massachusetts.

Children, born at Hampton:

    i.   MARY,[2] b. 2 Sept., 1639; m. Giles Fifield of Charlestown, Mass., later of Hampton. Samuel Adams, patriot and Governor of Mass., descends from this marriage.

    ii. ABRAHAM, twin, b. 2 Sept., 1639; killed by the Indians, 13 June, 1677; of Hampton; married and had issue.

    iii. LUKE, b. *circa* 1641; m. Hannah widow of Henry Cookery and dau. of Robert Long.

    iv. HUMPHREY, b. 22 Jan., 1642; d. y.

    v.   JAMES, b. 11 April, 1644; d. y.

    vi. TIMOTHY, b. 5 Oct., 1646; d. y.

    vii. JAMES, b. 5 Oct., 1647; of Hampton; married and had issue.

2. viii. DAVID.

    ix. ABIGAIL, b. 2 April, 1655; m. John Folsom of Exeter, N. H. General Nathaniel Folsom of the Continental Congress, 1774, was of this line.

Phila., and the conductor of the famous litigation to restrain the running of Sunday street cars, the case being entered in the Supreme Court Reports, as: Sparhawk *vs.* The Union Passenger Railroad. *Elizabeth*[6] *Sparhawk*, sister of the latter, married Gerald F. Dale and had, inter alia, the Rev. Gerald Fitzgerald Dale, late Presbyterian divine and missionary at Zahled, Syria, and Mrs. Mary S., wife of the Hon. Robert N. Wilson of Phila. late Judge of the Court of Common Pleas. *Catharine*[6] *Sparhawk*, another sister, married Jesse S. Kneedler, and had three sons: Howard Sparhawk Kneedler, Henry Martyn Kneedler, well-known manufacturers of Phila., and Major William Ludwig Kneedler, of Coronado, Cal., surgeon U. S. A. retired. *Samuel*[6] *Sparhawk*, a brother, married Sarah Axford Kneass, q. v.

* See "An Account of Part of the Family of Abraham Perkins of Hampton, N. H. who lived in Plymouth Colony, Mass.," by Hon. Joseph W. Porter, of Bangor, Maine, in *New England Historical and Genealogical Register*, vol. 50, pp. 34-40.

x. TIMOTHY, b. 2 or 29 July, 1657; d. y.
xi. SARAH, b. 7 or 26 July, 1659; living 1683.
xii. HUMPHREY, b. 17 May, 1661, of Hampton; married and had issue.

2. DAVID [2] PERKINS, ESQ. (*Abraham* [1]), born at Hampton, 28 February, 1653. In 1688 he purchased lands in and removed to the southern part of Bridgewater, in Plymouth Colony, and later built a mill there and started an iron forge. He was a man of high character, and, in his time, "the most noted man in the town" and its first representative to the General Court of Massachusetts after the union of the two Colonies, 1692, 1694, 1696, 1704-1707.* Full of years he died, at Bridgewater, in October, 1736.

His wife, Elizabeth, daughter of Francis Brown of Beverly, Mass., born 17 October, 1654; died at Bridgewater, 14 July, 1735.

Children, born in Beverly, except the youngest:

   i. MARY,[3] probably died young.
   ii. DAVID, m. 1 Feby., 1698, Martha, dau. of John and Sarah Howard. The settlement of his estate, 9 Aug., 1737, shows his heirs to be: widow Martha; children of eldest son John deceased; sons Abraham, David and Jonathan; daughters Sarah, Martha, wife of Dr. Joseph Byram, Mary, wife of Gideon Washburn, Elizabeth, wife of Solomon Leonard and Susanna widow of Samuel Allen.†
3. iii. NATHAN.
   iv. ABRAHAM, bpt. Beverly, 13 Jan., 1683; settled in South Kingston, R. I.; m. (1) Tabitha, dau. Nathaniel Niles; (2) Margaret Cross.
   v. THOMAS, b. Bridgewater, 8 May, 1688; d. there 5 June, 1761; m. Mary, dau. of James and Mary (Bowden) Washburn.

3. NATHAN [3] PERKINS (*David*,[2] *Esq.*, *Abraham* [1]), baptized in Beverly, Mass., 13 September, 1685; died in Bridgewater, circa 1727; married, at Bridgewater, 9 November, 1710, Martha, probably, daughter of Solomon Leonard. She married (2) 15 May, 1728, Isaac Hayward of Bridgewater. His children were all named in the will of their grandfather, David Perkins, Esq., 21 January, 1735.

Children, born in Bridgewater:

* *Province Laws of Mass.*, vol. viii, pp. 6, 45, 105; vol. ix, pp. 63, 115, 163.
† *Plymouth County Registry of Probate*, File No. 15554.

i. NATHAN,[4] b. 24 Aug., 1710; m. 2 Apr., 1752, Sarah, widow of Solomon Pratt, and had issue.
ii. SOLOMON, b. 30 June, 1712; d. 1742/3; m. 31 Dec., 1735, Lydia Sprague, who m. (2) James Keith of Bridgewater.*
4. iii. TIMOTHY.
iv. MARTHA, b. 10 Dec., 1717; m. 26 Sept., 1738, Samuel Edson, Jr., and had issue.
v. JAMES, b. 5 March, 1720; d. 11 April, 1795; m. Bethia Dunham, and had issue.
vi. SILENCE, b. 1723; living 21 Jan., 1735.

4. TIMOTHY [4] PERKINS (*Nathan,[3] David,[2] Esq., Abraham* [1]), was born in Bridgewater, 16 January, 1715, and died sometime after 15 March, 1768.† He resided in Bridgewater, South Precinct, and executed in 1741, sundry conveyances disposing of land that had belonged to his father ‡ and grandfather.‡

He married (1) 18 March, 1736, Susanna, daughter of Samuel ‖ and Abigail Washburn, born at Bridgewater, 13 March, 1714, and there deceased before, 6 October, 1753, the date of his second marriage to Zipporah, daughter of William and Experience Washburn.

Child:

5. i. NATHANIEL.[5]

5. NATHANIEL [5] PERKINS (*Timothy,[4] Nathan,[3] David,[2] Esq., Abraham* [1]), resided in the South Parish of Bridgewater, his homestead lands being partly in Bridgewater and partly in Easton. Between 6 May, 1785 and 19 October, 1801,§ he and wife Mary were parties to the sale of various lands in Bridgewater and Easton. He was a town officer of the former in 1789, 1791, 1792, and, after 1801, removed with his family to Winthrop, Maine.

He married, intentions declared 2 July, 1773, Mary, daughter of Joseph Alger, Jr.,** by his wife Naomi Hayward,†† born at Bridgewater, 9 September, 1754.

---

* *Plymouth Registry of Deeds*, Liber 39. f. 141.

† *Ibid.*, Lib. 54 ff. 207-8.

‡ *Ibid.*, Lib. 38 ff. 201, 202.

‖ A descendant in the fourth generation from Francis Cooke, a passenger on the historic *Mayflower*.

§ *Bristol County Registry of Deeds*, Libers 64, f. 136; 89, f. 463; 84, f. 140; 80, f. 423.

** *Ibid.*, Liber 71. f. 104.

†† A daughter of Elisha Hayward, of Bridgewater, by his second wife Bethia Snow, a descendant in ninth generation from Peter Brown, of the *Mayflower*.

Children, the first three recorded at Easton:

6. i. NATHANIEL.[6]
   ii. POLLY, b. at Easton, 5 April, 1778; m. Dean Howard of Easton.
   iii. NAOMI, b. at Easton, 13 Aug., 1780; m. Alfred Johnson of Reed-
        field, near Winthrop, Maine.
   iv. NATHAN.
   v. DEBORAH, m. John Burrows of Winthrop, Me.

6. NATHANIEL[6] PERKINS, JR. (*Nathaniel,*[5] *Timothy,*[4] *Nathan,*[3]
David,[2] *Esq., Abraham*[1]), was born 15 April, 1776, probably
in the South Parish of Bridgewater, his birth being recorded
at Easton. In 1800 he was surveyor of highways at Bridgewater, but, by 20 February, 1803, he had located at Winthrop,
Maine, being so described in a deed of that date.* Some few
years later he was lost at sea on a voyage to China.

He married, 5 July, 1794, Hannah, daughter of Edmund
Hayward † by his wife Anna Snell,‡ who was baptized in
West Bridgewater, 18 November, 1770, and died there, 3 June,
1837, having married (2) in 1821, John Snow.

Children, the first four born, probably, at West Bridgewater:

7. i. EDMUND[7] HAYWARD.
   ii. SUSAN, b. 27 July, 1797; d. 23 Sept., 1868; m. 1817, her cousin,
        Otis, son of Ebenezer Alger, b. 21 July, 1793; d. 25 July,
        1869. Resided at Cochesett, Mass., and had issue.
   iii. CAROLINE, m. 16 May, 1827, Josiah Vaughan Reed. Resided at
        New Bedford, Mass.
   iv. MELVIN OTIS, b. 5 May, 1802; d. 5 May, 1881; m., intentions
        dated 21 Aug., 1825, Mary Ann Willis of West Bridgewater.
        Resided at North Braintree. Issue: 1. *George.*[8] 2. *Martha
        Ann.* 3. *Marcia,* d. 4 Sept., 1916; m. Cyrus Williams.
        4. *Charles.* 5. *Edmund.* 6. *Jane.* 7. *Helen.*
   v. OWEN DUMMER, b. 6 April, 1804; d. 27 Dec., 1881; m. 30 April,
        1826, Mary Thomas of Hanson, Mass. Resided at East
        Bridgewater. Issue: 1. *Andrew W.,*[8] b. 1833; d. 19 Feb.,
        1904. 2. *Mary Jane.* 3. *Carolina.* 4. *Owen.*

7. EDMUND[7] HAYWARD PERKINS (*Nathaniel,*[6] *Jr., Nathaniel,*[5]
Timothy,[4] *Nathan,*[3] *David,*[2] *Esq., Abraham*[1]), born at West
Bridgewater, Massachusetts, 14 June, 1795, and died at
Quincy, Illinois, 13 November, 1884. He engaged in the
foundry business at South Boston, with his relative Cyrus

* *Plymouth County Registry of Deeds,* Liber 102, ff. 238-9.

† Edmund Hayward was a descendant in the fourth generation from Francis
Cooke, a passenger on the *Mayflower.*

‡ A daughter of Josiah Snell by his wife Abigail Fobes, a descendant of
John and Priscilla Alden, both passengers on the *Mayflower.*

Alger and subsequently these two were similarly engaged at Cochesett, West Bridgewater,* and at Providence,† Rhode Island, being at the latter place connected with George Earle and George Holmes.‡ In 1839 he located a claim or grant of one hundred and sixty acres of government lands near Hillsboro, Illinois, received in lieu of money or pension for service in the War of 1812, he having enlisted, when a lad of seventeen, in Captain Nathaniel Edson's Company of Massachusetts Militia. At Hillsboro he remained many years, removing finally to Quincy.

He married at Boston, 22 February, 1823, Hannah, daughter of Captain Josiah Sturtevant by his wife Mary Monroe, born at Pembroke, Massachusetts, 1 September, 1804; died 4 October, 1873.

Children:

   i. CHARLOTTE,⁸ d. y.

   ii. WILLIAM, b. 8 Aug., 1827; went West.

   iii. EDWIN R., b. 18 Jan., 1829; d. Quincy, Ill., 7 Jan., 1916; m. 31 Dec., 1850, Kitty M. Carter. Issue: 1. *Henry E.*,⁹ m. Ida Farnsworth. 2. *William T.* 3. *Nora E.*, m. Edward Dickhut of Quincy. 4. *Lucy*, m. Sidney Prince; resides at Fort Morgan, Col. 5. *Nellie R.*, m. E. B. Treat of Cheyenne, Wy. 6. *Mary J.* 7. *James F.* 8. *Sarah B.*, d. y. 9. *Kitty M.*, m. George S. Schaller of Quincy.

   iv. MARY S., b. 11 May, 1830; d. 26 Apr., 1880; m. 17 Feb., 1848, William H. Stephenson. Issue: 1. *James M.*,⁹ d. y. 2. *William N.*, of Coffeen, Ill. 3. *Martha J.*, m. Stephen Perry. 4. *George H.*, d. y. 5. *Edwin H.*, of Marshall, Okl. 6. *Robert S.* 7. *Charles W.*, of Hillsboro, Ill. 8. *Benjamin F.*, d. y. 9. *Harry P.*, d. y. 10. *George W.*, of Springfield, Mo. 11. *Chandler*, d. y. 12. *Carrie*, d. y.

   v. JAMES H., b. 1 Mar., 1832; d. 25 Dec., 1877; m. at Phila., Pa., Sarah Ann Jane Kirby. Issue: 1. *Mary Helen*,⁹ m. —— Taber.

   vi. LOUISA, d. y.

   vii. GEORGE HOLMES, b. Hillsboro, Ill., 28 Sept., 1839; d. Island Heights, N. J., 2 Feb., 1905; m. 17 Nov., 1870, Helen Christina, dau. of James Ritchie of Philadelphia, by his wife, Hannah Corson. Mr. Perkins, in 1863, in New York, entered into partnership with Mr. Joseph Le Comte, forming the firm of Le Comte and Perkins, manufacturers of tin containers for shipping kerosene to Europe. About 1866 he came to Philadelphia, where, after some changes, he became associated, in 1869, with the Atlantic Refining Company, as general man-

* Conveyed land in West Bridgewater to Melvin O. Perkins, under date of 4 Dec., 1830. *Plymouth County Registry of Deeds*, Liber 170, f. 252.

† Described as "of Providence, R. I.," made sale of lands in West Bridgewater by deed of 18 Oct., 1831. *Ibid.*, Lib. 252, f. 60.

‡ Afterwards Governor of Massachusetts.

ager, and, during his connection with this plant and its successor, the Standard Oil Company, he took out more than one hundred patents on machinery and processes for the manufacture of tin and other sheet-metal ware and for the convenient handling of petroleum oil. He was also a specialist on the microscopic study of paraffin and various other petroleum products. Among his most important patents, from a commercial viewpoint, were machines for closing seams on tin cans, nailing boxes, and uniting tinned plates by means of heat and pressure without the use of flux or solder. His most important scientific inventions were an instrument for measing viscosity, and an apparatus for examining the physical conditions of liquids at any given temperature. He was a member of the Masonic fraternity, the Franklin Institute, the American Society of Mechanical Engineers and the Germantown Cricket Club. Issue: *Emily Ritchie,*[9] b. 28 Sept., 1872; d. 16 June, 1918. 2. *George Howard,* m. Josephine Schock; resides in Cambridge, Mass. 3. *Edwin Alan,* m. Helen Chouteau Phinney; resides in Jamaica, L. I. 4. *Joseph Le Comte* of Philadelphia. 5. *Francis Everson,* b. 19 June, 1888; d. 7 Nov., 1916; m. Ethel McCormick of Albany, N. Y.

ISAAC PERKINS OF HAMPTON, NEW HAMPSHIRE.

ISAAC [1] PERKINS, born circa 1612, was among the recognized founders of New Hampshire and was freeman, at Hampton, in 1642. Neither will or settlement of his estate have been found, but he and wife Susanna, possibly daughter of Humphrey Wise * of Ipswich, are believed to have had twelve children,† of whom five became constructive factors in the colonies of East and West Jersey, Delaware, Maryland and Virginia. He died at Hampton, 13 November, 1685, and his widow accompanied her daughter, Rebecca Hussey, to New Castle County, Delaware, and there deceased in 1699, the administration of her estate being granted to John Hussey, 17 July, 1699.‡

Children, probably born at Hampton, order uncertain:

 i. LYDIA,[2] m. 17 Oct., 1659, Eliakim Wardell, who, after sharing the persecutions accorded to many of the Quakers of that day in New England, settled in Monmouth County, East Jersey, prior to 1667, where he was deputy in that year and in 1678, and High Sheriff in 1693. Through the marriage of his daughter, Lydia Wardell, to William Biddle the younger, 13 Dec., 1691, he became one of the forebears of the well known Biddle family of New Jersey and Philadelphia.

 ii. ISAAC, bapt. 8 Dec., 1639; drowned 30 Oct., 1661.

* *Boston Evening Transcript,* Sept. 26, 1917.

† *New England Historical and Genealogical Register,* vol. xii, p. 82.

‡ New Castle County, Delaware, *Probate Records.*

2. iii. JACOB.
   iv. REBECCA, m. 21 Sept., 1659, John Hussey,* who, by deed of
       1 July, 1695, purchased three hundred and forty acres of land
       near New Castle, Delaware, being then described as "late of
       Hamp Town in New Hampshire, near Piscatoway in New
       England." His will was probated 18 Feb., 1707.† He had
       a large family;‡ several of his grandchildren were members
       of the Sadsbury Meeting of Friends in Lancaster Co., Penna.,
       in 1737 and of the Warrington Meeting in York Co., in 1745.
   v. DANIEL, d. 1 Aug., 1662.
   vi. CALEB, m. 24 Apr., 1677, Bethia Philbrook, and remained at
       Hampton.
   vii. BENJAMIN, b. 17 Feb., 1650; d. 23 Nov., 1670.
   viii. SUSANNA, b. 21 Dec., 1652; m. (1) Isaac Buzwell of Salisbury;
       (2) William Fuller, Jr., of Hampton.
   ix. HANNAH, b. 24 Feb., 1656; m. James Philbrook.‖
   x. MARY, b. 23 July, 1658; m., probably, Isaac Chase of Hampton.
3. xi. EBENEZER.
   xii. JOSEPH, b. 9 Apr., 1661; m. Martha ——, who survived him;
       purchased land in Brandywine Hundred, New Castle Co., Del.,
       14 Oct., 1693,§ and there settled. His will, probated 19 Aug.,
       1707, constituted wife Martha executor and left bequests to
       children: *Joseph,[3] John, Caleb, Humphrey, Joshua, Marey*
       and *Marthay.* The three eldest were born at Hampton.**

2. JACOB [2] PERKINS (*Isaac* [1]), was baptized at Hampton,
New Hampshire, 24 May, 1640. In 1674 he was of Holmes
Hole, Martha's Vineyard, Massachusetts, and was the purchaser, 24 October, 1698, of three hundred and thirty acres on
the Delaware River, below Burlington, in West Jersey,†† where
he died in 1731, administration on his estate bearing date
18 May, 1731. He was a petitioner in 1704 for the Rev. Mr.
Talbot as rector for St. Mary's, Burlington, the latter having
there baptized his four children 20 November, 1703.‡‡

He married at Hampton, 30 December, 1669, Mary, daughter
of John Philbrick of Hampton.

* Son of Captain Christopher Hussey, member of Governor's Council of
Mass., 1680-85, and grandson of Rev. Stephen Bachiler, first minister at
Hampton.

† New Castle County, Delaware, *Calendar of Wills*, pp. 12-13.

‡ Among his present-day descendants on distaff lines are the Holcombs of
New Castle, Delaware, Clement Reeves Wainwright and Francis King Wainwright, Esqs., of Phila.

‖ The name was variously written in the early records : Filbrick, Philbrook.
Philbrick. It may have derived from the Greek " Phile "—lovely, and the
old English word—Brook.—*New Eng. Hist. and Gen. Reg.*, vol. xxxviii, p. 279.

§ *New Castle County Deeds*, Liber B1, f. 189.

** Charles Penrose Perkins, member of The Genealogical Society of Pennsylvania descends from this branch.

†† *New Jersey Archives*, 1st ser., vol. xxi, p. 442.

‡‡ *Publications of The Genealogical Society of Pennsylvania*, vol. ii, p. 242.

Children, born at Hampton:

i. ISAAC,[3] b. 18 Dec., 1671; received portion of his father's Burlington lands, in common with his brothers in 1711, before which time he has settled in Kent Co., Md., and there died in, or before 1746, leaving a son Wright Perkins. His wife, Elizabeth, was, possibly, a daughter of Joshua Wright [*] of Burlington Co., N. J., by his wife Elizabeth Empson.

ii. JACOB, b. 24 Dec., 1674; d. in Willingborough Township, Burlington Co., N. J., will proved, 7 Dec., 1731.[†] He and his wife, Sarah, who survived him, were evidently members of St. Mary's Church, Burlington, to which he left a legacy. Issue: 1. *Abraham*,[4] d. Apr., 1764; m. (1) Mary Simons; m. (2), license 4 December, 1733, Mrs. Sarah Gardener.[‡] 2. *Rebecca*. 3. *David*. 4. *Mary*. 5. *Ann*. 6. *Susanna*, m. Reuben Eldridge. *i. Hannah*, bpt. 7 Sept., 1710. 8. *Sarah*, m. George Munrow. 9. *Bathsheba*, bpt. 26 July, 1719; m. Daniel Parke. 10. *Rebecca*, m. Henry Nordyke. 11. *Martha*, m. — Vansciver.

iii. MARY, b. 10 Aug., 1678; m. 10 Dec., 1698, Robert Powell of Burlington Co., N. J., who died intestate, in Oct., 1706.

iv. BENJAMIN, b. 12 Aug., 1683; d. 5 July, 1755 and is buried at St. Mary's Burlington. He m., license 13 June, 1731, Elinor Cox. Their son, Major Jacob Perkins, member of the Committee of Observation of Burlington Co. in 1775, and Major in New Jersey Militia 1778 and 1779, died in Willingborough Township, 6 Oct., 1792, aged 61 years and 26 days.[||]

3. EBENEZER [2] PERKINS (*Isaac* [1]), was born at Hampton, New Hampshire, 9 December, 1659. On 14 October, 1693, he, being then described as "late of New England," purchased a portion of the "Bout" tract of land on the Delaware River, above Vertrecht Hook, in Brandywine Hundred, New Castle County, Delaware,[§] whereon he afterward resided. His will of 20 July, 1703, probated 16 September, following,[¶] named wife Mary and the children here following.

Children, the three eldest recorded at Hampton:

i. DANIEL,[3] b. June, 1685; d. at "White House Farm," near Chestertown, Md., in 1748. His marriage to Susanna Stan-

---

[*] *New Eng. Hist. and Gen. Register*, vol. xlvii, p. 484.

[†] *New Jersey Archives*, 1st ser., vol. xxx, p. 376.

[‡] The descendants of the second marriage, married into the Fennimore, Bispham and Ridgway families of Burlington Co., and among the present-day representatives thereof, are: Joseph R. Grundy, the well-known woolen manufacturer of Bristol and Philadelphia, and his sister, Miss Margaret Ridgway Grundy, a member of The Genealogical Society of Pennsylvania.

[||] Edwin Stanley Perkins, M. D., Lucius Scott Landreth and William Linton Landreth, Esqs., of Philadelphia, are descendants of Major Jacob Perkins.

[§] Scharf's *History of Delaware*, vol. ii, p. 900.

[¶] New Castle County, Delaware, *Probate Records*.

ton,* 1 May, 1715, is entered on the records of Shrewsbury Parish of which he was chosen a warden 15 April, 1723, and vestryman, 6 April, 1724. He was a prosperous miller and large land holder, as was attested by his will, proved 20 Apr., 1748, and that of his widow, Susanna, dated 22 Oct., 1758, probated 20 Feb., 1764,† both of which made liberal provision for their children ‡ therein named: *Ebenezer, Thomas, Daniel, Sarah, Susanna Day, Elizabeth* and *Martha.*§

ii. ABIGAIL, b. 11 Aug., 1689.
iii. JONATHAN, b. 10 May, 1691.
iv. ELIZABETH.
v. DAVID, settled in Kent Co., Md.; m. 18 Feb., 1723, Sarah Reding; had issue.
vi. ISAAC, m. circa 1723, Mary, dau. of Charles Booth and removed to the Shenandoah in Virginia; had large family.
vii. EBENEZER, settled in Kent Co., Md., will of 6 Jan., 1746, proved 16 Nov., 1748, left son Ebenezer to the care of the Cecil Meeting of Friends; left legacy to son-in-law, Francis Kinsey.

JOHN PERKINS OF IPSWICH, MASSACHUSETTS.

JOHN [1] PERKINS was baptized at Hillmorton, in Warwickshire, England, 23 December, 1583,** and was the son of Henry Perkins and the grandson of Thomas Perkins †† of that place. It is possible that a portion of his life had been spent, at Newent, in Gloucestershire, which would account for the long prevalent family tradition that he had been born there. At the age of forty-seven years he embarked for New England, with his wife and six children, in the ship Lyon of Bristowe, 1 December, 1630, and arrived at Boston, Massachusetts,

* Name incorrectly given Starton in Hanson's *Old Kent*, p. 189. See pp. 189-196 for further details.

† *Annapolis Wills*, Liber DD. No. 25. ff. 73-4: DD. No. 31, ff. 1190.

‡ The births of all the children, Martha excepted, are entered on the Shrewsbury Parish Register.

‖ These were the ancestors of many Marylanders of note, among them, Col. Isaac Perkins, a distinguished Revolutionary officer, and the late Hon. George Washington Thomas Perkins, United States Senator, 1826-1834, and Judge of Maryland Court of Appeals, 1834-1851.

§ Wright Medders Boyd of New York City, Lieut. Alvin Adams Boyd, late of Jacksonville, Fla., now over seas; Mrs. Henry Lane Williams of Minneapolis, Minn., Mrs. Robert Perry Cummins of Germantown, Phila., Mrs. Albert E. Shaw of Springfield, Mass., and Mrs. John Cooke Hirst of Philadelphia, the latter a life member of The Genealogical Society of Pennsylvania, are among the descendants of Martha Perkins, who became the second wife of Jonathan Turner (1738-1784), of Kent County, Md., and died in January, 1796.

** The Perkins Family in ye Olden Times, edited and privately printed by D. W. Perkins of Utica, N. Y., 1917.

†† Thomas Perkins of Hillmorton died in 1592, having had by his wife, Alice Kebble, children: Henry, d. 1609; John; William; Edward; Thomas; Luke, and Isaac.

5 February following. After a short stay in that town he removed, with the younger Winthrop, to Ipswich, which he represented as deputy to the General Court in 1636, held various town offices and trusts and occupied an eminently respectable position in that community. At his death in September, 1654, he was survived by wife Judith, three sons and three daughters and was the ancestor of at least seven early founders of distinct families of the Perkins name in Connecticut.

He married, at Hillmorton, 9 October, 1608, Judith, daughter of Michael Gater.

Children: all except the youngest recorded at Hillmorton.

    i.   JOHN,[2] bapt. 8 Nov., 1609; d. at Ipswich, 14 Oct., 1686; m. Elizabeth ——, who died 27 Sept., 1684; was quartermaster of Militia, 1670-1683. Through his son, Samuel,[3] he was the grandfather of Ebenezer [4] Perkins of Preston and Voluntown, Conn. and Coventry, R. I., and great-grandfather of James [5] Perkins and Abraham [5] Perkins, sons of Isaac,[4] who settled at Lyme, Conn., towards the close of the first quarter of the eighteenth century.

    ii.   ELIZABETH, bapt. 3 Mar., 1611; m. William Sargent of Amesbury, Mass.

    iii.   MARY, bapt. 3 Sept., 1615; m. Thomas Bradbury of Salisbury, Mass.

    iv.   ANN, bapt. 5 Sept., 1617; accompanied her parents to Mass.

    v.   THOMAS, bapt. 28 April, 1622; d. Topsfield, Mass., 7 May, 1686, leaving a large estate for that period; m. Phebe, dau. of Zacheus Gould and was the grandfather of Thomas Perkins of Enfield, Conn., who died there in 1709, aged forty-three years, leaving descendants.

2. vi.   JACOB, bapt. 12 Sept., 1624.

    vii.   LYDIA, bapt. at Boston, 3 Jan., 1632; m. Henry Bennett of Ipswich.

2. JACOB [2] PERKINS (*John, Esq.*), baptized at Hillmorton, 12 September, 1624; died at Ipswich, 29 January, 1700, "aged seventy-six years." Inheriting the principal part of his father's estate in Ipswich, he apportioned it among his own children before 1694. Of his sons, the three youngest, Matthew, Joseph and Jabez, went directly to Norwich, Connecticut, before the close of the seventeenth century, and there purchased twelve hundred acres in that portion afterwards known as the Newent Society, probably so named from Newent, in Gloucestershire, the supposed English habitat of the elder John Perkins. Matthew Perkins eventually returned to Ipswich, but his brothers remained at Norwich, married and left many descendants who attained distinction as physicians, clergymen and lawyers.

668

His first wife Elizabeth, died at Ipswich, 12 February, 1665. He married (2) Damaris, widow of Nathaniel Robinson of Boston.

Children, all born at Ipswich:

 i. ELIZABETH,[3] b. 1 April, 1650; m. Thomas Boreman of Topsfield.
 ii. JOHN, m. (1) Mary Fisk; (2) Elizabeth Prythatch; (3) Mary Hooper.
 iii. JUDITH, b. 11 July, 1655; m. Nathaniel Browne.
 iv. MARY, b. 14 May, 1658; m. (1) Thomas Wells; (2) John Annable.
3. v. JACOB, b. 3 Aug., 1662.
 vi. MATTHEW,[*] b. 23 June, 1665; was some years of Norwich, Conn., m. Esther Burnham; d. at Ipswich.
 vii. HANNAH, b. 11 Oct., 1670.
 viii. JOSEPH,[†] b. 24 June, 1674; d. Norwich, 4 or 6 Sept., 1726; m. Martha Morgan of Preston, Conn.
 ix. JABEZ,[‡] b. 15 May, 1677; d. Norwich, 15 Jan., 1741; m. (1) Hannah Lathrop of Norwich; (2) Charity Leonard; was captain of Norwich Train Band, 1721, *et seq.*

3. JACOB [3] PERKINS, JR. (*Sergeant Jacob,*[2] *John,*[1] *Esq.*), was born at Ipswich, 13 August, 1662, and died there in November, 1705. He married (1), 15 October, 1684, Elizabeth, daughter of John Sparks of Boston and Ipswich, by his wife Mary Sinnett,[||] who died 10 April, 1692. His second wife was Sarah Treadwell, by whom he had five children.[§]

* Jacob Perkins, who originated the substitution of steel-plate for copper-plate in fine engraving and printing, and who was associated in Philadelphia, some years from 1814, with the firm of Murray, Draper and Fairman bank-note engravers, was a great-grandson of Matthew Perkins, his father and grandfather bearing the same Christian name. He was born at Newburyport, Mass., 9 July, 1766, and died at London, England, 30 July, 1849; his device for cutting and heading nails at one operation; his elaboration and perfection of the steam gun; his invention of the pleometer and orthometer; his method of warming and ventilating rooms and holds of ships, and his new application of known principles to the improvement of the steam engine, are examples of the genius and inventive faculty which gave him high standing in the scientific world of his day.

† The late Samuel Huntington Perkins, Esq., and his son, the late Samuel Clarke Perkins, Esq., well known lawyers of Philadelphia descended through Joseph,[3] the line of descent being: Samuel Huntington,[6] Samuel,[5] Matthew,[4] Joseph,[3] Jacob,[2] John.[1]

‡ Maternally, the children of the late John H. Converse of Philadelphia descended from Captain Jabez [3] Perkins.

|| Daughter of Walter Sinnett who was of Milton, Mass., in 1638, and later of Boston. The famous "Liberty Tree," said to have been planted in 1646, and destroyed by the Tories in 1774, stood in his Boston houseyard. His name is perpetuated in the well-known romance, "A Woman of Shamut." See Mary E. Sinnott's *Annals of the Sinnott, Rogers, Coffin and Allied Families*, pp. 12-3.

§ For details of, see *The Family of John Perkins of Ipswich*, pt. iii, p. 10.

Children of Jacob, Jr., and Elizabeth (Sparks) Perkins, born at Ipswich:

  i. JACOB,[4] b. 15 Feb., 1685; m. Lydia ——; settled in Maine; left descendants.
4. ii. JOHN, b. 2 September, 1689.
  iii. ELIZABETH, b. 18 March, 1690; m. David Burnham.

4. JOHN [4] PERKINS (*Jacob*,[3] *Jr., Sergeant Jacob*,[2] *John*,[1] *Esq.*), born at Ipswich, 2 September, 1689; died New London, North Parish, Connecticut, *circa* December, 1758.

Upon reaching manhood he went to the vicinity of Norwich, Connecticut, doubtless influenced thereto by his uncles, Joseph and Jabez, and settled in the North Parish of New London, now Montville, adjoining Norwich. Between 1740 and 1758,* he was described as of "the North Society of Lyme" in sundry conveyances in which his wife, Lydia, was frequently a party. On 8 July, 1751, he and wife Lydia "in consideration of the love they bore their son, John Perkins, of New London, North Parish," conveyed the whole of that land which their father, Philip Mallsor, late of New London, North Parish, deceased, gave to his daughter Lydia Perkins, in and by his last will. Mr. Perkins died intestate, his estate being administered upon, by his widow, Lydia and son Joshua, 19 December, 1758. The inventory of his effects totalled £419 - 4 - 1, of which £323 was in realty.† In May 1761, the administrators memorialized the Connecticut Assembly for liberty to sell lands of said deceased, which was granted ‡ and on 19 March, 1763, two conveyances therefore were executed.‖

His first marriage has not been ascertained; he married (2), 27 May, 1727, Lydia, daughter of Philip Mallsor § of New London, North Parish, who was living at Hebron, Connecticut, as late as 17 October, 1778.

Lyme Land Records. Liber 7, f. 156; Lib. 9, f. 15; *New London Land Records*, Lib. 15, f. 230-1; Lib. 16, f. 211-12.

† *New London Registry of Probate.* Journ. no. 6, pp. 80, 134.

‡ *Conn. Colonial Records.* xi, p. 543.

‖ *Lyme Town Records*, Lib. 12, f. 211; Lib. 13, pp. 242-3.

§ Name indifferently written Malzer, Malser, Malsworth, and sometimes Marcy. His will of 25 May, 1751, named inter al. daughter Lydia Perkins and grandchildren, John, Philip, Jonathan and Richard Perkins.—*New London Registry of Probate*, Liber 1748-1753, ff. 234-6.

Child of John Perkins by first marriage:

  i. JOSHUA.[5]

Children of John and Lydia (Mallsor) Perkins, all, probably, born in North Parish, New London, order of birth uncertain:

5. ii. JOHN,[5] b. circa 1728.
   iii. JONATHAN, named in will of Philip Mallsor, 28 May, 1751; party to conveyance of 19 March, 1763.
   iv. PHILIP, named in aforesaid will; deceased before 19 March, 1763.
   v. LYDIA, married David Wood.
   vi. RICHARD, named in grandfather's will; deceased before 19 March, 1763.
   vii. MARTHA, married Timothy Minard.
   viii. SARAH, married Isaac Lamphire of Coventry, Connecticut.

5. JOHN [5] PERKINS (John,[4] Jacob,[3] Sergeant Jacob,[2] John,[1] Esq.), was born circa 1728, and reached his majority about 20 November, 1750, when he received from Philip Mallsor, his grandfather, a house and land in the township of New London.* There he remained until about 1761 when he removed to Hebron, in Connecticut, primarily to protect the property interest of his first wife. At Hebron, he made various purchases and sales of lands between 1764 and 1772,† the last conveyance being under date of 31 May, 1772, when he sold to Captain Benjamin Griswold, of Windsor, Connecticut, twenty acres with house and barn thereon standing. Some two years later, attracted by the possibilities offered by the Wyoming Valley, then under the jurisdiction of Connecticut, now in Pennsylvania, Mr. Perkins followed the "course of Empire" westward, and, during the Indian warfare of the Revolution was slain by the savages at Kingston, 7 November, 1778.‡

He married, first, at Hebron, 10 January, 1750, Sarah, daughter of John and Mary (Otis) Thompson,‖ who, born 8 March, 1725; died circa 1762. He married, second, circa 1764, Hepzibah Griswold, commonly called Ziba, daughter of Captain Benjamin Griswold § of Windsor, and widow of her

---

* New London Land Records, Liber xv, ff. 203-4; Lib. xix, f. 134.

† Hebron Land Records, Lib. v, ff. 44-5; 534-5.

‡ Miner's Wyoming, p. 246.

‖ Hebron Land Records, Lib. iv, f. 293; New London Land Records, Lib. xvi, ff. 177-8; Colchester Probate District, Lib. iii, ff. 18-20, 97-99, 247.

§ Will of Captain Benjamin Griswold recorded, Hartford Probate District, Liber xxi, ff. 227-9; 127 reverse side.

cousin, Phineas Griswold, born Windsor, 31 May, 1730. She was buried in the church yard of the Second Society of Windsor where her gravestone reads: "In Memory of Ziba, widow of John Perkins, who died 29 June, 1820, aged 90."

Children of John and Sarah (Thompson) Perkins:

   i.   Sarah,[6] b. New London, 7 Sept., 1751, m. Luman Long.
   ii.   Mary, m. at Hebron, 20 Aug., 1771, Elijah Mann.
   iii. Lydia, m. at Hebron, 18 Sept., 1780, David Skinner.
   iv. Martha.

Children of John and Ziba (Griswold) Perkins, order and place of birth uncertain:

   v.   John,[6] Jr., Revolutionary soldier; died 6 July, 1777.
   vi.   Aaron,* Revolutionary soldier, enlisted from Windsor in 1776, in Captain Robert Durkee's Independent Company of the Wyoming Valley, Connecticut Line; was in the skirmish at Millstone, N. J. and subsequently served against the Indians; Connecticut pensioner in Pennsylvania, under the Act of 1818; died at Kingston.
   vii. Griswold Perkins, bapt. 15 Feb., 1767; "died at Kingston, in Susquehanna, Pennsylvania;" estate of, administered upon, by his mother Mrs. Ziba Perkins, 7 Oct., 1786.†
   viii. David Perkins, b. 1 Jan., 1769; d. at Kingston, Penna., 8 June, 1854; m. Sarah, daughter of Thomas Ferrier of Amity, N. Y. On 25 March, 1791, he came into possession of various lots in Kingston, originally set off to his father, comprising some five hundred acres.‡ With his mother, Ziba Perkins of Windsor, Conn., he conveyed by deed of 22 March, 1808, certain land in Hebron township, Conn., willed to them by Benjamin Griswold of Windsor,‖ and on 4 Dec., 1820,§ he constituted John M. Miles of Hartford his attorney for the settlement "of the Estate of my mother, Ziba Perkins, late of Windsor." Among his descendants ** may be mentioned: the late Mrs. Lydia Atherton Henry, first wife of Rev. Winfield Scott Stites of Kingston; the late James Denton Hancock, Esq., of Franklin, Penna., and Thomas Henry Atherton, Esq., of Wilkes-Barre, Penna.

---

* Conveyed by deed of 7 May, 1822, land in Windsor set off from estate of late deceased mother, Ziba Perkins, bounded south on land distributed to David Perkins.—*Windsor Land Records*, Liber 28, f. 150.

† *Hartford Probate Records*, Lib. 23, f. 201.

‡ Meadow lot, no. 1 ; back lots, nos. 40, 27 ; town lot, no. 13, and two 4th division lots, nos. 26, 35.—*Luzerne Co. Registry of Deeds*, Liber 3, ff. 210, 138, 374.

‖ *Hebron Land Records*, Lib. 11, f. 80.

§ *Windsor Land Records*, Lib. 29, f. 16.

** For children of, see *Thomas Ferrier and some of his descendants*, by Elizabeth F. Lane of Elkhorn, Wisconsin, 1906.

PHILLIPS BIBLE RECORD.*

COURTESY OF MRS. STOCKTON TOWNSEND OF BRYN MAWR.

[The Bible bears the imprint, London, 1756. Thomas Baskett, Printer to the King's most Excellent Majesty; and by the Assigns of Robert Baskett, MDCCLVI.

The "Index" on first fly-leaf with baptisms of slaves on the reverse, is here given at the end.

The sketches of John Phillips are inter-leaved in the Bible at the beginning.]

JOHN PHILLIPS the 1st was the son of a Welsh curate who sent him to London, where he was bound to a trade or profession————

In the early part of the 17th century he was persuaded by a sailor boy to leave his master and secrete himself on board of a vessel and continued on the voyage, where he behaved so entirely to the satisfaction of his captain, that he induced his first master to transfer his indentures to him; he gradually rose to be mate and then captain. He became engaged to be married to a sister of an officer in one of the Royal deck-yards. About this time a vessel was to be sold at public sale which he thought he could buy to advantage—a brother of his wife undertook to furnish him with what money might be needed to make the purchase; on the strength of this he bought the vessel—afterwards his brother-in-law became unwilling to furnish him with the promised money—in this difficulty he applied to the merchants for whom he had sailed, these lent him the money he required, and now, in command of his own ship, he made several freighting voyages, the profits of which enabled him to pay the debt to the merchants. Being not on good terms with his wife's brother on account of the disappointment, he determined to leave England, to settle in America. Taking his wife on board he sailed for Barbadoes with a cargo in freight, when he discharged his cargo in Barbadoes, a slave ship from the coast of Guinea had disposed of all except the sick slaves, he bought them and sailed for Philadelphia with his purchase on board—he soon restored them to health. The mate of the vessel was also named Phillips, though no relation; this man knew that John Phillips intended to leave the sea and settle in Philadelphia, he proposed that John Phillips should establish a rope walk, and as he (the mate) had been by trade a rope-maker, he would act as his foreman and teach the negroes to work in the rope walk. Arriving in Philadelphia, as there was no rope walk here and as the plan promised well,

---

* Photostate copy of, in Collections of the Society, strictly followed.

John Phillips sold his vessel and bought a piece of ground extending from Front to Second St. (through which he afterwards laid out Poplar Lane). On this lot he built the rope walk and carried on this business during his life, after which his son succeeded him in the same vocation.

John Phillips the 1st left three children, John Phillips, Thomas Phillips and Margaret Phillips.

John Phillips married Rebecca Piewell * [sic.]; they had two children, one of whom died in early infancy, the other was William Phillips.

Thomas Phillips died unmarried.

Margaret Phillips married an Englishman by the name of Stocker, who after some years went back to England and never returned; her children were John Clements Stocker, Mrs. Nancy Potts and Mrs. Polly Miller.

William Phillips married Anna Smith, the daughter of Thomas W. Smith. William and Anna Phillips left ten children.

SOME INCIDENTS IN THE EARLY LIFE OF WILLIAM PHILLIPS.

William Phillips after completing his mercantile education in the counting house of George Meade (father of General Meade) loaded two ships somewhere about 1794 or 5 at the port of Philadelphia and sailed in one of them for Bordeaux where he arrived at such a time of famine that the flour on board his vessels sold for 55 silver French crowns a barrel, and when every inhabitant of the place had his daily ration of bread appointed by the Mayoralty so that he could procure no other, the necessary accompaniment to an invitation to dinner was "please bring your own bread with you."

Mr. Phillips had on board of his ships some barrels of Indian corn meal an article then entirely unknown in England and in the scarcity that prevailed it occurred to a philosopher who dealt in grain it would be a cheap and nutritious substitute for wheaten bread. So it was neatly put up in paper packages with "directions" and a small shanty on Cornhill rented for its sale—the meal sold rapidly the first day but on the opening of the second a riotous crowd collected with indignant cries that they had been cheated and insulted with horse-feed and to put the matter right in their fashion drove away the philosopher and his people, tore down the shanty and scattered the "yaller male" as they called it.

While in London Mr. Phillips boarded in the house with several other young Americans among whom were Mr. Daniel W. Coxe, Mr. Talbot and some other Virginians, quite ready for a lark—one of them had an idea agreeable to all the others, which was to go to Court after the newly invented equality fashion without submitting to the aristocratic formality of a presentation. The party went on the first occasion which was the "Queen's drawing room"—they did not carry their republican

---

* Pyewell.

674

principles however to go "sans culottes" but condescended to hire from the costumer second-hand Court Suits and Swords at an expense of a guinea a piece for that night only—in this glittering garb they were conveyed in sedan chairs to the entrance and fell into line with the other courtiers. They passed in the ring without any notice, but lingering in the room the Queen observed with royal quickness of eye that they were something new and strange and sent a page to investigate the Yankee Nation then in its extreme youth. They took the hint and vanished but were not deterred from returning to the ball that following evening. This was held in a place said my Mr. P. to have been very like St. Peter's church with its gallery on three sides. He was admitted to the gallery and from there observed the progress of the ball. The King and Queen entered with their attendants and took their seats or rather thrones under a canopy, and then the Royal Family followed in pairs and arranged themselves on each hand of their Parents. To understand this proceeding, or rather procession it must be remembered that at that time the Royal Pair had their quiver full of fifteen—the youngest at that time 13—in addition was the young Duke of Gloucester their cousin who afterwards married the Princess Mary. The ball was opened by the Prince of Wales (George the fourth) dancing a minuet with his elder sister followed by the Duke of Gloucester and the other Dukes of the troupe which was executed with great beauty and grace. In the meantime Mr. P. seated in the gallery was next to a gentleman who entered into conversation with him and seeing he was a stranger very politely told him he would be glad to give him the names of any person in the Court that he did not know. A gentleman happening to enter the ball-room at that time Mr. P. inquired who he was, his new friend told him that is Mr. Pitt, and observed that he must have been in London a very short time not to have known him and then went on to ask him[of]his own country. Mr. P. told him he was from Philadelphia when his new acquaintance seemed to be interested and told him that he had been in Philada some years ago and knew a great many persons there. He inquired about many of the ladies and among others was very particular about the Miss Chews, of whom Mr. P. gave him every information. His inquiring friend turned out to be Sir William Howe who commanded the English troops occupying Philada. in 1777.

Some years later when at a dinner in Philada. Mr. Coxe told this story an English gentleman at table doubted the possibility of such a-going to Court and a duel was only avoided by some friends getting Mr. Phillips to corroborate the narrative.

London, 1702 and 1706 *—John Phillips 1st and Anna his wife.

Children {
John Phillips 2nd married to Rebecca Pyewell—son William.

Margaret Phillips married to Anthony Stocker.
}

Children of Anthony and Margaret Stocker to wit

    John Clements Stocker—Anna Stocker—Mary Stocker.

---

* Years of birth of John and Anna Phillips.

John Clements Stocker was married in 1782 to Mary Katherine (Potts) Rutter daughter of Thomas and Martha (Potts) Rutter—he died Oct. 12, 1813; his wife died Nov. 28, of same year. His children were Anthony married to Elizabeth Clark of Portsmouth, N. H. he died Feby. 24, 1832—John Clements married to Caroline daughter of General Louis Tousard; he died July 28, 1833—Thomas Daniels born 1785, died 1790—Martha married to Robert Morton Lewis. She died Jany. 26, 1868—Mary Katherine born 1792 died 1793—Anna Maria married to Lawrence Lewis—died 1880—

Anna Stocker married 1778 to James Potts son of John and Ruth (Savage) Potts—he died in Philada. 10 Nov. 1788—his widow died 24 May, 1821—Children—Anthony, born 1779 died 1785—Maria married to George Poe in 1807 died at Pittsburg 1825—Clement born 1781 died unmarried. Andrew died unmarried at St. Thomas, W. I.—Mary Stocker married to John Miller—son Clement S—

W. S. P.

London. September ye 20th, 1730. Was Born John Phillips, about 9 oClock in the Evening.

Philadelphia. October ye 9th, 1737. Was Born Margarett Phillips, about 3 oClock in ye Evening.

Philadelphia. July ye 20th, 1739. Was Born John Phillips, about 7 oClock in the Morning.

Philadelphia. November 3d, 1740. Born William Phillips.

April ye 13th, 1742. William Phillips Departed this Life, aged one year, five months and 10 days.

Philadelphia. September 15th, 1743. Was Born Thomas Phillips at 4 oClock in ye Morning. . . . and died.

The above were all ye Children of John and Anna Phillips.

September ye 16th, 1748. Departed this Life, Anna Phillips, who died of a Yellow Fever, aged 42 Years, and being married 21 Years, 11 Months and one Day.

September ye 22d, 1762. Departed this Life John Phillips, who died of ye Yellow Jaundice, aged 60 Years—died at 12 oClock at Noon.

Philadelphia, Aprill ye 10th, 1766. This Evening, John Phillips, Son of John & Ann Phillips, marye'd Rebecca Pyewell, Daughter of William and Mary Katherene Pyewell. Was marye'd by ye Revern'd Jacob Duchee.

Philadelphia, November ye 13th, 1767, being Friday, Was borne a Daughter at 20 minutes past twelve oClock at Noon, of John & Rebbecca Phillips.

Ye 17th Day of December. The above Daughter was Christened by ye Revern'd Mr. Ric'd Petters and Called Margaret.

The 8th Day of August, 1760, dyed ye above Daughter Margaret at 7 oClock in ye Evening, aged 8 Months, Three Weeks & 5 Days.

Philadelphia, March the 14th, 1771 being Thursday was Born a Son at 6 oClock in the Evening of John & Rebbecca Phillips.

The 15th day of Aprill, 1771. The above Son was Christined by yᵉ Revern'd Jacob Duchee, & Called William.

Philadelphia, February the 26th, 1782 being Tuesday was Born a Son at 9 oClock in the Evening, of John & Rebbeca Phillips — the above Son was Christened by the Revern'd Doctor White, & Called John, April 3ᵈ, 1782 died when 6 mo. old.

Philadelphia, April 29th, 1799, being Monday. This day—was married, by the Revᵈ. Jaˢ. Abercrombie, William Phillips, son of John & Rebecca Phillips, to Anna Smith, daughter of Thomas W. & Eliza Smith.

Philadᵃ., February 23ᵈ, 1800, at 3 oClock P. M., was borne John Smith Phillips, son of William & Anna Phillips, & was christened by Rev. Jaˢ. Abercrombie.

Philadᵃ., December 23ᵈ, 1801, at 6 oClock A. M., was borne Elizabeth Phillips, daughter of William & Anna Phillips and was christened by Revᵈ. Jaˢ. Abercrombie, June, 1802.

Philadᵃ., Augt. 25, 1803. At 7 P. M. was borne Camilla Phillips, daughter of William and Anna Phillips, and Cristened by Rev. Jaˢ. Abercrombie.

William Smith Phillips, son of William & Anna Phillips, was born 7th October, 1805—Baptized by Revᵈ. Jaˢ. Abercrombie, May 14, 1806.

Emeline Phillips daughter of William & Anna Phillips was born 21st March, 1807 & baptized by Revᵈ. James Abercrombie, May 20, 1810.

Clements Stocker Phillips son of William & Anna Phillips was born 26th Nov., 1809 & baptized by Revᵈ. James Abercrombie May 20, 1810.

Anna Phillips daughter of William & Anna Phillips was born 21 Aprill, 1811, & baptized by Revᵈ. James Abercrombie May 30, 1812.

Clifford Smith Phillips son of William & Anna Phillips was born 21 May, 1813 & baptized by Revᵈ. James Abercrombie May 17, 1815.

Rebecca Phillips, daughter of William & Anna Phillips was born 28 July, 1815 & baptized by Revᵈ. Jackson Kemper June 9, 1816.

Caroline Phillips daughter of William & Anna Phillips was born Wednesday 27 June, 1821; baptized by Revᵈ. [—] Sheets.

Rebecca Phillips was Borne the 24th Day December at 4 oClock in the Morning 1741.

Departed this Life, John Phillips—April 27, 1806 aged 66 years, 8 months 19 days.

Departed this life, Rebecca Phillips, January 29, 1820 aged 78 years 1 mo. 5 days.

William Phillips, son of John & Rebecca Phillips, departed this life 24 August 1845—30 minutes past 4 oClock P. M. aged 74 years, 5 months, 10 days. (J. S. P.)

Philadelphia. October 17th, 1774—Was born Anna Smith, daughter of Thomas W. and Elizabeth Smith, whose maiden name was Clifford—

677

Feby. 10, 1856—Anna Smith above mentioned, married to William
Phillips departed this life in the 82nd year of her age—
May 26th, 1867—Rebecca Phillips—daughter of William and Anna
Phillips, departed this life, in the 51st year of her age.   J. S. P.
April 23d, 1868. Elizabeth Phillips, daughter of William and Anna
Phillips, departed this life, in the 68th year of her age—

> J. S. Phillips.

Clifford S. Phillips son of William & Anna Phillips, departed this
life the 3. December, 1868, in the 56th year of his age.   J. S.P.
1876, March 24 John Smith Phillips son of William and Anna
Phillips departed this life in the 77th year of his age.   W.S.P.
Another entry reads:
John Smith Phillips was born in Philadelphia 23 day of February
1800 at half an hour past three in the afternoon—This note was
made by Thomas W. Smith.

Elizabeth Phillips daughter of William and Anna Phillips was born in
Philadelphia, December 23d. 1801 at Half an Hour past Five o'clock in
the Morning.—This Note was made by Tho. W. Smith. The above are
the only entries in the Bible of Elizabeth Smith.

1879 January 24th. Clements Stocker Phillips son of William and
Anna Phillips, departed this life in the 70th year of his age—

> W. S. P.

1881 April 20. Emmeline Griffith daughter of William and Anna
Phillips departed this life in the 75th year of her age.   W. S.P.
Married May 5, 1825, by the Revd Mr. DeLancy, Camilla Phillips
Daughter of William & Anna Phillips to David Lewis Son of
David & Mary Lewis—
Married June 6th 1833, by the Revd. Dr. DeLancy, Emmeline Phil-
lips daughter of William & Anna Phillips to John P. Griffith
son of Robert E. & Mary Griffith—
Married Oct. 25t. 1838 by the Revd. Henry Morton Clements S. Phil-
lips son of Wm. & Anna Phillips to Mary C. Brinton daughter
of John & S. F. Brinton.
Married Nov. 15 1838 by the Revd. Dr. DeLancey Anna S. Phillips,
daughter of William & Anna Phillips to Adam May Stevenson
son of Cornelius & Mary Stevenson.
Married June 2nd 1846—by the Revernd W. H. Odenheimer Clifford
S. Phillips to Eliza Caroline daughter of Thomas A. Morgan.
Married October 5th 1848 by the Revd. Henry Morton William S.
Phillips Son of William and Anna Phillips to Frederica daughter of Edward * and Catharine Ingersoll.

---

* EDWARD INGERSOLL, ESQ., of the text, son of Honble Jared Ingersoll,
married, May 16, 1816, Catharine Ann Brinton, born June 4, 1796; died
April 22, 1866, daughter of John Hill and Sarah (Steinmetz) Brinton.
Vide Publications of The Genealogical Society of Pennsylvania, Volume
IX, pp. 53.
A note in the Bible mentions Edward Ingersoll as in the Second Troop,
Philadelphia City Cavalry, under Captain Benjamin Say, in 1820; and
his father as Adjutant in Regiment of Cavalry, 1810.

Married, 7th Novr. 1850, at the residence of Mrs. Anna Phillips, S. E. corner of Spruce & Eleventh Sts. by the Rev. Dr. M. A. D. W. Howe, Caroline, daughter of William and Anna Phillips, to John Barclay Biddle, M.D., son of Clement C. and Mary Biddle.

Philadelphia. Born Sep. 1st 1828—William Phillips Lewis son of David * & Camilla Lewis—Christened by Dr. Abercrombie while lying dangerously ill.

---

* DAVID LEWIS of the text, son of David and Mary (Darch) Lewis, born September 4, 1802; died April 27, 1895; married Camilla Phillips, born August 25, 1803; died July 21, 1887 [tombstone]. Had issue:

   i. WILLIAM PHILLIPS LEWIS, of the text; *d. s. p.* 18 June, 1906; Minister-in-Charge, Christ Church Chapel, Philadelphia, 1881 to 1895; married 17 June, 1868, at St. Mark's Church, by Rev. Walter Mitchell, to Sarah Morris Shober, born July 24, 1825; died June 29, 1917. No issue.

   ii. FRANCIS WALN LEWIS, of the text.

   iii. EDMUND DARCH LEWIS, of the text; died unmarried August 12, 1910; the widely known Philadelphia artist.

   iv. ANNA LEWIS, of the text; died at Lakewood, New Jersey, June 29, 1906; married (1) *q. v.* Samuel Emlen Randolph, who died December, 1872. Mrs. Randolph married (2) August 30, 1878, at St. Peter's by the Sea, Narragansett Pier, Rhode Island, Samuel Welsh, born September 3, 1803; died June 14, 1890. Issue by first marriage only: 1. *Philip Syng Physick Randolph,a q. v.*

   v. MARY DARCH LEWIS, of the text; died at Narragansett Pier, August 29, 1919; married, as of the text, Philip Syng Physick Conner, born May 14, 1837; died November 27, 1910. Issue: 1. *Camilla Conner,b q. v.* 2. *Edward Conner,c q. v.*

   vi. CLIFFORD LEWIS, of the text; died December 26, 1919; married, February 9, 1869, at St. Mark's Church, by Rev. William Phillips Lewis, Ella Eugenia Cozens, born October 23, 1846. Issue: 1. *David Lewis,* born December 12, 1869; baptized at St. Clement's Church; died November 2, 1925; married January 22, 1906, Lena Green Huneker, daughter of Thomas Green, died January 22, 1925; no issue. 2. *Clifford Lewis, Jr.,* born March 28, 1871; baptized at St. Clement's Church; married January 11, 1900, at Utica, New York, Isabel Marriner Kernan, born January 29, 1875, daughter of Nicholas E. Kernan of Utica and Harriet Ann Jenkins of Baltimore. Issue, born in Utica: i. ISABEL JENKINS LEWIS, born November 2, 1900. ii. CLIFFORD LEWIS, 3D., born September 8, 1904. iii. ELEANOR LEWIS, born March 16, 1907. 3. *William Burr Nash Lewis,* born December 29, 1872; baptized at Church of The Redeemer, Bryn Mawr; died unmarried, October 31, 1902. 4. *Eleanor Lewis,* born November 9, 1881; baptized at Christ Church Chapel by the Rev. William Phillips Lewis; died February 5, 1926; married June 6, 1907, Clifford Wheaton Vaughn of New York. No issue. (*See next page.*)

679

Born Aug. 19th 1832 (cholera summer) near Chester, Chester County, Francis Waln Lewis son of David & Camilla Lewis and died March 1833.

Philadelphia Born Oct. 17, 1835, E[d]mund D'Arch [sic.] Lewis son of David & Camilla Lewis. Christened by Dr. DeLancey St. Peter's Church.

Philadelphia Born April 21st 1837 Anna Lewis daughter of David & Camilla Lewis. Christened by Dr. DeLancey, St. Peter's Church.

Philadelphia Born Dec. 29 1839 Mary Darch Lewis daughter of David & Camilla Lewis in Pine St. Christened by Mr. Odenheimer St. Peter's Church.

Philadelphia Born June 18th 1843 S. E. corner Eleventh & Spruce the residence of his Grandfather Phillips, Clifford Lewis son of David & Camilla Lewis baptized in St. Luke's Church by Wm Spear.

---

a. PHILIP SYNG PHYSICK RANDOLPH, only child of Samuel Emlen and Anna (Lewis) Randolph, *supra,* born April 1, 1865; baptized by Rev. Mr. Davies; married (1) June 24, 1888, Hannah M. Fetherston; married (2) Josephine C. Watts. Issue by first marriage: i. *Dorothy Randolph,* born February 17, 1889; married (1) July 4, 1910, John R. Fell; married (2) September 2, 1924, Ogden L. Mills. Issue, surname *Fell:* 1. JOHN R. FELL, JR., born September 22, 1911; married December, 1931, Josephine Laimbeer. 2. DOROTHY R. FELL. 3. PHILIP SYNG PHYSICK FELL, born November 17, 1919. ii. *Philip Syng Physick Randolph, Jr.,* born February 7, 1890; married Madeleine Cochran; issue, surname *Randolph:* 1. PHILIP SYNG PHYSICK RANDOLPH, 3D., born February 17, 1921. iii. *Hannah Randolph,* born May 16, 1891; married Robert S. Hudson; issue, surname *Hudson:* ROBIN HUDSON. iv. *Emily Randolph,* born April 16, 1892; married July 4, 1913, Philip Stevenson; issue, surname *Stevenson:* 1. EMILIE STEVENSON. 2. PEGGY STEVENSON. 3. PHILLIS STEVENSON. v. *S. Emlen Randolph,* born May 17, 1894. vi. *L. Wister Randolph,* born 1896; married November 20, 1928, Mary D. Norris; issue, surname *Randolph:* 1. RICHARD RANDOLPH. 2. DOROTHY RANDOLPH.

c. EDWARD CONNER, son of Philip Syng Physick and Mary Darch (Lewis) Mary Darch (Lewis) Conner, *supra;* married at Octorara, July 3, 1889, Arthur Hale, born August 22, 1859, son of Rev. Edward Everett Hale of Boston. Issue: i. *Sybil Hale,* born May 3, 1890; died June, 1911; married November 2, 1904, Kurt Diederich; issue, surname *Diederich:* 1. CHILD, died young. 2. ELSA DIEDERICH, born January 6, 1908; married at Octorara, June 7, 1930, Jotham Johnson, born October 21, 1905.

c. EDWARD CONNER, son of Philip Syng Physick and Mary Darch (Lewis) Connor, *supra.,* born October 1, 1864; died Pinehurst, North Carolina, January 19, 1924; married (1) December 30, 1891, Frances Fetherston; married (2) November 6, 1911, Abbie Davis. Issue by first marriage: i. *Child,* died young. ii. *Edmund Darch Lewis Conner,* born November 30, 1899. Issue by second marriage: 1. DAVID SYNG PHYSICK CONNER, born March 6, 1914. 2. ALLEN BIDDLE CONNER, born April 18, 1922.

C. L.

May 2, 1847. All the above have gone through vaccination for whooping cough.

Married June 7th 1860 by the Revᵈ. Dʳ. Howe at the house of her father, Mary Darch Lewis to Philip S. P. Conner.

Married April 16, 1861, by the Revᵈ. Dʳ. Howe, at St. Luke's Church, Anna Lewis to S. Emlen Randolph.

Philadelphia Born Nov. 4, 1861, at 1911 Walnut St. Camilla Conner daughter of Philip S. P. and Mary D. Conner. Christened at Holy Trinity Church by Mr. Brooks.

July 28 [sic.] 1887 departed this life Camilla wife of David Lewis and daughter of Wm. and Anna Phillips in the 84 year of her age.

Sept. 13, 1888, departed this life Adam May Stevenson in the 82ⁿᵈ year of his age.

January 3, 1891 Departed this life William S. Phillips in the 86th year of his age.

April 23, 1891 Departed this life Frederica Phillips, wife of William S. Phillips, in the 70th year of her age.

Philadelphia Born Dec. 10, 1834 (in Front St. No. 200) Robert Eaglesfield Griffith * son of John P.† & Emmeline Griffith Christened by Dr. DeLancey, St. Peter's Church.

Philadelphia Born March 6, 1837 (in Spruce St., cor. of Eleventh) Anna Clifford Griffith,‡ daughter of John P. & Emmeline Griffith. Christened by Dr. DeLancey St. Peter's Church.

Philadelphia Born Augᵗ 17th 1839 Spruce St. Anna P. Stevenson § daughter of Adam May ‖ & Anna ¶ Stevenson. Baptized in St. Peter's Church by the Rev. Wᵐ. Odenheimer.

Philadelphia Born Jan. 14th 1842 Cornelius Stevenson,** in Spruce St. son of Adam May and Anna Stevenson, christened in St. Luke's Church by the Rev. Wᵐ. Spear.

---

* Robert Eglesfeld Griffith, or, as in text Eaglesfield, married Mary Howard Brice of Philadelphia. He died April 12, 1908. She died April 16, 1910.

† John Patterson Griffith, son of Robert Eglesfeld and Mary (Patterson) Griffith, was born January 8, 1802.

‡ Anna Clifford Griffith, of the text, died December 13, 1906.

§ Anna Phillips Stevenson, of the text, died unmarried February 13, 1914.

‖ Adam May Stevenson, born Philadelphia, November 11, 1806.

¶ Anna Smith Phillips died February 15, 1894.

** Cornelius Stevenson, of the text, died August 22, 1922; married Sarah Yorke, June 30, 1870. Mrs. Stevenson died November 14, 1921. Issue: 1. *William Yorke Stevenson,* born January 29, 1878; *d. s. p.* April 1, 1922; married in 1908, Christine Wetherill.

681

Born July 6th 1846 at the South East corner of Eleventh & Spruce Sts Rebecca Phillips Stevenson * daughter of Adam May and Anna Stevenson.

May 2-/1847. All the above have gone through vaccination for whooping cough.

Born April 3, 1849 at the South East corner of Eleventh & Spruce Sts. Elizabeth Clifford Stevenson † daughter of Adam May and Anna Stevenson. Christᵈ at St. Luke's Church by Revᵈ. M. A. DeWolf Howe.

Philadelphia Born April 19, 1847, 10 minutes before one P. M. 42 Pine St. William Morgan Phillips ‡ son of Clifford Smith and Eliza Caroline Phillips—Christᵈ by Wm. H. Odenheimer Rector of St. Peter's Church—

---

* REBECCA PHILLIPS STEVENSON, of the text, *d. s. p.* February 8, 1925; married, October 14, 1871, Frederick Thurston Mason, who died in 1917.

† ELIZABETH CLIFFORD STEVENSON, of the text, married October 19, 1876, John H. Easby, born August 14, 1844; died November 9, 1922. Issue: i. *May Stevenson Easby*, born September 15, 1878; married April 29, 1916, Henriette Large; issue: 1. MAY STEVENSON EASBY, JR., born February 29, 1920; died January 6, 1931. 2. GEORGE GORDON MEADE LARGE EASBY, born June 13, 1918.

‡ WILLIAM MORGAN PHILLIPS, of the text, died March 8, 1922; married June 5, 1873, Rebecca Chalkley Lewis, born November 28, 1849; died June 25, 1912; daughter of Joseph Saunders and Martha (Smith) Lewis. Issue: i. *Clifford Smith Phillips*, born March 11, 1874; married August 20, 1904, Anna Thompson, born January 25, 1884. Issue, surname *Phillips*: 1. WILLIAM MORGAN PHILLIPS, born May 20, 1905; married May 27, 1931, Elizabeth P. Colahan, born June 6, 1909. 2. VIRGINIA THOMPSON PHILLIPS, born January 17, 1917. ii. *Martha Lewis Phillips*, born March 31, 1876; married November 8, 1900, Edward George Trasel, born August 27, 1866; son of Edward George and Louisa (Laguerenne) Trasel. Issue, surname *Trasel*: 1. EDWARD GEORGE TRASEL, JR., born February 28, 1903; married April 20, 1931, Louise Holston Martin, born November 2, 1909, daughter of Charles Gold and Louise (Carrier) Martin of Springfield, Missouri. 2. MARIE LAGUERENNE TRASEL, born April 29, 1904; married May 16, 1925, Edward Wetherill Parrish, born February 12, 1904, son of Percival and Irma (Wetherill) Parrish; two children, surname *Parrish*: *Edward Wetherill Parrish*, born October 3, 1927, *Peter Trasel Parrish*, born June 14, 1930. 3. MARTHA PHILLIPS TRASEL, born May 11, 1906; married May 19, 1931, in Rome, Italy, Captain Cavaliere Grindo Fava; issue, one child, surname *Fava*: Rita Francesco Fava, born June 3, 1932. iii. *Joseph Lewis Phillips*, born February 15, 1879; married April 20, 1910, Louisa Bayard Hodge, born October 19, 1883. Issue, surname *Phillips*: 1. LOUISA BAYARD PHILLIPS, born January 22, 1911. 2. WALTER MASSEY PHILLIPS, born March 13, 1912. 3. MARY

Born 20th July, 1852, at Vancouver on the bank of the river Delaware, at 8 Oclock in the evening Harriet Morgan Phillips,* christened at All Saints' Church by Mr. Beasly on 22nd Sept—

Philadelphia Born Sepbr. 18th 1839 in Spruce St. Anna Clifford Phillips daughter of Mary C. & Clement S. Phillips † christened in St. James Church by the Rev. H. Morton.

Philadelphia Born August 30th 1841 6 O'clock in the morning George Brinton Phillips, son of Mary C. and Clement S. Phillips christened in St. James Church by the Rev. Henry Morton.

Philadelphia Born Oct. 21st 1844 William Brinton Phillips son of Mary C. and Clement S. Phillips. Christened by Dr. Morton, D.D. at St. James' Church.

Philadelphia Born Jany. 5th 1848 7 O'clock A. M., Clement S. Phillips,* Junr. Son of Clement S. Phillips & Mary C. Phillips. Christened in St. James' Church by the Rev. J. Bonner.

Philadelphia. Anna Clifford Biddle, eldest child of John B. and Caroline Biddle, was born at her father's house, N. E. corner of Spruce & Quince Sts., Wednesday, 17th September, 1851, at seven o'clock A. M. She was baptized by the Rev. Dr. Howe, at St. Luke's Church, Thursday, 25th March, 1852.

POWEL PHILLIPS, born April 4, 1914. 4. REBECCA LEWIS PHILLIPS, born October 15, 1916. 5. HARRIET MORGAN PHILLIPS, born November 2, 1919. 6. JOSEPH LEWIS PHILLIPS, JR., twin, born November 2, 1919.

* HARRIET MORGAN PHILLIPS, of the text, died June 14, 1926; married December 31, 1901, Walter Shelton Massey, born February 14, 1854; died May 29, 1909.

† CLEMENT STOCKER PHILLIPS, of the text, married, q. v., Mary Charlotte Brinton, born July 10, 1809; died June 5, 1885; daughter of John Hill and Sarah (Steinmetz) Brinton. Of their issue: i. *Ann Clifford Phillips*, of the text, died unmarried July 19, 1908. ii. *George Brinton Phillips*, of the text, died September 25, 1929; married January 3, 1883, Ellen Emlen Jones, daughter of Captain Benjamin and Harriet A. (Dans) Jones; had one child, ELEANOR EMLEN BRINTON PHILLIPS, born August 30, 1884; died September 16, 1889. iii. *William Brinton Phillips*, of the text, died unmarried January 28, 1926. iv. *Clement Stocker Phillips*, of the text, died October 20, 1925; married, November 15, 1881, Anna Clifford Biddle, q. v. died March 11, 1915, daughter of John Barclay and Caroline (Phillips) Biddle. Issue: 1. PHOEBE CAROLINE PHILLIPS, born March 22, 1883; married June 14, 1922, Alfred Coxe Prime, died March 2, 1926, son of Frederick and Laurette (de Tousard) Prime; two children, surname *Prime: Alfred Coxe Phillips Prime*, born July 30, 1923. *Phoebe Anna Prime*, born June 9, 1925.   P. C. P. P.

Harriet Biddle,* second child of John B. and Caroline Biddle, was born at the Paoli tavern, Chester co., Pa., Sunday, 8th August, 1852, at eleven o'clock P. M. She was baptized by the Rev. Dr. Howe, at St. Luke's Church, Philad^a—29th September, 1852.

William Phillips Biddle,† third child of John B. and Caroline Biddle, was born at his father's house, N. E. corner of Spruce & Quince Sts., Philad^a., Saturday, 17th December, 1853, at five o'clock P. M.

Clement Biddle,‡ fourth child of John B. and Caroline Biddle, was born at his father's house, N. E. corner of Spruce & Quince Sts., Philad^a., Monday, 11th December, 1854, at seven o'clock A. M.

Elizabeth Rebecca Biddle,§ fifth child of John B. and Caroline Biddle, was born at her father's house, N. E. corner Spruce & Quince Sts., Philad^a., December 9, 1856.

Caroline Biddle, sixth child of John B. and Caroline Biddle was born at her father's house, N. E. corner Spruce & Quince Sts., Philad^a. March 6, 1861.

Philadelphia Born April 2nd 1850 at half past 4 O'clock P. M. West side Schuylkill 9th Street 2nd door north from Pine Francis Clifford Phillips ||—son of William S. and Frederica Phillips—Christened by the Rev^d. Henry E. Montgomery at All Saints' Church Moyamensing, on the 6th October 1850.

Born May 23rd 1852 S. side of Pine St., 2nd house West of Sch^l. 6th Alfred Ingersoll Phillips, son of William S. and Frederica Phillips—Christened the same year in October, at the Church of the Mediator, by Rev^d. Arnott.

Married on the 30 June 1881—at Allegheny, Pennsylvania by the Rev. John Bakewell of Trenton New Jersey Francis Clifford

---

* HARRIET BIDDLE, of the text, married de Grasse Fox, born August 23, 1838; died September 30, 1906? Issue: i. *Sylvia de Grasse Fox*, born September 29, 1880; married Colonel Cecil Arthur Shaw of England, born June 10, 1871, British Army, D. S. O. ii. *Alice Maud Fox*.

† WILLIAM PHILLIPS BIDDLE, of the text, died February 24, 1923; married at Manila, Philippine Islands, April 12, 1908, Martha Reynolds Adger. No issue.

‡ CLEMENT BIDDLE, of the text, Commander U. S. N.; died June 5, 1933; married December 9, 1925, Anna Rutherford Pearson. No issue.

§ ELIZABETH REBECCA BIDDLE, of the text, married Samuel M. Miller of Philadelphia. Issue: i. *Charlotte Barclay Miller*, born September 3, 1878; died 15 April, 1890. ii. *Marion Spencer Miller*, born September 12, 1880; died February, 1881. iii. *John Biddle Miller*, born February, 1882; died young. iv. *Virginia Breckinridge Miller*, born July 5, 1883; married 23 May, 1911, Ralph Pemberton; no issue. v. *Elihu Spencer Miller, 3d.*, born July 21, 1884, married November 12, 1913, Rachel Coleman Lewis; issue: 1. ELIHU SPENCER MILLER, 4TH., born January 15, 1915.   P. C. P. P.

|| FRANCIS CLIFFORD PHILLIPS, of the text, died February 16, 1920.

Phillips to Sarah Ormsby Phillips, daughter of Ormsby and Anne S. [Phillips] * Phillips.

Born March 25 1884 Anne Ormsby daughter of above and died same day.

Born July 5, 1887 at the City of Allegheny Penna., Clifford Stephenson Phillips son of above.

Born June 13 1890 in Allegheny Frederick Ingersoll Phillips son of Francis C. Phillips & Sarah O. Phillips.

Married on the 17 June 1886 at Calvary Church Philada. by the Rev. Charles A. Dickey, Alfred Ingersoll Phillips † to Mary Colegate daughter of Richard C. and Elizabeth M. Woodruff Dale.

Born June 9, 1887 at Midnight Alfred Ingersoll Phillips ‡ son of above at 30 South 13th Street Philadelphia.

Born Tuesday July 23, 1889, at 9:40 P. M. at Crestnut Hill, Philadelphia Elizabeth Dale Phillips § daughter of Alfred I. and Mary C. Phillips.

Born Friday November 20, 1891, at 11:50 P. M. at Chestnut Hill, Philadelphia, Marguerite Fitzgerald Phillips || daughter of Alfred I. and Mary C. Phillips.

Born Monday, November 6, 1893, at Chestnut Hill Philadelphia at 9:55 P. M., Colegate Dale Phillips son of Alfred I. and Mary C. Phillips. Died the same day.

* * *

February ye 7th 1771 Was married a Negro Girll named Lucy to Fortune both belonging to John Phillips, by the Reverd. Mr. Peters.

March ye 28th 1771 Friday afternoon at 4 oClock was Borne a Negro Child, who was Christened by Mr. Peters & Named George.

November 6th 1772 Friday morning at 9 oClock, was Borne a Negro Child, who was Christened by Mr. Tho. Combes & Named Violet.

1774, April ye 13 Dyed Violet.

March 26, 1775, was borne a Negro Boy at 7 oClock in the morning, and was Christened by Reverend William White & named Fortune, and Dyed May ye 6th, 1777.

---

* The two Phillips families were unrelated.

† ALFRED INGERSOLL PHILLIPS, of the text, died August 15, 1914.

‡ ALFRED INGERSOLL PHILLIPS, JR., of the text, married June 21, 1915, Josephine Walbaum Neall. Issue: i. *Daniel Neall Phillips*, born September 10, 1916.

§ ELIZABETH DALE PHILLIPS, of the text, married August 9, 1912, George Fox, Jr. Issue: i. *Sylvia Fox*, born June 9, 1913.

|| MARGUERITE FITZGERALD PHILLIPS, of the text, married November 16, 1912, Stockton Townsend. Issue, surname *Townsend:* i. *Ann Ingersoll Townsend*, born June 28, 1915. ii. *Margot Fitzgerald Townsend*, born April 24, 1919. iii. *Marian Stockton Townsend*, born March 27, 1927.   M. F. P. S.

1778, April 30th was Borne Jack at one oClock P. M. Potts Grove. Christened by Reyernd Mr. White & Named Jack.

1780 September 17th was Borne a Negro Girll and Christend by ye Reverd Mr. White Decemb. 25, 1780 named Phillis.

George, who calls himself Brown was maryed to Anna Benton February 13th, 1800 by Revd. Mr. Jon[e]s, Baptist minister.

Was born William a Son of the above George & Anna, 27 January, 1801; christened by Revd. Absolem Jon[e]s.

Dyed, the above Child named William, August 4, 1801; buried by Absolem Jones.

Anna wife of Geo. Brown died 30 Aprill 1812.

George Brown died 27 November 1819.

George Brown married Charity Vance, 10 Aprill 1817.

1818 July 14 was borne a son of George & Charity, & Called George.

INDEX

WILLIAM PRESTON OF NEWCASTLE-UPON-TYNE
AND PHILADELPHIA.

By Charles S. Belsterling.

The surname of Preston in England is of great antiquity dating from the reign of Malcolm I of Scotland (A. D. 943 to 954). Before the compilation of Domesday Book, the estates of "Preston Richard" and "Preston Patrick" appear in an ancient preliminary survey comprising the lands then within that portion of the shire of York and later set off as county Westmoreland.

These two adjoining ancient manors may be termed the cradle of the Prestons. From the reign of King Henry II, when the custom of handing down a surname from father to son became established, they are shown to have been held by many succeeding generations of Prestons; in the case of the manor of "Preston Patrick," for an unbroken period of more than six hundred years. A long succession of persons bore the name of Richard de Preston and William de Preston from the time of King Henry II to that of Edward III.* From this parental stock are descended most of the Prestons whose names appear in the records of Great Britain, Ireland and America.

---

* *Transactions of the Cumberland and Westmoreland Antiquarian Society*, Second Series; Burke's *Landed Gentry*, London, 1852, Vol. 2, pp. 1066, *et seq.*

Sir Richard de Preston of the eleventh generation represented Westmoreland in Parliament during the reign of Edward III and was succeeded by his son Sir Richard. The son and heir of the latter, Sir John de Preston, was the last of the name to hold the two manors of " Preston Richard " and " Preston Patrick ". He also was a member of Parliament during the reign of Edward III. Space will not permit recounting the various methods by which the estates changed hands, nor how they were recovered several generations later.*

The branch of the Preston family with which this article is concerned, lived during the seventeenth century and earlier, in Newcastle-upon-Tyne and its environs. The family appears prominent in the Newcastle history as early as the middle of the fourteenth century. John de Preston was a bailiff of the towne in 1366 and 1368; keeper of the seal and collector of customs of the Port in 1359; collector of murage in 1362.† As late as the seventeenth century the family was there recognized as of the ancient family of Yorkshire heretofore called the cradle of the Prestons. "It may be truly said, Yorkshire has produced men for all things . . . as for the family of the Prestons of Newcastle-upon-Tyne, though they were removed from their native soil and much impaired in their estate, yet retained the spirit and mettle of their ancestors, they . . . carried like gentlemen and were accounted such amongst those who were truly so." ‡

No doubt, the Prestons of county Norfolk, England, known as the Beeston and Buckenham Prestons were of the same kin, for the reason that their arms are the same as those of the Newcastle-upon-Tyne and Philadelphia family: *Erm. on a chief sa., three crescents, or.*§

* *Cf.* Calendars of the Gormanston Registers. *Preston Family Genealogy of William Bowker Preston of Salt Lake City, Utah.*

† Early Newcastle Deeds, Surtees Society, Vol. 137, p. 217; Calendar of Patent Rolls 1358/61, pp. 181, 296; *ibid.*, 1361/4, p. 272; *ibid.*, 1364/7, p. 3.

‡ *Memoirs of Ambrose Barnes of Newcastle* — Surtees Society, Vol. 50, p. 24.

§ The Preston arms with its motto *"Lucem Spero Clariorem"* was assumed, under Royal License, by Lieutenant Colonel Sir Edward Hulton, D.S.O., M.C., who was created a Baronet in 1815. He was a son of Henry Hulton who married Elizabeth, daughter of Isaac Preston of Beeston, St. Lawrence, County Norfolk, on September 20, 1766. Colonel

The arms as described were used by the Preston family in Philadelphia upon its arrival there. The crescents may be found in the seal of Paul Preston, of whom presently, attached to his will of 1732 on file in the Registry of Wills, and the early generations employed the shield for a book plate, as shall appear later.

WILLIAM PRESTON, grandfather of William Preston, the Philadelphia emigrant ancestor, was church warden of the Parish of St. Andrew's, Newcastle-upon-Tyne, in the county of Northumberland. His signature appears on the Parish Register there in 1630. He was born *circa* 1596, and was admitted as a Freeman in the Weaver's guild in Newcastle in 1617. He died in Newcastle and was buried in St. Andrew's, March 3, 1643; about the year 1623 he married Elizabeth Watson.

Children of William and Elizabeth (Watson) Preston, all born at Newcastle-upon-Tyne and baptized in its parish Church of St. Andrew's:

2. i.   HENRY,[2] baptized February 29, 1624; married Jane Lawson.
   ii.   RALPH, baptized March 12, 1626; buried November 22, 1627.
   iii.   ANN, baptized March 23, 1627; married Ralph Ledgar, March 10, 1646.
   iv.   AMBROSE, baptized April 26, 1629; married Ann Turner, 1656.
   v.   JOHN, baptized November 20, 1631; buried August 26, 1645.
   vi.   MARGARET, baptized October 19, 1634; buried December 31, 1634.
   vii.   ALLES, baptized May 22, 1636.
   viii.   WILLIAM, baptized July 12, 1638.

2. HENRY [2] PRESTON (*William* [1]), baptized at St. Andrew's, Newcastle-upon-Tyne, February 29, 1624; was a member of the Guild of Weavers, made freeman May 1, 1645. His wife, Jane Lawson, whom he married at Newcastle, September 15, 1646, died after January 30, 1657.

Children of Henry and Jane (Lawson) Preston, all baptized at St. Andrew's:

Hulton assumed the name and arms of the Prestons when he was created a Baronet.

The Beeston Prestons of Norfolk were a prominent family. During the Civil Wars certain of them sided with and fought for the royal cause. William Preston, a Royalist, was taken prisoner by Cromwell at Lowescroft. Jacob Preston was falsely alleged to have been a Royalist and to have attended Charles I on the scaffold where he received from him an emerald ring. "The real Preston was Captain Robert Preston, who was watching the proceedings on behalf of the Parliament, and the Beeston family were essentially roundheads."—Rye's *Norfolk Hand Lists, First Series, No. 5.*

i. JANE,[3] baptized July 29, 1647.
3. ii. WILLIAM, baptized April 30, 1650; married Ann Taylor.
iii. THOMAS, baptized November 4, 1651.
iv. ELIZABETH, baptized November 4, 1651.
v. HENRY, baptized May 28, 1653.
vi. JOHN, born January 30, 1657; baptized February 5, 1657.

3. WILLIAM [3] PRESTON (*Henry,*[2] *William* [1]), baptized at Newcastle April 30, 1650; died in Frankford, Philadelphia, September 19, 1717.   He was educated at the Royal Grammar School of Newcastle-upon-Tyne, one of England's most prominent schools, founded in the reign of Henry VIII, and granted a charter by Queen Elizabeth in 1600.   Among its scholars who became famous may be named Admiral Lord Collingwood; Lord Eldon, Chancellor of England; Lord Stowell his brother; the poet Mark Akenside, and many others.

Like his father and grandfather, William Preston, was a member of the Guild of Weavers, having been made a Freeman in 1671.   Later he became a mason and builder.   This fact was doubtless the determining cause of his emigration to Pennsylvania.

Family tradition is responsible for the frequent statement that William Preston and his wife sailed from England in company with Francis Daniel Pastorius, Thomas Lloyd and some eighty other passengers, leaving 10th 4th mo. [June] 1683 and arriving 20th 6th mo. [August] 1683.   But the tradition is verified by two unassailable authorities: William Preston's entry * in the "Ould Preston Bible," elsewhere referred to, and by Pastorius in his *Bee Hive.*†

* "I left Ould England, with my wife and two children ye 10th of ye 4th month, 1683, and arrived in Pennsylvania ye 20th of 6th mo., 1683."

† "I prepared myself for this farthermost journey * * * Anno 1683, the 2nd of April I set out from Frankfort * * *.   The 4th day of May I sailed from Rotterdam * * *.   Came the 8th of ditto to London * * * went aboard of a ship which had the name of *America* (the captain whereof was Joseph Wasey) and being gone the 6th day of June from Gravesend, we arrived the 7th ditto at Deal and left England the *10th* of sd. month of *June* [*4th mo.*] and saw the 16th of August [6 mo] this new world, arriving the 18th ditto in the Bay of Delaware and the *20th* ditto at Philadelphia."

Watson also tells us that Pastorius, in the "Bee Hive" said further that "The fortunate day of our arrival on the 20th of 6th mo., 1683 * * *. I was as glad to land from the vessel every whit as St. Paul's shipmates were to land at Melita."

Among the passengers, says Pastorius, were Roman Catholics, Lutherans, Calvinists, Anabaptists, Episcopalians and only one Quaker. The Quaker referred to was undoubtedly Thomas Lloyd, as no record can be found that William Preston was a member of the Society of Friends in England. Besides, the minutes of the Society in Philadelphia show no record of a letter having been presented by him.

Also on the same ship was Joshua Tittery, a " servant to ye Society, broad Glass maker from New Cassle upon Tine." * The bringing of Joshua Tittery from Newcastle was the first definite step towards the manufacture of glass in Pennsylvania.

Likewise the coming of William Preston, a master builder of Newcastle was an important link in the preconceived plans for the building of the City of Philadelphia. It will be recalled that William Penn in the early days of the Colony was careful to select skilled artisans to ensure the excellence of the houses in durability and taste. By the year 1724 the master carpenters were numerous and important enough to compose a guild, patterned after The Worshipful Company of Carpenters of London founded in 1477, which ultimately resulted in the erection of Carpenters Hall, the home of the first Continental Congress.

Early upon his arrival we find William Preston receiving large grants of property.† On 15th 9 mo., 1684, he acquired from William Penn some 100 acres of land in Philadelphia, also city lot No. 1783; on 26th 2 mo., 1685, city lot No. 1897, and on 28th 3rd mo., 1685, he was *inter alia* granted some 1000 acres.

The earliest deed of record in Philadelphia bearing his name is dated 11th. 5th mo. 1691. It is a complicated document covering seven and one-half pages. The property, conveyed to Andrew Robeson and Charles Sander, was certain land situate along the Schuylkill River called Shumack Park. Among others William Preston appears as attorney for certain of the grantors; also Joshua Tittery, the aforesaid glass maker

* *The Pennsylvania Magazine of History and Biography*, Vol. VIII, p. 339.

† The originals of these land warrants are in the files of the Department of Internal Affairs of Pennsylvania, at Harrisburg. See also *Pennsylvania Archives*, 3rd Series, Vol. II, pp. 760, 764.

of Newcastle, is one of the grantors, with the consent of
Richard Townsend, millwright.

1685
Courtesy of The Historical Society of Pennsylvania.

Within two years after his coming to America, William
Preston was engaged as master builder in the construction of
the first permanent house of worship in Pennsylvania, Center
Square, antedating Merion Meeting House 1695, Christ
Church 1697, Holy Trinity, Old Swedes, Wilmington, 1699,
and Old Swedes, Wicaco, 1700. The building, planned in
1684, was to be of brick, size later determined 50 feet by 36
feet. Thomas Duckett and John Redman were appointed to
join with William Preston in carrying on the work. Samuel
Carpenter, Barnabas Wilcox and Alexander Beardsley were
appointed " to get the bricks, stone, etc., to the place to begin
work ". A committee was appointed in the summer of 1685
to draw on each subscriber for the paying of workmen in
provisions, etc., to the value of their subscriptions for the
building.*

* Minutes of Philadelphia Monthly Meetings, 9th 11 mo., 1682; 6th

William Preston early became a prominent member of the Society of Friends and appeared as witness to a marriage at Poquesink Creek, 6 mo. 2nd., 1684. In this year, at Quarterly Meeting, he was one of the representatives for Tackony and Poquesink.* Many similar appointments appear in succeeding years. From 1689 he was register of the Frankford Abington Monthly Meeting.† The minutes of Abington Meeting, 28th 6 mo., 1715, record that he and Daniel Pastorius were appointed "to attend ye Quarterly Meeting".‡

In 1692 his name is among the signers of "An early Petition of the Freeman of the Province of Pennsylvania to the Assembly " against the assessing and levying of certain taxes.§

The deed from Thomas ffairman, for the property upon which the Frankford Meeting House now stands, is in the handwriting of and witnessed by William Preston. The original is in the possession of the Historical Society of Frankford. The old meeting was Oxford Meeting until about 1800, when it was called Frankford Meeting. It belongs to Abington Quarterly Meeting. The minutes referred to show that he was an important factor in the building of this meeting house.

Not only was the integrity of William Preston and the high esteem in which he was held by his associates evidenced by the fact that he was entrusted with the affairs of the Society of Friends, including their financial matters and the construction of their meeting houses, but there are many additional proofs: He appraised the estate of Thomas Leary of Oxford in 1685, was executor of the estate of Thomas Livezey, 1691, one of

---

12 mo., 1682; 5th 6 mo., 1684; 1st 4 mo., 1685; 6th 5 mo., 1685; 12th 7 mo., 1685, in the hand of Samuel Preston. Samuel Preston came to Philadelphia from Maryland. He was a grandson of Richard Preston who arrived in Maryland in 1649, with seven of his family and entered land for seventy-three persons.—Edward D. Neill, *Founders of Maryland.*

* Philadelphia Quarterly Meeting Records, 2nd 10th mo., 1684.

† "At this meeting William Preston was to take ye Charge of ye Register Book, and to register such things as pertaine thereto. Ye 29th 2 mo., 1689." The minutes of this meeting also show that he had an important part in locating and building the meeting house.—*Cf. Minutes of Monthly Meetings*: 3rd 7 mo., 1683; 24th 7 mo., 1688; 29th 11 mo., 1698; 27th 9 mo., 1699.

‡ Marion Dexter Learned, *Life of Daniel Pastorius*, 221.

§ *The Pennsylvania Magazine of History*, 38, p. 500.

the trustees of the estate of Jonathan Livezey * 1698, and an executor of the will of John Lewis,† 1701, who gave his entire estate to "ye poor that is in necessity."

In 1692 he joined the ranks of George Keith who had also belonged to the Frankford or Oxford Meeting. One of the many notions of Keith was that it was entirely improper to have minister's galleries erected above the level of the seats of the other members of the Society. Accordingly, during the year 1692, William Preston and Robert Turner, went to the Old Front Street Meeting House, known as "Ye Bank Meeting House", and tore down the Minister's Gallery, their reason being that they had "a testimony against galleries". Turner continued to adhere to the Keithian doctrines, later going into the Episcopal Church. There is no indication in the minutes of the Abington Monthly Meeting or elsewhere, save the gallery episode, that William Preston was ever out of unity with Friends. His name appears throughout that trying period in the routine appointments of the meeting. The courteous apology he made was simply for the purpose of relieving his conscience and evidences a strong religious character. In acknowledging his error he asked forgiveness from Friends, the following being a copy of the original paper entitled "Condemnation to Clear the Truth":

"To ye quarterly meeting of ffriends in Philadelphia or to whomsoever it may concern:

Ffriends—Being sensible that I have brought trouble and groiffe upon ffriends in being concerned about pulling down ye gallery in ye front meeting house and being sensible of ye great love of ffriends in advising me to se unto the forwardness of ye said act and to condemn the same. Now these may signify for ye said action of mine, I am sorry it should so happen & for ye Truth's sake & Satisfaction of ffriends I do condemn it knowing & believing yt ye truth, admit of no violation, so hoping that this may give ffriends Satisfaction, desiring the love of ffriends as I hope I shall, in love to them whilst I draw breath.

Wm Preston

Frankford, 10/5/1696."

* Will proved 17th Dec., 1698.
† Will proved 16th July, 1701.

694

It is not here possible to outline the various ways in which William Preston rendered important and valuable service in the early development of Philadelphia County. He was instrumental in many surveys of its early townships. When the bridge crossing Mill Creek was washed away he was the leading spirit in opposing a change in the original road, which had paralleled the present Second Street and Frankford Avenue. On November 18, 1701 he was appointed by the Provincial Council a member of a committee of seven which stood for the old road; his fellow committeemen being Thos. Parsons, Joseph ffisher, Benj. Duffield, Robt. Adams, & Jno. Worral. The opposition committee which desired a new road consisted of: Grf. Jones, John Goodson, Samuel Richardson, Nicholas Waln, Robert Heath, Daniel Pastorius & Arnold Castell. The original report in favor of restoring the old road was accepted. It is in the hand-writing of William Preston and is in The Historical Society of Pennsylvania.

William Preston, designated in the monthly meeting as a yeoman, died in Frankford, Philadelphia, 19th 7 mo., 1717. In the words of his wife, Ann Taylor Preston, as recorded in the Ould Preston Bible: "My worthy husband William Preston departed this life ye 19th 7 month about half an hour after 9 o'clock in the morning, aged 67 years, 5 mos., lacking three days."

The Abington Monthly Meeting records his burial in the list of Oxford Burials, 1717. The action of Friends, covered by the entry from the minutes which appears in the footnote,* concerning the abolishment of marked gravestones, and

* "Quarterly Meeting held at Philada ye 2 of ye 7th mo., 1701: It was moved at this meeting by friends of Philad. mo. meeting that they being disatisfied with *Gravestones* or any other Sort of monuments over or About the Graves of friends bury ground have given their Sense and Judgment against It as *being needless.*

This Meeting Likewise are one with them therein believing It to be very needless and of evill tendency And therefor desires It may be recommended to the next yearly meeting for their Consideration that their may be generall order against it.

If they See Meet

Rowland Ellis	Richard Orme	*William Preston*
Thomas Walton	Thomas Story	Thomas Carpenter
Nich Walne And Antho: Morris		

and desired to Attend ye Service of ye next Yearly Meeting

A Copy of ye Minutes
Antho: Morris."

to which William Preston is a subscriber, is most unfortunate, from the viewpoint of posterity desiring to make research, since it is now impossible to ascertain the location of many graves of colonial ancestors who laid the foundations of our commonwealth.

The last will * and testament of William Preston, dated 29th 5 mo., 1714, is interesting as showing the customs of the day.† After payment of debts he gives to his eldest son, Amor, his "white broad-cloth coat, callominco vest, plush breeches," etc.: To his second son, Abel, "my dragett suit coat, vest and briches & stockings suitable," etc.: To Paul "my two cloaks, and all the remainder of my apparel, etc." The residue of the estate, moneys to be realized from sale of property, etc., is to be invested and the interest thereon, together with interest from bonds, etc., are to be held in trust for his wife.

The sundry household goods retained by widow Preston "being left her . . . amounting, as by an inventory may appear, to £94.5.4; the cash paid for coffin and digging grave was £8.9.1;" the wearing apparel for Amor, £11.14.0, and Paul, £5.0.0. Abel and Amor have cash "in hand on bonds" £25, and £37, respectively. The cash in hand on bonds due the estate amounted to £457.10.0.

William Preston married, September 10, 1672, Ann, daughter of Edward and Margaret Taylor, baptized at North Shields-upon-Tyne, England, July 18, 1651. Mrs. Preston accompanied her husband and two children to Pennsylvania and died at Frankford, Philadelphia, December 4, 1732. Her

* *Philadelphia Wills, Liber* D, No. 105, folio 80.

† The custom of willing specific articles was common among William Preston's early kin:

William Preston, of Twedemouth by will proved 31 March, 1582, gave "to George Crawford my man my armage sword and a pare of nisset britches of brode clothe * *; to John Rwelye * * a french crown for remembrance * *; to William Bell * * my books and my dagger * * ".

William Preston of Houghton, by will proved 1586, to "my said Sonne and Dorothy my daughter foure oxen equally between them. * * unto Agnes Simpson one black mare * * to Agnes my daughter one acre and a half of wheat and all my corn that is William Burdon's field, also I give her one graye meare and one graye fielie * * to my wife two kye and two loads of hay and I also give her sixty-six ewes * * unto Janey Burdon my servant two ewes * * all the rest of my goods to my wife and my daughter Agnes * *."

will, proved December 5, 1732, left estate to children Amor, Abel and Priscilla, daughter-in-law Elizabeth Preston and grand-child Mary Preston.

Children of William and Ann (Taylor) Preston, the first five born in North Shields-upon-Tyne, the others in Frankford, Philadelphia: *

    i.   HENRY,[4] born September 18, 1673; died, unmarried, in Philadelphia, 21 11 mo., 1707.†

    ii. BARBARY, born 8 mo., 1674, baptized St. Andrew's; died in England, 10 mo., 1675.

    iii. WILLIAM, born 25th 3 mo., 1678; died in England 13th 9 mo., 1681.

    iv. ELIZABETH, born 10th 5 mo., 1680; died in England, 12 mo., 1681.

    v.   REBECCA, born 10 mo., 1682, died in Philadelphia, 12th 7 mo., 1683.

4. vi. AMOR, born 7th 11 mo., 1684/5; married Esther Large.

    vii. ABEL, born 31st 11 mo., 1687/8; married first, October 8, 1712, Meribah Slocum of Shrewsbury, New Jersey, at house of Meribah Slocum; second, 21st 7 mo., 1731, Hannah Hudson of Philadelphia.

5. viii. PAUL, born 30th 9 mo., 1690; married Elizabeth (Oldman) Gilbert.

6. ix. PRISCILLA, born 27th 3 mo., 1693; married John Van Laer, Jr.

    x.   SARAH, born 21st 12 mo., 1695/6; predeceased her father.

    xi. PHOEBE, born 7th 7 mo., 1700; not named in father's will.

4. AMOR[4] PRESTON (*William,*[3] *Henry,*[2] *William*), born in Frankford, Philadelphia, January 7, 1684; died after November 29, 1732; married ‡ 6th 11 mo., 1710, Esther Large, and settled at Wicaco. After a time the little homestead was destroyed by forest-fires and the Prestons, on the invitations of friendly Indians, went to Hollekonk, in Buckingham, Bucks County. They both spoke Indian fluently,§ Mrs. Preston even serving as interpreter at an Indian treaty at Hollekonk. She died in Buckingham, at the home of her son, Paul.

---

* Unless otherwise stated, the genealogical data pertaining to this family is taken from the *Ould Preston Bible,* dated 1599, abstract of which may be found in the *Publications of the Genealogical Society of Pennsylvania,* vol. VII, p. 38 *et seq.* **

† Watson in his *Annals of Philadelphia* relates that Henry Preston was fined £5 by the Grand Jury for avoiding the duties of watchman and constable. "Among other respectable citizens thus fined," says Watson, "I noticed the names of Joseph Shippen, Abram Carpenter, George Claypole and Henry Preston."

‡ Falls Monthly Meeting: Certificate of clearness of marriage 8 mo. 30, 1710; " things are well " 10 mo. 6, 1710.

§ Henry D. Paxson, *Where Pennsylvania History Began,* 38.

**See Volume III of this work, pp. 649-651.

"1774—14 February, died in Bucks county, Mrs. Preston, at the advanced age of 100 years and upwards. She had seen Penn and his colonists at Philadelphia; had acted as his interpreter occasionally with the Indians. She possessed her memory and understanding till her last." *

Children † of Amor and Esther (Large) Preston, order of birth uncertain, and there may have been others:

  i. NATHAN,⁵ born 28 2 mo., 1711; died 24 April, 1787; ‡ married 28th 12 mo., 1737, MARY, daughter of John and Eleanor Hough, born 4th 7 mo., 1715; died 5th 1 mo., 1782. Issue: 1. *Mary Preston*, born 13 10 mo., 1739; died 7 7 mo., 1795. 2. *Martha Preston*, born 31 6 mo., 1743; died young. 3. *Eleanor Preston*, born 20th 3 mo., 1748.
  ii. MARY, died unmarried, November 13, 1782.
  iii. ELEANOR, married January 19, 1786, John Carey.
7. iv. PAUL, born 1724; married Hannah Scarborough Fisher.

5. PAUL ⁴ PRESTON (*William,*³ *Henry,*² *William* ¹), was born at Frankford, Philadelphia, 30th. 9 mo., 1690, and died there, November 9, 1732, his death being recorded on the Minutes of the Philadelphia Monthly Meeting. His probable burial was in Friends' ground, Arch Street, east of Fourth.

A leading iron worker of his day and vicinity, his will, proved December 5, 1732, shows a good estate, the inventory including large quantities of wrought iron, numerous plough shares, axes, tongs, shovels and anvils, also a number of slaves. Chattles, and movables appraised at £727.7.0.

At his residence in Philadelphia he exercised a gracious hospitality, kind to all classes and especially ministering to the necessities of the saints. Being appointed an elder, he was fervent in spirit in fulfilling the duties devolved on him, and his services in religious meetings were many. He was " careful in the intentions of religious meetings, and in the education of his children ". Thomas Chalkley, who considered Paul Preston's house as his Philadelphia home, gives testimony that on his dying bed he declared he: " had no

* Cf. Watson, *Annals,* i, 160, for tales told by Samuel Preston, son of Paul, of his grandmother, the aged Mrs. Preston; and *Davis' History of Bucks County.*

† Genealogical data furnished by Emma L. Rice of Newtown, Pennsylvania, a lineal descendant.

‡ "Buried at Plumstead, where the old meeting house stood, attended by a vast number of people, by which it appeared that he was a man well beloved as a minister of the Gospel."—*Publications of the Genealogical Society,* vol. iii, 47.

698

desire to live but to do good, and that it had been his care to keep a conscience void of offence towards God, and to all men which was his comfort." He therefor lived in good esteem with his friends and neighbors, much beloved for his kindnesses, and " when he deceased his loss was deeply felt ".*

Paul Preston

He married at Philadelphia Monthly Meeting, 22nd 2 mo., 1713, Elizabeth (Oldman) Gilbert, daughter of Thomas Oldman † and his wife Elizabeth Sikes,‡ and widow of Joshua Gilbert, who died in 1711. Among the thirty-seven witnesses

---

* Biographical Sketches of Ministers and Elders, *The Friend*, vol. 39, p. 348.

† The Oldmans were among the early Quaker families of Norfolk, England. In 1664, John Oldman of Watlington disclaimed Arms (Rye's *Norfolk Families*, p. 625). Thomas Oldman, the emigrant ancestor, sailed from Liverpool, England, 7 mo., 1683, on the *Morning Star*, of Chester, Thomas Hayes, master, and arrived in Philadelphia, 9th mo. 20, 1683 (see deposition of Thomas Oldman, Futhey and Cope, *History of Chester County, Pennsylvania*, p. 740). On 1st mo. 20th, 1687/8, he married Elizabeth Sikes at Lewes, Sussex County on Delaware, Pennsylvania. He was a man of property, member of Provincial Assembly of Pennsylvania from Sussex County, 1695-1697-1698, and Justice of Peace, 1695-1698. As a member of the Provincial Assembly was one of the signers of The Declaration of Fealty, Christian Belief and Test, a most remarkable historical document. The original of this document is in The Historical Society of Pennsylvania, dated September 10, 1695. The signers were all Quakers except John Farmer, a member of the Church of England. Among the signers were: Sam. Carpenter, Antho. Morris, Franc. Rawle, Edw. Shippen, David Lloyd and the other members of the Assembly. Thomas Oldman was also active in defense of the colony against the attacks of the French pirates in 1695.—Scharf's *History of Delaware*, vol. 11, 1235-1236. He died in Philadelphia, 11th mo. 21st, 1714. His wife, Elizabeth, died 6 mo. 23, 1724. The children of Thomas and Elizabeth Oldman were: 1. *Elizabeth*, above, born 1689; 2. *Thomas*, married Mary Garrett; 3. *Sarah*, married James Elfreth. Jane Oldman, a grand-daughter of Thomas Oldman, married Daniel Williams on March 27, 1746, North Meeting House, Philadelphia. He was a member of the Provincial Assembly, signer of the Non-Importation Act, and founder of Williamsport, Pennsylvania.

‡ Elizabeth Sikes, wife of Thomas Oldman, was a daughter of James and Elizabeth Sikes of Ouldham, Lancaster. James Sykes, in 1665, is

to the ceremony were: Anthony Morris, Thomas Chalkley, Hugh Durborrow, Joseph Drinker and Richard Waln.

Children of Paul and Elizabeth (Oldman) Gilbert Preston, order uncertain:

8. i.   WILLIAM,[5] born 1714; married Sarah Carlile.
ii.   RACHEL, died 15th 5 mo., 1715.
iii.   THOMAS, born 3d 10 mo., 1719. Thomas Preston was a druggist at the sign of the Golden Mortar, Second Street, between Chestnut and Market, opposite Black Horse Alley. He married Mary Lloyd at the house of Francis Cowl.
iv.   MARY, born 1724; married at Philadephia, 7th 4 mo., 1743, Samuel Lippincott, son of William Lippincott of Shrewsbury, New Jersey, where they settled. In 1747 they returned to Philadelphia but were transferred to Haddonfield; and thence, 10 mo., 1765, to Shrewsbury.
v.   BENJAMIN, buried 1728.
vi.   JOSEPH, born 1721. He is named in will of brother William, February 11, 1740.
vii.   HANNAH, born 1713, died 3 mo., 1718.
viii.   SARAH, died 3 mo., 1718.

6. PRISCILLA [4] PRESTON (*William,*[3] *Henry,*[2] *William* [1]), born at Frankford, Philadelphia, 27th 3 mo., 1693; married out of Meeting, September 13, 1713, John Van Laer, Jr., a Presbyterian. In 1735 their daughter, Ann [5] Van Laer, born 1716, married, as second wife, John Strangeways Hutton, an account of whom, by Charles Wilson Peale, is given in the *Columbian Magazine* for September, 1792, and whose portrait, from an oil painting by Peale, is reproduced in Watson's *Annals*. He was a son of John Hutton, born in Scotland, and grandson of Arthur Strangeways, of New York, who died in Boston at the age, it is said, of 101 years.

John Strangeways Hutton and his wife Ann [5] (Van Laer) Hutton are buried in the Third Presbyterian Churchyard of

recorded in Besse's *Sufferings of the Quakers*. At Marsden Monthly Meeting of Friends, Lancashire, 3d mo. 20, 1686, James Sikes gives notice of his intention to remove with his wife Elizabeth, his son Simon, and daughter Elizabeth, to America. The certificate of removal was granted by the same meeting, 4 mo. 17, 1686. Shortly after their arrival in Pennsylvania, his daughter Elizabeth, as stated above, married Thomas Oldman. James Sykes died in Lewis, in 1687. His wife, Elizabeth, having predeceased him there. The paternal ancestors of James Sykes are buried in the Sykes graveyard in Heyside, England. The children of James and Elizabeth Sikes, as entered on the Records of Marsden Meeting, were: 1. *Nathaniel*, b. 11 mo. 1, 1654/5; 2. *John*, b. 1 mo. 11, 1657/8; 3. *Simeon*, b. 11 mo. 18, 1659; 4. *Sylvanus*, b. 11 mo. 31, 1661; 5. *Elizabeth*, b. 7 mo. 15, 1664; 6, *James*, b. 6 mo. 3, 1669.

Philadelphia. The inscription on their tombstone reads: " In Memory of Ann Hutton, who died November 14th, 1788, Aged 72 years. Also, of John Hutton, who died December 23rd, 1792, Aged 108 years and 4 months." Of their sons: *George*[6] *Hutton* married August 11, 1760, Mary Moore. Their daughter Mary Hutton married John McMullin of Philadelphia, who left descendants of this and other surnames, among whom were the wives of the late Major-General William Scott Ketchum and Colonel Franklin Foster Flint. *John* [6] *Hutton* married October 6, 1764, Elizabeth Merritt. He died December 6, 1791, and his wife April 11, 1828, in the 80th year of her age. They are buried in St. Peter's Churchyard, Philadelphia. They left descendants living in Philadelphia, many of whom are mentioned in *Descendants of Jöran Kyn,* including their grandson Adjutant-Lieutenant John [8] Galt Hutton, who served in the War of 1812; and their grand-daughter, Lucinda [8] Ann Hutton, who married, October 27, 1842, John Swift Keen. Gregory [9] Barnard Keen, LL.D., 1844-1930, a son of this marriage, was one of the most talented descendants of William Preston the propositus, as well as one of Philadelphia's distinguished men of letters. For twenty years the Curator of The Historical Society of Pennsylvania, he had previously succeeded Frederick D. Stone as its Librarian. *Benjamin* [6] *Hutton* married Rebecca Plumsted, whose descendants are mentioned in *Chronicles of the Plumsted Family* by Eugene Devereux, and Keith's *Provincial Councillors of Pennsylvania.* In the former work, pp. 64, 65, it is erroneously assumed that William and Ann Preston came from the County of Norfolk, England, presumably because their arms were the same as the Prestons of that county. As heretofore shown, this particular Preston family came from Northumberland. The facts, however, are correctly stated in the article written by Gregory Bernard Keen, LL.D., concerning the Hutton, Plumsted and Devereux families.*

7. PAUL [5] PRESTON (*Amor,*[4] *William,*[3] *Henry,*[2] *William* [1]), born 1724, died in Buckingham, Bucks County, October 19, 1806. Following family example he was prominent in the religious body of which he was a member. From 1755 to 1777 he was clerk of Buckingham Meeting of Friends. By close application he became an excellent mathematician and linguist,

---

* *The Pennsylvania Magazine of History,* vol. 43, pp. 251 *et seq.*

and was county treasurer in 1768,* county surveyor, tax col-
lector and court translator of German.† He would appear to
have been school-master as well in or about 1750, since "Paul
Preston's school " is referred to in the *Journal* ‡ of John
Watson, Assistant Surveyor to the Commissioners of the
Province of Pennsylvania, whose friend he was.

He wrote considerable poetry as did his two daughters.
His most pretentious poem was *Solomoncis* in five or more
books,§ of which practically nothing has been preserved.   He
also wrote in verse an interesting narrative of *The Captivity
of Benjamin Gilbert and Family, by the Indians in 1780.*
Two stanzas illustrating the rhythm of the poem are cited

> " The all-protecting arm of Providence,
>   Can sweeten ev'ry bitter cup of grief;
> In all besetments is the best defence,
>   In every sorrow, the most sure relief.
>
> In poverty, the riches of the meek,
>   In pining hunger, cheers the fainting soul,
> Can with a wond'rous strength supply the weak,
>   Support the lame, and make the cripple whole."

A fine classical scholar he translated from the Latin *The
Works of Anicius Manlius Torquatus Severinus Boethius,*
concerning *The Consolation of Philosophy,* which his friends
published in 1808, together with the poem as a tribute to his
memory.   Though artificial and labored in style, the poem
shows a deep religious conviction and evidences in its choice
of language familiarity with the classics of the eighteenth
century.

The sonorous lines of the translation bear witness to his
knowledge of the Greek and Latin poets; the Works of
Boethius had many translators, among them Alfred the Great
and Queen Elizabeth.   Mr. W. V. Cooper, B.A., Kings College, Cambridge, later published a translation in the series
known as the Temple Classics.   A comparison of the latter
with Paul Preston's translation will show that the self-taught

* *Minutes of Pennsylvania Assembly.*

† Davis' *History of Bucks,* 270.

‡ *Pennsylvania Magazine of History,* Vol. 39, 1, *et seq.*

§ *Poets and Poetry of Bucks County,* by Gen. W. W. Davis.   A collection of papers read before the Bucks County Historical Society, Vol. I of
Publications of that Society.

THE

WORKS

OF

Anicius Manlius Torquatus Severinus Boethius,

CONCERNING THE

CONSOLATION OF PHILOSOPHY.

———◉✿◉———

WRITTEN ABOUT 1240 *YEARS AGO.*

———✿◉✿———

TRANSLATED FROM THE LATIN—BY
PAUL PRESTON,
A SELF-TAUGHT GENIUS OF THE COUNTY OF BUCKS.

———◆———

Published by his Friends as a Tribute to his Memory.

———◢◢●◢◢———

PRINTED AT DOYLESTOWN—BY
ASHER MINER.
1808.

(Copy in The Historical Society of Pennsylvania.)

scholar of nearly one hundred and fifty years ago caught the meaning and spirit of the original as well as the college-bred man of modern times.

He also left behind him a manuscript work on *Surveying* and still another which teaches the use to which a straight stick and compass can be applied. In 1787 his friend and former pupil, Jonathan Ingham, dedicated to him an English translation of the epitaph of Theocritus of Hippanox which is humbly inscribed to " my well esteemed friend and tutor Paul Preston. . . ."

Paul Preston

As before stated Paul Preston died in 1806, and is buried in the graveyard of Buckingham Meeting. Upon the stone marking his grave are the letters P. P. and the year, 1806. The Meeting House stands upon his old estate, in silent remembrance of this well-stored mind of the eighteenth century. The realty of Paul Preston included 127½ acres of land situated in Plumstead Township.*

He married, November 21, 1753, Hannah Scarborough Fisher, born April 13, 1727; died January 13, 1822.

Children of Paul and Hannah Scarborough (Fisher) Preston, born in Buckingham:

- i. DEBORAH,[6] born September 2, 1754; died unmarried, October 15, 1837.
- 9. ii. SAMUEL, born June 17, 1756; died December 8, 1834.
- iii. ANN, born March 3, 1758; died unmarried, January 4, 1845; a minister in Society of Friends.
- iv. NAOMI, born March 1, 1762; died December 9, 1845; married James Price.
- v. EUPHEMIA, born February 15, 1765; died unmarried, September 25, 1837.
- vi. PAUL, born March 10, 1767; died October 19, 1853.
- vii. SILAS, born June 20, 1769; died February 20, 1855; a prominent minister in Society of Friends; married Margaret, daughter of Francis and Eleanor Good, 4th 6 mo., 1796.

8. WILLIAM [5] PRESTON (*Paul,*[4] *William,*[3] *Henry,*[2] *William* [1]), born at Philadelphia, 1714; died there February 21, 1740. His was but a short life of twenty-six years. According to his will of February 11, 1740,† his home was on the "corner of the west side of Front Street ", with a lot of ground adjoining. From the inventory of his estate it would appear that he was a carpenter and builder, maintaining a shop apart from his home. Among his assets was a Negro boy, Caesar. This was the last slave owned by a William Preston of this branch.

William Preston

* *Bucks County Deeds*, Book No. 40.

† Proved February 24, 1740. Recorded *Liber* F, ff. 179, 194 Philadelphia Wills.

He married at Philadelphia, August 13, 1737,* Sarah, daughter of John † and Mary (Gladwin ‡) Carlisle of Burlington, New Jersey. This was a marriage "out of Meeting", satisfaction for which was made 24th 9 mo., 1738.

Child of William and Sarah (Carlile) Preston, born at Philadelphia:

10. i.   WILLIAM,[6] born 26th 10 mo., 1737; married Barbara Heisler.

9. HONORABLE SAMUEL [6] PRESTON (*Paul,*[5] *Amor,*[4] *William,*[3] *Henry,*[2] *William* [1]), born in Bucks County, Pennsylvania, June 17, 1756; died at Stockport, Wayne County, Pennsylvania, December 8, 1834. A staunch federalist, he was, by the appointment of Governor Thomas Mifflin in 1790, the first Associate Judge of Wayne County and served until 1803 when he resigned. He is recorded in the *History of Wayne Judiciary* as a Quaker, born in Bucks County and as the first man to engage in commerce on the Delaware River in Buckingham. As early as 1787, under the patronage of Henry Drinker, a wealthy Quaker of Philadelphia and a large land owner, he travelled through Wayne and Luzerne Counties seeking a proper site for a village. He named his chosen site Stockport and the township Buckingham.

He was a man of genius and a good mathematician. He built the first mills in Buckingham and by 1806 had cleared 130 acres of land. Iron and merchandise he brought up the Delaware River in Durham boats which were pulled by setting poles.

* The printed records of Christ Church give this marriage as that of William Reston and Sarah Carlile.

† JOHN CARLILE, born Spittlesfield, Stepney Parish, Middlesex, England, 13th 4 mo., 1678; died Burlington, New Jersey, in January, 1726; married, Burlington Meeting, 27th 5 mo., 1704, Mary Gladwin, who survived him, and removed with her daughter, Sarah, to Philadelphia bringing certificate to Meeting of Friends. He was a son of JOHN CARLILE of London, born 1648; married 29th 1 mo., 1671, Mary Goodwine, of Spittlesfield; son of JOHN CARLILE of London, born 1618; died 11th 3 mo., 1692; married April, 1647, Jane — —, born 1629; died 21 February, 1689.—*English Friends Records.* (Transcripts of, in Collections of The Genealogical Society of Pennsylvania.)

‡ MARY GLADWIN, daughter of Thomas and Mary Gladwin, was born at Burlington, July 1, 1685. The will of her father, dated December 19, 1694, proved January 5, following shows that her mother was already deceased.—*New Jersey Archives,* First Series, vol. 23, 188.

The fervent federalism of Judge Preston may best be gleaned from his famous charge to the grand jury of Wayne County, as printed in pamphlet form at Easton in 1800 and widely distributed at that time: *

" Therefore in this infant country, where the foundation of our political and moral character is yet to establish, a

prudential care is necessary to guard against all those surrounding evils, it is not only the duty of Jurymen but every individual citizen to discourage all such Seditions, murmurs and complaints against government and guard against every species of foreign influence, as the consequences are so pernicious to our welfare."

* A copy of this pamphlet and the Journals of Samuel Preston are in The Historical Society of Pennsylvania.

On the opposite page is reproduced the book plate of Judge Preston, as designed by his friend Benjamin West. It should be noted that it comprises the arms of the Beeston-Buckingham Prestons of Norfolk as well as those of the Prestons of Newcastle-upon-Tyne and Philadelphia, heretofore referred to.

The old Preston homestead at Wayne was erected more than one hundred and twenty-five years ago. It was built by Judge Preston, the first man who started an opening in the forests of that region, and has sheltered four generations. In the days of African slavery in this country it was known as a station of the "Underground Railroad", and afforded a safe retreat for scores of negro bondmen fleeing from servitude in the South to Canada. A contemporary wrote: "Knowing as I do the moral, social and intellectual excellencies of the Preston family, and making all due allowances for the frailties of human nature, truth compels me to say that I shall never look upon their like again." *

At his death in 1834, Judge Preston was survived by three sons and a daughter. Paul Silas Preston, the eldest of the sons, possessed an extensive library and was well acquainted with the classics. He was sheriff of the county from 1828, serving three years. In 1835, he was Register and Recorder. Having Quaker principles he was conscientiously opposed to slavery.

Judge Preston married, September 1, 1793, Marcia, daughter of Valentine and Marcia Jenkins of Dutchess County, New York. She died June 12, 1835, aged seventy-one years, six months and nine days.

Children of Hon. Samuel and Marcia (Jenkins) Preston, born at Stockport, Wayne County:

    i.   PAUL SAMUEL, married Henrietta Maria, daughter of Samuel R. Mogridge, who came from England; had issue.
    ii.   SAMUEL, died unmarried.
    iii. HANNAH, married Benjamin Randall; had issue.
    iv. WARNER MIFFLIN, died unmarried.

10. WILLIAM [6] PRESTON (*William,*[5] *Paul,*[4] *William,*[3] *Henry,*[2] *William* [1]), born Philadelphia, December 26, 1737; died in Northern Liberties, Philadelphia, October 6, 1820.

* Matthews' *History of Wayne, Pike and Monroe Counties, Pennsylvania*, pp. 520-529.

On 12th 5 mo., 1752, the following was written in the Preston Bible before referred to, " William Preston, his Bible that was his father's William, grandfather Paul Preston, great grandfather William Preston and great-great-grandfather Henry Preston." While this statement fixes the young owner's descent, it is perhaps incorrect as to the first owner of the honored volume which opens with the statement, "I [William Preston] left old England with my wife and two children the 10th 4 mo., 1683," and follows with *his* family record.

He became prominent as a boat builder, his yard being located in Northern Liberties. By his will, proved October 9, 1820, he disposed of a comparatively large estate to his immediate family.

During the Revolution William Preston served, first, in Captain Jesse Roe's company of Artillery Artificers, Continental Line, under command of General Knox; was later commissioned, April 7, 1777, lieutenant in Colonel Benjamin Flowers' Artillery Artificers Corps, Continental Line, and is named in a return of that Regiment, April 16, 1782.*

His marriage to Barbara Heisler of Germantown, September 17, 1758, was out of Meeting and "Satisfaction" was made to the Philadelphia Monthly Meeting 5th 10 mo., 1759, when "T. Elfreth was therefore desired to have it read at ye Bank" Meeting on Front Street, above Arch where his great grandfather destroyed the Minister's gallery in 1692. Barbara Preston died 30th 9 mo., 1798, during the yellow fever epidemic, and, with her son Joseph Preston, who died the same day, was buried in Friends' Ground at Fairhill.

Children of William and Barbara (Heisler), born in Philadelphia:

    i.   Mary,[7] died 9 mo., 1759.
    ii. Sarah, born 18th 10 mo., 1760; died February 2, 1763.
    iii. Hannah, born 17th 3 mo., 1763; died 1803; married, August 13, 1785, Daniel Murray. †
11. iv. William, born 12th 6 mo., 1765; Catharine Black.
    v. John, born 30th 3 mo., 1768.
    vi. Joseph, born 4th April, 1777; died 30 9 mo., 1798.

* *Pennsylvania Archives*, Fifth Series, vol. iii, 1086, 1094.

† For issue of this marriage, see *Publications*, vol. vii, 40.**

**See Volume III of this work, pp. 651.

11. WILLIAM [7] PRESTON (*William,*[6] *William,*[5] *Paul,*[4] *William,*[3] *Henry,*[2] *William* [1]), born Philadelphia 12th 6 mo., 1765; died there, October 4, 1819. With his father he was engaged in boat building but assumed the management of the business some ten years before his decease.

In the War of 1812 he was a member of the Northern Liberties' Volunteer Artillerists, commanded by Captain John Nagle, organized into a Batallion under Major A. M. Prevost, being in the service of the United States from September 8, 1814 to January 3, 1815.*

He married at Zion's Lutheran Church, Philadelphia, August 6, 1789,† Catharine, daughter of Frederick ‡ and

* *Pennsylvania Archives*, Sixth Series, vol. viii, 461, 463, 468.

† The original marriage certificate is in the Historical Society of Pennsylvania, the Rev. John Frederick Schmidt being the officiating clergyman. Because of patriotic utterances Mr. Schmidt was driven from Germantown during its occupancy by the British. Later he was sent to Zion Church, Philadelphia, where in December, 1799, he took part in the commemorative services on the death of Washington. According to the *Journal of Elizabeth Drinker*, Major General Henry Lee delivered an oration to 4000 persons assembled in the Church.

‡ George Frederick Swartz came to Philadelphia in the ship *Nancy*, Captain John Ewing, from Rotterdam, last from Cowes, and subscribed to the usual qualifications 27 September, 1752, signing as George Frederick Swartz (*Pennsylvania Archives*, Second Series, vol. xvii, 361-2). As George Frederick Swartz he married at Trinity, Oxford, August 5, 1755, Abigail Chester, who survived him. The original of this marriage certificate is in the possession of Mrs. Charles V. McLean of Philadelphia, a lineal descendant. Frederick Swartz served during the Revolution as a member of the Second Regiment of Pennsylvania Line under Colonel Haas. This regiment, first brought into the field December 24, 1776, suffered heavily at Brandywine and Germantown (*Pennsylvania Archives*, Fifth Series, vol. ii, 890). See also, Lineage Record No. 40110 of the Daughters of the American Revolution, and Records of the Sons of the Revolution in the State of New York.

In his will of 12 January, 1787, proved 19 January following, he described himself as " I, Frederick Black of Kensington in the County of Philadelphia, weak of body ". His worldly estate he bequeathed to Abigail his "dearly beloved wife" during widowhood, with remainder to his children and their children. In this connection, *cf. Philadelphia Deeds*, Book EF, No. 29, under date of 6 March, 1807.

709

Abigail (Chester) Black, born February 18, 1770; died April 13, 1856, and was buried in Monument Cemetery, Philadelphia.

Children of William and Catherine (Black) Preston, born in Philadelphia:

12. i. MARY,[8] born March 25, 1791; married (1) John Markley; (2) Maurice Starne.
   ii. ABIGAIL, born November 20, 1793; married Benjamin Addis Meredith, born October 24, 1782, son of Benjamin and Prudence (Lewis) Meredith; had issue.
   iii. WILLIAM, born October 23, 1797; died October 3, 1803. With this death the name of *William*, in the direct Preston line treated of, came to an end.
   iv. GEORGE, born February 14, 1801; died May 13, 1801.

12. MARY [8] PRESTON (*William,*[7] *William,*[6] *William,*[5] *Paul,*[4] *William,*[3] *Henry,*[2] *William* [1]), born in Philadelphia, March 25, 1791; died July 15, 1834; married (first) Second Presbyterian Church, Philadelphia, June 25, 1807, John Markley of Montgomery County, who died *circa* 1819. Mrs. Markley married (second) Maurice Starne.

Children of John and Mary (Preston) Markley, born in Philadelphia:

   i. ELIZA MARKLEY,[9] married William C. Stickney.
   ii. MATILDA MARKLEY, married Samuel L. Tomlin.
   iii. CATHERINE MARKLEY, born December 19, 1815; died July 14, 1886; married April 3, 1833, John Fonderlet Belsterling, Mayor of Northern Liberties, Philadelphia, 1845-1849; Solicitor, 1851. Issue: 1. *Emma Belsterling.* 2. *William Franklin Belsterling.* 3. *Mary Markley Belsterling.* 4 *Catherine Preston Belsterling.* 5. *John Jacob Belsterling.* 6. *Estella Belsterling.*
   iv. REBECCA MARKLEY, died after April 2, 1837.

Ellis Pugh, Quaker,
in Wales and Pennsylvania

GEORGE R. GRIFFITHS

"Notwithstanding, he was not one of the wise of this world, nor had human learning, yet he was made a profitable instrument to turn divers from vanity, and to exhort and strengthen many in their spiritual journey, in his native land and also in this country...."

Thus was Ellis Pugh, Quaker of Wales and Pennsylvania, described in the preface to his posthumously published book *Annerch ir Cymru . . .*. An unlettered Welsh lad, he early exhibited a spiritual depth which led him to become a Quaker minister in Wales about 1680. A vivid picture of the Wales in which the Friends' movement flourished and suffered and of Rowland Ellis and Ellis Pugh who later came to Pennsylvania is contained in a new Welsh book which has been translated into English.[1] It is a book which weaves fact and fancy together effectively to make these characters come alive.

Ellis Pugh has been a man of some mystery, being orphaned at the age of a few days in Merionethshire, Wales. Most of what we know of him comes from the biographical preface to *Annerch ir Cymru . . . .* He was born in the sixth month (that is, August under the old calendar) 1656 in the Parish of Dolgelley, Merionethshire, Wales. His father died before he was born and his mother, a few days after his birth. In his eighteenth year, about 1674, the preaching of John ap John so influenced him that he became a Quaker. A few years later, perhaps 1680, he became a minister of the Friends. Late in 1686 he left Wales with the Rowland Ellis company, arriving at Barbados in the first month (March) and continuing to Pennsylvania in the summer of 1687, a difficult voyage that consumed several months. His death came in Pennsylvania the 3rd day, 10th month, 1718 (i. e., 3 Dec 1718).

Many interesting questions arise. Who were his parents? Who raised the orphaned baby? Whom did he marry? And so on. He himself is strangely silent on all of these points. On a trip to Wales in 1974 one objective was to find answers to these questions. The first step, of course, in such a quest is to learn as much as possible about the subject in Pennsylvania and from sources available in the United States.

The Story in Pennsylvania

Several authors who have written on the Pennsylvania Quakers have made brief mention of Ellis Pugh, but such references have been fragmentary and sometimes apply to another Ellis Pugh. It is quickly apparent that two or even three Ellis Pughs (or Ellis ap Hugh in the Welsh patronymic form) occur in the Pennsylvania references. So it is that in colonial Pennsylvania Ellis Pugh, Quaker, of Dolgelley has remained ill-defined, obscured by the mists of time.

Those several references are of varying value. To the extent that valid sources and documents are cited, they narrow or pinpoint the field of further research. When they fail to so cite, they may still have value in providing clues for a specific search for corroborating facts and documentation.

Much of what has appeared in print has been based on the preface to his book, which he wrote shortly before his death, and which was published three years later. These facts were used by Charles Browning[3] and in Glenn's *Welsh Founders*.[4] They were expanded somewhat in a *History of Delaware County* to say that Ellis Pugh "with his wife Sina,*came* from *Brithdir* near Dolgelley, Merionethshire . . . settled in Radnor in 1686, but it is uncertain whether he ever owned any land" there; in 1706-7 he visited Wales; and for many years before his death he resided "within the verge of Gwynedd Monthly Meeting."[5] Another source, Maud Pugh,[6] has given Ellis' birthplace as Grath Gowen (which is probably the Garthgynfor mentioned on later pages) and says he settled first in Radnor Township, Chester County, and later was in Plymouth Township, Philadelphia County.

It has sometimes been said that Ellis Pugh married a widow with nine small children. Such a claim stretches credulity since, as will appear shortly, Ellis was probably married at age nineteen. A widow with nine children, on the other hand, could easily have been thirty. A lad of nineteen would be either very brave or foolhardy to take on a ready-made family of nine children. That story seems to be based on Glenn, who actually said: "As 'nine poor small children of Sina' are mentioned in their certificate, it is presumed that they were by a former huband." Ellis Pugh and his family did not emigrate until 1686. It now seems more likely that the nine small children were in fact those of Ellis than the previous children of a widowed Sina. Either way there is the problem of why the nine children do not all appear in later records, such as Ellis' will. Perhaps it is not unrealistic to suggest that some of them may have been among the victims of the harsh voyage from Wales.

Rowland Ellis and about 100 of his neighbors (including Ellis Pugh and family) from Dolgelley sailed in a Bristol ship from Milford Haven, South Wales, on the 16th day of the 8th month 1686. After a passage of 24 weeks, during which "many died through want," they arrived at Barbados, where the ship was detained six weeks.[8] Thus they arrived in Barbados in late March or early April 1687 and in Philadelphia about the middle of May.

Browning makes two references to Ellis Pughs who could not be our subject. The lineage is given of Ellis Pugh of Gwynedd Township, Pennsylvania, son of John ap Hugh (John Pugh) who came from Denbyshire, Wales. That could not be Ellis Pugh, Quaker, as the latter's father died in 1655 or 1656 in Wales. The unlikelihood that a Quaker minister would also be a Baptist rules out the Ellis Pugh who was in the Baptist Congregation of Welsh in Plymouth Township before 1703.

Browning also cites a deed by Richard Davies of Welshpool, Montgomeryshire, Wales, of acreage in his Pennsylvania grant to Ellis ap Hugh on 31 Jul 1682.[9] The initial reaction is to eliminate that Ellis ap Hugh because of the 1682 date. It must be remembered, however, that purchase of Pennsylvania land and immigration were not necessarily coincident. Rowland Ellis also made a large purchase from Richard Davies, but did not sail to Pennsylvania the first time until 1686. So, he may or may not be Ellis Pugh, Quaker. One source[10] says that Ellis ap Hugh "died aboard ship."

It is possible that the next two references by Browning are to Ellis Pugh, Quaker. Ellis Pugh received a legacy in the will of William Thomas of Radnor, dated the 18th day, 7th month, 1687, and proved the 4th day, 9th month, 1689. Around 1690 an Ellis Pugh of Merion Township was among the subscribers to shares of the Susquehanna Land Co.

Two further citations of Browning can be accepted with some confidence. In 1701 the Radnor Friends "met at the meeting house and at Rees Thomas's and Ellis Pugh's." Finally, 14th day, 5th month, 1720, Radnor Monthly Meeting records contain a minute with respect to printing the manuscript left by Ellis Pugh at his death. Twelve Friends of Haverford and Gwynedd considered the manuscript and recommended its publication. It is reputedly the first book in Welsh published in America.

Records of the late genealogist Gilbert Cope[11] say that Ellis Pugh was the son of John ap Hugh (John Pugh) of Gwynedd Township; was buried near Radnor Meeting House; married Sinah; and that their children were:

Ellin, born in Wales; married David Meredith [or Meredith David]
Ellis, born in Wales; married Mary Evans in 1708; died in 1711
Thomas, born in 1686 in Wales
John, born in Pennsylvania; married Jane Reese
Elizabeth, married Ellis Roberts
Job, born in 1693; married Phebe Miles Evan (widow)
Abraham, born in 1695; died in 1711

The sources utilized by Mr. Cope are not identified. A correspondent[12] says that Ellis and Sinah brought their certificate of membership, date the 25th day, 5th month, 1686, from Redstone Monthly Meeting, Pembrokeshire, Wales, to Radnor Monthly Meeting. What is puzzling about that is the fact that Redstone was a long way from Dolgelley.

Directly pertinent is the will of Ellis Pugh, recorded at Philadelphia.[13] Of Philadelphia, a mason, he mentions wife Sinah; sons Thomas, Job, and Ellis; daughter Ellen Davies; son-in-law Ellis Roberts; and granddaughters Katherine and Mary Meredith and Sinah Pugh. Son Job was named Executor. Named as overseers were son-in-law Meredith Davies, and friends David Meredith, John Moore, and Robert Jones. The witnesses were John Moore, William Griffith, Cadwalader Jones, and Robert Jones. The will was signed 29 Nov 1718, and proved 16 Mar 1718/19.

With this background, preparations were focused on the search to take place physically in the United Kingdom. Those included (1) familiarization with the three volumes of Smith and Gardner on *Genealogical Research in England and Wales*.[14] Volume 2 is particularly useful for its summary of the records on each county and the location of those records. Volume 3 has considerable merit for its examples of old alphabets and handwriting and its discussion of Latin names, terms, and numerals; (2) acquisition of *The Official List*, General Register Office, London, listing all offices which register vital statistics; (3) identification of appropriate parishes of the Church of Wales; (4) determination of probate jurisdictions in Merionethshire; (5) review of the holdings of the Society of Genealogists, London;[15] (6) study of a *Genealogical Atlas*.[16] Inclusion of such references in one's luggage can be quite useful. Some Welsh maps will also be needed but they can better be acquired overseas.

CENTRAL RECORDS IN LONDON

London, as the major air terminal, is the logical first stop for most genealogical research in England and Wales. The resources there include the Public Record Office (PRO), Chancery Lane, W.C.2; the General Register Office, Somerset House (by which it is better known), Strand, W.C., and its nearby annex, St. Catherine's House; the Society of Genealogists, 37 Harrington Gardens, S.W.7 (where a modest fee is charged non-members); the Department of Manuscripts, British Museum, W.C.; and the Library of Friends' House, Euston Road, N.W.1.

A visit to the PRO involves (a) signing in at a guard station; (b) registering at the main building for temporary research—where guidance on PRO holdings is also available; and (c) for a longer period than one day or for a return visit within one year, obtaining a letter of recommendation from the U. S. Embassy.

714

The Embassy will issue such a letter on presentation of a valid U. S. passport. A letter of recommendation from a genealogical or historical society in the United States will also be accepted. Such procedures take a little time at the PRO, but are not otherwise difficult. The delays must, of course, be taken into consideration in planning the time required at the PRO.

Some non-conformist (i. e., non-Church of England/Wales) records are located at the PRO. It does not, unfortunately, have a Quaker register for Merionethshire, nor any non-conformist registers for Merioneth for the period 1656-1686. Available also at the PRO are those wills which were filed with the Prerogative Court of Canterbury (PCC). That Court claimed sole jurisdiction when the deceased's estate was valued at more than five pounds and in two dioceses; also when those with property died at sea or overseas. The Index of PCC wills, which is located in a separate building but not far from the non-conformist registers, listed a will of a William Pugh, 1657, Radnor. When a requisition slip is filled out, an attendant will bring the will book promptly. A reading of the William Pugh will showed there was no bearing on Ellis Pugh.

At Somerset House and St. Catherine's House (the latter a couple of blocks away) are births, deaths, and marriages after 1 Jul 1837; hence they were not applicable to the 1656-1686 period of Ellis Pugh. The records are readily accessible, however. The Society of Genealogists has no church registers for Merionethshire. It should be emphasized that the above highlights major facilities and resources only, and by no means exhausts the scope of records to be found or their location in London.

FRIENDS' LIBRARY

At this point it became more critical to determine what might be in the Library of the Society of Friends on Euston Road. An advance letter had been written to the library but it was not necessary. There is, by the way, a modest library use fee. Personal there are courteous and helpful.

In addition to many works relating to Quakers and standard genealogical publications, the library includes registers of Monthly/Quarterly Friends' Meetings from many locations in England and Wales. Most pertinent to the search at hand was General Meetings of Herefordshire, Worcestershire, and Wales," but inspection showed there was nothing on Ellis Pugh, or Ellis ap Hugh or Ellis ap John for that matter. There are several possible names for the father of Ellis. Patronymics were still in use in Wales (even to some degree in Pennsylvania) in the middle and late 1600s. Ellis Pugh's children used the surname Pugh. The father of Ellis, on the other hand, might have had the Pugh surname, or Hugh as his Christian name, or even John—John ap Hugh—as one source already cited has said.

At the Library the Index to Friends' Meetings had this to say with regard to Merioneth:

"Monthly Meeting established 1668. In 1770 united as Montgomery and Merioneth Monthly Meeting. No records extant." [Underlining added].

That fact immediately and severely reduced hopes for a breakthrough on Ellis Pugh's background, especially on his marriage, which reasonably must have been a Quaker ceremony. The same Index with respect to Pembrokeshire Monthly Meeting said: "Records wanting 1668-1700," a crucial period in Ellis Pugh's life.

The index to Joseph Besse's *Sufferings*[18] for Wales and Warwickshire, included Rowland Ellis of "Dolgelly" and Pennsylvania, but not Ellis Pugh. Perhaps that is not surprising, for there is little indication that Ellis Pugh was a man of property. Hence, he was not likely to suffer the loss of such.

A microfilm of the North Wales Quarterly Meeting, 1668-1752, was in the Friends' Library, the original being in the County Record Office, Cardiff, Wales. It included the Minute Book at Dolobran (including Shropshire, Montgomery, and Merioneth), but a search of the 1674, 1680, 1686 time periods revealed no reference to Ellis Pugh.

Of much interest was a diary of John Kelsall.[19] An entry on page 62 reports: 29th of 10th Month 1706, Ellis Pugh lately from Merrion [*sic*] in Pennsylvania was at meeting. Ellis went the day after to Dolgelley. Rowland Ellis, Jr., who had landed from Philadelphia twelve months ago and Owen Roberts, second son of Hugh Roberts, lately from Pennsylvania, were with Ellis Pugh, all just come from London.

Page 83 has an entry for the 27th day, 4th Month 1708:

On the morrow Thomas Pot (from Penn.) went to Radnorshire intending in a little time for Bristol and thence take shipping for Pennsylvania along with Ellis Pugh.

The published series *Journal of Friends' Historical Society* contains some information on Redstone, which was a Meeting House near Narberth, South Wales. Friends' burials took place nearby at Trewern, parish of Llanddewy Velfry, Pembrokeshire. Trewern was the property of John Lewis, a few miles from Narberth.[20] Another entry[21] records that in 1668 "others from the neighborhood of Ruabon were presented at the preceding sessions as 'Quakers'." Among them were John ap John of Trevor and Thomas ap Pugh of Chirk. Also in Supplement 6: The Yearly Meeting in 1683 was held at Dolgyn, Merioneth; in 1685 it was held at Carthgynfor near Dolgelley.

In *The Friends' Library*, Vol. 3, 1839, is the life of Samuel Bownas. It refers to the Welsh Friend Ellis Pugh, saying that they went overseas together, with a Friend, Daniel Maud (apparently the ship's Master.) After a long passage they arrived at Portsmouth in the 10th month 1706 then went on to London.[21]

The Quaker history by Rev. Rees[22] sheds the following light on Ellis Pugh:

a. Merionethshire contributed more to Quakerism than any other Welsh county, considering its size, chiefly from Independents. Included were "Many of the ablest and wealthiest sons of Merionethshire...Dr. Edward Jones, Dr. Griffith Owen, Thomas and Robert Owen, Hugh Roberts, Ellis Pugh and others."

b. Quakerism flourished in the district of Dolgelley. Meetings were held at Dolgyn, Tyddyn y Garreg (or Tyddynygarreg, distant about two miles), Dewisbren and Tynyclawdd. Dolgelley supplied Pennsylvania with Griffith Owen, Robert Owen, Rowland Ellis, and Ellis Pugh.

c. Ellis Pugh, 1656-1718, minister, rendered distinguished service in Wales and Pennsylvania. He was "convinced" by "Sion ap Sion" as he affectionately called him (John ap John) in 1674. He married a widow, Sina, who had nine small children. (Except for Glenn, quoted earlier, no verification of this statement has been found.) In 1680 he began his public ministry, a stone mason by trade. His work at Dolgelley was hindered by persecutions. Families were scattered and the Church dwindled (from over 100 families) because of emigration. Many left for Pennsylvania and in 1686 Ellis Pugh, of Brithdir, Dolgelley, yeoman, followed with other Friends from Dolgelley. They reached Barbados in January and Pennsylvania early in the summer of 1687.

d. Ellis Pugh's book was published in Philadelphia in 1721 by Andrew Bradford. In the original Welsh edition (two copies of which are extant) a history of the author and testimony concerning him occupy pages i-x.

Rev. Rees also tells us that on the 27th day, 7th month of 1681 it was decided to hold the Yearly Meeting for Wales at Haverfordwest (Redstone). Redstone, near Narberth, about one mile north of Narberth Castle, Pembrokeshire, was once the center of great Quaker activity. The first Yearly Meeting for Wales was held there "5, ii, 1682." Tyddyn y Garreg, Merionethshire, he says was the house of Ellis Lewis.

In a 1732 English edition of Ellis Pugh's book, translated by Rowland Ellis (in 1727) and revised and corrected by David Lloyd, the testimony of the Monthly Meeting at Gwynedd, Philadelphia County, brings out another sorrow in his life. After Ellis Pugh's return to Pennsylvania from Wales in 1708, "three of his children, in the flower of their age, died within one month" of each other. From what we know of the children, this must have occurred in 1711.

The Friends' Library has a typescript biography of Ellis Pugh, for which neither author nor source was identified. An additional fact or statement merits attention. It is that Ellis Pugh settled first in Merion, Pennsylvania, then later purchased land in Plymouth Township. The land purchase has not been verified.

In view of the disappointing results at the Friends' Library it seemed opportune to leave London for Wales. Before leaving London, however, a visit to Her Majesty's Stationery Office to procure Welsh maps is recommended. The maps are available elsewhere but not with the wide selection offered at the Stationery Office. The Ordnance Survey Map Series is quite similar to those of the U. S. Geological Survey. The maps include a wealth of physical and man-made features. The 1:50,000 Series is to a scale of 1¼ inches to 1 mile. Sheet 124 is the Survey Map for Dolgellau (Dolgelley).

NATIONAL LIBRARY OF WALES

A pleasant drive or train ride to the west coast of central Wales will take you to the picturesque resort town of Aberystwyth, Cardiganshire. On spacious grounds on a hill overlooking the town, with a view of Cardigan Bay and the Irish Sea to the west, sits the National Library of Wales (NLW). It is the major genealogical and historical record facility of Wales.

In addition to vast published and manuscript holdings, the NLW has original parish registers for the earlier years for many parishes and Bishop's Transcripts of such registers for later years. Bishop's Transcripts are the copies which were required to be sent annually to the Bishop. The registers record separately marriages, births, and burials. Old calendar dates were used in the early entries. Also, in most of the earlier registers entries were inscribed in Latin. The NLW is accessible without charge. Its staff is both helpful and competent. The fact that it is the central repository for parish registers or Transcripts makes it the primary contact in lieu of individual churches.

But first it seems desirable to have some geographic and jurisdictional definitions. Brithdir, Garthgynfor, and Dolgelley,[24] for example, need to be understood in relation to one another. Brithdir and Islaw'rdref is now a civil parish of Merionethshire created in 1894 and comprised of the former townships of Brithdir Isaf (lower) and Brithdir Uchaf (upper) in Dolgelley (church) parish. Garthgynfor and Brithdir-isaf are townships in Brithdir. There is also a village by the name of Brithdir within Brithdir-isaf. Tyddyn y Garreg[25] is within the area of Garthgynfor. Thus, references to Brithdir and to Garthgynfor as the birthplace of Ellis Pugh are both correct. Dolgelley Parish, as church parish, dates from 1640.

The first point of reference for information on Ellis Pugh is the Dolgelley Parish Register, 1640-89. Entries of interest are listed below (in translation) in chronological order, many of them numbered to facilitate reference:

1654:   Baptisms: Elizabeth, d/o ———— ap Hugh and ———— (bt. 1 Apr and 9 May).
Richard, s/o John ap Hugh ap Hugh and Elizabeth, d/o Williams, 28 Feb.

	1656:	Baptisms:	David, s/o Lewis Pugh and Agnes, 20 Sep.
			Jane, d/o John Pugh and Elizabeth, 4 Oct.
	1657:	Baptisms:	John, s/o Hugh Pugh and Elin, 14 Aug.

(The above are included to show the Pugh/ap Hugh baptisms; none for **Ellis** shown.)

	1667:	Marriages:	John Pugh and Elizabeth William, ———— Jan.
1.	1672:	Baptisms:	Humphrey, s/o Ellis ap Hugh and Jane, 22 Sep.
2.	1673:	Baptisms:	Agnes, d/o Ellis ap Hugh of Brithdir and Elizabeth, 25 Jan.
	1674:	Burials:	Ellis Pugh, 11 Nov.
3.	1676:	Baptisms:	Ellin, d/o Ellis Pugh and Sina ————, 8 *Aug.*
4.	1677:	Baptisms:	Grace, d/o Ellis Pugh and Jane ————, 26 Sep.
5.	1678:	Burials:	Ellin Ellis, 24 Mar.
6.			Margaret, d/o Ellis, 28 Mar.
7.	1679:	Marriages:	Ellis ap Hugh and Catharine, d/o Hugh, 16 Jul.
8.	1681:	Baptisms:	Richard, s/o Ellis ap Hugh and Jane, 30 Oct.
9.	1682:	Burials:	Elizabeth, d/o Ellis, 25 Jul.
10.			John ap Ellis, 28 Jan.
11.	1684:	Burials:	Anna, d/o Ellis, 5 Jan.
12.			Catherine, infant of Ellis, 18 Mar.
13.	1685:	Burials:	Margaret, d/o Ellis, 31 May.
14.			Jane Ellis, infant, 10 Nov.
15.			Anthony ap Ellis, 21 Mar.
16.	1686:	Baptisms:	John, s/o Ellis Pugh and Jane, 25 Apr.
			Agnes, d/o Ellis, 18 Sep.

There were no marriages for 1671, 1672, 1673, or 1680. Burials were checked for 1655 (none) and 1656 (only two). Records of all appropriate years were read but had no other entries of interest. For example, in 1654, 1655, and 1656 there was no marriage which could conceivably be of the parents of Ellis Pugh.

The only marriage that comes close is item (7) but it is not Ellis Pugh, Quaker. Item (3) is the only baptism, for that matter the only record, clearly applicable to Ellis Pugh and Sina. Since Ellin was baptized in Aug 1676, Ellis and Sina were married probably in 1675, when Ellis was about nineteen. Glenn maintains that in Wales heirs to even small estates quite often married very early, boys at 14 to 16 and girls at 12 to 14.[28] Items (1), (4), (8), and (16) are all children of an Ellis Pugh (or ap Hugh) and Jane.

Note item (5), burial of Ellina Ellis in 1678. Is this a daughter of Ellis and Sina? Ellis and Sina had a daughter Ellin who grew to maturity. Items (6), (9), (10), (11), (12), (13), perhaps also (14), and (15) all involve burials of sons and daughters of an Ellis, but there is no way of knowing whether they were Ellis Pugh's. Item (2) seems so close to the target, the father being Ellis ap Hugh of Brithdir, but with a wife named Elisabeth it seems there was a fourth Ellis Pugh in the area (in addition to those with wives Sina, Jane, and Catharine).

With no burial in the parish record identifiable as the father of Ellis Pugh, it became necessary to consider probate records. Prior to 1858 the western half of Merioneth, including Dolgelley, fell under the jurisdiction of the Episcopal Consistory Court of Bangor. The balance of Merioneth was within the Episcopal Consistory Court of St. Asaph. The superior court was the Court of the Archbishop of Canterbury, already mentioned. The Bangor records were checked to no avail; specifically, Bangor Probate Registry, Calendar of Wills and Administrations, 1635-1699. The shadow over Ellis Pugh's records appeared once more. There was a "lapse" in the records for 1649-1659, inclusive. For St. Asaph there was also a lapse for 1649-1659. In an Index of PCC Administrations, Vol. II, was listed Pugh, John, in the ship *Swiftsure* in State Service at sea, 1655, f. 177. That is a possible father for Ellis Pugh which merits further investigation.

The NLW has marriage licenses for the Diocese of St. Asaph, 1616-1900, and for the Diocese of Bangor for 1757-1900, which is too late. As a long shot the former licenses were combed for 1672-1682, but with no productive results. Inspection of *Publications of the Merioneth Historical and Record Society* and the *List of Merioneth Manuscripts* was likewise fruitless.

DOLGELLEY, MERIONETHSHIRE

Situated in a valley on the river Afon Wnion is Dolgelley, a market town of Merionethshire, about 30 miles north of Aberystwyth. Few come nearer the image of a medieval town than Dolgelley. Were it not for the surfeit of modern automobiles, one could easily see Dolgelley as it must have been 1656-1686. Narrow streets hugging the sides of ancient buildings, frequent corners, twisting lanes, homes crowding the sidewalks, all contribute to the pervading quaintness.

The Merioneth County Record Office is located there, staffed by young archivists who take a genuine interest in the problems of inquiring visitors, Manuscript notes" contained several items worth citing: 1) Tyddyn y Garreg, in the township of Garthgynfor, around 1664 was owned by Owen Lewis Owen; 2) Ellis Pugh was born at Pen Rhos (Penrhos), a house near Tyddyn y Garreg; 3) a Friends' Monthly Meeting was held at Tyddyn y Garreg from 1678 to 1700; and 4) in 1690 (?)[*sic*] Ellis Pugh was an ordained minister of the church at Tyddyn y Garreg. Even though the date is wrong it suggests that Ellis Pugh was not at Redstone in 1686.

The Record Office also has a hand-written diary, author unnamed, which contained the following capsule of history. In 1668 those who became Quakers in Merioneth resided on lands once belonging to two Monasteries, the Strata Marcella and the Cymmes Abbey, and sequestered by Henry VIII in 1536. The family of Baron Owen (Owen *Lewis.* Owen. *Tyddyn* y Garreg)'swept the terrain" around Dolgelley and Llangwyn. Scores of relatives and dependents migrated with them and farmhouses were built on several estates. During the hundred years ending in 1646 several such small estates had been established, including Tyddyn y Garreg, and it was the owners of it that became Quakers in Merioneth.

The Abbey of Marcella was near Bala. During the Civil War a large number of Welsh joined Cromwell's army, many of them ancestors of Welsh Quakers in Pennsylvania. On the restoration of Charles II they were the greatest sufferers. There were, therefore, two distinct groups, in the Penlyn (Bala) area and the Dolgelley area.

One publication[28] contained records of hearth taxes in 1662 for Merioneth, too late for Ellis Pugh's father, but with several Hughs and ap Pughs listed. Other records and publications in the Record Office added to new data.

With directions from the archivist a visit was made to Tyddyn y Garreg, east of Dolgelley. The rather large house and adjoining barns are clearly old, typically Welsh, of solid stone, with few windows. A picture of the house is included in Glenn's book on Merion.[29] Inquiry of the present residents[30] failed to disclose any knowledge of Pen Rhos. In a nearby field is a Quaker cemetery, allegedly old, about 100 feet square in size. The cemetery is badly maintained and overgrown, as are nearly all in Wales—even those of Parish churches. Grass and weeds often reach 30 inches high. There were many stones in the Quaker cemetery, most of them difficult to read. The earliest legible stone bore a death date of 1849. The estate is perhaps a mile from the village of Brithdir, whose St. Marks Church was built in 1895.

The Rector of St. Mary's Parish (Church of Wales),[31] Dolgelley, kindly agreed to make his records available, but those for the time period consisted solely of copies of the originals, which, already inspected, are in the custody of the NLW.

A Brief Genealogy

In retrospect it may be seen that, in addition to some corroboration of previous stories, new information was primarily the 1676 baptism of Ellin, daughter of Ellis Pugh and Sina, and the naming of Pen Rhos on the *Tyddyn* y Garreg estate as Ellis Pugh's actual birthplace and home. Some new details of the 1706-08 visit to Wales were gained. On the negative side it was established that several series of crucial records are not extant.

Although Ellis Pugh's parents are not known, we can summarize our information about him, his wife and their descendants, based on sources already cited, as follows:

1. Ellis Pugh, b. Aug 1656, Tyddyn y Garreg, Dolgelley, Wales, m. Sina ———, d. near Philadelphia, 3 Dec 1718.

i. Ellin Pugh, bapt. 8 Aug 1676, Dolgelley, m. 22 Jan 1700 Meredith David, s/o David and Katharine Meredith. Their children took the surname Meredith.

ii. Ellis Pugh, b. Wales, m. 3 May 1708 Mary Evans, d/o Owen and Elizabeth Evans, d. 1711.

2. iii. Thomas Pugh, d. 1685, Merioneth, Wales, m. 23 Dec 1710 Jane Ann Roger, d/o Roger Robert, d. 1723, Merion, Pa. Several children, see below.

iv. John Pugh, b. 16 Dec 1688 in Pa., m. Jane Reese (d. 1760), d. 1711.

v. Elizabeth Pugh, b. Dec 1690, m. 1712 Ellis Roberts of Radnor, Pa., blacksmith, s/o Robert Ellis, dec'd.

vi. Job Pugh, b. 14 Jul 1693, m. 16 Sep 1731 Phebe Miles Evans (widow), d. 1751.

vii. Abraham Pugh, b. 17 Jul 1695, d. 1711.

2. Thomas Pugh, a mason like his father, left a will dated 3 May 1723 (Book D, #289), mentioning his brother Job and sons Jesse and Roger. Witnesses were John Roger, Thomas Ellis, Ellis Robert and Meredith David. It was proved by his wife Jane, 1 Oct 1723. Named as Trustees were Robert Jones of Merion, Meredith Davies, Robert Roger, Job Pugh and Ellis Roberts. His widow later married Isaac Malin. Children were:

3. i. Jesse Pugh, b. 16 Nov 1711 in Pa., m. Alice Malin, b. 29 Nov 1711.

ii. Roger Pugh, b. 1713, m. Sarah Handem, went to Kent Co., Del.

iii. Hannaniah Pugh, b. 1715 in Pa., m. 1740 Mary Davis.

iv. Michael Pugh, b. 1717 in Pa., m. Hannah Davis.

v. Katherine Pugh, b. 1721, m. 1) Benjamin Rhoads, 2) Jas. Travilla, went to York Co., Pa.

4. vi. Azariah Pugh, b. 1721, m. Hannah Beales (Bailes), b. 31 Mar 1729.

5. vii. Thomas Pugh, b. 1723, m. 1756 in York Co., Pa., Jane Lewis, d. 179.., Frederick Co., Va.

3. Jesse Pugh and his wife Alice Malin went to Frederick Co., Va. One son:

i. Thomas Pugh, b. 1731/2, m. Ann Wright.

4. Azariah Pugh and his wife Hannah Beales went first to Frederick Co., Va., and then about 1763 to Bush River, S.C. One son:

i. Ellis Pugh, b. 21 Mar 1748.

5. Thomas Pugh went to Frederick Co., Va., in 1770. He and his wife Jane Lewis had five children:

i. Jesse Pugh, m. 24 Jul 1786 Elizabeth Grey, d. 1830.

ii. Mahlon Pugh, b. 20 Oct 1762, m. *ca.* 1787 Hannah Arnold, d. 30 Mar 1829.

iii. Eli Pugh, m. 27 Apr 1795 Catherine Fisher, Frederick Co.

iv. Mishael Pugh, m. 1796 Margaret Lipscomb.

v. Ellis Pugh, m. Mary Reese.

POSTLUDE

There are in the course of history those who live with humility, but displaying such faith and character that their influence lives on. Such a man was Ellis Pugh.

"His conduct in his family, in his neighborhood and in the church, was meek, loving, and peaceable, and to edification; and his conversation innocent, chaste, and coupled with the fear of God, honorable among the friend and of good report among all people generally...."[22]

NOTES

1. Ellis Pugh, *Annerch ir Cymru*... *(A Salutation to the Britains, to call them from the many things, to the one thing needful...)* (Philadelphia, 1721).
2. Marion Eames, *The Secret Room* (Swansea, Wales, English edition, 1975).
3. Charles H. Browning, *Welsh Settlement of Pennsylvania* (Philadelphia, 1912).
4. Thomas A. Glenn, *Welsh Founders of Pennsylvania*, 2 vols. (Oxford, Pa., 1911-13).
5. George Smith, *History of Delaware County, Pennsylvania*... (Philadelphia, 1862), 494.
6. Maud Pugh, *Capon Valley—Its Pioneers and Their Descendants* 1698-1940, 2 vols. (n.p., 1948).
7. Glenn, *op. cit.*, 204.
8. Browning, *op. cit.*, 234.
9. *Ibid.*, 234ff for this and subsequent references to Browning in the next two paragraphs.
10. Handwritten diary, author unnamed, in possession of Merioneth County Record Office, Dolgelley.
11. In the Collections of GSP.
12. Correspondence in possession of a descendant.
13. Book D, p. 116.
14. David E. Gardner and Frank Smith, *Genealogical Research in England and Wales*, 3 vols. (Salt Lake City, 1956, 1959, 1964).
15. *Parish Register Copies, Part One Society of Genealogists Collection* (London, 1972), *Parish Register Copies, Part Two, Other Than the Society of Genealogists Collection* (London, 1971).
16. David E. Gardner, Derek Harland and Frank Smith, *A Genealogical Atlas of England and Wales* (Salt Lake City, 1960).
17. The records reviewed included: Marriages; Burials; Births; Supplement—Marriages and Burials, 1657-1776; and Supplement—Births, Burials and Marriages.
18. Vol. II, p. 603 of his *A Collection of the Sufferings of the People called Quakers*..., 2 vols. (London, 1753) shows entries for Rowland Ellis, pp. 756 and 761.
19. J. K. Kelsall, An Account of Friends Who Visited Dolobran Meeting; Since 2d Month 1701 (typescript, bound).
20. *Journal*, Vol. II, 45.
21. *Ibid.*, Supplement 6, pp. 12, 30.
22. Pp. 39-40.
23. Rev. T. Hardy Rees, *A History of the Quakers in Wales and Their Emigration to North America* (Carmerthen, 1925), *passim*.
24. In Welsh language, *brith* means mottled or speckled; *dir*, certain or necessary; *garth*, hill or enclosure; *dol*, meadow.
25. In Welsh language, *tyddyn* means farm or holding.
26. Glenn, *op. cit.*, xii.
27. Notes on the History of Early Quakers in the Neigbborhood of Dolgelley, typescript carbon, no author or source cited, Merioneth County Record Office, Dolgelley.
28. E. D. Jones, ed., *Journal of Merioneth Historical and Record Society*, II, 1953-6.
29. Thomas A. Glenn, *Merion in the Welsh Tract* . . . (Baltimore, 1970), facing 16, where it is described as "Property of Lewis Owen, 1678, and Meeting Place of Friends from 1664 to 1700."
30. Mr. Iowerth Price and family.
31. Glenn *Merion...*, *op. cit.*, has a picture of the church, facing 214.
32. Pugh, *Annerch ir Cymru*, *op. cit.*, preface.

Notes on the Ribaud Family
of Acadia and Philadelphia

Collected by

FERN DuCOMB KAHLERT

G ENEALOGICAL research in Pennsylvania families of French extraction presents many of the same problems encountered in research on families of Swiss or German origin. Surnames were spelled by English clerks as they were heard — phonetically — with the result that a single surname often appeared in a great variety of forms. The surname Ribaud is no exception; it is found under no less than a dozen different spellings, ranging from the simplest Rebo, through Reabeau, Ribau, Ribbau, Ribaux, Ribot, to its accepted form of Ribaud. Even that has sometimes been misinterpreted as Riband by those unfamiliar with eighteenth-century calligraphy!

Among the families of French extraction who came to Philadelphia in the eighteenth century were the so-called "French Neutrals" or Acadians of Nova Scotia. Dispersed through the Colonies in 1755 by the British for refusing to take the oath of allegiance to the Crown, these unfortunates, however, had been subjects of Great Britain since 1713, though exempted from bearing arms against France on taking the oath of fidelity to the British Crown. After the outbreak of the Seven Years' War the British, fearing these French-speaking inhabitants might act as a fifth-column by supporting French maneuvers, in July, 1755, ordered the immediate expulsion of all those who refused to take the oath of loyalty. Those destined for Pennsylvania arrived toward the latter part of November, 1755, and by the following spring were being dispersed through the countryside, their maintenance assigned to the Overseers of the Poor in the several counties.

Although many official records before the American Revolution refer to the "French Neutrals" as a body, there are few remaining notices of individuals. The registers of St. Joseph's Roman Catholic Church in Philadelphia occasionally noted that individuals were Acadians, but such notations were by no means consistent and, as the years progressed, finally disappeared entirely as the communicant members were absorbed into the local economy. Thus to trace any one Acadian family often pre-

724

sents insurmountable obstacles. No evidence has been found that Joseph Ribaud, subject of the following notes, was one of the French Neutrals, but as he did intermarry with an Acadian, he may very well have been one, in spite of family tradition.

In the notes of Wilson Mitchell DuComb, grandson of Vincent Du-Comb, is the statement that "Joseph Ribaud, my grandfather, was from Virginia, of the Jamestown Colony area. . . . he came to Philadelphia before the Revolution and was a sea trader. . . ." While search uncovered two men surnamed Ribeau and Ribot in Virginia very early, their connection with Joseph Ribaud, father-in-law of Vincent Du-Comb, has not as yet been established. The earliest reference to Joseph Ribaud is found in Philadelphia:

11 May 1761, married Joseph Ribau and Margaret Benoit. ("Marriages, St. Joseph's Roman Catholic Church, Philadelphia," *Records of the American Catholic Historical Society*, II [1886], 279, hereinafter cited as *ACHS*.)

According to the Reverend Robert A. Parsons, S.J., "The Benoit family [into which Joseph Ribaud married] was an Acadian family. They arrived with other Acadians in Philadelphia in 1755. As of 1763, there were three Benoits in Philadelphia: Joseph and Marie Benoit, most probably the father and mother of the above Margaret Benoit, and a widow, Madeleine Benoit. This information came from Fr. Hector J. Herbert, S.J., who has been collecting material all his life about the Acadians." That the Benoits were Acadians is confirmed by a communication, dated 3 May 1967, from W. I. Smith, Assistant Dominion Archivist at the Public Archives of Canada, Ottawa. He has written that on a list dated 20 June 1763, in Ministere des Affaires Etrangeres, correspondance politique, vol. 450, fol. 416V, "the names of Joseph Benoit and Marie Josephte Benoit appear on a list of Acadians in Pennsylvania. . . . The list indicates that they had their two children with them, but the names of the children are not given."

Further search in Philadelphia records has produced additional information on Joseph Ribaud and his family:

James Ribau, son of Joseph and Margaret Ribau, born 19 August, baptized 28 August 1763, by Father Harding. Sponsors: James and Sophia Robinson. ("Baptisms, St. Joseph's R. C. Church," *ACHS*, I [1884], 267.)

Philadelphia 2^d November 1771. Joseph Ribbau, Image Maker, a Wife & 3 Children . . . 5 in family. ("Account of the Number & Situation of the French Neutral Familys Now in this City," *The Pennsylvania Magazine of History and Biography*, XXIV [1900], 249-250.)

On this list of Acadians, Joseph Ribaud's family was one of twenty-two others, comprising in all seventy-eight individuals, considered by the

Overseers of the Poor as capable of maintaining themselves, and so not a charge on the public.

The following two items are of interest because of the later marriage of Joseph Ribaud to Mary Sennar:

License to marry, 11 November 1766, Francis Senner and Mary Harding. ("Names of Persons for whom Marriage Licenses were issued in the Province of Pennsylvania previous to 1790," *Pennsylvania Archives*, 2nd Series, II [1890], 220.)

Margaret Sennar, daughter of Francis and Mary Agatha Sennar, born 15 October, baptized 30 October 1774. Sponsors, Joseph and Margaret Ribau. ("Baptisms, St. Joseph's R. C. Church, *ACHS*, I, 341.)

With the advent of the Revolution, Joseph Ribaud appears to have abandoned "image-making" for a more active occupation, perhaps linked to an earlier one which he had pursued before he came to Philadelphia:

Brig *Lion*, 31 July 1777, Joseph Ribout, master. Owners, F. Daymon & Co. Crew: 200. Guns: 14. ("List of Armed Vessels from the Port of Philadelphia, 1776-1777 . . . ." *Pennsylvania Archives*, 5th Series, I, 609.)

From *Leaflet No. 3, Pennsylvania Navy, Division of Public Records,* published by the Pennsylvania Historical and Museum Commission at Harrisburg, it appears that "The relatively minor role of the Navy throughout the war can be explained in part by the activity of the Privateers. More than 400 of these armed but privately owned and operated vessels were licensed by Pennsylvania. Privateers preyed upon enemy shipping to the great profit of their owners and their crew. Since their profits were so large, the officers and men of Privateers received no public funds."

Francis Daymon, principal owner of the Brig *Lion*, is first noted in Philadelphia as master of French and Latin, proposing to open a school at his house in Front a few doors above Market Street, according to his announcement in the *Pennsylvania Journal*, 7 April 1773. By 1776, he was librarian "of the Public Library" — now the Library Company of Philadelphia — and was still keeping school, according to the same newspaper of 1 October 1776. The next year, he announced in the *Evening Post*, 25 March 1777, that he had a store in Water Street, a few doors above Market. He lived, however, in Front Street, the second door from the Coffee House, according to the *Pennsylvania Packet* of 23 July 1778.

How long Joseph Ribaud remained in Damon's employ is not known. His occupation is not given in the next recovered notice of Ribaud:

28 July 1779, married at Philadelphia, with license of the governor and dispensation from affinity, Joseph Ribaut, widower, to Mary Sennar. Witnesses: Anthony Groves, Andrew Lotier. ("Marriages, St. Joseph's R. C. Church," *ACHS*, IV [1893], 142.)

Francis Sinner had been assessed in Lower Delaware Ward, Philadelphia, early in 1779, on an estate rated at £5, according to the lists in *Pennsylvania Archives,* 3rd Series, XIV, 526. In this same ward, which extends from Locust to Walnut Streets, Joseph Ribaud's name appeared the following year on a Constable's Return in the Philadelphia Municipal Archives, City Hall as: Joseph Ribeau, Saylor [or Taylor], estate rated at £200. The same year and in successive years on other assessment lists, he was listed as:

1780: Joseph Ribeau, mariner, estate £2000, tax, £6.0.0.
1781: Joseph Ribeau, occupation rated at £50, tax, £0.10.0
1782: Joseph Ribeau, occupation rated at £80, tax, £0.8.4
1783: Joseph Ribeau, mariner, occupation £80 (*Pennsylvania Archives,* 3rd Series, XV, 226, 734; XVI, 294, 823.)

Francis, son of Francis and Mary Hubert, born 18 December 1782, baptized 1 January 1783. Sponsors: Joseph and wife Mary Ribau. ("Baptisms, St. Joseph's R. C. Church, *ACHS,* IV [1893], 46.)

Joseph Rebo, 505 Water Street. (Macpherson's *City Directory,* 1785, 111.)

Vincent Ducomb, hairdresser, and Rose Riband [*sic* — Ribaud] of the City of Philadelphia; license 12 November 1785; Bond £200. Bondsmen: Vincent Ducomb, Francois Serre. Witness: James Trimble. ("Marriage Licenses, 1784-1786," *Pennsylvania Archives,* 6th Series, VI, 291, 304.)

When the war ended, privateering was no longer feasible. Joseph Ribaud therefore returned to a more peaceable way of life. To ensure his position in the country it was advisable for him to proclaim his allegiance to the State, and before Plunket Fleeson he took the test of allegiance, agreeable to the Act passed 4 March 1786. His name and new occupation, and the date on which he took the test were entered as:

8 May 1786, Joseph Rebeaud, Shopkeeper of Philadelphia. ("List of the names and surnames of those who have given test of allegiance to this State . . . ," *Pennsylvania Archives,* 2nd Series, III [1890], 54.)

At the end of that year he either contemplated removing from the city, or expected to take a trip, for he announced in the *Pennsylvania Packet* for 25 December 1786, that

The subscriber, being about to leave this city, requests all persons who are indebted to him to pay immediately; and those who have any demands against him may receive payments by applying to JOSEPH RIBAUD, Church alley, Philadelphia. 23 December 1786.

In 1789, Joseph Ribaud was again assessed in Philadelphia. His personal estate was rated at £15; he was renting Peter Field's dwelling in Dock Ward, was rated at £149, and was paying an annual ground rent of £5 8s., which, rated at £54, was deducted from the £149, according to the entry on page 35 of the original Dock Ward Duplicate in the Municipal Archives. The following year in the First Census he was enumerated on Ninth Street between Walnut and Spruce, in the Southern District of the city (Dock Ward):

Joseph Reabeau, 1 male over 16, 1 female. (*Heads of Families at the First Census* . . . *1790: Pennsylvania* [Washington, D.C., 1908], 245.)

Married, 18 January 1791, Joseph Ribaud, Jr. and Nancy (or Ann) Cockran. Witnesses: Andrew Warner and James Gibson. (Transcript of records of Gloria Dei [Old Swedes'] Church, Philadelphia, II, 890, in Collections of the Genealogical Society of Pennsylvania [GSP].)

The elder Joseph Ribaud was apparently not assessed in Dock Ward in 1791, but according to the original duplicate for 1793, for that ward in the Municipal Archives, he (or his son) was listed on page 16 as "Joseph Ribaud, personal estate £20."

Buried Joseph Ribaux's [Jr.] child, Holy Trinity. (Burials August 1 to November 9, 1793, Yellow Fever Deaths in Philadelphia, 1793, 1797, 1798, 22, GSP.)

Although no record has been found of the death of the elder Ribaud's second wife Mary, it is possible she, too, succumbed to the plague, and that her death occasioned his removal from the city to the town of Lancaster.

17 November 1795, Peter Miller of Manchester Township, York County, Weaver, and Barbara his Wife, convey to Joseph Ribaud of the Borough and County of Lancaster, Merchant, for £270 in real Gold and Silver current lawful money, a Stone Messuage and two lots in Botts Town, Manchester Township, York County, situate on the North side of the great Road from the Borough of York to Frederick Town (now called King Street), Bounded Eastward with a 20 foot Alley, Northward with Reinhard Botts Land, Westward with Lots of Ground now in Tenure of Margaret Salome Spangler, and Southward with King Street, containing in Breadth East and West 65 feet and in Length or Depth 460 feet, Exclusive of an Alley called Carlisle Alley, which in the plan of the said Lots divides the hereby granted two Lots of Ground (whereby the one is called a Front Lot and the other a Back Lot) . . . which said Premises Everrard Harr and Wife Hannah conveyed to Peter Miller 1 September 1794. . . . Together with all Houses, Edifices and Buildings thereon Erected and Built . . . subject to the yearly payment of Twenty Shillings in Gold or Silver money Current to the Heirs and assigns of John Hagner deceased forever. . . .

Wit: George Lettman, J. Lukens   /s/ *in German*
Recorded 25 November 1795 in   Peter Müller
York Co. Deed Book LL, 140   *her*
                                   Barbara (X) Miller
                                   mark

A search by Mr. Charles J. Burgess of Gap, Pa., in the Lancaster County Court House and in the Historical Society in Lancaster failed to produce any evidence that Joseph Ribaud had actually ever lived in Lancaster. Deeds and the borough assessment lists contained no entries under his name or that of his son-in-law, Vincent DuComb. However, at York

Mr. Burgess found that the 1797 York County assessment list for Botts Town, Manchester Township, did list "Joseph Ribau" as having 1 lot, rated at $250, and one cow rated at $8, for a total valuation of $258 on which the tax was eighty-two cents. The entry included the notation there was a "stonehouse" on the premises. That year Joseph Ribaud acquired another piece of property:

27 June 1797, Henry Korbman, Yeoman, of the Borough of York and Catherine his Wife, convey to Joseph Ribaud of Botts Town, Manchester Township, York County, Gentleman, for the Sum of £171 in Gold or Silver lawful money of Pennsylvania, a certain Messuage, Tenement and Lot or piece of Ground on the East side of Water Street and South side of King Street in the Borough of York, Known on the General Plan of said Borough as Number 134, Containing in Breadth on Water Street 57 feet 6 inches and in length on King Street 250 feet to a twenty foot Alley, Bounded on the West by Water Street, on the North by King Street, on the East by the said Alley, and on the South by Lot Number 235, now in the tenure of George Sefrentz, being the same lot and premises which Peter Meyer and Martin Cronemiller, executors of the last will of Jacob Meyer, late of the Borough of York, deceased, conveyed 4 April 1797 to Henry Korbman. . . .
Wit: Jno. Morris, Jno. Morris, Jr.
Recorded 11 July 1797 in
York Co. Deed Book MM, 480

/s/ *in German*
Henrich Korbman
her
Catherine (X) Korbman
mark

Although Joseph Ribaud may have moved to this property in York, his children were still in Philadelphia. Six months after the purchase of the York house and lot, his daughter Catherine was married in Philadelphia:

Married 8 November (?) 1797, John Baptist Cadez, French, and Catherine Ribau, American. (Baptisms and Marriages, 1790-1806, Holy Trinity R. C. Church, Philadelphia, 139, GSP.)
Mary Rosina, daughter of John Baptist and Catherine Ribaud Cadez, born 11 August 1798, baptized 2nd of September. Sponsors: Anthony Lirou, Rose Ribaud DuComb. (*Ibid.*, 152)

Assessment records searched by Mr. Burgess in the York County Historical Society, show that in 1800 one George Hartman was tenant on "Reboes property" consisting of one house and one lot in the Borough of York. It was assessed at $150 on which the tax was nineteen cents. Thus, it would appear that Joseph had returned to Philadelphia, perhaps making his home with one of his children. Search in deeds failed to locate the sale of the Botts Town property which he must have sold prior to writing his will:

28 September 1801, In Nomini Domini, Amen, I Joseph Ribaud, late of Yorktown in the County of York in the Commonwealth of Pennsylvania, now of Philadelphia, being very sick and weak. . . . To Catherine McLaughlin who has attended me and kept my

House since five years and now lives at Abbotstown in the County of York [actually in Adams County] in a house I lately did hire, I bequeath $213.33 silver dollars as an acknowledgement of her kindness and attention to me and in full compensation of the same during the aforesaid Term. Also all the Household Furniture of whatsoever kind and also the Kitchen furniture now in aforesaid House at Abbotstown. Executor named below to sell and dispose of my aforesaid House and lot at Yorktown. The net proceeds of all real estate, and money I have on interest in the Hands of John Fry of Lancaster, Merchant, after payment of debts and legacy above, is to be equally divided between my three children, Rose Ribaud, wife of Vincent Ducomb, Joseph Ribaud, and Catharine Ribaud, wife of John Baptiste Catez. My Son-in-law Vincent Ducomb of Philadelphia to be sole executor. . . .

Wit: E. Perpignan   /s/ Joseph Ribaud
P. LeBarbier Duplessis
John Mease of Philadelphia, Gent., attests to the signature of Joseph Ribaud, being well acquainted with him and his hand writing.

The will was proved 8 October 1801, at Philadelphia and recorded in Will Book Y, 580, #88:1801. No inventory or settlement are included in the estate docket.

Addenda

Several deeds transferring real property to and from Joseph Ribaud were discovered too late to incorporate in the preceding notes. They are given below in abstracted form and furnish additional information about his life.

On 3 November 1783, William Ransted, cooper of Philadelphia, conveyed to Joseph Ribaud for £236 11s. 4d. one undivided third part of a messuage and lot on the east side of Front Street and west side of King (alias Water Street) in Philadelphia between Chestnut and Walnut Streets. (Recorded in Deed Book D-8, 267, 16 January 1784.) On the same day, Joseph Ribaud purchased at sheriff's sale the other two undivided third parts of the same premises, sold in execution as the estate of William Ransted. On 18 April 1785, Joseph Ribaud and his wife Mary sold this property, sixteen feet in breadth and extending thirty-four feet between Front and Water Street, to John Wood of Philadelphia, clock and watch maker. The consideration was £950 in "lawful Silver money of Pennsylvania." (Recorded 3 May 1785, in Deed Book D-12, 328, in which is recited the sheriff's sale of the property, first advertised for sale in the *Pennsylvania Packet*, 21 October 1783.)

Seven months later on 19 November 1785, Robert Duncan, Jr., late of Philadelphia but now of Richmond, Virginia, merchant, conveyed to Joseph Ribaud of Philadelphia for £1005 a messuage and lot on the west side of Second Street from Delaware and the north side of Vidall's Alley, the first alley south of Chestnut Street. (Recorded 24 January 1786, in Deed Book D-14, 526.) This property, twenty-seven feet in breadth on Second Street by sixty feet in depth along Vidall's Alley, on 9 December 1785, Ribaud mortgaged for £350 to Thomas Affleck, cabinet-maker of Philadelphia, who had sold the premises to Duncan 6 April 1784. On 19 December 1786, Joseph and Mary Ribaud conveyed the property to John Evans, merchant of Philadelphia, for the consideration of £500, and the payment of the mortgage monies and interest due to Affleck. (Recorded 1 February 1787, in Deed Book D-17, 443.)

On 7 June 1788, Peter Blanchard, innholder of the city, and his wife Mary, sold to Joseph Ribaud for £218 a two-story frame messuage and two lots of land in the square between Delaware Eighth and Ninth and Pine and Lombard Streets. The lot on which the house stood was on the west side of an alley called Blackberry Alley which ran from Pine to Lombard, had a frontage on the alley of forty-two feet and extended westward fifty-eight feet. The other lot was at the southeast corner of Blackberry Alley and an eight-foot alley called Blanchard's Alley, having a frontage on the first alley of sixty-two feet, and along the south side of Blanchard's Alley of ninety-eight feet. (Recorded in Deed Book D-21, 329.) Less than a month later on 1 July 1788, Ribaud bought from Charles White, merchant of Philadelphia, for £100 the two contiguous lots at the northwest corner of Delaware Eighth and Lombard Streets, each twenty-eight feet in front on Eighth by one hundred and eighty-eight feet on Lombard Street. (Recorded 19 July 1788, in Deed Book D-20, 313.)

In all of these transactions Joseph Ribaud was described as a merchant of Philadelphia. But on 31 August 1795, it was as Joseph Ribaud, Gentleman of Philadelphia, that he and his wife Mary sold for £900 the two-story frame messuage and lot on Blackberry Alley purchased from Blanchard, and all the "lot of ground and garden" at the northwest corner of Eighth and Lombard Streets he had purchased from Charles White, to Joseph Henzey, chair-maker of Philadelphia. (Recorded 1 September 1795, in Deed Book D-51, 415.)

From these records it is clear that Joseph Ribaud's wife Mary (who made her mark when they sold the various properties) was living as late as the first of September 1795. Whether she died in the yellow fever epidemic of that year, or after her husband purchased the house and lot in Botts Town, York County, the following November, has not as yet been resolved.

A STUDY OF THE RIGHTER-REITER FAMILIES
OF PHILADELPHIA COUNTY IN THE
EIGHTEENTH CENTURY

By Mildred Goshow

This study of the Righter-Reiter families of Philadelphia County was undertaken as a project in 1956-57 during the first Course in Genealogical Methods presented by this Society. Typed abstracts of the basic documents searched in the course of the project, consisting of 78 single-spaced pages of deeds, wills, church and cemetery records, tax lists, etc., are available for inspection in the Collections of the Society. The following article represents Miss Goshow's conclusions based on the material studied. While she has been interested in her own family's genealogy for many years, this is her first effort at presentation of such material in narrative form. We hope it will not be her last.

Among the very early settlers in Roxborough Township, Philadelphia County, was a certain Peter Righter. There is a tradition that he came from Germany in 1694 or somewhat later, as a member of the group of Pietists, who settled on the Ridge above the Wissahickon Creek, south of what is now known as Hermit Lane. Since there is no list of the persons who originally formed this group, or of those who joined them between 1694 and the death of Kelpius in 1708, when the community began to break up, there is no proof of whether a Peter Righter was or was not a member. Julius F. Sachse in his *German Pietists in Pennsylvania*,[1] accepts this tradition and states that it was from Phoebe Righter, widow of Daniel Righter, a grandson of Peter, that proof was obtained of the former tenure of her land by the " Mystic Brotherhood." The Pietist Community did not own the land on which it established itself. The Righters acquired the land years after the Community was scattered. The leaders of the Pietists were men of university education and considerable learning. If Peter Righter was one of them, he was an unlearned follower, for he could not write his name. The tradition further is that Peter Righter left the group very soon after his arrival here, married and raised a family. There is no record of the arrival of Peter Righter in America.

Peter Righter was certainly of German origin. While he could not write his name, his son, Bartholomew, could and signed his will in Ger-

---

[1] 206-210.

man script, " Barthol. Reiter." Some have suggested that the name was Richter. The Anglicized spelling, Righter, represents quite accurately the sound of the German Reiter, and not at all that of the German Richter. Variations in English spellings, such as Reighter, or Riter, also indicate Reiter as the German name.

The first record found of Peter Righter is the deed relating purchase, at sheriff's sale, 11 September 1725, of 80 acres of land, that had belonged to Matthew Holgate. This tract extended across Roxborough Township from the Schuylkill River to the Wissahickon Creek, 53 perches along the Creek, 40 along the River, south of the line of the present Hermit Lane. Sheriff Owen Roberts died before the actual conveyance of this land to Peter Righter was completed, but Peter seems to have taken possession at that time. On 23 January 1728, he sold 3 acres, a corner of this land on the east side of the road from Philadelphia to Plymouth, now Ridge Road, and at the northern end of the tract, to his son Bartholomew. It was not until 6 December 1728, that Sheriff Owen Owen, successor to Owen Roberts, on completion of payment of the price of 22 pounds by Peter, executed deeds to convey the land to him.[2]

It is evident that by this time Peter was married, and his family was growing up about him on his farm. No record of his marriage, of the name of his wife, or of the baptism of his children has been located. If Peter Righter adhered to any church after the break-up of the Pietist Community, or his departure from it, what church it may have been has not been determined.

Yeoman Peter Righter lived on his farm in lower Roxborough Township for 16 years longer. When John Hyatt prepared his list of landholders in Philadelphia County for Thomas Penn, Proprietor, in 1734, the returns for Roxborough Township included Peter Righter, 80 acres, Bartel Righter (" in corne ") 3 acres.[3] With the sale of 3 acres to Bartholomew (Bartel) the acreage for Peter should have been 77. 27 October 1741, Peter Righter, yeoman, sold his 77 acres of land for 60 pounds to his third son Michael.[4] Perhaps Peter was now too old to manage a farm, and lived out the few years left to him with his son. No wife was named in association with him in this sale of land, so it may be concluded that she died before this date.

[2] *Philadelphia County Deed Book* ADB-142, 485. All deeds, mortgages, wills and administrations cited hereinafter, unless otherwise designated, are Philadelphia County records.

[3] *Publications of the Genealogical Society of Pennsylvania*, Vol. 1 (1898), 181. The Genealogical Society of Pennsylvania will be cited hereafter as GSP.

[4] *Deed Book* H-9, 367.

Letters of administration were granted, 4 August 1744, to Bartholomew Righter " on the estate late of Peter Reighter, dec'd." No account or inventory of this estate is on file.[5] Bartholomew's account was to be filed 5 August 1745, when he may have been in his last illness, for he died that summer.[6]

Children of 1. Peter Righter:

2.   i.   Bartholomew Righter.
3.   ii.   Peter Righter.
4.   iii. Michael Righter.
5.   iv. George Righter.

There is no proof that this list is complete, nor of the order in which the children are listed, except that Michael was the third son. Bartholomew is placed first because he was the first to have land of his own, and was appointed administrator of his father's estate. Peter is included because of the tradition that Peter, the ferryman, was a brother of Michael. There is no proof that George was a son of Peter. It is assumed that he was because he lived in Roxborough Township, used the spelling Righter for his name, as did the others in the Roxborough family, and acquired land about the time a younger son might have done. There is certainly a probability that he belonged to the family.

---

[5] *Administration Book E*, 36 #65, 1744.

[6] This date for the death of the first Peter Righter, differs from that in previous studies. J. F. Sachse in his history of the German Pietists, and Joseph S. Miles in his *A Historical Sketch of Roxborough, Manayunk, and Wissahickon* (privately printed, 1940), have identified Peter Righter, the farmer and supposed member of the Pietist group, with Peter Righter, the ferryman, who died in 1776. Even before the record of administration of the estate of Peter Righter in 1744 was found it seemed improbable that Peter Righter, who immigrated as a mature man with the Pietist group in 1694 or shortly after, should embark on a strenuous occupation like that of ferryman, when he must have been close to 60 years of age (1741), or should live to 1776. In his history of the Pietists, Sachse gives biographical data on the few leaders of the group, whose names are known. These include: Johann Jacob Zimmerman, who died in 1694 at the age of 50, Johannes Kelpius, who died 1708, aged 35, Justus Falkner, who died 1723, aged 51, Daniel Falkner, who died 1741, aged 75, Johan Gottfried Seelig, who died 1745, aged 77, Henrich Bernhard Köster, who died 1749, aged 87, Conrad Matthai, who died 1748 (date of birth not given), and Christopher Witt, who died 1765, aged 90. It will be noted that 4 of the 8, for whom data are given, died in the 1740's, and only one lived beyond that decade. (Julius F. Sachse, *German Pietists of Provincial Pennsylvania*, passim). There is also a tradition that Peter the ferryman and Michael Righter were brothers. Horatio Gates Jones in the " Historical Sketch of Roxborough ", which he added as appendix to his *The Levering Family* (Philadelphia, 1858), stated on page 187, " Peter Righter, who owned ' Righter's Ferry ', on the Schuylkill, built a stone house on the banks of the Schuylkill above the Wissahiccon, and his brother Michael purchased a tract to the west ". Elsewhere Jones recorded that he was born in Peter Righter's house at the ferry, which his father had acquired by marriage to Esther Righter, granddaughter of Peter the ferryman. It is therefore concluded that Peter and Michael were both sons of the Peter Righter who died in 1744. The deed recording the sale of the first Peter's land states that Michael was his third son, and mentions his other son Bartholomew. If Michael and Bartholomew, thus proved to be brothers, were sons of Peter the ferryman, how is it that they were not mentioned in his will? His will mentions his sons Peter and John, and clearly implies by calling them elder and younger, that they were his only sons.

2. Bartholomew (Bartle, Barthol.) Righter (Reiter) was probably born shortly after 1700 in Roxborough Township, the son of Peter Righter, the emigrant. He learned the trade of cordwainer, and had sufficient education to be able to write his name in German script. On 23 January 1728, he purchased from his father 3 acres of land on the road leading to Holgate's Ford on the Wissahickon Creek, now probably Hermit Lane, a corner of his father's 80 acre farm. On 23 April 1736, he and his wife Elizabeth sold this lot, including a messuage, which he may have built on it, to John George Gager of Roxborough Township.[7] About two years later, on 4 January 1737/8, he purchased 250 acres of land from the Norris estate.[8] This tract was located in upper Roxborough, on both sides of the road from Plymouth to Philadelphia, now Ridge Road, extending north from approximately the present Port Royal Avenue to the present Manatawna Avenue, and east from the present Hagy's Mill Road to the Township Line Road. He built his new home there, and lived there the rest of his short life.

As in the case of his father, no church records of his marriage, or of the baptism of his children have been found. He was interested in a school in the neighborhood for his growing family, and was appointed to serve as trustee of the first school mentioned in Chestnut Hill, when in 1745, John Johnson granted a lot for school purposes on Paul's Mill Road (now Wise's Mill Road), about 800 feet west of the Wissahickon Creek, near the Roxborough Township line.[9] In August of 1744, he was appointed administrator of his father's estate. On 19 August 1745, " being weak in body," he made his will, devising his plantation and personal property to his wife Elizabeth for her use for life or until she remarried. Should she remarry, her share was to be 50 pounds, and the estate was to be held in trust till the children came of age. The land was then to be divided among the four sons, and the daughter Elizabeth was to receive 100 pounds on reaching age 18. He named his wife executrix, with Daniel Barrindoll executor. He signed his name to this will in German script, " Barthol Reiter." [10] The will was proved 20 September 1745. The exact date of death and place of burial have not been determined.

At the June 1757 term of the Court of Common Pleas, Sheriff James Coultas was ordered, with the help of a jury of 12 men, to partition the land of Bartle Righter among his four sons. The partition was approved September, 1757.[11]

---

7 Both these transactions are recorded in *Deed Book* I-13, 118.

8 *Deed Book* G-1, 205.

9 John J. MacFarlane, *History of Early Chestnut Hill* (Philadelphia, 1927), 72.

10 Will #30, 1745.

11 Recited in several deeds relating to this land, cited hereinafter. I did not locate the partition agreement.

The children of 2. Bartholomew and Elizabeth (———) Righter were:

6. i. John Righter.
7. ii. Jacob Righter.
8. iii. Peter Righter.
9. iv. Bartle Righter.
    v. Elizabeth Righter.

These are named in order as listed in Bartholomew's will, which may not have been the order of birth.

3. Peter Righter, Junior, son of Peter Righter the emigrant, was probably born in Roxborough Township in the first decade of the 18th century. The record of his independent business venture does not begin until 1741. In January of that year he was granted by John, Thomas, and Richard Penn, Proprietors, a patent for a ferry from his plantation on the east side of the Schuylkill in "Roxbury" Township to Lower Merion Township. The patent gave him the sole privilege of keeping a ferry at that place, and forbade all others from carrying passengers for 2 miles above and 2 miles below his ferry. This privilege was granted for 7 years, at a cost to Peter of 5 English silver shillings paid on the first of March, yearly. Peter was required to have at all times a boat or boats in good repair and sufficient persons or hands to give attention for ferrying passengers, horses, cattle and goods.[12] A ferry at this point, just above his mill is said to have been operated previously by Andrew Robeson.[13] The patent was renewed by John Penn, Proprietor, 11 October 1765,[14] and the ferry was maintained by Peter for the rest of his life, and after him by his son John. The location of the Righter Ferry is shown on "A Map of Philadelphia and Parts Adjacent" of 1752 by Scull and Heap, a short distance above the point where the Wissahickon Creek enters the Schuylkill River. On the map it is marked "Ferry," with a house on the Roxborough Township side of the river. A road, private till 1824, from "Wissahiccon" Road (now Ridge Road) extended along the river as far as the ferry. On the Lower Merion side the road to the ferry became known as Righter's Ferry Road, and still is so called, although it no longer reaches the river. What is now School Lane to Ridge Road gave access to the ferry from Germantown. The ferry was an important link in early communications between Lower Merion and Philadelphia, Ger-

---

[12] *Exemplification Book* 2, 637.

[13] *Pennsylvania Magazine of History and Biography* (hereinafter cited as *PMHB*), Vol. 50, 363, 364: Charles R. Barker's article ": The Stony Part of the Schuylkill, its Navigation, Fisheries, Fords, and Ferries," has a brief account of Righter's ferry.

[14] *Exemplification Book* 3, 518.

mantown and Lower Merion, as well as Roxborough and Lower Merion. It must have been a profitable enterprise, in which Peter was probably assisted by his 2 sons. The assessment for the Proprietary Tax of 1769 showed that he had one servant.[15]

The ferry patent of Peter Righter mentioned his plantation on the east bank of the Schuylkill River. Peter acquired the 77 acres in this plantation 4 August 1741, for 86 pounds, 12 shillings, 6 pence, from Thomas Bishop Vickris (Vicaris) of Chew Magna, Somerset County, England, through his attorney Richard Hockley, Philadelphia County, merchant. The land was located between the Schuylkill River and the Wissahickon Creek from the line near where Sumac Street now is, to a line 75 perches up the river. The section which reached the Wissahickon Creek was triangular with the broad base on the present Righter Street, then the road to Plymouth, and the narrow, blunted apex, 14 perches, on the Wissahickon Creek. The land rose steeply on the side of both river and creek to the Ridge. Included in the area to-day are the shops, formerly Pencoyd Iron Works on the River, Wissahickon Station on the Reading Railroad, Wissahickon Public School, and library, Northern Home for Children, and a considerable portion of the residential section of the Wissahickon area. Ridge Road, both the original, difficult route and the easier one adopted later up "Righter's Hill," crossed his plantation from the southwest to the northeast corner. A high rock cliff on Robeson's Hill, on the river side was set back from its east bank. Peter seemed to feel that his title was not sure, and 4 January 1742 he received a confirmation of the grant from George Thomas, Lieutenant Governor.[16] Peter built his stone house at the ferry on the river. He also acquired a lot of 9¾ acres in Lower Merion at the Merion side of his ferry.[17] He made further use of his river frontage in his shad fishery, an important business on the Schuylkill before the dam was built at Fairmount.

Peter Righter had married, but no record of his wife's name has been found. There is no record of his connection with any church. His oldest daughter was evidently born in 1741, and he had four other daughters and two sons. When in 1748 William Levering granted land for a public school in Roxborough, Peter Righter was named as one of the seven trustees.[18]

---

15 *Pennsylvania Archives*, 3rd Ser., Vol. XIV, 15, "Peter Righter, ferry, 74 acres, 2 horses, 3 cattle, 1 servant."

16 *Deed Book* G-2, 444; *Exemplification Book* 2, 639.

17 Recited in *Montgomery County Deed Book* 52, 395, H. G. Jones *et al.* to A. L. Anderson.

18 Deed not on record, but recited in *Deed Book* D-49, 476, when in 1771, additional land was donated.

10 January 1776 Peter Righter made his will, and died within a few days, for the will was proved 20 January 1776. His grave has not been located. Perhaps it was in the plot on the Levering farm, given to the community as the Roxborough Burial Ground, but there is no gravestone there for him. By his will, he devised to his eldest son Peter two lots of land, one on the east side of the Schuylkill, between the river and the Ferry Road, and one of 5 acres on the west side of the river. He instructed Peter to build a house on his land and provided that 100 pounds should be paid him when he did so. He gave Peter one half interest in his shad fishery. The residue of his lands, tenements and property he bequeathed to his younger son John. John was required to pay the money bequests to his oldest daughter Mary and his daughters Hannah, Rebecca, Sarah, and Margaret. He gave a case of drawers worth 8 pounds to Sarah and Margaret, and a large looking glass to Margaret. He named his son John and son-in-law Enoch Levering his executors. Since his wife was not mentioned, it is probable she died before he did.[19]

Children of 3. Peter Righter, Jr.

     i. Peter Righter. Very little about him has been found. Whether he carried out the instructions in his father's will to build a house on his land, was not determined. In his brother John's will, provision was made for the " legitimate " children of Peter to share in the estate in case John's daughter Esther died without issue. John seems to have acquired the land his father devised to Peter, for it was part of Esther's estate. There were three Peter Righters in Roxborough Township in this generation, and it is difficult to distinguish them. An incomplete assignment on a bond in the papers of an Owen Jones seems to relate to this Peter, for his brother John and brother-in-law Enoch Levering were mentioned in it.[20]

    ii. Mary Righter. She married Enoch Levering, the date of the marriage license being 10 September 1765.[21]

    iii. Hannah Righter. She married Aaron Levering, the date of the marriage license being 9 May 1763.[22] The history of the two Levering families has been traced by John Levering in his *Levering Family, History and Genealogy*.[23] This work states that Mary died 21 February 1794, aged 52 years, so that she was born in 1742, and that Hannah died 6 September 1806, aged 65, so that she was born in 1741, but Peter Righter mentioned in his will his oldest daughter Mary.

[19] *Will Book* Q, 240, #204, 1776.

[20] *GSP Genealogical Notes*, Vol. 9, 13.

[21] *PMHB* Vol. 40, 332, " Pennsylvania Marriage Licenses, 1762 to 1768."

[22] *PMHB* Vol. 40, 216, where her name is given as Ann Wrighter.

[23] Published by Levering Historical Association, 1897.

Aaron and Enoch Levering were brothers, and both moved from Roxborough to Baltimore.

    iv. Rebecca Righter. She was not mentioned in the will of her brother John, so may have died before 1790.

    v. Sarah Righter.

    vi. Margaret Righter.

10. vii. John Righter.

4. Michael Righter, third son of Peter Righter the emigrant, is the only one of the early Righters in Roxborough whose date of birth has been determined. Horatio Gates Jones, in his *Historic Notes of Olden Times in Roxborough and Manayunk*,[24] first printed in a local newspaper in 1859, stated that he had access to the graveyard book of the old Roxborough Burial Ground, of whose trustees the author's father, the Rev. H. G. Jones, was secretary, and that, although burials were made there before that date, the first entry was in 1786: "Michael Righter, Sen. aged 77 years and 5 months." Michael's gravestone has survived in fairly good condition. It gives the date of his death as July 1, 1786. He was therefore born about 1 February 1709. He was unable to write his name, making his mark on deeds and will.

He married Anna Catharina Geiger, daughter of John George Geiger of Roxborough Township, who may have been the John George "Gager," who, 23 April 1736, bought the 3 acre tract Michael's brother Bartholomew had acquired from his father. George Geiger by will, written 3 November 1747, left all his estate to "my well-beloved son-in-law Michael Righter." The will was probated 15 November 1747.[25] Catharina seems to have raised some objections, and then thought better of it, for a note on the will addressed to Mr. Plumstead, reads, "I hereby make known to you that I have no further objection to make agst. my late father's George Thuggers will receiv'd Probate but am willing it may receive its probate and pass the seal of your office forthwith." Her name or what seems to be an abbreviation of it, was signed in German script to this note.

On 4 August 1741, the same day Peter Righter made his purchase of land, Michael purchased, also from Thomas Bishop Vickris, for 80 pounds, 8 shillings, 9 pence, 71½ acres, adjoining Peter's tract in lower Roxborough Township.[26] This tract extended along the Wissahickon

---

24 The newspaper articles were clipped and pasted in a book, possibly by Mr. Jones, who was a secretary of the Historical Society of Pennsylvania, and the book was presented to the Society. It has no index. It is an excellent account of the first hundred years or so of Roxborough history. Hereinafter cited as Jones, *Historic Notes.*

25 Will #212, 1747.

26 *Deed Book* FTW-103, 365. This deed was not recorded until 1 April 1874.

Creek for 206 perches around the bend where the creek turns sharply southwest to flow towards the Schuylkill. To-day Lincoln Drive follows the course of the creek as far as this great bend. From the Creek his land extended to the old route of the high road through Roxborough, where Righter Street now is. He had only 29 perches on the high road.

On 27 October 1741, Michael bought from his father Peter Righter, for 60 pounds 77 acres of land on which his father had lived since 1725.[27] This tract extended from the Wissahickon Creek to the Schuylkill River, and adjoined what he had just purchased in the Vickris or Vicaris tract. The " high road " cut across it to the present Hermit Lane. He owned a plateau with an abrupt cliff on the river side and steep hill on the creek side. His land included the area where the German Pietistic Community, to which his father is said to have belonged, had its huts, including the cave made by Kelpius for his own use. In 1746 he built on the " high road " a stone house, which stood until a few years ago, in the triangle where Righter Street meets Ridge Road. Michael held all but about 4 acres of this land till his death. The 4 acres he sold 19 March 1744, to John George Bergman of Roxborough Township, tailor, for 21 pounds. Bergman secured the use of a 10 foot cartway on the north side of Michael's land for access to his 4 acres on the Wissahickon Creek from the Plymouth or Ridge Road.[28] Michael farmed the residue of the 148 acres as his means of livelihood for the rest of his life, and raised his large family there. When in 1771 William Levering granted land for the Roxborough School, Michael Righter was one of the 7 trustees named.[29] In 1777 to 1778, he, or his son Michael, was the assessor to determine the amount of damage done by the British in Roxborough Township during the British occupation of Philadelphia. On the assessor's list Michael claimed 39 pounds, 10 shillings damages, and his son Daniel 3 pounds.[30]

Michael made his will 29 January 1783. He added a codicil 29 June 1786, and the will was probated 18 July 1786. He had died 1 July 1786, and was buried in the Roxborough Burial Ground where he owned lot No. 62. His wife Catharina Geiger Righter survived him 10 years. She also is buried in the Roxborough Burial Ground, but her stone is not so well preserved as Michael's. The year of death was 1796. Michael, in his will, had provided that his wife " Caterina " was to have bed, bedstead, and bedding, 5 pounds in gold or silver, free use of her room with liberty

[27] Deed Book H-9, 367.

[28] Deed Book H-18, 423.

[29] Deed Book D-49, 476, 13 March 1771, William Levering to Michael Righter et al.

[30] PMHB, Vol. 25, (1901), 555, " Assessment of Damages Done by the British, 1777-1778." Jones gives these figures in his Historic Notes, 89-105.

of passing to and from it and wood for firewood brought to her door. Michael's house became the property of his son John, so his mother lived with him. The interest of one third part of the estate was to be paid to her by the children and grandchildren who inherited it, yearly, during her life.

The division of the estate among the 9 children who survived him, and the 5 children of his daughter Elizabeth, who had died before him, in equal shares either in land or money, was to be made by 3 persons, selected by his sons George, Michael, and John, each of them to choose " one discreet and reputable freeholder " to make the valuation and division. Those who received land were to pay money to those who got none as the said freeholders thought right.[31] The men chosen for this difficult task were Daniel Thomas and Matthew Holget, both of Germantown, and Anthony Cook of Roxborough Township. The Articles of Agreement, putting the results of their work in legal form, were signed 9 March 1787. The division of the land was a complicated one as it broke the tract into 11 lots. Seven children received land and each one had a lot on the " Reding " (Reading or Ridge) Road. John and Michael received lots extending from Ridge Road to the Schuylkill River. Peter, Caspar, Margaret, Daniel, and George shared the land between Ridge Road and the Wissahickon Creek, in the location of which a one perch wide lane, probably now Hermit Lane, was important, Margaret being the only one of the daughters to receive land. Daughters Catherine Levering and Mary Heft received 87 pounds, 2 shillings, 8½ pence each, and the five children of the third daughter Elizabeth Lare, dec'd, shared the same sum among them.[32]

The children of 4. Michael and Catharine (Geiger) Righter were:

      i. Caspar Righter. He was a blacksmith. 11 April 1794, he sold to Nicholas Kolp for 150 pounds the 2 lots he inherited from his father. He was then of Morris County, New Jersey.[33]

11. ii. George Righter. He was a wheelwright. 21 June 1787, he and his wife Rebecca sold his share of his father's estate for 150 pounds to David Mircle (Markle) of Roxborough Township. George was then of Brandywine Hundred, New Castle County, Delaware.[34]

---

31 *Will Book* T, 345, #205 of 1786.

32 *Deed Book* D-18, 632, Articles of Agreement.

33 *Deed Book* D-45, 16. In Parsippany, Morris County, New Jersey, there lived a Jasper Righter, 1739-1794, who is said to have been born in Roxborough. He served in 1776, as private, in Captain Israel Halsey's company, eastern battalion, Morris County, New Jersey militia. He married in 1769 Elizabeth Hopler, 1749-1809. Two of his descendants became members of the Daughters of the Revolution on the basis of his service. *DAR Lineage Book* 98, 264, 265, and 149, 256, 257. It seems probable that Caspar and Jasper were the same person, but no research was done to prove or disprove this.

34 *Deed Book* D-19, 220.

iii. Peter Righter. He may have been a cooper,[35] but it is difficult to distinguish the Peter Righters. There was no Peter Righter with 26 acres of land on the Tax Assessors' Lists for Roxborough Township in the Municipal Archives, probably because he seems to have sold his share of his father's land to his brother Michael, although no record of the sale was found, but Peter's land was part of the area owned by Michael as shown on the map made by John Hills in 1809. 24 September 1799, letters of administration were granted to Michael Righter on the estate of Peter Righter, dec'd. Charles Bower of Roxbury, cooper, and John Righter, of same place, farmer, were sureties for the 300 pound bond.[36] As Michael and John were his brothers, and Charles Bower's daughter was Michael's wife, this Peter Righter was probably Michael's son. In that case it may be that the Peter Righter on the tax assessors' lists for Roxborough Township for several years, as owner of 1½ acres and dwelling, and described in 1788 as a " fisherman " was Michael's son, for in 1800 the entry changes to Peter Righter, est.[37] There is, however, a possibility that this entry may relate to Peter's son Peter, because he inherited one half of his father's shad fishery. The census of 1790 lists 2 " Riters " named Peter in Roxborough Township. One of them is certainly Bartholomew's son Peter. The other may be either Peter's son or Michael's.[38] The spelling " Riter " was used in this census record, although all the Roxborough family used " Righter." Without information about their families, no correlation of the data in the 1790 census with the Peter Righters can be made.

12. iv. Michael Righter.
13. v. Daniel Righter.
    vi. John Righter. He probably died 1808. He was probably the John Righter who was on the tax assessors' lists as without property in 1781, 1782, 1783.[39] His wife was named Catharine. In 1787 he inherited the stone dwelling and 21 acres, 33 perches of land from his father. This land adjoined Michael's on the north, and extended from Ridge Road to the Schuylkill. It had two springs which Michael must be permitted to use, " alternately, that is to say 48 hours at a time and no more," with right to dig ditches to convey water to his lot.[40] His father also favored his youngest son John with a bequest of 10 pounds in gold and silver. The will specified that in the division of the land the freeholders selected should allot to John " my dwelling house and the land assigned to it, if he shall chuse to take it." In a codicil, he gave to John over and above his

[35] *Pennsylvania Archives*, 3rd Ser., Vol. XIV, 425, Provincial Tax, 1774, Roxborough Township.

[36] *Administration Book* K, 15, #294 of 1799.

[37] These assessors' lists are in the Municipal Archives in the basement of the Old Customs House, Philadelphia. Hereinafter cited as Roxborough Twp. Tax Lists.

[38] *Heads of Families: First Census of the United States, 1790, Pennsylvania*, Roxborough Township, 207, 208. (Hereinafter cited as *Heads of Families, 1790*.)

[39] *Pennsylvania Archives*, 3rd Ser., Vol. XVI, 30, 178, 650.

[40] Articles of Agreement, cited above.

share, a "horse and mare with gear belonging to them, my cart, plough, and harrow, and hay in the barn sufficient for the horses for one year." John's mother was bequeathed the use of a room in the house, but all the children who inherited land had to pay the interest on one third part to her yearly as long as she lived. While Margaret inherited land, it seems likely that she lived at the homestead, for she received, by the terms of the will, one of her father's cows and hay for her for one winter. John, Margaret and their mother shared the grain standing on the land at Michael's death.[41] John was listed as farmer on the assessors' lists for Roxborough Township. In 1790 he was listed as head of a family with 2 females, who may have been his wife and mother, or his mother and sister Margaret.[42] When the route of Ridge Road was changed from the very steep hill of what is now Righter Street, to the somewhat easier climb up "Righter's Hill" of the present route, John's house was separated from his land by the road. 1 April 1802, John and his wife Catharine sold the house and land for 500 pounds to John Kennedy and Robert Kennedy in order to pay a mortgage debt of 200 pounds with interest thereon to Sarah Woodrow. The right to use of springs and cartroad to the Schuylkill was reserved to the owner of the lot his brother Michael had inherited.[43] Robert Kennedy was an innkeeper, and it may be at this time that Michael's house became the "Plow Tavern." 15 June 1833 the house was bought by the Managers of the Poor of Roxborough Township as the local poor house.[44] In 1803, 1804, 1805, John Righter was described on the tax assessors' lists as schoolmaster, probably teacher of the Roxborough School, of which his brother Michael was one of the trustees. In 1806, the assessors described him as laborer with the same valuation, $208, as when he was schoolmaster.[45] 3 September 1808, letters of administration were granted to Catharine Righter on the estate of John Righter, farmer, dec'd. Thomas McCrea of Philadelphia, cooper, and Joseph Sorber of Northern Liberties, coachmaker, were sureties for the bond of $500.[46] Thomas McCrea was the husband of John's niece. No record has been found of John's children, if he had any.

vii. Catharine Righter. She was born 17 June 1732, and died 14 November 1808. She married Benjamin Levering, 2 April 1754.[47] Her descendants are traced in the Levering family histories by Horatio Gates Jones and John Levering. She and her husband were buried in the Roxborough Burial Ground, and their gravestones with dates are in good condition.

41 *Will Book* T, 345, #205, 1786.

42 *Heads of Families*, 1790, 207.

43 *Deed Book* EF-8, 169.

44 Jones, *Historic Notes*, 52.

45 Roxborough Twp. Tax Lists.

46 *Administration Book* K, 322, #173, 1808.

47 *Pennsylvania Archives*, 2nd Ser., Vol. VIII, 497, Marriage Records of the Swedes' Church (Gloria Dei), 1750-1810.

    viii. Mary Righter. She married ———— Heft.

    ix. Margaret Righter. She was the only one of the daughters who received land in the partition of Michael's estate in 1787. 8 August 1793, she sold this land to William White for 120 pounds. She was described in this deed as " spinster." [48]

    x. Elizabeth Righter. She died before her father made his will, 29 January 1783. Her 5 children, not named in the will, were to share her part of his estate. In the partition agreement, she was mentioned as Elizabeth Lare.

These children are listed in the order named in Michael's will, and not in order of birth. Catharine may have been the oldest. Five Righters, Michael, Daniel, George, John and Peter, served from Roxborough Township in the Philadelphia County militia, during the Revolution.[49] They could all have been Michael's sons, but may not have been. Michael and Daniel certainly were. John and Peter may have been Peter's sons, and George Righter also had a son George. It is certain that the Peter was not Bartholomew's son, because he was a member of the Society of Friends and did not serve.

5. George Righter was assumed to be a member of the Roxborough Township family for the reasons that have been given when the children of Peter Righter the emigrant were first listed in this article. The dates of his birth and death have not been found. He combined the occupations of farmer and weaver for he was sometimes described as one and sometimes as the other in deeds relating to him. He had sufficient education to write for he signed his name to all documents, and always spelled it " Righter," as did the other members of the Roxborough family. On 10 November 1746, he married Elizabeth Cumree (perhaps Gomry or Gumere).[50] Elizabeth could not write her name.

George Righter did not remain in Roxborough Township continuously throughout his life. His career was difficult to trace because of the existence of other George Righters contemporary with him, especially the George Reiter of Germantown Township, who also had a wife Elizabeth, and was a frequent investor in land. On 21 May 1747 George

---

[48] *Deed Book* D-37, 395.

[49] J. S. Miles, *Historical Sketch of Roxborough and Manayunk* (Philadelphia, 1940), 37. The account of the military operations in Roxborough Township is on pages 34-50. There is also an excellent account in Jones, *Historic Notes*.

[50] *GSP*, Vol. XIX, 308, " Register of Baptisms, 1701 to 1746, of the First Presbyterian Church of Philadelphia." The marriage was entered out of place among the baptisms. Also *Pennsylvania Archives* 2nd Ser., Vol. II, " Names of Persons to whom Marriage licences were issued in the Province of Pennsylvania, previous to 1790." For comment on this marriage, see *GSP*, Vol. XX, No. 2, " The Back Part of Germantown " by Hannah Benner Roach, note 73, p. 96. Since George Reiter of Cresheim also had a wife Elizabeth, there is some doubt as to which George married Elizabeth Cumree, but since he always used the German spelling, and was a Lutheran, it seems unlikely that it was George of Cresheim, who married her.

Righter of Roxborough Township purchased from John Conrad for 130 pounds, two tracts of land in Springfield Township, 26 acres, 120 perches together. This land was on the road from Plymouth to Philadelphia, and no great distance from the Roxborough Township line.[51] Three years later, 29 September 1750, George Righter of Roxborough Township, weaver, purchased from Cornelius Conrads and Priscilla his wife, for 365 pounds, two tracts of land, one of 55 acres, 110 perches in Roxborough Township, and one of 89 acres, with messuage, in Germantown Township. These were adjoining tracts on the township line.[52] The Roxborough tract was located between the township line and the tract Bartholomew Righter purchased in 1737. Bartholomew's deed[53] described his land as extending S.E. by S. 180 perches on the line of Mathias Conrads, from whom Cornelius had acquired it indirectly. While the Roxborough tract extended 180 perches on the township line, the Germantown Township tract extended 290 perches on the same line. George Righter held this land only a short time, and may never have lived on it. 24 May 1754, George Righter of Springfield, weaver, and Elizabeth his wife, sold most of it for 330 pounds to John Gumry. This sale included the whole of the tract in Germantown Township, and 18 acres, 110 perches of the tract in Roxborough Township. George retained the northern 37 acres of the latter.[54] Mrs. Hannah Benner Roach in her recent article on " The Back Part of Germantown," [55] expressed the opinion that John Gumry was George's brother-in-law. The deed of sale described the land as in John Gumry's " actual possession now being," and included a messuage on the Germantown Township tract. On 27 January 1758, George Righter mortgaged his two tracts in Springfield Township and the one in Roxborough Township to John Johnson, and 6 June 1763, John Johnson acknowledged payment of this debt.[56] On 8 March 1763, George, still of Springfield Township, bought from Bartle Righter for 269 pounds, 6 shillings, a tenement and two distinct tracts in Roxborough Township, 34¾ acres, 29 perches together.[57] One of these was

[51] *Deed Book* H-4, 404.

[52] *Deed Book* H-4, 497. The lot in Roxborough Township was part of the tract of 5000 acres, which after 1715, belonged to the Norris famliy. Joseph S. Miles in his excellent chapter on " First Settlers," in his *Historical Sketch of Roxborough and Manayunk* omitted reference to the sale of the part of this tract on the Germantown Township line to Mathias Conrads, from whose heirs Cornelius Conrads had purchased it. The deed for this transaction was not located. Mr. Miles does not locate the lot on his map illustrating this chapter.

[53] *Deed Book* G-1, 205.

[54] *Deed Book* IH-10, 434. This deed was not recorded until 1824.

[55] *GSP*, Vol. XX, 109.

[56] *Deed Book* H-8, 293. Mortgage.

[57] *Deed Book* H-19, 451.

on the Ridge Road and the road to Christopher Robin's Mill, now Port Royal Avenue. About this time he probably sold his land in Springfield and the Roxborough tract on the Germantown Township line, but these deeds have not been located. On 30 November 1764, he sold to Leonard Streepers the 10½ acres of woodland in Roxborough Township, the lot on the road to Christopher Robin's Mill, which he had purchased from Bartle Righter, a little over a year before.[58] This deed described him as " late of Springfield, now of Roxborrow Township." On 20 May 1766, he bought for 505 pounds from Jacob Righter, brother of Bartle, 20¼ acres in Roxborough Township.[59] George now owned approximately 45 acres of land on the west side of the road to Plymouth, now Ridge Road, in the upper section of Roxborough Township, part of the 250 acres his brother Bartholomew had purchased from the Norris estate in 1737. Tax records, both provincial or state, and local Roxborough Township assessors' lists showed that he lived on his 45 acres with dwelling to about 1784. On the local assessor's list for 1781 he was described as a " non-juror," which may indicate that he was a Mennonite or belonged to some other sect opposed to taking oaths.[60] He usually owned a couple of horses and cattle.[61] In 1784 George Righter, Senior, of Norriton Township, then Philadelphia County, but soon Montgomery, and Elizabeth his wife, sold their land in Roxborough Township.[62] It is probable that George was now getting old and retiring to live with his son. Although he was spoken of in these deeds as of Norriton Township, he actually never became a landowner there. It was his son George Junior, who purchased land in Norriton. No record has been found of when George and Elizabeth died, or of where they were buried. He had sold all of his real property, and there was no will or record of administration of an estate for him in either Philadelphia or Montgomery County.

George and Elizabeth (Cumree) Righter probably had only one child,

14.   i. George Righter, Junior.

6. John Righter, son of No. 2 Bartholomew and Elizabeth (————) Righter, was a minor when his father died in 1745. He received enough

---

[58] Deed Book H-20, 472.

[59] Recited in deed of sale of this land by George Righter to Harry Knauss, Deed Book D-21, 81.

[60] There was no George Righter in the card index of the Henshaw collection in the Friends Historical Library at Swarthmore College. This collection is hereinafter cited as FHL.

[61] Pennsylvania Archives, 3rd Ser., Vol. XIV, 15, 424, 695; Vol. XV, 136; Vol. XVI, 31, 177, 652. See also Roxborough Twp. Tax Lists.

[62] Deed Book D-13, 37: George Righter and Elizabeth to Adam Schneider; and Deed Book D-21, 81: same to Harry Knauss.

education to be able to write as indicated by his signature on deeds and will. He married twice, his first wife being Hannah Tunis, whom he married 26 February 1754.[63] She was the daughter of Anthony Tunis and his wife Bathsheba, of Germantown Township, later of Lower Merion Township. The Tunis family belonged to the Society of Friends. On 8th day, 11th month, 1754 at the Monthly Meeting held at Merion Meeting House, Hannah Righter brought acknowledgement in writing for her "outgoing in marriage." [64] On 11th day, 11th month, 1757, the Merion overseers proposed that John Righter be joined to this meeting.[65] When the 250 acres of his father's plantation in Roxborough were partitioned among the 4 sons, John's portion was a 40 acre tract with messuage on the easterly side of the road to Plymouth or Ridge Road. The house and tract of land he and Hannah sold 13 April 1761, for 300 pounds to his brother Peter. In this deed John was described as a house carpenter.[66] When this sale was made John was already living in Lower Merion Township, perhaps attracted by the residence there of his wife's family. 22 November 1760, he, described as yeoman, had purchased for 310 pounds from Hannah Harrison, 102 acres of land in Lower Merion Township.[67] This farm was located in Mill Creek Valley, and on the stream John built a dam and erected a stone grist and saw mill. Access to his property was by a road, still known as Righter's Mill Road, opened as a public road on his petition in 1763. In later years he changed his mill to paper manufacture, and it is as a "paper maker" that he described himself in his will.[68] In 1763 he bought 75 acres, 106 perches of land from Hannah Harrison,[69] 25 acres of which he sold to Jonathan Robeson, 1 August 1794.

63 *Pennsylvania Archives* 2nd Ser., Vol. VIII, 497: "Marriage Record of the Swedes' Church (Gloria Dei), 1750-1810," where her name is spelled Tanes.

64 FHL, *Radnor Minutes*, 1744-1758, 234. These minutes are on microfilm. Radnor, Merion and Haverford meetings formed one monthly meeting.

65 *Ibid.*, 336.

66 *Deed Book* H-18, 118.

67 *Deed Book* H-15, 160.

68 *PMHB*, Vol. 50 (1926), 13: Charles R. Barker, "Old Mills or Mill Creek, Lower Merion," gives an excellent account of John Righter's enterprises and difficulties as miller. His account is incorrect in one respect, as he describes John's brother Peter as the Schuylkill ferryman. John's brother was a farmer in upper Roxborough; the ferryman Peter was John's uncle. There were so many Peter Righters that confusion is difficult to avoid. There is in the main building of the Philadelphia Public Library, in the map room, a photostat of a map of Mill Creek District, prepared by Dr. Douglas Macfarlan, which shows the location of John Righter's mill. The location of his land is also shown on the *Record and Historical Map of Philadelphia and its Environs*, prepared in 1809 by John Hills, a copy of which is in the map room of the Historical Society of Pennsylvania.

69 Recited in *Montgomery County Deed Book 9*, 138: 1 August 1794 John Righter and Jane to Jonathan Robeson, when he sold part of this land.

In 1762 when Anthony Tunis died, he bequeathed by his will a lot of 1 acre, 114 perches on Plymouth Road in Germantown Township, to his daughter Hannah Righter, together with a legacy of 67 pounds to make her share of his estate equal to the 100 pounds given to her sisters. He made a special bequest of 20 shillings to such of his grandsons as were called by his name, a provision which benefited Hannah's son Anthony.[70] Not until 2 September 1796, after Hannah's death, was the lot in Germantown sold for 115 pounds, by her heirs to Christopher Heydrick.[71] Hannah was also a beneficiary under the will of her brother Joseph Tunis, who died in 1773.[72] The discharge to the executors of Joseph's will, signed 18 August 1775, shows that Hannah Righter received a one fifth share of the residuary estate of 1581 pounds, 10 shillings, 3 pence.[73] Young Anthony Righter was bequeathed by his Uncle Joseph " rights and property in Blockley and Merion united library."

In 1773 John's brother Bartle Righter came to live in Lower Merion on a tract of 46 acres, 60 perches, he bought from John.[74] A note on this deed showed that John had mortgaged this land to John Johnson of Germantown. At the close of the Revolution, for the Effective Supply Tax, John Righter's property was valued at 765 pounds, and in 1783, for the Federal Tax, included 100 acres, 3 cattle, 8 sheep, a grist mill.[75]

John remained a member of the Society of Friends until 1783, during most of this period being connected with Merion Meeting. On 30 October 1758 he secured a certificate of removal for himself, wife and family to Abington Monthly Meeting, and 29 December 1760, one was signed for him and his wife from Abington to Haverford Monthly Meeting, after the settlement of some complaint against him in case of property by John Roberts, miller, of Merion.[76] He did not produce this certificate of removal until the Monthly Meeting at Merion, 10 August 1764.[77] The minutes of the Monthly Meeting at Haverford Meeting House, 14 January 1783, have this entry, " Merion Preparative Meeting forwards a compleint that John Righter neglects attendance at meeting and frequent company keeping with a neighboring woman, wife of an-

---

70 *Will Book* M, 300, #173, 1763.

71 *Deed Book* D-77, 457.

72 *Will Book* P, 411 #288, 1773.

73 *Deed Book* I-15, 26: Discharge.

74 *Deed Book* H-18, 116.

75 *Pennsylvania Archives* 3rd Ser., Vol. XVI, 130, 592.

76 *GSP Collections*, " Records of Abington Monthly Meeting," 226, 262, 264, 274. Monthly Meeting will be hereinafter designated as MM.

77 FHL, *Minutes of Radnor MM, 1763-1772,* 58.

other man," and 8 April 1783, " Since he will not listen to advise and desires to separate from Friends he has disunited himself from religious fellowship until he sincerely condemns such conduct." [78] His daughter Hannah was disowned about the same time, having " become the mother of an illegitimate child." [79] Perhaps Hannah Tunis Righter had died before this date, and the restraining hand of wife and mother had been removed.[80]

After the death of Hannah, John married as his second wife Jane McAffee, daughter of William McAffee of Lower Merion.[81] When William McAffee died in 1793, he named his son Robert and son-in-law John Righter executors. Bartle Righter was one of the witnesses of the signature of this will.[82] The administration of this estate continued for the rest of John's life, entered into the provisions of his own will, and caused trouble for his wife as executrix of his will.

On 11 August 1808, John Righter made his will, but he lived on till 1824, when he must have been a very old man, perhaps 90 years of age. His children by Jane McAffee were minors at the time he wrote his will, and he made provision for their maintenance and education, as well as providing that " all money received or which shall be received " from Jane's father's estate, along with his own personal property should go to his wife Jane. She was also to have the rents and income of his real estate until the youngest child should reach 21. Then one half of the real estate was to be divided among his children, and the other half was to remain in his wife's hands till her death, when that also was to be divided among his children.[83]

The children of 6. John and Hannah (Tunis) Righter were:

15.   i. Anthony Righter.
      ii. Hannah Righter. She married Malcolm Guien, miller, of Lower Merion.
     iii. Sarah Righter. She married Frederick Bicking, Jr., papermaker, of Lower Merion. The Bicking family lived near the Righters.[84]

[78] FHL, *Minutes of Radnor MM, 1782-1784,* 5, 7, 8, 9, 11.

[79] *Ibid.* 13.

[80] There is nothing in the Records of the Friends to indicate that John Righter broke the rules of discipline by military service in the Revolution. Some of his descendants have claimed, in applications for membership in the Daughters of the Revolution, that he was the John Righter, who served in Captain Houlgate's company, 4th battalion, Philadelphia County militia, 1776, a Roxborough Township not a Lower Merion Township company. See *DAR Lineage Books,* #99021 and #104111. There were two John Righters in Roxborough Township, one of whom was more probably the member of Captain Houlgate's company.

[81] *PMHB* Vol. 52 (1928), 215: Charles R. Barker, "Colonial Taverns of Lower Merion."

[82] GSP Collections, *Abstract of Wills and Administrations of Montgomery County,* 1784-1822, Vol. I, 70.

[83] *Montgomery County Will* #5416.

[84] *Will Book* 3, 21 #108, 1809.

iv. Jane Righter. She married Joseph Bicking, papermaker, of "New Cochenhoppen" Township, Montgomery County, Pennsylvania.
v. Amelia Righter. She married Martin Proctor. John Righter by his will gave 5 shillings to his son-in-law Martin Proctor, and 10 pounds each to his grandchildren, heirs of his daughter Amelia Proctor.

The Records of Burials in Friends' Grave Yard at the Merion Meeting House, mentioned 3 other children in this family:

vi. John Righter, "son of John Righter, buried 5-13-1761."
vii. Mary Righter, "daughter of John Righter, buried 1-10-1766."
viii. "Jessey Righter, son of John Righter, buried 3-6-1766." [85]

Children of 6. John and Jane (McAffee) Righter were:

ix. John Righter. He was born about 1791, and married 17 November 1814, Euphemia Wilson, of Moorland, and died 1 May 1820, aged 29, leaving "an aged father and mother and 3 small children." [86]
16. x. William Righter.
xi. Charles Righter.

These children, except for the infants buried at Merion, are listed in the order they were named in John's will. The census of 1790 listed John Righter as head of a family in Lower Merion Township, with 2 males over 16, 2 males under 16, and 3 females. Anthony Righter was listed with a family of his own, including 3 males under 16, and 2 females.[87] The deed of sale of the lot in Germantown, Hannah Righter inherited from her father, showed that in 1796, daughters Sarah and Hannah were both married, and Amelia was still a spinster.[88]

When Jane Righter, executrix of the will of John Righter, filed her account of the settlement of his estate, 17 December 1832, exception was taken to the account by John Righter the younger, son of Anthony Righter, specifically to the amount she claimed as due to her from her father's estate. He also charged that Jane had violated the will by cutting timber on the land, and by sale of land. Testimony was heard by the Orphans Court, and Jane was upheld.[89]

---

[85] GSP Collections, *Records Relating to Radnor and Merion Meetings, Delaware County, Pa.*

[86] Montgomery County Historical Society Collections, *Lower Merion Records, 1820,* one of several notebooks of Margaret B. Harvey, contained these items on the marriage of John Righter, Jr. from the *Norristown Register,* 26 November 1814, and on his death from the same source, 24 May 1820.

[87] *Heads of Families,* Lower Merion Township, Montgomery County.

[88] *Deed Book* D-77, 457.

[89] *Montgomery County Orphans Court,* file #15515.

MICHAEL RIGHTER HOUSE

Erected by Michael Righter in 1746, S.E. corner Ridge Avenue and
Righter Street, Roxborough, Philadelphia County, the house was sold by
his son John Righter in 1802 and demolished in 1937.

From a sketch by Joseph S. Miles, 1924

7. Jacob Righter, son of No. 2 Bartholomew and Elizabeth (————)
Righter, was a cordwainer by trade, and had sufficient education to write
his name. His wife was named Sarah. In the partition of his father's
estate, he was allotted 66¼ acres on the west side of the Plymouth or
Ridge Road. He moved to the city of Philadelphia, and sold this land.
On 20 May 1766, he sold 20¼ acres to George Righter, probably his
uncle;[90] on 7 May 1771, he sold 15½ acres to Joseph Canous. In this
deed he was described as innkeeper of the City of Philadelphia.[91] On 27
August 1771, he sold 16 acres to Aaron Levering, being then cordwainer
of Philadelphia.[92] He must have remained in the city a short time, for he
was on various tax assessors' lists for Roxborough Township from 1774
on. As these lists showed that he owned only one acre with dwelling, he
must have sold the rest of his land, but no other deeds of sale were found
recorded in the period covered by this search. A tax list of 1780 described him as a "non-juror," a fact which may indicate that he was
connected with some sect opposed to oaths, but his name was not found
in the records of the Society of Friends. In 1796 and 1797, there were
two Jacob Righters, both cordwainers, on these assessors' lists. This may
indicate that Jacob had a son Jacob, whom he had taught his trade. The
census record for 1790 tallied the family of Jacob Riter in Roxborough
Township as 3 white males over 16, and 2 free white females, perhaps indicating 2 sons over 16 at that time and 1 daughter.[93] 1798 was the last
year the name of Jacob Righter appeared on the assessor's list for Roxborough Township. Whether he died then or moved away has not been
determined.[94]

Horatio Gates Jones in his *The Levering Family* related that Peter
Levering, son of Wickard and Elizabeth Levering, born 1764, married as
his first wife Elizabeth Righter, daughter of Jacob Righter. She died in
1796. Peter Levering, who lived in Montgomery County, died 8 February 1807, and was buried with his second wife at Roxborough.[95] He
listed their children as Jacob, Joseph, Benjamin, Sarah and Ann Elizabeth. Two of these children were named for their Righter grandparents.

8. Peter Righter, son of No. 2 Bartholomew and Elizabeth (————)
Righter, married Elizabeth Tunis, daughter of Anthony and Bathsheba
Tunis, and sister of Hannah, who had married his brother John. They

[90] Recited in deed of sale of this land by George Righter to Harry Knauss, *Deed Book* D-21, 81.
[91] *Deed Book* D-57, 57.
[92] *Deed Book* D-44, 441.
[93] *Heads of Families*, 1790, 207.
[94] Roxborough Twp. Tax Lists.
[95] Horatio Gates Jones, *The Levering Family* (Philadelphia, 1858), 49, 68.

were married in Friends meeting, 30th day, 10th month, 1759, Peter having joined the Society of Friends a short time before.[96] He was a joiner and yeoman, and lived all his life in the upper part of Roxborough Township. In September, 1757, he shared in the partition of his father's land, his share being located on the easterly side of Ridge Road. On 13 April 1761, he purchased 40 acres and messuage, which had been the share of his brother John.[97] This land, also on the easterly side of the Ridge Road, adjoined Peter's on the north. On 9 March 1763, he purchased 7 acres of his brother Bartle's share, adjoining his land to the south.[98] For the Proprietary Tax of 1769, he was assessed for 104 acres, 3 horses, 4 cattle,[99] and all subsequent tax lists gave 96 to 100 acres in his farm. Where occupation was given on the assessors' lists, he was described as yeoman or " joyner " or carpenter. In 1808, his property was described as 96 acres of land, 1 stone dwelling, 1 stone barn, 1 frame shop, valued at $2100, and 2 horses and 2 cows valued at $31. By 1811 the assessed value of this same property was $5616.[100]

When Anthony Tunis died in 1762, his daughter Elizabeth Righter was bequeathed 100 pounds. If Peter's son Anthony had been born by that date his legacy from his grandfather was 20 shillings, a bequest made to all his grandchildren named Anthony.[101] Elizabeth also was entitled to one fifth of the residuary estate of her brother Joseph, who died 10 years later.[102] When the executors under this will secured discharge from the obligation to the heirs, Peter Righter signed for his wife.[103]

As stated above, Peter Righter was a member of the Society of Friends. He attended the Plymouth Meeting, a few miles north of his farm on the Reading Road, having received a certificate of removal from Merion Meeting, 11th day, 10th month, 1763.[104] The tax assessor's list for Roxborough Township in 1781 indicated that he was " not qualified," that is had not taken the oath of allegiance to the Revolutionary government, and a " non-juror," that is opposed to the taking of any

---

[96] FHL, *Radnor MM, Record of Marriages, 1729-1763*, 247. The record of Peter's acceptance as a member is in the minutes of the MM at Haverford, 10th day, 7th month 1759, FHL, *Radnor Minutes, 1758-1763*, 37.

[97] *Deed Book* H-18, 118.

[98] *Deed Book* H-18, 116.

[99] *Pennsylvania Archives* 3rd Ser., Vol. XIV, 15.

[100] Roxborough Twp. Tax Lists.

[101] *Will Book* M, 300 #173, 1763.

[102] *Will Book* P, 411 #288, 1773.

[103] *Deed Book* I-15, 26: Discharge.

[104] FHL, *Minutes of Radnor MM, 1763-1772*, 25.

oaths,[105] so it can certainly be concluded that he was not the Peter Righter, who served in the military forces during the Revolution. The minutes of the Gwynedd Monthly Meeting, of which Plymouth Meeting was a member, showed that he was a loyal and active Friend. He was appointed to attend Quarterly Meeting in 1782; as overseer in Plymouth Meeting, 1782 to 1786; as member of a group to " have care of collecting the accounts of Friends suffering for our testimony against war " and advise and assist in cases of suffering or difficulty, 1782; a member of a new committee in 1783 to have care of the freed negroes; was appointed to distribute where " it may appear to be most useful," a number of treatises in the German language by J. Phips and Mary Brook, forwarded by the " Meeting for Sufferings " in Philadelphia, 1787; and from time to time investigated reports of misconduct on the part of Friends and remonstrated with them, for example, a committee to assist in cases of Friends in Plymouth " who neglect attendance at meeting, and take oath of allegiance and endeavor to convince them the error of their conduct, and inconsistency thereof with our peaceable principles." [106]

The census of 1790 listed 2 heads of families, named Peter Riter in Roxborough Township. Both households included 1 male over 16, and 1 under 16. One family had 1 female, and the other 2. It has not been determined which belonged to Peter of upper Roxborough, whose family at one time included 3 or 4 sons, and a daughter.[107]

Peter Righter made his will 2 October 1817, and it was probated 26 June 1819. His wife Elizabeth survived a few years, as she died shortly before April, 1822. Where they were buried has not been determined. Peter named his friend John Livezey as his executor. He gave his wife Elizabeth the privilege of living in his house, with household and kitchen furniture as the executor thought sufficient for her needs. All the rest of his moveable estate the executor was to sell at public vendue, and pay the proceeds in amounts he thought fit to Elizabeth, as she might need it. The executor was also to rent out his real estate, except the house and one half acre of land reserved for his wife. The wife was to be paid such part of the rent as the executor thought she needed yearly throughout her life. Firewood for her stove, hay and pasture for her cow were also to be provided. After her death the property was to be sold in lots at public or private sale. He cancelled the debt of $875 owed by his son John, deceased, and gave $250 each to the 9 children of John. He cancelled the

[105] Roxborough Twp. Tax Lists.

[106] GSP Collections, *Abstract of Minutes of the Gwynedd MM, 1714-1801*, see index for page references. Plymouth Meeting held MM with Gwynedd.

[107] *Heads of Families, 1790,* 207.

debt of $755 his son Joseph owed him and gave Joseph $3000, with the proviso, that, if Joseph died without issue, the sum was to be paid back for distribution among the grandchildren. He gave to Hannah Jones, daughter of his daughter Mary, deceased, $3000, and to Elizabeth, the daughter of his son Anthony, deceased, who had lived with him, $3000 to be paid when she reached age 18, and to Anthony's widow Rebecca $600. He gave $200 to his daughter-in-law, widow of his son John. The rest of his estate was to be divided equally among the grandchildren then living.[108]

On 5 April 1822, John Livezey, executor of Peter Righter's will, sold for $1134.12½, 13 acres and 13 perches of Peter's farm to Elizabeth, widow of John Righter, William Zorns of Abington Township, Montgomery County, and Mary, his wife (late Righter in right of Mary), Hannah Righter, Elizabeth Righter, and Sarah Righter, all of Roxborough Township.[109] Probably Mary, Hannah, Elizabeth and Sarah were 4 of the 9 children of Peter's son John. There should be other records of the settlement of this estate, but a brief search has not located them, except a report of John Livezey, executor, to the Orphans Court of a balance of $1285.00½ due the estate to be distributed.[110]

The children of 8. Peter and Elizabeth (Tunis) Righter were:

17.   i.   John Righter. He died before 1817, when his father made his will.
       ii.   Joseph Righter. He had no children when his father made his will in 1817. Joseph applied for a certificate to Exeter Meeting, and was granted it by the Gwynedd Monthly Meeting, 24 April 1792. On 31 March 1801 a certificate to Exeter was again signed for him.[111]
18.   iii.   Mary Righter.
19.   iv.   Anthony Righter.

These children are named in order as they were mentioned in Peter's will, which may not be the order of birth. Mary and John were born before October 11, 1763, for they were named in the certificate of removal from Merion Meeting, granted on that date. The Minutes of Gwynedd Monthly Meeting indicate that there may have been a son Peter, for, 28 June 1791, Peter Righter, Jr. requested a certificate of removal to Abington.[112]

---

108 *Will Book 7*, 30 #72, 1819.

109 *Deed Book* AM-33, 95.

110 *Orphans Court Book*, 28, 298, session of 15 September 1822.

111 GSP Collections, *Abstract of Minutes of the Gwynedd MM*, 1714-1801, 469, 470, 511, 537, 539, 540.

112 *Ibid.*, 463.

9. Bartholomew Righter, Jr., son of No. 2 Bartholomew and Elizabeth (———) Righter, seems always to have used Bartle as his name. His wife was named Charlotte. By occupation he was a blacksmith, and lived the greater part of his life in Lower Merion Township. He was born in Roxborough Township, and was a minor when his father died in 1745. When his father's 250 acre farm was divided among the 4 sons in 1757, he inherited 66¼ acres, most of it on the westerly side of the Ridge Road, and at the southern end of the tract. On 8 March 1753, he sold 34¾ acres in 2 distinct lots, one with tenement to George Righter, probably his uncle,[113] and the next day sold 7 acres, a tract on the easterly side of Ridge Road, for 49 pounds to his brother Peter.[114] He probably sold all his Roxborough land before 1769, the year of the first tax assessor's list for the township, for Bartle's name was not in that list. No deed was found recorded for the sale of the remaining 24½ acres. In the deeds for the sale of this land, no wife was named, so he probably married Charlotte after March, 1763. Perhaps he lived with John when he first went to Lower Merion, for on the tax assessor's list of 1769, his name was entered with John's grist and saw mill.[115] On 26 March 1773, he purchased for 235 pounds, 46 acres, 60 perches of land in Lower Merion Township, then Philadelphia County, from his brother John.[116] This tract in the Mill Creek area was part of the 75 acres John had bought from Hannah Harrison in 1763. Bartle's neighbor was Frederick Bicking, whose sons, Frederick and Joseph married John's daughters, Sarah and Jane. Most of this land Bartle held for the rest of his life, and on it probably had his blacksmith shop. Bartle's name was on the tax lists for Lower Merion Township in 1774 with 45 acres of land, 1 horse, 2 cattle, and 1780 his property had a valuation of 1500 pounds.[117] He was one of the heads of families listed in the 1790 census for Lower Merion, when his family included 1 male over 16, 2 males under 16, and 5 females. This may indicate that 2 of his sons and 4 daughters were born before 1790.[118] On 20 April 1792 Bartle and his wife Charlotte sold 13 acres, 21 perches of his land to Peter Bechtel. A note on this deed showed that John Johnson held a mortgage on the property.[119]

---

113 *Deed Book* H-19, 451.

114 *Deed Book* H-18, 116.

115 *Pennsylvania Archives* 3rd Ser., Vol. XIV, 101.

116 *Deed Book* D-36, 5.

117 *Pennsylvania Archives* 3rd Ser., Vol. XIV, 101, 357; Vol. XV, 64.

118 *Heads of Families*, 1790, 157.

119 *Montgomery County Deed Book* 7, 132.

Bartle Righter made his will, October, 1807, and probably died in 1809, for the will was probated 14 November 1809. It provided that his wife " Charlot " should hold for her use during her life all his estate, real and personal. He devised 25 pounds to each of his daughters to be paid when his youngest son should attain his 21st year. He gave his daughter Elizabeth his best feather bed, and 5 pounds to his grandson " Bartolamy Katch," when he should reach age 21. All the residue of his estate he gave to his 3 sons after the death of his wife. If the sons could not agree on the division of the land each was to choose a man, and these 3 with a surveyor were to make the partition, a drawing of lots to determine which portion each son should have. He appointed his son Rudolph and his friend George Jaret as executors. The inventory of his " goods and chattels," made 28 October 1809 by George Grow and John Cochran, included besides household articles, smith tools worth $40, and farm animals, crops and equipment to a total value of $502.25.[120] Charlotte Righter may have died early in 1819, for in May of that year the division of the land among the sons was made by Joseph Price, Jonathan Jones, and William Staddleman with John Elliott, surveyor. Of Bartholomew's 32 acres, 103 perches, Rudolph received a lot of 7 acres, 79 perches, together with buildings; Joseph 2 lots, one of 6 acres, 60 perches and one of 10 acres, 80 perches, and William 2 lots, one of 9¾ acres, 8 perches, and one of 2½ acres.[121]

The children of 9. Bartholomew and Charlotte (———) Righter were: (in the order mentioned in Bartle's will)

    i. Hannah Righter.
    ii. Mary Righter.
    iii. Rebecca Righter. She may have married Aaron Keech.[122]
    iv. Catharine Righter.
    v. Elizabeth Righter. She may have married William Fisher, 19 March 1818.[123] He was one of the administrators of the estate of her

[123] GSP Collections, *Marriages 1806-1853 by the Rev. Horatio Gates Jones, D.D., Pastor of Lower Merion Baptist Church.*

      brother William.

---

[120] *Montgomery County Will Book* 3, 170 and Will #5211. The original will is missing from his folder but the inventory is there.

[121] *Montgomery County Deed Book* 35, 751 and 36, 534: Releases.

[122] Horace H. Platt and William Lawton, *The History of Roxborough Lodge, No. 135, F and A Masons,* 1813-1913 (Philadelphia, 1913), 117. The biography of Past Master George Keech states that he was a native of Lower Merion, b. 29 August 1799, son of Aaron and Rebecca (Righter) Keech. " Bartolomy Katch," grandson mentioned in Bartle's will, may have been son of Aaron and Rebecca Keech. Bartle's spelling was defective as shown here in the spelling of his own first name. Aaron Keech was a member of Lower Merion Baptist Church, baptized 6 June 1829. Church records give date of his death as September, 1844. (GSP Collections, *Records of Lower Merion Baptist Church,* #101.) He left no will. Letters of Administration were granted to Henry Keech, 28 September 1844. (GSP Collections, *Abstract of Wills and Administrations Montgomery County,* 1828-1850, Vol. II, 362.

vi. William Righter. He was a blacksmith and lived in Lower Merion Township. He died in 1827, intestate. An inventory of his goods worth $31.57 was filed 27 August 1827. There was no mention of a wife in the releases he signed when his father's land was partitioned. On 3 May 1828, Joseph Righter and William Fisher, administrators of the estate of William Righter, sold for $810 the 2 lots he had received in the partition of his father's land. The Orphans Court had ordered this sale.[124]

20. vii. Rudolph Righter.
21. viii. Joseph Righter.

10. John Righter, son of No. 3 Peter Righter, was born 26 January 1753. He inherited from his father in 1776, most of his land in Roxborough and Lower Merion Townships, one half of the shad fishery, and the Schuylkill ferry. He operated the ferry and lived in the house at the ferry all his life. On 16 April 1777 he married Eleanor Bankson,[125] daughter of Peter and Esther (Linn) Bankson. The Bankson family was Swedish, the original form of the name being Bengtson. Peter Bankson was a shipwright, and his will named his wife, Esther, and daughter Elinor as beneficiaries of his estate.[126] John's wife died before he did, and was mentioned in his will in the bequest to his daughter Esther of " her late mother's wearing apparel, together with sundry articles of plate and mahogany household furniture which I got at our marriage." He was the tax assessor for Roxborough Township in 1779. In 1780 the assessor's list showed that he owned 81½ acres of land and dwelling in Roxborough Township, 9½ acres in Merion, 24 acres in Passyunk, 300 acres in Bedford County to a value in that time of inflation of 26,400 pounds. The properties in Merion, Passyunk, and Bedford County did not again appear on the lists, but he owned the lot in Merion as ferry terminal at the time of his death. In 1779 he had included 22 ounces of silver plate and a chair, (probably a sedan chair) along with horses, and cows.[127] He operated a farm as well as the ferry. During the British occupation of Philadelphia a redoubt was erected by them on a bluff on the east side of the Wissahickon Creek, so as to control the approach to the city by way of Ridge Road. It was manned by Hessians, who had a camp nearby, from which they made frequent raids for meat, grain and vegetables on Roxborough farms. The redoubt and camp were close to John Righter's

124 *Montgomery County Will*, file #15577, *Montgomery County Deed Book*, 44, 145.

125 *Pennsylvania Archives*, 2nd Ser., Vol. VIII, 216: " Record of Marriages at Chris᷈ ᷈hurch, Philadelphia, 1709-1806."

126 GSP Collections, *Genealogical Data* (M. Atherton Leach Collection) Vol. III, 6, 7.

127 Roxborough Twp. Tax Lists.

land and ferry. He was allowed 68 pounds, 17 shillings, 6 pence for damage done by the raiders on his property.[128]

In August of 1789 the first church in Roxborough Township was organized by 32 persons, most of them members of the First Baptist Church in Philadelphia, in a meeting at the schoolhouse. John Righter was a member of this group and was chosen a trustee,[129] but lived only a short time. He died 6 February 1790, aged 37 years, 10 days, and was buried in Roxborough Burial Ground.[130] His stone is well preserved, but there is none there for his wife. He made his will 3 January 1790, and it was proved 13 February 1790. In it he bequeathed 15 pounds towards building a Baptist Meeting House in Roxborough, exclusive of the 10 pounds he had already subscribed for that purpose. He bequeathed all his estate to his daughter Esther, and, considering her "infant estate," named Nathan Levering and Algernon Roberts her guardians. In case she should die before reaching legal age or without issue, he provided that his estate should be divided among the "legitimate" children of his brother Peter, and his sisters Mary, Hannah, Sarah, and Margaret.[131]

In 1786 the route of Ridge Road was changed from what is now Righter Street to the present route. The new route crossed John Righter's land, and Esther's guardians later collected 29 pounds for damage to her property. Since some people still used the old route, the guardians petitioned the court in March 1797 to close it. The court appointed a jury to view the situation and ordered the old road vacated.[132] Child of 10. John and Eleanor (Bankson) Righter was:

22.   i. Esther (Hester) Righter.

11. George Righter, son of No. 4 Michael and Catharine (Geiger) Righter, was a wheelwright. His wife was named Rebecca. At the time they sold his share of his father's estate, they lived in Brandywine Hundred, New Castle County, Delaware. The records of Old Swedes Church, Philadelphia, included among baptisms 2 children of George and Rebecca Righter:

i. Israel Righter, born 7 March 1764.
ii. Jesse Righter, born 18 July 1765.[133]

---

[128] PMHB Vol. XXV (1901), 555.

[129] Jones, Historic Notes, 110.

[130] The inscription on his gravestone is very clear, although that on his daughter's is almost illegible.

[131] Will Book U, 436 #175, 1790.

[132] Jones, Historic Notes, 65.

[133] GSP Collections, Old Swedes Church Gloria Dei, Philadelphia, Record of Baptisms, Marriages, 1750-1789, 100, 110.

There may have been other children. No search of New Castle County records has been made.

12. Michael Righter, son of No. 4 Michael and Catharine (Geiger) Righter, was born in 1748, and died July, 1819. He married Elizabeth Bower, daughter of Charles and Barbara Bower, of Roxborough Township.[134] In his will Charles Bower bequeathed his messuage and its household furniture to his wife Barbara, during her life, and after her death to his daughter Elizabeth Righter, and son-in-law Michael Righter, during their life, "making no waste or destruction thereon." On their deaths the estate was to be divided among the heirs of his daughter, Charles Righter to have 50 pounds, Michael Righter 20 pounds, and Catharine Righter 20 pounds more than an equal share with the rest of the heirs. The remainder of his lands he bequeathed to his son-in-law, Michael Righter, who was to pay all his debts. He signed his name to this will in German script. The will was proved 24 January 1807.[135] Tax assessors' lists for Roxborough Township showed that Charles Bower was a cooper, who owned 20 acres of land in addition to his dwelling. Charles and Barbara Bower were buried in Roxborough Burial Ground in the lot next to Michael and Elizabeth Righter, but the inscriptions on their stones are badly worn and illegible. Michael Righter combined the occupations of farmer and cooper, and tax assessors' lists showed that he was a storekeeper as well in 1788, 1789, 1791. His property in 1808 as given in the list for that year included 2 tracts of land, one of 20 acres with stone dwelling, stone barn, and shop, valued at $650, and one of 39½ acres with stone dwelling, frame stable, valued at $850. He also owned 2 horses and 3 cows. The assessors' list for 1787 credited Michael with 40 acres of land. Since he acquired only 16 acres, 58½ perches in the partition of his father's land in that year, it seems that he acquired his brother Peter's lot of 22 acres, 15 perches, immediately after partition was made. This transaction was not recorded, at least not at that time. John Hills' *Map of Philadelphia and Environs* (1809) showed that

---

134 A descendant of Michael Righter has claimed membership in the DAR on the basis of his service in the Revolution. She gives his dates as 1748-1819, Elizabeth's as 1757-1828, and the date of their marriage as 1775. At the time this record was made, their gravestones may not have been so badly worn. Her record states that Michael served as private in Captain John Levering's company, 7th battalion, Philadelphia County militia, 1781. (*DAR Lineage Book* 84, 133, 134 #83, 355.) I have a photostat from the card file on military service in the National Archives, which states that Michael was a private in Capt. Houlgate's Co. of Militia of the 4th Philadelphia County Batt'n commanded by Col. Henry Hill, on the muster roll from Dec. 17-19, 1776. Under the head of "State of Pennsylvania against United States for Depreciation on Pay of the Army," sum charged on Michael Righter's record 6 pounds 10 shillings, with the remark: "No proof of service." A note on his record stated that he was the only Michael Righter who served from Pennsylvania. This is not true, for there was a Michael Righter in Chester County, whose widow was awarded a pension on the basis of his services.

135 Will #10, 1807.

Michael owned Peter's lot. He owned no land previous to 1787.[136]
When Hermit Lane, the one perch wide cartway of the 1787 partition
agreement, was opened as a private road in 1794 Michael received 10
pounds for damage to his land, which the road crossed from the Wissahickon Creek to where it entered Daniel Righter's land.[137] It became a
public road 33 feet wide in 1804. On 4 April 1804 Michael Righter was
one of 13 trustees of the Roxborough Burial Ground, when Nathan
Levering granted additional land to the already walled in plot of 72
perches for that purpose.[138] This plot, originally the Levering family
burial ground on the Levering farm, is the oldest burial ground in Roxborough, where many of the early settlers were buried. It was located
back of the Roxborough Baptist Church property, the church drive giving access to it. On 4 April 1805, he was named as one of the 28 trustees
of the Roxborough School, when Abraham Levering granted an additional lot of land for the school.[139] Michael Righter died July, 1819, and
was buried in the Roxborough Burial Ground, where his grave and that
of his wife are still marked by gravestones. His will, made 4 April 1812,
was proved 28 August 1819. He bequeathed all his estate to his wife for
life or as long as she remained a widow. If she remarried the executors
were to pay to her interest of one third the estate yearly during her life.
On her death or remarriage $400 was to be paid to his son Charles, $20 to
his daughter Ann, and the residue to be divided among his 6 children,
daughters Catharine and Ann each to receive $100 less than each of the
4 sons. He appointed his sons Charles and Michael executors.[140]
The children of 12. Michael and Elizabeth (Bower) Righter were:

    i. Charles Righter. He married, 20 August 1821, Hester Albright.[141] He
        was a cooper by occupation.[142]
   ii. Catharine Righter. She married Thomas McCrea of Northern Liberties.[143]
  iii. Michael Righter. He was born 1785, and died 1826. He married
        Catharine Streitzel, 29 March 1810.[144] Catharine was born 30 Sep-
        tember 1793, daughter of John and Margaret (Levering) Streitzel,[145]

---

[136] Roxborough Twp. Tax Lists.

[137] Jones, *Historic Notes*, 71, 72.

[138] *Deed Book* EF-17, 434: Nathan Levering *et ux.* to Cornelius Holget.

[139] *Deed Book* EF-17, 309: Abraham Levering *et ux.* to Michael Righter *et al.*

[140] *Will Book* 7, 50 #95, 1819.

[141] GSP Collections, *Records of the German Reformed Church of Germantown.*

[142] Roxborough Twp. Tax Lists.

[143] *Deed Book* RLL-34, 339.

[144] GSP Collections, *Records of St. Michael's Lutheran Church*, Germantown.

[145] *DAR Lineage Book* 84, 133, 134.

and died 21 June 1877, aged 84. They were buried in Leverington Cemetery, Roxborough. Tax assessors' lists showed that Michael Righter, Jr. was also a cooper. In 1811, the first year the list indicated that he was a landowner, he owned 5 acres, a stone dwelling and frame stable, valued at $666.[146]

 iv. Samuel B. Righter.

 v. Ann Righter. She married Jacob Keely of Roxborough.[147] She was born 1794, and died 17 July 1857. Jacob Keely was born 9 February 1787, and died 19 February 1835.[148]

 vi. Jonathan Righter.

These are the 6 children named in Michael's will. There were 2 small children, described on gravestones as daughters of Michael and Elizabeth Righter, buried in their lot in Roxborough Burial Ground:

 vii. Barbara Righter.

 viii. Maria Righter.

13. **Daniel Righter**, son of No. 4 Michael and Catharine (Geiger) Righter, was born 1751, and died 1816. He married Phoebe Starne, daughter of Joseph Starne of Roxborough. She was born 2 October 1758, and died 10 June 1847, aged 88 years, 8 months, 8 days. They were buried in the Roxborough Burial Ground, and the dates were secured from their gravestones. Daniel was a weaver. He was listed as "journeyman weaver" in 1780 on the tax assessor's list for Roxborough Township, and thereafter as weaver. The Federal tax assessor for 1783 indicated that Daniel then lived on "widow Lake's est.," and owned 2 sheep.[149] In 1787 he received 2 lots in the partition of his father's land, 27 acres, 135 perches all together, his lots including the site of the Pietist Community of 1694, on the one perch wide lane, later called Hermit Lane. Location of his land was shown on Hills' *Map of Philadelphia and Environs*, 1809. In 1788 the tax assessor credited him with 27 acres and a dwelling worth 138 pounds. The dwelling is known to have been a log house, and was so described on the assessor's list of 1805, when he was also recorded as having a still. Between 1795 and 1798, he reduced his land holding to 18 acres, though no record of the deed was found in the period covered by this search. The assessor's list for 1808 gave his holding as 16 acres.[150] On 20 January 1817, letters of administration were

146 Roxborough Twp. Tax Lists.

147 *Deed Book* RLL-34, 339.

148 Gravestones, Roxborough Burial Ground.

149 *Pennsylvania Archives* 3rd Ser., Vol. XVI, 651. Ms. study of the Starne Family made by Joseph Starne Miles, now the property of his children.

150 Roxborough Twp. Tax Lists.

granted to John Righter and Jesse Righter to the estate of Daniel Righter, deceased. Joseph Starne of Roxborough Township, farmer, and Richard Roe were sureties for the $300 bond.[151] Phoebe Starne Righter lived on in the log house until 1847. There is a photograph of this log house in the collection of the Historical Society of Pennsylvania. After her death the surviving children sold the land.[152] From these deeds the list of children of Daniel and Phoebe (Starne) Righter was obtained. Their children were:

    i. John Righter, of Port Richmond, cooper, who married Sophia ———.
    ii. Jesse Righter, born 6 March 1793, died 6 December 1835 and buried in Roxborough Burial Ground. No issue.
    iii. Joseph Righter of Northern Liberties, cooper, born 10 July 1795, died 26 October 1849 and buried in same place.
    iv. Catharine Righter, married ——— Cully, and was a widow in 1847.
    v. Mary Righter, married ——— Allis, and was a widow in 1847. Probably she was the Mary Righter who, 11 October 1808, was married by the Rev. Horatio Gates Jones to Henry " Hollis," as listed on page 2 of the record of his marriages in the collection of the Genealogical Society of Pennsylvania.
    vi. Sarah Righter, who died before 6 December 1847.
    vii. Susan Righter, born 1800, and died 6 December 1877, and buried with her parents.

14. George Righter, Junior, son of No. 5 George and Elizabeth (Cumree or Gomry) Righter, married Christina or Christiana Roop, daughter of John and Elizabeth (Nice or Neis) Roop or Rupp.[153] He had sufficient education to be able to write his name, but Christina could not. George was a farmer. When his father sold his land in Roxborough Township in 1784, George, Jr., purchased for 900 pounds, from Jacob Auld, 111 acres of land, a plantation, which had once belonged to Nicholas Rittenhouse, in Norriton Township. The next day, he sold back to Jacob Auld a messuage and lot of 104 perches, from this farm on the Reading Road, which he had reserved for himself at the time of the sale.[154] They did not remain in Norriton Township long, for between 22 May 1786 and 1 April 1788, they sold their land there. He received 76 pounds more than he had paid in 1784.[155] Now George returned to

---

[151] *Administration Book* L, 369 #17, 1817.

[152] *Deed Book* AWM-50, 560 and *Deed Book* AWM-73, 46.

[153] S. K. Brecht, ed., *Genealogical Records of Schwenkfelder Families* (New York, 1923), 149. Also *Deed Book* RLL-52, 271: George Righter *et al.* to Cornelius Roop.

[154] *Montgomery County Deed Book* 3, 508 and 510.

[155] *Montgomery County Deed Book* 10, 534; and Book 4, 382 and 308.

Roxborough, where he purchased from John Barndoller for 600 pounds, a two story stone messuage and 2 adjoining lots of 64 acres, 140 perches, on the westerly side of the road to Plymouth or Ridge Road.[156]   This land was in upper Roxborough, not very far from the tract his father owned before 1784.   On this land George and Christina lived until his death.   They sold a small lot in 1797 to James Linson, cordwainer,[157] and 2 small lots in 1805,[158] and probably another in 1806, for the acreage on the tax assessors' lists for Roxborough Township went from 51 acres in 1805 to 45 acres in 1806.   These lists showed that he was a shop keeper from 1799 to 1802, and the property in 1805 included, besides his land and stone dwelling, a stone barn, and a log hatter's shop, 2 horses and 2 cows.[159]   11 April 1804, George with Christiana, along with other children of John Roop, dec'd, joined in the sale of a stone messuage and lot in Germantown Township, devised by will of John Roop, after the death of his wife Elizabeth, to his children.[160]

On 29 March 1810, George Righter made his will, by which the yearly interest of all his property was assigned to his wife for life or until she remarried.   If she remarried, she was to receive the interest on one third of his real estate.   He gave her all his goods and furniture, except his 8 day clock, which he reserved for one of his sons, the other son to have its value of $60, the choice to be agreed upon by them.   On the death or remarriage of his wife the estate was to be divided between the 2 sons.   He named his wife Christina and sons George and John as executors.   The will was proved 13 August 1810.[161]   In 1811 and 1812 Christina and her sons sold a messuage and 4 lots of their land in Roxborough.[162]   They probably sold all the property about this time.   In 1811 the tax assessor for Roxborough listed " Widow Righter, est." 45 acres, 1 stone dwelling, 1 stone barn, 1 log shop, 4½ acres, 1 stone dwelling, 1 stone shop.   In 1814, " Widow Righter, est." was listed with 1 dog, 1 horse, 3 cows.[163]

---

156 *Deed Book* D-21, 261. The Barndollar tract is located on the map in *Historical Sketch of Roxborough and Manayunk*, by J. S. Miles, 70.

157 *Deed Book* EF-9, 153: George Righter and Christina to James Linson.

158 *Deed Book* EF-20, 195: George Righter and Christina to Philip Lare; *Deed Book* EF-23, 93: same to John Shuster.

159 Roxborough Twp. Tax Lists.

160 *Deed Book* RLL-52, 271.

161 *Will Book* 3, 226 #88, 1810.

162 *Deed Book* GWR-13, 432: Christiana Righter *et al.* to William Smith; IC-20, 494: same to Stephen Davis; AWM-61, 396: same to Christopher Worth; AWM-61, 373: same to Michael Levering. These deeds show that the land was divided into small lots.

163 Roxborough Twp. Tax Lists.

The children of 14. George and Christina (Roop) Righter were:

    i. George Righter.
   ii. John Righter.

These sons were probably born before 1790, for the census of that year, named George " Riter," Jr. as head of family in Roxborough Township, with 2 free, white males under 16, and 1 free, white female, presumably Christina, in his household.[164]   The son George may be the George Righter, cordwainer, who made his appearance on the tax assessor's list for Roxborough Township in 1801, with a personal tax of $1. He owned a horse in 1803, and was assessed $1.25.

   15. Anthony Righter, son of No. 6 John and Hannah (Tunis) Righter, was a millwright of Lower Merion, later of Whitemarsh Township, Montgomery County, Pennsylvania. He married Elizabeth Taylor, daughter of Isaac and Catharine (Llewellyn) Taylor of Lower Merion.[165] On 13 June 1782, Anthony Righter, with " a birthright among the people called Quakers," was disowned for marrying out of meeting. He was also said to neglect attendance at meeting and to have paid fines in lieu of personal military service.[166] His sons Joseph and John were mentioned in documents relating to his rights in his father's estate.[167]
The children of 15. Anthony and Elizabeth (Taylor) Righter were:

     i. John Righter.
    ii. Morris T. Righter.
   iii. Isaac Righter.
   iv. Joseph Righter.
    v. Anthony Righter.
   vi. Richard Righter.
  vii. Mary Righter. She married ———— Pontzler.
 viii. Catharine Righter.
   ix. Elizabeth Righter. She married Michael Nuss.[168]

---

[164] *Heads of Families*, 1790, 207.

[165] *Will Book* S, 208 #196, 1782: will of Isaac Taylor; *Montgomery County Will* #6680: will of Catharine Taylor; *Montgomery County Miscellaneous Book* 3, 10.

[166] FHL, *Minutes of Radnor MM*, 1772-1782, 245, 257.

[167] *Montgomery County Miscellaneous Book* 3, 10: Power of Attorney, Anthony Righter and Elizabeth to their son John Righter. Richard Righter was one of the witnesses, 24 March 1827; same, 369: Anthony Righter to his son John Righter, 31 October 1831, assignment of rights in his father's estate. Peter Righter was a witness.

[168] There are accounts of this family in Elwood Roberts, ed., *Biographical Annals of Montgomery County, Pennsylvania,* (New York, 1904), biography of Horace B. Righter, Vol. I, 428, 429; of George W. Righter, Vol. II, 61; and Charles C. Righter, Vol. II, 506. These trace descendants of Anthony's son John Righter. I have not checked the information given there, as it goes beyond the scope of this study.

16. William Righter, son of 6. John and Jane (McAffee) Righter, died before January, 1832, when his minor children, over age 14, petitioned the Orphans Court for the appointment of a guardian. 17 January 1832, the Court appointed Daniel Nippes.[169] These children were:

  i. Maria Righter.
  ii. Jane Elizabeth Righter.

17. John Righter, son of No. 8 Peter and Elizabeth (Tunis) Righter, died before 1817, when his father made his will. His wife was named Elizabeth and may have been the daughter of Peter Phipps of Abington, whose will, written January, 1797, and proved 11 November 1797, provided a bequest of 100 pounds to his daughter Elizabeth Righter. The minutes of Gwynedd Monthly Meeting showed that John Righter requested a certificate of removal to Abington, 29 January 1788.[170] John and Elizabeth (Phipps ?) Righter had 9 children according to his father's will. Among them were:

  i. Mary Righter, who married William Zorns.[171]
  ii. Hannah Righter.
  iii. Elizabeth Righter.
  iv. Sarah Righter.

18. Mary Righter, daughter of No. 8 Peter and Elizabeth (Tunis) Righter, died before 1817, when her father made his will. 18 March 1788, the minutes of Gwynedd Monthly Meeting stated that the women had produced a certificate for Mary Righter to Abington, which was ap-

---

The same statement is given in all 3 biographies about the origin of the Righter family, and it is incorrect in several respects. The statement is, " The Righter family is of German origin, tracing the American ancestry to one of three brothers, who with two sisters, came to Philadelphia. One of them located in Lower Merion, settling on Mill Creek, where he owned a grist mill . . . The Righters were Friends, the two sisters being preachers in the Society." I have proved that John Righter, miller, of Lower Merion, was one of a family of four brothers and one sister, born in Roxborough Township, Philadelphia County, children of Bartholomew Righter, who was probably also born there. They were not Friends originally, John and Peter becoming Friends on marriage to members of the Society. I have been unable to find any records of the sister Elizabeth. Some of the descendants of this Anthony Righter were buried at St. Peter's Lutheran Church, Barren Hill, Montgomery County (GSP Magazine, Vol. XV, 16: " Gravestone Inscriptions St. Peter's Lutheran Church, Barren Hill, Montgomery County.")

169 Montgomery County Orphans Court file #15,517.

170 GSP Collections: Abstract of Wills and Administrations, Montgomery County, 1784-1822, Vol. I, 111, and Abstract of Minutes of Gwynedd MM, 433.

171 The card index of the W. W. Hinshaw collection at FHL contains this information: " Mary Righter (Dt. of John, dec'd, and Elizabeth) Phila. Co., Pa. married 1820-5-11 Zorns, William at Plymouth M.H." Deed Book AM-33, 95. These 4 children of John are named in this deed of sale of some of Peter's land.

proved and signed.[172]   Her husband was named Jones, and they had one daughter:

  i. Hannah Jones.

19. **Anthony Righter,** son of No. 8 Peter and Elizabeth (Tunis) Righter, also died before his father's will was made in 1817.   His wife was named Rebecca.   He was listed on the Roxborough Township tax assessors' lists in 1798 and 1799, as a carpenter.   It was probably of this Anthony Righter that the minutes of Gwynedd Monthly Meeting stated, 30 December 1800, "Plymouth informs that Anthony Righter hath accomplished his marriage with a woman not in membership and much neglects meetings.   John Wilson and Thos. Lancaster to visit him," and 24 February 1801, "Anthony Righter does not attend meetings or manifest any disposition to condemn his deviation.   Jos. Paul and David Shoemaker to prepare a testimony agst. him."   28 April 1801, Anthony Righter made no objection to the testimony against him.[173]   Anthony and Rebecca (———) Righter had one daughter:

  i. Elizabeth Righter, who lived with her grandparents at the time Peter made his will.

20. **Rudolph Righter,** son of No. 9 Bartholomew and Charlotte (———) Righter, was a house carpenter of Blockley Township, Philadelphia County, and Lower Merion Township, Montgomery County, Pennsylvania.   On 12 May 1814, he married Catharine Evans.[174]   He died, intestate, in 1823 or 1824.   On 6 February 1824, Isaac Warner and Joseph Righter filed an inventory of his goods, appraised at $61.51.   Catharine Righter, widow, renounced and Samuel Stern was appointed administrator, 16 February 1824.[175]   On 17 April 1826, Samuel Stearn, Administrator, sold a lot of 11 acres, 79 perches with messuage for $356.50.   This sale was made on order of the Orphans Court, as a result of a petition showing that Catharine, widow of Rudolph, did not have enough to maintain their minor children, John and Hugh.[176]   On 10 January 1827, Samuel Stearne, petitioned the Orphans Court to name guardians for John and Hugh Righter, minor children under 14, of Rudolph Righter,

[172] GSP Collections, *Abstract of Minutes of Gwynedd MM,* 435.

[173] *Ibid.,* 539, 540, 541, 542.

[174] GSP Collections, *Record of Marriages 1808-1853 by Rev. Horatio Gates Jones, Pastor of Lower Merion Baptist Church,* 5.

[175] *Montgomery County Will* #15,492.

[176] *Montgomery County Deed Book* 42, 97.

John Elliott, appointed previously, having died. The Court appointed Jacob Latch. A financial statement for the guardian was filed 31 March 1849.[177]

The children of 20. Rudolph and Catharine (Evans) Righter were:

> i. John Righter.
> ii. Hugh Righter.

21. Joseph Righter, son of No. 9 Bartholomew and Charlotte (————) Righter, was a blacksmith of the city of Philadelphia, and married Catharine ————. They had 2 children:

> i. Henry Righter.
> ii. Sophia Righter.

He sold part of the land inherited from his father in 1820 and 1828.[178] He died intestate 9 June 1832, and letters of administration were granted to Catharine Righter, 13 July 1832.[179] On 1 April 1841 Catharine sold a lot of 4 acres, with the permission of the Orphans Court, her petition stating that Joseph's personal estate was insufficient to maintain his minor children, Henry and Sophia.[180]

22. Esther (Hester) Righter, daughter of No. 10 John and Eleanor (Bankson) Righter, was born in 1777. She married the Rev. Horatio Gates Jones, of Chester County, Pennsylvania, 3 September 1801.[181] He was founder and pastor of the Lower Merion Baptist Church, but lived after his marriage in the Righter house at the ferry.[182] Esther died 29 December 1808, and was buried in the old Roxborough Burial Ground, near her father. Her gravestone is badly worn and almost completely illegible. The Rev. Horatio Gates Jones died 12 December 1853, and was buried in Leverington Cemetery, Roxborough, with his second wife, Deborah Levering Jones.

The children of the Rev. Horatio Gates and Esther (Righter) Jones were:

> i. John Righter Jones. He was born in 1803. He was a member of the Philadelphia bar, 1836 to 1847, and a Judge of the Court of Com-

---

[177] *Montgomery County Orphans Court* file #15,337.

[178] *Montgomery County Deed Book* 37, 186: 26 August 1820, Joseph Righter and Catharine to William Fisher; and 47, 218: 24 December 1828, Joseph Righter and Catharine to William Fisher.

[179] *Administration Book* O, 32.

[180] *Montgomery County Orphans Court* file #15539; *Montgomery County Deed Book* 71, 413: Catharine Righter, admx. to Morris Sibley.

[181] GSP Collections, *Record of Marriages, 1800-1851, collected by Thompson Westcott*, 3.

[182] Jones, *The Levering Family*, 61.

mon Pleas. He fell in battle near New Bern, North Carolina, 23 May 1863. He was Colonel of the 58th Regiment Pennsylvania Volunteers. " An accomplished Scholar, An Upright Judge, A brave Commander, A true Patriot, And a sincere Christian," says the inscription on his monument in Leverington Cemetery, Roxborough. He married Anne E. Clay, daughter of the Hon. Joseph Clay. She was born 26 July 1810, and died 26 August 1872.[183] No attempt was made to trace descendants.

    ii. Eleanor (Ellen) Marie Jones. She was born 18 November 1805. She was married in January, 1852 to the Rev. George Higgins, in Montgomery Baptist Church, Colmar, Pennsylvania. Ellen was the second wife of the Rev. George Higgins, who became pastor of Montgomery Baptist Church in 1850. In a history of the Church, prepared in 1895, there is a picture and biography of George Higgins, who was born in England, 16 December 1798, and died at Colmar, Pennsylvania, 9 March 1869, and was buried at the church there. Of his marriage to Ellen Jones the history stated, " It was celebrated on a bright, moonlight, winter evening in January, 1852, in the church, and, as the sleighing was good, the attendance was very large." There were no children by this marriage, but George Higgins had 6 by his first wife.[184]

    iii. Hester (Hetty) A. Jones. She was born at Roxborough 12 September 1807, and died at City Point, Virginia, 21 December 1864, " where she had gone with true Christian philanthropy and patriotism to devote herself to the care of our sick and wounded soldiers." [185] The Roxborough, Post of the G.A.R. was called the Hetty A. Jones Post.

These 3 children were baptized members of the Lower Merion Baptist Church, where their father was pastor.[186] They were named with their father in the deed of sale of the tract of land John and Peter Righter had owned in Lower Merion.[187]

One of the major purposes of this study was to discover what, if any, connection there was between this Roxborough Township family and the Reiter family of Germantown Township. No facts to prove such a connection were found. Possibilities are that Peter, the founder of the Roxborough family had a brother or another son, who became the founder of the Germantown family. Two documents were found relating to a John Reiter of quite early date. One of these was a warrant for

---

[183] Inscription on the monument in Leverington Cemetery, Roxborough, Philadelphia, Pa.

[184] Edward Mathews, *History of Montgomery Baptist Church* (Ambler, Pa., 1895), 32-35. There is a copy of this book at the Historical Society of Pennsylvania.

[185] Inscription on gravestone, Leverington Cemetery, Roxborough, where she was buried near her father.

[186] GSP Collections, *Records of Lower Merion Baptist Church 1808-1928*, 7 and 15.

[187] *Montgomery County Deed Book* 52, 395.

purchase of 15 acres in Philadelphia County, second day, fourth month 1714 by John Riter,[188] and the other of date 5 December 1745 was a mortgage held by Joseph Sims of Philadelphia on a small property in Germantown Township of Johanes Reiter, weaver.[189]   There was no evidence to link Johanes Reiter (he signed his name in German script) with the other family.   The first Reiter in the record of immigrants to Pennsylvania in the Colonial Period was one whose name was signed for him as Hans Mich. Rider.   He arrived 11 September 1728, on the Ship *James Goodwill* from Rotterdam via Deal.[190]   Provided that he brought his family with him, he could have been the founder of the Germantown Reiter family, but was too late for the Roxborough family.

In two respects the Germantown Reiters differed from the Roxborough family.   First, they retained the German spelling of the name through the first generation, while the Roxborough family almost immediately adopted the English spelling, Righter.   When in the second generation the Germantown family adopted an Anglicized spelling, they merely dropped the e and became Riters.   Second, the Germantown family was connected with the Lutheran Church, St. Michael's, in Mount Airy, but the connection of the Roxborough family was probably with one of the sects, and some of them, late in the eighteenth century, were Baptists.   Church records were lacking for most of the Roxborough family.   The names John, George and Michael occur in both families.

The first of the Germantown family was George Reiter, a farmer, who lived on a farm of about 35 acres (at the time of his will) in Cresheim, Germantown Township.   He was born 22 January 1727, and died 22 October 1794.   He married Elisabetha ————, who was born 25 February 1733, and died 26 December 1792.[191]   No record of his purchase of his farm in Cresheim was found, but he owned it before 1764, when he was described in a deed of that year as George Reiter of " Creesham." The tax record of 1783 recorded for him 36 acres, 5 horses, 2 cattle in Germantown Township.   Earlier tax records showed that he owned larger tracts: 1769-150 acres, 1774-300 acres, but, while listed with Germantown Township where George lived, these may include land he owned elsewhere.[192]   George invested extensively in land and purchased at various times land in Cheltenham, Springfield, Whitpain, and Whitemarsh Townships, and on Main Street in Germantown, and his will men-

188 *Pennsylvania Archives* 3rd Ser., Vol. III, 8, " Old Rights."

189 *Deed Book* G-7, 37.

190 Ralph Beaver Strassburger and William John Hinke, eds., *Pennsylvania German Pioneers*, (Norristown, 1934) Vol. I, 22.

191 GSP Collections, *Gravestone Inscriptions of St. Michael's Lutheran Churchyard, Germantown*, 18.

192 *Pennsylvania Archives* 3rd Ser., Vol. XIV, 94, 342, Vol. XVI, 564.

tioned 100 acres in Marborough Township, for which no deed was found.[193] He made his will 29 August 1794, and it was proved 22 November 1794. He devised his plantation in Germantown on which he had lived to his son George, his tract of 100 acres in Marlborough Township to his son Michael, 70 pounds to his granddaughter Elizabeth Dannanhour, 30 pounds to grandson Charles Dannanhour, 50 pounds to the Lutheran Church at " Beggartown,"[194] and the residue of his estate to be divided among his 8 children, as they may agree among themselves. The share of his daughter Eve was to be held in trust, interest to be paid her during her life, and principal to be divided among her children on her death. He named his son George and sons-in-law George Rex and Levi Rex executors.[195]

The children of George and Elizabeth (————) Reiter were:

i. Eva Catharina Reiter. She was born 27 February 1766, and married Christopher Hergesheimer, blacksmith, of Germantown.

ii. Johann Georg Reiter. He was born July 1768, and died 4 August 1833. He married Mary Rita Treichel, daughter of Elias Lewis and Mary Elizabeth Treichel of Northern Liberties, Philadelphia County.[196] Mary was born 26 April 1769, and died 2 June 1820. They were buried at St. Michael's Lutheran Church, Mount Airy. Their 6 children were baptized at St. Michael's.

iii. Johannes Reiter. He was born 13 July 1770, and probably died young, for he was not mentioned in his father's will.

iv. Michael Reiter. He was born 7 June 1772, and died 25 June 1845. He married Catharine E. Wunder, who died 11 March 1844 in her 70th year. They were buried in the Roxborough Burial Ground. He was a butcher at the time of his father's death.[197]

---

[193] *Deed Book* H-15, 275: 23 January 1762, Edward Shippen, Jr. *et ux.* to George Reiter. He sold part of this Cheltenham tract 27 August 1770. (*Deed Book* D-4, 50: George Reiter *et ux.* to Rynear Lukens) *Deek Book* D-1, 46: 15 September 1764, Frederick Altemus *et ux.* to George Reiter. He sold part of this Springfield tract to Andrew Hayberger, 7 December 1767 (*Deed Book* D-1, 53). *Deed Book* I-16, 4 and 6: 2 June 1775, Jonathan Davids *et ux.* to George Reiter. He still owned these adjoining tracts in Whitpain and Whitemarsh Townships when he died. The record of the second of these is defective in the Deed Book. *Deed Book* EF-9, 634: 4 May 1781, Christopher Meng *et ux.* to George Reiter. *Deed Book* D-38, 543: 20 March 1793, George Reiter *et ux.* to Moses Hill and Thomas Capner.

[194] Martin G. Brumbaugh in his *A History of the German Baptist Brethern in Europe and America* (Mount Morris, Ill., 1899), 166, relates a story of how this area, where St. Michael's Lutheran Church was located, came to be called Beggartown. The first house of worship of the Brethern was located there.

[195] *Will Book* X, 150 #103, 1794.

[196] *Deed Book* D-74, 32: 3 December 1798 George Riter *et ux.* to John Kessler.

[197] There is an account of this family in John W. Jordan, ed., *Colonial and Revolutionary Families of Pennsylvania* (New York, 1911), Vol. III, 1616-1621, and Vol. V, 250-257. George W. Riter, son of Michael and Catharine (Wunder) Riter, was a physician in Roxborough and prominent citizen. He served as Recorder of Deeds of Philadelphia County, 1824-1830, and was the GWR of the deed books. There is an account of him in the *History of the Roxborough Lodge No. 135 F and A Masons*, previously cited, 119. He was buried with his father and mother in the Roxborough Burial Ground, not far from the Michael and Catharine Righter and their family of the Roxborough Righters.

   v. Sara Reiter. She was born 27 October 1774, and died August 1775.

   vi. Margareta Reiter. She married William Zoll, innkeeper of Reading, Bucks County, Pennsylvania.

   vii. Elisabetha Reiter. She married Georg Bauer (Bower) of Reading, 12 January 1783.

   viii. Susanna Reiter. She married George Rex, blacksmith, of the Manor of Moreland, Montgomery County, Pennsylvania.

   ix. Catharina Reiter. She married Levi Rex, wheelwright, also of Moreland.

   x. Hanna Reiter. She married John Ashmead, coachmaker, of Germantown.

   xi. A daughter, who married Dannanhour and had 2 children, Elizabeth and Charles, mentioned in her father's will.

Except for those whose dates of birth were known from baptism records of St. Michael's Church, these children are not necessarily in order of birth. George in his will listed the 8 who survived him in the following order: George, Michael, Margaret, Eve, Elizabeth, Susanna, Catharine and Hanna.[198]

Records were found of a Reiter family in Upper Hanover Township, which may have been connected with the Roxborough or the Germantown families, but no proof of relationship was found. The record of this Upper Hanover family began with the purchase, 10 July 1749, of 142 acres of land in the township by George " Ryter." [199] On the tax assessor's list was George Michael Reiter (also spelled Riter and Righter) with a farm in 1769 of 300 acres.[200] His wife was named Catharine, and they had a large family. They were Lutherans, connected with St. Paul's Evangelical Lutheran Church at Red Hill, Pennsylvania.[201] George M. Righter made his will 20 April 1805, and it was proved 20 September 1805.[202] The 11 children as named in his will were:

   i. George Reiter. He died before his father.

   ii. Catharine Reiter. She married the Rev. John Conrad Reller, and was a widow when the will was made.

---

[198] GSP Collections, *St. Michael's Lutheran Church, Germantown, Record of Baptisms, Marriages and Burials*. Aside from the church records, information on this family was derived from the deeds resulting from the partition of the estate among the 8 surviving children: *Montgomery County Deed Book* 8, 475; Book 10, 62, 148; Book 20, 67; Book 22, 62. *Deed Book* EF-9, 636. In all of these the 8 children with their status as to marriage, were named.

[199] *Montgomery County Deed Book* 2, 626. Recorded 1786.

[200] *Pennsylvania Archives* 3rd Ser., Vol. XIV, 59.

[201] GSP Collections, *Records of St. Paul's Evangelical Lutheran Church, Red Hill, Penna.* See index for numerous entries on this family.

[202] *Montgomery County Will Book* 2, 482.

iii. Elizabeth Reiter. She married Conrad Wetzel, and died before her father.

iv. Eva Reiter. She married first Fredrick Sano and second Peter Heebner.

v. Margaret Reiter. She was blind from her youth.

vi. Mary Elizabeth Reiter. She married Peter Klein, and died before her father.

vii. Barbara Reiter. She married George Adam Blank.

viii. Michael Reiter.

ix. John Reiter.

x. Mary Reiter. She was the youngest daughter and had married the Rev. Frederick Wilhelm Geisenheimer.

xi. Peter Reiter, the youngest son.

Very little research was done on this family.

There was also a Reiter (or Riter, or Righter) family in Chester County, Pennsylvania, founded by a Michael Reiter, who is said to have emigrated from Saxony, Germany, and who had a wife Christiana. He served in the Revolution and died of wounds while a prisoner of the British.[203] No record of any connection of this family with the Reiters of Roxborough, Germantown, or Upper Hanover was found.[204]

---

203 *PMHB* Vol. 42 (1918), 352: Mrs. Harry Rogers, in " Pennsylvania Pensioners of the Revolution " quotes the record of the granting of a pension to Christiana Righter, 17 September 1793.

204 Records of this family are used as examples of methods of preparing a genealogy in Archibald F. Bennett's *A Guide for Genealogical Research* (Salt Lake City, Utah, 1956), 27-30; 76-83; 93-94.

Righter-Keech Records

THE following records supplement "A Study of the Righter-Reiter Families of Philadelphia County in the Eighteenth Century" by Mildred Goshow which appeared in Volume XXI (No. 1, 1958), 3-44, of this *Magazine*. Specifically they are records of the children and some of the grandchildren of No. 9 Bartholomew Righter, Jr., for whom see pages 27-29 of the above volume, and nicely substantiate Miss Goshow's deductions.[*]

Xerox copies of the originals, with other records, were sent to Miss Goshow by Richard B. Righter, 5540 Fair Oaks Street, Pittsburgh, Pa., 15217, in November, 1970. The originals, he stated, were on loose pieces of paper found in a nineteenth century Bible which had belonged to Mr. Righter's grandfather who, he believes, was a descendant of 15. Anthony Righter (see page 36 of the above volume).

Righter Records

Elizabeth Righter was born in the year 1764 December 11 Day
John Righter was born in the year 1768 January 24 [26?] Day
Hannah Righter was born in the year 1770 July 28 Day
William Righter was born in the year 1773 August 3 Day
Mary Righter was born in the year 1776 May 19 Day
Rebecca Righter was born in the year 1779 September 13 Day
William Righter was born in the year 1783 December 13 Day
Catherine Righter was born in the year 1787 Apriel 13 Day
Rudolph Righter was born in the year 1790 March 1 Day
John Jarret was born in the year 1791 June 3 Day
Joseph Righter was born in the year 1793 Apriel 6 Day
Elizabeth Righter was born in the year 1796 May 30 Day

Keech Records

Aaron Keech was born the 20th Day of november 1773
Rebecca [Righter] Keech was born the 13th Day of september 1779

[*Their Children*]

George Keech was born the 20th Day of August 1799
William Keech was born the 23rd Day of April 1801
John Keech was born the 2nd Day of May 1802
Mary Keech was born the 15th Day of August 1803
Bartholomew Keech was born the 20th Day of August 1804
Elizabeth Keech was born the 18th Day of September 1805

Martha J. Keech was born the 2nd Day of October 1806
Nathaniel Keech was born the 26th Day of January 1808
Henry G. Keech was born the 11th Day of February 1809
Charlotte W. Keech was born the 19th Day of January 1810
Catharine R. Keech was born the 1st Day of September 1811
Joseph Keech was born the 19th Day of September 1812
Maryann Keech was born the 7th Day of April 1814
Aaron Keech was born the 29th Day of August 1815
Jacob M. Keech was born the 8th Day of October 1816
John B. Keech was born the 28th Day of December 1817
Aaron Keech and Rebecca Righter was joined in the nuptual bonds of Matrimony the
    27 Day of March — 1798

[Deaths]

Mary Keech Departed this life the 5th Day of June 1804 Aged 9 months & 3 weeks
John Keech Departed this life the 9th Day of September 1807 Aged 5 years 4 months
    & 7 Days
Aaron Keech Departed this life the 19th Day of March 1816 — Aged 6 months & 8 Days
Nathaniel Keech Departed this life the 26th of July 1826 Aged 18 years & 6 months
Charlotte W. Sanders Departed this life the 20th of December 1824 Aged 24 years
    10 month & 24 Days
Elizabeth Tyson Departed this life the 12 Day of February 1835 Aged 29 years 4 months
    & 24 Days
Rebecca Keech Departed this life the 16 Day of April 1836 Aged 56 years 7 months
    & 3 Days
Aaron Keech Sr Departed this life the 27th Day of September 1844 Aged 70 Years
    10 months & 12 Days

THE RÜBENKAM FAMILY OF HESSEN,
Parent Stock of the Rubincam-Revercomb Family
of Pennsylvania and Virginia

BY MILTON RUBINCAM, F.A.S.G., F.N.G.S.

One of the difficulties in the field of Pennsylvania-German genealogy is the indentification of the pre-American home of the immigrant ancestor. Unless old family letters, diaries, Bible records, letters of manumission,[1] or other contemporary documents have survived to the present time, it is quite difficult to determine the locality in Germany where the search should commence.[2]

The clue to the European home of the Rubincam (Rubicam, Rubinkam, Rubencame) family of Pennsylvania, Delaware, Ohio, and elsewhere, and its southern branch, the Revercomb family of Virginia, West Virginia, Canada, and other places, was found in the record which John Wister, progenitor of one of Philadelphia's most distinguished families, entered in his Bible:

Anna Katharina Rüben-Kämin was born in Hesse-Cassel in the town of Wanfried,[3] February 25, 1709. She was daughter of Johann Philipp Ruben-Kamm, Pastor of the

---

[1] Letters of manumission were granted by the princes of the Holy Roman Empire to their subjects who wished to emigrate and who paid a stipulated fee. Such manumission documents identified the home in Germany and gave particulars about the emigrant, his family, and his property. As there were rigid rules against emigrating, however, many people desiring to settle in America did not apply for letters of manumission but slipped quietly away.

[2] Persistent and intelligent research often rewards the investigator even when direct evidence is lacking. The distinguished Austrian genealogist, Karl Friedrich von Frank, F.A.S.G., while searching for the home of Erasmus Rosenberger who lived in Hanover Twp., Lancaster (now Lebanon) Co., Pa., from 1743 until his removal to the Shenandoah Valley of Virginia in 1776, had only a general statement from a ship list on which to work. But by a careful and systematic search Dr. von Frank learned that this emigrant came from Schlüchtern, near Hanau (later a part of Hessen-Kassel), and traced his ancestry back to the last quarter of the 17th century. See Francis Coleman Rosenberger, "Erasmus Rosenberger of Shenandoah County and His German Origins," *The Virginia Magazine of History and Biography*, LXIII (January, 1955), 84-87.

[3] The country, known in early medieval times as Hessen centered around the Fulda, Werra, Eder and Lahn Rivers, forming part of the Frankish kingdom under the Merovingian monarchs and the Carolingian sovereigns. At the time of the Rübenkam emigration to America, six principalities, distinguished from each other by additional and hyphenated names, comprised Hessen and were part of the Holy Roman Empire: Hessen-Kassel, Hessen-Philippsthal, Hessen-Rheinfels-Rotenburg, Hessen-Rheinfels-Wanfried, Hessen-Darmstadt, and Hessen-Homburg. All of these were ruled by branches of the ancient House of Brabant; their ruling princes were called landgraves and their territories were known as landgraviates. The political division called Hessen-Rheinfels-Wanfried, the ancestral home of the Rübenkams, was a dependency of the more powerful landgraviate of Hessen-Kassel. As described in 1695, Hessen was bounded by Westphalia on the north, Thuringia on the east, the Abbey of Fulda and the Wetterau on the south, and by the Duchy of Westphalia, the counties of Hatzfeld and Wittgenstein, the Principality of Dillenburg, and the Countship of Solms on the West. See Jean-Baptiste d'Audiffret, *Histoire et Géographie, Ancienne et Moderne*, III, 32-322, for a fuller account of the area. Today Hessen lies directly west of the Eastern Zone of Germany. Wanfried, just inside the Western Zone, lies on the east bank of the Werra River. In 1693 it became the capital of the small landgraviate of Hessen-Rheinfels-Wanfried.

parish of Wanfried. After the death of the Father in 1726 [1725], at Berleburg in the countship of Wittgenstein, the Mother with her 6 children, 3 sons and 3 daughters, emigrated to Pennsylvania, and on the 10 November 1737, Anna Katharina intermarried with me, Johannes Wüster, and departed this life on 17 May 1770, between 5 and 6 o'clock in the afternoon, aged 61 years, 2 months, and 6 days. She bore 5 children, of whom 3 still survive. We lived and dwelt together 32 years, 5 months and 21 days, and I cherish the hope that she died in peace and bliss, so must it be. Amen! [4]

With the foregoing statement as a starting point, the present writer caused researches to be made in Germany a quarter of a century ago. Thanks to the interest and initiative of Kurt Holzapfel, Dipl. Ing., at Eschwege, Hessen; the late Dr. Carl Knetsch, Director of State Archives at Marburg; Fräulein Felice Rübencamp of Dresden, Saxony; Karl Friedrich von Frank, F.A.S.G., of Austria; *Kirchenrat* (Church Councillor) Eduard Grimmell of Kassel, Germany, and others, the pre-American genealogy of the Rubincam-Revercomb family has been reconstructed and is supported by documentary evidence.[5]

FRIEDRICH RÜBENKAM has heretofore been regarded as the first proved ancestor of the family. But in the fall of 1959 Kirchenrat Eduard Grimmell of Kassel discovered a clue to his parentage in the confirmation books of the Freiheitsgemeinde, a parish in the city of Kassel. The same record was examined early in 1961 by the writer's friend, John I. Coddington of Bordentown, New Jersey. The list of confirmations at Pentecost, 1609, included: *Frölich, Herman Rübenkams* S[ohn], 11 [*Jahre alt*].[6]

Mr. Coddington reviewed this record with Kirchenrat Grimmell as well as with Dr. Eckardt G. Franz, the new director of the State Archives at Marburg, depository of the Kassel parish registers prior to 1750. They all agreed that *Frölich*, or *Fröhlich*, meaning "joyous" or "happy," was an error on the part of the officiating clergyman who evidently meant to write "Friedrich." Dr. Franz stated that *Frölich* had not been given as a forename to a child since the Middle Ages. As the baptismal records of the Freiheitsgemeinde do not begin until 1600, neither Friedrich's birth nor his baptismal record are shown therein. But from his age at time of confirmation, it is evident he was born in or about 1598. Kirchenrat Grimmell and Mr. Coddington both state there can be no doubt that the 1609 record relates to the ancestor of the American family.[7]

---

[4] This Bible record was copied by the late Miss Frances A. Wister and forwarded on 19 Dec. 1932, to Maj. Louis Estell Fagan II, U.S.M.C., and by him transmitted to the writer 21 Aug. 1934.

[5] See *Archives of the Rubincam-Revercomb Family: German Documents*, (1959), collected by the author, copies of which are on file in most large libraries in the United States, including the Collections of the Genealogical Society of Pennsylvania, hereinafter cited as GSP.

[6] Konfirmationen in Festo Pentecoste, 1609, Freiheitsgemeinde registers, I, 274, column 1, line 19.

[7] Hermann Rübenkam apparently had another son Jacob who was confirmed at Christmas, 1614, as *Jacobe, Herman Rübenkams* S[ohn] 13 [*Jahre alt*]. *Ibid.*, 284, column 1, line 1.

Friedrich Rübenkam was apparently therefore about nineteen when he was matriculated at the University of Marburg, 3 December 1617. This is the oldest Protestant university, having been founded in 1527 by Landgrave Philipp the Magnanimous, of Hessen. Here, where Luther and Zwingli had disputed in 1529, Friedrich majored in theology under such distinguished Reformed (Calvinist) savants as Johannes Crocius, Raphael Egli, and Gregorius Schönfeld the Elder. His professor of Greek was Theodor Vietor, and he studied Hebrew under Professor Johannes Molther the Elder.[8]

He was graduated from Marburg in 1619 with the degree of Magister, equivalent to the English Master of Arts. He then served successively as a tutor in the noble families of Spede and von Hanstein at Frielingen, as assistant pastor at Niederaula, near Hersfeld[9] from 1623 to 1626, in the latter year succeeding to the pastorate at Frielingen upon the death of the incumbent, Ludovicus Waldenberger.

Probably it was at Frielingen that he married ANNA GERTRUD UNDERBERG, daughter of Nicolaus Underberg and his wife Anna Rickgans. The date of their marriage has not been determined, but the proof of Anna Gertrud's surname was found by Mr. Holzapfel in the Frielingen parish registers, wherein Rübencam himself wrote in 1632: *Socer meus Nicolaus Underberg obiit 5t 10bris,* "My father-in-law, Nicolaus Underberg, died 5th 10th month [December]."

Evidence relating to the Rickgans family was also unearthed by Mr. Holzapfel. In the *Währschaftsbuch,* or *Gerichtsbuch*—in which the transfers of real estate are recorded—of the Court of Justice at Abterode,[10] he found several documents, the earliest of which reads in abstracted form:

1651 Rickgansische Erben haben desvor ihre Mühle zu Abterode gelegen, die Thammühle genannt samt der dazu gehörigen Wiese vnd Flecken Landes H. Johann Philips Arnoldten, Vogt zu Frankershausen verkauft vor vnd umb 150 Thlr zu 32 alb. Demnach sich aber von gedachten Erben 4 Stemme beschweret ob wehre die mühle zu wohl-

---

[8] Marburg, on the Lahn River, is somewhat more than 65 air-miles southwest of Wanfried, and 60 miles north of Frankfurt. It was the principal town of what was sometimes called the Principality of Lahn in Upper Hessen. For the names of the professors under whom the Rübenkams studied at Marburg in the 17th century, see Franz Gundlach, "Catalogus Professorum Academiae Marburgensis," *Publications of the Historical Commission for Hessen and Waldeck,* XV (1927).

[9] A former Benedictine abbey, the Abbey of Hersfeld is beautifully situated on the Fulda at its confluence with the Geis and Haune Rivers, about 30 miles southwest of Wanfried. Frielingen, a village in the present Kreis Hersfeld about six miles southwest of Hersfeld, today has its post office at Kircheim. Niederaula is about three miles south of Kircheim.

[10] Abterode, a village in the present Kreis Eschwege, is about six miles northwest of Eschwege, the *Kreisstadt,* or chief town in the administrative subdivision called the *Kreis* or circle. It approximates a county seat. Eschwege itself is about five miles west of Wanfried, down the Werra on the west bank, and about 26 miles southeast of Kassel.

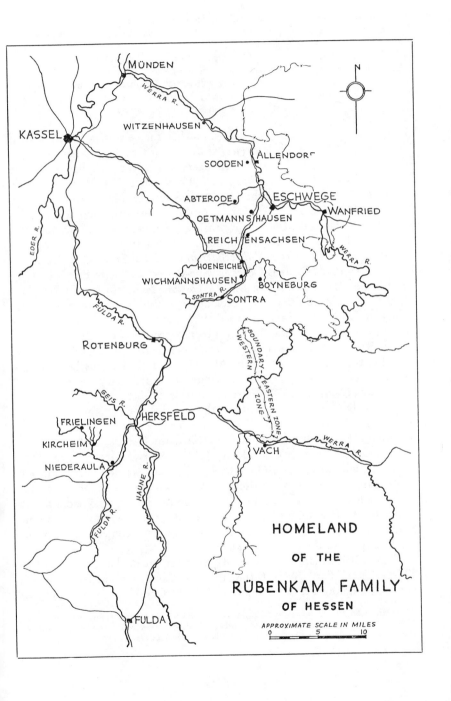

MÜNDEN

WERRA R.

KASSEL

WITZENHAUSEN

SOODEN • • ALLENDORF

ABTERODE • ESCHWEGE

EDER R. OETMANNSHAUSEN WANFRIED

REICHENSACHSEN

HOENEICHE WERRA R.

WICHMANNSHAUSEN

SONTRA R. BOYNEBURG

FULDA R. SONTRA

ROTENBURG

BOUNDARY-WESTERN EASTERN ZONE ZONE

GEIS R.

FRIELINGEN HERSFELD

KIRCHEIM VACH WERRA R.

NIEDERAULA

HAUNE R.

HOMELAND

OF THE

FULDA R. RÜBENKAM FAMILY

OF HESSEN

FULDA

APPROXIMATE SCALE IN MILES
0   5   10

feil verkaufft, als ist durch Unterhandlung der Obrigkeit die Sache in Güte dahin verglichen worden, das selbige 56 Thlr zum nachschuss von H. Vogten gegeben werden, worauf dan die Erben die Wehrschaft geboten.

Nicolas Gercke	wegen Nicolas Unterbergs stamm
Maria Stuntzin	vor sich selbst
Magnus Leimbach	wegen Friedrich Leimbachs stamm
Hans Rudeloff	wegen Johannis Curaei stamm
Hanss Lünne	wegen Simon Löbers stamm

According to this document, it appears that the heirs of a family named Rickgans sold their mill-dam (*wehre die mühle*) at Abterode to Mr. Johann Philipp Arnolt, bailiff of Franckershausen, for 150 thalers. These heirs were divided into five branches: (1) Nicolaus Gercke, representing Nicolaus Underberg's branch; (2) Maria Stuntzin, representing her own branch; (3) Magnus Leimbach, representing Friedrich Leimbach's branch; (4) Hans Rudeloff, representing Johannes Cureaus' branch; and (5) Hanss Lünne, representing Simon Löber's branch.

Another entry in the *Währschaftsbuch*, dated in 1669, to be noted later, shows that Nicolaus Gercke, wine-dealer, and wife Elisabeth were the heirs of Bernhard Rickgans, the *possible* father-in-law of Nicolaus Underberg. In addition, Mr. Holzapfel, searching the records of the Court of Justice at Bilstein, learned that among others subject to rent at Abterode, and living near to each other, were Nicolaus Underberg and Georg Rickgans, presumably a son of Bernhard. Mr. Holzapfel also found in the burial records of the Abterode church that Elisabeth, widow of Nicolaus Gercke, wagoner, was buried 20 February 1677, aged 92 years: *Elsa, Claus Gercke, Fuhrmanns relicta, 92 Jahre alt*.[11]

From these evidences, it *appears* that Bernhard Rickgans had six children: (1) Anna, wife of Nicolaus Underberg, who had at least two daughters, Elisabeth or Elsa, wife of Nicolaus Gercke, and Anna Gertrud, wife of Friedrich Rübenkam; (2) Maria, wife of a Stuntz; (3) a daughter, wife of Friedrich Leimbach, who had a son Magnus Leimbach; (4) a daughter, wife of Johannes Curaeus, who had a daughter, wife of Hans Rudeloff; (5) a daughter, wife of Simon Löber, who had a daughter, wife of Hans Lünne; (6) a son Georg. However, this reconstruction of the family of Friedrich Rübenkam's wife is conjectural only, and must be supported by record evidence.

Pastor Rübenkam and his family were caught in the whirlpool of the Thirty Years' War. By 1629 the Protestant cause, for which their hereditary ruler, Landgrave Wilhelm V, called The Constant, of Hessen-Kassel,

---

[11] Mr. Holzapfel also found the following burial record in the Abterode church registers: *Hedwig, Elisabeth Und bergs dochter, 10 Jahre alt*, "Hedwig, Elisabeth Und[er]berg's daughter, 10 years old." Their connection with the family of Nicholas Underberg has not been determined.

and his heroic wife Amalia Elisabeth, were fighting, seemed lost. The Catholic forces, led by Emperor Ferndinand II, gained the ascendance. On 6 March 1629, the Emperor issued the famous Edict of Restitution, in which he ordered the restoration of all ecclesiastical properties secularized since the Peace of Passau (1552), and directed Protestants to surrender to Catholics all benefices which had been appropriated contrary to the provisions of that treaty.

Hessen-Kassel was one of the Calvinist principalities at which the edict was aimed. Frielingen, under Rübenkam's pastoral care and situated within the territories of the historic Abbey of Hersfeld, consequently was seized by the enemy and placed under the rule of the Emperor's son, Archduke Leopold Wilhelm, who added the title of Abbot of Hersfeld to his many other ecclesiastical dignities. Rübenkam and his family took up their exile at Abterode, a few miles northwest of Eschwege. There the pastor spent two years in exile, and then a reversal of fortune carried him back to his parish chuch at Frielingen. Triumphantly he wrote in his church registers:

2do die 10bris Anno 1631, postquam papistae tribus fere annis in Abbatia Hersfeldensi floruerunt, illustrissimus atque potentissimus princeps Wilhelmus Hassiae Landgravius ibidem vi atque gladio jus suum obtinuit, nosque antea remotos pastores in pristinum quemlibet locum clementer restitui jussit, concionem primam habui dominica secunda adventus, facit deus ter opt. maximus ut omnia prospera ad nominis divini laudem atque ecclesiae salutem vergant.

Fridericus Rubecam p. tempore pastor Frilingae.

primo die ante nativit, Xi psalmos Davidis de Lobwasser canere incepimus initium factum cum psalmo 130 de profundis Ao. 1631.

(On 2 December 1631, after the Papacy had ruled in the Abbey of Hersfeld for almost three years, the Most Illustrious and Powerful Prince Wilhelm, Landgrave of Hessen, took possession by force and with the sword, and commanded that we preachers who had been previously driven away should be graciously restored to our former places. I held the first divine service on the second Sunday in Advent. God, thrice great and thrice good, has brought it about that everything turned out happily for the praise of His divine name and for the glory of the Church.

Friedrich Rübenkam, for the time being pastor at Frielingen.

On the first Christmas Day 1631, we all began to sing Lobwasser's Psalms of David, and began with Psalm 130: Out of the depths.) [12]

A year later in December 1632, his father-in-law Nicholas Underberg died at Frielingen, as noted above. The following 2 May 1633,

---

[12] Germans celebrated three days at Christmas, hence the "first Christmas Day" in 1631 was 24 December. Lobwasser was the author of a Hessian hymnal. The entry cited in the text was translated from Latin into German by Kurt Holzapfel, and from German into English by Dr. Albert H. Gerberich of Bethesda, Maryland.

Underberg's widow was one of the two godmothers of a daughter of Pastor Rübenkam, being referred to by him in the parish register as *socra mea,* "my mother-in-law."

Later that year the Rübenkams removed from Frielingen to Herolz, in the bishopric of Fulda, where they remained until 1635 when a sudden invasion of Croatians drove them out with great loss.[13] Once again they fled to Abterode. This year of 1635 was a tragic one for Pastor Rübenkam; in addition to the Croatian incursion, the plague swept the land and four members of his family succumbed to its ravages: Friedrich's little daughters Elisabeth and Anna Sibylla were both buried 5 October 1635; a certain Hans Caspar Rübecam, perhaps Friedrich's brother, was buried 30 October; and his mother-in-law, who had accompanied them on their flight, perished. The Abterode burial records show that on 14 October 1635 *Anna, Claus Underbergs relicta* was laid to rest.

Friedrich remained at Abterode for about another year, and then accepted a call to the ruined town of Wichmannshausen, where he was installed on 22 October 1636 as pastor by Inspector Caspar Josephi of Allendorf. Wichmannshausen, on the Sontra River[14] with a present population of 731 inhabitants, in the seventeenth century was an estate of the von Boyneburg family, with which Pastor Rübenkam's grandson, Johann Philipp, was to ally himself matrimonially.

Just three years later on 9 September 1639, Friedrich became pastor of nearby Oetmannshausen,[15] further up the river, where he passed the remainder of his life. The parish registers of the town do not commence until 1650, but the superintendent or bishop of his *classis* (ecclesiastical district), Johannes Hütterodt, kept a separate record in which he recorded that "Herr Rubekamp" and one of his sons both died on 3 April 1647. It is not clear whether their deaths were due to enemy action or from the plague, but it is quite likely they succumbed to the latter.

After Friedrich Rübenkam's death in 1647, his widow Anna Gertrud continued to live at Oetmannshausen. She was there in 1657 when her son Laurentius entered the University of Marburg, but three years later in 1660 the family had evidently removed to Eschwege, for in the Marburg matriculation records of that year her son Andreas was described as

---

[13] Herolz, in the present Kreis Schlüchtern, is less than two miles east of the town of Schlüchtern on the Kinzig River, and about 35 miles south of Frielingen. In 1635 Croatia, today a part of Yugoslavia, was partially occupied by Turks. Western Croatia, however, belonged to the Emperor, and it was from this section of the Holy Roman Empire that Ferdinand II brought these fierce fighters. They were brutal and ruthless, ravaging and burning pitilessly wherever they went.

[14] The Sontra is a tributary of the Werra River, joining it north of Eschwege. Wichmannshausen is about 10 miles upstream from the mouth of the Sontra.

[15] Oetmannshausen is barely three miles north of Wichmannshausen.

being from that place. Later the mother evidently returned to the town which had been her husband's last pastoral charge, for her burial record was found in the Oetmannshausen parish registers by the late Dr. Carl Knetsch: *1681 Gerdrut, Herrn Friderici Rübecams gewesen Pfarrers seeligen alhier relicta, den 11 Februarii,* "1681 Gertrud, widow of the deceased Mr. Friedrich Rübecam, pastor at this very place, 11 February."

Issue of Friedrich Rübenkam and his wife Anna Gertrud Underberg:

1. i. JOHANN GEORG RÜBENKAM, b. *ca.* 1626; d. 6 December 1680, of whom further.
   ii. ELISABETH RÜBENKAM, b. *ca.* 1631; bur. at Abterode 5 October 1635, aged 4 years.
   iii. ANNA SIBYLLA RÜBENKAM, b. *ca.* 1632; bur. at Abterode 5 October 1635, aged 3 years. A daughter, whose name was not given in the baptismal record, was bapt. at Frielingen 2 May 1633; godparents: the wife of Junker Johann Rudolf Spede "and my mother-in-law," (*atque socra mea*). This child might be identified with Anna Sibylla Rübenkam.
   iv. CHRISTOPH RÜBENKAM. The only evidence pertaining to the existence of this member of the family is found in the baptismal record of his nephew Christoph, son of Otto Beck, the husband of Rübenkam's sister Anna Gertrud.
   v. A son, unnamed, who d. at Oetmannshausen 3 April 1647.
2. vi. LAURENTIUS RÜBENKAM, d. 8 August 1681 at Eschwege, of whom further.
3. vii. ANDREAS RÜBENKAM, b. *ca.* 1642; d. 3 March 1698, ancestor of the Pennsylvania family, of whom further.
   viii. ANNA GERTRUD RÜBENKAM, b. at Oetmannshausen *ca.* 1644; conf. there at Easter, 1658, aged 14 years; bur. at Oetmannshausen 23 December 1732. She m. 1st, at the same place 15 October 1660, OTTO BECK, by whom she had issue, all bapt. at Oetmannshausen: 1. CHRISTOPH BECK, 19 February 1665; godfather: his uncle, Christoph Rübenkam. 2. JOHANN GEORG BECK, 24 February 1667; godfather: his uncle Johann Georg Rübenkam, Herr Rentmeister von Eschwege. Matric. at the University of Marburg 26 May 1696. 3. LAURENTIUS BECK, 11 July 1669; godfather: his uncle, Laurentius Rübenkam, pastor of Eschwege-Neustadt. Anna Gertrud (Rübenkam) Beck m. 2nd, also at Oetmannshausen 1 March 1682, JOHANNES WIDITZ of Datterode, bur. at Oetmannshausen 30 May 1696, by whom she had further issue: 4. CATHARINA JULIANA WIDITZ, bapt. at Oetmannshausen 19 February 1684; godmother: her mother's sister-in-law, *Catharina Juliana, Herrn Andreas Rübencambs, Pfarrer in der Neuenstadt zu Eschwege, Hausfrau.*

1. JOHANN GEORG RÜBENKAM, eldest son of Friedrich and Anna Gertrud Rübenkam, was born about 1626, probably at Frielingen. Nothing is known of his early life beyond the fact of his first marriage, at

a date unknown, to JULIANA MARGARETHA STÜCKRATH, baptized at Sontra 30 June 1633, the fifth child of Peter Stückrath (1596-1672) and his wife Catharina Schleidt.[16]

In 1667, when he was recorded as the godfather of his nephew Johann Georg Beck, he held the position of *Rentmeister*, or tax collector, of Eschwege, and still occupied that position two years later when his son Johann Peter Rübenkam entered the Hersfeld Gymnasium. At Rotenburg,[17] down the Fulda River from Hersfeld, on 26 March 1669 he borrowed 500 Reichsthalers in specie from Colonel Jost von Hundelshausen of Harmuthsachsen, for the use and on behalf of the Prince, presumably Landgrave Ernst of Hessen-Rheinfels. For the payment of this debt he pledged all of his property, wherever it might be or lie, with all of its benefits and privileges, as sureties naming not only himself but his mother, Gerdruth Rubekamin,[18] and Elizabeth, wife of the late Claus Gercke. As securities he listed his house, farm, garden and barns, as well as his fields and meadows, specifically listing the following pieces of property owned by him: one acre of land behind the Freiheit; one acre of the old farms (*ein acker ,alten Hoofe*) ; one acre along the Kupferbach—literally Copper Brook, apparently the name of a brook at or near Abterode; one acre on the Kupfergasse, probably a lane leading to the Copper Brook; one acre *uf der kalkrössen,* and three-quarters of an acre on the Mittelberg, a hill near Abterode, together with all of his goods and chattels, movable and immovable. The document was drawn up before the Salzgraf Coriarius, Tax-Collector Hupfelt of Sooden, a court official named Surbicke, and two witnesses. The sum borrowed was to be repaid annually in installments of 25 Reichsthalers on St. Martin's Day (11 November), the notice thereof to be issued a quarter of a year in advance.

The fact that Rübenkam named Elisabeth, widow of Claus Gercke, as one of his sureties is interesting, for it supports the theory advanced in the account of Pastor Rübenkam, that she was the sister of the pastor's wife, Anna Gertrud.

After the death of his first wife, Johann Georg Rübenkam married on 30 November 1675, ELIZABETH REXRODT, as his second wife. He died five years later on 6 December 1680, at which time he was *Bürgermeister,* or mayor, of Wanfried on the Werra.

---

[16] Protokolle der Kasseler Regierung, CB-8, Band 54 (1672), 521, 738. According to Mr. Holzapfel the Protokolle are abstracts of law suits and of judgements rendered on them. An entry under date of 15 May 1672, concerns a lawsuit over the estate of Peter Stückrath, among whose heirs were *die Kinder des Johann Georg Rübekam und dessen verstorbenen Ehefrau.*

[17] Rotenburg is down the Fulda, north of Hersfeld some 20 or more miles.

[18] In German, feminine surnames are formed by adding the suffix "-in" to the masculine form of the family name.

Issue of I. Johann Georg Rübenkam and his 1st wife Juliana Margaretha Stückrath:

    i. FRIEDRICH RÜBENKAM, conf. in 1674; d. at Eschwege 16 February 1676.[19]

    ii. JOHANN PETER RÜBENKAM. In 1669 entered the third class of the Gymnasium at Hersfeld.[20]

Issue of 1. Johann Georg Rübenkam by his 2nd wife Elisabeth Rexrodt:

    iii. KUNEGUNDA JULIANA RÜBENKAM, b. at Wanfried 3 January 1677.

    iv. JOHANN PAUL RÜBENKAM, b. 7 January 1679 at Wanfried, conf. in 1694; d. at Eschwege 24 December 1738. He m. 1st, at Eschwege 27 May 1711, ANNA GERTRUD BRILL, bapt. 31 August 1692; d. 15 April 1729, daughter of Martin Brill. Issue, all born at Eschwege: 1. JOHANN GEORG RÜBENKAM, bapt. 16 July 1712; godfather: Mr. Carl Rübenkam, steward at Vach. 2. MARTIN RÜBENKAM, bapt. 7 February 1715; godfather: Mr. Martin Brill; d. 25 May 1715. 3. MARIA ELISABETH RÜBENKAM, bapt. 15 April 1716; godmother: Mr. Martin Brill's daughter; m. 28 January 1742, JOHANNES REITZ, candidate in theology, son of Johann Adam Reitz, in the service of the school at Niddawitzhausen. 4 MARGARETHA ELISABETH RÜBENKAM, bapt. 6 April 1718; godmother: Georg Gemeling's wife; m. 6 June 1741, as his 2nd wife, ERNST CONRAD FIEDLER, master of the Clothworkers' Guild at Eschwege, and ensign in the local military company.[21] 5. CATHARINA ELISABETH RÜBENKAM, bapt. 7 September 1720; godmother: Lorentz Brill's wife; d. 8 December 1720. 6. CHRISTINA MARGARETHA RÜBENKAM, bapt. 23 December 1721; godmother: the daughter of Hieronymus Dircks, pastor at Eschwege-Neustadt; m. 13 June 1743, JOHANN WILHELM FRANCKE, judge at Biedenfeld. 7. ANNA ELISABETH RÜBENKAM, bapt. 21 June 1724; godmother: the wife of Mr. Langhans of Kassel. The parish registers note that on 1 November 1729, a daughter, not named, of Johann Paul Rübenkam, died. 8. CATHARINA ELISA-

---

19 Probably Johann Georg Rübenkam's son. His parentage is not stated in the recovered data from the Eschwege parish registers found by Mr. Holzapfel, but this is the only place to which he can presently be assigned.

20 This, the only data at present for him, is contained in a letter to the author from Frau Hildegard Schäfer-Mafry, Eisenach, Thuringia, 21 March 1950. It is taken from the "Schülerverzeichnis des Hersfelder Gymnasium von 1633-1704," edited by Philipp Hafner in *Die Stiftsruine, Zeitschrift für Vorgeschichte, Geschichte, Volks- und Heimatgeschichte,* No. 15, 120. The entry for the year 1669 reads: *516. Joh. Peter Rübencamm, quaestoris Eschwege, fil. III,* in translation stating that Johann Peter, son of the Rentmeister (Latin *quaestor*) at Eschwege, entered the third class of the Gymnasium at Hersfeld.

21 Dr. Erich Bartholomäus, "Die Meister der Eschweger Tuchmacherzunft seit 1637," *Hessische Familienkunde,* Band 2, Heft 10 (December, 1953), column 365.

BETH RÜBENKAM, bapt. 31 December 1726; godmother: Lorentz Brill's wife. 9. ANNA ELISABETH RÜBENKAM, bapt. 29 December 1728; m. 13 November 1748, JOHANN PHILIPP SCHREIBER, merchant. 9. CONRAD RÜBENKAM, bapt. 13 April 1729; godfather: Martin Brill's son; d. 17 September 1729. Johann Paul Rübenkam m. 2nd, 26 April 1731, ANNA MARIA (BRILL) SCHUHMANN, daughter of Johann Georg Brill and widow of Johann Gottfried Schuhmann. Issue: 11. ANTON FRIEDRICH RÜBENKAM, b. 31 March 1736; d. at Hannoverisch-Münden 29 November 1801; m. 20 June 1769; MARIE ELISA-BETH SELLING.[22]

v. KARL AUGUST RÜBENKAM, bapt. at Wanfried 7 July 1681. A baker by occupation, he probably was steward of an estate at Klein-vach, near Allendorf, for in 1712 the godfather of his nephew Jo-hann Georg Rübenkam (son of Johann Paul) was recorded as Herr Carl Rübenkam, steward at Vach. From 1742 to 1743 he was burgomaster of Wanfried, the same office held by his father.[23] The date of his death has not been found, nor has his wife's name been recovered. Issue credited to him in the Wanfried parish registers: 1. JOHANN CHRISTIAN RÜBENKAM, bapt. 26 April 1716; godfather: Christian Rohrbach of Sontra. 2. ANNA GERTRUD RÜBENKAM, bapt. 1 June 1718; godmother: Johann Paul Rüben-kam's wife; d. 19 March 1720. 3. KUNEGUNDA JULIANA RÜBENKAM, twin of the above, bapt. 1 June 1718; godmother: her father's sister, Kunegunda Juliana Rübenkam; m. 6 November 1742, JOHANN CHRISTOPH DANIEL. 4. MARIA ELISA-BETH RÜBENKAM, bapt. 17 February 1721; godmother: the wife of Johann Hermann Uckermann, wine dealer. 5. JOHANN HEIN-RICH RÜBENKAM, bapt. 3 November 1723; godfather: Johann Heinrich Hieronymus, Jr., baker. 6. MARIA CHRISTINA RÜ-BENKAM, m. 12 October 1752, THIMOTHEUS REXRODT.

2. LAURENTIUS RÜBENKAM, third son of Friedrich Rübenkam and Anna Gertrud Underberg, was godfather at the baptism 5 December 1654 at Oetmannshausen of Laurentius, son of Philipp Preijs. As *Laurentius Rubencam Othmanshusanus*, he was matriculated 27 January 1657 at the University of Marburg. Here he studied under his father's old master, Johannes Crocius, professor of theology, who died two years later; Sebastian Curtius (Kurtz), professor in ordinary of theology; Heinrich Duysing, professor in ordinary of Greek, and other Reformed scholars.

[22] This couple are the ancestors of the late distinguished German chemist, Dr. Robert Gottfried Heinrich Rübencamp (1858-1934), of Dresden, Saxony, and of his uncle Wilhelm Rübencamp who came to New York in the 1860's, married, and founded a family which still flourishes in the United States. Dr. Rübencamp's daughter, Fräulein Felice Rübencamp of Dresden, has been most helpful and interested in the prosecution of our researches in German records.

[23] Reinhold Strauss, in his *Chronik der Stadt Wanfried* (1908), 119, 123, erroneously calls him *Rübesam* and *Rübensam*.

786

In 1665 Rübenkam became assistant pastor at Eschwege-Neustadt, i.e., the "new town" of Eschwege, as distinguished from the older section, Eschwege-Altstadt, and a year later was appointed pastor. In 1670 he became pastor at the latter place, and then in 1672 was elevated to the dignity of Metropolitan of Eschwege. This title is now known in German Protestant churches as "Superintendent"; it corresponds generally to "Bishop" in other denominations. The State Archives at Marburg possess a letter written by Laurentius Rübenkam, dated 4 May 1675, wherein he recommended Jacobus Methe as assistant to the latter's father-in-law, Johann Heysse, who was then pastor at Oetmannshausen.[24]

The Metropolitan's death took place at Eschwege 8 August 1681. Opposite this date appears the single entry in the parish register: *H[err] M[agister] Laurentius Rübenkam, Metropolitanus.*

He married first, at Wanfried on 4 September 1666, ANNA GERTRUD MEISTERLINS (Meisterling) who died 9 January 1674. At Eschwege on 18 February 1675 he married second, CATHARINA MAGDALENA SCHREIBER, daughter of the princely Hessen-Rheinfels tax collector, Justus Heinrich Schreiber. She died 26 May 1694.

Issue of 2. Laurentius Rübenkam and his 1st wife Anna Gertrud Meisterlins:

    i. GUDE ELISABETH RÜBENKAM, bapt. 3 September 1667; godmother: the chief magistrate's wife; d. June, 1668.

Issue of 2. Laurentius Rübenkam and his 2nd wife Catharina Magdalena Schreiber:

    ii. CADTER MAGDALENA RÜBENKAM, bapt. 2 December 1675; godmother: the wife of the princely Hessian tax collector, Justus Heinrich Schreiber; d. 5 August 1676.

    iii. JOHANN HEINRICH RÜBENKAM, bapt. 10 December 1676; godfather: Mr. Johannes Kröschell, rector of Allendorf; conf. at Eschwege 1689. As *Johannes Henricus Rubenkambius Eschwegia-Hassus,* was matr. at the High School at Herborn, Countship of Nassau-Dillenburg, in 1692.[25]

---

[24] For full text of the Metropolitan's letter on behalf of Methe see *Archives of the Rubincam-Revercomb Family: German Documents, op. cit.,* Note 5 above, 17.

[25] Gottfried Zedler and Hans Sommer, *Die Matrikel der Hohen Schule und die Paedagogiums zu Herborn* (1908), 136. In 1693, with five other students at the High School, *Johann Henrich Rübenkamm von Eschwege aus Hessen* co-authored a learned theological dissertation entitled *Schriftmässige Untersuchung der Send-Schreiben an die sieben Gemeine in Asien,* (Biblical Inquiry of the Epistles to the Seven Communities in Asia). The title-page of the work, a photostat of which is in the author's collection, shows that the young authors studied under the famous Herborn professor, Dr. Heinrich Horche. The Nassauische Landesbibliothek (Nassavian State Library) at Wiesbaden, Hessen, has an original copy of the book.

iv. ANNA GERTRUD RÜBENKAM, bapt. 1 May 1678; godmother: her paternal grandmother, the widow of the deceased pastor Friedrich Rübenkam of Oetmannshausen; conf. at Eschwege in 1690.

v. JUSTUS HEINRICH RÜBENKAM, bapt. 27 August 1679; godfather: his maternal grandfather, Herr Rentmeister Justus Heinrich Shreiber; d. at Eschwege 11 January 1681.

4. ANDREAS RÜBENKAM, fifth son of Friedrich Rübenkam and his wife Anna Gertrud Underberg, and ancestor of the Pennsylvania family, was born at Oetmannshausen about 1642. He was confirmed there at Easter, 1654, at the age of twelve years. Later the family removed to Eschwege, from which place on 5 May 1660 he was matriculated at the University of Marburg as a theological student under the name of *Andreas Rubenkamm Eschwegensis*.

Nine years later on 7 June 1669, Andreas Rübenkam married CATHARINA JULIANA GLEIM who was born at Rotenburg about 1647, daughter of Pastor Balthasar Gleim and his wife Anna Margaretha Crollius. The Gleim ancestry of Andreas Rübenkam's wife has been traced with certainty to one Jacob Glime who was born at Eschwege about 1530. He was a *Lohgerbermeister* or master tanner, and was recorded as a householder at Eschwege in 1553. He had two sons, Curt Glime and Jacob Glime, the latter being an ancestor of the Hessian researcher, Kurt Holzapfel.

Curt Gliem (Glime, Gleim), son of Jacob, was born about 1565. A master tanner also, he lived in a section of Eschwege called Brühl, on a corner of the street called Flemmingsgasse. In 1606 his property was valued at 175 gulden. His son Hans Gleim, who followed in the family business of tanning, was born between 1590 and 1595. Before 1615 he married a girl named Anna Spilner; they were both dead before 1640.

Of their seven children, Balthasar (Baltzer) Gleim was born at Eschwege about 24 September 1616. On 9 April 1635 he was matriculated as a theological student at the University of Kassel which had temporarily replaced the University of Marburg during the Thirty Years' War.[26] He became rector of the Rotenburg School before 22 November 1646, when he was godfather to his nephew Balthasar, son of his brother Cyriacus Gleim. In July 1650, he was formally installed as pastor at Wanfried, on the Werra River, a position which he held at the time of his death a quar-

---

[26] Early in the Thirty Years' War, Marburg was captured by the forces of the landgrave of Hessen-Darmstadt, Lutheran ally of the Emperor. Landgrave Wilhelm V of Hessen-Kassel promptly founded a university at Kassel which existed until 1653, when the University of Marburg was restored to the control of Hessen-Kassel.

ter of a century later. He was buried at Wanfried on 23 December 1675, aged 59 years, 12 weeks, 5 days.[27]

On 17 July 1644, Balthasar Gleim married at Eschwege Anna Margaretha Crollius, by whom he had three children: Catharina Juliana Gleim, who married Andreas Rübenkam; Philipp Gleim (1649-1694), graduate of the Universities of Marburg, Bremen, Hanau, Helmstädt and Erfurt, judge and councillor at the Rotenburg Chancery; and Johannes Gleim (1653-1697), a graduate of the University of Marburg, and pastor at Wanfried, as his father's successor, from 1676 until his own death.[28]

The Crollius family first appears in the documents at Marburg in 1447 when Contz Krol (Konrad Krul) was recorded as a citizen in that famous town on the Lahn River. He died in 1455 or 1456. His son Henne (Heinrich) Kroll, citizen and woolenweaver at Marburg from 1455, was living as late as 1499. The latter's widow Cathrein (Krein, Crinchen) was still living in 1530. Their son Michel (Michael) Kroll, was living at Marburg in 1510 and 1514. His son Ebert (Eberhard) Kroll was a citizen and woolenweaver at Marburg from 1537. He was included in the *Musterungsliste,* or census of men of military age, in 1568. He died in 1585. Although Ebert's wife's name is unknown, the records of Marburg show that they had five children, of whom Matthaeus (Mebes, Möbus, Debes, Debus) Kroll was a citizen and woolenweaver at Marburg-Weidenhausen from 1586. In 1590 he paid *Geschoss* (account of municipal finances), was mentioned in a list of inhabitants in 1601, and in 1620 paid both *Geschoss* and *Bürgerschilling* (citizen-shilling, a tax). On 8 February 1620 Matthaeus Kroll sued the masters of the Weaver's Guild who sought to dispossess him of his market-stand. He was living as late as 1632. His wife's name was Elisabeth. Of their six children, Jacob Kroll, landlord of the inn *zum Adler* (At the Sign of the Eagle) at Marburg in 1618, married Margarethe Ruppersberg, by whom he had seven children. Of these, Heinrich Kroll, pastor of Breitenbach, was ancestor of a line of Hessian clergymen, and Burkhard Kroll was mentioned in 1645 as a cavalryman and saddler in the army of the Duke of Saxe-Weimar.

Johannes Kroll, another son of Matthaeus and Elisabeth, was born at Marburg in September 1599, and was confirmed there 16 April 1615.

---

[27] The genealogy of the Gleim family was reconstructed from original sources by Kurt Holzapfel, and published in 1953 by the author of this article in a short mimeographed paper, *The Family of Balthasar Gleim of Eschwege.*

[28] Sketches of Philipp and Johannes Gleim are in Friedrich Wilhelm Strieder, *Grundlage zu einer hessischen Gelehrten und Schriftsteller Geschichte seit der Reformation bis auf gegenwärtige Zeiten,* Band IV (1784), 424-425.

ESCHWEGE BEFORE THE GREAT FIRE OF 1637

From *Eschwege: Wegweiser durch Kreis und Stadt* (1959), 15

He was educated at Marburg and received his master's degree there in 1617. After holding school positions at Langenschwalbach and Nordenstadt, he became rector of the Eschwege School in 1629, and then assistant pastor at Eschwege-Neustadt in 1632. He was dean (bishop) and court preacher at Rotenburg from 1634 to 1653, and in the latter year became Metropolitan of Hersfeld. He was also rector of the Hersfeld Gymnasium (classical school). In 1656 Crollius, who had Latinized the name of Kroll in keeping with the custom of the times, was associated with Johannes Hütterodt, Metropolitan of Eschwege, in drawing up the school regulations of Landgrave Wilhelm VI of Hessen-Kassel. Two years later he became ill and never fully recovered, and in the summer of 1660 resigned the rectorship of the Gymnasium. He died at Hersfeld 19 October 1669, and was buried in *coemiterio inferiore* (*vulgo Frauenberg*), or the cemetery commonly called Frauenberg, no doubt on the hill of that name located outside the town of Hersfeld.

In 1619, after banns had been proclaimed on 13, 20 and 27 June, Johannes Crollius married Catharina Geiter, daughter of Benedictus Geiter of Breithard in the Taunus Mountains, Countship of Nassau-Weilburg. She was buried at Wanfried on 28 January 1681, aged 84 years. They had seven children: Philipp Thomas Crollius, a Rotenburg attorney; Anna Margaretha Crollius, wife of Pastor Balthasar Gleim and mother of Catharina Juliana (Gleim) Rübenkam; Wilhelm Jost Crollius, captain of Hessian militia, member of the town council, and five times mayor of Hersfeld (d. 1684); Johannes Crollius, II (1631-1696), Metropolitan of Sontra and ancestor of the late Dr. Carl Knetsch; Anna Catharina Crollius, wife of Mag. Johann Bernhard Wille (Willius), deacon at Hersfeld; a son born in 1636, died in 1637; and Johannes Laurentius Crollius (1641-1709), an eminent scholar, doctor of theology, rector of the University of Heidelberg (1692-1693), and rector of the University of Marburg in 1699.[29]

Andreas Rübenkam, affiliated through his marriage to Catharina Juliana Gleim, with this Crollius family, became assistant pastor at Eschwege-Neustadt, succeeding his brother Laurentius as pastor there in 1672 upon the latter's elevation to the Metropolitanate. Andreas' home on the market place (*Marktplatz*) is still standing; a snapshot of it is in the present writer's archives, thanks to the generosity of Mr. Holzapfel. He has also generously donated to the writer the signature portion of an original document dated at Eschwege 12 March 1680. The signatures are those of

29 Dr. Carl Knetsch, "Die Familie Crollius: Ein hessisches Theologengeschlecht," *Nachrichten der Gesellschaft für Familienkunde in Kurhessen und Waldeck*, 13. Jahrgang (August, 1938), 49-61; Milton Rubincam, "A Hessian Pedigree: Crollius of Marburg, Ancestral Line of Many American Families," *The American Genealogist*, XXVI (April, 1945), 225-234; additional information provided in recent years by Karl Friedrich von Frank.

Dr. Hieronymus Wetzell, Superintendent; Georg Heiderich Heilman, *Amtmann* (magistrate); M[agister] Laurentius Rübenkam, *Metropolitan und Pfarrer der Altstadt*; Andreas Rübenkam, *Pfarrer der Neustadt*; M[agister] Michael Wiskemann, deacon of Eschwege-Altstadt; Justus Heinrich Schreiber, Rentmeister, father-in-law of Laurentius Rübenkam; Johann Emerich Schreiber, *Rentschreiber*, or treasury clerk; Johannes Holzapfel, Bürgermeister, an ancestor of Kurt Holzapfel; and Johannes Glime (Gleim), Bürgermeister. The main portion of the document, which is in Mr. Holzapfel's private collection, deals with the settling of the church accounts in the classis of Eschwege. From these accounts it appears that the above-named gentlemen did not confine themselves entirely to business, for the records show that they consumed "quantities of wine." A convivial time must have been had by all!

Pastor Andreas Rübenkam died eighteen years later on 3 March 1698, at Eschwege, and was buried 9 March 1698. His widow Catharina Juliana survived him nearly a quarter of a century, dying at Eschwege 22 November 1722.

Issue of 3. Andreas Rübenkam and his wife Catharina Juliana Gleim:

4.   i. JOHANN PHILIPP RÜBENKAM, b. 20 April 1670; bur. 25 February 1725, of whom further.

    ii. JOHANN FRIEDRICH RÜBENKAM, b. at Wanfried 25 January 1672; d. at Eschwege 10 July 1739. Matr. at the University of Marburg 13 November 1688. Rector of the Eschwege School.

    iii. ANNA MARGARETHA RÜBENKAM, b. at Eschwege 4 November 1673; conf. there in 1686; m. 1 June 1699, HIERONYMUS WIGARD (Weychardus, Weichard) DIRCKS (Dirksen), bapt. at Eschwege 7 March 1664, son of Friedrich Dirksen [30] and his wife Catharina Elisabeth Behrmann (Bärmann); bur. at Eschwege 14 October 1727. Matr. at the University of Marburg in 1683, became a teacher in the Eschwege School in 1691, and was chosen *Konrector* of the school in 1697. He was assistant pastor at Eschwege from 1692, and pastor from 1706 until his death. He was the editor of at least two theological works.[31] Issue, all born at Eschwege: 1. ERNST ANDREAS DIRCKS, b. 11 March 1700; godfather: Herr Cappellan Andreas Knobel. Matr. at the University of Marburg in 1716. Was a lawyer at Eschwege. 2. CATHARINA MARGARETHA DIRCKS, b. 2 February 1702; d. at Berlin, Prussia, 11 July 1770; m. as his 2nd wife on 28 August 1725, JOHANN PHILIPP

---

[30] His family was originally from Brabant, now a Belgian province. Friedrich, of the fourth generation, was born at Bremen, but settled at Eschwege where he married in 1662. He held the office of burgomaster of Eschwege.

[31] See Strieder, *op. cit.*, Note 28 above, III (1783), for sketch of Hieronymus Wigard Dircks.

HEINIUS (Hein), b. at Kassel 6 January 1688; d. at Berlin 8 August 1775, aged 87.[32] 3. ERNST LUDWIG DIRCKS, b. 27 February 1704; godfather: Jacob Ernst Boclo. Served as a lieutenant in the army; later was a merchant at Bremen. 4. PHILIPP WILHELM DIRCKS, b. 31 August 1706; godfather: Pastor Johann Philipp Riebekam (Rübenkam), his uncle; matr. at the University of Marburg in 1724. 5. JOHANNA CATHARINA DIRCKS, b. 21 March 1709; godmother: her father's sister, Anna Catharina, wife of Burgomaster Johannes Goddefahrt of Witzenhausen. 6. JOHANN FRIEDRICH DIRCKS, b. 20 September 1712; godfather: Superintendent von Haxthausen of Allendorf; m. 28 October 1743, CATHARINA ELISABETH KALCKHOF, daughter of the apothecary, Joh. Heinrich Kalckhof. Was a lawyer by profession. 7. CATHARINA ELISABETH DIRCKS, d. or bur. 9 September 1718. Her birth or baptismal dates are not stated, but her paternal grandmother, Catharina Elisabeth Bärmännin, was her godmother.

iv. CATHARINA ELISABETH RÜBENKAM, b. at Eschwege 10 March 1676; d. there 2 June 1676.

v. JOHANN ANDREAS RÜBENKAM, b. at Eschwege 10 May 1677; conf. 1691; matr. at Marburg 9 June 1696; m. 23 April 1710, CATHARINA ELISABETH LÖBER. No further record recovered.

vi. MICHAEL WILHELM RÜBENKAM, b. at Eschwege 19 August 1680; conf. 1694; d. there 18 December 1734. Matr. at the University of Marburg 19 September 1696.

vii. MARIA JULIANA RÜBENKAM, b. at Eschwege 25 June 1684; d. there 5 July 1684.

viii. JOHANN KARL RÜBENKAM, b. at Eschwege 11 July 1686; d. there 19 April 1738.

ix. JOHANN GEORG PETER RÜBENKAM, b. at Eschwege 29 July, bapt. 7 December 1689; d. there 21 February 1766.

---

[32] Johann Philipp Heinius studied at the Schmalkalden Gymnasium and the University of Bremen, and became a professor at the University of Halle in 1712. He was awarded the degree of doctor of theology by the University of Frankfurt/Oder, and early in 1730 took up new duties as rector of the Joachimsthal Gymnasium at Berlin. He was elected a member of the Royal Accademy of Sciences (Königliche Akademie der Wissenschaften) at Berlin, 19 Apr. 1732. A member of the Historico-Philologico-Ecclesiastico-Oriental Class of the Academy, in 1744 he was appointed director of the newly-created Class of Philosophy. When he celebrated his jubilee as professor in 1762 a Latin ode was composed in his honor by a colleague. The following year he was honored by a long audience with Frederick the Great, King of Prussia, which touched on a variety of topics of mutual interest. His writings were not numerous. His Latin dissertations before the Royal Academy of Sciences were translated into French and published in the Memoirs of the Academy. He retired as rector from the Joachminsthal Gymnasium at 81, and lived quietly until his death. His first wife, whom he married in 1719, was a Fräulein Heiden who did not long survive the marriage. At present it is not known if Dr. Heinius had issue by her, but he is known to have had children by his second wife, Catharina Margaretha Dircks. One of his sons by her, Johann Philipp Heinius, was professor at Werder Gymnasium, and a daughter, Caroline Philippine Heinius (1738-1763) married in 1754 at the age of 16, as the 2nd of his four wives, Johann Friedrich Claessen, Kirchen-und Domrat (Church and Cathedral Councillor) of Berlin. Samuel Formey, "Éloge de M. Heinius," Nouveaux Mémoires de l'Académie Royale des Sciences et Belles-Lettres, Année MDCCLXXVI [1776], 62-67; Adolf Harnack, Geschichte der Königlich-Preussischen Akademie der Wissenschaften zu Berlin, Band III, 121; information from Karl Friedrich von Frank.

4. Johann Philipp Rübenkam, eldest son of 3. Andreas and Catharina Juliana (Gleim) Rübenkam, was born at Wanfried 20 April 1670. He is of special interest, for he was the last German ancestor of the Rubincam-Revercomb family. At the time of his birth there were living three grandparents: Anna Gertrud (Underberg) Rübenkam, widow of Friedrich; Pastor Balthasar Gleim of Wanfried and his wife Anna Margaretha Crollius; and one great-grandmother, Catharina (Geiter) Crollius, widow of the Metropolitan of Hersfeld, Johannes Crollius. His godfathers were his two uncles, Johannes and Philipp Gleim.

Under the name of *Johannes Philippus Rubencammius Eschwega-Hassus*, he was matriculated at the University of Marburg on 25 April 1687. His professors included Dr. Samuel Andreae, second professor in ordinary of theology; [33] Dr. Heinrich Duysing, third professor in ordinary of theology from 1685, then second and finally first professor in ordinary of theology, 1687; Thomas Gautier, founder of the French community at Marburg and fourth professor in ordinary of theology; Johannes May (Majus), professor of Greek and poesy, and of Oriental languages (except Hebrew); Maximilian Percelli, professor of eloquence and history, including profane and church history; [34] and Dr. Philipp Johann Tileman *genannt* (called, surnamed) Schenk, who became third professor in ordinary of theology in 1687, the year Rübenkam entered the university.

An explanation of the titles of Rübenkam's masters is in order. The "first professor in ordinary" lectured on the New Testament, the second on the Old Testament, the third on *Loci communes* and the *confessio Augustana*, and the fourth on the historical books of the Old Testament, Hebrew and Oriental languages. [35] These "professors in ordinary" were the regular professors who were entitled to take an active part in the administration of the university, and from among whom the rectors of the institution were chosen. "Professors in extraordinary" were not full ranking professors, and could not help to administer the university. The courses in "Systematic Theology," as they were called, included such sub-

---

[33] Dr. Samuel Andreae was the cousin of an ancestor of the late distinguished authority on the old families of New Netherland, William J. Hoffman, F.G.B.S., F.A.S.G.

[34] Maximilian Percelli, under whom Rübenkam studied church history, had an unusual career. He had formerly been a Catholic monk at Pressburg, and at one time was Italian and Latin secretary to the Bishop of Waitzen in Hungary. Converted to Calvinism at Zürich, he came to Marburg as a lecturer in philosophy in 1677, was appointed professor of practical philosophy (ethics and politics) in 1681, and from 1684 to 1694 held the Chair of Eloquence and History, including profane and church history. From 1694 until his death in 1703 he taught profane history only.

[35] Gundlach, *op. cit.*, Note 8 above, 21.

jects as dogma, Christian ethics, refutation of adversaries' errors, polemics, or the art of controversy, and theological disputes.[36]

The whereabouts of Johann Philipp Rübenkam after his graduation from Marburg, presumably about 1690, have thus far not been ascertained. But in 1692 his ruler, Landgrave Ernst of Hessen-Rheinfels, granted him the expectancy (succession) to the parish of Wanfried, then held by his uncle Johannes Gleim. In 1693 Landgrave Ernst died and was succeeded jointly by his two sons, Landgrave Wilhelm the Elder, at Rotenburg, and Landgrave Carl at Wanfried, who confirmed the expectancy.

Pastor Gleim died in 1697, and on 16 October of that year young Rübenkam at Wanfried addressed a petition to Landgrave Carl, whom he saluted as "Most Serene Prince, Most Gracious Prince and Lord." He reminded the landgrave of the expectancy granted to him and requested him to present his name to the Consistory at Kassel. "As Your Serene Highness may order as you choose in this matter," he concluded, "I have the utmost confidence that my petition will not be in vain and that just as you have favored me in the past you will now assist me to take the place of my deceased cousin [sic! uncle] which great favor I will, during all my lifetime, repay by my great respect and sense of duty toward you and your Princely House."

On 6 November 1697 Landgrave Carl, then in Vienna, formally approved the young minister's application. Landgrave Wilhelm, as co-ruler, also signified his willingness that Rübenkam should have the Wanfried parish. After the Hessen-Rheinfels Chancery, on 10 November, interposed no objection, the candidate's name was forwarded to the Consistory, and on 16 January 1698 Johann Philipp Rübenkam was officially installed as pastor of Wanfried.

The following year on 19 July 1699 at Reichensachsen, about four miles southwest of Eschwege, Johann Philipp Rübenkam married a 15-year-old girl, MARGARETHA CATHARINA SARTORIUS. She was baptized at Reichensachsen 26 February 1684, and was the younger, and eventually only surviving daughter of Matthias Sartorius, pastor at Wichmannshausen—where Johann Philipp's grandfather Friedrich Rübenkam had officiated between 1636 and 1639—and Sartorius's nobly born wife, Anna Juliana von Boyneburg genannt Hohenstein. Dr. von. Frank, who has done much work on the von Boyneburg family, informed the author that in those days, when a man attained the ministry, he was elevated to a social position "nearly equal to nobility," and therefore was eligible for

---

[36] *Ibid.*, 18.

the hand of a nobleman's daughter.[37] Otherwise the caste system was rigidly enforced.

Little is known about Pastor Sartorius. His name is the Latinized version of the German *Schneider,* meaning "tailor." When he was matriculated at the University of Marburg 24 March 1664, he was described as being "from Sontra" in Hessen-Kassel. He was already pastor at Wichmannshausen on 14 October 1680 when he married at Reichensachsen Anna Juliana von Boyneburg genannt Hohenstein. Two years later he was an unsuccessful candidate for the pastorate at Datterode. Some time during this period he added to his duties those of pastor of Hoheneiche, a nearby village. He died some time between Easter, 1694, when he was too ill to officiate at the confirmations held at that time, and 8 July 1694, when his successor was installed. His daughter was confirmed the following Easter, 1695, the record reading: *Margaretha Catharina Sartorin, Ehren M. Mathiae Sartorii [gewesener] Pfarrers zu Wichmanshausen, Tochter.*

If nothing is known about Sartorius's background, the same is not true for the antecedents of his wife. The House of Boyneburg [38] was one of the most powerful feudal families of Hessen; its annals extend back to the beginning of the twelfth century.[39] It threw out many branches, some of which are now extinct in the male lines, including the Boyneburg genannt Hohenstein branch to which Anna Juliana belonged which had been seated at Reichensachsen since the close of the fourteenth century.[40]

Anna Juliana's grandfather, Jost von Boyneburg genannt Hohenstein (1554–1619),[41] was a lieutenant-colonel in the army of Hessen-Kassel.

---

[37] The writer has collected a number of other cases in which 16th and 17th century clergymen of humble stock took their wives from noble families.

[38] The history of this family will be presented in detail by the author in a mimeographed monograph, *The House of Boyneburg,* upon completion of Mr. Coddington's researches in Germany.

[39] Baron Rudolf von Buttlar-Elberberg, in his *Stammbuch der althessischen Ritterschaft* (1888), states in his von Boyneburg tables, photostats of which are in the writer's collections, that according to Albrecht Freiherr von Boineburg zu Lengsfeld, the family was descended in the male line from Otto, Count of Nordheim and Duke of Bavaria in the 11th century, but this claim has not been proved satisfactorily. It is known, however, that the Nordheim counts did build and own Boyneburg castle, so that the claim is persuasive, at least.

[40] During the minority of Landgrave Philipp the Magnanimous, in the 16th century, Ludwig von Boyneburg was one of the ten regents of Hessen. In the following century, Baron Johann Christian von Boyneburg was one of the leading German statesmen and a friend of the philosopher, Leibnitz. For eight centuries the castle of Boyneburg, near Wichmannshausen, has been in the possession of this family, the present head of which, Kurt von Boyneburgk, has most graciously provided the author with pictures and information about the ancient fortress, once a favorite residence of Emperor Frederick I, called Barbarossa. The last male representative of the Boyneburg genannt Hohenstein branch was Johann Carl Dietrich von Boyneburg genannt Hohenstein (1729–1792), chief marshal at the court of Landgrave Friedrich II of Hessen-Kassel, the prince whose troops fought for England during the Revolutionary War.

[41] His father Jost von Boyneburg genannt Hohenstein, who died in 1589, was co-owner of Elberberg Castle in Kreis Fritzlar, Hessen. Married three times, he had sons by his first two wives: Catharina von Buttlar, mother of Jost, the younger, and a woman surnamed von Falken-Röhrda.

Married three times, by his second wife Anna von Hanstein-Bornhagen, he had a son Curt Leopold von Boyneburg genannt Hohenstein [42] who was born in 1609 and died at Reichensachsen 18 December 1673, aged 64 years, 4 months. About 1629 or 1630 he married his first cousin once removed, Sabine Sibylle von Boyneburg genannt Hohenstein,[43] born in 1611, who died, also at Reichensachsen, 28 March 1674, aged 63 years 3 weeks. They had at least three sons and four daughters, the youngest of whom was Anna Juliana, born at Reichensachsen in 1646, who married the above-noted Pastor Matthias Sartorius in 1680.

After Sartorius's death and the marriage in 1699 of their daughter Margaretha Catharina Sartorius to Pastor Johann Philipp Rübenkam, the Widow Sartorius went to live with the Rübenkams at Wanfried, east of the Werra River. There she died and was buried 1 February 1703. The entry in the Wanfried parish register, written by her son-in-law, conclusively identifies her as a member of the great von Boyneburg family:

Den 1 Februarii ist weiland H. Magistri Matthiae Sartorii gewesener Pfarrer zu Wichmannshausen und Hoheneiche nachgelassene Wittib Frau Anna Juliana geborene von Boÿneburg genant von Hohnstein zu Reichensachsen allheir begraben und alt worden 57 Jahre weniger 3 Monate. (1 February [1703] The widow of the late Herr Magister Matthias Sartorius, formerly pastor at Wichmannshausen and Hoheneiche, Mrs. Anna Juliana, born von Boyneburg genannt Hohenstein, of Reichensachsen, is buried in this very place, aged 57 years less 3 months.)

Little more is known of Johann Philipp Rübenkam's pastoral activities. On 31 August 1706, he was godfather to his nephew Philipp Wilhelm Dirksen, son of Pastor Hieronymus Wigard Dirksen and his wife Anna Margaretha Rübenkam. When in 1708 the town government of Wanfried issued a decree forbidding the use of snuff in church,[44] Johann Philipp Rübenkam may have had something to do with the issuance of

[42] Curt Leopold had an elder brother Adam who was the ancestor, in the female line, of the von Baumbach family which settled in Milwaukee about the middle of the 19th century; of a branch of the von Eschwege family which came to New York, and of Heintz von Eschwege, the present owner of the Reichensachsen estate, who has contributed much information on the von Boyneburgs of Reichensachsen.

[43] She was the daughter of Jost Christoph von Boyneburg genannt Hohenstein and his wife Sabine, daughter of Colonel Otto Georg von Scholley (1525/26-1583), commandant of the Kassel fortress. The latter was a son of Colonel Henning von Scholley, chamberlain to Landgrave Philipp the Magnanimous. A Brandenburger by birth, Col. v. Scholley had migrated to Hessen early in the 16th century and was present at the famous Diet of Worms in 1521, when Martin Luther defended himself against Emperor Charles V and the greatest princes and prelates of Germany. Jost Christoph von Boyneburg genannt Hohenstein was a son of Philipp von Boyneburg genannt Hohenstein (b. 1556) and his wife Christine von Kochberg, and a grandson of the elder Jost von Boyneburg genannt Hohenstein by his second wife, surnamed von Falken-Röhrda.

[44] Strauss, op. cit., Note 23 above, 103, "Verordnung welche des Tabakschnupfen in der Kirche verboten wurde."

the edict; consider how disconcerting it must have been to a preacher to have his congregation continually sneezing!

Be that as it may, Pastor Rübenkam administered to the spiritual needs of the Wanfrieders for nearly nineteen years. Toward the close of this period his health is said to have been undermined by overwork and his strict attention to duty. That at least is the statement made in a letter to the Hessen-Rheinfels Chancery at Rotenburg, dated 2 April 1716, by Landgrave Wilhelm the Younger, who had succeeded his father, Landgrave Carl, in 1711, and was now ruling jointly with his uncle, Landgrave Wilhelm the Elder. As Rübenkam's "recovery and convalescence are despaired of by all persons," the younger Wilhelm recommended as his successor one Georg Crause, then pastor at Dippach, in Kreis Bacharach in the Palatinate, who was a brother of his Highness's Chancellor Crause.

It appears, however, that an awkward situation had developed and that Rübenkam's illness may have been a "diplomatic" ailment, proposed as a smooth way to ease him out of his office. Under the terms of the Peace of Westphalia in 1648, the state religion of Hessen-Rheinfels had become the Reformed or Calvinist faith. All other religions were outlawed in the principality. The ruling family had turned Roman Catholic, but even so, they were required to defend Calvinism as the state church. But Johann Philipp Rübenkam, it seems, had come to the conclusion that the progressive faith known as Pietism, founded in 1670 by Philipp Jakob Spener, was superior to the strait-laced, dogmatic principles expounded by the Reformed Church. This we gather from Landgrave Wilhelm the Elder's stern letter to the Chancery on 7 December 1716:

> We have been reliably informed that the present Pastor Rübekam at Wanfried, after many remonstrances and exhortations, still refuses to conform to the Reformed religion as introduced into Hessen; that the Kassel Consistory has proceeded to remove the said pastor from his office, and at the same time, since his parochial office should not be vacant long, and it is Our duty to make the nomination, and our noble and friendly Cousin [*sic!* nephew] Landgrave Wilhelm the Younger desires that We nominate Georg Crause, brother of his Chancellor Crause, who is now pastor at Dippach in Kreis Bacharach in the Electoral Palatinate, We, therefore, give Our consent thereto. . . .

Much excitement was evidently caused by the situation at Wanfried, for there was at least one other candidate, besides Crause, for the job. Deacon Johann Christoph Lautermann, of Rotenburg, informed the Chancery in an undated letter that he had "received a reliable message from Kassel stating that the pastor of Wanfried, Rübenkam, has been removed from office because of his heterodoxy and great corruption, and that yesterday, being Sunday, he preached his last sermon." Lautermann then produced a rescript from Landgrave Wilhelm the Elder promising Lautermann the expectancy of the Wanfried parish; one can imagine the good deacon rolling his eyes heavenward as he piously and virtuously informed the Chancery that ". . . I have . . . so lived and conducted myself that I hope no complaint can be made against me."

A month later there was still uncertainty about Rübenkam's case. The Rotenburg Chancery wrote to the Kassel Consistory on 16 January 1717, "It has been announced that Pastor Ruebencamm of Wanfried has left the service and would be degraded. However, we have not yet received any notification and have no certainty of this occurrence." Rübenkam's departure from Wanfried, however, could not have taken place later than January.

He and his family moved westward, taking up their exile at Berleburg, on the Eder River, in the little neighboring state of Sayn-Wittgenstein-Berleburg, whose ruler, Count Casimir, was friendly to Pietists. There he died and was buried 25 February 1725. The church registers of the Evangelical Reformed community at Berleburg contain the record: *Anno 1725 d. 25ten Februarii ist alhier in der Stille begraben worden H.[err] Rübenkam, gewesener Prediger zu Wannfried in Hessen.*

Margaretha Catharina (Sartorius) Rübenkam remained in Berleburg with her children for well over a year after her husband's death. Then in the fall of 1726 with the children she joined a group of Wittgenstein emigrants going to Rotterdam, whence they sailed for England and finally for America. They landed in Philadelphia 2 December 1726.[45]

The Rübenkams settled in Bristol Township, Philadelphia County, where Margaretha Catharina died before 13 May 1727, when letters of administration on the estate of Margaret Catherine *Riebakamen* were granted to her eldest son "Frederick Wm Riebakam." [46] The inventory of her estate was made 12 June 1727 by three appraisers, two of whose signatures are indistinct: L—— Holzapple ——, Y—— C——, and John George. Fifty-two items were listed, including cash, wearing apparel, "a old Red Cow," "a Brindle Cow & Calf," "a Red Cow with brownish head," a saddle and bridle, iron hopples, a harrow with wooden tines, an iron stove, a black walnut table, seven "chears," a pewter dish, two pewter dishes and a basin, "a dozen & a half of plates," "a dozen & a half of spoons," "a little still" (nothing like home-made whiskey!), copper

---

[45] Information from Donald F. Durnbaugh, Instructor in History, Juniata College, Huntington, Pennsylvania, 1 March 1959. See also his article, "Johann Adam Gruber, Pennsylvania-German Prophet and Poet," *The Pennsylvania Magazine of History and Biography*, LXXXIII (1959), 382, hereinafter cited as *PMHB*.

[46] Estate of Margaretha Catharina Rübenkam: Philadelphia Administration Book C, 80, #68:1727. Wills, administrations and deeds cited hereinafter are Philadelphia records, unless otherwise noted.

kettles and teapots, two looking glasses, "a feather bed & billow case," a gun, four earthen mugs, eight drinking glasses, and "3 Window Curtains & other linen."

Issue of 4. Johann Philipp Rübenkam and his wife Margaretha Catharina Sartorius: [47]

1. FRIEDRICH WILHELM RÜBENKAM, b. *ca.* 1700-1702; d. in Bristol Township, apparently unmarried and without issue, before 7 August 1736 when letters of administration on his estate were granted to his brother Justus Rübenkam.[48]

ii. CATHARINA JULIANA RÜBENKAM, bapt. 4 October 1703; godmother: Catharina Agneta Crollius, daughter of the deceased Metropolitan of Sontra, Johannes Crollius II; bur. Upper Germantown burying ground 16 February 1774; m. 1st, at First Presbyterian Church, Philadelphia, 24 9m (November) 1727, JACOB COLLIDAY (Gallade, Galathe, Gollery, Colladay), b. *ca.* 1706; d. int. before 25 October 1750, when letters of administration on his estate were granted to his widow "Julianna Gallade." [49] Issue: 1. MARGRET CATHARINA COLLIDAY, b. 23 September 1728; d. young. 2. ANNA MARIA MAGDALENA COLLIDAY, b. 23 April 1731; d. 6 August 1764, aged 33; m. 7 November 1748, JOHN MELCHIOR MENG, b. 10 April 1726; d. 13 October 1812, bur. Germantown German Reformed churchyard.[50] 3. JACOB COLLIDAY, b. 15 April 1733; m. 8 April 1756, FRONICA WALTER. A wheelwright by trade, he was of Baltimore, Maryland in 1763.[51] 4. CATHARINE COLLIDAY, b. 30 May 1735; m. by license dated 5 October 1763, BALTES RESER (Razer) who was bur. 23 12m (December) 1773, in Germantown Friends'

---

[47] See Rubincam Family Papers, III, V, in GSP for extended genealogies of their descendants, and transcripts of documents (1446-1947) relating to them. The author is indebted to Hannah Benner Roach for additional supplemental data included below.

[48] Estate of Frederick William Rübenkam: Administration Book C, 328, #35:1736.

[49] Estate of Jacob *Gallada:* Administration Book F, 334, #27:1750. Jacob Colliday "was a Burger's Son of Manheim in Pfalz (a place so called) and came to this Country with his Mother very young . . . his Father died crossing the Ocean," according to Blasius Daniel Mackinet. See Note 55, below. "Maria Galete, wid., 38; Sarah Margaret, 7; Jacob, 4," are noted in the "List of Palatines Remaining at New York, 1710," in E. B. O'Callaghan, *The Documentary History of the State of New York* (Albany, 1860), III, 565.

[50] Melchior Meng, son of John Christopher Meng and wife Anna Dorothea Bauman of Germantown, m. 2nd, at Germantown German Reformed Church 22 Nov. 1765, Elizabeth Axe, and 3rd, at First (German) Reformed Church, Philadelphia 5 Apr. 1788, Elisabeth Lehman.

[51] Although Jacob Colliday, Jr.'s wife's name is variously reported as *Fern* or *Jane*, the original marriage license record entered in Richard Peters' Cash Book distinctly reads *Fronica.* It was as Frances (Franey, Fronica, Veronica) that she joined with Jacob Colliday in conveying to Blasius Daniel Mackinet property in Chestnut Hill 5 Aug. 1763. See Deed Book H-19, 211, and *Pennsylvania Genealogical Magazine,* XXI, 315. As Veronica, she is listed as the mother of Susanna, wife of John Swaze, b. 6 Mar. 1762; bapt. 28 Mar. 1785 at St. Michael's and Zion Lutheran Church, Philadelphia.

ground.[52] 5. SARAH COLLIDAY, b. 12 May 1737; m. at German Reformed Church, Philadelphia 10 January 1760, as his 2nd wife, ULRICH MENG, b. 11 June 1731; d. *ca.* 1790.[53] 6. WILLIAM COLLIDAY, b. 16 September 1738; d. 28 November 1823, aged 83, bur. Upper burying ground, Germantown; m. German Reformed Church, Germantown, 18 October 1765, HANNAH PASTORIUS, b. 17 November 1743; d. 11 July 1794, bur. Upper burying ground.[54] 7. SUSANNA COLLIDAY, b. 17 April 1741, perhaps the Susannah Colliday who was bur. 3 May 1816, in Upper burying ground, Germantown. Catharina Juliana (Rübenkam) Colliday, widow of Jacob, m. 2nd, as his 2nd or 3rd wife, BLASIUS DANIEL MACKINET (Macknet) who was bur. in Germantown Friends' ground 6th month (June) 1775.[55] No issue.

iii. JUSTUS WILHELM RÜBENKAM, bapt. 6 August 1705; godfather: Justus Walther Krause, bailiff at Kronberg; d. int. in Bristol Township, Philadelphia County before 21 December 1768, when letters of administration on his estate were granted to his widow and son-in-law John Gorgas; m. 1st, at First Presbyterian Church, Philadelphia, 5th 4m (June) 1735, KATHERINE CONREDS. No known issue. He m. 2nd, at same church, 2 2m (April) 1742, SUSANNA RITTEN-HOUSE, daughter of Peter Rittenhouse (*ca.* 1696-1748).[56] Issue: 1. ANN RÜBENKAM, b. 18 August 1745; bur. 4 April 1815 in St. Thomas' Episcopal churchyard, Whitemarsh Township, Montgomery County; m. as his 2nd wife, CHRISTIAN DONAT (Dunnat) [57] b.

---

[52] Baltes Reser's will, recorded in Will Book N, 340, #191:1774, names his wife Catherine and William Colliday executors. Reser's death notice in *Der Wöchentliche Pennsylvanische Staatsbote*, issue of 4 Jan. 1774, reports his age as 50 years. His widow operated a tavern at the northwest corner of Second and Race Streets in the house formerly occupied by Benjamin Franklin. See PMHB, XL (1916), 219 for their marriage license.

[53] Ulrich Meng, brother of the above-noted Melchior, and son of John Christopher Meng, was of Frederick County, Maryland in 1782. See *PMHB*, XXXII (1908), 112.

[54] William Colliday's will, written in 1818, is recorded in Montgomery County Will Book 6, 196; he had moved to Moreland Township about 1798 from Philadelphia.

[55] Will of Blasius Daniel Mackinet is recorded in Will Book Q, 180, #144:1775. Before his death Mackinet, at the request of his step-daughter Sarah Meng "living in Germantown," wrote an account of "her line of Nativity" which has survived to the present, and is in the possession of Sarah's descendant, Mrs. G. Rogers Harvey of Falls Church, Va. It confirms very closely the data found through German researches, and supplies the birth dates of the children of Catharina Juliana Rübenkam and her first husband Jacob Colliday. Mackinet's testimony regarding the character of the widow Margaretha Catharina (Sartorius) Rübenkam, with whom, as he said, he "was well acquainted," was "that she was a pious good Woman, led a Vertuous life & was an Ornament to her sex. The follies & pleasures of this World she despised & took upon her the . . . Cross of Christ. . . ."

[56] Estate of Justus *Revacum*, Administration Book H, 58, #70:1768. See Milton Rubincam, "Peter Rittenhouse of Cresheim," *National Genealogical Society Quarterly*, XXXI (1943), 42, for account of Peter Rittenhouse whose widow Ann subsequently married John Peter Heisler of Germantown.

[57] Christian Donat was a son of George Donat who was naturalized in 1734, as of Chester Co. *Pennsylvania Archives*, 2nd Series (1890), VII, 124. George Donat subsequently took up land in Springfield Twp., now Montgomery Co., where he died in 1761. Will Book M, 222, #124:1761. Barbara, first wife of Christian Donnit, was bur. in Germantown German Reformed churchyard 9 Sept. 1759, aged 16-10-0. The burial records of Christian and Ann (Rübenkam) Donat, as given in the transcript of the register of St. Thomas' Church, in GSP, differ from the transcript of their tombstones, published in this *Magazine*, XII, 254. The discrepancies are probably accounted for by the poor condition of the stones.

16 July 1740; bur. 6 April 1815 in St. Thomas' churchyard. 2. CATHERINE RÜBENKAM, d. or bur. 10 April 1815, aged 67-1-19; m. German Reformed Church, Germantown, 29 March 1764, HENRICH SCHÜTZ (Scheetz),[58] d. 7 October 1793, aged 51-5-7. Both bur. St. Michael's Lutheran Church, Germantown. 3. MARGARET RÜBENKAM, b. 2 May 1750; d. 24 September 1789; m. JOHN GORGAS, b. 1740; d. 30 October 1823. Both bur. Germantown Mennonite cemetery. 4. JULIANA RÜBENKAM, b. 27 March 1757; d. 9 January 1833; m. 30 March 1775, BENJAMIN GORGAS,[59] b. 19 February 1747; d. 23 October 1821. Both bur. Germantown Church of the Brethren cemetery. 5. SARAH RÜBENKAM, b. 7 July 1759; d. 4 March 1820; m. 11 March 1784, NATHAN LEVERING, b. 19 May 1745; d. 14 June 1812. Both bur. Roxborough Baptist cemetery. 6. SUSANNAH RÜBENKAM, m. *ca.* 1771, ANTHONY JOHNSON, sadler of Germantown, who d. 8 8m (August) 1823 in 78th year.[60] 7. DANIEL RÜBENKAM, d. 17 February 1832 in 67th year; m. ELIZABETH DULL who d. 19 December 1853, in 76th year. Both bur. Germantown Church of the Brethren.

iv. KARL (Charles) WILHELM RÜBENKAM, bapt. 5 May 1707; godfather: his uncle, theological candidate Michael Wilhelm Rübenkam; d. int. in Springfield Township, now Montgomery County, before 27 August 1748 when letters of administration on his estate were granted to his widow and brother Justus Rübenkam; m. BARBARA RITTENHOUSE, daughter of Peter Rittenhouse. She was dec'd by 12 September 1761, having m. James Stern as her 2nd husband.[61] Issue: 1. JUSTUS RÜBENKAM, m. St. Paul's Episcopal Church, Philadelphia, 30 September 1761, SARAH GIBBS. Lived in Moreland Township in 1769; in Warwick Township, Bucks County 1779-1787, and was in Warrington Township, same county in 1800. 2. JACOB RÜBENKAM, m. 20 October 1774, JEMIMA KEMP in Shenandoah County, Virginia.[62] 3. ANN RÜBENKAM, bur. 14

---

[58] Henry Schütz was the son of Gerhard Henrich Schütz (d. 1783, aged 81) who arrived in Philadelphia 27 Aug. 1739, on the snow *Betsie.*

[59] John and Benjamin Gorgas were sons of Johannes Gorgas and his wife Zytian Rittenhouse, daughter of Claus Rittenhouse, and first cousin of the above-noted Peter Rittenhouse.

[60] Anthony Johnson was a son of John Johnson, sadler of Germantown, who died in 1794. For the latter's will see Will Book X, 45, #33:1794. Anthony Johnson was reported to Abington Friends' Meeting 25 11m 1771 for marrying out to one not a member and without his parents' consent. See transcript of Abington Friends' Meeting Minutes, 513, GSP. He seems to have had only two children: *Justus Johnson,* and *Agnes Johnson* who m. 10 10m 1793, *Daniel Thomas, Jr.* For Anthony Johnson's will, see Will Book 8, 59, #122:1823. His death was reported in *Poulson's American Daily Advertiser,* issue of 19 Aug. 1823.

[61] Estate of Charles Rübenkam of Springfield Twp., Administration Book F, 190, #107:1748. By James Stern, Barbara (Rittenhouse) Rübenkam Stern had four children, surnamed Stern: Joseph, Elizabeth, Mary and Margaret.

[62] They were the ancestors of the Revercomb family of Virginia, West Virginia, Missouri, Canada, etc. See "The Noble Ancestry of the Revercomb Family," *The Virginia Magazine of History and Biography,* 68 (October, 1960), 454.

April 1798; m. Trinity Episcopal Church, Oxford Township, Philadelphia County, 16 March 1761, ANDREW REDHEFFER, d. 1817 in Springfield Township, Montgomery County. Both bur. St. Thomas' Episcopal churchyard. 4. CHARLES RÜBENKAM, d. Mill Creek Hundred, New Castle County, Delaware in 1811;[63] m. SUSANNA, surname unknown. 5. WILLIAM RÜBENKAM, dec'd before September 1781; m. ANNA, surname unknown, who m. 2nd, one Simon.[64] 6. PETER RÜBENKAM, living in Newlin Township, Chester County in 1819; m. HANNAH POTTS, living in the same township in 1830, aged between 70 and 80.[65]

v. ANNA CATHARINA RÜBENKAM, b. 25 February, bapt. 27 February 1709; godmother: Anna Catharina, wife of Johannes Goddefahrt, burgomaster of Witzenhausen; d. in Philadelphia 2 May 1770;[66] m. Philadelphia 10 November 1737, as his 2nd wife, JOHANNES WÜSTER (John Wister), bur. 1 2m 1789, aged 80. Issue: 1. JOHN WISTER, d. 24 1m 1739. 2. DANIEL WISTER, b. 4 February 1738/9; bur. 27 10m 1805, aged 66; m. 5 May 1760, LOWRY JONES,[67] b. ca. 1742; bur. 16 2m 1804. Both interred Friends' cemetery, Philadelphia. 3. WILLIAM WISTER, d. 7 6m 1742. 4. CATHERINE WISTER, b. 2 January 1742/3; d. 24 October 1797; m. 16 February 1761, SAMUEL MILES, b. 1 March 1739; d. in Cheltenham Township, Montgomery County 29 December 1805, aged 66.[68] 5. WILLIAM WISTER, b. 29 March 1746; d. in 1800, unmarried.

vi. JOHANNA CATHARINA RÜBENKAM, b. 31 May 1711; godmother: Johanna, wife of Jacob Wilhelm Uckerman. No further record.

vii. MARGARETHA CATHARINA RÜBENKAM, b. 5 July 1713; godmother: her paternal aunt, Anna Margaretha, wife of Hieronymus

---

[63] Charles Rübenkam moved to Delaware from Montgomery Co. about 1802. His will, recorded in New Castle Co. Will Book Q-1, 470, was dated 15 May 1810 and proved 13 December 1811.

[64] William and Ann Rübenkam had issue only two sons: *Johann Carolus (Charles) Ribekam*, b. 17 July, bapt. 18 Aug. 1768, at St. Michael's Lutheran Church, Germantown; godparents: Christofel Green and wife Anna Maria; and *Peter Rübenkam*, b. 1 Sept. 1770, bapt. 29 July 1774, at Germantown German Reformed Church, who d. int. 2 July 1799. Administration Book K, 9, #246:1799. See also Deed Book D-4, 149: 30 Sept. 1781, Andrew Redheffer *et al.* to Benjamin Gorgas.

[65] Descendants of Peter Rübenkam and wife Hannah Potts, daughter of Ezekial and Barbara Potts, settled in Ohio, Missouri, Maryland, Arizona, etc.

[66] In the Bible record quoted at the beginning of the text, Anna Catharina Rübenkam's husband, John Wister, gave 17 May 1770 as the date of her death. However, the *Pennsylvania Chronicle and Universal Advertiser* of Philadelphia, issue of Monday, 7 May 1770, reported that "On Wednesday last departed this life Mrs. Catherine Wister, the virtuous Consort of Mr. John Wister, of this City, Merchant; and on Thursday Evening her Remains, attended by a great Concourse of respectable Inhabitants, were deposited in Friends Burying Ground." Figuring back from Monday, 7 May, to the preceding Wednesday, gives 2 May 1770 as the date of her death.

[67] She was a daughter of Owen Jones and wife Susanna Evans.

[68] Samuel Miles, son of James Miles, was born in Whitemarsh, now in Montgomery Co. See *PMHB*, XLVI (1922), 72 and *Pennsylvania Archives*, 2nd Series (1880), X, 199 for biographical notices of his career.

Weichard Dirksen, pastor of Eschwege-Neustadt. Both John Wister and Blasius Daniel Mackinet stated that the Widow Rübenkam brought three daughters to America, but Mackinet, in an account written for one of her granddaughters, stated that the widow left "the eldest Daughter . . . in Germany in Berlinburgh [sic] where her Father died[.] She is married to a Merchant of that Place named Holtzklaus who—with Wife are, at this time dead. They have left Issue, one Daughter, who is marryed & lives in the . . . [undecipherable] . . . Mother died. Her Husband's name, is I believe, Reuschell." Unless there was an older daughter whose birth record has not been found as yet, it would appear that Mackinet must have meant that one of two "youngest" daughters, rather than the "eldest" daughter, had remained in Berleburg.

THE ACCOUNT WRITTEN BY BLASIUS DANIEL MACKNET

Whereas our Daughter Sarah Meng living in Germantown is desirous of knowing her line of Nativity, I therefore, through this make known unto her the same, so far as I have Knowledge of it.

Her Father was a Burger's Son of Manheim in Pfaltz (a Place so called) and came to this Country with his Mother very young; his Name was Jacob Colladay: his Father died crossing the Ocean. Her Mothers Name is Catharina Juliana, Father's Name Ribenkam, was born 1703 in Wasinfried in Hessia where her Father named Jnº Philip Ribenkam, was Preacher & preached the Gospel 19 years and his Father was Preacher at Eschwig (a Place so calld) Her Mothers Name was Magretta [sic] Catharine, a Ministers Daughter of Saxone in Hessia, her Fathers Name Sattorin, Her Mothers Name Anna Juliana of Luninburgh in Holstein. This may serve as a Memorendom, if perhaps sooner or later some of the Relations should come to this part of the World. Your Grand Mother, a Widow, came over with 6 grown Children in 1726, Viz. 3 Sons & 3 Daughters the eldest Daughter she left in Germany in Berlinburgh, where her Father died she is marryed to a Merchant of that Place, named Holtzklaus who—with his Wife are, at this time dead. They have left Issue, one Daughter, who is marryed & lives in the [undecipherable] Mother died. Her Husband's name, is I believe, Reuschell. Here follows a List of your Mothers Children born in this Country Viz—

1st	Margaret Catharina, born	1728	Sept 23	dead
2	Anna Maria	1731	April 23	
3	Jacob Colladay	1733	dº	15
4	Catharine	1735	May 30	
5	Sarah	1737	dº	12
6	William	1738	Sept 16	
7	Susanna	1741	April 17	

And Whereas I was well acquainted with your Grand Mother, I can give her the Testimony that she was a pious good Woman, led a Virtuous life, & was an Ornament to her Sex. The follies & pleasures of this World, she despisd, & took upon her the [undecipherable] Cross of Christ [rest of line undecipherable]

Blasius Daniel Macknet

CONCERNING THE NAME RÖVEKAMP-RÜBEKAMP

By Rudolph Rübecamp *

Names of the type *Rövekamp-Rübekamp* belong to the large group of word-formations composed of a German word plus the ending *Kamp* (Latin *campus*). They are common in the Low German Linguistic Area [1] between the Elbe and the Rhine Rivers, especially in the province of Westphalia and adjacent areas, where they serve as names for fields and towns. The Latin word *campus* was adopted in the form of *Kamp* in Low German at an early time to designate an enclosed field or piece of land belonging to an individual owner who tilled it,[2] as contrasted to an *Allmende*—common land belonging to the entire village.

So early as the eleventh century *Kamp* occurs in composition: documented in 1006 A.D.,[3] *Nitilcampum* signifies "a field overgrown with

---

* Dr. Rudolf Rübecamp studied at the University of Hamburg, stressing Romance languages, Latin and English. He earned his Ph.D. degree in 1930, and passed the state examination in 1932. At present he is a professor in the Hamburg-Eppendorf Gymnasium for Boys, teaching French, Spanish, and Latin. He is also "Professeur" in the Institut Francais of Hamburg. For some years he has been actively engaged in genealogical research on families named Rövekamp and Rübekamp. He and Mr. Milton Rubincam of Washington, D. C. have had active correspondence on the subject. In the brief article which Dr. Rübecamp has contributed he demonstrates how the genealogist can make use of philology, the science of words, especially names, and of statistical survey methods, such as the table of frequency of the occurrence of the name *Rövekamp-Rübekamp*.

[1] Ralph D. Owen: The terms "Low German" and "High German" have nothing to do with social distinctions; they are purely geographic terms. The coastal plain stretching from Holland to the mouth of the Elbe River is low ground. It includes part of the Low German Linguistic Area. The Dutch language of the Netherlands—until 1550 a part of the German empire—and a number of dialects in modern Germany are included in this linguistic group. While the dialects differ among themselves, they have much in common with English as it was spoken before the latter assimilated a large body of French words. The Angles, Saxons and Jutes who conquered Britain in 450 A.D., had come from this continental European coastal plain, and had carried their Low German dialects with them.

Middle and southern Germany, from Hessen in the north to Bavaria in the south, is high land; dialects in these areas are therefore called "High German" and constitute a High German Linguistic Area. Martin Luther's translation, about 1525, of the Bible into a composite form of High German, set the pattern for what soon became the standard language of all German lands. High German differs from Low German in three important ways. It uses the initial sound of *pf* for the Low German *p*; the initial sound of *s* or *z*, for the Low German *t*; and it uses a grammatical structure almost as complex as Latin. The definite article in standard High German has 24 forms to show gender, number or case; Low German has only two: *de* and *det*. English has only one: *the*.

High German	Low German	English
Pfund	Pund	pound
Pflanzë	Plantë	plant
essen	atten	eat
heiss (rhyme with ice)	hot	hot
zwei (rhyme with buy)	twee (rhyme with say)	two
Zeit (rhyme with kite)	Tiet (rhyme with seat)	tide, time

[2] Dr. Paul Cascorbi, edit., *Die Deutschen Familiennamen* (7th revised edition, Berlin, 1933), 286. This publication by the Bookstore of the Waisenhaus, Halle/Saale, treats German family names historically, geographically and linguistically.

[3] Adolf Bach, "Die deutschen Ortsnamen," *Deutsche Namenskunde* (Heidelberg, 1954), II, Band 1/2, paragraph 323.

nettles," hardly a compliment to its owner; in 1343,[4] *de Vulekamp,* "a bad field," is mentioned in the parish records of Bredenfleth on the Elbe, southwest of Hamburg. In addition *Kamp* regularly occurs in four combinations: (1) the location or quality of the field, as *Hogenkamp* (high), *Neukamp* (new); (2) what is grown in the field, as *Appelkamp* (apples), *Blomenkamp* (flowers), *Bökenkamp* (beech trees), *Ellerkamp* (alder trees), *Haverkamp* (oats), *Kleekamp* (clover), or *Röwekamp* (plants of the genus *beta,* hence beets, carrots and turnips); (3) what is located in the field, as *Kätenkamp* (a cottage), or *Mühlenkamp* (a mill); (4) the ownership of the field, as *Monekekamp* (monk's field) or *Ridderkamp* (knight's field).

In the cities and towns of the Low German Linguistic Area, such as Hamburg, Bremen, Münster, or Bielefeld, at the present time there are many names ending in "-kamp," some of them being family names, and others, street names.

In this same area there are numerous examples of the name "Rövekamp" or "Rübekamp" used to designate a landmark. De roevekamp in Hamburg records is mentioned as early as 1264, 1268, and 1288 [5] and is shown on maps of Hamburg in 1588, 1767, 1796 and 1824. It was located west of the present main railroad station. In Barmbeck, a suburb of Hamburg, Rübekamp Street, not referring to the roevekamp of 1264, has existed since 1900. A station of the elevated electric railway on that street bears the same name. Then in Oldenburg there is a street named Rövekamp; in Dissen, near Osnabrück, a street named Röwekamp; and Bremerhaven, Bielefeld and Dortmund each have a Rübenkamp Street.

The earliest instances of the name Rövekamp-Rübenkamp as a family name are documented in the fifteenth and sixteenth centuries, when city governments found it necessary for every individual to have a family name. Such instances are: Hartlef Rövekamp, 1446, in Osnabrück; Hans and Heinrich Rövekamp, 1465, in Einbeck, forty miles south of Hannover; Johann and Peter Rövekamp, 1581 in the parish of Bützfleth, southwest of Hamburg; Gerd Rubbenkamp (Ruwenkamp), 1494 and 1497, in Emden, near the mouth of the Ems River and the North Sea; Herman Rübekamp, 1585, in Weende, north of Goettingen; Johann Rübekamp, 1585, in Ischenrode, a district of Goettingen, Hannover; Joachim Rövekamp, died 1585 in Völksen, fifteen miles southwest of the city of Hannover; Johann and Thomas Rövekamp, 1585, in Völksen; Jo-

---

[4] Heinrich Borstelmann, *Familienkunde des Landes Kehdingen* (Hamburg, 1929), 2. This "Family History of the Area Kehdingen" was published by Zentralstelle für Niedersächsiche Familiengeschichte, the Central Organization for Low Saxon Family History.

[5] C. F. Gaedechens: *Historische Topographie der Freien und Hansëstadt Hamburg und ihrer nächsten Umbegung von der Entstehung bis auf die Gegenwart.* (Historical Topography of the Free and Hanseatic City of Hamburg and its immediate surroundings from the beginning to the present.) Published by W. Mauke Sons, Hamburg (1880), 47-48, 69.

hann Rövekamp, born *ca.* 1555 in Westfeld near Lübbecke, Westphalia; resided in 1585 at Nordstemmen, twenty miles south of the city of Hannover.[6]

In the seventeenth century, in addition to the Friedrich Rübenkam family of Hessen-Kassel which Mr. Milton Rubincam has so successfully traced, there is available information about two other families: that of Kort (Curt) Roefekamp (Rövekamp), who died in 1685 at Delmenhorst, southeast of Oldenburg;[7] and the Röwenkamp family of Sulingen and Bruchhausen,[8] places which lie about sixty and seventy miles northwest of Münster in Westphalia.

A recent survey of the Rövekamp-Röwekamp-Rübenkamp name in its various forms in thirty communities in Germany reveals several highly suggestive facts:

1. The original name is Low German: Rövekamp, Röwekamp. Its High German translation is Rübenkamp.

2. The Low German forms occurred 140 times; of these, Rövekamp appeared 35 times, and Röwekamp 91 times.

3. The High German forms occurred only twenty times; of these Rübekamp occurred five times, and Rübenkamp fifteen times.

3. In communities where it appeared ten or more times, it was found that the Low German forms occurred in Münster 29 times; in the Osnabrück area 17 times; in Essen ten times. The High German forms occurred in Mühlheim on the Ruhr ten times.

4. The center from which the name spread is the province of Westphalia, and particularly its capital, Münster, in the Low German Linguistic Area.

In the light of these findings, it would seem that anyone wishing to do further research on the progenitors of his Rövekamp, Röwekamp or Rübenkamp family would do well to concentrate on the area of Westphalia.

---

[6] Milton Rubincam, Outline of the History of the Rubincam, Revercomb Family.

[7] The baptisms of four of his children are recorded between 1660 and 1681. His descendants have been identified, some of whom as living in Hamburg, others in the United States.

[8] *Berend Hinrich Röwekamp* was one of three brothers who were born at Sulingen between 1670 and 1689. He probably practised the trade of cabinet-maker and joiner, and also cultivated a small piece of ground. His name appears in the list of *Ackerbürger* (citizens owning some acres of land). Because in 1710 the town burned and all its vital records were destroyed, to date it has been impossible to trace his ancestry. His son *Johann Hinrich Röwekamp*, b. 1709; d. 1761 in Sulingen, was also a cabinet-maker. His son, of the third generation, *Hinrich Wilhelm Röwekamp*, b. 1748, took up his father's trade. In 1780 he found a wife in Bruchhausen and settled there. Their son *Hinrich Wilhelm Röwekamp, Jr.*, b. 1788 in Bruchhausen; d. there in 1839, like his father and grandfather was a cabinet-maker by trade. *Anton Heinrich*, eldest son of Hinrich Wilhelm, Jr., was born in 1821 in Bruchhausen. He removed to Hamburg, became a citizen of Hamburg, and established a firm that manufactured chairs for the export trade. He died in 1871. He wrote his name either "Rübekamp" or "Rübecamp." He was the grandfather of the present writer. The family is still represented in Bruchhausen.

NOTES ON THE SCULL FAMILY OF NEW YORK, NEW JERSEY AND PHILADELPHIA.

CONTRIBUTED BY WILLIAM ELLIS SCULL.

PIETER JANSEN SCHOLL, the propositus of the Scull family of this monograph, was in New Amsterdam in 1661, where his name was indifferently written Schoel, Shull, Schuyl, Scholt, Skull. In March of that year he was a plaintiff with Abel Hardenbroeck in a suit at law against Coenraet Ten Eyck.*

On November 26, 1661, at his marriage to Margaretje, daughter of David Provoost,† he is described, on the records

---

* *Court Minutes of New Amsterdam,* iii, 275 *et seq.*

† DAVID PROVOOST, born Amsterdam, Holland, 10 August, 1608 ; came to New Amsterdam before April, 1639, perhaps with Governor Kieft and his company in March, 1638. He was a trader of the Dutch West India Company, 1640 ; commissary of provisions, tobacco inspector, commissary at Fort Good Hope, Hartford, Connecticut, where the Dutch maintained against the English a separate and independent government, 1642. He returned to New Amsterdam in 1647. He was schoolmaster, notary, attorney, counsellor, commissioner and commander of military forces. His name is at the head of the list, 2nd February, 1652, of the last Board of *Nine Men* who were, says Dr. O'Callaghan, "The immediate precursors of the Burgomasters and Scheppens, and of a municipal form of government in the City of New Amsterdam. They were the chosen representatives of the entire commonalty, and it was declared in their commissions that what they did should be the act of the whole people." They held their sessions in David Provoost's school-room. He was also a member of the Governor's Council and in 1654 was schout fiscal of the Brooklyn district ; and in May, 1655, schout or temporary secretary to the three Dutch towns, Breuckelen, Amersfoort [Flatlands] and Midwout [Flatbush], all of which were included in the Brooklyn district. He died 3 January, 1656, leaving a widow, Grietje or Margaretta Gillis. Her name is frequently spelled in the records:

of the Collegiate Dutch Church of New Amsterdam, as of the Hague.

At the Grand Church of the Hague, Pieter Jansen Scholl was baptized April 18, 1634, the son of Jan Pietersen Scholl and Annetje Claesdr van Soelen. He was preceded in Holland by three generations of Scholls and, in England, by a long line of ancestors whose patronymic was variously spelled Schuyl, Scholt, Schoel, Skull, Scull.

The Holland ancestors, proved by documentary evidence are briefly:

HARMEN SCHOLL, who, for a time of Brielle, a town just south of the Hook of Holland, purchased a house at the Hague in 1596, and there died in 1604. By his wife Maritgen Willems he had several children, among them:

PIETER HARMENSEN SCHOLL, born at Brielle; married Maria Matthysdr van Nyenhoven, 21 May, 1606, and, among other issue had:

JAN PIETERSEN SCHOLL, who was attached to the household of the Prince of Orange between 1640-1649, and deceased *circa* 1652. In 1647, he was appointed forrester of Etten and de Leur with Nicolaes Henric Smyers. The last occasion on which his signature is found, is in 1649, in connection with Dirck Claesr van Soelen, his brother-in-law. In 1652, Annetje Claesdr van Soelen, widow of Jan Pietersen Scholl, acknowledged house-rent debt to Cornelia Nies, widow of the late General Carel Nies. The baptismal Registers of the Grand Church, Hague, show several children of Jan Pietersen Scholl and his wife Annetje Claesdr as there baptized, and in 1634, Pieter Jansen Scholl, the propositus before mentioned.

Pieter Jansen Scholl of New Amsterdam took a more or less active part in the affairs of the little town. When in February, 1664, the burghers and inhabitants were taxed for the " fortification of the city " he was assessed 100 florins. A few months later the Dutch Colony passed under English

Jellis, Jellisen, Yllus and Yelsij. She was probably married in Holland and emigrated with her husband. She was the daughter of Gillis Jansen Verbrugge and Barbara Schut. In March, 1643, David Provoost gave to Gillis Jansen Verbrugge a power of attorney to receive an inheritance accruing to his wife by the decease of her uncle in France, of which country she was probably a native. She was living 29 July, 1701, when she acknowledged a deed to her son, Jonathan Provoost of a house and lot "on the east side of the great street, formerly called the Prince graft" [Broad Street].—*Cf.* Bergen's *Kings County Settlers; New York Genealogical and Biographical Record,* Volume VI, p. 3 *et seq.; Prévost-Provoost-Provost Family Record,* New York, 1895.

control, 4 September, 1664. About this time he resided on Hoogh straat * and may have continued there as late as 13 August, 1671, when his son David was baptized at New Amsterdam.† There is, however, some evidence to indicate that he was living in Brooklyn in 1667, as on 20 August, 1667, he and Denys Isaack Van Sartervelt, " honest persons " were witnesses to a deposition involving property. On 27 November, 1668, he sold a house and lot in Flatbush and was a party to a deed for land there, 27 August, 1677.‡

In 1673, his name appears on the Hempstead census as Peter Janse Schol § and at this Long Island settlement the remainder of his life was apparently spent. Of his homestead lands on the " south woods " he conveyed fifty acres to his " beloved son-in-law," Hendrick Mandeville, by deed of 14 June, 1684,‖ and died before 31 December, 1697.¶

The entry of his marriage to Margaritje Provoost, already alluded to, reads: 26 Novemb., 1661. Pieter Janszen Scholt, Uÿt den Hage, en Grietje Provoost, Uÿt't Vlacke bosch.** She was baptized at the New York Dutch Church, 24 February, 1641. According to Edwin R. Purple, in his *Sketch of David Provoost of New Amsterdam and Some of his Descendants,* a patent for 20 morgens, about 40 acres, located in Midwout, Flatbush, Long Island, was issued to her 9 May, 1660. It is possible that this patent was to her mother of the same name.

Children of Pieter Jansen and Grietje (Provoost) Scholt, the first four baptized at the New York Dutch Church. The sons, John and Peter, reverted to the English spelling of their surname, while David, and many of his descendants, adhered to the Dutch form.

1. i. ANNETJE,[2] baptized 16 July, 1662; died before 21 April, 1699; married, as first wife, Hendrick Mandeville, or de Mandeville, 18 July, 1680, a land owner at Hempstead and a patentee of Pacquenack or Pompton Plains, New Jersey. Through her

---

* *Court Minutes of New Amsterdam,* vol. V, 32, 222.

† *Records of the Reformed Dutch Church in New York.*

‡ Conveyances, Brooklyn, Kings County, book ii, 179. See *New York Genealogical and Biographical Record,* vol. LIV, 306.

§ Bergen, op. cit., 256.

‖ *Hempstead Town Records.*

¶ *Ibid.,* Liber D, 55. Printed Records, vol. ii, 171-2.

** *Records of the Reformed Dutch Church in New York.*

†† *New York Genealogical and Biographical Record,* vol. vi, 4.

son, David de Mandeville,* she had a line of descendants †
who had large land holdings on both banks of the Hudson as
far north as Poughkeepsie. Her great-granddaughter Hannah
Mandeville married Daniel Birdsall, and their family residence, the famous Birdsall House at Peekskill, is said to have
sheltered more American officers during the Revolution than
perhaps any other house in the Colonies.‡

   ii. GRIETJE, baptized 24 Sept., 1664.
2. iii. JOHN, baptized 15 Oct., 1666; died 8 April, 1748.
   iv. DAVID, bapt. 13 Aug., 1671; removed to the Raritan, New Jersey.
3. v. PETER, died Oct., 1739; married (2) Jane Mott.

2. JOHN [2] SCULL (*Peter Jansen* [1]), baptized at New Amsterdam, 15 October, 1666; died at Great Egg Harbor, 8 April,
1748.§ He sold his lands at Hempstead, Long Island, in 1691
and about 1695, possibly somewhat earlier, removed to West
Jersey. On 29 November of that year, being then described
as late of Long Island, he purchased of Thomas Budd of Philadelphia two hundred and fifty acres of land at Great Egg
Harbor in two lots, "one between the marsh next to the Sound,
Peter Cowanover and Patconck Creek; the other between said
marsh, Jonas Valentine and Patconck Creek." ‖ He acquired
other land and became identified with public affairs in the
young settlement. In May, 1701, he was appointed special
tax assessor for Egg Harbor.¶ On 26 January, 1717,** he was
commissioned Justice of the Peace and of the Courts of
Gloucester County and doubtless served many years in such
capacity.

This was the period of exodus from the Long Island towns
to the greater opportunities of the Delaware River and Jersey
coast-line. Of the pioneers some had the urge of the whaling
industry, one of the most lucrative of early eighteenth-century
avocations, whales being numerous from Sandy Hook to the
Capes of the Delaware. Others of the pioneers were members

* The Marquis de Chastelleux notes in his *Travels in North America* of 1780
that, "Approaching Pompton, I was astonished at the degree of perfection to
which agriculture is carried." Continuing, he draws especial attention to the
well-cultivated and fertile lands of "the Mandeville brothers, whose father
was a Dutchman and cleared the farms his sons now till."—Harland, *Some
Colonial Homesteads and their Stories.*

† See *Yellis Jansen de Mandeville of Garderen, Holland, and Greenwich Village on Manhattan Island, and Some of His Descendants: New York Genealogical and Biographical Record,* xxxviii, 284 *et seq.*

‡ Roebling, *Journal of the Reverend Silas Constant,* Philadelphia, 1901, 257.

§ *New Jersey Archives, First Series,* xxx, 422.

‖ *Ibid.,* 56, 59, 665.

¶ *Leaming and Spicer's Laws of New Jersey,* edition of 1758.

** *Publications of The Genealogical Society of Pennsylvania,* viii, 64.

811

of, or inclined to, the doctrines of the religious Society of
Friends. Indeed, this particular inclination may have been

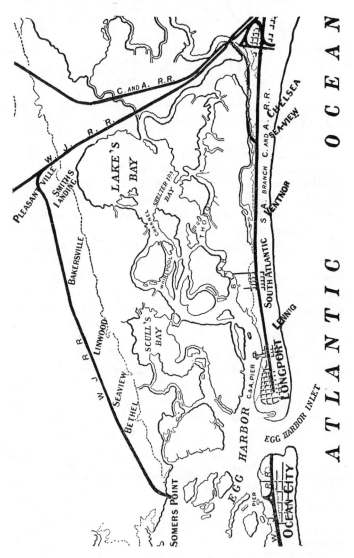

the primary cause of John Scull's removal. Friends meetings
were early established along the Jersey shore; that of Great
Egg Harbor in 1695, when John Somers, an extensive planter,

was made overseer, and Jonathan Adams, John Scull, Jonas Valentine and Peter Conover were in membership. In 1716, a Friends meeting house was built at Seaville, in Cape May County. The principal contributors from Gloucester County were John Somers and one [John] Scull. Known as the old Cedar Meeting House it is still standing.

John Fothergill, an eminent minister among Friends, visiting the provinces in 1722, writes that he "had a religious meeting at the house of John Scull, between Great Egg Harbor and Cape May, 7th 1 mo., 1722, which was well attended."

The Journal of John Chalkley also mentioned a meeting at John Scull's:

> From Cape May, we traveled along the sea-coast to Egg Harbor. We swam our horses over Egg Harbour river, and went ourselves in canoes, and afterwards had a meeting at Richard Somers' which was as large as could be expected, considering the people live at such a distance from each other.* The next meeting we had at John Scull's † [8th of the third month, 1726].

As early as 6th. first month, 1726/7, John Scull was made overseer of Great Egg Harbor meeting and first day services were ordered to be held at his house.

Whether by the pursuit of whaling,‡ or agriculture, or both, John Scull amassed a competence. This he disposed of by

* For many years after the first settlements on the ocean and river the only roads between them were the Indian trails. One of these started from Somers' Point and it was along this trail that visiting Friends were obliged to travel.

† Journal of Thomas Chalkley, 65.

‡ Dr. Daniel Coxe's Account of New Jersey, written about 1688, contains the statement:

"I have at the Expense of above Three thousand pounds settled a Towne and Established a ffishing for Whales which are very numerous about Cape May, both within the Bay and without all along the sea coast, which I am assured if well mannaged will bring in above £4000 per Annum all charges Defrayed." . . . . . .

"Because the only thing which has hindered our setting up this ffishery was want of salt, wee have lately sent over diverse ffrenchmen skillful in making salt by the sun in pitts or pans, whoe assure us that there are many convenient places upon the Coast over against the places of ffishing where millions of Bushell may be made at the Expense of 4 pence per Bushell."— *Biographical Notice of Doctor Daniel Coxe of London,* by Gideon Delaplaine Scull of Oxford, England, in *Pennsylvania Magazine of History,* vol. vii, 317-337.

The Boston News Letter of March 17 to 24, 1718, has this item: "We are told that the whale men catch'd six whales at Cape May and twelve at Egg Harbour."

will of 15 March, 1745,* giving to each of his children a proportionate share of his real and personal estate, and to his youngest sons, Recompense, Gideon and Isaiah, all his "Right to Absecom Beach." As a tribute to the business capacity of his wife he constituted her sole executor.

His wife, Mary Somers, who survived him, was in all probability, a sister of his neighbor, John Somers,† founder of the well known New Jersey family of that surname. His will named all of his children ‡ except David, who was then deceased.

Children of John Scull, order according to will:

    i. JOHN,³ removed to Cape May County, New Jersey.

4. ii. ABEL, married (1) —— Tonkin; (2) Martha Hughes.

    iii. PETER, removed to Tuckahoe, Cape May County; died intestate leaving good estate administered upon by brother, John Scull, "gentleman" of that county, 25 May, 1751.

    iv. DANIEL, married 14 June, 1731, Hannah Mannery; was collector of Egg Harbor; died intestate before 25 Nov., 1751, leaving widow, Hannah.

    v. BENJAMIN, removed to Cape May County.§

    vi. MARGARET, married Robert Smith.

5. vii. RECOMPENSE, married Phebe Dennis.

6. viii. GIDEON, married Judith Bellangee.

    ix. MARY, married (1) Jonas Wood of Great Egg Harbor; his will, proved 4 Nov., 1732, named issue; his widow married (2) 7 March, 1733, Abel Lee.

* New Jersey Archives, xxx, 422.

† John Somers, 1640-1723, said to have been a connection of John Lord Somers, Lord High Chancellor of England, and of Sir George Somers, discoverer of the Bermudas, was a native of Worcester. He early became a follower of George Fox and turned his attention to Penn's Holy Experiment on the Delaware. He purchased 500 acres of land in Pennsylvania and was in that Province on, or before, 8 September, 1682, when he witnessed Thomas Frame's will, the first to be probated at Philadelphia. He settled in Upper Dublin, now Somerton, but removed to Great Egg Harbor, New Jersey, about 1693. Here, in 1695, he purchased 3000 acres, which remained in his family's possession many years and was known as "Somerset Plantation," or Somers Point, from an early period, possibly from the establishment of the ferry, in 1693, across Great Egg Harbor River to Beesley's Point. Many years justice of the peace and of the Courts of Gloucester County, he also served in the memorable Assembly of 1708-9. Among the most noted of his descendants was Richard Somers, a Colonel of militia, Judge of the County Court, and an active Whig during the Revolution; also the latter's son, Richard Somers, a gallant naval officer, who lost his life in the historic affair before Tripoli, Africa, 4 September, 1804.

‡ We have the following melancholy Account, from Absecum on Egg-harbour, viz., That on the 7th of May past, at Night, Deborah the Wife of Nehemiah Nickerson, and Granddaughter of John Scull of the same place, with a Girl about 10 Years of Age, and a Negroe Boy, attempted to come on Shore in a Canoe, from the Beach, where they lived; but as appears by all Circumstances, they lost themselves in the Dark; and a great Storm happening at the same time, they put ashore on a small Island in the Marsh; where, their Canoe driving away, they all three unhappily perish'd. — The Pennsylvania Gazette, May 25 to June 1, 1738.

§ Descendants of the Scull brothers who settled in Cape May County are still resident in that county.

x. CATHARINE, married Amos Ireland of Egg Harbor; his will, proved 14 Jan., 1745, named issue.

xi. RACHEL, married (2) James Edwards.

xii. ISAIAH, married Ann ——. Issue: Abigail Scull.

xiii. DAVID, will dated 23 Sept., 1742, described him as of Great Egg Harbor; left real estate to brothers Recompense, Gideon and Isaiah; personalty to father, John Scull.

3. PETER [2] SCULL (*Peter Jansen* [1]), born, doubtless, on Long Island; died at Great Egg Harbor, New Jersey, between 28 August, 1739 and 8 October, of the same year, the dates respectively of his will and the inventory of his estate. He left Long Island for the greater opportunities of West Jersey where he purchased one hundred acres on the coast near Great Egg Harbor and adjoining Bear Swamp. At the time of this transaction, 10 August, 1700, he was described as of " near Great Egg Harbour." * He later added materially to his original land holdings and, at the time of his decease, his estate was close to a thousand acres.†

The name of his first wife has not been ascertained; he married (2), 20 February, 1731, Jane Mott who survived him.

Children of Peter Scull, order according to will:

i. PETER,[3] of Great Egg Harbor; will of 10 Feb., 1764; proved 22 March of same year, named wife Susanna to whom is given one-half of estate to bring up children. Issue: 1. *Peter Scull* who is to have one-half the estate, 2. *Samuel Scull*, 3. *Susanna Scull*, 4. *John Scull*, 5. *Nicholas Scull*, 6. *Hezekiah Scull*, 7. *James Scull*, 8. *Mary Scull*, 9. *Catharine Scull*.

ii. PHILIP, married (1) 14 Sept., 1737, Abigail Townsend; married (2) Elizabeth ——, who survived him. His will, executed 10 Aug., 1773; proved 7 Sept. following, described him as of Great Egg Harbor, named wife Elizabeth, and made Richard Somers and David Scull executors.

iii. SAMUEL, married (1) 14 Nov., 1745, Ruth Hickman. (2) Mrs. Hannah Steelman, who is named in his will of 3 June, 1774, proved 28 June, 1777, together with her children Nicodemus Steelman, Judith Steelman, Hannah Steelman, Christian Steelman.

iv. DANIEL, of Gloucester Township, Gloucester County, married Rachel ——, who is constituted executor in his will of 26 Jan., 1764, under which the following children are legatees. Issue: 1. *Jemima Scull*, 2. *Hannah Scull*, 3. *Jeane Scull*, 4. *Judith Scull*, 5. *John Scull*, 6. *David Scull*, 7. *Philip Scull*.

v. DAVID, married Hannah ——. His will of 20 Feb., 1784, proved 9 April, 1793, described him as of Great Egg Harbor, named wife Hannah, who, with David Somers, is constituted executor; son *David* and grandsons *Recompense Scull, David Scull* and *Daniel Scull*, sons of David Scull.

vi. JOHN, named in father's will.

vii. MARY, married Nathan Lake, son of John Lake of Egg Harbor.

---

* *New Jersey Archives*, second series, vol. xxi, 673.

† *Ibid.*, vol. xxx, 207, 422.

viii. PATIENCE, married Peter Truax of Gloucester.

ix. ELIZABETH, married 6 March, 1735, Joseph Townsend.

x. MARGARET, married 5 Jan., 1731, Charles Steelman. Issue: *Gartrey Steelman*, named in grandfather's will.

xi. ANN, died after 28 Aug., 1739.

4. ABEL [3] SCULL (*John,*[2] *Peter Jansen* [1]) born, possibly, on Long Island; died in Greenwich township, Gloucester County, New Jersey, in November, 1762. It was no doubt economic pressure that caused him to remove from Egg Harbor, where, however, he continued to hold the large cedar swamp noted in his will of 7 March, 1759.* In addition to his home plantation in Greenwich which he gave to his son Abel, he had another in Springfield township, Burlington County, which was devised to son Joseph. His two sons and brother-in-law Edward Tonkin were made executors of his will.

He married first ———— Tonkin; and secondly, 16 April, 1749, Martha Hughes, who survived him.

Children of Abel Scull; order according to will:

    i. ABEL,[4] of Greenwich, Gloucester County; married 1758, Martha, daughter of Samuel Shivers, and died without issue *circa* 1 Feby., 1763,† leaving a good estate.

    ii. MARY, married —— Doughty.

    iii. SARAH, married —— Hawkins.

    iv. JOSEPH, named in will.

    v. RACHEL, under age in 1759.

    vi. NAOMY, under age in 1759.

5. RECOMPENSE [3] SCULL (*John,*[2] *Peter Jansen* [1]) born at Great Egg Harbor; died there in September, 1792. In 1749 he was one of those to receive bounty for a wolf's head, animals of prey continuing to infest that region,‡ (*vide infra* under No. 6).

He married Phebe Dennis who, with son John, is constituted executor of his will of 21 March, 1786, proved 1 October, 1792.§

Children of Recompense and Phebe (Dennis) Scull, order according to will:

    i. JOHN,[4] married Sarah Somers. Issue: 1. *Sarah Ann Scull,* 2. *Wesley Scull,* 3. *Somers Scull,* 4. *Julia Ann Scull,* 5. *Rachel Scull,* 6. *Martha Scull,* 7. *Phebe Scull,* 8. *John Scull.*

    ii. SARAH, married (1) David Scull, (2) Reese Gwynne.

    iii. MARY, married —— Somers.

    iv. SOPHIA, said to have married twice.

* *New Jersey Archives,* vol. xxxiii, 377.   † *Ibid.,* 377.

‡ *Proceedings, &c. Surveyors' Association of West New Jersey,* 415.

§ Original will on file, Archives Department, Secretary of State's Office, Trenton, New Jersey.

6. GIDEON [3] SCULL (*John*,[2] *Peter Jansen* [1]), born at Great
Egg Harbor, 16 June, 1722; died there 6 December, 1776. As
late as 1753, Great Egg Harbor was the prey of panthers,
wolves and other wild animals destructive to life and the
pursuit of agriculture, and awards were ordered by the township for their capture. In this year Gideon Scull had a
bounty of one pound, ten shillings for two panthers' heads and
Andrew Griscom three pounds for a wolf's head.*

He improved and added to the considerable estate inherited
from his father and was recognized as one of the leading
citizens of the community. The following contemporaneous
evidence gives a pleasing picture of his upright walk before
his fellowmen that is worthy of preservation:

> A Testimony from the Monthly Meeting at Egg Har-
> bour and Cape May, concerning our Esteemed Friend
> Gideon Scull. He was born at Egg Harbour, the 16th
> day of 4 mo. 1722 of Religious parents, who educated
> him in the way of Friends. He was early convinced
> and became an example of plainness and sobriety and
> was of a steady upright life and conversation from his
> youth upwards, being a diligent attender of our Religious
> Meetings; and was a good degree exemplary in the station
> of an Elder many years; and about the 48th year of his
> age he received a gift of the Ministry in which we believe
> he was mostly faithful, as some of us were sensibly satis-
> fied of his Growth and improvement in the same. . . .
> He departed this life the 6th and was buried the 8th of
> the 12 mo. 1776, aged fifty four years, a Minister about
> six years.
>
> And we find freedom to add that he was a Loving
> Husband, a Tender parent, a sincere hearted Friend,
> who lived and died in good unity with Friends, and we
> have a well grounded hope he has entered into Everlast-
> ing Rest as a Reward of his faithful Labours.

From this it would appear that he had faith in that " creed
of creeds, the loveliness of perfect deeds."

He married at Little Egg Harbor Friends Meeting, in 1750,

---

* *Proceedings of the West Jersey Surveyors' Association*, 415.

Judith, daughter of James * and Margery † (Smith) Bellangee, born 26 March, 1729; named in her father's will of 9 March, 1781; was many years an Elder among Friends. With her sons James and Gideon she was an executor of her husband's will,‡ dated 17 June, 1776; proved 21 March, 1777.

Children of Gideon and Judith (Bellangee) Scull, born at Great Egg Harbor:

    i. JAMES,⁴ born 2 Oct., 1751; died 25 Aug., 1812; married in May, 1774, Susanna Leeds.§ Issue: 1. *Daniel Scull*, born 3 June, 1775; married Jemima Steelman. 2. *Gideon Scull*, born 30 Oct., 1777; married Alice Higbee. 3. *Dorcas Scull*, born 7 Oct., 1780; married (1) Samuel Ireland; (2) Jonas Leeds. 4. *Paul Scull*, born 2 April, 1783; married Sarah Steelman; had issue. 5. *James Scull*, born 25 March, 1786; married (1) Lorina Steelman; (2) —— Smith of Bristol, Penna. 6. *Susanna Scull*, born 25 Jan., 1789; married John Steelman. 7. *Hannah Scull*, born 20 June, 1792; married Edward Leeds. 8. *Joab Scull*, born 2 March, 1796; married Ann Stackhouse.

7. ii. GIDEON, married Sarah James.

    iii. PAUL, born 10 Dec., 1758; died 11 Dec., 1779.

---

* JAMES BELLANGEE, born 24 March, 1703; died in 1790; buried with wife in Friends grounds at Tuckerton; married at Little Egg Harbor Meeting, 6 Nov., 1727, Margery Smith. He was the son of Ive or Eve Bellangee, who produced certificate from Friends Meeting in Virginia to Meeting in Philadelphia, 26th 4 mo., 1696, and married 6 mo., 1696, Christiana, daughter of Nicholas and Hannah Delaplaine. In 1701 he purchased land in and removed to West New Jersey, his estate there lying on Old-man's Creek in Salem County, some twenty or more miles above John Scull's, where he died, between 2 Dec., 1719, and 10 May, 1720, the dates of the execution and probate of his will. *Cf. New Jersey Archives*, second series, vol. xxiii, 34, where his name is given as *Jene Bellange* instead of *Ive Bellange*. Ive Bellangee is said to have been the son of Theophilus de Bellangee, or Bellanger, a French Huguenot, who was shot during the dragonnades of Louis XIV, and whose wife and children fled to England and later to America.

James and Margery (Smith) Bellangee had eight children, of whom, three daughters, Phebe, Susanna and Ruth, married into the Ridgway family. Of the daughters, Phebe Bellanger, second wife of John Ridgway (1705-1775), was the mother of " Gentleman " John Ridgway (1755-1845), whose daughter, Sarah Ridgway, married Nicholas Waln; also mother of Jacob Ridgway (1768-1843), one of Philadelphia's merchant princes; and grandmother of Thomas Ridgway (1797-1887), thirty years president of Girard Trust Company, and of Madam Rush, whose large estate is represented in the Rush Library. *Cf.* Shourd, *History and Genealogy of Fenwick Colony;* Leach, *Old Philadelphia Families, under Ridgway.*

† Margery Smith, daughter of Thomas Smith of Cape May. *Proceedings of West Jersey Association*, 335.

‡ Recorded *Liber* 18, f. 253 *et seq.*, New Jersey Wills, Secretary of State's Office, Trenton.

§ DANIEL LEEDS, the great-grandfather of Susanna (Leeds) Scull, was the first surveyor-general of West New Jersey, and the compiler of the celebrated *Leeds' Almanac*, printed in 1687, by the famous printer William Bradford. His grandson, *Daniel Leeds*, father of Susanna (Leeds) Scull, was also a surveyor-general of New Jersey, under commission of 3 March, 1757.

iv. MARY, born 17 Nov., 1753; married David Bassett, Jr., born 17 Sept., 1753. Issue: 1. *Gideon Scull Bassett,* born 30 March, 1777. 2. *Mary Bassett,* born 8 Feb., 1779. 3. *Daniel Bassett,* born 31 Aug., 1781, died 7 Dec., 1782. 4. *David Bassett,* born 17 Nov., 1783.* 5. *Mark Bassett,* born 6 April, 1786. 6. *Judith Bassett.*

v. JUDITH, born 13 Jan., 1761; died 20 June 1786; married 8 Sept., 1779, David Offley, Jr., born Philadelphia, 20 Jan., 1756; died of yellow fever, serving his fellow men, 20 Oct., 1793. Lieut. *David Offley,* the only issue of this marriage, 1781-1838, was one of the three Commissioners who concluded the first treaty between the United States and Turkey, 1828; he married and had issue. Daniel Offley, Jr., married (2) 10 June, 1789, Ann Newbold, and had issue.†

vi. HANNAH, born 23 Dec., 1762; married David Davis. Issue: *Hannah Davis,* married George Hollingshead; had issue.

vii. RUTH, married Samuel Reeve. Issue: 1. *Joseph Reeve.* 2. *Martha Reeve.* 3. *Mary Reeve.* 4. *Samuel Reeve.* 5. *Rachel Reeve.* 6. *Martha Reeve,*‡ married —— Leeds. 8. *Ruth Reeve.*

* Records of Salem Meeting of Friends.

† For additional information of this line, *vide Descendants of Michael Offley: A Chart,* by the late Richard P. Tatum.

‡ An interesting letter, of no date, from Martha (Reeve) Leeds to David 5 Scull, gives a picture of the old Scull property, surroundings and family which is worthy of preservation. The writer was staying at Anscomb Cottage, Atlantic City and, taking a trip by rail to Somers Point made a brief call upon " Richard Somers, just at the Point, who lives in quite a large house with piazza and two balconies above overlooking the beautiful bay. The house is partly composed of a very hard glazed brick, the small windows, corner cupboard and the winding steep stairs made it very interesting to us to look at; Ann Somers the wife kindly took us upstairs to see the old chairs with canvas worked seats, showed us the portraits of the family and the old china, . . . we had but a short time to stay, taking the cars back to Leedsville, now called Linwood, which has a number of houses covering the whole ground of our Grandfather Scull's property. . . . to take us in his carriage first to see Grandfather Scull's house. We entered by the kitchen, a pretty comfortable sized room with a little Buttery back, and then went into the tiny sitting room and parlor with the planed beams overhead, perhaps they were of cedar, with the tiny mantel piece, and then went up the narrow winding stairs where thy father and our own mothers must have trod into the three little bed chambers, and then I thought how could all those men of noble forms, judging from thy father who was the only one I ever saw, four I believe, Uncles Gideon, James, Paul and Mark, and those six daughters, our beautiful Aunt Judith Offly, Mary Bassitt, Hanah Davis, Aunt Margery Leeds, my own dear mother, and Aunt Rachel Bolton. I say how they all have lived and slept in those tiny rooms " with the little windows " as Wood says, " where the sun came peeping in at dawn." But Sister says she remembers there was another part which was torn down. . . . then took us to the little graveyard, which has been reserved in the sale of the rest of the property, where repose the remains of various members of the Scull family. . . . it is pretty well overgrown but some cedars and a holly bush would make it look quite nice if it was cleaned up. I enclose thee a little branch of the holly. We there saw some tombstones, one having an inscription; I could not make out the date. . . . We then rode to the place where the Meeting House once stood where there is quite a nice graveyard now in possession of the Methodists who have a Meeting House near. Friends gave the ground to them, reserving the right of burial. . . . . It was on the road going to this place that the celebrated Daniel Offly dressed in regimentals and accompanied by Jonathan Evans, also a gay man, first saw our Aunt Judith,

viii. MARGERY, born 24 Feb., 1767; married 11 March, 1788, Daniel
Leeds of Leedsville, now Lenwood, Atlantic County, born 28
May, 1757; died 18 Oct., 1829, an Elder among Friends.
He was buried in the old Scull graveyard on his farm, near
his dwelling house. Issue: 1. *Judith Leeds*, married Nathan
Willits of Haddonfield. 2. *Gideon Leeds.* 3. *Josiah W.
Leeds.* 4. *Daniel Leeds.* 5. *Offley Leeds.* 6. *Benjamin Sykes
Leeds.* 7. *Japheth Leeds.* 8. *Margery Ann Leeds,* born 27
Aug., 1810; married Mark Saunders Bassett. 9. *Mary Bas-
sett Leeds,* born 3 Oct., 1813; married Edward Ritchie; had
issue.

ix. RACHEL, born 11 Oct., 1769; died Philadelphia, 10 June, 1818;
married 8 June, 1796, Samuel Bolton, son of Everard and
Deborah (Griscom) Bolton. Issue: 1. *Aquilla M. Bolton,*
born 11 March, 1797, married Christiana Aurand. 2. *Gidion
Bolton,* died young. 3. *Rachel Bolton,* died young. 4. *Sarah
Bolton,* born 11 Oct., 1801; died 7 Sept., 1852; married
Henry C. Corbit; had issue. 5. *Joseph Reeves Bolton,* born
17 Dec., 1803; died 15 Feby., 1883; married 2 Sept., 1828,
Sarah E. Jones. 6. *James Murray Bolton,* born 11 Feby.,
1806; died 27 Aug., 1846; married 9 Jan., 1833, Mary Eliza
English; had issue. 7. *Hannah Scull Bolton,* born 8 Sept.,
1807; died 22 April, 1851; married 1 Nov., 1827, Isaac Lloyd;
had issue. 8. *Samuel Bolton,* born 15 July, 1809; died 24
Aug., 1869; married 5 Dec., 1834, Hannah Saunders; had
issue.

x. MARK, born 20 Sept., 1773; died 16 Oct., 1808; married 2 June,
1794, Mary Banning. Issue: 1. *Mark Scull,* married Jane L.
Landrie; had issue. 2. *Amelia Scull,* married Micajah Reeve.
3. *Hannah Scull,* married Thomas Reeve. 4. *Sarah Scull,* died
unmarried. 5. *Lydia Scull,* died young. 6. *Ann Scull,* unmarried. 7. *Judith Scull.* 8. *Lydia Scull,* died unmarried.
9. *Paul Ebenezer Scull,* married Rhoda Tyler; had issue.

7. GIDEON [4] SCULL (*Gideon,*[3] *John,*[2] *Peter Jansen*[1]) born
at Great Egg Harbor, 27 April, 1756; died at Sculltown,
Salem County, 20 April, 1825. In early manhood he sold
his share of the paternal estate at Great Egg Harbor to his
brother, Mark Scull, and removed to what was then known
as Lockerton,* a settlement at the head of navigation on Oldman's Creek, eighteen miles from its mouth, and on the line

and being captivated with her beauty, soon after made proposals to her,
which were declined, but which when he became a converted man were
afterwards accepted, so Sister Ruth used to love to tell us. . . . Even in this
far off place the fashions of the day are followed and now the Railroad
brings them so near to Philadelphia it cannot be long before our Grandfather's
place of 500 acres perhaps, will vie with many others in the comforts and
elegancies of others near to Atlantic City and Philadelphia. . . . I hope thee
is right comfortable with thy dear family about thee, so pleasant just to be
waiting with such assurance for the call to depart which is far better for
the ready ones.

With love to Cousin Hannah and thy children,
I am very affectionately thy cousin,

M. R. LEEDS.

[Written about 1880.]

* Originally so named from the descendants of the Rev. Lars Karlsson Lock,
the early Swedish clergyman.

of Gloucester County. Here he became its leading merchant and was succeeded by his son in 1825. He owned a line of packet boats which operated between Sculltown and Philadelphia. He also built a blacksmith shop which was rented to various smiths, and the old forge was many years a land mark. In honor of the Scull family, prominent citizens and large property holders, the town was called Sculltown, but is now Auburn.*

Gideon Scull and his family were members of Pilesgrove Monthly Meeting of Friends, and his wife Sarah Scull was a recommended minister in the Society. In the division in Pilesgrove Meeting, 1827-1828, the Orthodox branch was weaker than that of the Hicksites and the old house of worship was formally transferred to the stronger group. Gideon Scull gave the land on which was erected the unpretentious frame meeting house still standing at Woodstown, on Union Street near Elm,† with reversion of the land to his descendants should the meeting house be no longer used for worship by the Orthodox branch of the Society.

He married, at Salem Meeting, 29 April, 1784, Sarah James, born 24 August, 1759; died 20 April, 1836; buried in Meeting-house graveyard at Woodstown; daughter of James James ‡ and his wife Abigail Lawrence.§ The children of

* *Cf.* Cushing and Sheppard, *History of the Counties of Gloucester, Salem and Cumberland, New Jersey,* 443.

† *Ibid.,* 460.

‡ JAMES JAMES, born in Phila., 19 Sept., 1729; died at Sculltown, 16 May, 1807; married at Newtown, L. I., 11 May, 1758, Abigail Lawrence, *q. v.* According to the Bible Record of Sarah (James) Scull, their children were: 1. *Sarah James,* above. 2. *Mary James,* b. 18 May, 1761; d. y. 3. *Hannah James,* b. 8 Sept., 1762. 4. *James James,* b. 2 May, 1764; m. Kerranhappuck Powell; removed to Sunbury, Georgia. 5. *Mary Hicks James,* b. 7 June, 1766; m. Daniel Harker of Phila. 6. *Samuel Lawrence James,* b. 5 June, 1768; m. Mary, dau. of Col. Edward Hall of Mannington, Salem Co., N. J.; their eldest dau. Clara Mary James, m. David Reeves of Bridgeton, N. J., who was subsequently of Phoenixville, Penna.

THOMAS JAMES, father of James James, died in Phila., 18 July [1768], "aged about 72 years," according to the Bible record of his son. He married Sarah ———, who was living as late as 31 May, 1762. Issue: 2. *Thomas,* b. 29 Jan., 1716. 3. *John,* b. 29 Mar., 1719. 4. *Hannah,* b. 24 Nov., 1722. 5. *Sarah,* b. 5 Mar., 1725; d. 14 July, 1756. 6. *James,* above, b. 19 Sept., 1729. This Bible record begins with the birth of Thomas, called "second son of Thomas James and Sarah"; and above the date of death of Thomas James, the father, is the entry: "born 1696."

§ ABIGAIL LAWRENCE, born Newtown, L. I., 14 May, 1737; died Woodstown, N. J., 16 May, 1770; was buried in Friends' ground. She was the daughter of *Samuel Lawrence,* 1689-1760, of Black Swamp, Queens Co., L. I. and his wife Mary Hicks, *q. v.* m. 1 Jan., 1717; granddaughter of *Major William Lawrence* of Flushing, L. I., died March, 1719/20 (member of Gov. Leisler's

this marriage became influential in different walks of life, several of the sons made their mark as successful business men.*

Children of Gideon and Sarah (James) Scull, born at Sculltown:

    i. ABIGAIL⁵ LAWRENCE, born 27 April, 1785; died young.

    i. ABIGAIL, born 14 Sept., 1786; died unmarried 5 Nov., 1867.

    iii. JAMES, born 24 Nov., 1788; died at sea 7 Oct., 1825.

8. iv. GIDEON, married Lydia Ann Rowan.

9.   v. PAUL, married Hope Kay.

    vi. OFFLEY, born 4 Dec., 1794; died 25 Nov., 1797.

    vii. SARAH, born 11 March, 1797; died unmarried 15 Feb., 1845.

10. viii. DAVID, married (1) Lydia Lippincott; (2) Hannah Davis Wood.

    ix. HANNAH, born 21 Sept., 1802; died 1 April, 1828; married 6 April, 1827, William Carpenter of Salem, born 21 Oct., 1802; died 13 April, 1889.

8. GIDEON⁵ SCULL (*Gideon,*⁴ *Gideon,*³ *John,*² *Peter Jansen*¹), born at Scultown, 22 October, 1790; died at Philadelphia 29 May, 1859. He was an enterprising business man and a member of the firm of Clement and Scull,† commission merchants on Market Street, Salem, New Jersey during the first quarter of the nineteenth century. Subsequently of Philadelphia, he was a wholesale merchant of the well-known firm of Scull and Thompson, being also identified with the Schuylkill Coal Company and other business enterprises. At

Council, Justice for Orange Co., N. Y.), and his wife Deborah Smith, married (license) June, 1680, daughter of Richard Smith the patentee of Smithtown, L. I.; great-granddaughter of Captain *William Lawrence*, who, baptized at St. Albans, Hertfordshire, England, 27 July, 1622, came to America in the ship *Planter*, 1635, and settled at Flushing, L. I., serving in various positions of trust: Magistrate, Sheriff, Captain of Foot. His ancestry has been traced to William Lawrence of St. Albans, who married 25 Nov., 1559, Katherine Beaumont.

MARY HICKS, wife of Samuel Lawrence, was the daughter of Col. *Thomas Hicks* (patentee of Little Neck, L. I., who died 28 Oct., 1712, having been many years prominent in Queens County as Captain, Lieut.-Colonel and Judge of the Courts), and his wife Deborah Whitehead, *q. v.* He was the son of Judge *Thomas Hicks* and his wife Mary Washburn; grandson of *John Hicks*, a patentee of Flushing, L. I. and his first wife Herodia Long, and great-grandson of *Robert Hicks*, who came to Plymouth, Massachusetts, in the ship *Fortune* in 1621. The ancestry of the latter is traced to a family of English gentry settled at Totworth, Gloucestershire, whose earliest known ancestor, Sir *Ellis Hicks*, was knighted at Poictiers in 1356 for bravery in capturing a set of colors from the French.—*New York Genealogical and Biographical Record*, vol. 38, 73.

MAJOR DANIEL WHITEHEAD, father of Deborah Hicks, 1646-1704, magistrate, ranger-general, member of New York Assembly, 1691 until his death, married Abigail, daughter of Thomas Stevenson, who died in 1717. His father, *Daniel Whitehead*, who died 16 November, 1668, aged 65 years, was a proprietor of Hempstead, L. I. in 1647.

* *Cf.* Sheppard and Cushing, *op. cit.*, 444.

† *Ibid.*

the time of his death and for some years preceding he resided on Spruce Street above Ninth in Portico Row.

He married Lydia Ann Rowan, only child of Dr. John Rowan * and his second wife, Lydia Ann (Tutness) Howell.

Children of Gideon and Lydia Ann (Rowan) Scull:

    i. CHARLES [6] PENROSE, died young.
    ii. THOMAS ROWAN, died young.
    iii. LYDIA, died unmarried.
    iv. GIDEON, died 28 June, 1899; was commissioned 3 August, 1861, Captain and Commissary of Subsistence, U. S. Volunteers; Colonel, 1 July, 1865, to 31 May, 1866; Brevet Major and Lieutenant Colonel Volunteers, 13 March, 1865, "for meritorious services in his department during the war; honorably mustered out 31 May, 1866. He married Anna Jertha Hedwig Seiler of Canton Berne, Switzerland. Issue: 1. *Max L. Scull.* 2. *Marjorie Scull*, married Bartlet H. Hayes. 3. *Guy H. Scull*, married Nancy Whitman. 4. *Dorothy Scull.*
    v. HARRIET, married Jacob Anthony of New York; had issue.
    vi. ANN PENROSE, married Robert Newlin. Issue: 1. *Cyrus Newlin.* 2. *Robert Newlin.* 3. *Charles Newlin*, married Agnes Hewson. 4. *Alfred Newlin.* 5. *Walter Newlin.* 6. *Anne Newlin*, married George H. Holt. 7. *William Verplanck Newlin.*
    vii. JACOB RIDGWAY, born 26 June, 1835; Haverford, 1853; married 3 May, 1865, Margaret Clevenstine.
    viii. ALFRED PENROSE, married Mary James Reeves, born 10 Jan., 1824; died 1893; dau. of David Reeves † of the Phoenixville iron works and his first wife Clara Mary James. Issue: 1. *Charles Scull.* 2. *Thomas Scull.* 3. *Nellie Scull*, married J. Boyd Nixon. 4. *Frederick Scull.* 5. *Margaret Scull.* 6. *Clara Scull.* 7. *Mary Scull*, married Samuel Wagner.
    ix. SARAH JAMES, married Nathaniel B. Curtis of Boston, Massachusetts, at one time president of Somerset Club. Issue: 1. *Nathaniel Curtis*, Harvard, 1877. 2. *Hamilton Curtis.* 3. *Philip Curtis*, married Mary Oliphant.
    x. MARGARET, married Nicholas Anthony. Issue: 1. *Emily Anthony*, married John Murray Forbes. 2. *Charles Anthony.* 3. *Henry Anthony.* 4. *Herbert Anthony.* 5. *Alfred R. Anthony.* 6. *Walter Anthony.* 7. *Helen Anthony*, married William Wisner. 8. *Margaret Anthony.*

9. PAUL [5] SCULL (*Gideon,*[4] *Gideon,*[3] *John,*[2] *Peter Jansen* [1]), born at Scultown, 4 September, 1792; died near Woodstown, 2 November, 1844. He settled on the Plainfield farm as it was called, about two miles from Woodstown, and was considered one of the foremost agriculturalists in the county, abreast with all the modern ideas of refertilization of the exhausted virgin soil. His premature death was regarded a public loss.

* Son of John Rowan of Philadelphia, brewer, will proved 6 Dec., 1759, and his wife Margaret Sharp.

† Cf. *Annals of the Sinnott, Rogers, Coffin, Reeves, Bodine and Allied Families*, Philadelphia, 1905, pp. 128-9.

He married 25 May, 1815, Hope, daughter of Isaac and Deborah Kay of Gloucester, New Jersey, born 11 June, 1789; died 1 September, 1868.

Children of Paul and Hope (Kay) Scull, born near Woodstown: *

> i. SARAH, born 19 Oct., 1816; married (1) 9 Nov., 1836, Biddle Reeves of Woodbury, (2) D. Cooper Andrews. Issue: 1. *Paul Scull Reeves*, born 10 Sept., 1837, of Philadelphia and Phoenixville; married Keturah Kreamer and had issue. 2. *Elizabeth Reeves*, born 4 Oct., 1839; died 28 Sept., 1857. 3. *Benjamin Reeves*, born 21 Aug., 1841; d. 6 Oct., 1847. 4. *Mary Scull Reeves*, born 27 July, 1843. 5. *Sarah Reeves*, born 9 Jan., 1846; died 27 July, 1865. 6. *Abby S. Reeves*, born 16 May, 1848. 7. *Biddle Reeves*, born 18 Nov., 1850; died 29 May, 1898; married Maria Carver. Issue: BIDDLE REEVES, who died 9 July, 1883, and was the fifth of his Christian name in direct descent.†
> ii. MARY, born 22 May, 1818; died unmarried.
> iii. ISAAC, born 2 July, 1820; married Susan Wood. Issue: 1. *Mary Scull*, b. 9 Oct., 1845. 2. *Paul Scull*, b. 7 Oct., 1848. 3 *Joseph W. Scull*, b. 22 Nov., 1852. 4. *Anna M. Scull*, b. 22 Nov., 1855. 5. *Louisa W. Scull*, b. 7 Nov., 1858. 8. *Susan H. Scull*, b. 24 April, 1861.
> iv. DEBORAH, born 7 Nov., 1822; married John H. Lippincott.

10. DAVID [5] SCULL (*Gideon,*[4] *Gideon,*[3] *John,*[2] *Peter Jansen*[1]), born at Sculltown, 8 December, 1799; died at his residence, 1516 Arch Street, Philadelphia, 24 December, 1884. While still a young man he left his native town for the wider opportunities of Philadelphia, where his business capacity and close application to his commission house, enabled him to acquire a competency and to retire from active control in favor of his sons.

In civic affairs he took a lively interest; was a director of the Bank of North America during the crucial period of the Civil War and reconstruction, 1860-1875, and a liberal contributor to the Pennsylvania Hospital. In membership with the Twelfth Street Meeting of Friends he was many years an overseer of meeting.

He married (1) 23 November, 1823, Lydia Lippincott, born at Moorestown, 16 September, 1801; died in Germantown, in August, 1854; daughter of Joshua Lippincott ‡ and

---

* Records of *Pilesgrove Friends Meeting.*

† Records Woodbury Meeting of Friends. *Cf. Annals of the Sinnot and Allied Families,* etc., 126, 132-3.

‡ JOSHUA [5] LIPPINCOTT, b. 23 Oct., 1774; m. 7 Nov., 1800, Esther Davis, He was descended from *Richard* [1] *Lippincott* of Devonshire, Eng., who emigrated to Massachusetts and was admitted a freeman at Boston 13 May, 1640. Embracing the principles of Friends he returned to Devonshire and resided

his wife Esther Davis.* He married (2) Hannah Davis Wood, who survived him and by whom there was no issue. His two marriages gave him the unusual distinction of celebrating two silver weddings.

at Stonehurst, Plymouth. In 1663 he came again to New England but removed to Shrewsbury, in East Jersey, where, occupying offices of trust he spent the last eighteen years of his life and died 25 Nov., 1683; his wife, Abigail, mother of his children, died 2 Aug., 1677; in 1677 he was a member of the first legislative assembly in East Jersey. *Restore 2 Lippincott*, his fourth child, b. Plymouth, Eng., 3 July, 1653; d. 20 July, 1741; m. (1) 6 Nov., 1674, Hannah Shattuck; (2) Martha Owen. His eighth child, *Jacob 3 Lippincott*, b. Aug., 1697; m. 1716, Mary Burr. Their son *Joshua 4 Lippincott* of Woolwich, Gloucester Co., N. J., m. (2) Rebecca, dau. of William Wilkins, and was the father of *Joshua 5 Lippincott* first above. — *Lippincotts of England and America*, edited from the Genealogical Papers of the late James S. Lippincott, Philadelphia, 1909.

* ESTHER DAVIS, 1778-1809, wife of Joshua Lippincott, was a daughter of *Jacob Davis*, 1734-1820, and Esther Wilkins, 1736-1785, his wife, married 1761, of Pilesgrove, Salem Co., N. J.; granddaughter of *David Davis*, justice of the Salem Co. Courts, and his wife Dorothy Cousins, and great-granddaughter of *John Davis* of Oyster Bay, L. I., who married, in 1680, Dorothea Gotherson and settled in Pilesgrove, West Jersey, in 1705. *Dorothea (Gotherson) Davis* was a daughter of Major Daniel Gotherson, an officer in the Parliamentary Army under Cromwell, citizen of London and author of several religious books and tracts, who died 1668. He married *circa* 1636, Dorothea Scott, who married (2) 1670, Joseph Hogben of Kent, England, and was of Oyster Bay, in 1680. She was a daughter of *Thomas Scott* of Egerton, Godmersham, Kent, who died 1635; author of two MSS. of 1626, now in the Bodleian Library, addressed to his kinsman, the Earl of Arundel, Earl Marshall of England. His lineage has been traced to Edward I, King of England. *Dorothea (Scott) Gotherson Hogben* of Egg Harbor and Scot's Hall, Godmersham, Kent, close to Canterbury, was a remarkable person, of ancient lineage. Having adopted the principles of Friends, Dorothea Gotherson held meetings in the name of the Scot's Congregation and, by her conversation and writings, strove to advance the cause. One of the latter, a pamphlet, printed in London, 1661, she presented to Charles II, under the title: *To all that are unregenerate, a Call to Repentance from dead works to Newness of Life.* Paternally, Dorothea Scot was descended from John Baliol, Lord of Barnard Castle, who, with his wife, Devorgilda, Countess of Huntingdon, founded Baliol College, Oxford, and was the father of John Baliol, King of Scotland, 1292-1296, and of William Baliol le Scot. The Scotts of Scot's Hall in Kent, claim to derive their surname and Scot's Hall from the family of John le Scot, last Palatine Earl of Chester and Earl of Huntingdon; through whom they likewise claim an uninterrupted descent from William Baliol le Scot. The mother of Dorothea Scott was Jane, daughter of *John Knatchbul* of Merscham Hatch, Esq., and her grandmother was *Lady Jane*, daughter of *Sir Thomas Wyatt* of Allington Castle, Kent, who headed the celebrated rebellion to place Lady Jane Gray upon the English throne and was executed for high treason April 11, 1554. His father, *Sir Thomas Wyatt*, the celebrated poet, 1503-1542, was the son of *Sir Henry Wyatt*, keeper of the Crown jewels under Henry VIII.—*Cf.* Gideon Deleplaine Scull, *Dorothea Scott, otherwise Gotherson and Hogben, of Egerton House, Kent*, &c.; to which is appended genealogical tables showing her descent from Charles Martel and William Baliol le Scot; see also James Renat Scott, *Memorials of the family of Scot, of Scot's-hall, in the County of Kent*, London, 1876, and Charles H. Browning, *Americans of Royal Descent*, Philadelphia, 1891, 237, 243, 373, 576.

Children of David and Lydia (Lippincott) Scull, born at
Sculltown:

    i. Gideon [6] Delaplaine, born 13 Aug., 1824; died Ilkley, York-
shire, England, 22 April, 1889; married at Leipsic, Saxony,
7 April, 1862, Anna, daughter of Thomas Holder, Esq. of
Temple Grafton, Yorkshire, England. Mr. Scull, Haverford,
Class of 1843, was a widely-known scholar, littérateur and
traveler, and many years resident in England. A frequent
contributor to magazines on historical subjects, he was the
author of *Genealogical Notes relating to the Family of Scull*,
London, 1876; *Memoir of W. G. Evelyn*, followed by *The
Evelyns of America*, compiled from family papers and other
sources, 1608-1805, Oxford, 1881; *Dorothea Scott*, otherwise
Gotherson and Hogben, of Egerton House, Kent, 1611-1680,
Oxford, 1883, and *Voyages of Peter Esprit Radisson, being
an Account of his Travels and Experiences among the North
American Indians from 1654 to 1684*, a volume of 400 pages
printed by the Prince Society. A work by him in manuscript,
compiled at Oxford, 1882, is in the library of the New Eng-
land Historic Genealogical Society of which he was a member.
It is entitled, *Sir William Browne, Knight, 1556-1610, and Sir
Nathaniel Rich, Knight, 1636. A Chapter of Family History*.
The work has a particular interest for the descendants of
Nathaniel Browne, an early settler of Hartford, Connecticut.
Issue: 1. *Walter Delaplaine Scull* of London, died in England training for air service in the Great War; an artist of
some merit. 2. *Edith Maria Lydia Scull*, died unmarried
shortly after her brother.

    ii. Caroline, died young.

    iii. Jane Lippincott Scull, married William Danforth Bispham.
Issue: 1. *David Scull Bispham, LL.D.*, Haverford, 1914, born
5 January, 1857; died New York City, 2 Oct., 1921; married
28 April, 1885, Caroline S. Russell and had issue. His important work, *A Quaker Singer's Recollections*, and magazine
articles on vocal music are well known; his reputation as a
singer was world-wide.

    iv. Hannah Scull, died unmarried.

11. v. David Scull, married Hannah Ellicott Coale.

    vi. Edward Lawrence Scull, born 7 March, 1846; died Surrey, Eng-
land, 14 June, 1884; Haverford, Class 1864; a recognized
minister of Friends Twelfth Street Meeting, Philadelphia;
married 26 Nov., 1879, Sarah Elizabeth Marshall. Issue: 1.
Edward Marshall Scull, born 7 Dec., 1880; married 26 May,
1914, Anne Price, daughter of Dr. Johnson of Chestnut Hill;
has issue. 2. *John Lawrence Scull*, born 11 Jan., 1883; married 1 Jan., 1907, Mary Rachel, daughter of Edward Bettle;
has issue.

    vii. Lydia Lippincott Scull, died unmarried.

    viii. Mary Scull, married Paschall Hacker.

11. David [6] Scull (*David*,[5] *Gideon*,[4] *Gideon*,[3] *John*,[2] *Peter
Jansen* [1]), born on the family estate at Sculltown, 17 January,
1836; died at his home, Leighton Place, Overbrook, Philadelphia, 22 November, 1907.

His early education was acquired at Westtown Boarding
School. In 1849, he entered the Introductory Department of
Haverford School and was graduated from Haverford College,

1854. During his college days, though enjoying the fulness of life and beauty, he began to show evidence of spiritual interests and serious concerns. This is well illustrated in an address, before the Loganian Society, given apparently in his senior year, in which he presents with considerable power the beauty of classical literature and its cultural value. "But," he concludes, "there is another literature and a higher, justly called sacred, which claims the attention of all. And the scholar who makes ancient (i. e. classical) literature alone the object of his attainments falls far short of the attainable standard of perfection. It is a treasure which he will share in common with the poor and lowly, a body of truths, which require not the soil of genius, or of talent, such as Plato and the heathen philosophers sought for but found not, such as even modern philosophers have sought in vain, who though they might speak in a hundred tongues would find themselves strangers to *one small voice* whose teachings would be unheeded and unknown."

Soon after leaving college he entered upon what proved to be a very successful career as a wool merchant, in which, from 1864 to 1884, he was joined with his brother, Edward L. Scull, in the business begun by their father. After the death of his brother he continued alone until 1891, when he retired. For fourteen years, from 1867, he was a director of the Girard National Bank; was one of the most active members of the group who organized the Mortgage Trust Company of Pennsylvania, and its vice-president from the incorporation in 1886; was also a manager of the Grandom Trust; and a director for some years of the Delaware and Chesapeake Canal. He was treasurer of the Law and Order Society for five years; a member of "The Committee of One Hundred"; a member of the Board of Managers of the William Penn Charter School; treasurer of Haverford College for eighteen years, and of the Philadelphia Dispensary for twenty-eight years. By appointment of the Founder he was a trustee of Bryn Mawr College, and served on many important committees.

Throughout his long life he remained a conscientious and devoted member of the Society of Friends, with which some of his ancestors had been identified for nearly three centuries. Following his decease Rufus M. Jones, in an estimate of the

827

life and character of David Scull for *The American Friend,* said:

> To me he was the consummate flower of American Quakerism in my generation. There were and are others who had a freer gift of utterance, a greater range of thought, a larger power of interpretation, but no one who has shown in fuller beauty that something which we call *spirit,* that indescribable thing called living personality . . . . .
>
> I do not need to say many words of his large generosity, for almost everybody knows of it. There have been hardly any movements in my time for the expansion of Quakerism, for the widening of education, for equipment to better service, to which he has not liberally contributed. Every Friends' college had received means from his hands, and on many of them he had bestowed much more than his funds—he had given his personal interest, counsel, prayers and patient labor. Haverford and Bryn Mawr Colleges especially, and the William Penn Charter School and *The American Friend* owe him a vast debt, beyond all estimate . . . .
>
> But no contribution he has made or left compares with that of his own life. God had given him a beautiful face, and He had made him, like Galahad, ' as good as he was beautiful.' There was a fine harmony of outer and inner, so that the whole impression was one of beauty.[*]

On 27 November, 1907, a few days subsequent to David Scull's death, President M. Carey Thomas of Bryn Mawr, delivered a memorial address to the students, in which, speaking of the decedent's relation to the college, she said:

> For nearly a quarter of a century, from its opening in 1885, until a week ago, he had spent and been spent in its service. He held successively, and sometimes simultaneously, the most laborious offices in the gift of the Trustees. He was secretary of the Board of Trustees for ten years, from 1885 to 1895; Chairman of the Committee on Buildings and Grounds for nineteen years, from 1885 to 1904; Vice-President of the Board of Trustees, from 1895 until his going abroad in 1904, and President of the Board of Trustees, and also President of the Board of Directors, from his return in 1906 until his death.

[*] See short biography in *Union with God,* D. Scull.

Every college building, after Taylor Hall and Merion Hall which were planned by the Founder of the College himself, was built under the supervision of David Scull as Chairman of the Trustees' Committee on Buildings and Grounds, Randor, Denbigh, the Pembrokes, Rockefeller, and the Library took their places in beautiful succession on the College campus, each in its appointed place.

Their harmonious arrrangement and unity of design are due in great part to David Scull's love of beauty, to his belief in following expert opinion, to his openmindedness, his readiness to be convinced; and above all to his great love for the College, and his single-hearted determination to give it the very best.

It was so in everything. He had no axes to grind, no enemies to defeat, no favourites to exalt. He loved everyone, and was loved by everyone capable of understanding his lovableness. He believed in everyone, and was believed in by everyone worthy of his belief. He was very gentle and courteous by grace and nature, but when he was sure that it was right to act—when the College was at stake—he was as bold as a lion.

His contributions to religious literature should not be overlooked, among these the most important are: a booklet on the *Ordinances*, 1908; *The Need of The Bible School to Supplement the Teaching in the Home and in the Ministry*, 1895; *Salvation in a Twofold Aspect*, 1896; *Communion and At-one-ment; Union with God;* 1902.

For many years he was an Elder in the Twelfth Street Meeting, Philadelphia, and he "was worthy to stand among the pillar Friends who have adorned the doctrine of inward Light and Grace." *

He married at Baltimore, 28 February, 1861, Hannah Ellicott Coale, daughter of William Ellis Coale † and his wife

---

* *Memoirs of David Scull*, Philadelphia, 1908, xx.

† WILLIAM 7 ELLIS COALE, born at "Wakefield," 25 September, 1795; died at Baltimore, Maryland, 30 September, 1865, was sixth in descent from *William 1 Coale*, who arrived in Virginia in 1618; he followed the teachings of George Fox; suffered imprisonment at Jamestown for conscience' sake; subsequently removed to Calvert County, Maryland, and died at St. Jerome in that county in July, 1669. *William 2 Coale*, his son, born in Virginia; died at Great Bonnerton, West River, Anne Arundel Co., Md., in February, 1678; was a prominent Friend of Cliff Meeting, West River; George Fox makes mention

Hannah Ellicott Carey,* born at Baltimore, 27 February, 1837; died at Philadelphia, 24 April, 1871, thus ending a union of peculiar beauty and happiness.

Child of David and Hannah Ellicott (Coale) Scull:

12. i. William 7 Ellis Scull, married Florence Moore Prall.

in his Journal of "a large and precious meeting at William Coale's." His third wife, Elizabeth, daughter of Philip and Sarah (Harrison) Thomas of West River, was the mother of his son, *Philip Coale,*3 born 6 September, 1673; died at "Portand Manor" on the Patuxent, after 16 July, 1718; married at West River Meeting, 6 April, 1697, Cassandra Skipwith, born 29 Oct., 1678, daughter of George Skipwith ** of "Silver Stone," Anne Arundel Co., and his wife, Elizabeth Thurston. The former is said to have been the youngest son of Sir Henry Skipwith, Bart., of Prestwould, Leicestershire; and the latter was the daughter of Thomas Thurston, who with his wife Bridget, daughters Elizabeth and Ann, and twenty servants settled in Maryland in 1676, having first visited Maryland and Virginia in 1658. His will, proved 13 April, 1693, named daughter, Elizabeth, wife of George Skipwith.†† Cassandra (Skipwith) Coale by will of 19 June, 1745, disposed of a large estate and made her son, *Skipwith Coale,* executor thereof. *Skipwith*4 *Coale* of Portland Manor, son of Philip and Cassandra (Skipwith) Coale, married Margaret, daughter of William and Margaret (Gill) Holland of Calvert Co., Md.; was Captain of militia and one of the "gentleman justices" of Baltimore County; removed to his plantation "Stone Hill," on the Susquehanna in Baltimore, now Harford Co., about 1737, and there died, having executed his will 31 August, 1755, and made his wife, Margaret, his executor. Their son *William*5 *Coale,* born 6 Dec., 1740, at Stone Hill, married (1) 7 Oct., 1761, Sarah, daughter of Isaac and Margaret (Lee) Webster of Baltimore Co., and died at his plantation "Travelers' Rest," Deer Creek, after March, 1805. His son, *Isaac*6 *Coale,* born at Travelers' Rest in 1765; married 7 Sept., 1786, at Darlington Friends Meeting House, Rachel, daughter of William and Mary (Goldhawk) Cox of Harford Co.; resided at Wakefield, Deer Creek, Harford Co., where he died *circa* 1825, and was the father of WILLIAM 7 ELLIS COALE of Baltimore.

** Discrepancies appear in various printed works as to the parentage of Cassandra Skipwith Coale. Some writers call her the daughter of Sir Gray Skipwith who died in Virginia in 1680, having emigrated to that province during the Cromwellian period. There is agreement, however, as to the descent of her grandfather, Sir Henry Skipwith of Prestwould, from Sir William Skipwith, Knt., of Ormsby, High Sheriff of Lincolnshire, whose wife Alice, was daughter of Sir Lionel Dymoke of the Dymokes, Kings Champion, who descended from Henry III of England.—*Cf. The Colonial Families of America,* vol. ii, 191; Lawrence Buckley Thomas, D.D., *The Thomas Book,* New York, 1896, 287-8.

†† Elizabeth (Thurston) Skipwith, widow of George Skipwith and mother of Cassandra (Skipwith) Coale, became the second wife of William Coale, the elder half-brother of Philip Coale. She married (3), as second wife, 29 June, 1704, Samuel Chew, merchant of Anne Arundel Co., whose will of 18 July, 1718, named grand-children-in-law, Cassandra and Elizabeth, daughters of Philip Coale and Cassandra, his wife. Mrs. Elizabeth (Thurston) Skipwith Coale Chew died 27 Feby., 1709/10. *Cf. The Thomas Book.*

* Hannah Ellicott Carey, born 7 August, 1795, wife of William Ellis Coale, was the daughter of James Carey (1751/2-1834), president of the first City Council of Baltimore and second president of the old Bank of Maryland, and his wife Martha Ellicott. The latter was eldest daughter of John Ellicott and his first wife, Leah Brown. About 1772 John Ellicott, and his brothers, Andrew Ellicott and Joseph Ellicott, sons of Andrew Ellicott (1708-1741) and his wife Ann Bye, removed from Bucks County, Pennsylvania, and bought lands and water rights on the Patapsco River, ten miles west of Baltimore, where Ellicott City now stands. Here the brothers, and their families after them, carried on an extensive milling business.

12. WILLIAM [7] ELLIS SCULL (*David,[6] David,[5] Gideon,[4] Gideon,[3] John,[2] Peter Jansen [1]*) was born at Philadelphia, 3 March, 1862. Acquiring his early education at Friends' Select School and William Penn Charter School, he was graduated from Haverford College, Class of 1883. He has spent much time in foreign and domestic travel, in philanthropic pursuits, civic betterment and church advancement. At one time vice-president of The John C. Winston Company, Publishers, Philadelphia; he is now a trustee of the Austen Riggs Foundation, Stockbridge, Massachusetts; editor *Westminster Abbey and The Cathedrals of England; Concerning a Cathedral proposed for the Diocese of Pennsylvania, including First Ten Years Founding the Cathedral Church of Christ;* a vestryman for thirty years of St. Asaph's Church, Bala, Pennsylvania; incorporator, vice-president, secretary and treasurer of Christ Church, Dark Harbor, Maine; proposer, incorporator and first Canon Registrar of the Cathedral Church of Christ of the Diocese of Pennsylvania; in 1923 started sanitariums in Bulgaria and Serbia for exiled Russians which at this date are being successfully operated; a director of the Delaware and Chesapeake Canal; a member of New Charter Committee of Philadelphia; a founder of the Tarratine and the Dark Harbor clubs; a member of the Philadelphia, Rittenhouse, Racquet, Radnor Hunt, Merion Cricket, Philadelphia Country, Bryn Mawr Polo, and Church clubs; The Historical Society of Pennsylvania, The Genealogical Society of Pennsylvania and a fellow of the American Geographical Society.

He married at Paterson, New Jersey, 16 February, 1887, Florence Moore Prall, daughter of Hon. Edwin Theodore Prall * of Paterson, New Jersey, and his wife, Rachel Moore

* EDWIN THEODORE PRALL, born at Staten Island, 11 November, 1821; died at Paterson; was sixth in descent from *Arent[1] des Prael,* or *Prall,* who came from Holland to New York in 1660; settled in Staten Island, where he purchased 160 acres of land and married (1) Maria, daughter of Peter and Francoise (du Bois) Billou of Staten Island, who died prior to 11 September, 1699. *Arent Prall* died shortly before the probate of his will, 4 Nov., 1725. His eldest son, *Peter[2] Prall* of Staten Island, married Maria Christopher, and died 27 Oct., 1748. *Abraham [3] Prall,* fourth son of the latter, born 13 Oct., 1706; inherited the homestead, "Morning Star," but subsequently removed to Northfield, and died 28 Sept., 1775, having married his cousin, Alida Hegerman, 9 May, 1731; born 6 Oct., 1702; died 15 Sept., 1781; daughter of Benjamin ** and Barentje Hegerman of Flatbush. Their youngest child, *Abraham [4] Prall,* born 11 Jan., 1740; died 6 May, 1820; married 22 May, 1768,

** *Cf.* Bergen's *Kings County Settlers* under Hegerman.

831

Thomson. Mrs. Scull is a member of the Acorn and Sedgeley clubs of Philadelphia, and of The Colonial Dames of America, Chapter II, Philadelphia.

Child of William Ellis and Florence Moore (Prall) Scull:

> Margaret [8] Ellis Scull, born 7 Oct., 1896; married 12 Sept., 1917, Alexander Biddle, son of Alexander Williams Biddle, M.D. and his wife Anne McKenna. He was born 4 April, 1893, and is a descendant of John Biddle, younger brother of William [3] Biddle who married Mary, daughter of Nicholas Scull, the Surveyor General of Pennsylvania. Issue: 1. *Alexander Williams Biddle,* born 4 March, 1919. 2. *David Scull Biddle,* born 23 April, 1925.

Mary, daughter of Daniel Stillwell †† and his wife Catharine (Larzelere) Johnson, born 28 May, 1749; died 25 April, 1811. *Daniel* [5] *Prall,* second son, born 25 March, 1773; died 16 Oct., 1817; married 22 Jan., 1794, Ann Mersereau, who died 17 April, 1813; daughter of Peter Mersereau ‡‡ and his wife Rebecca Lake. *William* [6] *Prall,* eldest son, born 27 April, 1795; died 16 Aug., 1825; married 26 Oct., 1815, Ann Egbert of Staten Island, born 9 June, 1792; died in Oct., 1853. Their son was *Edwin* [7] *Theodore Prall,* first named. A forthcoming work on Staten Island will contain an article on the Pralls of that place.

†† *Cf. ibid.,* 277-80, for line of descent: *Daniel* [5] *Stillwell* (1702-1760) ; *Col. Richard* [4] *Stillwell* (1677-1758) and Maria Golding; *Capt. Nicholas* [3] *Stillwell* (c. 1636-1715) and Mrs. Catharine Morgan; *Lieut. Nicholas* [2] *Stillwell* (c. 1600-1671) and Abigail Hopton; *John* [1] *Stillwell* of Surrey, England. Dr. John Stillwell is about to publish the Genealogy of the Stillwell Family, to which he has devoted years of research.

‡‡ PETER MERSEREAU, born 19 Jan., 1741, member of Committee of Safety, 1776; married 22 Oct., 1765, Rebecca Lake.—*Genealogy of the Lake Family;* Clute's *History of Staten Island; Register of Eglise Francoise* of New York.

CORRECTION

CORRECTION.—SCOTT-GOTHERSON-DAVIS-BASSETT. In the excellent account of the Scull family by the late William Ellis Scull, which appeared in the issue of the *Publications* of this Society for March, 1929, reference is made, page 230, to one "John Davis of Oyster Bay, Long Island, who married first in 1680, Dorothea Gotherson, and settled in Pilesgrove, West Jersey, in 1705." **

Among the references given for this statement are "*Dorothea Scott, otherwise Gotherson and Hogbien*" by Gideon D. Scull; and Charles H. Browning's *Americans of Royal Descent*, Philadelphia, 1891.*

An examination of these authorities shows that Browning depended upon Scull's book for his authority, and that definite reference to the time and place of the marriage claimed, is not given by Mr. Scull.

The third reference given, *Memorials of the Family of Scot of Scot's-hall in the County of Kent* by James R. Scott, London, 1876, is not available for reference.

The earliest known reference to this Gotherson-Davis marriage appears in Shourd's *History and Genealogy of the Fenwick Colony*, 1876, wherein is the statement, page 70, that

John Davis emigrated from Wales and settled on Long Island. He married Dorothea Gotherson, an English woman, reputed to have been very wealthy, and known to have been of royal descent.

He belonged to a sect called Singing Quakers and worshiped daily on a stump, and was very pious and consistent. He lived to the extreme old age of one hundred years. A number of years before his death, he removed his family to Pilesgrove Township, Salem County, New Jersey, near the present site of Woodstown. This was about 1705. All of the family became members of Friends' Meeting.

Shourd's is also authority for the statement that all of the children of John Davis were born on Long Island, and that his son Isaac Davis came to New Jersey before his father. John Davis is said to have married Dorothea Gotherson in 1680, and to have had by her the following named children, Isaac, John, David, and Malachi. Two daughters Hannah and Elizabeth died without issue. A daughter Abigail, sometimes spoken of as Abigail Elizabeth Davis, is said to have become the wife of Elisha Bassett of Salem. Later in this narrative it will be shown that this Davis-Bassett marriage is an error.

The foregoing statements next appear in a pamphlet of twenty-eight pages, with charts, published by Gideon D. Scull, at Oxford, England, in 1882. In 1883 Mr. Scull issued a larger volume of two hundred and sixteen pages, with charts, which is a mine of information concerning Dorothea Scott, otherwise Gotherson and Hogbien, but which gives no authority for the claimed marriage of her daughter to one John Davis of Oyster Bay, Long Island. The interest of Mr. Scull in this matter was personal, he being noted on one of the illustrating charts as a descendant of John Davis.

An examination of this pedigree shows that no evidence has yet been made available to prove: first, the Davis-Gotherson marriage; second, that therefore the royal descent indicated in the Scott charts may not be

---

* Pp. 233, 243, 373, 576.

**Page 825, this volume.

properly claimed by the Davis family of Salem County, New Jersey; third, that the commonly accepted account of said Davis family should be rewritten.

The royal pedigree claimed is that given in Browning's *Americans of Royal Descent*, 1891, page 257, and may only be accepted as tracing the pedigree of Dorothea (Scott) Gotherson, to Edward I. A portion of this pedigree is also used in *Magna Charta Barons* (1915), p. 286.

Stated briefly, the fact is, that in Browning's *Americans of Royal Descent* has been printed a royal pedigree, beginning with Edward I, King of England, and ending with David Davis of Salem County, New Jersey, and his sister, Abigail Davis, referred to as having married Elisha Bassett.

In the first edition of Gideon Scull's Dorothea Scott, 1882, no mention is made of the marriage of Abigail Davis to Elisha Bassett. The marriage is first indicated in the second and enlarged edition of 1883.

Reference to New Jersey Archives, First Series, Volume XXX, page 134 shows that Isaac Davis of Pilesgrove Township, Salem County, New Jersey, who made his will March 25, 1739, speaks of his daughter Abigail Bassett and of Elisha Bassett. Hence the Abigail Davis who married Elisha Bassett was the daughter of Isaac Davis and the grand-daughter of the John Davis heretofore spoken of as being her father.

Shourd's also states that Issac Davis came to Salem County before John Davis, his father, and that they both came from Long Island. The reference for the coming of the father, John Davis, is to be found on page 604 of the *Calendar New Jersey Records 1664-1703* (Archives, First Series, XX), where it is noted that on April 25, 1694, an assignment was made by John Haselwood to John Davis, late of longe Island, newyorkshire, of all his right and title in 200 acres of land.

In a deed of January 2, 1704, John Budd of Gloucester County, New Jersey, conveyed to John Davis and Isaac Davis, both of the Island of Nassau, in the Province of New York, yeomen, for the sum of eighty four pounds, seven hundred acres of land in the Western Division of New Jersey, each to receive three hundred and fifty acres.*

Of record at Trenton, New Jersey, is a deed poll of July 17, 1718, in which John Davis of Pilesgrove, Salem County, for 100 pounds sells to his two sons David and Malachi Davis of the same county, husband-men as " joint tenants in common and that there might be no advantage taken by survivorship " 237 acres of land in Pilesgrove Precinct, adjoining other land of the said John Davis and of Isaac Davis, are conveyed to each. Receipt of purchase dated 9th 2 mo., 1720.

The will of John Davis Jr., of Pilesgrove, dated 7, 3, 1734, shows he had children Thomas, John, Mary, Phebe and Charity. He directs that part of his plantation lying in Penns Neck and bought by him and his brother David of their Brother Malachi, be sold. That he had a wife named Eleanor, is shown by her signature to other papers.

The name of John Davis first appears in the records of Salem Monthly Meeting in 1729, and the first mentoin of a Dorothea Davis

---

* Salem, N. J., Old Deed Book, 1715-1797.

is in 1728. There is no doubt but that *this* Dorothea Davis is the wife of David Davis, and her maiden name appears to have been Cousins.

There is no certificate, or other record, to show where this John Davis Sr. came from, and there is no mention therein of the death of John Davis Sr., nor can any particular meeting record be ascribed with certainty to John Davis Jr., or to his father. Such, in general, is the situation which led to a checking of records * relating to the Scott-Davis pedigree as given by Scull and used by Browning and numerous other secondary authorities.

The result obtained by this research is discouraging. The most promising lead appeared in Volume XV, page 41, of the *New York Genealogical and Biographical Record*, where A. H. D. asked for information concerning one John Davis who, with his brother Thomas Davis, came to America from Kidderminster, England, resided for a time at Lynn, Massachusetts, then at New Haven, Connecticut, finally settling at East Hampton, Long Island. This request was followed in Volume XXVIII, page 62, by the announcement of a History of the Davis Family, descendants of John Davis, who died in East Hampton, Long Island, in 1705, by Albert H. Davis.

This particular John Davis is stated to have been born in England, 1612, and to have died at East Hampton, Long Island (Church Record), December 22, 1705. The name of his wife, who was also born in England, is not given. The names of the children were John, Hannah, and Thomas. Enough is therein noted to show that no John Davis of this Long Island family could have married a Dorothea Gotherson on Long Island, and removed to Pilesgrove Township, Salem County, New Jersey, in 1705.

References there are in the Long Island towns of Oyster Bay and Hempstead to other Johns Davis. But the most careful scrutiny and unbiased evaluation of the evidence presented leads but to the observation that nothing has yet appeared to confirm the Scott-Gotherson-Davis pedigree. What facts in Mr. Sculls' possession used to construct his charts, are' not now in evidence. Browning in referring to these charts as his authority, evidently took them at their face value.

Concerning the coming of Dorothea Gotherson to America, Scull states in his edition of 1883, page 31: " After the sale [of her English estate] in 1680, it would appear that Dorothea Gotherson and her children embarked in the autumn of that year for Oyster Bay, Long Island in America. Here her husband had, as early as 1633, purchased

---

* So far the works checked include: Americans of Royal Descent; Ellis, History of Gloucester, Salem and Cumberland Counties; Colonial Dames of Royal Decent; Sculls' Dorothea Scott, edition of 1882; Sculls' Dorothea Scott, 1883; Publications of The Genealogical Society of Pennsylvania; Printed Archives of New York and New Jersey; Publications of The New York Historical Society and The New York Genealogical and Biographical Society; New England Historical and Genealogical Register; Local Histories relating to Long Island and New England, not a few.

a few acres of land in that settlement. . . . John Richbell, merchant of Oyster Bay, sold 28th of August, 1633, to Daniel Gotherson his two dividends or allotments of land, containing together by estimate ten acres, situated in Oyster Bay, late in the occupation of Mark Meggs and Walter Scott.—Power of Attorney of Mrs. Gotherson to Governor Lovelace."

Long Island Friends Records, as published, show no Davis nor Gotherson references. It is possible, however, that the unpublished minutes might afford such references, but no checking of these have as yet been done by anyone making claim of descent from Dorothea Gotherson.—THOMAS BUTLER, Philadelphia.

MICHAEL SHINNICK OF THE NORTHERN LIBERTIES AND OXFORD TOWNSHIP, AND HIS SCHÖNECK-EGLER ANCESTRY

BY WALTER LEE SHEPPARD, JR., F.A.S.G.

In *The American Genealogist,* Volumes XVII, 79-86, and XIX, 45, 176, the writer presented a study of JOHANN MICHAEL SCHÖNECK and three generations of his descendants who used the spelling *Shinnick.* Since the appearance of those articles, further information regarding the antecedents of this emigrant have been supplied as a result of the able research of Dr. Karl Friedrich von Frank, F.A.S.G., of Austria. It has been thought worthwhile, therefore, to present this new information, with a short summary of the original article, in the study which follows.

HANS GEORG (JERG) SCHÖNECK, father of the above-mentioned Johann Michael Schöneck, was born and baptised at Klein-Sachsenheim, Württemberg,[1] on 15 January 1708, son of Bernhardt Schöneck,[2] a farmer of the same place, and his wife Elisabetha, daughter of Johann Jakob Kirn.[3] Hans George Schöneck became a shoemaker in Klein-Sachsenheim, but it was at Pfaffenhofen, Württemberg, that he married on Friday, 16 February 1734, SOPHIA AGATHA EGLER, born 3 April 1714,

---

[1] Klein-Sachsenheim, a village in the district Vaihingen, lies about 13 air-miles north of Stuttgart near a small tributary of the Neckar River. In 1883 it had 957 inhabitants. The parish and archival records of this place and others cited in the text were furnished by Dr. Karl Friedrich von Frank, Schloss Senftenegg, Post Ferschnitz, Niederösterreich. Certified copies are in the possession of the author.

[2] Bernhardt Schöneck, farmer, was the son of George Schöneck of Gross-Aspach, and d. in Klein-Sachsenheim 14 Feb. 1754, aged about 76 yrs, having m. there 21 Nov. 1702. Gross-Aspach lies about 9 miles east of the Neckar and due east of Klein-Sachsenheim about 15 miles.

[3] His daughter Elizabeth Kirn, wife of Bernard Schöneck, was b. and bapt. 29 Apr. 1677 at Gross-Sachsenheim south of the tributary of the Neckar. She d. at Klein-Sachsenheim 25 June 1715, aged 38. Her father, Johann (Hans) Jacob Kirn, who was b. and bapt. 31 Mar. 1651 and d. 5 Apr. 1696, aged 45 yrs., was the son of Jacob Kirn (Kurn), bapt. 26 June 1618, who m. at Gross-Sachsenheim 9 May 1647, Martha, daughter of Hans Würtemberger of Gross-Glattbach, a town some ten miles southwest of Klein-Sachsenheim. According to the town records of Gross-Sachsenheim, this elder Jacob Kirn on 13 Sept. 1652, apparently in a tavern brawl, stabbed one Peter Hamburger "in the back from the third rib upwards with a prohibited weapon." As a result of this injury Hamburger died on 22 September, and Jacob Kirn was ordered to be brought to trial at Stuttgart. He escaped, however, from his improperly guarded cell, using a drill to force the lock, and is thereafter lost to history, as he was not recaptured. One wonders what was considered a legal weapon for stabbing, and where he acquired a drill! He was a son of Martin Kirn of Beihingen, in the parish of Haiterbach, district Nagold, about 35 miles southwest of Stuttgart, who married 24 Aug. 1607, Rosina Roller of Pfalzgrafenweiler, 5 miles west of Beihingen, in district Freuenstadt. The younger Jacob Kirn m. Anna Maria Vischer, b. and bapt. 10 Aug. 1654; bur. 2 Feb. 1714 "aged about 60 years." She was the daughter of the assistant judge, Andreas Vischer, born in Marschalkenzimmern, about 14 miles south of Pfalzgrafenweiler, who d. 15 Feb. 1684, aged 66, by his second wife Susanna Fleischmann whom he m. 8 Apr. 1651. Her father Andreas Fleischmann of Klein-Sachsenheim, was described as "a soldier on the Hohentwiel," a famous fortress in district Tuttlingen, just north of the Swiss border.

"the legitimate daughter of Johann Martin Egler, forester at this place." The parish record shows that "banns were published on IV Epiphany [28 January], V Epiphany [4 February], and on VI Epiphany [11 February] 1734, all dates being New Style.

It was at Pfaffenhofen, a market town some eight air-miles northwest of Klein-Sachsenheim, near a tributary of the Neckar which supplied several mills, that the couple took up residence. Here the parish records contain the baptisms of four of their children, most of whom were born the day they were baptised:

i. JOHANN MICHAEL SCHÖNECK, b. 20 March 1735; bur. 22 November 1787, of whom further.

ii. ANNA BARBARA SCHÖNECK, bapt. 24 August 1736; bur. 5 July 1778, aged 42 years; m. at St. Michael's Evangelical Lutheran Church, Philadelphia, 5 March 1761, JOHANNES HEINRICH BAUER, a taylor by trade. They lived in the present 132 Elfreth's Alley from at least 1779 through 1785. Issue, all baptised at St. Michael's Lutheran Church: 1. CHARLOTTA BAUER, b. 2 October; bapt. 16 October 1763; sponsors: Johann Andreas Figner and wife Sophia Agatha. 2. JOHANN HEINRICH BAUER, b. 13 September; bapt. 21 October 1768; sponsors: Michael Schoeneck and wife Catharina. 3. JOHAN HEINRICH BAUER, b. 21 December, bapt. 26 December 1771; sponsors: " the father and mother-in-law Fagnerin." 4. MICHAEL BAUER, b. 6 April 1773; bapt. 18 April 1773; sponsors: Michael " Chenneck " and wife Catherina. 5. GEORGE BAUER, b. 6 October, bapt. 20 October 1776; sponsors: Michael " Schneck " and Catherina; bur. 18 November 1777. Johannes Bauer, widower, m. 2nd at St. Michael's, 29 October 1778, Catharina Schaeffer. Their descendants have not been followed.

iii. SABINA REGINA SCHÖNECK, bapt. 3 March 1739. Her name is crossed out in the family record of Pfaffenhofen parish, wherein each name is labelled " child." While the crossing out of the name may indicate this child died, it was standard practice to so mark names when a parishoner, or member of his family, moved away.[4]

iv. GEORGE FRIEDRICH SCHÖNECK, bapt. 31 May 1742. His name is also crossed off in the family's parish record.[5]

v. A son, name unknown,[6] deceased by 1794.

---

[4] Dr. von Frank supplied the information regarding the practice of crossing out names in parish registers.

[5] The transcript of records for St. Michael's Evangelical Lutheran Church, Germantown, in Collections of the Genealogical Society of Pennsylvania (hereinafter cited as GSP), note the burial on 17 Jan. 1777 of one Georg Schönig, aged 30. Except for the discrepancy of five years (perhaps an error), the entry may reflect the son Georg Friedrich Schöneck of the text. The same records also contain the baptism of one Maria Elisabetha Steinbrunner, daughter of Johannes Steinbrunner and wife Catherine, b. 27 Mar. 1757, bapt. 17 Apr. 1759, whose sponsor was Maria Elisabetha Schoenig, "the grandmother." Whether these entries are connected with the Schöneck family of this text has not been determined. See *The American Genealogist*, XVII, 79 for mention of other Schöneck immigrants.

[6] While this son may have died in infancy, there was a *Jacob Schenenck* listed as living in Montgomery Co., Pa., in the 1790 *Heads of Families* census, 159. He was head of a household which included 4 males under 16 years, 4 females over 16, and one slave.

Early in 1753 Hans George Schöneck, father of these children, petitioned the authorities in Pfaffenhofen for permission to emigrate to America. The parish register there shows that he, his wife Sophia Agatha, and their son Johann Michael Schöneck, now aged eighteen years, took communion for the last time at Pfaffenhofen on Easter Sunday (22 April) 1753. Neither Anna Barbara, then nearly seventeen years old, nor the three younger children listed above, took communion.

The Schöneck family, accompanied by Sophia Agatha's widowed father Johann Martin Egler, and her sister Margaretha Egler, travelled to Rotterdam, probably down the Neckar to its junction with the Rhine at Mannheim. At Rotterdam they took passage on the ship *Eastern Branch*, Captain James Nevin, bound for Philadelphia. After stopping at Plymouth en route to the new world, the family had arrived at Philadelphia by 3 October 1753, when the male passengers took and subscribed to the oaths of allegiance and abjuration before William Peters, Esq., at the Court House. The signers included both young Johann Michael Schöneck, who signed as "Johann Michel Schönek," and his grandfather Johann Martin Egler, who signed as "Joh. Marttin Egle."

Hans Georg Schöneck made his mark on the lists, the attendant clerks writing his name as "Johannes Sherney" on one list, and "Johanes Chirny" on another.[7] Dr. von Frank, who identified these last names as belonging to the father, has pointed out that either spelling would yield to the non-Germanic clerks the same sound as "Schöneck."

After his landing in Philadelphia, no further records have been found relating to Hans Georg Schöneck. Presumably he died shortly afterwards, for on 22 April 1754 his widow, as Sophia Agatha Egler, married as her second husband ANDREAS FÜGNER, born 25 August 1720, son of Andreas and Barbara Elisabeth Fügner, according to his burial record. The marriage was performed by the pastor of St. Michael's (later St. Michael's and Zion) Evangelical Lutheran Church in Philadelphia. Witnesses were Adam and Dorothea Merkel, and Christian and Dorothea Lubeman.[8]

---

[7] William J. Hinke, ed., *Pennsylvania German Pioneers* (Norristown, Pa., 1934), I, 585-588, Lists 213-A-B-C. Apparently Hans Georg Schöneck commonly went by his first name of Hans (Johannes), rather than by his second Christian name, as was more usual.

[8] The cornerstone for Zion Lutheran Church in Philadelphia was not laid until 1766, and the church not dedicated until 1769. Prior to this period the congregation was known as St. Michael's Evangelical Lutheran Church, Philadelphia, to distinguish it from the congregation in Germantown. Andreas Fügner, whose name appears on the ship lists as *Figener* and *Fygner*, had arrived in Philadelphia on board the snow

The newlyweds stood sponsors at St. Michael's on 23 August 1756 for Anna Maria, daughter of Michael and Anna Maria Rosnagle, and on 6 January 1765, for Andreas, son of Andreas and Ursula Spannagle. By 1769 they were living in Mulberry Ward in a house rented from the tavern-keeper John Wiseman. On the tax-lists that year, Sophia Agatha's husband was listed as "Andrew Figner, glover." By 1779 they had moved to the western part of the ward.[9] He died eight years later, aged a little over 67 years, and was buried 16 December 1787, according to the burial record of St. Michael's and Zion Church.

The burial record of his widow, in the registers of the same church, is under date of 30 September 1795; in translation it reads:

> Anna Sophia Agatha Fügner, born 11 April 1710. Parents: Johann Martin Egler and wife A. Barbara. Married 1st with Georg Schöneck in 1734, 3 sons, 2 daughters who are all dead; 2nd, in 1754 with Andreas Fügner. Died on the 28th of fever.[10]

Although the record does not so state, this was most probably yellow fever which was ravaging the city again that summer.

JOHANN MICHAEL SCHÖNECK, eldest son of Hans Georg Schöneck and his wife Sophia Agatha Egler, was baptised 21 March 1735 at Pfaffenhofen. His baptismal sponsors were Johann Adam Klein, a member of the town council; Philip Schaber, citizen and farmer; and Elisabeth Barbara, wife of J. Hans Jerg Thüringer, a shoemaker. The last-named sponsor may have been his father's partner, or perhaps the man to whom his father had been apprenticed.[11]

Good Hope, John Trump, Master, from Hamburg. He took the necessary qualifications 29 Sept. 1753. Pennsylvania German Pioneers, op. cit., I, 573-575, Lists 210-A-B-C. He appears to have been a widower with children, for St. Michael's registers show the burial on 6 Sept. 1758 of Johann Valentin, aged 7 years, son of Andreas Fügner. When this writer prepared the original Shinnick article for The American Genealogist, cited in the text, the original records of St. Michael's and Zion were not available to the public for inspection; searches and copies made by church officials were not always accurate. Since then the registers have been microfilmed and copies deposited in GSP which supplement the English translations of the early records made many years ago. After examination of the microfilm copies, Dr. von Frank pointed out that the abstract originally furnished the writer by the church, which gave Paulgros for Andreas Fügner, was incorrect.

[9] Pennsylvania Archives, 3rd Series, XIV, 204, 549, 826. See also the copy of the original tax list for 1769 which gives Fügner's landlord.

[10] The information contained in this burial record was no doubt furnished by her grandchildren, all of her own children having predeceased her, hence the discrepancy in her birth date of four years. The record is also the only place where the additional name of Anna appears. Dr. von Frank states it was not unusual for a girl to add to her given names that of one of her baptismal sponsors.

[11] Thüringer may have borne a close relationship to the Joh. Balthasar Thüringer "born at Paffenhoven in Giglingen Amt. Württemberg" in 1712, according to his burial record dated 22 Sept. 1777 in St. Michael's and Zion register, who arrived at Philadelphia and qualified 19 Sept. 1752, and to Joh. Ludwig Türringer, b. in Pfaffenhofen in 1703, "son of Joh. Georg Türringer and his wife Anna Catharina," who d. 13 Dec. 1777, according to the same register, and had qualified 27 Sept. 1752. Pennsylvania German Pioneers, op. cit., I, 480, 491, Lists 178-C and 186-C.

Although his father was not literate, Michael received some schooling, perhaps at the instance of his Egler grandparents, for he wrote his name in a clear and legible hand when he arrived with his parents on the *Eastern Branch* in 1753. Then only eighteen, there is no record of him for the next three years. But early in January 1757, just before his twenty-second birthday, he enlisted in Lord Jeffrey Amherst's Royal American Regiment of Foot. The regiment during the following three years took an active part in the French and Indian War, participating in the action at Louisburg in July 1758, at Ticonderoga and Crown Point a year later, and at Montreal in 1760. After the Treaty of Paris in 1763 concluded that war, the regiment saw further service against the Indians during Pontiac's conspiracy.

In how many of these actions Johann Michael Schöneck actually participated is not known, but his discharge, dated 3 August 1765, states that he served eight years and eight months.[12] It also gives the only personal description of him which has survived:

> By Captain James Marcus Prevost Commanding the First Battalion of His Majestys 60th or Royal American Regiment of Foot Whereof Sir Jeffrey Amherst is Col° in Chief These are to Certify that the Bearer hereof, Michael Jennick, born in Germany, aged Twenty Eight years and Six Months, Black Complexion Black Hair Brown Eyes five Feet four Inches high, has Served Honestly and Faithfully for the Space of Eight years and Eight Months as a soldier in the said Battalion in Captain Fizers Company, And He is hereby Discharged after having received all his Cloathing, Pay, Arrears and all Demands whatsoever, from the Time of his Inlistment, to this present Day of his Discharge, as appears by his Receipt on the back hereof. Given under my Hand and Seal at New York this third day of August 1765.

On the back of the discharge appears the receipt, with his clear signature:

> I Michael Jennick do Acknowledge to have Received my Pay, Arrears of Pay, Cloathing, and all Demands whatever, from the Time of my Inlistment to the present Day of my Discharge, and I do hereby Acquit my Colonial, Captain, and every other Officer from any Dues, Debts or Demands Whatsoever, As Witness my hand this third Day of August 1765 as also I have received three weeks pay to carry me home.
> /s/ Johann Michael Schöneck
> Witness
> Thomas Moss, Serj[t]

Michael Schöneck is next seen in Philadelphia ten months later. Here he married on 3 June 1766, ANNA HELENA PENZ, a widow, "born Thenerin from Darmbach in Canton Ottenwald." Less than a year later she died "in a hard confinement with a dead child, aged 39 years, 4 months less 6 days," and was buried 2 February 1767 in St. Michael's cemetery.

---

12 The discharge is reproduced in *The American Genealogist*, XVII, facing p. 80.

Michael Schöneck married second, on 9 June 1767, ANNA CATHA-
RINA HOLD, daughter of Johann Adam Hold (Holdt, Holtz) and his
wife Maria Christina Knochler (Knochel).[13] Michael and his second
wife lived at first in the Northern Liberties where on 31 March 1774 he
purchased a lot at the southwest corner of Second and Coats Street (now
Fairmount Avenue), which extended west to St. John's Street (now N.
American Street).[14]

When the Revolution started, he became an Associator in the local
militia and may have participated in the campaigns of the summers of
1775 and 1776 as part of the Flying Camp, records of which have not
survived. However, by December of the latter year, he was a member of
Captain Christopher Kucher's company, First Battalion Associators of
the City and Liberties, but had not turned out for service, possibly because he was active in the City Guards, where his military experience
would have been valuable in training the volunteers which comprised that
body. By early February 1777, he was a corporal in Captain Jacob
Bright's company of City Guards of the Northern District of Philadelphia, under Colonel Lewis Nichola. When the Militia Act of March
1777, went into effect, he was drafted with other men between 18 and 53
"capable of bearing arms," and found himself in the third class of Captain Anthony Leghner's company, Fifth Battalion, City Militia. They
were called into active service for two month's duty the end of July that
year, as the British approached Philadelphia; Michael, no doubt because
of his connection with the City Guards, paid a substitute to take his
place.[15]

In 1780 Michael and his family moved to Oxford Township, apparently to his father-in-law's farm, and in 1785 sold his property in the

---

13 A short sketch of Johann Adam Hold appears in *The American Genealogist*, XVII, 81, 82. To this
may now be added that his burial record in St. Michael's and Zion register, reads in translation: "17 January 1788, Adam Hold, born in Germany, 68 yrs, 5 mos, 5 ds old, [buried] in Oxford." This was Oxford Twp., Philadelphia Co., where his farm was, at the junction of Martin's Mill Road and Oxford Road.
Dr. von Frank identifies him as the Johann Adam Holdt who landed at Philadelphia from the *Robert and
Alice*, Martley Cusack, Master. He signed the ship lists with a mark "O" when he took the usual qualifications 24 Sept. 1742. *Pennsylvania German Pioneers, op. cit.*, I, 331, List 95-C. As many of the other
passengers were from the vicinity of Walldorf, near Heidelberg, and others were from Sohren in the Rhine-
land, according to Dr. von Frank, a search of the parish registers in both localiteis was undertaken, but
without result. Adam Holt's will, recorded in Philadelphia Will Book U, 73, #12:1788, was also signed
with the mark "O."

14 Recited in Philadelphia Deed Book D-23, 478: 3 Aug. 1785, Michael Sheneck to Conrad Seiffert.
See *Pennsylvania Archives*, 3rd Series, XIV, 396, 667; *ibid.*, XV, 108, 520; ibid., XVI, 12, 69, 182, 631
where his name is spelled Shineck, Shinick, Shinock, Shinnick, Shennack, Shenicks and Shennick.

15 *Pennsylvania Archives*, 6th Series, I, 12, 344, 583; Peters Papers, MS, Historical Society of Pennsylvania, VIII, 44. Family tradition states that he trained and drilled troops during the Revolution. The
interpretation of his Revolutionary service from extant records, as given in the text, was developed by
Hannah Benner Roach.

Northern Liberties for £500. A little over two years later he was dead at the age of 52. He was buried 22 November 1787, according to the records of St. Michael's and Zion Church. His widow Anna Catharina (Hold) Schöneck survived him four years and was buried 24 September 1791. Her burial record, in the same church register, states that she and her husband had "9 children, of which 2 sons and 4 daughters are still alive." Their children, as noted in St. Michael's and Zion registers, were:

i. JOHANN MICHAEL SCHÖNECK, b. 30 March, bapt. 10 April 1768; bur. 19 September 1769, aged 1 year 5 months.

ii. MARIA CHRISTINA SCHÖNECK, b. 6 January; bapt. 21 January 1770; m. 7 February 1791, GEORGE LUDWIG (Lewis) BENNER.

iii. JOHANN ADAM SCHÖNECK, b. 5 October, bapt. 27 October 1771; d. 6 April 1816; m. 4 May 1794, MARIA ELISABETH KEPPLER. For further data on their descendants see *The American Genealogist*, XVII, 84; *ibid.*, XIX, 45, 176, and *National Genealogical Society Quarterly*, XLVIII (March, 1961), 28-34.

iv. ELISABETH SCHÖNECK, b. 23 September, bapt. 17 October 1773; m. 1st, 9 May 1791, GEORG DIETRICH LEX; m. 2nd, before 1808, JOHN DORR.

v. ANNA CATHARINA SCHÖNECK,[16] b. 22 May, bapt. 4 June 1775; d. 6 September 1776, aged 1 year 3 month " of diarrhoea and vomiting."

vi. JOHANN JACOB SCHÖNECK, b. 22 January, bapt. 2 February 1777; d. 23 July 1842; m. 1st, 7 March 1799, ELISABETH KNORR, d. 25 June 1807; m. 2nd, 11 August 1808, HARRIET DIVERS who d. 26 August 1822; m. 3rd, 18 March 1827, Mrs. BARBARA (LAMMATT) BOWSER. For descendants see *The American Genealogist*, cited above.

vii. SOPHIA SCHÖNECK, b. 7 February, bapt. 27 February 1780; m. 30 January 1800, JACOB LENTZ as his 2nd wife. For further account of them see *National Genealogical Society Quarterly*, XLVIII (March, 1961), 28-34.

viii. ANNA CATHARINA SCHÖNECK, b. 4 July, bapt. 11 August 1782; bur. 14 August 1783, aged 1 year, 2 months, 8 days.

ix. ANNA BARBARA SCHÖNECK, b. 17 December 1783, bapt. 4 January 1784; m. before 1808, MICHAEL KNORR.[17]

---

16 The Anna Catharina Schöneck who married Johann Müller, reported in *The American Genealogist*, XVII, 84, as belonging to this family, is now shown to be incorrect. Perhaps she was connected with the family mentioned in Note 5, above.

17 Michael Knorr was a son of Bernard Knorr of Oxford Twp. See estate papers of Bernard Knorr, Philadelphia Administration #1:1817. Elisabeth Knorr, above-noted, who married Johann Jacob Schöneck in 1799, was probably the Elisabeth Knorr, daughter of Bernard Knorr and wife, bapt. 5 Apr. 1778 at St. John's (Höhn's) Reformed Church, Heidelberg Twp., Berks Co. See *Publications* of this Society, V, 70. This Bernard Knorr was a son of Hans Peter Knauer (Knorr) who qualified 14 Sept. 1751, (*Pennsylvania-German Pioneers, op. cit.*, I, 458, List 166-C), settled in Whitemarsh Twp., and died in 1771, (Philadelphia Will Book P, 142, #97:1771) leaving a widow Catherine Margaret; brother Melchior Knorr who had wife Catherine; and children: Christian, Margaret, wife of John Tolbert, Barnet (Bernard), Eve, George, Elisabeth and Peter Knorr. The writer is indebted to Hannah Benner Roach for the identification of this particular Knorr family which is not to be confused with the Germantown family of the same surname.

About the year 1700 one JACOB EGLER, then about fifty years old, came to Frauenzimmern,[18] three and a half miles east of Pfaffenhofen, to live. He was apparently a widower, and already the father of at least two children:

    i. ANNA MARIA EGLER who m. 5 June 1708 JACOB MOOSS.

    ii. JOHANN MARTIN EGLER, b. *ca.* 1685; d. after 3 October 1753, of whom further.

On 3 May 1701 the widower Jacob Egler married his second wife, MARIA MAGLADENA KÜGLER, "daughter of the magistrate of Michelbach." They had eight children, all baptized at Frauenzimmern, of whom the two who lived to marry and have issue were:

    iii. FRIEDRICH LUDWIG EGLER, a baker by trade, b. 20 January 1702; bur. 10 September 1726; m. 6 February 1725, ANNA CHRISTINA KRANNICH,[19] daughter of Jerg Krannich. She m. 2nd, 26 August 1727, Jerg Bach.

    iv. MARGARETHA ESTHER EGLER, b. 13 September 1707; d. 28 August 1791; m. 1st, 24 September 1726, JOHANN CUNRADT SCHEERLIN,[20] schoolmaster, who d. 31 August 1745. She m. 2nd, 3 May 1746, another schoolmaster, JOHANN JACOB, who d. 15 September 1791.

Jacob Egler was a "seignioral tenant farmer" and "ducal land steward" at Frauenzimmern when he died 1 April 1710. According to the parish register, his death occurred "between 3 and 4 o'clock in the evening and [he] was honorably interred on the 3rd following. His age was 60 years." His widow Maria Magdalena (Kügler) Egler, seven months later married on 18 November 1710, one Thomas Kull, and lived for twenty-two more years. She was buried 13 December 1732.

JOHANN MARTIN (Hans Martin) EGLER, son of the above Jacob Egler and his unknown first wife, on 11 February 1710, a scant two

---

The marriage connection of Michael Knorr with the Schöneck family is established in the 1808 settlement papers of the estate of Adam Hold. Therein the surviving children of Michael and Catherine Schöneck include Elisabeth, wife of John Dorr, Sophia, wife of Jacob Lentz, and Anna Barbara, wife of Michael Knorr. See Adam Hold estate papers, cited in Note 13 above.

[18] Jacob Egler's removal to Frauenzimmern about 1700 may have been occasioned by the unsettled times, just as earlier, during the Thirty Years' War, the Kirns had migrated from the vicinity of Beihingen eastward to Klein-Sachsenheim. During the last decades of the 17th century, French troops, under Louis XIV, had ravaged the Rhenish Palatinate and penetrated the duchy of Württemburg.

[19] They had one daughter, *Christina Magdalena Egler,* b. 3 Dec., bapt. 6 Dec. 1725, at Frauenzimmern.

[20] Their children, all bapt. at Frauenzimmern were: 1. *Christoph Cunrad Scheerlin,* 4 Apr. 1733. 2. *Ludovica Margaretha Scheerlin,* 27 June 1739. 3. *Johanna Louisa Scheerlin,* 5 Mar. 1741.

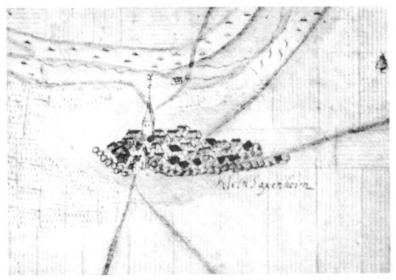

FRAUENZIMMERN AND KLEIN-SACHSENHEIM

Enlarged from seventeenth-century manuscript map: Kieser'sche Forstkarten, State Archives, Speyer.

months before his father's death, married ANNA CHRISTINA (SPIEGEL) GREIFF. Their marriage record at Pfaffenhofen describes the groom as "ducal forester at this place, the legitimate son of the ducal land-steward at Frauenzimmern, Jacob Egler." The bride, who had been baptised 14 April 1685 in Pfaffenhofen, was the daughter of Johann Remigius Spiegel and his wife Maria Agatha. The bride's first husband, whom she had married in Pfaffenhofen 16 November 1706, had been George Conrad Greiff, a tailor, son of Christian Greiff, assistant judge of Feuerbach.[21] Her second marriage lasted an even shorter time than the first, for less than a year after the ceremony she died at Pfaffenhofen, apparently without issue, on 26 January 1711, aged 25 years, 9 months.

After her death Johann Martin Egler found a second wife in the town of Löchgau, some seven miles southeast of Pfaffenhofen and about two miles west of the Neckar. On 3 November 1711, less than a year after his first wife's death, he married at Löchgau ANNA BARBARA PROGLI, daughter of Felix Progli (Pragli) and his wife Margaretha. The record of their marriage in the Löchgau register reads: *Die 3 9bris [1711] wurden copuliret, Johann Martin Egler, witwer v. Forstknecht zuo Pfaffenhofen, v. Anna Barbara, Felix Progglis, Burgers allhier Ehliche Dochter*, in translation, "On the 3rd day of November were joined Johann Martin Egler, widower annd forester in Pfaffenhofen, and Anna Barbara, the legitimate daughter of Felix Progli, citizen at this place." The Pfaffenhofen marriage entry varies slightly: *d. 3 Novembi zu Löchgaw, Johann Martin Egler, Wittwer und herrschaftlich Jäger allhier, Anna Barbara, Felix Bragners, Burgers zu Löchgaw, ehelicher Tochter.* Here the bride's name is given as "Bragner," apparently a Württemberger variation of the Swiss form of "Progli." This is substantiated by the Löchgau burial record of her father which states that "Felix Pragels, a citizen of Löchgau, born in Switzerland, died 30 July 1720, aged 65." According to the same record, her mother "Margaretha, widow of Felix Pragli, died of dysentery 29 October 1727."

Martin Egler took his new wife Anna Barbara back to Pfaffenhofen where their daughter Sophia Agatha Egler, who married Hans Jerg Schöneck, as previously noted, was born 3 April 1714. According to the parish record, Sophia Agatha's sponsors in baptism were "Sir Philipp Gottfried von Leutrum, son of the titled Sir First Commissioner of Woods and Forests in the preserve park; Anna, wife of Johann Balthasar Fabritius; and Christina, wife of Christoph Stuber." The father of von Leutrum, Sophia Agatha's baptismal sponsor, was "Master of Woods and Forest" of the Stromberg district from 1713 to 1717. Presumably her

---

[21] Feuerbach is just outside Stuttgart to the northwest.

father, Hans Martin Egler, "forester on foot [as distinct from mounted] in the Ebersbach wardenship, forest district of Stromberg," [22] was under his jurisdiction. Some twenty-five years later Egler no longer held this position. When his wife Anna Barbara (Progli) Egler died of consumption at Pfaffenhofen on 15 February 1739, aged 48 years, Hans Martin Egler was stated in her death record to be the "former ducal forester of this place."

No complete list of the other children of Egler and his wife Anna Barbara has been found for this record. However, in an undated communicant register of Pfaffenhofen, the family is listed as including his wife Anna Barbara, the daughter Margaretha (a communicant), as well as daughters Anna and Christina (unconfirmed), and presumed to be children. Apparently the list included only those members of the family then living at home.[23] As all these Egler names in this list had been crossed out, it would seem that the individuals had either died or moved away. Of them all, only Hans Martin and his daughter Margaretha Barbara are subsequently mentioned. While she obtained a permit to emigrate in 1753, none has been found for her father. It is assumed that she accompanied him, her sister Sophia Agatha Schöneck, and the latter's husband, Hans Georg Schöneck, on their voyage to Philadelphia on the *Eastern Branch*. Hans Martin reached port, since he signed the ship lists, but no further record of him has been found.[24] Perhaps, like his son-in-law, he died shortly after landing as a result of the rigors of the voyage.

TABLE OF WÜRTTEMBERG EVANGELICAL PARISH REGISTERS

Beihingen. Prior to 1808 in the parish of Haiterbach, district Nagold. Registers at Haiterbach: Baptisms from 1566, marriages from 1565, burials from 1636 to date. In 1883: 288 inhabitants.

Frauenzimmern. District Brackenheim. Baptisms from 1558, marriages from 1565, burials from 1614 to date. In 1883: 550 inhabitants.

Gross-Glattbach. District Vaihingen. Baptisms from 1647, marriages from 1707, burials from 1649 to date. In 1883: 753 inhabitants.

Gross-Sachsenheim. District Vaihingen. Baptisms, marriages and burials from 1562 to date. In 1883: 1304 inhabitants.

---

22 The forest district of Stromberg extended northwest from Löchgau some 15 miles.

23 The entry must have been made after 16 Feb. 1734, the date of Sophia Agatha Egler's marriage, since she was not included in the family list, and before 15 Feb. 1739, the date of her mother's death. If there were other living children, they presumably were grown and in homes of their own.

24 See *Pennsylvania German Pioneers*, Lists 213-A-B-C, as cited in Note 7, above. The published records of the Williams Township Lutheran congregation in Northampton County, *Pennsylvania-German Society Proceedings*, XVIII, show the baptism on 26 Jan. 1755, of Christina Magdalena, daughter of a Johann Martin *Egle* and wife Fredericka Albertina. Whether the Hans Martin Egler of the text was the same man as this Johann Martin Egle has not been determined. If he was the same, his third marriage, at the age of 69 or 70 years, almost certainly took place in Pennsylvania.

Hohentwiel. An enclave, district Tuttlingen. Records prior to 1732 at Tuttlingen, starting 1661. Local registers of baptisms 1734-66 and burials 1734-90 destroyed by fire in 1803.

Klein-Sachsenheim. District Vaihingen. Baptisms 1569-1655; 1673 to date. Marriages 1575-1685; 1693 to date. Burials 1591-1685; 1693 to date. In 1883: 957 inhabitants.

Löchgau. District Besigheim. Baptisms 1579-1679; 1693 to date. Marriages 1579-1679; 1716 to date. Burials 1579-1679; 1716 to date. In 1883: 1288 inhabitants.

Marschalkenzimmern. District Sulz. Baptisms from 1637, marriages from 1684, burials from 1682 to date. In 1883: 731 inhabitants.

Pfaffenhofen. District Heilbron. Baptisms, marriages and burials from 1558 to date. In 1883: 944 inhabitants.

Pfalzgrafenweiler. District Freudenstadt. Baptisms, marriages and burials from 1645 to date. In 1883: 1315 inhabitants.

THE SIMPSONS OF PAXTANG AND SUNBURY, PENNSYLVANIA

By George V. Massey II

The First and Second Generations.

Just at this spot the country is romantic. The name of the creek running thro' it, *Yellow-breeches* creek, may, indeed be unworthy of it. From hence the road lay thro' woods till the Susquehanna, and Harrisburg at a distance denoted that the ferry was at hand. I crossed the river about three and a half o'clock, surrounded by enchanting prospects. The ride to Middletown is along the eastern bank, and exhibits a striking sample of the *great*, in the opposite one, rising to a vast height, and wooded close to the water's edge for many miles. From this vast forest, and the expansive bed of the river navigable to its source for craft carrying two tons burden, the ideas of grandeur and immensity rush forcibly upon the mind, mixed with the desert-wildness of an uninhabited scene.

The first particular object on this road is Simpson's house, the owner of the ferry where I crossed. It is on a rock across the river.[1]

This house,[2] past which John Penn[3] rode on April 13, 1788, was that of " a gentleman of aristocratic bearing, yet much loved and respected by his neighbors."[4] A lieutenant at the siege of Quebec, Michael Simpson served throughout the Revolution with great credit, was later major-general of militia.[5] General Washington visited him overnight, at his house, October 23, 1794.[6]

---

[1] John Penn's Journal of a trip to Harrisburg, III, PMHB, 292-3.

[2] *Ibid.*, 293.

[3] John Penn (1729-95), grandson of William Penn (*Dict. of Amer. Biog.*).

[4] I, Egle's *Harrisburg Historical Register*, pp. 227-8.

[5] III, PMBH, 293.

[6] Helen A. Simpson's *Early Records of Simpson Families*, p. 177.

Sixty-eight years before John Penn's trip, a small band of Scots-Irish had come to settle (1720) [7] upon this scene of grandeur and immensity. Among these were John and Thomas Simpson from North Ireland, where, after the battle of Boyne, their father John had removed and died.[8]

The Indians called this part of the forest along the Susquehanna, where now spread Harrisburg and its suburbs, Paxtang, "where the waters stand " or " place of springs." [9]

Strict Covenanters, these men who built a log church, established a burying-ground soon after arrival. Here the Presbytery of New Castle sent the Reverend James Anderson and others, to preach.[10]

1. JOHN SIMPSON, the elder brother, born in 1680,[11] executed his will at Fishing Creek, when " very sick and weak though in perfect senses and memory." His estate, consisting of sums of money due him, was left to his executor Thomas Armstrong. This document was proved October 30, 1738, by Alexander Armstrong and William Bowman.[12] Contrary to Egle, his will is fair evidence that John left no children.[13]

2. THOMAS SIMPSON, the younger brother, born in 1683,[14] brought from Ireland his family, consisting, no doubt, of his wife, Jean and several children. His son Nathaniel and a daughter, Mrs. William Harper,[15] remained abroad.

A warrant for 200 acres in Paxtang Township was issued to Thomas Simpson March 22, 1733.[16] On May 21, 1735 he signed a petition for the building of a road to Philadelphia from Harris' Ferry.[17]

---

[7] Probably by 1716 (Egle's *Hist. of Dauphin Co., Pa.*, p. 394). Traditionally the Simpson brothers came in 1720 (monument at Paxtang Presbyterian Churchyard).

[8] III, Egle's *Notes and Queries*, 3d series, p. 209.

[9] G. P. Donehoo, *A History of Indian Villages, etc. in Pa.*, p. 146.

[10] Egle's *History of Dauphin County, Pa.*, p. 394.

[11] III, Egle's *Notes and Queries*, 3d series, p. 209.

[12] A-1, *Lancaster, Pa., Wills*, p. 33.

[13] III, Egle's *Notes and Queries*, 3d series, p. 209.

[14] *Ibid.*

[15] Son-in-law, Wm. Harper, in Ireland, will of Thomas Simpson, J-1, *Lancaster, Pa., Wills*, p. 247.

[16] Land Office, Harrisburg, Pa. (room 543), 39 S.

[17] Simpson's *Early Records of Simpson Families*, p. 163.

He likely seated land but, as was the case with the Scots-Irish at nearby Donegal, refused to apply, or pay quit-rents for some fifteen years after settling, until certain differences were adjusted with the proprietors.[18]

He did own a house, which he later willed to his wife, carried on the important business of smith, was a planter, and perhaps Indian trader. A glimpse of him and his family may be had from this rather full abstract of his will.

Of the township of "Packston", he was very sick and weak but of perfect mind and memory when on March 25, 1736, he bequeathed his soul to God. Then to Jean "may dearly beloved wife" all debts, and moveables of debts, cows, horses, mears and all household goods. He ordered 6 pounds to carry him out of debts and goods to be paid.

I do live may wife her hous to live in as long as she lives and ye garden in ye north sid of ye house, and ye cafe pasture, and two couse, 1 hors and them to be . . . mentioned and her to be soeported to fair on and all is to be . . . my son Samuel one of may . . . at ye doore.

I give may son Samuel may . . . and he is to give may wife 30 bushels of good wheat yearlay, as long as she lives.

I doe live my son Nathaniel a study and a hamer and 2 pear of tonges, a big vise and his third part of ye small tules.

My son Thomas ye other bige vise, and his third part of ye small tules.

I doe live my son Samuel ye anvell and ye belies and 2 pear of tongues and he is to pay may son Nathaniel 5 pounds of good money and if may son Nathaniel does not come to this country, may wife is to receive her part of tuls and money.

I doe live may grandson Jo . . . 1 gune, may grandson Thomas 1 gune, Andrew Boyed 1 gune.

I doe live may grandson Jo . . . 1 gune, may grandson Andrew Boyd 10 pounds of good money out of May estat, of my daughter . . . son and a gune I do live to may son in law in Ireland, William Harper.

Memorandum yet ye 15 line is entered lined.

Thomas Armstrong   Thomas Simpson
Joseph Hells.[19]

On November 21, 1772, Sarah Forster, late Sarah Armstrong, one of the daughters of Thomas Armstrong, late of "Paxton" Township, deceased, made oath in court that she was well acquainted with the handwriting of Thomas Armstrong, who subscribed his name as witness to

---

[18] Ellis and Evans *History of Lancaster County, Pa.,* p. 23.

[19] J-1, *Lancaster, Pa., Wills,* p. 247. (The original will could not be found. G.V.M. II.)

851

the written will of Thomas Simpson of the same township, deceased.[20]

Whether Thomas Simpson died when he was so very sick in March, 1736, or lived to the year 1772, when Sarah Forster testified concerning her father's signature, is hard to say. The docket does not show specifically that the will was ever probated. His residence, approximate age, family names leave little doubt that Thomas was first of this line in Paxtang.

At Paxtang Churchyard a monument is inscribed:

In memory of Thomas Simpson and his family who settled in Paxtang Anno Domini 1720.[21]

Children of Thomas Simpson of Ireland and Paxtang:

   i.   Nathaniel, resided out of the country, probably in Ireland, when in 1736 his father's will was executed. He may, however, have come to Pennsylvania soon after, for on March 17, 1737, there was warranted to one Nathaniel Simpson 150 acres in Paxtang Township on Spring Creek.[22] No patent was granted.

   ii.   A daughter, married William Harper, probably in Ireland, where he was residing March 25, 1736 when named in her father's will.

3. iii.   Samuel, born in 1708.

4. iv.   Thomas, born ca. 1710-14,[23] married Sarah and had issue, of whom John and Thomas were born before March 25, 1736, when their grandfather's will was executed. Of them further.

   v.   A daughter, married Mr. Boyd and had a son Andrew.

The Third Generation

3. SAMUEL SIMPSON was born in 1708.[24] A warrant for 100 acres in Drumore Township was issued to him February 4, 1741, but he seems not to have seated them.[25] Later 200 acres in Paxtang Township were warranted to him, April 21, 1753. When the survey was made in 1762 the grant was found to total 231 acres.[26] It adjoined the lands of Thomas

---

[20] *Ibid.*

[21] Simpson's *Early Recs. of Simpson Fams.*, p. 164.

[22] Land Office, Harrisburg, Pa., (room 543), warrants, p. 174.

[23] Simpson's *Early Recs. of Simpson Fams.*, pp. 165-6.

[24] III, Egle's *Notes and Queries*, 3d series, p. 209.

[25] Land Office, Harrisburg, Pa., warrants, p. 292.

[26] *Ibid.*, p. 776.

Simpson and William Kelso.[27] Here Samuel established his residence.

He was an ensign, 1747-48, in Captain Andrew Gregg's Company, Pennsylvania Associators, along the Susquehanna, later captain;[28] was called "gentleman" in certain land transfers.[29] He died in December, 1791, leaving a wife, Rebecca, and issue:[30]

    i.   Jean, born 1730.

    ii. Margaret, born 1732; married, October 4, 1752, William Augustus Harris, whose brother, John, founded Harrisburg. Their sons, John and Simpson, died without issue.

    iii. Sarah, born 1734 (or 1742), married in 1762 William Cooke, removed to Fort Augusta (now Sunbury), where Mr. Cooke was sheriff of Northumberland, 1772; a member of the Committee of Observation, the Provincial Convention, and served as colonel during the Revolution. He was later a member of the Assembly and an associate judge.

    iv. Samuel, born 1736.

    v. Rebecca, born 1738; married Thomas Cavet.

    vi. Nathaniel, born 1740; married Sarah.

    vii. Mary, born 1741; married Robert Taggart of Northumberland County.

IV. Assuming Thomas Simpson, in his will, named his sons by order of age, THOMAS SIMPSON, JR., was in such case, the youngest. He was therefore born about 1710-14.[31] His earliest proved transaction was in 1737, though he could have figured in that dated 1733/34.

From Thomas Penn, at the request of Thomas Simpson, of Lancaster County, March 22, 1733/34, a warrant was granted to take up 200 acres in Paxtang Township adjoining Lewis's land.[32] This tract, never surveyed, may have been for Thomas the father.

Three hundred acres were warranted Thomas, March 21, 1737, on a branch of Paxtang River.[33] The first land, however, to be surveyed for Thomas, Jr., was from a warrant for 150 acres issued February 20, 1737,

---

[27] A-86, *Copied Surveys*, J.W.L. by W.E.L., p. 228, Harrisburg, Pa., Land Office.

[28] Simpson's *Early Recs. of Simpson Fams.*, pp. 164-5.

[29] C-1, *Lancaster, Pa., Deeds*, p. 519, for 102¼ acres on Stoney Creek, Upper Paxton Township, bought in 1787 from James Buchanan by Samuel Simpson, which the latter sold.

[30] Simpson's *Early Recs. of Simpson Fams.*, pp. 164-7; III, *Egle's Notes and Queries*, 3d series, p. 209.

[31] Samuel, his elder brother, born 1706.

[32] *Lancaster, Copied Warrants*, S to 424, inclusive, no. 39, Harrisburg, Pa., Land Recs.

[33] *Warrants and Surveys*, p. 168, Harrisburg, Pa.

and laid out for 94½ acres in 1739 at Paxtang, adjoining his brother, Samuel.[34] This was evidently his residence.

Thomas Simpson paid Thomas and Richard Penn £266 February 21, 1760, for 380 Paxtang acres on the Susquehanna,[35] now part of the city of Harrisburg.[36]

Like his father, Thomas was a smith, operated a shop at his dwelling plantation.[37] It is not indicated with what kind of metal he and his father worked.

Thomas, with his brother Samuel and other inhabitants of Paxtang, petitioned the governor, July 22, 1754, for protection from the French and Indians whose fierce attacks on nearby settlements were causing great alarm.[38] Samuel had served as ensign and captain; Thomas's eldest son, John, was later lieutenant in these wars.[39]

When disorganization of the Presbyterians, because of the Old Side—New Side controversy, took place in the Paxtang and Derry churches, their minister, John Elder, supporting the Old Side, withdrew. He had come to Paxtang Church in 1738 and had replaced, in 1740, its original log structure with one of substantial limestone. The two congregations, wishing amity, again requested John Elder to take charge. This petition, dated September 26, 1754, was signed in bold hand by Thomas Simpson.[40] The Reverend Mr. Elder was not only his neighbor and friend, but his son-in-law as well, for he was married to Mary, Thomas Simpson's eldest daughter.[41] She sat in the first place on dignified settee heading rows of hewn-log pews, to hear her husband preach.[42]

" Weak in body but of perfect mind " was Thomas Simpson of Paxtang, when on December 24, 1760, he executed his will.

---

[34] A-86, *Copied Surveys*, J.W.L. by W.E.L., p. 229, Land Recs., Harrisburg, Pa.

[35] A-19, *Patents*, p. 418, Land Recs., Harrisburg, Pa.

[36] " A Connected Draft: of 29 tracts of land covering the city of Harrisburg," etc.

[37] Will of Thomas Simpson, 1761, Lancaster, Pa., vol. B-1, p. 383.

[38] Egle's *Hist. of Dauphin Co.*, Pa., p. 39.

[39] *Ibid.*, p. 55, May 4, 1758, 3 Bn. Pa. Reg. under Colonel Commandant James Burd.

[40] Egle's *Hist. of Dauphin Co.*, Pa., pp. 395-6. (Original petition at Dauphin Co. Historical Society.)

[41] Simpson's *Early Recs. of Simpson Fams.*, p. 171, (record of Paxtang and Derry Churches).

[42] Egle's *Hist. of Dauphin County*, Pa., p. 395.

After recommending his soul to God, his body to earth, to be buried in decent, Christian manner, he bequeathed to his dear wife her horse, saddle, bed, and furniture; ordered she live on the plantation he then occupied, if unsold, until son, Joseph, should come of age; that the said plantation be managed as usual by his children under his wife's direction and that she be maintained and " ye little ones " raised and provided for off its produce.

To his dear son, John, what money John was possessed of, John's horse, saddle, and the plantation the testator bought from Butler. That John have ye benefit of ye shop and tooles till son, Samuel, came of age, on condition he use the best of his skill and diligence to teach Samuel the smith trade and when Samuel was of age, the shop and tooles " in as good condition as they are in now," to be given up to Samuel. Samuel to be clothed and maintained by the produce of this plantation during apprenticeship.

To his dear sons, Thomas and Michael, the testator's tract of land on ye river side, the western end of that adjoining the river to Thomas, the opposite end to Michael, equally as to quantity and quality, (but) allow six acres of meadow-ground to be given out of Michael's share to Thomas, as may best suit both.

To his daughter, Rebecca, the black mare, a good saddle, and £12 paid by sons, Thomas and Michael, from their land within three years after their settling thereon.

He ordered his still and vessels thereunto belonging and whatever goods and chattels the family could spare, sold and bequeathed the money to son, William, (of which) £30, as soon as it could be called, put to interest for William's benefit 'till he arrived at maturity.

That his son, John, give son, Samuel, £5 as soon as his apprenticeship expired, to help Samuel set up his trade.

To his son Joseph, " this plantation viz, what is contained in ye patten, to come into his possession when he comes to age and I order that what plenisheing, household goods and furniture, excepting what may be judged merely necessary for the accommodation of a small Family, shall be then sold and all the cattle and horses, save only two horses and two milk cows, which I allow to my dear wife and that money arising from sd. sale, be divided among my sons viz Thomas, Michael, Samuel, William and Joseph as may be judged most wanted."

To dear wife, he left the Negro wench, Jude, to be hers for life, and at death to be disposed of at her pleasure. If she sees fit to sell her, ye money to her own use. To daughter, Rebecca, the Negro child, Betty. To sons, Elder and Kelso, £3 each, paid at the discretion of executors.

His dear wife and son, John, his only executors, were directed to take the management of his affairs and distribute and divide his estate according to the above directions.

Thomas Simpson signed with a shaky hand his will which was witnessed by James Houston, Samuel Forgey, and William Kerr. It was proved June 8, 10, 1761, at Lancaster, by the witnesses and Sarah and John Simpson.[43] Broken red wax seals affixed to the signatures of the testator and his son, John, show evidence of an impression now lost.[44]

---

[43] B-1, *Lancaster, Pa., Wills*, p. 383.

[44] Filing Case, Wills, S. 1731-72, 1761, Register's Office, Lancaster, Pa.

An inventory of the deceased's personal estate lists, among other items: 4 wagon horses, £52; 1 wagon, 2 chains, wagon cloth, £16; 1 riding horse, £12; 4 milk cows, 1 calf, £14; etc. Two brass candlesticks, 5s; 1 looking glass, 10s; 5 beds and furniture, £31; Delf Cheany and glasses, 5 silver teaspoons, £1, 13s; 1 gun, 1 pistol, £2; 17 sheep, 7 lambs, £10, 4s, etc. Total, £242, 17s. Appraised March 10, 1761, by Thomas Mages and Samuel Simpson. Proved at Lancaster, June 10, 1761, by Sarah and John Simpson, executors.[45]

In an unmarked grave Thomas lies at Paxtang Churchyard.[46] How long Sarah, his widow, lived after his will was proved, June 10, 1761, is not evident.

Children of Thomas Simpson and his wife Sarah:

i. Mary (born 1732; died 3 October, 1786, buried at Paxtang Churchyard) married 5 November, 1751, as his second wife, the Reverend John Elder.[47]

Mr. Elder, a graduate of the University of Edinburgh, was one of the most extraordinary men of interior Pennsylvania. Captain of mounted rangers, the famous "Paxtang Boys," during the French and Indian Wars, he was commissioned colonel of frontier blockhouses and stockades in 1763. Foremost in opposition to British tyranny, too old to fight in the Revolution, he raised troops, was on the Committee of Safety. When he received news that the British army had overrun Trenton, he went as usual on Sunday to the Paxtang Church, but omitted his sermon and instead, after a hasty prayer, exhorted the men present to support liberty and defend their country. In less than thirty minutes a company was formed, captained by his eldest son Robert.

The Hon. William Maclay, first Pennsylvania U. S. Senator, dictated the inscription on his tomb at Paxtang.[48]

By his second wife, Mary Simpson, he had eleven children, one of whom, Sarah, married General James Wallace, and left issue.[49]

ii. John was born March 2, 1733 on Paxton Creek, Paxton Township, Lancaster County, Pennsylvania; married, 1750, Ann Graham of Cumberland, who died in 1803, aged 57. He died March 22, 1804. On May 4, 1758 John

---

[45] Filing Case, Inventories, S. 1761-79, Register's Office, Lancaster, Pa.

[46] III, Egle's *Notes and Queries*, 3d series, p. 209.

[47] Simpson's *Early Recs. of Simpson Fams.*, p. 171.

[48] Biog. Sketch of Rev. John Elder (1706-92), pp. 483-4, Egle's *Hist. of Dauphin Co., Pa.*

[49] Mss. Sketch of Simpson Family by Charles V. Simpson, 1892, (descended from Jeremiah Simpson of Sunbury, Pa.), owned by Mrs. C. V. Simpson, 714 15th Street, Prospect Park, Pa.

Simpson was commissioned lieutenant in the Third Battalion of the Pennsylvania Regiment; served on the western frontier between 1758-'63 with British, regular Virginia, Maryland and Delaware forces. Licensed as Indian Trader in 1762, he removed in 1768 to Northumberland County where he bought and sold large land tracts. At Sunbury, facing the river, he built in 1796 a substantial stone house. He was appointed justice, 1775, 1776 and 1787; recorder and register of wills for Northumberland, 1777-98; captain of militia, 1776; paymaster in Colonel Cook's battalion and was a member of " Committee."

Thomas, the youngest of his six children, was a pioneer Pennsylvanian, Michigan printer, left among other descendents, Gardner Fred Williams, Esq., distinguished mining engineer, manager of DeBeers Mining Company and Thomas Hambly Beck, Esq., chairman of the board of Crowell-Collier Publishing Company.[50]

iii. Jean, born 1734; married William Kelso (1737-'88); died 20 February, 1777. Their tombs are at Paxtang Churchyard.

iv. Joseph, under age December 24, 1760, when his father's will was executed.

v. Samuel, under age in 1760 when his father's will was executed, was apprenticed to his brother John by that document.

vi. Thomas, born 1736, was " of Paxtang County Lancaster, gentleman," when on February 10, 1777, his will was executed (proved March 4, 1777). He divided a sizable estate among his wife Mary and their children: Michael (under 21), Thomas, Rebecca (under 18). He named his brother Michael Simpson and Joshua Elder, executors.[51]

vii. Michael, born at Paxtang in 1739-40,[52] has already been introduced. He was lieutenant under Arnold in the expedition against Quebec. As first lieutenant he commanded his company at the battle of Long Island; was promoted captain, December 1, 1776; saw action at Trenton, Princeton, Brandywine, Germantown and White Plains;[53] retired, January 1, 1781.[54]

While he did not join the Society of The Cincinnati, he is eligible as a *propositus*.[55] Dying without issue,[56] a collateral descendant is eligible to his

---

[50] *Lineage of Thomas Simpson of Paxtang* for Thomas Hambly Beck, Esq., by George V. Massey, II; chapters 3, 4.

[51] C-1, *Lancaster, Pa., Wills*, p. 384.

[52] Tombstone Inscriptions, Paxtang Presbyterian Churchyard, Mss. collection, Lancaster County Historical Society.

[53] I, Egle's *Harrisburg Historical Reg.*, p. 227.

[54] Linn and Egle, *Pa. in the War of the Rev.*, p. 231.

[55] *Original Members and Other Officers Eligible to the Society of the Cincinnati*, Metcalf. Simpson, Michael, Capt., retired January 17, 1781, 1st Regt. Pa. Continental Line.

[56] III, *Pa. Mag.*, p. 293.

claim, which, so far, has not been taken up.

To Colonel Henry he wrote, concerning Henry's account of the expedition through the wilderness in 1775, " perhaps the most arduous during the revolutionary war," that, " so far as he was concerned in the transactions related in the work, they are truly stated." His letter is printed as an introduction to Coloney Henry's record of that expedition.[57]

After the war Michael Simpson built a spacious stone house on the Susquehanna opposite Chamber's Ferry, which ferry, in conjunction with his own on the York side, he operated.[58] Though married three times he died without issue.[59]

General Simpson [60] of Fairview, county York, executed his will March 9, 1812. Ordered his tavern seat, with land, an 18-acre island opposite in the river and a small island with fishery sold within the year; bequeathed to his wife, Susanna, an annual income; cash legacies to nephews and nieces: Joseph Kelso (to compensate for medical services), Rebecca Kelso, Ann Stephen, Rebecca Awl (wife of Jacob), and children of nephew, Samuel Elder. To his nephew, Michael T. Simpson, all residue of estate at Fairview, including the ferry and privileges on either river shore; named him co-executor. Proved, August 16, 1813.[61]

He died, June 1, 1812, aged 73,[62] and, following instructions in his will, was buried in " his family burying place " at Paxtang Churchyard. A handsome monument marks the spot.[63]

viii. Rebecca.

ix. William was a private in Colonel Thompson's Battalion of Riflemen. He was wounded in front of Boston, August 27, 1775, and died a few days later.[64]

x. Elder.

xi. Kelso.

---

[57] XV, *Pa. Archives*, 2d series, p. 63.

[58] I, Egle's *Harrisburg Historical Reg.*, p. 227. His house destroyed by fire, 1883, *ibid.*

[59] III, *Pa. Mag.*, p. 293.

[60] *Ibid.*, major-general of Pa. Militia.

[61] N, *York, Pa., Wills*, p. 62.

[62] Tombstone Inscription Paxtang Presbyterian Churchyard. Mss. Collection Lancaster County Historical Society.

[63] His grand-nephew, John G. Simpson, visited the grave in 1845. (Article by Thomas Simpson of Saginaw, Mich. Mss. genealogy owned by Miss Mary Ann Simpson, Minor Street, West Chester, Pa.)

[64] X, *Pa. Archives*, 2d series, p. 41.

DESCENDANTS OF JAMES SMITH OF YORK, PENNSLYVANIA
A SIGNER OF THE DECLARATION OF INDEPENDENCE

By ROBERT M. TORRENCE

While the subject of this report has received considerable biographical notice, first in Sanderson, *Biography of the Signers of the Declaration,* 1827, he and his family have not been described genealogically in print. Thus, William H. Egle, M.D., in the *Pennsylvania Magazine of History and Biography,* (1880), volume IV, page 362:

SMITH, JAMES, of York County, was born in the north of Ireland, September 17, 1719. His father, John Smith, was a well-to-do farmer, but, induced by his brothers who had previously emigrated to this country and settled in Chester County, and having a large family, he came to Pennsylvania in 1729, locating on the west side of the Susquehanna (River) in what is now York County. He died in the neighborhood of York in 1761. His eldest son, George, studied law at Lancaster, but shortly after his admission to the bar (1740) was drowned in the Susquehanna while bathing. The third son, Arthur, was a farmer, and having a large family, removed to Western Pennsylvania prior to the Revolution. James, the second son, received a liberal education, having been placed under the charge of the Rev. Dr. Alison, Provost of the College of Philadelphia.* After completing his studies in Philadelphia,* he began that of law at Lancaster, where he was admitted to the bar in 1745. He subsequently went to the Cumberland Valley where he practised both law and surveying, remaining four or five years, and then permanently located at York. When the mutterings of the storm of the Revolution were heard, Mr. Smith became one of the firmest advocates for independence. He was chosen a member of the Provincial Deputies, July 15, 1774, and was the author of the "draught of instructions" to the Provincial Assembly. He was a member of the Provincial Convention of January 23, 1775; of the Provincial Conference of June 18, 1776; and of the Convention of 15th of July following. In 1775 he was commissioned colonel of the Frst Battalion of Associators of York County, and throughout the Revolutionary struggle was largely instrumental in organizing troops for the patriot army. In 1776 he was a delegate to the Continental Congress, and his name is affixed to the Declaration of Independence. He served in that body the following year, when he declined re-election. He was elected a member of the Assembly in 1779, and November 20, 1780, commissioned judge of the High Court of Appeals. The Supreme Executive Council appointed Col. Smith a brigadier-general of the Pennsylvania Militia,

---

* Correction. It is more likely that, as stated in the *Penna. Mag. Hist. and Biogr.,* VIII, 46-47, James Smith studied under the Rev. Francis Alison who came to New London, (a township in the southwest corner of Chester County, some 25 miles east of Smith's home in York County), as Presbyterian pastor in 1737 when Smith was aged 18. Alison was chosen master of the Presbyterian school founded there in 1744, and served until his removal in 1752 to Philadelphia as rector of the Academy, founded there in 1749 when Smith was aged 30! Alison was appointed *Vice* Provost of the College in Philadelphia in 1755, when Smith was 36! This correction applies also to the *Dict. Amer. Biogr.,* 1935, XVII, 283, and the *Biogr. Direct. Amer. Congr.,* 1950, p. 1828.

May 23, 1782, *vice* General Potter promoted. He was appointed one of the counsellors on the part of Pennsylvania in the controversy between that State and Connecticut, February 16, 1784. In the following year the Assembly elected him to Congress, in the place of Matthew Clarkson, resigned, but his advanced age obliged him to decline a re-election. Gen. Smith relinquished the practice of law in 1801, and from that period until his death lived in quiet retirement. He died at York on the 11th day of July, 1806. With an uncommonly retentive memory, with a vein of humor and a fund of anecdotes, his excellent conversational powers drew around him many who enjoyed his sharp wit and lively manners, and made his old age bright and genial. Gen. Smith married about 1760, Eleanor, daughter of John Armor, of New Castle, Delaware. She and two children survived him several years.

It is surprising to notice, since Colonel Smith was regarded as a man of wealth, under " Personal Valuations in the Borough of York, Penna." in the assessment list of 1783, the item " James Smith, Esq., lawyer, plate 72 pounds, 2 horses, total 715 Pounds." But in 1801, having a sufficiency of personal property, Colonel Smith relinquished his practice of the law. On 17 August 1805 a disastrous fire originating in the barn of John Hay, Esq., in York, destroyed a large number of the adjacent buildings, including the offices of James Smith, and his fine library and valuable personal papers were lost to posterity. It is fortunate that the Historical Society of York County, Penna., possesses what is purported to be the only authentic likeness of James Smith the Signer. It is the original Loessing-Hall engraving and it resembles in no respect that recently published in Dumas Malone's *Story of the Declaration of Independence*.

Monument of James Smith, Signer of the Declaration

The imposing monument in the English Presbyterian Churchyard in York, Penna., said to have been erected by his son James Smith Jr., but more likely by his son-in-law James Johnson, is inscribed:

(North side)   JAMES SMITH / One of the Signers of / the Declaration of Independence / died July 11, 1806, aged 93
(East side)   ELEANOR wife of James Smith
(South side)   MARGARET / wife of James Johnson / and daughter of James Smith /died January 18, 1838, aged 76 yrs. 8 mos. 4 days.
(West side)   JAMES JOHNSON / died December 15, 1848 / aged 84 years 10 days.

James Smith's residence was on the west side of South George Street, near the Public Square in York. At a later time it was occupied by W. C. Chapman, Esq. Later still, when it was about to be demolished, a large flat tombstone was found in the cellar, inscribed:

In perpetuum Rei Memoriam. Departed this life July 11, 1806, James Smith, Esq., at the advanced age of 93 years. An early warm and active friend in defence of the

JAMES SMITH OF YORK, PENNA., 1719–1806

A Signer of the Declaration of Independence

Etching by H. H. Hall, 1871, from copy by Benson J. Lossing of original drawing by Lewis Miller of York, Penna., 1800. Reproduction here by courtesy of the Historical Society of York County, to which the etching was presented by Grier Hersh, Esq., in December 1907.

Liberties of his country. This is therefore erected to show the feeling the worth attracted by his afflicted relatives and friends. In life esteemed, in death lamented. The Lord giveth and the Lord taketh away. Blessed be the name of the Lord.

"This tombstone formed one of the exhibits in the historic exhibition which was held in this building (James Smith's residence) prior to its demolition and as part of the Borough's Centennial Celebration. No one then knew and no one knows why Mr. Smith should have a monument over his grave and a tombstone in his cellar." *The York County Academy*, 1952. Probably the monument replaced the tombstone.

The Will of James Smith, Signer of the Declaration

"I, James Smith, the elder, of the Borough of York in Pennsylvania, do hereby give and devise unto my son James Smith, his heirs and assigns forever, all that lot of ground situate on the north side of my dwelling house and adjoining the alley, as the same is now under fence, and as to the rest residue and remainder of my Estate real and personal, of whatever it may consist, I will and devise the same to my beloved wife Eleanor Smith, to hold to her for and during the term of her natural life. Witness my hand and seal this twenty-fifth day of April 1806. (*Signed*) Jas. Smith (*seal*) Sealed and delivered in presence of us, Maxwell McDowell / Jno. Greer

York County: Before me Jacob Barnitz, Register for the Probate of Wills and granting Letters of Administration in and for the County of York, State of Pennsylvania, personally came Doctor Maxwell McDowell and John Greer, the two subscribing witnesses to the foregoing Instrument in writing and on their solemn oath do severally say that they were personally present and saw and heard the above named James Smith, Esqr., sign his name unto and seal and publish the foregoing as his last Will and Testament, and that at the time of the doing thereof he the said James Smith was of a sound and disposing mind memory and understanding to the best of their knowledge and belief, and that they subscribed their names thereto as witnesses in the presence of the said Testator and at his request and also in the presence of each other at the same time. Sworn & subscribed before me at York the seventeenth day of July A.D. 1806. J. Barnitz Regr. (*signed*) Maxwell McDowell / Jno. Greer * A true copy taken from & compared with the original at York. J. Barnitz, Regr. Letters of Administration with the Will annexed granted to James Smith Jr. November Court 1807 vacated the Letters granted to James Smith and awarded Letters De bonis non with the Will annexed to be granted to William Barber Esqr., after which, Octr. 14th 1814, Letters of Administration De bonis non with the Will annexed were granted to James Johnston. J. Barnitz, Regr." (Recorded in *York County Will Book L*, page 390, whence this transcript.)

Marriage of James Smith and Eleanor Armor

Sometime before June of 1760, James Smith, Esq., married ELEANOR ARMOR, who was born about 1739 and died 13 July 1818 according to a notice in the York *Recorder* of 21st. She was a daughter of John Armor

---

* This witness was probably the John Greer who was born in County Armagh, Ireland, in 1761, and died 19 April 1813 in York, Penna., married Susan Bailey who died 11 November 1808 aged 45, and both buried in the English (First) Presbyterian Churchyard in York.

who resided near New Castle, Delaware, and a niece of Thomas Armor,* a justice and surveyor who resided in York County, Penna., from some time previous to the Revolution, with whom she lived.

Children of James and Eleanor (Armor) Smith:

i. MARGARET SMITH born 14 May 1761; died 18 Jan. 1838 aged 76-8-4 according to monument inscription in Presb. Chyd. in York, Penna., and death notice in the York *Pennsylvania Republican* of 24th. She married on 13 Aug. 1805 in York JAMES JOHNSON, a merchant and land speculator of York, who was born 5 Dec. 1764 and died 15 Dec. 1848 aged 84-0-10 according to said monument and to the *Republican* of 20th and the *Gazette* of 26th. No issue. James Johnson was appointed the final administrator of Colonel James Smith's estate in 1814. His own Will, dated 31 Mar. 1848 and proved 18 Dec. 1848, names niece Mary M. Johnson execx. and his friend David G. Barnitz execr., devises money, land in Harford Co., Md., plantations in York Twp., York Co., Penna., and lots in the Borough of York, to nieces Anne and Sally Armor and nephew Robert Armor. Recorded in *York County Will Book no. 1*, page 209, whence this abstract.

ii. MARY SMITH born 20 April 1763, died 20 April 1840 aged 77 in Faun Twp., York Co., Penna., according to gravestone inscription in Presb. Chyd. in York and notice in the York *Gazette* of 21st and the York *Penna. Republican* of 22nd. She married, as his second wife, JAMES KELLY, a lawyer and member of Congress, who was born in 1760 and died 4 Feb. 1819 aged 59 according to the York *Recorder* of 9th. and the Hanover, Penna., *Guardian* of 5th. They had issue: 1-Elizabeth Smith Kelly bapt. 13 Mar. 1803 in the First Presb. Ch. of York, d. 23 or 26 Oct. 1831 according to the *Gazette* of 1st Nov., mar. 5 Oct. 1829 Samuel Hopkins of Baltimore, mercht., no issue; 2-Maria Kelly b. 1804, bapt. 27 Mar. 1811 aged 7 yrs., mar. about 1837 Elijah Vance but later resumed maiden name according to the report of the execrs. of estate of James Kelly decd. in the Wills Office of the Superior Court in Baltimore, and she mar. 2ndly. 11 Mar. 1845 William Henry Kurtz of York, Penna., who was b. 31 Jan. 1804 and d. 24 June 1868, a member of Congress, according to the York *Democratic Press* of 14th Mar. 1845, and she d. after 20 Aug. 1861 and probably before the date of his Will in which she is not mentioned, both buried in Prospect Hill Cem., York, her marker without dates, no issue; 3-James Kelly b. 1806,

---

* The Will of Thomas Armor of York Twp., York Co., Penna., dated 25 Nov. 1784 and proved 9 March 1785, names son Thomas, cousins Robert and Thomas Bigham, and appoints Robert Bigham executor.

A letter written and signed by James Smith, no date or addressee, ascribed to 1757, in the collections of the Historical Society of York County, Penna., concludes with: " P. S. If amidst your other business and amusements you should discover any female between 12 and 70 who you think would make a tolerable companion for life and might be obtained on reasonable terms, please to advertise me thereof and I shall be ready to make proper use thereof. Yrs. ut supra J. S."

bapt 27 Mar. 1811 aged 5 yrs., d. about 1835 according to the report of the execrs. of estate of James Kelly decd.; 4-Susanna Kelly b. 1807, bapt. 27 Mar. 1811 aged 4 yrs., d. about 1835 according to said report; 5-Carvel Kelly b. 1810, bapt. 27 Mar. 1811, d. 15 Aug. 1827 in Baltimore of pulmonary disease according to the *Recorder* of 21st.

iii. ELIZABETH SMITH born about 1765, died 6 September 1793, first wife of JAMES KELLY, abovesaid, according to the *Pennsylvania Herald* and the York *General Advertiser* of 11th.

iv. GEORGE SMITH " an attorney, born 24 April about 1767, died 12 February 1802," according to the register of the Rev. Robert Cathcart, First Presb. Ch. of York. It is supposed here that he was the George Smith who was admitted to the bar of York County on 6 April 1791. By Deed of 29 May 1805, James Smith, Sr., of the Town of York, Penna., Attorney-at-law, and Elinor his wife, of the first part, Margaret Smith, daughter of the said James and Elinor, of the second part, to James Smith, Junr., son of the said James Smith, Sr., of the third part; recital that George Smith, late of said Town of York, deceased, son of said James Smith, Sr., in his lifetime purchased at Sheriff's vendue a certain tract of land in Newberry Township, sold as the estate of Jacob Day, certain 150 acres, and afterwards sold one-half to William McClelland, that the said George Smith afterwards died intestate in possession of the other half thereof, whereupon the land descended to James Smith, Sr. during his lifetime and afterwards to said James Smith Jr.and his sister Margaret. By this tripartite Deed the parties abovenamed gave their undivided interests in said land to James Smith, Jr., for " natural love and affection " and one dollar. Recorded in *York County Deed Book 2-R*, page 438, whence this abstract. Letters of Administration upon the estate of George Smith late of the Borough of York, Penna., deceased, were granted 1 March 1802 to James Smith, Sr., his father, who gave bond of $1,000 with sureties Godfrey Lenhart and Jacob Obb. Recorded in *York County Bond Book 2-B*, page 30.

v. JAMES SMITH, JR., born about 1769, died in February 1812. The Will of James Smith Esq., of the Borough of York, County of York, Penna., dated 26 Oct. 1809 and proved 26 Feb. 1812, devises to cousins John Armor and Anna Armor his undivided half of two plantations in York Twp., the same in which my mother has a life estate; residue of estate real and personal to John Armor and Anna Armor, they to pay his just debts and legacies; to friend John Stroman Junr. " I give and bequeath my silver mounted sword and pistols, all my books, my scarlet coat and gin case or bottle case, the sword and pistols to be used in defense of his Country in case of necessity, and the bottles not to be filled too often unless it be with water, my dressing box and gun I leave to my cousin James Armor, my uniform I leave to Major John Brancire; " and appoints said John Stroman Junr. and John Armor execrs. Recorded in *York County Will Book M*, page 397, whence this abstract.

JOHN SOTCHER.

WILLIAM PENN'S STEWARD AT PENNSBURY MANOR.

BY JOSIAH GRANVILLE LEACH.

John Sotcher came to Pennsylvania with William Penn in the good ship Canterbury, in December, 1699, on the occasion of the Proprietary's last visit to his Province. Sotcher was, no doubt, well known to Penn in England, and accompanied him for the purpose of managing his affairs at his noted seat on the Delaware, known as Pennsbury Manor. A former Steward there had been James Harrison, Penn's much trusted friend, and a man highly honored in the Province, as is evidenced in his being chosen a member of the Provincial Council, one of the first justices of the peace and of the courts of Bucks County, and Chief Justice of the Provincial or Supreme Court.

Upon Sotcher's arrival in Pennsylvania, he took up his residence at Pennsbury, and was installed in the stewardship of the Manor. Among Penn's household was Mary Loftus, to whom Sotcher paid his addresses with the hearty approval of the Governor and Mrs. Penn, and, as the young couple had daily opportunities of meeting each other, it seems safe to assume that Sotcher's wooing soon won from Miss Loftus an acceptance of his hand and heart. Certain it is that he was successful in his suit before 4 September, 1701 as on that day he appeared at Falls Meeting, and after the custom of Friends, announced his intention of "taking Mary to wife." Previous to this date, Penn had determined to return with his family to England, and, being desirous of leaving Pennsbury in possession of Sotcher, he was present at the Meeting at which the latter declared his intentions, and expressed his desire to "see the marriage accomplished before he left the country," declaring "that the season hurried his departure." The usual action was then taken, and a committee appointed "to examine the matter" and report at the next meeting, Joseph Kirkbride and Mary Sirkett being named as the committee, and Phineas Pemberton, Joseph Kirkbride, Richard Hough, and Samuel Dark, were named as the committee to draw the marriage certificate. The Meeting re-assembled 8 October, 1701, when a letter from Governor and Mrs. Penn was read, consenting to the marriage, and a favorable report was received from the committee, whereupon the Meeting sanctioned the union.

The marriage ceremony took place at Pennsbury, and was attended by Penn and his family, and by many of the most distinguished persons in the Province. The marriage certificate bears date 16 October, 1701, and is witnessed by Penn, his wife Hannah, and daughter Letitia, and by the eminent James Logan, Secretary of the Province; Phineas Pemberton, Provincial Counsellor and Judge; Samuel Jennings, Governor of West New Jersey; Joseph Shippen, son of the then Mayor of Philadelphia, and many others of prominence. It was possibly the only marriage celebrated at Pennsbury, and General Davis states in his History of Bucks County, that "it is the only one Penn is known to have attended in this country."

Immediately after the marriage, Penn returned to England, leaving the bridal party in full possession of Pennsbury, where they had the direction of numerous servants and others employed on the manor. Penn sailed on the ship Dolmahoy, and while on ship-board he penned a letter of instructions to his worthy secretary, Logan, at the end of which he wrote: "Remember J. Sotcher and Pennsbury".

Penn's letters to Logan and others, from this time on, contain frequent mention of Sotcher. Shortly after his arrival in Europe, he learned of the death of Sotcher's brother, which fact he communicated to Sotcher, in a letter to Logan, dated at Kensington, 4th of 11th mo., 1701/2, saying:

"Let John Sotcher know that his brother is dead, and has left him £150 if he come in two years for it. He died above six months ago, so that he must come."

One week later, in another letter to Logan, he writes:

"I writ by an English ship last week—in short, not time to read it,—that if John and Mary come, his brother leaving him £150, if he come for it in two years, that Hugh be steward and gardener, and old Peter go to the garden when needful; and that Phineas Pemberton's wife and daughters see to the bedding and linen, once a month."

Sotcher went to England, and received his legacy, returning to Pennsylvania in August, 1702. Penn on learning of the safe return here of Sotcher, wrote that it was "glad tidings, the dangers on the seas considered."

When Sotcher's first child, Hannah, was born, Logan, realizing that Penn's family would be interested in the event, particularly as she had been named in honor of Mrs. Penn, wrote to Penn under date of 3d of 1st mo., 1702/3 "John Sotcher's wife has a fine girl named Hannah, six weeks old".

In a letter to Logan, dated London, 16 11mo; 1704/5, Penn writes:

"I had John Sotcher's letter, and desire him to go on as he has done.—my love to him and her [Mary] and the family". I was pleased with his account, but would have it yet more exact."

The following letters of Penn to Sotcher and his wife give unmistakable evidence of the friendship existing between them, and of the respect in which Sotcher was held by the renowned founder of Pennsylvania:

LOND. 12, 8 MO., 1705.

Honest John and Mary,—My reall love is to you, and desire you and your little ones preservation heartily, and I know so does my dear wife and loving mistress. We are all, through the Providence of God Lord's mercy, well, save little Hannah at Bristol, whose arme has a weakness. She is a sweete childe, as Thomas and little Margaret.

I doubt your care and good husbandry, and good housewifery, to make that place profitable to me, after the hundreds, yea thousauds, y^t have been sunk there from the beginning. Though if that could be lett, to one that would not misuse it, and you upon a plantation for my dear Johnnie, I should like it better, and pray tell James [Logan] so; for I think I have spent too much there already. Johnnie grows a fine childe, tall, briskey as a bird, his mother's limbs, but my countenance, and witty, as others say, and as healthy as any of them. Let me hear from you how Sam and Sue begin to be diligent. The Lord be with you, and all his humble and faithful ones, on both sides the water. Farewell: your reall friend,

WM. PENN.

LOND. 18, 3 MO., 1708.

John Sacher—Loving friend.—I had thy letter with satisfaction, and glad to hear of thy and family's welfare. I am glad to hear of the good condition of poor Pennsbury, beloved of us all, and there, in the will of God, we wish ourselves. If thou leaves it, give J. Logan an account of thy labor, as acres cleared, and fence, and of both plow and sow land. Likewise, deliver all ye linnen, and household stuff into his possession and care. I bless God, we are all alive and well, save our dear sweet Hannah, whom the Lord took four months ago, at 4 years, the wittiest and womanliest creature that her age could show, but his holy will be done. Thy loving friend,

WM. PENN.

To Honest Mary.—I had thine by our frd. Mary Dannester, with the pair of gloves to Johnnie, which both pleased and fitted him well. I was well pleased to heare of y^r well doing while at that place of my pleasure, poor Pennsbury, (which I like for a place better than any I have ever lived at, and I hope since 'tis lett, which to be sure James (Logan) does to our advantage,) it will be kept as it deserves, and be fitt to receive me, if the Lord please to make our way for our thither again. My dear father has been dangerously ill, which hurried me to Bristoll lately. There I saw thy brother, who has three children, and thrives in person and trade.

With true love to thee and thy husband, and honest friend Jane, remain thy friend, W. P.

About 1708 Sotcher gave up his stewardship, and withdrew from Pennsbury to an estate which he purchased at Bristol in the same county. Here, under the authority of the colonial government, he established a ferry across the Delaware to Burlington, New Jersey. His effort to secure the same is shown in the following extract from the records of the Provincial Council of Pennsylvania, under date of 31st of August 1709, as follows:

"John Sotcher of the County of Bucks, presented to the board an address or petition of the Magistrates of the said County, Grounded on divers Presentments of the Grand Juries of that County, complaining of the great want of a ferry over Delaware, from Bristol to Burlington, and requesting this board to authorize the said John Sotcher as the most proper person to keep the said ferry for the general accomodation of the Country there.

" Ordered, that it be first recommended to the House of Representatives, and it is hereby recommended to them, to agree on an act to be passed, for the establishing a ferry from Bristol to Burlington, in such manner as may give sufficient Encouragement to a fitt person to give it due attendance at all seasons, after wch the said John Sotcher shall be appointed to keep the same, as requested."

In Sotcher's day, as now, ferry privileges were important franchises, and were granted only to men of estate and good standing in the community, so that the action taken by the Provincial Council clearly indicates that Sotcher was known to and well regarded by the members of this distinguished body.

He is next heard of in 1712, when he was chosen by the good people of Bucks County, as one of their representatives in the Provincial Assembly, which trust he filled with such acceptance, that he was again chosen in 1715, and continuously thereafter until 1722. He was also prominent in the Society of Friends, and for seven years preceding his death, was an Elder of Falls Meeting. He died January 19, 1729, and his will, dated 6th of the previous December, was probated in Bucks County, February 26, 1729/30, of which his only son, Robert Sotcher, was made executor. By Mary Loftus he had four children, to wit:

1. Hannah Sotcher, born 25, 11th month, 1702; died probably in 1723; married in 1720, Joseph Kirkbride, Jr., a prominent citizen of Bucks County.

2. Mary Sotcher, born 18 September, 1704; died 22 November, 1778; married Mahlon Kirkbride, brother of Joseph, and equally prominent.

3. Robert Sotcher, born 3 September, 1706; died in 1753; married Mercy Brown.

4. Ann Sotcher, born 27 March, 1710; married in 1729, Mark Watson, a member of the Assembly and justice of the peace and of the courts.

* Does not include the "Newkirk" article, for which see pp. 477-497.

Alexander (cont.)
William 212
William 204, 213
William, Sr. 204, 212
Alexanders, (?) 203
Alger, Cyrus 662, 663
Ebenezer 662
Joseph, Jr. 661
Mary 661
Otis 662
Alison, (?) (Rev. Dr.)
859
Francis (Rev.) 859
Allaire, Alexander 147
Allard, Wyntje 533
Allen, (?) 78
Andrew 76
Ann 571
Samuel 660
William 571, 609, 610
Allenbach, Anna Maria 35
Allis, (?) 763
Allison, Joseph (Hon.)
182
Mary Elizabeth 608
Mary Perrine 182
Alspach, Reinhard 35
Alt, Heinrich 42
Altemus, Frederick 771
Alvey, Paul 227
Amherst, Jeffrey (Lord)
841
Jeffrey (Sir) 841
Anderson, Enoch 139
James (Rev.) 850
William (Maj.) 375
Wm. (Maj.) 375
Andra, Maria 191
Andreae, Samuel (Dr.) 794
Andrewes, Richard 553
Andrews, D. Cooper 824
Ebenezer 159
Edward 158
Elizabeth 158, 163
Enoch 139
Esther 159
Hannah 159
Isaac 158, 163
Jeremiah 158
John (Dr.) 107
Letitia 158
Mary 158
Sarah 158
Andriessen, Barbara 537
Andross, (?) 530
Edmund (Sir) 529
Andrus, Enoch 139
Annable, John 669
Anthony, Alfred R. 823
Charles 823
Dedrick 275
Emily 823
Helen 823
Henry 823
Herbert 823
Jacob 823
Margaret 823
Nicholas 823
Walter 823
Archdale, John 514
Arians, Wyntje 533
Ariens, Wyntje 533
Armitage, Caleb 103
Elizabeth 150
James 149, 150
Martha 150
Samuel 150
Thomas 150

Armor, Anna 864
Anne 863
Eleanor 860, 862-864
Elinor 864
James 864
John 860, 862-864
Robert 863
Sally 863
Thomas 863
Armstrong, Alexander 850
Sarah 851
Thomas 850, 851
Arnold, (?) 857
Benjamin 275
Hannah 722
Arnoldten, H. Johann
Philips 778
Arnolt, Johann Philipp
(Mr.) 780
Arnott, (?)(Rev.) 864
Arundel, (the Earl of) 825
Ashby, Mary 521
Ashcom, Charles 12
Ashcomb, (?) 12
Asheton, William 621 (See
ASSHETON)
Ashmead, John 772
Ashton (See also ASHETON,
ASSHETON)
(?) 557
Elizabeth 137
John 262
Thomas 134
William 621 (See
ASSHETON)
Ashworth, Agnes 26
Asprell, Mary 342
Aspril, Lydia 141, 342
Mary 14, 342
Sarah 141, 342
Asprill, Francis 141
Joseph 141
Mary 141
Sarah 141
Assel, Johann Adam 43
Katharina 43
Assheton, Frances 621,653
John 653
Mary 621
Philadelphia (the) 621
R. 626
Rachel 621
Robert 621, 656
Thomas 134
William 557
William (ASHETON,
ASHTON) 621, 653
Atherton, Lydia 672 (See
HENRY)
Thomas Henry 672
Atkinson, Andrew 86
Isaac 129, 130
James 203
Letitia 86
Thomas 86
Atwood, Annie Brown 118
William A. 119
Aubrey, Elizabeth 561
Letitia 563, 566, 574,
575
William 561
Audenried, Louise 371
Auld, Jacob 763
Aurand, Christiana 820
Austin, Edward 126, 137,
140
Elizabeth 135, 137
Hannah 140

Austin (cont.)
John 137
Mary 137
Samuel 137
Sarah 140
Thomas 137
William 137, 140
Avery, John 234,(Capt.) 3
Awl, Jacob 858
Rebecca 858
Axe, Elizabeth 800
Frederick 100, 104
Axford, Sarah 172
Ayquems, (?) 340
Baber, Peter 597
Philip 597
Bach, Jerg 844
Bachiler, Stephen (Rev.)
665
Bacon, David 60
Grace 149
Bailes, Hannah 722 (See
BEALES)
Bailey, Susan 862
Bainbridge, (?) 80, 82
Baker, Cicely 508
Jeremiah 136, 139
Juliana 568
Ruth 136, 137, 140
Ruth (Bowyer) Bonham
137
Samuel 59, 139
William 568
Bakewell, William 538
John (Rev.) 684
Bakhmeteff, G. 377
Balabrega, Catharine
Julia 573
Jacob 573
Juliana Catharine 573
Mary 573
Balch, Thomas Willing 77
Baldwin, (?) (Bishop) 75
John 282
Baliol, Devorgilda 825
John 825
Baliol le Scot, William
825
Ball, Eleanor 322, 323
Martha Corbin
(Tuberville) 369
Mottrom (Dr.) 369
Spencer Mottrom 369
Susannah 322
Thomas 322, 323
Ballinger, Henry 524
Susanna 547
Bally, William 321
Baltimore, (?) (Ld.) 211
(?) (Lord) 230, 231,
233, 234, 240, 242,
244
Cecelius (Lord) 230,233
Charles L 278
Frederick (Lord) 197
Bancroft, Blanche 642,643
W. C. (Lt. Col.) 642
W. C. (Lt.-Gen.) 653
Bane, Alex. 260
Alexander 255, 256, 258
Banke, Elsabeth 8
Bankson, Andrew 150
Eleanor 150, 758, 759,
768
Elinor 758
Elionar 150
Esther (Lynn) 150, 151
Hester 155

Berends, Claes 161
  Klass 161
Beresford, Christopher
    528
Bergman, John George 740
Berkley,(?) (Bishop) 87
Berndtz, Brandt 499
Bernts, Brandt 499
Berntsz, Altghen 501
  Bernt 501
  Brandt 499, 501
  Brant 501
  Claes 501
  Evertgen 501
  Geert 501
  Geertgen 501
  Gryt 501
  Reimer 501
  Reiner 501
  Renger 501
Berntz, Brandolph 499
  Brandolph (Brant) 500
Berry, Susannah
    (Middleton) 292
Bervard, (?) 220
Besk, Marg. 30
Bethell, Elizabeth 266
  Francis 266
  John 103
  John, Jr. 266
  Joseph 266
  Rose 266
  William 266
Bettle, Edward 826
  Mary Rachel 826
  William 373
Beuard, John 220
Bevan, Stephen 254
Bevard, (?) 220
Bewley, John 584
Bicking, Frederick 756
  Frederick, Jr. 749,756
  Joseph 750, 756
Bickingsale, Susanna 53
Biddle, (?) 78
  Alexander 832
  Alexander Williams 832
  Anna Clifford 683
  Caroline 684
  Clement 684
  Clement C. 137, 679
  Clement C. (Col.) 658
  David Scull 832
  Edward 76, 77
  Elizabeth Rebecca 684
  Emily Duncan 108
  Harriet 684
  John 832
  John B. 683, 684, 686
  John Barclay 679, 683,
    684
  Julia (Montgomery) 108
  Lydia Spencer 108
  Mary 679
  Nicholas (Capt.) 78
  Owen 573
  Sarah Duncan 108
  Thomas Montgomery 108
  William 506, 664, 832
  William MacFunn 108
  William Phillips 684
Bidle, Katherine 554
  Richard 553, 554
Bigger, Elizabeth 283
  James 283
Bigham, Robert 863
  Thomas 863
Biles, William 128

Billinge, Edward 506
Billou, Maria 831
  Peter 831
Bingaman, Catharine A.110
Bingham, William 572
Binney, Barnabas (Dr.) 541
Binny, Andrew 177
Birch, Jane 304
Birckhead, Angelina
    Matilda 304
  Anne (Harrison) 303
  Christian (Harris) 303
  Christopher 303
  Edward 303
  Eliza Ann 303
  Elizabeth 324
  Elizabeth (Middleton)
    303
  Franklin Middleton 304
  Isabella Sarah 304
  Jennie 304
  John 303
  Mary Elizabeth 304, 308
  Middleton 304
  Nehemiah 303
  Oliver H. 304
  Sarah (Hutchins) 303
  William 303
  William Nehemiah 304
Bird, William 297
Birdsall, Daniel 811
Bisans, Joh. Thomas 337
Bishop, Henry 227, 232
  Paul 104
Bispham, David Scull 826
  William Danforth 826
Bissans, Maria 337
Bisshans, Thomas 337
Bittenbender, Christopher
    191
Bitting, Henry 195
Black, Catharine 708-710
  Frederick 709, 710 (See
    also SWARTZ)
  John 367
  Lydia 367
  Mary 357, 367, 379
  William 169
Bladen, Ann 361, 382
  William 206
Blaine, Ephraim (Col.)109
  Harriet S. 377
Blakey, William 128
Blanchard, Mary 731
  Peter 731
Blank, George Adam 773
Bloomer, George C. 377
Blyth, Catrin 49
  Christian 49
  Samuel 49, 50
  William 49
Boardman, George Dana
    (Rev.) 72
Boarman, (?) (Maj.) 311
Boclo, Jacob Ernst 793
Bodine, Isaac 331
Boesche, Henry 308
Boethius, Anicius Manlius
    Torquarus Severinus
    702, 703
Bohl, Johann Peter 35
  Peter 35
Bohler, Anna Catharina
    192
Bollings, Isaac 350
Bolton, Aquilla M. 820
  Everard 820
  Gidion 820

Bolton (cont.)
  Hannah Scull 820
  James Murray 820
  Joseph Reeves 820
  Rachel 820
  Rachel (Aunt) 819
  Samuel 820
  Sarah 820
Bond, James 158
Bonham, Catharine 139
  Ephraim 138, 139
  Ruth 135, 138, 139
  Ruth (Bowyer) 139
  Samuel 126, 138, 139
Bonner, J. (Rev.) 683
Bonsall, Mary 263
  Rachel 263
  Richard 263
Booth, Charles 667
  Mary 667
Boreman, Thomas 669
Borhans, Jans 327
Borie, (?) 73
Boswell, Jno. 291
Boteler, Henry
Botts, Reinhard 728
Bouchelle, Peter 214
Boughton, Richard 275
  Richd 275
Boulton, Edward 140
Bowden, Mary 660
Bowen, Anne 116
  Burkett 116
  Edward 594
  Frances Stella (?) 594
  Gulielma Maria Penn 594
  Jane (Mrs.) 116
  Janet Penn 594
  John 594
  John A. B. Penn 594
  John Alexander Barclay
    Penn 594
  John Ivor Erskine Penn
    594
  Peter 594
Bower, Barbara 760
  Charles 742, 760
  Elizabeth 760, 761
  Georg 772 (See BAUER)
Bowie, Elizabeth 363
  Eversfield (Capt.) 363
Bowlby, Thomas 162
Bowling, Thomas 138
Bowman, Elizabeth 236
  Henry 236
  William 850
Bownas, Samuel 716
Bowser, Barbara (Lamatt)
    (Mrs.) 843
Bowyer, Benjamin 131, 133
  Elizabeth 134, 137, 140
  Esther 120, 121, 123,
    124, 134, 140, 141
  Esther (Hester) 137
  Esther (King) 140
  Hannah 134
  John 120-123, 125, 126,
    129-136, 140, 142,
    157, 160
  John, Jr. 121, 123, 124,
    131, 132, 144, 156
  John, Sr. 123
  Martha 122, 134, 136
  Mary 133, 134
  Rebecca 133, 134, 138
  Ruth 134, 139
  Sarah 124, 125, 130,
    134, 135-137, 142,

Bowyer (cont.)
  Sarah (cont.) 143, 160
  Sarah (Hastings) 136
  Thomas 122, 133, 134
  William 124, 131, 136
Boyd, (?) (Mr.) 852
  (?) (Simpson) 852
  Alvin Adams (Lt.) 667
  Andrew 851, 852
  Esther 138
  Wright Medders 667
Boyden, John 320
  William 280, 282
Boyear, Jan 122
  Rebecca 133
Boyed, Andrew 851
Boyer, Elizabeth 137
  Hannah 122
  John 122
  Matilda 371
  Sarah 135
  Thomas 133
Boyle, Esther 138
Boyte, Ann 138
  Esther 137, 138
  Esther (Hester) 138
  Hester 135, 138
  John 138
  Lucy 138
  Philip 126, 137, 138
  Sarah 138
  William 138
Bradbury, Thomas 668
Bradford, Andrew 717
  William 818
Bradley, Abigail 217
  Priscillya 314
Bradshaw (of Pendleton)
  620
  Anne 557, 621
  Frances 557, 621
  Francis 553, 554, 619,
    620
  James 557, 559, 621
  John 557, 559, 621
  Laurence 620
  Lawrence 557
  Mary 557, 621, 622
  Rachel (Penn) 557
  Ralph 557, 620 (See
    Randall), 621, 626
  Randall (otherwise
    Ralph) 620
  Raphe 620, 621
  Rebecca 557, 621
  Robert 557, 621
  Sarah 264, 557, 621
  Sarah (Levi) 264
  Thomas 264
  William 557, 559, 621
Bradway, Edward 93, 127
  Mary 93
Brady, Caroline 187
  Thomas F. 187
  Thomas F., Jr. 187
Braetscher, Barbara 31
Bragner, Anna Barbara 846
Brainard, (?) 378
Braithwaite, Joane 92, 93
  William 92
Brancire, John (Maj.) 864
Brand, Christiana 196
Brandt, Randolph (Capt.)
  279, 280
Brandts, Geertgen 500
  Gerritgen 501
Brannyn, Darby 342
Branson, William 350, 351

Brants, Geertien 499
Brasey, Thomas 266
Bratscher, Heinrich 37
  Jacob 37
Braun, Sarah Elizabeth
  336
Braund, Henry (Dr.) 643
Bravard, (?) 220, 221
Breckinridge, John C.
  (Gen.) 304
Bredin, Elizabeth 111
  Joseph 111
Bregy, F. Amedee (Judge)
  182
Brenneman, Catharine 114
Brent, Robert 311
Brentnal, Hannah 57
Brett, George 285
  Susannah 285
Breuard, John 220
Brevard, (?) 206, 218,
  220, 221
  Adam,210, 218, 219,221,
    224
  Ann 222
  Benjamin 218, 219, 222
  Clarissa 22
  David 222
  Elizabeth 218, 219, 222
  James 222
  Jane 222
  Jean 219
  John 209, 210, 214,217,
    224
  John, Jr. 220, 222
  John, Sr. 220, 221
  Joshua 222
  Mary 222
  Rachel 222
  Rebecca 222
  Rhoda 222
  Robert 218, 219, 222
  Sarah 222
  Thomas 222
  Zebulon 218, 219, 222
Brewer, Robert Noak (?)
  581
Brice, Mary Howard 681
Brick, John 97
Bridges, Emily 365, 379
  Jemima 365
  Mary 365, 366
  Robert 365
Bright, Jacob (Capt.)
  842
Brill, Anna Gertrud 785
  Anna Maria 786
  Johann Georg 786
  Lorentz 785, 786
  Martin 785, 786
  Martin (Mr.) 785
Brinkloe, Comfort 236
  Daniel 236
Brinton, Catharine Ann
  678 (See INGERSOLL)
  John 678
  John Hill 678, 683
  Mary C. 678, 683
  Mary Charlotte 683
  S. F. 678
Briscoe, Emma 370
Brittan, Lyonel 128
Broadhead, Daniel (Capt.
  533
Brodhead, Daniel 535
  Elber Howe 377
  Richard (Capt.) 533
Bromley, John 377

Brook, Mary 754
Brooke, (?) 169
  Basil 136
  Bowyer 136, 137
  Bowyer, Jr. 137, 139
  Bowyer, Sr. 139, 140
  Elizabeth 135, 136
  Harriet 137
  John 136
  Mary 136, 137, 370
  Priscilla 118
  Reese 137, 139
  Roger 126, 134, 136,
    137, 139
  Saml 117
  Samuel 118
  Sarah 136
  Sarah (Bowyer) 136
Brookholding, Philadelphia
  624, 625
  Thomas 624, 625
Brooks, (?) (Mr.) 681
  Caroline Amelia 184
  David 260
  Eleanor D. 184
  George 354
  Jane 353
  John Head 184
  Napoleon Bonaparte
    Kneass 184
  William 151
Broughton, Amy 518
Brown, David 212
  Elizabeth 660
  Francis 660
  Geo. 686
  George 686
  Leah 830
  Mercy 870
  Peter 550, 661
  Thomas 364
  Thomas, Sr. 364
  William 686
Browne, Mary 136
  Nathaniel 669, 826
  Nina Florence 376
  Peter 59, 137
  Priscilla (Coats)
    Parrock 137
  Ross 376
  Will 655
  William (Sir) 826
Browning, Edward H. 586
  Horatio 305
Brownlie, Annie Watson
  176
Browns, (?) 203
Bruard, John 205, 219
Bruce, Comfort 238
Bruder, Joh. Heinrich 35
Bruner, Sarah 338, 339
Bryan, George (Hon.) 175,
  176
  Margaretta Sybilla 175
  Rosea 375
  William 288
Brydges, James 652
Bub, Catharina 190
  Georg Adam 190
Buchanan, (?) (Pres.) 310
  James 853
Bucher, Eva Rosina 45
Buchon, (?) 32
Buck, Charles E. (Rev.)
  306
Bucker, Frances 523
Buckley, Anthony M. 63
  Arthur Henry Rede (Maj.)

877

Cope (cont.)
David 117
Jane 117, 118
Coppock, Jane (Owen) 258
Jonathan 258, 259
Rachel 258, 259
Corbit, Henry C. 820
Corcoran, Mary Irma
(Sister) 5
Cornelis, Gerrit 498
Jannetgen 501
Jannichgen 499
Jantgen 499
Mattheus 498
Cornelisse, Chieltje 498,
500
Deuws 500
Geertien 499, 500
Geertruy 499
Gerrit 498, 499
Jan 500
Mattheus 498, 500
Cornelissen, Disje 498,
500
Gerrit 500
Mattheus 500
Cornellisen, Gerrit 498
Cornelusdr, Jannichgen
500
Cornman, John 546
Cornog, Catherine 68
Cornwall, Emily 639
James 639
Cornwallis, (?) 168
Corslett, (?) 11
Corsley, (?) 11
Richard 11
Corson, Hannah 663
Stillwell F. 184
Virginia Adele 184
Coryell, George 302
Costoms, Mary 522
Cotton, (?) (Esq.) 587
Coulbourne, William
(Capt.) 228
Coulston, William 249
Coulstone, William 248
Coultas, James (Sheriff)
735
Courts, John 277, 287,
317
Cousins, Dorothea 835
Dorothy 825
Coventry, William (Sir)
559
Coverd, (?) 206
Cowan, Walter (Lt.) 636
Cowanover, Peter 811
Cowl, Francis 700
Cowherd, Francis 64
Cox, Deborah 339
Elinor 666
Grace 571
James 571
John 199
Joseph 503
Mary 503
Rachel 830
William 830
Coxe, Daniel (Dr.) 813
Daniel (Gov.) 126
Daniel W. (Mr.) 674,
675
Coyle, Emeline 550
John 550
Coyne, Margaret 310
Cozens, Ella Eugenia 679
Crabb, Helen 362

Crabb (cont.)
Martha 362
Thomas 362
Craft, Maudlin 14
Sarah 14
William 14
Crafte, William 9
Crager, Mary 266
Craig, Cynthia 68
Daniel 68
Thomas 215
Cramer, Johannes 550
Crause, Chancellor 798
Georg 798
Craven, Alfred 187, 376
Alfred, Jr. 187
Alfred Edmiston 376
Alfred W. 361, 368
Alfred Wingate 369,376,
383
Alice 376
Ann Evelina 361
Ann Mary 361, 382, 383
Anna Maria 369
Anna Truxtun 376
Augustus Carter 376
Caroline 187
Catharine 362
Charles E. 361
Charles Edmiston 369,
376
Charles Henderson 376
Edmund (Edwin) 188
Elijah (Revd.) 362
Elijah R. 376
Elijah Richardson (Rev.)
376
Ellin Travers 376
Emily Henderson 376
Emma Matilda 188
Eveline 362
Evelyn Tingey 376
Frederick B. 375
Gershom (Dr.) 361, 368
Hannah T. 361, 362
Hannah (Tingey) 368
Hannah Tingey 374
Henry Smith 376
Ida 376
Isaac 362
Ishi B. 188
Ishi Bullman 188
Ishi Hunt 187
Louis Stevenson 376
Louise Harriet 187
MacDonough 376
Margaretta Tingey 368,
383
Maria Forrest 376
Mary 376
Mary Augusta 376
Minna 376
Rebecca 362
Rebecca (Quick) 361,
368
Robert 376
Sarah E. (Landreth)
376
T. A. M. 369
Thomas 187, 362
Thomas T. 361, 375
Thomas Tingey 368,
369, 383
Thomas Tingey, Jr. 376
Tunis 361, 362, 368,
375, 376, 380, 383
Tunis A. M. 361
Tunis Augustus 383

Craven (cont.)
Tunis Augustus
Macdonough 369
Tunis T. 362
Virginia 188, 376
William Walling 187
Crawford, George 696
Cremorne, (?) (Lady) 565,
625, 626 (See also
FREAME)
(?) (Lord and Lady) 625
(?) (Viscountess) (the
Right Honorable Phila-
delphia Hannah) 626
Cress, Henry 104
Crinchen, Cathrein (See
KREIN) 789
Crispin, (?) (Capt.) 621
M. Jackson 621
Silas 10, 11, 13
William 11, 557, 621
William (Capt.) 621
Croasdale, William 128
Crocius, Johannes 778,
786
Crockett, Richard 225,
227, 241
Croft, Maudlin 9
Sarah 9
William 9
Crofte, William 9
Crollius, (?) 791
Anna Catharina 791
Anna Margaretha 788,
789, 791, 794
Catharina Agneta 800
Johannes 791 (See also
KROLL)
Johannes, II 791, 800
Johannes Laurentius 791
Philipp Thomas 791
Wilhelm Jost 791
Crompton, Margaretta 625
Richard 625
Susanna Margaretta 625
Cromwell, (?) 228, 623,
689, 720, 825
Oliver Eaton 377
Cronemiller, Martin 729
Croning, Lysbeth 329
Croome, Peter (Lt.) 650
Crosbie, (?) (Viscount)
582
William 582
Crosby, (?) 11
Ann Cornelia 371
Catharine (Beale) 371
Christiana 371
Christiana (Richards)
371
James 128
John Pierce 363, 371
Mary John 371
Nathaniel Davis 371
Pierce 371
Croslett, (?) 11
Crosley, (?) 11
James 128
Cross, Margaret 660
Samuel 610
Crozer, Samuel A., Jr.
377
Crukshank, John 156
Mary 156
Cuerton, Eliza 260
Elizabeth 256, 261, 262
Jane 256
Margaret 256, 257

886

Hopler, Elizabeth 741
Hopson, John 49
Hopton, Abigail 832
Horche, Heinrich (Dr.) 787
Hord, Daniel 67
Horn, Henry (Hon.) 167, 171
  John Henry 167
Horte, John 556
Horter, Catharine 177
  Catharine (Wise) 177
  George 177
Horton, William H. 171
Hough, Eleanor 698
  John 698
  Mary 689
  Richard 866
Houlgate, (?) (Capt.) 749, 760
House, Edward M. (Col.) 310
Houston, Buchanan 305
  Daniel 50
  James 855
  Jane 50
  John 48-50
  Margaret E. 48
  Martha 49, 50
  William 50
Houtz, Christian 545
Howard, (?) 51, 52
  Alice 56, 58, 63, 66, 68, 71
  Ann 305
  Benjamin 51
  C. P. 67
  Caleb 59, 60, 62
  Caleb N. 62
  Caleb Newbold 63
  Charles 56, 59, 63, 67
  Charles P. 64-66, 71
  Charles Pitt 59, 63-65, 67, 69, 71
  Charles Powell 63
  Dean 662
  Debby 63
  Deborah 56, 59, 62, 66, 67, 71
  Deborah Newbold 63
  Edith 59, 61, 62
  Edith (Newbold) 61
  Edith Newbold 62, 63
  Edmund 204
  Eliza 63
  Elizabeth 59, 71
  Elizabeth Buckley 63
  Emma Buckley 63
  Grace 53, 55, 56, 69, 71
  Grace (Beeks) 55, 56
  Jane 65
  Joanna 53, 54, 71
  John 52-60, 63, 64, 67, 68, 71, 660
  Joshua 71
  Luke 56, 59, 71
  Martha 660
  Mary 53, 54, 71, 172
  Sarah 56, 58-60, 62, 71, 660
  Sarah (Bunting) 56, 59, 60, 63, 67
  Sarah Newbold 63
  Sophia Weston 305, 306
  Susanna 54
  Susannah 57
  Thomas 51-53, 55,

Howard (cont.)
  Thomas (cont.) 57-62, 67, 69-71, 305
  William 315
Howarth, Elizabeth 648
  Frederick 648
Howe, (?) (Gen.) 101, 168
  (?) (Rev. Dr.) 680, 683, 684
  M. A. D. W. (Rev. Dr.) 679
  M. A. DeWolf (Rev.) 682
  William (Sir) 675
Howell, Daniel 125, 145
  Francis Butler 649
  Dorothy Frances 649
  Lydia Ann (Tutness) 823
Howison, Henry L. (Capt.) 308
Howland, John 605
Hubbell, Lizzie 119
Huber, (?) 27-31
  Abraham 37, 38
  Adam 33
  Adolf 32
  Andreas 35
  Anna 36, 37
  Anna Barbara 38, 45
  Anna Christina 38
  Anna Katharina 40, 41, 44, 45
  Anna Katharine 39
  Anna Margareta 38, 40, 43, 45
  Anna Margarete 45
  Anna Maria 28, 39, 43-46
  Anna Maria Katharina 38
  Barbara 36, 37
  C. 47
  Catharina 36
  Catharine 36
  Charlotte Luise 44
  Christian 36
  Ciriacus 38, 40, 41, 43, 45, 46
  Clara Elisabeth 39, 42
  Clara Elizabeth 40
  Daniel 35
  Elisabeth 30
  Elisabeth Barbara 45
  Elizabeth 30
  Eva Elisabeth 42
  Eva Margareta 40, 41
  Eva Margareta (Linn) 40
  Franz Karl 47
  Fredrika Elisabeth 45
  Friedrich 46
  Fronegg 36
  Georg 37
  George 35
  Hans 31, 36-40, 42, 43, 45, 46
  Hans Bartholomaus 38, 39, 42
  Hans Georg 39
  Hans Heinrich 37
  Hans Jacob 37
  Hans Jobst 40
  Hans Rudolf 30
  Heinrich 33, 34, 36, 40, 44
  Heinrich, Jr. 40
  Heinrich Philipp 32, 38

Huber (cont.)
  Henry 33, 34, 44
  Jacob 37
  Joh. Georg 43
  Joh. Werner (Dr.) 30
  Johann 34, 35
  Johann Adam 33, 34, 39, 42, 44
  Johann Andreas 39
  Johann Bernhard 45
  Johann Carl 45
  Johann Caspar 43, 45, 46
  Johann Conrad 45
  Johann Georg 39, 43, 45
  Johann George 40
  Johann Heinrich 34, 39, 40, 43, 44
  Johann Jacob 34, 39, 42, 44, 45
  Johann Konrath 33, 41, 43
  Johann Michael 44
  Johann Nicol 33
  Johann Nikolaus 38, 43, 44
  Johann Paul 41, 43
  Johann Peter 39, 40, 42, 43, 45, 46
  Johann Philipp 33, 38, 39, 40, 41, 42, 44-47
  Johannes 34, 37, 38, 42, 45
  John 44
  John Caspar 45
  John Jacob 30
  Jorg 37
  Juliann Catherin 44
  Jurgan 35
  Karl 46
  Karl Theodor 46
  Kaspar 46
  Katharina Margareta 46
  Luise 47
  Magdalena 36
  Margarethe 36
  Maria 47
  Maria Barbara 42
  Maria Dorothea 42, 45
  Maria Elisabeth 41, 43-45
  Maria Elizabeth 33, 44
  Maria Elizabetha 33
  Maria Katharina 39, 42, 43, 46
  Maria Sibilla 41
  Martin 31, 32, 35-40, 42, 43, 45, 46
  Mauritius 37
  Moritz 37
  Nickel 33
  Peter 31
  Philip 46
  Philipp 44
  Philipp Lorenz 46
  Phillipp 33
  Rosina Luise 45
  Rudolf 40
  Sophie Margarete 46
  Susanna 37, 47
  Valentin 47
  Verena 36, 37
  Veronika 36, 37
  Wilhelm 47
  Zilliox 38, 40
  Zilljacob 38, 40, 41
Hubert, Francis 727
  Mary 727
Huberter, (?) 35

Kroll (cont.)
Debus (See Matthaeus) 789
Ebert (Eberhard) 789
Elisabeth (?) 789
Heinrich 789
Henne (Heinrich) 789
Jacob 789
Johannes 789, 791
Matthaeus (Mebe, Mobus, Debes, Debus) 789
Mebe (See Matthaeus) 789
Michel (Michael) 789
Mobus (See Matthaeus) 789
Krom, (?) 330
Elisabet 329
Elisabet Willemsen 326, 329, 330
Lysbeth 329
Krook, Max (Dr.) 605
Kroschell, Johannes (Mr.) 787
Krul, Konrad (also Contz Krol) 789
Kubler, Christina 192
Friedrich 192
Kucher, Christopher (Capt.) 842
Kugler, Maria Magdalena 844
Maria Magladena (?) 844
Kull, Thomas 844
Kunst, Cornelis Borents 539
Kunst, Jacomyntje 533, 539
Kurn, Jacob 837 (also KIRN)
Kurtz, Betsy 336
George 336, 337
Margaretha 336
Peggy 336
Sebastian (See CURTIUS) 786
William Henry 863
Kymbel, Joannetta Maria 167
Kyn, Joran 701
Labouchere, John 638
Mary Francis 638
Lackland, John 5
Lafayette, (?) (Gen.) 548
Laguerenne, Louisa 682
Laimbeer, Josephine 680
Lake, (?) (Widow) 762
John 815
Nathan 815
Rebecca 832
Lamatt, Barbara 843 (See BOWSER)
Lamb, Louise 310
Lambert, John 260
Lampater, John 337
Sarah 336
Lamphire, Isaac 671
Lancaster, Edward 508
Joseph 311
Thos. 767
Landreth, Lucius Scott (Esq.) 666
William Linton (Esq.) 666
Landrie, Jane L. 820
Lane, (?) (Capt.) 363
Barbara (Brook) 363
Edward 122

Lane (cont.)
Rebecca 544
Samuel 544
Walter 203
Langhans, (?) (Mr.) 785
Langhorn, R. 559
Langston, Thomas 145
Lardner, Frances 623, 624
Hannah 570, 571, 623, 624
John (Dr.) 570
Lynford 571
Lare, Elizabeth 741, 744
Philip 764
Large, Esther 697, 698
Henriette 682
John 130, 355
Larzelere, Catharine 832
Latch, Jacob 768
Lathrop, Hannah 669
Latrobe, B. H. 360
Lautermann, Johann Christoph (Deacon) 798, 799
Law, (?) 360
Lawrence, Abigail 821
John 569
Margaret 200
Mary 572
Richard 553
Samuel 821, 822
William 822
William (Capt.) 822
William (Maj.) 821,822
Lawrie, Gawen 506, 514
Lawson, Jane 689
Lawson-Smith, Anthony Michael 650
Michael (Sq. Ldr.) 650
Layfield, Naomi 2
Naomi Hinman Roades Fasset 2
Thomas 2, 203
Thomas, Jr. 2
Lea, J. Henry 554
Leach, Jesse (Judge) 304
Mary Ann 304
Leader, Elizabeth 343
Leah, Jacob 276
Leahy, Anthony John Hallifax 648
Christopher Michael 648
Jonathan Edmund 648
Michael Roland 648
Philippa Sarah 648
Learned, Frank 376
Leary, Thomas 693
Leavergood, Adam 195, 196
Anna Maria 195
Catharina 195
Catharine 196
Christina 195, 196
Daniel 195
Elizabeth 195, 196
Jacob 195, 196
John 195, 196
Mathias 196
Peter 195, 196
Le Comte, Joseph (Mr.) 663
Ledgar, Ralph 689
Lee, (?) 88, 89
Abel 814
Geo. 292
Henry (Maj. Gen.) 709
James 58
Margaret 830
Leebegoot, Adam 194

Leebegoot (cont.)
Anna 194
Jacob 194
Johan Pieter 194
Maria 194'
Susanna 194, 195
Ulrich 194
Leech, Nathan 621
Thomas 146, 151, 154
Leeds, (?) 819
Benjamin Sykes 820
Daniel 508, 818, 820
Edward 818
Gideon 820
Japheth 820
Jonas 818
Josiah W. 820
Judith 820
M. R. 820
Margery (Aunt) 819
Margery Ann 820
Mary Bassett 820
Offley 820
Susanna 818
Lees, Joseph 264
Lefevor, (?) 92
Ann 92
Hipolite 91, 92, 93
Hipolite, Jr. 92
Mary 91, 92
Leghner, Anthony (Capt.) 842
Lehman, Elisabeth 800
Lehnmann, (?) 13
Philip Theodore 13
Le Huray, Anne Elizabeth 187
Charles 187, 188
Eleanora 187
Elizabeth 186, 187
Emilia Caroline 187, 188
George 187
Harriet 188
Julia 187, 188
Nich, Sr. 186
Nicholas 186-188
Nicholas, Jr. 187
Sophia 187, 188
Leibnitz, (?) 796
Leibundgut, (?) 194
Leimbach, Friedrich 780
Magnus 780
Leisler, (?) 530, 534
(?) (Gov.) 821
Lemetra, Isaac 332
Lemon, Hickford 277
Lenhart, Godfrey 864
Lenix, Ann 129, 130
Richard 130
William 129, 130
William, Jr. 130
Lens, Johann Jacob 189
Lentz, Anna Margaretha 191
Catharine 191
Christiann 191
Elizabeth 191
Georg 191
George 190, 191, 193
Henrietta 191
Jacob 843, 844
Johann Jacob 189, 190
John 191
Sophia, Jr. 193
William 191
Lenz, Anna Maria 189, 190, 192, 193
Anna Maria (Loffler) 191

Lenz (cont.)
Christina Magdalena 191
Elisabetha 190
Georg 189, 192
Georg Adam 190
Gottlieb 190
Hans Jacob 189, 191
Jacob 189-191
Joh. Daniel 191
Joh. Geo. 191
Joh. Georg 192
Johann 190
Johann Jacob 189-192
Lielia (Lydia) 190
Margaretha 190
Maria Catharina 190
Leonard, Charity 669
Martha (?) 660
Solomon 660
le Scot, John 825
William Baliol 825
Lesley, Caroline 376
Leslie, Frank 188
Lester, Hannah 148
Lettman, George 728
Letton, Mary 304
Mary (Willett) 304
Michael 304
Levengood, Ulrich 195
Levergood, Jacob 195
Ulrich 195
Leverich, Charles P. 109
Henry 109
Levering, Aaron 738, 739, 752
Abraham 761
Ann Elizabeth 752
Benjamin 743, 752
Deborah 768
Elizabeth 752
Enoch 738, 739
Jacob 752
John 103, 738, 743
John (Capt.) 760
Joseph 752
Margaret 761
Michael 764
Nathan 759, 761, 802
Peter 752
Sarah 752
Wickard 752
William 737, 740
Le Vert, (?) (Madame) 612
Ann Lea (Metcalf) 612
Claude (Dr.) 612
Cornelia Henrietta 612
Henry Strachey (M. D.) 612
Le Verte, Claude (Madame) 595, 612
Lewen, Agnes 620
Lewis, (?) 379
(?) (Mrs.) 99
Andrew (Genl.) 375
Ann 354, 373, 377
Anna 679-681
Betty 375
Charles W. 108
Clifford 679, 680
Clifford, Jr. 679
Clifford, 3rd 679
Daniel 247
David 365, 373, 678-681, 686
Edmund (D'Arch) 680
Edmund Darch 679
Eleanor 679
Eli 373

Lewis (cont.)
Elizabeth 314, 316, 373
Ellis 373, 717
Francis Waln 679, 680
George 365
Isabel Jenkins 679
Jane 722
John 694, 716
Joseph Saunders 682
Joshua 373
Lawrence 365, 676
Lydia 373
Mary 117, 373, 678
Mary Darch 679-681
Mary (Pyle) 354, 373
Nathaniel 373
Phoebe 373
Prudence 710
Rachel Coleman 684
Rebecca Chalkley 682
Robert 354, 359, 373, 547
Robert, Sr. 373
Robert Morton 676
Saml 117
Samuel, Jr. 266
Sarah 239
Susannah (Susan) 239
William 373
William Burr Nash 679
William Irvine 108
William Phillips 679
William Phillips (Rev.) 679
Wrexam 239
Lewman, Sarah 297
Lex, Georg Dietrich 843
Liebegut, Jacob 196
Liebegut, Adam 194, 196
Albrecht 194
Anna 195
Anna Margaretha 194
Catharine 196
Christina 196
Hans Adam 194
Hans Jacob 194
Hans Peter 194
Henry 196
Jacob 196
John 196
Maria Catharina 194
Peter 196
Philip 196
Ulrich 194-196
Liebenugh, Adam 196
Liebgut, Peter 195
Lieuw, Philip 329
Lincoln, Abraham 536
Mordecai 536
Lindauer, John 185
Louise 185
Linden, Maria Elisabeth 39
Lindsay, Bertram Alexander 595
Eleanor Charlotte (?) 594, 595
Lindsey, Edmund 315
Linn, (?) (Mrs.) 146
Esther 758
Eva Margareta 40
Johann Nikolaus 40
Joseph 147
Maria 41
Maria Magdalena 39, 40
Linson, James 764
Linton, Robert 217, 221
Lipincott, Freedom 524

Lipincott (cont.)
Mary (Custin) 524
Samuel 524
Lipingcott, Freedom 522
Lippincott, (?) 523
Abigail 522, 825
Deborah (Cooper) 148
Freedom 514, 522-524
Jacob 825
James S. 825
John H. 824
Judith 524
Lydia 822, 824, 826
Mary 524
Mary "Custin" 525
Remembrance 523
Restore 825
Richard 522, 824, 825
Samuel 700
William 700
Lippincotts, (?) 507
Lippingcott, Freedome 523
Lipscomb, Margaret 722
Lirou, Anthony 729
Lishman, Alfred 642
Doris Faith 642 (See HARRYMAN)
Liston, William 212, 213
William (Rev.) 213
Livezey, John 754, 755
Jonathan 694
Thomas 545, 693
Livingood, Peter 195
Ulrich 195
Livingston, Robert R. 569
Ljungstedt, Hannah Milnor (Mrs. Robinson) 275
Llewellyn, Catharine 765
Griffith Robert Poyntz 645
Hermione Poyntz 645
Lloyd, David 77, 127, 699, 717
Isaac 820
John 247
Mary 700
Thomas 690, 691
Lobdell, Samuel 359, 384
Lober, (?) 780
Catharina Elisabeth 793
Simon 780
Lobwasser, (?) 781
Lock, Lars (Rev.) 348
Lars Karlson (Rev.) 820
Lodge, Elizabeth 323, 324
Joanna (O'Neale) 324
William 323, 324
Loffler, Anna Maria 189-191
Johann Georg 192
Johann Melchior 189, 191
Theodorus Friedrich 192
Loftus, Mary 865-869
Logan, J. 868
James 503, 632, 655, 656, 866-868
William 154
Lokier, Ann 625
Lomax, C. 276
Cleborne 277
London, Ambrose 229
Long, Aline Hester 649
Charles Poore 649
Charles Poore (Maj.) 644
Frederick Farwell 550
Hannah 659
Herodia 822

Middleton (cont.)
Benjamin Franklin
(cont.) 324, 325
Caroline 301
Casandra 296
Catherine Hyatt 301
Catherine Mary 307
Catherine Mary (Eliot)
325
Charity 285, 289
D. Wesley, Jr. 308
Daniel 293, 294
Daniel Wesley 303, 306
Daniel Wesley, Jr. 307
David 297
Edith 308
Edward 283, 325
Eleanor 288, 292, 294,
295, 298
Electius 296, 302, 325
Elinor 285
Eliza. 318
Eliza M. 365
Elizabeth 285, 289,
290, 292, 300, 303,
306, 315, 324
Elizabeth Greenleaf
307
Elizabeth Jane 296
Elizabeth (Teares) 289,
292, 293, 313, 314
Elizabeth (Ward) 292
Ellen 306
Ellen Ross 325
Emeline 298
Erasmus J. 305, 306
Erasmus J., Jr. 306
Erasmus Johnson 301,
303, 305, 306
Erasmus Johnson, Jr.
306, 325
Esther 301
Francis Elizabeth 298
Francis G. 325
Frank E. 310
Frank Eliot 307-310
Frank Eliot, Jr. 310
Frederic A. 309
Frederic Andrew 309
Frederick Eliot 310
George Elmer 309
Grace Cordelia 309
Hannah (Johnson) 302,
305-307
Hannah Johnson 308
Harriet E. 325
Harry 310
Hatton 285
Helen 305
Heneritta 286, 291
Heniretta 286, 291
Henrietta 286
Henry Clay 301
Henry Oscar 308
Holland 288, 292
Horace Madison 307
Horace P. 302
Horatio 292
Hugh 90, 93-95, 288,
291-295, 297, 298,
321
Hugh C. 275, 313
Hugh Calhoun 292
Hugh Teare 292
Ignatius 285, 297
Isaac 291, 294, 295,
301
Isaac S. 301

Middleton (cont.)
Isaac Smallwood 294-
298, 320, 321
Isabel 309
J. Benjamin 325
James 285, 289, 290,
296, 301, 302, 305-
307
James Howard 306
Jefferson 309
Jennie 298
Jesse 305, 325
Jesse Riggs 304
Joel 298
John 90, 94, 282, 284,
285, 289, 292, 298
John Clark 310
John H. 325
John W. 325
Johnson van Dyke 307,
325
Lemuel J. 301
Lemuel James 303, 307,
309, 310
Lemuel James, Jr. 307
Lurenna 298
Margaret Haines
(Thompson) 325
Marian 305
Martha 285
Mary 90, 94, 276-278,
284, 285, 292-294,
321
Mary Ann (Leach) 308
Mary (Coghill) 294,
297
Mary Isabel 308
Mary (Poppleton)
Pledger 94
Mary T. 304
Mary Virginia 306
Mary (Wheeler) 279,
285, 286
Matilda 300, 324
May 308
Mitchell 293
Nellie 301
Newton 310
Nora 308
Norah 302
Oscar 304
Penelope 285
Philadelphia Adelia
292
Rachel 297
Reuben 301
Reuben Franklin 304
Richard 325
Richard Ross 306
Robert 275-286, 288-
292, 294
Robert, Jr. 276
Robert, Sr. 276
Robt. 277, 278
Rose Florence 309
S. Isaac 295
Samuel 288, 290-292,
294-296, 298-301,
303-305, 324, 325
Samuel Caleb 301, 304,
308, 325
Samuel Eliot 307, 308
Samuel Ward 292
Sarah 285
Smallwood Coghill 296
Smith 285
Sophia Weston 306
Sophie Belle 310

Middleton (cont.)
Susannah 285
Thomas 275, 284, 285,
289, 290, 298
Thomas Howard 306
Thomas J. 308, 324
Thomas Jefferson 298,
299, 301, 304, 324,
325
William 279, 284-298,
313, 315, 317, 318,
321
William, Jr. 288, 292-
295, 320
William, Sr. 288, 293,
294, 297
William Eliot 308, 310
William Morris 291
William O'Neale 300,
324
William Whitwell 310
Wm. 277
Wm. O'N. 300
Zachariah 292
Miers, Jacob 147
Michael 147
Mifflin, Thomas 545
Miflin, Thomas (Gov.) 705
Migdoll, Sarah 339
Milbourn, Tabitha 224
Miles, James 803
John Kneass 184
John M. 672
John Sexton 184
Joseph Starne 762
Phebe (?) 713 (See
EVAN)
Phebe 722 (See EVANS)
Samuel 545, 803
Milhous, Hannah 504
James 503
John 503
Joshua 504
Joshua V. 504
Robert 504
Sarah 504
Thomas 503, 504
William 504
Milledoler, Philip (Rev.)
371
Miller, Abraham 326, 334,
335
Barbara 728
Catharine 326, 334, 335
Charlotte Barclay 684
Christiana 334, 335
Clement S. 676
Daniel 19
Ebenezer 158
Elihu Spencer, 3rd
684
Elihu Spencer, 4th
684
Elizabeth 326, 335
Hendry 331
Henry 326, 331-335
James T. 371
Jan 326
John 158, 326, 332,
333, 676
John Biddle 684
John T. 544
Jost 326, 327, 333-
335
Lewis 861
Marion Spencer 684
Mary 326, 327, 334,
335

900

Nagle, John (Capt.) 709
Neall, Josephine Walbaum 685
Nedham, Charles Sewell (Capt.) 593
  Iris Eleanor Burgoyne 593 (See DEANE)
Neill, Charles 323
  Henrietta 323
  William 107
Neiman, Charles 196
Neis, Elizabeth 763 (See NICE)
Nelson, (?) 80
Neville, Joseph 197
Nevin, James (Capt.) 839
Nevins, Isabella 210
  William 210
Newbold, (?) (Widow) 109
  Ann 520, 819
  Caleb 60
  Edith 60, 63
  Elizabeth Irvine 109
  Emily (Bonnie) Duncan 109
  Esther (Lowndes) 109
  Esther Lowndes 109
  Francis 2
  James 2
  John (Capt.) 2
  Lettice 520
  Margaret (Daisy) Ellis Irvine 109
  Mary Middleton 109
  Michael 61, 109, 520
  Naomi 2
  Naomi Hinman Roades Fasset Layfield 2
  Samuel 63
  Sarah (Haines) 60
  Thomas (Dr.) 109
Newcomb, Gulielma Maria 624
  Gulielma Maria Frances 625
  John 566
  William Hawkins 624, 625
Newkirk, Adamson Bentley 389
  Caroline E. 390
  Garrett 390
  Rachel 390
  Samuel 390
  Thomas Jefferson 389
Newlin, Alfred 823
  Anne 823
  Charles 823
  Cyrus 823
  Robert 823
  Walter 823
  William Verplanck 823
Newman, George S. 67
  Gertrude Alder (Mrs.) 310
Nice (or NEIS), Elizabeth 763, 764
Nichol, John 560
  John (See NICOL) 652
  Margaret 560
Nichola, Lewis (Col.) 842

Nicholas (cont.)
  Owen 255, 259
  Samuel 252, 270
Nicholdson, Anne 97
  Samuel 97
Nichols, Joseph 93
  Sarah 325
Nicholson, Abel 96
  Abell 97
  Alice Lord 55
  Ann 97
  Anne 97
  Elizabeth Abbott 97
  Francis 530
  Hannah 97
  John 90, 96, 97
  John Armytage 577, 634, 638
  Joseph 97
  Katherine 577, 638
  Mary 97
  Ruth 97
  Samuel 97
  Sarah 90, 98
  Sarah (Powell) 98
  William 97
  William Newcome 633, 634
Nickerson, Deborah (?) 814
  Nehemiah 814
Niclas, Gertrudt 499
Nicol (NICHOL), John 652
  Margaret 652
Nicola, Lewis (Col.) 170
Nicolls, (?) (Col.) 526, 527
  (?) (Gov.) 527
  Richard (Col.) 529
  Richard (Sir) 526
  William (Rev.) 579
Nies, Carel (Gen.) 809
  Cornelia 809
Nieukirk, (?) 330
  (?) (Mrs.) 335
  Catherine (Burroughs) 390
  Cornelius 326, 333, 334, 335
  Cornelius (Col.) 327
  Matthew 390
  William Brooks 390
Nieuwkerk, (?) 386
Niles, Nathaniel 660
  Tabitha 660
Nippes, Daniel 766
Nixon, Frank 504
  George 503, 504
  George, III 504
  J. Boyd 823
  James 503, 504
  James, Jr. 504
  Jean 504
  Mary 504
  Richard Milhous 503, 504
Noble, Ellen (Ross) (Mrs.) 305
Noland, (?) 107
Nordheim, Count of (Otto) 796
Nordyke, Henry 666
Norris, Isaac 132, 148
  Joseph 259
  Mary D. 680
Norton, Thomas 151
Norwood, Sarah (Hutchinson) 151, 155

Notley, Thomas 232
Nottingham, (?) 519
  Hannah 520
  John 517, 520, 521
  Judith 520, 521
  Mary 520, 521
  Sam 520
  Susanna 518-521
  Thomas 520, 521, 523
  William (Capt.) 538
Noy, Nicholas 514
Nuss, Michael 765
Obb, Jacob 864
Odenheimer, (?) (Mr.) 680
  W. H. (Rev.) 678
  Wm. (Rev.) 681
  Wm. H. 682
O'Donnel, Owen 216
O'Dwire, Edwin 207
Oelife, (?) 507
Offley, David, Jr. 819
  David (Lt.) 819
  Michael 819
Offly, Daniel 819
  Judith (Aunt) 819, 820
Ogden, Isaac C. 176
Ogle, Marie 377
Olave, (?) 507
Oldman, Ann 157
  Elizabeth 697 (See GILBERT), 699, 700
  Jane 699
  John 699
  Joseph 125, 151, 153, 157, 162
  Mary 157
  Sarah 157, 158, 699
  Thomas 157, 699, 700
  Thomas, Jr. 157
Olif, Martha 509
Olife, (?) 507
  Ann 516
  Joyce 511
  Richard 511
  Roger 510
  Thomas, Sr. 516
Oliffe, Ann 509, 511, 512
  Anne 511, 512
  Benjamin 509
  Doily 512
  Dorothy 512
  Elizabeth 509, 511
  Francis 509, 510, 511
  Hannah 509
  Henry 509, 510
  John 509, 511
  Joyce 511-515
  Mary 509, 511
  Richard 509-512, 515, 516
  Sarah 509
  Thomas 508-516
  Thomas, Sr. 509-511, 515, 516
  William 511
Oliphant, Anthony David 652
  Bruce Kingsley 652
  David Kingsley 652
  James Robert 652
  K. I. P. (Lt. Col.) 652
  Mary 823
Olive, (?) 507
  Ann 509, 510, 512
  Benjamin 507-510
  Benjamin, Sr. 510
  Elizabeth 509, 510
  John 509, 510

Nicholas, Anthony 270
  John 270
  Margaret (Moore) 270, 274
  Martha 270
  Mary 270

908

Rashleigh (cont.)
 John Cosmo Stuart 638
 Jonathan 577, 637, 638,
  644, 649
 Jonathan Onley 644
 Margaret Anne 650
 Mary Anna 638
 Mary Vivien 650
 Morwenna 650
 Peter 650
 Peter Carelton 650
 Philip Stuart 650
 Richard Harry 650
 Susanna Jane 650
 William Francis 650
 William Stuart 644, 649
Rastall, John 554, 626
 Margaret 554, 556
Ratcliff, Edward 131
Rawle, Franc. 699
 Francis 249
 William, Jr. (Capt.)
  171
Rawlins, John Fawset
 Herbert 568
Razer, Baltes 800 (See
 RESER)
Reab, Lawrence Augustus
 Rigail 612
Reabeau, Joseph 728
Reachert, John 190
Read, Blair Beale 377
 Edith Ross 377
 Emily Truxtun 377
 F. P. Blair 377
 George 377
 George, 3rd (Hon.) 377
 Gertrude Parker 377
 Louisa Ridgeley Dorsey
  377
 Mary Anna 377
 Sarah 125, 148
 William 370
 William Thompson 377
Reade, (?) (Maj. Gen.)
 641
 Evelyne Helen Revell
  634
 Hubert Granville 635
 John Page 576, 634, 640
 Mary Spencer Revell
  641, 646
 Raymond Nathaniel
  Northland Revell 635,
  640, 641, 646
 Revell 641
Rebeaud, Joseph 727
Rebo, Joseph 727
Redheffer, Andrew 103,
 803
Reding, Sarah 667
Redman, Daniel (Col.) 12
 John 692
 John C. 299
Reed, Joseph 580
 Josiah Vaughan 662
 Margaret 199
 William B. 181
Rees, (?) (Rev.) 717
 David 258, 259
 Edward 251, 257
 Elizabeth 75
 Evan 544
 John 249
 Rachel 259
 Rachel (Coppock-Moore)
  259
 T. Hardy (Rev.) 723

Reese, David 259
 Ellis 722
 Hannah 137
 Jane 713, 722
 Rachel 259
Reeve, Agnes 518
 Anne 518
 Joseph 819
 Martha 819
 Mary 819
 Micajah 820
 Rachel 819
 Richard 518
 Ruth 819
 Samuel 819
 Thomas 820
Reeves, Abby S. 824
 Benjamin 824
 Biddle 824
 David 821, 823
 Elizabeth 824
 Mary James 823
 Mary Scull 824
 Paul Scull 824
 Sarah 824
Regniers, Jacob 532
Reiff, George 542
Reighter, Peter 734
Reily, Jno 352
 John 352, 504
Reis, Rosina 337
Reiter, (?) 772
 Barbara 773
 Barthol 735
 Barthol. 733
 Catharina 772
 Catharine 772
 Catharine (?) 772
 Christiana (?) 773
 Elisabetha 770, 772
 Elizabeth 744, 771,773
 Eva 773
 Eva Catharina 771
 Eve 771
 George 744, 770, 771,
  772
 George Michael 772
 Hanna 772
 Johanes 770
 Johann Georg 771
 Johannes 771
 John 769, 770, 773
 Margaret 773
 Margareta 772
 Mary 773
 Mary Elizabeth 773
 Michael 770-773
 Peter 773
 Sara 772
 Susanna 772
Reitz, Johann Adam 785
 Johannes 785
Reller, John Conrad
  (Rev.) 772
Remmie, Elizabeth 583
Remy, John 211
Reser (RAZER), Baltes
 800, 801
Reston, William 705 (See
 PRESTON)
Reuschell, (?) 804
Revacum, Justus 801
Revell, Thos. 515
Rex, George 771, 772
 Levi 771, 772
Rexrodt, Elizabeth 784,
 785
 Thimotheus 786

Reymond, John 282
Reynaud, Victorine 378
Reynolds, (?) 112
 Elizabeth 381
 James (Dr.) 108
 John, Sr. 381
Rhoades, Margaret 238
Rhoads, (?) 1
 Adam 268
 Benjamin 722
 Danl J. 117
 John 233
 Joseph 269
 Mary 114
 Samuel 56, 269
Rhodes, (?) 1
 John, Sr. 231
 William A. 588
Rhys, Elizabeth 75
Riband, Rose 727
Ribau, Catherine 729
 James 725
 Joseph 725-727, 729
Ribaud (See also REABEAU,
 REBEAUD, REBO, RIBAND,
 RIBAU, RIBAUX, RIBBAU,
 RIBOT, RIBOUT)
 Catharine 730
 Catherine 729
 Joseph 725-731
 Joseph, Jr. 728
 Rose 729, 730
Ribaut, Joseph 726
Ribaux, Joseph, Jr. 728
Ribbau, Joseph 725
Ribeau, Joseph 727
Ribekam, Johann Carolus
 (Charles) 803
Ribenkam, Catharina
 Juliana 804
 Jno Philip 804
Ribout, Joseph 726
Rice, Emma L. 698
Rich, Nathaniel (Sir) 826
 Sylvester N. 547
Richards, Eliza 239
Richardson, (?) 160
 Francis 159, 160
 John 159
 Joseph 159, 160
 Letitia (Swift) 159
 Samuel 695
 W. R. (Rev.) 604
 William 210, 211
Richbell, John 836
Richman, Harman 326, 335
Rickgans, (?) 780
 Anna 778, 780, 782
 Bernhard 780
 Georg 780
 Maria 780
Rider, Hans Mich. 770
Ridgely, Nicholas 96, 98
 Rachel 98
Ridgelys, (?) 96
Ridgway, Jacob 818
 John 818 ("Gentleman")
 Sarah 818
 Thomas 818
Ridley, Charles William
  (Rev.) 634
 Fanny Louisa Pole 634
 Henry Nicholson 634
 Mary Louisa 634
 Oliver Matthew (Rev.) 577,634
 Oliver Stuart (Rev.) 634
Riebakam, Frederick Wm.799
Riebakamen, Margaret
  Catherine 799
Riebekam, Johann Philipp 793

Rogers (cont.)
  William (Rev.) 101, 356
Rohrbach, Christian 786
Roller, Rosina 837
Ronaldson, James 177
Rooke, Margaret 8
Roop, Christina (or
  Christiana) 763-765
  Cornelius 763
  John 763 (Also RUPP),
  764
Rooper, Georgina 576,
  636, 643
  John Bonfoy 576, 636
Roosa, Albert Heymans 533
  Albert Heymans (Capt.)
  533
  Neeltje 533
Rooth, Richard (Sir) 560
Roots, (?) 1
  Jan (Dr.) 1
Rosenberger, Erasmus 776
Rosier, Notley 311
Rosnagle, Anna Maria 840
  Michael 840
Ross, Ellen 306
  George 547
  Henry Pawling 547
  Richard 305, 306
  Richard L. 306
  Sarah 595, 596
  Thomas 547
  William H. 595
Rossell, Francis 129
Rotgers, Cornelis 499
Roth, William Lewis 171
Rothmuller, George Peter
  41
  Karl Ludwig 41
Rovekamp, Curt (Kort) 807
  Hans 806
  Hartlef 806
  Heinrich 806
  Joachim 806
  Johann 806, 807
  Kort (Curt) (See
  ROEFEKAMP) 807
  Peter 806
  Thomas 806
Rowan, John 823
  John (Dr.) 823
  Lydia Ann 822, 823
Rowekamp, Anton Heinrich
  807
  Berend Hinrich 807
  Hinrich Wilhelm 807
  Hinrich Wilhelm, Jr.
  807
  Johann Hinrich 807
Rowland, Benjamin 147
  John 128, 238
Royden, William 123
Rozer, Benjamin 275
  Benjamin (Col.) 281
Rubbenkamp (RUWENKAMP),
  Gerd 806
Rubecam, Friderici 783
  Friedrich 783
  Gerdrut 783
  Gertrud 783
Rubecamp, Anton Heinrich
  807
  Rudolf (Dr.) 805
  Rudolph 805
Rubekamin, Gerdruth 784
Rubekamp, (?) (Herr) 782
  Anton Heinrich 807
  Herman 806

Rubekamp (cont.)
  Johann 806
Rubencam, Fridericius
  781
  Friedrich 778
  Hans Caspar 782
  Laurentius 786
Rubencambs, Andreas
  (Herrn) 783
  Catharina Juliana (?)
  783
Rubencamm, Joh. Peter 785
Rubencammius, Johannes
  Philippus 794
Rubencamp, Felice
  (Fraulein) 777, 786
  Robert Gottfried
  Heinrich (Dr.) 786
  Wilhelm 786
Rubenkam, (?) 783, 785
  (?) (H.(err)) 799
  (?) (Pastor) 780, 782,
  784, 798, 799
  (?) (Widow) 804
  Andreas 782, 783, 788,
  789, 791, 792, 794
  Andreas (Pastor) 792
  Ann 801-803
  Anna (?) 803
  Anna Catharina 803
  Anna Elisabeth 785,
  786
  Anna Gertrud 783, 786,
  788
  Anna Margaretha 792,
  797, 803
  Anna Sibylla 782, 783
  Anton Friedrich 786
  Cadter Magdalena 787
  Carl (Herr) 786
  Carl (Mr.) 785
  Catharina Elisabeth
  785, 786, 793
  Catharina Juliana 800,
  801
  Catherine 802
  Charles 802, 803
  Charles Wilhelm (See
  Karl) 802
  Christina Margaretha
  785
  Christoph 783
  Conrad 786
  Daniel 802
  Elisabeth 782, 783
  Frederick William 800
  Friedrich 777, 778,
  780, 781-783, 785,
  786, 788, 794, 795,
  807
  Friedrich Wilhelm 800
  Frolich 777
  Gude Elisabeth 787
  Herman 777
  Hermann 777
  Jacob 777, 802
  Jacobe 777
  Johann Andreas 793
  Johann Christian 786
  Johann Friedrich 792
  Johann Georg 783-786
  Johann Georg Peter 793
  Johann Heinrich 786,
  787
  Johann Karl 793
  Johann Paul 785, 786
  Johann Peter 784, 785
  Johann Philipp 782,

Rubenkam (cont.)
  Johann Philipp (cont.)
  792, 794, 795, 797-
  799
  Johann Philipp (Pastor)
  793 (See RIEBEKAM),
  798, 799
  Johanna Catharina 803
  Juliana 802
  Justus 800, 802
  Justus Heinrich 788
  Justus Wilhelm 801
  Karl August 786
  Karl (Charles) Wilhelm
  802
  Kunegunda Juliana 785,
  786
  Laurentius 782, 783,
  786, 787, 791
  Laurentius (Magister)
  792
  Margaret 802
  Margaretha Catharina
  803
  Margaretha Elisabeth
  785
  Maria Christina 786
  Maria Elisabeth 785,
  786
  Maria Juliana 793
  Martin 785
  Michael Wilhelm 793,
  802
  Peter 803
  Sarah 802
  Susanna (?) 803
  Susannah 802
  William 803
Rubenkambius, Johannes
  Henricus 787
Ruben-Kamin, Anna
  Katharina 776, 777
Ruben-Kamm, Johann Philipp
  776, 777
Rubenkamm, Andreas 788
  Johann Henrich 787
Rubesam (RUBESSAM), (?)
  786 (See RUBENKAM)
Rubincam (See also
  REVACUM, REVERCOMB,
  RIBEKAM, RIBENKAM,
  RIEBAKAM, RIEBAKAMEN,
  RIEBEKAM, ROEFEKAMP,
  ROVEKAMP, ROWEKAMP,
  RUBBENCAMP, RUBECAM,
  RUBECAMP, RUBEKAMIN,
  RUBEKAMP, RUBENCAM,
  RUBENCAMBS, RUBENCAMM,
  RUBENCAMMIUS, RUBEN-
  CAMP, RUBENKAM, RUBEN-
  KAMBIUS, RUBEN-KAMIN,
  RUBEN-KAMM, RUBENKAMM,
  RUBESAM, RUEBENCAMM)
  RUWENKAMP)
  Milton 776, 791, 801, 805,807
Rudeloff, Hans 780
Ruebencamm, (?) (Pastor)
  799
Ruhl, Anna 192
  Hans 192
Rule, Elizabeth 198
Rumsey, William 92
Runnels, (?) 349
Rupp, John 796 (See ROOP)
Ruppersberg, Margarethe
  789
Rush, (?) (Madame) 818
Russell, (?) 628

911

912

913

916

921